T5-AOM-099

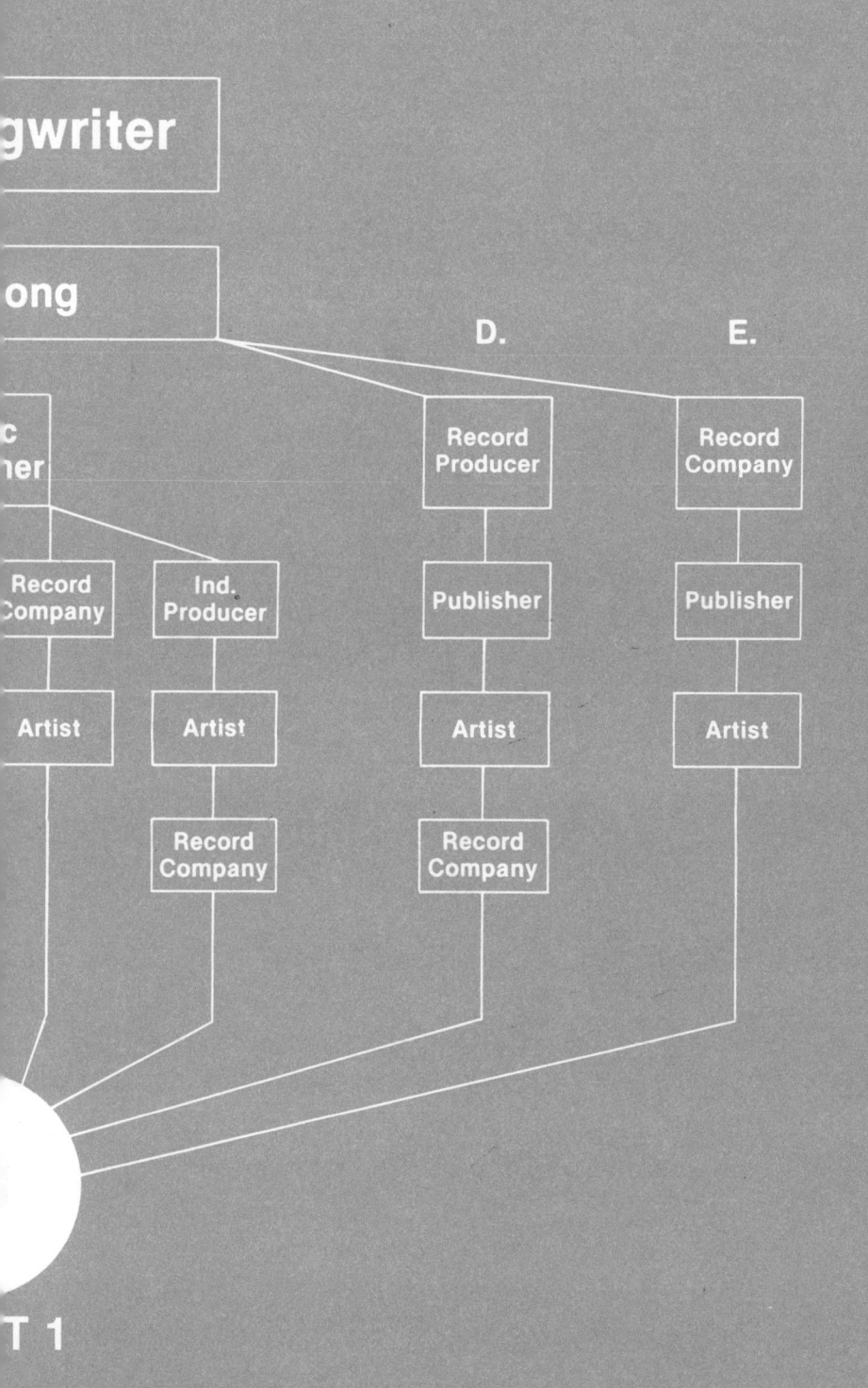

gwriter

ong

D.

E.

Record Producer

Record Company

Record Company

Ind. Producer

Publisher

Publisher

Artist

Artist

Artist

Artist

Record Company

Record Company

T 1

# 1984 SONG WRITER'S MARKET™

## WHERE TO SELL YOUR SONGS

Edited by Barbara Norton Kuroff

**Writer's Digest Books**
Cincinnati, Ohio

Distributed in Canada by Prentice-Hall of Canada Ltd., 1870 Birchmount Road, Scarborough, Ontario M1P 2J7, and in Australia and New Zealand by Bookwise (Aust.) Pty. Ltd., 101 Argus Street, Cheltenham, V1C 3192, Australia.

Songwriter's Market. Copyright © 1983. Published by Writer's Digest Books, 9933 Alliance Rd., Cincinnati, Ohio 45242. Printed and bound in the United States of America. All rights reserved. No part of this book may be reproduced in any manner whatsoever without written permission from the publisher, except by reviewers who may quote brief passages to be printed in a magazine or newspaper.

International Standard Serial Number 0161-5971
International Standard Book Number 0-89879-123-5

# Contents

## The Profession

- **1** Introduction
- **3** Using Your Songwriter's Market
- **5** Writing for the Local Alternative Music Markets
    - **6** Advertising Agencies
    - **8** Audiovisual Markets
    - **9** Writing for Local Performers
    - **9** Writing for the Musical Theater

## The Markets

- **11** Music Publishers
    - **21 Close-up:** Stan Hertzman, Manager/Producer/Publisher
    - **67 Close-up:** Steve Kipner, Songwriter/Performer
    - **79 Close-up:** Andy Goldmark, Songwriter/Publisher
    - **95 Close-up:** Amy Grant, Performer
    - **113 Close-up:** Mike Reid, Songwriter/Performer
    - **118 Close-up:** Alfie Davison, Songwriter/Performer
- **124** Record Companies
    - **130 Close-up:** Rick James, Performer
    - **171 Close-up:** Helen Hudson, Songwriter/Performer
    - **192 Close-up:** Brian Ross, Producer/Publisher
- **206** Record Producers
    - **211 Close-up:** Ron Blackwood, Producer/Publisher
    - **229 Close-up:** David Mackay, Producer
    - **259 Close-up:** Tom Snow, Songwriter/Publisher/Performer
- **261** Advertising Agencies
- **283** Audiovisual Firms
    - **285 Close-up:** Alan and Marilyn Bergman, Lyricists
- **296** Managers & Booking Agencies
- **343** Play Producers & Publishers
    - **345 Close-up:** Stephen Schwartz, Composer/Lyricist
    - **355 Close-up:** Jeff Jones, Composer/Arranger/Musician

# Services & Opportunities

- **357** Contests and Awards
- **360** Organizations and Clubs
  - **365 Close-up:** Doug Thiele, Songwriter
- **368** Publications of Interest
- **372** Workshops

# Appendix

- **375** The Business of Songwriting
  - **375** The Structure of the Music Business
  - **376** Submitting Your Songs (By Mail)
  - **377** Submitting in Person
  - **377** The Money
  - **378** Copyright
  - **379** Record Keeping
  - **379** The Rip Offs
  - **380** Co-writing
  - **380** Alternatives

  ### Special Features
  - **381** Contracts
  - **387** Overview of the AGAC Popular Songwriters Contract
  - **388** The AGAC Popular Songwriters Contract
  - **399** Home Demos that "Sell" Songs
  - **401** How to Be a Music Market Detective

# Glossary
**405**

# Index
**409**

# The Profession

## Introduction

Change.

It's the only thing that remains the same in the music business. New companies form; old ones merge or go out of business altogether; executives and recording artists play musical chairs from one company to another, from one part of the country to another, or even from one continent to another; and musical tastes vary as regularly as seasons or hemlines.

Here at *Songwriter's Market*, we spend every working day of every year just keeping up with all the changes in the music industry. This, our sixth edition of *Songwriter's Market*, reflects the most recent changes in the music industry and tells you the things you *must* know to get your songs to the people who can get them published and recorded.

This book contains over two thousand markets for your songs: music publishers, record companies, record producers, advertising agencies, audiovisual firms, play producers, and managers. Over five hundred of these markets appear in *Songwriter's Market* for the first time and this year we have marked all the new listings with an asterisk for your quick reference. Listings that appeared in last year's edition have been updated with the most current information for inclusion in this edition.

The people listed in this book want to hear your songs. They told us so. That's why they're in this book.

Today's music knows no geographic boundaries. That's why this year *Songwriter's Market* has gone international. Among our new listings are over one hundred publishers, record companies, and record producers located in Australia, England, New Zealand, and even Scotland and Wales. All of these companies either already work with songwriters in other countries or say they welcome an opportunity to do so.

There's much more in *Songwriter's Market*, however, than just thousands of valuable markets for your songs. In an article written especially for *Songwriter's Market*, James Dearing, author of *Making Money Making Music*, tells you how to make money and build a reputation with your songs—right in your home town: writing jingles for advertising agencies, music for audiovisual firms, musicals for community theater groups, and songs for local performing and recording artists.

In "Contracts," in the Appendix of this book, Bob Leone, Director of Special Projects for the American Guild of Authors and Composers (AGAC), gives specific information on what a publishing contract should and should not contain. He even includes a copy of the valuable AGAC contract, along with a descriptive overview of its features. In addition, Leone gives information you need to know about other contracts a songwriter might be asked to sign: recording, production, management, and collaboration agreements.

## 2  Songwriter's Market '84

"How to Be a Music Market Detective," also in the Appendix, gives step-by-step tips on how to get your material to the recording artists, the one important song market whose addresses can't be found in directories.

There's lots of glitter in *Songwriter's Market* too, but glitter of a very useful kind. In the Close-ups throughout the book, you'll hear advice directly from songwriters, producers, performers, and other industry people.

No matter where you live, if you are a songwriter, this book was compiled for you. *Songwriter's Market* is your up-to-date guide to the changing music industry, a roadmap that can take your songs over hundreds or even thousands of miles, through doors and onto the desks and tape players of the people who can make your dream of songwriting success come true. Read it, enjoy it, but most of all, use it.

*—Barbara Norton Kuroff*

# Using Your Songwriter's Market

To most effectively use *Songwriter's Market*, read the section introductions *first*. Each gives a brief overview of the market area and can help you decide if it's a field of songwriting you'd be interested in working with. Any special information and phraseology found within the listings will also be mentioned.

Then, *study* the listings, keeping these facts in mind:

- The information you are reading came directly from representatives of the companies listed. It is reported exactly as they gave it to us.
- All correspondence and submissions should be addressed to the contact person named in the listing.
- All mail should contain a stamped, self-addressed envelope (SASE); submissions to listings in foreign countries should include a self-addressed envelope (SAE) and International Reply Coupons (IRC).
- "Does not accept unsolicited material" means you should never submit anything before you query *and* receive permission to submit.
- "Query" means to contact the company by phone or mail *before* submitting anything.
- The types of music, the number of songs you may include in the submission, and the way you should submit your songs are stated in each listing. Your close attention to the exact specifications of a particular listing will help assure your success.
- The year the company was established will be given only for companies established in 1981 and after. The risk is sometimes greater when dealing with new companies. So far as we know, all are reputable but some are unable to compete with larger, older companies. Many do survive, however, and become very successful. And most all new companies are wide open to material from new songwriters.
- An asterisk appears before the names of companies listed in this book for the first time.
- Figures given (e.g., number of songs published, released or produced per year or number of new songwriters published per year) are approximations to help you determine a market's activity and its openness to material from new songwriters.
- The length of time companies say they need to report back to songwriters on submissions is also approximate. Publishers especially go through periods of unbelievably heavy loads of submissions. If a market doesn't respond within several weeks after the time frame given in its listing, follow up with a brief, friendly letter giving detailed information about your submission: Include your name, address and phone number; titles of songs submitted; type of demo submitted; and date of submission.
- The Glossary in the back of this book will explain unfamiliar terms you might encounter while reading the listing.

- Although every listing in *Songwriter's Market* is updated, verified or researched prior to publication, some changes are bound to occur between now and the time you contact any listing.
- Listings are based on editorial interviews and questionnaires. They are *not* advertisements, *nor* are markets reported here necessarily endorsed by the editor.
- Looking for a particular market? Check the Index. If you don't find it there, it is because 1) It's not interested in receiving material at this time. 2) It's no longer in business or has merged with another company. 3) It charges (counter to our criteria for inclusion) for services a songwriter should receive free. 4) It has failed to verify or update its listing annually. 5) It has requested that it not be listed. 6) We have received reports from songwriters about unresolved problems they've had with the company.
- A word of warning. Don't pay to have your song published and/or recorded, or to have your lyrics—or a poem—set to music. Read "The Rip Offs" and "Contracts" (both located in the Appendix to this book) to learn how to recognize and protect yourself from the *songshark*. *Songwriter's Market* reserves the right to exclude any listing which does not meet its requirements.

# Writing for the Local Alternative Music Markets

BY JAMES DEARING

Have you ever read an article about popular songwriting that *didn't* warn against devastating odds, and the awesome degree of talent, luck, and perseverance that you as a songwriter need to "make it?" No? Then this may be a "first."

Fortunately, there are some alternate markets for songwriters that—when grouped together—offer just as much room for creativity, notoriety, and (yes!) money as writing popular music. You'll still need talent and perseverance, but the luck required and those formidable odds are greatly reduced. Best of all, these "other" ways to make money writing music are jobs you can find right now, in your own home town. The local alternatives include selling music (jingles) for television and radio advertisements to sponsors, advertising agencies and recording studios; writing musical soundtracks for audiovisual companies and businesses; writing songs for local entertainers to perform and record; and writing plays (musicals) for community theaters, playhouses, and school drama departments.

## The Pro's and Con's

Writing for alternative markets won't be the answer to *all* of your dreams. There are some trade-offs involved. For example, watching the debut of the musical you toiled over after months—maybe even *years*—will satisfy your creative needs, but it won't do much for your monetary needs. Realistically, you may not even cover your expenses of paper and typewriter ribbons.

On the other hand, you can make a bundle of money writing and producing local advertising jingles, but your creative desires may be caged-in by the substantial structural constraints inherent in this style of writing. Realize that local alternatives for songwriters fall into one of these categories: They're either creatively satisfying or monetarily satisfying. Luckily, these categories are not mutually exclusive. After you build up your credits as a local playwright, you'll be qualified to begin making money writing musicals on a larger scale; and as a local jingle writer, you'll be able to take more artistic chances and greater creative liberties with assignments.

Of the popular songwriting alternatives mentioned—writing jingles for advertising, soundtracks for audiovisual films, songs for local performers, and musicals for local theaters—local job availability varies considerably. Each metropolitan area has thousands of potential jingle accounts, hundreds of businesses and agencies in need of songwriters for AV production, and many bands and entertainers who will consider original material for performances. Outlets for theatrical performances are usually more limited. Each local market, however, is hungry for new writers.

Local markets, just like major markets in the music centers, want top-quality material. Clearly, they don't always get what they want, as evidenced by the proliferation of unprofessional television commercials, but don't assume you can "get by" with writing mediocre material. (In fact, musically untrained advertising agency copywriters are more to blame for dull commercials than are songwriters.) Your job is to make the right impression. Take the extra time to polish your material. Prove your worth immediately!

---

**James Dearing** *is the author of* Making Money Making Music (No Matter Where You Live), *Writer's Digest Books, and has written for several musician and songwriter magazines. Dearing has also led workshops for songwriter and musician organizations in New York, Pennsylvania, Missouri, Illinois, Colorado, and California, and performs as a professional musician.*

An advantage of working locally is that some situations are "team oriented." You might be hired as an in-house writer with a studio, and collaborate with the producer while juggling feedback from an ad agency director about what his client wants. Or, you may be working with the public relations officer of a large company, trying to incorporate the business' philosophy into a slide show soundtrack. This atmosphere of camaraderie is in stark contrast to the nomadic existence a songwriter can encounter while lost in New York City or Los Angeles, trying to impress publishers and record company personnel.

At the same time, this advantage of working together can become a disadvantage when you learn that you don't have the final say on your creation—the sponsor does! Some of the people you'll work with locally won't know a sharp from a flat; yet, if you're to work with them, you'll need to accommodate them.

Another advantage of working as a local songwriter is the versatility it affords. You'll have distinct career options. You can build up your track record until you're ready to crack the Big Time, or you can plot your career with the intent of staying local, and carve out a very comfortable living as you become more and more successful, thus eliminating any need to move to a hectic megatropolis.

## Advertising Agencies: The Industry

The advertising field offers songwriters the greatest money-making opportunities locally. The dollar volume to be spent on television and radio ads in 1985 is projected to be 29 *billion* dollars. There are advertisers everywhere, and they're willing to spend from $500-$10,000 for a *local* advertising concept. How much of the budget you make depends on what you do, and how many ways the budget is being divided.

Music rental firms, which stock enormous libraries of prerecorded background music, present a very serious threat to songwriters. A major part of your sales pitch to prospective buyers must emphasize why the soundtrack you'll provide is better than prerecorded music. For instance, if they hire you, you'll be able to tailor the soundtrack to the video and voice messages the client wants to project, rather than the client having to arrange the film to match parts of the music. The use of prerecorded or "canned" music instead of jingle writers and musicians is widespread on a local scale. Radio stations and advertising agencies are notorious for selling a client on a block of air time, and then recycling music from albums to create the ads. Production of ads from these "borrowed" composites is usually poor; the result can be even worse when ad agency or media station copywriters try to create jingles! Untrained in the craft of songwriting, melodies and lyrics both are usually unimaginative and poorly structured.

Distasteful as the above facts about the advertising industry might be, they can work to the advantage of creative, productive songwriters. By first taking time to analyze what advertising is (or should be) and then exhibiting both creativity and dependability, you'll be able to win clients.

## Jingles: The Theory and the Craft

Advertising is the practice of persuasion. Since you'll be expected to write persuasive lyrics, it's a good idea to know a bit about advertising.

Advertisements are an appeal to human needs. These needs have been neatly defined and categorized by Dr. Abraham Maslow, communications specialist and researcher. According to Maslow, the most basic needs are *physical needs*, such as sleep, food, thirst, and sex. Physical needs are very intense, and must be fulfilled before a person can "move up" to worrying about *safety needs*, such as security and comfort. Higher still are *love needs*, such as being accepted by others and participating in groups. The next need is *self esteem*, when people seek recognition, achievement, and prestige. The highest is *self actualization needs*, when people do things purely for the challenge of accomplishment or creative desire.

Keep these need levels in mind when writing lyrics to jingles. Different clients want to appeal to different consumers. A jingle for a safari tour agency might effectively appeal to an appreciation of the wilderness (self actualization); a jingle for a luxurious restaurant could appeal to an image of success and wealth (self esteem); a jingle for a low-income housing development might best appeal to basic physical needs. Study jingles on TV and radio and compare the product they're selling with the "need level consumer" the lyrics are addressing.

The age of the consumers that the jingle is written for is important. You don't write a hard rock jingle if the sponsor is selling motorhomes or diamond rings.

The public perception of businesses and services is also important. A fast food restaurant jingle shouldn't be slow, just as a jingle for a store selling beds and reclining chairs shouldn't be fast.

Most commercials are divided into a "front," a "bridge," and a "tag." The front is the attention-grabber. This is where your jingle will fit. During the bridge, your jingle will continue playing softly in the background, with the announcer's "sell" message in the foreground. The front (your jingle) is really just a device to fool the listener or viewer into remaining attentive during the sell message. The last part of a commercial, the tag, is a brief summation of the sell message. Commercial length varies from 60 seconds to five seconds (in which case only a quick sell message is used). Rarely does the jingle itself ever exceed 20 seconds in length.

There are some general rules of writing jingle lyrics: Use familiar words; be economical with what you have to say; write in the present tense; concentrate on one singular idea; avoid cliches; and write for listeners on a one-to-one basis using personal pronouns. When the jingle is recorded, make sure the lyrics are perfectly understandable.

You can write either lyrics or melody first. "I sit down with a pencil and start kicking around variations on their old commercial, unless the agent says to come up with something completely new," says one successful jingle writer. "I write down possible hooks and then choose the best one, set it to an appropriate rhythm, and then set a melody."

An excellent step-by-step guide to writing jingles is Antonio Teixeira, Jr.'s *Music To Sell By*, available from Berklee Press, 1265 Boylston Street, Boston, Massachusetts, 02215.

## Selling: Yourself and Your Work

There are three types of working arrangements commonly encountered by jingle writers:

1. After dropping off a demo tape with an advertising agency, the songwriter will get a call from the advertising director when he has a client whose image fits the songwriter's style.

2. When a client contacts the studio directly about making a commercial, an overburdened recording studio producer will call a songwriter who has previously written and produced a jingle at the studio.

3. An ambitious, sales-minded songwriter contacts a local client directly, asking if he would be interested in listening to a new commercial on speculation for his business/organization/political campaign. The songwriter writes and records the jingle, and the client buys it.

To get that first jingle assignment, you've got two choices: Either drop off demo tapes with ad agencies, or begin writing jingles on speculation for sponsors. Writing "on spec" can also lead to getting jobs through recording studios.

To get your name on file with local ad agencies, you'll need to write several 20-second jingles which show your versatility in style. Remember: If your jingles all sound similar in tempo, instrumentation, vocals, and style, the agent will only call you when that particular type of assignment comes up. Also remember to get your hooks up front: establish clearly the jingle theme and the product or service you're advertising.

When your demo tape is the best you honestly feel it can be, you're ready to begin marketing strategy. Thumb through the telephone book Yellow Pages and call the firms listed under "Advertising Agencies." Ask if they'd listen to your demo jingle tape. If they will listen and like what they hear, they'll call you when an assignment they think you can handle becomes available. Additional names and addresses of agencies along with specific clients of each may be obtained from *The Standard Directory of Advertising Agencies* (National Register Publishing Company). Also check the Advertising Agencies section of this book for names, addresses and submission policies of companies in or near your home town.

The assignments you'll get will vary considerably. Sometimes you'll be asked to rewrite an established jingle from a pop melody to a new wave melody. At other times you'll be left to create something completely new. The assignment may call for only one 30-second commercial; or—for a much larger budget—a total package concept, which might include 60-second and 30-second spots, with a 10-second section the sponsor can lift out, and a 5-second lift out hook (or logo).

In any case, you'll probably receive ideas from the director or agency copywriters about the image the client is striving for, and what information should be pushed in the jingle (either service, low prices, quality, etc.) All this information will come to you in a "fact sheet" from the agency.

Besides input from the director and copywriters, the sponsor will often volunteer his two cents about how the final jingle should sound. A major part of jingle writing is remaining amiable with all parties concerned, and realizing that even though the others may all be tone deaf, their contributions may still be valid. Never forget who is paying you!

In theory, jingle writers only sell advertising rights to each jingle for one advertising campaign; after that, a reuse fee is supposed to be negotiated. In reality, however, the agency or sponsor paying you calls the shots. Most likely, you'll be offered a lump sum, and be expected to relinquish all rights to the jingle. The one right you may be able to retain is use of the melody for turning it into a popular song. Local advertisers will usually give you popular song rights, since any further air play of the melody will only make their commercials more popular, thus (theoretically) selling more goods.

Make sure the contract you're signing stipulates that this is a local advertisement, and will not be syndicated nationally. If the ad will be syndicated, you're entitled to a much larger payment.

## Making Your Own Markets

The best method to get started locally is to solicit sponsors yourself, thus circumventing the agency. If you have a home recording studio, you can also circumvent the independent recording studio. Working on your own is preferred by many jingle writers, since it allows greater creative flexibility and—if budgeted carefully—pays more money.

"Most business owners are flattered when I ask if I can make them a spot on spec," says Mike, a jingle writer. "Once they hear the name of their company on the cassette they get excited."

After getting the go-ahead from a client, write the jingle and convince some musician friends to help you record a tape. Do it at home if possible. Only after the client has heard your jingle and agrees to finance it should you reserve studio time and begin the jingle session. Have the client pay the studio directly. In this way, the studio will realize your worth as a jingle writer *and* as a producer. Again, this "double duty" can double your pay, and lead not only to studio referrals, but also word of mouth jobs from the client.

## Audiovisual Markets

The audiovisual field is another home town market that offers songwriters many money-making opportunities. I know one songwriter who is on salary creating film soundtracks for the University of California at Davis. Another songwriter/friend has established herself as a freelance audiovisual songwriter by selling her services to businesses for instructional and informational slide shows. The jobs are out there; it's up to you to record a top-notch tape showing your versatility, and then make contacts with the people in charge of audiovisual production in schools, government, business and industry, advertising agencies, libraries, associations, and organizations. Besides these sources, you'll want to meet people at audiovisual production companies, since these people are always looking for dependable songwriters and musicians to enhance their products.

You'll increase your chances of getting the job if you play several instruments. Synthesizers in particular can add a lot to an AV soundtrack. You can, of course, go into a studio with musicians you've hired, but your personal profit margin will suffer.

Since the musical bed is strictly background in an AV production, be careful about overwriting and overplaying. Respect the power of silence to emphasize points being made either with pictures or by the speaker.

AV soundtracks pay well, typically $200-1,000 for local projects. And local AV writing credits can be your ticket to working for national audiovisual companies. Check the "Audiovisual Companies" section of the Yellow Pages for names of AV firms in your town. Also check the Audiovisual Firms section in this book for AV firm listings that include specifics on submitting your material.

## Writing for Local Performers

Whether you're interested in writing pop, country, rock, religious, or any other kind of music, it's wise to begin testing your product in your own community. Local outlets such as concert halls, nightclubs, schools, and churches and other organizational groups give you the chance to gather vital feedback from the public about your material.

You probably won't receive any money for material you write for these local markets. But if you want to eventually place your songs with recording artists, publishers, record companies, or artist managers, you can increase your chances of success by contacting local musicians and singers in nightclubs and giving them lyric sheets and/or tapes of your songs for them to perform. Then, while listening to your songs being performed, ask yourself the following questions:

1. How does the audience respond to my song?
2. Does the audience response equate with the mood I'm trying to create?
3. If your song is written of the popular music market, is the hook as strong and catchy as those of copy songs the band is playing?
4. Is the tempo and feel what I had in mind? Or is the band overplaying in parts and underplaying in others, speeding up or slowing down, until the integrity of my song is lost?

Remember as you answer these questions that you are not judging the band but *your* material. This is a testing ground for your songs, an opportunity for you to elicit feedback of your material from the audience, the band, and even (if you're honest) from yourself. This is all to help you when you're ready to record and mail or hand-carry tapes to publishers, artists or record companies.

Of course, there's always the chance that the local band singing your song will garner a recording contract. That would be fortunate, but don't count on it happening. Use audience reaction to help you focus your songwriting and recording production abilities.

## Writing for the Musical Theater

Writing musicals is a wholly distinct style of writing, but the same basic steps of beginning in your own home town and building a reputation before trying to market your material on the national level is recommended. Your markets are high school and college drama departments, and community, children's, church and other organizational theater groups. Like writing popular music for local musicians, theatrical writing on the local level pays little if any money. If you receive any money, it'll be a modest payment for each performance of the play, or a small percentage of ticket sales.

"My first two shown were children's musicals," one songwriter told me. "I had taken my own kid to one of these shows, and I thought, 'Hey, I could do that!' Working with those kids was a blast, but I didn't get paid anything."

This is the way of local theater. You must be willing to write for free in order to accumulate newspaper reviews, which, when sent with query letters or complete scripts to the producers listed in the Play Producers & Publishers section of *Songwriter's Market*, will turn heads and open doors. For now, your aim should be to compile reviews of your works. Naturally, all this time writing for local theaters will allow your talent to mature. You'll learn the ins and outs of theater production, and how to discipline yourself to write, write, write. Here are 10 suggestions for launching your theatrical writing career:

1. *Drown yourself in musicals.* Analyze what elements make a hit, and what makes a flop. On trips to the nearest big city, catch a show. Compare full-blown productions with the high school musical down the street. Often, bigger isn't better.

2. *Involve yourself with a theatrical company or department.* This practical experience will give you a sense of what ideas work and why, and how much is realistically possible for small theaters to handle. Getting involved now will also give you your first contacts when you're ready to submit a manuscript.

3. *Start now.* Jot down ideas and plots. What is it that you want to say? How many characters will you need? What will the moral (the take-away) be?

4. *The songs belong to the story.* The story doesn't belong to the songs! Your songs must be an integral, vital part of the story, not just an enhancement.

5. *Write what you know.* Aim for basic emotions and experiences that the audience will be able to relate to. Don't be afraid to research your subjects—realism is a fundamental of a good play.

6. *Keep costs down.* Plan and write with small budgets in mind. You're not on Broadway. You're aiming for colleges, dinner theaters and community centers. Keep casting to a minimum, and arrange the music so that a small combo can make it sound right.

7. *Write simple lyrics.* Your songs don't have to be profound ideological statements. The great majority of hits are themes on love.

8. *Invite a broad acceptance.* A play is an attempt at communication. To limit your potential audience limits the play's chance to get your message across (and limits the chance for making any money).

9. *The play should be able to stand alone.* It's fun to get caught up in props and special effects aimed at awing the audience, but you can't disguise a flop, no matter how fancy the decoration.

10. *Stay in tune with the industry.* The Theater Communications Group publishes a list called Information for Playwrights (355 Lexington Ave., New York NY 10017). You can also get useful information by joining the American Theatre Association (ATA, 1029 Vermont Ave. NW, Washington DC 20005), which publishes various theater and membership directories; and the Dramatist's Guild (234 W. 44th St., New York NY 10036), which publishes a newsletter that covers, as do the other periodicals mentioned here, contests, producers, markets and trends.

## The Future

The most revolutionary trend in composing and songwriting is electronics. Digitally-encoded synthesizers, coupled with microcomputers and piano keyboards, are fast becoming more affordable. For local songwriters, whether writing for the theater, local performers, audiovisual agencies or businesses, or writing for the jingle market, these new instruments will allow the writer to create the whole product without hiring musicians or renting studio time. And besides saving money, they offer the songwriter a new time-efficient way to compose and arrange. All you'll need is creativity, and the initiative to tap the song markets right in your own home town.

# The Markets

## Music Publishers

Music publishers represent the largest single market for songwriters. The reason is simple: songs are the music publisher's business. The publisher is the songwriter's connection in the music business, the middle man who has the contacts and the know-how to put your songs to work. The music industry relies on publishers to supply a steady flow of fresh, creative material. The publisher constantly "shops" songs to the A&R directors of record companies, to independent producers, and even directly to recording artists, getting cuts on new songs and covers on those that have been recorded.

The publisher not only places songs. He also takes care of the business end of publishing: song registration, demo-making, lead sheet preparation, and mechanical royalty payments to the songwriter. The publisher's handling of these time-consuming but necessary functions frees the songwriter to spend more time in his creative function of writing songs.

The importance of the music publisher to both amateur and seasoned songwriters cannot be overstated. Smart publishers are always on the lookout not just for a terrific song, but for talented songwriters who can continue to supply their catalog with marketable material. If a publisher sees potential in your songs he can work with you to nurture your talent—making suggestions, pointing out your weaknesses and strengths, teaming you with a co-writer, and encouraging you through periods of self-doubt about your abilities as a writer. (See the Close-up of hit songwriter Mike Reid in this section for more on the important role his publisher, Milsap Music, has played in his career.)

If a publisher has enough money in his budget and enough faith in your songs, he may even offer you an exclusive songwriting contract and pay you periodic advances against future royalties your songs might generate. For information on contracts between publisher and songwriter, see "Contracts" in the Appendix of this book.

If there is a trend today, it is that, no matter what their preference in types of music, publishers demand quality. Today's publisher looks for strong lyrics and well-constructed melodies, songs that keep the listener's attention for more than a few seconds, songs that a person will hear on the radio once or twice, then whistle or sing on his way to buy the records.

Many of today's publishers are looking for songs with "crossover" potential—ones that are not readily classified as rock or country or R&B, for instance. Such songs are not only easier for a publisher to place (more markets), but, once recorded, they generate greater income to both publisher and songwriter through increased airplay, more live performances, and a higher number of record sales.

Many publishers, however, are open to specialized types of music such as Spanish, reggae, punk rock, and new wave; this year we're seeing requests for rapper and techno-pop. Some publishers are even looking for music as specialized as polkas, waltzes, old-time country, novelty songs and more. Even disco, which has been declared dead by some companies, is still in demand by others. Christian music, especially contemporary Christian songs with special appeal to teenagers and young adults, continues to be increasingly popular with publishers. (See the Close-up of multi-award-winning songwriter/singer Amy Grant in this section.)

This year our geographic marketplace for songs has expanded too. Appearing in this section for the first time—as well as in the Record Companies and Record Producers sections—are a number of companies located in England, Australia and New Zealand. Each has expressed a willingness to work with songwriters from the US; most already have worked successfully with US songwriters. Others indicate in their listings that they have not yet, but would be willing to listen to material from US songwriters. Listings for foreign publishers also state whether royalites are paid directly to US songwriters or through a US publishing affiliate (and some companies use either method, depending on individual circumstances).

The international music marketplace is more important today than ever before, and certainly one that aspiring songwriters should not overlook. Australian songwriter Steve Kipner, for instance, had a million-seller hit in Europe before becoming famous in the US for hits such as Olivia Newton-John's "Physical" (see the Close-up of Kipner in this section).

With so many options, your only problem will be which publishers to contact. Read each listing carefully. Notice what types of music they publish, what songs they've placed, and the names of the artists who've recorded them.

The geographic index at the end of this section will quickly refer you to publishers in Australia, England and New Zealand. It also lists, geographically, publishers in the US music centers of Los Angeles, Nashville and New York. Use this information to quickly locate publishers in those cities. Or use the index to make contacts and organize your itinerary before you travel to a music center so you can make the most of your valuable time while you are there.

To keep up week-by-week on which companies are publishing the hits, check charts in *Billboard* and *Cash Box*.

Some companies we contacted did not give us the information needed for a listing. The names of those companies appear at the very end of this section along with a synopsis of their reasons for not listing and a note on how to contact them.

Additional names and addresses of publishers can be found in the *Billboard International Buyer's Guide*, though it contains no submission information.

If there is a publisher whose name you can't find either among the listings in this section, or in the "Quiet Types" at the end of this section, see "How to Be a Music Market Detective" in the Appendix of this book. There you can learn how to successfully track down any publisher, record company, record producer, or even recording artist you think might be interested in your songs.

**ABLE MUSIC, INC.**, Box 308, Vansant VA 24656. Affiliates: Modoc Music and ASAI Records. Music publisher. BMI. Publishes 200 songs/year; publishes 50 new songwriters/year. Pays standard royalty. Pays staff writers $100/week plus royalties to develop new material.
**How to Contact:** Submit demo tape and lyric sheet. Prefers cassette with 3-6 songs on demo. SASE.
**Music:** Bluegrass, church/religious, C&W, MOR and top 40/pop. Recently published "Angel in Disguise" and "Your Song," recorded by Roy John Fuller (C&W).

**ACOUSTIC MUSIC, INC.**, Box 1546, Nashville TN 37202. (615)242-9198. Affiliates: Lawday Music Corp. (BMI), Daydan Music Corp. (ASCAP), and Allmusic Inc. (ASCAP). Administrator: Nancy Dunne. Music publisher. BMI. Publishes 35-50 songs/year. Pays standard royalties.
**How to Contact:** Call or write first, then submit demo tape and lyric sheet. Prefers 7½ ips reel-to-reel or cassette with 2-3 songs on demo. SASE. Reports in 1 month.

**Music:** C&W; folk; MOR and gospel. Recently published "Come to Me" (by Gene Price), recorded by Aretha Franklin; "Ready to Take My Chances" (by Dewayne Orender and Helen Cornelius), recorded by Oak Ridge Boys/MCA Records; "You've Got a Friend in Me" (by Lamar Morris and D. Orender), recorded by Faron Young/MCA Records; and "Holidays" (by D. Orender), recorded by Patti Page.

**\*ACE ADAMS MUSIC, ADAM PUERTAS MUSIC**, Box 214, Co. Op. City Station, Bronx NY 10475. (212)379-2593. Affiliates: Ace Adams Music (BMI), Adam Puertas (ASCAP), Billace Music (SESAC). A&R Directors: Joe or Ace Adams. Music publisher, record company and record producer. Member NMPA. Publishes 100 songs/year; publishes 12 new songwriters/year. Pays standard royalty.
**How to Contact:** Write or call first about your interest, arrange personal interview or submit demo tape and lyric sheet. Prefers 7½ ips or cassette with 4-8 songs on demo. SASE. Reports in 2 weeks.
**Music:** Mostly R&B, C&W and dance; also children's, progressive and top 40/pop. Recently published "Zoot Zoot Zoot" (by Ace Adams), recorded by Tiny Tim/Ra Jo Records (children's/Christmas); and "Honky Tonk" (by Ace Adams), recorded by Roy Clarke, James Brown/King Records (dance).

**ALDOUS DEMIAN PUBLISHING, LTD.**, Radio City Station, Box 1348, New York NY 10101. (212)375-2639, (212)824-7842. Vice President: Harold Weber. Music publisher, record company, record producer, management firm and record distributor. Member New York Music Task Force, Inc. Publishes 50 songs/year; publishes 6 new songwriters/year. Pays standard royalty.
**How to Contact:** Submit demo tape and lyric sheet. Prefers "best quality metal or chrome" cassette with 3-10, "preferably 5" songs on demo. "Include resume, photo (if possible) and brief statement of goals." SASE. Reports in 4-6 weeks.
**Music:** C&W, dance-oriented, easy listening, folk, gospel, jazz, MOR, progressive, Spanish, R&B, rock (specialty), top 40/pop and new wave. Recently published "Starting Fresh," "Classified" and "Executive on Display" (by Joe Meyers Dorf), recorded by Joe Yussi/Pear Records (rockabilly/trilogy); "Don't You Know I Love You?" (by Tommy Acosta), recorded by Paul Ferrar/Pear Records (pop/MOR); "Angel In Black Leather" (by Phyllis Lee), recorded by Phyllis Lee and Lightning Force/Orange Records; "J Train" (by Don Huston), recorded by Dawn Huston & Campaign featuring River; and "Rock & Roll Crucifix" (by T. Acosta), recorded by T. Acosta/Acosmic-Orange Records (10-song rock opera).

**\*ALEPH-BAZE MUSIC & STRANGELAND MUSIC**, 7419 Clybourn Ave., Sun Valley CA 91352. (213)765-2774. Executive Vice President: Raymond Jarr. Music publisher. ASCAP, BMI. Publishes 50 songs/year; publishes 5 new songwriters/year. Pays standard royalty.
**How to Contact:** Submit demo tape and lyric sheet. Prefers cassette with 2-6 songs on demo. SASE. Reports in 1 month.
**Music:** Mostly easy listening; also C&W, gospel, Spanish, R&B, rock (country), soul and top 40/pop. Recently published "You Inspire Me" (by Raymond Soular), recorded by R. Soular/Kapri Records (gospel); "Love Is the Only Thing You Need" (by R. Soular); and "Fun Fun Fun" (by R. Shaw), both recorded by Angela Shaw (soft rock).
**Tips:** "The song must have a good story and a good melody—something different to tell the public."

**ALEXIS**, Box 532, Malibu CA 90265. (213)858-7282. Affiliates: Marvelle (BMI), Lou-Lee (BMI) and D.R. Music (ASCAP). President: Lee Magid. Music publisher, record company, and record and video producer. ASCAP. Member AIMP. Publishes 40 songs/year; publishes 5 new songwriters/year. Pays standard royalty.
**How to Contact:** Submit by mail demo tape and lyric sheet. Prefers cassette with 1-3 songs on demo. "Try to make demo as clear as possible—guitar or piano should be sufficient. A full rhythm and vocal demo is always better." SASE. Reports in 1 month.
**Music:** Bluegrass, blues, church/religious, C&W, dance-oriented, folk, gospel, jazz, Spanish and R&B. Recently published "Jesus Is Just Alright" (by Art Reynolds), recorded by Doobie Brothers/WB Records (rock gospel), "Something About the South" (by Al Abajian), recorded by Becky Bishop/CMI Records (rhythm rock), "This Ole Man of Mine" (by B. Bishop), recorded by Becky Bishop/LMI Records (rock-a-billy); and "Don't You Know" (by Bobby Worth), recorded by Della Reese and Jerry Vale.

**ALJONI MUSIC CO.**, Box 18918, Los Angeles CA 90018. (213)935-7277. Affiliate: Hallmarque Musical Works, Ltd. (ASCAP). General Manager: Al Hall, Jr. Music publisher and record producer. BMI. Publishes 12 songs/year; publishes 4 new songwriters/year. Pays standard royalty.
**How to Contact:** Submit demo tape and lyric sheet. Prefers 7½ ips reel-to-reel or cassette with 5-10 songs on demo. "Songs should have good melody, slick lyrics, nice chord progressions, etc." Does not return unsolicited material. Reports in 1 month.
**Music:** Jazz, R&B, rock (soft), soul and top 40/pop. Recently published "You're Gonna Lose Me" (by

J. Morrisette, C. Faulkner and A. Hall, Jr.), recorded by Freddie Hubbard/Fantasy Records (R&B); "I'm Yours" (by C. McDonald and A. Hall, Jr.), recorded by F. Hubbard/Fantasy Records (jazz/pop); and "Bip Bam" (by William Brown), recorded by Bill Brown/Brownstone Records (R&B/pop).

**AL-KRIS MUSIC**, Box 4185, Youngstown OH 44515. (216)793-7295. Professional Manager: Richard Hahn. Music publisher, record company and record producer. BMI. Publishes 8 songs/year; publishes 4 new songwriters/year. Pays standard royalty.
**How to Contact:** Query letter first. Submit demo tape and lyric sheet. Prefers cassette with 3-5 songs on demo. SASE. Reports in 3 weeks.
**Music:** Children's, C&W, folk, gospel, MOR and top 40/pop. Recently published "Prom Night" (by Don Yalleck), recorded by the B-Minors/Ikon Records; "Teach Me Lovely Lady" (by Hahn), recorded by Jim Stack/Peppermint Records (C&W); and "Help Me I'm Falling" (by Hahn), recorded by Kirsti Manna/Genuine Records.
**Tips:** "Submission package must be neat and the demo tape must be of decent quality."

\***ALPHA-ROBINSON MUSIC**, 19176 Mitchell, Detroit MI 48234. (313)893-9370. President: Juanita Robinson. Music publisher. ASCAP. Publishes 6 songs/year. Pays standard royalty.
**How to Contact:** Submit demo tape and lyric sheet. Prefers cassette with 2-4 songs on demo. SASE. Reports in 1 month; "longer if we're out of town."
**Music:** Mostly top 40/pop; also MOR and R&B.

**ALTERNATIVE DIRECTION MUSIC PUBLISHERS**, Box 3278, Station D, Ottawa, Ontario, Canada K1P 6H8. (613)820-6066. President and Director of Publishing: David Stein. Music publisher. Estab. 1980. PROCAN. Pays standard royalty. "I am flexible with a writer who has previous success. I attempt to publish between 6-10 new writers a year."
**How to Contact:** Submit demo tape. Prefers cassette with 2-4 songs on demo. SASE if sent within Canada; American songwriters send SAE and $1 for postage and handling. Reports in 6 weeks.
**Music:** Top 40, rock, pop, electro-pop, funk/R&B, country and crossover.
**Tips:** "Before sending out your songs ask yourself whether your hooks and lyrics are as strong as what you hear on the radio. If they are not, go back and rewrite or rework the song. Also make certain the song sounds "contemporary."

\***AMALGAMATED TULIP CORP.**, 117 W. Rockand Rd., Box 615, Libertyville IL 60048. (312)362-4060. President: Perry Johnson. Music publisher, record company and record producer. BMI. Publishes 20 songs/year; publishes 20 new songwriters/year. Pays standard royalty.
**How to Contact:** Submit demo tape and lyric sheet or write about your interest. Prefers cassette with 3-5 songs on demo. SASE. Reports in 1 month.
**Music:** Mostly hard rock; also top 40, MOR; blues, C&W and easy listening progressive. Recently published "This Feels Like Love To Me," by Sermay (top 40); "All He Wants," by Mike Boone (progressive); and "How Is It a Pretty Girl Like You Has Never Been Kissed," by Chacksfield (progressive).
**Tips:** "We're aggressive and work a song."

**AMERICAN BROADCASTING MUSIC, INC.**, 4151 Prospect Ave., Los Angeles CA 90027. (213)663-3311, ext. 1389 or 1557. Affiliate: ABC/Circle Music, Inc. (BMI). Director: Georgett Studnicka. Music publisher. ASCAP. Member NMPA. Publishes 30 songs/year; publishes 6 new songwriters/year. Pays standard royalty. Sometimes hires staff writers for TV themes.
**How to Contact:** Submit demo tape and lyric sheet or arrange interview to play demo tape. Prefers cassette with 2-4 songs on demo. SASE. Reports in 3 weeks.
**Music:** C&W, easy listening, jazz, MOR and top 40/pop. "Our copyrights number over 2,000 at this time, but consist mainly of TV themes."

\***AMERICAN ENTERTAINMENT GENERAL**, Suite 503, 8730 Sunset Blvd., Los Angeles CA 90069. (213)652-1230. Professional Manager: John Diego. Music publisher and personal management company. Estab. 1981. Member AIMP, CCC. Pays standard royalty.
**How to Contact:** Submit demo tape and lyric sheet. Prefers cassette with 1-3 songs on demo. SASE. Reports in 3 weeks.
**Music:** Mostly C&W and pop; also MOR, Spanish, R&B, rock (soft) and top 40.

\***AMERICUS MUSIC**, Box 314, Hendersonville TN 37075. (615)824-8308. Affiliate: Stars and Stripes Music (BMI). President: D.L. Riis. Music publisher. ASCAP. Publishes 15-20 songs/year; publishes 6 new songwriters/year. Pays standard royalty.
**How to Contact:** Submit demo tape and lyric sheet. Prefers cassette with 1-5 songs on demo. SASE. Reports in 3 weeks.
**Music:** Mostly C&W; also bluegrass, easy listening, gospel, R&B and top 40/pop.

## Music Publishers 15

*AMI, 111 Free Hill Rd., Hendersonville TN 87075. (615)822-6786. Affiliate: Bridger Publishing. Vice President: Kenneth Bridger. Music publisher, record company and record producer. BMI. Publishes 30 songs/year; publishes 24 new songwriters/year. Pays standard royalty.
**How to Contact:** Submit demo tape and lyric sheet. Prefers cassette with 2-5 songs on demo. SASE. Reports in 3 weeks.
**Music:** Mostly C&W; also classical, easy listening and gospel.

**AMIRON MUSIC**, 20531 Plummer St., Chatsworth CA 91311. (213)998-0443. Affiliate: Aztex Productions. Manager: A. Sullivan. Music publisher, record company, record producer and manager. ASCAP. Publishes 2-4 songs/year; publishes 2-4 new songwriters/year. Pays standard royalty.
**How to Contact:** Submit demo tape and lyric sheet. Prefers 7 1/2 ips reel-to-reel or cassette with any number songs on demo. SASE. Reports in 3 weeks.
**Music:** C&W, easy listening, MOR, progressive, R&B, rock and top 40/pop. Recently published "Midnite Flite" (by Frank and C. Ball), recorded by Papillon/AKO Records (MOR); "Better Run" (by G. Bonar), recorded by Newstreet/Dorn Records (rock); and "Look In My Eyes" (by P. Newstreet), recorded by 7 artists and released in Australia.
**Tips:** Send songs with "good story-lyrics."

*ANDERSONG MUSIC, 165 Wolverhampton Rd., Sedgley, DY31QR, England. 44-09073-2211. Affiliate: Heavy Metal Music. Managing Director: Paul Birch. Music publisher, record company and record producer. MCPS, PRS, PPL. Member BPI and IFPI. Publishes 150 songs/year; publishes 50 new songwriters/year. Pays negotiable royalty.
**How to Contact:** Submit demo tape. Prefers 7 1/2 or 15 ips reel-to-reel, cassette or record with 1 song to a complete album on the demo. Does not return unsolicited material. Reports in 1 month.
**Music:** Rock (all types). Recently published songs written by Frank Bornemann and Zeeb Parkes, recorded by Eloy/Heavy Metal Worldwide Records and Witchfinder/Heavy Metal Records.
**Tips:** "Send a product that is finished or as near finished as possible."

**ANDUSTIN MUSIC**, Box 669, Woodstock NY 12498. (914)679-6069. Affiliates: Graph (ASCAP) and Small Fortune (BMI). Contact: Professional Manager. Music publisher and record producer. ASCAP. Publishes 20 songs/year; publishes 2 new songwriters/year. Pays standard royalty.
**How to Contact:** Submit demo tape and lyric sheet. Prefers cassette with 1-3 songs on demo. SASE. Reports in 3 weeks.
**Music:** Rock and top 40/pop. Recently published "Rock And Roll Love Song" (by Tim Moore), recorded by the Bay City Rollers (rock); "Second Avenue" (by Tim Moore), recorded by Art Garfunkel (rock); and "Steal Away" and "Saturday Night" (by Robbie Dupuis), recorded by R. Dupree/Oozle Records (rock).

**ANODE MUSIC**, Box 11967, Houston TX 77016. (713)694-2971. President: Freddie Kober. Music publisher, record company, record producer, and recording studio (Honeybee). BMI. Publishes 10 songs/year; publishes 2 new songwriters/year. Pays standard royalty.
**How to Contact:** Submit demo tape and lyric sheet. Prefers cassette with 1-3 songs on demo. SASE. Reports in 2 weeks.
**Music:** Gospel and soul. Recently published "That Means So Much to Me" (by Freddie Kober), recorded by Mel Starr, Z.Z. Hill/Freko Records (love ballad); "My Baby Can" (by Freddie Kober), recorded by Mel Starr/Freko Records (disco); and "Shake the Funk Out of It" (by Freddie Kober), recorded by Contage'us (disco).
**Tips:** "Songs should have good lyrics and melody; if fast, a strong bass line."

**APON PUBLISHING CO.**, Box 3082, Steinway Station, Long Island City, NY 11103. Manager: Don Zemann. Music publisher, record company and record producer. ASCAP. Publishes 250 songs/year. Pays according to special agreements made with individual songwriters.
**How to Contact:** Call first about your interest, then submit demo tape and lyric sheet. Prefers 15 ips reel-to-reel or cassette with 1-12 songs on demo. SASE. Reports in 1 month.
**Music:** Classical, dance-oriented, easy listening, folk and international. Recently published "Polka Fever" (by Slawko Kunst), recorded by Czech Brass/Apon Records (polkas); "Russian Gypsy Melodies" (by Sandor Lakatos), recorded by Hungarian Gypsy Orchestra/Apon Records (gypsy tunes); and "Czech Songs" (by Alojz Skolka), recorded by Budvarka Ensemble/Apon Records (folk/pop).
**Tips:** "We are sub-publishers for pop music from overseas."

**APPLE-GLASS MUSIC**, A division of American Music Company, Box 8604, Madison WI 53708. Professional Manager: Daniel W. Miller. Music publisher and recording studio (Legend). BMI. Publishes 10-25 songs/year. Pays standard royalty.
**How to Contact:** Submit demo tape and lyric sheet. Prefers "professionally produced" 7 1/2 ips reel-to-

reel or cassette with 1-3 songs on demo. "We suggest songwriter's name, address and song titles be typed on labels affixed to tape reel (or cassette) and box for identification." SASE. Reports in 6 months. "Our contracts do not feature reversion clauses and we do not offer advances on unearned royalties."
**Music:** Bluegrass, C&W, polka, gospel and top 40/rock.

**APRIL/BLACKWOOD MUSIC CANADA, LTD.**, 1121 Leslie St., Don Mius, Ontario, Canada L1U 2V8. (416)447-3311. Affiliate: Worldwide Corp. Copyright Administrator: Sandra Carruthers. Music publisher. CAPAC, PROCAN. Member CARAS.
**How to Contact:** Submit demo tape and lyric sheet. Prefers cassette with 2-5 songs on demo. SASE. Reports in 2-3 weeks.
**Music:** C&W, easy listening, MOR, rock and top 40/pop. Recently published "Physical" (by S. Kipner and T. Shaddick), recorded by Olivia Newton-John (MOR); "Believe It or Not" (by Mike Post), recorded by Joey Scarbury (MOR); and "Turn Me Loose" (by Paul Dean and Mike Reno), recorded by Loverboy (rock).

**ARCADE MUSIC CO.**, Arzee Recording Co., 3010 N. Front St., Philadelphia PA 19133. (215)426-5682. Affiliates: Valleybrook (ASCAP), Rex Zario Music (BMI) and Seabreeze Music (BMI). President: Rex Zario. Music publisher, booking agency and record company. ASCAP. Publishes 100-150 songs/year. Pays standard royalty.
**How to Contact:** Submit demo tape and lead or lyric sheet. Prefers 7½ or 15 ips reel-to-reel or cassette with 5-10 songs on demo. SASE. Reports in 1 month.
**Music:** Bluegrass, C&W, easy listening, folk, gospel, rock 'n roll (fifties style) and top 40/pop. Recently published "Why Do I Cry Over You" (by DeKnight and Keefer), recorded by Bill Haley/Arzee Records (C&W); "Hand Clap For Jesus" (by Rodney Harris), recorded by Gospel Blenders/Arzee Records (gospel); and "I Couldn't See The Tears" (by Miller and Marcin), recorded by Dee Dee Marcin/Arzee Records (C&W).

**ARISTA MUSIC PUBLISHING GROUP**, (formerly Arista-Interworld), 8304 Beverly Blvd., Los Angeles CA 90048. (213)852-0771. Affiliates: Arista Music, Inc. (ASCAP), Careers Music, Inc. (BMI), and A-Plus Music, Inc. (SESAC). Contact: General Professional Manager: Linda Blum. Professional Managers: Judy Stakee, Tom Sturges. Music publisher. BMI and ASCAP. Member NMPA. Hires staff writers. Pays per individual contracts.
**How to Contact:** Submit demo tape and *neat* lyric and lead sheets. Prefers cassette with 2 songs on demo. SASE imperative. Reports in 1 month, "depending on backlog of submissions."
**Tips:** "All material is listened to, so if it's a hit!. . ."

**ART AUDIO PUBLISHING CO.**, 9706 Cameron St., Detroit MI 48212. (313)893-3406. President: Albert M. Leigh. Professional Manager: Dolores M. Leigh. Music publisher and record producer. BMI. Pays standard royalty.
**How to Contact:** Submit demo tape, lead sheet and lyric sheet. Prefers cassette with 1-3 songs on demo. SASE. Reports in 2 weeks.
**Music:** Disco, easy listening, R&B, soul, rock, C&W, gospel and top 40/pop.
**Tips:** "Basically we are interested only in new product with a strong title; a love story expressive of soul, excitement, taste; heavy lead singer delivering emotional sound. All lyrics are up-front, words clearly understandable."

**ASC MUSIC CO.**, 168 Water St., Binghamton NY 13901. (607)722-7259. President: David Lebous. Music publisher. ASCAP.
**How to Contact:** Query by mail. Prefers cassette with minimum 3 songs on demo. SASE. Reports in 3 weeks.
**Music:** C&W, MOR, rock and top 40/pop.

**ASILOMAR/DREENA MUSIC**, 80 8th Ave., New York NY 10011. (212)757-8805. Vice President and Creative Manager: Ron Beigel. Music publisher. ASCAP and BMI. Member NMPA. Publishes 100 songs/year, publishes 15 new songwriters/year. Pays standard royalty.
**How to Contact:** Submit demo tape and "always include lead or lyric sheet." Prefers cassette with 1-3 songs on demo. SASE. Reports in 1 month.
**Music:** C&W, easy listening, R&B, rock and top 40/pop. Recently published "Still in Saigon" (by Dan Daley), recorded by Charlie Daniels/Epic Records (rock), "Goodbye Sweet Virginia" (by B. Minasian and B. Rich) and "Reins of Love" (by D. McCarthy and D. Miller), recorded by Rodney Lay (country rock).
**Tips:** "Make sure the demo is clear and clean, write with the 'top ten' sound in mind."

## Music Publishers

**ATJACK MUSIC**, 4050 Buckingham Rd., Los Angeles CA 90008. (213)290-2262. Music publisher and record producer. BMI.
**How to Contact:** Submit demo tape and lyric sheet. Prefers cassette. SASE. Reports in 3 weeks.
**Music:** Gospel, jazz, R&B, soul and top 40/pop.

**ATTIC PUBLISHING GROUP**, Suite 3, 98 Queen St. E., Ontario, Canada M5C 1S6. (416)862-0352. Affiliates: Pondwater Music (CAPAC), Abovewater Music (PROCAN), Big Bay Music (PROCAN), Downchild Music (CAPAC) and Triumphsongs (CAPAC). President: Al Mair. Music publisher and record company. Publishes 50 songs/year; publishes 15 new songwriters/year. "We publish recording artists only—no exclusive songwriters." Pays standard royalty.
**How to Contact:** Call professional manager first about your interest, then submit demo tape and lyric sheet. Prefers cassette with 1-4 songs on demo. SAE and International Reply Coupons. Reports in 3 weeks or longer.
**Music:** Blues, MOR, rock and top 40/pop. Recently published "The Homecoming" (by Hagood Hardy), recorded by H. Hardy/Attic Records (pop instrumental); "Shot Gun Blues" and "Almost" (by Donny Walsh), recorded by The Blues Brothers/WEA Records (blues); and all songs by rock groups Triumph, Godoo, Anvil, Tios Bopcats, Chain Reaction, and Teenage Head.

**ATV MUSIC CORP.**, 6255 Sunset Blvd., Hollywood CA 90028. (213)462-6933. Affiliates: Maklen Music (BMI), Welbeck Music (ASCAP), and Comet Music (ASCAP). Music publisher. BMI. Member NMTA, CCC, and Harry Fox Agency. Publishes hundreds of songs/year; publishes 4 new songwriters/year. Hires staff writers. Pays standard royalty.
**How to Contact:** Write or call first about your interest. Prefers cassette with 4 songs on demo. Refuses unsolicited material. SASE. Reports in 1 month.
**Music:** Bluegrass, blues, children's, church/religious, C&W, dance-oriented, easy listening, folk, gospel, jazz, MOR, progressive, R&B, rock, soul and top 40/pop. Recently published "Hit Me With Your Best Shot" (by Eddie Schwartz), recorded by Pat Benatar (rock); "He's So Shy" (by Cynthia Weil and Tom Snow), recorded by Pointer Sisters (R&B); and "Just Once" (by Barry Mann and C. Weil), recorded by Quincy Jones (R&B).
**Tips:** "Know what's charting. ATV is looking for songs that can be placed with people that are currently charting. Have had success with ballads. Lyrics must be good."

**ATV MUSIC CORP.**, 888 7th Ave., New York NY 10019. (212)977-5680. General Professional Manager: Marv Goodman. Music publisher.
**How to Contact:** Submit demo tape and lyric sheet. Prefers cassette with 2-3 songs on demo. SASE. Reports in 3 weeks.
**Music:** Rock and top 40/pop.

**ATV MUSIC CORP.**, 1217 16th Ave. S., Nashville TN 37212. (615)327-2753. Affiliates: Welbeck Music (ASCAP), Venice Music (BMI) and MacLen Music (BMI). General Manager: Byron Hill. Professional Manager: Bernard Walters or Barry Sanders. Music publisher. BMI, ASCAP. Member CMA, NARAS and NMPA. Pays standard royalties.
**How to Contact:** Arrange personal interview *only*; "do not mail tapes." Prefers cassette with 1-3 songs on demo.
**Music:** Mostly country and pop; also MOR, R&B, rock, soul and gospel. Recently published "Scarlet Fever" (by Dekle), recorded by Kenny Rogers/EMI/Liberty Records; "Touch Me" (by Al Downing), recorded by Tom Jones/Mercury Records; and "Lucille" (by A. Collins and R. Penninan), recorded by Waylon Jennings/RCA Records (all country).
**Tips:** "Be extremely selective. Submit material with hit single potential. Write strong ideas—be different."

**AUDIO ARTS PUBLISHING**, 5617 Melrose Ave., Hollywood CA 90038. Affiliate: Madelon (BMI). Contact: Madelon Baker. Music publisher and record company. ASCAP. Member AIMP and NMPA. Pays standard royalty.
**How to Contact:** Submit cassette and lyric sheet with 1-4 songs on demo. SASE.
**Music:** Country, gospel, soul and top 40/pop.

***AURA RECORDS & MUSIC LTD.**, 1 Kendall Place, London, W1H 3AG, England. 44-01-486-5288. Managing Director: Aaron Sixx. Music publisher and record company. Member MCPS, PRS, Phonographic Performance Ltd. Publishes 25 songs/year; publishes 3 new songwriters/year. Pays standard royalty; royalties to US songwriters through US publishing affiliate.
**How to Contact:** Submit demo tape and lyric sheet. Prefers cassette with 2-10 songs on demo. SAE and IRC. Reports in 1 month.

**Music:** Progressive, rock and top 40/pop. Recently published "Graveyard Groove" (by Krupa/Cheri), recorded by the Revillos/Epic Records, Aura Records (top 40/pop); "God Given Right" (by Lee Fardon), recorded by Lee Fardon/Aura Records (rock); and "Drama of Exile" (by Nico), recorded by Nico/Aura Records (progressive).

**AUTOGRAPH MUSIC**, 601 E. Blacklidge Dr., Tucson AZ 85705. (602)882-9016. Professional Manager: Joe Bidwell. Music publisher. BMI. Publishes 20 songs/year; publishes 4 new songwriters/year. Pays standard royalty.
**How to Contact:** Submit demo tape and lyric sheet. Prefers cassette with 1-3 songs on demo. Returns unsolicited material only with SASE. Reports in 3 weeks.
**Music:** C&W and top 40/pop. Recently published "Time" (by E. Forrest), recorded by Two Horse/BIRC Records (Latin rock); Road To Ruin" and "I Can Still Remember" (by D. Stitt), recorded by Rick Skinner/Bug Records (C&W); "I Live On Heartaches" (by D. Stitt), recorded by Kenny Durell/Custom Records (C&W), also recorded; by Eddie Golden/BIRC Records (C&W); and "Josie's Her Name" (by D. Stitt), recorded by D. Stitt/BIRC Records (C&W).
**Tips:** "Songs with strong hooks or themes most likely to be signed."

**AVILO MUSIC**, 880 NE 71st St., Miami FL 33138. (305)759-1405. Affiliates: Oliva Music (SESAC). President: Carlos Oliva. Music publisher, record company and record producer. BMI. Member NARM. Publishes 70 songs/year; publishes 10 new songwriters/year. Pays standard royalty.
**How to Contact:** Submit demo tape and lyric sheet. Prefers cassette with any number songs on demo. SASE. Reports in 2 weeks.
**Music:** Dance-oriented, Spanish and rock. Recently published "Pa-Pun" (by O. Valdes), recorded by Group Alma/Alhambra Records (salsa/rock); "Se Que Pretendes" (by M. Palacio), recorded by Judge's Nephews/Common Cause Records (ballad); and "La Diferencia," recorded by Mary Pacheco.
**Tips:** "Songs should have a strong hook, simple melody and sense-making lyrics."

*****AXBAR PRODUCTIONS**, Box 12353, San Antonio TX 78212. (512)735-3322. Affiliate: Axbar Productions and Axe Handle Music (ASCAP). Business Manager: Joe Scates. Music publisher, record company, record producer and record distributors. BMI. Member CMA. Publishes 30-40 songs/year; publishes 11 new songwriters/year. Pays standard royalty.
**How to Contact:** Submit demo tape and lyric sheet or arrange personal interview. Prefers 7½ ips or cassette with 1-5 songs on demo. SASE. Reports ASAP, but "we hold the better songs for more detailed study."
**Music:** Mostly country; also blues, MOR and rock (soft). Recently published "I Get High on Music" (by M. Nesler), recorded by Mark Nesler/AXBAR Records (country); "Falling Back in Your Arms" (by Jerry Blanton), recorded by Carla Neet/AXBAR Records (country/pop); and "Heaven on My Mind" (by Daryl Hall/Ray Sanders), recorded by Mark Chesnutt/AXBAR Records (country).

**B.C. ENTERPRISES OF MEMPHIS, INC.**, 726 E. McLemore Ave., Memphis TN 38106. (901)947-2553. Affiliates: Colca Music (BMI), Insight Music (BMI), and Epitome Music (BMI). Administrative Assistant: Nat Engleberg. Music publisher, record company and record producer. BMI. Publishes 10 songs/year; publishes 1 new songwriter/year. Pays standard royalty.
**How to Contact:** Write first about your interest. Prefers cassette with 1-3 songs on demo. SASE. Reports in 1 week.
**Music:** Blues, black gospel, R&B and soul. Recently published "Selfrising Flour" (by Byron and Brandon Catron), recorded by Ironing Board Sam (blues); and "You Must Be Gravity" (by Claudette Catron), recorded by Sir Henry Ivy/Brian Manor Records (R&B).

*****B & D PUBLISHING**, Box 838, Enterprise AL 36331. Vice President: Michael Bryan. Music publisher, record company and record producer. BMI. Pays standard royalty.
**How to Contact:** Write first about your interest; submit demo tape and lyric sheet. Prefers cassette with 3-5 songs on demo. SASE. Reports in one month.
**Music:** Mostly rock, top 40, R&B; also MOR and rockabilly. Recently published "Radio Free Boogie" (by Lenon Xenon), recorded by Grasshoppers (rock/funk).

**BABY HUEY MUSIC**, 2308 Elliott Ave., Nashville TN 37204. (615)834-3481. Affiliate: Krimson Hues Music (BMI). Professional Manager: Mark Stephan Hughes. Music publisher. ASCAP. Member NSA, GMA and IMU. Publishes 30 songs/year; publishes 10 new songwriters/year. Pays standard royalty.
**How to Contact:** Submit demo tape and typewritten lyric sheet. Cassette only with 3 songs on demo. SASE. Reports in 4 weeks.
**Music:** C&W, gospel, MOR, R&B, rock and top 40/pop. Recently published "Everything's Not

## Music Publishers 19

Enough" (by Rolle, Michelli, Sharp and Hughes), recorded by Frankie Sanchez/Charta Records (MOR); and "Lady Like You" (by Ray and Hughes), recorded by Bill Schleuter/LaJon Records (ballad).
**Tips:** "We are looking for strong singles with good catchy hooks and tight lyrics. Submit professional demo."

**BAL & BAL MUSIC PUBLISHING CO.**, Box 369, LaCanada CA 91011. (213)952-1242. President: Adrian Bal. Music publisher, record company and record producer. ASCAP. Member AGAC and AIMP. Publishes 2-4 songs/year; publishes 2 new songwriters/year. Pays royalty per AGAC contract.
**How to Contact:** Submit demo tape and lyric sheet. Prefers cassette with 3 songs on demo. SASE. Reports in 1 month.
**Music:** Mostly MOR; also blues, church/religious, C&W, easy listening, jazz, R&B, rock, soul and top 40/pop. Recently published "Los Angeles" (by Rich Martin), recorded by Bob Ryer/Bal Records (MOR); and "Song of the Pasadena Rose Parade" (by Jack Heinderich), recorded by B. Ryer/Bal Records (swing).
**Tips:** "Songs should be commercial; purchased by 9- to 18-year-old group."

**BAND OF ANGELS, INC.**, Suite 400, 1420 K St. NW, Washington DC 20005. (202)347-1420. Affiliate: Heaven's Gate Music (ASCAP). Director of Publishing: Yolanda McFarlane. Music publisher and record company. BMI. Member NMPA and BMA. Publishes 10-16 songs/year; publishes 3 new songwriters/year. Pays standard royalty.
**How to Contact:** Submit demo tape and lyric sheet. Prefers cassette with 3-6 songs on demo. "Include name, address and telephone number *on tape*." Reports in 2 weeks.
**Music:** Dance-oriented, R&B, soul and top 40/pop. Recently published "Remote Control" and "I Want It" (by N. Mann, B. Beard and C. Fortune), recorded by The Reddings/B.I.D. Records (R&B).

***BARSONGS LIMITED**, 4, Cheniston Gardens, Kensington, London, W8 6TQ, England. 44-01-937-2252. Music publisher and record producer. Estab. 1982. MCPS, PRS, MPA. Publishes 50 songs/year; publishes 3 new songwriters/year. Pays negotiable royalty.
**How to Contact:** Submit demo tape and lyric sheet. Prefers cassette with 1-4 songs on demo. SASE. Reports in 1 month.
**Music:** Mostly pop, rock and adult contemporary; also dance-oriented, jingles, progressive, R&B and soul. Recently published "Don't Take Away" (by J. Gregg), recorded by J. Gregg/Polydor Records (AOR/MOR); "It Should Have Been You" (by J. Gregg), recorded by Jonathan Gregg/Polydor Records (AOR); "Legends" and "Train Ride" (by K. McCulloch & A. Barson), recorded by Profit/Hansa Records (pop); and "To Hell With Him" (by Macaluso/Molinary), recorded by Taka Boom/PRT Records.
**Tips:** "We require strong melodies and good lyrics that are widely appealing, i.e., think globally, not only locally. Uptempo pop or ballads preferred. Don't kill your song by overproducing the demo tape."

**BARUTH MUSIC**, Suite 101, 8033 Sunset Blvd., Hollywood CA 90046. (213)840-0490. Branch office: 3628 W. 159th St., Cleveland OH 44111. (216)671-5302. Professional Manager: Jain Baruth. Music publisher, record company, record producer, management firm and promoter. ASCAP. Pays standard royalty.
**How to Contact:** Submit demo tape and lead sheet. Prefers cassette with 2-3 songs on demo. SASE. Reports in 4 weeks.
**Music:** Folk; progressive; R&B; rock; and top 40/pop. Recently published "Soothe Me" (by David Baruth), recorded by Quartz/Music Adventures Records (rock); "This Time to the End" (by Eddie Pecchio), recorded by Great Lakes Band/Music Adventures Records (pop); and "I'm So Positive" (by David Baruth), recorded by BBB/Music Adventures Records (inspirational)."

***BASS CLEF MUSIC**, 141 South Ave., Fanwood NJ 07023. (201)322-6226. Contact: Michael W. Thomas. Music publisher. Estab. 1981. BMI. Publishes 28 songs/year; publishes 2 new songwriters/year. Pays standard royalty.
**How to Contact:** Submit demo tape and lyric sheet. Prefers 7½ ips reel-to-reel or cassette with 2-8 songs on demo. SASE. Reports in 3 weeks.
**Music:** Mostly R&B, dance-oriented and top 40. Recently published "Do It" (by Mike "T"), recorded by Mike "T"/Golden Pyramid Records (rap); and "Wanna Dance" (by Mike "T"), recorded by Lavias/Golden Pyramid (soul/R&B).

**BEARCE PUBLISHING**, 7635 Telephone Rd., Leroy NY 14482. Contact: Kenny or Jim Bearce. Music publisher, record company and record producer. Estab. 1980. ASCAP. Publishes 25 songs/year; publishes 2 new songwriters/year. Pays standard royalty.
**How to Contact:** Submit demo tape and lyric sheet. Prefers 7½ ips reel-to-reel or cassette with 2-5

songs on demo. "Demo tape should be clean with lead vocal, piano or guitar, bass, and light percussion." SASE. Reports in 1 month.
**Music:** Children's, dance-oriented, MOR, rock (country), top 40/pop and new wave.

*****BEARSONGS**, 190 Monument Rd., Birmingham, B16 8UU, England. 44-021-454-7020. Professional Manager: Jim Simpson. Music publisher, record company and record producer. MCPS, PRS. Publishes 25 songs/year; publishes 2 new songwriters/year. Pays 60-70% of performance and mechanical royalties to songwriters; royalties paid directly to US songwriters.
**How to Contact:** Submit demo tape and lyric sheet. Prefers reel-to-reel or cassette with your "best" songs on demo. SAE and IRC. Reports in 2 weeks.
**Music:** Blues, jazz, R&B and soul.

*****BEAUTIFUL DAY MUSIC**, 15 Glenbury Lane, Brookville NY 11545. (516)626-9504. Branch: 22240 Schoenborn St., Canoga Park CA 91304. (213)883-4865. Contact: Tom Ingegno (New York); Mike Frenchik (California). Music publisher and record producer. BMI. Publishes 10-20 songs/year; publishes 4 new songwriters/year. Pays standard royalty.
**How to Contact:** Submit demo tape and lyric sheet. Prefers cassette with minimum of 3 songs on demo. SASE. Reports in 3 weeks.
**Music:** R&R and top 40/pop. Recently published "Breaking My Heart" (by Ingegno, Monaco and Frenchik); "Tonight" (by Fullerton); and "You Don't Remember Me" (by Ingregno), all recorded by Thrills (all R&R).

**BEE MOR MUSIC**, Suite 2129, 1100 Glendon, Los Angeles CA 90024. (213)208-7871. Affiliate: Pepper & Salt Music/ASCAP. Vice President and General Manager: Morey Alexander. Music publisher, record company, record producer and management firm. BMI. Member NARAS. Publishes 20-50 songs/year; publishes 5-10 new songwriters/year. Pays standard royalty.
**How to Contact:** Submit demo tape and lyric sheet. Prefers cassette with 4-8 songs on demo. Does not return unsolicited material. Reports in 1 week.
**Music:** Mostly R&B, country and pop; also blues, dance-oriented, jazz, soul and top 40. Recently published "Paradise Express" (by Mitch DeMattoff), recorded by Aurora Borealis/Red Hot Records (jazz fusion); "I Love You Mom" (by Ray Dewey and Jimmy George), recorded by R. Winters/Polygram Records (ballad); and "Fight for the Funk" (by R. Winters), recorded by R. Winters/Polygram Records (funk R&B).

**BEECHWOOD**, 6255 Sunset Blvd., Hollywood CA 90028. (213)469-8371. Affiliates: Screen Gems (BMI) and Cole Gems (ASCAP). Music publisher. BMI and ASCAP. Member NMPA. Publishes several songs/year. Hires staff writers.
**How to Contact:** Call first about your interest. Prefers cassette and lyric/lead sheet. Refuses unsolicited material. SASE. Reports in 1 month.
**Music:** MOR, rock and top 40/pop.

**BEECHWOOD MUSIC**, 1207 16th Ave. S., Nashville TN 37212. (615)320-7700. Music publisher. BMI, ASCAP. Not currently accepting outside material.

**BEECHWOOD MUSIC CORP.**, 1370 Avenue of the Americas, New York NY 10019. (212)489-6740. Professional Manager: Paul Tannen. Music publisher and record company (Capitol and EMI Records). BMI. Hires staff writers.
**How to Contact:** Call first about your interest to see if they are accepting material, then submit demo tape and lyric sheet. Prefers cassette with 1-3 songs on demo.
**Music:** All kinds.

**BELWIN-MILLS PUBLISHING CORP.**, 1776 Broadway, New York NY 10019. (212)245-1100. Affiliates: Deshon Music Inc. (BMI)/Mills Music (ASCAP), Belwin-Mills Publishing Corp. (ASCAP) and American Academy of Music (ASCAP). Professional Manager: Robin Feather. Member NMPA. Publishes 100 songs/year; publishes 15 new songwriters/year. Pays standard royalty.
**How to Contact:** Submit demo tape and lyric sheet. Prefers cassette with 1-3 songs on demo. SASE.
**Music:** Mostly top 40; also C&W, easy listening, MOR, progressive, R&B, rock, and pop. Recently published "Cynical Girl" (by Marshall Crenshaw), recorded by M. Crenshaw/Warner Bros. Records (pop/rock); "Caravan" (by Duke Ellington), recorded by Little Steven and the Disciples of Soul/EMI Records; "Sweet Lorraine" (by Burwell and Parish), recorded by Uriah Heep/Polygram Records; and "Shakin' All Over" (by J. Kidd), recorded by Lisa Bade/A&M Records.
**Tips:** "Submit the clearest sounding demo possible."

# Close-up

**Stan Hertzman**
Manager/Producer/Publisher

While working from 1962-1967 on a double major in marketing/management and psychology from the University of Cincinnati, Stan Hertzman was also working as part of a popular Cincinnati rock band. "I was just an average singer, guitar player and keyboardist," says Hertzman. "My real strength, even then, was in organization and business. I had much more interest in managing the band and in getting bookings."

When the person who was managing the Beatles offered Hertzman and his fellow band members an opportunity to move to New York City and record on Columbia Records, it was Hertzman who said no. "I just couldn't see dropping out of college and changing my lifestyle. That wasn't what I wanted. That's still not what I want. If I can't be in the music business and stay here in Cincinnati, I don't want to be in it at all."

Today as president of music conglomerate Hal Bernard Enterprises, Hertzman lives in Cincinnati but often travels to music centers—and non-music centers—to make contacts and represent the artists and songwriters he works with: Illinois-based Adrian Belew, Florida-based Danny Morgan, and up-and-coming avant-garde groups like The Raisins, The Young Invaders and The Adults.

Even with his busy schedule, Hertzman says he listens to every demo tape he receives—"boxes full"—often playing them on his car's tape deck while traveling. "The biggest mistake I see songwriters make on demos," says Hertzman, "is that they simply don't work hard enough. They try to slide by with mediocre tunes that are only whimsical attempts at songwriting, just hoping somebody out there will think it's great. What they should do is write a few songs and work on them until they really *are* great, instead of writing lots of tunes that are just average."

Hertzman admits songwriters are at a psychological disadvantage. "The music business is loaded with negative response, and it takes a very healthy-minded person to keep writing when his songs aren't getting recorded."

Don't let negative response slow you down, or positive response make you too confident advises Hertzman. "If one day fifty people say they hate your music, that doesn't necessarily mean you're not a good songwriter. And, if the next day fifty people say they love your music, that doesn't necessarily mean your songs are the best. Just keep writing—every day. A songwriter is like a runner who must run to strengthen his cardiovascular system. If he stops running, his system will grow sluggish again. To get strong and stay strong, a writer must keep writing."

**QUINT BENEDETTI MUSIC**, Box 2388, Toluca Lake CA 91602. (213)985-8284. Affiliates: Ann-Ben Music (BMI) and Mi-Dav-An-Mark Music (ASCAP). Contact: Quint Benedetti. Music publisher, record producer and artist manager. Pays standard royalty.
**How to Contact:** Submit demo tape and lyric sheet. Prefers cassette with 2-6 songs on demo. Submit Christmas songs no later than July 15. SASE. Reports in 1 month "or sooner."
**Music:** Musical comedy and Christmas songs. Recently published "Christmas Is for Children" and "Christmas Presents."

**\*BERANDOL MUSIC LTD.**, 11 Saint Joseph St., Toronto, Ontario, Canada M4Y 1J8. (416)924-8121. General Manager: Barbara Kroetsch. Music publisher, record company, record producer and distributor. BMI. Member CMPA, CIRPA, CRIA. Pays negotiable royalty.
**How to Contact:** Submit demo tape and lyric sheet; arrange personal interview. Prefers musical scores or cassette with 4-6 songs on demo. SASE. Reports in 1 month.
**Music:** Mostly top 40, MOR, choral, children's and classical; also bluegrass, blues, church/religious, C&W, dance-oriented, easy listening, gospel, jazz, MOR, progressive, R&B, rock and soul.

**HAL BERNARD ENTERPRISES, INC.**, Box 6507, 2181 Victory Pkwy., Cincinnati OH 45206. (513)861-1500. Affiliates: Sunnyslope Music (ASCAP), Bumpershoot Music (BMI), Apple Butter Music (ASCAP), Saiko Music (ASCAP), TYI Music (ASCAP) and Smorgaschord Music (ASCAP). Administrates Troutman's Music Co. (BMI). President: Stan Hertzman. Music publisher, record company and management firm. Pays negotiable royalty.
**How to Contact:** Submit demo tape and lyric sheet. Prefers cassette with 3 songs on demo. SASE. Reports in 1 month.
**Music:** Rock, R&B and top 40/pop. Recently published "Do It Roger" (by R. Troutman and L. Troutman), recorded by Roger/Warner Bros. Records (soul); "Dance Floor" (by R. Troutman and L. Troutman), recorded by ZAPP/Warner Bros. Records (soul); "The Lone Rhinoceros" (by Adrain Belew), recorded by A. Belew/Island Records (progressive); "Your Song Is Mine" (by Fetters, Nyswonger and Toth), recorded by Mighty High/MCA Records (rock); "Eastern Avenue River Railway Blues" (by Mike Reid), recorded by Jerry Jeff Walker/Elektra Records (pop/country); "Like A Falling Star" (by C. Fletcher), recorded by Blaze/Epic Records (rock); "Slave" (by Arduser, Close, Arduser), recorded by Darts/Reckless Records (rock), and "Icy Blue" (by Charlie Fletcher), recorded by C. Fletcher/Buddah/Arista Records.
**Tips:** "Cast your demos. If you as the songwriter can't sing it—don't. Get someone who can present your song properly, use a straight rhythm track and keep it as naked as possible. If you think it still needs somthing else, have a string arranger, etc. help you, but still keep the *voice up* and the *lyrics clear*."

**BETTER-HALF MUSIC CO.**, c/o Estate of Jacqueline Hilliard, Howard E. Guedalia, Executor, David's Way, Bedford Hills NY 10507. Music publisher, record producer and record company. ASCAP. Publishes 10 songs/year. Pays standard royalty.
**How to Contact:** Submit demo tape and lead sheet. Prefers cassette with 1-3 songs on demo tape. SASE. Reports in 1 month.
**Music:** C&W, bluegrass, blues, children's, easy listening, jazz, MOR, R&B, rock, soul and top 40/pop. Recently published "Come Live With Me, Angel" (by Hilliard/Ware), recorded by Marvin Gaye and Tamla/Motown Records (soul); "Instant Love" (by Hilliard/Ware), recorded by Main Ingredient, Lean Ware and Tamla/RCA Records (soul); and "Rolling Down a Mountainside" (by Hilliard/Ware), recorded by Main Ingredient/RCA Records and Isaac Hayes/STAX Records (soul).

**BIG HEART MUSIC**, Suite 309, 9454 Wilshire Blvd., Beverly Hills CA 90212. (213)273-7020. Affiliate: Wooden Bear Music (ASCAP). Managing Director: Randy Bash. Music publisher. BMI. Member NMPA.
**How to Contact:** Submit demo tape and lead or lyric sheet. Prefers 7½ ips reel-to-reel or cassette with 3 songs on demo. SASE. Reports in 2 weeks.
**Music:** C&W, MOR, soul and top 40/pop.

**BIG MIKE MUSIC**, Big Mike Productions, Suite 2-W, 408 W. 115th St., New York NY 10025. (212)222-8715. Manager: Bill Downs. Music publisher. ASCAP, BMI. Publishes 20 songs/year, publishes 10 new songwriters/year. Pays standard royalty.
**How to Contact:** Submit demo tape and lead sheet. Prefers cassette with 2-3 songs on demo. "Must have clean lead sheet and good demo with instrumental background. We will not accept tapes with vocal only." Does not return unsolicited material. Reports in 4 weeks.
**Music:** R&B, rock and soul. Recently published "Love Should Be A Crime" (by Tommie Munddy); "Don't Let Him Move In" (by Joellyn Cooperman); and "Stand-by Lover" (by Brad Smiley), all re-

corded by Dolly Gilmore/Vampp Records.
**Tips:** "Keep trying even after refusals. Most of the time a producer is looking for a song for now without a thought of the future."

**\*BIG SECRET MUSIC LTD.**, Havoc House, Cods Hill, Beenham, Reading, Bershire RG7 5QG, England. 44-0735-213623. Chairman: Guy Fletcher. Music publisher and recording studio. PRS. Member MPA. Publishes 20 songs/year. Has not yet, but would listen to songs from US writers. Pays negotiable royalty. Royalties paid directly to US songwriters or through US publishing affiliate.
**How to Contact:** Submit demo tape and lyric sheet. Prefers 15 ips reel-to-reel with 4 maximum songs on demo. SAE and IRC. Reports in 1 month.
**Music:** Mostly AOR and MOR; also rock (country crossover) and top 40/pop. Recently published "Lady, Put the Light Out" (by Guy Fletcher and Doug Flett), recorded by Joe Cocker; "Save Me" (by G. Fletcher and D. Flett), recorded by Louise Mandrell; and "Amity" (by G. Fletcher and D. Flett), recorded by Oakridge Boys.

**\*BIG SPLIFF MUSIC**, The White House, N. Lopham, DISS, Norfolk, England. 44-0379-88-693. Contact: Peter Shertser. Record company and record producer. MCPS, PRS, Phonographic Performance Ltd. Publishes 10-30 songs/year; publishes 3 new songwriters/year. Pays 50-75% of performance and mechanical royalties to songwriters; royalties paid directly to US songwriters or through a US publishing affiliate.
**How to Contact:** Write first. Prefers cassette with 2 songs on demo. SAE and IRC. Reports in 2 weeks.
**Music:** Mostly blues; also R&B. Recently published "Annie Maybe" (by T. Key & J.J. Malone), recorded by Trayce Key & J.J. Malone/Red Lightin Records (blues/R&B); "It Came On Time" (by R. Guines), recorded by R. Guines/Red Lightin Records (blues/R&B); and "A Hell of a Night" (by R. Guines & J. Sample), recorded by R. Guines/Red Lightin Records (blues/R&B).

**\*BILLETDOUX MUSIC PUBLISHING**, Box 11960, Chicago IL 60611. (312)561-0027. Production Manager: Mary Freeman. Music publisher, record company and record producer. BMI. Publishes 10 songs/year; publishes 3 new songwriters/year. Pays standard royalty.
**How to Contact:** Submit demo tape and lyric sheet. Prefers cassette with 3-6 songs on demo. SASE. Reports in 1 month.
**Music:** Mostly R&B; also blues, C&W, gospel, jazz, MOR, rock (pop, country and hard), soul and top 40/pop. Recently published "I Wanna Be With You" (by Rich Dumas), recorded by Mickey Dee/GRV Records (R&B); "I'm Gonna Love You" (by Randy Terry), recorded by R. Terry/GRV Records (country rock); and "Journey to Beyond" (by D. Kirk), recorded by Duncan Kirk/GRV Records (crossover rock).

**\*BIOGRAPH RECORDS, INC.**, Box 109, Canaan NY 12029. (518)392-3400. Affiliate: Caplin Music (BMI). President: Arnold S. Caplin. Music publisher, record producer and record company. ASCAP. Pays standard royalty.
**How to Contact:** Write or call first about your interest. Prefers 7½ ips reel-to-reel with 6 songs minimum on demo. SASE. Reports in 1 month.
**Music:** Bluegrass, blues, folk and jazz. Recently published "Sally, Where'd You Get Your Whiskey?" (by Gary Davis), recorded by G. Davis/Biograph Records (rock/blues); and "Now Is The Time" and "Line In the Track" (by Dan Smith), recorded by D. Smith/Biograph Records (folk).

**\*BLACK & WHITE MUSIC CORPORATION LIMITED**, 9 Devonport, 23 Southwick St., London W2, England. 44-01-402-9650. Director: Tim Knight. Music publisher and record producer. Estab. 1981. MCPS, PRS. Member of MPA. Publishes 30 songs/year; publishes 6 new songwriters/year. Pays negotiable royalty.
**How to Contact:** Submit demo tape and lyric sheet. Prefers cassette with 3-6 songs on demo. SAE and IRC. Reports in 1 month.
**Music:** Mostly top 40/pop; also dance-oriented, progressive, R&B, rock (hard) and soul. Recently published "Judge Dredd" and "You You You" (by Loose Talk), recorded by Loose Talk/Jet Records (pop); and "Natural High" (by Charles McCormick), recorded by Captain Sky/Philly World Records (pop).

**BLACK STALLION COUNTRY PUBLISHING**, Box 2250, Culver City CA 90230. (213)419-8142. President: Kenn Kingsbury. Music publisher and book publisher *Who's Who in Country & Western Music*. BMI. Member ACM, CMA, CMF. Publishes 2 songs/year; publishes 1 new songwriter/year. Pays standard royalty.
**How to Contact:** Submit demo tape and lyric sheet. Prefers 7½ ips reel-to-reel or cassette with 2-4 songs on demo. SASE. Reports in 1 month.

**Music:** Bluegrass, C&W and top 40/pop.
**Tips:** "Be professional in attitude and presentation. Submit only the material you think is better than anything being played on the radio."

**BLACKWOOD MUSIC**, Box 17272, Memphis TN 38117-0242. (901)767-2220. President: Ron Blackwood. Music publisher, record company and record producer. BMI. Publishes 500 songs/year; publishes 27 new songwriters/year. Hires staff writers. Pays standard royalty.
**How to Contact:** Submit demo tape and lyric sheet. Prefers cassette with 1-5 songs on demo. Does not return unsolicited material. Reports in 1 month "only if we use the songs."
**Music:** Bluegrass, children's, choral, church/religious, C&W, easy listening, gospel, MOR, R&B, rock, soul and top 40/pop.

**BLUE ISLAND PUBLISHING**, Unit 3, 1446 N. Martel, Los Angeles CA 90046. (213)851-3733. Affiliates: Bob Fleming Music (BMI) and Dahlhouse Publishing (ASCAP). General Manager: Bob Gilbert. Music publisher, record company and record producer. ASCAP. Publishes 50 songs/year. Pays standard royalty.
**How to Contact:** Submit demo tape and lyric sheet. Prefers cassette with 3-6 songs on demo. "Submit only your best single-oriented songs to fit top 40 format. Easy to understand songs with strong hooks and good lyrics make it." SASE. Reports in 3 weeks.
**Music:** C&W, MOR, rock and top 40/pop.

**BLUE UMBRELLA MUSIC PUBLISHING CO.**, 3011 Beach 40th St., Brooklyn NY 11224. (212)372-6436. Contact: Kadish Millet. Music publisher. ASCAP. Publishes 25 songs/year; publishes 3 new songwriters/year. Pays standard royalty.
**How to Contact:** Submit demo tape and lead sheet. Prefers cassette with 1-10 songs on demo. "Wrap cassette well; some cassette boxes have fairly sharp edges and break through envelope. I want a lead sheet (not lyric sheet) and accurate info on who owns the copyright at the time of submission." SASE. Reports in 2 weeks.
**Music:** Country. "I want only country songs with double entendre (sexy, adult type) lyrics such as 'Behind Closed Doors,' 'Almost Persuaded,' 'Here Comes My Weekend Friend,' 'Help Me Make it Through the Night,' 'Sleepin' Single in a Double Bed,' and 'Teach Me to Cheat.' "

**BO GAL MUSIC**, Box 6687, Wheeling WV 26003. (614)758-5812. Affiliate: Green Up Music (BMI). President: Bob Gallion. Music publisher and record company. BMI. Pays standard royalties.
**How to Contact:** Submit demo tape. Prefers reel-to-reel tape. SASE. Reports in 1 month.
**Music:** Bluegrass, blues, church/religious, C&W, folk, gospel, MOR and top 40/pop. Recently published "The Next Time" (by Don Sniffin), recorded by Patti Powell/Arby Records (MOR); and "Looks Like You're Going Anyway" (by Sniffin), recorded by Powell/Arby Records (MOR).

***BOCU MUSIC LTD.**, 1 Wyndham Yd., Wyndham Place, London W1H 1AR, England. 44-01-402-7433/4/5. Managers: Howard Huntridge and Carole Broughton. Music publisher. MCPS, PRS, Photographic Performance Ltd. Member of MPA. Publishes 3 new songwriters/year.
**How to Contact:** Submit demo tape and lyric sheet with stamped, addressed envelope. Prefers 7½ reel-to-reel or cassette with 6 songs on demo. SAE and IRC. Reports in 1 month.
**Music:** Mostly top 40/pop; also blues, dance-oriented, easy listening, MOR, R&B, rock and soul. Recently published "Physical" (by Steve Kipner), recorded by Olivia Newton John; "Winner Takes It All" (by Abba), recorded by Abba; and "Heart Attack" (by S. Kipner), recorded by Olivia Newton John.
**Tips:** "Be selective; send good demo of songs with good melodies and interesting themes."

***BOGGY DEPOT MUSIC**, 10051 Greenleaf, Santa Fe Spring CA 90670. (213)946-3193. President: Overton Lee. Music publisher, record company, record producer and video producer. BMI, ASCAP. Publishes 10 songs/year. Pays standard royalty.
**How to Contact:** Submit demo tape and lyric sheet. Prefers cassette with 1-3 songs on demo. Does not return unsolicited material. Reports in 3-4 months.
**Music:** Mostly country; also bluegrass, blues and gospel. Recently published "How Many Heart Aches," recorded by Alan Lee Blackwell/O.L. Records (C&W); "Cry Baby Baby Cry," recorded by Johnny Blankenship/O.L. Records (C&W/rock); and "It May Be Tonight," recorded by Gene Davis/O.L. Records (C&W).

**BOSS TWEED MUSIC**, Box 23, Sun Valley CA 91352. (213)982-2174. Contact: J. Eric Freedner. Music publisher and record company. BMI. Publishes 4 songs/year; publishes 1 new songwriter/year. Pays standard royalty.

**How to Contact:** Write first about your interest, then submit demo tape and lyric sheet. Prefers 7½ ips reel-to-reel or cassette with 2-5 songs on demo. SASE. Reports in 3 weeks.
**Music:** Folk, rock (country and novelty) and novelty/humor. Recently published six novelty songs written and recorded by Larry Treadwell/Zzyzx Records; "Vallo The Pirate" (by Tim Mockler), recorded by J. Eric Freedner/Zzyzx Records (humor); and "Medfly Stomp" (by J.E. Freedner), recorded by J.E. Freedner/Zzyzx Records (humor).
**Tips:** "Include tape, lyric sheets, return envelope, and a letter with any other information."

**BOURNE MUSIC**, 437 Fifth Ave., New York NY 10016. (212)679-3700. Office Manager: Al Tuckman. Affiliate: Murbo Music (BMI). Music publisher and record producer. ASCAP. Member NMPA. Publishes 10 songs/year. Pays standard royalty.
**How to Contact:** Submit demo tape, lead sheet and lyric sheet. Prefers 7½ ips reel-to-reel or cassette with 3-4 songs on demo. SASE. Reports in 6 weeks.
**Music:** Mostly A/C, rock, R&B and country; uses all types. Published "San Antonio Rose"(by Bob Wills), recorded by Ray Price and Willie Nelson/CBS Records (country); and "Love Letters in the Sand" (by Nick Kenny, Charles Kenny and J. Fred Coots), recorded by John Schneider.

**TOMMY BOYCE & MELVIN POWERS MUSIC ENTERPRISES**, 12015 Sherman Rd., North Hollywood CA 91605. (213)875-1711. President: Melvin Powers. Music publisher and record company. ASCAP.
**How to Contact:** Submit demo tape and lyric sheet. Prefers cassette with 3 songs on demo. SASE. Reports in 1 month.
**Music:** C&W and MOR. Recently published "Willie Burgundy" (by Tommy Boyce and Melvin Powers), recorded by Teresa Brewer (MOR); "Mr. Songwriter" (by T. Boyce and M. Powers), recorded by Sunday Sharpe (C&W); and "Who Wants a Slightly Used Woman?" (by T. Boyce and M. Powers), recorded by Connie Cato (C&W).
**Tips:** "Before you send your songs to a publisher, have a *professional* (musician, singer) listen to them. Get their professional critique. New songwriters waste a lot of time and money which they should be using on courses in song and lyric writing and workshops. Then test your songs against those on the radio. Do they measure up? I'd recommend collaboration as the best source of instant feedback and critique."

**BRANCH INTERNATIONAL MUSIC**, Box 31819, Dallas TX 75231. (214)750-0720. A&R Director: Mike Anthony. Music publisher. BMI. Publishes 20 songs/year. Pays standard maximum royalty.
**How to Contact:** Submit demo tape and lead or lyric sheet. Prefers 7½ ips reel-to-reel with 1-4 songs on demo. SASE. Reports in 1 month.
**Music:** C&W and gospel. Recently published "Tough Act To Follow" (by V. Stovall and B. Palmer), recorded by Billy Parker/SCR Records (C&W); "You're a Woman" (by Dugg Collins), recorded by DeWayne Bowman/Yatahey Records (C&W); "The Closest Thing to You" (by J. Hudson), recorded by DeWayne Bowman/Yatahey Records; and *Cajun Paradise*, by Craig Saileau/Yatahey Records.

**BRANDWOOD MUSIC, INC.**, Box 24214, Nashville TN 37202. (615)292-3593. President: Ansley R. Fleetwood. Music publisher. BMI. Publishes 30 songs/year; publishes 4 new songwriters/year. Pays standard royalty.
**How to Contact:** Submit demo tape and lyric sheet. Prefers cassette with 2-5 songs on demo. "Demo songs with voice and one instrument, not full band. Use high-quality tape; make sure all lyrics can be understood." SASE. Reports in 3 weeks.
**Music:** C&W, MOR and top 40/pop. Recently published "Just Good Ol' Boys" (by A. Fleetwood), recorded by Moe Bandy and Joe Stampley/Columbia Records (C&W); "Freight Train Boogie" (by Terry McMillan), recorded by T. McMillan/RCA Records (C&W); "I've Aged Twenty Years in Five" (by C. Gordon), recorded by George Jones/Epic Records (C&W).

**BRAVE NEW MUSIC**, Suite 1116, 6253 Hollywood Blvd., Hollywood CA 90028. (213)466-3534. President: Daniel Friedman. Music publisher. BMI. ASCAP affiliate in organization. Publishes 12 songs/year; publishes 5 new songwriters/year. Pays standard royalty.
**How to Contact:** Write first about your interest. Prefers cassette with 1-4 songs on demo. "Good tape quality is greatly appreciated." SASE. Reports in 1 month.
**Music:** Choral, country, dance-oriented, easy listening, rock and top 40/pop.
**Tips:** "Write commercial *coverable* songs, make good demos. Give serious thought to lyrics. Have a coöperative attitude."

**BREAKTHROUGH QUALITY MUSIC**, Box 354, Durham CT 06722. (203)349-9637. Affiliate: Second Listen Music (BMI). Professional Manager: Michael Frost. Music publisher. ASCAP. Publishes 5-10 songs/year; publishes 4 new songwriters/year. Pays standard royalty.

**How to Contact:** Submit demo tape and lyric sheet. Prefers 7½ ips reel-to-reel or cassette with 1-3 songs on demo. SASE. Reports in 1 month.
**Music:** C&W, easy listening, MOR and top 40/pop.

**BROAD RIVER PUBLISHING CO.**, Dyer Rt., Cowen WV 26202. (304)226-3424. Secretary: Gladys Spearman. Music publisher and record company. BMI. Publishes 2 songs/year; publishes 2 new songwriters/year. Pays standard royalty.
**How to Contact:** Submit demo tape and lyric sheet. Prefers cassette with 3-6 songs on demo. "Be sure cassette tape is clear. Songs should have meanings based on the word of God." SASE. Reports in 1-3 months.
**Music:** Church/religious and gospel. Recently published "Come, Lord Jesus" (by Tena Shull), "Get Behind Me Satan" and "Why Should I Worry or Fear" (by Gladys and Ernest Spearman), recorded by The Singing Spearman's/New Dawning Records (gospel).

**BROADMAN PRESS**, 127 9th Ave. N., Nashville TN 37234. (615)251-2500. Music Editor: Mark Blankenship. Music publisher. SESAC, ASCAP and BMI. Publishes 200 songs/year.
**How to Contact:** Submit demo tape and lead sheet. Prefers reel-to-reel or cassette with 1-10 songs on demo. SASE. Reports in 6 weeks.
**Music:** Choral, church/religious and gospel. "We publish all forms of sacred music including solo/choral for all ages, and instrumental for handbell, organ, piano, recorder and orchestra."

**BROOKLYN COUNTRY MUSIC**, Suite 1705, 150 E. 39th St., New York NY 10016. (212)889-3754. A&R Director: Zhaba Jay. Music publisher, record producer, record company and management company. ASCAP. Publishes 100 songs/year; publishes 3 new songwriters/year. Pays standard royalty.
**How to Contact:** Submit demo tape and lyric sheet. Prefers 7½ ips reel-to-reel or cassette with 2-5 songs on demo. "Do not send rating cards. We will *not* answer enclosed post cards rating material, singer, etc. and will contact writer only if interested." Does not return unsolicited material.
**Music:** Blues; country rock (uptown & downtown styles); and R&B. Recently published "Two People on the Wrong Side of the Door" (by V. Jay and D. Roberts), recorded by Valerie Jay/Brooklyn Country Records (country); "Outside the Law" (by V. Jay and D. Roberts), recorded by Valerie Jay and Danny Roberts/Musicland Express U.S.A. Records (country rock); and "Evil Mama" (by Keith Fredericks), recorded by Danny Roberts/Musicland Express U.S.A. Records (country rock).

**BROOKS BROTHERS PUBLISHERS**, 311 Margo Lane, Nashville TN 37211. (615)834-4124. Manager: Jake Brooks. Music publisher. BMI. Publishes 12 songs/year; publishes 2 new songwriters/year. Pays standard royalty.
**How to Contact:** Submit vocal/guitar/piano demo tape and lyric sheet. Prefers cassette with 1-3 songs on demo. "Print clearly." SASE. Reports in 2 weeks.
**Music:** C&W (western, western country, country). Recently published "This Cowboy's Hat" (by Jake Brooks), recorded by Porter Wagoner/Warner/VIVA Records (country); "If I Had You" (by J. Brooks); "Crazy & Lonely" (by Jeff Moore), recorded by J. Moore/Goldust Records; and "In My Lady's Eyes" and "Moonshine Dreamer" (by David Ruthstrom), recorded by D. Ruthstrom/Goldust Records (country/pop).
**Tips:** Looking for "heavy lyrics."

**BROWN MOON/BRITTELL MUSIC**, Box 19274, Houston TX 77215. Manager: Dirk Greene. Music publisher. ASCAP, BMI. Publishes 20 songs/year. Pays standard royalty.
**How to Contact:** Submit demo tape and lyric sheet. Prefers 7½ ips reel-to-reel or cassette with 3-6 songs on demo. Include photos and biographical material. Does not return unsolicited material. Reports in 2 months.
**Music:** C&W ("cross-over potential only—no hardcore"); rock; and top 40/pop. "We are interested in commercial, well-structured songs. Send only if you are convinced you have a classic." Recently published "Deliver" (by Kim Martin); "How Can I Tell Her" (by Steven Beasley); and "A Better Man" (by Jon Stone).

**ALBERT E. BRUMLEY & SONS**, Powell MO 65730. (417)435-2225. Affiliate: Hartford Music (SESAC). President: Bob Brumley. Music publisher. SESAC. Publishes 25-50 songs/year; publishes 5-10 new songwriters/year. Pays standard royalties.
**How to Contact:** Submit demo tape and lead sheet. Prefers cassette with 3-4 songs on demo. SASE. Reports in 3 weeks.
**Music:** Choral, church/religious, C&W and gospel.

**BRUT MUSIC PUBLISHING**, 1345 Ave. of the Americas, New York NY 10105. (212)581-3114. Vice President: Stan Krell. Music publisher. ASCAP. Pays standard royalty.

**Music Publishers** **27**

**How to Contact:** Submit demo tape and lyric sheet. Prefers cassette. SASE. Reports as soon as possible.
**Music:** Easy listening, MOR, rock and top 40/pop. Recently published "Now That We're in Love" (by Sammy Cahn and George Barrie), recorded by Steve Lawrence; and "Every Day Is New Year's Eve" and "What Becomes of Love" (by S. Cahn and G. Barrie).

***BULLET MANAGEMENT/ITS A HIT PRODUCTIONS**, Box H, Harvard MA 01451. (617)456-8111. A&R Director: Stephen Bond Garvan. Record producer. ASCAP. Publishes 10 songs/year; publishes 3 new songwriters/year. Pays standard royalty.
**How to Contact:** Submit demo tape and lyric sheet; write about your interest. Prefers 7½ ips reel-to-reel or cassette with 3 songs on demo. Does not return unsolicited material. Reports in 1 month.
**Music:** Mostly R&R, pop/rock and country rock; also C&W. Recently published "Are You Afraid of Falling (by A. Estes), recorded by Estes Boys/Would'n Shoe Records (pop); "Save The Whales (by C.J. McDonald), recorded by Allen Estes/Greenpeace Records (pop); and "Keep on Singing" (by Dean Adrien), recorded by D. Adrien/L'orient Records (pop).
**Tips:** "We are looking for professional hook, structure and presentation."

**BURIED TREASURE MUSIC**, 524 Doral Country Dr., Nashville TN 37221. Affiliate: Captain Kidd Music (BMI). Nashville repesentative for the Gilley's Publishing Group; Points West Music (BMI), and Red Rose Music (ASCAP). Executive Producer: Scott Turner. Music publisher and record producer. ASCAP. Publishes 75 songs/year; publishes 10-15 new songwriters/year. Pays standard royalty.
**How to Contact:** Submit demo tape and lead sheet. Prefers cassette with 1-4 songs on demo. SASE. Reports in 2 weeks.
**Music:** Country, progessive country, moderate rock, ("no punk"); some MOR. Recently published "We Make a Great Country Song" (by Denny Ray Lamson) and "Here I Am Again" (by M. Medskey and B. Riley), recorded by Bobby Lewis/Ventura Records (country); and "Minstrel Man" (by D.R. Lamson), recorded by Oasis.
**Tips:** "*Don't* send songs in envelopes that are 15''x20'', or by Registered Mail. It doesn't help a bit. Say something that's been said a thousand times before . . . only say it differently."

**BUSH/LEHRMAN PRODUCTIONS**, 928 Broadway, New York NY 10010. (212)505-7300. Professional Managers: Ted Lehrman, Libby Bush. Music publisher and record producer. ASCAP. Publishes 5 songs/year. Pays standard royalty.
**How to Contact:** Submit demo tape and lyric sheet. Prefers 7½ ips reel-to-reel or cassette with 2-4 songs on demo. Reports in 6 weeks. "Please enclose self-addressed stamped envelope."
**Music:** MOR, rock, R&B, dance, C&W and adult contemporary.
**Tips:** "Send us potential hit singles material only, no album cuts. Strong hooks; positive lyrics; medium and up-tempo songs; clean, listenable demo. Doesn't have to be complicated."

**BUTTERMILK SKY ASSOCIATES**, 515 Madison Ave., New York NY 10022. (212)759-2275. President: Murray Deutch. Vice President: Stu Cantor. Music publisher. BMI and ASCAP. Member NMPA. Publishes 100 songs/year; publishes 20 new songwriters/year. Pays standard royalties.
**How to Contact:** Arrange personal interview or submit demo tape and lyric sheet. Prefers cassette with 3 songs maximum on demo. Does not return unsolicited material. Reports in 3 months. "Include SASE with solicited submissions."
**Music:** R&R, dance, MOR, R&B, and top 40/pop. Recently published "Tryin' to Get to You" (by McCoy/Singleton), recorded by Phil Seymour/Boardwalk Records; and "I've Had It," recorded by Louise Goffin/Electra-Asylum Records.

**CACTUS MUSIC AND GIDGET PUBLISHING**, 5 Aldom Circle, West Caldwell NJ 07006. (201)226-0035. Contact: Jim Hall or Gidget Starr. Music publisher, record company and record producer. ASCAP. Publishes 10 songs/year; publishes 15 new songwriters. Pays standard royalty.
**How to Contact:** Write or call first about your interest, submit demo tape and lyric sheet, or arrange personal interview. Prefers 7½ ips reel-to-reel or cassette with 4 songs minimum on demo. Does not return unsolicited material. Reports in 1 month.
**Music:** Mostly C&W, rock and gospel; also bluegrass, blues, easy listening, R&B and top 40/pop. Recently published "Old Foggy Town" (by Doc Hopkins), recorded by Jim Hall/Tar Heel Records (gospel); "Airport In the Sky" (by Hicks and Boline), recorded by Hicks/Pentecostaltone Records (bluegrass gospel); and "Baby Let's Go Out" (by Harris, Hall, Shields and Starr), recorded by Hall/Tar Heel Records.

**CALIGULA, INC.**, 60 Pearl St., New York NY 10004. Contact: Professional Manager. Music publisher. ASCAP. Publishes 10 songs/year. Pays standard royalty.

**How to Contact:** Write first about your interest. "No unsolicited material please." Prefers cassette with 4 songs on demo. SASE. Reports in 1 month.

**CALVARY RECORDS, INC.**, 142 8th Ave. N., Nashville TN 37203. (615)244-8800. Affiliates: Songs of Calvary (BMI), Music of Calvary (SESAC) and LifeStream Music (ASCAP). Producer: Nick Bluno. Music publisher and record company.
**How to Contact:** Submit demo tape and lyric sheet. Prefers cassette with 1-3 songs on demo. SASE. Reports in 3 weeks.
**Music:** Church/religious, contemporary Christian and gospel.

**CALWEST SONGS/LEE ANDERSON ENTERPRISES**, 1509 Broadway, Bellingham WA 78225. (206)676-9961. Contact: Bob Wood. Music publisher and record company. BMI. Pays standard royalty.
**How to Contact:** Write first about your interest, then submit demo tape and lyric sheet. Prefers cassette with 2-4 songs on demo. SASE.
**Music:** Bluegrass, blues, children's, C&W, easy listening, folk, gospel, R&B, rock (country) and top 40/pop.

**CAMERICA MUSIC**, 489 5th Ave., New York NY 10017. (212)682-8400. Affiliate: Camex Music (BMI). Professional Manager: Mike Corbett. Music publisher and production firm. ASCAP. Publishes 50 songs/year; publishes 20 new songwriters/year. Pays standard royalty.
**How to Contact:** Submit demo tape and lyric sheet. Prefers cassette with 1-4 songs on demo. "Songs should have great hooks, interesting chord changes, classic melodies and conversational lyrics." SASE. Reports in 8 weeks.
**Music:** Mostly dance-oriented rock; also easy listening, folk, jazz, MOR, R&B, rock, soul and top 40/pop. Recently published "Wish We Were Heroes" (by Austin Gravelding), recorded by Kenny Dale/Capitol Records (country/pop); "It Hurts Too Much" (by Eric Carmen), recorded by Robert Gordon/RCA Records (rock); and "Change of Heart" (by Eric Carmen), recorded by Donna Fargo/Warner Bros. Records (pop rock).

**THE CAMERON ORGANISATION, INC.**, 822 Hillgrove Ave., Western Springs IL 60558. (312)246-8222. Branch: 2700 Cahvenga E., Los Angeles CA 90068. Affiliates: Monona Music (BMI), Watertoons Music (BMI), Hoochie Coochie Music (BMI), Skafish Music (BMI) and Rathsino Publishing (BMI). President/Manager: Scott A. Cameron. Music publisher. BMI. Publishes 2-10 songs/year; publishes 1 new songwriter/year. Pays standard royalty.
**How to Contact:** Submit demo tape and lead sheet. Prefers 7½ ips reel-to-reel or cassette with 1-3 songs on demo.
**Music:** Mostly blues; also progressive, rock, soul and top 40/pop. Recently published "Got to Love You Baby" (Hoochie Coochie Music), recorded by The Blues Band/RCA, Limited Records; "Champagne and Reefer" and "The Blues Had a Baby and They Called It Rock and Roll," recorded by Muddy Waters/Watertoons/Blue Sky (CBS) Records; "Earthquake and Hurricane" (by Willie Dixon/Hoochie Coochie Music), recorded by Tina Turner/United Artist Records; and "Built for Comfort" (by W. Dixon), recorded by Hoyt Axton (blues/rock), for 20th Century Fox film *Heart Like a Wheel*.

**GLEN CAMPBELL ENTERPRISES, LTD.**, Suite 2530, 1900 Avenue of the Stars, Los Angeles CA 90067. (213)553-8434. Publishing company. BMI. ASCAP.
**How to Contact:** Submit demo tape and lead sheet. Prefers cassette with 1-3 songs on demo. SASE.
**Music:** All types.

**CAN YOU HEAR ME MUSIC**, Box 14243, San Francisco CA 94114. (415)824-3676. Contact: R. Hanrahan. Music publisher and record producer. BMI. Publishes 5 songs/year; publishes 5 new songwriters/year. Pays 85% royalty to songwriters.
**How to Contact:** Call first about your interest. Prefers cassette with 5 songs maximum on demo. SASE. Reports in 1 month.
**Music:** R&B (ska), rock (new wave) and experimental.

**CANAL PUBLISHING, INC.**, #4, 6325 Guilforo Ave., Indianapolis IN 46220. (317)255-3116. Vice President: Terry Barnes. Music publisher. BMI. Publishes 50-100 songs/year; publishes 5-10 new songwriters/year. Usually pays standard royalty.
**How to Contact:** Submit demo tape and lyric sheet. Prefers cassette with 1-4 songs on demo. SASE. Reports in 1 month.
**Music:** Country, easy listening, MOR, rock and top 40/pop. Recently published "Dancin' Shoes" (by Carl Storie), recorded by Nigel Olsen, the Faith Band and Michael Clark (ballad); and "You're My Weakness" (by John Cascella), recorded by the Faith Band (top 40/pop).

## Music Publishers

**\*CANDLESTICK PUBLISHING CO.**, 582 Armour Circle NE, Atlanta GA 30324. (404)875-8272. Affiliate: Dream Merchant Music (BMI). Partners: Larry King, R.B. Hudmon, Gwen Kesler. Music publisher. BMI. Pays standard royalty.
**How to Contact:** Submit demo tape and lead sheet. Send cassette with 1-6 songs on demo. SASE. Reports in 1-2 months.
**Music:** Rock, soul, country and top 40/pop. Recently published "How Can I Be a Witness?," "If You Don't Cheat on Me;" "Holdin' On;" and "Searching For Your Love" recorded by R.B. Hudmon (soul).

**CAN'T STOP MUSIC**, Can't Stop Productions, Inc., Suite 302, 65 E. 55th St., New York NY 10022. (212)751-6177. Affiliate: Stop Light Music (ASCAP). President: Maximilian Dahan-Lavelle. International Manager: Hope Goering. Manager: Russell Sidelsky. Music publisher and production company. BMI. Publishes 15 songs/year; publishes 4 new songwriters/year. Pays 30-50% royalty.
**How to Contact:** Submit demo tape. Cassette only. SASE. Reports in 8 weeks.
**Music:** Disco, easy listening, rock, soul and top 40/pop. Recently published "5 O'Clock in the Morning" (by J. Morali, VP Band, H. Belolo, D. Frederiksen), recorded by Village People/RCA Records (mid-tempo pop); "Action Man" (by J. Morali, VP Band, H. Belolo, D. Frederiksen), recorded by Village People/RCA Records (pop rock); and "I'll Do My Best" (by M. Malavasi, G. Salerni, A. Thornton), recorded by Ritchie Family/RCA Records (dance).
**Tips:** "We prefer no more than 3 titles on each submission."

**\*CAPITOL STAR ARTIST ENT., INC.**, 1159 Jay St., Box 11276. Rochester NY 14613. (916)328-5565. Director: Don Redanz. Music publisher, record company and record producer. BMI. Publishes 4 songs/year. Pays standard royalty.
**Music:** Bluegrass, church/religious, C&W and gospel.

**\*CAP-ORION MUSIC PUBLISHING CO. INC.**, Box 1235, New Rochelle NY 10802. (914)834-5676. Affiliates: Caduceus Music Ltd. (BMI), Chez D Music (ASCAP), and Lynnie Bear Music (BMI). Professional Manager: David Saperstein. Music publisher, record company and record producer. BMI. Publishes 10 songs/year; publishes 2 new songwriters/year. Pays standard royalty.
**How to Contact:** Submit demo tape and lyric sheet. Prefers cassette with 1-3 songs on demo. SASE. Reports in 1 month.
**Music:** Mostly rock; also top 40/pop. Recently published "Struck by Lightnin' " (by D. Chimela), recorded by Rat Race Chain/Crescent Records (pop); "Forever" (by Vigil, Resnick, Zepol), recorded by Wowii/Cartoon Records (pop); and "Waitin' Line" (by Lanza and Messina), recorded by Spyder's Gang/Scepter Records (rock).

**DON CASALE MUSIC, INC.**, 377 Plainfield St., Westbury NY 11590. (516)333-7898. President: Don Casale. Music publisher.
**How to Contact:** "Call or write (SASE) before submitting.

**CASTALIA MUSIC**, Box 11516, Milwaukee WI 53211. President: Jim Spencer. Music publisher, record company and record producer. BMI. Publishes about 36 songs/year; publishes 10 new songwriters/year. Pays standard royalty.
**How to Contact:** Write first about your interest or submit demo tape and lyric sheet. Prefers cassette with 1-6 songs on demo. SASE. Reports in 1 month.
**Music:** All types. Recently published "Open Your Window" (by Matelic and Spencer), recorded by Jim Spencer/Fair Wind Records (R&B ballad); "Color Appreciation" (by Glenn Rehse), recorded by Plasticland/Scadillac Records (rock); and "Stars Are Right" (by Mark Schneider), recorded by The Red Ball Jets/Better Records (rock).

**CATALPA PUBLISHING CO.**, 2609 NW 36th St., Oklahoma City OK 73112. (405)942-0462. Professional Manager: Bobby Boyd. Music publisher, record company and record producer. BMI. Publishes 100 songs/year; publishes 6 new songwriters/year. Pays standard royalty.
**How to Contact:** Write first about your interest, then submit demo tape and lyric sheet. Prefers 7½ ips reel-to-reel with 3-12 songs on demo. Does not return unsolicited material. Reports in 2 weeks.
**Music:** C&W, R&B, rock, soul and top 40/pop.

**\*CATS WHISKERS MUSIC LTD.**, 320, Queens Rd., London, SE14, England. 44-01-639-7198. Affiliate: Rondor Music (London) Ltd. General Manager: John Drummer. Music publisher, record producer and production company. PRS. Publishes 50-60 songs/year; publishes 3 new songwriters/year. Has not yet, but would listen to songs from US songwriters. Pays negotiable royalties; royalties paid directly to US songwriters.

## 30  Songwriter's Market '84

**How to Contact:** Submit demo tape and lyric sheet. Prefers cassette for demo. SAE and IRC. Reports in 1 month.
**Music:** Mostly dance-oriented, rock and novelty; also children's, MOR, progressive, R&B, soul and top 40/pop. Recently published "Don't Call Me Chicken Head" (by Crendy/April/Dummer/Nevin), recorded by True Life Confessions/Speed Records (dance); "If I Can't Have You" (by Bibi/April/Dummer), recorded by True Life Confessions/Speed Records (rock); and "Sex Slave" and "Housewives Choice" (by Bibi/April), recorded by John Dummer & Helen April/A&M Records (novelty).

**CBS SONGS**, 1015 16th Ave. S, Nashville TN 37212. (615)329-8100. Affiliates: April Music (ASCAP), Blackwood Music Inc (BMI). Manager: Judy Harris. Member NMPA and NMA. Music publisher. Does not accept unsolicited material.

**CHAPIE MUSIC**, Chapman Recording Studios, 228 W. 5th St., Kansas City MO 64105. (816)842-6854. Owner: Chuck Chapman. Music publisher and record company. BMI. Publishes 25 songs/year; publishes 25 new songwriters/year. Pays standard royalty.
**How to Contact:** Submit demo tape. Prefers cassette with 3 songs minimum on tape. SASE. Reports in 1 month.
**Music:** Mostly country; also bluegrass, choral, church/religious, classical, disco, easy listening, folk, gospel, jazz, MOR, progressive, rock, soul and top 40/pop. Recently published "Sometimes Takes A Woman" (by Greg Camp), recorded by G. Camp/Fifth Street Records; "These Days" (by Norman Jolly), recorded by Jolly Brothers/Fifth Street Records; and "Love Thief" (by Don Quinn), recorded by D. Quinn/Fifth Street Records.
**Tips:** Be "short and to the point."

**\*CHAPPELL & CO. (AUST.) PTY LTD.**, 99 Forbes St., Woolloomooloo, Box KX250 Kings Cross, Sydney, NSW, 2011, Australia. 61-02-356-3322. Professional Managers: Jennifer Wright and Robert DuRose. Music publisher. Member AMCOS, APRA and Australian Music Publishers Association Pty., Ltd. Pays negotiable royalty; royalties paid directly to US songwriters or paid to US songwriters through US publishing affiliate.
**How to Contact:** Write first; submit demo tape and lyric sheet. Prefers cassette with 1-5 songs on demo. SAE and IRC. Reports in 2 weeks.
**Music:** Blues, children's, C&W, dance-oriented, easy listening, folk, jazz, MOR, R&B, rock, soul and top 40/pop. Recently published "True Love" (by Billy Field & Tom Price), recorded by B. Field/WEA Records (soft rock); "The Queen & Me" (by Eric McCusker), recorded by Mondo Rock/WEA Records (rock); and "No Time" (by E. McCusker), recorded by Mondo Rock/WEA Records (rock).
**Tips:** "Submit good commercial, clear demos."

**\*CHARISMA MUSIC PUBLISHING CO. LTD.**, 90 Wardour St., London, W1, England, 44-01-434-1351. Head of Publishing: Rob Gold. Music publisher and record company. MCPS, PRS, Phonographic Performance Ltd. Member PPL, PRS, British Video Association. Publishes 50 songs/year; publishes 6 new songwriters/year. Hires staff writers. Pays negotiable royalty; royalties paid directly to US songwriters.
**How to Contact:** Submit demo tape and lyric sheet. Prefers cassette with 1-6 songs on demo. "We want strong melodies and outstanding lyrics." SAE and IRC. Reports in 1-2 weeks.
**Music:** Mostly rock; also blues, modern contemporary, dance-oriented, folk, R&B, soul and top 40/pop. ("Coverable songs important.") Recently published "He Knows Ya Know" (by Fish), recorded by Mariccion/EMI Records (hard rock); "Market Square Herpes" (by Fish), recorded by Mariccion/EMI Records (hard rock); and "Night Nurse" (by Gregory Isaacs), recorded by Gregory Isaacs/Island Records (reggae).
**Tips:** "Don't submit too many songs in one go."

**CHARTBOUND MUSIC PUBLICATIONS, LTD.**, Suite 204, 1508 Harlem, Memphis TN 38114. (901)274-2726. Executive Director: Reginald Eskridge. Music publisher and recording studio. ASCAP. Member NMPA (pending), BMA, NARAS, MSMA and The Blues Foundation. Publishes 2-4 songs/year; publishes 3 new songwriters/year. "We plan to employ songwriters on salary to exclusively write for our company within the next 12-18 months." Pays standard royalty.
**How to Contact:** Call or write first about your interest, then submit demo tape and lyric sheet. Prefers 15 and 7½ ips reel-to-reel or cassette with 1-5 songs on demo. "Only submit unpublished songs for our consideration. Submit only your best. Big demo production is not necessary, but it helps." SASE. Reports in 3 weeks.
**Music:** Dance-oriented, MOR, R&B, soul and top 40/pop. Recently published "Am I Going to be the One" and "Never be the Same"(by Vaneese Thomas), recorded by Colors/Becket Records (top 40/pop); "Show Me That One More Time" (by Daniel Boga, Willie Mitchell, George Jackson and Billi Always), recorded by Billy Always/Waylo Records (R&B/soul).

## Music Publishers 31

**\*CHASCOT MUSIC PUBLISHING**, Box 3161, Atlanta GA 30302. President: Charles E. Scott. Music publisher, record company and record producer. BMI. Publishes 25 songs/year. Pays standard royalties.
**How to Contact:** Submit demo tape and lead sheet. Prefers cassette. SASE. Reports in 3 weeks.
**Music:** Blues, disco, gospel, R&B, soul and top 40/pop. Recently published "Do It Again," by John Weber (blues); "Come On, Try It," by Bobby Lewis (R&B); and "Pay My Bills," by Janet Steinberg (pop).

**C. CHASE MUSIC PRODUCTIONS**, Division of Chase Dominion Limited. 83 Kneeland Ave., Binghamton NY 13905. (607)797-1190. Director: Dr. Clarence W. Chase. Music publisher and music printer specializing in hymns; gospel, popular and vocal music; children's songs and lead sheets. ASCAP. Publishes 10 songs/year; publishes 1 new songwriter/year. Pays minimum standard royalty.
**How to Contact:** Write first about your interest. Prefers 7 1/2 ips reel-to-reel or cassette with 1-3 songs on demo and lead sheet. Does not return unsolicited material. Reports "as time allows."
**Music:** Children's, choral, church/religious, classical, C&W, folk, gospel and MOR. Recently published "Farewell Alma Mater" (by James Alteri); "Heaven's Roses Have No Thorns" (by Matie Ferguson) (traditional hymn); "I Am Me" (by Bernard Cervini) (hymn anthem); "Slipping Through My Fingers" (by C.W. Chase and Carolyn L. Houck) (C&W); and "Heaven on My Mind" and "Anytime" (by C.W. Chase).
**Tips:** "Write songs in everyday language that the ordinary person can identify with. So many times we receive hymns that are nothing more than three verses of worn-out religious cliches. Have a central theme when hymn-writing (e.g., Heaven, the Cross, Love of God, etc.)"

**\*CHATTERBOX MUSIC**, Suite 200, 20 Music Square W, Nashville TN 37203. (615)244-5900. President: Andy DiMartino. General Manager of Publishing: Stefan Nordin. Music publisher, record company and record producer. BMI, ASCAP. Publishes 50-250 songs/year; publishes 3 new songwriters/year. Pays standard royalty.
**How to Contact:** Submit demo tape and lyric sheet. Prefers cassette with 1-5 songs on demo. SASE. Reports in 3 weeks.
**Music:** Mostly up-tempo pop/country, top 40 and C&W; also dance-oriented, easy listening, MOR and rock. Recently published "Pepsi Man" (by Bill Addison), recorded by Bobby Mackey (C&W); "In the Heat of the Night" (by Gary T'To), recorded by G. T'To (top 40); and "United States of Japan" (by D. Hudson), recorded by Scafell Pike (top 40).
**Tips:** "We are looking for songs that can be placed with artists who are currently on the charts in US and Europe."

**CHEAVORIA MUSIC CO.**, 1219 Kerlin Ave., Brewton AL 36426. (205)867-2228. Affiliate: Bait String Music (ASCAP). Songwriter: Roy Edwards. Producer: Shannon Edwards. Music publisher, record producer and management firm. BMI. Publishes 15 songs/year; publishes 10 new songwriters/year. Pays standard royalties.
**How to Contact:** Query or submit demo tape and lead sheet. Prefers cassette with 2-5 songs on demo. SASE. Reports in 3 weeks.
**Music:** Mostly country, R&B, MOR; also disco, easy listening, progressive, soul and top 40/pop. Recently published "I've Changed to Your Kind of Life" (by Ruby Wilson); "Empty Promises" (by Bobbie Roberson); and "Let Me Go" (by B. Roberson), all recorded by B. Roberson/Bolivia Records (C&W); "Always and Forever" (by Jim Portwood), recorded by J. Portwood (country); "Music Inside" (by Nelson Trout), recorded by Roy Edwards (MOR); and "Make Me Forget" (by Horace Linsley), recorded by B. Roberson.

**CHERIE MUSIC CO.**, 3621 Heath Ln., Mesquite TX 75150. (214)279-5858. Contact: Jimmy Fields. Music publisher, record company and record producer. BMI. Publishes 30 songs/year; publishes 10-15 new songwriters/year. Pays standard royalty.
**How to Contact:** Submit demo tape and lyric sheet. Prefers 7 1/2 ips reel-to-reel or cassette with 5 songs on demo. SASE. Reports in 2 months.
**Music:** Mostly country; also bluegrass, church/religious, easy listening, progressive country, R&B, rock (hard) and top 40/pop.
**Tips:** "Do not over produce—let us hear the melody and lyrics."

**CHERRY LANE MUSIC PUBLISHING CO., INC.**, 110 Midland Ave., Port Chester NY 10573. (914)937-8601 and (212)824-7711. (New York Tie-line). Affiliated and/or administered companies: Windstar Music (ASCAP), Accabonac Music (ASCAP), Jolly Rogers Publishing (ASCAP), M-3 Music (ASCAP), Cappy Music (ASCAP), Cherry Wood Music (ASCAP), Hemlane Music (ASCAP), Cherry River Music (BMI), Windsea Music (BMI), Milton Okun Publishing (BMI), Mar-Ken Music

(BMI), Chicken Key Music (BMI), Third Son Music (ASCAP), Birdwing Music (ASCAP), Rainy Now Music (ASCAP), Sparrow Song (BMI), World Artist Music Co., Inc., (BMI), Group 7 Music (BMI), Cherry Blossom Music Co. (SESAC), and His Eye Music (SESAC). Music publisher. ASCAP. Member NMPA. Pays standard royalties.
**How to Contact:** "We do not accept unsolicited material."
**Music:** Easy listening, folk, MOR, inspirational and top 40/pop. Publishers of John Denver, Kenny Rogers, Steve Glassmeyer, Bill & Taffy Danoff, Tom Paxton, David Mallett, Jonathan Carroll, Margot Kunkel and Michael Dailey.

*****CHERRY RED MUSIC LTD.**, 53 Kensington Gardens Square, London, W2 4BA, England, 44-01-229-8854. General Manager: Theo Chalmers. Music publisher. MCPS, PRS. Publishes 500 songs/year. Pays negotiable royalty to songwriters; royalties paid directly to US songwriters.
**How to Contact:** Submit demo tape and lyric sheet. Prefers cassette with 2 songs on demo. Does not return unsolicited material. Reports in 1 month.
**Music:** Mostly electronic pop, dance-oriented, and punk; also classical. Recently published "Waves" (by Arthur and Luscombe), recorded by Blancmange (ballad); "Perfect" (by Matt Johnson); recorded by the Time (dance rock); and "Cattle and Cane" (by McLennan and Forster), recorded by the Go-Betweens (pop).
**Tips:** "Be non-derivative."

**CHESTNUT MOUND MUSIC**, Box 213, Hendersonville TN 37075. (615)822-1360. Affiliate: Pleasant View Music (ASCAP). Contact: Eddie Crook. Music publisher, record company and record producer. BMI. ASCAP. Publishes 30 songs/year; publishes 10 new songwriters/year. Pays standard royalty.
**How to Contact:** Write or call first about your interest, then submit demo tape and lyric sheet. Prefers cassette with 2-4 songs on demo. Does not return unsolicited material.
**Music:** C&W and gospel.

**CHINWAH SONGS/BIRTHRIGHT MUSIC**, 3101 S. Western Ave., Los Angeles CA 90018. (213)258-8011. Affiliate: House of Talley (BMI). General Manager: Leroy C. Lovett. Music publisher. SESAC, ASCAP. Member RIAA, NSG. Publishes 25-30 songs/year; publishes 5 new songwriters/year. Pays standard royalty.
**How to Contact:** Write first about your interest, then submit demo tape and lyric sheet. Prefers cassette with 3-5 songs on demo. SASE. Reports in 3 weeks.
**Music:** Gospel, inspiration and contemporary, church/choral, also MOR and Spanish. Recently published "Feels Like Fire" (by Gabriel Hardeman), recorded by Delegation/Birthright Records; "Love Will Rise" (by Michael Orr), recorded by Book of Life/Birthright Records (both contemporary gospel); and "Help Me to Stand" (by Albert Hartdige), recorded by Voices of Watts/Savoy Records (inspirational gospel).
**Tips:** "We look for 'good' lyrics as well as a fair or strong hook (something to make you remember the tune). A good presentation always helps convince the listener."

**CHIP 'N' DALE MUSIC PUBLISHERS, INC.**, 2125 8th Ave., S, Nashville TN 37204. (615)363-6002. Affiliates: Door Knob Music (BMI) and Lodestar Music (SESAC). President: Gene Kennedy. Vice President: Karen Jeglum. Music publisher. ASCAP. Member NSAI, CMA, NMPA, and ACM. Publishes 200 songs/year; publishes 100 new songwriters/year. Pays standard royalty.
**How to Contact:** Submit demo tape and lyric sheet (include SASE) or arrange personal interview. Prefers 7½ ips reel-to-reel or cassette with 1-4 songs on demo. SASE. Reports in 1-3 weeks.
**Music:** C&W, MOR and gospel. Recently published "Hold Me" (by Harry Shields), recorded by David Rogers/Music Masters Records (modern country).

**CHRIS MUSIC PUBLISHING**, 133 Arbutus Ave., Box 396, Manistique MI 49854-0396. Affiliate: Saralee Music (BMI). President: Reg B. Christensen. Music publisher and record company. BMI. Publishes 50 songs/year; publishes 10-15 new songwriters/year. Pays standard royalty.
**How to Contact:** Query, then submit cassette *only* with 2-5 songs on demo and lyric sheet. "No fancy, big band demo necessary; just one instrument with a clean, clear voice. Copyrighted material only. Send registration number. If not registered with Copyright office, let us know what you've done to protect your material." SASE. Reports in 1 month or ASAP.
**Music:** Bluegrass, C&W, gospel, MOR, rock (acid & hard), and soul. Recently co-published "Diamonds and Pearls," recorded by the Paradons/K-Tel Records (R&B); "Nashville Nut," recorded by Jay Savant (C&W); and "Ask Me No Questions," recorded by Bill Woods (C&W).
**Tips:** "The writer should indicate if he has a certain singer in mind. Also, we publishers have info on up and coming recording sessions of most well known recording artists (and pay big money to get this in-

fo.)" We can analyze your suggestion to see if a number of auditioners come up with a majority opinion which agrees with your analysis."

**CHROMEWOOD MUSIC**, Box 2388, Prescott AZ 86302. (602)445-5801. Affiliates: Hollydale Music (ASCAP) and Winteroak Music (ASCAP). Publishing Division President: Gaye Ellen Foreman. Music publisher. BMI. Publishes 30 songs/year; publishes 8 new songwriters/year. Pays standard royalty.
**How to Contact:** Submit demo tape and lyric sheet. Prefers cassette with 3-5 songs on demo. SASE. Reports in 3 weeks.
**Music:** C&W, easy listening and rock (country). Recently published "Out on the Road Again" (by M.D. Morgan), recorded by M.D. Morgan/Big Wheels Records (country); "Truckin' Woman" (by J. Pannell), recorded by J. Pannell/Big Wheels Records (country); and "Straw Hats and Stetsons" (by M.D. Morgan), recorded by Michael Hollister Morgan/Quarter Moon Records (country).

**THE CHU YEKO MUSICAL FOUNDATION**, Box 10051, Beverly Hills CA 90213. (213)761-2646. Branch: Box 1314, Englewood Cliffs NJ 07632. Affiliates: Broadway/Hollywood International Music Publishers. Messages: (201)567-5524. Producer: Doris Chu. Music publisher, record company, record producer, video and film producer. ASCAP, BMI. Publishes 10-20 songs/year; publishes 2-7 new songwriters/year. Pays negotiable royalty (up to 10% of profits).
**How to Contact:** Submit demo tape and lyric sheet. Prefers cassette with any number songs on demo. SASE. Reports in 1 month.
**Music:** Mostly musicals; also pop/rock, R&B, C&W and R&R. "Complete musicals preferred." Recently published "81 Proof," recorded on CYM Foundation Records; "Here's to L.A." (by Samovitz, Everest, Skyer, etc.), recorded by Paul Wong/The CYM Foundation Records (MOR); and "The Gun Control Tango" (by John Everest), recorded by various artists/The CYM Foundation Records (satiric).
**Tips:** Interested in complete musicals, and top 40/pop, rock, R&B, C&W, MOR, religious-oriented songs. "Co-publishers welcome."

**CIANO PUBLISHING**, Box 263, Hasbrouck Heights NJ 07604. (201)288-8935. President: Ron Luciano. Music publisher, record company and record producer. BMI. Publishes 12 songs/year. Pays standard royalty.
**How to Contact:** Query, submit demo tape and lead sheet or submit acetate disc and lead sheet. Prefers 7½ ips reel-to-reel, cassette or acetate with 2-6 songs on demo. SASE. Reports in 1 month.
**Music:** Disco, easy listening, MOR, R&B, rock, soul and top 40/pop. Recently published "Lucky" (by T. Galloway), recorded by Lucifer/Legz Records (rock n roll); "Fly Away" (by Philip Mitchell and Barron and Susan Sillars), recorded by Lucifer/Tiara Records (folk); and "Love's a Crazy Game" (by Joseph M. Leo and Paul Cannarella), recorded by Lucifer (top 40/disco).

***CITY PUBLISHING CO.**, 3966 Standish Ave., Cincinnati OH 45213. (513)793-8191. President: Roosevelt Lee. Music publisher, record company and record producer. Estab. 1981. BMI. Publishes 8 songs/year. Pays standard royalty.
**How to Contact:** Write first about your interest; submit demo tape and lyric sheet. Prefers cassette with maximum of 4 songs on demo. SASE. Reports in 1 month.
**Music:** Mostly C&W, R&B and soul. Recently published "Love City Part 1&2" (by Ronald Lee), recorded by Larry Daley/WES World Records (soul); and "Come Home to Me" (by Mike Ellis), recorded by M. Ellis/Key Records (C&W).

**CLARK MUSIC PUBLISHING**, Clark Musical Productions, Box 299, Watseka IL 60970. President: Dr. Paul E. Clark. Music publisher, booking agency and record company. BMI. Publishes 10-20 songs/year. Pays standard royalties.
**How to Contact:** Submit demo tape and lead sheet. Prefers cassette with 1-3 songs on demo. SASE.
**Music:** Church/religious, C&W, easy listening and gospel.

***CLARUS MUSIC, LTD.**, 340 Bellevue Ave., Yonkers NY 10703. (914)591-7715. President: Mrs. S. Fass. Music publisher, record company and record producer. ASCAP. Member MENC, NYSSMA, RIAA. "We publish children's records and material." Publishes 2 new songwriters/year. "Royalties paid are based on various reasons (plays, songs, etc.)."
**How to Contact:** Submit demo tape and lyric sheet and script. Prefers 7½ ips reel-to-reel or cassette with 4-10 songs on demo. SASE. Reports in 1-3 months.
**Music:** Children's.

**BRUCE COHN MUSIC**, Box 359, Sonoma CA 95476. (707)938-4060. Affiliates: Flat Lizard Music (ASCAP), Maybe Music (ASCAP), Quark Music (BMI), Skunkster Publishing (ASCAP), Snug Music

(BMI), Noodle Tunes (BMI), Pants Down Music (BMI), Spikes Music (BMI), Soquel Songs (ASCAP), Tauripin Tunes (ASCAP), Windecor Music (BMI) and R.P. Winkelman Tunes (ASCAP). Manager/Owner: Bruce Cohn. Music publisher and management firm. Publishes 10-20 songs/year.
**How to Contact:** Query. SASE.
**Music:** MOR; rock; soul; and top 40/pop. Recently published "It Keeps You Running" and "Taking it to the Streets" recorded by the Doobie Brothers (pop).

**COLLBECK PUBLISHING CO.**, 4817 Karchmer, Corpus Christi TX 78415. (512)854-7376. President: Gary Beck. Music publisher, record producer, record company and recording company. BMI. Publishes 10-100 songs/year.
**How to Contact:** Submit demo tape and lyric sheet. Prefers cassette with "as many songs as possible" on demo tape. SASE. Reports in 3 weeks.
**Music:** Pop and country.

*****BARRY COLLINGS MUSIC LTD.**, 15 Claremont Rd., Westcliff On-Sea, Essex, England. 44-702-43464. Telex: 242241 REF181 Orbit. Affiliates: Hilda Music, Orbit Music, Amusement Music (PRS) (MCPS), Orbit Records and Amusement Records. Managing Director: Barry Collings. Music publisher and record company. MCPS, PRS, Phonographic Performance Ltd. Member MPA and BPI. Publishes 50 songs/year; publishes 20 new songwriters/year. Pays standard royalty ("although some agreements rise to 60% over a period of time and we have clauses allowing 75% after several hits").
**How to Contact:** Submit demo tape and lyric sheet. Prefers cassette with 1-12 songs on demo. SAE and IRC. Reports in 3 weeks.
**Music:** Mostly MOR and pop; also dance-oriented, R&B, rock (all types) and soul. Recently published "Hazel Eyes" (by Ray Dorset), recorded by Mungo Jerry/Stagecoach Records (pop).
**Tips:** "Keep on submitting titles to us."

**CONNEL PUBLISHING**, 130 Pilgrim Dr., San Antonio TX 78213. (512)344-5033. Affiliate: J.C.E. Publishing Company (ASCAP). Owner: Jerry Connell. Record company, music publisher, record producer and booking agency. BMI. Publishes 75 songs/year; publishes 50 new songwriters/year. Pays standard royalties.
**How to Contact:** Query, submit demo tape, submit acetate disc, or submit lead sheet. Prefers 7½ or 15 ips reel-to-reel or cassette with 1 song on demo. Does not return unsolicited material. Reports in 2 weeks.
**Music:** Bluegrass, church/religious, C&W, disco, easy listening, folk, gospel, jazz, MOR, R&B, rock and top 40/pop. Recently published "Heaven" (by Joe Brown), recorded by J. Brown/Cherokee Records (C&W); "Streets of San Antonio" (by Mike Lord), recorded by M. Lord/Cherokee Records (C&W); and "Hundred Dollar Boots" (by Ronnie Mason), recorded by R. Mason/Cherokee Records (C&W).

**COPYRIGHT SERVICE BUREAU LTD.**, 221 W. 57 St., New York NY 10019. (212)582-5030. Vice President of Administration: Ms. Jeri R. Spencer. Music publisher. BMI, ASCAP and SESAC.
**How to Contact:** Submit demo tape and lyric sheet. Prefers cassette with 5 songs on demo. "Include a note in your submission and follow up with a letter." Does not return unsolicited material. Reports in 6 weeks.
**Music:** All types.

**COTILLION MUSIC, INC.**, 75 Rockefeller Plaza, New York NY 10019. (212)484-8132. Affiliate: Walden Music, Inc. (ASCAP). Professional Administrator: Bonnie Blumenthal. Music publisher. Member NMPA.
**How to Contact:** Does not return unsolicited material.
**Music:** Contemporary and rock.

**COUNTERPOP MUSIC GROUP**, (formerly O.A.S. Music Publishing), 3140 E. Shadowlawn Ave., Atlanta GA 30305. (404)231-9888. Affiliates: O.A.S. Music Publishing (ASCAP), Andgold Music Publishing (BMI), and Counterpop Music Publishing (BMI). Catalog Administrator: Vicui Tunstall. Music publisher. Publishes 15 songs/year; publishes 3 new songwriters/year. Pays standard royalty.
**How to Contact:** Submit demo tape and lyric sheet. Prefers cassette with 1-3 songs on demo. "We like strong repetitive hooks." SASE. Reports as soon as possible.
**Music:** C&W, easy listening, MOR, R&B, rock, soul and top 40/pop. Recently published "The Woman in Me" (by Susan Thomas), recorded by Crystal Gayle/CBS Records (MOR).

**COUNTRY CLASSICS MUSIC PUBLISHING CO.**, 105 Burk Dr., Oklahoma City OK 73115. (405)677-6448. Affiliates: Sunny Lane Music. (ASCAP), Compo Music Publishing (BMI), and Deva-

ney Music Publishing (BMI). General Manager: Sonny Lane. Music publisher, record company and record producer. ASCAP, BMI. Publishes 8 songs/year; publishes 2 new songwriters/year. Pays standard royalties.
**How to Contact:** Submit demo tape. Prefers cassette with 2-6 songs on demo. SASE. Reports in 3 weeks.
**Music:** Mostly church/religious and C&W; also easy listening, gospel; MOR and top 40/pop. Recently published "You Still Got It" (by Daryl Hall and Ray Sanders), recorded by Larry James/Dee Jay Records (country); "Jesus Is the Best Thing That Ever Happened to Me" (by Yvonne DeVaney), recorded by Wanda Jackson/Vine Records (religious); and "Do It Like Your Daddy Told You To" (by Gary McCray), recorded by Kentucky/JMP (Jamtangen) Records (country—recorded in Sweden, released in the Scandinavian countries).
**Tips:** "Write a simple melody with strong lyrics and make a good demo tape."

**COUNTRY LEGS MUSIC**, 1577 Redwood Dr., Harvey LA 70058. (504)367-8501. Affiliate: Golden Sunburst Music (BMI). Manager: George Leger. Music publisher, record company, record producer, record distributor and promoter. ASCAP. Member CMA. Publishes 12-15 songs/year; publishes 1-2 new songwriter/year. "We spend a lot of time trying to develop new writers." Pays standard royalty.
**How to Contact:** Submit demo tape and lyric and lead sheet. Prefers 7½ ips reel-to-reel or cassette with 3-5 songs on demo. SASE. Reports in 1 month or ASAP.
**Music:** Mostly country (ballad or two-step style); also gospel, progressive country and R&B. Recently published "Let's Put Christ in Christmas Again" (by George Leger), recorded by G. Leger/Sunset Records (country Christmas); "I Don't Care It Don't Matter Anymore" (by Larry Maynard), recorded by L. Maynard/Sunburst Records (country pop); and "Oh Lonely Heart" (by Kenneth Adams), recorded by Sonny Fears/Sunset Records (country).
**Tips:** "Take time to write one good song instead of ten bad ones and pitch to one publisher at one time."

**COUNTRY STAR MUSIC**, 439 Wiley Ave., Franklin PA 16323. (814)432-4633. Affiliates: Kelly Music Publications (BMI) and Process Music Publications (BMI). President: Norman Kelly. Music publisher and record company. ASCAP. Publishes 15-20 songs/year; publishes 5-10 new songwriters/year. Pays standard royalty.
**How to Contact:** Submit demo tape and lyric sheet. Prefers 7½ ips reel-to-reel or cassette with 1-4 songs on demo. SASE. Reports in 2 weeks.
**Music:** Mostly country; also bluegrass, easy listening, folk, gospel, MOR and top 40/pop. Recently published "Siempre" (by Marvin Geyer), recorded by Doc Holiday/Country Star Records; "My Love Rolls Over" (by Valerie Anderson), recorded by V. Anderson/Country Star Records; and "Late Last Night" (by Bill Ayers), recorded by B. Ayers/Country Star Records (all country).
**Tips:** "Send only your best songs—ones you feel are equal to or better than current hits."

**COUSINS MUSIC**, 211 Birchwood Ave., Upper Nyack NY 10960. (914)358-0861. Affiliate: Neems (ASCAP). President: Lou Cicchetti. Music publisher and record producer. BMI. Publishes 5-10 songs/year; publishes 6 new songwriters/year. Pays standard royalty.
**How to Contact:** Submit demo tape and lyric sheet. Prefers 7½ or 15 ips reel-to-reel or cassette with any number of songs on demo. SASE. Reports in 2 weeks.
**Music:** Mostly country; also rock. Recently published "Barbara-Ann" (by F. Fassert), recorded by the Regents, Jan & Dean, the Beach Boys, etc. (rock); and "Your Honor" (by J.O. Daniel), recorded by Koko/West Side Records (country).
**Tips:** "Most artists are writing their own material and most labels will not entertain new ideas or material from new writers. You must somehow get label attention. We do this with a good professional demo produced by us and circulated among the few creative producers and A&R people still seeking new talent."

**COVERED BRIDGE MUSIC**, 615 Durrett Dr., Nashville TN 37211. (615)833-1457. Affiliates: Town Square (SESAC) and Iron Skillet (ASCAP). General Manager: Bill Wence. Music publisher. BMI.
**How to Contact:** Submit demo tape and lyric sheet. Prefers cassette only, maximum 2 songs on demo. SASE. Reports in 2 weeks. "Send us your best song. Use a quality, clear tape. Don't bother sending 10 or 15 songs on one tape."
**Music:** Country. Recently published "Marriage on the Rocks" (by Carl Struck), recorded by C. Struck/Rustic Records (country); "Quicksand" and "I Wanna Do It Again" (by Bill Wence), recorded by B. Wence (country).

***COWBOY JUNCTION PUB. CO.**, Highway 44 West, Lecanto FL 32661. (904)746-4754. President: Elizabeth Thompson. Music publisher and record producer. BMI.

**How to Contact:** SASE. Reports "when ever we get a chance."
**Music:** Mostly C&W; also bluegrass. Recently published "The Story of Barney Clark," "Flea Market Cowboy," and "Le High Valley" (by Boris Max Patuch), recorded by Buddy Max/Cowboy Junction Records (country).

**CRAZY CAJUN MUSIC, INC.**, 5626 Brock St., Houston TX 77023. (713)926-4431. Affiliate: Swamp (ASCAP). Contact: Huey P. Meaux. Music publisher, record producer and record company. BMI. Pays standard royalty.
**How to Contact:** Write first about your interest, then submit demo tape and lyric sheet or arrange personal interview to play demo tape. Prefers cassette with 1-4 songs on demo. SASE. Reports in 1 month.
**Music:** Blues, C&W crossover, disco, easy listening, folk, gospel, MOR, progressive, R&B, rock, soul and top 40/pop. Recently published "The Rains Came" recorded by Freddie Fender/ABC Records (country pop).

**CREAM PUBLISHING GROUP**, 8025 Melrose Ave., Los Angeles CA 90046. (213)655-0944. Affiliates: Butter Music (BMI), Churn Music (ASCAP). Professional Manager/Staff Song Writer: Marty Sadler. Music publisher. BMI, ASCAP. Member NMPA. Publishes 150 songs/year; publishes 50 new songwriters/year. Pays standard royalty. Sometimes secures songwriters on salary basis. Catalogs 4,000 songs/year.
**How to Contact:** Submit demo tape and lyric sheet. Prefers cassette with maximum 4 songs on demo. "Include lyrics and as much information as possible and songs that could be done by more than 2 artists." SASE. Reports in 1 week.
**Music:** Bluegrass, blues, church/religious, C&W, disco, easy listening, folk, gospel, jazz, MOR, progressive, R&B, rock (hard and soft) and top 40/pop. Recently published "Happy Birthday, Darlin'" (by Chuck Howard), recorded by Conway Twitty/MCA Records.

**CREATIVE CORPS.**, Suite E, 6607 W. Sunset, Hollywood CA 90028. (213)464-3495. Affiliates: Driving Music (ASCAP) and Visual Songs (BMI). President: Kurt Hunter. Music publisher and record producer. BMI, ASCAP. Member AIMP. Publishes 10 songs/year; publishes 2 new songwriters/year. Pays standard royalty.
**How to Contact:** Submit demo tape and lyric sheet. Prefers cassette with 1-5 songs on demo tape. SASE. Reports in 4 months.
**Music:** C&W (with cross-over potential), R&B, rock, soul and top 40/pop. Recently published "Come and Love Me" (by N. Mezey), recorded by Dandy/Warner Curb Records (country); "Dancin' Wheels" (by N. Mezey, R. Pollack and L. Keen), recorded on Columbia House Records (disco); and "N.O.-.L.A." (by J. Selk and A. Del Zoppo), recorded by Chuck Francour/EMI Records (rock).
**Tips:** "Songs must be creative with strong hook-chorus."

**CREEKSIDE MUSIC**, 100 Labon St., Tabor City NC 28463. (919)653-2546. President: Elson H. Stevens. Music publisher, record company, record producer and promotions. BMI. Publishes 50 songs/year; publishes 10 new songwriters/year. Pays standard royalty.
**How to Contact:** Call first about your interest, then submit demo tape and lyric sheet or arrange personal interview to play demo tape. Prefers 7½ ips reel-to-reel or cassette with 1-3 songs on demo. SASE. Reports in 1 month.
**Music:** Mostly country; also bluegrass, gospel, rock (country and hard) and black music. Recently published "Pages of My Mind" (by Glen Todd), and "Nightime Lady" (by Mitchell Todd), recorded by T. Jay Jon/Seaside Records (country); and "Cheap Imitation" (by J.C. Batchelor), recorded by The Musickmakers/Seaside Records (country).
**Tips:** "Send only songs with strong punch."

***CREOLE MUSIC LTD.**, 91-93 High St., Harlesden, London, England. 44-01-965-9223. Publishing Manager: David Brooks. Music publisher, record company and record producer. MCPS, PRS, Phonographic Performance Ltd. Member MPA. Publishes 150 songs/year; publishes 8 new songwriters/year. Pays negotiable royalty; royalties paid directly to US songwriters. Submit demo tape and lyric sheet. Prefers cassette with 2-6 songs on demo. SAE and IRC. Reports in 3 weeks.
**Music:** Mostly rock and disco; also C&W, easy listening R&B and soul. Recently published "This Heart of Mine," by The Wonders; "I Believe in You," by Nina Shaw; and "Single Handed," by Sharon Haywood.

**CRIMSON DYNASTY**, Crimson Dynasty Record Corp., Box 271, Jenkintown PA 19046. President: Stan Peahota. Music publisher, record company and recording studio. ASCAP. Publishes 18-20 songs/year; publishes 4 new songwriters/year. Offers cash advance against royalty. Sometimes hires staff writers.

**How to Contact:** Submit demo tape and lead sheet. Include photo and resume. Prefers 7½ ips reel-to-reel, cassette, 8-track cartridge or disc. SASE. Reports in 3 weeks.
**Music:** Blues; C&W; easy listening and novelty.
**Tips:** "All submissions will be reviewed. We are looking for songs that Muhammad Ali, Frank Sinatra or the Beatles would sing if they were to listen to them. That is the style we want."

**THE EDDIE CROOK COMPANY,** Box 213, Hendersonville TN 37075. (615)822-1360. Affiliates: Chestnut Mound Music (BMI) and Pleasant View Music (ASCAP). Contact: Eddie Crook. Music publisher, record company and record producer. BMI and ASCAP. Publishes 15 songs/year; publishes 10 new songwriters/year. Pays standard royalty.
**How to Contact:** Submit demo tape and lyric sheet or arrange personal interview. Prefers cassette with 1-3 songs on demo. Does not return unsolicited material. Reports in 1 month.
**Music:** Gospel. Recently published "I've Already Won the War" (by Tommy Alexander), recorded by Happy Goodmans/Word Records; "Sunrise in the Morning" (by Vaughn Thacker), recorded by Florida Boys/Word Records; "I'm Tired of Living in a World of Sin" (by Naomi Rudd), recorded by The Lewis Family/Canaan Records.

**CUDE & PICKENS PUBLISHING,** 519 N. Halifax Ave., Daytona Beach FL 32018. (904)252-0381. A&R Director: Bobby Lee Cude. Music publisher, record company and record producer. BMI. Publishes 25-50 songs/year. Pays standard royalty.
**How to Contact:** Write first about your interest. "We are not accepting any new writers at this time." Prefers cassette with 1-6 songs on demo. SASE. Reports as soon as possible.
**Music:** C&W, easy listening, gospel, MOR, top 40/pop and Broadway Show. Recently published "Tallulah! Tallulah!" (musical tribute to Tallulah Bankhead); "Los Angeles Town" (Los Angeles Commemorative bicentennial song); "Come to the Islands of the Caribbean" (island song); and "It's Twelve O'Clock! Do You Know Where Your Children Are?"

**V&M CUTLER MUSIC CO.,** Box 43, Chatsworth CA 91311. (213)886-7746. Manager: Max Cutler. Music publisher. ASCAP. Member Harry Fox Agency. Publishes 7 songs/year; publishes 2 new songwriters/year. Pays standard royalty.
**How to Contact:** Write first about your interest. Prefers cassette and lead and lyric sheet with 3-5 songs on demo. "Keep voice up and lyrics clear." SASE. Reports in 3 weeks.
**Music:** Mostly top 40/pop ballads; also blues, easy listening, MOR and R&B. Recently published "Runaway Girl," "He's a Gambler," and "I Don't Belong" by Victoria-Diane Cutler/Liasou Records (ballads).
**Tips:** "Both lyric and music must be outstanding, and easy to follow. Try catering to 21-35 year olds. Write a meaningful slow ballad."

***CYHOEDDIADAU SAIN,** Llandwrog, Caernarfon, Swynedd, LL54 5TG, United Kingdom. 44-0286-831-111. Directors: Hefin Elis and Dafydd Iwan. Music publisher, record company, record producer and record distributors. MCPS, PRS, Phonographic Performance Ltd. Member APRS. Publishes 150 songs/year; publishes 12 new songwriters/year. Has not yet, but would listen to songs from US songwriters. Pays 6¼% of retail price of album to songwriters, prorated per number of songs.
**How to Contact:** Submit demo tape and lyric sheet. Prefers cassette with 1-5 songs on demo. SAE and IRC. Reports in 1 month.
**Music:** Mostly choral (Welsh language); also children's, church/religious, classical, C&W, folk and MOR. Recently published "Chwarae'n Troi'n Chwerw" (by Caryl Ifans & Myfyr Isaac), recorded by Bando/Sain Records (MOR); "Cerddwn Ymalen" (by Dafydd Iwan), recorded by Dafydd Iwan & Arlog/Sain Records (folk); and "Y Dref Wen" (by Tecwyn Ifan), recorded by Llanelli Male Choir/Sain Records (choral).
**Tips:** "Songs should be relevant to the scene in Wales."

***DAN THE MAN MUSIC PUB. CO.,** 3094 W. 101 St., Cleveland OH 44111. (216)631-6553. President: Daniel L. Bischoff. Music publisher, record company and record producer. Estab. 1982. ASCAP. Publishes 20 songs/year; publishes 10-12 new songwriters/year. Pays standard royalty.
**How to Contact:** Submit demo tape and lyric sheet. Prefers cassette or record with 2-4 "of your best" songs on demo. SASE. Repots in 3 weeks.
**Music:** Mostly country, top 40, love songs and novelty; also easy listening, folk, R&B and soul. Recently published "Just a Simple Bouquet" and "Our Love Will Not Fade," by Johnny Wright/Dan the Man Records (C&W); and "Job-Less" by Dan the Man/Dan the Man Records (novelty).
**Tips:** "We like catchy songs and very good love songs."

**DANA PUBLISHING CO.,** 824 83rd St., Miami Beach FL 33141. (305)865-8960. President: Walter Dana. Music publisher, record company and record producer. BMI. Pays standard royalty.

**How to Contact:** Write first about your interest. Prefers 7½ or 15 ips reel-to-reel or cassette. SASE.
**Music:** Classical and Polish.

**DANBORO PUBLISHING CO.**, Box 2199, Vancouver, British Columbia, Canada V6B 3V7. (604)669-3195. Affiliate: Synchron Publishing (CAPAC). President: John Rodney. Music publisher and record company. BMI. Publishes 25-35 songs/year. Pays standard royalties.
**How to Contact:** Submit demo tape. Prefers 7½ ips reel-to-reel with 2-6 songs on demo. "Be selective. Send only the best songs. Identify tapes fully." SAE and IRC. Reports in 1 month.
**Music:** C&W, easy listening, MOR, rock and top 40/pop. Recently published "The Commander," by Elmer Gill and E. Lockjaw Davis; and "I Can't Hear for Listening," by E. Gill; and "For Gigi," by Lockjaw Davis.

**DAVID MUSIC**, 1650 Broadway, New York NY 11021. (212)247-2159. Affiliates: Felicia Wynne Music (BMI), Sarah Music (ASCAP). President: Morton Wax. Music publisher and record company. BMI. Pays standard royalty.
**How to Contact:** Submit demo tape and lyric sheet. Prefers cassette. Does not return unsolicited material. Reports as soon as possible.
**Music:** All kinds.

**DAVIKE MUSIC CO.**, Box 8842, Los Angeles CA 90008. (213)292-5138. Contact: Isaiah Jones. Music publisher. ASCAP. Publishes 3 songs/year; publishes 1 new songwriter/year. Pays standard royalty.
**How to Contact:** Query first, submit demo tape and lyric sheet or arrange personal interview to play demo tape. Prefers 7½ ips reel-to-reel or cassette. SASE. Reports in 1 month.
**Music:** Mostly gospel, pop; also blues, choral, church/religious, disco, easy listening, folk, gospel, MOR, R&B, soul, and top 40. Recently published "Stand" (by Don Herron); recorded by the Voices of Watts/Savoy Records; "Jesus Is Coming in Glory" (by Andre Oliver and Isiah Jones), recorded by Bobby Glenn/Godwil Records; "Halleujah! Praise the Lord" (by A. Oliver and I. Jones), recorded by Desiree Oliver/Godwil Records; "He'll Lead You On to the Light" and "God Loves Me" (both by A. Oliver and I. Jones), "Deliverance" (by I. Jones), and "God Is Everywhere" (by James Hinton and I. Jones), all on Godwill Records.
**Tips:** "Send lead sheet with demo."

**DAWN TREADER MUSIC**, 2223 Strawberry, Pasadena TX 77502. (713)472-5563. Affiliates: Shepherd's Fold Music (BMI), Straight Way Music (ASCAP) and Dawn Treader Music (SESAC). President: Darrell A. Harris. Music publisher. Publishes 100 songs/year. Pays standard royalty.
**How to Contact:** Submit demo tape and lyric sheet. Prefers cassette with 3 songs maximum on demo. "We would like as much background information as possible on the writer and his or her musical activities." SASE. Reports in 1 month.
**Music:** Contemporary gospel; and top 40/pop. "We are looking for well-constructed songs with a solid Christian lyrical content." Recently published "More Power to Ya," by Petra/Star Song Records; "The Sacrifice," by Wayne Watson/Milk & Honey Records; "Only One Lord," by Dallas Holm and Praise/Green Tree Records; and "Every Single Step," by Michael James Murphy/Milk & Honey Records.

***DAZIA MUSIC PUBLISHING COMPANY**, 13033 W. McNichols, Detroit MI 48235. (313)342-9692. Professional Manager: Jacqueline Harris. Music publisher, record company, record producer and production company. Estab. 1981. BMI. Publishes 8 songs/year; publishes 2 new songwriters/year. Pays standard royalty.
**How to Contact:** Write first about your interest; submit demo tape and lyric sheet. Prefers 7½ ips or cassette with 1-4 songs on demo. Put adequate postage on both the outside (mailing) envelope and the SASE or submissions will not be returned. SASE. Reports in 1 month.
**Music:** Mostly R&B and pop; also children's, dance-oriented, easy listening and soul. Recently published "Do Me Baby Do Me" (by Cortez Harris and J. Williams), recorded by Somerset/Dazia Records (dance/R&B); "Concentrate on Love" (by C. Harris and J. Williams), recorded by Alicia Myers/MCA Records (R&B); "Do Anything For You" (by C. Harris), recorded by Somerset/Dazia Records); and "I'm In Love With You" (by C. Harris), recorded by Somerset/Dazia Records (ballad).

**DE WALDEN MUSIC INTERNATIONAL, INC.**, #1911, 6255 Sunset Blvd., Hollywood CA 90028. (213)462-1922. Affiliates: Chriswald Music, Inc. (ASCAP), Father Music (BMI). Managing Director: Christian de Walden. Music publisher and record producer. BMI, ASCAP. Publishes 100 songs/year; publishes 2-3 new songwriters/year. Pays standard royalty.
**How to Contact:** Arrange personal interview if in the area or submit demo tape and lyric sheet. Prefers cassette with 1-5 songs on demo. SASE. Reports "as soon as possible."
**Music:** Country (pop), easy listening, MOR, Spanish, soul and top 40/pop. Recently published

"I.O.U." (by A. Roberts/K. Chater), recorded by Lee Greenwood (country crossover); "Afterall" (by A. Roberts/T. Arney), recorded by Pussycat (country crossover); and "Don't Let Go" (by L. Macaluso), recorded by Hornettes (pop).
**Tips:** "Songs *must* have great hooks."

**DEERCREEK PUBLISHING CO.**, 232 Jefferson Bldg., Greenfield OH 45123. (513)981-3978. President: Clay Eager. Music publisher, record producer, booking agency and advertising bureau. BMI. Pays standard royalties.
**How to Contact:** Query or submit demo tape. Prefers reel-to-reel with 1-12 songs on demo. SASE. Reports in 1 month.
**Music:** Bluegrass, church/religious, C&W, folk and gospel.

**DELIGHTFUL MUSIC LTD.**, 1733 Broadway, New York NY 10019. (212)757-6770. Affiliate: Double F Music (ASCAP). Vice-President: Martin Feig. Music publisher and record company. BMI. Hires staff writers. Pays standard royalty.
**How to Contact:** Submit demo tape and lyric sheet. Prefers cassette as demo. SASE. Reports in 2 months.
**Music:** R&B and top 40/pop. Recently published "Let's Go Dancin' " (by Amir Bayyan, James Taylor and Kool The Gang), recorded by Kool & The Gang.

**LOU DeLISE PRODUCTIONS**, 2001 W. Moyamensing Ave., Philadelphia PA 19145. (215)271-0803. Music Director: Lou DeLise. General Manager: Norman Rosen. Music publisher and record producer. BMI. Member AGAC and AF of M. Publishes 12 songs/year; publishes 2-4 new songwriters/year. Pays standard royalty.
**How to Contact:** Submit demo tape and lyric sheet. Prefers cassette with 1-3 songs on demo. SASE. Reports in 1 month.
**Music:** C&W; dance; MOR; rock; R&B; and top 40/pop. Recently recorded "Searchin for Love" (by Hotchkis and Terry), recorded by Bruce McFarland (pop); "Love Jones" (by U. Fay and T. Adams), recorded by Ray Eskridge (R&B); "Lover Come to Me" (by Fay, James and DeLise), recorded by Ray Eskridge (R&B).

**DERBY MUSIC**, Las Vegas Recording Studio, 3977 Vegas Valley Dr., Las Vegas NV 89121. (702)457-4365. Mailing Address: Box 42937, Las Vegas NV 89116. President: Hank Castro. Affiliates: Ru-Dot-To Music (BMI), She-La-La Music (SESAC) and Hankeychip Music (ASCAP). Music publisher and recording studio. (She-La-La Music/SESAC). Publishes 10-20 songs/year; publishes 4-5 new songwriters/year.
**Music:** Bluegrass, blues, C&W, easy listening, gospel, jazz, MOR, progressive, R&B, rock, soul and top 40/pop. Recently published "Right in the Middle of Forever" (by Ron Fuller), recorded on ECR Records (country disco).

**DIAMOND IN THE ROUGH MUSIC**, 1440 Kearny St. NE, Washington DC 20017. (202)635-0464. Vice President A&R: Rodney Brown. Music publisher, record company and record producer. BMI. Publishes 50 songs/year. Pays standard royalties.
**How to Contact:** Submit demo tape. Prefers 7½ ips reel-to-reel or cassette with 2-4 songs on demo. SASE. Reports in 1 month.
**Music:** Disco, R&B and soul. Recently published "You've Got What It Takes" (by Rodney Brown), recorded by Bobby Thurston (disco).

**DIAMONDBACK MUSIC**, 10 Waterville St., San Francisco CA 94124. Administrator: Joseph Buchwald. Music publisher. BMI. Publishes 6 songs/year; publishes 1 new songwriter/year. Pays standard royalty.
**How to Contact:** Submit demo tape and lead sheet. Prefers cassette with 3-6 songs on demo. SASE. Reports "as soon as possible."
**Music:** Ballads and MOR. Recently published "Miracles," (by Balin), recorded by Balin/RCA Records (love ballad); "Hearts," and "Do It for Love" (by Barish), recorded by Balin/EMI Records (love ballads).

**DIVERSIFIED MUSIC, INC.**, Box 17087, Nashville TN 37217. (615)754-9400. Affiliates: Millstone (ASCAP), Almarie (BMI) and Juina (SESAC). Professional Manager: Gene Vowell. Music publisher. Publishes 200 songs/year; publishes 10-12 new songwriters/year.
**How to Contact:** Call first about your interest and arrange personal interview to play demo tape. Prefers cassette with 1-2 songs on demo. "Include lyric sheet." SASE. Reports in 1 month.
**Music:** Bluegrass, C&W, easy listening, folk, gospel, MOR, progressive and top 40/pop.

**HUGH DIXON MUSIC, INC.**, 292 Lorraine Dr., Montreal/Baie d'Urfe, Quebec, Canada H9X 2R1. (514)457-5959. Affiliates: Dicap Music (CAPAC) and Dipro Music (PROCAN). President: Hugh D. Dixon. Executive Assistant: C.M.A. van Ogtrop. Music publisher, record company and recording studio. Pays standard royalty.
**How to Contact:** Submit demo tape and lyric sheet. Prefers cassette with 2-5 songs on demo. SAE and IRC. Acknowledgement upon receipt. Reports in 1 month.
**Music:** "Inspirational, uplifting, introspective, cosmic, spiritual, philosophical, metaphysical lyrics that can be marketed in a country/soft rock or avant-garde/futuristic format." Also producers/distributors of spoken word and meditation environment recordings.

**DOC DICK ENTERPRISES**, 16 E. Broad St., Mt. Vernon NY 10552. (914)668-4488. President: Richard Rashbaum. Music publisher and management firm. BMI. Publishes 6 songs/year; publishes 4 new songwriters/year. Pays standard royalties.
**How to Contact:** Query, submit demo tape and lead sheet, submit acetate disc, or submit acetate disc and lead sheet. Prefers cassette with 1-4 songs on demo. SASE. Reports in 2 weeks.
**Music:** Mostly R&B and top 40/pop; also disco and soul. Recently published "Everybody Get Off" and "Romance at a Disco (by Ken Simmons), recorded by Daybreak/Prelude Records (R&B); and "Run to Me" and "Love Is Serious Business" (by Alfie Davison), recorded by Daybreak/Salsoul Records (R&B).

**DON-DEL MUSIC/DON-DE MUSIC**, 15041 Wabash Ave., S. Holland IL 60473. (312)339-0307. President: Donald De Lucia. Music publisher, record producer and record company. BMI and ASCAP. Pays standard royalty.
**How to Contact:** Submit demo tape and lyric sheet. Prefers 7½ ips reel-to-reel with 4-6 songs on demo. SASE. Reports in 1 week.
**Music:** C&W, rock and top 40/pop.

**DONNA MARIE MUSIC**, c/o American Creative Entertainment Ltd., Suite 818, 1616 Pacific Ave., Atlantic City NJ 08401. (609)347-0484. President: Danny Luciano. Associate Producer: Armand Cucinotti. Music publisher, record company and record producer. ASCAP. Publishes 6 songs/year; publishes 3 new songwriters/year. Pays standard royalty.
**How to Contact:** Submit demo tape and lyric sheet. Prefers 7½ ips reel-to-reel or cassette with 4-8 songs on demo. "No 8-tracks." SASE. Reports in 6 weeks.
**Music:** MOR, R&B, rock, soul and top 40/pop.

**DONNA MUSIC PUBLISHING CO.**, Box 113, Woburn MA 01801. (617)933-1474. General Manager: Frank Paul. Music publisher, record company, record producer, management firm and booking agency. BMI. Publishes 50-75 songs/year. Pays standard royalties.
**How to Contact:** Submit demo tape and lead sheet. Prefers cassette with 3-6 songs on demo. "We will listen to tapes but will not return material. If we believe a song has potential, we will contact the songwriter." Reports in 1 month.
**Music:** C&W, easy listening, gospel, MOR, R&B, rock, soul and top 40/pop. Recently published "Happy Happy Birthday Baby," recorded by Mango Sylvia and Gilbert Lopez/Casa Grande Records (R&B).

**DOOMS MUSIC PUBLISHING CO.**, Box 2072, Waynesboro VA 22980. (703)949-0106. Contact: John Major, Margie Major. Music publisher and record company. BMI. Pays on royalty basis.
**How to Contact:** Submit demo tape. Prefers cassette. SASE. Reports in 3 weeks.
**Music:** Bluegrass, C&W, easy listening, gospel and MOR. Recently published "So Good to be Loved" (by James Melvin), recorded by J. Melvin (country).

**DOOR KNOB MUSIC PUBLISHING, INC.**, 2125 8th Ave. S., Nashville TN 37204. (615)383-6002. Affiliates: Chip 'N' Dale Music Publishers, Inc (ASCAP); and Lodestar Music (SESAC). President: Gene Kennedy. Vice President: Karen Jeglum. Music publisher. BMI. Member NMPA, NSAI, CMA and ACM. Publishes 200 songs/year; publishes 100 new songwriters/year. Pays standard royalty.
**How to Contact:** Submit demo tape and lyric sheet or arrange personal interview. Prefers 7½ ips reel-to-reel or cassette with 1-4 songs on demo. SASE. Reports in 6 weeks.
**Music:** C&W, MOR and gospel. Recently published "When a Woman Cries" (by Betty Duke and Sammy Lyons), recorded by David Rogers/Republic Records (modern country); and "A Thing or Two on My Mind" (by Max Fagan), recorded by Gene Kennedy and Karen Jeglum/Door Knob Records.

**DRAGON FLY MUSIC**, 219 Meriden Rd., Waterbury CT 06705. (203)754-3674. Contact: Ralph Calabrese. Music publisher and record producer. BMI. Publishes 4 songs/year; publishes 2 new songwriters/year. Pays standard royalties.

## Music Publishers 41

**How to Contact:** Submit demo tape or demo tape and lead sheet. Prefers 7½ ips reel-to-reel with 3-6 songs on demo. SASE. Reports in 1 month.
**Music:** Disco, rock, soul and top 40/pop. Recently published "Don't Want to Live Without You," "My Baby's Gone" and "Bad, Bad Girl" (by R. Calabrese), recorded on ABC Records; and "Going Nowhere Fast" (by R. Calabrese), recorded on London Records (top 40/pop).

**DRAGON INTERNATIONAL MUSIC,** Box 8263, Haledon NJ 07508. (201)942-6810. President: Samuel Cummings. Music publisher, record producer and record company. BMI. Publishes 4 songs/year; 5 new songwriters/year.
**How to Contact:** Query. Prefers 7½ ips reel-to-reel or cassette with 3-5 songs on demo. SASE. Reports in 1 month.
**Music:** Reggae and soul. Recently published "Being a Woman" (by Sam Cummings and Rudolph Richards), recorded by Yolanda Brown/April Records (disco); "Disco Fever" (by Clive Waugh and S. Cummings), recorded by Rhonda Durand/April Records (disco); and "Best Time of My Life" (by Paul Davidson), recorded by Davidson/April Records (easy listening).

**\*THE DRAKE MUSIC GROUP,** 809 18th Ave. S., Nashville TN 37203. (615)327-3211. Affiliates: Petewood Music (ASCAP) and Window Music Pub. Co. Inc. (BMI). Professional Manager: Ron Cornelius. Music publisher and record producer. BMI, ASCAP, SESAC. Member NMA, CMA, GMA. Publishes 75-100 songs/year; publishes 1-2 new songwriters/year. Hires staff writers. Pays standard royalty.
**How to Contact:** Write or call about your interest. Prefers cassette with 2-4 songs on demo. SASE. Reports in 3 weeks.
**Music:** Mostly country and gospel; also church/religious, C&W, easy listening, MOR and top 40/pop. Recently published "Amazing Grace," recorded by B.J. Thomas (gospel); "Whatever Happened to Old Fashioned Love," recorded by B.J. Thomas (country); and "If Drinkin' Don't Kill Me," recorded by George Jones (country).

**DUANE MUSIC, INC.,** 382 Clarence Ave., Sunnydale CA 94086. (408)739-6133. Affiliate: Morhits Publishing (BMI). President: Garrie Thompson. Music publisher. BMI. Publishes 10-20 songs/year; publishes 1 new songwriter/year. Pays standard royalty.
**How to Contact:** Submit demo tape and lead sheet. Prefers cassette with 1-4 songs on demo. SASE. Reports in 1 month.
**Music:** Blues, C&W, disco, easy listening, rock, soul and top 40/pop. Recently published "Little Girl," recorded by Ban (rock); "Warm Tender Love," recorded by Percy Sledge (soul); and "My Adorable One," recorded by Joe Simon (blues).

**DUPUY RECORDS/PRODUCTIONS/PUBLISHING, INC.,** Suite 200, 10960 Ventura Blvd., Studio City CA 91604. (213)980-6412). President: Pedro Dupuy. Estab. 1981. Music publisher, record company and record producer. ASCAP. Member AGAC. Publishes 50 songs/year; publishes 4 new songwriters/year. Hires staff writers. Pays standard royalty.
**How to Contact:** Write or call first about your interest, arrange personal interview or submit demo tape and lyric sheet. Prefers cassette with 2-4 songs on demo. SASE. Reports in 1 month.
**Music:** Mostly R&B and pop; also easy listening, jazz, MOR, soul and top 40. Recently published "Livin' for Your Love," and "Show Me the Way" (by Gordon Gilman), recorded by G. Gilman/Dupuy Records (R&B).
**Tips:** Songs should have "very definitive lyrics with hook."

**DYNAMO PUBLISHING CO.,** 484 Lake Park Ave., Box 6, Oakland CA 94610. (415)482-4854. A&R Director: Dan Orth. Music publisher, record company and record producer. BMI. Member SRS. Publishes 2 songs/year; publishes 1 new songwriter/year. Pays standard royalty.
**How to Contact:** Write or call first about your interest, then submit demo tape and lyric sheet. Prefers cassette with 1-3 songs on demo. SASE. Reports in 1 month.
**Music:** C&W, easy listening, folk, MOR, R&B, rock (hard, soft, pop), top 40/pop and new wave. Recently published "Cruisin' the Strip" and "Hard-Boiled" (by Dan Orth and Phil Phillips), recorded by P. Phillips (hard rock); and "It Takes More" (by P. Phillips), recorded by P. Phillips (pop rock).

**E.L.J. RECORD CO.,** 1344 Waldron, St. Louis MO 63130. (314)803-3605. President: Eddie Johnson. Vice President: William Johnson. Music publisher and record company. BMI. Publishes 8-10 songs/year; publishes 2 new songwriters/year. Pays 5-10% royalty.
**How to Contact:** Submit demo tape or submit demo tape and lead sheet. Prefers 7½ ips reel-to-reel or cassette with 4 songs on demo. SASE. Reports in 2 weeks.
**Music:** Blues, easy listening, soul and top 40/pop. Recently published "Morning Star" (by Jim Jones),

recorded by J. Jones (gospel); "Jive Me" (by Joe Smith), recorded by J. Smith (R&B); and *Rock House Annie* on E.L.J. Records.

**EAGLE ROCK MUSIC CO.**, 5414 Radford Ave., North Hollywood CA 91607. (213)760-8771. President: Mort Katz. Music publisher. ASCAP. Member AGAC, ACM, CMA. Publishes 12 songs/year; publishes 3 new songwriters/year. Pays standard royalty.
**How to Contact:** Submit demo tape and lyric sheet. Prefers cassette with 2-3 songs on demo. SASE. Reports in 3 weeks.
**Music:** C&W, easy listening, gospel and MOR. Recently published "Where Do Pets Go When They Die" (by M. Katz and R. Katz), recorded by Angels of Love/Magic Eye Records (gospel); "How to Shape Up Your Tush" (by M. Katz), recorded by Genevieve Marie/Magic Eye Records (pop); and "Something Deep Inside Me" (by M. Katz), recorded by Jane Quisenberry/Magic Eye Records (country).
**Tips:** "In today's competitive market the song has to be a knock-out! Don't write just to write. Write to sell!"

**EARLY BIRD MUSIC**, Waltner Enterprises, 14702 Canterbury, Tustin CA 92680. (714)731-2981. President: Steve Waltner. Music publisher and record company. BMI. Publishes 12 songs/year; publishes 3 new songwriters/year. Pays standard royalty on mechanicals.
**How to Contact:** Submit demo tape and lead sheet. Prefers cassette with 2-4 songs on demo. SASE. Reports in 3 weeks.
**Music:** C&W, easy listening, MOR and top 40/pop.

**EARTH AND SKY MUSIC PUBLISHING, INC.**, Box 4157, Winter Park FL 32793. President: Ernest Hatton. Music publisher. BMI. Publishes about 100 songs/year; publishes 15 new songwriters/year. Pays standard royalty.
**How to Contact:** Write first about your interest or submit demo tape and lyric sheet. Prefers 7½ ips reel-to-reel with 1-3 songs on demo. "We're looking for a very good demo recording with proof of copyright and lead sheet." SASE. Reports in 1 month.
**Music:** Mostly pop and easy listening adult contemporary; also bluegrass, church/religious, C&W, jazz, MOR, progressive, R&B, rock and top 40. Recently published "Morning Light" (by R. Lester), recorded by Stallion Band/LCS Records (country); "Late Night Lullaby" (by J. McIntosh), recorded by J. McIntosh/Earth and Sky Records (adult contemporary); "Goodby Lady Jane" (by N. Kubick), recorded by Transatlantic/LCS Records (mellow rock); "This Dream Is Mine" (by Hatton and Hurley), recorded by Scott Collins/Earth and Sky Records (pop); and "Together Again" (by Hatton and Davies), recorded by Sandy Contella/LCS Records (pop).
**Tips:** "Send copyrighted material with very good demo and lead sheet."

**EARTHSCREAM MUSIC PUBLISHING CO.**, Suite A, 2036 Pasket, Houston TX 77092. (713)688-8067. Contact: Jeff Johnson. Music publisher, record company and record producer. BMI. Publishes 15-25 songs/year. Pays standard royalties.
**How to Contact:** Submit demo tape and lyric sheet. Prefers cassette with 2-5 songs on demo. SASE. Reports in 1 month.
**Music:** Blues, rock and top 40/pop. Recently published "White Lies" (by Pennington-Wells), recorded by The Barbara Pennington Band (pop-rock); "Anywhere You Go" (by Steve Carr), recorded by Mary Ann Kakos (MOR); "The Drifter" (by S. Carr), recorded by S. Carr (MOR); and "Honky Tonkin' Time" (by Ron Collier), recorded by R. Collier (country).

**DON EDGAR MUSIC**, 2312 Jasper, Fort Worth TX 76106. (817)626-3448. Contact: Don or Darrell Edgar. Music publisher and sheet music jobber and retailer. BMI. Publishes 2-5 songs/year; publishes 1 new songwriter/year. Pays standard royalty. Sometimes employs songwriters on salary basis "for professional arrangement of accepted works for publication. Payment is made per song depending upon complexity and length. Professional arrangers are always needed for a variety of music."
**How to Contact:** Submit demo tape, lyric sheet and "legible" lead sheet if possible. Prefers cassette or 45 record with 1-4 songs on demo. "Submit no more than 4 compositions without further invitation." Reports "no later than 5 weeks with personal reply. Nothing is returned without SASE."
**Music:** Protestant church/religious; country; easy listening; gospel (especially quartet); progressive; R&B (Spanish OK); and top 40/pop. Recently recorded "Think of Him" (by Esther Hendrick), recorded by Chuck Wagon Gang/Columbia Records (gospel); "Without the Lord" (by John D. Montroy), recorded by Tinsley Trio/Triangle Records (religious); and "Fill Up My Glass" (by Jim Hulsey), recorded by Jim Hulsey/Chevell Records (country).

## Music Publishers 43

*LES EDITIONS LA BOBINE, 408 St. Gabriel, Montreal, Quebec, Canada H2Y 2Z9. (514)866-2021. Affiliate: Edition Bobinason (PROCAN). President: Yves Godin. Music publisher, record company and record producer. BMI and ASCAP. Publishes 20 songs/year; publishes 4 new songwriters/year. Pays standard royalty.
**How to Contact:** Submit demo tape and lyric sheet. Prefers cassette with 5 songs on demo. SAE and IRC. Reports in 2 weeks.
**Music:** Dance-oriented, easy listening, rock and top 40/pop. Recently published "If You Can Count" (by Cesarez), recorded by Bobinason/DJ Records (electro/pop); "Snap" (by Beau Flash), recorded by Focus/DJ Records (electro/rock); and "SQS Anonyme" (by Dwight Druick), recorded by Bobinason/DJ Records (pop/rock).

EDITIONS NAHEJ, 5514 Isabella, Montreal, Quebec, Canada H3X 1R6. (514)487-0859. Affiliates: Valcor (CAPAC), Yiddish (CAPAC), Zapiti (CAPAL), Nahej (PROCAN), Kif-Kif (PROCAN) and Shoubidouwa (PROCAN). President: Jehan V. Valiquet. Music Publisher and record company. PROCAN. Publishes 25 songs/year; publishes 10 new songwriters/year. Pays standard royalty.
**How to Contact:** Submit demo tape and lyric sheet. Prefers cassette with 3 songs minimum on demo. SAE and IRC.
**Music:** Children's (French), MOR and top 40/pop.

EL CHICANO MUSIC, 20531 Plummer St., Chatsworth CA 91311. (213)998-0443. A&R Director: A. Sullivan. Music publisher, booking agency and record company. ASCAP. Pays standard royalty.
**How to Contact:** Submit demo tape and lead sheet. Prefers 7½ ips reel-to-reel. SASE. Reports in 3 weeks.
**Music:** Bluegrass; blues; C&W; disco; easy listening; jazz; MOR; progressive; rock; soul; and top 40/pop. Recently published "Dancing Mama" (disco); "Just Cruisin' " (MOR); and "Ron Con-Con" (Latin rock).

EN AVANT MUSIC CO., Box 381585, Memphis TN 38138. (901)761-3709. Affiliate: Robert Shindler Music Co. (BMI). President: Robert Shindler. Music publisher and record producer. ASCAP. Member NSAI. Publishes 30 songs/year; publishes 2 new songwriters/year. Pays standard royalty.
**How to Contact:** Submit demo tape and lyric sheet. Prefers cassette with 3-4 songs on demo. Does not return unsolicited material. Reports in 1 month.
**Music:** R&B, rock (hard, pop, R&B), soul and top 40/pop. Recently published "You Can Be Loved Again" (by Sam Bryant), recorded by S. Bryant/Epic Records (top 40); "I Can't Do Without Your Love" (by Robert Shindler), recorded by S. Bryant/Epic Records (R&B); and "You Mean That Much To Me" (by Tom Jones III and S. Bryant), recorded by Larry Rasberry/Mercury Records (pop rock).

*ENCHANTMENT MUSIC CO., Box 998, Mesilla Park NM 88047. (505)524-1889. Affiliate: Brooks Bros. Publishers (BMI). Contact: Emmit H. Brooks. Music publisher and record company. BMI. Publishes 20 songs/year; publishes 7 new songwriters/year. Pays standard royalty.
**How to Contact:** Submit demo tape and lyric sheet. Prefers cassette with 1-3 songs on demo. SASE. Reports in 1 month.
**Music:** Mostly C&W, MOR, top 40/pop and rock; also bluegrass, easy listening, folk, and Spanish. Recently published "Crazy and Lonely" (by Jeff Moore), recorded by J. Moore/Goldust Records (MOR); "Rock 'n Roll Party" (by Danny Scott), recorded by Voltz/Goldust Records (rock); and "She's Hollywood (D. Scott and Darvin Lamm), recorded by Voltz/Goldust Records (rock).

ENGLISH MOUNTAIN PUBLISHING CO., 332 N. Brinker Ave., Columbus OH 43204. (614)279-5251. Script Manager: Jetta Brown. Music publisher, record company, record producer, management firm and booking agency. BMI. Pays standard royalties.
**How to Contact:** Query, arrange personal interview, submit demo, submit demo tape and lead sheet, submit lead sheet, or arrange in-person audition. Prefers 7½ or 15 ips reel-to-reel or cassette. Does not return unsolicited material.
**Music:** Bluegrass; blues; church/religious; C&W; folk; gospel; MOR; and top 40/pop. Recently published "Way Back in West Virginia" and "Each Side of the River" (by Kae and Walt Cochran), recorded by W. Cochran/Holly Records (C&W); and "I Already Know" (by M. Cordle and W. Cochran), recorded by Cochran/Holly Records (C&W).

ENTERTAINMENT CO. MUSIC GROUP, 40 W. 57th St., New York NY 10019. (212)265-2600. Music publisher and record producer.
**How to Contact:** Submit cassette and lyric sheet with maximum 1 song on demo. Does not return unsolicited material. Reports in 1-3 months.
**Music:** C&W, MOR, R&B, pop and top 40/pop.

**44** Songwriter's Market '84

**EPOCH UNIVERSAL PUBLICATIONS, INC.**, 10802 N. 23rd Ave., Phoenix AZ 85029. (602)864-1980. Affiliates: NALR (BMI), Epoch Music Corp. (ASCAP), Epoch Universal Publications, Ltd. (Canada). Executive Vice President: David Serey. Music publisher, record company and record producer. BMI. Publishes 100-300 songs/year; publishes 20 new songwriters/year. Hires staff writers. "Position filled at this time, but resumes may be sent to be kept on file." Pays standard royalty.
**How to Contact:** Submit demo tape and lyric sheet. Prefers 7½ ips reel-to-reel or cassette with minimum 3 songs on demo. SASE. Reports in 1 month.
**Music:** Children's, choral, church/religious, classical, gospel and liturgical. Recently published "Here I Am, Lord" (by Dan Schutte), recorded by St. Louis Jesuits/NALR Records (liturgical); "Land of Love" (by Marcy Tigner), recorded by Little Marcy/Sounds of Hope Records (children's); and "The Ones I Love" (by Carey Landry), recorded by C. Landry/NALR Records (liturgical).
**Tips:** "Songs should be strong but simple enough for congregational singing, preferably in a liturgically setting."

**EQUA MUSIC**, 1800 Mowry Ave., Fremont CA 94538. (415)794-6637. Affiliate: Mepro Music (BMI). President: Warren M. Johnson. Music publisher and record company. ASCAP. Member CMA. Publishes 10-15 songs/year; publishes 5 new songwriters/year. Pays standard royalty.
**How to Contact:** Submit demo tape and lyric sheet. Prefers cassette with 3-6 songs on demo. SASE. Reports in 3 weeks.
**Music:** C&W. Recently published "No Place to Hide" (by Kay Savage), and "Goin' Home Alone" (by Gail Zeiler), recorded by G. Zeiler/Equa Records (C&W ballad); and "It Ain't My Concern" (by G. Zeiler) recorded by G. Zeiler/Equa Records (C&W uptempo).

*****EQUINOX MUSIC (AVI Music Publishing Group)**, #1212, 7060 Hollywood Blvd., Hollywood CA 90028. (213)462-7151. Affiliates: Bel-Canto Music (ASCAP), Forsythe Music (ASCAP), and Norfolk Music (BMI). Managing Director, A&R: Seth Marshall III. Music publisher, record company, record producer, and artist management. BMI, SESAC. Publishes 100-200 songs/year; publishes 20-25 new songwriters/year. Pays standard royalty or as specified in individual contracts.
**How to Contact:** Submit demo tape and lyric sheet. Prefers cassette with any amount of songs on demo. SASE. Reports "when we get to it."
**Music:** Mostly jazz, gospel, country, R&B and rock ("in that order"); also dance-oriented and top 40/pop. Recently published "Tainted Love" (by Ed Cobb), recorded by Soft Cell/Sire Records (rock/pop); "Take A Look Inside My Heart" (by David Benoit), recorded by D. Benoit/AVI Records (jazz fusion); "Cocomotion" (by W. Michael Lewis and L. Rinder), recorded by El Coco/AVI Records (disco); and "Downhill From Here" (by J. Kranzdorf and R. Bakalyan), recorded by Whole Wheat/AVI Records (rock).

*****ESSEX MUSIC OF AUSTRALIA PTY. LTD.**, Uniline House, 5/13 Northcliff St., Milsons Point, Sydney, NSW, 2061, Australia. 61-02-922-4100. Affiliates: Buckwood Music of Australia Pty, Ltd., Cromwell Music of Australia Pty. Ltd., Arwin Music of Australia Pty., Ltd., David Platz Music of Australia Pty., Ltd.; all APRA affiliated. Affiliates/US: The Richmond Organization (TRO); ASCAP, BMI. Professional Manager: John Morrison. Music publisher. APRA, Australasian Mechanical Copyright Owners Society, Ltd. Member AMPAL. Publishes 6 new songwriters/year. Pays standard royalty; royalties to US songwriters paid through US publishing affiliate.
**How to Contact:** Submit demo tape and lyric sheet. Prefers cassette with 3-6 songs on demo. SAE and IRC. Reports in 2 weeks.
**Music:** C&W, easy listening, folk, MOR, R&B, rock and top 40/pop. Recently published "Big City Talk" (by Marc Hunter), recorded by M. Hunter/Polygram Records (pop/rock); "Romantically Inclined" (by John Hanlon/Mike Harvey), recorded by J. Hanlon/Polygram Records, New Zealand (ballad); and "Losing Your Touch" (by Robin Sinclair), recorded by Tina Cross/Laser Records (pop).
**Tips:** "Send good quality and clear demos, and resume of current activities, etc."

*****ETUDE/BAKCAN**, 121 Meadowbrook Dr., Somerville NJ 08876. (201)359-3110. Coordinator: Ronnie Mack. Producer: Tony Camillo. Music publisher, record company and record producer. BMI.
**How to Contact:** Submit demo tape and lyric sheet. Prefers reel-to-reel or cassette with maximum of 3 songs on demo. Does not return unsolicited material. Reports in 1 month.
**Music:** R&B, rock, soul and top 40/pop.

**FAIRCHILD MUSIC PUBLISHING**, 13112 N. Halcourt, Norwalk CA 90650. (714)554-0851. Contact: Jerry Wood. Music publisher. BMI. Publishes 6-10 songs/year. Pays standard royalty.
**How to Contact:** Submit demo tape and lyric sheet. Prefers 7½ ips reel-to-reel or cassette with 1-4 songs on demo. SASE. Reports in 2 weeks.
**Music:** C&W, easy listening and MOR. Recently published "Many Are the Colors" and "I Won't Be

## Music Publishers 45

There'' (by Roy Dee), recorded by R. Dee/Tribal Records (country); "99 Years" (by Ron Hayden), recorded by R. Hayden/Tribal Records (country); "Mine Is Yours to Share" and "Put Back the Pieces of My Heart" (by Wanda Davis), recorded by W. Davis/Tribal Records (country); and "Genuine Gold Plated Boy Scout Knife" and "Fairy Tales and Roses" (by Jeanne Taylor), recorded by J. Taylor/Tribal Records (country).

**FAME PUBLISHING CO., INC.**, Box 2527, Muscle Shoals AL 35660. Affiliate: Rick Hall Music (ASCAP). Publishing Manager: Walt Aldridge. Music publisher and record producer. BMI. Publishes 150 songs/year; publishes 6 new songwriters/year. Pays standard royalty.
**How to Contact:** Submit demo tape. Prefers cassette with 1-3 songs on demo. "Please include legible lyrics." No tapes returned. SASE. Reports in 6 weeks. "No phone calls."
**Music:** R&B, top 40/pop and country. Recently published "There's No Gettin Over Me" (by Brasfield/Aldridge), recorded by Ronnie Milsap/RCA Records (top 40/country cross; "Till You're Gone" (by Brasfield/Aldridge), recorded by Barbara Mandrell/MCA Records (top 40/country cross); and "The Man With the Golden Thumb" (by Henderson/McGuire), recorded by Jerry Reed/RCA Records (top 40/country cross).

**FERRY BOAT MUSIC**, Rt. 2, Box 133, Burton WA 98013. (206)463-2850. Affiliate: Thea Music (BMI). President: Bob Krinsky. Music publisher, record company and record producer. ASCAP. Publishes 20 songs/year; publishes 5 new songwriters/year. Pays standard royalty.
**How to Contact:** Submit demo tape and lyric sheet. Prefers cassette with 1-3 songs on demo. "Include cover letter stating the purpose for submission as well as examples of artists for whom you believe the material is appropriate." Does not return unsolicited material. Reports in 1 month.
**Music:** Mostly blues, jazz, and rock; also top 40/pop. Recently published "Life Goes On" (by Diane Schour), recorded by D. Schour/First American Records (jazz/blues); "Modernman" (by Rick Smith), recorded by Lonesome City Kings/First American Records (rock); and "No Sleep Tonight" (by R. Smith), recorded by R. Smith (rock).
**Tips:** "Special market material should be very strong. Otherwise, send top drawer hits please."

**FIRELIGHT PUBLISHING**, c/o SRS, 6772 Hollywood Blvd., Hollywood CA 90028. (213)764-3980. Professional Manager: Doug Thiele. Music publisher. ASCAP. Member California Copyright Conference and Academy of Country Music. Not currently accepting material.
**Music:** C&W, MOR, R&B, rock (any) and top 40/pop. Recently published "Almost in Love" (by Parks and Thiele), recorded by Dolly Parton/RCA Records (ballad); "Dancin' Like Lovers" (by Herbstritt and Thiele), recorded by Mary Macgregor/RSO Records (ballad); and "Sailing Ship Majestic" (by Thiele), recorded by Mike Asquino/Red Cloud Records (country pop).
**Tips:** "Songs should have positive themes, highly memorable hooks and substantive but conversational lyrics. I'm after simple ideas, straight forwardly expressed and universally applicable. If your song moves listeners to tears and they remember the title easily, I want to hear it."

**FLIN-FLON MUSIC**, 102 Veteran's Ave., Mullen NE 69152. (308)546-2294. General Manager: L.E. Walker. Music publisher. BMI. Pays standard royalty.
**How to Contact:** Submit demo tape and lyric sheet. Prefers 7½ ips reel-to-reel or cassette with 1-3 songs on demo. SASE. Reports in 1 month.
**Music:** Bluegrass, disco, folk, R&B, C&W, contemporary, gospel and soft rock. Recently published "Nine Twenty Train" (by Randy Robinson), recorded by WDLJ/Flin-Flon Records (MOR); "All Thru the Night" (by Jeanie Snyder), recorded by WDLJ/Flin-Flon Records (country); and "Hello Ba-bay" (by Earl Walker), recorded by Group/Varsity Records (jazz).

***THE FLYING MUSIC COMPANY LTD.**, 1, Lower James St., London, W1, England. 44-01-734-8311. Director: Paul K. Walden. Music publisher and record company. Estab. 1982. MCPS, PRS, Phonographic Performance Ltd. Member MPA. Publishes 60-70 songs/year; publishes 2 new songwriters/year. Pays negotiable royalty; royalties paid directly to US songwriters.
**How to Contact:** Submit demo tape and lyric sheet. Prefers cassette with 2-6 songs on demo. "Background information on the writer is useful." Reports in 1 month.
**Music:** Mostly top 40/pop; also dance-oriented, progressive, rock (soft and pop) and soul. Recently published "Magic Touch" (by David Courtney & Stephen Kalinich), recorded by Odyssey/RCA Records (pop); "We've Got Ourselves In Love" (by D. Courtney & S. Kalinich), recorded by Leo Sayer/Chrysalis Records (pop); and "Like a Stone" (by Paul French), recorded by Voyager (pop).

**FOCAL POINT MUSIC PUBLISHERS**, 922 McArthur Blvd., Warner Robins GA 31093. (912)923-6533. Manager: Ray Melton. Music publisher and record company. BMI. Publishes 8 songs/year; publishes 1 new songwriter/year. Pays standard royalty.

**46** Songwriter's Market '84

**How to Contact:** Submit demo tape and lead sheet. Prefers cassette with 2-4 songs on demo. SASE.
**Music:** Country, gospel and old-style rock. Recently published "Tribute to George Jones" (by Wayne Holcomb/Steve Jacobs), recorded by W. Holcomb/R-M Records (country); "My Family Reunion" (by W. Holcomb/Steve Jacobs), recorded by W. Holcomb/R-M Records (country); and "He's Big Enough" (by Charles Dennis), recorded by C. Dennis/Gospel Voice Records (gospel).
**Tips:** "Let the publisher know you're in the business as an entertainer or serious songwriter."

**FORREST HILLS MUSIC, INC.**, 1609 Roy Acuff Pl., Nashville TN 37203. (615)244-1060. Affiliates: Ash Valley Music (ASCAP) and Roadrunner Music (BMI). Music publisher. BMI. Member NMPA. Publishes 20-22 songs/year; publishes 1-2 new songwriters/year. Pays standard minimum royalty.
**How to Contact:** Submit demo tape and lyric sheet. Prefers reel-to-reel. SASE. Reports in 4 weeks.
**Music:** C&W, easy listening, MOR and top 40/pop. Recently published "Alabama Rose," (by B.R. Reynolds, D. Bretts, and G. Stewart), recorded by Joe Sun/Ovation Records (country); "Hollywood," (by G. Stewart, W. Carson), recorded by Alabama/RCA Records (country); and "It's True," (by C. Anderson, M.B. Anderson and G. Stewart), recorded by Terri Gibbs/MCA Records (country).

**FOURTH CORNER MUSIC (SESAC)**, 2140 St. Clair St., Bellingham WA 98226. (206)733-3807. Affiliates: Heartstone Music (BMI) and Silverstone Music (ASCAP). Director, Catalog Promotions: Renie Peterson. Music publisher, record company and record producer. Member NSAI and GMA. Publishes 10 songs/year; publishes 3 new songwriters/year. Pays standard royalty.
**How to Contact:** Write first about your interest, then submit demo tape and lyric sheet. Prefers cassette with 1-4 songs on demo. "Must be a good, clear demo, SASE is a must!" Reports in 3 weeks.
**Music:** C&W and gospel. Recently published "Movin' On Up" and "I'm Not the Same" (by Jose Nardone), recorded by J. Nardone/Love/Peace/Service Records (gospel).
**Tips:** "Study AM radio in your market as only songs which compete can get furthered for recording. Songs and demos need to be top-notch. We do not accept anything unless there is a place for it on a record we will be producing, or if we feel we can further it to known artists. In other words, we will not tie-up anyone's songs unless they can be used."

**FREE & SHOW MUSIC**, 652 Hilary Dr., Tiburon CA 94920. (213)822-7629. President: Ron Patton. Music publisher. Estab. 1981. ASCAP. Publishes 12 songs/year; publishes 5 new songwriters/year. Pays standard royalty.
**How to Contact:** Write first about your interest, then submit demo tape and lyric sheet. Prefers cassette with 1-3 songs on demo. "Demos should be well-recorded. State why you're sending the tape and which artists might record your song." SASE. Reports in 3 weeks.
**Music:** C&W, dance-oriented, easy listening, MOR, R&B, rock, soul and top 40/pop. Recently published "Video Game" (by Joe Borowski), recorded by Michael Jeff/Baywest Records (new wave); "Carry On, Carrie Ann" (by Laurie Roberts, Ron Patton and Michael Peyser), recorded by M. Jeff/Baywest Records (top 40/pop).

**FRICK MUSIC PUBLISHING CO.**, 404 Bluegrass Ave., Madison TN 37115. (615)865-6380. Contact: Bob Frick. Music publisher, record company and record producer. BMI. Publishes 50 songs/year; publishes 1 new songwriter/year. Pays standard royalty.
**How to Contact:** Call first about your interest, then submit demo tape and lyric sheet. Prefers 7½ ips reel-to-reel or cassette with 2-10 songs on demo. SASE. Reports in 1 month.
**Music:** C&W, gospel, rock and top 40/pop. Recently published "I Can't Help Myself" (by Bob Frick), recorded by Ray Darby (country) and also recorded by Bob Scott (country/gospel); and "Soul Searcher" (by B. Frick), recorded by B. Scott and Henry Slaughter (gospel).

**FRIENDLY FINLEY MUSIC**, 103 Westview Ave., Valparaiso FL 32580. (904)678-7211. Affiliate: Shelly Singleton Music (BMI). Owner: Finley Duncan. President: Bruce Duncan. Music publisher, record company and record producer. BMI. Publishes 10-15 songs/year. Pays standard royalties.
**How to Contact:** Query, arrange personal interview, or submit demo tape and lead sheet. Prefers cassette or 7½ ips reel-to-reel tape with 3-5 songs on demo. "Send what you consider your best, and at least one of what you consider your worst." SASE. Reports in 1 week.
**Music:** C&W; disco; easy listening; MOR; R&B; rock; soul; and top 40/pop. Recently published "1-

---

**Market conditions are constantly changing! If this is 1985 or later, buy the newest edition of *Songwriter's Market* at your favorite bookstore or order directly from Writer's Digest Books.**

800 Blues" and "Time Flies When You're Having Love" (by Bert Colwell), recorded by Bert Colwell/Country Artists Records (C&W); "That's Why They Call It a Love Song" (by Bert Colwell), recorded by Willie Morrell/Country Artists Records (C&W); and "If the World Should End Tomorrow" (by Gumms, Andrews, Duncan), recorded by Willie Morrell/Country Artists Records (C&W).

**FROZEN INCA MUSIC**, Suite 201, 450 14th St., Atlanta GA 30318. (404)873-3918. President: Michael Rothschild. Music publisher and record company. BMI. Publishes 15 songs/year; publishes 14 new songwriters/year. Pays standard royalty.
**How to Contact:** Write or call first about your interest, then submit demo tape and lyric sheet. Prefers 7½ ips reel-to-reel or cassette with 4-10 songs on demo. SASE. Reports in 1 month.
**Music:** Blues, dance-oriented, jazz, MOR, progressive, Spanish, R&B, rock, soul and top 40/pop. Recently published "Baya-Baya" (by David Earle Johnson and John Abercrombie) and "Frozen Moments" (by Dan Wall), both recorded by D.E. Johnson, J. Abercrombie and D. Wall (jazz); and "Magical Eyes" (by Tim Miller), recorded by T. Miller (pop).

**FULL CYCLE MUSIC PUBLISHING CO.**, 80 E. San Francisco St., Santa Fe NM 87501. (505)982-2900. President: Reno Myerson. Music publisher, record company, record producer and record manufacturer and distributor. BMI, ASCAP. Publishes 1 new songwriter/year. Pays standard royalty.
**How to Contact:** Arrange personal interview to play demo tape or submit demo tape and lyric sheet. Prefers cassette with 4-10 songs on demo. SASE. Reports in 1 month.
**Music:** Bluegrass, blues, C&W, folk, jazz, R&B, rock (hard, country) and soul. Recently published "Many" (by Joey Bradley), recorded by Juice/Full Circle Records (reggae).

**FUNKY ACRES MUSIC CO.**, Suite 2E, 145 W. 55th St, New York NY 10019, (212)245-7179; Rt. 2, Box 133, Burton Vashon Island WA 98103, (206)463-2850. Affiliates: Thea Music (BMI), Hip Notic Music (BMI), Ferry Boat Music (ASCAP) in Washington. Contact: Warren Baker (New York), Robert Krinsky (Seattle). Music publisher. ASCAP. Publishes 5 new songwriters/year. Pays standard royalty.
**How to Contact:** Submit demo tape, lyric sheet, and lead sheet if available. Prefers cassette with 3 songs maximum on demo. Does not return unsolicited material; will contact songwriter only if interested.
**Music:** C&W, disco, MOR, R&B, rock, soul and top 40/pop.
**Tips:** "Suggest artists for whom you think your songs are appropriate. We rely on personal contacts to get songs directly to the artists and producers. The songwriter is our greatest asset, we look to develop them to the fullest."

**FYDAQ MUSIC**, 240 E. Radcliffe Dr., Claremont CA 91711. (714)624-0677. Affiliates: Jubilation Music (BMI), and Cetacean (ASCAP). President: Gary Buckley. Music publisher and production company. BMI. Member ACM, CMA, GMA, NARAS, Audio Engineering. Publishes 30-40 songs/year.
**How to Contact:** Submit demo tape and lead or lyric sheet. Prefers 7½ ips reel-to-reel or cassette with 1-4 songs on demo. SASE. Reports in 3 weeks.
**Music:** C&W, easy listening, gospel, MOR, progressive, rock (country), soul and top 40/pop. Recently published "You're Smiling Again" recorded by Rick Buche/Paradise Records (pop); "My Only Love" recorded by Dusk/Fubar Records (top 40); "Grandpas Song" recorded by Jerry Roark (gospel); "How Many Times" recorded by Finley Duke (gospel); "Working Man's Prayer" recorded by Jody Barry/Majega Records (gospel); "Better Get Right" recorded by Crownsmen/Manna Records (gospel); "Is It Right," "Touch Me Now," "It's All Right" and "What You Doin' to Me" recorded by Borderline/Majega Records (rock/top 40); "She Comes to Me Softly"/"Without You" recorded by Borderline/Quikstar Records (top 40/pop); "Still in the Game" recorded by Michael Noll/Gottabehit Records (top 40/pop); and "It's A Long Lonesome Walk," recorded by Finley Duke/Majega Records.

**G.G. MUSIC, INC.**, Box 374, Fairview NJ 07022. (201)941-3987. Affiliate: Wazuri Music (BMI). President: Linwood Simon. Music publisher and artist management company. BMI. Pays standard royalty.
**How to Contact:** Submit demo tape and lyric sheet. Prefers cassette with 1-2 songs on demo. SASE. Reports in 3 weeks.
**Music:** Dance-oriented, R&B, rock (light), soul and melodies. Recently published "America" (by Linwood M. Simon), recorded by Gloria Gaynor/Atlantic Records (pop); "For You My Love" (by L. Simon), recorded by G. Gaynor/Atlantic Records (MOR); and "I Can Take the Pain" (by G. Gaynor), recorded G. Gaynor/Polygram Records (rock).
**Tips:** "The writer should understand that he must recognize all the elements needed to make a hit record: strong lyrics, good hook and an overall progressive and commercial sound the buying public can relate to. Love songs are 90% of records sold."

**\*CHRIS GABRIELLI**, 203 Culver Ave., Charleston SC 29407. (803)766-2500. Assistant Manager: Chris Gabrielli. Music publisher, record company and record producer. BMI. Publishes 25 songs/year; publishes 6 new songwriters/year. Pays standard royalty.
**How to Contact:** Submit demo tape and lyric sheet; call about your interest. Prefers cassette with 3 songs on demo. SASE. Reports in 1 week.
**Music:** Mostly R&B; also blues, rock, soul and beach music. Recently published "Tell You For the Last Time" and "Be Young Be Foolish" (R&B).

**AL GALLICO MUSIC CORP.**, Suite 507, 9255 Sunset Blvd., Los Angeles CA 90069. (213)274-0165. Affiliates: Algee (BMI), Altam (BMI) and Easy Listening (ASCAP). Air Assistant: Kevin Magowan. Music publisher. BMI. Member NMPA. Payment differs from song to song. Hires staff writers.
**How to Contact:** Submit demo tape and lead sheet. Prefers cassette with 1-3 songs on demo. SASE for return of material. Reports in 2 weeks.
**Music:** C&W, easy listening and top 40/pop. "We're very strong in contemporary country and crossover material." Recently published "Swingin' " (by John Anderson and Loinel Delmore), recorded by J. Anderson/Warner Bros. Recods (country crossover); "Jose Cuervo" (by Cindy Jordan), recorded by Shelly West/RIVA-Warner Bros. Records (country); "The Ride" (by Gary Gentry and J.B. Detterline), recorded by David Allen Coe/Columbia Records (country); and "Back on the Chain Gang" (by Chrissie Hynde), recorded by The Pretenders/Warners-SIRE Records (top 40).
**Tips:** "Be aware of the artists we work with and the artists who record outside material. Study their styles. Study the songs being played on the radio; they're being played because a number of people believed in them and said yes. Come up with fresh ideas and titles; vivid, sincere, relationship-oriented lyrics; melodic, catchy melodies; tight structures and contemporary chords and feel. Remember the music industry is based on, and needs, great songs."

**AL GALLICO MUSIC CORP.**, 1111 17th Ave. S., Nashville TN 37212. (615)327-2773. Music publisher. BMI and ASCAP. Pays standard royalty.
**How to Contact:** Submit demo tape and lyric sheet or "arrange to leave tape at office for our staff to listen to." Prefers cassette with 3 songs on demo. SASE. Reports in 3 weeks.
**Music:** Country. Recently published "Swingin' " (by Lynell A. Delmore), recorded by John David Anderson; "Taking It Easy" (by Billy and Mark Sherrill), recorded by Lacy J. Dalton; and "It's Hard to Be the Dreamer" (by Joe Chambers, Larry Jenkins and Conway Twitty), recorded by Donna Fargo.
**Tips:** "Be prepared to leave tapes at our office."

**GALYN MUSIC**, 233 Penner Dr., Pearl MS 39208. (601)939-6616. 939-5975. Affiliate: NyLag Music. Contact: George W. Allen. Music publisher, record company and record producer. BMI. Member NSAI, CMA. Publishes 30-50 songs/year; publishes 5 new songwriters/year. Pays standard royalty.
**How to Contact:** Submit demo tape and lyric sheet, write or call about your interest or arrange personal interview. Prefers 7½ ips reel-to-reel or cassette with 2-6 songs on demo. "Be sure the vocal is up front and the lyrics are tight and tell a story." SASE. Reports in 3 weeks.
**Music:** Bluegrass, blues, C&W, gospel, MOR, progressive, R&B, rock, soul and top 40/pop. Recently published "So In Love Again" (by Jackie Pearson), recorded by J. Pearson/Shu-Qua-Lok Records (pop); "Just Let Me Love You" (by Ted Holman), recorded by T. Holman/Acorn Records (country); and "Play Me a Cheating Song" (by George Allen), recorded by Keith Lamb/Acorn Records (country).
**Tips:** "Send only the best you have. Make sure the lyrics are tight with the vocals up front. You don't need a big production—guitar or piano with vocal will do fine. If we hear something we think is hit material we will make a first class demo tape at our expense on material we publish."

**\*GAMMILL-MURPHY MUSIC**, 2913 95th St., Lubbock TX 79423. (806)745-5992. A&R Director: Bill Gammill. Music publisher, record company and record producer. Estab. 1982. BMI. Publishes 10 songs/year; publishes 2 new songwriters/year. Pays standard royalty.
**How to Contact:** Submit demo tape and lyric sheet. Prefers cassette with 1-3 songs on demo. SASE. Reports in 2 weeks.
**Music:** Mostly contemporary Christian; also church/religious and gospel. Recently published "Learning How to Fly" (by Russ Murphy), recorded by Bill Gammill and Russ Murphy (contemporary Christian); "Starting From Scratch" (by B. Gammill and R. Murphy), recorded by B. Gammill and R. Murphy (contemporary Christian); and "Do You Love Him?" (by B. Gammill), recorded by B. Gammill and R. Murphy (contemporary Christian).
**Tips:** "We are looking for material that is original, fresh and theologically sound."

**GARRETT MUSIC ENTERPRISES**, Suite 1019, 6255 Sunset Blvd., Hollywood CA 90028. (213)467-2181. Publisher: Randy Cate. Music publisher and production company. BMI. ASCAP. Member NMPA.
**How to Contact:** Prefers cassette with 2 songs on demo. SASE "for returns. No lyrics only."

**Music Publishers** **49**

**\*GARRON MUSIC**, Kirkland Park Studios, Lethame Rd., Strathaven, Glasgow ML10 6EE, Scotland. 44-0357-21130. Director: Bill Garden. Music publisher and record producer. PRS, Phonographic Performance Ltd. Publishes 5 songs/year; publishes 3 new songwriters/year. Pays standard royalty.
**How to Contact:** Submit demo tape and lyric sheet. Prefers cassette with 3-6 songs on demo. SAE and IRC. Reports in 1 month.
**Music:** Mostly C&W, MOR and folk; also dance-oriented, easy listening, gospel, jazz, R&B and top 40/pop. Recently published "Our Anniversary" (by Garden), recorded by Flo Stevens (MOR); "Nashville Hall of Fame" (by Wilson), recorded by Tug Wilson (C&W); and "Soccoro Connection" (by Harley), recorded by Passport (pop).

**GIL GILDAY PUBLISHING CO.**, Box 600516, North Miami Beach FL 33160. (305)945-3738. Affiliates: Farjay (BMI) and Sancti (SESAC). Executive Director: J. "Gil" Gilday. A&R Director: Rufus Smith. Music publisher, record company and record producer. ASCAP. Publishes 60-100 songs/year; publishers 10-15 new songwriters/year. Pays standard royalties.
**How to Contact:** Submit demo tape and lead sheet. Prefers 7½ ips reel-to-reel or cassette with 1-3 songs on demo. "Make sure name and address are listed." SASE. Reports in 1 month, "sooner if possible."
**Music:** Church/religious, C&W, easy listening, gospel, MOR and top 40/pop. Recently published "Father's Prayer," recorded by the Blackwood Brothers (MOR/gospel); "Pussy Cat Song," recorded by Connie Vannet (C&W); "You & Me" (by J. Rostacy), recorded by Don C. Davis (MOR); "What's Happening" and "Posey Petals" (by W. Cartier), recorded by Duke Snider (rock/R&B); and "So All Alone," recorded by Don C. Davis (MOR).

**GLEN EAGLE PUBLISHING COMPANY**, 64 New Hyde Park Rd., Garden City NY 11530. Contact: P. Noonan or F. Curran. Music publisher and record company. Estab. 1981. BMI. Pays standard royalty.
**How to Contact:** Write first about your interest, then submit demo tape and lyric sheet. Prefers cassette with 1-4 songs on demo. SASE. Reports in 3 weeks.
**Music:** Church/religious, folk and Irish. Recently published "From the Shannon to the Clyde" (by Pat Roper), recorded by P. Roper and Tommy Doyle/Rego Records (folk); and "Come With Me Molly" (by Jesse Owens), recorded by J. Owens/Rego Records (folk).

**GOD'S WORLD**, 27335 Penn St., Inkster MI 48141. (313)595-8247. Affiliates: Manfield Music (BMI), Stephen Enoch Johnson Music (ASCAP). President: Elder Otis G. Johnson. Music publisher, record company and record producer. SESAC. Member American Mechanical Rights Association, GMA, BMA, NARAS. Publishes 50 songs/year; publishes 6 new songwriters/year. Pays standard royalty.
**How to Contact:** Write first about your interest, submit demo tape and lyric sheet; call about your interest and arrange personal interview to play demo tape. Prefers 7½ ips reel-to-reel or cassette with 3 songs on demo. SASE. Reports in 1 month.
**Music:** Church/religious, C&W, easy listening, gospel and jazz. Recently published "Walk in the Sunlight of My Love" and "Lo He Comes Quickly" (by Dorothy W. Butler), recorded by the National Conventions of Choirs/Savoy Records; and "Pentecost Power" (by Otis G. and Shirley A. Johnson), recorded by Elder Otis G. Johnson; "There's Never Been a Wonder Like My Jesus" (by David Beecher); and "I Will Still Rejoice and Follow You" and "As A Man and A Woman, How Rich Your Life Can Be," recorded by Marcella Ratliff.

**GOLD STREET, INC.**, Box 124, Kirbyville TX 75956. (409)423-2234. President: James L. Gibson. Vice President A&R: Robbie Gibson. Music publisher and record company. ASCAP, BMI. Publishes 20 songs/year; publishes 3 new songwriters/year. Pays standard royalty.
**How to Contact:** Submit demo tape and lyric sheet. Prefers cassette with 1-4 songs on demo. "Send us your demos using either a rhythm track or a complete arrangement with strings, etc. We like to hear your ideas on tape, though we may not necessarily use them as you hear them." SASE. Reports in 1 month.
**Music:** Gospel, all types. Recently published "I Need You" (by James Gibson); "The Third Day" (by Steve Mattoxx); "Lonely Times" (by Debbie Scruggs); "Rainmaker" (by Richard Ebert); and "Sonshine" (by R. Gibson).

**GOLDEN DAWN MUSIC**, 26177 Kinyon Dr., Taylor MI 48180. (313)292-5281. President: Peggy La Sorda. Music publisher and record company. BMI. Publishes 10 songs/year; publishes 2 new songwriters/year. Pays standard royalty.
**How to Contact:** Write first with SASE, then submit demo tape and lyric sheet. Original unpublished material only. Prefers 7½ ips reel-to-reel or cassette with 1-4 songs on demo. SASE. Reports in 3 weeks.

**Music:** C&W, dance-oriented, easy listening, folk, gospel, MOR, top 40/pop and gospel.
**Tips:** "Material should reflect today's market."

**GOLDEN GUITAR MUSIC,** Box 40602, Tucson AZ 85717. Affiliate: Enterprize Music (ASCAP). President: Jeff Johnson. Music publisher. BMI. Publishes 10-15 songs/year. Pays standard royalty.
**How to Contact:** Submit demo tape and lyric sheet. Prefers 7½ or 15 ips reel-to-reel or cassette with 2-6 songs on demo. SASE. Reports in 1 month.
**Music:** Mostly country; also bluegrass, church/religious, gospel and light rock. Recently published "Willy's Boy" (by Jeff Johnson), recorded by Brenda D./Half Moon Records (country); "Wearing a Smile of a Clown" (by Jerry Haymes), recorded by J. Haymes/Umpire Records (country); and "What's This World Coming To?" (by J. Johnson), recorded by Jeff Johnson/Dewl Records (country/religious).
**Tips:** "Make an effort to submit a good quality demo—not necessarily complicated but clear and clean."

**GOPAM ENTERPRISES, INC.,** #13C-W, 11 Riverside Dr., New York NY 10023. (212)724-6120. Affiliates: Upam Music (BMI), Zawinul Music (BMI), Taggie Music Co. (BMI), Jodax Music Co. (BMI), Semenya Music (BMI), Margenia Music (BMI), Turbine Music (BMI), Appleberry Music (BMI), Kae-Lyn Music (BMI), Jillean Music (BMI), Jowat Music (BMI), John Oscar Music, Inc. (ASCAP), Bi-Circle (BMI), Tri-Circle (ASCAP), Dillard Music and Pril Music (BMI). Managing Director: Laurie Goldstein. Music publisher. BMI. Member NMPA. Pays standard royalties.
**How to Contact:** Query or submit demo tape and lead or lyric sheet. Prefers cassette with 1-3 songs. "Primarily interested in jazz and jazz related compositions." SASE. Reports as soon as possible.
**Music:** Blues; easy listening; jazz; R&B; soul; and pop.

**GORDON MUSIC CO., INC.,** #103, 12111 Strathern St., Hollywood CA 91605. (213)768-7597. Affiliates include Marlen (ASCAP), JesBy (ASCAP), Tor (ASCAP), Dave (ASCAP), Bernie (ASCAP) and Sunshine (BMI). President: Jeff Gordon. Music publisher. ASCAP. Publishes 12 songs/year; publishes 3 new songwriters/year. Pays standard royalty.
**How to Contact:** Call first about your interest and arrange personal interview to play demo. Prefers cassette with 5-12 songs on demo. Does not return unsolicited material. Reports in 1 week.
**Music:** Mostly rock; also children's, choral, church/religious, C&W, jazz and top 40/pop. Recently published "It's All Natasha's Fault," and "Run Silent: Run Deep" (by T. Mockley and T. Lloyd), recorded by Failsafe/Paris Records (R&R); and "Toy Parade" (by M. Lenrad, D. Kahn and M. Green), recorded by Rupert Holmes/Boardwalk Records.
**Tips:** "All material should be recorded on nothing less than a 4-track. The better the quality of sound the better chance of picking up the song."

**GOSPEL CLEF,** Box 90, Rugby Station, Brooklyn NY 11203. (212)773-5910. President: John R. Lockley. Music publisher. BMI. Pays standard royalty.
**How to Contact:** Write first about your interest. Prefers cassette with 2 songs on demo. "All songs submitted to our company should have a positive and direct reverence for God, Jesus, and the spirit of the Lord, etc." SASE. Reports in 1 month.
**Music:** Church/religious and spiritual. Recently published "My God Is Able" (by Elder J.R. Lockley, Jr), recorded by Glorytones/Gospel Records, Inc. (spiritual); "You've Got a Friend When He Is Jesus" (by Ann Moncrief), recorded by Elder J.R. Lockley/Gospel Records, Inc. (spiritual); and "Nothing but the Name of Jesus" (by Elder J.R. Lockley, Jr), recorded by The Lockley Family/Gospel Records, Inc. (spiritual).

**THE GRAND PASHA PUBLISHER,** 5615 Melrose Ave., Hollywood CA 90038. (213)466-3507. Affiliates: Sasha Songs, Unlimited (BMI), The Pasha Music Co. (ASCAP). Present: Spencer Proffer. General Manager: Carol Peters. A&R Director: Lyn Corey-Benson. Music publisher, record company and record producer. Publishes 100 songs/year; publishes 4 new songwriters/year. Pays standard royalty.
**How to Contact:** Call first about your interest. Prefers cassette with 2-4 songs on demo. SASE. Reports in 3 weeks.
**Music:** Rock and top 40/pop.

**GRAVENHURST MUSIC,** 1469 3rd Ave., New Brighton PA 15066. (412)843-2431, and 847-0111. Promotion Director: Roz Miller. President: Jerry Reed. Music publisher and record company. BMI. Publishes 30-50 songs/year. Pays standard royalty.
**How to Contact:** Submit demo tape and lead and lyric sheets. Prefers 7½ ips reel-to-reel or cassette with 1-3 songs on demo. SASE. Reports in 3 weeks.
**Music:** Blues, C&W, disco, easy listening, MOR, rock and soul. Recently published "Dancin' Man," recorded by Q (pop); and "Alone," recorded by the JBC Band (soul).

## Music Publishers 51

**GRAWICK MUSIC**, Box 90639, Nashville TN 37209. (615)321-3319. Affiliates: Mester (BMI) and James Hendrix (ASCAP). President: James Hendrix. Music publisher and record company. BMI. Publishes 20 songs/year; publishes 6 new songwriters/year. Pays standard royalty.
**How to Contact:** Submit demo tape and lyric sheet. Prefers cassette with 3-4 songs on demo. SASE. Reports in 1 month.
**Music:** Church/religious, gospel, R&B and top 40/pop. Recently published "Love, Sweet Love" (by Bettye Shelton), recorded by B. Shelton/Carrie Records; "The Jam" (by Dicky Marable), recorded by Spice/Carrie Records (R&B); "Who Knows" (by J. Hendrix), recorded by Cornell Blakely and produced by Berry Gordy, Jr. (R&B); and "Can It Be" (by Eric Von), recorded by the E-Z Band (pop).

*__GREATER SONGS__, Box 38, Toowong, Brisbane QLD, 4066, Australia. 61-07-370-7078. Manager: David Leary. Music publisher. Estab. 1982. APRA, AMCOS. Publishes 15 songs/year; publishes 1 new songwriter/year. Has not yet, but would listen to songs from US songwriters. Pays standard royalty; royalties paid to US songwriters through US publishing affiliate.
**How to Contact:** Submit demo tape and lyric sheet. Prefers cassette with 2-10 songs on demo. SAE and IRC. Reports in 2 weeks.
**Music:** Bluegrass, children's, C&W, easy listening, MOR, rock (hard and country) and top 40/pop. Recently published "Misty Mountain" (by D. Leary), recorded by Maria Dallas/Grevillen Records (country rock); "Cowboy Heroes" and "In a Sailboat With You" (children's).
**Tips:** "Do not over-develop melody line, choose lyrics carefully, and try to tie title of song to strongest melody phrase."

**GROOVESVILLE MUSIC**, 15855 Wyoming, Detroit MI 48238. (313)861-2363. Affiliates: Conquistador (ASCAP) and Double Sharp (ASCAP). Director: Will Davis. Music publisher, record company and record producer. BMI. Member NMPA. Publishes 25 songs/year; publishes 5 new songwriters/year. Pays standard royalties.
**How to Contact:** Query, submit demo tape and lyric sheet. Prefers cassette with 1-2 songs on demo. SASE. Reports in 4 weeks.
**Music:** Disco, easy listening, MOR, progressive, R&B, rock, soul and top 40/pop. Recently published "In the Rain" (by Tony Hester), recorded by Blue Magic/Atlantic Recording; "I've Been Born Again" (by D. Davis and J. Dean), recorded by Glenn Frey/Elektra/Aslyum/Nonesuch Records; "You've Got It" (by L.J. Reynolds), "You & Me" (by William Brown), "Special Effects" (by Calhoun and Stegall), and *Travelin*, all recorded by L.J. Reynolds/Capitol Records.

**FRANK GUBALA MUSIC**, Hillside Rd., Cumberland RI 02864. (401)333-6097. Contact: Frank Gubala. Music publisher and booking agency.
**How to Contact:** Submit demo tape or submit demo tape and lead sheet. Prefers cassette. Does not return unsolicited material. Reports in 1 month.
**Music:** Blues, disco, easy listening, MOR and top 40/pop.

*__GULE RECORD__, 7046 Hollywood Blvd., Hollywood CA 90028. (213)462-0502. Vice President: Harry Gordon. Music publisher, record company and record producer.
**How to Contact:** Submit demo tape or submit acetate disc. Prefers 7½ ips reel-to-reel tape with 2 songs on demo. SASE.
**Music** C&W, gospel, R&B, rock, soul and top 40/pop.

**HALBEN MUSIC PUBLISHING CO.**, Suite 38, 4824 Cote des Neiges Rd., Montreal, Quebec, Canada H3V 1G4. (514)739-4774. Affiliate: Rainy River Music Limited (PROCAN). President/Professional Manager: Ben Kaye. Music publisher and record producer. CAPAC. Publishes 100 songs/year; publishes 6 new songwriters/year. Pays standard royalty.
**How to Contact:** Submit demo tape and lyric sheet. Prefers 7½ ips reel-to-reel or cassette with 2-3 songs on demo. SAE and International Reply Coupons. Reports in approximately 1 month.
**Music:** Blues, easy listening, MOR, R&B, rock (hard, country), soul and top 40/pop. Recently published "Loven' You Once is Never Enough" (by Larry Whitley), sung by Toni Bellin as the U.S. entry in the Seoul Song Festival '83; "You Should Have Been" (by Norman Lang and Camille Langlois) recorded by Norman Lang/RCA Records (contemporary rock); and "La Vie A Fait de Toi, Une Femme" (by Daniel Malfara and J.P. Allaire), recorded by Gilles Girard and Super Classels/WEA Records (ballad).
**Tips:** "Songs should have a good story line and a strong hook in chorus or bridge and be 2½-3½ minutes long. Simple piano/vocal or guitar/vocal is acceptable—don't over-arrange the idea."

**HALNAT MUSIC PUBLISHING CO.**, Box 37156, Cincinnati OH 45222. (513)531-7605. Affiliate: Saul Avenue Publishing (BMI). President: Saul Halper. Music publisher. (ASCAP). Member NMPA. Publishes 6 songs/year; publishes 3 new songwriters/year. Pays standard royalty.

**How to Contact:** Submit demo tape and lyric sheet. Prefers cassette with 2-4 songs on demo. SASE. Reports in 2 weeks.
**Music:** Bluegrass, blues, C&W, gospel, R&B and soul. Recently published "Kansas City," recorded by the Beatles (rock); "Ain't Never Seen So Much Rain Before," recorded by Christine Kittrell (soul); and "Meet Me at the Station" (by R. Davis, J. Railey and G. Redd), recorded by Freddy King (rock).

**HAMMAN PUBLISHING, INC.**, Rt. 1, Box 195A, Dean Rd., Maitland FL 32751. (305)677-0611. President: Glenn Hamman. Music publisher, record company and record producer. BMI. Publishes 35 songs/year; publishes 10-15 new songwriters/year. Pays standard royalty.
**How to Contact:** Submit demo tape and lyric sheet or arrange personal interview. Prefers cassette with 2-3 songs on demo. "Please make sure all works are copyrighted before sending." SASE. Reports in 1 month.
**Music:** Church/religious, C&W, easy listening, gospel, jazz, MOR and R&B. Recently published "Blastoff Columbia" (by Jerry Rucker); "My Shoes Keep Walking Back to You" (by Lee Ross, Bob Whills); and "Eveready Pair of Arms" (by Jane Crouch, Joan Hager); all recorded by Silver Pelican Records (country).

**HANSEN-O'BRIEN MUSIC**, (formerly O'Brien Publishing Co.), Suite 8, 234 5th Ave., Redwood City CA 94063. (415)367-0298. President: E.J. O'Brien. Music publisher, record company and record producer. Estab. 1981. BMI. Publishes 10 songs/year; publishes 3 new songwriters/year. Pays standard royalty.
**How to Contact:** Submit demo tape and lyric sheet. Prefers cassette with 3-6 songs on demo. SASE. Reports in 2 weeks.
**Music:** Bluegrass, blues, C&W, MOR, R&B, rock and top 40/pop. Recently published "Devil in Her Eyes" (by E.J. O'Brien), recorded by The Hanson Brothers/O'Brien Records (crossover country); "Give It Up" (by Paul Hanson), recorded by P. Hanson/Duck Records (rock); and "The Devils Dues" (by E.J. O'Brien and P. Hanson), recorded by P. Hanson/O'Brien Records (C&W).

**HAPPY DAY MUSIC CO.**, Box 602, Kennett MO 63857. Affiliate: Lincoln Road Music (BMI). President: Joe Keene. BMI. Pays standard royalty.
**How to Contact:** Submit demo tape and lead sheet. Prefers reel-to-reel or cassette. SASE. Reports in 2 weeks.
**Music:** Gospel and religious. Recently published "I'm Going Up," recorded by the Inspirations (gospel); and "Glory Bound," recorded by the Lewis Family (gospel).

**HARD TEN MUSIC**, 1720 Lake St., Glendale CA 91201. (213)257-0454. Managing Director: Jennifer Bensi. Music publisher. Estab. 1983. ASCAP. Pays standard royalty.
**How to Contact:** Submit demo tape and lyric sheet. Prefers 7½ ips reel-to-reel or cassette with 1-3 songs on demo. "A simple demo will do; elaborate productions are not necessary." SASE. Reports in 3 weeks.
**Music:** Mostly rock, top 40/pop, new wave and hi-tech material; also jazz, MOR, progressive, R&B and soul.

**HARRISON MUSIC CORP.**, Suite 807, 6253 Hollywood Blvd., Hollywood CA 90028. (213)466-3834. Affiliates: Beethoven Music (ASCAP) and Lathe Music (BMI). Professional Manager: Tad Maloney. Music publisher. ASCAP. Member NMPA, AIMP. Pays standard royalty.
**How to Contact:** Arrange personal interview to play demo tape. Prefers 7½ ips reel-to-reel or cassette with 3-5 songs on demo with lead sheet or lyric sheet. Does not accept or return unsolicited material. Reports in 1 week.
**Music:** Blues; children's; church/religious; classical; easy listening; gospel; jazz; MOR; R&B; rock (country and pop); and top 40/pop. "Our requirements are a good tune and lyric that is well-constructed, with no slang or vogue words. We look ahead many years in order to properly work a song, and have found that something articulate works better in the long run. All of our standards are constantly being recorded—re-released etc." Published "Don't Get Around Much Anymore" (by Bob Russell and Duke Ellington), recorded by Willie Nelson/CBS Records (standard); "He Ain't Heavy, He's My Brother" (by Bob Russell and Bobby Scott), recorded by Neil Diamond.
**Tips:** "Get professional training and understand writing from an assignment point-of-view, not an intensely personal one."

**JOHN HARVEY PUBLISHING CO.**, Box 245, Encinal TX 78019. President: John Harvey. Music publisher and record producer. BMI. Member Harry Fox Agency. Publishes 24 songs/year; publishes 2 new songwriters/year. Pays standard royalty.
**How to Contact:** Submit demo tape and lyric sheet. Prefers cassette with 3-6 songs on demo. Will ac-

cept reel-to-reel at 7 1/2 ips. Will return material with return postage. Include brief resume. No query necessary. Reports in 2 weeks.
**Music:** Country, children's, easy listening, gospel, folk, Latin, instrumental, polkas and waltzes. Recently published "Another Time" (by Johnny Gonzalez), recorded by J. Gonzalez/CBS Records (country); "Palabras de Un Hijo" (by John Harvey), recorded by Bernardo y Sus Compadres/Dina Records); and "Mi Deseo" (by J. Harvey), recorded by J. Harvey/Peerless Records (Latin).
**Tips:** "Make demo as clear-sounding as possible, even if simple. Make all other enclosed material, such as lyric sheets, bios, etc., neat. Send the best material you have. Buy bulk cassettes at low price for demos, and let publishers keep your tape for future reference. This increases chances of your song being reviewed more than once. Needs are changing constantly."

**HAYSTACK PUBLISHING COMPANY**, Box 1528, Shreveport LA 71165. (318)742-7803. Affiliate: Hayseed Publishing Company (BMI). President: David Kent. Music publisher, record producer and record company. ASCAP. Publishes 25 songs/year; published 2 new songwriters in 1979 who were "contract artists with the Louisiana Hayride." Pays standard royalty.
**How to Contact:** Write first about your interest. Prefers cassette with 2-3 songs on demo. SASE. Reports in 3 weeks.
**Music:** C&W; gospel; and MOR. Recently published "Here He Comes" and "Goin' Fishin' " (by Micki Fuhrman), recorded by M. Fuhrman on Canaan Records (gospel); and "Don't You Think It's Time" (by Lee Marres), recorded by L. Marres/La Hayride Records (country).

**HEAVEN SONGS**, 9502 Harrell St., Pico Rivera CA 90660. (213)692-1472. Contact: Dave Paton. Music publisher, record company and record producer. BMI. Publishes 30-50 songs/year; publishes 10 new songwriters/year. Pays standard royalty.
**How to Contact:** Submit demo tape and lyric sheet. Prefers 7 1/2 ips reel-to-reel or cassette with 3-6 songs on demo. SASE. Reports in 2 weeks.
**Music:** C&W, dance-oriented, easy listening, folk, jazz, MOR, progressive, R&B, rock, soul and top 40/pop. Recently published "Tears Away" (by Bill Craig), recorded by Retvos/Hollyrock Records (dance/rock); "Someone Kind" (by B. Craig), recorded by B. Craig/Hollyrock Records (dance/rock); and "She Collects Hearts" (by Mark Anderson), recorded by Heaven/Hollyrock Records (dance).
**Tips:** Looking for "better quality demos."

***HEDLEY MUSIC GROUP**, 71 Rutland Rd., Chesterfield, Derbyshire, S40 1ND, England. 44-0246-79976. Affiliates: Michael James Music, Hardwick Music, March Music, Hedley Songs and Vehicle Music. Director: Tony Hedley. Music publisher, record company and record producer. MCPS. Member MPA. Publishes 2 new songwriters/year. Has not yet, but would listen to songs from US songwriters. Pays negotiable royalty; royalties paid directly to US songwriters or through US publishing affiliate.
**How to Contact:** Write first; submit demo tape and lyric sheet. Prefers cassette with 1-4 songs on demo. Tapes should be clearly labeled. SAE and IRC. Reports in 2 weeks.
**Music:** Mostly pop and folk; also C&W, rock (all types) and soul. Recently published "Fiddlers Green" (by John Conolly), recorded by over forty acts including George Hamilton IV, the Dubliners, Max Boyce, the Yetties, De Hofner (top German band).
**Tips:** "We are looking for country/pop crossover and rock material for existing artists. We also would like to acquire masters."

**HELIOS MUSIC CORPORATION**, 221 W. 57th St., c/o Copyright Service Bureau, Ltd., New York NY 10019. (212)581-0280. Affiliates: Monsapec Music, Inc. (BMI) and Glamorous Music, Inc. (ASCAP). President: Claus Ogerman. Music publisher. BMI. Publishes 90 songs/year. Pays standard royalty.
**How to Contact:** Submit demo tape and lyric sheet. Prefers cassette with 1-3 songs on demo. Does not return unsolicited material.
**Music:** Classical and jazz.

**HELPING HAND MUSIC LTD.**, 9229 58th Ave., Edmonton, Alberta, Canada T6E 0B7. (403)436-0665. Director A&R: R. Harlan Smith. Music publisher, record company, record producer and management firm. PROCAN. Publishes 50 songs/year. Pays standard royalties.
**How to Contact:** Submit demo tape, or submit demo tape and lead sheet. Prefers cassette with 3-5 songs on demo. Would also like "a written statement verifying that publishing is available internationally on the material submitted." Does not return material. Reports in 90 days.
**Music:** C&W; easy listening, MOR, and top 40/pop. Recently published "Easy Feelin Dream" (by R.H. Smith/S. Mooney), recorded by R. Harlan Smith and Chris Nielsen/Royalty Records (country); "Hootch, Heartache & Hallelujah" (by S. MacDougall), recorded by Laura Vinson & Red Wyng/Royalty Records (country/rock); "Too Much of a Lady" (by G. Fjellgaard), recorded by Larry Gustafson/

Royalty Records (country/rock); "Branded My Heart" (by L. Vinson), recorded by Laura Vinson & Red Wyng/Royalty Records (country); and "Take Your Time" (by D. Charney and C. Nielsen), recorded by Chris Nielsen/Royalty Records (country).

**THE HERALD ASSOCIATION, INC.**, Box 218, Wellman Heights, Johnsonville SC 29555. (803)386-2600. Affiliates: Silhouette Music (SESAC), Bridge Music (BMI), Heraldic Music (ASCAP) and Huffman Publishing (BMI). Director: Erv Lewis. Music publisher, record company and record producer. Member GMA. Publishes 15-20 songs/year; publishes 4 new songwriters/year. Pays standard royalty.
**How to Contact:** Submit demo tape and lyric sheet. Prefers cassette with 4-6 songs on demo. SASE. Reports in 2 months.
**Music:** Church/religious and gospel. Recently published "Nashville Without Jesus" (by Erv Lewis and Jerry Arhelger), recorded by Jerry Arhelger/Herald Records (gospel); "Life Giving Song" (by Sandy Bond), recorded by the Impacts/Mark Five Records (gospel); and "Here Comes That Joy Again" (by E. Lewis), recorded by Faye Yates (gospel).
**Tips:** "Avoid trite, overused phrases. Strive for fresh ways to say the same things, unusual rhyme, etc. Build strong hook and payoff lines into the songs. Send good tape. If we cannot hear the song above background noise, its chances are slim."

*****HIGHEST PRAISE PUBLISHING**, Box 1869, Hollywood CA 91042. (213)564-1008. Contact: Philip Nicholas. Music publisher, record company and record producer. Estab. 1981. BMI. Member NARAS, GMA. Publishes 20 songs/year; publishes 3 new songwriters/year. Pays standard royalty.
**How to Contact:** Submit demo tape and lyric sheet. Prefers cassette with 2-4 songs on demo. SASE. Reports in 1 month.
**Music:** Gospel. Recently published "God's Woman" (by P. Nicholas), recorded by P. Nicholas (gospel); "Generations" (by S. Jackson), recorded by P. Nicholas (gospel); and "Little Birdie" (by T. McFadden and P. Nicholas), recorded by P. Nicholas (gospel).

*****HIGHWAY MUSIC**, 6A Foregate St., Astwood Bank, Redditch, Worcester, B96 6DW, England. 44-0527-89-3737. General Manager: John Zollman. Music publisher and record company. MCPS, PRS and Phonographic Performance Ltd. Publishes 80 songs/year; publishes 2 new songwriters/year. Has not yet, but would listen to songs from US songwriters. Pays 50% of performance and mechanical royalties.
**How to Contact:** Submit demo tape and lyric sheet. Prefers cassette with 1-6 songs on demo. SAE and IRC. Reports in 1 month.
**Music:** Mostly folk, "but we are encouraging our existing writers and looking at new material in the MOR and AOR areas;" also easy listening and adult oriented rock. Recently published "Valley of Strathmore" (by A.M. Stewart), recorded by Silly Wizard/Shanachie Records, US; Highway Records, U.K. (folk); and "John O'Dreams" (by Bill Caddick), recorded on Aeocus Records, US (folk/MOR).

**THE HIT MACHINE MUSIC CO.**, subsidiary of Diversified Management Group, Box 20692, San Diego CA 92120. (714)277-3141. President: Marty Kuritz. Music publisher and record company. BMI. Publishes 10-20 songs/year. Pays standard royalty.
**How to Contact:** Submit demo tape and lead sheet. Prefers cassette with 3 songs on demo. SASE. Reports in 1 month.
**Music:** MOR, rock (soft), soul and top 40/pop. Recently published "I've Got Everthing I Need" and "I Wasn't Born Yesterday," recorded by Quiet Fire.

*****HOLY SPIRIT MUSIC**, Box 31, Edmonton KY 42129. (502)432-3183. President: W. Junior Lawson. Music publisher and record company. BMI. Member GMA, International Association of Gospel Music Publishers. Publishes 10 new songwriters/year; publishes 2 new songwriters/year. Pays standard royalty.
**How to Contact:** Submit demo tape and lyric sheet; call about your interest or arrange personal interview. Prefers 7½ ips reel-to-reel or cassette with any number of songs on demo. SASE. Reports in 3 weeks.
**Music:** Mostly Southern gospel; also MOR, progressive and top 40/pop. Recently published "Through Gates of Splendor" (by Marilyn K. Bowling), recorded by The Helmsman (Southern gospel); "Victory Ahead" (by Judy C. North), recorded by The Happy Travelers (Southern gospel); and "Canaanland Is Just in Sight" (by Jeff Gibson), recorded by The Florida Boys (Southern gospel).
**Tips:** Send "good clear cut tape with typed or printed copy of lyrics."

**HOOSIER HILLS PUBLISHING**, 1309 Celesta Way, Sellersburg IN 47172. (812)246-2959. Contact: Buddy Powell. Music publisher, record company and record producer. BMI. Publishes 10 songs/

year; publishes 10 new songwriters/year. Pays standard royalty.
**How to Contact:** Submit demo tape and lyric sheet. Prefers 7½ ips reel-to-reel or cassette with 2-4 songs on demo. SASE. Reports in 2 weeks.
**Music:** Bluegrass, C&W and gospel.

**HOT GOLD MUSIC PUBLISHING CO.**, Box 25654, Richmond VA 23260. (804)225-7810. President: Joseph J. Carter Jr. Music publisher, booking agency and record company. BMI. Publishes 10 songs/year; publishes 2 new songwriters/year. Pays standard royalty.
**How to Contact:** Submit demo tape. Prefers cassette with 1-3 songs on demo. SASE. Reports in 60 days.
**Music:** Mostly pop and R&B; also rock, soul and top 40. Recently published "How Long Will I Be a Fool" (by Willis L. Barnet), recorded by the Waller Family/Dynamic Artists Records (pop/soul); "Get Up Everybody" (by Ronnie R. Cokes), recorded by Starfire/Dynamic Artists Records (funk/soul); and "I Believe in You" (by Joseph J. Carter Jr.), recorded by Waller Family/MCA Records (pop/R&B); and "Sooner or Later, Baby" (by J.J. Carter Jr).

**HOUSE OF DIAMONDS MUSIC**, Box 449, Cleburne TX 76031. (817)641-3029. Publisher: Jan Diamond. Music publisher. BMI. Member, CMA.
**How to Contact:** Submit demo tape and lyric sheet. Prefers cassette.
**Music:** C&W, folk, gospel, MOR, progressive, country rock and top 40/pop.

***HUNTLEY STREET PUBLISHING**, 100 Huntley St., Toronto, Ontario, Canada M4X 2L1. (416)961-8001. Publishing Director: Bruce W. Stacey. Music publisher. Estab. 1981. PROCAN. Publishes 30 songs/year. Pays standard royalty.
**How to Contact:** Write first about your interest. Prefers cassette with 2-3 songs on demo. SAE and IRC. Reports in 1 month.
**Music:** Children's, contemporary church/religious and gospel.

**I.A.M. MUSIC**, 17422 Murphy Ave., Irvine CA 92719. (714)751-2015. Vice President Record Production: Paul Freeman. Music publisher, record company, mastering and record producer. ASCAP, BMI. Member NARAS, AIMP, GMA. Publishes 75-100 songs/year; publishes 1-2 new songwriters/year. Pays standard royalty; some writers for hire with publishing companies.
**How to Contact:** Submit demo tape and lyric sheet. Prefers cassette with 3 or more songs on demo. SASE. Reports in 2 months.
**Music:** All types. Recently published "Higher Power" (by Denny Correll), recorded by Darrell Mansfield and the Imperials/Word Records; "The Witness" and "He Set Free" (by D. Correll), recorded by D. Correll/Word Records (all gospel).
**Tips:** "Submit audible tapes with good quality lead sheets."

***IFFIN MUSIC PUBLISHING CO.**, Suite #215, 38 Music Square E., Nashville TN 37203. (615)254-0825. Professional Manager: Charlie Bragg. Music publisher. Estab. 1982. BMI. Pays standard royalty.
**How to Contact:** Submit demo tape and lyric sheet. Prefers cassette with 1-3 songs on demo. SASE. Reports in 1 month.
**Music:** C&W, gospel and MOR.
**Tips:** "We are a new company trying to establish a catalog, and are just beginning to pitch to record producers."

***IMAGE MUSIC PTY., LTD.**, 137 Moray St., South Melbourne, Victoria, 3205, Australia. 61-3-699-9999. US: Mason & Sloane, 1299 Ocean Ave., Santa Monica CA 90401. Affiliates/Australia: Rainbow Music (APRA) and Haven Music (APRA). Affiliates/US: American Image Music (BMI) and American Rainbird Music (ASCAP). Director: John McDonald. Music publisher, record company and record producer. APRA, AMCOS, Phonographic Performance Co. of Australia Ltd. Member AMPAL. Publishes 30-40 songs/year; publishes 8 new songwriters/year. Pays standard royalty; royalties paid directly to US songwriters ("if signed to our Australian company"), or through US publishing affiliate ("if songwriter is signed to our US company").
**How to Contact:** Submit demo tape and lyric sheet. Prefers cassette with 3-6 songs on demo. "Concentrate on quality rather than quantity: strong melodic hooks (choruses), and meaningful lyrics that tell a story. Forget obvious rhymes. Make good demos—pay attention to playing and singing." "We will not return material unless instructed to do so. Foreign submissions will not be returned unless postage is paid in advance." SAE and IRC. Reports in 1 week.
**Music:** Country, dance-oriented, folk, MOR, rock (all kinds) and top 40/pop. Recently published "Oh How She Loves Me" (by Richard Bennett & Larry Williams), recorded by Bluestone/Avenue Records,

Australia (top 40/pop); "Thinking of You" (by Lee Conway), recorded by Gary Holton & Casino Steel/Polygram Records, Europe (top 40/pop); and "Coleraine" (by David Hampson), recorded by the Cobbers/Festival Records, Australia and New Zealand (country).

**\*INCIDENTAL MUSIC**, 4th Floor, 50 Newton St., Manchester, M1 2EA, England. 44-061-236-9849. A&R Representative: Richard Boon. Music publisher and record company. MCPS, PRS, PPL. Publishes 30 songs/year; publishes 4 news songwriters/year. Pays standard royalty; royalties to US songwriters paid through MCPS, PRS and their affiliates.
**How to Contact:** Submit demo tape and lyric sheet. Prefers cassette with 2-5 songs on demo. SAE and IRC. Reports in 1 month.
**Music:** Mostly pop, rock and jazz; also blues, dance-oriented, easy listening, MOR, progressive, R&B, soul and punk. Recently published "Discipline" (by God's Gift), recorded by God's Gift/New Hormones Records (hardcore); "You'll Never Never Know" and "Violette," (Dislocation Dance), recorded by Dislocation Dance/New Hormones Records (pop).

**INTERPLANETARY MUSIC**, 7901 S. La Salle St., Chicago IL 60620. (312)224-0396. President: James R. Hall III. Vice President: Henry Jackson. Music publisher, booking agency and record company. BMI. Publishes 30 songs/year; publishes 10 new songwriters/year. Pays standard maximum royalty.
**How to Contact:** Submit demo tape or arrange personal interview. Prefers cassette. SASE. Reports in 3 weeks.
**Music:** Disco; soul; and top 40/pop. Recently published "Girl, Why Do You Want to Take My Heart?", recorded by Magical Connection (pop); and "You Blew My Mind This Time," recorded by Joe Martin (soul/pop/easy listening).

**\*I'VE GOT THE MUSIC COMPANY**, Box 2631, Muscle Shoals AL 35662. (205)381-1455. Affiliates: Song Tailors Music Co. (BMI), Terry Woodford Music (ASCAP) and Creative Source Music (BMI). Professional Manager: Richard Butler. Music publisher, record producer and video production company (Flying Colors Video). BMI, ASCAP. Publishes varied number of songs/year. Hires staff writers. Pays standard royalty.
**How to Contact:** Submit demo tape and lyric sheet. Prefers cassette with 1-3 songs on demo. SASE for returned material. Reports ASAP.
**Music:** Mostly top 40/pop; also C&W, dance-oriented, easy listening, MOR, progressive, R&B, rock and soul. Recently published "After I Cry Tonight" (by Phillip Mitchell), recorded by Lanier & Co./LARC-MCA Records (ballad); "Minimum Love" (by Mac McAnally and Jerry Weller), recorded by M. McAnally/Geffen Records (top 40/pop); and "Old Flame" (by M. McAnally and Donny Lowery), recorded by Alabama/RCA Records (country).

**JACKPOT MUSIC**, 133 Walton Ferry, Hendersonville TN 37075. (615)824-2820. Affiliates: Eager Beaver Music and His Word Music. President: Clyde Beavers. Music publisher, record producer, record company and studio. BMI, ASCAP and SESAC. Pays standard royalty.
**How to Contact:** Call first about your interest, then submit demo tape and lyric sheet. Prefers 7½ ips reel-to-reel or cassette with 1-3 songs on demo. SASE. Reports as soon as possible.
**Music:** Bluegrass, children's, church/religious, C&W, folk and gospel.

**JACLYN MUSIC**, 249 Hermitage Ave., Nashville TN 37210. (615)242-2220. President: Jack Lynch. Music publisher and record company. BMI. Affiliate: Nashville Music Sales, Jaclyn Recording Co., Nashville Bluegrass Recording Co. and Nashville Music Club. Publishes 12 songs/year. Pays standard royalty.
**How to Contact:** Query, then submit demo tape and lyric sheet. Prefers lyric sheet and cassette with 1-12 songs on demo. SASE. Reports in 1 week.
**Music:** Bluegrass, church/religious, C&W, and gospel. Recently published "Just One in a Crowd" (by Jack Lynch); "Nashville Wildcat" (by Pat Osborne), both recorded by Pat Osborne/Jalyn Records; and "Tornado Strut" (by Tom Cordell), recorded by Tom Cordell/Jayln Records.
**Tips:** "Make good demo tape and send good typed lyric sheet. Many tapes and lyric sheets we receive are inferior."

**JAMES BOY PUBLISHING CO.**, Box 128, Worcester PA 19590. (215)424-0800. President: Mr. J. James. Music publisher. BMI. Pays standard royalty.
**How to Contact:** Submit demo tape and lyric sheet. Prefers cassette with any number songs on demo. Reports in 1 month.
**Music:** C&W, dance-oriented, easy listening, folk, gospel, MOR, R&B, top 40/pop and soul.

## Music Publishers 57

**DICK JAMES MUSIC, INC.**, 24 Music Square E., Nashville TN 37203. (615)242-0600. Affiliates: Cookaway Music (ASCAP), Dejamus Music (ASCAP), Maribus Music (BMI), Daramus Music (ASCAP) and Yamaha. General Manager: Arthur Braun. Professional Manager, Mike Hollandsworth. Music publisher. BMI. Member NMPA. Publishes 20,000 songs/year: publishes 25 new songwriters/year worldwide.
**How to Contact:** Submit demo tape and lead sheet. Prefers cassette with 1-3 songs on demo. SASE. Reports ASAP.
**Music:** C&W; easy listening; MOR; rock (country and hard); soul; R&B; and top 40/pop. Recently published "We Said Good-by" (by Roger Greenaway and Geoff Stephens), recorded by Crystal Gayle (C&W); and "Heartbreaker," recorded by Pat Benatar.

**JANELL MUSIC PUBLISHING/TIKI ENTERPRISES, INC.**, 792 E. Julian St., San Jose CA 95112. (408)286-9840 or (408)286-9845. Affiliates: Janell (BMI) and Tooter Scooter Music (BMI). President: Gradie O'Neal. Secretary: Jeannine Osborn. Music publisher and record company. BMI. Publishes 75 songs/year; publishes 6 new songwriters/year. Pays standard royalty.
**How to Contact:** Submit demo tape with lead or lyric sheet. Prefers cassette with 3 songs on demo. SASE. Reports in 2 weeks.
**Music:** C&W, easy listening, gospel, MOR, rock (soft or hard), soul and top 40/pop. Recently published "Hard Times Are Here" (by Cal and Joyce Hyden), recorded by Joe Richie (country); "Vide Video" (by C. and J. Hyden), recorded by Jeannine Osborn/Rowena Records (rock); and "My Lifeline" (by Pam Landrum), recorded by P. Landrum/PDL Records (pop).

***DOUG JANSEN MUSIC**, 1st Floor, Suite 6/73, Miller St. North, Sydney, New South Wales, 2060, Australia. 61-4362907. Affiliates: Network Publishing, Shogun Music and Desert Fox Music. Managing Director: Doug Jansen. Music publisher and record producer. APRA, AMCOS. Member AMPA. Pays standard royalty; royalties paid directly to songwriter or through US publishing affiliate.
**How to Contact:** Submit demo tape and lyric sheet. Prefers cassette with 1-8 songs on demo. Does not return unsolicited material. Reports in 1 month.
**Music:** Mostly top 40; also MOR and rock. Recently published "She's a Gypsy" (by T. Dempsey), recorded by Col. Joye (top 40); "Queen of the Silver Star" (by T. Dempsey), recorded by Bill S. Boyd (top 40); and "A Sucker for that Old R&R" (by G. Bruno), recorded by Jade Hurley (top 40).

***JASON MUSIC/MOORESIDE MUSIC**, Soho St., London, W1, V6HR, England. 44-01-437-2245. Managing Director: David Marcus. Music publisher, record company and record producer. BMI, MCPS, PRS, PPL. Publishes 10 songs/year. Has not yet, but would listen to songs from US songwriters. Pays standard royalty; royalties paid directly to US songwriters.
**How to Contact:** Write first. Prefers cassette with 2-4 songs on demo. SAE and IRC. Reports in 1 month.
**Music:** Mostly MOR and dance-oriented; also blues, C&W, easy listening and R&B.

***JAY JAY PUBLISHING**, 35 NE 62nd St., Miami FL 33138. (305)758-0000. Contact: Walter Hagiello. Music publisher, record company and record producer. BMI. Member NARAS. Publishes 15-25 songs/year. Pays standard royalty.
**How to Contact:** Submit demo tape and lyric sheet. Prefers 15 ips reel-to-reel with 2-6 songs on demo. SASE. Reports in 1 month.
**Music:** Mostly polkas and waltzes; also C&W and easy listening.

**JEMIAH PUBLISHING**, Box 2501, Columbia SC 29202. (803)754-3556. Professional Manager: Myron Alford. Music publisher, record producer and artist management firm. Estab. 1981. BMI. Publishes 5-10 songs/year; publishes 4 new songwriters/year. Pays standard royalty.
**How to Contact:** Submit demo tape and lyric sheet. Prefers 7½ ips reel-to-reel or cassette with 1-4 songs on demo. SASE. Reports in 1 month.
**Music:** Mostly R&B; also gospel, MOR, C&W, rock (top 40), soul and top 40/pop. Recently published "Enjoy with Me" (by E. Jackson, M. Alford and R. Hoefer, Jr.), recorded by Midnight Blue/Enjoy Records (R&B); "Wishing" (by M. Alford, D. Bailey, E. Jackson, R. Hoefer, Jr. and D. Hodge, Jr.), and "Feel It and Groove Together" (by D. Hodge, Jr., E. Jackson and M. Alford), both recorded by Midnight Blue/Samarah Records (R&B); and "Reaching Out" and "Filth" (by J. Campbell, G. Parsons, E. Robinson, Jr., J. Duffir, K. Brown, G. Hackett, K. Hubbert), recorded by Private Stash (formerly Southside Coalition).

**JERJOY MUSIC**, Box 3615, Peoria IL 61604. (309)673-5755. Professional Manager: Jerry Hanlon. Music publisher. BMI. Publishes 4 songs/year; publishes 3 new songwriters/year. Pays standard royalty.
**How to Contact:** Submit demo tape and lyric sheet. Prefers cassette with 4-8 songs on demo. SASE. Reports in 2 weeks.

**Music:** C&W. Recently published "Love Has Gone Away" (by D. Moody), recorded by Jerry Hanlon (country ballad); "Hey, Little Dan" (by A. Simmons), recorded by J. Hanlon (country); and "Scarlet Woman" (by J. Hanlon and J. Schneider), recorded by J. Hanlon (country).

**JERO MUSIC LTD.**, Suite 11, 2309 N. 36th St., Milwaukee WI 53210. (414)445-4872. President: Marvell Love. Music publisher, record company and record producer. BMI. Publishes 6 songs/year; publishes 2 new songwriters/year. Pays standard royalty.
**How to Contact:** Submit demo tape and lyric sheet. Prefers cassette with 3-5 songs on demo. SASE. Reports in 1 month.
**Music:** Mostly soul; also gospel, R&B and top 40/pop. Recently published "Class A" (by the Majestics), recorded by the Majestics/New World Records (rapper); "Key to Love" (by the Majestics), recorded by the Majestics/New World Records" (ballad); and "I Call Him" (by James Mitchell), recorded by Masonic Wonders/More-Love Records (gospel).

**JIBARO MUSIC CO., INC.**, Box 424, Mount Clemens MI 48043. (313)791-2678. President/Professional Manager: Jim Roach. General Manager: Ann Roach. Music publisher and production company. BMI. Pays standard royalty.
**How to Contact:** Submit demo tape and lead sheet. Prefers cassette with 1-4 songs on demo. SASE. Reports in 2 weeks.
**Music:** Disco, jazz, MOR and soul. Recently published "Casanova Brown," recorded by Gloria Gaynor (disco/soul); "Thank God You're My Lady," recorded by the Dells (ballad); "I Dig Your Music," recorded by the Dramatics (disco/soul); and "You're My Super Hero" and "Super Heros Theme" (both by Jim Roach), both recorded by Everlife/CRC Records (pop).

**JMR ENTERPRISES**, 1014 16th Ave. S., Nashville TN 37212. (615)244-1630. Affiliates: Kelly & Lloyd Music (ASCAP), Mick Lloyd Music (SESAC), Street Song Music (ASCAP) and Jerrimick Music (BMI). Professional Manager: Kenny Jones. Music publisher, record producer and record company. ASCAP. Member CMA, NSAI and NARAS. Publishes 150 songs/year; publishes 20 new songwriters/year. Pays standard royalty.
**How to Contact:** Submit demo tape and lyric sheet. Prefers cassette with 1-3 songs on demo. SASE. Reports in 1 week.
**Music:** C&W, easy listening, gospel, MOR, progressive, church/religious, R&B, rock and top 40/pop. Recently published "Take Your Time in Leavin' " (by Jerri Kelly), recorded by Loretta Lynn/MCA Records (C&W); "Isn't Leavin' Me Enough" (by Larry Stallings and Kay Savage), recorded by Dave Rowland/Elektra Records (C&W); "Walk Me Cross the River," recorded by Jerri Kelly/Carrere Records (C&W/MOR/pop); and "Fool By Your Side," recorded by Dave Rowland & Sugar (country gold).

**LITTLE RICHIE JOHNSON MUSIC**, 913 S. Main St., Belen NM 87002. (505)864-7441. Manager: Joey Lee. Music publisher, record company and record producer. BMI. Publishes 25 songs/year; publishes 15-20 new songwriters/year. Pays standard royalty.
**How to Contact:** Submit demo tape and lyric sheet. Prefers 7½ ips reel-to-reel or cassette with 6-8 songs on demo. SASE. Reports in 2 weeks.
**Music:** C&W, gospel and Spanish. Recently published "Let It Be" (by Nadine Moore), recorded by Carol Roman/LRJ Records (C&W); "I Just Want to Be Free" (by Carol Roman), recorded by Carol Roman/LRJ Records (C&W); and "Sweet Freedom" (by Nadine Moore), recorded by Carol Roman/LRJ Records (C&W).

**JON MUSIC**, Box 233, 329 N. Main St., Church Point LA 70525. (318)684-2176. Owner: Lee Lavergne. Music publisher and record company. BMI. Publishes 10-20 songs/year; publishes 6 new songwriters/year. Pays standard royalty.
**How to Contact:** Submit demo tape. Prefers 7½ ips reel-to-reel or cassette with 2-6 songs on demo. SASE. Reports in 2 weeks.
**Music:** Mostly country; also rock and soul. Recently published "Broken Hearts" and "I Can Play Too" (by Doris Bijeaux), recorded by D. Bijeaux/Lanor Records (country); and "Suicide Ride" (by Glenn Thibodeaux), recorded by G. Thibodeaux/Lanor Records (rock).

**JONAN MUSIC**, 342 Westminster Ave., Elizabeth NJ 07208. Office Manager: Helen Gottesmann. Music publisher. ASCAP. Publishes 60 songs/year.
**Music:** Only publishes material of artists recording on Savoy Records. Recently published "Calvary" and "Meditation" (by Sylvia G. Wayman); "Can You Feel Him Moving?," "He's Coming Back" and "I'm Satisfied" (by Milbert McKenzie); "God is Everything We Need," "He That Hath an Ear, Let Him Hear" and "Oh Lord Who Shall Abide" (by Andrew Cooper); "He's Real" by Barbara Best; "Hold On" by Lois Tillery; and "What a Wonder the Lord Has Done" (by Moses and M. McKensize).

Music Publishers **59**

***JORIN**, Bente Record, 382 Central Park W., New York NY 10025. (212)749-2267. President: Jon Shaka. Music publisher. ASCAP. Pays standard royalty.
**How to Contact:** Submit demo tape and lyric sheet. Prefers cassette with 3-5 songs on demo. SASE. Reports in 1 month.
**Music:** R&B and soul.

**K AND R MUSIC, INC.**, 19 Frontenac Rd., Box 616, Trumansburg NY 14886. (607)387-5775. Reviewer: Christine Dwyer. Music publisher and record company. ASCAP. Publishes 40-50 songs/year; publishes 3 new songwriters/year. Pays standard royalty.
**How to Contact:** Submit demo tape and lyric sheet. Prefers cassette with 6-12 songs on demo. SASE. Reports in 1 month.
**Music:** Mostly church/religious and folk; also children's. Recently published "Follow Me" (by Ray Repp); recorded by R. Repp/K&R Records (MOR/religious); "Change My Heart" (by Mary Lu Walker), recorded by M.L. Walker/K&R Records (children's); and "We are Singing" (by Tom Shade), published in *Life Songs Hymnal* (folk/religious).
**Tips:** "We are interested in music that is singable."

**KACK KLICK, INC.**, Mirror Records, Inc., 645 Titus Ave., Rochester NY 14617. (716)544-3500. Vice President: Armand Schaubroeck. Manager: Kim Simons. Music publisher and record company. BMI. Publishes 20 songs/year; publishes 4-12 new songwriters/year. Pays standard royalty.
**How to Contact:** Submit demo tape. Prefers cassette. Include photo. SASE. Reports in 2 months.
**Music:** MOR, progressive, rock, top 40/pop and new wave. Recently published *Here Are the Chesterfield Kings*, recorded by the Chesterfield Kings; *Over the Rainbow*, by Don Potter; and "I Shot My Guardian Angel" (by Armand Schaubrock), recorded by A. Schaubrock/Mirror Records.

**KAMAKAZI MUSIC CORPORATION**, 314 W. 71st St., New York NY 10023. (212)595-4330. Professional Manager: Miles J. Lourie. Music publisher. BMI. Pays standard royalty.
**How to Contact:** Submit demo tape and lyric sheet. Prefers cassette with 2-3 songs on demo. SASE. Reports in 4-6 weeks.
**Music:** Progressive, rock/country crossover, R&B, rock and top 40/pop.

**KARJAN MUSIC PUBLISHING CO.**, Box 205, White Lake NY 12786. (914)583-4471. President: Mickey Barnett. Music publisher, record company and record producer. SESAC. Member CMA. Publishes 25 songs/year; publishes 4 new songwriters/year. Pays standard royalty.
**How to Contact:** Submit demo tape and lyric sheet. Prefers cassette with 1-3 songs on demo. SASE. Reports in 3 weeks.
**Music:** Blues, C&W, easy listening, MOR, R&B and top 40/pop.

**KAT FAMILY MUSIC PUBLISHING**, B-130, 5775 Peachtree Dunwoody Rd. NE, Atlanta GA 30342. (404)252-6600. President: Joel A. Katz. Music publisher. BMI. Publishes 30-50 songs/year. Pays standard royalty.
**How to Contact:** Submit demo tape and lyric sheet. Prefers cassette with 2-4 songs on demo. SASE. Reports in 1 month.
**Music:** Rock; pop; country; MOR; R&B; and contemporary gospel.

**KATCH NAZAR MUSIC**, Rose Hill Group, 2929 New Seneca Turnpike, Marcellus NY 13108. (315)673-1117. Affiliate: Bleecker Street Music (BMI). A&R Director: Vincent Taft. Music publisher. ASCAP. Publishes 6-15 songs/year; publishes 2 new songwriters/year. Pays standard royalty.
**How to Contact:** Submit demo tape and lyric sheet. Prefers cassette with 1-4 songs on demo. "Please be selective. Songs should be melodic and have 'un-busy' music; strong, realistic lyrics; a beginning, middle and end." SASE. Reports in 2 weeks.
**Music:** Mostly rock and top 40/pop; also C&W, dance-oriented, jazz and R&B. Recently published "She's the One" (by Mike Crissan), recorded by Tickets (rock); "Ocean Algae" (by Sudan Baronian), recorded by Taksim (jazz); and "Skytrain" (By Zarm), recorded by Zarm (dance).

**JOE KEENE MUSIC CO.**, Box 602, Kennett MO 63857. Affiliates: Lincoln Road Music (BMI) and Cone Music (BMI). President: Joe Keene. Music publisher. BMI. Publishes 12-20 songs/year; publishes 3-4 new songwriters/year. Pays standard royalty.
**How to Contact:** Submit demo tape and lead sheet. Prefers reel-to-reel or cassette. SASE. Reports in 2 weeks.
**Music:** Mostly country; also rock and easy listening. Recently published "Working All Day and Loving All Night" and "Nobody Can Do It Like Me" (by Joe Keene), recorded by J. Keene/KSS Records (country); "Don't Start Something You Can't Finish" (by J. Keene), recorded by Terry Ray Bradley/

B&B Records (country/rock); and "My Baby Loves Me" (by Diana Sutton), recorded by Diana Foxe/ KSS Records (pop).

**\*KEENY-YORK PUBLISHING**, Box 121, Waterville OH 43566. (419)535-7900. Affiliate: Park J. Tunes (ASCAP). Contact: Doug Larue. Music publisher, record company, record producer and film producer. BMI. Publishes 50 songs/year; publishes 4 new songwriters/year. Pays standard royalty.
**How to Contact:** Submit demo tape and lyric sheet. Prefers cassette with 5-10 songs on demo. Include photo and one-page resume. SASE. Reports in 1 month.
**Music:** Mostly top 40/pop; also C&W, easy listening and MOR. Recently published "Where Do We Go From Here" (by J. Petrone), recorded by Kathy White/Jamestune Records (pop); "Wintersong" (by M. Shaw), recorded by Jackass Flatts (C&W); "Pigskin Blues" (by M. Shaw), recorded by MDS (C&W); "Theme from Limelight" (by Dan Faehnle); and "Since You've Been Gone," by Michael Drew Shaw (tribute to J.F.K.); easy listening and MOR.
**Tips:** "We are now producing *Limelight*, a nightly musical variety show for cable syndication. We are also working with Belle Star on a new album project."

**KELLY & LLOYD MUSIC**, 1014 16th Ave. S, Nashville TN 37212. (615)244-1630. Affiliates: Mick Lloyd Music (SESAC) and Jerri Music (BMI), part of JMR Enterprises. President: Mick Lloyd. Music publisher, record producer and record company. ASCAP. Publishes 150 songs/year; publishes 12 new songwriters/year. Pays standard royalty.
**How to Contact:** Submit demo tape and lyric sheet. Prefers cassette with 1-4 songs on demo. SASE. Reports in 1 week. "Submit a clear tape and lyrics."
**Music:** "I'm as Much of a Woman" (by Jerri Kelly), recorded by DeDe Church/Little Giant Records (country); "Fool By Your Side" (by Bobby Cox), recorded by Dave Rowland & Sugar/Elektra Records; "Take a Chance on Love" (by Byron Gallimore), recorded by D. Rowland & Sugar/Elektra Records; "Life on the Road" (by Mick Lloyd), recorded by D. Rowland & Sugar/Elektra Records (country); and "Take Your Time in Leavin" (by J. Kelly), recorded by Loretta Lynn/MCA Records.

**GENE KENNEDY ENTERPRISES, INC.**, 2125 8th Ave. S., Nashville TN 37204. (615)383-6002. Affiliates: Chip 'n Dale (ASCAP), Door Knob Music (BMI), Lodestar (SESAC), Bekson (BMI) and Kenwald (ASCAP). President: Gene Kennedy. Vice President: Karen Jeglum. Music publisher; and independent producer, distributor and promoter.
**How to Contact:** Query or arrange personal interview. Prefers cassette or 7½ ips reel-to-reel with 1-3 songs on demo. "Tape should be accompanied by lyrics." SASE. Reports in 2-5 weeks.
**Music:** Bluegrass; C&W; gospel; MOR.

**KICKING MULE PUBLISHING/DESK DRAWER PUBLISHING**, Box 158, Alderpoint CA 95411. Manager: Ed Denson. Music publisher and record company. BMI. Member NAIRD. Publishes 120 songs/year; publishes 10 new songwriters/year. Pays standard royalties.
**How to Contact:** Write first about your interest. Prefers cassette with 1-3 songs on demo. Does not return unsolicited material. Reports "as soon as possible."
**Music:** Bluegrass (flatpicking); blues (fingerpicking); and folk (guitar/banjo only). "We publish only material released on our albums. Since we record virtuoso guitar and banjo players, virtually the only way to get a tune published with us is to be such a player, or to have such a player record your song. We don't publish many 'songs' per se, our entire catalog is devoted 95% to instrumentals and 5% to songs with lyrics. As publishers we are not in the market for new songs. This listing is more of a hope that people will not waste their time and ours sending us blue-sky demos of material that does not relate to our very specialized business." Recently published "The Sweeper" (by George Gritzbach), recorded by Gritzbach/KM Records (folk); "Thunder On The Run" (by Stefan Grossman), recorded by Grossman/KM Records (guitar instrumental); and "Pokerface Smile" (by Robert Force), recorded by Force & D'Ossche (country).

**\*LORNA KIRTLAND MUSIC LTD.**, 93 Hainault Road, Chigwell, Essex, England. 44-500-9846. Director: Lorna Kirtland. Music publisher. Estab. 1983. PRS. "I listen to any song which is professionally done."
**How to Contact:** Submit demo tape and lyric sheet. Prefers cassette with maximum 2 songs on demo. "Send an excellent demo—no calls, please." SAE and IRC. Reports in 3 weeks.
**Music:** Mostly top 40/pop; also rock (no heavy), soul and ballads.

**KITCHEN TABLE MUSIC**, Box 861, Edmonton, Alberta, Canada T5J 2L8. (403)477-6844. Affiliates: Gimbleco West Music/PROCAN; Stony Plain Music/CAPAC, and Eyeball Wine Music/CAPAC. Managing Director: Holger Petersen. Music publisher, record company and record producer. PRO-

CAN. Member CIRPA and CARAS. Publishes 50 songs/year; publishes 5 new songwriters/year. Pays standard royalty.
**How to Contact:** Submit demo tape and lyric sheet. Prefers cassette with 1-4 songs on demo. SAE and IRC. Reports in 3 weeks.
**Music:** Bluegrass, folk, MOR, progressive, rock and top 40/pop. Recently published "Misty Mountain" (by Ferron), recorded by Ferron/Stony Plain Records (folk); "Running Start" (by Larry Pink), recorded by Crowcuss/Stony Plain Records (rock); and "The Matrimonial Blues" (by Paul Hann), recorded by Paul Hann/Stony Plain Records (folk).

**KRPCO MUSIC**, 4926 W. Gunnison, Chicago IL 60630. (312)545-0861. President: Ray Peck. Music publisher, record company, record producer and record distributor. BMI, ASCAP. Publishes 12-16 songs/year; publishes 5 new songwriters/year. Pays standard royalty.
**How to Contact:** Submit demo tape and lyric sheet. Prefers cassette with 4-6 songs on demo. SASE. Reports in 1 month.
**Music:** All types. Recently published "Boy I Need You" (by Nadine Herman), recorded on Stang Records; and "John Lennon," recorded by Torn Orphans/Kiderian Records.

**LA LOU MUSIC**, 711 Stevenson St., Lafayette LA 70501. (318)234-5577. President: Carol J. Rachou, Sr. Music publisher, record company (La Louisianne), record producer, recording studio and distributing company. BMI. Publishes 50-60 songs/year. Pays standard royalty.
**How to Contact:** Submit demo tape and lyric sheet. Prefers 7½ ips reel-to-reel or cassette with 1-6 songs on demo. "If possible, we would like variations of each song (tempos, styles, keys, etc.)." SASE.
**Music:** "We are primarily interested in Cajun French songs." Also bluegrass, blues, church/religious, C&W, folk, gospel, jazz, MOR, progressive, R&B, rock, top 40/pop, comedy and French comedy. Published "Lache Pas La Patate" (by C.J. Trahan), recorded by Jimmy C. Newman/La Louisianne Records (Canjun/French); "When the Saints Go Marching In" (in Cajun French and English by Jimmy C. Newman/La Louisianne Records); and "Sweet Cajun Love Song" (by Eddy Raven), recorded by Eddy Raven/La Louisianne Records (Cajun French/English).

**LACKEY PUBLISHING CO.**, Box 269, Caddo OK 74729. (405)367-2798. President: Robert F. Lackey. Music publisher and record producer. BMI. Publishes 10-12 songs/year; publishes 6-8 new songwriters/year. Pays standard royalty.
**How to Contact:** Submit demo tape. Prefers 7½ ips reel-to-reel tape with 1-10 songs on demo. SASE. Reports in 2 weeks.
**Music:** Mostly country and MOR; also bluegrass, blues, church/religious, easy listening, folk, gospel, progressive, R&B and top 40/pop. Recently published "Summer Sun" and "Teenager in Love" (by Franklin Lackey), recorded by Sherry Renae/Cannonball Records (MOR); "Mary Lou" (by F. Lackey), recorded by Mike Hall/Cannonball Records (R&B); "Red River Rose" (by Mike Hall), recorded by Mike Hall/Uptown Records (country); "Mississippi River Take Me Home" (by Frank Lackey), recorded by Frank Lackey/Uptown Records (MOR); "Going to Louisiana" (by Mike Hall), recorded by Mike Hall/Uptown Records (MOR); and "Through Baby's Eyes" (by F. Lackey), recorded by F. Lackey/Uptown Records (country).
**Tips:** "Have accompaniment of 3 or more musicians."

**LADD MUSIC CO.**, 401 Wintermantle Ave., Scranton PA 18505. (717)343-6718. President: Phil Ladd. Music publisher, record company and record producer. BMI. Publishes 4 songs/year. Pays standard royalty.
**How to Contact:** Query or submit demo tape and lead sheet. Prefers cassette with minimum 2 songs on demo. SASE. Reports in 3 weeks.
**Music:** Children's, C&W, easy listening, R&B, rock and top 40/pop. Recently published "Piano Nelly," (by Bobby Poe), recorded by Bobby Brant/Whiterock Records(rock); and "Miss Lucy" (by Poe), recorded by Big Al Downing/Whiterock Records (rock).

**LADERA MUSIC PUBLISHING**, Worldway Postal Center, Box 91120, Los Angeles CA 90009. (213)641-0178. President: Philip Sonnichsen. Chairman: Edward "Lalo" Guerrero. Music publisher, record company and record producer. Estab. 1981. BMI. Pays standard royalty.
**How to Contact:** Write first about your interest or submit demo tape and lyric sheet. Prefers cassette or reel-to-reel. SASE. Reports in 1 month.
**Music:** "We are a Chicano/Latin-oriented company. New material may be in English or Spanish."

**LANCE JAY MUSIC**, Box 62, Shiloh TN 38376. (901)689-5141. Vice President: Carol Morris. Music publisher. ASCAP. Affiliate: Carol Faye Music. BMI. Works with songwriters on contract.

**How to Contact:** Submit demo tape and lead sheet. Prefers 7½ ips reel-to-reel or cassette with 2-4 songs on demo. SASE. Reports in 1 month.
**Music:** Bluegrass, C&W and gospel. Recently published "Cole Bell," "Living Ain't Been Easy," and "Tomorrow."

**JAY LANDERS MUSIC**, Suite 920, 9255 Sunset Blvd., Los Angeles CA 90069. (213)550-8819. President: Jay Landers. Music publisher and record producer. ASCAP. Member OCMP. Publishes 30 songs/year; publishes 2-3 new songwriters/year. Pays standard royalty.
**How to Contact:** Query, or submit demo tape and lyric sheet. Prefers cassette with 1-3 songs on demo. SASE. Reports within 4 weeks.
**Music:** Easy listening, MOR, pop, rock, and top 40/pop. Recently published "Coming In and Out of Your Life" (by Bobby Whiteside and Richard Parker), recorded by Barbara Streisand; "Mirror, Mirror" (by Michael Sembello), recorded by Diana Ross; "The Air That I Breathe" (by Albert Hammond), recorded by the Hollies (MOR/pop), and "99 Miles From LA" (by A. Hammond/Hal David), recorded by Johnny Mathis.

**STUART LANIS MUSIC, INC.**, 1273½ N. Crescent Hts. Blvd., Los Angeles CA 90046. (213)550-4500. Affiliate: Peter Piper Publishing (ASCAP). A&R: Stuart Lanis. Music publisher, record producer and record company. BMI. Publishes 15-20 songs/year. Pays standard royalty.
**How to Contact:** Submit demo tape and lyric sheet. Prefers cassette with 3-6 songs on demo. SASE. Reports in 3 weeks.
**Music:** Children's, church/religious, classical, easy listening, gospel, MOR and top 40/pop.

**LARDON MUSIC**, Box 200, River Grove IL 60171. General Manager: Larry Nestor. Music publisher. BMI. Publishes 8-10 songs/year; publishes 0-1 new songwriters/year. Pays standard royalty.
**How to Contact:** Submit demo tape and lead sheet. Prefers 7½ ips reel-to-reel or cassette with a maximum of 3 songs on demo. SASE. Reports in 2 weeks.
**Music:** Children's (educational material as used on *Sesame Street* and *Captain Kangaroo*), country and pop. Recently published "I Can't Sleep You Off," "Love Me or Trade Me," and "Whiskey River" (by Larry Nestor), recorded by Johnny Cooper (country and pop).
**Tips:** "Video segment to match up with songs can be very helpful, especially in trying to hook up with children's shows."

*****LAREO MUSIC, INC.**, 425 Park Ave., New York NY 10022. (212)371-9400. Los Angeles: 606 N. Larchmont Blvd., Los Angeles CA 90004. Vice President: Norman Weiser (New York). Creative Director: Richard Weiser (Los Angles). Music publisher. Estab. 1981. BMI, ASCAP, SESAC. Member NMPA. Publishes 350-500 songs/year; publishes 12 new songwriters/year. Pays standard royalty.
**How to Contact:** Submit demo tape and lyric sheet or arrange personal interview. Prefers 7½ ips reel-to-reel or cassette with 1-4 songs on demo. SASE. Reports ASAP.
**Music:** Mostly jazz, black gospel, Latin, country and pop; also blues, choral, church/religious, dance-oriented, easy listening, MOR, progressive, Spanish, R&B, rock (all kinds) and soul. Recently published "Go" (by Shirley Caesar), recorded by Shirley Caesar/Word Records (gospel); "Adicto" (by Oscar De Fontana and V. Saens), recorded by Oscar De Fontana/Fonsa Records (Latin); and "Southern Fried" (by Bill Anderson), recorded by Bill Anderson/Vanguard Records (country).

**LARKSPUR MUSIC PUBLISHING**, Box 1001, Soquel CA 95073. General Manager: Jon Hutchings. Music publisher, record company, record producer and sound reenforcement company. BMI. Member Billboard's Association of Publishers/Producers. Pays standard royalty.
**How to Contact:** Submit demo tape and lyric sheet. Prefers cassette with 3-5 songs on demo. "Include 8x10 photo and bio." SASE. Reports "after material is reviewed; time varies."
**Music:** R&B, rock and top 40/pop.

**LAUGHING BIRD SONGS PUBLISHING CO.**, Box 3144, Covina CA 91723. (213)967-1451. President: Angelo Roman, Jr. Music management and production consultant. ASCAP. Pays standard royalty. Publishes 3-4 new songwriters/year.
**How to Contact:** Submit demo tape and lyric sheet. Prefers cassette with 1-3 songs on demo. SASE. Reports in 1 month. Note: "We usually work with material from artists we regularly deal with."
**Music:** Mostly top 40; also C&W, easy listening, MOR, rock and pop.

**LAZAR MUSIC**, Box 77, Center Square PA 19422. (215)635-6921. Affiliate: Ron "Mr. Wonderful's Music". President: A. Gravatt. Music publisher and record company. Estab. 1981. BMI. Pays negotiable royalty.
**How to Contact:** Write first about your interest, then submit demo tape and lyric sheet. Prefers cassette with 1-4 songs on demo. SASE. Reports in 1 month.

**Music:** Dance-oriented, jazz, MOR, progressive, R&B, rock, soul and top 40/pop. Recently published "Tight Money" (by T. Walker and A. Gravatt), recorded by CE Rock/Lazer Records (R&B/pop); and "I Want You (So Bad)" (by R. Lewis and A. Gravatt), recorded by Latita/Lazer Records (pop).
**Tips:** "Be sure that the music and lyrics truly have hit potential."

\*LE MATT MUSIC, LTD., c/o Stewart House, Hillbottom Rd., Highwycombe, Bucks, England. 44-0491-36301. Affiliate: Lee Music, Ltd. Contact: Ron or Cathrine Lee. Music publisher, record company and record producer. MCPS, PRS. Member MPA. Publishes 50 songs/year; publishes 15 new songwriters/year. Pays standard royalty; royalties paid directly to US songwriters or through US publishing affiliate.
**How to Contact:** Submit demo tape and lyric sheet. Prefers 7½ or 15 ips reel-to-reel, cassette or video (if possible) with 1-3 songs on demo. Make sure name and address are on reel or cassette. SAE and IRC. Reports in 3 weeks.
**Music:** Bluegrass, blues, C&W, dance-oriented, easy listening, MOR, progressive, R&B, rock (any type), soul and top 40/pop. Recently published "I Do Love You" (by Keatly), recorded by Penny Arcade/PVK Records; "I'm Only Looking" (by Daniel Boone), recorded by D. Boone/Swoop Records; "I'm a Rep" (by Bowman), recorded by the Chromatics/Grenoville Records; *The Chromatics* (by Bowman), recorded by the Chromatics/Grenoville Records; and "I Hate School," "Questions" and *Suburban Studs* (by Hunt), recorded by the Surburan Studs/Pogo Records.

\*ALFRED LENGNICK & CO. LTD., Purley Oaks Studios, 421A Brighton Rd., South Croydon, Surrey, CR2 6YR, England. Music publisher. MCPS, PRS, MRS. Pays standard royalty; royalties paid directly to US songwriters.
**How to Contact:** SAE and IRC.
**Music:** Choral, church/religious, classical, folk and MOR.

**LILLENAS PUBLISHING CO.**, Box 527, Kansas City MO 64141. (816)931-1900. Affiliates: Beacon Hill Music (SESAC) and Faith Music (SESAC). Director: Ken Bible. Music Editor: Lyndell Leatherman. Music publisher and record producer. SESAC. Pays standard royalty.
**How to Contact:** Submit lead sheet. "A demo tape is helpful, but not necessary." Prefers cassette with 1-5 songs on demo. SASE. Reports in 2-8 weeks.
**Music:** Church/religious and gospel. Publishes primarily choral music, approximately 12 books/recordings per year, plus approximately 30 anthems. Also publishes some children's music, vocal solos, vocal ensembles and instrumentals.

**LINEAGE PUBLISHING CO.**, Box 211, East Prairie MO 63845. (314)649-2211. Professional Manager: Tommy Loomas. Music publisher, record producer and record company. BMI. Pays standard royalty.
**How to Contact:** Query before submitting demo tape and lyric sheet. Prefers cassette with 2-4 songs on demo. SASE. Reports in 1 month.
**Music:** C&W; easy listening; MOR; country rock; and top 40/pop. Recently published "Country Boy" (by Alden Lambert), recorded by Lambert/Capstan Records (country); "Dawn" (by Hank Waring), recorded by Waring/Jalyn Records (country); and "Best of All" (by Tommy Loomas), recorded by Mary Nichols/Onie Records (MOR).

**LITTLE JOE MUSIC CO.**, 604 Broad St., Johnstown PA 15906. (814)539-8117. Owner: Al Page. Music publisher. BMI. Publishes 12-24 songs/year; publishes 2 new songwriters/year. Pays standard royalty.
**How to Contact:** Submit demo tape and lead sheet. Prefers 3¾ ips reel-to-reel with 2-4 songs on demo. SASE. Reports in 2 weeks.
**Music:** Bluegrass, church/religious, C&W, folk and polkas. Recently published *Orthodox Catholic Choir*; *Catholic Church Choir* (Roman Catholic music); *Orthodox Greek Catholic Choir* (religious); and *Organ* (instrumental).

**LITTLE OTIS MUSIC**, 101 Westchester Ave., Port Chester NY 10573. (914)939-1066. General manager: Judy Novy. Music publisher and record producer. BMI. Publishes 15 songs/year; publishes 2 new songwriters/year. Pays standard royalties.
**How to Contact:** Submit demo tape and lead sheet. Prefers cassette with 1-5 songs on demo. SASE. Reports in 1 month.
**Music:** MOR; R&B; rock; soul; and top 40/pop. Recently published "Play It the Fair Way" (by T. Masi, soul/R&B), and "Rainmaker" (by G. Siano, soul/R&B), all recorded by Johnny Sundance.

**LITTLE THINGS MUSIC**, #322, 2300 Henderson Mill Rd. NE, Atlanta GA 30345. (404)493-1210. Affiliate: July Child Music (ASCAP). Contact: Jim Oliver. Music publisher, record company and record

producer. Estab. 1981. BMI. Publishes 2-3 songs/year; publishes 3 new songwriters/year. Pays standard royalty.
**How to Contact:** Submit demo tape and lyric sheet. Prefers cassette with 3 songs on demo. SASE. Reports in 3 weeks.
**Music:** Children's, church/religious, C&W, gospel and R&B.

**LODESTAR MUSIC**, (Division of Gene Kennedy Enterprises, Inc.), 2125 8th Ave., S., Nashville TN 37204. (615)383-6002. Affiliates: Chip 'N' Dale Music Publishers, Inc. (ASCAP) and Door Knob Music Publishing, Inc. (BMI). President: Gene Kennedy. Vice President: Karen Jeglum. Music publisher. SESAC. Member NSAI, CMA and ACM. Publishes 20 songs/year; publishes 10 new songwriters/year. Pays standard royalty.
**How to Contact:** Submit demo tape and lyric sheet or arrange personal interview. Prefers 7½ ips reel-to-reel or cassette with 1-4 songs. SASE. Reports in 1-3 weeks.
**Music:** C&W, MOR and gospel. Recently published "You're Still the One (Who Makes My Life Complete)" (by James Britt/Ervan James/Bobby Young), recorded by Douglas/Door Knob Records and Gene Kennedy and Karen Jeglum/Door Knob Records (MOR).

**LONE LAKE SONGS, INC.**, 93 N. Central Ave., Box 126, Elmsford NY 10523. President: Ron Carpenter. Music publisher. ASCAP. Publishes 25 songs/year; published 23 new writers in 1982. Hires staff writers: "should be established musicians and able to arrange and to write material for certain projects, such as commercials."
**How to Contact:** Submit demo tape, submit demo tape and lead sheet, or submit lead sheet. Prefers cassette with 1-6 songs on demo. "Do not send original copies of masters." SASE. Reports in 1 month.
**Music:** Bluegrass, C&W, disco, easy listening, folk, gospel, MOR, rock (mellow), soul and top 40/pop.

**LOOK HEAR MUSIC**, 24548 Pierce, Southfield MI 48075. (313)559-7630. President: Bruce Lorfel. Music publisher and record company. BMI. Publishes 10-20 songs/year; publishes 5 new songwriters/year. Pays standard royalty.
**How to Contact:** Submit demo tape and lyric sheet. Prefers cassette with 1-3 songs on demo. SASE. Reports in 1 month.
**Music:** MOR, rock and top 40/pop. Recently published "We're Gonna' Rock" (by Cochran, Edwards, Sarkisian, Volin and Warren); "Dreamin' " (by Warren); and "Can't Think Right" (by Edwards), all recorded by The Look/Plastic Records (rock).

**THE LORENZ CORPORATION**, 501 E. 3rd St., Dayton OH 45401. Affiliates: Lorenz Publishing Company and Sonshine Productions (publishes monthly sacred music periodicals for youth and adult choirs as well as piano and organ periodicals); Sacred Music Press (publishes in octavo form "a more stylized type of sacred music for church and school choirs"); Triune Music/Triangle Records Cantus (Trigon); Heritage Music Press and Roger Dean. Music Editor: Gene McClusky. Music publisher. BMI, ASCAP and SESAC. Member NMPA, MPA and CMPA. Publishes 200 songs/year; publishes 10 new songwriters/year. Pays standard royalty.
**How to Contact:** Send manuscripts and demo tapes. SASE. Reports in 1 month.

**LORENZ CREATIVE SERVICES**, 824 19th Ave. S., Nashville TN 37203. (615)329-1429. Affiliates: Triune Music, Inc. (ASCAP), Timespann Music (BMI), Nova Press (SESAC), Many Hats Music (ASCAP), Stone Bluff Music (SESAC), Sunshine Productions, and 19th Street Music (BMI). President: Elwyn Raymer. Operations Manager: Lisa Keeling. Music publisher and production company. ASCAP, NMPA, CMPA. Publishes 100 songs/year; publishes 5-10 new songwriters/year. Pays negotiable royalty.
**How to Contact:** Submit demo tape and lyric sheet. Prefers cassette with 2-4 songs on demo. SASE. Reports in 3 months.
**Music:** Children's, choral, church/religious, classical and gospel.
**Tips:** "Have copies of lead sheets/manuscripts and tapes available to leave with us."

*__LOS ANGELES INTERNATIONAL MUSIC__, Box 209, 102 Burbank Dr. B, Toledo OH 43695. President: Florence Lloyd. Music publisher. ASCAP. Member NMPA. Publishes 30 songs/year; publishes 8 new songwriters/year. Hires staff writers; pays negotiable salary "depending on expectations and music of songwriter." Pays standard royalty.
**How to Contact:** Submit demo tape and lyric sheet. Prefers 7½ ips reel-to-reel, cassette or demo records with 3-6 songs on demo. "Send only best songs with as much attention to music as to lyrics. Include lead sheets and/or arrangements. Sound and creativity are very important." Does not return unsolicited material. Reports in 3 weeks.

## Music Publishers 65

**Music:** Recently published "This Ole Heart" (by Cynthia Jones and Arron Tolbert), recorded by Backlash/Walking Tall Records; "Fair Game" (by Jimmy Lloyd Jr/Terry Snodgrass), recorded by Raymond Alexander/Fast Flight Records; "Give Me Some Credit" (by Carl Smith), recorded by La Que/Future Shock Records; "Who's Backstabbing Who?" (by Gregory Austin), recorded by La Que; and "Love Projection" (by Robert Slack), recorded by Unique Pleasure.
**Tips:** "Have a good knowledge of music and what sounds are becoming hit records. We prefer songwriters who are dedicated to the belief that songs are salable in today's market."

**LOWERY MUSIC CO., INC.**, 3051 Clairmont Rd. NE, Atlanta GA 30329. (404)325-0832. Affiliates: Brother Bill's Music (ASCAP), Low-Sal Inc. (BMI) and Low-Twi Inc. (BMI). Member CMA, NARAS and NMPA. Contact: Professional Director. Music publisher and record producer. BMI. Member NMPA. Publishes 20-30 songs/year; publishes 10 new songwriters/year. Pays standard royalties.
**How to Contact:** Submit demo tape and lyric sheet. Prefers cassette with 1-4 songs on demo. SASE. Reports in 2 weeks.
**Music:** Contemporary Christian, top 40, R&R and C&W.

**HAROLD LUICK & ASSOCIATES MUSIC PUBLISHER**, Box B, Carlisle IA 50047. (515)989-3679. President: Harold L. Luick. Music publisher, record company, record producer and music industry consultant. BMI. Publishes 20-25 songs/year; publishes 10 new songwriters/year. Pays standard royalty.
**How to Contact:** Write or call first about your interest, arrange personal interview or submit demo tape and lyric sheet. Prefers cassette with 3-5 songs on demo. SASE. Reports in 3 weeks.
**Music:** Bluegrass, C&W, dance-oriented, easy listening, gospel, MOR, R&B, country rock-a-billy and top 40/pop. Recently published "For a Little While" (by T. Neil Smith), recorded by Blue Sky Band/Studio 2000 Records (country); "Pop Corn Song" (by Kenny Hofer), recorded by Kenny Hofer/4 Leaf Records (dance-oriented); and "Yankee Duke" (by Darrell C. Thomas), recorded by D.C. Thomas/DTC Records (country).
**Tips:** "Know the difference between a *tune* and a *song*. Submit only songs. Make decent 'dubs.' It is not a matter of *luck*, but a matter of being prepared when *luck* comes along. If you are unlucky then you have been unprepared. Submit only your *best* works."

**JIM McCOY MUSIC/ALEAR MUSIC**, Box 574, Sounds of Winchester, Winchester VA 22601. (703)667-9379. Affiliate: New Edition Publishing. Contact: Jim McCoy. Music publisher, record company, record producer and management firm. BMI. Publishes 50 songs/year; publishes 25 new songwriters/year. Pays standard royalty.
**How to Contact:** Submit demo tape and lead sheet. Prefers 7½ ips reel-to-reel or cassette with 5-10 songs on demo. SASE. Reports in 1 month.
**Music:** Bluegrass, church/religious, C&W, folk, gospel, progressive and rock. Recently published "Going with Jesus" (by Fred Fox), recorded by Middleburg Harmonizers (gospel); "Lost in Austin" (by Panama Red), recorded by Del Davidson (country); and *Jim McCoy Sings*, recorded by Jim McCoy (country).

**MACHARMONY MUSIC**, Suite 5C, 400 W. 43rd St., New York NY 10036. Director: Walter Herman. Music publisher. ASCAP. Publishes 6 songs/year. Pays standard royalty.
**How to Contact:** Submit demo tape and lyric sheet. Prefers cassette with 1-3 songs on demo. SASE. Reports in 1 month.
**Music:** Rock (pop, hard and soft). Recently published "Secret Lover," by R. Barlett/Date Line International Records (rock); "Pretenders" and "Face in Your Crowd," by Mac Bryde and Bartlett/Date Line International Records (rock).

**MAINROADS PUBLISHING**, 100 Huntley St., Toronto, Ontario, Canada M4Y 2L1. (416)961-8001. Publishing Director: Bruce W. Stacey. Music publisher and record company. CAPAC. Publishes 75 songs/year; publishes 1 new songwriter/year. Pays standard royalty.
**How to Contact:** Submit demo tape and lyric sheet or write about your interest. Prefers cassette with 3-5 songs on demo. SAE and IRC. Reports in 1 month.
**Music:** Children's, choral, church/religious and gospel.

**MALACO, INC.**, Box 9287, Jackson MS 39206. (601)982-4522. Producer: James Griffin. President: Tommy Couch. Producers: Tommy Couch and Wolf Stephenson. Vice President: Wolf Stephenson. Music publisher, record producer and record company. BMI. Publishes 60 songs/year. Pays standard royalty.
**How to Contact:** Submit demo tape and lyric sheet. Prefers cassette with 1-5 songs on demo. Does not return unsolicited material.

Music: Blues; disco; easy listening; gospel; MOR; R&B; rock; soul; and top 40/pop. Recently published "Groove Me" (by King Floyd), recorded by the Blues Brothers.

**MANFIELD MUSIC**, Holy Spirit Records, 27335 Penn St., Inkster MI 48141. (313)862-8220 or 562-8975. President: Elder Otis G. Johnson. Music Director: Ted Thomas. Music publisher, record producer and record company. BMI. Publishes 50 songs/year; publishes 5 new songwriters/year. Pays standard royalty.
How to Contact: Query or submit demo tape and lyric sheet. Prefers 3¾ or 7½ ips reel-to-reel or cassette with 3 songs minimum on tape. Include phone number. SASE. Reports in 1 month.
Music: Church/religious and gospel. Recently published "To Be With You" (by Otis G. Johnson), recorded by Otis G. Johnson/ASPRO Records; "Life is Beautiful" (by Alison Simone and George Johnson), recorded by George Johnson/ASPRO Records; "Ask the Lord" (by Marion L. Lang), recorded by Sonlight/ASPRO Records; "Let's Help Them See the Light" (by Craig T. Erquhart), recorded by Sonlight/ASPRO Records; and "Sing From the Center World" and "Ladybug," recorded by Karen Bauchard/ASPRO Records.

**MANNA MUSIC, INC.**, 2111 Kenmere Ave., Burbank CA 91504. (213)843-8100. Affiliates: Gaviota Music (BMI), Hollyville Music (SESAC) and Nashwood Music (ASCAP). President: Hal Spencer. Music publisher and record company. ASCAP. Member NMPA. Hires staff writers.
How to Contact: Submit demo tape or submit demo tape and lead sheet. Prefers cassette with 1-5 songs on demo. Does not return unsolicited material. Reports in 2 weeks.
Music: Choral; church/religious; and gospel. Published "How Great Thou Art," recorded by Elvis Presley (religious); "Sweet, Sweet Spirit," recorded by Pat Boone (religious); and "His Name Is Wonderful," recorded by Norma Zimmer (religious).

**MARIELLE MUSIC CO.**, Box 842, Radio City Station, New York NY 10019. Branch: Box 11012, Chicago IL 60611. (312)266-9616. Music publisher and record producer. BMI. Pays standard royalty.
How to Contact: Submit demo tape and lyric sheet. Prefers cassette with any number songs on demo. Does not return unsolicited material. Reports in 3 months.
Music: C&W, easy listening, jazz, MOR, R&B, rock, soul and top 40/pop.

**MARMIK MUSIC, INC.**, 135 E. Muller Rd., East Peoria IL 61611. (309)699-7204. President: Martin Mitchell. Music publisher and record company. BMI. Publishes 50-100 songs/year; publishes 10 new songwriter/year. Pays standard royalty.
How to Contact: Query, submit demo tape, or submit demo tape and lead sheet. Prefers reel-to-reel or cassette with 2-10 songs on demo. "With first submission, include an affidavit of ownership of the material." SASE. Reports in 2 weeks.
Music: Blues, church/religious, C&W, easy listening, gospel and MOR. Recently published "Good Times Blues" (by Roy Harder), recorded by Jack Greeley/Musi-Mation Records (country); "All My Love" (by Mike Mitchell), recorded by Jack Greeley/Musi-Mation Records (MOR); and "A Song in Your Heart" (by Darlene Hunt), recorded by D. Hunt/Musi-Mation Records (religious).

**MARSAINT MUSIC, INC.**, 3809 Clematis Ave., New Orleans LA 70122. (504)949-8386. A&R Director: M.E. Sehorn. Music publisher. BMI. Pays standard royalty.
How to Contact: Submit demo tape and lyric sheet. Prefers cassette with 3-5 songs on demo. SASE. Reports in 1 month.
Music: Blues, gospel, jazz, R&B and soul. Recently published "Released" (by Allen R. Toussaint), recorded by Patti Labelle/CBS Records (soul); "Southern Nights" (by A.R. Toussaint), recorded by Glen Campbell (country); songs recorded by Ramsey Lewis/CBS Records (progressive jazz) and Eric Gale/CBS Records (progressive jazz).

**\*MARSHALL STREET MELODIES**, 8102 Polk St. NE, Minneapolis MN 55432. (612)784-7458. President/General Manager: Michael S.J. Gapinski. Music publisher and record company. Estab. 1982. BMI. Member MSA. Publishes 4-8 songs/year. Pays standard royalty.
How to Contact: Write first about your interest. Prefers cassette with 1-3 songs on demo. "Include clear and concise sheet music and *separate* lyric sheets." Does not return unsolicited material. Reports in 2 weeks.
Music: Mostly slow dance; also disco. Recently published "Magic in Her Eyes" (by Michael Gapinski), recorded by Michael Sylvester/Marshall Street Melodies Records (easy listening/pop); "I Was A Fool" (by M. Gapinski), recorded by M. Sylvester/Marshall Street Melodies Records (top 40/pop); and "Ain't Gonna Give Up" (by M. Gapinski), recorded by M. Sylvester/Marshall Street Melodies Records (new wave/top 40).
Tips: "We only need slow dance and funk-type dance songs."

# Close-up

**Steve Kipner**
Songwriter/Performer

In the late seventies, Australian songwriter/performer Steve Kipner, living in England, wrote songs—in English—that were translated into Italian and Spanish and sold millions of copies in Europe, Mexico and South America. "Because of that success, I started to get a lot of covers by entertainers in non-English speaking countries, but not in America," Kipner recalls.

Now, living in Los Angeles, Kipner is a complete international success as the co-writer of "Physical" and "Heart Attack," recorded by Olivia Newton-John and "My Potential New Boyfriend," recorded by Dolly Parton as well as songs for Sheena Easton, Cher, The Hollies, Stephen Stills, Englebert Humperdinck, Amy Holland, Manhattan Transfer, Juice Newton, Paul Anka, America and other top artists.

Kipner warns songwriters to be wary of getting "caught in the trap of trying to write a song for a specific artist, a hit for *somebody*. Instead, write songs for *anybody*. Include things on the demo—a guitar part, for instance—not to attract a particular artist, but because they are the best things for that particular song. That way, the end product will have its own personality. And if it's good, it will attract a *lot* of different types of artists."

Kipner says he's often surprised at who ends up recording his songs. "Not that we were doing it for the Pointer sisters, but when we were working on 'My Potential New Boyfriend,' we did get the feeing that it would be a great song for them. I would never have imagined that Dolly Parton would end up recording it. Just like I would never have imagined a girl singing 'Physical,' let alone, Olivia Newton-John."

Kipner had thought "Physical" would be a perfect song for Rod Stewart. Even though he had known Newton-John since their Australian days, Kipner says "If I were going to have played songs for Olivia, I would have played different ones than 'Physical'."

Lee Cramer, Olivia Newton-John's producer, just happened to hear "Physical" through the wall of a Hollywood recording studio where Kipner was playing it, newly demoed, for his own producer. Cramer loved the song and played it for Olivia who loved it too.

Kipner's best piece of advice to writers is: "Do it because you're enthusiastic about it, not because you want to be a successful songwriter or make a lot of money. Songwriting is my job, but it is also my hobby, what I *like* to do. If I wasn't getting paid to do it, I'd be doing it for free."

**MARULLO MUSIC PUBLISHERS**, 1121 Market St., Galveston TX 77550. (713)762-4590. President: A.W. Marullo, Sr. Music publisher, record company and record producer. BMI. Publishes 24 songs/year; publishes 8 new songwriters/year. Pays standard royalty.
**How to Contact:** Submit demo tape and lyric sheet. Prefers 7½ ips reel-to-reel or cassette with 4-6 songs on demo. SASE. Reports in 1 month.
**Music:** C&W, soul and top 40/pop. Recently published "Girl I Never Had" (by Bobbe Brown), recorded by Brown Bros./Paid Records (C&W); "Alimony Blues" (by Michael Claughton), recorded by Michael John/Red Dot Records (C&W); and "We'll Make Believe Again," written and recorded by Kemberly and Michael John/Red Dot Records (C&W).

**ANDY MARVEL MUSIC**, 8 Pasture Ln., Roslyn Heights NY 11577. (516)621-4307. Affiliates: Bing, Bing, Bing Music (ASCAP), Andysongs (BMI), Droopy Tunes (BMI). President: Andy Marvel. Music publisher, record company and record producer. Estab. 1981. ASCAP. Publishes 30 songs/year; publishes 10 new songwriters/year. Pays standard royalty.
**How to Contact:** Submit demo tape and lyric sheet or arrange personal interview to play demo tape. Prefers 7½ ips reel-to-reel or cassette with 3-5 songs on demo. SASE. Reports in 2 weeks.
**Music:** C&W, MOR and top 40/pop. Recently published "Learning to Live with a Heartache" (by Andy Marvel and Sheree Sano), and "Love Will Never be the Same Without You" (by A. Marvel and Don Levy), both recorded by John Wesley Shipp/Jamie Records (MOR ballads); and "I Surrender My Heart to You" (by A. Marvel and Meg Raben), recorded by Jerri Bokeno/Ricochet Records (pop/rock).

**MASTERLEASE MUSIC PUBLICATIONS**, Box 234, St. Louis MO 63166. (314)296-9526. President: Bob Bax. Music publisher and record company. BMI. Publishes 3 songs/year. Pays standard royalty.
**How to Contact:** Write first about your interest, then submit demo tape and lyric sheet. Prefers cassette with 2-6 songs on demo. Does not return unsolicited material. Reports in 1 month.
**Music:** Bluegrass, blues, church/religious, C&W, gospel, Spanish and R&B.

**MASTER'S COLLECTION PUBLISHING & T.M.C. PUBLISHING**, Box 189, Station W, Toronto, Ontario Canada M6M 4Z2. (416)746-1991. President: Paul J. Young. Music publisher and record company. PROCAN, CAPAC. Member CIRPA. Publishes 100 songs/year; publishes 40 new songwriters/year. Pays standard royalty.
**How to Contact:** Write first about your interest. Prefers cassette with 3-6 songs on demo. Does not return unsolicited material. Reports in 1 month.
**Music:** Christian/religious and pop/rock. Recently published "Crown of Glory" (by Ruth Fazal) and "One City Stands" (by Andrew Donaldson), on The Master's Collection Records; and "Christmas Is" (by Frank Hargreaves), recorded by His Ambassadors/The Master's Collection Records (Christmas).

*****MATTHEWS MUSIC PTY., LTD.**, 7 Denison St., Rozelle, New South Whales, 2039, Australia. 61-02-82-0669. Director: Phil Matthews. Music publisher, record company and record producer. APRA, AMCOS. Member AMPA. Publishes 100 songs/year; publishes 5 new songwriters/year. Has not yet, but would listen to songs from US songwriters. Pays standard royalty; royalties paid directly to US songwriters or paid to US songwriters through a US publishing affiliate.
**How to Contact:** Submit demo tape and lyric sheet. Prefers cassette with 5-10 songs on demo. SAE and IRC. Reports in 1 month.
**Music:** Country and top 40/pop. Recently published "Our Lips Are Sealed" (by Hall), recorded by Go-Go's (pop); "WOT" (by Capt. Sensible), recorded by Capt. Sensible (pop); and "Imperial Bedroom" (by Elvis Costello), recorded by Elvis Costello (rock).

*****MAUI MUSIC**, 87 Wilson St., Hawera, Taranaki, New Zealand. 64-8-7537. Affiliates: Maui Records (APRA); Maui Music (AMCOS) and Josephine & Ephraim Music. Manager: Barletta Prime. Director: Dalvanius Prime. Music publisher, record company and record producer. APRA, AMCOS. Publishes 25-30 songs/year (Maori language) and 10-20 songs/year (English); publishes 2 new songwriters/year. Has not yet, but would listen to songs from US songwriters. Pays standard royalties set by the New Zealand government after 40% sales tax.
**How to Contact:** Write first; submit demo tape and lyric sheet. Prefers cassette as demo. Include bio and photo. SAE an IRC. Reports in 1 month.
**Music:** Mostly MOR; also blues, C&W, dance-oriented, easy listening, R&B, rock, soul, top 40/pop and ethnic, e.g. Indian. Recently published "Can't You See I'm a Fool Over You", recorded by Prince Tui Teka/RCA Records (C&W); and "Checkmate on Love," and "Voodoo Lady," recorded by Dalvanius & the Fascinations/Festival Records (soul), all written by Dalvanius and Barletta Prime.

**MCA MUSIC**, MCA, Inc., 70 Universal City Plaza, Universal City CA 91608. (213)508-4550. Affiliates: Leeds Music (ASCAP), Duchess Music (BMI), Music Corporation of America (BMI), and MCA Music (ASCAP). Music publisher. ASCAP. Member NMPA. Publishes numerous songs/year; publishes 5 new songwriters/year. Pays standard royalties. Hires staff writers.
**How to Contact:** Submit demo tape and lead sheet or demo tape and lyric sheet. Prefers cassette with 1-3 songs on demo. SASE. Reports in 1 month.
**Music:** Blues; easy listening; jazz; MOR; R&B; rock; soul; country and top 40/pop. Recently published "I'm in Love," recorded by Evelyn King.

*****MCA MUSIC AUSTRALIA PTY., LTD.**, 23 Pelican St., Darlinghurst, Sydney, New South Wales, 2010, Australia. 61-02-267-6088. Affiliate: Chris Gilbey Pty., Ltd. Director: Ben Teh. Professional Manager: Stephen Walters. Music publisher and record producer. APRA and AMCOS. Member AMPAL, Ltd. Publishes 6 new songwriters/year. Hires staff writers. Pays standard royalty; royalties paid to US songwriters through US publishing affiliate.
**How to Contact:** Submit demo tape and lyric sheet. Prefers 7½ ips reel-to-reel or cassette. SAE and IRC. Reports in 2 weeks.
**Music:** Mostly top 40/pop, rock and country; also MOR. Recently published "Lady, What's Your Name" (by Jon Kennett and Dave Skinner), recorded by "Swanee"/WEA Records (top 40/pop); "I'm a Punk" (by Morling/Ingram/Lennon/Mulray/Sterling), recorded by Doug Mulray & the Rude Band/EMI Records (top 40/pop comedy); and "Every Little Bit of Australia" (by Rod Boucher), recorded by Slim Dusty/EMI Records (country).

**ME MUSIC**, Box 1010, Hendersonville TN 37075. (615)329-9492. Affiliate: Mel-Dee Music (BMI). General Manager: Dee Mullins. Music publisher, record company (Melodee) and record producer (Melodee Ent.). ASCAP. Member AFM, AFTRA. Publishes 30-40 songs/year; publishes 2 new songwriters/year. Pays standard royalty.
**How to Contact:** Write or call first about your interest, then submit demo tape and lyric sheet or arrange personal interview to play demo tape. Prefers cassette with 1-4 songs on demo. SASE. Reports in 1 month.
**Music:** Bluegrass, C&W, folk, gospel, MOR, rock (country) and top 40/pop.

**MEDIA CONCEPTS, INC./MCI MUSIC**, 52 N. Everts, Elanford NY 10523. (914)699-4003. Affiliate: Sunsongs Music (BMI). Professional Manager: Chip Rigo. Music publisher and record producer. BMI, ASCAP. Publishes 50 songs/year; publishes 15 new songwriters/year. Pays standard royalty.
**How to Contact:** Submit demo tape and lyric sheet. Prefers cassette with 3-6 songs on demo. SASE. Reports in 3 weeks.
**Music:** C&W, dance-oriented, easy listening, R&B, rock (all styles) and top 40/pop. Recently published "Just Want You Around" (by M. Berman), recorded by Sunrise/Arista Records (pop rock); "Never Gonna' Stop" (by Herman Eng), "Stood Up" (by Lisa Tyler) and "Cut Too Deep" (by John Stevens), recorded by Jailbait (rock); and "Run to Me" (by Alfie Davison), recorded by Daybreak.

**MEDIA INTERSTELLAR MUSIC**, Box 20346, Chicago IL 60620. (312)778-8760. Professional Manager: V. Beleska. Music publisher. BMI. Publishes 20-40 songs/year. Also "joint ownership plans, where a songwriter becomes co-publisher. Expenses and profits are shared. We *don't* charge the songwriter for our services as publisher. We cannot consider any material, however, without first receiving a written query (don't phone) describing yourself and your songs in some depth. The letter should explain your background, type of songs written and why songs are unique enough to be listened to."
**How to Contact:** "Inquire first, describing yourself and songs available." Prefers 7½ ips reel-to-reel, cassette or disc with 1-5 songs on demo. SASE. Reports in 2-8 weeks.
**Music:** Avant-garde; C&W; disco; easy listening; MOR; progressive; rock; soul; and top 40/pop. Recently published "All for You," and "The Show Never Ends," recorded by Christopher (MOR/rock); and "Tricentennial 2076," recorded by Vyto B (avant-garde).

**MEGA-STAR MUSIC**, 200 W. 51st St., New York NY 10019. (212)245-3939. Vice President and General Manager: Barry Yearwood. Music publisher and record producer. BMI. Publishes 12 songs/year; publishes 10 new songwriters/year. Pays standard royalty.
**How to Contact:** Submit demo tape and lyric sheet. Prefers cassette with 4-8 songs on demo. Does not return unsolicited material. Reports in 1 month.
**Music:** Mostly R&B and dance; also gospel, jazz, MOR, progressive, rock, soul and top 40/pop. Recently published "Dancing to the Beat" (by Henderson and Whitfield), recorded by Park Place (dance); and "Party Nights" (by Howie Young), recorded by Carol Douglas/Plateau Records (all dance).
**Tips:** "We look for clever vocals and strong hooks."

**\*MEMNON, LTD.**, Box 98, Forest Hills NY 11375. (212)261-1111. Cable: MEMNON NEW YORK. Affiliate: Tithonus Music, Ltd. (ASCAP). President: K.Z. Purzycki. Music publisher. ASCAP. Member Harry Fox Agency, Inc. Publishes 17 songs/year; publishes 2 new songwriters/year. Pays standard royalty.
**How to Contact:** Submit demo tape and lyric sheet. Prefers cassette with 3-5 songs on demo. SASE. Reports in 1 month.
**Music:** Choral, C&W, easy listening and MOR. Recently published "All My Life" (by Angelo Vess), recorded by Sound Alternative/Memnon Records (top 40/pop); "Only a Fool" (by Angelo Vess), recorded by Sound Alternative/Memnon Records (MOR); "Music Inside" (by Cosmo Carrozza and Nelson Trout), recorded by Roy Edwards/Bolivia Records (MOR); and "We Can Make It Together" (by Larry Baxter & Ralph Miles), recorded by R. Edwards/Bolivia Records (country).
**Tips:** "Be familiar with songs currently being played, but don't be afraid of submitting something a bit different. Songs must have good melody with appropriate lyrics which won't sound dated a decade from now."

**MEMPHIS MANAGEMENT MUSIC**, Box 17272, Memphis TN 38187-0272. (901)767-2220. (Blackwood Music/Memphis Management Corp.) Contact: Ron Blackwood. Music publisher, record company, record producer and record promoter. BMI, ASCAP. Publishes 100 songs/year; publishes 10 new songwriters/year. Pays standard royalty.
**How to Contact:** Submit demo tape and lyric sheet. Prefers cassette with 1-5 songs on demo. Does not return unsolicited material. Reports in 1 month "only if we're interested in the material."
**Music:** C&W, gospel, MOR and top 40/pop.

**MERCANTILE MUSIC**, Box 2271, Palm Springs CA 92263. (619)320-4848. Affiliate: Blueford Music (ASCAP). President: Kent Fox. Music publisher and record producer. Publishes 12 new songwriters/year. Pays standard royalty.
**How to Contact:** Submit demo tape and lyric sheet. Prefers cassette with 3-12 songs on demo. SASE. Reports in 1 month.
**Music:** C&W; easy listening; rock; MOR; and top 40/pop.

**MERIT MUSIC CORP.**, (formerly Music Publishing Corp.), 815-18th Ave. S., Nashville TN 37203. (615)327-0518. Affiliates: Singletree Music, Barnwood Music (BMI), Joiner Music (ASCAP) and Doubletree Music (SESAC). Manager: Dave Burgess. Music publisher. BMI and ASCAP. Pays standard royalty.
**How to Contact:** Write first about your interest." Prefers cassette with 3 songs on demo. SASE. Reports in 3 weeks.
**Music:** Country, MOR, rock and top 40/pop. Recently published "Power of Positive Drinking," recorded by Mickey Gilley/CBS Records (country); "Girls Get Prettier at Closing Time," recorded by Mickey Gilley/CBS Records (country); and "Dock of the Bay," recorded by Ottis Redding (soul/pop/MOR).

**\*MERTIS MUSIC CO.**, 8130 Northlawn, Detroit MI 48204. (313)934-0106. Vice President: Olivia John. Music publisher and record company. BMI. Publishes 40-50 songs/year; publishes 2 new songwriters/year. Pays standard royalty.
**How to Contact:** Submit demo tape and lead sheet. Prefers cassette with 4-8 songs on demo. SASE. Reports in 1 month or ASAP.
**Music:** Mostly gospel, pop and R&B; also jazz. Recently published "You Don't Know" (by Mertis John), recorded by Lorene Thompson/MEDA Records (gospel); "I'm Guilty" (by Michael McKay), recorded by Lorene Daniels/MEDA Records (gospel); and "Keep on Moving" (by Joe Hunter and Mertis John), recorded by Buddy Lamp/MEDA Records (pop).

**MICHAVIN MUSIC**, 1260 North F. St., Pensacola FL 32501. Manager: Vincent L. Smith III. Music publisher, record producer and music arranger.
**How to Contact:** Query. Prefers cassette.
**Music:** Disco, jazz, R&B, soul and top 40/pop.

**MID AMERICA MUSIC**, (a division of Ozark Opry Records, Inc.), Box 242, Osage Beach MO 65065. (314)348-3383. Affiliate: Tall Corn Publishing (BMI). General Manager: Lee Mace. Music publisher. ASCAP. Publishes 25 songs/year. Pays standard royalty.
**How to Contact:** Arrange personal interview or submit demo tape and lead sheet. Prefers 7½ ips reel-to-reel or cassette with 1-3 songs on demo. "Tape should be of good quality, and the voice should be louder than the music." SASE. Reports in 3 weeks.
**Music:** Bluegrass, children's, church/religious, C&W, disco, easy listening, gospel, MOR and rock.

Music Publishers **71**

Recently published "Never Asking for More," (by Rod Johnson), recorded by Graham Fee/Fee-Line Records (MOR); "Losing the Blues" (by Steve and Juli Ann Whiting), recorded by S. Whiting/KRC Records (MOR); and "Iowa a Place to Grow" (by S. Whiting), recorded by S. Whiting/KRC Records (MOR).

**MIDEB MUSIC**, 1501 Broadway, New York, NY 10036. (212)786-7667. Affiliate: Twin Music (BMI). President: Sam Weiss. Vice President: Daniel Glass. Music publisher and record company. ASCAP. Publishes 20 songs/year. Hires staff writers
**How to Contact:** Query. Prefers 7½ ips reel-to-reel or cassette with 1-3 songs on demo. SASE. Reports in 2 weeks.
**Music:** Blues, disco, easy listening, MOR, progressive, R&B, rock, soul and top 40/pop. Recently published "Keep on Dancin" (by Eric Matthew and Gary Turnier), recorded by Gary's Gang (pop); "Ain't That Enough for You" (by John Davis), recorded by John Davis and the Monster Orchestra (disco); "Just How Sweet Is Your Love," recorded by Rhyze; "This Beat is Mine," recorded by Vicky "D"; and "We'll Make It," recorded by Mike and Brenda Sutten.

**THE MIGHTY THREE MUSIC GROUP**, 309 S. Broad St., Philadelphia PA 19107. (215)546-3510. Affiliates: Assorted Music (BMI), Bell Boy Music (BMI), Downstairs Music (BMI), Razor Sharp Music (BMI), Rose Tree Music (ASCAP) and World War Three Music (BMI). President: Earl Shelton. Vice President of Publishing Administration: Constance Heigler. Contact: Professional Manager: William Lacy. Music publisher. BMI and ASCAP. Member NMPA. Publishes 100 songs/year; publishes 6 new songwriters/year. Pays standard royalty. Sometimes offers advance: "If a writer is signed to us exclusively, we offer him advances recoupable against writer royalties after songs have been recorded and released."
**How to Contact:** Submit demo tape and lyric sheet. Prefers cassette with 1-3 songs on demo. "Must provide large SASE for return." Reports in 8 weeks.
**Music:** C&W, disco, easy listening, folk, gospel, jazz, MOR, progressive, rock (hard, country), soul and top 40/pop. Recently published "Swing That Sexy Thing," by Carl Carlton/International Records; and "Your Body's Here with Me" (by Gilbert, Sigler and Sigler), recorded by The O'Jays/Philadelphia International Records (gospel); and "God Said It" (by Gamble and Womack), recorded by The 5 Blind Boys of Alabama/Peace International Records.

**MIGHTY TWINNS MUSIC**, 9134 S. Indiana Ave., Chicago IL 60619. (312)660-9717. General Manager: Rone Scott. Music publisher and record producer. BMI. Member NMPA. Publishes 2-3 songs/year; publishes 2-5 new songwriters/year. Pays standard royalty.
**How to Contact:** Submit demo tape and lyric sheet. Prefers cassette with 2-4 songs on demo. SASE "only if you want material returned." Reports in 1 month.
**Music:** Mostly top 40 and gospel; also children's, church/religious and R&B. Recently published "Do Yourself a Favor" (by M.T. Scott), recorded by Beautiful Zion Choir (gospel); "You'll Never Know (by L. Bates), recorded by Ramsey Lewis (soul/R&B); and "Be Nice to Me" (by D. Johnson and R. Scott), recorded by Danny Johnson/First American Records (R&B).
**Tips:** Looking for "good hot songs with hot hooks."

**BRIAN MILLAN MUSIC CORP.**, Suite 1212, 3475 St. Urbain St., Montreal, Quebec, H2X 2N4 Canada. President: Brian Millan. Music publisher and record producer. ASCAP. Publishes 100 songs/year; publishes 5-6 new songwriters/year. Pays standard royalty.
**How to Contact:** Submit demo tape and lead sheet. Prefers cassette only with 1-4 songs on demo. SAE and IRC. Reports in 2 weeks.
**Music:** C&W, MOR, top 40, rock, new wave, instrumental, soul, dixieland and children's. Recently published "If We Never Call It Love," by Ke Rieme/CBS Records (MOR); "Say Something Nice," by Chiarelli-Spilmon/Ariola Records (C&W); and "Forever More My Love," by Chiarelli-Spilmon/Rediffusion Records, England (MOR).
**Tips:** "Mail us your best songs. Only the material itself has any weight—not the writer's name."

**MIMIC MUSIC**, Box 201, Smyrna GA 30080. (404)432-2454. Affiliates: Skip Jack Music (BMI) and Stepping Stone (BMI). Manager: Tom Hodges. Music publisher, record producer, record company and management company. BMI. Publishes 20 songs/year. Pays standard royalty.
**How to Contact:** Submit demo tape and lyric sheet. Prefers cassette with 3-10 songs on demo. SASE. Reports in 2 weeks.
**Music:** Bluegrass, blues, church/religious, C&W, easy listening, gospel, MOR, R&B, rock, soul and top 40/pop. Recently published "Please Tell Her to Wait" (by Norman Skipper), recorded on Capitol Records (country); "Good Ole Country Music" (by Helen Humphries), recorded on British Overseas Records (country); and "Take Away the Roses" (by Burke-Bailey), recorded on British Overseas Records (country).

**MIRACLE-JOY PUBLICATIONS**, Box 711, Hackensack NJ 07601. (201)488-5211. President: Johnny Miracle. Vice President: Aileen Joy. Music publisher and record company. BMI.
**How to Contact:** Submit demo tape or submit demo tape and lead sheet. Prefers 7½ ips reel-to-reel or cassette with 2-6 songs on demo. SASE. Reports in 2 weeks.
**Music:** Children's, church/religious, C&W, easy listening, folk and gospel. Recently published "Pizzaman," recorded by Tiny (novelty); "Memories I Hold of You," recorded by Sam Starr (C&W); and "The Ashes Are Still Warm," recorded by Al and Carrol (C&W).

**MR. MORT MUSIC**, 44 Music Square E., Nashville TN 37203. (615)255-2175. Affiliate: Jason Dee Music (BMI). President: Charles Fields. Music publisher, record company and record producer. ASCAP. Publishes 50 songs/year; publishes 6 new songwriters/year. Pays standard royalty.
**How to Contact:** Submit demo tape and lead sheet. Prefers 7½ ips reel-to-reel or cassette with 1-4 songs on demo. SASE. Reports in 2 weeks.
**Music:** Blues, C&W, easy listening, MOR and top 40/pop. Recently published "Ruby Red" (by Jason Dee), recorded by The Four Guys; and "Love to Love" (by Jim Eastwood), recorded by B.G. Rice.

**MOBY DICK RECORDS**, 573 Castro St., San Francisco CA 94114. (415)864-2519. President: Bill Motley. Music publisher, record company and record producer. Estab. 1980. ASCAP. Publishes 15 songs/year; publishes 4 new songwriters/year. Hires staff writers; pays $200/week. Pays standard royalty.
**How to Contact:** Call first about your interest, then submit demo tape and lyric sheet or arrange personal interview to play demo tape. Prefers 7½ ips reel-to-reel or cassette with 2-3 songs on demo. SASE. Reports in 3 weeks.
**Music:** Dance-oriented, R&B and disco.

**IVAN MOGULL MUSIC CORP.**, 625 Madison Ave., New York NY 10022. (212)355-5636. President: Ivan Mogull. Music publisher. ASCAP, BMI and SESAC. Member NMPA. Publishes 10-30 songs/year. Pays standard royalty.
**How to Contact:** Submit demo tape and lyric sheet. Prefers 7½ ips reel-to-reel or cassette. SASE. Reports in 2 weeks. Must enclose SASE.
**Music:** Rock and top 40/pop. Publisher of all Abba hits.

*****MONARD MUSIC**, 10622 Commerce Ave., Tujunga CA 91042. (213)353-8165. Affiliate: Pencott Publishing (BMI). Contact: Kent Washburn. Music publisher, record company and record producer. ASCAP. Member NARAS, GMA. Publishes 15 songs/year; publishes 1 new songwriter/year. Pays standard royalty.
**How to Contact:** Submit demo tape and lyric sheet. Prefers cassette with 2-4 songs on demo. SASE. Reports in 1 month.
**Music:** Mostly R&B; also gospel, jazz, soul and top 40/pop. Recently published "Resurrection" (by Terry Lupton), recorded by Paul Davis/Spirit Records (gospel); "Don't Burn No Bridges" (by R. Anderson), recorded by Hypnotics/EMKAY Records (R&B); and "Ain't No Flys" (by R. Matthews), recorded by R. Matthews/Spirit Records (gospel).

**MONKEY MUSIC, INC., A Monkey Business Company**, Box 21288, Nashville TN 37221. (615)646-3335. Affiliates: Ape's Hit Music (BMI), Deaf Monkey Music (ASCAP) and Song Doctors. Director of Publishing/A&R: Debbie Newfeldt. Music publisher. Publishes 50 songs/year; publishes 5-10 new songwriters/year. Pays standard royalty.
**How to Contact:** Submit demo tape and lyric sheet. Prefers 7½ ips reel-to-reel or cassette with 3-5 songs on demo. "Lyric and/or lead sheet must be submitted with tape along with SASE. Do not submit lyric and/or lead sheet only." Reports in 1 month.
**Music:** C&W, easy listening, MOR, progressive, rock (hard and country) and top 40/pop.

*****MONONA/WATERTOONS/HOOCHIE COOCHIE/SKAFISH MUSIC**, Suite 4103, 2700 Cahuenga E., Los Angeles CA 90068. (213)851-6228. Vice President: Nancy Meyer. Music publisher. BMI. Publishes 2-3 songs/year. Pays standard royalty.
**How to Contact:** Call first about your interest. Prefers cassette with 1-4 songs on demo. SASE. Reports in 3-4 months.
**Music:** Mostly blues; also R&B and rock. Recently published "Built for Comfort" (by Willie Dixon), recorded by Hoyt Axton for the film "Heart Like A Wheel" (blues/rock); and "Blues Had a Baby and They Named It Rock & Roll" (by Muddy Waters), recorded by various artists and for the film "Get Crazy"/Sherwood Productions (blues/rock).
**Tips:** "We are looking for professional artists/writers who have already had songs published and recorded."

## Music Publishers 73

**MONTGOMERY PUBLISHING**, 8914 Georgian Dr., Austin TX 78753. (512)836-3201. Affiliate: Jo-Rae Music (BMI). General Manager: Shirley A. Montgomery. Music publisher, record company, record producer and booking agency. BMI. Publishes 25 songs/year; publishes 3 new songwriters/year. Pays standard royalty.
**How to Contact:** Submit demo tape and lyric sheet. Prefers cassette with 1-3 songs on demo. SASE.
**Music:** C&W. Recently published "Someone Wrote A Love Song" (by Jess DeMaine), recorded by J. DeMaine/Darva Records; "You Are Everything" (by Judi Tigert), recorded by Suzanne Carlson/Darva Records; and "Dark Lighted Barrooms" (by Steve Douglas), recorded by S. Douglas/Demon Records (all C&W).

\***MONTINA MUSIC**, Box 702, Snowdon Station, Montreal, Quebec, Canada H3X 3X8. Affiliate: Sabre Music (CAPAC). Professional General Manager: David P. Leonard. Music publisher. PROCAN. Member MIEA. Pays standard royalty.
**How to Contact:** Submit demo tape and lyric sheet. Prefers 15 or 7½ ips reel-to-reel, cassette, phonograph record or videocassette. Does not return unsolicited material.
**Music:** Mostly top 40; also bluegrass, blues, C&W, dance-oriented, easy listening, folk, gospel, jazz, MOR, progressive, R&B, rock and soul.

**DOUG MOODY MUSIC**, Mystic Music Centre, 6277 Selma Ave., Hollywood CA 90028. President: Doug Moody. Music publisher, record company and record producer (music library for TV, film, etc.). BMI. Member NMPA. Publishes 100 songs/year; publishes 50 new songwriters/year. Pays standard royalty.
**How to Contact:** Submit demo tape and lyric sheet. Prefers cassette with 1-2 songs on demo. SASE. Reports as soon as possible.
**Music:** "We are now looking for punk, hardcore and heavy metal—we need an aggressive young sound."

**MOON JUNE MUSIC**, 5821 SE Powell Blvd., Portland OR 97206. President: Bob Stoutenburg. Music publisher.
**How to Contact:** Submit demo tape. Prefers 7½ ips reel-to-reel or cassette with 2-10 songs on demo. SASE. Reports in 1 month.

**THE MORGAN MUSIC GROUP**, Box 2388, Prescott AZ 86302. (602)445-5801. Affiliates: Holydale (ASCAP), Winteroak (ASCAP) and Chromewood (BMI). President/Publishing: Gaye Ellen Foreman. Music publisher, record company and record producer. BMI, ASCAP. Publishes 50-75 songs/year; publishes 5-10 new songwriters/year. Pays standard royalty; $25-250 advance given against royalties.
**How to Contact:** Submit demo tape and lyric sheet. Prefers cassette with 3 songs on demo. SASE. Reports in 1 month.
**Music:** C&W, rock (country) and top 40/pop (country). Recently published "Run She Will" (by Greer and Morgan), recorded by Garry Greer/Big Wheels Records; "Out on the Road Again" (by M.D. Morgan), recorded by M.D. Morgan/Big Wheels Records; and "CB Blues" (by George Rawls), recorded by G. Rawls/Big Wheels Records (all C&W).

**MORRIS MUSIC, INC.**, Suite 319, 9255 Sunset Blvd., Hollywood CA 90069. Affiliates: Sashay Music (ASCAP), Steve Morris Music (BMI), Morrisongs (ASCAP). Administered by Chrysalis. Professional Manager: Alison Witlin. Music publisher. BMI. Publishes 50 songs/year. Pays standard royalty.
**How to Contact:** Arrange personal interview, submit demo tape or submit demo tape and lead sheet. Prefers cassette with 1-3 songs on demo. SASE. Reports in 2 weeks.
**Music:** New music, progressive, C&W, rock, soul and top 40/pop. Recently published "Sandy Beaches" (by John Jarvis & Delbert McClinton), recorded by Steve Cropper (rock); "Mountain of Love" (by Harold Dorman), recorded by Charlie Pride (country); "I'm Not Ready Yet" (by Tom T. Hall), recorded by George Jones (C&W); and "I Can't Turn My Heart Away" (by John Jarvis) recorded by Art Garfunkel (pop ballad).

**MORRISON HILL MUSIC**, 227 Union St., Lodi NJ 07644. (201)471-2770. Affiliate: Monja-Hearn Music (BMI). Manager: Joseph A. Sterner. Music publisher. ASCAP. Publishes 20 songs/year. Publishes 5 new songwriters/year. Pays standard royalty; uses AGAC contract.
**How to Contact:** Write or call first about your interest. "We prefer to discuss how-to-submit with prospective writers by mail or phone." SASE. Reports in 2 weeks.
**Music:** Mostly country (all types); also bluegrass, blues (country), folk, gospel (contemporary), R&B and rock (country).
**Tips:** "We are looking for talented songwriters, not 'one-song' writers. We will inform those who in-

quire, and are accepted, what we want and how we want it. We are publishers and song-pluggers. We also manage professional groups. Be professional and businesslike in your dealings with publishers and it will carry over into your writing. A writer, who is a professional craftsperson, is always rewarded."

*MOTORBEAT MUSIC, 765 Bennaville, Birmingham MI 48009. (313)540-4532. President: Scott Forman. Music publisher. Estab. 1981. BMI. Publishes 25 songs/year; publishes 5 new songwriters/year. Pays standard royalty or 75% (co-publishing).
**How to Contact:** Submit demo tape and lyric sheet or call about your interest. Prefers 7½ips reel-to-reel or cassette with 3-6 songs on demo. SASE. Reports in 3 weeks.
**Music:** Mostly progressive rock and dance-oriented rock; also rock, soul and top 40/pop. Recently published "Broken Haloes" (by Dave Adamson), recorded by Rhythm Corps/Transcity Records (progressive rock); "Solidarity" (by G. Apro, D. Adamson, R. Lousin, M. Persh and B. Schultz), recorded by Rhythm Corps/Transcity Records (top 40 rock); and "I Hate Science" (by M. Graffe & J. Lawniczak), recorded by Trainable/Transcity Records (progressive rock).
**Tips:** "Make demos as professional as possible."

**MOUNTAIN RAILROAD MUSIC**, Box 1681, Madison WI 53701. (608)256-6000. Music publisher, record producer and record company. President: Stephen Powers. ASCAP. Publishes 6-10 songs/year; publishes 2 new songwriters/year. Pays standard royalty.
**How to Contact:** Submit demo tape and lyric sheet. Prefers cassette with 1-3 songs on demo. SASE. Reports in 1 month.
**Music:** Mostly pop and folk; also C&W, progressive, rock and reggae. Recently published "Walk Me Round Your Garden" (by Dick Pinney), recorded by Michael Johnson/EMI-America Records (pop); "Rollin' Home to Rockford" (by Ron Holm), recorded by Emery Christiansen/Mountain Railroad Records (country-rock); and "Phenomenon of Love" (by Dick Pinney), recorded by Free Hot Lunch!/Mountain Railroad Records (pop).

*MOUNTAIN WILLIE MUSIC, SWEET BERNADETTE, TWO SISTERS, #308, 14055 Cedar Rd., Cleveland OH 44118. (216)932-1990. Vice President and General Manager: Robert Porrello. Music publisher, record company and record producer. Publishes 30 songs/year; publishes 10 new songwriters/year. Pays standard royalty.
**How to Contact:** Submit demo tape and lyric sheet. Prefers reel-to-reel with 2-4 songs on demo. SASE. Reports in 2-4 weeks.
**Music:** Mostly top 40 and rock; also children's, C&W, dance-oriented, R&B and soul. Recently published "Groove Your Blues Away" (by Paul Richmond, Darryl Ellis and Dunn Pearson, Jr), recorded by APB/Our Gang Entertainment Records (R&B); and "Do You Still Love Me" (by Paul Richmond), recorded by APB/Our Gang Entertainment Records (R&B).

*MULTIMEDIA MUSIC GROUP, 110 21st Ave. S., Box 120479, Nashville TN 37212. (615)327-2532. Affiliate: Music Vendor (ASCAP). General Manager: Cliff Williamson. Music publisher, record producer and television production company. Estab. 1982. BMI. Member CMA and NARAS. Publishes 122 songs/year; publishes 6 new songwriters/year. Hires staff writers. Pays standard royalty.
**How to Contact:** Submit demo tape and lyric sheet. Prefers cassette with 3 songs on demo. SASE. Reports in 1 week.
**Music:** Mostly country and pop; also bluegrass, C&W, MOR, R&B, rock, soul and top 40/pop. Recently published "Rich Man" (by Ed Mattson), recorded by Terri Gibbs/MCA Records (country); "Wild Turkey" (by Moffatt and Sebert), recorded by Lacy J. Dalton/CBS Records (country); "Levis to Calvin Klein" (by Runyeon and Lathrop), recorded by Brenda Lee/MCA Records (country); and "Are We Breaking Up" (by Mitchell and Wells), recorded by Joe Simon/Spring Records (R&B).

**MUSEDCO PUBLISHING CO.**, Box 5916, Richardson TX 75080. (214)783-9925. Contact: Dick A. Shuff. Music publisher. BMI. Member SRS and AFM. Publishes 12-15 songs/year; publishes 1-2 new songwriters/year. Pays royalties based on gross receipts from distributor or "work for hire" on each song.
**How to Contact:** Query by phone or letter giving background. Submit demo tape and lyric sheet. Prefers cassette with 2-3 songs on demo. SASE. Reports in 1 month.
**Music:** Choral, church/religious, C&W, and gospel. Recently published "He is the Answer" and "Teach Me," by Fargason and Shuff (choral-religious); and "You Walk With Me," by Fargason and Shuff (piano collection).
**Tips:** "Send positive songs, songs that inspire and that appeal to choral groups—2-3 of your best and no more. The recording should be of good quality."

*MUSIC ANNO DOMINI, Box 7452, Grand Rapids MI 49510. (616)241-3787. Director: Hans Altena. Music publisher, record company and management agency. SESAC. Publishes 20 songs/year;

publishes 2 new songwriters/year. Pays standard royalty.
**How to Contact:** Submit demo tape and lyric sheet. Prefers cassette with 1-4 songs on demo. SASE. Reports in 1 week.
**Music:** Mostly contemporary Christian rock and MOR; also gospel. Recently published "No Violence" (by James Ward), recorded by James Ward/A.D. Records (contemporary Christian); "Mourning to Dancing" (by James Ward), recorded by James Ward and the Lambs & Lion/Berison Records (contemporary Christian); and "I Know Jesus Gonna' Keep Me," recorded by the New City Choir/A.D. Records (contemporary Christian/choral).
**Tips:** "I look for intelligent, creative, honest lyrics with daring arrangements."

**MUSIC CONCEPTS INTERNATIONAL**, 9348 Santa Monica Blvd., Beverly Hills CA 90210. (213)550-6255. Affiliate: Adamsongs (ASCAP) and Pzazz Music (BMI). President: Steve Bedell. Music publisher. BMI, ASCAP. Member NMPA, AIMP and NARAS. Publishes 20 songs/year; publishes 4 new songwriters/year.
**How to Contact:** Submit demo tape and lyric sheet. Prefers 7½ or 15 ips reel-to-reel or cassette with 3-5 songs on demo. SASE. Reports in 2 weeks.
**Music:** MOR, R&B, rock (soft) and top 40/pop. Recently published "Don't Call It Love" (by Tom Snow and Dean Pitchford), recorded by Kim Carnes/EMI Records (pop/rock); "Harder Than Diamond" (by Evan Pace and Scott Lipsker), recorded by Chubby Checker/MCA (rock); and "Never Say Never" (by Jay Asher and D. Pitchford), recorded by Linda Clifford/Capital Records (R&B).

**MUSIC COPYRIGHT HOLDING CORPORATION**, Box 767, Radio City Station, New York NY 10101. A&R Director: Mark Simon. Music publisher, record producer and management firm. ASCAP, BMI and SESAC. Publishes 18 songs/year. Pays standard royalty.
**How to Contact:** Submit demo tape and lead sheet. Prefers cassette with 3-6 songs on demo. Does not return unsolicited material. Reports in 6-8 weeks.
**Music:** Mostly jazz, gospel and country; also bluegrass, blues, children's, church/religious, easy listening, folk, R&B and soul.

**MUSIC CRAFTSHOP**, Box 22325, Nashville TN 37202. (615)385-0900. Affiliates: Hit Kit Music (BMI), Phono Music (SESAC) and Sunbuilt (ASCAP). Music publisher. ASCAP. Publishes 300 songs/year; publishes 150 new songwriters/year. Pays standard royalties.
**How to Contact:** Query or submit demo tape and lyric sheet. Prefers 7½ ips reel-to-reel with 1-3 songs on demo. SASE. Reports in 1 week.
**Music:** C&W, MOR and pop.

**MUSIC DESIGNERS**, 241 White Pond Rd., Hudson MA 01749. (617)890-8787. Affiliates: Mutiny Music and EMI Music. President: Jeff Gilman. Music publisher, record company and production company. BMI. Pays standard royalties.
**How to Contact:** Submit demo tape and lead sheet. Prefers 7½ ips reel-to-reel or cassette with 1-6 songs on demo. SASE. Reports in 3 weeks.
**Music:** Children's, C&W, disco, folk, MOR, progressive, rock, soul and top 40/pop. Recently released "Man Enough," recorded by No Slack (pop/R&B); "Why Don't We Love Each Other?," recorded by the Ellis Hall Group (pop/R&B); "Breaker 1-9," recorded by the Back Bay Rhythm Section (disco); and "I Love You," recorded by Nicolette Larson.

**MUSIC FOR PERCUSSION, INC.**, 170 NE 33rd St., Fort Lauderdale FL 33334. (305)563-1844. Affiliate: Plymouth Music (ASCAP). Contact: Bernard Fisher, Fran Taber. Music publisher. BMI.
**How to Contact:** Submit demo tape and lead sheet. Prefers 7½ ips reel-to-reel. "Be sure that the tapes submitted are carefully labeled with title, name and address of composer." SASE. Reports in 1 month.
**Music:** "We are interested primarily in choral music."

*****MUSIC MANAGEMENT**, Box 4705, Arlington VA 22204. (703)522-2718. Affiliates: One Language Music (BMI), Dee Dee's Music (BMI), Triumph Music (BMI), Old Virginia Music (ASCAP). Professional Manager: Janice Connor. Music publisher and record company. BMI, ASCAP. Publishes 30-40 songs/year; publishes 6 new songwriters/year. Pays standard royalty.
**How to Contact:** Submit demo tape and lyric sheet. Prefers cassette with 1-4 songs on demo. "No elaborate arrangements on demos; just highlight melody and lyrics." SASE. Reports in 3 weeks.
**Music:** Top 40/pop, soul and MOR. Recently published "I'm Gonna Love You" (by Sam Conjerti), recorded by S. Conjerti/Ear Witness Records (MOR); "Last Days of Rock 'n' Roll (by John Eggers), recorded by The Rumblers/Ear Witness Records (top 40); and "Pump It Baby" (by Bobby Warner), recorded by The Mercury Band/RWP Records (soul).
**Tips:** "Write dynamic lyrics."

**MUSIC PUBLISHING CORPORATION/CREAM PUBLISHING GROUP**, 8025 Melrose Ave., Los Angeles CA 90046. (213)655-0944. Affiliates: Singletree Music Company (BMI), Doubletree Music (SESAC), Harken Music (BMI), Lariat Music (ASCAP), Latigo Music (ASCAP), Sage & Sand Music (SESAC), Rawhide Music Company (BMI), Barnwood Music (BMI), and Joiner Music (ASCAP). Administers Hank Williams Jr.'s Bocephus Catalog. Professional Manager/Staff Song Writer: Marty Sadler. Music publisher. BMI. ASCAP. Member NMPA. Publishes 150 songs/year; publishes 50 new songwriters/year. Pays standard royalty. Sometimes secures songwriters on salary basis. Catalogs 4,000 songs/year.
**How to Contact:** Submit demo tape and lyric sheet. Prefers cassette with maximum 4 songs on demo. "Include lyrics and as much information as possible and songs that could be done by more than 2 artists." SASE. Reports in 1 week.
**Music:** Bluegrass, blues, church/religious, C&W, easy listening, folk, gospel, jazz, MOR, progressive, R&B, rock (hard and soft) and top 40/pop.

**MUSIC RESOURCES INTERNATIONAL CORP.**, 5th Floor, 21 W. 39th St., New York NY 10018. (212)869-2299. Affiliate: Clearinghouse Music (BMI). President: Andy Hussakowsky. Music publisher, record label (Cleaninghouse Records) and record producer. ASCAP. Publishes 20-30 songs/year; publishes 2-3 new songwriters/year. Pays standard royalty.
**How to Contact:** Submit demo tape and lyric sheet. Prefers cassette with 1-3 songs on demo; "master quality only." SASE. Reports in 3 months.
**Music:** Mostly black and top 40/pop; also C&W, dance-oriented, R&B, rock and soul. Recently published "The Doo Wop Song" (by Fox and Mozian), recorded by Denny Green/Midsong Records; "Superhero" (by J. Roach), recorded by Everlife/Clearinghouse Records (R&B/disco); and "The Lover" (by J. Rage), recorded by Rage/Clearinghouse Records (R&B).
**Tips:** "MRI has negotiated leases with Buddah, Polydor, Polygram, Casablanca, AVI and other major labels. We also represent Mark James co-writer of "Always on My Mind," "Moody Blue," "Suspicious Minds" and other hit songs."

**\*MUSINFO PUBLISHING GROUPE, INC.**, 5514 Isabella St., Montreal, Quebec, Canada H3X 1R6. (514)484-5419. General Manager: Jehan V. Valiquet. Music publisher, record company, record producer, promotion and marketing consultants. Estab. 1982. PROCAN, CAPAC. Publishes 150 songs/year; publishes 10 new songwriters/year. Pays standard royalty.
**How to Contact:** Submit demo tape and lyric sheet. Prefers cassette for demo. SASE. Reports in 1 month.
**Music:** Mostly dance-oriented and top 40/pop in French; also children's, folk, MOR and Spanish. Recently published *L'Amour*, recorded by Jean Francois Michael/Able Canada Records (MOR LP); *Makof* (by Makof), recorded by Makof/Trans Canada Records (MOR LP); and *Paris France* (by Ecama), recorded by Paris France Transit/Trans Canada Records (dance LP).

**MUSTEVIC SOUND INC.**, 193-18 120th Ave., New York NY 11412. (212)527-1586. President: Brenda Taylor. Music publisher, record producer and record company. BMI. Publishes 7-9 songs/year; publishes 3-4 new songwriters/year. Pays standard royalty.
**How to Contact:** Write first about your interest. Prefers cassette with 3 songs maximum on demo. SASE. Reports in 1 month.
**Music:** Jazz. Recently published "Empty Streets" (by Brandon Ross), recorded by New Life/Mustevic Records (jazz rock); "Nova" (by S. Reid), recorded by Steve Reid/Mustevic Records (jazz instrumental); and "Rose Is" (by L. Walker), recorded by Les Walker/Mustevic Records (jazz instrumental).

**\*NANCY JANE PUBLISHING CO.**, 1102 Virginia St. SW, Lenoir, NC 28645. (704)758-4170. President: Mike McCoy. Music publisher, record company and record producer. Estab. 1982. BMI. Publishes 4 songs/year. Pays standard royalty.
**How to Contact:** Submit demo tape and lyric sheet. Prefers cassette with 1-4 songs on demo. SASE. Reports in 1 month.
**Music:** Mostly C&W, religious, gospel, R&B, outlaw C&W and bluegrass. Recently published "Music City" (by Mike McCoy), recorded by M. McCoy/Legend Records (C&W); "Old Fashion Preacher" (by M. McCoy), recorded by M. McCoy/Legend Records (gospel); and "Cinderella" (by Mike McCoy), recorded by M. McCoy/Legend Records (C&W).

**\*NARROWROAD RECORDS/MUSIC**, Box 3664, Davenport IA 52808. A&R Manager: Gary Unger. Music publisher and record company. BMI.
**How to Contact:** Write or call first about your interest or arrange personal interview to play demo tape. Prefers 7½ or 15 ips reel-to-reel or cassette with 4-10 songs on demo. Include a resume listing previous work. SASE. Reports in 1-3 months.

**Music:** Mostly pop/religious and gospel. Recently published "Jesus Took Me In" (by Paul Gregory), recorded by P. Gregory/Narrowroad Records (pop/religious); "In Jesus Name," by Gary Unger; and "One Day Too Late," by Betty Parsons/Narrowroad Records.

**NASHCAL MUSIC**, 3746 Mount Diablo Blvd., Lafayette CA 94546. (415)283-7624. Affiliates: Bobby Fischer Music (ASCAP) and Bobby's Beat (SESAC). Contact: Chris Blake. Music publisher, record company, record producer and promotion firm. BMI. Member CMA, NSAI and FICAP. Publishes 25 songs/year; publishes 5 new songwriters/year. Pays standard royalty.
**How to Contact:** Submit demo tape and lyric sheet. Prefers cassette with 2-3 songs on demo. "We review material as time permits and return with SASE *if* time permits." Reports ASAP.
**Music:** Modern country. Recently published "City Boy" (by Bob Rodin and C. Blete), recorded by Moe Bandy/Columbia Records; "Mama" (by C. Blete and B. fischer), recorded by Dotsy/Tanglewood Records; and "Girl Don't Ever Get Lonely" (by C. Blete and B. Fischer), recorded by Moe and Joe/Columbia Records (all country).

*****NELTER MUSIC PUBLISHING**, Box 3072, Brooklyn NY 11202. (212)774-1008. President: Wallace D. Garrett. Music publisher, record company and record producer. Estab. 1982. BMI. Pays standard royalty.
**How to Contact:** Submit demo tape and lyric sheet. Prefers cassette with 3-5 songs on demo. "Ballads *must* have good lyrics." SASE. Reports in 1-3 months.
**Music:** Mostly R&B, soul and dance; also C&W, jazz, Spanish, rock and punk-funk.

*****NERVOUS PUBLISHING**, 4/36 Dabbs Hill Lane, Northout, Middlesex, London, England. 44-01-422-3462. Managing Director: Roy Williams. Music publisher, record company and record producer. MCPS, PRS and Phonographic Performance Ltd. Publishes 50 songs/year; publishes 8 new songwriters/year. Pays standard royalty; royalties paid directly to US songwriters.
**How to Contact:** Submit demo tape and lyric sheet. Prefers cassette with 3-10 songs on demo. "Include letter giving your age and mentioning any previously-published material." SAE and IRC. Reports in 2 weeks.
**Music:** Mostly rockabilly; also blues, C&W, R&B and rock (50s style). Recently published "Rockabilly Guy" (by Bloomberg), recorded by Polecats/Mercury Records (rockabilly); "Marie Celeste" (by Bloomberg/Rooney/Scorer/Lehrman), recorded by Polecats/Mercury Records (rockabilly); and "Lumere Urban" (by Ball and Veitch), recorded by Doug Veitch/Drum Records (cajun).

**NEVER ENDING MUSIC**, Box 58, Glendora NJ 08029. Affiliates: Hot Pot Music (BMI) and Record Room Music (ASCAP). General Manager: Eddie Jay Harris. Music publisher and record company. BMI.
**How to Contact:** Write about your interest, then submit demo tape and lyric sheet. SASE (on solicited material only). Refuses unsolicited submissions.

**NEVERLAND MUSIC PUBLISHING CO.**, 225 E. 57th St., New York NY 10022. (212)888-7711. Affiliates: Baseball Music Publishing Co. (ASCAP), Force Feed Music Publishing Co. (ASCAP), Earl Music (ASCAP) and Peg Music (BMI). President and General Manager: Earl Shuman. Music publisher. BMI. Member NMPA. Publishes 15 songs/year; publishes 2 new songwriters/year. Pays standard royalty.
**How to Contact:** Submit demo tape and lyric sheet or arrange personal interview to play demo tape. Prefers 7½ ips reel-to-reel or cassette with 1-4 songs on demo. SASE. "Writer should inquire about submitted material in 2 weeks."
**Music:** C&W, easy listening, R&B, rock (all types) and top 40/pop. Recently published "Two Out of Three Ain't Bad" (by Jim Steinman), recorded by MeatLoaf/Epic Records (rock ballad); "Paradise by the Dashboard Light" (by J. Steinman), recorded by MeatLoaf/Epic Records (story rock novelty); and "People Who Read *People Magazine*" (by Kinky Friedman), recorded by Rovers/Epic Records (country/pop).
**Tips:** "You must have a great song—it helps if it is presented on a strong demo."

*****NEW MUSIC ENTERPRISES**, 46 Alexandra Crescent, Bromley, Kent, BR1 4EU, England. 44-01-460-6584. Affiliates: Wilhelm Music, Arhelger Music, Silhouette Music, Bridge Music, Eric Anders Music, Sherebiah Music, Clancy Music and Jimmy Payne Music. Manager: Paul Davis. Music publisher and record company. MCPS, PRS. Subpublishes 50 songs/year; publishes 20 new songwriters/year. Pays standard royalty; royalties to US songwriters and through US affiliate.
**How to Contact:** Write first; submit demo tape and lyric sheet. Prefers cassette with any number of songs on demo. SAE and IRC. Reports in 3 weeks.
**Music:** All forms of contemporary Christian music (bluegrass, children's, gospel, country, MOR and

soul). Recently published "Breaker Breaker Sweet Jesus" (by Jerry Arhelber), recorded by Thrasher Brothers/Word Records (country gospel); "I'm Going On for Jesus" (by Rick & Rosemary Wilhelm), recorded by Dave Oldham/Benson Records (inspirational); and "God Is the Foundation" (by Chip Hardy), recorded by Jimmy Payne/Word Records (country gospel).
**Tips:** "Songs should have good Christian message and be relevant to everyday living."

**NEWCREATURE MUSIC**, 108 Berkley Dr., Madison TN 37115. (615)868-3407. President: Bill Anderson, Jr. Music publisher, record company, record producer and radio and TV syndication. BMI. Publishes 25 songs/year; publishes 1 new songwriter/year. Pays standard royalty.
**How to Contact:** Submit demo tape and lyric sheet. Prefers 7½ ips reel-to-reel or cassette with 4-10 songs on demo. SASE. Reports in 1 month.
**Music:** C&W, gospel, jazz, R&B, rock and top 40/pop. Recently published "Fear Not" (by J.C. Yates), recorded by Joanne Cash/Kola Records (gospel); and "Praises Unto the Lord" (by B. Anderson, Jr. and D.D. Morris), gospel theme song for syndicated radio program.

**NEWPORT BEACH MUSIC**, 17422 Murphy Ave., Irvine CA 92714. (714)730-1309. Vice President Record Production: Paul Freeman. Music publisher, record company, mastering and record producer. ASCAP and BMI. Member NARAS, AIMP, CMA. Publishes 75-100 songs/year; publishes 1-2 new songwriters/year. Pays standard royalty; some writers for hire with publishing companies.
**How to Contact:** Submit demo tape and lyric sheet. Prefers cassette with 3 or more songs on demo. SASE. Reports in 2 months.
**Music:** All types. Recently published "Higher Power" (by Denny Correll), recorded by Darrell Mansfield & The Imperials/Word Records; and "The Witness" and "He Set Free" (by D. Correll), recorded by D. Correll/Word Records (all gospel).
**Tips:** "Audible tapes with good quality, lead sheets."

**NEWWRITERS MUSIC**, Suite 200, 43 Music Square E., Nashville TN 37203. (615)244-1025. Affiliate: Timestar Music (ASCAP). National Promotion Director: Chuck Dixon. Music publisher, record company and record producer. BMI. Publishes 200 songs/year; publishes 17 new songwriters/year. Pays standard royalty.
**How to Contact:** Write first about your interest or submit demo tape and lyric sheet. Prefers cassette with 1-4 songs on demo. "Use clean tape!" SASE. Reports in 1 week.

**NICK-O-VAL MUSIC**, Suite IA, 254 W. 72nd St., New York NY 10023. (212)873-2179. Associate Director: Ms. Tee Alston. Music publisher and record producer. ASCAP.
**How to Contact:** Submit demo tape and lyric sheet. Prefers cassette with 2 songs on demo. SASE. Reporting time depends on schedule.
**Music:** R&B.
**Tips:** "This is the publishing company of Nick Ashford and Valerie Simpson. The material you submit has to compete with their songs—it must be great!"

*****JOSEPH NICOLETTI MUSIC**, Box 2818, Newport Beach CA 92663. California International Records & Video. Vice President: Cheryl Nicoletti. Music publisher, record company and record producer. ASCAP. Member NARAS, AFTRA and SAG (Harry Fox Agency/ASCAP). Publishes 2-3 songs/year. Pays standard royalty.
**How to Contact:** Write about your interest or submit demo tape and lyric sheet. Prefers cassette with 1-4 songs on demo. SASE. Reports in 1 month.
**Music:** MOR, rock (new wave, pop, classical), top 40/pop and rockabilly. Recently published "Let's Put the Fun Back in Rock 'n' Roll" (by J. Nicoletti), recorded by Freddie Cannon & The Belmonts/A&M Records (pop rock); and "Children Are the Future" (by Nicoletti), recorded by Joseph Nicoletti (ballad).
**Tips:** "Publishing should be open, demo should be of good quality and the writer should have a strong belief in the material he sends."

**NISE PRODUCTIONS INC.**, Suite 101, 413 Cooper St., Camden NJ 08102. (215)963-3190. Affiliate: Logo III Records. President: Michael Nise. Music publisher, record company, recording studio and production company. BMI. Publishes 10-20 songs/year. Pays standard royalty.
**How to Contact:** Submit demo tape. Prefers cassette with 3 songs on demo. SASE. Reports in 1 month.
**Music:** Children's, church/religious, C&W, dance-oriented, easy listening, folk, gospel, jazz, R&B, rock, soul and top 40/pop. Now recording William Sackett and his radio orchestra.

**NONPAREIL MUSIC**, 9th Floor, 11 W. 17th St., New York NY 10011. (212)924-9338. President: Andy Goldmark. Music publisher. ASCAP. Publishes 50 songs/year. Hires staff writers; pays $10,000 and up/year for exclusivity. Pays standard royalty.

# Close-up

**Andy Goldmark**
Songwriter/Publisher

Although still a young man, songwriter/publisher Andy Goldmark has been in the mainstream of the music industry for over thirteen years. He left Yale University in 1972 to make his debut album for Warner Brothers Records, where he stayed on the staff of Warner Brothers Music from 1973-1976. After that, he recorded an album for A&M Records and signed a writing contract with Irving/Almo Music. From 1979-1981 he wrote for Walden Music (part of Atlantic Records). Since then he has ventured out on his own, not only as a writer but as the president of his own publishing company, Nonpareil Music (see the listing in this section).

When submitting to him or to any other publisher, Goldmark advises songwriters: "Take advantage of your chance by giving it your best shot. Send *only* songs you feel are great for today's top artists. As the industry goes through its current pains, publishers rely on only the *best* songs for their catalogs. It's a tight squeeze now to get any song onto any album. So, as a publisher, I need to be 150% sure of and committed to what I am selling."

Other than quality, what does Goldmark look for when reviewing material for his publishing catalog? "I can't really say what it is that turns me on to a song. So much of what makes a song great is undefinable. It is something—anything—that grabs me. It is a lyric and a melody that draws me right into the heart and the heat of the song. I look for songs like 'Yesterday' by the Beatles, songs which are beautifully simple, yet timeless. I look for songs that will be recorded by many artists over the years, ones that are open to endless interpretations."

The demo—your showcase for your songs—should, in Goldmark's estimation, "say it all." As far as production, instrumentation, voices, etc., on the demo, he says it's up to you, the songwriter, to decide what you want your song to say. "Use as much as you feel is necessary to show the song in its best possible light."

Goldmark also advises songwriters not to let rejection keep them from continuing to write and submit. "Everyone stumbles and falls, but if you fall in the right direction—if you learn from your rejection—you can't lose. Songwriting starts with the blank page and an open heart. Add experience to these basic ingredients, and each time you've finished writing a song, you'll be a better songwriter. All else will fall into place."

**How to Contact:** Submit demo tape and lyric sheet. Prefers cassette with 3-5 songs on demo. SASE. Reports in 1 week.
**Music:** Mostly pop; also C&W, MOR and R&B. Recently published "Ace High Love" (by Andy Goldmark & Henry Gaffney), recorded by Marshall Tucker Band/Warner Brothers Records (pop/country); "She's Got You Running" (by Andy Goldmark & Jim Ryan), recorded by Mickey Thomas/Electra Asylum Records (pop/rock); and "Heart Over Head Over You" (by Andy Goldmark & Robin Batteau), recorded by Bette Midler/Atlantic Records (pop).
**Tips:** "Take your best shot only with songs you feel are great for today's top artists."

**\*NORTH RANCH MUSIC,** 2974 Parkview Dr., Thousand Oaks CA 91362. (805)497-4738. Affiliate: Flying Lady Music (ASCAP). President: Don Perry. Music publisher and record producer. BMI. Member NARAS. Publishes 6-8 songs/year; publishes 2 new songwriters/year. Pays standard royalty.
**How to Contact:** Submit demo tape and lyric sheet. Prefers cassette with 2-4 songs on demo. SASE. Reports in 1 month.
**Music:** Mostly soft rock and country; also MOR, R&B and top 40/pop. Recently published "I Wrote It In a Song" and "She Cheers Me Up" (by Bob Summers and Penny Askey), recorded by Thom Pace/Capitol Records (soft rock); and "I Used to Be Her" and "First Good Song" (by Lyndsey Edwards), recorded by L. Edwards/Monument Records (country).
**Tips:** "Don't over-produce demos. Do your homework on artists and producers and cast songs to their style."

**NORTHERN COMFORT MUSIC,** 10 Erica Ave., Toronto, Ontario, Canada M3H 3H2. (416)923-5717. Affiliate: Sacro-Iliac Music (PROCAN). President: J. Allan Vogel. Music publisher and record producer. CAPAC. Member LMPA. Publishes 16-20 songs/year; publishes 1 new songwriter/year. Pays standard royalty.
**How to Contact:** Submit demo tape and lyric sheet. Prefers 7½ ips reel-to-reel or cassette with 3-5 songs on demo. SAE and IRC. Reports in 3 weeks.
**Music:** Mostly contemporary pop/rock (uptempo and/or ballads); also jazz, MOR, progressive, R&B and soul. Recently published "One Night Stand" (by J. Vogel), recorded by Rhona Jill (pop/rock).
**Tips:** "Be honest. Write contemporary hit material. Write about city life and make it danceable."

**NOTABLE MUSIC CO. INC.,** 161 W. 54th St., New York NY 10019. (212)757-9547. Affiliate: Portable Music Co., Inc. (BMI). General Manager: Eric Colodne. Music publisher. ASCAP. Member NMPA. Publishes 50-75 songs/year. Pays standard royalty.
**How to Contact:** Call first about your interest. Prefers cassette with 3-5 songs on demo. SASE. Reports in 1 month.
**Music:** Disco, easy listening, jazz, MOR, R&B, soul and top 40/pop. Recently published "If My Friends Could See Me Now" (by Cy Coleman and Dorothy Fields), recorded by Linda Clifford/Warner Records (slow disco); "Colors of My Life" (by Cy Coleman and Mike Stewart), recorded by Perry Como/RCA Records (MOR); "Let Me Be Your Fantasy" (by Neil Sheppard and Mitch Farber), recorded by Love Symphony Orchestra (disco/top 40); and "Never" (by C. Coleman, B. Comden and A. Green), recorded by Buddar and The Body Shop (disco/soul).

**NOTEWORTHY PUBLISHING CO.,** 7802 Express St., Burnaby, British Columbia, Canada V5A 1T4. (604)421-3441. Manager: Paul Yardshuk. Music publisher, record company, record producer and record manufacturer. BMI, PROCAN. Publishes 250 songs/year; publishes 25 new songwriters/year. Pays standard royalty.
**How to Contact:** Submit demo tape and lyric sheet. Prefers cassette with 10-12 songs on demo. SAE and IRC. Reports in 1 week.
**Music:** Church/religious and gospel. Recently published "I'm Gonna Live" (by Bruce Wright), recorded by Tunesmith/Servant Records; "In the Spirit of the King" (by Hank Laake), recorded by Tunesmith/Hank Laake Records; and "Find Your Heart a Home" (by N. Mann), recorded by Tunesmith/Barnabas Records (all gospel rock songs).
**Tips:** "We look for people who can sing their own songs."

**NRP MUSIC GROUP,** 11th Floor, 160 E. 56th St., New York NY 10022. (212)758-3267. A&R Director: Fred Bailim. Music publisher and record company. BMI, ASCAP. Publishes 10-12 songs/year; publishes 2 new songwriters/year. Pays standard royalty.
**How to Contact:** Submit demo tape and lyric sheet. Prefers cassette with 3-5 songs on demo. SASE. Reports in 1 week.
**Music:** Dance-oriented, R&B, soul and top 40/pop.

**NU-TRAYL PUBLISHING CO.,** 10015 W. 8 Mile Rd., Franksville WI 53126. (414)835-4622. Contact: Tommy O'Day. Music publisher, record company and record producer. ASCAP. Publishes 10

songs/year; publishes 3 new songwriters/year. Pays standard royalty.
**How to Contact:** Submit demo tape and lyric sheet. Prefers 7½ ips reel-to-reel or cassette with 1-3 songs on demo. SASE. Reports in 1 month.
**Music:** C&W, MOR, rock & top 40/pop. Recently published "I Heard a Song Today" (by T. O'Day and J. Marvel), "Kiss Your Past Goodby" (by Peter Richerson), and "Todays Woman" (by T. O'Day and B. Perice), all recorded by T. O'Day/Nu-trayl Records (C&W).

**O.A.S. MUSIC GROUP**, 805 18th Ave. S., Nashville TN 37203. (615)327-3900. Affiliates: Arian Publications (ASCAP), Onhisown (BMI) and Shadowfax Music (BMI). Administrator: Stallion Music. Director: Steve Singleton. Music publisher. Member NMPA. Pays standard royalty.
**How to Contact:** Arrange personal interview for any Monday, or submit demo tape and lyric sheet. Prefers 7½ ips reel-to-reel or cassette with 3-4 songs on demo. SASE. Reports in 3 months.
**Music:** Bluegrass, blues, C&W, disco, easy listening, MOR, progressive, rock, soul and top 40/pop. Recently published "With You" recorded by Charly McCain; "The Faithful Kind" recorded by Percy Sledge and "Could I Have This Dance," recorded by Anne Murray.

**OAK SPRINGS MUSIC**, Rt. 5, Box 382, Yakima WA 98903. (509)966-1193. President: Hiram White. Music publisher. BMI. Publishes 15 songs/year; publishes 3 new songwriters/year. Pays standard royalty.
**How to Contact:** Submit demo tape and lead sheet. Prefers cassette with 1-4 songs on demo. "Keep it simple (voice and guitar), with no promo material." SASE. Reports in 1 month.
**Music:** Bluegrass, blues, C&W, disco, folk, MOR, progressive and rock. Recently published "Prueba de Amor" (by Fiden cio Villarrcal), recorded by Ruben Cortez/Aquila de plata (salsa); "Yard Sale," recorded by Larry Merrit/Tell International Records (C&W); "La Rochelle," recorded by Larry Merrit/Tell International Records (C&W); and "Mr. Pruitt's Apple Farm," by Mike Wolters/Tell International Records (C&W).

**OAKRIDGE MUSIC RECORDING SERVICE**, 2001 Elton Rd., Haltom City TX 76117. (817)838-8001. President: Homer Lee Sewell. Music publisher and record company. BMI. Publishes 5 songs/year. Charges for some services: "If the writer is under contract to me, I don't charge for demos, etc. Otherwise, I do charge."
**How to Contact:** Query by mail. Prefers 7½ ips reel-to-reel or cassette with 3 songs on demo. "Send parcel post and mark the box 'Don't X-ray'." SASE. Reports in 1 month.
**Music:** Bluegrass, church/religious, C&W and gospel. Recently published "Crazy World We Live In" (by Karen Huff); "13 Steps" (by Charlie Sewall); "Ambush/If You Really Want Me To, I'll Go" (by Don Hudson); and *Praise He the Lord* (by Robert Swift).

*****OAKWOOD MUSIC**, Reed Ave., Canterbury, Kent, CT1 1ET, England. 01-44-0227-50033. Contact: Managing Director. Music publisher and record producer. Estab. 1982. MCPS, PRS. Publishes 30 new songs/year. Pays standard royalty; royalties paid directly to US songwriters.
**How to Contact:** Submit demo tape and lyric sheet. Prefers cassette with 1-4 songs on demo. SAE and IRC. Reports in 1 month.
**Music:** Mostly pop; also dance-oriented.

**MICHAEL O'CONNOR MUSIC**, Box 1869, Studio City CA 91604. (213)762-7551. Affiliate: O'Connor Songs (ASCAP). Contact: Michael O'Connor. Music publisher. BMI. Member NMPA, AIMP. Publishes 25 songs/year; publishes 5 new songwriters/year. Hires staff writers; pays $175-325/week. Pays standard royalty.
**How to Contact:** Submit demo tape and lyric sheet. Prefers cassette with 1-6 songs on demo. SASE. Reports in 1 month.
**Music:** C&W, easy listening, R&B, rock, soul and top 40/pop. Recently published "You Never Gave Up on Me" (by Leslie Pearl), recorded by Crystal Gayle/CBS Records (pop/country); "Guys Like You Give Love a Bad Name" (by Larry Cox and Bill Purse), recorded by Donna Washington/Capitol Records (R&B), also recorded by Stacy Lattisaw/Atlantic Records (R&B); "Girls Can Get It" (by L. Pearl), recorded by Dr. Hook/Polygram Records (pop); "If the Love Fits Wear It" (by Leslie Pearl and Phil Redrow), recorded by L. Pearl/RCA Records (pop); and "When Love Goes Right" (by Diane Warren), recorded by Stevie Woods/Atlantic Records (R&B).
**Tips:** "We are looking for songs that have a clever title, hopefully revolving around the subject of love; great lyric images—the kind of lyric you find on a greeting card; and have unique ways of expressing ideas that would strike a responsive chord in the public."

**MARY FRANCES ODLE RECORDING & PUBLISHING CO.**, Box 4335, Pasadena TX 77502. (713)645-4345. President: Mary Frances Odle. Promotion: Mace McGregor and Frances Rollins. Music publisher, booking agency and record company. BMI. Publishes 8-10 songs/year. Pays standard royalty.

**How to Contact:** Submit demo tape or submit demo tape and lead sheet. Prefers 7½ ips reel-to-reel or cassette with 5 songs minimum on tape. SASE. Reports in 2 weeks.
**Music:** Mostly easy listening and C&W; also blues, church/religious, gospel, MOR, rock and soul. Recently published "You Get Drunk on Wine," by Jim Coleman (C&W); "I See Satan," recorded on Odle Records (religious); and "My Lady Never Lets Me Down," by Bobby Fuller/Odle Records (easy listening).

**\*TRISHA O'KEEFE MUSIC, LTD.**, 19 Acre Lane, London, SW2, England. 44-01-274-0164. Director: Trisha O'Keefe. Music publisher, record company and record producer. MCPS, PRS and Phonographic Performance Ltd. Member MPA, ILA. Publishes 10 songs/year; publishes 4 new songwriters/year. Pays 60-70% of performance and mechanical royalties to songwriters; royalties paid directly to US songwriters.
**How to Contact:** Submit demo tape and lyric sheet. Prefers cassette with 2-10 songs on demo. SAE and IRC. Reports in 1 month.
**Music:** Mostly top 40, soul, rock, C&W and dance; also easy listening, gospel, jazz, MOR, R&B, new wave, novelty and AOR. Recently published "Music Is Our Freedom" (by Julie Amiet and P. Saberton), recorded by J. Amiet (Latin/jazz); "Tonight" (by T. O'Keefe), recorded by J. Amiet (ballad); and "The On 'n' On Song" (by P. Little), recorded by Precious Little (disco).

**OKISHER MUSIC**, Box 20814, Oklahoma City OK 73156. (405)751-8954. President: Mickey Sherman. Music publisher, record company and record producer. BMI. Member OCMA. Publishes 4 new songwriters/year. Pays standard royalty.
**How to Contact:** Submit demo tape and lyric sheet. "Enclose press kit or other background information." Prefers 7½ ips reel-to-reel or cassette with 1-3 songs on demo. Does not return unsolicited material. Reports in 1 month.
**Music:** Blues, C&W, easy listening, jazz, MOR, R&B and soul. Recently published "Constantly Amazed" (by Allen Spears), recorded by Stoney Edwards/Music America Records (country MOR); "Cocaine Blues" (by Mickey Sherman), recorded by Janjo/Seeds Records (modern blues); "You Got to Marry Me" (by Charles Burton), recorded by Janjo/Seeds Records (country); "Dallas Swing" (by Benny Kubiak), recorded by B. Kubiak/Seeds Records (country); and "Sally Jane" (by Bill Lendrum), recorded by Tony Albert/ LRJ Records (country).

**\*OKOBOJI MUSIC**, Box 100, Spirit Lake IA 51360. (712)336-2859. President: John Senn. Music publisher, record company and record producer. BMI. Publishes 15 songs/year. Pays standard royalty.
**How to Contact:** Submit demo tape and lyric sheet. Prefers 7½ or 15 ips reel-to-reel or cassette with 1-5 songs on demo. SASE. Reports in 1 month.
**Music:** Mostly country; also church/religious, gospel and top 40/pop.

**OLD BOSTON PUBLISHING**, 180 Pond St., Cohasset MA 02025. (619)942-1191. Writer Relations: Claire Babcock. Music publisher, record company and record producer. BMI. Publishes 10 songs/year; publishes 2 new songwriters/year. Pays standard royalty.
**How to Contact:** Call first about your interest. Prefers 7½ ips reel-to-reel or cassette with 1-3 songs on demo. Does not return unsolicited material.
**Music:** Recently published "Scollay Square" (by RIK Tinory), recorded on Old Boston Records (dixie/nostalgia).

**\*OLD HOME PLACE MUSIC**, 8705 Deanna Dr., Gaithersburg MD 20879. (301)253-5962. President: Wayne Busbice. Music publisher, record company and record producer. BMI. Member Country Music Association. Publishes 20-30 songs/year; publishes 6 new songwriters/year. Pays standard royalty.
**How to Contact:** Write about your interest. Prefers cassette with 3-5 songs on demo. "We prefer songwriters to have recommendation of an established artist." SASE. Reports in 1 month.
**Music:** Mostly bluegrass; also C&W. Recently published "Fiddlers' Potpourri" (by Carl Nelson), recorded by Carl Nelson/WEBCO Records (bluegrass); "Lost Without You" (by Wayne Busbice), recorded by Buzz Busby/WEBCO records (bluegrass); and "Amtrak Express" (by Darrell Sanders), recorded by Darrell Sanders/WEBCO Records (bluegrass).

**\*OLOFSONG MUSIC**, 6 Heath Close, London, W5, England. 44-01-991-0993 or 2208. Contact: Jan Olofsson. Music publisher, record company and record producer. BMI, MCPS, PRS. Publishes 4 new songwriters/year. Pays negotiable royalty; royalties paid directly to US songwriters or through US publishing affiliate.
**How to Contact:** Submit demo tape and lyric sheet. Prefers 7½ ips reel-to-reel with 3-12 songs on demo. SAE and IRC. Reports in 3 weeks.

**Music:** C&W, easy listening, MOR, rock, soul and top 40/pop. Recently published "Della and the Dealer" (by Hoyt Axton), recorded by H. Axton (C&W); "In a Broken Dream" (by Bentley), recorded by Rod Stewart; and "Lavender Blue" (by Olofsson), recorded by Mac Kissoon.

**O'LYRIC MUSIC**, Suite 8, 11833 Laurelwood Dr., Studio City CA 91604. (213)506-5473. Affiliate: O'Lyrical Music (ASCAP). President: Jim O'Loughlin. Music publisher and record producer. BMI. Member California Copyright Conference. Publishes 30-50 songs/year; publishes 4 new songwriters/year. Hires staff writers; pays $15,000/year—"only duty expected is songwriting. Writers paid by royalties earned and by advances."
**How to Contact:** Submit demo tape and lyric sheet. Prefers cassette with 1-3 songs on demo. SASE. Reports as soon as possible.
**Music:** C&W, dance-oriented, easy listening, jazz, MOR, progressive, R&B, rock, soul and top 40/pop. Recently published *B.Y.O.B.*, recorded by Sister Sledge; "38 Special," recorded by Ronnie McDowell; "Spare Hearts," recorded by T.G. Shepherd; "You Can't Lose What You Never Had," recorded by Lynn Anderson. O'Lyric Music was also music supervisor for the Embassy-released film "Zapped," starring Scott Baio.

**ON THE WING MUSIC PUBLISHING CO.**, 12024 Riverside Dr. E., Windsor, Ontario, Canada N8P 1A9. (519)735-7769. President: Jim Thomson II. Music publisher, record company and record producer. PROCAN. Publishes 12 songs/year; publishes 1 new songwriter/year. Pays standard royalty.
**How to Contact:** Arrange personal interview to play demo tape or submit demo tape and lyric sheet with bio. Prefers cassette with 4 songs minimum on demo. "If you are submitting more than 1 style, submit at least 2, preferably 3, songs in each style. I want to know something about the songwriters and artists with whom I work. Send a short bio; include membership in professional organizations, outside interests and things about which you have strong convictions—abortion, religion, social issues, world hunger, etc. Lyrical depth, without sexual suggestiveness and obscenity are a definite plus." SAE and IRC. Reports in 3 weeks "but only if interested, due to volume."
**Music:** Mostly rock and MOR; also bluegrass, blues, children's, church/religious, classical, C&W, easy listening, folk, gospel, jazz, progressive, Spanish, R&B, soul and top 40/pop. Recently published "I've Got Jesus" (by Jim Thomson II), recorded by Preflyte/Skylight Records (gospel); "I Saw It on the Tube" (by J. Thomson II), recorded by Jim Thomson II/Skylight Records (folk rock); and "Old Gypsy Moon" (by J. Thomson II), recorded by Preflyte/JLTII Records (top 40 pop).

**ONEIDA MUSIC PUBLISHING CO.**, 760 Blandina St., Utica NY 13501. (315)735-6187. President: Stanley Markowski. Music publisher. BMI. Publishes 25 songs/year; publishes 6 new songwriters/year. Pays standard royalty.
**How to Contact:** Submit demo tape and lyric sheet. Prefers reel-to-reel or cassette with "no limit" of songs on demo. SASE. Reports in 1 month.
**Music:** All types. Recently published "Bowling Ball Blues" (by John Piazza), recorded by Joe Angerosa.

**ORCHID PUBLISHING**, Bouquet-Orchid Enterprises, Box 18284, Shreveport LA 71138. (318)686-7362. President: Bill Bohannon. Music publisher and record company. BMI. Member CMA. Publishes 8-10 songs/year; publishes 3 new songwriters/year. Pays standard royalty.
**How to Contact:** Submit demo tape and lead sheet. Prefers 7½ ips reel-to-reel or cassette with 3-5 songs on demo. SASE. Reports in 1 month.
**Music:** Church/religious ("B.J. Thomas, etc.—contemporary gospel"); C&W ("Dolly Parton/Kenny Rogers type material"); and top 40/pop ("Rick Springfield/Oak Ridge Boys type material"). Recently published "Lie to Me" (by L. Bearden and B. Bohannon); "One More Trip" (by B. White and Bohannon), recorded by Bohannon/Paula Records; "The Touch of You" (by B. Bohannon), recorded by Adam Day/Bouquet Records; and "I Need You Today" (by B. Bohannon and S. Wilson), recorded by S. Wilson/Bouquet Records (all C&W).

**OTTO PUBLISHING CO.**, 7766 NW 44th St., Sunrise FL 33321. (305)741-7766. President: Frank X. Loconto. Music publisher. Estab. 1982. ASCAP. Publishes 12 songs/year; publishes 3 new songwriters/year. Pays standard royalty.
**How to Contact:** Submit demo tape and lyric sheet. Prefers cassette with 1-4 songs on demo. SASE. Reports in 1 month.
**Music:** Mostly C&W; also MOR. Recently published "Paranda" (by Frank X. Loconto), recorded by Accents 1 & 2/Guava Duff Records (calypso) and "Let's Get With It America" (by Mary Jane Sullivan & F.X. Loconto), recorded by Mary Jane/ICI Records (patriotic).

**RAY OVERHOLT MUSIC**, 112 S. 26th St., Battle Creek MI 49015. (616)963-0554. A&R Director: Mildred Overholt. Manager: Ray Overholt. Music publisher. BMI. Publishes 25 songs/year; publishes 10 new songwriters/year. Pays 10-25% royalty. "We also use the standard songwriter's contract at the going rate."
**How to Contact:** Submit demo tape and lead sheet. Prefers cassette with 1-3 songs on demo. SASE. Reports in 3 weeks.
**Music:** Church/religious and gospel. Recently published "Tell My Daddy" (by R. Overholt), recorded by Becky Overholt/Artists Records (ballad hymn); "Another Day's Gone By" (by R. Overholt), recorded by Dodson Family/Crusade Records (country gospel); and "Lord, How Long" (by R. Overholt), recorded by Cathedrals/Word Records (country gospel).
**Tips:** "We desire songs with a country gospel touch—songs that tell a story with a Biblical message or theme."

**LEE MACES OZARK OPRY MUSIC PUBLISHING**, Box 242, Osage Beach MO 65065. (314)348-2702. Affiliates: Tall Corn Publishing (BMI) and Mid America Music Publishing (ASCAP). General Manager: Lee Mace. Music publisher, record company and record producer. Publishes 12 songs/year. Pays standard royalty.
**How to Contact:** Arrange personal interview or submit demo tape and lead sheet. Prefers 7½ ips reel-to-reel or cassette with 2-4 songs on demo. SASE. Reports in 2 weeks.
**Music:** Bluegrass; blues; church/religious; C&W; gospel; and R&B. Recently published "Younger Than Tomorrow" (by M. Sexton), recorded by Mark Sexton (pop/country); "I Can't Sell My Self" (by D. Thomas), recorded by Darrel Thomas (country); "Farrahs Faucet" (by Jack Selover), recorded by Lorance Aubrey (country); "Waylon Sing To Mama" (by D. Thomas), recorded by D. Thomas/Ozark Opry Records (country); and "Don't Say No to Me Tonight" (by Don and Dick Addrisi), recorded by M. Sexton/Sun De Mar Records (pop/country).

**PACKAGE GOOD MUSIC**, 1145 Green St., Manville NJ 08835. Contact: Marc Zydiack. Music publisher. BMI.
**How to Contact:** Submit demo tape. Prefers cassette with 3 songs minimum on tape. SASE. Reports in 1 month.
**Music:** Easy listening, folk (progressive), MOR, progressive, rock and top 40/pop. Recently published "There's No Place like You" (country rock); "Frosty the Dopeman" (progressive folk); "Nymphomaniac Blues," recorded by Marc Zydiak; and "Let's Start a Punk Rock Band," recorded by Professor Marx (punk rock).

**PALAMAR MUSIC PUBLISHERS**, 726 Carlson Dr., Orlando FL 32804. (305)644-3853. Affiliate: MuStaff Music Publishers (BMI). President: Will Campbell. Music publisher and record company. BMI. Publishes 4-20 songs/year; publishes 2-5 new songwriters/year. Pays standard royalty.
**How to Contact:** Submit demo tape and lead sheet. Prefers 7½ ips reel-to-reel with 3-6 songs on demo. SASE. Reports in 1 week.
**Music:** Bluegrass, church/religious, C&W, gospel and MOR. Recently published "Dust" (by E.D. Linebarger), recorded by Big Dan Starr/Decade Records (gospel); "Third Finger Left Hand" (by E.D. Linebarger), recorded by Big Dan Starr/Decade Records (popular); and "I've Come Here to Do Some Drinking" (by W. Campbell), recorded by Will Campbell/Decade Records (country).
**Tips:** "Submit songs that are cleverly written with punch. I also like simple demos that are clearly recorded."

**PAVILLION PRODUCTIONS/PROMOTION, INC.**, Suite 44F, 322 W. 57th St., New York NY 10019. (212)247-6854. President: John Luongo. Music publisher, record promotion, record producer and management office.
**How to Contact:** Submit demo tape, lyric sheet and biography. Prefers cassette. Does not return unsolicited material. Reports in 4 weeks.
**Music:** Progressive, R&B, rock, soul and top 40/pop. Recently published *You're Too Late*, recorded by Fantasy (R&B); *Ready for Love*, recorded by Silverado (rock); *Zulu*, recorded by the Quick (R&B); *Run, Run, Run*, recorded by Funkapolitan (AOR); *Back Track*, recorded by Certone (R&B); and *Art In America*, by Art In American (AOR).

***PAYTON PLACE PUBLISHING**, Suite 803, 7302 Mullins, Houston TX 77081. (713)776-9219. Affiliate: Clarity Publishing. President: I.P. Sweat. Music publisher and record producer. Estab. 1982. BMI.
**How to Contact:** Write or call first about interest; submit demo tape and lyric sheet. Prefers cassette with 1-2 songs on demo. SASE.
**Music:** Mostly C&W; also bluegrass, blues and dance-oriented.

## Music Publishers 85

**PEER-SOUTHERN ORGANIZATION**, 6777 Hollywood Blvd., Hollywood CA 90028. Affiliates: Charles K. Harris Music Publishing (ASCAP), La Salle Music (ASCAP), Melody Lane (BMI), Panther Music (ASCAP), Peer International (BMI), Pera Music (BMI), RFD Music (ASCAP) and Southern Music (ASCAP), Professional Manager: Roy Kohn. Music publisher and production company. Member NMPA. Pays standard royalty; 5¢/sheet on sheet music.
**How to Contact:** Write first about your interest; unsolicited tapes not accepted.
**Music:** C&W; disco; easy listening; MOR; rock; and top 40/pop.

**PEER-SOUTHERN ORGANIZATION**, 1740 Broadway, New York NY 10019. (212)265-3910. Affiliates: Peer International Corporation (BMI) and Southern Music (ASCAP). Ch. of Board: Monique I. Peer. President: Ralph Peer II. Vice President: Mario Conti. Creative Director/East Coast: Holly Green. Professional Manager: Roy Kohn. Music publisher. Member NMPA. Publishes 500 songs/year. Pays standard royalty.
**How to Contact:** Submit demo tape and lyric sheet. Prefers cassette with 1-5 songs on demo. SASE. Reports in 1 month.
**Music:** Bluegrass, choral, classical, C&W, disco, easy listening, MOR, progressive, R&B, rock, soul and top 40/pop. Published "Blue Moon of Kentucky," recorded by Elvis Presley.

**PEER-SOUTHERN ORGANIZATION**, 7 Music Circle N., Nashville TN 37203. (615)244-6200. Affiliates: Charles K. Harris Music (ASCAP), La Salle Music (ASCAP), Melody Lane (BMI), Panther Music (ASCAP), Peer International (BMI), Pera Music (BMI), RFD Music (ASCAP) and Southern Music (ASCAP). Director of Nashville Operations: Merlin Littlefield. Member NMPA. Pays standard royalty.
**How to Contact:** Query or submit demo tape and lead sheet. Prefers 7½ ips reel-to-reel or cassette wth 1-4 songs on demo. SASE. Reports in 1 month.
**Music:** C&W, contemporary gospel, MOR, R&B, rock and top 40/pop. Recently published "Georgia On My Mind" (by H. Carmichael), recorded by Willie Nelson; "Since I Don't Have You" (by J. Staaton), recorded y Art Garfunkle (top 40); "Last Blue Yodel" (by J. Rodgers), recorded by Ernest Tubb; "Miss the Mississippi and You," recorded by Crystal Gayle; "Music Is My Way of Life," recorded by Patti LaBelle; and "Maybe I'll Cry Over You" (by E. Britt), recorded by Arthur Blanch.

**PEER-SOUTHERN ORGANIZATION**, Suite 300, 180 Bloor St. W., Toronto, Ontario, Canada N56 2V6. Managing Director: Matthew Heft. Music publisher. PROCAN and CAPAC.
**How to Contact:** Submit demo tape. Prefers cassette with 1-3 songs on demo. SAE and IRC. Reports in 1 month.
**Music:** Bluegrass, blues, children's, choral, church/religious, classical, C&W, disco, easy listening, folk, gospel, jazz, MOR, progressive, rock, soul and top 40/pop.

***PEGASUS MUSIC**, 27 Bayside Ave., Te Atatu, Auckland, 8, New Zealand. Professional Manager: Ginny Peters. Music publisher and record company. APRA. Publishes 6 songs/year. Has not yet, but would listen to songs from US songwriters. Pays 3-5% to artists on contract and standard royalty to songwriters; royalties paid directly to US songwriters.
**How to Contact:** Submit demo tape and lyric sheet. Prefers cassette with 3-5 songs on demo. SAE and IRC. Reports in 1 month.
**Music:** Mostly C&W; also bluegrass, easy listening and top 40/pop.

**PELIPERUS MUSIC CO.**, 4142 Benton Blvd., Kansas City MO 64130. (816)861-0852. Branch office: 10424 St. Andrews Pl., Los Angeles CA 90047. (213)755-9494. Professional Manager: Byron Motley. Music publisher. Estab. 1981. ASCAP. Member AGAC, BMA. Publishes 15 songs/year; publishes 5 new songwriters/year. Pays standard royalty.
**How to Contact:** Submit demo tape and lyric sheet. Prefers cassette with 2-5 songs on demo. Does not return unsolicited material, "but we will send letter if we decide to pass material on." Reports in 2 weeks.
**Music:** Mostly top 40/pop and MOR; also easy listening, gospel and soul. Recently published "We Were Love" (by Byron Motley & Carol Aubrey), recorded by Natalie Nugent/Holton Records (top 40/pop); "Didn't We Love" (by B. Motley), recorded by Jonathan Sentel/Rainbow Records (MOR); "No One Left" (by B. Motley & John Braden), recorded by N. Nugent/Holton Records (top 40/pop); and "I Must Be Dreamin'  (by B. Motley & Lance Winkler), recorded by N. Nugent/Holton Records (top 40/pop).
**Tips:** "I look for strong lyricists with versatile styles."

**PENNY PINCHER PUBLISHING, INC.**, Box 780, Oakwood VA 24631. Affiliate: Loose Jaw Productions. President: R.J. Fuller. Music publisher and record producer. BMI and ASCAP. SESAC. Mem-

ber of "most all" professional organizations. Publishes 50 songs/year; publishes 35 new songwriters/year. Pays standard royalty.
**How to Contact:** Submit demo tape and lyric sheet. Prefers cassette with 2-5 songs on demo. "We would like a biography." Also enclose photos. SASE. Reports in 1 month.
**Music:** Bluegrass, blues, C&W, folk, gospel, MOR, R&B, rock and top 40/pop. Recently published "Giving Up Getting Over You" and "Out of Hand" by Roy John.
**Tips:** "Study the charts, get good hooks and turn arounds, use effective and not childish rhyme, be patient giving publisher all the time he wants, use return envelope, write, write and write—practice makes perfect!"

**\*PEOPLE CITY MUSIC PUBLISHING INC.**, Suite 600, 1055 Wilson Ave., Toronto, Ontario, Canada M3K 1Y9. (416)630-2973. Affiliate: Lonsong Music Inc. (CAPAC). President: Frank Longo. Music publisher, record company and record producer. PROCAN. Member CARAS. Publishes 5 songs/year; publishes 1 new songwriter/year. Pays standard royalty.
**How to Contact:** Submit demo tape and lyric sheet. Prefers cassette with 1-3 songs on demo. "Enclose SASE." Reports in 2 weeks.
**Music:** Mostly R&B and pop; also dance-oriented, easy listening and R&B. Recently published "You've Got No-One," recorded by Patti Jannetta/Janta Records (pop/rock); "Coast to Coast," recorded by The Longo Brothers; "Easy Life" (by F. Longo and L. Longo), recorded by Jim Mancel/People City Music Records (pop); "In the Middle of the Night" (by D. Longo, L. Longo, F. Longo), recorded by Jill Nogell/People City Music Records (R&B/pop); and "The Nightlife" (by D. Longo, L. Longo, F. Longo), recorded by Wayne St. John/People City Music Records (R&B).
**Tips:** "Send 1-3 songs (only your best) on a cassette with lyric sheets and SASE."

**PERLA MUSIC**, 20 Martha St., Woodcliff Lake NJ 07675. (201)391-2486. President: Gene A. Perla. Music publisher, record producer and record company. ASCAP. Publishes 12 songs/year; publishes 2 new songwriters/year. Pays 75%/25% split.
**How to Contact:** Call first about your interest. Prefers cassette. SASE.
**Music:** All types. Recently published "Korinna" (by Gene Perla), recorded by Elvin Jones/McCoy Tyner Records (ballad); "Bunny Honey" (by G. Perla), recorded by E. Jones/Trio Records (50's R&R); and "Bahama Mama" (by G. Perla), recorded by G. Perla/P.M. Records (reggae).

**\*PERMANENT POP MUSIC**, Box 1406, Brea CA 92621. (714)595-6925. President: Ray Paul. Music publisher and record producer. BMI. Publishes 10-15 songs year; publishes 2 new songwriters/year. Pays standard royalty.
**How to Contact:** Submit demo tape and lyric sheet; arrange personal interview to play demo tape. Prefers cassette or records with 3-5 songs on demo. "Please submit any press kits, bios and photos." SASE. Reports in 3-4 weeks.
**Music:** Mostly top 40/pop, rock ("no hard rock") and dance-oriented rock; also easy listening, MOR and progressive. Recently published "How Do You Know?" (by Ray Paul), recorded by R. Paul/Permanent Press Records (rock/pop); "Complicated Girl" (by D. Cook and R. Werner), recorded by Puppet Rulers/Permanent Press Records (rock/top 40); "Keep It Confidential" (by R. Paul), recorded by R. Paul/Permanent Press Records (rock/top 40); "Hold It" and "Tears (Little Darlin')" (by R. Paul), recorded by R. Paul and RPM/Muscle Recordworks Records (both rock/top 40).

**DON PERRY PRODUCTIONS**, 2974 Parkview Dr., Thousand Oaks CA 91362. (805)497-4738. Affiliates: North Ranch Music (BMI), Flying Lady Music (ASCAP). Director of Music Publishing: Don Perry. Music publisher and record producer. BMI and ASCAP. Publishes 50 TV and film scores/year; publishes 4-5 new songwriters/year. Pays standard royalty.
**How to Contact:** Prefers demo tape and lyric sheet to be submitted by mail. SASE. Reports in 1 month.
**Music:** Bluegrass, blues, children's, C&W, disco, easy listening, MOR, progressive, R&B, country rock, soul and top 40/pop. Recently produced "Butterfly" soundtrack on Applause Records. Recently published "Too Hot to Sleep" by Sylvester/Fantasy Records; and "I Used to Be Her," by Lyndsey Edwards/Monument Records.

**PHILIPPOPOLIS MUSIC**, 12027 Califa St., North Hollywood CA 91607. President: Milcho Leviev. Music publisher and record company. BMI. Member GEMA, NARAS. Publishes 5 songs/year. Pays standard royalties.
**How to Contact:** Query. Prefers cassette with 1-3 songs on demo. SASE. Reports in 1 month.
**Music:** Jazz and classical. Recently published "Music for Big Band and Symphony Orchestra" (by Milcho Leviev), recorded by M. Leviev/Trend Records (classical); "Bulgarian Boogie" (by M. Leviev) recorded by M. Leviev/Trend Records (jazz); "Women's Dance" (by M. Leviev), recorded by Free Flight/Palo Alto Records (fusion); "A Heartbeat" (by M. Leviev), recorded by Free Flight/Palo Alto

Records (jazz); and "Emy" (by M. Leviev), recorded by Free Flight (jazz).
**Tips:** "Treat music as an art form."

**PHONETONES,** 400 Essex St., Salem MA 01970. (617)744-7678. Logistics Co-Ordinator: Edsel Ferrari. Music publisher and record company. Estab. 1981. ASCAP. Publishes 3 new songwriters/year. Pays standard royalty.
**How to Contact:** Submit demo tape and lyric sheet. Prefers cassette with 2-4 songs on demo. SASE. Reports in 1 month.
**Music:** Rock, pop and new wave. Recently published "We Run Ourselves," (by Mare Mchugh), recorded by Tweeds/Eat Records (rock); "And Many Many More," (by Erik Lindgren), recorded by Original Artists/Eat Records (DOR); "The Press Conference," (by Rose and Egendorf), recorded by Newshounds/Ragun Records (novelty); and "Slippin' Away" (by Bob Holmes), recorded by Rubber Rodeo/Eat Records (new wave C&W).

*****PILGRIM INTERNATIONAL LTD.,** Suite 6V, 4140 Union St., Flushing NY 11355. (212)939-4538. Affiliate: Pilgrim/Hibiscus Music (ASCAP). President: John Pilgrim. Music publisher and management company. Estab. 1981. ASCAP. Publishes 10-20 songs/year; publishes 1 new songwriter/year. Pays standard royalty.
**How to Contact:** Write first about your interest; submit demo tape and lyric sheet. Prefers cassette with 3-6 songs on demo. SASE. Reports in 2 weeks.
**Music:** Mostly top 40/pop, dance-oriented and easy listening; also C&W, gospel, MOR and R&B.
**Tips:** "Looking for songs with strong lyrics and songs that can be placed with artists who are currently charting."

**PINE ISLAND MUSIC,** #308, 9430 Live Oak Place, Ft. Lauderdale FL 33324. (305)472-7757. Affiliates: Lantana Music (ASCAP) and Twister Music (ASCAP). President: Jack P. Bluestein. Music publisher, record company and record producer. BMI. Publishes 10-20 songs/year; publishes 2 new songwriters/year. Pays standard royalty.
**How to Contact:** Submit demo tape and lyric sheet. Prefers cassette with 1-3 songs on demo. SASE. Reports in 1 month.
**Music:** Mostly C&W and pop; also gospel and MOR. Recently published "I Wake Up and It Rains" (by Joe McDonald), "Gotta Keep Movin' " (by Tom Roush), and "A Miracle In You" (by Tom Lazarus), all recorded by Gary Oakes and Lou Garcia/Twister Records (country pop).

*****PINEAPPLE MUSIC PUBLISHING CO.,** 1311 Candlelight Ave., Dallas TX 75116. (214)298-9576. Affiliate: Big State Music Pub. Co. (BMI). President: Paul Ketter. Music publisher, record producer and record company. ASCAP. Publishes 20-30 songs/year. Pays standard royalty.
**How to Contact:** Submit demo tape and lyric sheet. Prefers cassette with 1-8 songs on demo. SASE. Reports in 3 weeks.
**Music:** C&W, folk, country MOR, progressive country and "strong" pop. Recently published "Bar after Bar" (by F. Feliccia and F. Raffa), recorded by Bunnie Mills/Sagittar Records (honky tonk country); "Only a Woman" (by D. Baumgartner), recorded by Bunnie Mills/Sagittar Records (C&W/ballad); and "Theodore" (by D. Gregory and G. Puls), recorded by Dave Gregory/Sagittar Records (children's Christmas); and "I Wanna Say 'I Do'," recorded by P.J. Kamel/Sagittar Records.
**Tips:** "We only want to hear from writers who have written 100 or more songs. Please do not send us songs that have been already rejected by others."

*****PIXIE MUSIC CO. LTD.,** 10 St. Mary's Hill, Stamford, PE9 2DP, England. 44-0780-51736. Managing Director: Ken Cox. Music publisher, record company and record producer. MCPS, PRS and Phonographic Performance Ltd. Publishes 20 songs/year; publishes 3 new songwriters/year. Pays standard royalty; royalties paid directly to US songwriters.
**How to Contact:** Submit demo tape and lyric sheet. Prefers cassette with 2-6 songs on demo. SAE and IRC. Reports in 2 weeks.
**Music:** Mostly top 40/pop; also C&W and soul (uptempo). Recently published "All You Got Your Ears On" (by R. Ryan), recorded by R. Ryan/Buffalo Records (C&W/CB); "Pig of the Year" (by J. Cooke), recorded by M. Taylor/Weasel Records (pop); and "Somewhere-Nowhere" (by C. Grey), recorded by Vision/Downtown Records (pop).

**THE PLEIADES MUSIC GROUP,** The Barn, N. Ferrisburg VT 05473. (802)425-2111. Affiliates: Pleiades Music (BMI), Other Music (ASCAP), Grimes Creek (ASCAP) and On Strike Music (BMI). A&R Director: Bob Peskin. Music publisher. BMI, ASCAP. Member NAIRD. Publishes 100 songs/year; publishes 6 new songwriters/year. Pays standard royalty.
**How to Contact:** "We are not currently seeking unsolicited material."

**POLKA TOWNE MUSIC**, 211 Post Ave., Westbury NY 11590. President: Teresa Zapolska. Music publisher, record company, record producer and booking agency. BMI. "We review all music once a month."
**How to Contact:** Submit demo tape and lead sheet. Prefers cassette with 1-3 songs on demo. SASE for return of material. Reports in 1 month.
**Music:** Polkas and waltzes.

**POSITIVE PRODUCTIONS**, Box 1405, Highland Park NJ 08904. (201)463-8845. President: J. Vincenzo. Music publisher and record producer. BMI. Publishes 5 songs/year. Payment negotiable.
**How to Contact:** Submit demo tape and lyric sheet. Prefers 7½ ips reel-to-reel with 2-4 songs on demo. SASE. Reports in 1 month.
**Music:** Children's; easy listening; folk; and MOR. Recently published "Two Timer", and "Ash Wednesday," recorded by Wooden Soldier (MOR).

**POWER-PLAY PUBLISHING**, 1900 Elm Hill Pike, Nashville TN 37210. (615)889-8000. Contact: Mark Mathis. Music publisher and record company. BMI. Pays standard royalty.
**How to Contact:** Arrange personal interview. Prefers 7½ ips reel-to-reel with 2 songs on demo. SASE. Reports in 1 month.
**Music:** Bluegrass, blues, C&W, disco, easy listening, folk, gospel, R&B, rock, soul and top 40/pop.

**POWHATAN MUSIC PUBLISHING**, Box 993, Salem VA 24153. (703)387-0208. Affiliate: Double Jack Publishing (BMI). President: Jack Mullins. Music publisher and record company. BMI. Publishes 42 songs/year; publishes 4 new songwriters/year. Pays standard royalty and "if established, more".
**How to Contact:** Submit demo tape and lyric sheet. Prefers 7½ ips reel-to-reel with 2-4 songs on demo. SASE. Reports in 1 month ("no review").
**Music:** Bluegrass, C&W, R&B and top 40/pop.

**PRESCRIPTION CO.**, 70 Murray Ave., Port Washington NY 11050. (516)767-1929. President: David F. Gasman. Music publisher, record company and record producer. BMI. Pays standard royalty.
**How to Contact:** Call or write first about your interest, then submit demo tape and lyric sheet. Prefers cassette with any number songs on demo. Does not return unsolicited material. Reports in 1 month.
**Music:** Bluegrass, blues, children's, C&W, dance-oriented, easy listening, folk, jazz, MOR, progressive, R&B, rock, soul and top 40/pop. Recently published "You Came In," "Rock 'n' Roll Blues"(rock) and "Seasons" (by D.F. Gasman), all recorded by Medicine Mike/Prescription Records (country).
**Tips:** "Songs should be good and written to last. Forget fads—we want songs that'll sound as good in 10 years as they do today. Organization, communication, and exploration of form is as essential as message (and sincerity matters, too)."

**JIMMY PRICE MUSIC PUBLISHING**, 1662 Wyatt Parkway, Lexington KY 40505. (606)254-7474. President: James T. Price. Music publisher, record company, record producer and music printer. BMI. Publishes 7 new songwriters/year. Pays standard royalty.
**How to Contact:** Submit demo tape and lyric sheet. Prefers 7½ ips reel-to-reel with 1-6 songs on demo. SASE. Reports in 1 month.
**Music:** Bluegrass, blues, church/religious, C&W and gospel. Recently published "Country Waltz" (by James T. Price), recorded by K. Wade/Sun-Ray Records (waltz); "Where the Music Plays Sweetly" (by Charles Stephens), and "Beautiful Love" (by J.T. Price), both recorded by C. Stephens/Sun-Ray Records (country).

***PRIORITY/PREFERENCE MUSIC-CBS SONGS**, 3310 W. End Ave., Nashville TN 37203. (615)383-6000. Manager, Music Publishing: Dennis Worley. Music publisher and record company. Estab. 1981. BMI, ASCAP. Publishes 25 songs/year; publishes 3 new songwriters/year.
**How to Contact:** Submit demo tape and lyric sheet. Prefers cassette with 3-5 songs on demo. Does not review unsolicited material.
**Music:** Mostly gospel; also choral and church/religious. Recently published "New Lives for Old" (by Gary Driskell), recorded by Wayne Watson/Milk & Honey Records (gospel); "Come & See" (by Bob Bennett & Michael Aguilar), recorded by B. Bennett/Priority Records (gospel); and "Bless Your Name" (by Cindy, Becky & Nancy Cruse), recorded by The Cruse Family/Miority Records (gospel).

**PRITCHETT PUBLICATONS**, 38603 Sage Tree St., Palmdale CA 93550. Branch Office: 171 Pine Haven, Daytona Beach FL 32014. (904)252-4849. President: L.R. Pritchett. Vice Presidents: Charles Vickers, Ed Crawley. Branch: 17 Pine Haven, Daytona Beach FL 32014. Affiliate: Alison Music (ASCAP). Music publisher, record producer and record company. BMI. Member NSG. Publishes 30 songs/

year; publishes 1 new songwriter/year. Pays standard royalty.
**How to Contact:** Submit lead sheet; "If we're interested, then a demo tape will be requested." SASE. Reports in 1 month.
**Music:** Blues, church/religious, classical, C&W, disco, easy listening, folk, gospel, jazz, progressive, R&B, rock, MOR, soul and top 40/pop.

**PROPHECY PUBLISHING, INC.**, Box 4945, Austin TX 78765. (512)452-9412. Affiliate: Black Coffee Music (BMI). Administrates Chicken Fried Music, Floating Tones, and Steven Fromholz Publishing. President: T. White. Music publisher. ASCAP. Member NMPA. Publishes 200-300 songs/year. Pays standard royalty, less expenses; "expenses such as tape duplicating, photocopying and long distance phone calls are recouped from the writer's earnings."
**How to Contact:** Submit demo tape and lyric sheet. Prefers cassette with 1-3 songs on demo. Does not return unsolicited material. "No reply can be expected, unless we're interested in the material."
**Music:** Bluegrass, blues, classical, C&W, disco, easy listening, folk, gospel, jazz, MOR, progressive, rock, soul and top 40/pop. Recently published "Everybody's Goin' on the Road," recorded by Hoyt Axton (C&W); "Busha-Busha," recorded by Arthur Brown (rock); and "When the World Comes Crashing Through," recorded by Private Lives (rock).

**PUBLICARE MUSIC, LTD.**, Nashville Sound, Inc., 9717 Jensen, Houston TX 77843. (713)695-3648. Director of Copyright Affairs: Jim D. Johnson. Affiliate: Pubit Music (BMI). Music publisher, record company and production company. ASCAP. Member NMPA. Pays 50-75% royalty. Publishes 10-20 songs/year. Hires staff writers: pays according to individual situation.
**How to Contact:** Submit demo tape and lead sheet. Prefers cassette with 2-4 songs on demo. SASE. Reports in 3 weeks.
**Music:** C&W, disco, MOR, progressive, rock and top 40/pop. Prefers songs that have market crossover potential.

**PUBLISHING VENTURES, INC.**, (formerly Extra Money Music), Suite 264, 1290 Avenue of the Americas, New York NY 10019. (212)399-0090. Affiliates: King King Music (BMI), Gary Bonds Music (BMI), Son of Kong Music/ASCAP. Managing Director: Andrea Starr. Music publisher. Estab. 1982. ASCAP. Publishes 15 songs/year; publishes 4 new songwriters/year. Pays standard royalty.
**How to Contact:** Submit demo tape and lyric sheet. Prefers cassette with 1-3 songs on demo. Does not return unsolicited material. Reports in 3-8 weeks.
**Music:** Rock, top 40/pop and R&B; also ballads, C&W and MOR. Recently published "Turn the Music Down" and "Bring Her Back" (by Gary Bonds and Laurie Anderson), recorded by Gary U.S. Bonds/EMI Records (pop/rock).
**Tips:** Looking for "radio-oriented hit singles with strong hooks and interesting lyrics and titles."

**GERALD W. PURCELL ASSOCIATES**, 964 Second Ave., New York NY 10022. (212)421-2670, 2674, 2675 and 2676. President: Gerald Purcell. Music publisher. BMI, ASCAP. Member CPM, CMA, NARM. Publishes 50 songs/year; publishes 4 new songwriters/year. Pays standard royalty.
**How to Contact:** Submit demo tape with maximum of 3 songs, lyric sheet and clear lead sheet. Prefers cassette. SASE. Reports as soon as possible.
**Music:** Country.

**PYRAMID RECORDS**, Box 140316, Nashville TN 37214. (615)889-6675. Music publisher and record company. BMI.
**How to Contact:** Submit demo tape and lead sheet. Prefers 7½ ips reel-to-reel or cassette. SASE. Reports in 2 weeks.
**Music:** C&W and gospel. Recently released "Christmas Time in Heaven (by Bob Pauley), recorded by Jimmy Kish; and "Life's Railway to Heaven" (by C.D. Tillmare), recorded by J. Kish.

**QUALITY MUSIC PUBLISHING**, 380 Birchmount Rd., Scarborough, Ontario, Canada M1K 1M7. (416)698-5511. Affiliates: Shediac Music (CAPAC), Broadland Music (PROCAN), Eskimo/Nuna Music (CAPAC), Rycha Music (PROCAN), Old Shanty Music (CAPAC) and Sons Celestes Music (CAPAC). General Manager: Nadine Langlois. Music publisher and record company. PROCAN. Publishes 200 songs/year; publishes 10 new songwriters/year. Pays standard royalty.
**How to Contact:** Submit demo tape and lead sheet. Prefers 7½ ips reel-to-reel or cassette with 2-5 songs on demo. SAE and IRC. Reports in 1 month.
**Music:** C&W, disco, gospel, MOR, progressive, rock (country or hard) and top 40/pop. Recently published "Harmonium," recorded by Harmonium (top 40/pop); "Try It Out" (by Gino Soccio), recorded by G. Soccio/RFC/Atlantic Records; and "Set Me Free" (by G. Soccio), recorded by Karen Silver/RFC Records (disco/pop).

**QUEEN OF HEARTS**, 6105-A Youree Dr., Shreveport LA 71005. (318)861-05679. Music Publisher: George Clinton.
**How to Contact:** Submit demo tape and lyric sheet. Prefers cassette as demo. SASE. Reports in 6-8 weeks.
**Music:** C&W, gospel and rock.

**QUINONES MUSIC CO.**, 1344 Waldron, St. Louis MO 63130. President: Eddie Johnson. Music publisher. BMI. Publishes 8-12 songs/year; publishes 2-3 new songwriters/year. Pays standard royalty.
**How to Contact:** Submit demo tape and lyric sheet. Prefers cassette with 3 songs on demo. SASE. Reports in 2 weeks.
**Music:** Blues, church/religious, gospel, R&B, soul and top 40/pop.

**RAC RACOUILLAT MUSIC ENTERPRISES**, Suite B, 7934 Mission Center Ct., San Diego CA 92108. (714)296-9641. Affiliate: Mal & Rac Music Enterprises (ASCAP). President: Robert "Rac" Racouillat. Music publisher, record company and record producer. BMI. Member Songwriters Organizations National Group, Songwriters of San Diego Association. Publishes 30-50 songs/year; publishes 14 new songwriters/year. Pays standard royalty.
**How to Contact:** Submit demo tape and typed lyric sheet. Prefers cassette with 3-5 songs on demo. SASE. Reports in 2 weeks.
**Music:** C&W, dance-oriented, easy listening (A/C), MOR (A/C), new wave, R&B, rock (soft) and top 40/pop. Recently published "Bike Hustle" (by Robert "Rac" Racouillat), recorded by Bebe and Donnie Singer (pop/dance-oriented); "Kiss Your Past Good-by" (by Peter Richardson), recorded by Gary Hanley (country/pop); "That's a Lot of Lovin' for $1.69" (by P. Richardson), recorded by Joe Trucks (country/pop); and "You're My Kind of People" (by Robert "Rac" Racouillat), recorded by Frank Joseph.

**RAINFIRE MUSIC**, 15217 Otsego, Sherman Oaks CA 91430. (213)784-0388. Contact: Professional Manager. Music publisher, record company and record producer. BMI. Member of NARAS, ACM. Publishes 20-40 songs/year; publishes 15 new songwriters/year. Pays standard royalty. Submit demo tape and lyric sheet. Prefers cassette with 2-3 songs on demo. SASE. Reports in 2 weeks.
**Music:** C&W, easy listening, MOR, progressive, R&B, rock, soul, top 40/pop and disco. Recently published "Lovers and Losers" (by Penta & Noshkin), recorded by Katie Phillips (C&W); "In the Beginning" (by Silver & Greenspan), recorded by Karen Silver (disco) and "Love Diet" (by Joe Cannon), recorded by Rita Jenrette (pop).
**Tips:** "We look for songs with a catchy hook and at least 4 progressions within the body."

**RAVEN MUSIC**, 4107 Woodland Park N., Seattle WA 98103. (206)632-0887. President: Ron Ellis. Music publisher. BMI. Publishes 12-15 songs/year. Pays standard royalty.
**How to Contact:** Write first about your interest. Prefers cassette with 2-6 songs on demo. SASE. Reports in 2 weeks.
**Music:** Children's (educational and worship), church/religious (worship and liturgical) and easy listening (Christian message-oriented or very positive). Recently published "There's a Time There's a Moment," "With All My Heart," "Life Is You," "Gentle Rains," "Songs For Our Children" and "Starlight" (by Ellis & Lynch) recorded for Raven Music (liturgical/worship).
**Tips:** "Our field is contemporary Christian and music for worship and praise. Songs must be generally singable by large groups, for worship in the hymn tradition but with contemporary style (strong melodic lines with scripture-based lyrics)."

**RAYBIRD MUSIC**, Suite 303, 457 W. 57th St., New York NY 10019. (212)245-2299. Affiliates: Kips Bay Music (ASCAP), TaJah Music (BMI). President: Ray Passman. General Manager: Teddy Charles. Music publisher. BMI. Publishes 6 songs/year; publishes 2 new songwriters/year. Pays standard royalty.
**How to Contact:** Write first about your interest. Prefers cassette with 3-5 songs on demo. SASE. Reports in 2 weeks.
**Music:** Jazz. Recently published "Cliches" (by Harold Danco, Holli Ross and Ray Passman), recorded by Meredith D'Ambrosio/Palo Alto Records (blue waltz ballad); "De-Bop Live" (by H. Ross, R. Passman and Miles Davis), recorded by Mark Murphy/Muse Records (be-bop ballad); and "Down St. Thomgs4irst about your interest. Prefers cassette with 3-5 songs on demo. SASE. Reports in 2 weeks.
**Music:** Jazz. Recently published "Cliches" (by Harold Danco, Holli Ross and Ray Passman), recorded by Meredith D'Ambrosio/Palo Alto Records (blue waltz ballad); "De-Bop Live" (by H. Ross, R. Passman and Miles Davis), recorded by Mark Murphy/Muse Records (be-bop ballad); and "Down St. Thomas Way" (by Herb Wasserman), recorded by R. Passman/Muse Records (calypso).

Music Publishers  **91**

***RBI RECORDS/ROWALBA PUBLISHING**, c/o Rob Warren, #209, 39 E. 12th St., New York NY 10003. (212)673-9456. President: Rob Warren. Music publisher, record company and record producer. Estab. 1981. BMI, ASCAP. Publishes 20-30 songs/year; publishes 3 new songwriters/year. Pays standard royalty.
**How to Contact:** Write about your interest with a description of the kind of material being created; submit demo tape and lyric sheet. Prefers cassette with 1-6 songs on demo. "Send SASE if material should be returned." Reports in 1 month.
**Music:** Mostly pop, top 40 and new wave; also blues, R&B, rock and soul. Recently published "Anything You Want" (by R. Warren/A. Basi), recorded by Chiclettes/RBI Records (pop/new wave); "Lover's Call" (by R. Warren), recorded by Chiclettes/RBI Records (pop/new wave); and "Lisa's in Love" (by L. Matthews/A. Basi), recorded by Chiclettes/RBI Records (pop/new wave).
**Tips:** "Songs must be very melodic, very catchy and memorable and have a good beat—must be top 40 material. We prefer suitability for a female vocal duo (or solo). Should have new wave feel, but remain commercially viable (ballads, however are OK). We're looking for sounds similar to Human League, Flock of Seagulls, Police, Men at Work, Duran Duran, Haircut 100, Go-Go's, Joe Jackson, Scandal, Rolling Stones, early Beatles, 60s British sound and Motown sound."

**RCS PUBLISHING CO.**, 5220 Essen Lane, Baton Rouge LA 70808. (504)766-3233. Affiliates: Layback Music (BMI) and Impulsivo (ASCAP). President: Cyril C. Vetter. Music publisher, record company and record producer. ASCAP. Pays standard royalty.
**Music:** C&W, MOR, R&B, rock, soul and top 40/pop.

**\*RED BUS MUSIC INTERNATIONAL, LTD.**, 48 Broadley Terrace, London, NW1, England. 44-01-258-0324. Managing Director (International): Eliot N. Cotton. Music publisher, record company and record producer. MCPS, PRS, Phonographic Performance Ltd. Member MPA. Publishes 40 songs/year; publishes 5 new songwriters/year. Pays standard royalty; royalties paid to songwriter through US publishing affiliate.
**How to Contact:** Submit demo tape and lyric sheet. Prefers cassette for demo. SAE and IRC. Reports in 3 weeks.
**Music:** Dance-oriented, MOR, rock and top 40/pop.

**RED TENNIES MUSIC**, 816 N. La Cienega, Los Angeles CA 90069. (213)657-4521. President: Dale Gonyea. Music publisher. BMI. Pays standard royalty.
**How to Contact:** Submit demo tape and lyric sheet. Prefers cassette with 1-3 songs on demo. Does not return unsolicited material. Reports as soon as possible.
**Music:** Top 40/pop and comedy.

**JACK REDICK MUSIC PUBLISHING CO.**, Rt. 1, Box 85, Georgetown SC 29840. (803)546-7139. Affiliate: Wagon Wheel Records (BMI). Manager: Jack Redick. Music publisher. BMI.
**How to Contact:** Submit demo tape. Prefers cassette with 1-6 songs on demo. "We will be glad to review any records, cassettes or reels if postage is enclosed with SAE. Do not send originals. For review of new, uncopyrighted material, send songs on cassette with return postage."
**Music:** Gospel, country or rockabilly. Recently published "This Man Named Jesus," by Gospel Echo; "Devil in Disguise," by The Oasis; "What Must I Do to Prove My Love for You," by Ray Jones; "Show Me the Stairway," by Ray Wilson; and "Dear Dad," by Jack Redick.
**Tips:** "Send songs of today. Always send your best with voice and lyrics up front and music in the background so it can be understood."

**JIM REEVES ENTERPRISES**, Drawer I, Madison TN 37115. (615)868-1150. Affiliates: Ma-ree Music, Inc. (ASCAP) and Tuckahoe Music (BMI). Professional Manager: Lee Morgan.

**REN MAUR MUSIC CORP.**, 663 5th Ave., New York NY 10022. (212)757-3638. Affiliate: R.R. Music (ASCAP). President: Rena L. Feeney. Music publisher and record company. BMI. Member AGAC and NARAS. Publishes 6-8 songs/year. Pays 4-8% royalty.
**How to Contact:** Submit demo tape and lead sheet. Prefers cassette with 2-4 songs on demo. SASE. Reports in 1 month.
**Music:** R&B, rock, soul and top 40/pop. Recently published "Do It to Me and I'll Do It to You" and "Once You Fall in Love" (by Billy Nichols), recorded by Rena/Factory Beat Records; and "Lead Me to Love" (by Brad Smiley), recorded by Carmen John/Factory Beat Records (ballad/dance).
**Tips:** "Send lead sheets and a good, almost finished cassette ready for producing or remixing."

**\*GARY REVEL MUSIC**, 1551 N. Western Ave., Los Angeles CA 90027. (213)467-6647 (Go-Songs). President: Linda Revel. Music publisher. ASCAP. Publishes 20 songs/year; publishes 4 new songwriters/year. Pays standard royalty.

**How to Contact:** Write or call about your interest; submit demo tape and lyric sheet. Prefers cassette with 1-12 songs on demo. SASE. Reports in1 month.
**Music:** Mostly top 40/pop; also blues, children's, church/religious, C&W, rock and rockabilly. Recently published "Pac Man on Her Mind" (by Gary Revel and Joe Yore), "Wouldn't It Be Nice" (by G. Revel), and "Lovin' Wine" (by G. and Linda Revel), all recorded by Gary Revel/Tops Records (top 40).

**\*WM. REZEY MUSIC CO.,** Box 1257, Albany NY 12201. (518)438-4333. President: Wm. Rezey. Music publisher and record producer. BMI. Publishes 15 songs/year; publishes 2 new songwriters/year. Pays standard royalty.
**How to Contact:** Submit demo tape and lyric sheet. Prefers cassette with 3 songs on demo. SASE. Reports in 3 weeks.
**Music:** Mostly rock and top 40; also church/religious and R&B. Recently published "Gotta Find a Job" (by Gary Tash), "That Girl Is Leaving You" (by Daley and Tash), and "No Place to Go" (by Sagendorf, Rivera and Tash), all recorded by Emerald City Band.

**RHYTHMS PRODUCTIONS,** Whitney Bldg., Box 34485, Los Angeles CA 90034. Affiliate: Tom Thumb Music (ASCAP). President: Ruth White. Music publisher and record company. ASCAP. Member NARAS, AFM. Publishes 3-4 LPs/year. Pays negotiable royalty.
**How to Contact:** Submit lead sheet with letter outlining background in educational children's music. Prefers cassette. SASE. Reports in 1 month.
**Music:** "We're only interested in children's songs for the education market. Our materials are sold primarily in schools, so artists/writers with a teaching background would be most likely to understand our requirements." Recently published "Musical Math" and "Musical Reading," (by D. White and R. White), recorded by Gris and Sotello/Tom Thumb Records (children's educational); and several volumes of the series "Action Songs" (by J. Mandel and others), recorded by Mandel/Tom Thumb Records (children's educational).

**RMS TRIAD PUBLISHING,** 6267 Potomac Circle, West Bloomfield MI 48033. (313)661-5167. Affiliates: RMS (ASCAP), Triad (BMI). Contact: Bob Szajner. Music publisher, record company and record producer. ASCAP. Member NMPA and AR of M. Publishes 3 songs/year; publishes 1 new songwriter/year. Pays negotiable royalty.
**How to Contact:** Write first about your interest. Prefers cassette with 2-4 songs on demo. SASE. Reports in 3 weeks.
**Music:** Jazz. Recently published "Flying Horace," "Meeting Competition," "Extra Light," and "Reminiscence" (all by Bob Szajner), recorded by Triad/RMS Records (mainstream jazz instrumentals).

**\*ROBJEN MUSIC,** Box 186, Cedarburg WI 53012. (414)673-5091. Publisher: Robert Wiegert. Music publisher, record company and record producer. BMI. Publishes 50 songs/year; publishes 1 new songwriter/year. Pays standard royalty.
**How to Contact:** Write first about your interest; submit demo tape and lyric sheet. Prefers 7½ ips reel-to-reel or cassette with 1-3 songs on demo. SASE. Reports in 1 month.
**Music:** "Right now we are looking for contemporary Christian music." Recently published "I Believed In You" by Bob Wiegert and Cathy Bemis/Abacus Records (pop); "I Think It's Gonna Rain" by B. Wiegert ad B. Armatoski/Abacus Records (MOR/country); and "I'd Be Satisfied" by Bob Wiegert, Cathy Bemis and Katie McGivin/Abacus Records (pop).

**\*ROCKEN RYTHMN PUBLISHING,** Box 12752, Memphis TN 38182-0752. (901)276-2113. A&R Director: Bill Lusk. Music publisher, record company and record producer. BMI. Member MIM, TBF. Publishes varied number of songs/year; publishes 2 new songwriters/year. Pays standard royalty.
**How to Contact:** Submit demo tape and lyric sheet. Prefers cassette with 1-4 songs on demo. "Specify number of songs on the tape." SASE, but "We would like the option of keeping tape on file." Reports in 1 month.
**Music:** Mostly rock, pop, R&B and blues; also MOR, soul and top 40/pop. Recently published "Where You Want Me" and "Straight and Narrow Line" (by B. Lusk and T. Fosko), recorded by B. Lusk.

**ROCKET PUBLISHING,** 125 Kensington High St., London, W8 3NT, England. 44-01-938-1741.
**How to Contact:** Submit demo tape and lyric sheet. Prefers cassette with 1-5 songs on demo. "Please include lyric or lead sheets, your name, address, phone number, and International Reply Coupons." Does not return unsolicited material. Reports in 1 month.
**Music:** Disco, R&B and rock. Recently published "Empty Garden" (by Elton John and Bernie Taupin), recorded by E. John; and "Blue Eyes" by E. John and Gary Osbourne.

Music Publishers **93**

**ROCKMORE MUSIC**, 1733 Carmona Ave., Los Angeles CA 90019. (213)933-6521. Music publisher and record company. Contact: Willie H. Rocquemore. BMI. Publishes 4 songs/year; publishes 2 new songwriters/year. Pays 10% royalties USA; 50% foreign countries.
**How to Contact:** Submit demo tape and lyric sheet. Prefers 7½ ips reel-to-reel with 4 songs maximum on demo. SASE. Reports in 1 month.
**Music:** Blues, dance, R&B, soul and top 40/pop. Recently published "I Can't Complain" (ballad), "Let's Just Fake It for Tonight" (R&R), and "Summer Lovers" (MOR), recorded by Jennifer Jayson/Rockin! Records.
**Tips:** "Listen to radios POP songs."

**ROCKY BELL MUSIC**, Box 3247, Shawnee KS 66203. (913)631-6060. Affiliates: White Cat Music (ASCAP); Comstock Records; and Murual Management Association. Professional Manager: Frank Fara. Producer/Arranger: Patty Yeats Parker. Music publisher, record company, record producer and management firm. BMI. Member CMA, GMA, ACME, MACE, BCCMA, BBB. Publishes 60 songs/year; "75% of our published songs are from non-charted and developing writers." Pays standard royalties.
**How to Contact:** Arrange personal interview or submit demo tape. Cassette only with 1-5 songs on demo. SASE. Reports in 2 weeks.
**Music:** C&W. Recently released *A Part of Me* (by Eric Bach and Andrew Wolf), recorded by Don TeBeaux; "The Last Desperado" (by Allen Green), recorded by Buddi Day; "From Where I Sit I Can See Where I Stand" (by Dusty McKinney), recorded by Gary Mahnken; "Oklahoma Memories" (by Max Reinhart and Charlie Beth), recorded by Reg Watkins and Lori Kristin; "Falling Apart at the Seams" (by Charles Kennedy and Inez Polizzi), recorded by D. TeBeaux; and "Photographs" (by Dave Kalman), recorded by Roman Gregory.
**Tips:** "We need up-tempo tunes especially in both country and gospel fields. Also need tunes by Canadian writers since we work both US and Canadian markets/artists."

**ROCKY'S RAGDOLL PUBLISHING**, Box 13781, 205A Television Circle, Savannah GA 31406. (912)927-1761. President: David M. Evans. Music publisher. BMI. Member CMA, NSAI. Publishes 8-12 songs/year; publishes 1-2 new songwriters/year. Pays standard royalty.
**How to Contact:** Submit demo tape and lyric sheet. Prefers cassette with 1-5 songs on demo. SASE. Reports in 3 weeks.
**Music:** C&W, rock (new wave, country) and top 40/pop. Recently published "Running Around" (by D. Maxwell-M. Price), recorded by Ronnie Sullivan/Brandwood Records (country); "Maybe Next Time Around" (by J. Roberson), recorded by Jeff Willis (country); and "Monday Night Cheatin' " (by J. Roberson and A. Fleetwood), recorded by Moe Bandy/Columbia Records (country).
**Tips:** "Songs should have simple lyric, good hook, sing along melody."

**ROHM MUSIC**, 10 George St., Box 57, Wallingford CT 06492. (203)265-0010. Affiliate: Trod Nossel Artists Records and Management (BMI). A&R Director: Doug Snyder. President: Thomas Doc Cavalier. Music publisher. BMI. Publishes 35-50 songs/year.
**How to Contact:** Submit demo tape. Prefers cassette with 1-4 songs on demo. SASE. Reports in 1 month."
**Music:** Rock, soul, R&B and top 40/pop. Recently published "This Guy's Got Trouble" and "Tidal Wave" (by Robert Elliott), recorded by The B. Willie Smith Band/TNA Records; and "They Don't Love You (Like I Do)" (by Christine Ohlman), recorded by C. Ohlman and the Soul Rockers.

*****RONDOR MUSIC (AUSTRALIA) PTY., LTD.**, 570 Military Rd., Mosman, Sydney, NSW 2088, Australia. 61-9696266. Managing Director: Bob Aird. Music publisher. APRA, Australasian Mechanical Copyright Owners Society. Member AMPAL, Country Music (Australia), Songwriters Association. Publishes 3 new songwriters/year. Pays negotiable royalty; royalties paid to US songwriters through US publishing affiliate.
**How to Contact:** Submit demo tape and lyric sheet. Prefers 15 ips reel-to-reel with 4-10 songs on demo. "Good quality demos are obviously more effective." Does not return unsolicited material. Reports in 3 weeks.
**Music:** Mostly C&W and top 40; also dance-oriented, MOR and rock. Recently published "Our Love Is on the Faultline" (by Reece Kirk), recorded by Crystal Gale; "One Perfect Day" (by Roger Hart-Wells), recorded by the Little Herdes; and "Choir Girl" (by Don Walker), recorded by Cold Chisel.

**ROOTS MUSIC**, Box 111, Sea Bright NJ 07760. President: Robert Bowden. Vice President: Jean Schweitzer. Music publisher. BMI. Publishes 2 songs/year; publishes 2 new songwriters/year. Pays standard royalty.
**How to Contact:** Submit demo tape and lyric sheet. Prefers cassette with any number songs on demo. "I

only want inspired songs written by talented writers." SASE. Reports in 1 month.
**Music:** Mostly country; also church/religious, classical, folk, MOR, progressive, rock (soft, mellow) and top 40/pop.

**BRIAN ROSS MUSIC**, 7120 Sunset Blvd., Hollywood CA 90046. (213)851-2500; 662-3121. Affiliates: Thrush (BMI), New High (ASCAP) and IMC (ASCAP). President/Professional Manager: Brian Ross. Music publisher, record company, record producer and worldwide music representatives and administrators. BMI; also member of all foreign performance societies. Member CCC, AIMP, NARAS. Publishes 70-200 songs/year; publishes 35 new songwriters/year. Sometimes hires staff writers; pays about $1,000-1,500/month as an advance against future royalties from songs. Pays standard royalty.
**How to Contact:** Submit demo tape and lyric sheet. Prefers cassette with 1-6 songs on demo. Print your name on both cassette and cassette box. SASE. Reports in 1 week.
**Music:** Mostly top 40/pop, contemporary and MOR; also disco, new wave and techno-pop. Recently published "Talk Talk" (by Sean BonniWell), recorded by Alice Cooper (new wave); "I'm on Fire" (by Robert Jason), recorded by Barry White (R&B ballad); and "Makin' Love" (by R. Jason), recorded by Didi Anthony (R&B ballad).
**Tips:** "Be unique, innovative and extraordinary. Let us know about you as a person so that we have a background on your creative ability. If you play an instrument, perform your own material. Also, tell us who you think should record your song."

**ROTHSTEIN MUSIC, LTD.**, 720 E. 79th St., Brooklyn NY 11236. (212)444-3283. Affiliate: Adam Jan Music (ASCAP). President: Sharon Rothstein. Music publisher. Estab. 1981. BMI. Member NMPA. Publishes 20 songs/year; publishes 3 new songwriters/year. Pays standard royalty.
**How to Contact:** Submit demo tape and lyric sheet. Cassette only with 2-4 songs on demo. SASE. Reports in 1 month.
**Music:** C&W, easy listening, MOR, R&B, rock and top 40/pop.

**ROUND SOUND MUSIC**, 1918 Wise Dr., Dothan AL 36303. (205)794-9067. President: Jerry Wise. Music publisher. BMI. Member CMA, GMA. Publishes 10-20 songs/year, publishes 5-10 new songwriters/year. Pays standard royalty.
**How to Contact:** Write first about your interest, then submit demo tape and lyric sheet. Prefers 7½ ips reel-to-reel or cassette with 1-6 songs on demo. SASE. Reports in 1 month.
**Music:** C&W, easy listening, MOR, rock, soul and top 40/pop.
**Tips:** "Songs must be commercial."

**ROWILCO**, Box 8135, Chicago IL 60680. (312)224-5612. Professional Manager: R.C. Hillsman. Music publisher. BMI. Publishes 8-20 songs/year.
**How to Contact:** Arrange personal interview or submit demo tape and lyric sheet. Prefers 7½ or 15 ips quarter-inch reel-to-reel with 4-6 songs on demo. Submissions should be sent via registered mail. SASE. Reports in 3 weeks.
**Music:** Blues, church/religious, C&W, disco, easy listening, gospel, jazz, MOR, rock and top 40/pop.

**ROYAL FLAIR PUBLISHING**, 106 Navajo, Council Bluffs IA 51501. (712)366-1136. Music publisher and record producer. BMI. Publishes 15-20 songs/year; publishes 3 new songwriters/year. Pays standard royalties.
**How to Contact:** Query. Prefers cassette with 2-6 songs on demo. SASE. Reports in 1 month.
**Music:** Old time country. Recently published "I Like It Raw" (by Bob Everhart); "Jack Darby" (by B. Everhart); and "These Eyes" (by B. Everhart/Oliver Armstrong), all recorded by B. Everhart/Folkways Records (neo-country).
**Tips:** "Song definitely has to have old-time country flavor with all the traditional values of country music. No sex, outlandish swearing, or drugs-booze type songs are acceptable."

**RUBICON MUSIC**, 8319 Lankershim Blvd., North Hollywood CA 91605. (213)875-1775. Affiliate: Dunamis Music (ASCAP) and Piro Music (ASCAP). Vice President/Music Publishing: Teri Piro. Professional Manager: Teri Piro. Music publisher. Members NMPA, ASCAP, BMI. Publishes 50 songs/year; publishes 10 new songwriters/year. Pays standard royalty.
**How to Contact:** Submit demo tape and lyric sheet. Cassette with maximum 3 songs on demo. SASE. Reports in 1 month.
**Music:** Choral; church/religious; C&W; disco; easy listening; folk; gospel; jazz; MOR; progressive; R&B; rock; soul and top 40/pop. Recently published "Holding onto Yesterday" (by David Pack and Joe Puerta), recorded by Ambrosia/20th Century Fox Records (pop); "How Much I Feel" and "The Biggest Part of Me" (by David Pack), recorded by Ambrosia/Warner Bros. Records (pop); "Sometimes Alleluia," (by Chuck Girard), recorded by Chuck Girard/Good News Records (contemporary gospel); "You're the Only Woman," (by David Pack), recorded by Ambrosia/Warner Bros. Records (pop).

# Close-up

**Amy Grant**
Performer/Songwriter

In 1983, at the age of 21, contemporary Christian singer Amy Grant's album *Age to Age* won her a Grammy (Best Contemporary Album) and three Dove Awards (Artist of the Year, Best Album of the Year, and Best Album Cover).

Grant's music career had started years before that, however. She grew up in Houston—later Nashville—listening to the sounds of such singers as Carol King and James Taylor. By the age of 14 she was serious enough about music to begin writing songs. At 15, a tape of songs she had written landed her a recording contract with Word Records in Nashville.

Since then, Grant has not only finished high school but attended Vanderbilt University. She also performs annually at over 80 concerts across the country as well as making appearances with groups such as the Bill Gaither Trio and the Billy Graham Crusade.

Grant, who describes her music as pop with Christian lyrics says: "People have been talking about the same personal experience of walking with Christ for centuries. Today it needs to be said in new and different ways."

Her advice to songwriters wishing to write about the Christian experience is good advice for any songwriter wanting to write about *any* experience. (She is in fact married to songwriter Gary Chapman who penned the country hit "Finally," recorded by T.G. Sheppard.)

"Less is more," says Grant. "If you can state an idea simply, more people will understand it. Pick a concise topic—*one* feeling or *one* thought. Figure out exactly what you are trying to say, and then say it in one sentence. Then, think of a very *hooky* way to express that idea and build your song around that hook.

"A song is rarely more than three minutes long, and maybe only fifteen lines. You must somehow capture your feeling—get your message across—in that three minutes and in those fifteen lines. As you write your song, keep checking and rechecking lines to make sure what you've written is pointing to where you want the song to go."

Grant also advises songwriters "never assume a song has gotten through (to the person you're playing it for) after the first pitch. You never know what kind of a day the person you're playing a song for has had. He just might not be in the frame of mind to be receptive and able to hear what your song is saying. But, if you really believe a song is fantastic, it is important that you keep on pitching it."

Amy Grant accepts her success gratefully, and humbly: "I do what I do because of the love of Christ." It is that attitude toward music and career that most characterizes the Christian music field.

—*Dean Kuroff*

**RUSTRON MUSIC PUBLISHERS**, 200 Westmoreland Ave., White Plains NY 10606. (914)946-1689. Director: Rusty Gordon. Professional Manager: Ron Caruso. Music publisher. BMI. Member AGAC, AFTRA, Harry Fox Organization. Publishes 10-25 songs/year; publishes 6-10 new songwriters/year. Pays standard royalty; uses AGAC contract.
**How to Contact:** Arrange personal interview or submit demo tape and lead or lyric sheet. Prefers cassette or 7½ ips reel-to-reel. "Put leader between all songs and at the beginning and end of the tape. Use a tape box. Label it." SASE. Reports in 10 weeks.
**Music:** C&W (contemporary or story songs), disco, easy listening, folk (folk-rock), MOR, rock (pop or soft) and top 40/pop (originals only). Recently published "Rhythm of the Music" (by Gordon and Caruso), recorded by Lois Britten/Rustron Records (pop/disco); "Piece of the Pie" (by Gordon and Caruso) (salsa/disco) and "El Amor" (by Camilo Aceuedo) (Spanish ballad), recorded by Christian Camilo/Rustron Records and Alhambra International (Spanish ballad); and "Love in the Music" (by Gordon and Caruso), recorded by Dianne Mower/Rustron Records (pop/rock).
**Tips:** "Write strong hooks, unpredictable melodies and interesting chord changes. We want 2½- to 3½-minute well-crafted songs with unusual and interesting concepts, commercially marketable for today's sound."

**S.M.C.L. PRODUCTIONS, INC.**, 450 E. Beaumont Ave., St. Bruno, Quebec, Canada J3V 2R3. (514)653-7838. Affiliates: A.Q.E.M. Ltee (CAPAC), Bag Enrg. (CAPAC), C.F. Music (CAPAC), Big Bazaar Music (CAPAC), Sunrise Music (CAPAC), Stage One Music (CAPAC), L.M.S. Ltee (CAPAC), ITT Music (CAPAC), Machine Music (CAPAC) and Dynamite Music (CAPAC). President: Christian Lefort. Music publisher and record company. CAPAC. Publishes 100 songs/year.
**How to Contact:** Submit demo tape and lead sheet. Prefers 7½ ips reel-to-reel with 4-12 songs on demo. SAE and IRC. Reports in 1 month.
**Music:** Dance, easy listening, MOR and top 40/pop. Recently published "Put Your Feet to the Beat," recorded by the Ritchie Family/Able Records (disco); and "Take a Chance," recorded by Queen Samantha/Able Records (disco).

**S & R MUSIC PUBLISHING CO.**, 39 Belmont, Rancho Mirage CA 92270. (619)346-0075. Contact: Dolores Gulden. Affiliates: Meteor Music (BMI) and Boomerang Music (BMI). ASCAP. Member AIMP and NMPA. Publishes 100 songs/year; publishes 50 new songwriters/year. Pays standard royalty.
**How to Contact:** Submit demo tape and lyric sheet. Prefers 7½ ips reel-to-reel or cassette with 1-4 songs on demo. SASE. Reports in 2 weeks.
**Music:** "We are mostly interested in lyrics or melodies for instrumentals." Recently published "A Touch of Love" (by Buddy Merrill), recorded by B. Merrill (MOR); "My Easy Side" (by Kirby Hamilton), recorded by K. Hamilton (jazz); and "Banyan Bay" (by Chet Demilo) (MOR).

**THE S.R.O. PUBLISHING GROUP,** (formerly Core Music Publishing), 189 Carlton St., Toronto, Ontario, Canada M5A 2K7. (416)923-5855. Affiliates: Core Music Publishing (CAPAC), Mark-Cain Music (CAPAC) and Brandy Music (BMI). Vice-President: Pegi Cecconi. A&R Director: Val Azzoli. Music publisher with affiliated management, record and production companies. CAPAC. Member CMPA. Publishes 20-30 songs/year; publishes 1 new songwriter/year. Pays standard royalty.
**How to Contact:** Submit demo tape with bio material. Cassettes *only* with maximum of 3 songs on demo. SAE and IRC. Reports in 6 weeks. Does not accept unsolicited material.
**Music:** Progressive, rock and top 40/pop. Recently published "New World Man" (by Lee/Lifeson/Peart), recorded by Rush/Polygram Anthem Records (Canada) (rock); "Hold On" (by Ian Thomas), recorded by Santana/CBS Records; and "Right Before Your Eyes" (by Ian Thomas), recorded by America/Capitol Records.

*****SABRE MUSIC**, Box 702, Snowdon Station, Montreal, Quebec, Canada H3X 3X8. Affiliate: Montina Music (CAPAC). Professional General Manager: D. Leonard. Music publisher. CAPAC. Member MIEA. Pays standard royalty.
**How to Contact:** Submit demo tape and lyric sheet. Prefers 7½ or 15 ips reel-to-reel, cassette or record as demo. Does not return unsolicited material.
**Music:** Mostly top 40; also blues, C&W, dance-oriented, easy listening, folk, gospel, jazz, MOR, progressive, R&B, rock, soul and pop.

**SAFMAR PUBLISHING CO.**, Box 978, Mooresville NC 28115. (704)663-4892. Manager: Jack Safrit. Music publisher. BMI. Publishes 10 songs/year. Pays standard royalty.
**How to Contact:** Submit demo tape and lyric sheet or write or call first about your interest. Prefers cassette with 2-5 songs on demo. SASE. Reports in 2 weeks.
**Music:** Mostly C&W; also bluegrass, gospel and beach. Recently published "Good Ole Country Music," "Goodbye Forever," and "Cold Hearted Woman" (by Martin & Safrit), recorded by Craig Martin (country).

Music Publishers **97**

**SASHA SONGS, UNLTD. & THE GRAND PASHA PUBLISHER**, Division of The Pasha Music Org., Inc., 5615 Melrose, Hollywood CA 90038. (213)466-3507. President: Spencer D. Proffer. General Manager: Carol Peters. Send material to Lyn Corey-Benson, A&R Director. Music publisher, record production company and independent label distributed by CBS. BMI. Publishes 60 songs/year; publishes 3-4 new songwriters/year. Pays standard royalty.
**How to Contact:** Write first about your interest. Prefers cassette with 2-3 songs on demo. SASE. Reports in 3 weeks.
**Music:** Mostly rock and top 40/pop; also progressive. Recently published "Take a Little Bit" (by S. Proffer, et al), recorded by Eddie Money/Columbia Records (top 40/pop); "Mental Health" (by K. DuBron, et al), recorded by Quiet Riot/Pasha Records (rock); and "Eden's Gate" (by Billy Thorpe, et al), recorded by B. Thorpe/Pasha Records (rock progressive).
**Tips:** "Don't forget the hook."

*****SASNRAS MUSIC**, 902 Pinecone Trail, Anderson SC 29621. (803)225-0833. General Manager: Ann Simmons. Music publisher, record company and recording studio. Estab. 1981. BMI. Member CMA, NSAI, NAIRD. Publishes 10-20 songs/year. Pays standard royalty.
**How to Contact:** Submit demo tape and lyric sheet. Prefers cassette with 3-6 songs on demo. "Please label your tape with your name, whether stereo or mono, side A or B, home or studio demo, and include a separate tape schedule listing song titles in playing order." Does not return unsolicited material. Reports in 3 weeks "if interested."
**Music:** Mostly C&W, blues and folk; also easy listening, gospel, jazz, MOR, R&B and rock & roll (50s and 60s). Recently published "Walkin' Joe," "Yes Tennessee, I Love You" and "The Late Letter" (by Roger Alan Simmons and Ann Simmons), recorded by Roger Simmons/Rogersound Records.

*****SAUL AVENUE MUSIC PUBLISHING**, Box 37156, Cincinnati OH 45222. (513)891-2300 or 891-2301. President: Saul Halper. Music publisher. BMI. Member NMPA. Publishes 4 songs/year; publishes 1 new songwriter/year. Pays standard royalty.
**How to Contact:** Submit demo tape and lyric sheet. Prefers cassette with 4 songs on demo. SASE. Reports in 3 weeks.
**Music:** Bluegrass, blues, gospel and R&B.

**SAVGOS MUSIC, INC.**, 342 Westminster Ave., Elizabeth NJ 07208. Affiliate: Jonan Music (ASCAP). Office Manager: Helen Gottesmann. Music publisher. ASCAP. Publishes 150 songs/year; publishes 50 new songwriters/year. Pays standard royalty—50% of mechanical.
**Music:** Publishes only material of artists recording on Savoy Records. Recently published "Deliverance" (by J. Cleveland), recorded by James Cleveland & Cleveland Singers; "Know He Can, Believe He Will" (by Wm. A. Taylor), recorded by J. Cleveland with World's Greatest Gospel Stars Vol. II; "Christ Won't Fail" (by J. Cleveland), recorded by The Craig Brothers; "I Found All That I Need in the Lord" (by Ernest Franklin), recorded by Rev. Ernest Franklin; "I'm Glad to be Here" (by Patricia Punch), recorded by Albertina Walker; "You Can Depend On God" (by David Allen), recorded by The Pentecostal Community Choir; and "Jesus Brought Joy" (by Sullivan Pugh), recorded by The Consolers.

**SCARLET STALLION MUSIC**, Box 902, Provo UT 84603. Contact: Professional Manager. Personal management and concert promotion company. BMI. Publishes 30 songs/year. Pays standard royalty.
**How to Contact:** Submit demo tape and lyric sheet. Prefers cassette with 4-6 songs on demo. SASE. Reports in 3 weeks.
**Music:** C&W (crossover to pop), folk, MOR, rock and top 40/pop. Recently published "Tonight" (by Tom Ivers), recorded by Tyrant (rock/pop); "Arizona Highways" (by Bill Tuddenham), recorded by Dave Boshard (country/pop); and "How Long Has It Been" (by D. Boshard), recorded by D. Boshard (pop/MOR).

**SCHABRAF MUSIC**, 5000 Eggleston Ave., Orlando FL 32810. Affiliates: Solo Gratia (SESAC) and Immunity (ASCAP). President: Eric T. Schabacker. Music publisher, record producer, and recording studio (Bee Jay Studios). BMI. Publishes 20 songs/year; publishes 10 new songwriters/year. Pays standard royalty.
**How to Contact:** Submit demo tape and lyric sheet. Prefers cassette with 1-4 songs on demo. SASE. Reports in 2 weeks.
**Music:** Dance-oriented, easy listening, MOR, progressive, rock, soul, top 40/pop and contemporary Christian. Recently published "Who Loves You" (by Jonathan Fitzwilliam), recorded by Xavier (top 40).

**SCOTTI BROTHERS MUSIC PUBLISHING**, 2114 Pico Blvd., Santa Monica CA 90405. (213)450-4143. Affiliate: Flowering Stone (ASCAP) and Holy Moley (BMI). Professional Managers:

Jeff Harrington and Jeff Penning. Music publisher and record company. BMI, ASCAP. Member NMPA, AIMP, RIAA and CMA. Publishes 40 songs/year; publishes 2 new songwriters/year. Pays standard royalty.
**How to Contact:** Submit demo tape and lyric sheet. Prefers cassette with 1-2 songs on demo. Does not return unsolicited material; "we report only if we're interested."
**Music:** Mostly top 40/pop and country; also easy listening, MOR and rock. Recently published "Eye of the Tiger" (by J. Peterick and F. Sullivan), recorded by Survivor/Scotti Bros.-CBS Records (rock); "Natural Love" (J. Harrington and J. Pennig), recorded by Petula Clark/Scotti Bros.-CBS Records (country-pop); and "Them Good Ol' Boys Are Bad" (J. Harrington and J. Pennig), recorded by John Schneider/Scotti Bros.-CBS Records (country).

**SCREEN GEMS/COLGEMS/EMI MUSIC, INC.**, 1370 Avenue of the Americas, New York NY 10019. (212)489-6740. Affiliate: Colgems (ASCAP). Contact: Professional Manager. Music publisher and record company (Capitol and EMI). BMI. Hires staff writers.
**How to Contact:** Call first about your interest to see if they are accepting material, then submit demo tape and lyric sheet. Prefers cassette with 1-3 songs on demo.
**Music:** All kinds.

**SCULLY MUSIC CO.**, The Sunshine Group, 800 South 4th St., Philadelphia PA 19147. (215)755-7000. Affiliate: Orange Bear Music (BMI). Assistant to President: Michele Quigley. Music publisher and record production company. Member AGAC. Publishes 40 songs/year; publishes 20 songwriters/year. ASCAP. Pays standard royalties.
**How to Contact:** Submit demo tape and lead sheet or disc and lyric sheet. Prefers 7½ ips or cassette with 1-4 songs on demo. SASE. Reports in 1 month.
**Music:** Mostly dance, pop, R&B; also MOR, top 40 and rock. Recently published "The Flute" (by Walter Kahn and Julie Carter), recorded by Pipedream/CBS/Epic Records; "Dr. Jam" (by Mark Miller, Joe Loris, Reuben Cross and W. Kahn), recorded by Men At Play/Sunshine Records; and "You Don't Know What You Got" (by Tom Uzzo, Debbie Stevens and W. Kahn), recorded by Karen Young/Boardwalk Records.

**SEA CRUISE PRODUCTIONS**, Box 1830, Gretna LA 70053. Affiliates: Sea Cruise Music (BMI), Briarmeade Music (ASCAP), Keeta Music (BMI). President/General Manager: Ken Keene. Music publisher, record company, record producer, public relations firm and talent management firm. BMI, ASCAP. Member CMA, NSAI, ACM. Publishes 50 songs/year; publishes 10 new songwriters/year. Pays standard royalty.
**How to Contact:** Submit demo tape and lyric sheet. Prefers 7½ ips reel-to-reel or cassette with 1-10 songs on demo. SASE. Reports in 1 month.
**Music:** Blues, children's, C&W, easy listening, gospel, MOR, R&B, rock, soul and top 40/pop. Recently published "Country Goose" (by Johnny Pennino), recorded by J. Pennino/Sonor Records (country/rock); "Lonely Street" (by Ken Keene and Tom Pallardy), recorded by F. Ford, by F. Ford/Briarmeade Records (ballad/top 40); and "Heaven & Hell" (by F. Ford/Briarmeade Records (blues/top 40).

***SEISMIC MUSIC**, 31 Nassau Ave., Wilmington MA 01887. (617)658-8391. Engineer: Larry Feeney. Music publisher, record company and record producer. ASCAP. Publishes 3 songs/year; publishes 6 new songwriters/year. Pays standard royalty.
**How to Contact:** Write first about your interest; submit demo tape and lyric sheet. Prefers cassette with 2 songs on demo. Does not return unsolicited material. Reports in 1 month.
**Music:** Mostly rock; also bluegrass, blues, C&W, dance-oriented, easy listening, folk, jazz, MOR, progressive, R&B and top 40/pop. Recently published "She'll Drive You Crazy" (by Coulston, Conohan, Giancola), recorded by Wild Turkey/Destiny Records (R&B); and "Push It to the Limit" (by Marc O'Brien), recorded by The Wages/Destiny Records (rock/pop).

**SEPTEMBER MUSIC CORP.**, 250 W. 57th St., New York NY 10019. (212)581-1338. Affiliate: Galahad Music, Inc. President: Stanley Mills. Music publisher. BMI and ASCAP. Member NMPA. Pays standard royalty.
**How to Contact:** Submit demo tape and lyric sheet. Prefers 7½ ips reel-to-reel or cassette with 3 songs maximum on demo. SASE. Reports in 1 month.
**Music:** All types. Recently published "Barbara's Daughter," recorded by Patti Page/Plantation Records; "Dance Little Bird," on GNP Records/Mirus Records; "Rock and Roll You're Beautiful," recorded by B.J. Thomas/Cleveland International Records; and "Paddington and Friends" and "The Songs of Paddington" on Kid Stuff Records.
**Tips:** "Good choruses and lyrics are most important. The song must be different, idea-wise, and tell a complete story."

**SEYAH MUSIC**, Master Audio, Inc., 1227 Spring St. NW, Atlanta GA 30309. (404)873-6425. Affiliates: Paydirt Music (ASCAP) and Lyresong Music (BMI). President: Babs Richardson. Music publisher and recording studio. BMI. Publishes 20 songs/year; publishes 1-2 new songwriters/year. Pays standard royalty.
**How to Contact:** Submit demo tape. Prefers cassette with 2-3 songs on demo. SASE. Reports in 1 month.
**Music:** C&W, disco, gospel, R&B, soul and top 40/pop. Recently published *Great News*, (by Troy Ramey), recorded by T. Ramey and the Soul Searchers/Nashboro Records (black gospel); "Try Jesus," recorded by T. Ramey (gospel); and "Tea Cups and Doilies," (by Mac Frampton), recorded by M. Frampton/Triumvirate Records (Broadway show type).

**SHAWNEE PRESS, INC.**, Delaware Water Gap PA 18327. (717)476-0550. Affiliates: Harold Flammer, Inc. (ASCAP), Glory Sound, Templeton Music (ASCAP), Malcolm Music (BMI) and Choral Press (SESAC). Director of Publications: Lewis M. Kirby Jr. Music publisher and record company. ASCAP. Member NMPA, MPA, CMPA. Publishes 150-200 songs/year; publishes 25 new songwriters/year. Pays royalty negotiated at the time of purchase.
**How to Contact:** Submit demo tape and lead sheet or submit lead sheet. Prefers cassette. SASE. Reports in 2 months.
**Music:** Children's, choral, church/religious, classical, easy listening, folk, gospel, MOR and top 40/pop. "Shawnee Press is primarily a publisher of choral and instrumental music for educational or religious use." Published "Black and White" (by Robinson and Arkin), recorded by Three Dog Night/ABC-Dunhill Records (top 40); "This Is My Country" (by Raye and Jacobs), recorded by Anita Bryant/Columbia Records (patriotic); "Let Me Call You Sweetheart" (by Whitson and Friedman), recorded by Mitch Miller/Columbia Records (easy listening/pop); and "If I Had My Way" (by Kendis and Klein), recorded by the Mills Brothers/Brunswick Records (pop).
**Tips:** "Send material for review suitable for use in schools or churches or for publication/recording for gospel market. Primarily interested in choral music."

**LARRY SHAYNE ENTERPRISES**, #222, 6362 Hollywood Blvd., Hollywood CA 90028. (213)462-1603. Affiliate: Workers Union Music (BMI). Music publisher, record producer and record company. ASCAP. Member NMPA. Publishes 50 songs/year. Pays standard royalty.
**How to Contact:** Query by phone, then submit demo (cassette) and lyric sheet. "I will not return cassettes unless SASE is enclosed." Reports in 2 weeks.
**Music:** Easy listening, jazz, MOR, contemporary rock and top 40/pop. Published "Ode To Billy Joe," "Girl Talk," "Chorus Line" (by Marvin Hamlisch) and "Pink Panther" and "Peter Gunn" (by Henri Mancini).

**SHELTON ASSOCIATES**, 2250 Bryn Mawr Ave., Philadelphia PA 19131. (215)477-7122. A&R Director: Leo Gayton. Adminstrator: Richard Jackson. Music publisher. BMI. Publishes 12 songs/year; publishes 8 new songwriters/year. Pays standard royalty.
**How to Contact:** Submit demo tape. Prefers 7½ ips reel-to-reel or cassette with 3-5 songs on demo. SASE. Reports in 3 weeks.
**Music:** Mostly R&B, top 40; also dance, easy listening, MOR, progressive, R&B, rock, soul and top 40/pop. Recently published "Craving" (by G. Harris), recorded by Giles Crawford (pop); "Do the Funk" (by C. Bevdree), recorded by Galaxy (R&B); "Ain't This Love?" (by R. Covington), recorded by Dream Merchants (R&B); and "Bus Stop" (by Eugene Curry and Fred Bright); recorded by the Lambchops (R&B).

***SHETLAND SOUND**, Box 120023, Nashville TN 37212. Affiliate: Little David Music (BMI). Contact: President. Music publisher and record producer. ASCAP and BMI. Member NMA. Publishes 12 songs/year. Pays standard royalty.
**How to Contact:** Write first about your interest. Prefers cassette with 2-3 songs on demo. SASE.
**Music:** Country.

**SIDEWALK SAILOR MUSIC**, Box 423, Station F, Toronto, Ontario, Canada M4Y 2L8. Affiliates: Etheric Polyphony (CAPAC), Scales of My Head Music (PROCAN), Cumulonimbus Music (PROCAN). Professional Manager: Allen Shechtman. Music publisher and record producer. Member CAPAC, CARAS, CIRPA. Publishes 8-10 songs/year; publishes 1 new songwriter/year. "We recoup any costs from publisher's income, then split publisher's side of income on a 25-75% basis with songwriter (25 percent)."
**How to Contact:** Submit demo tape and lyric sheet. Prefers 7½-15 ips reel-to-reel or cassette with 3 songs on demo. "Check your songs before you send them to anyone. Make sure they are your best ef-

forts and have been reworked to make them as accessible as possible." SAE and IRC. Reports in 3 months.
**Music:** Progressive, AOR, electronic, pop and country. Recently published "I'm Dancing Alone" (by Lloyd Landa), recorded by M. Evans (pop/C&W); "Open Up Our Hearts" (by L. Landa), recorded by Irene Atmay and Jesse Collins (R&B ballad); and "The River Song" (by L. Landa), recorded by I. Atmay (pop ballad).

**SILHOUETTE MUSIC,** Box 218, Wellman Heights, Johnsonville SC 29555. (803)386-2600. Affiliates: Bridge Music (BMI) and Heraldic Music (ASCAP). Director: Erv Lewis. Music publisher and record company. SESAC. Member GMA. Publishes 15-40 songs/year; publishes 3 new songwriters/year.
**How to Contact:** Submit demo tape and lyric sheet. Prefers cassette with 3-6 songs on demo. "Record the tape on one side only, as we use mono equipment on playback." SASE. Reports in 2 months.
**Music:** Church/religious and gospel. Recently published "He Is" (by Jerry Arhelger), recorded by Jerry Arhelger/Herald Records (gospel); "Jesus Can" (by Erv Lewis), recorded by Sydna Taylor/Herald Records (gospel); and "Hold On Children" (by Erv Lewis), recorded by Judith Friday/Herald Records (gospel).

**SILICON MUSIC PUBLISHING CO.,** 222 Tulane St., Garland TX 75043. President: Gene Summers. Vice President: Deanna L. Summers. Public Relations: Steve Summers. Music publisher. BMI. Publishes 10-20 songs/year. Pays standard royalty.
**How to Contact:** Submit demo tape. Prefers cassette with 1-2 songs on demo. Does not return unsolicited material.
**Music:** C&W, MOR and rock. Recently published "Mister Misery" (by Chuck Hall), recorded by C. Hall/Wilco Records; "Hangover Blues" (by Bill Kelly and Bill Ashley), recorded by Jonny Reb/Domino Records; "Taxation, Inflation and Depreciation" (by Herb Wilson), recorded by H. Wilson/Domino Records; "Hot Pants" (by Dea Summers, Bill Smith and Dan Edwards), recorded by Gene Summers/W&G Records (Australia); "Baby Please Tell Me Why" (by John Rathburn and D. Summers); and "Sid, Johnny, Joe, Mac & Me" (by G. Summers).
**Tips:** "We are very interested in 50s rock and rockabilly *original masters* for release through overseas affiliates. If you are the owner of any 50s masters, contact us first! We have releases in Holland, Switzerland, England, Belgium, France, Sweden, Norway and Australia. We have the market if you have the tapes. In conjunction with Domino Records and overseas affiliates, we have established the National Rockabilly Hall of Fame. All candidates for induction consideration should be directed to: Awards and Induction Committee; c/o Silicon Music, BMI."

**SILVER BLUE PRODUCTIONS, LTD.,** 220 Central Park S., New York NY 10019. Affiliate: Silver Blue Music (ASCAP) and Oceans Blue Music (BMI). President: Joel Diamond. Music publisher and record producer.
**How to Contact:** Submit demo tape and lead sheet. Prefers cassette with 3 songs on demo. SASE. Reports in 3 weeks "only if we are interested in the material."
**Music:** Top 40/pop and AC. Recently published "After the Lovin' " and "This Moment in Time" (by Richie Adams and Alan Bernstein), recorded by Englebert Humperdink (AC and top 40/pop); and "Let's Just Stay Home Tonight" (by Lottie Golden and Richard Scher), recorded by Helen Reddy.

**SHELBY SINGLETON MUSIC INC.,** 3106 Belmont Blvd., Nashville TN 37212. (615)385-1960. Affiliates: Prize (ASCAP), Green Isle (ASCAP) and Green Owl (BMI). Professional Manager: Sidney Singleton. Music publisher and record company. BMI. Member NMPA. Publishes 200 songs/year; publishes 10 new songwriters/year. Pays standard royalties.
**How to Contact:** Submit demo tape and lyric sheet. Prefers cassette. SASE. Reports "as soon as possible.".
**Music:** C&W, easy listening, easy rock and top 40/pop.

**SIRLOIN MUSIC PUBLISHING CO.,** Suite 303, 14045 S. Main, Houston TX 77035. (713)641-0793 or (713)645-5391. President: Roger L. Cummings. Music publisher. BMI. Member AGAC. Publishes 36 songs/year; publishes 4 new songwriters/year. Pays standard royalty.
**How to Contact:** Submit demo tape and lyric sheet. Prefers cassette with 3-6 songs on demo. SASE. Reports in 1 month.
**Music:** Blues, C&W, gospel, jazz, R&B, rock, soul and top 40/pop. Recently published "Let's Get On Down" (by Steve Cummings), recorded by Friction/Happy Beat Records (top 40); "Let Me Add Sunshine" (by Roger Cummings), recorded by Ralph Lowe/Columbine Records (country); and "She's Right On Time" (by R. Cummings), recorded by Richey Cee/Fox Century Records (soul).

**SIVATT MUSIC PUBLISHING CO.**, Box 7172, Greenville SC 29610. (803)295-3177. President: Jesse B. Evatte. Music publisher and record company. BMI. Publishes 20 songs/year; publishes 5 new songwriters/year. Pays standard royalty.
**How to Contact:** Submit demo tape and lead sheet. Prefers cassette with 2-6 songs on demo. SASE. Reports in 1 month.
**Music:** Bluegrass, church/religious, C&W, easy listening, folk and gospel. Recently published "L-O-V-E" (by Johnny Halloway), recorded by the Gospel Jubilee (gospel); and "His Bride" (by David Abbott), recorded by Abbott/Mark Five Records (gospel).

*****MACK SMITH MUSIC**, 814 W. Claiborne St., Box 672, Greenwood MS 38930. (601)453-3302. Contact: Mack Allen Smith. Music publisher and record company. BMI. Pays standard royalty.
**How to Contact:** Submit demo tape and lead or lyric sheet. Prefers cassette with 1-5 songs on demo. SASE. Reports in 1 month.
**Music:** C&W, rock and top 40/pop. Recently published "If I Could Get One More Hit" (by Mack Allen Smith), recorded by James O'Gwynn/Plantation Records (country); and "Angel Face Body Full of Sin" and "Who the Heck is Bob Wills?" (by Smith), recorded by M.A. Smith/Ace Records (country).

**SNAPFINGER MUSIC**, Box 35158, Decatur GA 30035. Affiliate: Hand Clappin' Music (ASCAP). Contact: Don Bryant. Music publisher. Publishes 12 songs/year; various number of new songwriters/year. Pays standard royalty.
**How to Contact:** Submit demo tape and typed lyric sheet. Prefers cassette with 1-2 songs on demo. SASE. Reports in 1 month.
**Music:** Mostly country, R&B, pop; also easy listening, gospel, MOR, rock and top 40. Recently published "Women's Liberation" (by John Farley) and "In a Class by Myself" (by Louis Brown), both recorded by Don Bryant (country); and "Destination Love" (by Corky Threadkill), recorded by Curtis Reed (R&B).

**SNOOPY MUSIC**, 3156 Gifford Lane, Coconut Grove FL 33133. Director of A&R: Jim Rudd. Music publisher, record company, record producer and recording studio. BMI. Member AFTRA. Publishes 1-5 songs/year; publishes 3 new songwriters/year. Pays standard royalty.
**How to Contact:** Submit demo tape and lead sheet. Prefers cassette with 1-3 songs on demo. SASE. Reports in 3-4 weeks.
**Music:** Country rock and adult contemporary.

**SONE SONGS**, 10101 Woodlake Dr., Cockeysville MD 21030. General Manager: George Brigman. Music publisher. BMI. Publishes 10-20 songs/year; publishes 1-2 new songwriters/year. Pays standard royalty.
**How to Contact:** Submit demo tape and lyric sheet. Prefers 7½ ips reel-to-reel with 1-6 songs on demo. SASE. Reports in 3 weeks.
**Music:** Blues, C&W, disco, easy listening, folk, gospel, jazz, MOR, progressive, R&B, rock, soul and top 40/pop. Recently published "Nashville" and "Lovin' You" (by Brigman and Amos), recorded by J. Butterworth/Equinox Records (country); and "My Cherie," "Blowin' Smoke" and "Drifting" (by Brigman), recorded by Split/Solid Records (rock, jazz).

**SONG FARM MUSIC**, Box 24561, Nashville TN 37202. (615)242-1037. President: Tom Pallardy. Music publisher and record producer. BMI. Member NSAI. Publishes 2-3 songs/year; publishes 1-2 new songwriters/year. Pays standard royalty.
**How to Contact:** Submit demo tape and lyric or lead sheet. Prefers cassette with 2 songs on demo. SASE. Reports in 1 month.
**Music:** C&W, crossover and top 40/pop. Recently published "After Every Goodbye" (by Tom and Jo Pallardy), recorded by Lisa Ward/Whitehorse Records (positive/uptempo); "Only You Can Stop the Rain" (by T. Pallardy), recorded by Jerry Hopper (country; and "Another Heartache" (by Annette Lumsden), recorded by Carl Finney (country).
**Tips:** "Material should be submitted neatly and professionally with as good quality demo as possible. Songs need not be elaborately produced (voice and guitar/piano are fine) but they should be clear. Songs must be well constructed, lyrically tight, good strong hook, interesting melody, easily remembered; i.e., commercial!"

*****SONG OF SONGS MUSIC**, Box 219, Langhorne PA 19047. (215)757-4144. Director: Barbara Riffe. Music publisher. Estab. 1981. ASCAP. Publishes 5 songs/year; publishes 1 new songwriter/year. Pays standard royalty.
**How to Contact:** Submit demo tape and lyric sheet. Prefers cassette with 2-4 songs on demo. SASE. Reports in 3 weeks.

**Music:** C&W, easy listening, folk, jazz, MOR, Spanish and top 40/pop. Recently published *A Collection of Jazz*, by Pedro Iturralde (a song folio for college and university distribution).

**SONG TAILORS MUSIC CO.**, Box 2631, Muscle Shoals AL 35660. (205)381-1455. Affiliate: I've Got the Music (ASCAP). General Manager: Kevin Lamb. Music publisher. BMI. Publishes 100 songs/year. Pays standard royalty.
**How to Contact:** Submit demo tape and lead sheet. Prefers 7½ or 15 ips reel-to-reel or cassette with 1-3 songs on demo. SASE. Reports "as soon as possible."
**Music:** Blues, C&W, dance, easy listening, folk, jazz, MOR, progressive, rock, soul and top 40/pop. Recently published "Get It Up" (by Byrne and Brasfield), recorded by Ronnie Milsap/RCA Records (pop); "Slippen Up Slippin Around" (by Wyrick and Woodford), recorded by Christy Lane/United Artist Records (country); "Here Comes the Hurt Again" (by Johnson), recorded by Manhattan/CBS Records (R&B); "Old Flame" (by Lowery and McAnally), recorded by Alabama Band; "Hold Me Like You Never Had Me" (by Byrne and Brasfield), recorded by Randy Parton; "It's My Job" (by McAnally), recorded by Jimmy Buffet; and "That Didn't Hurt Too Bad" (by Byne and Brasfield), recorded by Dr. Hook.

**SONGLINE MUSIC**, 1909 Clemson Dr., Richardson TX 75081. (214)235-4653. Contact: Eddie Fargason. Music publisher and record producer. BMI. Member GMA. Produces 6 songs/year; publishes 4 new songwriters/year. Pays standard royalty.
**How to Contact:** Submit demo tape and lyric sheet. Prefers 7½ ips reel-to-reel or cassette with 1-3 songs on demo. SASE. Reports in 1 month.
**Music:** C&W (pop), gospel, MOR, progressive, R&B and top 40/pop. Recently published "Prop Up Your Brother (On The Leaning Side)," (by Baker/Shuff/Fargason), recorded by Gary Lanier/Hisong Records (gospel); and "Light the Light," (by Fargason), recorded by G. Lanier/Hisong Records (gospel).
**Tips:** "Send only those songs you feel are your most commercial. We are very interested in *positive pop* material."

**SONGS FOR TODAY, INC.**, Suite 409, 50 E. 42nd St., New York NY 10017. (212)687-2299. Affiliates: Sublime Music (BMI), Fresh Memory Music, (ASCAP), Songs for Today, Ltd. (PRS). Vice President: H. Kruger. Music publisher and record company. SESAC. Member Mechanical Copyright Protection Society. Publishes 50 songs/year; publishes 5 new songwriters/year. Pays standard royalty.
**How to Contact:** Submit demo tape and lyric sheet. Prefers 15 ips reel-to-reel or cassette with 1-4 songs on demo. Does not return unsolicited material. Reports in 2 weeks
**Music:** C&W, easy listening, MOR, R&B, soul and top 40/pop.

**SONGS FROM THE BOX**, 5180-B Park Ave., Memphis TN 38119. (901)761-5074. Affiliate: Voice of Paradise (ASCAP). President: Mark Blackwood. Contact: Sparrow Holt. Music publisher, record company and record producer. BMI. Publishes 25 songs/year. Pays standard royalty.
**How to Contact:** Submit demo tape and lyric sheet. Prefers cassette. "Be sure that *both* demo tape and lyric sheet are provided." Does not return unsolicited material. Reports in 1 month.
**Music:** Gospel and contemporary Christian. "We are primarily interested in contemporary and MOR Christian style songs." Recently published "I'm Following You" (by Debi Cox), recorded by Blackwood Brothers/Voice Box Records (Christian); "Life Time Friend" (by D. Cox), recorded by Larry Orrell/Voice Box Records (Christian); "Credit Where Credit Is Due" (by M. Sparrow Holt), recorded by Sparrow/Voice Box Records (Christian); and "We Come to Worship" (by Denny Darrow), recorded by Blackwood Brothers/Voice Box Records (MOR Christian).
**Tips:** "We like a well-structured song with a good hook, strong lead line and fundamental Christian lyric."

**SORO PUBLISHING**, 1322 Inwood Rd., Dallas TX 75247. (214)638-7712. President: Bob Cline. Music publisher. SESAC, TMA. Publishes 20 songs/year; publishes 5 new songwriters/year. Pays standard royalty.
**How to Contact:** Submit demo tape and lyric sheet. Prefers cassette with 2-6 songs on demo. SASE.
**Music:** Contemporary church/religious and gospel. Recently published "If You Need a Touch" (by David Vrnado), and "Heaven's City Limits" (by Kent Carnley), both recorded by Becky Fender/Rainbow Records (contemporary Christian); and "Serve Him" (by K. Carnley), recorded by Bob Thompson/Rainbow Records (contemporary Christian).
**Tips:** "Submit a clear, professional demo tape, and any references or credits to demonstrate a proven track record."

***SOUND IMAGE PUBLISHING**, 6556 Wilkinson, North Hollywood CA 91606. (213)762-8881. Affiliate: Sound Image Publishing (BMI). Vice President: David Chatfield. Music publisher, record

company, record producer and video company. ASCAP. Member NARAS. Publishes 60 songs/year; publishes 3 new songwriters/year. Pays standard royalty.
**How to Contact:** Submit demo tape and lyric sheet. Prefers cassette with 2-6 songs on demo. Does not return unsolicited material. Reports in 1 month.
**Music:** Mostly rock; also dance-oriented, R&B and top 40/pop. Recently published "Sandy" (by Mike Lombardo), recorded by The Secrets (techno-pop); "She Don't Love You" (by George Faber), recorded by G. Faber & Stronghold (R&B/pop); and "Jah Rastafari" (by Reggie Butler), recorded by Jah Moon (reggae).

**SOUTHERN CRESCENT PUBLISHING**, 121 N. 4th St., Easton PA 18042. (215)258-5990. Branch: #5J, 320 W. 30th St., New York NY 10000. (212)564-3246. Affiliate: Ripsaw Record Co. President: James H. Kirkhuff Jr. (Easton). Vice President: Jonathan Strong (New York). Music publisher. BMI. Publishes 5-10 songsyear. Pays standard royalty.
**How to Contact:** Submit demo tape and lyric sheet. Prefers cassette. SASE.
**Music:** Bluegrass, C&W and rockabilly. Recently published "Feelin' Right Tonight" (by Tex Rubinowitz), recorded by Tex Rubinowitz/Ripsaw Records (rockabilly); and "Knock-Kneed Nellie" (by W.C. Hancock Jr.), recorded by Billy Hancock/Ripsaw Records (rockabilly).

**SOUTHERN WRITERS GROUP USA**, Box 40764, Nashville TN 37204. Office Manager: Buzz Cason. Music publisher. BMI, ASCAP. Member NMPA. Publishes 150 songs/year; publishes 1-2 new songwriters/year. Pays standard royalty.
**How to Contact:** "We are not soliciting outside material at this time, and we ask that songwriters not contact us until further notice." Does not return unsolicited material.
**Music:** Blues, C&W, dance, easy listening, folk, jazz, MOR, progressive, R&B, rock, soul and top 40/pop. Recently published "Bluer than Blue" (by Randy Goodrum), recorded by Michael Johnson/EMI (pop); and "She Believes in Me" (by Steve Gibb), recorded by Kenny Rogers/Liberty Records (country/pop).

**SPARROW/BIRDWING MUSIC**, 8025 Deering, Canoga Park CA 91304. (213)703-6599. Affiliates: Birdwing Music (ASCAP), Sparrow Song (BMI), and His Eye Music (SESAC). Director of Publishing: Phil Perkins. Music publisher, record company and record producer. Member CMPA. Publishes 50-100 songs/year; publishes 5 new songwriters/year. Pays standard royalty.
**How to Contact:** Write or call first about your interest, then submit demo tape and lyric sheet. Prefers cassette with 1-3 songs on demo. "A lead sheet is helpful, and a typewritten lyric sheet is essential. Also include a list of qualifications and credentials." SASE. Reports in 3-4 months.
**Music:** Mostly contemporary Christian; also children's, church/religious and choral.

**BEN SPEER MUSIC**, 54 Music Square W., Box 40201, Nashville TN 37204. (615)329-9999. Affiliates: Emmanuel Music (ASCAP), My Father's Music (BMI). Song Promotion: Robin Mew. Music publisher. SESAC. Member GMA. Publishes 50 songs/year; publishes 11 new songwriters/year. Pays standard royalty.
**How to Contact:** Submit demo tape and lyric sheet. Prefers cassette with 1-3 songs on demo. SASE. Reports in 4-6 weeks.
**Music:** Church/religious and gospel. Recently published "I'm Standing on the Solid Rock" (by Harold Lane), recorded by The Speer Family; and "One More Hallelujah" (by Dave Clark), recorded by The Speer Family and The Florida Boys.
**Tips:** "Lyrics should be *unique* and have deep spiritual meaning."

**SPIRIT AND SOUL PUBLISHING CO.**, Box 7574, Tulsa OK 74105. (918)587-1515. President: Ben Ferrell. Director of Publishing: Jim Rhodes. Music publisher, record company and record producer. Estab. 1981. ASCAP. Publishes 50 songs/year. Pays standard royalty.
**How to Contact:** Arrange personal interview to play demo tape or submit demo tape and lyric sheet. Prefers cassette with no more than 3 songs. SASE. Reports in 3 weeks.
**Music:** Traditional and contemporary gospel. Recently published "El Shaddai" (by Ben Ferrell), recorded by Marv Martin/Castle Records (praise/worship); "I've Been Redeemed" (by B. Ferrell), recorded by The Agape Singers/House of Kings Records (country); and "Bug Off Bug" (by Mike McClenagan), recorded by M. Martin/Castle Records (contemporary country).

---

**The asterisk (*) before a listing indicates that the listing is new in this edition. New markets are often the most receptive to freelance contributions.**

**104** Songwriter's Market '84

**\*STAGE ONE MUSIC**, 22 Madeira Grove, Woodford, Essex, England. 44-01-505-1110. A&R Manager: John Bassett. Music publisher and record company. MCPS, PRS. Member MPA. Publishes 20 songs/year; publishes 8 new songwriters/year. Pays 50-75% of performance and mechanical royalties to songwriters; royalties paid directly to US songwriters or through US publishing affiliate.
**How to Contact:** Submit demo tape and lyric sheet. Prefers cassette with 1-4 songs on demo. SAE and IRC. Reports in 1 month.
**Music:** Mostly pop; also dance-oriented, easy listening and MOR. Recently published "We Know It's Diana" (by Kamen), recorded by Boys Next Door/WEA Records (pop); "Tropicana" (by Harroon), recorded by Cold Hand Band/BK Records (pop); and "Ska'D for Life" (by Doyle and Bassett), recorded by Ska-Dows/Cheapskate Records.

**WADE STALEY MUSIC**, Box 5712, High Point NC 27262. (919)885-0263. President: W.C. Staley. Music publisher, record company and record producer. BMI. Publishes 35 songs/year. Pays standard royalty.
**How to Contact:** Submit demo tape and lyric sheet. Prefers cassette with 3-7 songs on demo. SASE. Reports in 1 month.
**Music:** Bluegrass, church/religious, C&W, folk, gospel, MOR, R&B, rock, soul and top 40/pop.

**STARFOX PUBLISHING**, Box 13584, Atlanta GA 30324. (404)872-6000. President: Alexander Janoulis. Vice President, Creative: Oliver Cooper. General Manager: Hamilton Underwood. Music publisher. BMI. Publishes 30 songs/year. Pays 25-50% royalty. Does not charge for services.
**How to Contact:** Submit demo tape and lyric sheet. Prefers reel-to-reel or cassette with 2-3 songs on demo. Does not return unsolicited material. Reports "as soon as possible."
**Music:** Blues, C&W, disco, MOR, progressive, rock and top 40/pop. Recently published "Streets of Babylon," and "Take It or Leave It," (by Mike Warren, John and David Dryden), recorded by Starfoxx/Hottrax Records (rock); and "Cherie" (by Mark and David Watson), recorded by The BOP/Hottrax Records (new wave).

**STARTIME MUSIC**, Box 643, LaQuinta CA 92253. (714)564-4823. Affiliate: Yo Yo Music (BMI). President: Fred Rice. Record producer, record company and music publisher (Yo Yo Music/BMI). ASCAP. Releases 2-12 singles/year; publishes 4-6 new songwriters/year. Pays standard royalty.
**How to Contact:** Submit demo tape and lead sheet. Prefers cassette with 1-2 songs on demo. SASE. Reports in 6 weeks.
**Music:** Mostly novelty; also country, rock and top 40/pop. Recently published "White Lady" (by Bent Myggen), "Somebody Cares" (by Don and Lucretia Dominquez), and "Love Is Just a Touch Away" (by Anthony Grenek), all recorded by Rob Carter (MOR/contemporary singles).
**Tips:** "A song has to be built on 'flesh and blood'—the rhythm is the skeleton, the musical theme is the flesh and the lyrics are the blood (the soul)."

**STONE ROW MUSIC CO.**, 2022 Vardon, Flossmoor IL 60422. President: Joanne Swanson. Music publisher. BMI. Publishes 3 songs/year. Pays standard royalty.
**Music:** Mostly top 40; also women's and electronic music. Recently published "When I Got Your Letter," "I'm In Love" and "When You Kissed Me Today" by J. Swanson (top 40).
**Tips:** "Send a quality melody—something catchy with intelligent music."

**\*STONEBESS MUSIC CO.**, 163 Orizaba Ave., San Francisco CA 94132. (415)334-2247. President: W.C. Stone. Music publisher. BMI. Publishes varied number of songs/year. Pays standard royalty.
**How to Contact:** Submit demo tape and lyric sheet; arrange personal interview to play demo tape. Prefers 7½ ips reel-to-reel as demo.

**STRAWBERRY PATCH**, Box 7417, Marietta GA 30065. President: Diane Pfeifer. Music publisher. ASCAP. Member NSAI, Advisory Board of Southern Writers, Atlanta Songwriters Association. Publishes 10 songs/year. Pays standard royalty.
**How to Contact:** Submit demo tape and lyric sheet. Prefers cassette with 3-4 songs on demo. SASE, "if return wished." Reports in 2 weeks.
**Music:** Mostly C&W; also easy listening, MOR and top 40/pop. Recently published "Perfect Fool" (by Diane Pfeifer), recorded by Debbie Boone/Warner-Curb Records (pop/country); "Missin' You All by Myself" (by D. Pfeifer), recorded by Frizzell & West/Warner-Viva Records (country); and "Play Something We Could Love To" (by D. Pfeifer), recorded by D. Pfeifer/Capitol Records (pop/country).

**\*STREET TUNES LTD.**, 81 Harley House, Marylebone Rd., London, NW1, England. 44-01-486-1816. Professional Manager: John Glover. Music publisher, record company, record producer and artists manager. MCPS, PRS, Phonographic Performance Ltd. Publishes 50-75 songs/year; publishes 15

## Music Publishers 105

new songwriters/year. Pays standard royalty; royalties paid directly to US songwriters or through US publishing affiliate.
**How to Contact:** Write or call first; submit demo tape and lyric sheet. Prefers 7½ ips or cassette with 3-5 songs on demo. "Send good quality demo." SAE and IRC. Reports in 2 weeks.
**Music:** Mostly rock, progressive, film and background music; also blues, dance-oriented, R&B, soul and top 40/pop. Recently published "Young Idea" (by Nicky Moore), recorded by Samson/Polydor Records; "Girl" (by R. Archer and L. Archer), recorded by Stampede/Polydor Records; and "Visions of Africa" (by P. Bonas and B. Graham), recorded by Zen Attack/Street Tunes (rock).

**JEB STUART MUSIC CO.**, Box 6032, Station B, Miami FL 33123. (305)547-1424. President: Jeb Stuart. Music publisher, record producer and management firm. BMI.
**How to Contact:** Query or submit demo tape and lead sheet. Prefers cassette or disc with 2-4 songs on demo. SASE. Reports in 1 month.
**Music:** Blues, church/religious, C&W, disco, gospel, jazz, rock, soul and top 40/pop. Recently published "We've Got to Change the Plan," "Baby Let's Get Together Tonight," "You Better Believe It Baby," and "Saucy Music" by Jeboria Stuart (jazz/pop/R&B).

**SUGARPLUM MUSIC CO.**, 1022 16th Ave. S., Nashville TN 37212. (615)255-5711. Affiliates: Gingham Music Co. (ASCAP), Calico Music Co. (SESAC). Administrative Assistant: Joe Allen. Music publisher. BMI. Member NMPA, CMA, NARAS and NSAI. Pays standard royalty.
**How to Contact:** Submit demo tape and lyric sheet. Prefers 7½ ips reel-to-reel or cassette with 1-3 songs on demo. SASE. Reports in 3 weeks.
**Music:** C&W, easy listening, MOR and country/pop. Recently published "Girls, Women & Ladies," "When You Fall in Love, Everything's a Waltz," "Love's Found You and Me" (*Maverick* Theme) and "Last Cowboy Song" by Ed Bruce/MCA Records (country); "Hand of the Man," recorded by B.J. Thomas/Myrrh Records; and "The Last Thing She Said," recorded by Ray Price.

**SULZER MUSIC**, Dave Wilson Productions, 3505 Kensington Ave., Philadelphia PA 19134. (215)744-6111. Affiliates: Arzee Music (ASCAP), Asterisk Music (BMI), Rollercoaster Records (ASCAP), Rex Zario Music (BMI), Seabreeze Music (BMI), Wilson/Zario Publishers (BMI), Jack Howard Publishers (BMI), and Arcade Music (ASCAP). President: Dave Wilson. Vice President: Claire Mac. Publishes 100-150 songs/year; publishes 10 new songwriters/year. BMI. Pays standard royalties.
**How to Contact:** Submit demo tape or submit demo tape and lead sheet. Prefers 7½ or 15 ips reel-to-reel cassette with 6-10 songs on demo. SASE. Reports in 1 month.
**Music:** C&W, easy listening, folk, top 40/pop and pop country.

**SU-MA PUBLISHING CO., INC.**, Box 1125, Shreveport LA 71163. (318)222-0195. Publishing Manager: Ms. Donnis Lewis. Music publisher. BMI. Publishes 75 songs/year. Pays standard royalty.
**How to Contact:** Submit demo tape or submit demo tape and lead sheet. Prefers 7½ ips reel-to-reel, cassette or 8-track cartridge. SASE. Reports in 1 month.
**Music:** C&W, gospel and soul.
**Tips:** "All songs must contain both lyrics and melody."

**SUN-BEAR CORPORATION**, 1650 Broadway, New York NY 10019. (212)226-4278. Affiliates: EMI, Watnabe, Shinko, Siegel, Castle, Peer-Southern, Pascal and ATV. A&R Directors: Ezra Cook, Steve Loeb. Music publisher and record producer. Pays standard royalty.
**How to Contact:** Write first about your interest, then submit demo tape and lyric sheet or arrange personal interview to play demo tape. Prefers 7½ ips reel-to-reel with 1-3 songs on demo. Does not return unsolicited material. Reports in 1 month.
**Music:** C&W, easy listening, MOR, rock, soul and top 40/pop. Recently published "Rock City" and "Warrior" (by Guy Speranza and Mark Reale), recorded by Riot/Eurodisc Ariola Records (rock); "It's a Shame" (by D. Sumrall), recorded by Sumrall/Pie Records; "One Step Away" (by J. Gordon), recorded by Spinners/Atlantic Records; and "By Your Side" (by S. Loeb and B. Arnell), recorded by Ben Vereen/Buddah Records.

**SUNBONNET PUBLISHING CO.**, (formerly Beantown Publishing Co.), 910 E. Maxwell St., Pensacola FL 32503. (904)438-2763. President: Earl Lett. Music publisher, record company and record producer. BMI. Member CMA. Publishes 5 songs/year; publishes 2 new songwriters/year. Pays standard royalty.
**How to Contact:** Write first about your interest. Prefers cassette demo. Does not return unsolicited material. Reports in 1 month.
**Music:** Mostly country; also R&B, soul and top 40/pop. Recently published "Room #2," "Almost All the Time," and "You're Gettin Better" (by E. Lett), recorded by Florida Bill/Sunbonnet Records (country).

**SUNBURY/DUNBAR MUSIC CANADA, LTD.**, 2245 Markham Rd., Scarborough, Ontario, Canada M1B 2W3. Affiliate: Dunbar Music Canada, Ltd. (PROCAN). President: Jack Feeney. Music publisher. CAPAC, PROCAN. Member CMPA and CARAS. Publishes 100 songs/year; publishes 5 new songwriters/year. Pays standard royalty.
**How to Contact:** Submit demo tape and lyric sheet. Prefers cassette with 3-5 songs on demo. SAE and IRC. Reports in 1 month.
**Music:** Country, pop and MOR. Recently published "Till The Morning Comes" (by R. Macdonald, W. Salter, C. Daniels), recorded by Roberta Flack/WEA Records (jazz/pop); "Like Nothing Ever Happened" (by K. Fleming, D. Morgan), recorded by Sylvia/RCA Records (country/pop); and "The Sands of Tune" (by J. Carter and G. Shakespear), recorded by Band of the Blackwatch/RCA Records (traditional).
**Tips:** "Have songs with good quality and commercial viability. Professional presentation of music—i.e., good productions and sounds."

*****SUNDOWNER MUSIC (AUSTRALASIA) PTY., LTD.**, Box 440, Toorak, Victoria, 3142, Australia. 61-03-240-8577. Contact: Barry Coburn or Genevieve Leeds. Music publisher. APRA, AMCOS. Member AMPAL. Publishes 100 songs/year; publishes 5 new songwriters/year. Pays negotiable royalty; royalties paid directly to US songwriters.
**How to Contact:** Submit demo tape and lyric sheet. Prefers reel-to-reel or cassette as demo. Lyric sheets not required but should be available on request. SAE and IRC. Reports in 2 weeks.
**Music:** Bluegrass, C&W, MOR, rock (all types) and top 40/pop. Recently published "Shoop Shoop Diddy Wop Cumma Cumma Wang Dang" (by Murray Grindlay and Mark Ackerman), recorded by M. Grindlay/White Label Mushroom Records; and "No Account Cowboy" (by David Hampson), recorded by Caulton/J&B Records (contemporary country).

**SUNSHINE COUNTRY ENTERPRISES, INC.**, Box 31351, Dallas TX 75231. (214)690-8875. Producer: "The General." A&R: Mike Anthony. Music publisher and record company. BMI.
**How to Contact:** Submit demo tape and lead sheet. Prefers 7½ ips reel-to-reel with 1-4 songs on demo. SASE. Reports in 1 month.
**Music:** C&W and gospel. Recently published "Spin My Heart Around Again," recorded by DeWayne Bowman (C&W); "Pride Was the First to Go," recorded by DeWayne Bowman (C&W); "Sixth of June," recorded by Dick Hammonds (C&W); and "Let a Fool Take a Bow," recorded by Dick Hammonds (C&W).

**SWEET POLLY MUSIC**, Box 521, Newberry SC 29108. (803)276-0639. Studio Manager: Polly Davis. Producer: Hayne Davis. Music publisher and record producer. BMI. Publishes 20-30 songs/year.
**How to Contact:** Submit demo tape and lyric sheet. Prefers 7½ ips reel-to-reel or cassette with 4-8 songs on demo. "Include brief bio, list experience, credits etc. Express a desire to actively work on helping to produce/promote material. We are looking for professional writer/co-producer especially." SASE. Reports in 2 weeks.
**Music:** C&W (contemporary), easy listening, MOR, rock and top 40/pop. Recently published "Rainy Days" (by Hayne Davis), recorded by Raw Material (country rock); "Down To the Lovin'" and "Back in 1956," (by H. Davis), recorded by Sugar & Spice (bubblegum/disco).

**SWEET SINGER MUSIC**, The Mathes Company, Box 22653, Nashville TN 37202. Affiliate: Star of David (SESAC) and Sing Sweeter Music (ASCAP). President: Dave Mathes. BMI. Member CMA, GMA, NMPA, NARAS and AFM. Publishes 30-100 songs/year; publishes 6-20 new songwriters/year. Pays standard royalty.
**How to Contact:** Submit demo tape and lyric sheet. Prefers 7½ ips reel-to-reel with 3-5 songs on demo. "Enclose $1 to help defray postage and handling."
**Music:** Mostly country, gospel; also bluegrass, blues, C&W, disco, easy listening, gospel, MOR, progressive rock (country), soul, top 40/pop and instrumental. Recently published "Simple Love Song" (by Pelleteri, Mathes, Bass), recorded by DeAnna/Rising Star Records (MOR); "If the Man on the Street Were You" (by Verlin Chalmers), recorded by Roy Drusky (gospel/country); "Livin' on the Lovin' Side of Life" (by Dorothy Hampton/Larry Pearre), recorded by Jimmy Gateley (country); and "Moonlight Honky Tonkin" (by Warner Mack/David McCaskell), recorded by W. Mack (country).
**Tips:** Needs "well-thought out lyrics, resulting from rewriting until satisfied that the song is as good as the top ten songs on the chart."

**SWEET SWAMP MUSIC**, Red Kill Road, Fleischmanns NY 12430. (914)254-4565. President/General Manager: Barry Drake. Music publisher, booking agency, record company and management firm. BMI. Publishes 25 songs/year. Pays standard royalty.

Music Publishers **107**

**How to Contact:** Submit demo tape and lead sheet. Prefers cassette with 3-5 songs on demo. SASE. Reports in 1 month.
**Music:** Bluegrass; blues; C&W; easy listening; folk; MOR; progressive; rock (hard or country) and top 40/pop. Recently published ''Fallen Star,'' ''Blues For Hobo Joe'' and ''Beg, Steal or Borrow'' (by Barry Drake), recorded by B. Drake/Catskill Mountain Records.

**SWEET TOOTH MUSIC PUBLISHING**, 2716 Springlake Ct., Irving TX 75060. (214)259-4032. General Manager: Kenny Wayne Hagler. Music publisher, record company, record producer, recording artist and traveling musician. BMI. Publishes 10-15 songs/year; publishes 5 new songwriters/year. Pays standard royalty.
**How to Contact:** Submit demo tape and lyric sheet. Prefers 7½ ips reel-to-reel or cassette with 3-4 songs on demo. SASE. Reports in 1 month.
**Music:** Mosty C&W; also blues, C&W, MOR, R&B, rock, soul and top 40/pop. Recently published '' 'Bout a Broken Heart'' (by Mike Jeffrey), recorded by M. Jeffrey/Night Records (C&W); and ''Green Eyes'' and ''You Give Me Vibrations'' (S. Luray), recorded by Reign/Candy Records.
**Tips:** ''Compare all songs with the hits of today. Make sure the song has a good hook and is commercially appealing.''

*****TABITHA MUSIC, LTD.**, 39 Cordery Rd., St. Thomas, Exeter, Devon, EX2 9DJ, England. 44-0392-79914. Affiliate: Dice Music. Managing Director: Graham Sclater. Music publisher and record producer. MCPS, PRS. Member MPA. Publishes 30-50 songs/yar; publishes 6 new songwriters/year. Pays negotiable royalty; royalties paid directly to US songwriters.
**How to Contact:** Submit demo tape and lyric sheet. Prefers cassette with 1-4 songs on demo. SAE and IRC. Reports in 2 weeks.
**Music:** Mostly MOR and pop; also C&W, dance-oriented, Spanish, rock, soul and top 40. Recently published ''Can't Get Enough of You'' (by D. Sanger), recorded by Key West/Epic Records (pop); ''Grizzly Bear Boogie'' (by A. Ross), recorded by Shades/Pye Records (R&R); and ''Animals'' (by A. Smith), recorded by Earthshake/King Records, Japan (heavy rock).

**TAL MUSIC, INC.**, 16147 Littlefield, Detroit MI 48538. (313)863-3787. President: Edith Talley. Vice President A&R: Harold McKinney. Music publisher and record company. BMI. Publishes 4 songs/year. Pays standard royalty.
**How to Contact:** Submit demo tape, arrange personal interview, submit demo tape and lead sheet or submit lead sheet. Prefers 7½ ips reel-to-reel or cassette. SASE. Reports ASAP.
**Music:** Choral, church/religious, C&W, dance, easy listening, gospel, jazz, rock, soul and top 40/pop. Recently published ''E.R.A.'' and ''Pocket'' (by Tommy McGee), recorded by T. McGee/TMG Records (R&B disco); ''Stay With Me'' (by T. McGee and Larry Rhodes), recorded by T. McGee/TMG Records (ballad); and ''Now That I Found You'' (by T. McGee and Melvin Forrest), recorded by T. McGee/TMG Records (ballad).
**Tips:** ''Make sure the songs are on a quality demo and that lyrics are properly structured to flow with one idea.''

*****DALE TEDESCO MUSIC CO.**, 17043 Romar St., Northridge CA 91325. (213)885-0775. Affiliates: Dale Tedesco Music (BMI) and Tedesco Tunes (ASCAP). President: Dale T. Tedesco. Music publisher. Estab. 1981. BMI, ASCAP. Member AIMP. Publishes 20-40 songs/year; publishes 12-18 new songwriters/year. Pays standard royalty.
**How to Contact:** Submit demo tape and lyric sheet. Prefers cassette with 1-3 songs on demo. SASE. Reports in 2 weeks.
**Music:** Mostly top 40, R&B and pop; also C&W, dance-oriented, easy listening, folk, jazz, MOR, rock and soul.

*****TELEVOX MUSIC**, #5, 11887 Ellice St., Malibu CA 90265. (213)457-5475. Affiliate: Headstack Music (ASCAP). Professional Manager: Ray Blair. Music publisher. Estab. 1981. BMI. Member AIMP. Publishes 3 songs/year. Pays standard royalty.
**How to Contact:** Submit demo tape and lyric sheet. Prefers cassette with 1-3 songs on demo. SASE. Reports in 2 weeks.
**Music:** Mostly rock and new wave; also C&W, dance-oriented, progressive, R&B, soul and top 40/pop. Recently published ''He Could Be the One'' (by Bobby and Larson Paine), recorded by Josie Cotton/Elektra Records (top 40); and ''No Pictures of Dad'' (by James Gittridge), recorded by Josie Cotton/Elektra Records (ballad/pop).

**THINK BIG MUSIC**, 901 Kenilworth Rd., Montreal, Quebec, Canada H3R 2R5. (514)341-6721. Affiliate: Big Fuss Music (PROCAN). President: Leon Aronson. Music publisher, and record producer.

CAPAC. Publishes 50 songs/year; publishes 2 new songwriters/year. Pays standard royalty.
**How to Contact:** Submit demo tape and lead sheet. Prefers cassette with 6 songs on demo. SAE and IRC. Reports in 1 month.
**Music:** Mostly top 40/pop; also dance-oriented and pop-rock.

**THIRD STORY MUSIC, INC.**, Suite 1500, 6430 Sunset Blvd., Los Angeles CA 90028. (213)463-1151. President: M. Cohen. Music publisher. BMI. Member AIMP. Publishes 100 songs/year; publishes 3 new songwriters/year. Pays standard royalty.
**How to Contact:** Submit demo tape and lyric sheet. Prefers cassette with 1-3 songs on demo. Does not return unsolicited material. Report in 2 weeks.
**Music:** Disco, R&B, rock and top 40/pop. Recently published "Everybody's Talkin'," recorded by Fred Neil/Elektra Records; "Hey Joe," recorded by Jimi Hendrix; and "Ol' 55," recorded by Tom Waits/Elektra Records.
**Tips:** "Send simple demos; nothing elaborate."

**THIRD STORY MUSIC, INC.**, 3436 Sansom St., Philadelphia PA 19104. (215)386-5987. Affiliates: City Surfer and TSR, Inc. President: John Wicks. Vice President: Scott Herzog. Contact: Alexandra Scott. Music publisher, record company and record producer. ASCAP. Publishes 15 songs/year; publishes 8 new songwriters/year. Pays negotiable royalty.
**How to Contact:** Submit demo tape and lyric sheet. Prefers cassette with 1-4 songs on demo. SASE. Reports in 1 month.
**Music:** Blues (rock), choral (gospel), church/religious, C&W, dance-oriented, easy listening, gospel, jazz, MOR, R&B, rock (all kinds), soul and top 40/pop.

**3 H'S MUSIC**, 1103 Neff Ave. S., West Covina CA 91790. (213)919-5055. President: Henry Oakes. Music publisher, record company and record producer. ASCAP. Publishes 3 songs/year; publishes 1 new songwriter/year. Pays standard royalty.
**How to Contact:** Write first about your interest. Prefers cassette with 2 songs on demo. SASE. Reports in 1 week.
**Music:** Children's, choral, church/religious, classical, C&W, dance-oriented, easy listening, folk, gospel, MOR and Spanish. Recently published "City of the Angels" and "Raquel" (by Oakes), (pop/MOR).

*****TOM TOM PUBLISHING CO.**, Box 566, Massena NY 13662. (315)769-2448. Affiliate: Bop Talk Music (ASCAP). Vice President: Thomas Gramuglia. Music publisher and record company. Pays standard royalty.
**How to Contact:** Submit demo tape. Prefers 7½ ips reel-to-reel with 1-12 songs on demo. SASE. Reports in 1 month.
**Music:** Jazz and folk.

**TOMPAUL MUSIC CO.**, 628 South St., Mount Airy NC 27030. (919)786-2865. Owner: Paul E. Johnson. Music publisher and record company. BMI. Publishes 75 songs/year; publishes 20 new songwriters/year. Pays standard royalties.
**How to Contact:** Submit demo tape and lead sheet. Prefers 7½ ips reel-to-reel with 3-5 songs on demo. SASE. Reports in 1 month.
**Music:** Bluegrass, church/religious, C&W, easy listening, folk, gospel, MOR, rock (country), soul and top 40/pop. Recently published "I Surrender Dear" (by Bobby L. Atkins), recorded by Chet Atkins/R.C.A. Records (pop instrumental); and "Fire on the Mountain" and "End of a Dream", (by Paul E. Johnson), recorded by Blue Ridge Mountain Boys/Stark Records (bluegrass)

**TOPSAIL MUSIC**, 71 Boylston St., Brookline MA 02147. (617)739-2010. Affiliate: Mutiny Music. International subpublisher: EMI Music. President: Fred Berk. Music publisher, recording company and production company. BMI. Pays standard royalties.
**How to Contact:** Submit demo tape or lead sheet. Prefers reel-to-reel or cassette with 1-6 songs on demo. SASE. Reports in 3 weeks.
**Music:** C&W, rockabilly, progressive, rock, soul and top 40/pop. Recently published "Man Enough," recorded by No Slack (pop/R&B); "Why Don't We Love Each Other?," recorded by the Ellis Hall Group (pop/R&B); and "Breaker 1-9," recorded by the Back Bay Rhythm Section (disco).

**TOULOUSE MUSIC PUBLISHING CO., INC.**, Box 96, El Cerrito CA 94530. Executive Vice President: James Bronson, Jr. Music publisher, record company and record producer. BMI. Member AIMP. Publishes 1 new songwriter/year. Hires staff writers. Pays standard royalty.

## Music Publishers 109

**How to Contact:** Submit demo tape and lyric sheet. Prefers cassette with 2-4 songs on demo. SASE. Reports in 1 month.
**Music:** Bluegrass, gospel, jazz, R&B and soul.

**TRANSATLANTIC MUSIC**, Box 1998, Beverly Hills CA 90213. President: Fred de Rafols. Music publisher. BMI. Publishes 30-50 songs/year. Payment negotiable.
**How to Contact:** Submit demo tape and lead sheet. Prefers cassette with 2 songs on demo. SASE. Reports in 3 weeks.
**Music:** Rock, new wave, top 40/pop, punk and international. Recently published "Next" and "Love You No More," recorded by J.D. Drews/MCA Records; and "Sex is a Bottomless Pit" and "Boiling in the Melting Pot" recorded by The Nobodys/Whatever Records.

**TREE PUBLISHING CO., INC.**, 8 Music Square W., Nashville TN 37203. (615)327-3162. Affiliates: Cross Keys Publishing (ASCAP), Twittybird Music Publishing (BMI), Uncanny Music (ASCAP), Warhawk Music (BMI), Tree/Harlan Howard Songs (BMI), Kentree Music (BMI), Stairway Music (BMI) and Meadowgreen Music (ASCAP). President and Chief Officer: Buddy Killen. Contact: Donna Hilley. Professional Managers/Song Pluggers: Dan Wilson, Terry Choate and Tom Long. Music publisher. Member NMPA.
**How to Contact:** Call first "to see if we're currently accepting material," then submit demo tape. Prefers cassette with 1-3 songs on demo. "Voice and guitar or piano accompaniment is sufficient. There is no need to have full orchestra or band on track. We just need to hear the words and melody clearly." SASE. Reports in 10-12 weeks. "We will not return material unless proper postage is on return envelope."
**Music:** Country, MOR, rock (hard or country), soul, top 40/pop and contemporary Christian.

**TRUSTY PUBLICATIONS**, Rt. 1, Box 100, Nebo KY 42441. (502)249-3194. President: Elsie Childers. Music publisher and record company. BMI. Member CMA and NSAI. Publishes 8-10 songs/year; publishes 3-4 new songwriters/year. Pays standard royalties.
**How to Contact:** Submit demo tape and lead sheet. Prefers 7½ ips reel-to-reel or cassette with 2-4 songs on demo. SASE. Reports in 1 month.
**Music:** Mostly country and country/pop; also blues, church/religious, disco, easy listening, folk, gospel, MOR, soul and top 40. Recently published "Hard Knocks" and "These Shoes" (by Don Cottrell), recorded by Tim Emery & Legacy (country/rock); and "Last Love Song" (by T. Emery), recorded by T. Emery & Legacy (country/ballad).

**\*TSR, INC. & CITY SURFER MUSIC**, 3436 Sansom St., Philadelphia PA 19104. (215)386-5998. A&R Staff: Scott Herzog and Alexandra Scott. Music publisher, record company, record producer and recording studio. ASCAP. Member NMPA. Publishes 3 new songwriters/year. Pays standard royalty.
**How to Contact:** Submit demo tape and lyric sheet. Prefers cassette with 2-3 songs on demo. "We like quality studio tapes." SASE. Reports in 1 month.
**Music:** Mostly MOR and easy listening; also C&W, dance-oriented, gospel, rock, soul, top 40/pop, funk, rap and salsa.
**Tips:** "Submit only current commercial hit material directed with a particular artist in mind—no album cuts."

**TUMAC MUSIC PUBLISHING**, Rt. 1, Box 143, Senola GA 30276. (404)599-6935. Affiliate: Shandy Guff (BMI). Professional Manager: Phil McDaniel. General Manager: Joe McTamney. Music publisher, record producer and record company. ASCAP. Publishes 6 songs/year. Pays standard royalty.
**How to Contact:** Submit demo tape and lyric sheet. Prefers cassette with 1-3 songs on demo. SASE. Reports in 3 weeks.
**Music:** C&W, dance, easy listening, jazz (country), MOR, rock (adult/country), top 40/pop and R&B. Recently published "A Spinner of Rainbows" (by Sheehy and McTamney), recorded by Roni Stoneman/Spin Check Records (MOR); "Why Couldn't I Just Love You" (by Beneteau and McTamney), recorded by Ron Perrault/Lauric Records (MOR); and "In Love with Today" recorded by Connie Johnson/Century Seven Records.
**Tips:** "Listen to what is being recorded. Learn to rewrite songs that are incomplete and continuously rejected."

**\*TUTCH MUSIC PUBLISHING**, 25 Bob Hill Rd, Ridgefield CT 06877. (203)438-5366. Professional Manager: Richie Kidd. Music publisher, record company and record producer. BMI. Member CMA, CSA. Publishes 10-15 songs/year; publishes 4 new songwriters/year.
**How to Contact:** Write first about your interest. Prefers cassette with 2 songs on demo. SASE. Reports in 2 weeks.

**Music:** Mostly country and pop; also dance-oriented, MOR, R&B and rock. Recently published "Texas Heartache #1" (by Paul Hotchkiss), recorded by Mickey Gilley/Epic Records (country); "Wheeler Dealer" (by M. Terry and P. Hotchkiss), recorded by Gerri Roth/Aura Records (rock); "Heartache Express" (by P. Hotchkiss and M. Terry), recorded by M. Gilley/Epic Records (country); "Jenny Rae" (by M. Terry and P. Hotchkiss), recorded by Wendel Atkins/Gilley Records (country/pop); "Fishaholic" (by Ray Giantic), recorded by Sawback Sally/Tutch Records (country); "Queen of the Mansion" (by P. Hotchkiss/Bob Royce), recorded by Maureen Hutchinson/Jato Records; "Love was Meant to Be" (by M. Terry), recorded by Country Touch/Axbar Records (country); and "Nashville Plastic" (by P. Hotchkiss/M. Terry), recorded by Hutcher Bros./Red Horse Records (country rock).
**Tips:** "Songs should have good solid lyrics with a message; good vocal on the demo."

**\*TWIST AND SHOUT MUSIC**, Suite B 41, Alderbrook Rd., Clapham South, London, SW12, England. 44-01-673-3240. Affiliate: Shout and Scream Music (PRS, MCPS). Managing Director: Clive Solomon. Professional Manager: Brad Day. Music publisher. Estab. 1981. MCPS, PRS. Publishes a varied number of songs/year; publishes 6 new songwriters/year. Has not yet, but would listen to songs from US songwriters. Royalties paid directly to US songwriters.
**Music:** Submit demo tape and lyric sheet. Prefers cassette with 2-4 songs on demo. SAE and IRC. Reports in 1 month.
**Music:** Mostly new wave and post punk; also electronic, progressive, rock, soul and top 40/pop. Recently published "The Quarter Moon" (by J. Dmochowski), recorded by The V.I.P.'s/Gem-RCA Records; "Part-Time Punks" (by D. Treacy), recorded by TV Personalities/Rough Trade Records; and "Hanging Around" (by A. Conway), recorded by Toni Basi/Radialchoice Records.
**Tips:** "We are keener to work with new radical, creative artists than conventional songwriters. Our pet hates include boring US MOR FM rock."

**TYNER MUSIC**, #115, 38 Music Square E., Nashville TN 37203. (615)244-4224. Affiliate: Longshot Music (SESAC) and Timberjack Music (BMI). President: Harrison Tyner. Music publisher. ASCAP. Publishes 75-100 songs/year. Pays standard royalty. Hires staff writers; pays $75-300/week.
**How to Contact:** Submit demo tape and lyric sheet to Sue Tyner, Executive Vice President. Prefers 7½ ips reel-to-reel or cassette with 4-7 songs on demo. "No registered mail accepted." SASE. Reports in 2 months.
**Music:** C&W, easy listening, MOR and top 40/pop.

**\*TYSCOT, INC.**, 3403 N. Ralston Ave., Indianapolis IN 46218. (317)926-6271. Affiliates: Clark Publishing (BMI), Linell Music (ASCAP). Vice President/General Manager: Rick Clark. Music publisher, record company and record producer. ASCAP. Publishes 30 songs/year; publishes 5 new songwriters/year. Pays standard royalty.
**How to Contact:** Submit demo tape and lyric sheet. Prefers cassette with minimum of 4 songs on demo. SASE. Reports in 1 month.
**Music:** Mostly gospel and soul; also church/religious, dance-oriented, jazz, R&B and top 40/pop. Recently published "Hold Out" (by Robert Turner), recorded by Robert Turner & Silver Hearts/Tyscot Records (gospel); "I Wish" (by Terry Huff), recorded by T. Huff/Circle City Records (R&B); and "Flam" (by R. Griffin, B. Carhee & L. Paul), recorded by Ricky Clark/Circle City Records (soul/dance).

**ULTIMA THULE MUSIC PUBLISHING CO.**, Box 20604, Sacramento CA 95820. (916)446-6301. A&R Administrative Consultant: Almerritt Covington. Music publisher, record company, record producer and consultants. BMI. Publishes 2 songs/year.
**How to Contact:** Submit demo tape and lyric sheet. Prefers cassette with 6-10 songs on demo. "Leave 4-6 seconds of leader tape between songs." SASE. Reports in 6 weeks.
**Music:** Church/religious, C&W, easy listening, gospel, jazz, MOR, R&B, rock (soft), soul and top 40/pop.

**UNIVERSAL STARS MUSIC**, Rt. 3, Box 5B, Leerville LA 71446. Affiliate: Headliner Music. National Representative: Sherree Stephens. Music publisher. BMI. Publishes 12-24 songs/year; publishes 1 new songwriter/year. Pays standard royalty.
**How to Contact:** Submit demo tape and lyric sheet. Prefers cassette with 1-6 songs on demo. Does not return unsolicited material. Reports in 1 month, if interested.

**Music:** Bluegrass, church/religious, C&W, folk, gospel and top 40/pop. Recently published *Jesus Came All the Way*, recorded by Sherrie Scott (religious LP); *Oh, Lord Save Me*, recorded by Melodie Scott (gospel LP); and *Praise Him*, recorded by J.J. & Sherrie Stephens (religious single and LP).

**UNREGULATED MUSIC**, Box 81485, Fairbanks AK 99708. (907)456-3419. President: Michael States. Music publisher, record company and record producer. BMI. Publishes 25 songs/year; publishes 8 new songwriters/year. Pays standard royalty.
**How to Contact:** Submit demo tape and lyric sheet. Prefers cassette with 2-5 songs on demo. "Include a statement of your goals." SASE. Reports in 1 month.
**Music:** Gospel, black gospel and new wave gospel. Recently published "Whose Birthday Is It?" (by M. Beggs), recorded by M. Beggs/Unregulated Records (reggae/gospel); "Jesus Is the Light of the World" (by W. Watson), recorded by W. Watson/Unregulated Records (soul/gospel); and "The King Ain't Dead" and "Crumble and Die" (by Paul Porter), recorded by P. Porter/Lift Records (new wave/gospel).

*****UPSTART MUSIC**, 2210 Rapier Blvd., Arlington TX 76013. (817)461-8481. Affiliate: Pantego Sound (BMI). President: Charles Stewart. Music publisher, record company and record producer. BMI. Member NARM. Publishes 100 songs/year; publishes 3 new songwriters/year. Pays standard royalty.
**How to Contact:** Submit demo tape and lyric sheet. Prefers cassette with 1-6 songs on demo. Place name and phone number on cassette. SASE. Reports in 3 weeks.
**Music:** Mostly country; also blues, R&B and rock. Recently published "Play Together Again Again" (by Abbott & Stewart), recorded by Buck Owens & Emmylou Harris/Warner Brothers Records (country); "I Won't Be Sleepin' Alone" (by Abbott & Stewart), recorded by Gene Watson/Capitol Records (country); and "If This Is Freedom" (by Abbott & Stewart), recorded by Joe Stampley/CBS Records (country).

**URSULA MUSIC**, 108 Morning Glory Lane, Manheim PA 17545. Affiliates: Welz Music (ASCAP), Florentine Music (BMI) and Wynwood Music (BMI). President/Professional Manager: Joey Welz. Music publisher, record company and booking agency. BMI. Member AFM. Publishes 15-25 songs/year; publishes 2-4 new songwriters/year. Pays standard royalty.
**How to Contact:** Submit demo tape and lead sheet. Prefers cassette with 4-8 songs on demo. Does not return unsolicited material. "We hold until we need material for a session, then we search our files."
**Music:** C&W, dance, MOR, rock and top 40/pop. Recently published "I Remember Rock 'n' Roll," and "In My Car," (by J. Welz and G. Granahan); and "American Made Rock 'n' Roll" (by J. Welz), all recorded by J. Welz.

**VAAM MUSIC**, Suite C-114, 3740 Evans St., Los Angeles CA 90027. (213)664-7765. Affiliate: Pete Martin Music (ASCAP). President: Pete Martin. Music publisher and record producer. BMI. Publishes 8 new songwriters/year. Pays standard royalty.
**How to Contact:** Submit demo tape and lyric sheet. Prefers 7½ ips reel-to-reel or cassette with 1-4 songs on demo. SASE. Reports in 1 month.
**Music:** C&W, easy listening, MOR, rock (general), soul and top 40/pop.

**VADO MUSIC**, 2226 McDonald Ave., Brooklyn NY 11213. (212)946-4405. Affiliate: Romona Music (ASCAP). Music publisher. ASCAP. Publishes 20 songs/year; publishes 5 new songwriters/year. Pays standard royalty.
**How to Contact:** Submit demo tape and lyric sheet. Prefers cassette with 4 songs on demo. SASE. Reports in 3 weeks.
**Music:** Gospel, jazz, R&B, rock and soul. Recently published "I Am Somebody" (by Alex Alexander), recorded by Alexander/Jody Records (disco); "The Feeling I Have Inside for You," recorded by Ed Hailey/Jody Records (disco); and "Double Dealing Daddy," recorded by G. Black/Jody Records (rock).

**JERRY VAMPLE PUBLISHING CO.**, Box 23152, Kansas City MO 64141. President: Jerry Vample. Music publisher, record company and record producer. BMI. Publishes 15 songs/year; publishes 15 new songwriters/year. Pays standard royalty.
**How to Contact:** Write first about your interest, then submit demo tape and lyric sheet. Prefers 7½ ips reel-to-reel or cassette with 2-4 songs on demo. SASE. Reports in 1 month.
**Music:** Church/religious, easy listening and gospel.

**VECTOR MUSIC**, c/o Drake Music Group, 809 18th Ave. S., Nashville TN 37203. (615)327-3211. Affiliate: Belton Music (ASCAP). Contact: Rose Drake. Music publisher. BMI. Member NMPA. Pays standard royalty.

**How to Contact:** Submit demo tape and lyric sheet. Prefers cassette with 2 songs on demo. SASE. Reports in 1 month.
**Music:** C&W, easy listening, MOR and country rock. Recently published "East Bound and Down" (by Dick Feller and Jerry Reed), recorded by J. Reed (country/pop); "Ragamuffin Man" (by Stewart Harris), recorded by Donna Fargo (country); and "The Man with the Golden Thumb" (by Bud McGuire and Billy Henderson), recorded by J. Reed (country).

**\*VERON MUSIC/WORLD ACCLAIM MUSIC**, Unit 10, 3500 Glen Erin Dr., Mississauga, Ontario, Canada L5L 1W6. (416)820-7788. General Manager: Veronica Mataseje. Music publisher, record company, record producer and music industry consultants. PROCAN, CAPAC. Publishes 6 songs/year; publishes 2 new songwriters/year. Pays standard royalty.
**How to Contact:** Submit demo tape. Prefers cassette with 1-4 songs on demo. SASE. Reports in 1 month.
**Music:** Mostly C&W and top 40/pop; also MOR. Recently published "Little League in Heaven" (by George Wells), recorded by Orval Prophet/Acclaim Records (C&W); and "Annie" and "Westward Bound" (by V. Mataseje), recorded by Julie Ann/16th Avenue Records (MOR).
**Tips:** Needs "good lyrics. Watch what is being charted in the major trades."

**\*THE VIRGINIA ARTS PUBLISHING COMPANIES**, Box 800, Louisa VA 23093. (703)967-2245. Affiliate: Notegun Music (BMI). Creative Director: Paul Brier. Music publisher, record company, record producer, recording studio and jingle producer. BMI. Publishes 15 songs plus background scores of TV shows/year; publishes 3 new songwriters/year. Pays standard royalty.
**How to Contact:** Submit demo tape and lyric sheet. Prefers 7½ or 15 ips reel-to-reel or cassette with 2-4 songs on demo. SASE. Reports in 2 weeks.
**Music:** Mostly children's; also top 40, bluegrass, C&W, dance-oriented, jazz, rock, TV and film scoring. Recently published "Powerhouse," by Paul Brier (theme song for PBS TV series); "Footsteps," by P. Brier (theme song for PBS TV series); and "A Simple Song," by Fred P. Karns (used on TV, top 40).
**Tips:** "Because so much of our material goes into TV for children, we look for natural, flowing, conversational lyrics with universal appeal."

**VOKES MUSIC PUBLISHING**, Box 12, New Kensington PA 15068. (412)335-2775. President: Howard Vokes. Music publisher, record company, booking agency and promotion company. BMI.
**How to Contact:** Submit demo tape and lead sheet. Cassette only. SASE. Reports "a few days after receiving."
**Music:** Bluegrass, C&W and gospel. Recently published "Your Kisses and Lies," "Keep Cool but Don't Freeze," "Judge of Hearts," "Born without a Name," "I Was a Fool" and "Tomorrow Is My Last Day."

**\*WARNER BROS. MUSIC AUSTRALIA PTY., LTD.**, 319B Penshurst St., Willoughby, NSW 2068, Australia. 61-02-406-5322. Affiliates US: Warner Brothers Muci Corp. (ASCAP), Warner-Tamerlane Publishing Corp (BMI). Managing Director: John Bromell. Music publisher. APRA, AMCOS. Member AMPAL. Publishes 100 songs/year; publishes 20 new songwriters/year. Will listen to songs submitted by US songwriters, but only when submitted through US publishing affiliates. Pays negotiable royalty; royalties paid to US songwriters through US publishing affiliates.
**How to Contact:** Submit demo tape and lyric sheet. Prefers cassette with 2-4 songs on demo. SAE and IRC. Reports in 2 weeks.
**Music:** Mostly rock; also easy listening and top 40/pop. Recently published "Without You" (by Bernie Lynch), recorded by Eurogliders/Polygram Records (top 40/pop); "U.S. Forces" (by Moginie/Garrett), recorded by Midnight Oil/CBS Records (rock); and "Spellbound" (by Richard Clapton), recorded by R. Clapton/WEA Records (rock).

**\*KENT WASHBURN PRODUCTIONS**, 10622 Commerce Ave., Tujunga CA 91042. (213)855-0525. Affiliates: Monard Music (ASCAP) and Pencott Publishing (BMI). Contact: Kent Washburn. Music publisher and record producer. Publishes 20 songs/year; publishes 3 new songwriters/year. Pays standard royalty.
**How to Contact:** Submit demo tape and lyric sheet. Prefers cassette with 1-5 songs on demo. SASE. Reports in 1 month.
**Music:** Church/religious, contemporary gospel, R&B, soul and top 40/pop. Recently published "Don't Burn No Bridges" (by Romain Anderson), recorded by Jackie Wilson/Brunswick Records (R&B); "Resurrection" (by Washburn and Lupton), recorded by Paul Davis/Spirit Records (gospel); and "You Don't Even Know My Name" (by Kelly), recorded by Free Love/EMKAY Records (R&B).

# Close-up

**Mike Reid**
Songwriter/Performer

"There's just one way to be a songwriter—that's just to do it," says Mike Reid whose successes include the Ronnie Milsap number one hits "Inside" and "Stranger in My House." Reid "did it"—made his commitment to songwriting—by giving up a successful career in professional football to move to Nashville, a move he certainly doesn't regret.

"I think often that it would have been nice had I come to Nashville earlier," says Reid. "Coming to this town made me think about what I was trying to accomplish as a songwriter. So often before when I wrote a song I was simply following my emotional response to one thing or another. Whether good or bad, when you write songs like that, they are from a terribly personal point of view. But coming to Nashville made me realize I really wanted to write songs for people, not just for myself. Nashville gave me great respect for songwriters who can say interesting things to a whole lot of people—and that's the challenge of good, commercial, heartfelt songwriting."

Being even more specific about Nashville, Reid says, "The best thing that's happened to me in this town was meeting Rob Galbraith, Ronnie Milsap's publishing manager." Reid credits his publisher, Milsap Music, with his growth and success as a writer. A good publisher, he says, is "one who understands what you're trying to do and has the same musical head and heart that you have.

"A good publisher can show you where you are going wrong on a good song idea, or where the strengths lie within the idea. He can give you the input to help you make a better song. He can also help you move on to something else when you are so lost in the song you can't see it's not such a good idea after all."

Reid sees each new song he writes as a unique creation. Likewise, he sees the demo for each song as something that should be created especially for that song. "I mistrust anybody who says demos should be 'one' thing. You as the writer must understand the music that you've written. Take two steps back and ask 'what's the *best* way for me to show this song?' It makes little sense, for example, to have a fully-produced demo on a ballad. It's more important that you, the writer, deliver the song with the proper heart and soul. But even on a 'groove' song where you should have rhythm tracks and even other instruments, still keep it simple. If not, you can end up spending a lot of money for nothing."

Reid also views each new song as an exercise in becoming better at his craft. He advises all songwriters to "simply write as often as you can. I'm a firm believer that you have to write a lot of bad songs before the good ones start coming out."

**WATERHOUSE MUSIC, INC.**, 526 Nicollet Mall, Minneapolis MN 55402. (612)332-6575. Director of Operations: Gary Marx. Music publisher and record producer. BMI. Publishes 2 new songwriters/year. Pays negotiable royalty.
**How to Contact:** Call first about your interest, submit demo tape and lyric sheet. Prefers cassette with 3-10 songs on demo. "Include promo material and cover letter." SASE. Reports in 1 month.
**Music:** Blues, dance-oriented (mainstream), folk (rock), R&B, rock, soul and top 40/pop. Recently published "Up from the Alley" (by Lamont Cranston Band), recorded by Lamont Cranston Band/Waterhouse Records (rock); "My Babe" (Roy Buchanan version), recorded by Little Walter/Waterhouse Records (rock); and "Times of Our Lives" (by Rex Fowler), recorded by Aztec Two-Step/Waterhouse Records (rock/top 40 ballad).

**WATONGA PUBLISHING CO.**, 2609 NW 36th St., Oklahoma City OK 73112. (405)942-0462. Music publisher. ASCAP. Pays standard royalty.
**How to Contact:** Submit demo tape and lyric sheet. Prefers 7½ ips reel-to-reel as demo.
**Music:** C&W, R&B, rock, soul and top 40/pop.

*****WATTS CITY PRODUCTIONS**, 11211 Wilmington Ave., Los Angeles CA 90059. (213)566-9982. President/Producer: Joe Fornis. Music publisher, record company and record producer. ASCAP. Publishes 10 songs/year; publishes 2 new songwriters/year. Pays standard royalty.
**How to Contact:** Submit demo tape. Prefers cassette with 4-12 songs on demo. SASE. Reports in 3 weeks.
**Music:** R&B, soul and top 40/pop.

*****JEFF WAYNE MUSIC PUBLISHING, LTD.**, Oliver House, 8/9 Ivor Place, London, NW1 6BY, England. 44-01-724-2471. Affiliate/U.K.: Littlechap Music, Ltd. Affiliate/US: Ollie Record Productions, 551 Fifth Ave., New York NY 10017. Managing Director: Jeff Wayne. Music publisher, record company, record producer, recording studios and record promotion. PRS. Publishes 500 songs/year; publishes 6 new songwriters/year. Pays 50% of performance and mechanical royalties; royalties paid to US songwriters through US publishing affiliate (CBS Songs/April Music).
**How to Contact:** Submit demo tape and lyric sheet. Prefers cassette with 3-6 songs on demo. Include photo and biographical material. SASE. Reports in 1-3 months.
**Music:** Mostly rock and pop; also R&B and soul. Recently published "Remember My Name" (by Stevie Lange and Gary Bell), recorded by S. Lange/RCA Records (rock); "Matador" (by Jeff Wayne), recorded by J. Wayne/CBS Records (pop); and "Leave Your Number" (by John Altman and Mitch Dalton), recorded The Mutams/RCA Records (rock).
**Tips:** "Demos should be of high quality, both vocally and instrumentally."

*****WEB IV MUSIC PUBLISHING**, 2107 Faulkner Rd. NE, Atlanta GA 30324. Contact: Nancy Mitchell. Music publisher. Pays standard royalty.
**How to Contact:** Submit demo tape and lyric sheet. "Please don't call." Prefers cassette with 3-4 songs on demo. SASE. Reports in 1 month.
**Music:** R&B, rock and top 40/pop.

**WEEZE MUSIC CO. & DOUBLE HEADER PRODUCTIONS**, Suite 4N, 61 Jane St., New York NY 10014. (212)929-2068. Contact: Steve Scharf. Music publisher and record producer. BMI. Publishes 3 songs/year; publishes possibly 1 new songwriter/year. "No advance—if song is recorded by me, the publishing is either 100% or split 50%-50%."
**How to Contact:** Call first about your interest and then submit demo tape and lyric sheet. Prefers 7½ ips reel-to-reel or cassette with maximum 4 songs on demo. SASE.
**Music:** Mostly R&B and R&R; also top 40/pop and adult contemporary.
**Tips:** Looking for "strong melody, intelligent lyrics and a good attitude as a person."

*****RON WEISER PUBLISHING**, 6918 Peach Ave., Van Nuys CA 91406. (213)781-4805. Contact: Ron Weiser. Music publisher, record company and record producer. BMI. Publishes 30-50 songs/year; publishes 6 new songwriters/year. Pays standard royalty.
**How to Contact:** Submit demo tape and lyric sheet. Prefers cassette for demo. Does not return unsolicited material. Reports in 1 month.
**Music:** Mostly rockabilly; also C&W and R&B. Recently published "Marie Marie" (by D. Alvin), recorded by Blasters (rockabilly); "The Newest Wave" (by R. Campi), recorded by Ray Campi (rockabilly); and "Tennessee & Texas," recorded by The Magnetics (rockabilly).

*****WELCHY GRAPE PUBLISHING**, 991 Oak St., West Barnstable MA 02668. (617)362-4908. President: Mike Welch. Music publisher, record company and record producer. BMI. Publishes 12 songs/year. Pays standard royalty.

**How to Contact:** Submit demo tape and lyric sheet or write about your interest. Prefers cassette or record with 10 songs on demo. SASE. Reports in 1 month.
**Music:** C&W, easy listening, folk, folk rock, MOR, rock (country and hard). Recently published "Everybody Knows" (MOR single); "Turning Point" (rock single); and "Rainy Nights and Candle Light" (MOR/crossover) (all by Mike Welch), all recorded by M. Welch and the Renovations Band/W/G Records.

**THE WELDEE MUSIC COMPANY,** Box 561, Wooster OH 44691. Affiliates: Red Swan Music (BMI) and Spangle Music (BMI). General Manager: Quentin W. Welty. Music publisher. BMI. Member CMA, NARAS. Publishes 12-15 songs/year; publishes 1 new songwriter/year. Pays standard royalty.
**How to Contact:** Submit demo tape. Prefers 7½ ips reel-to-reel with 1-5 songs on demo. "Mono or full-track only." SASE. Reports in 2 weeks.
**Music:** Bluegrass, C&W, folk and gospel. Recently published "Take Your Shoes Off Moses," recorded by the Lewis Family (C&W); "Multiply the Heartaches," recorded by G. Jones and M. Montgomery (C&W); and "Unkind Words," recorded by Kathy Dee (pop/C&W).
**Tips:** Songs must be 'commercial' for today's market."

**WESJAC MUSIC,** 129 W. Main St., Box 743, Lake City SC 29560. (803)394-3712. General Manager: W.R. Bragdton Jr. Music publisher and record company. BMI. Publishes 3 songs/year; publishes 1 new songwriter/year. Pays standard royalty.
**How to Contact:** Submit demo tape and lead sheet or submit lead sheet. Prefers 7½ or 15 ips reel-to-reel with 2 songs minimum on tape. SASE. Reports in 1 month.
**Music:** Church/religious and gospel. Recently published "I'm Glad I Wasn't Made by Man" (by Handy McFadden and W.R. Bragdton), recorded by Gospel Songbirds/Wesjac Records (gospel); and "I Can't Stop Loving God" and "My Soul is Heaven Bound" (by William Nelson), both recorded by Traveling Four/Wesjac Records (gospel).
**Tips:** Likes "good material and good cooperation in the matter."

**WEYAND MUSIC PUBLISHING,** 297 Rehm Rd., Depew NY 14043. (716)684-5323. Proprietor: C.D. Weyand. Music publisher. ASCAP. Member NMPA. Pays negotiable royalty.
**How to Contact:** "Only fully written piano arrangements will be considered. Please—no *lead* sheets. SASE a must. All material submitted must be complete and copyrighted by the person(s) making submission." SASE. Reports in 1-3 months.
**Music:** Mostly classical; also bluegrass, blues, C&W, easy listening, R&B and top 40/pop. Recently published "Around the Bend," "Never Cry," "Words at Parting", "With You," "Why Can't You?" and "It's the Only Way" (all by Weyand), all recorded on DaCar Records; "We Care," "Song For Freedom" (songs for hostages in Iran), *The '80s Song Folio*, "A Thousand Stars," "Prelude in C Minor," "Prelude Op. 28-No. 7" (by Chopin with variation by Weyand) and "Meditation" (classical), all by Weyand.
**Tips:** "Write for complete catalog. Instrumental and orchestral works must be of a professional nature when recorded on tape or on cassette and must include a full 'conductor' score for proper review."

**WHITE CAT MUSIC,** Box 3247, Shawnee KS 66203. (913)631-6060. Affiliate: Rocky Bell Music (BMI). Music publisher. Professional Manager: Frank Fara. Producer: Patty Parker. Publishes 60 songs/year; "75% of our published songs are from non-charted and developing writers." Pays standard royalty.
**How to Contact:** Arrange personal interview or submit demo tape. Cassette only with 1-5 songs on demo. SASE. Reports in 2 weeks.
**Music:** Mostly pop and country; also C&W and contemporary gospel. Recently published "I Was Wrong" (by Craig Fleishman and Jon Granet), recorded by Roman Gregory/Highrise Records; "Christmas Without You" (by David Mulcey and Bob Howard), recorded by Don TeBeaux; "Still Be a Me & You" (by Larry Baxter and Nelson Trout), recorded by D. TeBeaux; "She Learned Everything She Knows from a Cheating Man" (by Ken Wesley), recorded by Bill Hersh; "The Song of Reno at Night" (by Inez Polizzi and Phil Coley), recorded by D. Tebeaux/Comstock Records (pop-country); "Love Me Tonight" (by David Rackley), recorded by Buddi Day/Comstock Records (country crossover); and "Here Come the Lines" (by Donette Wollston), recoded by Reg Watkins and Lori Kristin/Comstock Records (traditonal country).
**Tips:** Needs "good clean demo (uptempo modern country), and Canadian writers."

**WHITE CLAY PRODUCTIONS, INC.,** 1103 Elktan Rd., Newark DE 19711. (302)368-1211. Affiliates: White Clay Music (BMI) and Straight-Face Music (ASCAP). A&R Director: E. Michael Fisher. BMI. Publishes 14 songs/year; publishes 3 new songwriters/year. Pays standard royalty.

**How to Contact:** Submit demo tape and lyric sheet. Prefers cassette as demo. SASE. Reports in 3 weeks.
**Music:** Dance-oriented, country, jazz, progressive, R&B, rock and new wave.

**WILL-DU MUSIC PUBLISHERS,** 833 N. Orange Grove Ave., Los Angeles CA 90046. (213)653-8358. Affiliate: Deliver Music Pub. Co. (BMI). General Manager: Lou Dulfon. Music publisher and management company. BMI. Member AGAC. Publishes 6-8 songs/year for European markets. Pays standard royalty.
**How to Contact:** "We have a full complement of writers."
**Music:** R&B, rock, rock soul and top 40/pop. Recently published *Screamin' the Blues* (by Screamin' Jay Hawkins), album recorded by Red Lightnin' Records, published in UK by Big Spliff Music; and "Monkburry Moon Delight" (by Linda and Paul McCartney) published by Deliver Music.

**DON WILLIAMS MUSIC GROUP,** Suite 1106, 1888 Century Park. E., Los Angeles CA 90067. (213)556-2458. Affiliates: Redstripe Music (BMI), Pacific View Music (ASCAP) and Wishbone Music (ASCAP). Contact: D.W. Hathaway. Music publishing/administration and record production. BMI and ASCAP. Publishes 40 songs/year. Pays standard royalty.
**How to Contact:** Submit demo tape and lyric sheet. Prefers cassette with 2-3 songs on demo. "List name, address and telephone number on package." SASE. Reports in 4-6 weeks.
**Music:** Progressive C&W, easy listening, jazz, MOR, R&B, rock, soul, disco and top 40/pop. Recently published "Just Can't Win Them All," "Read Between the Lines" and "Steal the Night" (by Trevor Veitch), recorded by Stevie Woods/Cotillion Records.

*****WILSING MUSIC PUBLISHERS,** Rt. 3, Box 100-N, Stuart VA 24171. (703)694-6128. Contact: Frank W. Singleton. Music publisher and record company (Spinn Records). BMI. Pays standard royalty.
**How to Contact:** Submit demo tape and lyric sheet. Prefers 7½ or 15 ips reel-to-reel or cassette as demo. SASE. Reports in 1 month.
**Music:** Mostly C&W; also bluegrass, church/religious, folk and gospel. Recently published "Unclaimed Soldier" and "Live Here with the Blues" (by Tommy Riddle), recorded by T. Riddle/Spinn Records (country).

**LUTHER WILSON MUSIC CO.,** Box 2664, Kansas City KS 66110. (913)621-1676. Contact: Luther Wilson Jr. Music publisher, music copying and record company (LWJ Records). Estab. 1982. ASCAP. Publishes 60-80 songs/year; publishes 2 new songwriters/year. Pays standard royalty.
**How to Contact:** Submit demo tape and lyric sheet. Prefers cassette with minimum of 4 new songs on demo. SASE. Reports in 3 weeks.
**Music:** Mostly top 40 and R&B; also bluegrass, blues, C&W, dance-oriented, easy listening, folk, gospel, jazz, MOR, rock and soul. Recently published "Don't Say A Word" (by Vickie Chiney and Luther Wilson Jr.), recorded by Steve Fuller/NeeseCo Records (easy listening); "Don't Let Me See Your Face" (by Fawna Taylor and L. Wilson, Jr.), and "I Really Love You" (by Lawrence Greene and L. Wilson, Jr), both recorded by Wilson, Taylor and Greene/LWJ Records (top 40/R&B).
**Tips:** "Use good quality tapes and get voice out front. We openly encourage songwriters to send us material. Send only the songs with strong catchy hooks and lyrics."

**WINDOW MUSIC PUBLISHING CO., INC.,** 809 18th Ave. S., Nashville TN 37203. (615)327-3211. Affiliates: Tomake Music (ASCAP), Speak Music (BMI), Ernest Tubb Music, Inc. (BMI) and Petewood Music (ASCAP). Office Manager: Rose Trimble. Music publisher. BMI. Publishes 300 songs/year. Pays standard royalty.
**How to Contact:** Not currently accepting outside material.
**Music:** C&W, easy listening, gospel, rock and top 40/pop. Recently published "If Drinkin' Don't Kill Me (Her Memory Will)" (by Rick Beresford and Harlan Sanders), recorded by George Jones/Epic Records (C&W); and "I'll Be There," recorded by Gayle Davis/Warner Brothers Records (C&W).

**WISHBONE, INC.,** Box 2631, Muscle Shoals AL 35662. (205)381-1455. Affiliates: Song Tailors Music Co. (BMI), Terry Woodford Music (ASCAP), I've Got the Music Co. (ASCAP) and Creative Source Music (BMI). Professional Manager: Richard Butler. General Manager: Kevin Lamb. Music publisher, record producer, studio and video production company (Flying Colors Video). BMI, ASCAP. Publishes a varied number of songs/year. Hires staff writers. Pays standard royalty.
**How to Contact:** Submit demo tape and lyric sheet. Prefers cassette with 1-3 songs on demo. SASE for returned material. Reports ASAP.
**Music:** Mostly top 40/pop; also C&W, dance-oriented, easy listening, MOR, progressive, R&B, rock and soul. Recently published "Hug Me, Squeeze Me" (by Brandon Barnes and Calvin Frost), recorded

by Debra Hurd/Geffen Records (top 40/pop); "Minimum Love" (by Mac McAnally & Jerry Wexler), recorded by M. McAnally/Geffen Records (top 40/pop); and "Old Flame" (by M. McAnally & Donny Lowery), recorded by Alabama/RCA Records (country).

**WOODRICH PUBLISHING CO.**, Box 38, Lexington AL 35648. (205)247-3983. Affiliate: Mernee Music (ASCAP). President: Woody Richardson. Music publisher and record company. BMI. Publishes 20 songs/year; publishes 5 new songwriters/year. Pays 50% royalty less expenses.
**How to Contact:** Submit demo tape. Prefers 7½ ips reel-to-reel or cassette with 2-4 songs on demo. SASE. Reports in 1 month.
**Music:** Mostly black gospel and country; also bluegrass, blues, choral, church/religious, C&W, easy listening, folk, gospel, jazz, MOR, progressive, rock, soul and top 40/pop. Recently published "If God Should Go on Strike" (by Wash Hobson, Jr), recorded by The Hobson Family (black gospel); "Packing Up" (by D. Stockton), recorded by The Sentry Men (southern gospel); and "Surrender Hill" (by Lynn Cramer and Ted Mack), recorded by L. Cramer (country).
**Tips:** "Send a good demo and include a lyric sheet, but written music is not necessary."

*****WOOMERA MUSIC PTY., LTD.**, 17 Radford Rd., Reservoir, Victoria 3073, Australia. Affiliate/US: Jaspar Music. Affiliate/Canada: Banff & Melbourne Music. Director: Ron Gillespie. Music publisher and record company. APRA, AMCOS. Member AMPA. Will listen to songs submitted by US songwriters, but only when submitted through US publishing affiliates. Pays standard royalty; royalties paid to US songwriters through US publishing affiliate.
**How to Contact:** Submit demo tape and lyric sheet. Prefers cassette with 2-5 songs on demo. Does not return unsolicited material. Reports in 1 month.
**Music:** Mostly C&W; also folk and top 40/pop.

**WORD MUSIC**, Division of Word, Inc., Box 1790, Waco TX 76796. (817)772-7650. Affiliates: Rodeheaver (ASCAP), Myrrh (ASCAP), Dayspring (BMI) and The Norman Clayton Publishing Co. (SESAC). Music Editors: Ken Barker, Bill Wolaver and Gary Rhodes. A&R Dept.: Bubba Smith, Word Records, Suite 302, 2300 Hillsboro Rd., Nashville TN 37212. Music publisher and record company. ASCAP. Member GMA. Publishes 25 songs/year; publishes 1-3 new songwriters/year.
**How to Contact:** Submit demo tape and lead sheet. Prefers cassette with 1-3 songs on demo. SASE. Reports in 10 weeks.
**Music:** Mostly choral anthems and octaves; also children's, choral, church/religious and gospel. "Songs of a commercial, solo nature should be submitted to the A&R department of our record company." Recently published "Hosanna" (by Tricia Walker), recorded by Joni Eareckson/Word Records (contemporary/MOR); "Corner Stone" and "John 3:17" (by Leon Patillo), recorded by L. Patillo/Myrrh Records (contemporary).
**Tips:** "Lead sheets, or final form—anything submitted—should be legible and understandable. The care that a writer extends in the works he submits reflects the work he'll submit if a working relationship is started. First impressions are important."

*****WORK MUSIC PUBLISHING COMPANY**, Suite 2, 1390 Sherbrooke W., Montreal, Quebec, Canada H3G 1J9. (514)844-2877. Affiliate: Level-S-Music (ASCAP). President: Paul Klein. Music publisher, record company and record producer. Estab. 1981. BMI. Publishes 20 songs/year; publishes 5 new songwriters/year. Hires staff writers; pays $100/week advance against royalties. Pays standard royalty.
**How to Contact:** Submit demo tape and lyric sheet. Prefers cassette with 1-4 songs on demo. Does not return unsolicited material. Reports in 1 month.
**Music:** Mostly dance-oriented; also soul. Recently published "Cold Fire" (by R. Dabney and L. Davis), recorded by Gypsy Lane/Musicworks Records (dance); "Sneakin'" (by L. Richardson, A. Felder and J. Freeman), recorded by Joe Freeman/Musicworks Records (dance); and "Everytime" (by R. Dabney and L. Davis), recorded by Little Dabs/Musicworks Records (dance).

*****REX ZARIO MUSIC**, 3010 N. Front St., Philadelphia PA 19133. (215)426-5682. Affiliates: Jack Howard Publishing (BMI), Seabreeze Music (BMI), Valley Brook Publishing (ASCAP), Arcade Music Co. (ASCAP). Production Manager: Lucky Taylor. Music publisher, record company and record producer. BMI. Publishes 15-25 songs/year. Pays standard royalty.
**How to Contact:** Submit demo tape and lyric sheet. Prefers 7½ ips reel-to-reel or cassette with 4-6 songs on demo. SASE. Reports in 1 month.
**Music:** C&W, MOR, R&R and bluegrass. Recently published "Night Wine" (by Lucky Taylor, Doris Frye, Rex Zario and Jesse Rogers), recorded by J. Rogers/Arcade Records (MOR); "Go Man Go, Get Gone" (by L. Taylor, D. Frye and R. Zario), recorded by R. Zario/Rollercoaster Records in England (C&W); and "Worlds Apart" (by Ray Whitley and R. Zario), recorded by R. Whitely/Arzee (C&W).

# Close-up

**Alfie Davison**
Songwriter/Performer

"I really feel that writers and artists, like any creative people, have the responsibility to use their God-given talent to spread messages of good will to people." The responsibility songwriter/performer Alfie Davison talks about means "Identifying the things that are truly important to you, grasping what is important to other people, then writing and singing about those things. Be a commentator on the times you live in. Develop a philosophy and write about the things you feel."

Davison's "philosophy" was formed as a young man growing up in New York City. "Like a lot of people who grew up in the late sixties, I was influenced by the sounds from Motown, especially Stevie Wonder." At sixteen, Davison began his own music career as a disc jockey where he learned two things that have proven helpful in his own music career: "what makes a record popular, and how to turn on an audience."

The first song Davison wrote, "Who's Gonna Love Me," was recorded by the Imperials, went to the top ten on song charts in England, and gave him his first charted song in the US. Since then he has recorded his own material both on RCA and Mercury Records. His songs have also been recorded by Gloria Gaynor, Ralph Carter, and McPhadden and Whitehead, among others, and covered by artists in England, France, Belgium and Japan.

Not only a successful songwriter/performer, Davison also teaches reading to New York high school students. "Teaching is good because it keeps me in touch with that part of the market that buys records," says Davison. "I can hear what they listen to and what they buy and how it relates to their own lives. I hear students using the same expressions in their everyday language that they've picked up from currently-popular songs. That's why I feel it is especially important that young people be given good, positive images and messages in songs."

Davison considers himself a student too—a student of his craft of songwriting. Not only is he occasionally a speaker at the Ted Lehrman/Libby Bush Songwriter Seminars and Workshops in NYC (see listing in the Workshops section of this book), but he has also been a student of the workshop. "A workshop is a good place to have your material bounced around, to get other points of view, and to meet collaborators," says Davison. In fact, Davison co-wrote "Love is a Serious Business" with Lehrman, a song that was not only recorded by Davison on Mercury Records, but also recorded and released in England by Grace Kennedy.

Davison has an optimistic outlook for his own future as well as that of other young, aspiring songwriters and performers. "Not that anyone should try to imitate them, but there *is* another Lennon-McCartney somewhere, and there *is* another Stevie Wonder somewhere. I'm hopeful that the time is drawing near when these new writers and artists will get their chance to influence the music industry."

# Geographic Index

The US section of this handy geographic index will quickly give you the names of publishers located in the music centers of Los Angeles, Nashville and New York. The International section lists, geographically, markets for your songs in Australia, England and New Zealand.

Find the names of companies in this index, and then check listings within the Music Publishers section for addresses, phone numbers and submission details.

## UNITED STATES

### LOS ANGELES

Alexis
Aljoni Music Co.
American Broadcasting Music, Inc.
American Entertainment General
Arista Music Publishing Group
ATJACK Music
ATV Music Corp.
Audio Arts Publishing
Baruth Music
Bee Mor Music
Beechwood
Big Heart Music
Black Stallion Country Publishing
Blue Island Publishing
Tommy Boyce & Melvin Powers Music Enterprises
Brave New Music
Glen Campbell Enterprises, Ltd.
Chinwah Songs/Birthright Music
The Chu Yeko Musical Foundation
Davike Music Co.
De Walden Music International, Inc.
Dupuy Records/Productions/Publishing, Inc.
Eagle Rock Music Co.
Equinox Music
Firelight Publishing
Al Gallico Music Corp.
Garrett Music Enterprises
Gordon Music Co.
The Grand Pasha Publisher
Gule Record
Harrison Music Corp.
Highest Praise Publishing
Ladera Music Publishing

Jay Landers Music
Stuart Lanis Music, Inc.
Manna Music, Inc.
MCA Music
Monona/Watertoons/Hoochie Coochie/Skafish Music
Doug Moody Music
Morris Music, Inc.
Music Concepts International
Music Publishing Corporation/Cream Publishing Group
Michael O'Connor Music
O'Lyric Music
Philippopolis Music
Red Tennis Music
Gary Revel Music
Rhythms Productions
Rockmore Music
Brian Ross Music
Rubicon Music
Sasha Songs, Unltd. & The Grand Pasha Publisher
Larry Shayne Enterprises
Sound Image Publishing
Televox Music
Third Story Music, Inc.
Transatlantic Music
VAAM Music
Watts City Productions
Ron Weiser Publishing
Don Williams Music Group

### NASHVILLE

Acoustic Music, Inc.
Americus Music
AMI
ATV Music Corp.
Baby Huey Music
Beechwood Music
Brandwood Music, Inc.
Broadman Press

Brooks Brothers Publishers
Buried Treasure Music
Calvary Records, Inc.
CBS Songs
Chatterbox Music
Chestnut Mound Music
Chip 'N' Dale Music Publishers
Covered Bridge Music
Diversified Music, Inc.
Door Knob Music Publishing, Inc.
The Drake Music Group
Bobby Fischer Music
Forrest Hills Music, Inc.
Frick Music Publishing Co.
Al Gallico Music Corp.
Grawick Music
Iffin Music Publishing Co.
Jackpot Music
Jacklyn Music
Dick James Music, Inc.
JMR Enterprises
Kelley & Lloyd Music
Gene Kennedy Enterprises, Inc.
Lodestar Music
Lorenz Crative Services
Merit Music Corp.
Mr. Mort Music
Monkey Music, Inc.
Multimedia Music Group
Music Craftshop
Newcreative Music
Newwriters Music
O.A.S. Music Group
Peer-Southern Organization
Power-Play Publishing
Priority/Preference Music-CBS Songs
Pyramid Records
Jim Reeves Enterprises
Shetland Sound
Shelby Singleton Music Inc.
Song Farm Music

Southern Writers Group USA
Ben Speer Music
Sugarplum Music Co.
Sweet Singer Music
Tree Publishing Co., Inc.
Tyner Music
Vector Music
Window Music Publishing Co., Inc.

## NEW YORK

ACE Adams Music, Adam Puertas Music
Aldous Demian Publishing, Ltd.
APON Publishing Co.
Asilomar/Dreena Music
ATV Music Corp.
Beechwood Music Corp.
Belwin-Mills Publishing Corp.
Big Mike Music
Blue Umbrella Music Publishing Co.
Bourne Music
Brooklyn Country Music
Brut Music Publishing

Bush/Lehrman Productions
Buttermilk Sky Associates
Caligula, Inc.
Camerica Music
Can't Stop Music
Copyright Service Bureau Ltd.
Cotillion Music
David Music
Delightful Music Ltd.
Entertainment Co. Music Group
Funky Acres Music Co.
Gopam Enterprises, Inc.
Gospel Clef
Helios Music Corporation
Jorin
Kamakazi Music Corporation
Lareo Music, Inc.
MacHarmony Music
Marielle Music Co.
Mega-Star Music
Memnon, Ltd.
Mideb Music
Ivan Mogull Music Corp.
Music Copyright Holding Corporation
Music Resources International Corp.

Mustevic Sound Inc.
Nelter Music Publishing
Neverland Music Publishing Co.
Nick-O-Val Music
Nonpareil Music
Notable Music Co. Inc.
NRP Music Group
Pavillion Productions/Promotion, Inc.
Peer-Southern Organization
Pilgrim International Ltd.
Publishing Ventures, Inc.
Gerald W. Purcell Associates
Raybird Music
RBI Records/Rowalba Publishing
Ren Maur Music Corp.
Rothstein Music, Ltd.
Screen Gems/Colgems/EMI Music, Inc.
September Music Corp.
Silver Blue Productions, Ltd.
Songs for Today, Inc.
Sun-Bear Corporation
Vado Music
Weeze Music Co. & Double Header Productions

# INTERNATIONAL

## AUSTRALIA

Chappell & Co. (AUST.) Pty., Ltd.
Essex Music of Australia Pty. Ltd.
Greater Songs
Image Music Pty., Ltd.
Doug Jansen Music
Matthews Music Pty., Ltd.
MCA Music Australia Pty., Ltd.
Rondor Music (Australia) Pty., Ltd.
Sundowner Music (Australasia) Pty., Ltd.
Warner Bros. Music Australia Pty., Ltd.
Woomera Music Pty., Ltd.

## ENGLAND

Andersongt Music

Aura Records & Music Ltd.
Barsongs Limited
Bearsongs
Big Secret Music Ltd.
Big Spliff Music
Black & White Music Corporation Limited
BOCU Music Ltd.
Cats Whiskers Music Ltd.
Charisma Music Publishing Co. Ltd.
Cherry Red Music Ltd.
Barry Collings Music Ltd.
The Flying Music Company Ltd.
Hedley Music Group
Highway Music
Incidental Music
Jason Music/Mooreside Music
Lorna Kirtland Music Ltd.
Le Matt Music, Ltd.

Alfred Lengnick & Co. Ltd.
Nervous Publishing
New Music Enterprises
Oakwood Music
Trisha O'Keefe Music, Ltd.
Olofsong Music
Pixie Music Co. Ltd.
Red Bus Music International, Ltd.
Rocket Publishing
Stage One Music
Street Tunes Ltd.
Tabitha Music Ltd.
Twist and Shout Music
Walden Music
Jeff Wayne Music Publishing, Ltd.

## NEW ZEALAND

Maui Music
Pegasus Music

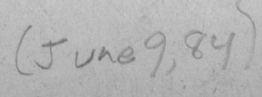

* = recent success in Hot 100 (June 9, 84)

Music Publishers **121**

## The Quiet Types

In preparing *Songwriter's Market 1984*, we contacted all major American and Canadian music publishers at least once—and in some cases, two or three times. Most responded. Some, however, did not give us information for one of the following reasons:
- They are not actively seeking new artists or material from songwriters.
- They *will* listen to material, but believe that they receive sufficient material without listing in *Songwriter's Market*.
- They are a branch office that concentrates on marketing or other business endeavors, and leaves selection of artists and songs to branches in other cities.
- They work only with artists or songwriters recommended to them from other sources.
- They are staffed with inhouse songwriters.
- They don't have a staff large enough to handle the increased number of submissions a listing would create.
- They are concerned with copyright problems that might result if they record a song similar to one they've reviewed and rejected.
- They have once listed with another songwriter directory and were deluged with inappropriate submissions.

Though some of the following firms will review material, we suggest that you *not* send demo tapes. Write a brief query letter describing your material and asking about the company's current submission policies. Always use a self-addressed, stamped envelope or post card for such queries (see sample reply form in "The Business of Songwriting").

Abkco Music, Inc., 1700 Broadway, New York NY 10019.
Acuff-Rose Publishing Inc., 2510 Franklin Rd., Nashville TN 37204.
Al-Bo Music Co., 37 Odell Ave., Yonkers NY 10701.
Almo (see Rondor).
Alpha Music Inc., 40 E. 49th St., New York NY 10017.
American Broadcasting Music Inc., 1330 Avenue of the Americas, New York NY 10019.
American Cowboy, 14 Music Circle E., Nashville TN 37203.
Atlantic Music (see Criterion Music Corp.).
Baray & Honeytree, 49 Music Square E., Nashville TN 37203.
Earl Barton Music Corp., 1121 S. Glenstone, Springfield MO 65804.
The Benson Co., Inc., 1816 Hayes St., Nashville TN 37203.
Bicycle Music Co., 8756 Holloway Dr., Los Angeles CA 90069.
Boxer Music, Box 120501, Nashville TN 37212.
Buckhorn Music Publishing Co., Inc., Box 120547, Nashville TN 37212.
Buddah Music, 1790 Broadway, New York NY 10019.
Burlington Music Corp., 539 W. 25th St., New York NY 10001.
CBS Songs, 1515 Broadway, New York NY 10036.
Cedarwood, 39 Music Square E., Nashville TN 37203.
Chappell Music Co., 11 Music Circle S., Nashville TN 37203.
Chappell Music Co., 810 7th Ave., New York NY 10019.
Chicago Music Publishing, c/o Greene & Reynolds, Suite 1424, 1900 Avenue of the Stars, Los Angeles CA 90067.
Chrysalis Music Corp., 115 E. 57th St., New York NY 10022.
Coal Miners Music, Inc., 7 Music Circle N., Nashville TN 37203.
Martin Cohen, Suite 1500, 6430 Sunset Blvd., Los Angeles CA 90028.
Bruce Cohn Music, Box 359, Sonoma CA 95476.
Combine Music Group, 35 Music Square E., Nashville TN 37203.
Contention, Box 824, Nashville TN 37202.

Criterion Music Corp., 6124 Selma Ave., Hollywood CA 90028.
Daksel/Seldak Music Corp., 65 W. 55th St., New York NY 10019.
Dawnbreaker Music Co., 216 Chatsworth Dr., San Fernando CA 91340.
Debdave Music Inc., Box 140110, Nashville TN 37214.
Famous Music Corp., 6430 Sunset Blvd., Los Angeles CA 90028.
Famous Music Corp., 2 Music Circle S., Nashville TN 37203.
Famous Music Corp., 1 Gulf & Western Plaza, New York NY 10023.
Fate Music, 1046 Carol Dr., Los Angeles CA 90069.
Fermata International Melodies, Suite 916, 6290 Sunset Blvd., Hollywood CA 90028.
Frebar Music Co., 5514 Kelly Rd., Brentwood TN 37027.
Larry Gatlin (see Combine).
Gaucho Music, 161 W. 54th St., New York NY 10019.
Gold Hill Music, Inc., 5032 Lankershim Blvd., North Hollywood CA 91601.
The Goodman Group, 110 E. 59th St., New York NY 10022.
Hall of Fame Music Co., Box 921, Beverly Hills CA 90213.
Hope Publishing Co., 380 S. Main Place, Carol Stream IL 60187.
House of Gold Music, Inc., Box 120967, 1614 16th Ave., S., Nashville TN 37212.
Intersong Music, Inc., Suite 1904, 6255 Sunset Blvd., Hollywood CA 90028.
Irving/Almo (see Rondor).
Island Music/UFO Music, Inc., 6525 Sunset Blvd., Hollywood CA 90028.
Jobete Music Co., Inc., 6255 Sunset Blvd., Hollywood CA 90028.
Kirshner/CBS Music Publishing, 8961 Sunset Blvd., Los Angeles CA 90069.
Kirshner/CBS Music Publishing, 1370 W. 55th St., New York NY 10019.
Koala, 6253 Hollywood Blvd., Los Angeles CA 90028.
Edwin H. Morris & Co., 39 W. 54th St., New York NY 10019.
MCA Music, 1106 17th Ave. S., Nashville TN 37212.
MCA Music, 445 Park Ave., New York NY 10022.
MPL Communications Inc., (see Edwin H. Morris & Co.).
Muscle Shoals Sound Publ'g Co., Inc., Box 915, 1000 Alabama Ave., Sheffield AL 35660.
Music City (see Combine Music Group).
Participation House Music, Inc., 1348 Lexington Ave., New York NY 10028.
George Pincus & Sons, 1650 Broadway, New York NY 10019.
Raydiola Music, Box 5270, Beverly Hills CA 90210.
Riva Music Publishing Group, 232 E. 61st St., New York NY 10021.
Rodsongs (see Rondor).
Rondor Music International, Inc., 1358 N. La Brea Ave., Hollywood CA 90028.
Rose Bridge (see Earl Barton).
Sabal (see Mel Tillis).
Sawgrass Music Publishers (see Mel Tillis).
Screen Gems-EMI Music, Inc., 6255 Sunset Blvd., Hollywood CA 90028.
Screen Gems-Colgems-EMI Music Inc., 1207 16th Ave. S., Nashville TN 37212.
Shade Tree Music Inc., Box 500, Bella Vista CA 96008.
Shapiro Bernstein, 10 E. 53rd St., New York NY 10022.
Silverline Music, Inc., 329 Rockland Rd., Hendersonville TN 37075.
Southern Nights (see Combine Music Group).
Stone Bridge (see Bicycle Music Co.).
Mel Tillis Music, 1520 Demonbreun St., Nashville TN 37203.

## Music Publishers 123

Virgin (see Chappell).
Warner/Tamerlane Music, 9200 Sunset Blvd., Los Angeles CA 90069.
Warner/Tamerlane Music, 75 Rockefeller Plaza, New York NY 10019.
Warner/Tamerlane Music, 44 Music Square W., Nashville TN 37203.

# Record Companies

Unlike the music publisher whose only business is songs, the record company must be many things to many people. The record company not only provides the recording facilities—studio, equipment, technicians, etc.—but also secures artists, producers and musicians; and manufactures, distributes and promotes new records and tapes. All this can add up to thousands of dollars invested into one song.

The recording industry, then, is big business with big expenses. To stay in business record companies must always be conscious of the "bottom line," which means they must be selective about the songs and artists they choose to record. This need for the best can work to the advantage of unknown songwriters, however. Even though most record companies look to publishers for songs—many even have their own publishing branch—the A&R man doesn't care *who* you are or *where* you came from as long as you have the song he's looking for!

Unlike the publisher who listens to songs knowing he can shop them to many artists and many record companies, the A&R director listens to new songs with specific artists in mind—those artists recording on his company's label. This is bad for the songwriter in the sense that it narrows the reviewer's persective of your material's worth (to him, anyway). This is to your advantage, however, if you have a song you think would suit one of his artists. Also, the A&R man will usually know right away—and let you know right away—whether he can or cannot use your material.

Playing your songs for the A&R director of a record company can be especially beneficial if you are an artist or group who writes your own material. A&R men not only look for songs for the artists they record, but they also look for new and exciting talent to record on their label. (For information on contracts between a record company and a recording artist, see "Contracts" in the Appendix of this book.) If you are in this songwriter-performer category, include with your demo a photo (professional—no snapshots), a biography (typewritten, neat, concise, and emphasizing previous performance experience), and also clippings of any performance reviews.

Appearing in this section for the first time—as well as in the Music Publishers and Record Producers sections—are companies located in England, Australia and New Zealand. Each has expressed a willingness to work with songwriters and artists from the US (most already have). Some indicate in their listings that they have not yet, but would be willing to listen to material from US songwriters. Listings for foreign companies also state whether royalties are paid directly to US songwriters and artists, or through a US affiliate (and some companies use either method, depending on individual circumstances).

The geographic index at the end of this section will quickly refer you to publishers in Australia, England and New Zealand. It also lists, geographically, record companies in the US music centers of Los Angeles, Nashville and New York. Use this information to quickly locate publishers in those cities. Or use the index to make contacts and organize your itinerary *before* you travel to a music center so you can make the most of your valuable time while you are there.

*Billboard* and *Cash Box* charts give the names of top recording artists and the labels on which they record. Additional names and addresses of record companies can be found in the *Billboard International Buyer's Guide*, though it contains no submission information.

Some companies we contacted did not give us the information needed for a listing. The names of those companies appear as "Quiet Types" at the very end of this section, along with a synopsis of their reasons for not listing and a note on how to contact them.

If there is a record company whose name you can't find either among the listings in this section, or in the "Quiet Types" at the end of this section, see "How to Be a Music Market Detective" in the Appendix of this book. There you can learn how to successfully track down any record company, music publisher, record producer, or even recording artist you think might be interested in your songs.

**A&M RECORDS, INC.**, 1416 N. La Brea, Hollywood CA 90028. (213)469-2411. Record company. Releases 84 singles and 56 albums/year. Works with artists and songwriters on contract.
**How to Contact:** "Direct all material through a publisher." SASE.
**Music:** C&W, dance, easy listening, folk, jazz, MOR, progressive, R&B, rock, soul, and top 40/pop. Recently released *Ghost in the Machine*, by the Police (rock LP); *Dare*, by the Human League (rock LP); and *The Dude*, by Quincy Jones (jazz/R&B LP).

**A&M RECORDS INC.**, 595 Madison Ave., New York NY 10022. (212)826-0477. East Coast Manager: Hernando Courtright. Record company.
**How to Contact:** Submit demo tape. Prefers cassette with 1-5 songs on demo. SASE. Reports in 1 month.
**Music:** Dance, progressive, R&B, rock and top 40/pop. Recently released *Mr. Roboto*, by Styx; *Famous Last Words*, by Supertramp; and *Singles*, by Squeeze.

**A&M RECORDS OF CANADA, LTD.**, 939 Warden Ave., Scarborough, Ontario, Canada M1L 4C5. (416)752-7191. A&R Coordinator: Michael Godin. Record company and music publisher; Almo/CAPAC, ASCAP, Irving/PROCAN, BMI. Member CRIA. Works with artists on contract. Pays statutory rate to publishers for each record sold.
**How to Contact:** Submit demo tape and lyric sheet. Prefers cassette with 3-5 songs on demo. "Be aware of the time it takes to listen and respond. Be patient." SAE and IRC. Reports in 1 month.
**Music:** Progressive, rock (hard) and top 40/pop. Recently released *Ghost in the Machine*, by Police; *Kilroy Was Here*, by Styx; and *Cuts Like a Knife*, by Bryan Adams (all rock LPs). Other artists include Payola$, Peter Pringle, Fist and Eddie Schwartz.
**Tips:** "Listen to the new records being released regularly and be aware of what you are competing with for radio airplay, sales, concerts, video, etc."

*****ABACUS**, Box 186, Cedarburg WI 53012 (414)673-5091. Labels include Abacus and New Dawn Records. Producer: Bob Wiegert. Record company, record producer and music publisher (RobJen Music). Works with musicians on salary for in-house studio work; songwriters on contract. Pays negotiable royalty to artists on contract; statutory rate to publishers for each record sold.
**How to Contact:** Write first about your interest; submit demo tape and lyric sheet. Prefers 7½ ips reel-to-reel or cassette with 1-3 songs on demo. SASE. Reports in 1 month.
**Music:** "If the song is commercial we will use it." Recently released "I Believe In You," by Cathy Bemis (pop single); "Alabama," and "I Think It's Gonna Rain," by Stills & Scott (country rock singles). Other artists include Katie Mcgivin.

**ACCLAIM RECORDS, INC.**, Unit 10, 3500 Glen Erin Dr., Mississauga, Ontario, Canada L5L 1W6. (416)820-7788. President/General Manager: Veronica Mataseje. Record company, record producer and music publisher (Veron Music/PROCAN and World Acclaim Music/CAPAC). Estab. 1981. Member CMA, CARAS. Releases 12-15 singles and 5 albums/year. Works with songwriters on contract. Pays negotiable royalty to artists on contract; statutory rate (Canadian) to publishers for each record sold.
**How to Contact:** Call first about your interest. Prefers cassette with 2-5 songs on demo. SASE, "but I prefer not to have to return material." Reports in 3-4 weeks.
**Music:** Mostly contemporary country, also gospel, rock (country) and top 40/pop. Recently released "Dance with Me Molly" and "Tommy," by Tommy Hunter (country singles); and "Ease My Mind," by Iris Larratt (country/pop single). Other artists include Orval Prophet.
**Tips:** "We look for international appeal in an artist or song."

*****ACI INTERNATIONAL/GROOVESONG RECORDS**, Division of Echord Communications Industries, Box 3664, Davenport IA 52808. (309)794-1968. Labels include Groovesong and ACI Int. National Promotion Director: Gary Unger. Assistant A&R Manager: David Blumer. Record company. Estab. 1983. Releases 7 singles and 2 albums/year. Works with musicians and artists on contract or salary; songwriters on royalty contract; also negotiates co-production agreements and master leasing. Pays 10¢/single and 50¢/album to artists and 4¢ to producers for each record sold; statutory rate is 4¢ mechanical royalty rate to publishers for each record sold.
**How to Contact:** Write or call first about your interest; arrange personal interview. Prefers 7½, 15 or 30 ips reel-to-reel or cassette with 4-8 songs on demo. SASE. Reports in 8-10 weeks.
**Music:** Mostly dance-oriented, top 40 and pop/rock; also easy listening. Recently released "Lucky in Love," and "Love's Lifes Waiting," by Paul Gregory (pop singles); "Stepping Stone" b/w "Alive Again," by Dave Weiner (pop/AC/country singles); "Don't You Believe?," by D. Coulter (pop single); and "Long Long Time" and "Give A Care," by Alan Hale (pop singles). Other artists include Union, Gary Unger, Betty Parsons and Union Pacfic Band.

## 126 Songwriter's Market '84

**AFERTON RECORDS**, Box 2315, Springfield IL 62705. (217)528-7355. A&R Director: Kenneth A. White. Record company and music publisher (Satchitananda Publishing/BMI). Releases 10 singles and 8 albums/year. Works with musicians on salary; artists and songwriters on contract. Pays statutory rate to publishers for each record sold.
**How to Contact:** Submit demo tape and lyric sheet. Prefers cassette with 3-5 songs on demo. SASE. Reports in 1 month.
**Music:** Jazz, progressive, rock and top 40/pop. "We are not locked in to these categories and will consider any form of music if it is very good and if we can deal with it." Recently released *A Thought Away*, by Satchitananda (progressive jazz rock LP); *The Aferton Project*, by The Aferton Project (pop/rock LP); "Crazy Women," by Boe Perry (pop single); and "Nowhere," by Jill Kennedy (pop single).

*****ALAB**, Box 838, Enterprise AL 36331. President: Danny Bryan. Record company, record producer and music publisher (BD Publishing/BMI). Works with musicians and artists on contract; songwriters on royalty contract. Pays standard royalty to artist; statutory rate to publishers for each record sold.
**How to Contact:** Write first about your interest; submit demo tape and lyric sheet. Prefers cassette with 3-5 songs on demo. SASE. Reports in 1 month.
**Music:** Mostly top 40/pop, rock and MOR; also church/religious, C&W, easy listening, gospel, jazz, progressive, R&B and rockabilly. Recently released "Radio Free Boogie," by The Grasshoppers (rock/funk single). Other artists include Lovecraft, The Modern, Lenon Xenon and the Kinfolks (rockabilly).

**ALEAR RECORDS**, Box 574, Sounds of Winchester, Winchester VA 22601. (703)667-9379. Labels include Master Records, Winchester Records and Real McCoy Records. Secretary: Bertha McCoy. Record company, music publisher (Jim McCoy Music, Clear Music, New Edition Music/BMI), record producer and recording studio. Releases 20 singles and 10 albums/year. Works with artists and songwriters on contract; musicians on salary. Pays 2% minimum royalty to artists; statutory rate to publishers for each record sold.
**How to Contact:** Submit demo tape and lead sheet. Prefers 7½ ips reel-to-reel or cassette with 5-10 songs on demo. SASE. Reports in 1 month.
**Music:** Bluegrass, church/religious, C&W, folk, gospel, progressive and rock. Recently released "One More Time" by Earl Howard (country/single); "He Didn't Become Famous" by Jim McCoy (country/single); *Gospel Greats*, by Carroll County Ramblers (bluegrass gospel/LP). Other artists include Alvin Kesner, Jubilee Travelers, Jim McCoy, and Middleburg Harmonizers.

**AMALGAMATED TULIP CORP.**, 117 W. Rockland Rd., Libertyville IL 60048. (312)362-4060. Labels include Dharma Records. Director of Publishing and Administration: Mary Chris. Record company and music publisher. Works with musicians on salary; artists and songwriters on contract. Pays royalty to artists and songwriters on contract.
**How to Contact:** Submit demo tape. Prefers cassette with 2-5 songs on demo. SASE. Reports in 1-3 months.
**Music:** Rock (progressive and easy listening) and top 40/pop. Recently released "Another Trip to Earth," by Gabriel Bondage (progressive rock single); and *Corky Siegel*, by Corky Siegel (folk LP). Other artists include Conrad Black (rock).

**AMBIENTE MUSIC PRODUCTIONS, INC.**, Worldway Postal Center, Box 91120, Los Angeles CA 90009. (213)641-0178. Labels include Global Perspective. President: Philip Sonnichsen. Chairman: Edward "Lalo" Guerrero. Record company, record producer and music publisher (Ladera Music Publishing/BMI). Estab. 1981. Deals with artists and songwriters. Pays statutory rate to publishers for each record sold.
**How to Contact:** Write first about your interest, or submit demo tape and lyric sheet. Prefers cassette or reel-to-reel. SASE. Reports in 1 month.
**Music:** "We are a Chicano/Latin-oriented company. New material may be in English or Spanish."

**THE AME CORPORATION**, Suite 108, 3701 Twin Lakes Ct., Baltimore MD 21207. (800)638-5700. In MD-(301)521-5012. President: Edward Astri. Record company, record producer and music publisher (David Astri Publishing, Inc.). Estab. 1982. Releases 25-40 singles and 40+ albums/year. Works with artists and songwriters on contract. Pays 4-15% royalty to artists on contract or buys material outright.
**How to Contact:** Submit demo tape and lyric sheet. Prefers 15 or 30 ips reel-to-reel or cassette with 6-12 songs on demo. SASE. Reports in 1 month.
**Music:** Mostly rock (pop/rockabilly), C&W and top 40/pop; also bluegrass, church/religious, classical, gospel, progressive, Spanish and R&B. Recently released "Lou's Blues," by Patrick Williams (black/crossover single); *Dreams & Themes*, by P. Williams (progressive/pop LP); *Blondes*, by John Stewart

(rock/pop LP); *Friend, Lover, Wife*, by Johnny Paycheck (country LP); *Steppenwolf*, by Wolftracks (rock/pop LP); and "This Time We're Winning," by Little Anthony (pop single).
**Tips:** "Flexability and cooperation promote success. Don't like the 'temperamental artist' type."

**AMERICAN MUSIC COMPANY/CUCA RECORD AND CASSETTE MANUFACTURING COMPANY**, Box 8604, Madison WI 53708. Labels include American, Cuca, Jolly Dutchman, Age of Aquarius, Top Gun, Sound Power and Night Owl Records. Vice-President: Daniel W. Miller. Record company and music publisher (American Legend Music/ASCAP and Apple-Glass Music/BMI). Works with artists and songwriters on contract. Pays 10% royalty to artists on contract; 50% royalty to songwriters on contract.
**How to Contact:** Submit demo tape, photo and complete information. Prefers reel-to-reel tape (but will accept cassettes) with 2-20 songs on demo. SASE. "No calls, please." Reports within 6 months.
**Music:** "Old time" (polkas, waltzes), bluegrass, folk and ethnic. Recently released "Hupsadyna," by Styczynski (ethnic single); *Polka 76*, by Meisner (ethnic LP); and "Muleskinner Blues," (million-seller) by the Fendermen (rock single).
**Tips:** "Cuca has an extensive catalog and is known as "America's leading line of ethnic and old-time music." Artists may have a superior chance of having their material released on Cuca, American or affiliated labels, if they present *studio-quality* tapes of *all original* material."

*****AMI**, 111 Free Hill Rd., Hendersonville TN 37075. (615)822-6786. Labels include B&B. Vice President: Kenneth Bridger. Record company, record producer and music publisher (Bridger Publishing). Estab. 1981. Releases 22 singles and 6 albums/year. Works with artists and songwriters on contract; musicians on salary for in-house studio work. Pays 3-10% royalty to artists on contract; statutory rate to publishers for each record sold.
**How to Contact:** Submit demo tape and lyric sheet; call about your interest or arrange personal interview. Prefers reel-to-reel or cassette with 2-5 songs on demo. SASE.
**Music:** Mostly C&W; also classical, easy listening, gospel and top 40/pop. Recently released "Friday Night Feelin," and "Today My World Slipped Away," by Vern Gosdin (singles); and "Could It Be I Don't Belong Here Anymore," by Margo Smith (single). Other artists include Shannon Leigh, Terry Aden, Rich Lander, Terri Hart, Terry Ray Bradley and Kim Bridger.

**AMIRON MUSIC/AZTEC PRODUCTIONS**, 20531 Plummer St., Chatsworth CA 91311. (213)998-0443. Labels include Dorn Records and Aztec Records. General Manager: A. Sullivan. Record company, booking agency and music publisher (Amiron Music). Releases 2 singles/year. Works with artists and songwriters on contract. Pays 10% maximum royalty to artists on contract; standard royalty to songwriters on contract; pays statutory rate.
**How to Contact:** Submit demo tape and lead sheet. Prefers 7½ ips reel-to-reel or cassette. SASE. Reports in 3 weeks.
**Music:** Bluegrass, blues, C&W, dance, easy listening, folk, gospel, jazz, MOR, rock ("no heavy metal") and top 40/pop. Recently released "Blood from My Hand" and "It Feels Good," by Quicksand (R&B/disco singles); and "Act of Mercy," by Abraxas (top 40/pop single). Other artists include Jacqueleen Clifford and Sandy Benton.
**Tips:** "Be sure the material has a hook; it should make people want to make love or fight. Write something that will give a talented new artist that edge on current competition."

**ANAMAZE RECORDS**, Suite 2A, 1802 Ocean Pkwy., Brooklyn NY 11223. (212)627-8499. President/A&R Director: Cosmo Ohms. Record company and record producer. Works with musicians on salary; artists on contract. Pays 3½% minimum royalty to artists on contract.
**How to Contact:** Write first about your interest. Prefers cassette with 3 songs maximum on demo. SASE. Reports in 1 month.
**Music:** New wave and future-oriented rock; and top 40/pop. Recently released "Humans Being Humans," "We Can Have a Party," and *Summer Volcano*, by Startoon.

**LEE ANDERSON ENTERPRISES**, 415 N. Main St., St. Clair MO 63077. (314)629-1123. Labels include Country Capers, Belltone, Sports and Greenbush. Record company and music publisher (Calwest Songs/BMI).
**How to Contact:** Write first about your interest, then submit demo tape and lyric sheet to Bob Wood, Calwest Songs (BMI), 1509 Broadway, Bellingham WA 78225. (206)676-9761. Prefers cassette with 2-4 songs on demo. SASE.
**Music:** Bluegrass, blues, church/religious, C&W, easy listening, folk, gospel and R&B.

*****ANDREA RECORD CO.**, Old Antrim Rd., Hancock NH 03449. Creative Director: Dick Nevell. Record company. Works with artists on contract; musicians on salary for in-house studio work. Pays

statutory rate to publishers for each record sold.
**How to Contact:** Submit demo tape and lyric sheet. Prefers cassette with minimum 6 songs on demo. SASE. Reports in 1 month.
**Music:** Recently released "Jane," by Dick Nevell (C&W single); *Snooze*, by D. Nevell (mixed LP); and *Live At The Marble Palace*, by Canterbury Folk (folk LP).

**ANTHEM RECORDS OF CANADA**, 189 Carleton Ave., Toronto, Ontario, Canada M5A 2K7. (416)773-4371. Managing Director: Tom Berry. Press & Publicity: Marilyn Harris. Record company. Releases 5-10 singles and 4-8 albums/year. Works with artists on contract. Pays 5-16% royalty to artists on contract.
**How to Contact:** Submit demo tape.
**Music:** Top 40 and AOR. Recently released *Signals*, by Rush/AOR Records (top 40/LP); "New World Man," by Rush/AOR Records (top 40 single); and *Kim Mitchell*, by K. Mitchell (top 40 EP). Other artists include Coney Hatch, Ian Thomas, Moe Koffman and the Boys Brigade.

**APON RECORD COMPANY, INC.**, 44-16 Broadway, Box 3082, Long Island City, NY 11103. (212)721-5599. Contact: Don Zemann. Record company, record producer and music publisher (Apon Publishing Company/ASCAP). Releases 15 albums/year. Works with artists and songwriters on contract. Pays according to special agreements made with individual songwriters; statutory rate to publishers for each record sold.
**How to Contact:** Call first about your interest, then submit demo tape and lyric sheet. Prefers 15 ips reel-to-reel or cassette with 1-12 songs on demo. SASE. Reports in 1 month.
**Music:** Church/religious, classical, dance-oriented, easy listening, folk and international. Recently released *Polka Fever*, by Slawko Kunst, (polka LP); *Russian Gypsy Melodies*, by Sandor Lakatos (gypsy tunes LP); and *Budvarka*, by Alojz Skolka Ensemble (folk/pop LP).

**APRIL RECORDS**, Box 8263., Haledon NJ 07508. (201)942-6810. Labels include Alsaman, Arch, Kela, Afro and Cummings Records. Vice President: Gauntiet Cummings. Record company, music publisher (Dragon International Music) and record producer. Releases 3 singles and 1 album/year. Works with artists and songwriters on contract. Pays standard royalty to artists and to songwriters on contract; statutory rate to publishers for each record sold.
**How to Contact:** Submit demo tape and lyric sheet. Prefers 7½ ips reel-to-reel with 3-5 songs on demo. SASE. Reports in 1 month.
**Music:** Dance, reggae and soul. Recently released *Africa Stands Alone*, by Culture (reggae LP); *Africa Shall Stretch Forth Her Hands* and *Small Street at Her Hands*, by the Mighty Threes (reggae LPs); and "Being A Woman", by Yolanda Brown and Rhonda Durand (disco single).

**AQUARIUS RECORDS**, 6265 Cote de Liesse Rd., St. Laurent, Quebec, Canada H4T 1C3. (514)735-5303. A&R/Promotion Director: Keith Brown. Record company and music publisher (Slalom/PRO, Crescent/CAPAC). Member CRIA and CIRPA. Releases 5-10 singles and 3-5 albums/year. Works with artists on contract. Pays statutory rate to publishers for each record sold.
**How to Contact:** Submit demo tape and lyric sheet or arrange personal interview. Prefers cassette with 2-10 songs on demo. SASE "only for mailings within Canada. We will pay return mail on international submissions." Reports in 1 month.
**Music:** Rock (hard, adult contemporary). Recently released *Power Play*, by April Wine (AOR LP); "Enough Is Enough," by April Wine (single); and *Code Breaker*, by Morse Code. Other artists include Corey Hart and Silver Darts.
**Tips:** "We strongly prefer working rock bands (as opposed to 'studio' projects)."

**AQUILA RECORDS**, Box 600516, North Miami Beach FL 33160. (305)945-3738. Labels include Gil's Funny Records, U.K., and Laurel Records. Executive Director: J. Gilday. Record company, music publisher (Gil Gilday Publishing/ASCAP, Farjay Music/BMI and Sancti Publishing/SUBAC) and record producer. Releases 23 singles and 5 albums/year. Pays 50% royalty to artists on contract; pays statutory rate to publishers for each record sold.
**How to Contact:** Submit demo tape and lead sheet. Prefers 7½ ips reel-to-reel tape with 2 songs on demo. "Please include simple piano vocal." SASE. Reports in 3 weeks.
**Music:** Disco, gospel, MOR and top 40/pop. Recently released *Quietman*, recorded by Lou Paoli (MOR). Other artists include Don C. Davis and Mark Palmor.

**ARBY RECORDS**, Box 6687, Wheeling WV 26003. (614)758-5812. President: S.P. Tarpley. Record company. Works with artists on contract. Pays 6% royalty to artists and songwriters on contract.
**How to Contact:** Submit demo tape. Prefers 7½ ips reel-to-reel with 2 songs minimum on tape. Does not return unsolicited material. Reports in 1 month.

**Music:** Bluegrass, blues, church/religious, C&W, easy listening, folk, gospel, MOR and progressive. Recently released "Looks Like You're Going Anyway" and "The Next Time," by Patti Powell (country/MOR singles); and "Stranger on the Bridge," by George Elliott (C&W single).

**ARGUS RECORD PRODUCTIONS**, Box 58, Glendora NJ 08029. (609)939-0034. Labels include Argus and Record Room Records. General Manager: Eddie Jay Harris. Office Manager: Linda Holland. Record company.
**How to Contact:** Submit demo tape and lead sheet. Prefers cassette with 1-2 songs on demo. SASE. Does not return unsolicited material. Reports in 1 month.
**Music:** Children's; church/religious; dance; rock; and top 40/pop. Recently released "In the 80's," by Daniel Hartman (country rock single).

*__ARIANA RECORDS__, 8924 E. Calle Norlo, Tucson AZ 85710. (602)885-5931. President: James M. Gasper. Vice President: Thomas M. Dukes. Record company, record producer and music publisher (Myko Music). Estab. 1981. Releases 2 singles and 2 albums/year. Works with artists and songwriters on contract; musicians on salary. Pays 50% royalty to artists on contract; statutory rate to publishers for each record sold.
**How to Contact:** Submit demo tape and lyric sheet. Prefers 7½ ips reel-to-reel or cassette with 3-5 songs on demo. SASE. Reports in 1 month.
**Music:** Mostly R&B, pop rock, R&R and rockabilly; also easy listening, rock and top 40/pop. Recently released "Loving You," by Mark Newland Band (R&R single); "Jump Start My Heart," by The Wellingtons (pop rock single); and "Sweet Virgins," by Madison-Jet (pop rock single).
**Tips:** "Listen to the radio."

**ARISTA RECORDS INC.**, 1888 Century Park E., Suite 1510, Los Angeles CA 90067. (213)553-1777. Labels include Arista, Buddha, Ariola, GRP, Savoy, Jive Records and Project 3 Records. A&R Directors: Bud Scoppa, Bob Feiden and Michael Barackman. Record company. Works with artists on contract.
**How to Contact:** Submit demo tape. Prefers cassette. SASE. Reports "as soon as possible."
**Music:** Dance, easy listening, folk, jazz, MOR, progressive, R&B, rock (primarily), soul and top 40/pop. Recently released *Another Grey Crea*, recorded by Graham Parker/Project (LP/single); *Pelican West*, recorded by Haircut (AOR LP/singles). Other artists include Barry Manilow, Greatful Dead, Al Stewart, Aretha Franklin, Allman Brothers, Raydio, Jennifer Warnes, Phylis Hymen, Dionne Warwick, Hiroshima, Gil Scott Heron, Average White Band, Michael Henderson, Melissa Manchester and Monty Python.
**Tip:** "Minimum standards should be adhered to. Demos don't have to be fancy—just understandable."

*__ARISTA/ARIOLA RECORDS__, 3 Cavendish Sq., London, W1M 9HA, England, 44-01-580-5566. Labels include Arista, Ariola, Hansa, West End (UK only) and Old Bell catalog; Arista Records in the US. Contact: A&R Department. Record company and music publisher (Arista/Careers Music). Releases 100 singles and 30 albums/year. Works with artists on contract. "Each artist is exclusive." Royalties paid to US songwriters and artists through US publishing or recording affiliate.
**How to Contact:** Submit demo tape and lyric sheet. Prefers cassette with 3-5 songs on demo. SAE and IRC. Reports in 1 month.
**Music:** Mostly dance-oriented music; also jazz, MOR, R&B, rock, soul and top 40/pop. Recently released *Heartbreaker*, by Dionne Warwick (MOR/top 40 LP and single); "Love On Your Side," by Thompson Twins (dance single); and *SKY 5*, by SKY (progressive LP and single). Other artists include Stray Cats, Dave Edmunds, Fashion, Haircut 100, Lotus Eaters, Sal Paradise, Lizzie Welch, Uropa Lula, Beat and Blues Band.
**Tips:** "Send material that is original with commercial appeal. Most of our artists are self contained. Rarely do we seek outside material and we look for artists who are both songwriters and performers."

**ARLO RECORDS**, 7635 Telephone Rd., Leroy NY 14482. Contact: Kenny or Jim Bearce. Record company, record producer, music publisher (Bearce Publishing/ASCAP) and recording studio. Releases 4 singles and 2 albums/year. Works with artists and songwriters on contract; musicians on salary for in-house studio work. Pays 2½-7% royalty to artists on contract; negotiable rate to publishers for each record sold.
**How to Contact:** Submit demo tape and lyric sheet. Prefers 7½ ips reel-to-reel or cassette with 2-5 songs on demo. "Include a well-organized promo package with tape, lead sheet, photo and resume." SASE. Reports in 1 month.
**Music:** Children's, dance-oriented, MOR, rock (country), top 40/pop and new wave. Recently released "Cry Cry Darlin," by J. Alexander (country single); *Music from a Candy Box*, by L.B. Lynch (church LP); and *North Forest Springs to Life*, by Bearce & Bearce (variety pop/country rock LP).

# Close-up

**Rick James**
Performer/Songwriter

Rick James has been called sexy, belligerent, and outrageous. His corn-rowed, shoulder-length braids and flashy costumes are not the total of the man, however. There's creative genius, whether performing—turning on packed house crowds—or writing songs that come from the introspective part of James that the crowds don't see. The combination of his inward and outward extremes add up to Rick James, one of a kind in an industry where just maintaining an identity is often the greatest accomplishment of all.

James, actually James Johnson, was born and raised in Buffalo, New York. He lived in a music community that spawned such talents as Neil Young; Joni Mitchell; Blood, Sweat & Tears' leader David Clayton Thomas; and early members of The Buffalo Springfield and Steppenwolf groups.

"My encouragement," says James, "always came from my mother." His mother, Betty Gladden, nearly single-handedly raised eight children, says James, and she did it with the primary employment of being a numbers' runner.

Genius, be it songwriting, performing, or any creative bent, is often spawned—or at least nurtured—by misfortune. James' now well-publicized background included growing up as a precocious kid, growing out of delinquency, and then going AWOL from the Navy. But it left him with a dream of becoming two things—a star and a millionaire. It also left him with the drive to accomplish that dream.

In 1978, James was signed as a staff writer for Motown, where he also released his debut album, *Come Get It*, which went platinum. He followed it with *Busting Out of L Seven* and *Fire It Up* which went platinum and gold respectively.

But it was his fifth Motown album, *Street Songs*, termed "*an arresting set of punk funk*," with James' vivid lyrical interpretations of street life, that catapulted his career.

What does James want to do now that he's seemed to have already done it all? "Motion pictures, more writing, and producing." He has already written a treatment for a musical penned *Alice in Wonderland*. He's also begun work on his autobiography which he hopes will become a motion picture. He'll star of course, because he admits, "Nobody can play me, but me."

**ART ATTACK RECORDS, INC.**, Box 31475, Ft. Lowell Station, Tucson AZ 85751. (602)881-1212. Contact: William Cashman. Record company, music publisher (Cardio Music/BMI) and record producer. Member RIAA. Releases 2 singles and 2 albums/year. Works with artists on contract; mechanical rate negotiable.
**How to Contact:** Submit demo tape and lyric sheet. Prefers cassette with 3-10 songs on demo. "We are interested in the artist's performance abilities and would need to see photos and biographical materials as well as to hear the music." Does not return unsolicited material. Reports in 1 month.
**Music:** Rock, jazz and progressive. Other artists include Chris Buck Group, Troupe Deluxe, Crown Glass, and Randy Orange.
**Tips:** "Be creative."

**ARTEMIS RECORDS, LTD.**, Box 110, Howard Beach NY 11414. (212)738-4806. President: John Giamundo. Record company and music publisher. Works with artists and songwriters on contract. Payment negotiable.
**How to Contact:** Submit demo tape. Prefers 7½ or 15 ips reel-to-reel, or disc. SASE.
**Music:** Classical; disco; easy listening; folk; jazz; MOR; progressive; rock; soul; top 40/pop; and reggae.
**Tips:** "Send copyrighted material only. Enclose SASE if you wish us to return your product after review. We will not necessarily comment on unsolicited material."

**ASSOCIATED RECORDING COMPANIES**, 2250 Bryn Mawr Ave., Philadelphia PA 19131. (215)477-7122. Labels include Pearl Harbor, Jaguar and Jenges Records (Shelton Associates/BMI). A&R Directors: Ted Brown, Leo Gaton. Administrator: Richard Jackson. Record company and music publisher. Releases 12 albums and 7 singles/year. Works with artists and songwriters on contract. Pays 6-9% royalty to artists on contract; standard royalty to songwriters on contract; statutory rate to publishers for each record sold.
**How to Contact:** Submit demo tape. Prefers 7½ ips reel-to-reel or cassette with 3-5 songs on demo. SASE. Reports in 2 weeks.
**Music:** Mostly R&B and top 40; also easy listening, MOR, soul and pop. Recently released "Craving," by Giles Crawford (pop single); "Bus Stop," by Lambchops (R&B single); and "Do the Funk," by Galaxy (R&B single). Other artists include George Guess, Looper, Dream Merchants and Vee Vee.
**Tips:** "Looking for artists with a finished product. Very high royalty rate."

**ATLANTIC RECORDING CORP.**, 9229 Sunset Blvd., Los Angeles CA 90069. (213)278-9230. Labels include Atco and Custom Records. Works with artists on contract.
**How to Contact:** Submit demo tape. Prefers cassette or 7½ ips reel-to-reel with 3-5 songs on demo. SASE. Reports in 2 weeks.
**Music:** Blues, disco, easy listening, folk, jazz, MOR, progressive, R&B, rock, soul and top 40/pop.

**ATTIC RECORDS, LTD.**, 624 King St. W, Toronto, Ontario, Canada M5V 1M7. (416)862-0352. Labels include Attic and Basement. President: Al Mair. Record company and music publisher (Attic Publishing Group). Member CARAS, CRIA. Releases 25 singles and 30 albums/year. Works with artists and songwriters on contract. Pays statutory rate to publishers for each record sold.
**How to Contact:** Call first about your interest or submit demo tape and lyric sheet. Prefers cassette with 3-5 songs on demo. SAE and IRCs. Reports in 3 weeks.
**Music:** Blues, MOR, rock and top 40/pop. Artists include Anvil, Bobcats, Nylons, Downchild, The Lincolns, Steppenwolf and Kamahl.

**AUDIO FIDELITY ENTERPRISES INC.**, 45 E. Milton, Rahway NJ 07065. (201)388-5000. Labels include Audio Fidelity, Audio Rarities, Personality Series, First Component Classical, Chiaroscuro, Image, Thimble and Karate Records. Vice President Publishing: Roslyn D. Kern. Record company. Works with artists on contract. Pays negotiable royalty.
**How to Contact:** Call first about your interest, then submit demo tape and lyric sheet. Prefers cassette or record as demo. SASE. Reports in 2 weeks.
**Music:** Classical, dance, easy listening, jazz, MOR, progressive, rock and top 40/pop.

*****AVI RECORDS, INC.**, +1212, 7060 Hollywood Blvd., Hollywood CA 90028. (213)463-7151. Labels include AVI Records. A&R Managing Director: Seth Marshall III. Record company, record producer, music publisher (Equinox Music/AVI Music Publishing Group) and artist management firm. RIAA. Releases 10 singles and 50 albums/year. Works with artists and songwriters on contract; musicians on salary; songwriters on royalty contract. Pays 10-20% (of wholesale sales) to artists on contract; statutory or negotiated rate "for medley usage/low budget, etc."

**132** Songwriter's Market '84

**How to Contact:** Submit demo tape and lyric sheet. Prefers cassette as demo. SASE. Reports "when we get to it."
**Music:** Mostly jazz, gospel, R&B, and rock/disco; also dance-oriented and top 40/pop. Recently released "Tainted Love," by Soft Cell (rock LP and single); "Cocomotion," by El Coco (disco LP and single); "Downhill from Here," by 100% Whole Wheat (rock LP and single); and "Take a Look Inside My Heart," by J. Benoit (jazz LP and single). Other artists include Gloria Jones, Dominick Allen, Supermax, Oliver Sain, Michael Martin, Paul Delicato and S.S.T.

*****AXBAR RECORDS,** Box 12353, San Antonio TX 78212. (512)735-3322. Labels include Axbar, JA-TO and Charro. Producer: Joe Scates. Record company, record producer, music publisher (Axbar Productions/BMI and Axe Handle Music/ASCAP) and distributors of country music products. CMA. Releases 12-15 singles and 3-6 albums/year. Works with artists and songwriters on contract; musicians on salary. Pays 8% maximum royalty to artists on contract; statutory rate to publishers for each record sold.
**How to Contact:** Submit demo tape and lyric sheet ("country and crossover only—no hard rock, reggae, etc."). Prefers 7½ ips reel-to-reel or cassette with 1-5 songs on demo. "Send us only your best shots." SASE. Reports ASAP, "but don't rush us."
**Music:** Mostly country; also blues, western, MOR and soft rock. Recently released "Bitter Winds of Time," by Ronnie Hughes (modern country single); "Today Just Ain't the Day," by Mark Nesler (country single); and *A Twin Fiddles Album*, by Hank Singer & Ron Knuth (traditional country LP). Other artists include Juni Moon, Mark Chesnutt, Carla Neet, Ray Sanders, Perry Jones, George Chambers, The Davenports, Joe's Studio Band, Keith Adams and Ken Pollard.

*****AZRA RECORDS,** Box 411, Maywood CA 90270. (213)589-2794. Labels include Not So Famous David's Records, Condor Classics and Erika Records. Artist Development: David T. Richards. Record company. Releases 5 singles and 5-10 albums/year. Works with artists on contract. "Artists usually carry their own publishing." Pays 10-20% royalty (wholesale) to artists on contract; statutory rate to publishers for each record sold.
**How to Contact:** Submit demo tape and lyric sheet. Prefers cassette with 3-12 songs on demo. Include bio and photo. SASE. Reports in 2 weeks.
**Music:** Mostly heavy metal and novelty tunes. Recently released *Kiss Me L.A.*, by Angelyne (pop/dance LP); "Special Forces," by Special Forces (hard rock 12" EP); and *Warriors*, by various L.A. bands (rock LP, colored vinyl). Other artists include Centaurus, Rise, Sharks, Mad Man Jack and Raiders of the Lost Surf.
**Tips:** "We prefer groups that have been together a minimum of 6 months and solo artists who can write for specific projects."

**B & C MUSICAL SERVICES,** Box 19265, Las Vegas NV 89132. Labels include BRIC. Vice President: Chic Carron. Record company and music publisher (Dimba Music/ASCAP).
**How to Contact:** Write first about your interest (SASE).
**Music:** Bluegrass, C&W, easy listening, rock (country rock).
**Tips:** "Be professional in your contacts with the company."

**BACKSTREET RECORDS,** (division of MCA Records), 70 Universal City Plaza, Universal City CA 91608. (213)508-4590. A&R Director: B.J.B. Barnao. Record company. Releases 8-10 singles and 8 albums/year. Works with artists on contract. Pays statutory rate to publishers for each record sold.
**How to Contact:** Submit demo tape and lyric sheet. Prefers cassette with 2 songs on demo. SASE. Reports in 1 month.
**Music:** Dance-oriented, progressive, rock and top 40/pop. Artists include Tom Petty and the Heartbreakers, Cat People and Nils Lofgren.

*****BAGATELLE RECORD COMPANY,** 400 San Jacinto St., Houston TX 77002. (713)225-6654. President: Byron Benton. Record company, record producer and music publisher (Floyd Tillman Music Co.). Releases 20 singles and 10 albums/year. Works with songwriters on contract; musicians on salary for in-house studio work. Pays negotiable royalty to artists on contract.
**How to Contact:** Submit demo tape and lyric sheet. Prefers cassette for demo. SASE. Reports in 2 weeks.
**Music:** Mostly C&W; also gospel. Recently released "This is Real," by Floyd Tillman (C&W single); "Lucille," by Sherri Jerrico (C&W single); and "Everything You Touch," by Johnny Nelms (C&W single). Other artists include Jerry Irby, Bobby Beason, Bobby Burton, Donna Hazard, Danny Brown and Sonny Hall.

*****BAL RECORDS,** Box 369, La Canada CA 91011. (213)952-1242. President: Adrian Bal. Record company, record producer and music publisher (Bal & Bal Music). Releases 1 single/year. Works with

artists and songwriters on contract. Pays 10% minimum royalty to artists on contract; statutory rate to publishers for each record sold.
**How to Contact:** Submit demo tape and lyric sheet. Prefers cassette with 3 songs on demo. SASE. Reports in 1 month.
**Music:** Blues, church/religious, C&W, easy listening, jazz, MOR, R&B, rock, soul and top 40/pop. Recently released "Los Angeles," by Rich Martin (ballad single); and "Song of the Pasadena Rose Parade," by Jack Heinderich (swing single).

**\*BAM-CARUSO RECORDS**, 4 Liverpool Rd., St. Albans, Herts, England. 44-0727-32109. Labels include Waldo's Records. General Manager: Phil Smee. Record company and music publisher (Waldo's Music). Releases 10 singles and 6 albums/year. Works with artists on contract; musicians on salary for in-house studio work. Pays 2-12% royalty to artists on contract; pays 6¼% to publishers for each record sold. Royalties paid directly to US songwriters and artists.
**How to Contact:** Submit demo tape and lyric sheet plus photos if possible. Prefers cassette with minimum 2 songs on demo. SAE and IRC. Reports in 1 month.
**Music:** Mostly 60s music—new psychodelic bands, beat groups, R&B, etc.; also folk, progressive, rock and soul. Recently released "The Whale Zoo," by Clive Pig & The Hopeful Chinamen (rock single); "Back in Time for Tea," by Nick Haeffner (rock single); *From the House of Lords*; *The Psycheochic Snarl* and *The 45 Minute Technicolor Dream*, all by various artists (60s psychedelic LPs).
**Tips:** "We specialize in compilations of small bands. We will consider any good song or band that shows promise."

**\*BBW RECORDS**, Box 262, Livingston NJ 07039. (201)994-1195. A&R Director: Dave Taylor. Estab. 1981. Member RIAA, NARAS, Big Bands' '80's. Releases 2 singles and 2 albums/year. Works with artists on contract. Pays 7-9% royalty to artists on contract; statutory rate to publishers for each record sold.
**How to Contact:** Submit demo tape and lyric sheet. Prefers cassette with 5-7 songs on demo. Include bio. SASE. Reports in 3 weeks.
**Music:** Mostly jazz and big band; also MOR and top 40/pop. Recently released *Best of Both Worlds*, by Rich Szabo (big band LP); "Jumpin' On the Bandstand," by R. Szabo (pop single); and "Ikyat," by Rich Acciavatti (fusion single).

**BEARSVILLE RECORDS**, Box 135, Bearsville NY 12409. (914)679-7303. Contact: Donald Schmitzerle. Record company and music publisher. Works with artists and songwriters on contract.
**How to Contact:** Submit demo tape and lyric sheet. Prefers cassette with maximum 2 songs on demo. SASE. Reports as soon as possible.
**Music:** Rock and top 40/pop. "No disco."

**BEE GEE/BIRTHRIGHT RECORDS-Distributors, Inc.**, 3101 S. Western Ave., Los Angeles CA 90018. (213)258-8011 or 731-0907. Vice President/General Manager: Leroy C. Lovett. A&R/Company Producer: Michael D. Trammel. Record company and music publisher (Chinwah Songs/SESAC, Birthright Music/ASCAP, House of Talley/BMI). Member RIAA and NSG. Releases 10-12 albums/year.
**How to Contact:** Submit demo tape. Prefers cassette with 1-4 songs on demo. SASE. Reports in 2-3 weeks.
**Music:** Gospel, inspirational, contemporary, pop-oriented, gospel, Spanish, some MOR. Recently released *Feels Like Fire*, by Gabriel Hardeman (gospel-pop LP); *Live with the Symphony*, by Edwin Hawkins/Singers (gospel LP); and *He Will Provide*, by Biblical Gospel Singers (gospel LP).

**BEE HIVE JAZZ RECORDS**, 1130 Colfax, Evanston IL 60201. (312)328-5593. Producer: Susan L. Neumann. Record company, music publisher and record producer. Works with musicians on salary; artists and songwriters on contract. Pays 50% royalty to artists on contract; standard royalty to songwriters on contract.
**How to Contact:** Write or call about your interest, submit demo tape and lyric sheet or arrange personal interview to play demo tape. SASE. Reports in 1 month.
**Music:** Jazz only. Recently released *Baritone Madness*, by Nick Brignola (jazz LP); *Fire & Filibree*, by Curtis Fuller (jazz LP); and *Neo/Nistico*, by Sal Nistico (jazz LP).

**BELIEVE IN A DREAM RECORDS, INC. (B.I.D.)**, Suite 400, 1420 K St. NW, Washington DC 20005. Director of Publishing: Yolanda McFarlane. Record company and music publisher (Band of Angels, Inc. and Heaven's Gate Music). Member RIAA. Releases 2 singles and 2 albums/year. Works with artists and songwriters on contract. Pays negotiable royalty to artists on contract; statutory rate to publishers for each record sold.

**How to Contact:** Submit demo tape and lyric sheet. Prefers cassette with 3-6 songs on demo. "Include name, address and telephone number *on tape*." SASE. Reports in 2 weeks.
**Music:** Dance-oriented, R&B, soul and top 40/pop. Recently released "Remote Control," by The Reddings (R&B single); *The Awakening*, by The Reddings (R&B LP); and "Groovy Freaks," by the Real Thing (dance-oriented 12" single).

*****BENTE RECORD**, 382 Central Park West, New York NY 10025. (212)749-2268. Co-President: John Blount. Record company and music publisher (Jonrin). Releases 4 singles and 5 albums/year. Works with artists and songwriters on contract; musicians on salary. Pays negotiable royalty to artists on contract; statutory rate to publishers for each record sold.
**How to Contact:** Submit demo tape and lyric sheet. Prefers cassette with 3-5 songs on demo. SASE. Reports in 1 month.
**Music:** R&B, soul.

*****BGS PRODUCTIONS LTD.**, Newtown St., Kilsyth, Glasgow, G65 0JX, Scotland. 44-0236-821-81. Labels include Country Music Records, BGS and Chord. Director: Dougie Stevenson. Record company, record producer and music publisher (Garron Music). Member ARRS, PPL, MCPS. Releases 6 singles and 20 albums/year. Works with artists and songwriters on contract. Pays 3-10% royalty to artists on contract; 6¼% to publishers for each record sold. Royalties paid to US songwriters and artists through US publishing or recording affiliate.
**How to Contact:** Submit demo tape and lyric sheet. Prefers cassette with 3-6 songs on demo. SAE and IRC. Reports in 1 month.
**Music:** Mostly C&W, MOR and folk; also dance-oriented, easy listening, gospel, jazz, R&B and top 40/pop. Recently released *Reunion 81*, by Clyde Valley Stompers (traditional jazz LP); *Live At Eden Court*, by Alasdair Gillies (Scottish LP); and *Favourite Memories of Mine*, by Sydney Devine (country LP). Other artists include Addie Harper, Bryan Taylor, Grant Frazer, Mike Clark, Stuart Anderson and Flo Stevens.
**Tips:** "We are more interested in artists who make live appearances."

*****BIG BEAR RECORDS**, 190 Monument Rd., Birmingham, B16 8UU, England. 44-021-454-7020. Labels include Big Bear, Truckers Delight and Grandstand Records. A&R Director: Jim Simpson. Record company, record producer and music publisher (Bearsongs). Releases 12 singles and 6 albums/year. Works with artists and songwriters on contract. Pays 8-10% royalty to artists on contract; 6¼% to publishers for each record sold. Royalties paid directly to the songwriters and artists or through US publishing or recording affiliate.
**How to Contact:** Submit demo tape and lyric sheet. Prefers 7½ or 15 ips reel-to-reel or cassette as demo. SAE and IRC. Reports in 2 weeks.
**Music:** Blues, jazz, R&B and soul. Artists include Roy Ree & Energee, The Gangsters, Muscles and many jazz and bluesmen.

**BIG MIKE MUSIC**, 408 W. 115th St., New York NY 10025. (212)222-8715. Labels include Right On! and Big Mike Records. Manager: Bill Downs. Record company and music publisher. Releases 5 singles and 3 albums/year. Works with artists and songwriters on contract. Pays standard royalty.
**How to Contact:** Submit demo tape and lead sheet. Prefers cassette with 1-2 songs on demo. SASE. Reports in 1 month.
**Music:** Soul, pop and "boy-girl relationship" type songs. Recently released *Making Love to the Sound of Music*, by Dolly Gilore (soul/pop LP); and "In the Heat of the Night," by James Lee Williams and Evelyn Wright. Other artists include Tommie Mundy and Baby Knockers.

**BIG WHEELS/QUARTER MOON RECORDS, INC.**, Box 2388, Prescott AZ 86302. (602)445-5801. Contact: Michael D. Morgan. Record company, record producer and music publisher (The Morgan Music Group). Member CMA, NARAS. Works with artists and songwriters on contract. Pays 6%-"open" royalty to artists on contract; statutory rate to publishers for each record sold.
**How to Contact:** Submit demo tape and lyric sheet only. Prefers cassette with 3 songs on demo. SASE. Reports in 1 month.
**Music:** C&W, rock (country) and pop/country. Recently released *Song of the American Trucker*, by various artists (country LP and singles). Artists include Tim Schumacher, Garry Greer, Judy Pannell, George Gordon and Michael Hollister Morgan.

**BIOGRAPH RECORDS, INC.**, Box 109, Canaan NY 12029. (518)392-3401. Labels include Biograph, Melodeon, Center and Historical Records. President: Arnold S. Caplin. Record company, music publisher and record producer. Works with musicians on salary; artists and songwriters on contract. Pays 4% minimum royalty to artists on contract; standard royalty to songwriters on contract.

**How to Contact:** Write or call first about your interest. Prefers 7½ ips reel-to-reel with 6 songs minimum on demo. SASE. Reports in 1 month.
**Music:** Bluegrass, blues, folk and jazz. Recently released *American Dreamer*, by Oscar Brand and The Secret Band (contemporary/folk); *Tenors, Anyone?*, by Stan Getz, Wardell Gray, Zoot Sims and Paul Quinichette; *Lullaby of Broadway* (LP) and *Get Nung*, by the Kneeningy Band. Other artists include Nick Seeger, Dan Smith, Allan Block and New Sunshine Jazz Band.

**BIRC RECORDS,** 601 E. Blacklidge, Tucson AZ 85705. (602)882-9016. President: Joe Bidwell. Record company and music publisher (Autograph Music/BMI). Works with musicians and songwriters on contract. Releases 10 singles and 4 albums/year. Pays standard royalties to songwriters on contract; statutory rate to publishers for each record sold.
**How to Contact:** Submit demo tape and lyric sheet. Prefers cassette with 1-3 songs on demo. SASE. Reports in 3 weeks.
**Music:** C&W, top 40/pop and duets. Recently released "I Smile (But You Know It Ain't Easy)" b/w "I'm Into Something Good," by Erin Brooks; "Tonight You Might Find a Friend" b/w "Here Today and Gone Tomorrow," by Duncan Stitt; and "The Natchez Trace" b/w "Last Call for Alcohol," by Don Shipley (all country singles). Other artists include Dennis Kidd and Jack Baron.

**BLIND PIG RECORDS,** 208 S. 1st St., Ann Arbor MI 48103. (313)428-7216. Contact: Jerry Del Giudice. Record company, record producer and music publisher (Viper Music/BMI). Member NAIRD. Releases 3-6 albums/year. Works with artists on contract. Pays negotiable royalty to artists on contract; negotiable rate to publishers for each record sold.
**How to Contact:** Submit demo tape and lyric sheet. Prefers cassette with songs on demo "unless artist has finished master tape (LPs only); then send copy of complete tape. Include any other promo/press material, including recent itineraries." SASE. Reports in 2-3 months.
**Music:** Blues, R&B (40s, 50s) and rock (rockabilly). Recently released *Everybody Needs It*, by Ellen McIlwaine and Jack Bruce (rock/rhythm LP); *It's All Rock & Roll*, by Steve Nardella (rock/rockabilly LP); and "Drinking TNT and Smoking Dynamite," by Buddy Guy and Jr. Wells.

**BLUE ISLAND RECORDS,** 1446 N. Martel, Unit 3, Los Angeles CA 90046. (213)851-3733. Label includes BOB. Contact: Bob Gilbert. Record company, record producer and music publisher (Blue Island Publishing). Releases 5 singles/year. Works with artists and songwriters on contract. Pays 12% royalty to artists on contract; statutory rate to publishers for each record sold.
**How to Contact:** Submit demo tape and lyric sheet. Prefers cassette with 3-6 songs on demo. SASE. Reports in 3 weeks.
**Music:** C&W, MOR, rock and top 40/pop.
**Tips:** "I review *every* song presented. So many in this industry only listen to selected songs per tape. I listen to all songs because you never can tell who will present the next hit song."

**BLUE SKY RECORDS,** 745 5th Ave., New York NY 10151. (212)751-3400. Record company. Releases 4 singles and 4 albums/year. Works with musicians on contract; pays statutory rate to publishers for each record sold.
**How to Contact:** Prefers cassette with 3 songs maximum on demo.
**Music:** Blues; R&B; rock and top 40/pop. Recently released *Instant Replay* and *Relight My Fire* by Dan Hartman (top 40/album/single).
**Tips:** "Submit single oriented material, good hooks, radio and mainstream appeal."

**BOLIVIA RECORDS,** 1219 Kerlin Ave., Brewton AL 36426. (205)867-2228. Labels include Known Artist. President: Roy Edwards. Record company, record producer and music publisher (Cheavoria Music Co.). Releases 8 singles and 4 albums/year. Works with artists and songwriters on contract; musicians on salary for in-house studio work. Pays royalty to artists on contract; statutory rate to publishers for each record sold.
**How to Contact:** Write first about your interest, then submit demo tape and lyric sheet. Prefers cassette with 3-5 songs on demo. SASE. Reports in 1 month.
**Music:** C&W, easy listening, MOR, R&B and soul. Recently released "Make Me Forget," by Bobbie Roberson (country/MOR single); "Always and Forever," by Jim Portwood (country single); and "Music Inside," by Ray Edwards (MOR single).
**Tips:** "Write good songs, with a good meaning and sing a good song with a good feeling."

**BOOT RECORDS, LTD.,** 1343 Matheson Blvd. W., Mississauga, Ontario, Canada L4W 1R1. (416)625-2676. Labels include Boot, Cynda, Generation, Boot Master Concert Series and Boot International Records. General Manager: Peter Krytiuk. President: Jury Krytiuk. Record company and music publisher (Morning Music Ltd./CAPAC). Releases 40 singles and 20 albums/year. Works with musi-

cians on contract. Pays statutory rate to publishers for each record sold. "We operate on a lease basis with the artist paying the cost of the session."
**How to Contact:** Submit demo tape. Prefers 7½ or 15 ips reel-to-reel or cassette with 3-6 songs on demo. "Prefers some originals and some standards." SASE. Reports in 1 week.
**Music:** Mostly classical, polka and easy listening; also bluegrass, C&W, dance, folk, MOR, rock, reggae and top 40/pop. Recently released *Little Bird Dance*, by Walter Ostanek (polka LP); *Spirit Child*, by Willie Thrasher; and "L.O.V.E. is a 4-Letter Word," by Glenn Chipkar (top 40 single). Other artists include The Garrison Brothers, Sandy Mason, The Emeralds and Kelita Harverland.
**Tips:** "We have really increased our concentration on distribution in Canada. Should an artist manufacture their product we would definitely be interested in the distribution."

**BOUQUET RECORDS**, Bouquet-Orchid Enterprises, Box 18284, Shreveport LA 71138. (318)686-7362. President: Bill Bohannon. Record company and music publisher (Orchid Publishing/BMI). Releases 3-4 singles and 2 albums/year. Works with artists and songwriters on contract. Pays 5% royalty to artists on contract; pays statutory rate to publishers for each record sold.
**How to Contact:** Submit demo tape and lead sheet. Prefers 7½ ips reel-to-reel or cassette with 3-5 songs on demo. SASE. Reports in 1 month.
**Music:** Church/religious (prefers country gospel); C&W (the type suitable for Barbara Mandrell, Dolly Parton, Linda Ronstadt, etc.); and top 40/pop (the type suitable for Kenny Rogers, the Oak Ridge Boys, etc.). Recently released "Gonna Be a Brighter Day," by Bill Bohannon (country single); "Eyes of a Fool," by Bandoleers (C&W single); and "Thank You for Being You," by Adam Day (C&W single).
**Tips:** "Submit material that relates to what is currently being charted. A strong story line will help."

**BOYCE & POWERS MUSIC**, 12015 Sherman Rd., North Hollywood CA 91605. (213)875-1711. President: Melvin Powers. Record company and music publisher. Releases 12 singles/year. Works with songwriters on contract.
**How to Contact:** Submit demo tape and lyric sheet. Prefers cassette or disc with 3 songs minimum on demo. SASE. Reports in 1 month.
**Music:** C&W and MOR. Recently released "Who Wants a Slightly Used Woman?", by Connie Cato (country single); "Mr. Songwriter," by Sunday Sharpe (country single); and "Willie Burgundy," by Teresa Brewer (MOR single).

**BOYD RECORDS**, 2609 NW 36th St., Oklahoma City OK 73112. (405)942-0462. President: Bobby Boyd. Record company and music publisher. Releases 12 singles and 4 albums/year. Works with artists and songwriters on contract. Pays negotiable royalty to artists on contract; statutory rate to publishers for each record sold.
**How to Contact:** Submit demo tape and lyric sheet. Prefers 7½ ips reel-to-reel with 3-12 songs on demo. "Do not send anything that has to be returned." Reports in 2 weeks "if we like it."
**Music:** C&W, R&B, soul and top 40/pop. Recently released "Say You Love Me (One More Time)," by Dale Ward (C&W single); "There's No Way to Measure Love," by Dale Greear (C&W single); "Snap Your Fingers," by Debbie Smith (top 40 single); "One Teardrop at a Time," by Tina Camarillo (pop/C&W single); "Flip the Switch," by Cherie Greear; "Legends Never Die," by Jim Whitaker (pop single); and "We Miss You Red Souvine," by Marvin Ray (country LP and single). Other artists include Faye Haley and Bobby Barnett.

**BRANCH INTERNATIONAL RECORDS**, Box 31819, Dallas TX 75231. (214)750-0720. A&R: Mike Anthony. Record company. Works with artists and songwriters on contract. Pays 6-8% royalty to artists on contract; standard royalty to songwriters on contract.
**How to Contact:** Submit demo tape and lyric sheet. Prefers cassette with 3-5 songs on demo. SASE. Reports in approximately 1 month.
**Music:** C&W and gospel. Recently released "No Satin Sheets to Cry On," by Janet Cave; and "Old Man on the Square," by Charlie Seybert. Other artists include George Brazzel, Digger Wyatt and Jack Wyatt.

**BREAD 'N HONEY RECORDS**, Box 3391, Ventura CA 93006. (805)644-1821. Contact: Mark Craig. Record company, record producer and music publisher (Bread 'N Honey/ASCAP, and Honeybread/BMI). Releases 5-6 albums/year. Member GMA. Pays statutory rate to publishers for each record sold.
**How to Contact:** Submit demo tape and lyric sheet. Prefers cassette as demo. SASE. Reports in 3 weeks.
**Music:** Gospel. Recently released *Hymns for Classic Guitars*, by Rick Foster (gospel LP); *More Hymns for Classic Guitars*, by R. Foster (gospel LP); and *Kathie Sullivan*, by Kathie Sullivan (gospel LP). Other artists include Kathie Lee Johnson, Dave Fullen and Michael Redman.

**BRIARMEADE RECORDS**, Box 1830, Gretna LA 70053. Labels include Burlap, Keeta, Keene and Sonor Records. President: Ken Keene. Vice President: Frankie Ford. Record company, music publisher (Briarmeade Music/ASCAP and Keeta Music/BMI) and record producer. Member CMA and NSAI. Releases 10 singles and 3 albums/year. Works with artists and songwriters on contract. Pays 5-7% royalty to artists on contract; standard royalty to songwriters on contract.
**How to Contact:** Submit demo tape and lyric sheet. Prefers 7½ ips 5" or 7" reel-to-reel or cassette with 2-5 songs on demo. "If artist or group has record LP available, it can be submitted, disregarding 5 song maximum. Artist/group should also send complete promo package with photos, biography, records/tapes and references." SASE. Reports in 1 month.
**Music:** Blues, children's, church/religious, C&W, disco, easy listening, gospel, MOR, R&B, country rock, soul and top 40/pop. Recently released "Country Goose," by Johnny Pennino (sax international single); "Desperado," by Frankie Ford (pop vocal single); "Twelfth of Never," by Narvel Felts (country single). Other artists include Denny Barberio, The Briarmeade Singers, Marilyn Strothcamp, Larry Swift, Tom Pallardy, Phil EnLoe, Majik Dust and Matt Lucas.

**BSO RECORDS, INC.**, Main office: Via C. Modestino, 64 Paternopoli 83052 (Avellino) Italy. 39-0827-71073. US office: 2595 Carrell Ln., Willow Grove PA 19090. (215)674-0562. President and General Manager: Sal Barbieri. A&R Manager: Raffaele Barbieri. US Office Manager: Ciro Schiano. "All the tapes must be sent to our main office in Italy." Record company and music publisher (Conypol Music/BMI). Releases 15 singles and 8 albums/year. Works with songwriters on contract; musicians on salary for in-house studio work. Pays standard royalty to artists on contract; statutory rate to publishers for each record sold.
**How to Contact:** Submit demo tape and lyric sheet. Prefers 7½ ips reel-to-reel or cassette with 1-4 songs on demo. "Use a straight rhythm track; keep lyrics clear and voice up." SASE. Reports in 1 month.
**Music:** C&W, dance-oriented, easy listening, MOR, progressive, R&B, soft rock, soul, top 40/pop. Recently released *Feeling Good*, by Sal Barbieri (dance LP); "Beatrice," by S. Barbieri (top 40 singles) and "Nostalgia," by Gus Manvel (pop single). Other artists include Bianca, La Dolce Vita and Doris McCain.

**BUDDAH RECORDS, INC.**, (formerly Roulette Records), 18th Floor, 1790 Broadway, New York NY 10019. Labels include Routlette, Pyramid and A&R Records. Director: Phil Kahl.
**How to contact:** Submit demo tape and lyric sheet. Prefers 7½ ips reel-to-reel or cassette with 1-3 songs on demo. SASE. Reports in 1 month.
**Music:** Blues, choral, C&W, dance, easy listening, folk, jazz, MOR, progressive, R&B, rock, soul and top 40/pop.

**BULLDOG RECORDS**, Suite 1301, 50 E. 42nd St., New York NY 10017. (212)687-2299. Labels include Ember and Bulldog Records. Head of A&R: Howard Kruger. President: J.S. Kruger. Record company. Works with artists and songwriters on contract. Pays 5-8% royalty to artists on contract; standard royalty to songwriters on contract.
**How to Contact:** Submit demo tape and lead sheet. Prefers cassette with 2-6 songs on demo. SASE. Reports in 1 month.
**Music:** Dance, soul and top 40/pop. Recently released "Fabulous Babe," by Kenny Williams (European pop single); *Glen Campbell Live in Concert*; "How Can You Tell You Got It," by David Soul; and "Monies Too Tight To Mention," by Valentine Brothers.
**Tips:** "We operate more in Europe than in the US, so allow time for material to flow overseas."

**BUSCH COUNTRY RECORDS**, 1002 W. Busch Blvd., Tampa FL 33612. (813)935-6289. Contact: Randall Bethencourt. Record company and music publisher (Busch Country Publishing and Rhythm and Rhyme Music). Member RIAA. Releases 3-5 singles and 1-2 albums/year. Works with songwriters on contract; musicians on salary for in-house studio work. Pays 3-10% royalty to artists on contract; statutory rate to publishers for each record sold.
**How to Contact:** Submit demo tape and lyric sheet. Prefers reel-to-reel or cassette with 3-5 songs on demo. SASE. Reports in 6 weeks.
**Music:** C&W. Artists include Randy Wade, Bobby Hess and Amanda Lynn.

**CADENCE JAZZ RECORDS, LTD.**, Cadence Bldg., Redwood NY 13679. (315)287-7852. Labels include Cadence Blues Records. Producer: Bob Rusch. Record company and record producer. Releases 10-15 albums/year. Works with artists on contract. Pays negotiable royalty to artists on contract; statutory rate to publishers for each record sold.
**How to Contact:** Submit demo tape. Prefers cassette. SASE. Reports in 1 week.
**Music:** Blues and jazz. Recently released *Beaver Harris Live at Nyon*, by Harris (jazz LP); *Saheb Sarbib*

*Live at the Public Theatre*, by Sarbib (jazz LP); and *Skizoke*, by Frank Lowe (jazz LP). Other artists include Larry Gelb, Barbara Donald, Dwight James, Hugh Brodie and J.R. Monterose.

**CALIFORNIA INTERNATIONAL RECORDS & VIDEO**, Box 2818, Newport Beach CA 92663. President: Joseph Nicoletti. Creative Director: Cheryl Nicoletti. Record company, record producer and music publisher (ASCAP). Member NARAS, AFTRA AND SAG. Releases 2-3 singles/year. Works with musicians on salary; artists and songwriters on contract. Pays 3-5% royalty to artists on contract; statutory rate to publishers for each record sold.
**How to Contact:** Write first about your interest, then submit demo tape and lead sheet. Prefers cassette with 1-3 songs on demo. SASE. Reports in 1 month.
**Music:** Mostly rock-oriented (new wave, pop, classical) and great ballads; also MOR, top 40/pop and rockabilly. Recently released "Let's Put the Fun Back in Rock 'n Roll," by Freddie Cannon and the Belmonts (pop/rock single). Other artists include Joseph Nicoletti.

**CANDY RECORDS,** 2716 Springlake Ct., Irving TX 75060. (214)259-4032. Labels include Sweet Tooth, Lil' Possum and Holli Records. General Manager: Kenny Wayne Hagler. Record company, record producer and music publisher (Sweet Tooth Music/BMI). Releases approximately 4 singles and 5 albums/year. Works with artists on contract. Pays 5% royalty to artists on contract; statutory rate to publishers for each record sold.
**How to Contact:** Submit demo tape and lyric sheet. Prefers 7½ ips reel-to-reel or cassette with 3-4 songs on demo. "Send only quality material." SASE. Reports in 1 month.
**Music:** Mostly C&W and rock; also soul, blues and top 40/pop. Recently released "Green Eyes", by Reign (country rock single); *In Mothion*, by Kenny Wayne & The Komotions (top 40 LP); and " 'Bout a Broken Heart," by Michael Jeffrey (country single). Others artists include Carter Holcomb.

**CAPITOL RECORDS**, 1370 Avenue of the Americas, New York NY 10019. (212)757-7470. Vice President, East Coast A&R: Bruce Garfield. Record company and music publisher (Screen Gems).
**How to Contact:** Submit demo tape and lyric sheet. Prefers cassette with 4 songs on demo. SASE. Reports in 3 months.
**Music:** All types.

**CAPITOL RECORDS, INC.**, 1750 N. Vine St., Hollywood CA 90028. (213)462-6252. Contact: John Gold. Record company. Releases 170 singles/year. Works with artists.
**How to Contact.** Submit demo tape. Prefers cassettes with 4 songs on demo. "Have an agent, manager or publisher submit material for you and submit the best-quality demo you can afford." SASE. Reports in 4-6 weeks.
**Music:** Progressive rock, rock, new wave. Recently released *Missing Persons*, by Missing Persons (rock LP). Other artists include The Tubes and Billy Squier.

***CAPITOL STAR ARTISTS ENT. INC.**, 1159 Jay St., Box 11276, Rochester NY 14611. (216)328-5565. Director: Don Redanz. Record company, record producer and music publisher (Red Plow). Releases 20 singles and 4 albums/year. Works with artists and songwriters on contract; musicians on salary for in-house studio work.
**How to Contact:** Submit demo tape and lyric sheet. Prefers 7½ ips reel-to-reel or cassette with 4 songs on demo. SASE. Reports in 2 weeks.
**Music:** Mostly C&W; also bluegrass, church/religious and gospel. Recently released "Dust on Mother's Bible," by Tony Starr (C&W single). Other artists include Don Bailes and Gladys Smith.

***CAPSTAN RECORD PRODUCTION**, Box 211, East Prairie MO 63845. (314)649-2211. Contact: Archie Corlew. Record company, music publisher and record producer. Works with artists on contract. Pays 3-5% royalty to artists on contract.
**How to Contact:** Write first about your interest, then submit demo tape and lyric sheet. Prefers cassette with 2-4 songs on demo. SASE. Reports in 1 month.
**Music:** C&W, easy listening, MOR, country rock and top 40/pop. Recently released "Dry Away the Pain," by Julia Brown (easy listening single); and "Country Boy," by Alden Lambert (country single). Other artists include Shuri Castle and the Burchettes.

**CAROUSEL RECORDS, INC.**, 1273½ N. Crescent Hts. Blvd., Los Angeles CA 90046. (213)550-4500. A&R: Stuart Lanis. Record company, music publisher and record producer. Works with musicians on contract.
**How to Contact:** Submit demo tape and lyric sheet. Prefers cassette with 3-6 songs on demo. SASE. Reports in 3 weeks.
**Music:** Children's, country, church/religious, classical, easy listening, gospel, MOR, and top 40/pop.

**Record Companies** **139**

**CARRIE RECORDS CO.**, Box 90639, 902-42nd Ave., N., Nashville TN 37209. (615)321-3319. Labels include Ricare and Lanrod Records). President: James Hendrix. Record company and music publisher (Grawick Music). Releases 8 singles and 4 albums/year. Works with songwriters on contract. Pays 2-4% royalty to artists on contract; statutory rate to publishers for each record sold.
**How to Contact:** Submit demo tape and lyric sheet. Prefers cassette with 3-4 songs on demo. SASE. Reports in 1 month.
**Music:** Church/religious, gospel, R&B, and top 40/pop. Recently released "An Everlasting Love," and "My Life and Song," by Keith Chism; and "Can It Be" and "The Beat," by the E-Z Band. Other artists include Cornelius Grant, Ellison Family, Michael Hunter and P-Wee & The Psalmsters.

**CASA GRANDE RECORDS**, Box 113, Woburn MA 01801. (617)933-1474. Labels include Don-Mar Records and Strawhut Records. Manager: Frank Paul. Record company, record producer and music publisher (Donna Music Publishing Company and Antone Music Publishers). Amount of releases/year varies. Works with artists and songwriters on contract. Pays 3% minimum royalty to artists on contract.
**How to Contact:** Submit tape and lyric sheet. Prefers cassette with 3-6 songs on demo. SASE. Reports as soon as possible.
**Music:** Children's, C&W, easy listening, folk, gospel, MOR, Spanish, R&B, rock, soul and top 40/pop. Recently released *Happy Birthday Baby*, by TuneWeavers (R&B LP and single).

***CASINO RECORDS**, 536 E. St. Louis Ave., Las Vegas NV 89104. (702)731-2322. Labels include Casino and Great Lakes. President: Lou Ragland. Record company, record producer and music publisher (Lamora Music). Estab. 1982. Member ACEC. Release 5 singles and 5 albums/year. Works with artists and songwriters on contract. Pays 6½-12% royalty to artists on contract; statutory rate to publishers on contract.
**How to Contact:** Submit demo tape and lyric sheet. Prefers cassette with 4-8 songs on demo. "Please type lyrics." SASE. Reports in 2 weeks.
**Music:** Mostly C&W and soul; also easy listening, MOR and top 40/pop. Recently released "This Is the Night for Loving," by G.L.O. (top 40 single); "Didn't I Tell You," by Lou Ragland (soul single); and *Take a Chance on Love*, by L. Ragland (soul/easy listening LP). Other artists include Doris Troy, Janis Carter, Bobby Wade, JJ Bryantt and the Sexey Saxses.

**CASTALIA RECORDS/A MAJOR LABEL**, Box 11516, Milwaukee WI 53211. Labels include Fair Wind Records and Balloon Records. President: Jim Spencer. Promotion Director: Dave Luhrrsen. Record company, record producer, and music publisher (Castalia Music/BMI). Releases 2 singles and 2-6 albums/year. Works with artists and songwriters on contract; musicians on salary for in-house studio work. Pays statutory rate to publishers for each record sold.
**How to Contact:** Submit demo tape and lyric sheet or write first about your interest. Prefers cassette with 1-6 songs on demo. SASE. Reports in 1 month.
**Music:** All types. Recently published "Sunset Lady," by Marvell Love (R&B single); *Put Your Trust in God*, by Phebe Holmes and Darrell Hines (gospel LP); *Doctor Yah Yah*, by Suspence (blues/rock single); and "Thought I Wasn't Gonna Make It Back," by the Viceroys (R&B single).

**CASTLE MUSIC, INC.**, Box 7574, Tulsa OK 74105. (918)587-1515. Labels include Castle Records, House of Kings Records. President: Ben Ferrell. Record company, record producer and music publisher (Spirit & Soul Publishing Co./ASCAP, Mighty Song Publishing Co./BMI). Estab. 1981. Releases 15 albums/year. Works with artists and songwriters on contract. Pays 3-10% royalty to artists on contract; statutory rate to publishers for each record sold.
**How to Contact:** Arrange personal interview to play demo tape. Prefers cassette with 2-10 songs on demo. SASE. Reports in 3 weeks.
**Music:** Choral, gospel (contemporary) and MOR. Recently released *Sent By the Great I Am*, by Followers of Christ (contemporary/black LP); *Ha Ha Ha on the Devil*, by Ron Perty (contemporary LP); and *Lovin' Eyes*, by Marv Martin (MOR LP). Other artists include Doyle Tucker, Gary Copeland, Jerome Johns, Paul and Susan Hansen, Everitt and Ferrell and The Gospel In Concert Band.

***CBS RECORDS**, 17-19 Soho Square, London WI,England. 44-01-734-8181. Affiliates/U.K.: CBS, Epic and Innervision. Affiliate/U.S.: CBS, Inc. A&R Manager: Dave Novik. Record company and music publisher (CBS Songs/April Music Ltd.). Member all major music organizations. Works with artists and songwriters on contract. Pays negotiable royalty to artists on contract; negotiable rate to publishers for each record sold. Listens only to material submitted by songwriters and artists from England.
**How to Contact:** Submit demo type and lyric sheet. Prefers cassette with 2-5 songs on demo. SASE. Reports ASAP.
**Music:** Mostly top 40/pop, rock, soul and R&B; also dance-oriented, easy listening and progressive. Recently released *Total Eclipse of the Heart*, by Bonnie Tyler (top 40/pop/rock); *Bad Boys*, by Wham

(top 40/pop/dance-oriented); *Thriller*, by Michael Jackson (top 40/pop/dance-oriented); and *Cargo*, by Men at Work (top 40/pop/rock).

**CHA-CHA RECORDS**, 15041 Wabash Ave., S. Holland IL 60473. (312)339-0307. Labels include Cha-Cha (rock) and Cap (C&W). President: Donald L. De Lucia. Record company, record producer, and music publisher (Don-Del Music/BMI and Don-De/ASCAP). Releases 2 singles and 2 albums/year. Works with artists on contract. Pays 3%/record to artists on contract; statutory rate to publishers for each record sold.
**How to Contact:** Submit demo tape and lyric sheet. Prefers 7½ ips reel-to-reel with 4-6 songs on demo. SASE. Reports in 1 week.
**Music:** C&W, rock, and top 40/pop. Recently released *99 Chicks*, by Ron Haydock and the Boppers (rock LP). Other artists include Don Glasser and Lois Castello.

*****CHAPMAN RECORDS**, 228 W. 5th St., Kansas City MO 64105. (816)842-6854. Contact: Chuck Chapman. Record company and music publisher. Releases 6-15 singles and 3-5 albums/year. Works with artists on contract. Pays negotiable royalty. Charges for some services: "We charge for recording services for music that we don't publish."
**How to Contact:** Submit demo tape. Prefers cassette with minimum 3 songs on demo. SASE. Reports in 1 month.
**Music:** Bluegrass, choral, church/religious, classical, C&W, dance, easy listening, folk, gospel, jazz, MOR, progressive, rock, soul and top 40/pop. Recently released "Somewhere Down in Texas," by Norton Canfield (country single); *Telephone to Glory*, by Frank Frazier (gospel LP); *Western Electric*, by Pott Country Band (country LP); "Standard Question, by Phil Neal; and "Horsehot and Gun Powder," by Bob Reeder.

**CHARADE RECORDS**, 1384 E. Sequoia Ave., Tulare CA 93274. (209)686-2533. Labels include Tadarab Records. President: Raymond A. Baradat. Record company and music publisher (Baradat Music/BMI). Releases 3 singles and 2 albums/year. Works with musicians on salary; artists and songwriters on contract. Pays 4-6% royalty to artists on contract; statutory rate to publishers for each record sold.
**How to Contact:** Submit demo tape and lyric sheet. Prefers 7½ ips reel-to-reel or cassette with 1-4 songs on demo. SASE. Reports in 1 month.
**Music:** C&W, dance, jazz, rock (soft), soul and top 40/pop. Recently released "Damn You Tule Fog," by Don LeBaron (pop single); "Goodbye Elaine," by John Keith (rock single); and "Hand Jive," by The Charades (soul single). Other artists include Bob Dennison, Gene Short, Ray Baradat, Jr., Melanie Hankins, and Randie Coulter.

**CHARTA RECORDS**, 44 Music Square E., Nashville TN 37203. (615)255-2175. Labels include Sun-Rize Records. President: Charles Fields. Record company, music publisher and record producer (Mr. Mort Music/ASCAP, Jason Dee Music/BMI). Member BMI. Releases 30 singles and 6 albums/year. Works with artists and songwriters on contract; musicians on salary. Pays 4-7% royalty to artists on contract; standard royalties to songwriters on contract.
**How to Contact:** Submit demo tape and lead sheet. Prefers 7½ ips reel-to-reel or cassette with 1-4 songs on demo. SASE. Reports in 2 weeks.
**Music:** Blues, C&W, easy listening, MOR and top 40/pop. Artists include Jessey Higdon, Eddie Rivers, Sam Hall, Bobby G. Rice and Bobby Wayne Loftis.

*****CHATTAHOOCHEE RECORDS**, 5300 Sepulveda Blvd., Van Nuys CA 91411. (213)788-6865. Contact: Chris Yardum. Record company and music publisher (ETNOC/CONTE). Member NARAS. Releases 4 singles/year. Works with artists and songwriters on contract.
**How to Contact:** Submit demo tape and lyric sheet. Prefers cassette with 2-6 songs on demo. SASE. Reports in 2-3 weeks.
**Music:** Top 40/pop.

**CHEROKEE SOUND RECORDING/NEW DAWNING RECORDS**, Dyer Rt., Cowen WV 26206. (304)226-3424. Secretary: Gladys Spearman. Record company and music publisher (Broad River Publishing Co./BMI). Releases 1 album/year. Works with artists and songwriters on contract. Pays royalty to artists on contract.
**How to Contact:** Submit demo tape and lyric sheet. Prefers cassette with 3-6 songs on demo. "Be sure cassette tape is clear. Songs should have meaning based on the word of God." SASE. Reports in 1-3 months.
**Music:** Church/religious and gospel. Recently released *Best of Spearman's*, *Lifting up Jesus*, and *Holding on to the Rock*, by The Singing Spearman's (gospel LPs).

**CHRISTY RECORDS**, 726 Carlson Dr., Orlando FL 32804. (305)644-3853. Labels include Decade Records and Green Leaf Records. President: Will Campbell. Record company and music publisher (Palamar Music Publishers/BMI). Releases 5 singles and 2-5 albums/year. Works with artists and songwriters on contract.
**How to Contact:** Submit demo tape or submit demo tape and lead sheet. Prefers 7½ ips reel-to-reel with 3-6 songs on demo. SASE. Reports in 1 week.
**Music:** Bluegrass, church/religious, C&W, gospel and MOR. Recently released "Don't I Know You?", by Don Rader (country single); "Homespun Mem'ries," by Nelson Young (bluegrass single); and "I Get Lonely," by Larada Collins (MOR single).

**CHRYSALIS RECORDS, INC.**, 645 Madison Ave., New York NY 10022. (212)758-3555. Contact: Brendan Bourke. Record company and music publisher. Member NARAS. Releases 10 singles and 25 albums/year. Works with musicians on salary; artists and songwriters on contract. Pays negotiable royalty to artists on contract; standard royalty to songwriters on contract.
**How to Contact:** Call before submitting demo tape. Prefers 7½ or 15 ips reel-to-reel or cassette with 3-4 songs on demo. Include photo and bio. SASE.
**Music:** Rock (general) and top 40/pop. Recently released *Get Nervous*, by Pat Benatar; *Desperate*," by Divinyls; *Quartet* by Ultravos and *True*, by Spandau Ballet. Other artists include Charlie Dore, Rory Gallagher, Ian Hunter, Billy Idol, Jethro Tull, Leo Kottke, Linx, The Specials, Stiff Little Fingers and Robin Trower.

**THE CHU YEKO MUSICAL FOUNDATION**, Box 10051, Beverly Hills CA 90213. (213)761-2646. Affiliate: Box 1314, Englewood Cliffs NJ 07632. (201)224-5811. Messages: (201)567-5524. Labels include The Chu Yeko Musical Foundation, Take Home Tunes! Record Co., and Original Cast Records, and Broadway Baby Records. Producer: Doris Chu. Record company and music publisher (Broadway/Hollywood International Music Publishers/ASCAP). Releases 5-10 album/year. Works with songwriters on contract. Pays 1-10% royalty to artists on contract; statutory rate to publishers for each record sold.
**How to Contact:** Submit demo tape and lyric sheet. Prefers cassette with any number of songs on demo. SASE. Reports in 1 month.
**Music:** All types. Recently released *King of Hearts*, by Millicent Martin, Don Scardino and the original cast (LP); *81 Proof*, by the original cast (LP); *Ka-Boom!*, by the original cast (musical LP); and *Fly with Me*, by the original cast (musical LP).
**Tips:** "A produced original musical group or singer in Los Angeles area, with financial backing, would increase an artist's or songwriter's chance of working with us."

*****CLARUS MUSIC, LTD.**, 340 Bellevue Ave., Yonkers NY 10703. (914)591-7715. President: S. Fass. Records company, record producer and music publisher. Member MENC, NYSSMA, RIAA. Releases 1-2 albums/year. Works with artists and songwriters on contract. Pays current royalty rate to artists on contract; statutory rate to publishers for each record sold.
**How to Contact:** Submit demo tape and lyric sheet plus typed script. Prefers 7½ips reel-to-reel or cassette with 4-10 songs on demo. SASE. Reports in 1-3 months.
**Music:** Children's.

**CLAY PIGEON RECORDS**, Box 20346, Chicago IL 60620. (312)778-8760. Labels include Clay Pigeon International and Patefonas Records. President: V. Beleska. A&R Director: Rudy Markus. Record company. Releases 3-5 singles and 2-5 albums/year. Works with musicians on salary; artists and songwriters on contract. "Royalties on records start at 2% of retail. All acts negotiate with us individually. Four percent is common. Royalties paid to publishers are often at 2¢ per selection, per record sold."
**How to Contact:** "Inquire by mail first (do not phone), describing yourself and your material in some depth. We cannot consider any material without a written query." Prefers 7½ ips reel-to-reel, cassette or disc with 1-5 songs on demo. SASE. Reports in 2-8 weeks.
**Music:** Avant-garde, new wave, MOR, progressive, rock and top 40/pop. Recently released "Tribe of Dolls," by Vyto B (modern rock single); "Band That Never Made It," by Bena Neva Mada (modern rock single); and "I'm Sure Now," by Seetz Executive (MOR ballad).
**Tips:** "Cover letter should explain songwriter's background, type of songs written and why songs are unique enough to be listened to."

**CLEARINGHOUSE RECORDS CORP.**, 5th Floor, 21 W. 39th St., New York NY 10018. Nashville: 13 Music Square, Nashville TN 37205. (615)254-9248. (212)869-2299. Labels include CRC Records and MRI Records. President: Andy Hussakowsky. A&R Director: Gene O'Brien. Record company and music publisher. Releases 10 singles and 5 albums/year. Works with musicians on contract. Pays 5-12% royalty to artists on contract; statutory rate to publishers for each record sold. "We are interested in dis-

tribution of finished masters for US and foreign releases."
**How to Contact:** Submit demo tape and lead sheet. Prefers cassette with 1-3 songs on demo. SASE. Reports in 2 months.
**Music:** Mostly pop, R&B and C&W; also dance and rock. Recently released "Just One More Time," by Johnny Pinna and Salvation; *The Lover*, by Jimmy Raye (LP); "You're My Super Hero," by Everlife; and "Crazy Little Mamma," by Freddy Frogs and BMT'S. Other artists include the Boppers (Sweden). Other artists include Kenny Krystal, Ray Davis, Mark James, J.D. Cash, Star Rider and Rockin' Reggie.

*****CLOUDBURST RECORDS**, Box 31, Edmonton KY 42129. (502)432-3183. President: Rev. Junior Lawson. Record company and music publisher (Holy Spirit Music). Releases 3 singles and 4 albums/year. Works with songwriters on contract. Pays 4¢ royalty to artists on contract.
**How to Contact:** Submit demo tape and lyric sheets; call about your interest or arrange personal interview. Prefers 7½ ips reel-to-reel or cassette for demo. SASE. Reports in 3 weeks.
**Music:** Mostly southern gospel; also C&W, gospel, MOR and progressive. Recently released *Introducing the Cornerstones* and *Extra! Extra!*, by The Cornerstones (southern gospel LPs); and *Old-Fashioned Ways*, by the Sounds of Joy (southern gospel LP). Other artists include The New Apostles and The Helmsmen.

**COAST TO COAST RECORDS**, Box 5339, FDR Station, New York NY 10022. (212)751-7078. A&R Director: Nancy Ruehs. Record company and music publisher (Frankly Music/BMI, J.D. Music/ASCAP). Releases 2 albums/year. Works with musicians on contract and songwriters on salary.
**How to Contact:** Submit demo tape and lyric sheet. Prefers cassette with 2-3 songs on demo. Does not return unsolicited material. Reports in 2 weeks.
**Music:** Disco, MOR and R&B. Artists include Duke Jupiter and William Robinson.

**COMMON CAUSE RECORDS**, 880 NE. 71st, Miami FL 33138. (305)759-1405. Labels include Common Cause Records. President: Carlos Oliva. Record company, record producer and music publisher (Avilo Music/BMI, Oliva Music/SESAC, Santa Clara Music/ASCAP). Member NARM. Releases 10 singles and 10 albums/year. Works with artists on contract. Pays 10-15% royalty to artists on contract; statutory rate to publishers for each record sold.
**How to Contact:** Submit demo tape and lyric sheet with biographical data or resume. Prefers cassette as demo. SASE. Reports in 6 weeks.
**Music:** Dance-oriented, MOR, Spanish and rock. Recently released *Friends*, by Friends, *Paco-Paco*, by Paco-Paco; and *Hay Carino*, by Clouds (all Latin contemporary LPs). Other artists include Mary Pacheco, Marco Rizo, Nelson Galanos, and Orquesta La Tremenda.

**COMPO RECORD AND PUBLISHING CO.**, Box 15222, Oklahoma City OK 73115. (405)677-6448. Branch office: Suite 219, 38 Music Square E., Nashville TN 37203. President: Yvonne De Vaney. General Manager: Sonny Lane. Record company and music publisher (Country Classics Music/BMI). Releases 4 singles and 1-2 albums/year. Works with artists and songwriters on contract. Pays 5% minimum royalty to artists and songwriters on contract; statutory rate to publishers for each record sold.
**How to Contact:** Submit demo tape and lead sheet. Prefers cassette with 4-8 songs on demo. SASE. Reports in 3 weeks.
**Music:** C&W, gospel, MOR and top 40/pop. Recently released "Just for a Moment (I Almost Forgot You Were Mine)" b/w "God Made an Angel (When He Made Me You)," and "Teach Me to Live Without You" b/w "I'm Just Fool Enough," by Yvonne DeVaney (country singles); and "Take Me Back into Your World" b/w "Do It Like Your Daddy Told You to," by Gary McCray (country single). Other artists include Wes Onley.

**COMSTOCK RECORDS LTD.**, Box 3247, Shawnee KS 66203. (913)631-6060. Canadian distribution on Highrise & Comstock Records. Production Manager/Producer: Patty Parker. President: Frank Fara. Record company, music publisher (White Cat Music/ASCAP, Rocky Bell Music/BMI), record producer and management and promotions firm. Releases 24-30 singles and 2-4 albums/year. Works with artists and songwriters on contract; musicians on salary. Pays 6% retail minimum royalty to artists on contract; standard royalty to songwriters on contract; pays statutory rate to publishers for each record sold.
**How to Contact:** Arrange personal interview or submit demo tape. Prefers cassette with 1-5 songs on demo. "Enclose stamped return envelope if cassette is to be returned." Reports in 2 weeks.
**Music:** Mostly contemporary or pop/country; also C&W and contemporary gospel. Recently released *A Part of Me*, by Don TeBeaux (C&W LP and single); *Long Time Comin'*, by O'Roark Brothers (C&W LP and single); *Lucky Caller #3*, by Doc and Dustry (C&W LP and single); "Pretty Lady," by Guy Shan-

non (C&W single); "Hung Up on You," by Anne Lord (C&W single); "I've Already Left You in My Mind," by Mercey Brothers (C&W single); "Blessed Baby Jesus," by Trudy Buck Rogers (Christmas single); "Christmas without You," by D. TeBeaux (C&W Christmas single); and "The Last Desperado" by Buddi Day (C&W single). Other artists include Bill Hersh.
**Tips:** "Send up tempo country in the modern vein."

**COSMIC RECORDS OF CANADA**, 292 Lorraine Dr., Montreal, Quebec, Canada H9X 2R1. (514)457-5959. Labels include Elevator Records, Fresh Records, Meta Records, Hexagon Records, Les Disques Pamplemousse (French) and Happinessville Records. President: Hugh Dixon. Record company (Hugh Dixon Music, Inc). Releases 10 singles and 3-5 albums/year. Works with artists and songwriters on contract. Pays 4-7% royalty to artists on contract; statutory rate to publishers for each record sold.
**How to Contact:** Submit demo tape and lyric sheet. Include biography and photos if possible. Prefers cassette with 2-5 songs on demo. SAE and IRC.
**Music:** Recently released "Love in the Rain," "Night Riders," "All It Takes Is You and Me," "Got It Made," "The Spark" and "Can You Take Any More?" Artists include Danielle Vallee, Glen and Doug, Time Capsule, Muffet, Peep and Horner and Sue Jesse.
**Tips:** "Want strong melodies that are memorable combined with meaningful lyrics. Lyrics should present a high conscious level perspective along spiritual ideals. Want love songs, songs of overcoming difficulties and perseverance and determination, motivational and inspirational songs and songs that express the heart of being. Any type of musical packaging considered."

**COUNTERPART CREATIVE STUDIOS**, 3744 Applegate Ave., Cincinnati OH 45211. (513)661-8810. President: Shad O'Shea. Record company, music publisher (Hurdy Gurdy Music Co., Counterpart Music/BMI) and jingle company. Member RIAA. Releases 24 singles and 6 albums/year. Works with musicians on salary; artists and songwriters on contract. Pays 5% royalty to artists on contract; statutory rate to publishers for each record sold.
**How to Contact:** Submit demo tape. Prefers 7½ ips reel-to-reel with 1-2 songs on demo. SASE. Reports in 1 week.
**Music:** Bluegrass, blues, children's, choral, church/religious, classical, C&W, dance, easy listening, folk, gospel, jazz, MOR, progressive; rock, funk, soul and top 40/pop. Recently released "McLove Story," by Shad O'Shea/Plantation Records; "Hot Fun in the Summertime," by Dayton/Capitol Records; "Treak Zoid," by Midnight Star/Warner Bros. Records; and "Ready for the Saddle," by David Anderson/Fraternity Records.

**COUNTRY INTERNATIONAL**, 1010 17th Ave. S., Nashville TN 37212. (615)327-4656. Vice President, Promotion: Tom Dean. Record company. Works with artists and songwriters on contract; musicians on salary for in-house studio work. Pays statutory rate to publishers for each record sold.
**How to Contact:** Submit demo tape and lyric sheet. Prefers 7½ ips reel-to-reel or cassette with 1-4 songs on demo. SASE. Reports in 2 weeks.
**Music:** C&W.

**COUNTRY STAR, INC.**, 439 Wiley Ave., Franklin PA 16323. (814)432-4633. Labels include Country Star, Process and Mersey Records. Contact: Norman Kelly. Record company and music publisher (Country Star/ASCAP, Process and Kelly/BMI). Releases 15-20 singles and 3-5 albums/year. Member AFM and AFTRA. Works with artists and songwriters on contract; musicians on salary for in-house studio work. Pays 6% royalty to artists on contract; statutory rate to publishers for each record sold.
**How to Contact:** Write first about your interest. Prefers 7½ ips reel-to-reel or cassette with 1-4 songs on demo. SASE. Reports in 2 weeks.
**Music:** Mostly country; also bluegrass, C&W, easy listening, folk, MOR, rock and top 40/pop. Recently released "Siempre," by Marvin "Doc" Holiday (C&W single); "Hand Him Down to Me," by Junie Lou (C&W single); and "Radar," by Rose-Marie (rock single). Other artists include Bonnie Baldwin, Junior Norman, Al Fravir, Eddie Doyle, Patty Cottrill, Joe Keys, C. Starr, Shirley Hitzeman, God's Children, Denver Bill, Virge Brown, Valerie Anderson, and the Glen Lucas Family.

**COURRIER RECORDS**, 1650 Broadway, New York NY 11021. (212)247-2159. Labels include Overseas Wax. President: Morton Wax. Record company, record producer and music publisher (David Music, Inc./BMI). Estab. 1982. Works with artists and songwriters on contract. Pays standard royalty to artists on contract; statutory rate to publishers for each record sold.
**How to Contact:** Submit demo tape and lyric sheet. Prefers cassette. Does not return unsolicited material. Reports ASAP.
**Music:** All kinds.

## 144 Songwriter's Market '84

**CREATIVE SOUND, INC.**, Box 607, Malibu CA 90265. Labels include Sonrise and Creative Sound Records. President: Bob Cotterell. Record company. Releases 10 albums/year. Works with musicians on contract. Payment varies.
**How to Contact:** Submit demo tape or submit demo tape and lead sheet. Prefers cassette or 8-track cartridge. SASE.
**Music:** "Contemporary Christian music. We're looking for good finished masters."

*****CREOLE RECORDS LTD.**, 91/93 High St., Harlesdew, London, NW10, England. 44-01-965-9223. Labels (England): Creole, Ecstacy, Dynamic, Polo, Cactus, Replay, Blast from the Past. Labels (US): Creole Music, Inc. Managing Director (record demos): Bruce White. Publishing Manager (publishing demos): David Brooks. Record company, record producer and music publisher. BPI, PPC. Releases 30-40 singles and 12-20 albums/year. Works with artists and songwriters on contract. Pays 10-16% royalty to artists on contract; 6¼% to publishers for each record sold.
**How to Contact:** Submit demo tape and lyric sheet. Prefers cassette with 2-4 songs as demo. SAE and IRC. Reports in 2 weeks.
**Music:** Mostly pop and dance; also R&B. Recently released "Can't Run from Love," by Maxine Singleton (dance single); *White Sky*, by Peter Green (blues LP); and "Keep on Walking," by Rod (dance single). Other artists include the Pinkees, Pete McDonald, City IQ, Liquid Gold, Ellie Hope, Adrian Baker, Bob Puzey (writer), Terry Hanton and Enigma.

*****CRESCENT RECORDS/CARTOON RECORDS**, Box 1235, New Rochelle NY 10802. (914)834-5676. A&R Director: McNamara. Record company, record producer and music publisher (Cap-Orion Music). Releases 2-4 singles and 1 album/year. Works with artists and songwriters on contract. Pays negotiable royalty to artists on contract; statutory rate to publishers for each record sold.
**How to Contact:** Submit demo type and lyric sheet. Prefers cassette with 1-3 songs on demo. SASE. Reports in 1 month.
**Music:** Mostly rock and pop; also MOR, R&B and soul. Recently released "Struck by Lightnin'," by Rat Race Choir (pop single); "Forever," by Wowii (rock single); and "Right On," by Spyder Turner (R&B single). Other artists include Precious and Beth Ames.

*****CRIMSON DYNASTY RECORDS CORP.**, B-271 Cedar and West Ave., Jenkintown PA 19046. (215)757-8022. Labels include Aurora Borealis, Avalanche, Bronto Sauraus, California Mud Slide, Crimson Dynasty, Crystal Blue Flame, Debtors Prison, Dragon, Dungeon, Dynasty, Earth Quake, Earth-Tremmor, Enchanted Knight, Flame, Golden Hawk, Hologram, Hurricane, Knight, Lightning, Misty Blue, Operation Golden Hawk, Poltergeist, Sinbad, Thunder Lizzard, Tornado, Typhoon, Volcano, Volcanus and Zansabar. A&R Director: Destiny Knight. ASCAP. Releases 12 singles and 5 albums/year. Works with artists and songwriters on contract; musicians on salary. Pays 5-10% royalty to artists on contract; negotiated rate to publishers for each record sold.
**How to Contact:** Submit demo tape and lyric sheet. "If we are not interested in a submitted tape, we automatically forward it to other record companies we think might be interested in the product." Prefers cassette with 3-5 songs on demo. SASE; returns material "if specifically requested."
**Music:** Mostly country; also bluegrass, easy listening, R&B and rock (Elvis-type sound).
**Tips:** "The first ten seconds of the demo tape must be exciting or interesting."

**"CRYIN IN THE STREETS" RECORD COMPANY**, Box 2544, Baton Rouge LA 70821. (504)924-6865 (24 hours). Director: E.K. Harrison. Recording studio (Ebb Tide) and production company (Jimmy Angel Production, Inc.). Labels include Ebenezer's Gospel Records, Inc., Church of Gospel Ministry Records, Inc., Showcase Records, Inc. and R.C.O. Records. Releases 12 singles and 3 albums/year. Works with artists and songwriters. "We also deal in old-but-solid-gold records in every field dating back to the 50s, 60s and 70's and are searching for old master tapes of singles and albums to buy or lease." Pays 10-12% royalty to artists on contract; statutory rate to publishers for each record sold.
**How to Contact:** Submit demo tape and lyric sheet of new material or submit list or cassette of oldies. SASE. Reports in 2 weeks.
**Music:** Soul, country, rock, gospel, jazz, pop and oldies. Recently released "Butterfly" by Marie (rock single); *Ebb Tide Presents*, by various artists (LP); and "Oh, Babe," by Betsy Davidson (country single). Other artists include George Perkins, Willie Joe, Jimmy Angel, Greg Schmidt, Richard Jones, Willie D and the Mighty Serenades.

*****CURTISS RECORDS**, Box 4740, Nashville TN 37216. (615)859-0355. President: Wade Curtiss. Record company and producer. Releases 6-20 singles and 2-5 albums in 1980. Works with artists and songwriters on contract. Pays 8¢/record royalty to artists on contract; 2½¢/record royalty to songwriters on contract.

**How to Contact:** Submit demo tape and lead sheet. Prefers 7½ ips reel-to-reel with 2-8 songs on demo. SASE. Reports in 3 weeks.
**Music:** Bluegrass, blues, C&W, disco, folk, gospel, jazz, rock, soul and top 40/pop. Recently released "Book of Matches," by Gary White; and "Rompin' " and "Punsky," by the Rhythm Rockers.

**DA CAR RECORDING**, 297 Rehm Rd., Depew NY 14043. (716)684-5323. Proprietor and Producer: C.D. Weyand. Record company and music publisher (Weyand Music Publishing/ASCAP). Member NMPA and Harry Fox Agency. Works with artists and songwriters on contract as negotiated; pays negotiated rate.
**How to Contact:** Submit professional demo tape. Prefers 7½ ips reel-to-reel on 5-inch reel with 1-5 songs on demo. Prefers leader tape between songs on cassette with 1-5 songs on demo. "Full piano arrangement must be included with tape or cassette. With orchestral or instrumental works—full score is a *must* for proper review of material. Only copyrighted material will be listened to; all other will be returned." SASE. Reports in 1 month.
**Music:** Classical, dance, easy-listening and jazz.
**Tips:** "Keep vocal distinct and out front. Full band required. We favor arrangements featuring strings. No electronic sounds. SASE a must!"

**DALLAS STAR RECORDS**, 9646 Rylie Rd., Dallas TX 75217. Executive Vice President: G.W. Moore. Record company, record producer and music publisher (Tiffanie Miko Music/BMI). Member CMA and TMA. Releases 8 singles and 5 albums/year. Works with musicians on salary for in-house studio work and songwriters on royalty contract. Pays 4-9½% royalty to artists on contract; statutory rate to publisher for each record sold.
**How to Contact:** Call first about your interest, then submit demo tape and lyric sheet. Prefers cassette with 2-5 songs on demo. SASE. Reports in 1 month.
**Music:** Country and modern country, gospel and rock (no heavy, metal or punk, new wave). Recently released "Cold Stone Wall," by Krys Christiana (modern country single); "One Night Stanley," by Jerry Abbott (modern country single); and "You," by Terri Lynn (modern country single). Other artists include Doc Holiday, Dallas Stash, Bobby Hibbitts, Justise Wells and Ben Wasson.

*****DAN THE MAN RECORDS CO.**, 3094 W. 101 St., Cleveland OH 44111. (216)631-6553. President: Daniel L. Bischoff. Record company, record producer and music publisher (Dan The Man Music Publishing Co./ASCAP). Estab. 1982. Releases 6-10 singles and 1-3 albums/year. Works with artists and songwriters on contract. Pays statutory rate to publishers for each record sold.
**How to Contact:** Submit demo tape and lyric sheet. Prefers cassette with 2-4 songs on demo. SASE. Reports in 3 weeks or sooner.
**Music:** Mostly country, top 40 and soul love songs; also C&W, easy listening, folk, R&B, rock and novelty. Recently released "Our Love Will Not Fade," by Johnny Wright (C&W single); "Reaganomics," by Dan the Man (novelty single); "Just A Simple Bouquet," by J. Wright (country single); and "Iran Crisis," "Collect," "E.T. Interview" and "Buzzard Man," by Dan the Man (all novelty singles).
**Tips:** Looking for "novelty records, catchy tunes."

**DANCE-A-THON RECORDS**, Station K, Box 13584, Atlanta GA 30324. (404)872-6000 and 872-4000. Labels include Banned, Hotlanta, Hottrax and Spectrum Stereo Records. President: Aleck Janoulis. Vice President/A&R Director: Oliver P. Cooper. Record company and music publisher. Releases 10-12 singles and 2-4 albums/year. Works with artists and songwriters on contract. Pays "3½-7% on 90% sold" to artists on contract.
**How to Contact:** Submit tape and lyric sheet. Prefers 7½ ips reel-to-reel or cassette with 1-3 songs on demo. "Demo tapes can be submitted with voice and either guitar or piano accompaniment only. A master should be sent only after a letter is submitted and replied to." Does not return unsolicited material.
**Music:** C&W, disco, easy listening, MOR, rock (new wave and C&W) and top 40/pop. Recently released *The Square Root of Two*, by the Night Shadows (60s re-issue LP); and *Nockum Nekkid (rock LP)* and "Disco Rock" (rock single), both by Starfoxx; *Text Specimens* by various artists (LP); and *Invasion of the Acid-Eaters*, by the Night Shadows (rock LP).
**Tips:** "Specialty service started for new artists—the 'Test Specimen' series of LP's features several new artists per record. Excellent for starting a track record in the music business. Write for details."

*****DANSAN RECORDS**, 14 Soho St., London, W1V 6HB, England. 44-01-437-2245. Labels include Dansan, Leisure, 'O'Liver "D" and Blank Records. Managing Director: David Marcus. Record company, record producer and music publisher (Jason Music, Mooreside Music). Releases 4 singles and 8-10 albums/year. Works with artists and songwriters on contract. Pays 2-15% royalty to artists on contract; pays royalty for each record sold "as laid down by MCPS." Royalties paid to US songwriters

and artists through US publishing or recording affiliate. Has not yet, but would listen to material from US songwriters and artists.
**How to Contact:** Write first. Prefers cassette for demo. Does not return unsolicited material. Reports in 1 month.
**Music:** Mostly dance-oriented and MOR; also C&W, easy listening and R&B. Recently released *Play It Again Bryan*, by Bryan Smith (MOR LP); *Andy's Dance Party*, by Andy Ross (MOR LP); and *Dancing Guitars*, by Bert Weedon (MOR LP).

**DATE LINE INTERNATIONAL RECORDS**, Suite 5c, 400 W. 43rd St., New York NY 10036. A&R Director: Jane A. Eaton. Record company, record producer and music publisher (MacHarmony Music/ASCAP and Tteltrab Music/BMI). Releases 5 singles and 3 albums/year. Pays statutory rate to publishers for each record sold.
**How to Contact:** Submit demo tape and lyric sheet. Prefers cassette with 1-3 songs on demo. SASE. Reports in 1 month; returns "only with SASE."
**Music:** Rock (hard and soft) and top 40/pop. Recently released *A Feeling's Coming over Me*, by Phyllis MacBryde (pop LP); and "Hey, Cab Driver" and "I Want to Know You," by Roger and the Ramjets (dance).

**DAWN PRODUCTIONS**, 108 Morning Glory Ln., Manheim PA 17545. Labels include Bat, LeFevre, Canadian American Recordings, Grafitti, Music Machine, Music City, Palmer and Vermillion Records. President: Joey Welz. Record company, booking agency and music publisher. (Ursula Music/BMI and Welz Music/ASCAP). Releases 4 singles and 2 albums/year. Works with artists and songwriters on contract. "We lease the record to a major label, who is responsible for paying the royalties."
**How to Contact:** Submit demo tape and lead sheet. Prefers 7½ ips reel-to-reel or cassette with 6-12 songs on demo. Does not return unsolicited material. "We hold it until we need material for a session, then we search our files."
**Music:** C&W, dance, easy listening, folk, MOR, rock and top 40/pop. Recently released "I Remember Rock and Roll," "In My Car," and *American Made Rock 'n Roll*, by Joey Welz.

*****DAWN PROMOTIONS AND AGENCY, LTD.**, 186 Casterton Rd., Stamford, Lincs, PE9 2XX, England. 44-0780-51736. Labels include Soul Stop (up-tempo soul); Buffalo (country) and Weasel (pop). Managing Director: Ken Cox. Record company, record producer, music publisher (Pixie Music Co.) and entertainment agency. Member EAA. Releases 8-10 singles and 1 album/year. Works with artists and songwriters on contract; musicians on salary for in-house studio work. Pays 8-12% to artists on contract; pays statutory rate to publishers for each record sold. Royalties paid to US songwriters and artists through US publishing or recording affiliate.
**How to Contact:** Submit demo tape and lyric sheet. Prefers cassette with 2-4 songs on demo. SAE and IRC. Reports in 2 weeks.
**Music:** Mostly soul (up-tempo); also C&W and top 40/pop. Recently released "What," by Judy Street (pop/soul single); "Nine Times Out of the Ten," by Muriel Day (pop/soul single); and "All You Got Your Ears On," by Ron Ryan (CB/country single). Other artists include Jed Ford (country) and Corrine Gillies (pop).

*****DAZIA RECORDS**, 13033 W. McNichols, Detroit MI 48521 (313)342-9696. Labels include Dazia. Business Manager: Jacqueline Harris. Record company, record producer, music publisher (Dazia Music) and production company. Estab. 1982. Releases 8 singles/year. Works with artists and songwriters on contract. Pays negotiable royalty to artists on contract.
**How to Contact:** Write first about your interest; submit demo tape and lyric sheet. Prefers 7½ ips reel-to-reel or cassette with 1-4 songs on demo. Include photo and bio. SASE. Reports in 1 week.
**Music:** Mostly R&B and top 40/pop; also children's, C&W, dance-oriented, easy listening, gospel and soul. Recently released "Do Me Baby Do Me," by Somerset (dance-oriented single and 12"). Other artists include Cortez Harris and Assuage.

**DEKA RECORDS**, Box 5712, High Point NC 27262. (919)885-0263. Labels include Mecca, Rose. President: W.C. Staley. Record company, record producer and music publisher (Oak Hollow Music, Staley Music Publishing). Releases 10 singles and 25 albums/year. Works with artists and songwriters on contract; musicians on salary for in-house studio work. Pays negotiable royalty to artists on contract; statutory rate to publishers for each record sold.
**How to Contact:** Submit demo tape and lyric sheet. Prefers cassette with 3-7 songs on demo. SASE. Reports in 1 month.
**Music:** Bluegrass, church/religious, C&W, folk, gospel, MOR, R&B, rock, soul and top 40/pop. Recently released *Here and Now*, by Blueridge Rangers (bluegrass LP). Other artists include Harvesters, Deacons, Apostil of Song, Carolina Rangers, Jim Green Singers, Mickey Hawks, Wade Carlton, Tucker Williams, Johnny Lee and Larry Solomon.

**DE-LITE RECORDS**, 1733 Broadway, New York NY 10019. (212)757-6770. President: Gabe Vigorito. Record company and music publisher (Delightful Music Ltd.). Releases 10 singles and 4-5 albums/year. Works with artists on contract.
**How to Contact:** Submit demo tape and lyric sheet. Prefers cassette as demo. SASE. Reports in 1-2 months.
**Music:** R&B and top 40/pop. Recently released *Something Special*, by Kool & The Gang (R&B/pop LP); and *Second Cup*, by Coffee.

*****DELTA SOUND RECORDS**, 814 W. Claiborne St., Box 672, Greenwood MS 38930. (601)453-3302. Labels include Cindy Boo Records. Contact: Mack Allen Smith. Record company and music publisher (Mack Smith Music/BMI). Releases 3-10 singles and 2-6 albums/year. Works with artists and songwriters on contract. Pays 3-5% royalty to artists on contract; standard royalty to songwriters on contract.
**How to Contact:** Submit demo tape and lead or lyric sheet. Prefers cassette with 1-5 songs on demo.
**Music:** C&W, rock and top 40/pop. Recently released "All The Praises" (country single) and *We Gotta Rock Tonight* (country LP), by Mack Allen Smith.
**Tips:** "Submit songs that have strong lyrics with a good hook. I think a song should tell a story people can relate to."

*****DESTINY RECORDS**, 31 Nassau Ave., Wilmington MA 01887. (617)658-8391. Engineer: Larry Feeney. Record company, record producer and music publisher (Seismic Music). Releases 3-5 singles and 1 album/year. Works with artists and songwriters on contract; musicians on salary for in-house studio work. Pays negotiable rate to artists on contract; statutory rate to publishers for each record sold.
**How to Contact:** Write first about your interest; submit demo tape and lyric sheet. Prefers cassette with maximum 2 songs on demo. Does not return unsolicited material. Reports in 1 month.
**Music:** Mostly rock; also bluegrass, blues, church/religious, C&W, dance-oriented, easy listening, folk, jazz, MOR, progressive, R&B, soul and top 40/pop. Recently released "Push It to the Limit," by The Wages (pop/rock single); "She'll Drive You Crazy," by Wild Turkey (R&R single); and *The Kingdom of Simitz*, by the Kingdom of Simitz (rock/jazz LP).

*****DHARMA RECORDS**, 117 W. Rockland Rd., Box 615, Libertyville IL 60048. (312)362-4060. Labels include Future and Homexercise. Vice President: Rick Johnson. Record company, record producer and music publisher (Amalgamated Tulip Corp.). Releases 2 singles and 1 album/year. Works with artists and songwriters on contract. Pays negotiable royalty to artists on contract; statutory rate to publishers for each record sold.
**How to Contact:** Submit demo tape and lyric sheet or write about your interest. Prefers cassette with 3-5 songs on demo. SASE. Reports in 1 month.
**Music:** Mostly hard rock; also easy listening, MOR, progressive rock and top 40/pop. Recently released *Corky Siegel*, by Corky Siegel (folk-country LP); *Dancexercise*, by Johnson & Poole (exercise LP); and "Last Chance," by Gabriel Bondage (progressive rock single).

**DIMENSION RECORDS**, Box 17087, Nashville TN 37217. (615)754-9400. A&R Producer: Ray Pennington. Record company and music publisher (Diversified Music/ASCAP, Almanie Music/BMI, Millstone Music, Julina Music/SESAC). Releases 15 singles and 3 albums/year. Works with musicians and songwriters on contract; pays statutory rate to publisher for each record sold.
**How to Contact:** Arrange personal interview to play demo tape. Prefers 7½ ips reel-to-reel with maximum 4 songs on demo. SASE. Reports in 1 month.
**Music:** Primarily country, progressive and traditional; also bluegrass; easy listening, folk, gospel, MOR and top 40/pop. Recently released "The Fool in Me," and "Innocent Lies," by Sonny James; and "One Away from One," and "Too Many Heartaches," by Billy Walker. Other artists include Peggy Foreman and Dave Kirby.

**DOMINO RECORDS, LTD.**, Ridgewood Park Estates, 222 Tulane St., Garland TX 75043. Labels include Front Row Records. Contact: Gene or Dea Summers. Public Relations/Artist and Fan Club Coordinator: Steve Summers. Record company and music publisher (Silicon Music/BMI). Releases 5-12 singles and 2-8 albums/year. Works with artists and songwriters on contract. Pays negotiable royalties to artists on contract; standard royalty to songwriters on contract.
**How to Contact:** Submit demo tape. Prefers cassette with 1-3 songs on demo. Does not return unsolicited material. SASE. Reports ASAP.
**Music:** C&W, R&B, rock (soft) and 50s material. Recently released "Stagger Walk," by Fabulous Capris (R&B single); "Grand Ole Opry Queen," by Linda Plowman (C&W single); and "Hayrick Mountain," by Margie Louise (C&W single).
**Tips:** "If you own masters of 1950s rock and rock-a-billy, contact us first! We will work with you on a

percentage basis for overseas release. We have active releases in Holland, Switzerland, Belgium, Australia, England, France, Sweden, Norway and the US at the present. We need original masters. You must be able to prove ownership of tapes before we can accept a deal. We're looking for little-known, obscure recordings. We have the market if you have the tapes!"

**DOOR KNOB RECORDS**, 2125 8th Ave., S., Nashville TN 37204. (615)383-6002. Labels include Society Records. President: Gene Kennedy. Vice President: Karen Jeglum. Director of Promotion: Joe Carroll. Record company, record producer, music publisher (Door Knob Music, Publishers Inc., Chip 'N' Dale Music Publishers and Lodestar Music), independent distribution and promotion firm. Member CMA. Releases 25 singles and 2 albums/year. Pays 4-7% of 90% of records sold; statutory rate to publishers for each record sold.
**How to Contact:** Submit demo tape and lyric sheet or arrange personal interview. Prefers 7½ ips reel-to-reel or cassette with 1-4 songs on demo. SASE. Reports in 1-4 weeks.
**Music:** C&W and MOR. Recently released "Green Eyes" and "Back in Debbie's Arms," by Tom Carlile; and "A Thing or Two on My Mind," by Gene Kennedy and Karen Jeglum. Other artists include Kris Carpenter, Shirley Parker and Thomas Riley.

**DORN RECORDS**, 20531 Plummer St., Chatsworth CA 91311. (213)998-0443. Labels include DORN, AKO and ATEC Records. Manager: A. Sullivan. Record company, record producer and music publisher (AMIRON Music/ASCAP). Releases 4 singles and 1 album/year. Works with songwriters on contract. Pays 5-10% royalty to artists on contract; statutory rate to publishers for each record sold.
**How to Contact:** Submit demo tape and lyric sheet. Prefers 7½ips reel-to-reel or cassette as demo. SASE. Reports in 3 weeks.
**Music:** Blues, C&W, dance-oriented, easy listening, MOR, progressive, Spanish, R&B, rock and top 40/pop. Recently released *Newstreet*, (rock LP and single); and "Better Run" (pop/rock single), by Newstreet. Other artists include Lista Brown, El Chicano, Zell Black, Zaral, AKO, Johnny Forever, One Flite Up, Debbie Rockwell, Pyramid and Monica Lewis.

**DUPUY RECORDS/PRODUCTIONS/PUBLISHING, INC.**, Suite 200, 10960 Ventura Blvd., Studio City CA 91604. (213)980-6412. President: Pedro Dupuy. Record company, record producer and music publisher (Dupuy Publishing, Inc./ASCAP). Estab. 1981. Releases 5 singles and 5 albums/year. Works with artists and songwriters on contract; musicians on salary for in-house studio work. Pays negotiable rate to publishers for each record sold.
**How to Contact:** Write or call first about your interest, arrange personal interview or submit demo tape and lyric sheet. Prefers cassette with 2-4 songs on demo. SASE. Reports in 1 month.
**Music:** Easy listening, jazz, MOR, R&B, soul and top 40/pop. Artists include Gordon Gilman and Ronnie Logean.
**Tips:** Needs "very definite lyrics with hook."

**DYNAMIC ARTISTS RECORDS**, Box 25654, Richmond VA 23260. (804)225-7810. President: Joseph J. Carter Jr. Record company, music publisher, booking agency, management firm and production firm (Hot Gold Music Publishing Co./BMI). Releases 4 singles and 2 albums/year. Works with musicians on salary: artists and songwriters on contract; statutory rate to publishers for each record sold. Pays 7-10% royalty to artists on contract.
**How to Contact:** Submit demo tape. Prefers cassette with 1-3 songs on demo. SASE. Reports in 60 days.
**Music:** Mostly soul and pop; also dance and rock. Recently released "Without You Tonight," by Waller Family (ballad single); *Love Moods*, by Waller Family (soul and pop LP); and "Sooner or Later," by Dave Webb (pop single). Other artists include the Dynamic Soul Orchestra, Flaming Cavaliers, and Starfire.

**DYNAMITE**, 5 Aldom Circle, West Caldwell NJ 07006. (201)226-0035. Labels include Dynamite, Deadwood, Tar Heel, True Love, Cactus, Peek Records and Deadwood-Dynamite cassette tapes. Contact Jim Hall or Gidget Starr. Record company, record producer and music publisher. Works with artists and songwriters on contract. Pays 5% royalty to artists on contract; statutory rate to publishers for each record sold.
**How to Contact:** Submit demo tape and lyric sheet or write first about your interest. Prefers 7½ ips reel-to-reel or cassette with 5 songs on demo. Does not return unsolicited material. Reports in 2 weeks.
**Music:** Bluegrass, blues, C&W, gospel and rock. Artists include Doc Hopkins and Tune Twisters, Sal Franco, Alice Faye and Charlie Bailey.

**E.L.J. RECORD CO.**, 1344 Waldron, St. Louis MO 63130. President: Eddie Johnson. Record company, record producer and music publisher (Quinones/BMI). Works with musicians on salary; artists

and songwriters on contract. Releases 6 singles and 3 albums/year. Pays 3% minimum royalty to artists on contract; statutory rate to publisher for each record sold.
**How to Contact:** Submit demo tape or submit demo tape and lead sheet. Prefers 7½ ips reel-to-reel or cassette with 4 songs on demo. SASE. Reports in 2 weeks.
**Music:** Blues, church/religious, R&B, soul and top 40/pop. Recently released "Rocks in Your Pillow" and "When the Light of the Candle," both by Bobby Scott (R&B singles); and "Who Am I," by Eddie Johnson (top 40 single). Other artists include Joe Buckner, LeRoy Harris, Vivian Harper and Bill Shank.

**\*EASY CHAIR RECORDS**, 2913 95th St., Lubbock TX 79423. (806)745-5992. President: Bill Gammill. Record company, record producer and music publisher (Gammill-Murphy Music). Estab. 1982. Releases 1 single and 1 album/year. Works with artists on contract. Pays 7-15% royalty to artists on contract; statutory rate to publishers for each record sold.
**How to Contact:** Submit demo tape and lyric sheet. Prefers cassette with 1-3 songs on demo. SASE. Reports in 2 weeks.
**Music:** Mostly contemporary Christian; also church/religious and gospel. Recently released "Learning How to Fly," by Gammill & Murphy (contemporary Christian single); and *Starting From Scratch*, by Gammill & Murphy (contemporary Christian album).

**EAT RECORDS**, 400 Essex St., Salem MA 01970. (617)744-7678. Labels include Neat and Dial-Tone. A&R Director: Edsel Ferrari. Record company, record producer and music publisher (Phonetones). Member NAIRD. Releases 3 singles and 3 albums/year. Works with artists and songwriters on contract. Pays statutory rate to publishers for each record sold.
**How to Contact:** Submit demo tape and lyric sheet. Prefers cassette with 2-4 songs on demo. SASE. Reports in 1 month.
**Music:** Dance-oriented, R&B, rock, pop and new wave. Recently released *She Had to Go*, by Rubber Rodeo (wave LP). Other artists include Tweeds, Men & Volts, The Incredible Casuals, The Original Artists, and Human Sexual Response.

**ECHO RECORDS**, 824 83rd St., Miami Beach FL 03141. (305)865-8960. Record company, record producer and music publisher (Dana). Releases 2 singles and 1 album/year. Pays statutory rate to publishers for each record sold.
**How to Contact:** Write first about your interest. Prefers 7½ or 15 ips reel-to-reel or cassette as demo. SASE. Reports in 1 week.
**Music:** Classical and Polish.

**ECLIPSE RECORDS**, 118 5th St., Box 176, Taylorsville NC 28681. (704)632-4735. Contact: Harry Deal. Record company, music publisher and record producer. Works with artists and songwriters on contract.
**How to Contact:** Submit demo tape and lyric sheet. Prefers cassette with 2-3 songs on demo. SASE. Reports in 2-3 weeks.
**Music:** C&W, dance, folk, MOR, R&B, rock, soul and top 40/pop.

**EDUCATOR RECORDS, INC.**, Box 490, Wayne PA 19087. (215)423-5960. President and Musical Director: Bart Arntz. Record company and music publisher. Releases 33 singles and 14 albums/year. Works with musicians on salary; artists and songwriters on contract. Pays negotiable royalty to artists on contract; standard royalty to songwriters on contract.
**How to Contact:** Submit demo tape. Prefers 7½ ips reel-to-reel or cassette with 3-8 songs on demo. "Tape must be clearly audible. We are constantly seeking strong instrumentals of all types of music. We are also interested in license agreements on finished masters." SASE. Reports in 3 weeks.
**Music:** Children's (character songs), disco, soul and show music of the '30s and '40s. "We are primarily a dance record company (tap, jazz and ballet). We also produce R&B material." Recently released *Jazz Moves*, by Ron Daniels (jazz dance LP).

**\*EMKAY RECORDS**, 10622 Commerce Ave., Tujunga CA 91042. (213)353-8165. Contact: Kent Washburn. Record company, record producer and music publisher (Monard Music/ASCAP, Pencott Publishing/BMI). Releases 2-3 singles and 1-2 albums/year. Works with artists and songwriters on contract. Pays 5-12½% royalty to artists on contract; statutory rate to publishers for each record sold.
**How to Contact:** Submit demo tape and lyric sheet. Prefers cassette with 2-4 songs on demo. SASE. Reports in 1 month.
**Music:** Mostly R&B and soul; also gospel, jazz, soul and top 40/pop. Recent releases *A Life In a Day*, by Justin Thyme (jazz LP); *Free Love*, by Free Love (R&B LP); and "Don't Burn No Bridges," by Hypnotics (R&B single).

**ENTERPRIZE RECORDS**, 3623 McCann Rd., Longview TX 75605. (214)757-1839. Contact: Jerry Haymes. Record company and music publisher (Golden Guitar/BMI and Enterprize Music/ASCAP). Works with artists and songwriters on contract. Pays statutory rate to publishers for each record sold.
**How to Contact:** Submit demo tape and lyric sheet. Prefers reel-to-reel and cassettes. SASE. Reports as soon as possible.
**Music:** Bluegrass, C&W, gospel and MOR. Recently released "Island of Dreams," and "Love You More Than I Can Say," by Brenda D. (MOR single); and "Smile of a Clown", by Jerry Haymes (C&W single). Other artists include The Pages and Jeff Johnson.

**EPOCH UNIVERSAL PUBLICATIONS, INC.**, 10802 N. 23rd Ave., Phoenix AZ 85029. (602)864-1980. Labels include North American Liturgy Resources (NALR), Livingsong Records, affiliated with Sounds of Hope Records. A&R Director: Paul Quinlan. Record company, record producer and music publisher (Epoch Music Corp./ASCAP, North American Liturgy Resources/BMI). Member NARAS, GMA, CBA, NCGA. Releases 10-20 albums/year. Works with artists and songwriters on contract; musicians on salary for in-house studio work. Pays negotiable royalty to artists on contract; statutory rate to publishers for each record sold.
**How to Contact:** Submit demo tape and lyric sheet. Prefers 7½ ips reel-to-reel or cassette with 3-20 songs on demo. SASE. Reports in 1 month.
**Music:** Children's, choral, church/religious, classical, gospel and liturgical. Recently released *Lord of Light*, by St. Louis Jesuits (liturgical LP); *Christmas with Friends*, by Ed McMahon and Doc Severinsen (seasonal LP); and *Land of Love*, by Marcy Tigner (children's). Other artists include Carey Landry, The Dameans, Michael Joncas, Pat Boone, Tom Kendzia, Jerry Goebel, Tom Conry, Abraham Kaplan, Don Reagan, Paul & Timothy, Grayson Brown, Joe Zsigray, Ed Gutfreund, Paul Quinlan, Ellis and Lynch, Deanna Edwards.
**Tips:** "Songwriters and artists should be able to write or record songs that have been used successfully in liturgical celebrations, concerts or generally inspire the listener. Artists should be willing to give concerts."

**EQUA RECORDS**, 1800 Mowry Ave., Fremont CA 94538. (415)794-6637. President: Warren M. Johnson. Record company and music publisher (Equa Music/ASCAP, Mepro Music/BMI). Member CMA. Releases 4-5 singles/year. Works with artists and songwriters on contract. Pays statutory rate to publishers for each record sold.
**How to Contact:** Submit demo tape and lyric sheet. Prefers cassette with 3-6 songs on demo. SASE. Reports in 3 weeks.
**Music:** C&W. Recently released "No Place to Hide," "It Ain't My Concern" and "Goin' Home Alone," by Gail Zeiler (C&W singles).

*****ESQUIRE RECORDS TALENT LTD.**, 185A, Newmarket Rd., Norwich, Norfolk, NR4 6AP, England. 44-0603-51139. Labels include Starlite and Titan. Director: Peter Newbrook. Record company and music publisher (Esquire Music Co.). Releases 3 singles and 10 albums/year. Works with artists on contract. Pays negotiable royalty to artists on contract; 6¼% to publishers for each record sold. Royalties paid to US songwriters and artists through US publishing or recording affiliate. Has not yet, but would listen to material from US songwriters and artists.
**How to Contact:** Write first. Prefers cassette for demo. SAE and IRC. Reports in 1 month.
**Music:** Mostly jazz; also MOR and R&B. Artists include Cleo Laine, Teddy Wilson, John Dankworth and Mary Lou Williams.

**ETS RECORD CO.**, Box 932. Honolulu HI 96808. Contact: A&R Department. Record company. Works with musicians on contract. Pays standard royalty to artists and songwriters on contract.
**How to Contact:** Write first about your interest. Prefers 7½ ips reel-to-reel with 1-2 songs on demo. SASE. Reports in 1 week.
**Music:** C&W; and easy listening.

**F&L RECORDS**, Suite #902, 50 Music Square W., Nashville TN 37203. (615)329-2228. Labels include Progress Records. General Manager: Bobby Fischer. Record company, record producer, music publisher (Bobby Fisher Music Group), national promoter and distributor. Member NSAI, CMA, CPA, FICAP. Releases 10 singles/year. Works with artists and songwriters on contract. Pays maximum royalty to artists on contract; statutory rate to publishers for each record sold.
**How to Contact:** Submit demo tape and lyric sheet. Prefers cassette with 2-3 songs on demo. SASE. Reports "when time permits."
**Music:** C&W and progressive. Recently released "Storm of Love," "Right Back Loving You Again," "Better Off Blue" and "Stumblin' In" by Chantilly. Other artists include Danny White, Linda Nail and Wyvon Alexander. "We distribute the records of Dottsy, Johnny Carver and Johnny Russell for Tanglewood Records."

## Record Companies 151

**FACTORY BEAT RECORDS, INC.**, 663 5th Ave., New York NY 10022. (212)757-3638. Labels include RER, Ren Rome and Can Scor Productions, Inc. President: Rena L. Feeney. Record company, record producer and music publisher (Ren-Maur Music Corp.). Member NARAS, BMI and AGAC. Releases 4 singles and 2 albums/year. Works with musicians on salary for in-house studio work. Pays 4-12% royalty to artists on contract; statutory rate to publishers for each record sold.
**How to Contact:** Submit demo tape and lyric sheet only. Prefers cassette as demo. SASE. Reports in 3 weeks.
**Music:** R&B, rock, soul and top 40/pop.

**\*FAMOUS DOOR PUBLISHING CO./T.M. INTERNATIONAL RECORDS**, Box 16608, Milwaukee WI 53216 or 4526 Crittenden Ave., Indianapolis IN 46205. (414)461-0602. Contact: Odell or Cardell Tillman. Record company and music publisher. Releases 5 singles and 3 albums/year. Works with artists on contract; musicians on salary for in-house studio work. Pays statutory rate to publishers for each record sold. .
**How to Contact:** Submit demo tape and lyric sheet. Prefers cassette with 4 songs on demo. SASE. Reports ASAP.
**Music:** Mostly soul; also bluegrass, gospel, jazz and R&B. Recently released *Sorceress*, by Joanne Tardy (R&B LP); *Crazy Love* and *Music Makes Me High*, by Joanne Tardy (bluegrass LPs).

**FAMOUS DOOR RECORDS**, Box 92, Station A, Flushing NY 11358. (212)463-6281. Contact: Harry Lim. Record company. Member NARAS. Releases 6 albums/year. Works with artists on contract. Pays 5% maximum royalty to artists on contract; statutory rate to publishers for each record sold.
**How to Contact:** Write first about your interest. Prefers cassette with 3 songs minimum on demo. SASE. Reports in 1 month.
**Music:** Jazz. Recently released *Street of Dreams*, by The Ross Tompkins Trio; *Roarin' Back into New York, New York*, by The Bill Watrous Quartet; and *Hail to the Chief: Butch Miles Salutes Count Basie*, by The Butch Miles Octet. Other artists include Glenn Zattola, Danny Stiles and Dick Cary.
**Tips:** Looking for "good instrumentals."

**FANFARE RECORDS**, Box 2501, Des Moines IA 50315. (515)285-6564. President: Art Smart Stenstrom. Record company and music publisher (Love Street Publishing/BMI). Releases 1 album/year. Works with artists on contract. Payment negotiable; pays statutory rate to publishers for each record sold.
**How to Contact:** Not currently reviewing new material.
**Music:** Rock and top 40/pop. Recently released *Colt .45*, by Colt .45 (country rock LP); and *Sailing on Fantasies*, by Silver Laughter (top 40 LP).

**FANTASY/PRESTIGE/MILESTONE/STAX RECORDS**, 10th and Parker, Berkeley CA 94710. (415)549-2500. Associate A&R Director: Phil Jones. Record company. Works with artists and songwriters on contract.
**How to Contact:** Submit demo tape. Prefers cassette as demo. SASE. Reports in 3 weeks.
**Music:** R&B, soul, jazz and top 40/pop. Recently released *Azymuth*, by Azymuth (jazz LP); and *Shock*, by Shock (R&B LP).

**FAR EAST RECORDS**, 4810 SW 69th Ave., Miami FL 33155. (305)665-5701. Labels include Far East and Fusion Records. President: Rich Piccolo. Record company, record producer and music publisher (Anitya Songs). Releases 5 singles and 4-5 albums/year. Works with artists and songwriters on contract; musicians on salary for in-house studio work. Pays 4-6% royalty to artists on contract; statutory rate to publishers for each record sold.
**How to Contact:** Submit demo tape and lyric sheet. Prefers cassette with 3 songs on demo. SASE. Reports in 3 weeks.
**Music:** Jazz, MOR, progressive, R&B, rock, soul and top 40/pop and reggae. Recently released *Rajas & Lions*, by Rajas & Lions (reggae LP and single); and *Build My World*, by RLP Group (pop-jazz LP).

**FARR RECORDS**, Box 1098, Somerville NJ 08876. (201)725-3850. Contact: Candace Campbell. Record company and record producer. Member RIAA. Releases 30 singles and 30 albums/year. Works with artists and songwriters on contract. Pays negotiable royalty to artists on contract; statutory rate to publishers for each record sold.
**How to Contact:** Submit demo tape and lyric sheet. Prefers cassette with 4 songs on demo. SASE. Reports in 2 weeks.
**Music:** C&W, dance-oriented, easy listening, folk, MOR, rock, soul and top 40/pop.

**\*50 STATES RECORDS & TAPES**, Box 314, Hendersonville TN 37075. (615)824-8308. A&R Director: Johnny Howard. Record company, record producer and music publisher (Chap's Music). Re-

leases 12 singles and 6 albums/year. Works with artists and songwriters on contract. Pays negotiable royalty to artists on contract; statutory rate to publishers for each record sold.
**How to Contact:** Submit demo tape and lyric sheet. Prefers cassette with 1-5 songs on demo. SASE. Reports in 3 weeks.
**Music:** Mostly country and top 40; also bluegrass and gospel. Recently released "England, America Loves You," by Fabulous Fryers (country/pop single); *You Lay So Easy On My Mind*, by Jack Paris (country/pop LP); and "Keep Your Hands Off My Baby," by Sharry Hanna (country/pop single).

**FLOWERS RECORDS**, Rt. 1, Box 120F, Swoope VA 24479. (703)885-3309. Contact: Charles A. Flowers. Record company, music publisher and recording studio. Works with musicians on salary; songwriters on contract. Pays standard royalties to songwriters on contract.
**How to Contact:** Call first about your interest. Prefers 7½ ips reel-to-reel. SASE. Reports in 1 week.
**Music:** Bluegrass, blues, classical, C&W, easy listening, folk, gospel, jazz, progressive, R&B, rock and top 40/pop. Recently released "You Make Me Feel So Good," by Barbara Flowers (country single); *Upward Way*, by S. Cook (gospel LP); "Lost Your Love Forever," by R. Call (easy listening single); and "The Way It's Meant to Be," by J. Campbell (country single). Other artists include Shenandoah Valley Crusaders, Greg Everhart and Southern Hospitality.

*****THE FLYING RECORD COMPANY LTD.**, 1 Lower James St., London, W1, England. 44-01-734-8311. Director: Paul K. Walden. Record company and music publisher (The Flying Music Company, Ltd.). Estab. 1981. Member MPA, PPL. Releases 12 singles and 2-3 albums/year. Works with musicians and songwriters on contract. Pays negotiable royalty to artists on contract; statutory rate to publishers for each record sold. Royalties paid directly to US songwriters and artists.
**How to Contact:** Submit demo tape and lyric sheet. Prefers 7½ or 15 ips reel-to-reel cassette with 3-6 songs on demo. SAE and IRC. Reports in 1 month.
**Music:** Mostly top 40/pop; also progressive, soft rock and soul. Recently released "Like a Stone," and "Halfway Motel," by Voyager (pop singles); and "Magic Touch," by Leroy Simmons (pop/soul single). Other artists include Paul French, D'Arc, Springwater and Whiplash.

**FORCE RECORDS**, Box 25664, Chicago IL 60625. (312)583-1507. Contact: Ed Kammer. Record company and music publisher (Tripoli Music/BMI). Releases 3-4 singles and 1-2 albums/year. Works with artists on contract. Pays negotiable royalty; statutory rate to publishers for each record sold.
**How to Contact:** Submit demo tape and lyric sheet. Prefers 7½ ips reel-to-reel or cassette with 4 songs minimum on demo. Does not return unsolicited material. Reports in 6 weeks.
**Music:** Dance-oriented, easy listening, rock (hard and pop) and top 40/pop. Recently released "Texas," by The Myth (AOR single); and "Outlaw," by Chaos (pop rock single). Other artists include George Michael.
**Tips:** "Have a viable act and be open to material suggestions. Also keep an open mind as far as producer goes."

**FOREVER RECORDS**, Box 40772, Nashville TN 37204. (615)256-2242. Labels include Chenaniah and Mustard Seed Records. Record company, record producer and music publisher (Chenaniah Music/SESAC, Derron Music/ASCAP, Re'Generation Publications and Spring Hill Publishing Group). Member NARAS. Releases 2 singles and 12 albums/year. Works with songwriters on contract. Pays statutory rate to publishers for each record sold.
**How to Contact:** Call first about your interest. Prefers cassette with 2-5 songs on demo. SASE. Reports in 1 month.
**Music:** Children's, choral, church/religious, easy listening, gospel and MOR. Recently released *Hymns in Velvet*, by Re'Generation (inspirational LP); *Christmas in Velvet/Volume II*, by The Re'Generation (Christmas LP); *Miles & Webb*, by Kevin Miles and Rick Webb (inspirational LP); and *Music of the People*, by The Larry Mayfield Orchestra and Singers (sacred choral LP). Other artists include Neil Madsen, Ben Markley, Jance Wacker, and Free Spirit.

**415 RECORDS**, Box 14563, San Francisco CA 94114. (415)621-3415; 522-9828. Director, A&R: Chris Knab. Record company and music publisher (Very Safe Music/BMI and Even Safer Music/ASCAP). Releases 6 albums/year. Works with artists on contract.
**How to Contact:** Submit demo tape. Prefers cassette only with 1-5 songs on demo. SASE. Pays statutory rate to publishers for each record sold.
**Music:** New wave rock. Recently released *Heartbeat & Triggers*, by Translator (415/Columbia Records); *Benefactor*, by Romeo Void (415/Columbia Records); *Good as Gold*, by The Red Rockers (415 Records); and *The White EP*, by Pop-O-Pies (415 Records). Other artists include New Math, Roky Erickson and the Aliens, and the Units.

**Record Companies** **153**

**FRANNE RECORDS**, Box 8135, Chicago IL 60680. (312)224-5612. Labels include Superbe Records. A&R Director/Executive Producer: R.C. Hillsman. Record company, music publisher and producer. Works with artists and songwriters on contract. Pays 3½% royalty to artists and songwriters on contract.
**How to Contact:** Arrange personal interview or submit demo tape and lead sheet. Prefers 7½ or 15 ips quarter-inch reel-to-reel or cassette with 4-6 songs on demo. "By registered mail only." SASE. Reports in 3 weeks.
**Music:** Church/religious, C&W, disco, gospel, jazz, MOR, rock and top 40/pop. Recently released "He's Love" and "You Better Get Right," by Allen Duo (gospel singles).

**FRECKLE RECORDS**, Pioneer Sq., Box 4005, Seattle WA 98104. (206)682-3200. Record company and music publisher (Reilly & Maloney Music/BMI). Member NAIRD. Releases 2-3 singles and 2 albums/year. Works with artists on contract. Pays statutory rate to publishers for each record sold.
**How to Contact:** Call first about your interest. SASE.
**Music:** Folk and contemporary. Recently released "Ballad of the 49er Faithful," by Reilly & Maloney (novelty single); *The Harvest Is In*, by David Maloney (contemporary LP); and *Good Company*, by Reilly & Maloney.

**FREKO RECORDS**, Box 11967, Houston TX 77016. (713)694-2971. President: Freddie Kober. Record company, record producer and music publisher (Anode Music/BMI). Releases 2 singles/year. Works with songwriters on contract. Pays negotiable royalty to artists on contract; statutory rate to publishers for each record sold.
**How to Contact:** Submit demo tape and lyric sheet. Prefers cassette with 1-3 songs on demo. SASE. Reports in 2 weeks.
**Music:** Gospel and soul. Recently released "Shake the Funk out of It", by Contage'us (disco single) and "That Means So Much to Me", by Mel Starr (love ballad single).

**FULL CIRCLE RECORDS**, 80 E. San Francisco St., Santa Fe NM 87501. (505)982-2900. President: Reno Myerson. Record company, record producer and music publisher (Full Cycle Music Publishing Co./BMI, ASCAP). Works with artists and songwriters on contract; musicians on salary for in-house studio work. Pays 20-50% of net royalty to artists on contract; statutory rate to publishers for each record sold.
**How to Contact:** Submit demo tape and lyric sheet. Prefers cassette with 4-10 songs on demo. SASE. Reports in 1 month.
**Music:** Bluegrass, blues, C&W, dance-oriented, folk, jazz, progressive, R&B, rock and soul. Recently released *Love From The Heart*, by Lisa Gilkysan; *Armchair Cabaret*, by Big Sky Mudflat; and *Welcome Back*, by Geromino Black.

*****FULL SAIL RECORDS**, Full Sail Productions, 71 Boylston St., Brookline MA 02147. (617)739-2010. President: Fred Berk. (Topsail Music/BMI). Releases 10 singles and 3 albums/year. Works with artists and songwriters on contract. Pays 5-7% royalty to artists on contract; standard royalties to songwriters on contract; statutory rate to publishers for each record sold.
**How to Contact:** Submit demo tape. Prefers 7½ ips reel-to-reel or cassette with 1-10 songs on demo.
**Music:** C&W, rockabilly, rock, soul and top 40/pop.

**FUN CITY RECORDS CO.**, 281 W. 6th St., Mansfield OH 44902. Executive Producer: Larry Rawls. Record company and record producer. Releases 4 singles/year. Works with songwriters on contract. Pays 10¢-30¢/record sold to artists on contract; statutory rate to publishers for each record sold.
**How to Contact:** Submit demo tape and lyric sheet. Prefers cassette with 3-5 songs on demo. Does not return unsolicited material. Reports in 3 weeks.
**Music:** Mostly R&B and top 40/pop; also contemporary gospel. Recently released "Love So Divine" and "Let's Stay Together," by Rawls Brothers (R&B/ballad singles); "Ready for De Funk," by Larry Rawls (R&B/top 40 single); and "Sunshine," by Shellis Payne (pop single).

**GAMMA RECORDS, LTD.**, Suite 804, 3575 Blvd. St. Laurent, Montreal, Quebec, Canada H2X 2T7. (514)842-1788. A&R Director: Daniel Lazare. Record company and music publisher. Works with artists and songwriters on contract. Pays negotiable royalty.
**How to Contact:** Submit demo tape and lyric sheet.

**GAMMON RECORDS**, Box 14243, San Francisco CA 94114. (415)824-3676. Labels include Walking Dead. Record company, record producer and music publisher (Can You Hear Me Music/BMI). Releases 2-3 singles and 2-3 albums/year. Works with artists on contract.

**How to Contact:** Call first about your interest. Prefers cassette with 3-5 songs on demo. SASE. Reports in 1 month.
**Music:** R&B (SA), rock (general) and experimental.

**GCS RECORDS,** 1508 Harlem Suite 206, Memphis TN 38114. (901)274-2726. Labels include Del-A-Ron Records and Great-Day Records. A&R Directors: Daniel Boga and Larry Henderson. Record company and music publisher. Releases 3 singles and 2 albums/year. Works with artists on record contract and musicians on salary for in-house studio work. Pays 4-6% royalty to artists on contract; statutory rate to publishers for each record sold.
**How to Contact:** Submit demo tape and lyric sheet, write or call about your interest or arrange personal interview. Prefers 7½ or 15 ips reel-to-reel or cassette with 3-5 songs on demo. SASE. Reports in 1 month.
**Music:** Gospel, R&B, rock, soul and top 40/pop. Recently released "My Anna" and "If You Say You Care," by Ron Smith (top 40/pop singles); and "Cookie" and "Band Command," by Cabari (R&B singles).

**GHOST RECORDS,** 1905 Pesos Place, Kalamazoo MI 49008. (616)375-2641. Labels include Ghost and Jobie Records. President: Don Jobe. Record company. Releases 5-8 singles and 2 albums/year. Works with artists and songwriters on contract.
**How to Contact:** Submit demo tape and lead sheet. Prefers 7½ ips reel-to-reel. SASE. Reports in 1 month.
**Music:** Mostly country rock; also easy listening, rock, soul, top 40/pop and country/western. Recently released "Nadine" by the Ghosters (top 40 single); and "Bendin' Over Backwards," by Dan Stersic and The Country Squires (C&W single). Other artists include Jim Hollberg and the Tru-Tones.

**GLAD-HAMP RECORDS INC.,** 1995 Broadway, New York NY 10023. (212)787-1223. A&R: Charlie Mack. Record company. Works with artists and songwriters on contract. Pays 5-15% royalty to artists on contract; standard royalty to songwriters on contract.
**How to Contact:** Submit demo tape and lyric sheet. Prefers 7½ ips reel-to-reel or cassette with 2-4 songs on demo. SASE. Reports in 1 month.
**Music:** Jazz, R&B and soul. Recently released *Lionel Hampton Big Band Live*, *Chameleon* and *Outrageous* by Lionel Hampton and Friends (jazz LPs); and "School Daze," by Brothers Unique (12" rap).

**GLOBAL RECORD CO.,** 133 Arbutus Ave., Box 396, Manistique MI 49854-0396. President: Reg B. Christensen. Record company and music publisher (Chris Music/BMI and Sara Lee Music/BMI). Works with artists and songwriters on contract. Pays 10% royalty to artists on contract.
**How to Contact:** Submit demo and lyric or lead sheet. Cassette only with 2-5 songs on demo. "If songs are copyrighted, give number and date. If not copyrighted tell what, if anything you've done to protect them." SASE. Reports in 1 month.
**Music:** Bluegrass, C&W, gospel, MOR, acid and hard rock and soul.

**GOLD GUITAR RECORDS,** 1450 Terrell, Beaumont TX 77701. (713)832-0748. President: Don Gilbert. Record company, record producer and music publisher (Don Gilbert Music/BMI). Releases 10 singles/year. Works with songwriters on contract; musicians on salary for in-house studio work. Pays 8-15% royalty to artists on contract; statutory rate to publishers for each record sold.
**How to Contact:** Submit demo tape and lyric sheet. Prefers 7½ ips reel-to-reel or cassette with 2-10 songs on demo. SASE. Reports in 1 month.
**Music:** C&W and MOR. Recently released "Five Rooms of Memories" and "The Other One," by Don Gilbert (country singles). Other artists include Sherry Black, George Lee and Scottie.

**GOLD STREET, INC.,** Box 124, Kirbyville TX 75956. (713)423-2234. Labels include Gold Street. Vice President A&R: Robbie Gibson. Record company and music publisher. Releases 3 or more singles and 2 or more albums/year. Works with artists and songwriters on contract; pays minimum 10% royalty to artists on contract; statutory rate to publishers for each record sold.
**How to Contact:** Submit demo tape and typed lyric sheet. Prefers cassette with 2-4 songs on demo. SASE. Reports ASAP.
**Music:** Gospel, all types. Recently released "I Need You," "Sonshine," and "The Third Day," by The Third Day (religious singles); and *Brighter Days*, by The Gibsons (religious LP).
**Tips:** "We only consider sincere, hard working groups who are willing to grow with us. We are a small independent label on the grow with a bright future."

**GOLDBAND RECORDS,** Box 1485, Lake Charles LA 70602. Labels include Folk-Star, Tek, Tic-Toc, Anla, Jador and Luffcin Records. President: Eddie Shuler. Record company and record producer.

## Record Companies 155

Works with artists and songwriters on contract; musicians on salary for in-house studio work. Pays 3-5% royalty to artists on contract; standard royalty to songwriters on contract.
**How to Contact:** Submit demo tape and lyric sheet. Prefers cassette with 2-6 songs on demo. SASE. Reports in 2 months.
**Music:** Blues, C&W, easy listening, folk, R&B, rock and top 40/pop. Recently released *Katie Webster Has the Blues* (blues LP) and "Things I Used to Do" (blues single), by Katie Webster; "Waiting For My Child," by Milford Scott (spiritual single); "Gabriel and Madaline," by Johnny Jano (cajun country single); and "Cajun Disco," by the La Salle Sisters (disco single). Other artists incude Jimmy House, John Henry III, Gary Paul Jackson, Junior Booth, Rockin Sidney, Ralph Young, Tedd Dupin, R. Sims, Mike Young and Everett Brady.

**GOLDUST RECORD CO.**, 115 E. Idaho Ave., Las Cruces NM 88001. (505)524-1889. Contact: Emmit H. Brooks. Record company, music publisher (Enchantment Music/BMI) and recording studio. Member CMA. Releases 8-12 singles and 8 albums/year. Works with artists and songwriters on contract; musicians on salary for in-house studio work. Pays 4-6% royalty to artists on contract; standard royalty to songwriters on contract; statutory rate to publishers for each record sold.
**How to Contact:** Submit demo tape. Prefers cassette with 1-5 songs on demo. "We do not wish to review material which has been previously released." Send SASE if return of material is requested. Reports in 1 month.
**Music:** C&W, easy listening, MOR, rock (soft or country), top 40/pop and fiddle instrumentals. Recently released "Crazy and Lonely," by Jeff Moore (country single); *Twin Fiddles*, by Tammy and Junior Daugherty (country instrumental LP); *Shock Treatment*, by Voltz (rock LP); *The Clay Mac Band in Austin*, by Clay Mac Band (country LP); and "Mississippi" by Dana Bivens (country single). Other artists include Hyram Posey, Wes Nivens, David Ruthstrom, Dick Jonas, Jake Brooks, Raintree, Claudia Jones, Desperados, Breeze, Terry Lee and Bill Lendrom.

*****GRANDVILLE RECORD CORP.**, Box 11960, Chicago IL 60611. (312)561-0027. Executive Producer/President: Clifford Rubin. Record company, record producer and music publisher (Billetdoux Music/BMI). Releases 5 singles and 2 albums/year. Works with artists and songwriters on contract; musicians on salary for in-house studio work. Pays 3-6% royalty to artists on contract; statutory rate to publishers for each record sold.
**How to Contact:** Submit demo tape and lyric sheet. Prefers cassette with 3-6 songs on demo. SASE. Reports in 1 month.
**Music:** Mostly R&B; also blues, C&W, gospel, jazz, MOR, rock, soul and top 40/pop. Recently released "I Wanna Be With You," by Mickey Dee (R&B single); "I'm Gonna Love You," by Randy Terry (country/rock/pop single); and *Journey to Beyond*, by Duncan Pryce Kirk (AOR LP). Other artists include Shannon Band, Emmett Beard, Main Foundation and the Hardy Brothers.
**Tips:** "We want commercial hooks with lyrics that are to the point as well as universal."

*****GRASS ROOTS RECORD & TAPE/LMI RECORDS**, Box 532, Malibu CA 90265. (213)858-7282. Labels include LMI Records. President: Lee Magid. Record company, record producer and music publisher (Alexis/ASCAP, Marvelle/BMI). Member AIMP, NARAC. Releases 4 singles and 4 albums/year. Works with artists and songwriters on contract. Pays 2-5% royalty to artists on contract; pays negotiable royalty to publishers for each record sold.
**How to Contact:** Submit demo tape and lyric sheet. Prefers cassette with 3 songs on demo. "Please, no 45s." SASE. Reports in 1 month minimum.
**Music:** Mostly R&B, C&W, blues and gospel; also bluegrass, children's, Spanish and rock. Recently released *First Shot Live*, by Becky Bishop (C&W LP); *Hear Me Now*, by Ernie Andrews (R&B LP); and *Boss Man of the Blues*, by Joe Turner (blues LP). Other artists include Gloria Lynne, Arthur Prysock, Carl Bean and Addie.

*****GREAT SOUTHERN RECORD CO., INC.**, Box 13977, New Orleans LA 70119. (504)482-4211. Labels include New Orleans Sound® and Bayou Blue. President: John Berthelot. Record company, record producer and music publisher (John Berthelot & Associates/ASCAP, Storyville Publishing Co./BMI). Member NARAS, MIEA, AFM. Releases varied number of singles and albums/year. "We specialize in artists in New Orleans and Louisiana." Pays 6-8% royalty to artists on contract; statutory rate to publishers for each record sold.
**How to Contact:** Submit demo tape and lyric sheet. Prefers cassette with 1-2 songs on demo. Reports in 6 months-1 year; "be patient if I don't answer right away."
**Music:** Mostly R&B, Cajun, rockabilly, ballads and Zydeco; also blues and C&W. Artists include Tucker McDaniel and Kivi Santamaria.
**Tips:** "I don't make decisions about record release quickly. I specialize in New Orleans artists (various types of music) and Louisiana Cajun/Zydeco artists, and only record with artists who live and perform primarily in this region (touring periodically)."

**GULE RECORD**, 7046 Hollywood Blvd., Hollywood CA 90028. (213)462-0502. National Sales Manager: Harry Gordon. Record company, music publisher and record producer. Releases 20 singles and 10-15 albums/year.
**How to Contact:** Submit demo tape or submit acetate disc. Cassette only with 2 songs minimum on demo. SASE. Reports in 1 week.
**Music:** C&W, R&B and top 40/pop.

**HALPERN SOUNDS**, 1775 Old County #9, Belmont CA 94002. (415)592-4900. President: Steven Halpern. Record company and record producer. Releases 3 albums/year. Works with artists and songwriters on contract. Pays 1-10% royalty to artists on contract.
**How to Contact:** Submit demo tape and lyric sheet. Prefers cassette with 4-6 songs on demo. SASE. Reports in 3 months.
**Music:** Easy listening, MOR and "music for health and relaxation." Recently released *Star Children*, by Ingo Swan and Steven Halpern (top 40 LP); *Prelude*, by S. Halpern (relaxing LP); and *Comfort Zone*, by S. Halpern (soothing LP).

**HANSEN-O'BRIEN MUSIC**, Suite 8, 234 5th Ave., Redwood City CA 94063. (415)367-0298. President: E.J. O'Brien. Record company, record producer and music publisher (O'Brien Publishing Co.). Estab. 1981. Releases 10 singles and 2 albums/year. Works with artists and songwriters on contract. Pays 2.5-15% royalty to artists on contract; statutory rate to publishers for each record sold.
**How to Contact:** Submit demo tape and lyric sheet. Prefers cassette with 3-6 songs on demo. SASE. Reports in 2 weeks.
**Music:** Bluegrass, blues, C&W, MOR, R&B, rock and top 40/pop. Recently released "Devil in Her Eyes," by Paul Hanson (crossover single); "Not at Home to the Blues," by P. Hanson; and "Fallen Angels, Juke Box Queens," by Hanson Brothers (both C&W singles).

**HAPPY BEAT RECORDS**, Suite 303, 14045 S. Main, Houston TX 77035. (713)641-0793 or 645-5391. Labels include MSB Records. President: Roger L. Cummings. Record company, music publisher (Sirloin Music Publishing/BMI), promotion and distribution firm. Releases 4 singles and 2 albums/year. Works with artists and songwriters on contract; musicians on salary for in-house studio work. Pays negotiable royalty to artists on contract; negotiable rate to publishers for each record sold.
**How to Contact:** Submit demo tape and lyric sheet. Prefers cassette with 3-6 songs on demo. "Artists should include photo." SASE. Reports in 1 month.
**Music:** Blues, dance-oriented, jazz, R&B, rock, soul and top 40/pop. Recently released "Disco With Me," by Steve Cummings (dance single); and "Let's Get On Down," by Friction (soul/funk single). Other artists include Carl Adams, Carl Stewart and Invasion.

**HAPPY DAY RECORDS, INC.**, 800 N. Ridgeland, Oak Park IL 60302. (312)848-3322. Vice President: Vince Ippolito. Record company, music publisher and record producer.
**How to Contact:** Submit demo tape and lyric sheet. Prefers 7½ ips reel-to-reel or cassette with 1-3 songs on demo. SASE.
**Music:** MOR, progressive, R&B, rock, soul and top 40/pop. Recently released "Fightin' Jane," by Frank Pisani (MOR/country single).

**HARD HAT RECORDS AND CASSETTES**, 519 N. Halifax Ave., Daytona Beach FL 32018. (904)252-0381. Labels include Hard Hat, Maricao, Blue Bandana and Indian Head. President: Bobby Lee Cude. Record company, record producer and music publisher (Cude & Pickens Publishing/BMI). Releases 12 singles and 6 albums/year. Works with artists and songwriters on contract; musicians on salary for in-house studio work. Pays standard royalty to artists on contract; statutory rate to publishers for each record sold.
**How to Contact:** Write first about your interest. Prefers cassette with 1-6 songs on demo. SASE.
**Music:** C&W, easy listening, gospel, MOR, top 40/pop and Broadway Show. Recently released "Tallulah! Tallulah!" (Broadway show tune); "Los Angeles Town," (Los Angeles Bicentennial Song); "Country Blues," "Death Row," "Me and My Guitar," and "Country Cookin'," by Blue Bandana Country Band.

**HARD-BOILED RECORDS**, 484 Lake Park Ave., Box 6, Oakland CA 94610. (415)482-4854. A&R Director: Dan Orth. Record company, record producer and music publisher (Dynamo Publishing Co./BMI). Releases 1 single/year. Works with artists and songwriters on contract; musicians on salary for in-house studio work. Pays 10-50% royalty to artists on contract; statutory rate to publishers for each record sold.
**How to Contact:** Write or call first about your interest, then submit demo tape and lyric sheet. Prefers cassette with 1-3 songs on demo. SASE. Reports in 1 month.
**Music:** C&W, easy listening, folk, MOR, R&B, rock (hard, soft, pop), top 40/pop and new wave. Re-

cently released "Cruisin' the Strip," by Phil Phillips (hard rock single); and "It Takes More," by P. Phillips (pop rock single).
**Tips:** "We are interested in anyone with extraordinary songwriting or musical talent."

**HEART RECORDS & TAPES OF CANADA LTD.**, Box 3713, Station B, Calgary, Alberta, Canada T2M 4M4. (403)230-3545. President: Ron Mahonin. Member of CARAS, CIRPA, CMRRA, CRIA. Record company, record producer, music publisher (Have A Heart Music/PROCAN and Lovin' Heart Songs/CAPAC). Releases 10 singles and 2-3 albums/year. Works with musicians on salary; artists and songwriters on contract. Pays negotiable royalty to artists and songwriters on contract; pays statutory rate to publishers for each record sold.
**How to Contact:** Submit demo tape and lyric sheet. Prefers cassette with 1-4 songs on demo. International Reply Coupons or $1 to handle postage. Reports in 1 month.
**Music:** C&W, easy listening, MOR, progressive, rock and top 40/pop. Recently released *America's Gone Country*, by Rick Morgenstern (country LP); *The Kids*, by The Kids (pop LP); *My Love*, by Ron Mahonin (MOR LP); and "He's #1," by The Kids (pop single). Other artists include James Lee Hitchner, Even Steven, Fay Stevens, Black Gold Country and Ted Miller.
**Tips:** "Send commercially oriented material."

*****HEAVY METAL RECORDS**, 165 Wolverhampton Rd., Sedgley, West Midlands, DY31QR, England. 44-09-073-2211 or 3356. Labels include Heavy Metal Records, Heavy Metal Worldwide and Revolver. Contact: Paul Birch. Record compay, record producer and music publisher (Anersong Music and Heavy Metal Music). Member BPI, MCPS, PRS, PPL and IFPI. Releases 10 singles and 20 albums/year. Works with artists on contract. Pays 6¼% to publishers for each record sold. Royalties paid directly to US songwriters and artists or through US publishing or recording affiliate.
**How to Contact:** Submit demo tape; no lyric sheets. Prefers cassette with maximum 3 songs as demo. "Include photo if looking for label deal. Please remember to write name and phone number on tape as well as box." Does not return unsolicited material.
**Music:** Mostly heavy metal; also progressive and rock. "We're looking for heavy metal in the style of Asia, Genesis, Toto and AC/DC." Recently released *Lonesome Crow*, by the Scorpions (heavy metal LP); *Death Penalty*, by Witchfinder General (hard rock LP); and *Planets*, by Eloy (melodic rock LP).

**THE HERALD ASSOCIATION, INC.**, Box 218, Wellman Heights, Johnsonville SC 29555. Labels include Herald, Klesis and Mark Five Records. Director: H. Ervin Lewis. Record company, music publisher and record producer. Member GMA. Releases 2-3 singles and 8-10 albums/year. Works with artists and songwriters on contract. "Several songwriters are under exclusive contract." Musicians on salary for in-house studio work. Pays 4-6% royalty to artists on contract; statutory rate to publishers for each record sold.
**How to Contact:** Submit demo tape and lyric sheet. Prefers cassette with 4-8 songs on demo. "Plainly mark outside of package with contents and identify each demo and lead sheet with name and address." SASE. Reports in 2 months.
**Music:** Choral; church/religious; and gospel. Recently released *God's Not Finished with Me*, by Carman (contemporary gospel LP); *Images*, by Rick Eldridge (contemporary gospel LP); and *Covenant Man*, by Lewis Moore (contemporary gospel LP).

*****HIGHWAY RECORDS LTD.**, 6A Foegate St., Astwood Bank, Redditch, Worcester, B96 6BW, United Kingdom. 44-0527-893737. UK Labels include Highway, Leader and Trailer Records, US labels include Shanachie and Rounder Records. Director: John Zollman. Record company, record producer and music publisher (Highway Music). Member MCPS. Releases 5-10 albums/year; "singles will be a new market for us." Works with artists and songwriters on contract; musicians on salary for in-house studio work. Pays 2-10% royalty to artists on contract; 6¼% to publishers for each record sold; "sometimes" buys material outright. Royalties paid directly to US songwriters and artists or paid via MCPS. Has not yet but would listen to material from US songwriters and artists.
**How to Contact:** Submit demo tape and lyric sheet. Prefers cassette with 1-6 songs on demo. SAE and IRC. Reports in 1 month.
**Music:** Mostly folk; also easy listening, MOR and comedy. Recently released *Wild and Beautiful*, by Silly Wizard (folk LP); *By the Hush*, by Andy M. Stewart (folk LP); and *Kites*, by Dave Walters (easy listening/folk LP).

**HOLLYROCK RECORDS**, 9502 Harrell St., Pico Rivera CA 90660. (213)692-1472. A&R Director: Dave Paton. Record company, record producer and music publisher (Heaven Songs/BMI). Releases 2 singles and 4 albums/year. Works with artists and songwriters on contract; musicians on salary for in-house studio work. Pays negotiable royalty to artists on contract; statutory rate to publishers for each record sold.

**How to Contact:** Submit demo tape and lyric sheet. Prefers 7½ ips reel-to-reel or cassette with 3-6 songs on demo. SASE. Reports in 2 weeks.
**Music:** C&W, easy listening, folk, jazz, MOR, progressive, rock and top 40/pop. Recently recorded *For Heavens Sake* and *Earthbound*, by Heaven (rock LPs).

**HOLY SPIRIT RECORDS, INC.**, 27335 Penn St., Inkster MI 48141. (313)595-8247. Labels include Jesus Only, Ware, God's World and Aspro Records. Contact: Elder Otis G. Johnson or Patricia Jones. Record company, music publisher (Manfield Music/BMI, Stephen Enoch Johnson Music/ASCAP and God's World Music/SESAC) and record producer. Releases 5 singles and 5 albums/year. Works with artists and songwriters on contract. Pays 5-10% royalty to artists on contract; statutory rate to publishers for each record sold.
**How to Contact:** Write or call first about your interest, then submit demo tape and lyric sheet. Prefers 7½ ips reel-to-reel or cassette with 3 songs on demo. SASE. Reports in 1 month.
**Music:** Church/religious, C&W, easy listening, gospel and jazz. Recently released *To Be With You*, by Otis G. Johnson; and "Sing from the Center World," and "Ladybug" by Karen Bouchard. Other artists include Marcella Ratliff, Isaac Jenkins, Joe Gothard, George Johnson, Linda Strong and Angela Snodgrass.

*****HULA RECORDS INC.**, Box 2135, Honolulu HI 96805. (808)847-4608. Labels include Hawaii Call's Music Group, Inc. and Surfside Records, Inc. President: Donald P. McDiarmid III. Record company, record producer and music publisher (Kona-Kai Distribution Co.). Releases 5 albums/year. Works with artists on contract. Pays statutory rate to publishers for each record sold.
**How to Contact:** Submit demo tape and lyric sheet. Prefers cassette for demo. SASE. Reports in 1 week.
**Music:** Hawaiian.

**HUNGARIA RECORDS, INC.**, Box 2073, Teaneck NJ 07566. (201)836-4869. General Manager: Stephen Kotansky. Record company and record producer. Releases 2-3 albums/year. Works with artists on contract. Payment negotiable.
**How to Contact:** Write first about your interest. Prefers cassette with 1 song on demo. SASE. Reports in 1 month.
**Music:** Hungarian and Eastern European folk music only. Recently released *HRLP 001*, by Kallo's Zoltan (Hungarian folk LP); *HRLP 002*, and *HRLP 004*, by Teka Ensemble (Hungarian folk music/LP); and *HRLP 003*, by Kodaly Quartet.

*****IGL AUDIO**, Shore Acres, Box 100, Spirit Lake IA 51360. (712)336-2859. President: John Senn. Record company, record producer and music publisher (Okoboji Music). Releases 10 singles and 6 albums/year. Works with artists and songwriters on contract; musicians on salary for in-house studio work. Pays 8% maximum royalty to artists on contract; statutory rate to publishers for each record sold.
**How to Contact:** Submit demo tape and lyric sheet. Prefers cassette with 1-5 songs on demo. SASE. Reports in 1 month.
**Music:** Mostly modern country (rock/pop) and church/religious; also gospel and top 40/pop. Recently released "Love Tender Love," by DJ & the Runaways (country single); and *American Heritage*, by American Heritage (religious LP). Other artists include Vegas and Becky Weber.
**Tips:** "We are looking for both up-tempo and slower-type country, pop and gospel songs with strong modern lyrics and melodies."

**IMPACT RECORDS/NIGHT FOOD MUSIC**, Box 15537, Long Beach CA 90815. (213)498-1674. President: Danny Holloway. Record producer, music publisher and management firm.
**How to Contact:** Submit demo tape. Prefers cassette with 3-6 songs on demo. SASE. Reports in 2 weeks.
**Music:** Mostly d372e-oriented; also R&B, rock (new wave) and pop. Works primarily with solo singers and rock groups. Artists include King Cotton, Billy Bizeau and Question 16.

**JALYN RECORDING COMPANY**, 249 Hermitage Ave., Nashville TN 37210. (615)242-2220. President: Jack Lynch. Record company, music publisher and distributor (Jaclyn Music, BMI). Releases 6 singles/year and 6 albums/year. Works with artists on contract. Pays 5-10% royalty to artists on contract; statutory rate to publishers for each record sold.
**How to Contact:** Write or call first about your interest. Prefers cassette with 1-12 songs on demo and lyric sheet. SASE. Reports in 1 week.
**Music:** Bluegrass, church/religious, C&W and gospel. Recently released *Old Time Religion*, by Ernest Carter (bluegrass LP); *On and On*, by The Mountain Echoes (LP); *Black Headed Woman*, by Eddy Howard and Jack Lynch (LP); and *Bluegrass & Black Diamonds*, by Jack Lynch & the Nashville Travelers. Other artists include Tommy Cordell and Pat Osborne.

## Record Companies 159

**JAMAKA RECORD CO.**, 3621 Heath Ln., Mesquite TX 75150. (214)279-5858. Labels include Felco, Candlestick, Plano and Texas Tea. Contact: Jimmy Fields. Record company, record producer and music publisher (Cherie Music/BMI). Releases 10 singles and 2 albums/year. Works with artists and songwriters on contract; musicians on salary for in-house studio work. Pays royalties to artists on contract; statutory rate to publishers for each record sold.
**How to Contact:** Submit demo tape and lyric sheet. Prefers 7½ ips reel-to-reel or cassette with songs on demo. "A new singer should send a good 7½" tape with at least 4 strong songs, presumably recorded in a professional studio." SASE. Reports in 2 months.
**Music:** Bluegrass, church/religious, C&W, easy listening, progressive country, R&B, rock (hard) and top 40/pop. Recently released *Heart Achin' Blues*, by Suzan Stotts (progressive country LP); and "Your Convenience," by Bobby Crown (country single). Other artists include Boots and His Buddies, George McCoy, Joe Bill, Saucers, V-Notes, The Carmacks, Billy Taylor, Bobby Crown, The Twisters, Jimmy Fields and Straight Jackets.
**Tips:** "Songs should have strong lyrics, with a good story, whether country, rock or pop."

***JAY JAY PUBLISHING**, 35 NE 62nd St., Miami FL 33138. (305)758-0000. Contact: Walter Hagielio. Record company, record producer and music publisher (BMI). Pays standard royalty.
**How to Contact:** Submit demo tape and lyric sheet. Prefers 15 ips reel-to-reel with 2-6 songs on demo. SASE. Reports in 1 month.
**Music:** Mostly polkas and waltzes; also C&W and easy listening.

**JERSEY COAST AGENTS, LTD.**, 72 Thorne Place, Hazlet Township NJ 07734. (201)787-3891. Labels include Karass, Granfalloon, Anomaly, Stonehedge, Output, Middle Class and BMA Records. President: Joe McHugh. Vice President, A&R: D.W. Griffiths. Record company, booking agency, music publisher (Pork Pine/BMI) and management firm. Member NARAS. Releases 0-2 singles and 4-8 albums/year. Works with musicians and artists on contract. Pays varying royalty percentages that are "higher than average."
**How to Contact:** Call or write describing material first. Prefers cassette with 3-4 songs on demo. SASE. Reports "as soon as work load permits."
**Music:** Bluegrass, folk, progressive and rock. Recently released *Conspiracy, Vol. V, Live*, by Conspiracy; *Working Man's Banjo*, *Jersey Tomatoes*, and *Hopeless Passion*, by D.W. Griffiths; *Late Night Garage*, by Late Night Garage; and *Guitar*, by Bob Harris.

**JEWEL RECORD CORP.**, 728 Texas St., Box 1125, Shreveport LA 71163. (318)222-0673. President: Stanley J. Lewis. Executive Vice President: F.R. Lewis. National Promotion Director: Ms. Donnis Lewis. Record company and music publisher.
**How to Contact:** Submit demo tape or submit demo tape and lead sheet. Prefers 7½ reel-to-reel, cassette or 8-track cartridge. SASE. Reports in 1 month.
**Music:** C&W, gospel and soul.

***JIVE RECORDS**, Zomba House, 165-167 Willesden High Rd., London, NW10, England. 44-01-451-3044. Affiliate US: Zomba Enterprises, Inc., Zomba House, 1348 Lexington Ave., NY 10028. Contact: A&R Director. Record company, record producer and music publisher (Zomba Music Publishers Ltd.). Releases 15 singles and 5 albums/year. Works with artists and songwriters on contract. Royalties paid to US songwriters and artists through US publishing or recording affiliate.
**How to Contact:** Submit demo tape and lyric sheet. Prefers cassette with 1-3 songs on demo. SASE. Reports in 2 weeks.
**Music:** Mostly R&B, soul and rock; also dance-oriented and top 40/pop. Recently released *A Flock of Seagulls*, by A Flock of Seagulls (rock LP); and "Magic Wand," by Whodini (R&B/rap single). Other artists include Roman Holiday, Richard Jon Smith, Stevie Lange and Q-Feel.

**JODY RECORDS**, 2226 McDonald Ave., Brooklyn NY 11223. (212)946-4405. Labels include Atlas and Jody Records. A&R Director: Mick Marlett. Record company. Releases 30 singles and 20 albums/year. Works with artists and songwriters on contract; musicians on salary for in-house studio work. Pays standard royalty to artists on contract; statutory rate to publishers for each record sold.
**How to Contact:** Submit demo tape and lyric sheet. Prefers 7½ ips reel-to-reel or cassette with 2-4 songs on demo. SASE. Reports in 2 weeks.
**Music:** C&W, dance-oriented, gospel, jazz, MOR, progressive, R&B and rock. Recently published "I Am Somebody," by Alex Alexander (disco single); "Do the Hammer," by Eddie Hailey (R&R single); and "Love Just Laughed at Me Again," by A. Alexander (R&R). Other artists include Gloria Black and Tony Graye.

**JRM RECORDS**, Box 993, Salem VA 24153. (703)387-0208. Label includes Dominion. President: Jack Mullins. Record company and music publisher (Powhatan Music and Double Jack Publishing). Re-

leases 8 singles and 10 albums/year. Works with artists and songwriters on contract. Pays 5-15% to artists on contract; statutory rate to publishers for each record sold.
**How to Contact:** Submit demo tape and lyric sheet. Prefers 7½ ips reel-to-reel with 2-4 songs on demo. SASE. Reports in 1 month.
**Music:** Bluegrass, C&W and R&B. Recently released "Girl", by Simpson Allen (pop-country single); "Oh What a Feeling", by Robin Glass (top 40 single); and "B.T. Boogie", by Wayne Craig (top 40 single). Other artists include Jim Earnes, Shenandoah Cut Ups and Wildfire.

**K AND R RECORDS**, 19 Frontenae Rd., Box 616, Trumansburg NY 14886. (607)387-5325. Reviewer: Christine Dwyer. Record company, record producer and music publisher. Releases 3-5 albums/year. Pays 5% royalty to artists on contract; statutory rate to publishers for each record sold.
**How to Contact:** Submit demo tape and lyric sheet. Prefers cassette with 6-12 songs on demo. SASE. Reports in 1 month.
**Music:** Children's and church/religious (folk, MOR). Recently released *Share the Sunlight*, by Mary Lu Walker (children's LP); *Antioch*, by Antioch (folk/religious LP); and *By Love Are We All Bound*, by Ray Repp (MOR/religious LP). Other artists include Bea Verdi, Prezio Brothers and Sunshine.

*****KAPRI RECORDS, INC.**, 7419 Clyboun Ave., Sun Valley CA 91352. (213)765-2774. Vice President of A&R: Chris Soular. Record company (Aleph Base Music and Strange Land Music). Releases 5 singles and 1 album/year. Works with artists and songwriters on contract; musicians on salary for in-house studio work. Pays 4-5% royalty to artists on contract; statutory rate to publishers for each record sold.
**How to Contact:** Submit demo tape and lyric sheet. Prefers cassette with 3-6 songs on demo. SASE. Reports in 1 month.
**Music:** C&W, easy listening, gospel, Spanish, R&B, rock, country rock and top 40/pop. Recently released "Stranger in a Strange Land," by Angelea Shaw (easy listening LP and single); "Taking Away My Heart," by Estee Rox (rock LP and single); and "You Inspire Me," by Raymond Soular (gospel LP and single). Other artists include Heaveniareas, Spice of Ice, R.C. Kettle, Follow Up and CC Band.

**KAT FAMILY RECORDS**, Suite B-130, 5775 Peachtree Dunwoody Rd. NE, Atlanta, GA 30342. (404)252-5800. President: Joel A. Katz. Vice President/General Manager: Mike Sullivan. Record company. Fee derived from sales royalty.
**How to Contact:** Submit demo tape and lyric sheet. Prefers cassette with 5-10 songs on demo. SASE. Reports in 1 month.
**Music:** Rock, top 40/pop and contemporary gospel. Recently recorded Darts (British do-wop band); Smashers, James Anderson, Marc Speer, William Bell, Bertie Higgins, Major Lance and Unipop.

**K-D MUSIC CO. DIVISION OF KDP, INC.**, 111 Valley Rd., Wilmington DE 19804-1397. (302)655-7488. A&R: Ed Kennedy. General Manager: Shirley Kay. Record company. Releases 6 albums/year. Works with artists and songwriters on contract; musicians on salary for in-house studio work. Payment negotiable. Charges for some services: to "outside producers or publishers only."
**How to Contact:** Submit demo and lead sheet. Prefers acetate disc or pressing. SASE. Reports in 2 weeks. Will accept audio tape, cassette or VTR.
**Music:** Bluegrass, blues, children's, choral, church/religious, classical, C&W, easy listening, folk, gospel, jazz, MOR, rock and top 40/pop. Recently released *Autumn Leaves*, by Bill Andrews (rock LP).

**KEYNOTE RECORDS**, Box 4185, Youngstown OH 44515. (216)793-7295. Executive Producer: Richard M. Hahn. Record company, record producer and music publisher (Al-Kris Music/BMI). Releases 5 singles and 2 albums/year. Works with artists and songwriters on contract. Pays 3-5% royalty to artists on contract; statutory rate to publishers for each record sold.
**How to Contact:** Query by letter first. Submit demo tape and lyric sheet. Prefers cassette with 3-5 songs on demo. "Must have decent quality tape and clear lead or lyric sheet." SASE. Reports in 3 weeks.
**Music:** Children's, C&W, folk, gospel, MOR and top 40/pop. Recently released "Here Come the Browns", by Kardiak Kids (MOR single); "Jubilee" and "His Lovin'", by Cycles (top 40 single); "Help Me I'm Falling," by Kirsti Manna (MOR ballad singe). Other artists include Phil Hickman, Jim Stack, The B-Minors, and Ken Crosslin.

**KICKING MULE RECORDS, INC.**, Box 158, Alderpoint CA 95411. (707)926-5312. Labels include Sonet USA and Transatlantic USA Records. Head of A&R: Stefan Grossman. Record company and music publisher (Kicking Mule Publishing/BMI, Desk Drawer Publishing/ASCAP). Member NAIRD. Releases 12 albums/year. Works with artists on contract. Pays 10-16% royalty to artists on contract; standard royalty to songwriters on contract.

**How to Contact:** Submit demo tape. Prefers reel-to-reel or cassette with 3-5 songs on demo. SASE. Reports in 1 month.
**Music:** Bluegrass, blues and folk. Recently released *Mooncoin*, by Mickie Zekley (Irish traditional LP); *New York Banjo Ensemble Plays Gershwin* (pop music LP); *Blue Hula Stomp*, by Bob Brozman (pop music blues LP). Other artists include Michael Rugg, Neal Hellman, Bert Jansch, John Renbourn, Stefan Grossman, John James, Happy Traum, Fred Sokolow, Bob Stanton, Bob Hadley, Leo Wijnkamp, Jr., Mark Nelson, Lea Nicholson and Hank Sapoznik.
**Tips:** "We are a label mostly for instrumentalists. The songs are brought to us by the artists but we contact the artists because of their playing, not their songs. First, listen to what we have released and don't send material that is outside our interests. Secondly, learn to play your instrument well. We have little interest in songs or songwriters, but we are quite interested in people who play guitar, banjo, or dulcimer well."

**KIDERIAN RECORD PRODUCTS**, 4926 W. Gunnison, Chicago IL 60630. (312)545-0861. Labels include Homestead, Newbary, Sonic Wave, Virgin Vinal, Trinity, Tempe and Stang Records. President: Ray Peck. Record company, record producer and music publisher (KRPCO). Releases 25-30 singles and 5-6 albums/year. Works with artists and songwriters on contract; musicians on salary for in-house studio work. Pays statutory rate to publishers for each record sold.
**How to Contact:** Submit demo tape and lyric sheet. Prefers cassette with 4-6 songs on demo. Reports in 1 month.
**Music:** Bluegrass, blues, children's, choral, classical, C&W, dance-oriented, easy listening, folk, gospel, jazz, MOR, progressive, Spanish, R&B, rock, soul, top 40/pop and new wave. Recently released *Gary Cross Live*, by Gary Cross (C&W LP and single); *Rich Rags Syncopated Love*, by Rich Rags (new wave LP and single); and *Tricky Zingers*, by Creme Soda (power pop LP and single). Other artists include Boyz (Paul), Tom Petreli, The 80's, Ray Peck, The Trouble Boys, Wall Street, Pirate, Mammoth, Nadine Herman and Torn Orphan.

**KING OF KINGS RECORD CO.**, 38603 Sage Tree St., Palmdale CA 93550. A&R Director: Leroy Pritchett. Record company and music publisher. Releases 1 album/year. Pays statutory rate to publishers for each record sold.
**How to Contact:** Submit lead sheet only. SASE. Reports in 1 month.
**Music:** Church/religious and gospel. Recently released *Another Dawn*, and *Heaven Is Just over the Hill* (gospel LPs), and *Charles Vickers Does Disco*, (disco LP) by Charles Vickers.

**KING-J RECORD CO.**, (subsidiary of Joe King Productions, Inc.), 80 Yesler, Seattle WA 98104. (206)622-8358. Labels include New Meadows and Cora Records. Contact: Joe King. Record company and music publisher (Joe King Music/BMI). Releases 10 singles and 3 albums/year. Works with musicians on salary for in-house studio work and songwriters on contract.
**How to Contact:** Submit demo tape and lyric sheet. Prefers cassette with 6-8 songs on demo. SASE. Reports in 2 weeks.
**Music:** C&W. Recently released "Old Whiskey," by Avery Family (country single); "Speachless," by Lloyd Green (country single); and "Statue of a Fool," by Albert Young Eagle (country single).

**SID KLEINER MUSIC ENTERPRISES**, 3701 25th Ave. SW, Naples FL 33999. (813)455-2696. Labels include Musi-Poe, Top-Star, This Is It, Token, and Country-King Records. Contact: Sid Kleiner. Record company and consulting firm to music industry. Releases 10 albums/year. Works with musicians and songwriters on contract. Charges for some services: "We may, at our option, charge *actual* production expense. We are not get-rich-quickers or rip-off artists. But we are too small to pay all of these bills!"
**How to Contact:** Submit demo tape and lead sheet. Prefers cassette. SASE, "otherwise materials aren't returned." Reports in 3 weeks.
**Music:** Bluegrass, C&W, easy listening, folk, jazz, and "banjo and guitar soloists and features." Recently released *Burd Boys on Stage* and *Chartbusters and Other Hits* (country LPs), by the Burd Boys; and *Find a Simple Life*, by Dave Kleiner (folk/rock LP). Other artists include Sid Kleiner.

**KNEPTUNE INTERNATIONAL RECORDS**, 10850 Riverside Dr., Suite 302, North Hollywood CA 91602. (213)763-5000. Canadian office: Box 5236, Vancouver, British Columbia Canada V6B 4B3. President: Kenny Harris. Record company. Member NARAS. Releases 6 singles and 4 albums/year. Works with musicians on contract. Pays 5-18% royalty to artists and songwriters on contract; statutory rate to publishers for each record sold.
**How to Contact:** Submit tape and lead sheet; "only finished masters considered." Prefers cassette with 6-12 songs on demo. SASE. Reports in 1 month.
**Music:** Classical, C&W, jazz and MOR. Recently released *Dallas* (TV show score), by John Parker

(adult contemporary single/LP); "I've Got Your Key," by Jamie Donald (country single); and *Mozart Serenade in B-Flat*, by Toronto Chamber Winds (classical LP). Other artists include Larry Moore, J.C. Purcell and Mary Murphy.

**L.M.I. (LEE MAGID, INC.)**, Box 532, Malibu CA 90265. (213)858-7282. President: Lee Magid. Record company, record producer and music publisher (Alexis Music/ASCAP, Marvelle Music/BMI, and Lou-Lee Music/BMI). Releases 8 singles/year and 4 albums/year. Works with artists, songwriters and self-contained groups on contract. Pays 2½-5% royalty to artists on contract; standard royalty to songwriters on contract. Pays negotiable rate to publishers for each record sold.
**How to Contact:** Submit demo tape and lyric sheet. Prefers cassette with 3-4 songs on demo. SASE. Reports in 3 weeks.
**Music:** Mostly country, R&R, pop and jazz; also blues, gospel, R&B and soul. Recently released *First Shot—Live*, by Becky Bishop (country rock LP); *Hear Me Now*, by Ernie Andrews (jazz/pop LP); and "Truckstop Waitress," by B. Bishop (country single). Other artists include "Rags" Waldorf Band, Lyn Turner, Sandy Landers, Art Reynolds and Rene Heredia.
**Tips:** "Send a good clear demo. Try to get some financial help to back up talent."

**L.P.S. RECORDS, INC.**, 2140 St. Clair St., Bellingham WA 98226. (206)733-3807. Labels include Love/Peace/Service (gospel) and LPS (C&W). President: Renie Peterson. Record company, record producer and music publisher (Fourth Corner/SESAC), Heartstone Music/BMI and Silverstone Music/ASCAP). Member AFM and MPT. "We are only doing custom work at the present time." Pays statutory rate to publishers for each record sold.
**How to Contact:** Submit demo tape and lyric sheet. Prefers cassette with 3 songs on demo. SASE. Reports in 3 weeks.
**Music:** Mostly gospel; "we'd like to get some good C&W." Recently released *There Is A Way*, by Jose Nardone (gospel LP). Other artists include Neil G. Vasburgh, Claudette Dykstra, Mike French, Tina Allen, Marty Bowen Gloria Davon and Cloud of Witnesses.
**Tips:** Songwriters should have "mastery of craft. Write fresh songs with no forced rhymes. Nothing trite."

**LA LOUISIANNE RECORDS**, 711 Stevenson St., Lafayette LA 70501. (318)234-5577. Labels include Tamm and Belle. President: (Mr.) Carol J. Rachou, Sr. Record company, record producer, recording studio and music publisher (La Lou Music/BMI). Releases 10-20 singles and 4-6 albums/year. Works with artists and songwriters on contract. "We also deal with promoters, managers, agents, etc." Pays statutory rate to publishers for each record sold.
**How to Contact:** Submit demo tape and lyric sheet. Prefers 7½ ips reel-to-reel or cassette with 1-6 songs on demo. "If possible, submit different musical variations of songs (tempos, styles, keys, etc.)." SASE.
**Music:** Primarily produces Cajun/French but also produces some blues, church/religious, classical, C&W, folk, gospel, jazz, MOR, progressive, R&B, rock, top 40/pop, comedy, French comedy and instrumental. Recently released *Lache Pas La Patate* (Gold record in Canada), by Jimmy C. Newman (French Cajun LP); *A Cajun Tradition Vol. 2*, by Nathan Abshire (French Cajun LP); *Cajun Fiddle*, by Rufus Thibodeaux (Cajun/country LP); *That Cajun Country Sound*, by Eddy Raven (French and English Cajun/country LP); and *Authentic French Music*, by Ambrose Thibodeaux (traditional Cajun LP). Other artists include Vin Bruce, Aldus Roger, Merlin Fontenot, L.J. Foret, Blackie Forestier, The Dusenbery Family, Alex Broussard, Bud Fletcher.

**LADD MUSIC CO.**, 401 Wintermantle Ave., Scranton PA 18505. (717)343-6718. Labels include White Rock Records. President: Phil Ladd. Record company, music publisher and producer. Releases 12-24 singles and 1-3 albums/year. Works with artists and songwriters on contract. Pays negotiable rate to artists on contract; 4% royalty to songwriters on contract.
**How To Contact:** Submit demo tape and lead sheet. Prefers cassette with 1-6 songs on demo. SASE. Reports in 2 weeks.
**Music:** Blues, children's, choral, C&W, easy listening, MOR, rock, soul and top 40/pop. Recently released "Miss Lucy," by Big Al Downing (rock single); and "Once in Awhile," by Clyde Stacy (MOR single).

**LAKE COUNTRY RECORDS**, Box 88, Decatur TX 76234. (817)627-2128. President: Danny Wood. Releases 5 singles/year. Works with artists and songwriters on contract. Pays 7-12% royalty to artists on contract; statutory rate to publishers for each record sold.
**How to Contact:** Write first about your interest. Prefers 7½ ips reel-to-reel with 1-4 songs on demo. SASE. Reports in 1 month.
**Music:** Bluegrass and C&W. Recently released "Trusting Love", by Ronnie Mac (C&W single); "Day

Dreams", by Larry Quinten (C&W single); and "It's Not That Easy", by Larry Wampler (C&W single).

**LANDMARK (AUDIO OF NASHVILLE)**, 108 Berkley Dr., Madison TN 37115. (615)868-3407. Labels include Looking Glass, Smokehouse. Producers: Bill Anderson, Jr. or D.D. Morris. Record company, record producer and music publisher (Newcreature Music/BMI). Releases 4 singles and 4 albums/year. Works with artists and songwriters on contract; musicians on salary for in-house studio work. Pays statutory rate to publishers for each record sold.
**How to Contact:** Submit demo tape and lyric sheet. Prefers 7 1/2 ips reel-to-reel or cassette with 4-10 songs on demo. SASE. Reports in 1 month.
**Music:** C&W, gospel, jazz, R&B, rock and top 40/pop. Artists include Little Richard and Sheri Hare.

**LANDSLIDE RECORDS**, 450 14th St. NW, Atlanta GA 30318. (404)873-3918. President: Michael Rothschild. Record company and music publisher (Frozen Inca/BMI). Member NARAS. Releases 2 singles and 5 albums/year. Works with artists and songwriters on contract. Pays 5-15% royalty to artists on contract; statutory rate to publishers for each record sold.
**How to Contact:** Write or call first about your interest, then submit demo tape and lyric sheet. Prefers 7 1/2 ips reel-to-reel or cassette with 4-10 songs on demo. SASE. Reports in 1 month.
**Music:** Mostly progressive and dance-oriented; also blues, jazz, MOR, Spanish, R&B, rock, soul and top 40/pop. Recently released *Isles of Langerham*, by The Late Bronze Age (progressive LP); *Dancing Under the Streetlights*, by The Brains (progressive/new music LP); and *Middle of the Night*, by Bruce Baxter (pop/new music LP). Other artists include David Earle Johnson, Defuser, The Heartfixers, Curlew, Maggie Ree and Dan Wall.
**Tips:** "Don't be afraid to go to extremes in presenting your work."

**LANOR RECORDS**, 329 N. Main St., Box 233, Church Point LA 70525. (318)684-2176. Labels include Lanor and Joker Records. Contact: Lee Lavergne. Record company and music publisher. Works with artists and songwriters on contract. Pays 3.5% royalty to artists on contract.
**How to Contact:** Submit demo tape. Prefers 7 1/2 ips reel-to-reel or cassette with 2-6 songs on demo. SASE. Reports in 2 weeks.
**Music:** Mostly country; also rock, and soul. Recently released "Pretty Poison" and "She's Walking," by Charles Mann (country singles); and "Something to Do," by Paul Marx (country single). Other artists include Doris Bijeaux, Glenn T. and Aldus Roger.

**\*LAR-JO RECORDS, INC.**, 1911 Winton St., Middletown OH 45042. (513)425-6716. President, A&R: Jo Barbara Falcone. Record company, record producer and music publisher (Jo-Lar Music). Estab. 1982. Releases 6 singles and 2 albums/year. Works with artists and songwriters on contract. Pays 2-3% royalty to artists on contract; statutory rate to publishers for each record sold.
**How to Contact:** Submit demo tape and lyric sheet; write or call about your interest or arrange personal interview. Prefers cassette or 16-track master with 3-6 songs on demo. SASE. Reports in 1 month.
**Music:** Blues, classical, C&W, easy listening, gospel, jazz, progressive, R&B, soul and country rock. Recently released "Tasty," by Larry & Jo (single and LP).

**\*LASALLE RECORDING CO.**, 8959 S. Oglesby Ave., Chicago IL 60617. (312)375-4276. Labels include Fay, LaSalle and Planet Records. Vice President: Armond Jackson. Record company, music publisher and booking agency. Works with musicians and songwriters on contract. Pays 1%/record per side royalty to artists and songwriters on contract.
**How to Contact:** Submit demo tape, or submit demo tape and lead sheet. Prefers 7 1/2 ips reel-to-reel or cassette with 12 songs minimum on tape. SASE. Reports in 2 weeks.
**Music:** Blues, church/religious, gospel and top 40/pop. Recently released "Midnight Shuffle," by Jump Jackson (R&B single).

**\*LASER RECORDS**, 55 Grove St., Birchgrove (Box 38, Balmaiw), Sydney, NSW 2041, Australia. 61-02-8187590. Labels/Australia: Laser, Studio One, Biog Mouth and Reg Leg. Labels/US: Dorn Records, Aztec Productions and A.K.O. Manager: Lynne Wood. Record company, record producer and music publisher (Laser Music Pty, Ltd.). Member APRA, AMPAL. Releases 15-38 singles and 5-10 albums/year. Works with artists and songwriters on contract; musicians on salary for in-house studio work. Pays 5-8% royalty to artists on contract; 5% to publishers for each record sold. Royalties paid directly to US songwriters and artists or through US publishing or recording affiliate.
**How to Contact:** Submit demo tape and lyric sheet. Prefers 7 1/2 or 15 ips reel-to-reel, cassette or video cassette with 5-10 songs on demo. SAE and IRC. Reports in 2 weeks.
**Music:** Mostly rock ballads, beat ballads, new wave pop, US rock, pop classics, heavy rock, girly and European pop; also dance-oriented. Recently released "Losing Your Touch," by Tina Cross (dance rock

single); *Paul Madigan*, by Paul Madigan (country rock LP); and *The Squeeze Is On*, by Squeeze (new wave pop LP). Other artists include Dark Tan, Deborah Gray, Unaware Flying Colours, Roxy Rollers and Peggy Flee.

**\*LE MATT MUSIC LTD.**, c/o Stewart House, Hill Bottom Rd., Highwycombe, Buckinghamshire, England. 44-0525-220400 or 0494-36301/36401. Labels include Swoop, Genouille, Pogo and Check Records. Contact: Ron or Cathrine Lee. Record company, record producer and music publisher (Le Matt Music, Ltd., Lee Music, Ltd., and Pogo Records, Ltd.) Member MPA. Releases 12 singles and 12 albums/year. Pays negotiable royalty to artists on contract; MCPS rates to publishers for each record sold. Royalties paid to US songwriters and artists through US publishing or recording affiliate.
**How to Contact:** Submit demo tape and lyric sheet. Include bio and photo. Prefers 7½ or 15 ips reel-to-reel, cassette or video cassette with 1-3 songs on demo. SAE and IRC. Reports in 3 weeks.
**Music:** Bluegrass, blues, C&W, dance-oriented, easy listening, MOR, progressive, R&B, rock, soul and top 40/pop. Recently released "I Do Love You," by Penny Arcade (MOR single); "I'm Only Looking," by Daniel Boone (reggae single); "I'm a Rep" and *The Chromatics*, by The Chromatics (R&R single and LP); *Suburban Studs*, "I Hate School" and "Questions," by the Suburban Studs (new wave LP and singles). Other artists include Emmitt Till, Touche, Orphan, Nightmare, Jonny Moon and Ian "Sludge" Lees.

**\*LEGEND RECORDS AND PROMOTIONS**, 1102 Virginia St. SW, Lenoir NC 28645. (704)758-4170. Labels include Legend Records. President: Mike McCoy. Record company, record producer and music publisher (Nancy Jane Publishing). Estab. 1982. Releases 1 single and 1 album/year. Works with songwriters on contract. Pays 10% maximum royalty to artists on contract; statutory rate to publishers for each record sold.
**How to Contact:** Submit demo tape and lyric sheet. Prefers cassette with 1-4 songs on demo. Reports in 1 month.
**Music:** Mostly C&W, church/religious, gospel, R&B and outlaw C&W; also bluegrass. Recently released "Music City," and "Cinderella," by Mike McCoy (C&W singles); and "Old Fashion Preacher," by M. McCoy (gospel single).
**Tips:** "Analyze your songs very carefully and write with the times; lyrics must be good; story should sound real."

**TY LEMLEY MUSIC(ASCAP)**, 430 Pearce Rd., Pittsburgh PA 15234. (412)341-0991. Labels include Tymena Music. President: Ty Lemley. Vice President: Tolmena Lemley. General Manager: Bud Lemley. Member AFTRA, AGVA, CMA AFM. Record company and record producer. Works with artists and songwriters on contract; musicians on salary for in-house studio work. Pays maximum royalty to artists on contract; statutory rate to publishers for each record sold.
**How to Contact:** Submit demo tape and lyric sheet. Prefers cassette or 45 demo record. Reports in 1 month.
**Music:** C&W, MOR, easy listening and top 40. Recently released "One Day at a Time," by Ty Lemley (MOR single); and "Me and You," by T. Lemley (rock single).

**LITTLE DAVID RECORDS, INC.**, Suite 1037, 8033 Sunset Blvd., Los Angeles CA 90046. (213)876-9602. President: Monte Kay. Labels include Hidden Records. Record company. Works with artists and songwriters on contract.
**How to Contact:** Query. SASE.
**Music:** Blues, dance, easy listening, folk, jazz, MOR, progressive, R&B, rock, soul and top 40/pop. Recently released *An Evening With Two Grand Pianos*, by Hank Jones and John Lewis (jazz LP).

**THE LITTLE GIANT RECORD COMPANY**, 1014 16th Ave. S., Nashville TN 37212. (615)244-4360. President: Roy Sinkovich. General Manager: Mick Lloyd. Promotion Director: Kenny Jones. Record company, music publisher (JMR Enterprises), and record producer. Member CMA, FICAP, NARAS and NSAI. Releases 12 singles and 4 albums/year. Works with songwriters on contract; musicians on salary for in-house studio work. Pays 5½-7½% royalty to artists on contract; statutory rate to publishers for each record sold.
**How to Contact:** Submit demo tape and lyric sheet. Prefers cassette with 1-4 songs on demo. SASE. Reports in 4 weeks.
**Music:** C&W, easy listening, MOR, progressive, R&B, rock and top 40/pop. Recently released "Come On Out To California" by Billy Seacow. Other artists include Melissa Prewitt and The Nashville Machine.

**LITTLE GIANT RECORDS**, Box 205, White Lake NY 12786. (914)583-4471. Label includes Killer Records. A&R Director: Mike Pell. Record company, record producer and music publisher (Karjan Mu-

sic Publishing Co./SESAC). Releases 6 singles and 6 albums/year. Works with artists and songwriters on contract. Pays standard royalty to artists on contract; statutory rate to publishers for each record sold.
**How to Contact:** Submit demo tape and lyric sheet. Prefers cassette with 1-3 songs on demo. SASE. Reports in 3 weeks.
**Music:** C&W, easy listening, MOR, R&B and top 40/pop. Recently released *Presenting T. Barry Kaminski* (MOR LP); *Country Songs and Dreams* by Chuck Wilson (C&W LP); and *You Requested This* by Mickey Barnett (MOR LP). Other artists incude Bobby Gold, The Third Edition, Jason Ross, Kenny Adams and Amanda.

*****LOCK RECORD CO.**, 163 Orizaba Ave., San Francisco CA 94132 (415)334-2247. Labels include Loadstone and Open Records. Director: W.C. Stone. Record company and music publisher. Releases 4-8 singles/year. Works with artists and songwriters on contract; musicians on salary for in-house studio work. Pays flat fee of 4¢/record sold or 80% to artists on contract; statutory rate to publishers for each record sold.
**How to Contact:** Submit demo tape and lyric sheet; arrange a personal interview or "arrange to have us listen to a live performance." Prefers 7½ ips reel-to-reel or session tape with 1-5 songs as demo. Reports in 2 weeks.
**Music:** Mostly R&B; also blues, dance-oriented, easy listening, jazz, hard rock and soul. Recently released *Trying To Become A Millionaire*, by the California Playboys.
**Tips:** "All tunes written by an artist or group must be registered with the copyright office and the owner must have a copy of the registration when making an agreement to record or assign a master tape to us."

**LOGO III**, Suite 101, 413 Cooper St., Camden NJ 08102. (215)276-0100. President: Michael Nise. Labels include Phoenix 413. Record company, music publisher and record producer. Works with artists and songwriters on contract, musicians on salary for in-house studio work. Pays standard royalty to artists on contract; statutory rate to publishers for each record sold. Payment negotiable.
**How to Contact:** Submit cassette with 1-3 songs on demo. SASE. Reports in 1 month.
**Music:** Children's, church/religious, C&W, dance, easy listening, folk, gospel, jazz, R&B, rock, soul and top 40/pop. Recently released "The Mork and Mindy Theme," by Sunburst (dance single). Other artists include William Sackett and His Radio Orchestra.

**LONGHORN RECORDS**, (formerly Club of Spade Records), Box 1995, Studio City CA 91604. (213)656-0574. Contact: Lil Rodell and Harvey Appell. Record company and music publisher (Udder Publishing/BMI). Releases 6 singles and 6-15 albums/year. Works with artists and songwriters on contract and individual basis; musicians on salary for in-house studio work.
**How to Contact:** Submit record or demo tape, arrange personal interview, or submit demo tape, record and lead sheet. Prefers 15 ips reel-to-reel or cassette with 10-20 songs on demo. SASE. Reports in 3 weeks.
**Music:** Mostly C&W; also bluegrass, western swing and folk. Recently released "Then and Now," by Kenny Roberts; "The Legendary," by Pee Weeking; "31st Street Blues," by Bob Wills and Tommy Duncan; and "Lucky U Ranch," by Sons of the Pioneers. Other artists include Johnny Bytheway and Hardrock Gunter.

**LUCIFER RECORDS, INC.**, Box 263, Hasbrouck Heights NJ 07604. (201)288-8935. Branch: Box 263, Brigantine NJ 08203. (609)266-2623. President: Ron Luciano. Record company, booking agency and music publisher. Works with artists and songwriters on salary and contract.
**How to Contact:** Arrange personal interview. Prefers cassette with 4-8 songs on demo. SASE. Reports in 3 weeks.
**Music:** Dance, easy listening, MOR, rock, soul and top 40/pop. Recently released "I Who Have Nothing," by Spit-N-Image (rock single); "Lucky," and "Smoke Ya," by Legz (rock single); and "Loves a Crazy Game," by Voyage (disco/ballad single). Other artists include Diamond Jym, Charles Lamont and Lucifer.

**LUNA RECORDS CO.**, 434 Center St., Healdsburg CA 95448. (707)433-4138. Labels include Luna, Lugar, Yuriko and Sony Records. President: Abel De Luna. Record company, booking agency and music publisher (Yema Publishing/ASCAP and Luna Publishing/BMI). Releases 30 singles and 20 albums/year. Works with artists and songwriters on contract. Pays 8% royalty to artists on contract; statutory rate.
**How to Contact:** Submit demo tape and lead sheet. Prefers cassette with 5-10 songs on demo. Does not return unsolicited material. Reports in 3 weeks.
**Music:** Children's and Latin. Recently released "El Solitario," by Los Pasteles Verdes (Spanish 45 and LP); "Que Me Entierren Cantando," by Los Huracanes Del Norte (Spanish 45 and LP); and "Te Vas O Quedar Liorando," by La Banda Int'de Ray Camacho (Spanish 45 and LP). Other artists include Los

Luceritos de Michoacan, Los Astros, Los Buhos, Tany Ponce, Grupo Santa Maria, Los Flamantes Del Norte, and Los Errantes Del Norte.

**M.R.C. RECORDS**, Box 2072, Waynesboro VA 22980. (703)949-0106. Labels include MRC, Lark and Echo Records. Contact: John or Margie F. Major. Record company, music publisher and recording studio.
**How to Contact:** Submit demo tape and lyric sheet. Prefers cassette tapes. SASE. Reports in 2 weeks.
**Music:** Bluegrass, C&W, dance, easy listening, gospel, MOR, rock (country, hard), soul and top 40/pop.
**Tips:** "Don't submit songs with tunes purchased from advertisements."

***MAGNUM FORCE RECORDS AND MUSIC LTD.**, Coronation Suite, Shepperton Studio Centre, Shepperton, Middlesex, TW170QD, England. 44-09328-60363. Labels include Magnum Force and Blue Moon. Label Manager: Sue Witham. Record company and music publisher (Magnum Force Music). Member BPI, MCPS, PRS and PPL. Releases varying number of singles and 20 albums/year. Works with artists and songwriters on contract. Pays negotable rate to artists, negotiable rate to publishers for each record sold. Royalties paid directly to US songwriters and artists or through US publishing or recording affiliate.
**How to Contact:** Submit demo tape and lyric sheet. Prefers 15 ips reel-to-reel or cassette with 2-6 songs on demo. SAE and IRC. Reports ASAP.
**Music:** Mostly 50s R&R; also C&W, R&B and rock. Recently released *Dressed in Black* by Gene Vincent (R&R LP); *Unleashed*, by The Blue Caps (R&R LP); and *At the Rockhouse*, by Shakin' Stevens (R&R LP). Other artists include Strollers, Johnny & The Roccos, The Fantoms, Garth Hewitt and Lyndon Needs.
**Tips:** "Be aware of our catalog requirements. Good demos and top lines, if possible."

**MAJEGA RECORDS**, 240 E. Radcliffe Dr., Claremont CA 91711. (714)624-0677. President: Gary K. Buckley. Record company. Works with artists and songwriters on contract;musicians on salary for in-house studio work. Pays negotable royalty to artists on contract; standard royalty to songwriters on contract; statutory rate to publishers for each record sold.
**How to Contact:** Submit demo tape or submit demo tape and lead sheet. Prefers 7½ ips reel-to-reel or cassette with 1-4 songs on demo. SASE. Reports in 3 weeks.
**Music:** C&W, easy listening, gospel, MOR, rock (country or pop) and top 40/pop. Recently released *To God, with Love* and *Country Love*, recorded by Jerry Roark (gospel/C&W LPs); "Songwriter," (pop single) and *Buche*, by Rick Buche (top 40 LP); *Steppin' Out*, by The Gospelmen (gospel LP); "Our America," by June Wade and the Country Congregation (country/gospel single); "Is It Right," "Touch Me Now," "It's Alright," and "What You Doin' to Me," by Borderline (top 40 singles); and *Sky's the Limit* by Michael Noll (top 40 LP).

***MAJOR LABEL RECORD CO.**, Box 651, Worthington OH 43085. (614)846-2026. President: Richard H. Deitch. Record company and music publisher (XC Music Publishing/ASCAP). Releases 1 single/year. Works with artists and songwriters on contract. Pays negotable royalty to artists on contract; statutory rate to publishers for each record sold.
**How to Contact:** Submit demo tape and lyric sheet. Prefers cassette with 1-6 songs on demo. SASE.
**Music:** Country, MOR, rock, top 40/pop and new wave. Recently released "War Museum", by XL (rock single).

**MALACO RECORDS**, Box 9287, Jackson MS 39206. (601)982-4522. Labels include Chimneyville Records. Producers: Wolf Stephenson, Tommy Couch. Record company, music publisher and record producer. Works with artists and songwriters on contract and salary. Pays standard royalty.
**How to Contact:** Submit demo tape and lyric sheet. Prefers cassette with 1-5 songs on demo. SASE. Reports in 1 month.
**Music:** R&B music only. Recently released "Talk to Me," by Dorothy Moore (R&B single); *Groove Me*, by Fern Kinney (disco single and LP); and *Let's Do It Together*, by James Bradley (R&B single and LP). Other artists include Freedom, Jewel Bass, Natural High, Z.Z. Hill and Denise Lasalle.

**MANQUIN**, Box 2388, Toluca Lake CA 91602. (213)985-8284. Labels include Quinto Records. Contact: Quint Benedetti. Record company, music publisher, record producer, management firm and public relations firm. Works with artists and songwriters on contract. Pays standard royalty to artists and songwriters on contract.
**How to Contact:** Query or submit demo tape and lead sheet. Prefers cassette with 2-3 songs on demo. SASE. Reports in 1 month.
**Music:** Complete Broadway musicals, seasonal and Christmas songs only.

**Record Companies 167**

*MARMIK, 135 E. Muller Rd., East Peoria IL 61611. (309)699-7204. President: Martin Mitchell. Record company and music publisher. Releases 20-25 singles and 6-10 albums/year. Works with musicians and songwriters. Pays negotiable royalty. Sometimes buys material from songwriters outright; payment negotiable.
**How to Contact:** Query, submit demo tape, or submit demo tape and lead sheet. Prefers reel-to-reel or cassette with 2-10 songs on demo. "With first submission include an affidavit of ownership of material." SASE. Reports in 2 weeks.
**Music:** Mostly MOR and country; also blues, children's, choral, church/religious, easy listening, and gospel. Recently released "Follow Me," by Frank Radley (country singer); "Sun Don't Shine No More," by Joanne and Marty (country single); and *Now Playing*, by Joanne and Marty (MOR LP). Other artists include Jo Ann Standridge a Manny McPike.
**Tips:** "Don't imitate."

**MARULLO MASTER LEASING CO.**, 1121 Market, Galveston TX 77550. (713)762-4590. Labels include Red Dot and Rotab. President: A.W. Marullo, Sr. Record company, record producer and music publisher (Marullo Music/BMI). Releases 12 singles and 2 albums/year. Works with artists and songwriters on contract. Pays 10% royalty to artists on contract; statutory rate to publishers for each record sold.
**How to Contact:** Submit demo tape and lyric sheet. Prefers 7½ ips reel-to-reel or cassette with 4-6 songs on demo. SASE. Reports in 1 month.
**Music:** C&W and top 40/pop. Recently published "Girl I Never Had," "Take It or Leave It" and "Clinging Vines," by Brown Brothers (C&W singles). Other artists include Michael John and Kimberly.

**MARVEL RECORDS CO.**, 852 Elm St., Manchester NH 03101. Labels include Banff, Marvel, Rodeo International, W&G and Melbourne Records. Executive Director: James N. Parks. Record company and music publisher (Jaspar Music Publishing Co., Ltd./BMI, Melbourne Music Publishing Co., Ltd./ASCAP). Member IRMA. Releases 8 singles and 8 albums/year. Works with artists and songwriters on contract; musicians on salary for in-house studio work. Payment to artist negotiable; pays statutory rate to publishers for each record sold.
**How to Contact:** Submit lead sheet.
**Tips:** "All of our artists are relatively new artists from Australia, Canada and the U.K. They are released here in the U.S.A. only after strong success in their own countries."

**MASTER TRAK SOUND RECORDERS**, (formerly Modern Sound Studios), Miller Building, 415 N. Parkerson, Box 1345, Crowley LA 70526. (318)783-1601. Labels include Master-Trak, Showtime, Kajun, Cajun Classic, Blues Unlimited, Wilwood and Par T. Contact: Jay Miller. General Manager and Chief Engineer: Mark Miller. Recording studio and record companies. Works with artists on royalty basis; musicians on salary for in-house studio work. Pays 4% and 5% artist royalty. (No studio charges to contract artists.) Studio available on hourly basis to the public. Works with musicians on salary; artists and songwriters on contract. Pays 4-5% royalty to artists on contract. Charges for some services: "We charge for making audition tapes of any material that we do not publish."
**How to Contact:** Submit demo tape and lead sheet. Prefers 7½ ips reel-to-reel. SASE. Reports in 1 month.
**Music:** Blues, church/religious, C&W, dance, folk, gospel, MOR, progressive, rock and soul. Recently released *L. Broussard*, by the Lagniapee Gang; *Cajun Fiddling & Singing Now & Tommorrow*, by Hadley Castille; and *Camey Doucet Introduces Pierre & The Squirrely Squirrels*, by Camey Doucet.

**THE MASTER'S COLLECTION LIMITED**, Box 189, Station W, Toronto, Ontario Canada M6M 4Z2. (416)746-1991. Labels include Sharon, T.M.C., The Master's Collection, Pilgrim and Little Pilgrim. President: Paul J. Young. Record company and music publisher (T.M.C. Publishing/CAPAC and Master's Collection Publishing/PROCAN). Member CIRPA. Releases 3-6 singles and 10-12 albums/year. Works with artists and songwriters on contract. Pays 2%-10% royalty to artists on contract; statutory rate to publishers for each record sold.
**How to Contact:** Write first about your interest. Prefers cassette with 3-6 songs on demo. Does not return unsolicited material. Reports in 1 month.
**Music:** Mostly Christian gosepl ("any style"); also church/religious. Recently released *The King Is Coming*, by Gene Choi (instrumental LP); *Nobody's Children*, by McKenzie-Prokop (Christian rock LP); and *We're Gonna See You*, by His Ambassadors (Christian light pop LP). Other artists include Rick Piche, Mark Moore, Wiz Bryant and Gene MacLellan.

**MCA RECORDS**, 27 Music Square E., Nashville TN 37203. (615)244-8944. Contact: A&R Department. Record company. Releases 60 singles and 30 albums/year. Works with artists on contract.

**How to Contact:** Query. Prefers 7½ ips reel-to-reel with 2-4 songs on demo. SASE.
**Music:** Recently released "Ya'll Come Back Saloon," by the Oak Ridge Boys (country single); "I Believe in You," by Don Williams (country single); "If Loving You Is Wrong," by Barbara Mandrell (country single); and "Somebody's Knockin'," by Terri Gibbs.

**MCA RECORDS,** 10 E. 53rd St., New York NY 10022. (212)888-9700. Labels include Lark, Churchill, Black Label and Sparrow. Vice President and General Manager/East Coast: Bob Sener. Works with musicians on contract.
**How to Contact:** Submit demo tape and lyric sheet. Prefers cassette with maximum 4 songs on demo. SASE. Reports in 3 weeks.
**Music:** MOR, rock and top 40/pop. Recently released *Bernadette Peters*, by B. Peters (AOR LP).

***MCP/DAVISOUND,** Box 521, By-Pass 76, Newberry SC 29108. (803)276-0639. Labels include Mother Cleo, Cleo and Cub Records. Producer/Director: Hayne Davis. Studio Manager: Polly Davis. Record company, music publisher (Sweet Polly Music/BMI), recording studio, and production company producing music for films, features and commercials. "MCP is a unique, small (but multifaceted) company engaged in numerous activities for the communications/entertainment industry." Releases 6 singles and 2 albums/year. Works with artists and songwriters on contract; musicians on salary for in-house studio work. "We also work with co-producers, supplying our facility and talent for outside use for a front fee. We hire talent (vocalists, musicians and writers) of varying types, styles and capabilities at varying intervals, depending on the requirements and frequency of the work project and the individual's capabilities." Charges for some services: offers studio facilities for rental by "outside" songwriters, producers and publishers.
**How to Contact:** Submit demo tape and lead sheet. Prefers cassette with 2-8 songs on demo. "We are not responsible for return of tapes, lead sheets, etc. on unsolicited material. If, however, appropriate packaging and return postage are included, we make every effort to return materials and notify the sender by personal letter." SASE. Reports in 2 weeks.
**Music:** C&W (modern country), disco, easy listening, MOR, rock and top 40/pop. Recently released "Sheila," by James Meadows (modern country single); "Too Far Gone," by Curt Bradford (modern country single); and *Cooks in 1 Minute*, by the J. Teal Band (rock LP).

***MDS-NORTHCOAST,** Box 121, Waterville OH 43566. (419)535-7900. Labels include MDS, Northcoast, Heritage, Jamestune, Purple Gwano and Toledo. Assistant to the President: D. LaRue. Record company, record producer and music publisher (Keeny-York, Park J. Tunes). Releases 6 singles and 2 albums/year. Works with artists and songwriters on contract. Pays negotiable royalty to artists; statutory rate to publishers for each record sold.
**How to Contact:** Submit demo tape and lyric sheet. Prefers cassette with 5-10 songs on demo. SASE. Reports in 1 month.
**Music:** Mostly pop; also C&W, easy listening and MOR.

***MEDA RECORD CO.,** 8130 Northlawn, Detroit MI 48204. (313)934-0106. West Coast: 8569 Horner, Los Angeles CA (213)657-2649. A&R Director: Joe Hunter. Record company, record producer and music publisher (Mertis Music Company). Releases 4 singles and 4 albums/year. Works with artists and songwriters on contract. Pays 4-12% royalty to artists on contract; statutory rate to publishers for each record sold.
**How to Contact:** Submit demo tape and lyric sheet. Prefers cassette with 4-8 songs on demo. SASE. Reports in 1 month.
**Music:** Mostly gospel, R&B and pop; also jazz and top 40. Recently released "You Don't Know," by Lorine Thompson (gospel single); "I'm Guilty,." by Lorene Daniels (gospel single); and "Keep On Moving," by Buddy Lamp (pop single). Other artists include Amos Pope.

**MELODEE RECORDS,** Box 1010, Hendersonville TN 37075. (615)329-9492. General Manager: Dee Mullins. Record company, record producer, music publisher (Dee Mullins Music/ASCAP, Mel-Dee Music/BMI), and promotion and distribution firm. Member NARM, Music Expo, MIDEM. Releases 10-20 singles and 20-30 albums/year. Works with artists and songwriters on contract; musicians on salary for in-house studio work. Pays standard royalty to artists on contract; statutory rate to publishers for each record sold.
**How to Contact:** Write or call first about your interest, then submit demo tape and lyric sheet or arrange personal interview to play demo tape. Prefers cassette with 1-4 songs on demo. SASE. Reports in 1 month.
**Music:** Bluegrass, C&W, folk, gospel, MOR, rock (country) and top 40/pop. Recently released "Over" and "Giving Up Easy," by Leon Everette (C&W singles); *I Don't Want to Lose*, by L. Everette (C&W LP); and "There Lies the Difference" by Dee Mullins. Other artists include Jo Countess, Polly Ford, Rommie Osbahr and Hank Marshall.

**\*MEMNON RECORDS**, Box 84, Glen Cove NY 11542. General Manager: Katherine Swier. Music publisher (Memnon, Ltd.). Releases 3 singles and 1 album/year. Works with songwriters on contract. Pays 3-6% royalty to artists on contract; statutory rate to publishers for each record sold.
**How to Contact:** Submit demo tape and lyric sheet. Prefers cassette with 3-5 songs on demo. Include photograph and bio. SASE. Reports in 1 month.
**Music:** Mostly classical, C&W and easy listening; also dance-oriented and top 40/pop. Recently released "All My Life," by Sound Alternative (top 40/pop single); and "Don't Leave Me," by Krystof (top 40/pop single).

**MERCANTILE RECORDS**, Box 2271, Palm Springs CA 92263. (619)320-4848. President: Kent Fox. Record company, record producer and music publisher. Works with artists on contract.
**How to Contact:** Submit demo tape and lyric sheet. Prefers cassette with 3-12 songs on demo. SASE. Reports in 1 month.
**Music:** C&W, easy listening, rock and top 40/pop.

**\*MESSAGE RECORDS**, Box 1869, Hollywood CA 90028. (213)564-1008. Producers: Philip Nicholas and Kent Washburn. Record company, record producer and music publisher (Highest Praise Publishing/BMI). Estab. 1981. Member NARAS, GMA. Releases 2 albums/year. Works with artists and songwriters on contract. Pays 5-50% of gross royalties to artists on contract; statutory rate to publishers for each record sold.
**How to Contact:** Submit demo tape and lyric sheet. Prefers cassette with 3-4 songs on demo. SASE. Reports in 1 month.
**Music:** Mostly gospel; also choral and church/religious. Recently released *Tell the World*, by Nicholas (gospel LP). Other artists include Rodney Friend.

**MICHAL RECORDING ENTERPRISES**, Box 2194, Memphis TN 38101. (901)774-5689. Labels include Gospel Express, Six Sisters, Del My and Bishop Records. President: Bishop J.B. Cole. Vice President: Michal Cole. Record company, music publisher (Michal's Music/SESAC, My Son's/BMI) and booking agency. Releases 8 singles and 5 albums/year. Works with musicians and songwriters on contract. Pays 4% royalty to artists on contract; 2½% royalty to songwriters on contract; pays statutory rate to publishers for each record sold.
**How to Contact:** Submit demo tape. Prefers 7½ ips reel-to-reel or cassette. SASE. Reports in 2 months.
**Music:** Blues, church/religious, gospel and soul. Recently released *In Search of the Blues*, by Larry David (blues LP); *Phone Call from Heaven*, by The Bishop (gospel LP); and *Reunion*, by Miss-Nightingales (gospel LP). Other artists include Lula Calling, Gospel Song Birds and Miss Nighty Gales.

**MILLENNIUM RECORDS**, 1697 Broadway, New York NY 10019. (212)974-0200. President: Jimmy Ienner. Record company and music publisher. Works with musicians and songwriters on contract.
**How to Contact:** Call first then submit demo tape, lyric sheets and any biographical data to Melanie Fox. Prefers cassette with 3-5 songs on demo. SASE.
**Music:** Rock and MOR. Artists include Tommy James, Bruce Cockburn, Franke and the Knockouts, Don McLean, Chilliwack and Roadway.

**MIRROR RECORDS, INC.**, 645 Titus Ave., Rochester NY 14617. (716)544-3500. Labels include Mirror and House of Guitars Records. Vice President: Armand Schaubroeck. Record company and music publisher. Works with artists and songwriters on contract; musicians on salary for in-house studio work. Pays 33% royalty to artists on contract; negotiable royalty to songwriters on contract.
**How to Contact:** Submit demo tape. Prefers 7½ ips reel-to-reel or cassette. Include photo with submission. SASE. Reports in 2 months.
**Music:** Folk, progressive, rock and punk. Recently released "Over the Rainbow," by Don Potter; and *Here Are the Chesterfield Kings*, by the Chesterfield Kings. Other artists include Jerry Porter, and Kack Klick.

**MOBY DICK RECORDS**, 2354 Market St., San Francisco CA 94114. (415)864-2519. Production: Stan Morriss. Record company, record producer and music publisher (Moby Dick Publishing/ASCAP). Releases 30 singles and 15 albums/year. Works with artists and songwriters on contract; musicians on salary for in-house studio work. Pays 8-15% royalty to artists on contract; statutory rate to publishers for each record sold.
**How to Contact:** Submit demo tape and lyric sheet or arrange personal interview to play demo tape. Prefers 7½ ips reel-to-reel or cassette with 2-3 songs on demo. SASE. Reports in 3 weeks.
**Music:** Dance-oriented, R&B and disco. Recently released *Disc Charge*, by Boystown Gang (disco LP and single); *Hit N' Run Lover*, by Carol Jiana (dance LP and single); and "Step by Step," by Peter Grifith (disco single).

***MONTACE RECORDS**, 1221 Bainbridge St., Philadelphia PA 19147. (215)545-2282. President: Alan Rubens. Record company, record producer and music publisher (Front Wheel Music). Releases 12 singles and 5 albums/year. Works with artists and songwriters on contract. Pays statutory rate to publishers for each record sold.
**How to Contact:** Submit demo tape and lyric sheet. Prefers cassette with minimum of 1 song on demo. SASE. Reports in 3 weeks.
**Music:** Mostly R&B and dance; also soul, rock and top 40/pop. Recently released "Starry Eyed," by Mandric.

**MONTICANA RECORDS**, Box 702, Snowdon Station, Montreal, Quebec, Canada H3X 3X8. (514)345-4142. Labels include Dynacom and Monticana Records. General Manager: David P. Leonard. Record company, record producer, and music publisher (Montina Music/BMI). Member MIEA. Works with artists and songwriters on contract. Pays negotiable royalty to artists on contract; statutory rate to publishers for each record sold.
**How to Contact:** Submit demo tape and lyric sheet. Prefers 7½ or 15 ips reel-to-reel, phonograph record or videocassette (VHS). Does not return unsolicited material.
**Music:** Mostly top 40, blues, C&W, dance-oriented, easy listening, folk, gospel, jazz, MOR, progressive, R&B, rock and soul.

**\*MOON SHINE RECORDS**, 20 Music Square West, Nashville TN 37203. (615)244-5900. President: Andy Di Martino. General Manager of Publishing: Stefan Nordin. Record company, record producer and music publisher (Chatterbox Music Publishing, Chatterbox Music/ASCAP, Double Dice Music/BMI). Member RIAA. Releases 15-25 singles and 5-10 albums/year. Works with artists and songwriters; musicians on salary for in-house studio work. Pays statutory rate to publishers for each record sold.
**How to Contact:** Submit demo tape and lyric sheet. Prefers cassette with 1-5 songs on demo. SASE. Reports in 3 weeks.
**Music:** Mostly crossover country and top 40; also dance-oriented, easy listening, MOR, R&B and rock. Recently released "Took It Like A Man," and "Lonely Heart," by Cedar Creek (crossover/country singles); "Pepsi Man," by Bobby Mackey (country single); and *United States of Japan*, by Scafell Pike (pop LP). Other artists include Garry Valentine, Gary T'to, Rick Michaels, Steve Slayton, Stargazer, Iceland and Stars & Bars.
**Tips:** "We are always looking for artists and songs with international chart potential."

**MORNINGSTAR RECORDS**, Box 213, Hendersonville TN 37075. (615)822-1360. Labels include Moringstar, Harvest, Regency and NECP. Contact: Eddie Crook. Record company, record producer and music publisher (Chestnut Mound Music/BMI). Releases 10 singles and 30 albums/year. Works with artists and songwriters on contract. Pays negotiable royalty to artists on contract; statutory rate to publishers for each record sold.
**How to Contact:** Write or call first about your interest. Prefers cassette with 2-4 songs on demo. Does not return unsolicited material. Reports in 1 month.
**Music:** Gospel.

**\*MOUNTAIN RAILROAD RECORDS, INC.**, Box 1681, Madison WI 53701. (608)256-6000. President: Stephen Powers. Record company, record producer and music publisher (Mountain Railroad Music). Member NARM, NAIRD, NARAS. Releases 5 singles and 5 albums/year. Works with artists and songwriters; musicians on salary for in-house studio work. Pays 6-12% royalty to artists on contract; statutory rate to publishers for each record sold.
**How to Contact:** Submit demo tape and lyric sheet. Prefers cassette with 1-3 songs on demo. SASE. Reports in 1 month.
**Music:** Mostly pop, rock and folk; also blues, children's, C&W, jazz, progressive, top 40/pop and reggae. Recently released *Every Corner Dance*, by Spooner (rock LP); *Roy Rogers Meets Albert Einstein*, by Snopek (jazz-rock-classical LP); and *Wa-Ha Music*, by Free Hot Lunch! (pop LP). Other artists include Gamble Rogers, Betsy Kaske, Tom Paxton, Josh White, Jr, and Jim Kweskin.
**Tips:** "Artists should build an audience via live appearances."

**\*MUSIC A.D. RECORDS**, Box 7452, Grand Rapids MI 49510. (616)241-3787. Contact: Hans Altena. Record company, music publisher (Music Anno Domini/SESAC) and management agency. Releases 2 singles and 2 albums/year. Works with songwriters on contract. Pays 6-9% royalty to artists on contract; statutory rate to publishers for each record sold.
**How to Contact:** Submit demo tape and lyric sheet. Prefers cassette with 1-4 songs on demo. SASE. Reports in 1 week.
**Music:** Mostly contemporary Christian rock and MOR and contemporary choral; also gospel and rock. Recently released *No Violence*, by James Ward (contemporary Christian LP & single); *Fun Raiser!*, by

# Close-up

**Helen Hudson**
Songwriter/Performer

"I don't think you can aim for the top of the ladder before you hit each rung. I think you've got to keep your eye on the rungs," says songwriter/performer Helen Hudson, now on a national concert tour of college campuses.

For her, climbing the *rungs* means experiencing life, writing and practicing daily, seeking objective criticism, and pursuing her own pop/folk/rock style.

"All the songs I've heard that are bad are usually bad because the person writing them had nothing to say." She says songwriters should write about what they know, not about a love or Paris they've never experienced.

Hudson not only sings and plays guitar and piano, but also writes all the songs she performs and records. Last year's concert tour to 100 colleges—for which she won the Campus Entertainer of the Year Award for solo artist—proved to be "a tremendous ground for writing." In addition to this year's tour, she is working on a second album.

Nine years ago as a novice songwriter/performer, she never imagined the hard work that goes into a music career. "You never really break in," she says. "You just keep working at what you do and keep knocking on doors."

Knocking on doors—and not taking "no" for an answer—makes the difference between whether people will someday hear your songs or your voice. "There are a lot of people who are far greater talents than I or anybody else in the business, but you'll never hear from them because they didn't have the intestinal fortitude it takes to stick to the business mess of it."

It was L.A. talent nights five and six times a week that eventually led to Hudson's appearance on a national television special, the recording of two singles, her album "Playing for Time," and the concert tours.

Forty percent of becoming a successful songwriter/performer stems from talent, Hudson believes; sixty percent from business acumen, like advertising, promotion, and a good manager and agent. But even with talent and promotion, to succeed a songwriter or performer must have a big portion of good old-fashioned grit. "If songwriters could be granted one wish, it would be that they would have enough pain to make them feel (the struggle) but not so much that they give up."

With about 300 songs to her credit, Hudson never gives up on her *climb* toward the top. "That's the beauty of writing and performing," she says. "I think there's a magic; you keep thinking, 'well, maybe tomorrow, *maybe tomorrow*,' so you keep going."

—*Paula Deimling*

Salmond & Mulder (contemporary Christian LP & single); and *Songs of the New City*, by New City Choir (contemporary choral LP). Other artists include Snapshot.

**MUSIC ADVENTURES RECORDS, INC.**, Suite 101, 8033 Sunset Blvd., West Hollywood CA 90046. Cleveland Office: 3628 W. 159th St., Cleveland OH 44111. Labels include Ohio Records. Vice President A&R: Jhon Baruth. Record company, music publisher, record producer, management firm and promoter. Releases 5 singles and 1-3 albums/year. Works with artists on contract. Pays 10-20% royalty to artists on contract; standard royalties to songwriters on contract.
**How to Contact:** Submit demo tape and lead sheet. Prefers cassette with 2-3 songs on demo. SASE. Reports within 4 weeks.
**Music:** Folk, progressive, R&B, top 40/pop, and inspirational. Recently released "With You in My Eyes," by Coyote (country rock single); "Disco Rapist," by the Other Half (rock single); "This Time to the End," by Great Lakes Band (pop rock single); "Now I'm Asking," by BBB (pop rock single); and *I'm So Positive*, by BBB (LP).

**MUSIC CITY RECORDS**, 108 Morning Glory Lane, Manheim PA 17545. (717)299-1600. Labels include Bat, LeFevre, Disc-go, Palmer and Canadian American Records. A&R Director: Joey Welz. President: Jimmy Velvet. Works with artists on contract. Pays 2-5% royalty.
**How to Contact:** Submit demo tape and lyric sheet. Prefers cassette with 4-8 songs on demo. "Interested in leasing finished masters. Have it arranged in a style—rock, pop, country, etc." Does not return unsolicited material. Holds submitted material for consideration.
**Music:** C&W, dance, easy listening, MOR, rock and top 40/pop. Recently released "Bring Back the Music" b/w "The Hawk Talks," by Bill Haley's Comets with Joey Welz; "We Should Be in Love," by Joey Welz (pop/country single); "It's You,"' by Jimmy Velvet (pop/country single); "Rippin' Em' Off," by the New Wave Comets (punk single); and *American Made Rock n Roll*, by J. Welz (rock LP). Other artists include Randy Boykin, Gary Conaham, Roy Smith, Gerry Granaham and Solor System.

**MUSICANZA CORPORATION**, 2878 Bayview Ave., Wantagh NY 11793. (516)826-2735. Record company and music publisher (ASCAP). Works with artists and songwriters on contract.
**How to Contact:** Submit lead and lyric sheet. SASE. Reports in several months.
**Music:** "We will only accept original children's songs; we publish them ourselves." Recently released *Dolly Dimples*, by many artists (children's LP); and *Yeaster Bunny*, by many artists (children's LP).

**MUSTEVIC SOUND, INC.**, 193-18 120th Ave., New York NY 11412. (212)527-1586. Producer: Steve Reid. Record company, music publisher (Mustevic Sound Publishing/BMI) and record producer. Member BMA and SIRMA. Releases 2-6 albums/year. Works with artists and songwriters on contract. Pays 12-25% to artists on contract; standard royalty to songwriters on contract; statutory rate to publishers for each record sold.
**How to Contact:** Write first about your interest. Prefers cassette with 1-3 songs on demo. SASE. Reports in 3 weeks.
**Music:** Jazz. Recently released *Rhythmatism*, by Steve Reid (jazz LP); *Visions of Third Eye*, by New Life (jazz LP); and *Odyssey of the Oblong Square*, by Steve Reid (jazz LP). Other artists include Charles Tyler, Brandon Ross, David Wertman, Les Walker, Artthur Blythe, and Brandon Ross.

**\*MYSTIC OAK RECORDS**, 1727 Elm St., Bethlehem PA 18017. (215)865-1083. Talent Coordinator: Bill Byron. Record company and record producer. Releases 2-6 singles and 2-12 albums/year. Works with artists on contract. Pays negotiable royalty to artists on contract; statutory rate to publishers for each record sold.
**How to Contact:** Write about your interest. Prefers 15 ips reel-to-reel or cassette with 3-6 songs on demo. Include bio and performance information. SASE. Reports in 1 month.
**Music:** Mostly sythetic pop, new wave, experimental; also folk and top 40/pop. Recently released *Set the Trend*, by Trendsetters (new wave LP). Other artists include Office Toys, Psychic Warriors, and Steve Brosky and the BBC.
**Tips:** "Be professional in all respects and work toward being able to formulate "hit" songs."

**MYSTIC RECORDS, INC.**, Doug Moody Productions Inc., 6277 Selma Ave., Hollywood CA 90028. (213)464-9667. Labels include Mystic, Solar, Clock, Elmundo de la Musica (Latin), and Mystic Sound Records. President: Doug Moody. Coordinator: Nancy Faith. Record company, music publisher and production firm. Also originates film and TV music and syndicated radio show. Releases 20 singles and 8-10 albums/year. Works with artists and songwriters on contract; musicians on salary for in-house studio work. Pays standard rates; some advances.
**How to Contact:** Submit demo tape or submit demo tape and lead sheet to Doug Moody Productions. Prefers cassette. Reports in 1 month. SAE, Attn: Nancy Faith.

**Record Companies 173**

**Music:** Blues, C&W, easy listening, gospel (modern, rock or pop), MOR, rockabilly, soul, top 40/pop and "spoken word plays (up to 1 hour)." Has own 16 track recording and video facilities.
**Tips:** Mystic also releases collector item records limited editions in picture disc or shaped records.

**NASHBORO RECORDS**, 1011 Woodland, Nashville TN 37206. (615)227-5081. Labels include Creed, Ernie's, Kenwood, Excello, Abet, Mankind and Nasco Records. Vice President/A&R: John Jossey. Record company. Pays standard royalty to artists and songwriters.
**How to Contact:** Submit demo tape and lyric sheet. Prefers reel-to-reel demos. "Please include address and phone number." SASE. Reports in 1-2 months.
**Music:** Gospel. Recently released *Ain't No Stopping Us Now*, by Gospel Keynotes (gospel LP) and *There Is No Hope For This World*, by Bobby James and New Life Singers (gospel LP).

*****NERVOUS RECORDS**, 4/36 Dabbs Hill Lane, Northholt, Middlesex, England. 44-01-422-3462. Label includes Nervous. Managing Director: R. Williams. Record company, record producer and music publisher (Nervous Publishing and Zorch Music). Member MCPS, PRS, PPL. Releases 5 singles and 6 albums/year. Works with artists and songwriters on contract. Pays 3-10% royalty to artists on contract; 6½% to publishers for each record sold. Royalties paid directly to US songwriters and artists or through US publishing or recording affiliate.
**How to Contact:** Submit demo tape and lyric sheet. Prefers 4-15 songs on demo. SAE and IRC. Reports in 2 weeks.
**Music:** Mostly R&R and rockabilly; also R&B. Recently released "Rockabilly Guy," by Polecats (rockabilly single); and *Boogie Disease*, by Deltas (rockabilly LP). Others artists include Restless, Ricochets, Dynamite, Frantix, Buzz and the Flyers, Rockin' Johnny, Scotty Robbins, Bonneville, Flip-Out, Shakin' Quiffs, Syn-dicate and Paladins.
**Tips:** Looking for "unusual new material within the basic musical rock 'n' roll/rockabilly/psychobilly format."

**NEW ENGLAND RECORD COMPANY**, Drawer 520, Stafford TX 77477. President: Daniel Andrade. Record company, record producer and music publisher (Andrade Publishing Company/BMI). Releases 4 singles and 2 albums/year. Works with artists and songwriters on contract; musicians on salary for in-house studio work. Pays 5-10% royalty to artists on contract; negotiates rates to publishers for each record sold.
**How to Contact:** Submit demo tape and lyric sheet. Prefers 7½ ips reel-to-reel or cassette with 2-5 songs on demo. SASE. Reports in 2 months.
**Music:** Church/religious, C&W and top 40/pop. Recently released *A Lonely Stranger* and *Hank Williams Is Singing Again*, by Hank The Drifter (country LPs); "Hank Williams Ghost," by Hank The Drifter (country single); and "Tribute to Hank Williams," by Hank The Drifter (country cassette).

*****NEW HORMONES**, 4th Floor, 50 Newton St., Manchester, M1 2EA, England. 44-061-236-9849. A&R Representative: Richard Boon. Record company and music publisher (Incidental Music). Member PPL, PRS, MCPS. Works with artists and songwriters on contract. Pays 50% of profit to artists on contract; 6¼% to publishers for each record sold. Royalties paid to US songwriters and artists through US publishing or recording affiliate.
**How to Contact:** Submit demo tape and lyric sheet. Prefers cassette with 2-5 songs on demo. SAE and IRC. Reports in 1 month.
**Music:** Mostly pop, rock and jazz; also dance-oriented, progressive and top 40/pop. Recently released *Danger Came Smiling*, by Ludus (jazz LP); "Rosemary," by Dislocation Dance (pop single); and "Discipline," by God's Gift (hardcore single). Other artists include Eric Random, Diagram Brothers and Biting Tongues.

*****NEW MUSIC ENTERPRISES**, 46 Alexandra Crescent, Bromley, Kent, BR14E&, United Kingdom. 44-01-460-6584. Labels/England: New Music, Herald, Pilot and Fig Tree. Labels/US: Herald. Manager: Paul Davis. Record company and music publisher (New Music Enterprises). Member PRS, MCPS. Releases 20 albums/year. Works with artists on contract; also licenses foreign albums. Pays negotiable royalty to artists on contract; statutory rate for each record sold. Royalties paid to US songwriters and artists through US publishing or recording affiliate.
**How to Contact:** Write first. Prefers cassette with 2-4 songs on demo. SAE and IRC.
**Music:** Mostly "Christian music of all styles if contemporary (i.e., non-classical);" also bluegrass, C&W, easy listening, MOR and rock. Recently released *Travelin' On*, by Jerry Arhelger (country LP); and *Personally* by The Samuelsons (gospel LP). Other artists include Linda Hargrove Bartholohew, Erv Lewis, Judy Herring, Rosemary Wilhelm, Roland Friday and Eric Anders.

**NEW WORLD RECORDS**, Suite 11, 2309 N. 36th St., Milwaukee WI 53210. (414)445-4872. Labels include New World and More-Love Records. President: Marvell Love. Record company, music

publisher (Jero Limited/BMI) and record producer. Releases 3-5 singles and 1-2 albums/year. Works with artists and songwriters on contract; musicians on salary for in-house studio work. Pays 3-5% royalty to artists on contract: standard royalties to songwriters on contract; statutory rate to publishers for each record sold.
**How to Contact:** Submit demo tape and lyric sheet. Prefers cassette with 3-5 songs on demo. SASE. Reports in 3 weeks.
**Music:** Mostly R&B; also gospel, soul and top 40/pop. Recently released "Class A," by the Majestics (rapper); "Key to Loe," by the Majestics (ballad); and "I Call Him," by James Mitchell and the Majestic Wonders (gospel).

**NIRVANA RECORDS**, 1145 Green St., Manville NJ 08835. A&R Director: Marc Zydiak. Record company, record producer and music publisher (Package Good Music/BMI).
**How to Contact:** Prefers 7½ ips reel-to-reel or cassette with a minimum of 3 songs on demo. SASE. Reports in 1 month.
**Music:** Easy listening, folk, progressive, rock and top 40/pop. Recently released "Frosty the Dopeman," by Marc Zydiak (LP/single); "Let's Start a Punk Rock Band," by Professor Marx (single); and *No Place like You*, by Marc Zydiak (LP).

**NORTH AMERICAN LITURGY RESOURCES**, 10802 N. 23rd Ave., Phoenix AZ 85029. (602)864-1980. Labels include NALR and Sound of Hope. Music Editor: Henry Papale. Record company, record producer and music publisher (NALR/BMI). Releases 5-8 albums/year. Works with artists on contract; musicians on salary for in-house studio work. Pays statutory rate to publishers for each record sold.
**How to Contact:** Submit demo tape and lyric sheet. Prefers cassette with 5-12 songs on demo. SASE. Reports in 1 month.
**Music:** Children's, choral, church/religious, liturgical and Christian rock and inspirational. Recently released *Light of the World*, by Tom Kendzia (Christian rock LP); *By Name I Have Called You*, by Rev. Carey Landry (Christian LP); *The Time Has Come*, by Pat Boone (Christian LP); *On Eagle's Wings*, by Michael Joncas (Catholic LP); and *Reach For the Rainbow*, by Sheldon Cohen (choral LP). Other artists include St. Louis Jesuits, The Dameans, Tutti Camarata, Ellis and Lynch, Abraham Kaplan and Tom Conry.
**Tips:** "Be familiar with our recordings. Free catalogs and brochures supplied on request."

**NUCLEUS RECORDS**, Box 111, Sea Bright NJ 07760. President: Robert Bowden. Secretary: Jean Schweitzer. Record company and music publisher (Roots Music/BMI). Member AFM (US and Canada). Releases 1 single/year. Works with songwriters on contract. Pays up to 6-10% royalty for each record sold.
**How to Contact:** Submit demo tape and lyric sheet. Prefers cassette with any number songs on demo. SASE. Reports in 1 month.
**Music:** Mostly country; also church/religious, classical, folk, MOR, progressive, rock (soft, mellow) and top 40/pop. Recently released "Pressure Cooker" and "Vibrating Love," by Jean Schweitzer (pop/country single).

*****O.L. RECORDS, INC.**, 10051 Greenleaf, Santa Fe Spring CA 90670. (213)946-1524. President: Overton Lee. Record company, record producer, video production and music publisher (Boggy Depot, Overton Lee Music). Releases 6 singles and 2 albums/year. Works with artists and songwriters on contract. Pays statutory rate to publishers for each record sold.
**How to Contact:** Submit demo tape and lyric sheet. Prefers cassette with 1-3 songs on demo. Reports in 3-4 months.
**Music:** Mostly C&W and bluegrass; also blues and gospel.

*****OAKWOOD AUDIO PRODUCTIONS**, 75 Strode Pk Rd., Hernebay, Kent CT6 7JQ, England. (02)2734066. Director: Graeme Quinton-Jones. Record producer and music pubisher (Oakwood Music). Member PRS, MCPS. Works with artists and songwriters on contract. Pays 4-10% royalty to artists on contract.
**How to Contact:** Submit demo tape and lyric sheet. Prefers cassette with 1-4 songs on demo. SAE and IRC. Reports in 1 month.
**Music:** Mostly top 40/pop; also C&W, easy listening, MOR and R&B.

*****OAT WILLIE PRODUCTIONS**, 69 Engert Ave., Brooklyn NY 11222. (212)782-7183. Labels include Oat Willie and Stark Raving Mod. President: Debra Chiusano. Vice President: Jim Carney. Record company and record producer. Estab. 1982. Works with artists on contract; musicians on salary for in-house studio work. Pays 4½-8% royalty to artists on contract; statutory rate to publishers for each record sold.

**How to Contact:** Submit demo tape and lyric sheet. Prefers cassette with 1-3 songs on demo. SASE. Reports in 1-3 months.
**Music:** Mostly top 40/pop; also C&W, dance-oriented, easy listening, R&B and rock (all types). Recently released "I Just Wanna Dance," "I Really Don't Think So," and "Violent Due to Environment," by the N.Y. Ravers (wave/pop singles). Other artists include D. Blacque & Spook Rock and Hopping Mad.

**OHIO RECORDS**, Box 655, Hudson OH 44236. (216)650-1330. Label includes Deco. A&R Director: Russ Delaney. Record company, record producer and personal manager. Member BMI, RIAA, CMA, FICAP. Releases 2 singles and 1 album/year. Pays standard royalty; pays statutory rate to publishers for each record sold.
**How to Contact:** Submit demo tape and lyric sheet. Prefers cassette with 6 songs minimum on demo. Tapes returned only with SASE. Reports in one month. "Sometimes we hold material until we're ready for a session."
**Music:** Country. Recently released "Can You Go Back to That Ole Jukebox" (country single); "Taste of the Blues," (country single); and *He e e re's Ethel*, (country LP) by Ethel Delaney.
**Tips:** "I manage several artists who also write on the Ohio label and on occasion we do look for good commercial material from outside writers."

**OLD HAT RECORDS**, 3442 Nies, Fort Worth TX 76111. (817)834-3879. Labels include Old Hat Records. President: James Michael Taylor. Record company, booking agency, music publisher (Royal T Music/ASCAP) and production company. Member TMA. Releases 4 singles and 2 albums/year. Works with artists and songwriters on contract.
**How to Contact:** Submit demo tape, arrange personal interview, submit demo tape and lead sheet. Prefers 3¾ or 7½ ips reel-to-reel or cassette with 6-12 songs on demo. SASE. Reports in 1 month.
**Music:** Children's, choral, C&W, folk, rock and top 40/pop. Recently released *Water Under the Bridge*, by Texas Water (country LP); *Texas Rain*, by Texas Water (country/progressive LP); *First Unk*, by Bob French (folk LP); and "What To Do with the Pictures," by James M. Taylor (C&W single).

*****ORBIT RECORDS**, 15 Clremont Rd., Westcliff-on-Sea, Essex, SS0 7DX, England. 44-0702-43464. Labels include Orbit and Amusement. Managing Director: Barry Collings. Record company and music publisher (Barry Collings Music Ltd.). Member MPA, British Phonographic Industry Ltd. Releases 12 singles and 6 albums/year. Works with artists and songwriters on contract. Pays 8-16% royalty to artists on contract; 6¼% to publishers for each record sold. Royalties paid directly to US songwriters. Has not yet but would be willing to listen to material from US songwriters and artists.
**How to Contact:** Submit demo tape and lyric sheet. Prefers cassette with 3-12 songs on demo. SASE. Reports in 2 weeks.
**Music:** Mostly top 40/pop and soul; also children's, C&W, dance-oriented, easy listening, folk, MOR, R&B and rock (all types). Recently released "Do You Love Me" by Drama (pop single); *Black Bottom*, by Troggs (pop LP); and *Greatest Hits*, by Ray Dorset and Mungo Jerry (pop LP). Other artists include Vanity Fare, Siera, Wayne Fontana, Foundations, "plus many newly-signed young groups."

**LEE MACE'S OZARK OPRY RECORDS, INC.**, Box 242, Osage Beach MO 65065. (314)348-3383. Labels include Kajac, Ven Jence, Vision, KRC and Red Rock Records. General Manager: Lee Mace. Record company, music publisher and record producer. Works with artists and songwriters on contract; musicians on salary for in-house studio work. Pays 3-8% royalty to artists on contract: standard royalty to songwriters on contract.
**How to Contact:** Arrange personal interview or submit demo tape and lead sheet. Prefers 7½ ips reel-to-reel or cassette with 2-4 songs on demo. SASE. Reports in 2 weeks.
**Music:** Bluegrass, blues, church/religious, C&W, gospel and R&B. Recently released "Waylon Sing to Mama," by Darrell Thomas (country single); and *Lee Mace 25 Years*, by the Ozark Opry (country LP).

**P.M. RECORDS, INC.**, 20 Martha St., Woodcliff Lake NJ 07675. (201)391-2486. President: Gene A. Perla. Record company, music publisher (Perla Music/ASCAP) and record producer. Works with artists on contract.
**How to Contact:** Call first about your interest. Prefers cassette. SASE.
**Music:** All types. Recently released *A Very Rare Evening*, by Nina Simone (pop LP); *Heads Up*, by Stone Alliance (fusion LP); and *On The Mountain* by Elvin Jones (jazz LP). Other artists include Bernie Senensky, Jan Hammer, John Abercrombie, Steve Holt and Nina Sheldon.

**PARASOUND, INC.**, Suite 414, 680 Beach St., San Francisco CA 94109. (415)673-4544. President: Bernie Krause. Vice Presdient: Gary Remal. Record company and music publisher. Releases 1-3 singles and 1-3 albums/year. Works with artists and songwriters on contract. Payment negotiable.

**How to Contact:** Submit demo tape and lead sheet. Prefers 7½ ips reel-to-reel or cassette with 3-6 songs on demo. SASE. Reports in 3 weeks.
**Music:** Top 40/pop, new wave, jazz and electronic. Recently released *Citadels* by Bernie Krause (jazz-fusion LP).

**PCRL/DISQUES FLEUR, INC.**, 2364 Sherbrooke E., Montreal, Quebec, Canada H2K 1E6. (514)526-2831. Labels include Sterling, Quatre Saisons, Foreign Exchange, Boitadisc, Mayerling, Collection and Previll. Professional Manager: Carole Risch. Record company, record producer, and music publisher (Crisch Music/PROCAN and Notre Musique/CAPAC). Member ADISQ. Releases 25 singles and 10 albums/year. Works with artists and songwriters on contract. Pays 4%-16% royalty to artists on contract; statutory rate to publisher for each record sold.
**How to Contact:** Submit demo tape and lyric sheet. Prefers 15½ ips reel-to-reel or cassette with 3-7 songs on demo. SAE and International Reply Coupons. Reports in 3 weeks.
**Music:** Easy listening, MOR (ballads), rock and top 40/pop. Recently produced *C'est Magnifique*, by Santa Esmeralda (rock/latin American LP); *Un Coup d'Amour*, by Richard Cocciante (MOR LP); and "T'es Plus Une Star," by C. Michel (top 40/pop single). Other artists include Bernard Blane, Deveze, Diane Juster, Julie Arel, Alain Delorme, Michel Murty, Marie-France Paquin, Marie Myriam, Herbert Leonard and Mia Rochos.

**PEPP RECORDS**, 11800 Mayfield Ave., Los Angeles CA 90049. (213)820-5061. President: Rick Rhodes. Record company, record producer and music publisher (Captain Nemo Music). Member NARAS. Works with artists and songwriters on contract. Pays standard royalty to artists on contract; statutory rate to publishers for each record sold.
**How to Contact:** Submit demo tape and lyric sheet. Prefers cassette with 4-10 songs on demo. SASE. Reports in 1 month.
**Music:** Top 40/pop. Recently released "One More Miracle," by Rick Rhodes (pop single); and "It's All Downhill from Here" by R. Rhodes and Jerry Robinson (pop single). Other artists include Bob Roden and Aaron Weiner.

*****PERMANENT PRESS RECORDS**, Box 1406, Brea CA 92621. (714)595-6925. Labels include Permanent Press Records. A&R Director/Producer: Ray Paul. Record company, record producer and music publisher (Permanent Pop Music/BMI). Estab. 1981. Releases 3 12" singles and EPs and 2-4 albums. Works with artists and songwriters on contract. Pays 3-5% royalty to artists on contract; statutory rate to publishers for each record sold.
**How to Contact:** Submit demo tape and lyric sheet; arrange for personal interview. Prefers cassette or other records with 3-5 songs on demo. "Include any press material along with photos and bios." SASE. Reports in 3 weeks to 1 month.
**Music:** Mostly rock, top 40/rock and dance-oriented 80s music; also easy listening, MOR and R&B. Recently released "How Do You Know?," by Ray Paul (top 40/pop rock single); and "Complicated Girl," by Puppet Rulers (rock/top 40 single). Other artists include Memo and Nick Name.
**Tips:** "Believe in your music but be aware of today's market. Keep abreast of the music business and in touch with the current music scene by reading the trade charts, etc."

*****PEYTON RECORDS**, A Division of J.P.M. Industries, 3750 Bordeaux Dr., Northbrook IL 60062. (312)498-2751. Contact: Artists Relations. Record company, record producer and music publisher (J.P.M. Publishing). BMI. Member AES. Releases 4-7 singles and 4-7 albums/year. Works with artists and songwriters on contract; musicians on salary for in-house studio work. Pays negotiable royalty to artists on contract.
**How to Contact:** Write first about your interest; submit demo tape and lyric sheet. Prefers cassette with 2-4 songs on demo. "Don't get caught up in production; just make the art work." SASE. Reports in 2 weeks.
**Music:** Top 40/pop. Recently released "Track," and *Introducing Bellwether*, by Bellwether (pop). Other artists include Doug Frankle and John Keating.

*****PHILO RECORDS, INC.**, The Barn, N. Ferrisburg VT 05473. (802)425-2111. Labels include Philo and Fretless. A&R Co-ordinator: Bob Peskin. Record company and music publisher (Pleiades Music Group). Member NAIRD. Releases 10 albums/year. Works with artists on contract. Pays 6-13% royalty to artists on contract; statutory rate to publishers for each record sold.
**How to Contact:** Write first about your interest. Prefers cassette with 3-6 songs on demo. SASE. Reports in 1 month.
**Music:** Mostly folk and jazz; also bluegrass, classical, rock and top 40/pop. Recently released *Testimony* by Ferron (folk LP); *Elements*, by M. Egan and D. Gottlieb (jazz LP); and *Kilimanjaro Two* by Kilimanjaro (jazz LP).

## Record Companies 177

**PLANTATION RECORDS**, 3106 Belmont Blvd., Nashville TN 37212. (615)385-1960. Labels include Sun International and SSS Records. Contact: A&R Director. Record company and music publisher. Pays standard royalty.
**How to Contact:** Query first, then submit demo tape. Prefers cassette. SASE. Does not accept unsolicited material. Reports ASAP.
**Music:** Bluegrass, blues, C&W, dance, easy listening, folk, gospel, jazz MOR, progressive, R&B, rock, soul and top 40/pop.

**PLASTIC RECORDS**, 24548 Pierce, Southfield MI 48075. (313)559-7630. Labels include Chaos. President: Bruce Lorfel. Record company and music publisher (Look Hear Music/BMI). Releases 2 singles and 2 albums/year. Works with artists and songwriters on contract. Pays negotiable royalty to artists on contract; statutory rate to publishers for each record sold.
**How to Contact:** Submit demo tape and lyric sheet. Prefers cassette with 1-3 songs on demo. SASE. Reports in 1 month.
**Music:** MOR, rock and top 40/pop. Recently published *We're Gonna' Rock*, by The Look (rock LP).

**PLEIADES MUSIC**, The Barn, N. Ferrisburg VT 05473. (802)425-2111. Labels include Philo and Fretless Records. Vice President: Bill Schubart. Record company and music publisher (The Pleiades Music Group/BMI, Other Music, Inc./ASCAP). Member NARAS, NAIRD. Releases 6-10 albums/year. Works with artists and songwriters on contract. Pays variable royalty to artists on contract; 50% royalty to songwriters on contract; pays negotiable royalty to publishers.
**How to Contact:** Submit demo tape. Must be cassette with 3-5 songs on demo. Reports in 1 month. No returns without SASE.
**Music:** Folk, jazz and classical. Recently released *Elements* by Mark Egan and Danny Gottlieb (jazz LP); *Testimony* by Ferron (pop/folk LP); *Live at Symphony Hall* by the New Black Eagle Jazz Band; and *Kilimanjaro Two* by Kilimanjaro (pop/jazz LP). Other artists include: Mary McCaslin, Jean Redpath, Utah Phillips, Do'a, Dave Van Ronk, Priscilla Herdmann, Bill Staines and Lui Collins.

**POLKA TOWNE RECORDS**, 211 Post Ave., Westbury NY 11590. President: Teresa Zapolska. Record company, music publisher, record producer and booking agency. Works with artists and songwriters on contract.
**How to Contact:** Submit demo tape. Prefers cassette with 1-3 songs on demo. SASE for report and SASE for return of cassette. "We review music once a month."
**Music:** Polkas and waltzes.

**POLYGRAM RECORDS**, 810 7th Ave., New York NY 10019. (212)399-7051. Contact: A&R Director. Record company. Works with artists on contract.
**How to Contact:** Submit demo tape and lead sheet. Prefers 7½ or 15 ips reel-to-reel or cassette. SASE.
**Music:** Rock, R&B and top 40/pop. Recently released *Something Special*, by Kool & the Gang (R&B); *Great White North*, by Bob and Doug McKenzie (comedy); and *Chariots of Fire*, by Vangelis (soundtrack). Other artists include The Waitresses, Novo Combo, Bar-Kays, Yarbrough and Peoples, Bobby Caldwell, J.J. Cale, Scorpions, Cameo, Benny Mardones and Moody Blues.

**PRAISE INDUSTRIES CORP.**, 7802 Express St., Burnaby, British Columbia, Canada V5A 1T4. US Branch: Unit C5, 1308 Meador St., Bellingham WA 98225. (206)671-9562. Labels include New Born, Little People, Faith, Horizon, Tunesmith, Country Oak and Quest Records. Manager: Paul Yaroshuk. Record company, music publisher and studio (Noteworthy Publishing Co./BMI). Releases 60 singles and 24 albums/year. Works with artists and songwriters on contract. Pays 10% royalty to artists on contract; pays 2¾% in Canadian rate to publishers for each record sold.
**How to Contact:** Submit demo tape. Prefers reel-to-reel with 12 songs on demo. SAE and IRC. Reports in 2 weeks.
**Music:** Bluegrass, children's, choral, church/religious, C&W, folk and gospel. Recently released *Rockin' Revival*, by Servant (gospel rock LP); *Till You Came In*, by Abraham & Moses (contemporary LP); and *Midnight Fire*, by Randell Waller (gospel rock LP). Other artists include Joane Cash Yates, Heir Born, Free Way and Homespun.

*****PRECIOUS RECORDS**, 19 Acre Lane, London, SW2, England. 44-01-274-0164. Director: Trisha O'Keefe. Record company, record producer and music publisher (Trisha O'Keefe Music Ltd.). Member PRS, MCPS, ILA. Releases 6 singles and 2-3 albums/year. Works with artists and songwriters on contract. Pays 10-12% royalty to artists on contract; 6¼% royalty to publishers for each record sold. Royalties paid directly to US songwriters and artists.
**How to Contact:** Submit demo tape and lyric sheet. Prefers cassette with 2-10 songs on demo. SAE and IRC. Reports in 1 month.

**Music:** Mostly top 40/rock, C&W and dance; also easy listening, gospel, jazz, MOR, soul and R&B. Recently released "You've Gotta Be A Hustler," by Sue Wilkinson (novelty single); "Music Is Our Freedom," by Julie Amiet (Latin/jazz single); and "The On 'N' On Song," by Precious Little (disco single). Other artists include China Rogue (hard rock), and Sadie Nine (AOR/pop).

**PRELUDE RECORDS**, Suite 403, 200 W. 57th St., New York NY 10019. Contact: A&R Director. President: Marvin Schlachter. Record company and music publisher. Releases 20 singles and 10-15 albums/year. Works with artists on contract; pays statutory rate to publishers for each record sold.
**How to Contact:** Submit demo tape. Prefers 7 1/2 ips reel-to-reel or cassette. SASE. Reports in 3 weeks.
**Music:** Dance and soul; "material with a strong pop crossover potential, whether dance, R&B, or dance-oriented rock." Recently released "You're the One for Me," by D-Train; "Must Be the Music," by Secret Weapon; and "Gonna Get Over You," by France Joli (all dance singles). Other artists include Lorraine Johnson, Kumano, Musique, Passion, Saturday Night Band, Sharon Redd, Gayle Adams, The Strikers, Bobby Thurston, Nick Straker Band, U.N. and Theo Vaness.

**THE PRESCRIPTION CO.**, 70 Murray Ave., Port Washington NY 11050. (516)767-1929. President: David F. Gasman. Record company, record producer and music publisher (Prescription Co./BMI). Releases a varying number of singles and albums/year. Works with artists and songwriters on contract. Pays statutory rate to publishers for each record sold.
**How to Contact:** Call or write first about your interest, then submit demo tape and lyric sheet. Prefers cassette with any number of songs on demo. Does not return unsolicited material. Reports in 1 month.
**Music:** Bluegrass, blues, children's, C&W, dance-oriented, easy listening, folk, jazz, MOR, progressive, R&B, rock, soul and top 40/pop. Recently released "You Came In" b/w "Seasons" (pop/country single) and "Rock 'n Roll Blues," (rock single) by Medicine Mike.

***PRIMERO RECORDS**, #145, 4414 Centerview, San Antonio TX 78228. (512)734-7785. Contact: Melanie Clark. Record company and music publisher (Babcock North Music/BMI). Estab. 1981. Releases varying number of singles/year. Works with artists on contract. Pays negotiable royalty to artists on contract; negotiable royalty to publishers for each record sold.
**How to Contact:** Submit demo tape and lyric sheet. Prefers cassette with 2-5 songs on demo. SASE. Reports ASAP.
**Music:** Mostly country; also easy listening. Recently released "Just Once," by John Wesley Ryles (country single); "All My Lovin'," by Mundo Earwood (country single); and "Nickles Worth of Heaven," by Brian Collins (country single).

***PRIORITY RECORDS/CBS**, 3310 W. End Ave., Nashville TN 37203. (615)383-6000. Labels include River Song and Discos Priority Records. Manager, Music Publishing: Dennis Worley. Record company and music publisher (Priority Music/ASCAP, Preference Music/BMI). Estab. 1981. Member GMA, NARAS. Releases 15 singles and 20 albums/year. Works with artists and songwriters on contract.
**How to Contact:** Submit demo tape and lyric sheet. Prefers cassette with 3-5 songs on demo. Does not review unsolicited material.
**Music:** Mostly gospel; also choral and church/religious. Recently released *Matters of the Heart*, by Bob Bennett (gospel LP); *Some-O-Dat*, by Carman (gospel LP); and *The Cruse Family*, by The Cruse Family (gospel LP). Other artists include Cynthia Clawson, David & the Giants, B.J. Thomas, Johnny Rivers and Patrick Henderson.

***PRODUCTION CONNECTION, INC.**, 408 St. Gabriel, Montreal, Quebec, Canada H2Y 2Z9. (514)866-2021. Labels include Focus, Bobinason, Vierge and Horizon. President: Yves Godin. Record company, record producer and music publisher (Les Editions LaBobine). Releases 15 singles/year. Works with artists on contract. Pays 4-8% royalty to artists on contract; statutory rate to publishers for each record sold.
**How to Contact:** Submit demo tape and lyric sheet. Prefers cassette with minimum 5 songs on demo. SASE. Reports in 2 weeks.
**Music:** Dance-orients, easy listening, rock and top 40/pop. Recently released "If You Can Count," by Cesarez (electro pop single); "Snap," by Beauflash (electro rock single); and "SOS Anonyme," by Dwight Druick (pop rock single).

**QUALITY RECORDS**, 380 Birchmount Rd., Scarborough, Ontario, Canada M1K 1M7. (416)698-5511. Domestic (owned) labels include Quality, Celebration, Birchmount and Ringside. Director of Business Affairs: Nadine A. Langlois. Record company, record producer and music publisher (Quality Music Publishing). Member CRIA, CIRPA, CMPA. Works with artists and songwriters on contract. Pays 7%-10% royalty to artists on contract; statutory rate to publishers for each record sold.

**How to Contact:** Submit demo tape and lyric sheet. Prefers 7½ ips reel-to-reel or cassette with 3-10 songs on demo. SAE and IRC. Reports in 2 weeks.
**Music:** Dance-oriented, MOR, progressive, rock (hard metal rock and roll) and top 40/pop. Recently released *Outline*, by Gino Soccio (dance-oriented LP); *Instructions*, by the Instructions (top 40 LP); and *Frank Soda*, by F. Soda (metal rock LP). Other artists include Ronnie Hawkins, Karen Silver and Bentwood Rocker.

**QUANTUM RECORDS, LTD.**, 170A Baldwin St., Toronto, Ontario, Canada M5T 1L8. A&R Director: Mike Alyanak. Record company. Releases 10 singles and 8 albums/year. Works with artists and songwriters on contract; musicians on salary for in-house studio work. Pays 6-10% royalty to artists on contract; statutory rate to publishers for each record sold.
**How to Contact:** Submit demo tape and lyric sheet. Prefers cassette with 2-6 songs on demo. SAE and IRC. Reports in 3 weeks.
**Music:** Dance-oriented, rock (all types) and top 40/pop. Recently released *Taking Off*, by Harlow (dance-oriented LP and single); *Quick as Silver*, by Vezi (pop rock LP and single); and *Foreign Movie*, by Rex Chainbelt (new wave rock LP and single). Other artists include Keith McKie, Brandy, Billy Reed, Belinda Metz and Bob Rapson.

**QUINTO RECORD PRODUCTIONS**, Box 2388, Toluca Lake CA 91602. (213)985-8284. Labels include Quinto, Suzi, Fun, Top 'n' Bottom and Clovermint Records. Contact: Quint Benedetti. Record company, music publisher and demo producer. Works with songwriters on contract. Pays standard royalty.
**How to Contact:** Submit demo tape and lyric sheet. Prefers cassette with 2-4 songs on demo. SASE. Reports in 1 month.
**Music:** Musical comedy and Christmas songs only. "We are presently scouting for new musical comedy material for possible recording and stage production locally." Recently released *Chocalonia*, by original cast (rock musical LP); *The Lavender Lady*, by Agnes Moorehead (one-woman show LP); and *Topsy or Sorry about That Harriett*, by the original cast (LP). Other artists include Sheri Decartier.

**R.E.F. RECORDS**, 404 Bluegrass Ave., Madison TN 37115. (615)865-6380. Contact: Bob Frick. Record company, record producer and music publisher (Frick Music Publishing Co./BMI). Releases 10 albums/year. Works with artists and songwriters on contract. Pays 3-5¢ royalty to artists on contract; statutory rate to publishers for each record sold.
How to Contact: Call first about your interest, then submit demo tape and lyric sheet. Prefers 7½ ips reel-to-reel or cassette with 2-10 songs on demo. SASE. Reports in 1 month.
**Music:** C&W, gospel, rock and top 40/pop. Recently released *Release Me*, by Bob Scott; *Bob Scott Picks on Henry Slaughter*, by B. Scott and H. Slaughter; and *I Can't Help Myself*, by B. Scott and family (all gospel LPs). Other artists include Scott Frick, Larry Ahlborn, Francisco Morales, Candy Coleman, and Peggy Beard.

*****RA JO INTERNATIONAL**, Box 214, Co. Op. City Station, Bronx, NY 10451. (212)379-2593. Labels include Ra Jo. A&R Directors: J. and Ace Adams. Record company, record producer and music publisher (Ace Adams Music, Adam Puertas Music). Member RIAA, NMPA. Releases 4 singles and 2 albums/year. Works with artists and songwriters on contract; musicians on salary for in-house studio work. Pays negotiable royalty to artists on contract; statutory rate to publishers for each record sold.
**How to Contact:** Write or call first about your interest; arrange a personal interview; submit demo tape and lyric sheet. Prefers cassette with 4-8 songs on demo. SASE. Reports in 2 weeks.
**Music:** Mostly R&B and country; also children's, dance-oriented, progressive and top 40/pop. Recently released "Zoot, Zoot, Zoot," by Tiny Tim (children's Christmas LP).

**RAINBOW SOUND INC.**, 1322 Inwood Rd., Dallas TX 75247. (214)638-7712. President: Bob Cline. Record company, music publisher (Soro Publishing/SESAC, Rainsound Music/ASCAP), record producer and record pressing plant. Member TMA. Releases 3-4 singles and 5-6 albums/year. Works with artists and songwriters on contract. Pays 5% royalty to artists on contract; standard royalty to songwriters on contract; statutory rate to publishers for each record sold.
**How to Contact:** Submit demo tape and lyric sheet. Prefers cassette with 2-6 songs on demo. SASE. Reports in 2 weeks.
**Music:** Contemporary church/religious and gospel. Recently released *If You Need a Touch*, by Beckey Fender (contemporary Christian LP); "Star Studded Nights" and "Three Way Love," by The Shoppe (country singles).
**Tips:** "Submit a clear, professional demo tape, and any other credits or references."

*****RAINFIRE RECORDS**, 15217 Otsego St., Sherman Oaks CA 91403. President: Lou Penta. Record company, record producer, music publisher (Rainfire Music/BMI) and recording studio. Member

NARAS, ACM. Releases 2 singles and 1 album/year. Works with artists and songwriters on contract. Pays negotiable royalty to artists on contract.
**How to Contact:** Submit demo tape and lyric sheet. Prefers cassette with 2-5 songs on demo. SASE. Reports in 1 week.
**Music:** Mostly MOR; also C&W, dance-oriented, rock and top 40/pop. Recently released "Country Soul," by Country Canyon Band (country single); and "Video Games," by Sunny (new wave single). Other artists include Rita Jenrette and Rhonda Silver.

**RAVEN RECORDS**, 1918 Wise Dr., Dothan AL 36303. (205)793-1329. Labels include Studio Four Records. President: Jerry Wise. Record company and music publisher (Round Sound Music/BMI). Member CMA and GMA. Releases 3-6 singles and 5-10 albums/year. Works with artists and songwriters on contract. Pays 2-20% royalty to artists on contract; standard royalty to songwriters on contract; pays statutory rate to publishers for each record sold.
**How to Contact:** Write first about your interest, then submit demo tape and lyric sheet. Prefers 7½ ips reel-to-reel or cassette with 1-6 songs on demo. SASE. Reports in 1 month.
**Music:** C&W, easy listening, MOR, rock, soul and top 40/pop.

*****RBI/RECORD BREAKERS INTERNATIONAL**, #209, 39 E. 12th St., New York NY 10003. (212)673-9456. President: Rob Warren. Record company, record producer and music publisher (Rowalba). Estab. 1981. Releases 2-3 albums/year. Works with artists and songwriters on contract; musicians on salary for in-house studio work. Pays negotiable royalty to artists on contract; statutory rate to publishers for each record sold.
**How to Contact:** Submit demo tape and lyric sheet; write about your interest, specifying type of material. Prefers cassette with 1-6 songs on demo. SASE. Reports in 1 month.
**Music:** Mostly top 40/pop and new wave; also R&B, rock and soul. Recently released *Anything You Want*, by The Chiclettes (8-song cassette tape). Other artists include Tom Nielsen and Joanna & The Passionettes.

**RCA RECORDS**, 6363 Sunset Blvd., Los Angeles CA 90028. (213)468-4000 or 468-4165. A&R/West Coast: Paul Atkinson. A&R/East Coast: Dan Loggins. Record company. Works with artists and songwriters on contract. Not currently accepting unsolicited material.
**Music:** Classical, dance, jazz, progressive, R&B, rock, soul and top 40/pop.
**Tips:** "We're interested in a simple demo with piano and voice for songs. The same applies for artists, but get vocals out front."

*****RCI RECORDS, INC.**, Box 126, Elmsford NY 10523. (914)592-7983. Vice President National Promotion: Ray Roberts. Record company, distribution and promotional services to other independent record labels. Releases 12-25 singles and 4 albums/year. Works with artists on contract. Pays 7-10% royalty to artists on contract; statutory rate to publishers for each record sold.
**How to Contact:** Submit demo tape and lyric sheet; call about your interest. Prefers cassette with 2-6 songs on demo. SASE. Reports in 1 month.
**Music:** Mostly country and top 40; also jazz, MOR, R&B, rock (all types) and soul. Recently released "Lonely Hearts," by Sneed Brothers (country single); *I'll Be Alright*, by Tommy Piersol (country single & LP); and *You Can't Fall in Love When You're Cryin'*, by Mary Lou Turner (country single & LP). Other artists include Tukanon, Donna Stark, Bethany, Don Krenc, De De Upchurch, Bill Wence, Charlie Bandi, Ron Carpenter and Anthony Beye Lorie.
**Tips:** "New ideas and very original material are needed. More concern should be taken with the songs and artists rather than how good the recording studio can make them sound using electronic equipment. Clean song lyrics with a powerful message will make someone stop and listen."

**RECORD COMPANY OF THE SOUTH (RCS)**, 5220 Essen Lane, Baton Rouge LA 70808. (504)766-3233. President: Cyril E. Vetter. Record company, music publisher and record producer. Works with musicians on salary; artists and songwriters on contract. Pays 3-7% royalty to artists on contract; standard royalty to songwriters on contract.
**How to Contact:** Submit demo tape and lyric sheet. Prefers cassette (7½ ips reel-to-reel OK) with 1-10 songs on demo. SASE. Reports in 1 month.
**Music:** C&W, MOR, R&B, rock (hard and country), soul and top 40/pop. Recently released "Suddenly Single," by Butch Hornsby (country single); *Don't Take It Out on the Dog*, by Butch Hornsby (country LP); and *Safe with Me*, by Irma Thomas (pop single and LP). Other artists include Luther Kent, Gregg Wright and Floyd Brown.

*****RED BUS RECORDS (INTERNATIONAL) LTD.**, 48 Broadley Terrace, London, NW1, England. 44-01-258-0324. Labels/England include Excaliber, R&B and Red Bus. Labels/US include MCA.

Managing Director: Eliot N. Cohon. Record company, record producer and music publisher (Red Bus Music, Int.). Releases 24 singles and 4 albums/year. Works with artists and songwriters on contract; musicians on salary for in-house studio work. Pays negotiable royalty to artists on contract; negotiable rate to publishers for each record sold. Royalties paid directly to US songwriters and artists.
**How to Contact:** Submit demo tape and lyric sheet. Prefers cassette with 2-6 songs on demo. SAE and IRC. Reports in 3 weeks.
**Music:** Mostly top 40/pop; also dance-oriented, easy listening, jazz, MOR, R&B, rock and soul. Recently released "Just An Illusion," and *In The Heat of the Night*, both by Imagination (pop single and LP). Other artists include Neil Lockwood, Steve Voice, Savanna, Kelly Marie, Roy Hamilton, Splash Down and Touch Down.

**\*RED HORSE RECORDS**, Box 163, W. Redding CT 06896. (203)438-5366. Labels include Tutch and Red Kastle. Professional Manager: R. Kidd. Record company, record producer and music publisher (Tutch Music Publishing/BMI). Member CMA and CSA. Releases 4-5 singles and 1 album/year. Works with songwriters on contract; musicians on salary for in-house studio work. Pays 4-10% royalty to artists on contract; statutory rate to publishers for each record sold.
**How to Contact:** Write first about your interest. Prefers cassette with minimum 2 songs on demo. SASE. Reports in 2 weeks.
**Music:** Mostly country and top 40/pop; also dance-oriented, easy listening, R&B and rock. Recently released "Queen of the Mansion," by Maureen Hutchinson (country/pop single); "Wheeler Dealer," by Gerri Roth (rock/top 40 single); and "I'm the One," by Gerry Malone (MOR single). Other artists include Patti Terri, Malone and Hutcher, Fran Taylor, Country Touch, Hutcher Brothers and Kristian Bivona.

**REGO IRISH RECORDS & TAPES, INC.**, 64 New Hyde Park Rd., Garden City NY 11530. (516)328-7800. A&R Director: P. Noonan. Record company and music publisher (Glen Eagle Publishing Co.). Releases 2-3 singles and 10 albums/year. Works with artists and songwriters on contract. Pays negotiable royalty to artists on contract; statutory rate to publishers for each record sold.
**How to Contact:** Submit demo tape and lyric sheet. Prefers cassette with 1-4 songs on demo. SASE. Reports in 3 weeks.
**Music:** Church/religious, folk and Irish. Recently released *A Musical Taste of Ireland*, by Paddy Noonan (instrumental LP); *Write It Down*, by Hal Roach (comedy LP); and *Portrait In Green*, by Noonan, Hegarty and O'Shea (variety LP). Other artists include Louis Browne, Eamon Kelly, Pat Roper, Al Logan, Patrick O'Hagan, Carmel Quinn, Jesse Owens, Ann and Francie Brolley and Jimmy Kennedy.

**RELEASE RECORDS**, Box 234, St. Louis MO 63026. (314)296-9526. Labels include Bluebrass Records. President: Bob Bax. Record company and music publisher (Masterlease Publishing Co./BMI). Releases 1 single/year. Works with songwriters on contract. Pays 2-8% royalty to artists on contract; statutory rate to publishers for each record sold.
**Music:** Bluegrass, blues, church/religious, C&W, gospel, Spanish and R&B.

**RELIX RECORDS, INC.**, Box 94, Brooklyn NY 11229. (212)645-0818. Promotions Director: G. Saunders. Record company. Estab. 1981. Releases 2 singles and 2 albums/year. Works with artists on contract. Pays negotiable royalty to artists on contract; negotiable rate to publishers for each record sold.
**How to Contact:** Write first about your interest, then submit demo tape and lyric sheet. Prefers 7½ ips reel-to-reel or cassette with 1-4 songs on demo. SASE. Reports in 1 week.
**Music:** Bluegrass and rock (San Francisco). Recently released *Jack-O-Roses*, and *Promontory Rider*, by Robert Hunter (rock LPs).

**\*REVOLUTIONRECORDS**, 3156 Gifford Ln., Coconut Grove FL 33133. (305)448-2735. Labels include FatCat. Director: Jim R. Rudd. Record company, record producer, music publisher (Snoopy Music/BMI) and management consultant. Member BMI, AFTRA. Releases 1-2 singles and 1-2 albums. Works with artists and songwriters on contract. Pays 10-50% royalty to artists on contract; statutory rate to publishers for each record sold.
**How to Contact:** Submit demo tape and lyric plus lead sheet. Prefers cassette with 1-3 songs on demo. SASE. Reports in 1 month.
**Music:** Blues, C&W, easy listening, jazz, MOR, R&B and rockabilly. Recently released "The Clown," by Toni Bishop (A/C single); and "Cocaine Train," by Sundown Express (C&W single). Other artists include Ken Jinks, Kim Russell and Spinnaker.

**REVONAH RECORDS**, Box 217, Ferndale NY 12734. (914)292-5965. Contact: Paul Gerry. Record company and booking agency. Releases 5-10 singles and 4-6 albums/year. Works with artists and song-

writers on contract. Pays statutory rate to publishers for each record sold.
**How to Contact:** Submit demo tape and lead sheet or arrange personal interview. Prefers reel-to-reel, cassette or 8-track cartridge. SASE. Reports in 1 month.
**Music:** Bluegrass, C&W, folk and gospel. Recently released *Red Rector*, by Red Rector (bluegrass LP); *No Doubt about It*, by Curley Seckler (bluegrass LP); and *Bluegrass Unleashed*, by The Dog Run Boys (bluegrass LP). Other artists include Mac Martin, the Shenandoah Cutups, Stacy Phillips, Simon St. Pierre, Gene Elders, Fred Pike, Roger Bellow, Del McCoury, The Stuart Family, Mountain Grass, Walter Hensley, Clinton King, Jerry Oliano and The Gospelites.
**Tips:** "Songwriter should have working knowledge of how a song should be written and good melody."

**RFC RECORDS**, Suite 1001, 161 W. 54th St., New York NY 10019. President: Ray Caviano. Record company. Works with artists on contract.
**How to Contact:** Submit demo tape and lyric sheet. Prefers cassette with 1-5 songs on tape. SASE. Reports in 3 weeks.
**Music:** Dance and R&B. Recently released "Dancer," by Gino Soccio (disco single); *The Glow of Love and Miracles*, by Change (R&B/disco LP); and "Smack Dab in The Middle," by Janice McClain (disco single). "RFC is primarily a disco label, interested in progressive, high-energy dance music in all its forms." Other artists include Karen Silver.

**RICHEY RECORDS**, 7121 W. Vickery, Fort Worth TX 76116. (817)731-7375. Labels include Ridge Runner, Flying High, and Grass Mountain Records. President: Slim Richey. Record company and music publisher (Ridgerunner Publishing/ASCAP and Grass Mountain Publishing/BMI). Releases 2 singles and 12 albums/year. Works with artists and songwriters on contract; musicians on salary for in-house studio work. Pays 6% royalty to artists on contract; standard royalty to songwriters on contract.
**How to Contact:** Submit demo tape and lead sheet. Prefers cassette as demo.
**Music:** Recently released *Texas Boogie Blues*, by Ray Sharpe (pop LP). Other artists include Tennessee Gentlemen and Alan Munde.

**RICOCHET RECORDS, LTD.**, 8 Pasture Ln., Roslyn Heights NY 11577. (516)922-6980. President: Andy Marvel. Record company, record producer and music publisher (Bing, Bing, Bing Music/ASCAP, Droopy Tunes/BMI). Estab. 1981. Works with artists and songwriters on contract. Pays statutory rate to publishers for each record sold.
**How to Contact:** Submit demo tape and lyric sheet or arrange personal interview to play demo tape. Prefers 7½ ips reel-to-reel or cassette with 3-5 songs on demo. SASE. Reports in 2 weeks.
**Music:** C&W, MOR and top 40/pop. Artists include Leslie Oren, Harold Evans, Roland Pope, Dana Carew, Steve Elkins and Ethan Hurwitz.

**RIGHT ON RECORDS**, Suite 2W, 408 W. 115th St., New York NY 10025. (212)222-8715. Labels include Big Mike Records. Manager: Bill Downs. Record company and music publisher. Works with artists on contract. Pays standard royalty.
**How to Contact:** Submit demo tape and lead sheet. Prefers cassette with 3 songs on demo. Does not return unsolicited material.
**Music:** R&B, rock, soul and new wave. "We're interested in master tapes (originals) for European releases." Recently released "The Redhead," by G.G. Turner (new wave single); "Dance Little Children," by Ad Libs (disco/soul single); *Seen on TV*, by Radio Romance; *Ground Zero*, by Nu-Clear Energy; and *Outa Control*, by True. Other artists include Chris Bartley, Dolly Gilmore and Jerry Brown and the Beyond Group.

**RIPSAW RECORD CO**, 121 N. 4th St., Easton PA 18042. (215)258-5990. Branch: Suite 1003, 4545 Connecticut Ave. NW, Washington DC 20008. (212)564-3246. President: Jim Kirk (Easton). Vice President: Jonathan Strong (DC). Record company (Southern Crescent Publishing/BMI) Releases 6 singles/year. Works with artists and songwriters on contract. Payment negotiable with artists on contract; standard royalty to songwriters on contract; statutory rate to publishers for each record sold.
**How to Contact:** Submit demo tape and lyric sheet or "invite us to a club date to listen." Prefers cassette. SASE.
**Music:** Bluegrass, C&W and rockabilly. Recently released "Feelin' Right Tonight," by Martha Hull (R&R single); and "Get with It," by Johnny Seaton (rockabilly single). Other artists include Billy Hancock and Tex Rubinowitz.
**Tips:** "Keep it rockabilly."

**RMS TRIAD RECORDS**, 6267 Potomac Circle, West Bloomfield MI 48033. (313)661-5167. Labels include RMS and Triad Records. Contact: Bob Szajner. Record company, record producer and music publisher (RMS Triad Publishing/ASCAP). Member BMA, RIAA, NARAS and NAIRD. Releases 3 al-

bums/year. Works with artists on contract. Pays negotiable royalty; statutory rate to publishers for each record sold.
**How to Contact:** Write first about your interest. Prefers cassette with 2-4 songs on demo. SASE. Reports in 3 weeks.
**Music:** Jazz. Recently released *Jazz Opus 20/40*, *Sound Ideas* and *Afterthoughts*, by Triad (jazz LPs). Other artists include Frank Isola, Roy Brooks, Ray McKinney and Ed Pickens.

**ROBBINS RECORDS**, Rt. 3, Box 5B, Leesville LA 71446. Labels include Headliner Stars Records. National Representative: Sherree Scott. Record company and music publisher (Headliner Stars Music and Universal Stars Music/BMI). Releases 6 singles and 2-6 albums/year. Works with artists and songwriters on contract. Pays standard royalty to artists on contract; statutory rate to publishers for each record sold.
**How to Contact:** Submit demo tape and lyric sheet. Prefers cassette with 1-6 songs on demo. Does not return unsolicited material. Reports only if interested.
**Music:** Bluegrass, church/religious, C&W, folk, gospel, and top 40/pop. Recently released *Jesus Came All The Way*, by Sherree Scott (religious LP); *Oh, Lord Save Me*, by Melodie Scott (gospel LP); and *Praise Him*, by J.J. & Sherrie Stephens (religious single LP). Other artists include Renee Scott.

**ROB-LEE MUSIC**, Box 1338, Merchantville NJ 08109. (215)561-5822. Labels include Castle, TCB, Jade, Rock Island and Camden Soul Records. Vice President/A&R: Bob Francis. Record company and record producer. Member RIAA. Releases 15-20 singles and 3-4 albums/year. Works with artists and songwriters on contract. Pays 4-6% royalty to artists on contract; standard royalty to songwriters on contract; pays 5¢/song or 1¢/minute to music publishers for each record sold.
**How to Contact:** Submit demo tape and lyric sheet. Prefers 7½ ips reel-to-reel or cassette with 2-8 songs on demo. "Include biography and photos if possible." SASE. Reports in 2 weeks.
**Music:** Mostly funk; also C&W (country rock), dance, jazz, progressive, rock and top 40/pop. Recently released "Ain't No Thing" by Phoenix (R&B/funk single); "Me & My Horse" by the All Stars (R&B single); and "Wide Open" by Adrienne Wett (R&B/funk). Other artists include Full House, Big El, TCB Band, Snow, Heavy Weather, James "Grumpy" Brogidalo and the Orlons.

***ROCKEN MUSIC CORP.**, Box 12752, Memphis TN 38182-0752. (901)276-2113. Labels include Rocken Rythmn Records. President: Bill Lusk. A&R Director: Mike Noland. Record company, record producer, music publisher (Rocken Rythmn/BMI) and management, promotion and booking agency. Member Music Industries of Memphis and The Blues Foundation. Releases varying number of singles and albums/year. Works with artists and songwriters on contract; musicians on salary for in-house studio work. Pays negotiable rate to artists on contract; statutory rate to publishers for each record sold.
**How to Contact:** Submit demo tape and lyric sheet. Prefers cassette with 1-4 songs on demo. "Specify the number of songs on the tape." SASE, "but we would like the option to keep tape on file." Reports in 1 month.
**Music:** Mostly rock, pop and R&B; also blues, MOR, soul and top 40. Recently released "Where You Want Me," by Bill Lusk (pop single); and "Straight and Narrow Line," by B. Lusk (R&B single). Other artists include Rick Malchow and Sharon Smith.

**ROCKIN! RECORDS**, 1733 Carmona Ave., Los Angeles CA 90019. (213)933-6521. Labels include Rockmore Records. Manager: Perry Rocquemore. A&R Director: Willie H. Rocquemore. Record company, music publisher (Broadcast Music/BMI) and record producer. Member RIAA. Releases 4 singles and 1 album/year. Works with artists and songwriters on contract. Pays standard royalty; pays statutory rate to publishers for each record sold.
**How to Contact:** Submit demo tape and lyric sheet. Prefers 7½ ips reel-to-reel or cassette with 4 songs maximum on demo. SASE. Reports in 1 month.
**Music:** Country, rock, ballad and top 40/pop. Recently released "I Can't Complain," "Let's Just Fake It for Tonight," "Hello Good Times," and "Summer Lovers," all by Jennifer Jayson. Other artists include Jennifer Well.
**Tips:** "Listen to top forty hits on radio."

***ROGERSOUND RECORDS**, 902 Pinecone Trail, Anderson SC 29621. (803)225-0833. Labels include Rogersound, Sagebrush, Parlor, and Lazy River. General Manager: Ann Simmons. Record company, music publisher (Sasnras Music/BMI) and recording studio. Estab. 1981. Releases 5 singles and 2 albums/year. Works with artists and songwriters on contract; musicians on salary for in-house studio work. Pays negotiable royalty to artists on contract; statutory rate to publishers for each record sold.
**How to Contact:** Submit demo tape and lyric sheet. Prefers cassette with 3-6 songs on demo. "You may submit bio-resume, copies of any newspaper articles pertaining to you or your songs, and photos or records for our files. These will not be returned." Reports in 3 weeks "if interested."

**184** Songwriter's Market '84

Music: C&W, blues and folk; also easy listening, gospel, jazz, MOR, R&B and 50s-60s rock and roll. Recently released "Walkin' Joe (folk single), "Runaway" (rock and roll single); and *Roger Simmons*, recorded by Roger Simmons (C&W LP). Other artists include Ann Simmons.

*ROLLIN' ROCK RECORDS, 6918 Peach Ave., Van Nuys CA 91406. (213)781-4805. Labels include Rockabilly Rebel, Rockabilly Uprising. Contact: Ron Weiser. Record company, record producer and music publisher (Ron Weiser Publishing, Rockin' Ronny Music). Releases varied number of singles and 4-5 albums/year. Works with artists and songwriters on contract; musicians on salary for in-house studio work. Pays 4-7% royalty to artists on contract; statutory rate to publishers for each record sold.
**How to Contact:** Submit demo tape and lyric sheet. Prefers cassette as demo. Does not return unsolicited material. Reports in 1 month.
Music: Mostly rockabilly, 50s R&B and R&R; also C&W and R&B. Artists include Ray Campi & His Rockabilly Rebels, The Blasters and American Music.

*RONDERCREST LTD., 296 High Road, Lond, W41PA, England. 44-01-747-1695. Labels include Brickyard, Loose, Crucial and Foot 'n' Mouth. Talent Acquirer: Pete Bite. Record company, record producer, music publisher (Loose Music, Keswick Music) and exporter. Member MCPS, PRS, BPI, IFPI. Releases 6-15 singles and 3-10 albums/year. Works with artists and songwriters on contract. Pays negotiable royalty to artists on contract; 6¼% to publishers for each record sold. Royalties paid directly to US songwriters and artists.
**How to Contact:** Submit demo tape and lyric sheet. Prefers cassette with 1-4 songs on demo. SAE and IRC. Reports in 3 weeks.
Music: Mostly top 40, heavy rock and pop; also C&W, dance-oriented and jazz (funk). Recently released "Hold On," by Xero (rock single); and "Mahatma Ghandi Knew," by John Richardson (top 40 single). Other artists include Pete Bite (top 40); Nan Tuck Five (progressive); and Outasight (folk).
**Tips:** "We are interested in lease tape deals mainly. Submit finished master."

*ROOFTOP RECORDS, Box 669, Wilderville OR 97543. (503)474-1987. President: Jim Palosaari. Record company, music publisher (Beatitunes Music) and artist booking agency. Estab. 1982. ASCAP. Member GMA, CBA. Releases 6 singles and 8 albums/year. Works with artists and songwriters on contract. Pays 6-14% royalty to artists on contract; statutory rate to publishers for each record sold.
**How to Contact:** Write first about your interest; submit demo tape and lyric sheet. Prefers cassette with 2-5 songs on demo. Does not return unsolicited material. Reports in 1 month.
Music: Mostly gospel rock; also children's, MOR, progressive, R&B, top 40/pop and contemporary. Recently released *World of Sand*, by Servant (gospel rock LP); *Simple Direction*, by Loyd Thogmartin (R&B LP); and *Always, Robyn*, by Robyn Pope (MOR LP). Other artists include Mac Frampton (concert pianist); Shelter (art rock); and Sandie Brock (top 40).

ROUGH TRADE, INC., 326 6th St., San Francisco CA 94103. (415)621-4186. Labels include Factory, Instant, Smash Trade. Contact: Steve Montgomery. Record company, record producer, music publisher, distributor, wholesaler, retail and mail order house. Releases 5 singles and 10 albums/year. Works with artists and songwriters on contract. Pays 15-85% royalty to artists on contract; statutory rate to publishers for each record sold.
**How to Contact:** Submit demo tape and lyric sheet. Prefers cassette with 3-6 songs on demo. "Write your phone number and address on everything." SASE. Reports in 1 month.
Music: Blues, dance-oriented, progressive, rock, top 40/pop and new wave. Recently released *Movement*, by New Order (progressive rock/top 40 LP); *Behind the Magnolia Curtain*, by Panther Burns (blues LP); *Odyshape*, by Raincoats (progressive LP); and *Sound of the Sand*, by David Thomas (progressive LP). Other artists include Toiling Midgets.

ROUNDER RECORDS CORP., 1 Camp St., Cambridge MA 02140. (617)354-0700. Contact: Marian Leighton. Record company. Works with artists and songwriters on contract. Pays 7% minimum royalty to artists on contract; standard royalty to songwriters on contract.
**How to Contact:** Submit cassette with 4-6 songs on demo. SASE. "Please don't call. We will try to provide a response within 4-6 weeks."
Music: Bluegrass; blues; children's; C&W; folk; R&B; and rock. Recently released *More George Thorogood & The Destroyers*, by George Thorogood & The Destroyers (rock/R&B LP); and *Full Moon on the Farm*, by Norman Blake (guitar LP). Other artists include John Hammond, Tony Rice, J.D. Crowe, Guy Van Duser, Artie Traum & Pat Alger, Michael Hurley, Hazel Dickens, Jerry Douglas, Mark O'Connor, Sleepy La Beef, Johnny Copeland, Steve Young, Bela Sleck, The Johnson Mountain Boys, and Butch Robins.

*ROYAL RECORDS, 27 Argyle Rd., Ilford, Essex, 1G1 3BH, England. Labels/England include Penthouse, B.K., Royal. A&R Director: Jane Adams. Record company and music publisher (Stage One

Music). Member APRS. Releases 6 singles and 2 albums/year. Works with artists and songwriters on contract. Pays 8-14% royalty to artists on contract; 6¼% royalty to producers for each record sold. Royalties paid directly to US songwriters and artists or through US publishing or recording affiliate. Has not yet but would listen to material from US songwriters and artists.
**How to Contact:** Submit demo tape and lyric sheet. Prefers cassette with 1-3 songs on demo. SAE and IRC. Reports in 3 weeks.
**Music:** Mostly MOR and pop; also dance-oriented, easy listening and drum corps. Recently released "Rocking With My Radio," by Lesley Jayne (pop single); "Never Gonna Lose Me," by Sax Maniax (pop single); and *Oversaved*, by S. Maniax (pop LP). Other artists include Ska-Dows, Cold Hand Band, Gatecrashers, Allsorts and Eye Spy Club.

**ROYAL T MUSIC**, 3442 Nies, Fort Worth TX 76111. (817)834-3879. Labels include Old Hat. President: James Michael Taylor. Record company, music publisher (Royal T Music/ASCAP) and booking agency. Member TMA. Releases 4 singles and 2 albums/year. Works with artists and songwriters on contract.
**How to Contact:** Submit demo tape and lead sheet. Prefers 7½ ips reel-to-reel or cassette with 6-12 songs on demo. SASE. Reports in 1 month.
**Music:** Children's, choral, C&W, folk, MOR, rock and top 40/pop. Recently released *Water Under the Bridge*, by Texas Water (country/pop LP); and *The Mansfield Tapes*, by James Michael Taylor (folk, country LP).

**ROYALTY RECORDS OF CANADA, LTD.**, 9229 58th Ave., Edmonton, Alberta, Canada T6E 0B7 (403)436-0665. Contact: R. Harlan Smith. Record company, music publisher, record producer and management firm. Releases 12-15 singles and 4-6 albums/year. Works with songwriters on contract; musicians on scale. Pays standard royalties.
**How to Contact:** Arrange personal interview, submit demo tape, or submit demo tape and lead sheet. Prefers cassette with 3-5 songs on demo. "Also include a written statement verifying that publishing is available internationally on the material submitted." Does not return material. Reports in 90 days.
**Music:** C&W, easy listening, MOR and top 40/pop.

**RUSTIC RECORDS**, 615 Durrett Dr., Nashville TN 37211. (615)833-1457. President: Jack Stillwell. Record company. Works with artists and songwriters on contract. Pays royalty to artists on contract; statutory royalty to songwriters on contract.
**How to Contact:** Submit demo tape with lyric or lead sheet. Cassette only with 2 songs on demo. SASE. Reports in 3 weeks.
**Music:** C&W. Recently released "Breakaway," "Quicksand," and "I Wanna Do It Again" by Bill Wence (country single). Other artists include Jack Stillwell and Carl Struck.

*****RUTLAND RECORDS**, 7 Rutland Rd., Chesterfield, Derbyshire, S40 1ND, England. 44-0246-79976. Labels include Rutland Records. Director: Tony Hedley. Record company, record producer, music publisher (Hedley Music Group/MCPS) and promotions company. Releases 4 singles and 2 albums/year. Works with artists and songwriters on contract. Pays negotiable royalty to artists on contract; 6½% to publishers for each record sold. Royalties paid directly to US songwriters and artists or through US publishing or recording affiliate. Has not yet but would listen to material from US songwriters and artists.
**How to Contact:** Write first; submit demo tape and lyric sheet. Prefers cassette with 1-4 songs on demo. SAE and IRC. Reports in 2 weeks.
**Music:** Mostly pop and rock (hard and country); also folk, progressive, soul and top 40/pop; "we want to also expand into country music." Artists include Dagaband and Bitch.
**Tips:** "We are looking for good country material suitable for UK artists as well as chart potential pop and rock."

*****RWP RECORDS GROUP**, Box 4705, Arlington VA 22204. (703)522-2718. Labels include Ear Witness, RWP and Philipe. A&R Director: Robert Wardrick. Record company, music publisher (Music Management/ASCAP, BMI). Member Independent Labels Association. Releases 10-15 singles and 3-5 albums/year. Works with artists and songwriters on contract; musicians on salary for in-house studio work. Pays 3-10% royalty to artists on contract; statutory rate to publishers for each record sold.
**How to Contact:** Submit demo tape and lyric sheet. Prefers cassette with 4 songs on demo. "Artists should include a short bio and photos." SASE. Reports in 3 weeks.
**Music:** Mostly soul, MOR and top 40; also dance-oriented and progressive. Recently released *Last Days of Rock*, by The Rumblers (top 40 LP); and "A Million Years", by Mercury Band (soul single). Other artists include Tom Newman, Sam Conjerti, Barbara Williams and Glass House.

**\*SAIN (RECORDIAU) CYF**, Llandwrog, Caernarfon, Gwynedd, LL54 STG, Wales. 44-0286-831-111. Labels include Tryfan, Welsh Teldisc, Ty Ar Y Graig. Directors: Hefin Elis and Dafydd Iwan. Record company, record producer, music publisher (Cyhoeddiadau Sain) and record distrbutor. Member APRS. Releases 10 singles and 40 albums/year. Works with artists and songwriters on contract. Pays 4-10% royalty to artists on contract; 6¼% to publishers for each record sold, pro rated per song. Has not yet, but would listen to material from US songwriters and artists.
**How to Contact:** Submit demo tape and lyric sheet. Prefers cassette with 1-5 songs on demo. SAE and IRC. Reports in 1 month.
**Music:** Mostly choral (Welsh language); also children's, church/religious, classical, C&W, folk, MOR and rock. Recently released *Ychydig Hedd*, by Trebor Edwards (MOR LP); *Shampiw*, by Bando (rock LP); and *Pan Ddaw'r Nos*, by Llanelli Male Choir (choral LP). Other artists include Omega, Ail Symudiad, Ar Log, Dafydd Iwan, Tecwyn Ifan, Ficar, Derec Brown, Margaret Williams, Cilmeri, Pendyrus Choir, Brythoniaid Choir and Rhos Choir.
**Tips:** "Music should be relevant to the 'scene' in Wales."

**SALSOUL RECORDS**, 401 5th Ave., New York NY 10016. (212)889-7340. Executive Vice President: Ken Carey. Record company and music publisher (Lucky Three/BMI, Salsoul/ASCAP). Releases 40-60 singles and 20-25 albums/year. Works with artists and songwriters on contract. Payment negotiable.
**How to Contact:** Submit demo tape and lyric sheet. Prefers cassette with 3-4 songs maximum on demo. "May or may not return unsolicited material." Reports in 3 weeks.
**Music:** Dance, R&B, rock, soul and top 40/pop.

**SAM RECORDS**, 1501 Broadway, New York NY 10036. (212)786-7667. Vice President: Daniel S. Glass. Record company, music publisher and record producer. Works with artists on contract. Payment negotiable.
**How to Contact:** Call first about your interest, then submit demo tape and lyric sheet. Prefers 7½ ips reel-to-reel or cassette with 1-3 songs on demo. SASE. Reports in 2 weeks.
**Music:** Blues, dance, folk, MOR, progressive, R&B, rock, soul and top 40/pop. "We are eagerly looking for artists in R&B and new rock." Recently released *Keep On Dancin'*, by Gary's Gang (disco pop LP); "Love Magic," (pop single) and *Ain't That Enough for You*, by John Davis With The Monster Orchestra (pop LP); "Let's Do It," by Convention; "Don't Stop," by K.I.D.; and "Just How Sweet Is Your Love," by Rhyze.

**SANDCASTLE RECORDS**, 157 W. 57th St., New York NY 10019. (212)582-6135. Labels include Tara and Coby Records. President: Mark Cosmedy. Record company. Releases 10-14 singles and 7-10 albums/year. Works with artists and songwriters on contract. Payment negotiable.
**How to Contact:** Submit demo tape and lead sheet. Prefers 7½ ips reel-to-reel or cassette with 2-4 songs on demo. SASE. Reports in 1 month.
**Music:** C&W, easy listening, folk, jazz, MOR, progressive, rock and top 40/pop.

**SAPPHIRE RECORD CO.**, 2815 Octavia St., New Orleans LA 70115. (504)866-3478. Labels include Ludukay and Sapphire. Contact: Lou Welsch. Record company and music publisher (Sapphire Music Publishers/BMI). Member CMA. Releases 1 single/year. Works with artists and songwriters on contract. Pays standard royalty to artists on contract; statutory rate to publishers for each record sold.
**How to Contact:** Call to arrange interview to play demo tape. Prefers cassette with 4 songs on demo. SASE. Reports in 3 weeks.
**Music:** Blues, C&W, jazz, R&B, soul and top 40/pop. Recently released "Mardi Gras Mambo," by Hawketts (oldie single). Other artists include Mike Lord.

**SAVOY RECORDS**, 342 Westminister Ave., Box 279, Elizabeth NJ 07208. Contact: Helen Gottesmann, Milton Biggham. Record company and music publisher (Savgos Music, Inc./BMI, Jonan Music, Inc./ASCAP and Arisav Music, Inc./SESAC). Member RIAA. Releases 60 albums/year. Pays statutory rate to publishers for each record sold.
**How to Contact:** Query. Reports in 2 weeks.
**Music:** Gospel and traditional gospel. Recently released "Ye Have Dwelled In This Mountain Long Enough," by the New York State Mass Choir of GMWA; "The Little Wooden Church On The Hill," by Rev. Leroy Liddell; "Hallelujah 'Tis Done," by James Cleveland & Los Angeles Chapter of GMWA: "I'm Packing Up, Getting Ready," by Rev. Ernest Franklin; "Pass It On by The Fourth of May" and "Nobody But Jesus," by The Philadelphia Mass Choir; "There's A Blessing On The Way," by The Triboro Mass Choir; "I Can See Clearly Now," by The O'Neal Twins; "He Keeps On Making A Way," by Rev. Isaac Douglas; "You Don't Know How Good God's Been To Me," by the Charles Fold Singers; "Deliverance," by J. Cleveland & The Cleveland Singers; and "I Found A Friend," by The Gospel Music Workshop Mass Choir.

**Record Companies** **187**

**SCARAMOUCHE RECORDS**, Drawer 1967, Warner Robins GA 31099. (912)953-2800. Director: Robert R. Kovach. Record company and record producer. Releases 4 singles and 1 album/year. Works with artists and songwriters on contract. Pays 3-5% royalty to artists on contract; pays statutory rate to publishers for each record sold.
**How to Contact:** Submit demo tape and lyric sheet. Prefers 7½ ips reel-to-reel or cassette with 3-5 songs on demo. SASE. Reports in 1 month.
**Music:** Blues, C&W, easy listening, R&B, rock, soul and top 40/pop. Recently released "Easy on Your Feet," by Justice (dance/easy listening single). Other artists include Napoleon Starke.
**Tips:** "To be different makes the difference."

**SCENE PRODUCTIONS**, Box 1243, Beckley WV 25801. (304)252-4836. Labels include Rising Sun and Country Road Records. Executive Professional Manager Producer: Richard L. Petry. Record company, record producer and music publisher (Purple Haze Music/BMI). Member of AFM. Releases 1-2 singles and 1-2 albums/year. Works with artists and songwriters on contract. Pays 3-5% royalty to artists on contract; standard royalty to songwriters on contract; statutory rate to publishers for each record sold. Charges "initial costs, but is conditionally paid back to artist."
**How to Contact:** Write first about your interest, then submit demo tape and lyric sheet. Prefers cassette with 2-5 songs on demo. SASE. Reports in 1 month.
**Music:** Mostly pop and country; also MOR, light and commercial rock and top 40. Recently released *Premiere*, by Tim Brophy (pop/LP); and "Can't Get Over Losing You"and "Home Sweet West Virginia" by Dave Runion (country single). Other artists include Bob McCormick and Imagene Floyd.
**Tips:** "Songs should be well-thought-out and well-constructed—songwriting is a craft."

***SCRATCH RECORDS LTD.**, Rock City, Shepperton Studios Centre, Shepperton, Middlesex, England. 44-09328-66531. Labels/England: Scratch, Rock City. Labels/US : Plateua. Managing Director: Brian Adams. Record company, record producer and music publisher (Rock City Music, Ltd.). Member APRS, MCPS, PRS. Releases 6 singles and 2 albums/year. Works with artists and songwriters on contract. Pays negotiable rate to artists on contract; negotiable rate to publishers for each record sold. Royalties paid directly to US songwriters and artists or through a US publishing or recording affiliate. Has not yet, but would listen to material by US songwriters and artists.
**How to Contact:** Submit demo tape and lyric sheet. Prefers 15 ips reel-to-reel or cassette with 1-3 songs on demo. SASE. Reports in 1 month.
**Music:** Mostly top 40/pop; also MOR, rock (heavy) and comedy. Recently released "Go, Now," and "Say You Don't Mind," by Denny Laine (pop singles); and *Jim Davidson Live,*" by D. Laine (comedy LP).

**SEA CRUISE PRODUCTIONS**, Box 1830, Gretna LA 70053. Labels include Briarmeade, Keeta, Keene, Sonor (Sound of New Orleans Records), Burlap, Speedy. President: Ken Keene. Record company, record producer, music publisher (Briarmeade Music/ASCAP, Sea Cruise Music/BMI, Keeta Music/BMI), talent management firm and public relations firm. Member NSAI, CMA, ACM. Releases 10-20 singles and 5+ albums/year. Works with artists and songwriters on contract. Pays 4-6% royalty to artists on contract; statutory rate to publishers for each record sold.
**How to Contact:** Submit demo tape and lyric sheet. Prefers 7½ ips reel-to-reel or cassette with 1-10 songs on demo. SASE. Reports in 1 month.
**Music:** Blues, children's, C&W, easy listening, gospel, MOR, R&B, rock, soul and top 40/pop. Recently released *Raw and Rare*, by Frankie Ford (MOR/pop LP); *Saxy Country Soul*, by Johnny Pennino (country/pop LP); and "Country Goose," by J. Pennino (country/pop single). Other artists include Matt Lucas and Jimmy Payne.

**SEASIDE RECORDS**, 100 Labon St., Tabor City NC 28463. (919)653-2546. President: Elson H. Stevens. Record company, record producer, music publisher (Creekside Music/BMI) and promotion company. Releases 20 singles and 2-4 albums/year. Works with songwriters on contract; musicians on salary for in-house studio work. Pays 4-10% royalty to artists on contract; 2¾-4¢ to publishers for each record sold.
**How to Contact:** Write or call first about your interest, then submit demo tape and lyric sheet. Prefers 7½ ips reel-to-reel, cassette or 8-track tape with 2-3 songs on demo. SASE. Reports in 1 month.
**Music:** Mostly country; also bluegrass, folk, gospel, rock (country, hard) and beach music. Recently released "Nighttime Lady," by T. Jay Jon (country single); "Beach Fever," by Fat Jack Band (beach music single); and "Cheap Imitation," by The Musicmakers (country single). Other artists include Mitch Todd, Sheila Gore, Copper Creek, Glenn Todd, Wilma Watts, The Escorts and Country Cut-ups.
**Tips:** "Only artists who possess commercial quality and are ready and willing to work need contact us."

**SEEDS RECORDS**, Box 20814, Oklahoma City, OK 73156. (405)751-8954. Labels include Homa. Record company, record producer and music publisher (Okisher Publishing/BMI). Releases 20-30 sin-

gles and 10-15 albums/year. Works with artists and songwriters on contract. Pays negotiable royalty to artists on contract; statutory rate to publishers for each record sold.
**How to Contact:** Submit demo tape and lyric sheet. Prefers cassette with 1-3 songs on demo. Does not return unsolicited material. Reports in 1 month.
**Music:** Blues, C&W, easy listening, jazz, MOR, R&B and soul. Recently released *Cocaine Blues*, by Janjo (blues LP); *Bad Case of the Blues*, by Janjo (easy listening LP); and "Dallas Swing," by Benny Kubiak (country single). Other artists include Stoney Edwards, Tony Albert and Charley Shaw.

**SHILOH RECORDS**, Box 62, Shiloh TN 38376. (901)689-5141. President: W.R. Morris. Record company. Labels include Majesty Records. Releases 10-15 singles and 5-8 albums/year. Works with artists on contract. Payment negotiable. Charges for some services. "We charge if an artist wants record produced and we feel material is not suitable for our market."
**How to Contact:** Submit demo tape and lead sheet. Prefers 7 1/2 ips reel-to-reel or cassette with 2-4 songs on demo. SASE. Reports in 1 month.
**Music:** C&W, gospel and bluegrass. Recently released "Anything," by Earl Green.

**SHORT PUMP RECORDS**, Short Pump Associates, Box 11292, Richmond VA 23230. (804)355-4117. President: Ken Brown. Vice President: Dennis Huber. Record company and production company. Releases 3 singles and 2 albums/year. Works with musicians on percentage; artists and songwriters on contract. Pays 12% royalty to artists on contract.
**How to Contact:** Submit demo tape and lead sheet. Prefers cassette with 3-6 songs on demo. SASE. Reports in 2 weeks.
**Music:** R&R. Recently released *Two B's Please* (LP); and "Candyapple Red," and "Brite Eyes," by the Robbin Thompson Band (rock). Other artists include Good Humor Band, Train Ride and RTB's.

**SHU-QUA-LOK RECORDS**, 233 Penner Dr., Pearl MS 39208. (601)939-6616. Labels include Acorn and So-Len. Contact: George W. Allen. Record company, record producer and music publisher (Galyn Music/BMI). Member NSAI, CMA. Releases 10 singles and 1 album/year. Works with artists and songwriters on contract; musicians on salary for in-house studio work. Pays standard royalty to artists on contract; statutory rate to publishers for each record sold.
**How to Contact:** Submit demo tape and lyric sheet, write or call about your interest or arrange personal interview. Prefers 7 1/2 ips reel-to-reel or cassette with 2-6 songs on demo. "Be sure the vocal is up front and the lyrics are tight and tell a story." SASE. Reports in 3 weeks.
**Music:** Bluegrass, blues, C&W, gospel, MOR, progressive, R&B, rock, soul and top 40/pop. Recently released "Play Me a Cheating Song," by Keith Lamb (country single); "Please Don't Lead Me On," by Jackie Pearson (MOR single); "Just Let Me Love You," by Ted Holman (country single) and "Pleasant State of Mind," and "Reminiscing" by Bobby Sauls. Other artists include Cathy Capton, Debbie Gooch, David Dunn and Larry Jenkins.

**SILVER PELICAN RECORDS**, Dean Rd., Rt. 1, Box 195A, Maitland FL 32751. President: Glenn Hamman. Record company, record producer and music publisher (Hamman Publishing, Inc./BMI). Member AFM. Releases 4-6 singles and 2-3 albums/year. Pays 5-7% royalty to artists on contract; statutory rate to publishers for each record sold.
**How to Contact:** Submit demo tape and lyric sheet or arrange personal interview. Prefers cassette with 2-5 songs on demo. "Please make sure all work is copywritten before submitting." SASE. Reports in 1 month.
**Music:** Church/religious, C&W, easy listening, gospel, jazz, MOR and R&B. Recently released "Blastoff Columbia," by Roy McCall (country single); *Flying High with Tony Albert*, by Tony Albert (country LP); and "Eveready Pair of Arms," by Robyn Young (country single). Other artists include Flora Maclin and Brad Wolf.

**SINGSPIRATION MUSIC/RECORDS**, 1415 Lake Dr., Grand Rapids MI 49506. (616)459-6900. Labels include New Dawn and Milk n' Honey Records. Director of Music Publications: Don Wyrtzen. National Music Coordinator: Forrest Coe. Director of Record Dept.: Phil Brower. Record company and music publisher (ASCAP, SESAC). Member GMA, NARAS. Releases 10 singles and 10-15 albums/year. Works with musicians on salary; artists and songwriters on contract. Pays 5% royalty to artists on contract; statutory rate to publishers for each record sold.
**How to Contact:** Not currently reviewing new material. Does not return unsolicited material. Reports in 2 months.
**Music:** Church/religious, Christian contemporary, gospel and MOR. Recently released *New Lives for Old*, by Wayne Watson; *Legacy*, by Michael Card; and *It's Alright Now*, by Harvest. Other artists include Twila Paris, Bill Pearce, Michael James Murphy and Gary Rand.

**SIRE RECORDS**, 3 East 54 St., New York NY 10022. (212)832-0950. A&R Director: Michael Rosenblatt. Record company.

**How to Contact:** Submit demo tape and lyric sheet. Prefers cassette as demo. SASE. Reports in 1 month.
**Music:** All types. Recently released *The Pretenders*, by The Pretenders (rock LP).

**SIVATT MUSIC PUBLISHING CO.**, Box 7172, Greenville SC 29610. (803)295-3177. Labels include Pioneer, Brand-X and Accent Records. President: Jesse B. Evatte. Secretary: Sybil P. Evatte. Record company and music publisher. Publishes 4-10 singles and 11-25 albums/year. Works with artists and songwriters on contract. Pays standard royalty to artists and songwriters on contract.
**How to Contact:** Submit demo tape and lead sheet. Prefers cassette with 2-6 songs on demo. SASE. Reports in 1 month.
**Music:** Bluegrass, choral, church/religious, C&W, easy listening, folk and gospel. Recently released *Down Home Singing*, by the Roy Knight Singers (country gospel LP); *Sincerely*, by Joyce and the Rogers Brothers (gospel LP); and *Down Home Guitar*, by Bob Dennis (instrumental gospel LP).

**SKYLIGHT RECORDS**, 12024 Riverside Dr. E., Windsor, Ontario, Canada N8P 1A9. (519)255-7067. Labels include JLT Records. President: Jim Thomson II. Record company, record producer and music publisher (On the Wing Music Publishing Co./PROCAN). Releases 3 singles and 2 albums/year. Works with songwriters on contract. Pays statutory rate to publishers for each record sold or first recording will be negotiable.
**How to Contact:** Submit demo tape; biography and lyric sheet or arrange personal interview. Prefers cassette with 4 songs on demo; "submit at least 2 of each style; if submitting more than 1 style, preferably 3 songs." SAE and IRC. Reports in 2 weeks "but only if interested due to volume."
**Music:** Mostly rock and MOR; also bluegrass, blues, children's, church/religious, classical, C&W, easy listening, folk, gospel, jazz, MOR, progressive, Spanish, R&B, soul and top 40 pop. Recently released "Old Gyspy Moon," by J. Thomson II (top 40 single); *Preflyte Row*, by Preflyte (rock LP); and *Filling the Void*, by J. Thomson II (MOR LP).
**Tips:** "I work with artists and songwriters who have a sense of purpose other than just music behind what they do. Send bio outlining motivations, convictions and goals, and we may end up working together."

**SLASH RECORDS**, Box 48888, Los Angeles CA 90048. (213)937-4660. Labels include Ruby, Big International, Slash and Warner. A&R Director: Chris Desjardins. Record company and music publisher. Releases 5 singles and 6-10 albums/year. Works with artists on contract. Pays negotiable royalty to artists on contract; statutory rate to publishers for each record sold.
**How to Contact:** Submit demo tape and lyric sheet. Prefers cassette with 3-5 songs on demo. "Material will be returned on request." SASE. Reports in 1 month.
**Music:** C&W, R&B, rock, soul, top 40/pop, rockabilly, new wave and punk. Recently released *Nonfiction*, by the Blasters; and *Sundown*, by Rank & File.

*****SMI RECORDS, CORP.**, Suite 6, 353 W. 48th St., New York NY 10036. Labels include Will Power and On Time Records. Director, Marketing and Promotions: David Nelson Askew. Record company, record producer, music publisher (Get Rich Music/BMI, Stay Rich Music/ASCAP) and management firm. Member BMA, NARM, NAIRD, SIRMA. Releases 12 singles and 6 albums/year. Works with artists and songwriters on contract. Pays negotiable royalty to artists on contract; negotiable rate to publishers for each record sold.
**How to Contact:** Submit demo tape and lyric sheet; write about your interest. "No rough demo—only completed demos or masters." Prefers 7½ ips reel-to-reel or cassette with 1-3 songs on demo. SASE. Reports in 4-6 weeks.
**Music:** Mostly good up-temo funky dance music; also dance-oriented, R&B, soul, urban contemporary dance tunes and rap music. Recently released "Love Is Callin," by Omega (rap single); "Reality" by the Romantic Lovers (rap single); and "Style," by A/OK (dance single). Other artists include The Bangies, Kenny Bee, Dawn, Cold Crushers, T. Stark, G-Force and Melody Brothers.

**SOLID GOLD RECORDS**, 180 Bloor St. W., #400, Toronto, Ontario, Canada M5S 2V6. (416)960-8161. Vice President: Neill Dixon. Record company and music publisher (Solid Gold Publishing, 18 Karat Gold Music). Releases 5-12 singles and 5-8 albums/year. Works with artists and songwriters on contract. Pays statutory rate to publishers for each record sold.
**How to Contact:** Submit demo tape and lyric sheet. Prefers cassette with 3-5 songs on demo. Reports in 1 month only if interested.
**Music:** C&W, rock and top 40/pop. Recently released "My Girl," by Chilliwalk (pop/rock/top 40 single); "I Believe," by Chilliwalk (top 40 single); and *Toronto Headon*, by Toronto (rock LP). Other artists include Headpins, The Good Brothers and Girlschool.

**SOLID RECORDS**, Apt. M, 10101 Woodlake Dr., Cockeysville MD 21030. A&R Director: George Brigman. Record company, music publisher and record producer (Sone Songs/BMI). Releases 1-2 singles and 1 album/year. Works with musicians on salary; artists and songwriters on contract. Pays 5-20% royalty to artists on contract; standard royalty to songwriters on contract.
**How to Contact:** Submit demo tape and lyric sheet. Prefers 7½ ips reel-to-reel with 1-6 songs on demo. No cassettes. SASE. Reports in 3 weeks.
**Music:** Mostly hard rock and progressive rock; also blues, C&W, easy listening, jazz and heavy metal rock. Recently released *I Can Hear the Ants Dancin*, by Split (rock LP); and *The Return of the Young Pennsylvanians* (compilation LP). Other artists include the Mascara Snake, Russ Nixon and Buckwheat.

**SONATA RECORDS**, 4304 Del Monte Ave., San Diego CA 92107. (714)222-3346. President: Paul DiLella. Record company and music publisher. Member RIAA. Works with artists and songwriters on contract. Pays 5% royalty to artists on contract; 2¢/record to songwriters on contract.
**How to Contact:** Submit demo tape and lead sheet or submit lead sheet. Prefers 7½ ips reel-to-reel or cassette with 6-12 songs on demo. SASE. Reports in 1 month.
**Music:** Church/religious, classical, C&W, dance, easy listening, gospel, MOR, rock and top 40/pop. Recently released "My Tropic Isle," by Cathy Foy (Hawaiian single). Other artists include Paul Dante.

*****SOUL SOUNDS UNLIMITED RECORDING CO.**, Box 24240, Cincinnati OH 45224. President: Alvin Don Chico Pettijohn. Record company and music publisher. Works with artists and songwriters on contract. Pays negotiable royalty to artists and songwriters on contract. Charges for some services: "we will make demo tapes for songwriters for their own use. If we feel that a writer or musician is best suited for our needs in the recording field, we will offer a recording contract."
**How to Contact:** Submit demo tape. Prefers 15 ips reel-to-reel, cassette or 8-track cartridge. SASE. "All tapes will become the property of Soul Sounds if return postage is not included." Reports in 3 weeks.
**Music:** Dance and soul. Recently released "Loving You," by the Devotions (easy listening/soul single); and "Need a Lot of Woman," by Henry R. Kyles (easy listening single).

*****SOUND IMAGE RECORDS**, 6556 Wilkinson, N. Hollywood CA 91606. (213)762-8881. Labels include Sound Image and Harmony. President: Martin J. Eberhardt. Record company, record producer, music publisher (Sound Image Publishing) and video company. Member NARAS. Releases 12 singles and 6 albums/year. Works with artists and songwriters on contract; musicians on salary for in-house studio work. Pays 5-10% royalty to artists; statutory rate to publishers for each record sold.
**How to Contact:** Submit demo tape and lyric sheet. Prefers cassette with 3-6 songs on demo. Include photo and bio. Does not return unsolicited material. Reports in 1 month.
**Music:** Mostly mainstream rock; also dance-oriented, R&B, top 40/pop, reggae and techno-pop. Recently released *The Secrets*, (techno-pop LP); *George Faber & Stronghold*, (R&B/pop LP); and *Jah Moon*, (reggae LP).

*****SOUND SOUTH RECORDS**, 203 Culver Ave., Charleston SC 29407. (803)766-2500. Assistant Manager: Chris Gabrielli. Record company, record producer and music publisher (Sound South Publishing). Releases 12 singles and 6 albums/year. Works with songwriters on contract. Pays 50-70% royalty to artists on contract.
**How to Contact:** Submit demo tape and lyric sheet; call about your interest. Prefers reel-to-reel or cassette with a minimum of 3 songs on demo. Reports in 1 week.
**Music:** Blues, R&B, rock, soul and top 40/pop. Recently released *Greatest Hits*, by Tams (LP); and *Greatest Hits*, by Cornelius Brothers (LP).

**SOUNDS OF HOPE, INC.**, Box 35083, Phoenix AZ 85069. (602)864-1980. President: Bruce Bruno. Record company and music publisher. Releases 2 albums/year. Works with artists and songwriters on contract; musicians on salary for in-house studio work. Pays negotiable royalty to artists on contract; statutory rate to publishers for each record sold.
**How to Contact:** Submit demo tape and lyric sheet. Prefers 7½ ips reel-to-reel or cassette with 2-12 songs on demo. SASE. Reports in 1 week.
**Music:** Children's, church/religious and gospel. Recently released *Christmas with Friends*, by Ed McMahon and Doc Severinson (Christmas LP); and *Land of Love*, by Marcy Tigner (children's LP).
**Tips:** "We are a young label, with a Grammy nomination for our first record. Artists need not have a track record, but they must be serious."

**SOUNDS OF WINCHESTER**, Box 574, Winchester VA 22601. (703)667-9379. Labels include Alear, Winchester and Real McCoy Records. Contact: Jim or Bertha McCoy. Record company, music

publisher (Jim McCoy Music, Alear Music and New Edition Music/BMI) and recording studio. Releases 20 singles and 10 albums/year. Works with artists and songwriters on contract; musicians on salary for in-house studio work. Pays 2% royalty to artists and songwriters on contract, statutory rate to publishers for each record sold.
**How to Contact:** Submit demo tape or arrange personal interview. Prefers 7½ ips reel-to-reel with 4-12 songs on demo. Does not return unsolicited material. Reports in 1 month.
**Music:** Bluegrass, C&W, gospel, rock (country) and top 40/pop. Recently released "One More Time," by Earl Howard (country single); *Thank You Jesus*, by Jubilee Travelers (gospel LP); and "String Along;" by Dave Elliott (country single). Other artists include Jim McCoy, Carroll County Ramblers and Alvin Kesner.

**SPRING RECORDS**, 161 W. 54th St., New York NY 10019. (212)581-5398. Contact: A&R Department. Record company. Works with artists and songwriters on contract; musicians on salary for in-house studio work.
**How to Contact:** Submit demo tape and lyric sheet. Prefers masters.
**Music:** R&B only. Recently released *Hard Times*, by Millie Jackson (R&B LP); and *Is This the Future?*, by Fatback Band (R&B LP).

**THE STACY-LEE**, Box 711, Hackensack NJ 07602. (201)488-5211. Labels include Banana, Inner Circle, Joy, Lions Den, Lotus, Lybra, Riot, Vanishing Point, S.A.M. Record company, record producer and music publisher (Miracle-Joy/BMI). Works with artists and songwriters on contract; musicians on salary for in-house studio work.
**How to Contact:** Submit demo tape and lyric sheet. Prefers cassette with 1-6 songs on demo. SASE. Reports in 3 weeks.
**Music:** Children's, church/religious, C&W, easy listening, folk, gospel and MOR.

**STANDY RECORDS, INC.**, 760 Blandina St., Utica NY 13501. (315)735-6187. Labels include Kama Records. President: Stanley Markowski. Record company and music publisher (Oneida Music). Works with artists and songwriters on contract. Pays standard royalty to artists on contract; statutory rate to publishers for each record sold.
**How to Contact:** Submit demo tape and lyric sheet. Prefers 7½ ips reel-to-reel or cassette. SASE. Reports in 1 month.
**Music:** All types. Recently released "I Believe in America", by Tiny Tim (pop single); "Baby I'm Possessed by You," by Dawn Bouck (pop single); and "We'll Build A Bungalow", by Norris The Troubador (pop single).

**STAR JAZZ RECORDS, INC.**, 5220 SW 8th St., Fort Lauderdale FL 33317. (305)581-4310. Producer: Will Connelly. Record company. Works with musicians on salary for in-house studio work. Payment negotiable.
**How to Contact:** Write first about your interest. Prefers cassette. "There are no limits on amount of material, but recommend limiting time to 15 minutes. If we like what we hear, we'll ask for more." Does not return unsolicited material. "We will return material submitted as a result of pre-inquiry." Reports in 2 weeks.
**Music:** Dixieland jazz (20s-40s). Recently released *Justice Makes Love*, by Tom Justice (jazz LP); *Jazz You Like It*, by Biscayne Jazz Band (jazz LP); and *Swingin' Free*, by Sundance (jazz LP).

**STAR SONG RECORDS**, 2223 Strawberry, Pasadena TX 77502. (713)472-5563. President: Darrell A. Harris. Record company, music publisher and record producer. Works with artists and songwriters on contract; musicians on salary for in-house studio work. Pays negotiable royalty to artists on contract; standard royalty to songwriters on contract.
**Music:** Contemporary gospel. Recently released *Never Say Die*, by Petra (cntemporary gospel LP); and *Vigil*, by Kemper Crabb (contemporary gospel LP). Other artists include Craig Smith and Steve and Annie Chapman.

**STARBORN RECORDS**, Box 2950, Hollywood CA 90078. (213)662-3121 (office); 850-2500 (studio). Producer: Brian Ross. Record company, record producer, music publisher (Brian Ross Music/BMI, Thrush Music/BMI, IMC Music/ASCAP and New High Music/ASCAP); and worldwide record promotion, distribution, marketing and merchandising firm. Member AF of M, AFTRA, AIMP, CCC, NARAS and NARM. Releases 25-50 singles and 15-25 albums/year. Works with artists and songwriters on contract. Pays 50% "of all money earned by Starborn Records to artists and songwriters on contract"; statutory rate to publishers for each record sold.
**How to Contact:** Submit demo tape and lyric sheet. Prefers cassette with 1-6 songs on demo. "Print your name and address clearly on tape box *and* cassette. Include photo and short biography." SASE. Reports in 1 week.

# Close-up

**Brian Ross**
Producer/Publisher

"I spend approximately four months of every year outside the US developing relationships with record companies all over the world for the purpose of soliciting record contracts on behalf of my artists," says Brian Ross. Ross, President of L.A.-based Starborn Records International, Brian Ross Productions, and Brian Ross Music, is pictured here arriving in Cannes, France for the annual international music industry exposition MIDEM.

"The record industry is a 10 billion dollar-a-year industry *worldwide*," says Ross. "The US only accounts for forty percent of that business. I'm quite comfortable doing business internationally, going for the part of the market that is not in the US."

Ross came from a musical family; his father was a studio musician playing on sessions behind such greats as Frank Sinatra. Following the musical tradition, Ross studied classical music from age five, but at age twelve began playing in rock and roll bands. Then in 1966 he produced his first record, a session for the Music Machine, a group he'd found playing in an L.A. bowling alley. "We must have rehearsed ten thousand times," Ross recalls. "But that way I knew my budget, relatively small then, would carry me far. Once we were in the studio at RCA, there were no costly, time-wasting questions or experiments. All we had to do was lay down the tracks."

Today, Ross says, "I'm everything that is necessary to take a brand new act from the street level to a total entity. I am both a producer and a publisher, but, to complement that, I am also a creative and administrative individual. I wear those hats interchangeably as needed to service my artists and songwriters."

Ross who receives 750-1,500 tapes a week, says, "But first, I am a producer. Whatever I listen to, I listen to with the ears of a producer. I'm listening for something that is unique, innovative and extraordinary. I'm particularly looking for somebody who is a trend-setter, not a trend-follower. I don't want to cash in on somebody else's trends—I want to create the trends."

As for the necessity of living in a music center, Ross says: "I don't think success is indigenous to where one lives geographically. I think of myself as a clearinghouse for songs and artists, not only those from anywhere in the US, but from all parts of the world. Once I have a rapport with a client, I can do my job for them no matter where they live. It would be a rather cramped California if it were mandatory that every singer and songwriter and musician had to physically move to L.A. We'd probably all sink into the ocean."

**Music:** Mostly top 40/pop contemporary "with great hooks and good melodies and chord changes;" also all other types. Recently released "I'm on Fire," by The Muglestons (top 40/pop single); "Making Love," by Didi Anthony (top 40/pop single); "I Wish You the Best," by Robert Jason (MOR/top 40/pop single); and *Talk Talk*, by the Music Machine (new wave LP). Other artists include John Elias, Gary Rose, Papillon, the Brian Ross Orchestra and Biener & Scott.

*STARBURST RECORDS INC.**, Box 3072, Brooklyn NY 11202. (212)774-1008. President: Wallace D. Garrett. Record company, record producer and music publisher (Nelter Music Publishing Co.). Estab. 1982. Releases 3-4 singles and 2 albums/year. Works with artists and songwriters on contract; musicians on salary for in-house studio work. Pays standard royalty to artists on contract; statutory rate to publishers for each record sold.
**How to Contact:** Submit demo tape and lyric sheet or "we will attend showcases where songwriters and artists are performing." Prefers cassette with 3-5 songs on demo. SASE. Reports in 1-3 months.
**Music:** Mostly R&B, soul and dance; also C&W, jazz, Spanish and rock.
**Tips:** "We are looking for songs that touch the heart, songs so beautiful they will bring a tear to the eye. Dance-oriented songs must have good hooks, something that will make you hum it after you've heard it once."

**STARGEM RECORDS, INC.**, 43 Music Square East, Nashville TN 37203. (615)244-1025. President and A&R Director: Wayne Hodge. Record company, record producer and music publisher (Newwriters Music/BMI and Timestar Music/ASCAP). Works with artists and songwriters on contract; musicians on salary for in-house studio work. Pays 5-15% royalty to artists on contract; statutory rate to publishers for each record sold.
**How to Contact:** Write first about your interest, then submit demo tape and lyric sheet. Prefers 7½ ips reel-to-reel or cassette with 1-4 songs on demo. "Have clear recording and use new tape." SASE. Reports in 2 weeks.
**Music:** C&W (modern and MOR).

**STARK RECORDS & TAPE CO.**, 628 South St., Mount Airy NC 27030. (919)786-2865. Labels include Stark, Hello, Pilot and Sugarbear. Contact: Paul E. Johnson. Record company and music publisher (Tompaul Music Company/BMI, Broadcast Music). Releases 30 singles and 45 albums/year. Works with artists and songwriters on contract. Pays 10% royalty to artists on contract; statutory rate to publishers for each record sold.
**How to Contact:** Submit demo tape and lead sheet. Prefers 7½ ips reel-to-reel with 3-5 songs on demo. SASE. Reports in 1 month.
**Music:** Bluegrass, church/religious, C&W, folk, gospel, rock (country) and top 40/pop. Recently released "Fire on the Mountain" and "Pony Express" by Blue Ridge Mountain Boys (bluegrass singles); *I Surrender Dear*, by Chet Atkins (pop/instrumental LP); and "Bought Me a Farm in the Country" and "Wrong Side of Town," by the Country Cousins (country singles). Other artists include Bruce Evans, Jim Hodges, Eddie Johnson, Paul E. Johnson, Alan Westmoreland, Bobby L. Atkins, Randy Scott, Ralph E. Hill and Johnny Long.

**STARMAN RECORDS**, Box 20604, Sacramento CA 95820. (916)446-6301. President: Almerritt V. Covington. Record company, record producer and music publisher (Ultima Thule Music Publishing Co./BMI). Releases 1 single and 1 album/year. Works with artists on contract; musicians on salary for in-house studio work. Pays 20% residual to artists on contract; statutory rate to writers for each record sold.
**How to Contact:** "Submit SASE for material request form;" then submit demo tape and lyric sheet. Prefers cassette with 6-12 songs on demo. "Please type titles, leave leader space between songs and index numbers." SASE. Reports in 6 weeks.
**Music:** Church/religious, C&W, easy listening, gospel, jazz, MOR, R&B, rock (soft), soul and top 40/pop. Artists include Ray Raymond, Freddie Williams, New Testament Choir and Sunlight.

*STARTIME MUSIC**, Box 643, LaQuinta CA 92253. (714)564-4823. President: Fred Rice. Record producer and music publisher (Yo Yo Music/BMI). ASCAP. Releases 2-12 singles/year. Pays standard royalty.
**How to Contact:** Submit demo tape and lead sheet. Prefers cassette with 1-2 songs on demo. SASE. Reports in 6 weeks.
**Music:** Mostly novelty; also country, rock and top 40/pop. Recently released "White Lady," "Somebody Cares," and "Love Is Just a Touch Away," recorded by Rob Carter (MOR/contemporary singles).
**Tips:** "A song has to be built of 'flesh and blood—the rhythm is the skeleton, the musical theme is the flesh and the lyrics are the blood (the soul). Don't write a song, write a record! Must have *provocative* title, *repetitive* musical theme with *simple* word phrase lyrics, *identifiable* melody line, and, lastly, should have a *different sound*."

**Songwriter's Market '84**

*STREET TUNES LTD., 81 Harley House, Marylebone Road, London, NW1, England. 44-01-883-0775. Labels include Street Tunes and Techno Discs. A&R Manager/Producer: Steve Rowles. Record company, record producer, music publisher (Street Tunes, Ltd.) and artists management. Member PRS, MCPS. Releases 3 singles and 6 albums/year. Pays 8-14% royalty to artists and songwriters on contract; statutory rate to publishers for each record sold. Royalties paid to US songwriters and artists through US publishing or recording affiliate. Has not yet, but would listen to material from US songwriters and artists.
**How to Contact:** Submit demo tape and lyric sheet. Prefers 7½ ips reel-to-reel or cassette with 3-5 songs on demo. SAE and IRC. Reports in 2 weeks.
**Music:** Mostly rock and progressive; also dance-oriented, R&B, soul and top 40/pop. Recently released *Leaves in the Wind* and *Koss*, by Paul Kossoff (rock LPs); and *Endangered Species*, by Black Alice (rock LP). Other artists include Click, Nicky Moore, Nick Battle, Famous Names, Zen Attack, Shephard's Way and Fermulae One.

**SUN INTERNATIONAL CORP.**, 3106 Belmont Blvd., Nashville TN 37212. (615)385-1960. Labels include Plantation Records and SSS International Records. Professional Manager: Shelby Singleton. Record company, record producer and music publisher (Shelby Singleton Music, Prize Music). Member RIAA and NARAS. Releases 30 singles and 25 albums/year. Works with artists and songwriters on contract. Pays 8-15% royalty to artists on contract; statutory rate to publishers for each record sold.
**How to Contact:** Submit demo tape and lyric sheet. Send cassette along with self-addressed envelope. Prefers cassette with 1-3 songs on demo. SASE. Reports in 1 month.
**Music:** C&W, easy listening, MOR, easy rock and top 40/pop. Artists include Norris Treat, Orion, Rita Remington, Patti Page and Charlie Walker.
**Tips:** "Present professional demo along with lyrics and explanation of career-goals. Artists should have a working band."

**SUNBONNET RECORDS**, (formerly Beantown Records), 910 E. Maxwell St., Pensacola FL 32503. (904)438-2763. President: Earl Lett. Record company, record producer and music publisher (Beantown Publishing Co.). Member CMA. Releases 5 singles and 2 albums/year. Works with artists and songwriters on contract.
**How to Contact:** Write first about your interest. Prefers cassette demo. Does not return unsolicited material. Reports in 1 month.
**Music:** Mostly C&W; also R&B, soul and top 40/pop. Recently released "Room #2," "Almost All the Time," and "You're Gettin' Better," by Florida Bill (country singles). Other artists include Professor Lett and Earl Lett.

**SUN-RAY RECORDS**, 1662 Wyatt Pkwy., Lexington KY 40505. (606)254-7474. Labels include Sun-Ray and Sky-Vue Records. President: James T. Price. Record company and music publisher (Jimmy Price Music Publisher/BMI). Releases 9 singles/year. Works with songwriters on contract; musicians on salary for in-house studio work. Pays statutory rate to publishers for each record sold.
**How to Contact:** Submit demo tape or submit demo tape and lead sheet. Prefers 7½ ips reel-to-reel with 2-6 songs on demo. SASE. Reports in 3 weeks.
**Music:** Bluegrass (sacred or C&W), church/religious, C&W and gospel. Recently released "Truck Driver's Rock," by Virgil Vickers (single); "All Them Wifes," by Harold Montgomery (single); and "Flat Top Box," by Tommy Jackson (single). Other artists include James Mailicote, Charles Hall and Kenny Wade.
**Tips:** "We need songs with a good story along with rhyme and meter."

**SUNSET RECORDS, INC.**, 1577 Redwood Dr., Harvey LA 70058. (504)367-8501. Labels include Sunburst Records. President: George Leger. Record company, record producer, and music publisher (Country Legs Music/ASCAP and Golden Sunburst Music/BMI). Member CMA. Releases 5 singles/year. Works with artists and songwriters on contract. Pays 5% royalty to artists on contract.
**How to Contact:** Submit demo tape and lyric and lead sheet. Prefers 7½ ips reel-to-reel or cassette with 3-5 songs on demo. "Artists—send tape of vocal abilities and desires." SASE. Reports in 1 month.
**Music:** C&W, gospel, progressive country and R&B. Recently released "A Snowman for Christmas," by George Leger (country/Christmas single). Other artists include Larry Maynard.

**SUNSHINE SOUND ENTERPRISES, INC.**, 7764 N.W. 71st St., Miami FL 33166. (305)592-1014. Contact: Preliminary Screening Committee. Manager: Sherry Smith. Record company and music publisher. Releases 10-50 singles and 5-25 albums/year. Works with artists and songwriters on contract. Pays 4% minimum royalty to artists on contract; standard royalties to songwriters on contract.
**How to Contact:** Submit demo tape and lead sheet. Prefers cassette with 1-3 songs on demo. SASE. Reports in 6-8 weeks. "No reports issued unless material is accepted or unless we wish additional material for review."

Music: Dance, progressive, rock, soul and top 40/pop. Recently released "Dance Across the Floor," "Spark" and "Is It In" by Jimmy "Bo" Horne (R&B/pop/disco singles).

*THE SURREY SOUND RECORD LABEL LTD., 70 Kingston Rd., Leatherhead, Surrey, England. 44-3723-79444. A&R Director: Mike Cobb. Record company, record producer and music publisher (Sesame Songs, Ltd.). Member PRS (Sesame Songs Ltd.). Works with artists and songwriters on contract. Pays 6-8% royalty (first year) to artists on contract; 6-25% to publishers for each record sold. Royalties paid directly to US songwriters and artists. Has not yet, but would listen to material from US songwriters and artists.
How to Contact: Submit demo tape and lyric sheet. Prefers cassette with 1-5 songs on demo. SAE and IRC. Reports in 3 weeks.
Music: Mostly rock (hard and country) and top 40/pop; also dance-oriented, easy listening, MOR, R&B and "anything unusual or gimmicky." Recently released *Contact You*, by Fay Ray (rock LP); "Are You Waiting," by Angie Rox (modern pop single); and "McEnroe," by Vic Ropejump (gimmick single). Other artists include Energy (English rock band), Reactors (English rock), and Mike Carter (MOR).
Tips: "We are an independent company and although we have a lot of experience in producing rock, we are always looking for something new and different. It doesn't matter how different—we'll *always* listen."

SUSAN RECORDS, Box 4740, Nashville TN 37216. (615)865-4740. Labels include Denco Records. A&R Director: Russ Edwards. Record company and music publisher. Releases 2-20 singles and 1-5 albums/year. Works with artists and songwriters on contract. Pays 6¢/record to artists on contract. Buys some material outright; payment varies.
How to Contact: Submit demo tape and lead sheet. Prefers 7½ ips reel-to-reel with 1-6 songs on demo. SASE. Reports in 2 weeks.
Music: Blues, C&W, dance, easy listening, folk, gospel, jazz, MOR, rock, soul and top 40/pop.

*SWEET CITY RECORDS, 28001 Chagrin Blvd., Cleveland OH 44122. (216)464-5990. Labels include Sweet City and BMO. President: Catll Madutli. Record company, record producer, music publisher (BEMA Music, AMEB Music) and manager. Releases 8 singles and 4 albums/year. Works with artists and songwriters on contract; musicians on salary for in-house studio work. Pays 2-5% royalty to artists on contract; statutory rate to publishers for each record sold.
How to Contact: Submit demo tape and lyric sheet. Prefers cassette with 2-3 songs on demo. SASE. Reports "only when interested."
Music: Mostly R&B and rock; also church/religious, dance-oriented, gospel and soul. Recently released "Ah! Leah," by Donnie Iris (rock single); "Mandolay," by La Plavour (dance 12" single); and "He Can't Love You," by Michael Stancey (rock/pop single). Other artists include Karen Jackson (a/c), Swankk (R&B), Primary Colors (rock) and B.E. Taylor (rock).

TAKE HOME TUNES, Box 1314, Englewood Cliffs, NJ 07632. Lables include Broadway Baby and Original Cast Records. Contact: Doris Chu Yeko. Branch office: Box 10051, Beverly Hills CA 90213. (213)761-2646 and 998-9839. Record company and music publisher (The Chu Yeko Musical Foundation/BMI, Broadway/Hollywood International Music Publishers/ASCAP). Releases 8-10 albums/year. Works with artists and songwriters on contract. Royalty payment varies for artists on contract; pays 5-10% royalty to songwriters on contract.
How to Contact: Submit demo tape. Prefers cassette. SASE. Reports in 1 month.
Music: Mostly children's and Broadway-type show tunes; also pop, rock, R&B, C&W and MOR. Recently released *King of Hearts*, by Millicent Martin and Don Scardino; *Bring Back Birdie*, by Donald O'Connor and Chita Rivera; *81 Proof* and *Housewives Cantata*, by the Original cast (musical LPs).
Tips: "A produced original musical singer or group appearing in Los Angeles area with financial backing would increase an artist's or songwriter's chance of working with us."

TELESON-AMERICA, 62 Fairfax St., Somerville MA 02144. (617)776-2146. Labels include Grand Orgue, Motette-Ursina and Solist. Record company. Releases 20-30 albums/year. Works with artists on contract.
How to Contact: Write first about your interest. Prefers 7½ or 15 ips reel-to-reel as demo. SASE. Reports in 4 months.

---

**Market conditions are constantly changing! If this is 1985 or later, buy the newest edition of *Songwriter's Market* at your favorite bookstore or order directly from Writer's Digest Books.**

**Music:** Church/religious and classical (pipe organ). Artists include Pierre Labric, Marie-Andree Morisset-Balier, Heinz Bernhard Orlinski, Jean Langlais, Almut Rossler, Michel Morisset, Gunther Kaunzinger, Marie-Louise Jacquet-Langlais, Gaston Litaize, Hermann Harrassowitz, Johannes Ricken, Rosalinde Haas, Daniel Roth, Jean-Jacques Grunewald and Paul Wisskirchen.

**TELL INTERNATIONAL RECORD CO.**, Rt. 5, Box 368-A, Yakima WA 98903. (509)966-6334. President: Jerry Merritt. A&R Director: Hiram White. Record company. Works with artists on contract. Pays standard royalty to artists on contract.
**How to Contact:** Submit demo tape and lead sheet. Prefers cassette with 1-4 songs on demo. SASE. Reports in 1 month.
**Music:** Bluegrass, blues, C&W, disco, folk, jazz, MOR and rock. Recently released "Billie Joe" and "Georgia Wine," by Barbara Jean Taylor (C&W singles); and "I'm Too Shy," by Penny Stadler (C&W single).

*****TEROCK RECORDS**, Box 4740, Nashville TN 37216. (615)865-4740. Labels include Terock, Susan, Denco, Rock-A-Nash-A-Billy. Manager: S.D. Neal. Record company, record producer, and music publisher (Heavy Jamin' Music/ASCAP). "We also lease masters." Member ASCAP, BMI. Releases 4 singles and 3 albums/year. Works with artists and songwriters on contract. Pays 5-8% royalty to artists on contract; standard royalty to songwriters on contract.
**How to Contact:** Submit demo tape and lyric sheet. Prefers 7½ ips reel-to-reel or cassette with 3-6 songs on demo. SASE. Reports in 3 weeks.
**Music:** Mostly C&W and rockabilly; also bluegrass, blues, easy listening, folk, gospel, jazz, MOR, progressive, Spanish, R&B, rock, soul and top 40/pop. Recently released "That's Why I Love You," by Dixie Dee (C&W); "Born to Bum Around," by Curt Flemons (C&W); and "Big Heavy," by the Rhythm Rockers (rock).

**3 G'S INDUSTRIES**, 5500 Troost, Kansas City MO 64110. (816)361-8455. Labels include NMI, Cory, 3 G's and Chris C's Records. President: Eugene Gold. Record company and music publisher (3 G's Music Co., Gid-Gad Music/BMI). Releases 2 singles and 4 albums/year. Works with artists and songwriters on contract. Pays 3-5% royalty rate to artists on contract; standard royalty to songwriters on contract; statutory rate to publishers for each record sold.
**How to Contact:** Submit demo tape and lyric sheet. Prefers cassette with 4-6 songs on demo. SASE. Reports in 1 month.
**Music:** Mostly R&B and gospel; also jazz, MOR and soul. Recently released "Baby We Can Make It," by Ronnie and Vicky (R&B EP); "You Left Me at a Bad Bad Time," by Suspension (soul EP); and *City People* by Max Groone (jazz LP).

**TNA RECORDS**, 10 George St., Box 57, Wallingford CT 06492. (203)269-4465. A&R Director: Douglas Snyder. Record company, record producer, music publisher (Rohm Music, Linesider Music, BIG Music) and personal management. Releases 2-4 albums/year. Works with artists and songwriters on contract. Pays 15-75% royalty to artists on contract; statutory rate to publishers for each record sold.
**How to Contact:** Submit demo tape and lyric sheet. Include statement of goals and purposes. Prefers cassette with 2-6 songs on demo. SASE. Reports in 2 weeks.
**Music:** Mostly rock and soul; also blues, dance-oriented, R&B and top 40/pop. Recently released *The B. Willie Smith Band* and *World's Favorite Songs* by B. Willie Smith (R&B LPs); and *Bob Mel*, by B. Mel (rock/pop LP). Other artists include Christine Ohlman and the Soul Rockers.
**Tips:** "Artists and songwriters should have high code of ethics coupled with enthusiasm. Being in Connecticut area helps with communication in management and direction."

**TOUCHE RECORDS**, Box 96, El Cerrito CA 94530. Executive Vice President: James Bronson, Jr. Record company, record producer (Mom and Pop Productions, Inc.) and music publisher (Toulouse Music Co./BMI). Member AIMP. Works with artists and songwriters on contract; musicians on salary for in-house studio work. Pays statutory rate to publishers for each record sold.
**How to Contact:** Submit demo tape and lyric sheet. Prefers cassette with 2-4 songs on demo. SASE. Reports in 1 month.
**Music:** Bluegrass, gospel, jazz, R&B and soul. Artists include Les Oublies du Jazz Ensemble.

*****TRANSCITY RECORDS**, 765 Bennaville, Birmingham MI 48009. (313)540-4532. Labels include American Hotel. President: Scott Forman. Record company and music publisher (Motorbeat Music/BMI). Estab. 1981. Releases 5 singles and 10 albums/year. Works with artists and songwriters on contract. Pays 6-15% royalty to artists on contract; 3-4¢ to publishers for each record sold.
**How to Contact:** Submit demo tape and lyric sheet or call about your interest. Prefers 7½ ips reel-to-reel or cassette with 3-6 songs on demo. SASE. Reports in 3 weeks.

**Music:** Mostly dance-oriented rock and new music rock; also progressive and soul. Recently released *Pacquet De Cinq*, by Rhythm Corps (new music/rock mini LP); *The Automatix*, by the Automatix (top 40 rock mini LP); and "The Whip," by The Urbations (R&B/Ska/new music single). Other artists include Figures on a Beach, Circuit Two and Via Satellite.

**TREND RECORDS**, Box 201, Smyrna GA 30081. (404)432-2454. Labels include Trendsetter, Atlanta and Stepping Stone Records. President: Tom Hodges. Record company, music publisher, record producer and management firm. Releases 6-10 singles and 2-8 albums/year. Works with artists on contract. Pays 5-7% royalty to artists on contract: standard royalty to songwriters on contract.
**How to Contact:** Submit demo tape and lead sheet. Prefers cassette with 3-6 songs on demo. SASE. Reports in 3 weeks.
**Music:** Bluegrass, C&W, gospel, MOR, rock and soul. Recently released *Feet*, by Jim Single (C&W single and LP), "Sugar Daddy," by Frank Brannon (C&W single); and "Kennesaw Get Your Guns." Other artists include Jo Anne Johnson.

**TRIANGLE RECORDS, INC.**, 824 19th Ave. S., Nashville TN 37203. Product Coordinator: Lynn Phillips. Executive Vice President: Elwyn Raymer. Record company and music publisher (Triune Music/ASCAP, Timespan Music/BMI, Nova Press/SESAC). Releases 3-6 singles/year and 2-5 albums/year. Works with artists and songwriters on contract. Pays negotiable royalty to artists on contract; statutory rate to publishers for each record sold.
**How to Contact:** Submit demo tape and lead sheet. Prefers 7½ ips reel-to-reel or cassette with 1-3 songs on demo. SASE. Reports in 2 months.
**Music:** Children's, choral, church/religious, classical and gospel. Recently released *Finest Hour*, by Cynthia Clawson (sacred MOR LP). Other artists include Bob Bailey, Ragan Courtney and Tina English.

**TRUCKER MAN RECORDS**, Centerline Rd., Cruz Bay, St. John VI 00830. (809)776-6814. Manager: Amory Saunders. Labels include One Number 18 Records. President: Llewellyn Adrian Sewer. Record company, music publisher, record producer, management firm and booking agency (Trucker Man Music/BMI). Releases 5-20 singles and 2-10 albums/year. Works with musicians on salary; artists and songwriters on contract. Pays 5-10% royalty to artists on contract; standard royalties to songwriters on contract.
**How to Contact:** Submit demo tape and lead sheet, or submit lead sheet. Prefers cassette with 2-4 songs on demo. SASE. Reports in 3 weeks.
**Music:** Church/religious, dance, R&B, soul and top 40/pop. Recently released *Soca by Bus*, by Lord Ranger; *The World Needs Love*, by Star Shield; *Born Again* and *World*, by Eddie and the Movements; and *Ambush Them*, by Reality. Other artists include Ras Abijah and Imaginations.

***TRUE NORTH RECORDS**, The Finkelstein Management Co. Ltd., Suite 2B, 98 Queen St. E, Toronto, Ontario, Canada M5C 1S6. (416)364-6040. Professional Manager: Jehanne Languedoc (Shan). Record company, management company, record producer, music publisher (Mummy Dust Music) and production company. Member CIRPA, CMPA, PROCAN, CAPAC. Releases approximately 11 singles and 4 albums/year. Works with artists on contract. Pays negotiable royalty to artists on contract; negotiable rate to publishers for each record sold.
**How to Contact:** Call about your interest. Prefers cassette with 2-4 songs on demo. Include bio. SASE. Reports in 1 month but demo tape will not be returned.
**Music:** Top 40/pop. Recently released *For Those Who Think Young*, and *Shaking the Foundations*, both by Rough Trade (pop LPs); *Humans*, *Inner City Front*, *The Trouble With Normal*, and "Dancing in the Dragons Jaws," all by Bruce Cockburn (pop LPs and single). Other artists includes Murray McLauchlan and Tony Kosinec.

**TRUSTY RECORDS**, Rt. 1, Box 100, Nebo KY 42441. (502)249-3194. President: Elsie Childers. Record company and music publisher (Trusty Publications/BMI). Member NSAI, CMA. Releases 2-3 singles/year. Works with artists and songwriters on contract. Pays 2% royalty to artists on contract; statutory rate to publishers for each record sold.
**How to Contact:** Submit demo tape and lead sheet. Prefers 7½ ips reel-to-reel or cassette with 2-4 songs on demo. SASE. Reports in 1 month.
**Music:** Mostly country; also blues, church/religious, dance, easy listening, folk, gospel, MOR, soul and top 40/pop. Recently released "Why I Shot the Sheriff," and "The State Police & The Money Man Band," by Southern Comfort (country singles). Other artists incude Jamie Bowles, Tim Emery & Legacy, Tracy White and Randy Hudson.
**Tips:** "Send clear sounding demos."

**TSR, INC.**, 3436 Sansom St., Philadelphia PA 19104. (215)386-5998. Vice President, Promotion: Rodney Burton. Director of Promotion: Alexandra Scott. Record company, record producer and music publisher (Third Story Music, City Surfer Music, Inc.). Releases 3 singles and 10 albums/year.
**How to Contact:** Submit demo tape and lyric sheet. Prefers cassette with 1-4 songs on demo. SASE. Reports in 1 month.
**Music:** Blues (rock), choral (gospel), church/religious, C&W, dance-oriented, easy listening, gospel, jazz, MOR, R&B, rock (all kinds), soul and top 40/pop.

**TYMENA MUSIC**, 430 Pearce Rd., Pittsburgh PA 15234. (412)341-0991. Labels include Tolrone and TyLemley Music (ASCAP). President: Ty Lemley. Vice President: Tolmena Lemley. General Manager: Bud Lemley. Record company and record producer. BMI. Member AFM, AFTRA, AGVA, CMA. Works with artists on contract. Pays standard royalty to artists on contract; statutory rate to publishers for each record sold.
**How to Contact:** Submit demo tape or 45 record and lyric sheet. Prefers cassette as demo. SASE. Reports in 1 month.
**Music:** C&W, easy listening, MOR and top 40/pop. Recently released "Offer Me Your Love," by Ty Lemley (top 40/pop single); "Me and You," by T. Lemley (rock single); "Ramblin' Ways," by T. Lemley (country single); and "One Day At a Time," by T. Lemley (MOR single).

*****TYSCOT RECORDS**, 3403 N. Ralston Ave., Indianapolis IN 46218. (317)926-6271. A&R Director: Brenda Carhee. Record company, record producer and music publisher (Tyscot, Inc./ASCAP, Clark Publishing/BMI). Releases 6 singles and 3 albums/year. Works with artists and songwriters on contract. Pays negotiable royalty to artists on contract.
**How to Contact:** Submit demo tape and lyric sheet. Prefers cassette with 4 songs on demo. SASE. Reports in 1 month.
**Music:** Mostly gospel and soul; also church/religious, dance-oriented, jazz and R&B. Recently released *Hold Out*, by Robert Turner (gospel LP); "Flam," by Ricky Clark (dance-oriented 12''); and "I Wish" b/w "Come on Around," by Terry Huff (soul single). Other artists include Truth and Devotion, The Bishop's Choir, Pentecostal Ambassadors, Christ Church Radio Choir and Circle City Band.

**UNIVERSAL-ATHENA RECORDS**, Box 3615, Peoria IL 61614. (309)673-5755. A&R Director: Jerry Hanlon. Record company and music publisher (Jerjoy Music/BMI). Works with artists and songwriters on contract; musicians on salary for in-house studio work. Pays statutory rate to publishers for each record sold.
**How to Contact:** Submit demo tape and lyric sheet. Prefers cassette with 4-8 songs on demo. SASE. Reports in 2 weeks.
**Music:** C&W. Recently released *Memories*, by Jerry Hanlon (country LP). Other artists include Robby Hull.

**UNREGULATED RECORD CO., INC.**, Box 81485, Fairbanks AK 99708. (907)456-3419. Labels include Lift Records. President: Michael States. Record company, record producer and music publisher (Unregulated Music/BMI). Releases 3 singles and 3 albums/year. Works with artists and songwriters on contract. Pays negotiable royalty to artists on contract; statutory rate to publishers for each record sold.
**How to Contact:** Submit demo tape and lyric sheet. Prefers cassette with 2-5 songs on demo. SASE. Reports in 1 month.
**Music:** Gospel (avant garde, soul, reggae). Recently released *Beat the Cynics*, by Cynics (new wave gospel LP); and *Christmas with Jesus*, by Lily of the Valley Choir (new wave/black gospel LP). Other artists include Marty Beggs, Paul Porter, Spoon, Pat Fitzgerald, Robyn Hood, Richard Jesse and the Movement.

*****UPSTART RECORDS**, 2210 Rapier Blvd., Arlington TX 76013. (817)461-8481. Labels include Made In Texas. President: Charles Stewart. Record company, record producer and music publisher (Upstart Music/BMI). Estab. 1982. Member NARM. Releases 4 singles and 4 albums/year. Works with artists and songwriters on contract; musicians on salary for in-house studio work. Pays 6.5-8% royalty to artists on contract; statutory rate to publishers for each record sold.
**How to Contact:** Submit demo tape and lyric sheet. Prefers cassette with 1-6 songs on demo. "Have name, address and phone number on cassette." SASE. Reports in 3 weeks.
**Music:** Mostly C&W; also blues, R&B and rock. Recently released *Aerobics Country*, by Pam Pilarcik (exercise LP); and *Country Dance Lessons*, by Weldon & Laree Bryant (instructional LP). Other artists include Danny Wood.

*****URBAN ROCK RECORDS**, 427 W. 51st St., New York NY 10019. (212)246-7516. Operations Director: Keith Carlos. Record company, record producer and music publisher (Cousin Ice). Releases 6

singles and 6 albums/year. Works with artists on contract. Pays negotiable royalty to artists on contract; statutory rate to publishers for each record sold.
**How to Contact:** Submit demo tape and lyric sheet. Prefers 7½ ips reel-to-reel or cassette with 5-10 songs on demo. SASE. Reports in 1 month.
**Music:** Mostly soul; also dance-oriented, jazz (fusion), rock (contemporary) and top 40/pop. Recently released *Cousin Ice*, by Cousin Ice (fusion LP); "Catch Your Glow," by Cousin Ice (top 40 single); and "Last Chance," by Splashband (dance single). Other artists include Diva Gray.
**Tips:** "Submit a feeling, not just a formula."

**VAMPLE RECORD, INC.**, Box 23152, Kansas City MO 64141. Labels include Vamp Recording Co., JerryCo Records. President/General Manager: Jerry Vample. Record company, record producer and music publisher (Jerry Vample Publishing Co./BMI). Releases 4 singles and 2 albums/year. Works with artists and songwriters on contract. Pays standard royalty to artists on contract; statutory rate to publishers for each record sold.
**How to Contact:** Submit demo tape and lyric sheet. Prefers 7½ ips reel-to-reel or cassette with 2-4 songs on demo. SASE. Reports in 1 month.
**Music:** Church/religious, easy listening and gospel.

**VELVET PRODUCTIONS**, 517 W. 57th St., Los Angeles CA 90037. (213)753-7893. Labels include Velvet, Kenya, Normar and Stoop Down Records. Manager: Aaron Johnson. Record company, booking agency and promoter. BMI. Releases 3 singles and 2 albums/year. Works with artists and songwriters on contract. Pays 5% royalty to artists on contract.
**How to Contact:** Submit demo tape, arrange personal interview, submit demo tape and lead sheet, or submit lead sheet. Prefers cassette with 3-5 songs on demo. SASE. Reports in 2 months.
**Music:** Blues, gospel, rock, soul and top 40/pop. Recently released "I Wanna Be Loved" and "How I Wish," by Arlene Bell (disco singles); "Love Stealing Ain't Worth the Feeling," by Chuck Willis (blues single); and "Two Sides to Every Coin," and "It's About Time I Made a Change," by A. Bell.

**\*VENTURE/TONY CAMILLO**, 121 Meadowbrook Dr., Somerville NJ 08876. (201)359-5110. Labels include Venture. Coordinator: Ronnie Mack. Record company, record producer and music publisher (Etude, Barcaw). Releases 50 singles and 10 albums/year. Works wth aritists and songwriters on contract; musicians on salary for in-house studio work. Pays negotiable royalty to artists on contract; negotiable rate to publishers for each record sold.
**How to Contact:** Submit demo tape and lyric sheet. Prefers reel-to-reel or cassette wth maximum 3 songs on demo. SASE. Reports in 1 month.
**Music:** R&B, rock, soul and top 40/pop. Recently released "Midnight Train," by G. Knight.

**VILLAGE RECORDS, INC.**, #4, 6325 Guilford Ave., Indianapolis IN 46270. (317)251-5878. Vice President/General Manager: Terry Barnes. Record company and music publisher (Canal Publishing). Member AFM. Releases 5-10 singles and 4-5 albums/year. Works with artists and songwriters on contract. Pays statutory rate to publishers for each record sold.
**How to Contact:** Submit demo tape and lyric sheet. Prefers cassette with 1-4 songs on demo. SASE. Reports in 1 month.
**Music:** Country, easy listening, MOR, rock and top 40/pop. Recently released *Rock N Romance*, by Faith Band (top 40/pop LP); "Dancin Shoes," by Faith Band (ballad single); *Sweet Music*, by Roadmaster (rock LP); and "Wolly Bully," by Adam Smasher (rock single).

**VOICE BOX RECORDS**, 5180-B Park Ave., Memphis TN 38119. (901)761-5074. President: Mark Blackwood. Record company, record producer and music publisher (Song From The Box/BMI, Voice Of Paradise/ASCAP). Releases 10 singles and 6 albums/year. Works with artists and songwriters on contract. Pays 50% royalty to artists on contract; statutory rate to publishers for each record sold.
**How to Contact:** Submit demo tape and lyric sheet. Prefers cassette. "Be sure that *both* demo tape and lyric sheet are provided." Does not return unsolicited material. Reports in 1 month.
**Music:** Christian. "We record and produce primarily Christian MOR style of music and artists." Recently released *I'm Following You*, and *We Come to Worship*, by Blackwood Brothers (both Christian singles and LPs); *Conclusions*, by Larry Orrell (Christian single and LP); "Life Time Friend," by L. Orrell (Christian single;) "Vessel of Love," by Lindy Hearne; and "Lord I Need Your Love," by Geanne Johnston.

**VOKES MUSIC PUBLISHING & RECORD CO.**, Box 12, New Kensington PA 15068. (412)335-2775. Labels include Vokes and Country Boy Records. President: Howard Vokes. Record company, booking agency and music publisher. Releases 8 singles and 5 albums/year. Works with artists and songwriters on contract. Pays 2½-4½¢/song royalty to artists and songwriters on contract.

**How to Contact:** Submit demo tape and lead sheet. Cassette only. SASE. Reports in 2 weeks.
**Music:** Bluegrass, C&W and gospel. Recently released *Songs of Broken Love Affairs* and *Tears at the Grand Ole Op'ry*, by Howard Vokes; *Hank Williams Isn't Dead*, by Denver Duke and Jeffery Null; *Ballad of Johnny Horton*, by Hank King, Jimmy Parker, Larry Dale and Rudy Thacker; and *Billy Wallace Sings His Hits*, by B. Wallace.

***W&G RECORD PROCESSING CO., PTY.**, 17 Radford Road Reservoir, Victoria, 3073, Australia. 61-03-4604522. Labels include W&G and Gem. Affiliates/US: Melbourne Records and Jaspar Music. Director: Ron Gillespie. Record company, record producer and music publisher (Woomera Music Pty.). Works with artists on contract. Pays 3-7½% royalty to artists on contract; 6% to publishers for each record sold. Royalties paid to US songwriters and artists through US publishing or recording affiliate. Willing to listen to songs submitted by US songwriters and artists only when submitted through US affiliates.
**How to Contact:** Write first. Prefers cassette with 1-3 songs on demo. SAE and IRC. Reports in 1 month.
**Music:** Mostly MOR; also children's, choral, church/religious, C&W, dance-oriented, easy listening, folk, gospel, rock and top 40/pop.

**WALTNER ENTERPRISES**, 14702 Canterbury, Tustin CA 92680. (714)731-2981. Labels include Calico and Daisy. President: Steve Waltner. Record company and music publisher (Early Bird Music/BMI). Releases 6-8 singles and 2 albums/year. Works with musicians and songwriters on contract. Pays 5-10% royalty to artists on contract; standard royalty to songwriters on contract; pays statutory rate to publishers for each record sold.
**How to Contact:** Submit demo tape and lead sheet. Prefers 7½ ips reel-to-reel or cassette with 2-4 songs on demo. SASE. Reports in 3 weeks.
**Music:** C&W, easy listening, MOR and top 40/pop. Recently released "Will You Be Here in the Morning," by Jason Chase (country/pop single); "Country's Here to Stay," by Steve Shelby (country single); and "Slim & Lefty," by Lester Cash (country novelty single).

**WAM MUSIC CORP., LTD.**, 901 Kenilworth Rd., Montreal, Quebec, Canada H3R 2R5. (514)341-6721. Labels include WAM and Disques Pleiade Records. President: Leon Aronson. Record company, music publisher and record producer. Works with artists and songwriters on contract. Pays 5% minimum royalty to artists on contract; standard royalty to songwriters on contract.
**How to Contact:** Query or submit demo tape and lead sheet. Prefers 7½ ips reel-to-reel tape with 1-4 songs on demo. SAE and IRC. Reports in 3 weeks.
**Music:** Dance, MOR, rock and top 40/pop. Recently released "Savin' It Up," by Marty Butler (MOR single); and *Entre Nous*, by Diane Tell (pop LP). Other artists include Basic Black and Pearl, Carlyle Miller and 1945.

**WARNER BROTHERS RECORDS, INC.**, 3300 Warner Blvd., Burbank CA 91510. (213)846-9090. Contact: A&R Coordinator. Record company. Works with artists and songwriters on contract.
**How to Contact:** Submit demo tape. Prefers 7½ ips reel-to-reel or cassette as demo. SASE. Reports in 8 weeks.
**Music:** Bluegrass, blues, children's, choral, church/religious, C&W, disco, easy listening, folk, gospel, jazz, MOR, progressive, R&B, rock, soul and top 40/pop.

***WATTS CITY RECORDS**, 11211 Wilmington Ave., Los Angeles CA 90059. (213)566-9982. Labels include Watts City and Melatone. President/Producers: Joe Fornnis. Record company, record producer and music publisher (Watts City Productions/ASCAP). Releases 5 singles and 2 albums/year. Works with artists and songwriters on contract. Pays 6% royalty to artists on contract; statutory rate to publishers for each record sold.
**How to Contact:** Submit demo tape and lyric sheet. Prefers cassette with 4-12 songs on demo. SASE. Reports in 3 weeks.
**Music:** R&B, soul and top 40/pop.

***WEA MUSIC OF CANADA, LTD.**, 1810 Birchmount Rd., Scarborough, Ontario, Canada M1P 2J1. (416)291-2515. Labels include Warner Bros., Elektra, Atlantic Reprise, Sire, Bearsville, ECM, Geffen, Island, Qwest, Asylum, Nonesuch, Solar, Atco, Mirage, Rolling Stones and Swan Song. A&R Manager: Bob Roper. Record company and music publisher (Don Valley Music, Home Cooked Music). Member CRIA, CARAS. Releases 250 singles and 300 albums/year. Works with artists on contract. Pays negotiable royalty to artists on contract; negotiable rate to publishers for each record sold.
**How to Contact:** Submit demo tape and lyric sheet. Prefers cassette with 4-6 songs on demo. Include photos, bio and any other pertinent information. SASE. Reports in 1 month.

**Music:** Mostly rock and top 40/pop; also classical, country, dance-oriented, easy listening, folk, jazz, MOR, progressive, R&B and soul. Recently released *Hello, I Must Be Going*, by Phil Collins (rock LP); *Trans*, by Neil Young (MOR/folk); and *Another Page*, by Christopher Cross (top 40/pop LP).

*WEBCO RECORDS & RECORDING STUDIO, 8705 Deanna Dr., Gaithersburg MD 20879. (301)253-5962 or 251-1285. President: Wayne E. Busbice. Record company, record producer and music publisher (Old Home Place Music). Member CMA. Releases 4-6 singles and 8 albums/year. Works with artists and songwriters on contract. Pays 40% royalty (after costs) to artists on contract; statutory rate to publishers for each record sold.
**How to Contact:** Write about your interest. Prefers cassette with 3-5 songs on demo. SASE. Reports in 1 month.
**Music:** Mostly bluegrass; also C&W. Recently released *Buzz Busby-A Pioneer of Tradition with Bluegrass*, by Buzz Busby (bluegrass LP); *Carl Nelson & His Fiddle on Pine Lake*, by Carl Nelson (fiddle & bluegrass LP); and *The Bluegrass Sounds of Buzz Busby*, by B. Busby (bluegrass LP). Other artists include Darrell Sanders, Blackthorn Stick, The Grass Reflection, Bill Rouse & The Uptown Grass Band, Brooke Johns and Jack Finchton & The Dixie Grass.

**WESJAC RECORD ENTERPRISES,** 129 W. Main St., Box 743, Lake City SC 29560. (803)394-3712. A&R Director: W.R. Bragdton Jr. Record company and music publisher (Wesjac Music/BMI). Releases 3 singles/year. Works with artists on contract; musicians on salary for in-house studio work. Pays 5% royalty to artists and songwriters on contract; pays statutory rate to publishers for each record sold.
**How to Contact:** Submit demo tape and lead sheet. Prefers 7 3/8 or 15 ips reel-to-reel with 2 songs minimum on tape. SASE. Reports in 1 month.
**Music:** Church/religious and gospel. Recently recorded "If You Want See Jesus" and "We Call Him Jesus," by The Exciting Linen Singers (singles); "In Your Hands" and "Walk on and Let It Alone," by Jeremiah Ensemble (singles); and "The New Testament Fulfill the Old Testament" and "Forgive and Be Forgiven," by Evangelist Katie Gamble and The True Gospel Singers (singles). Other artists include The Burgess Sisters and Royal Travelers.

*W/G RECORD CO., 991 Oak St., West Barnstable MA 02668. (617)362-4908. Labels include Welchy Grape Records. President: Mike Welch. Record company, record producer and music publisher (WelchyGrape Publishing). Releases 2 singles and 1 album/year. Works with songwriters on contract.
**How to Contact:** Submit demo tape and lyric sheet or write about your interest. Prefers cassette or records with 10 songs on demo. SASE. Reports in 1 month.
**Music:** C&W, easy listening, folk/rock, MOR, rock (country and hard) and top 40/pop. Recently released *Renovations*, by Mike Welch (MOR LP); *Resurgence*, (MOR/rock LP); "Everybody Knows," (MOR single); and "Turning Point," (rock single) all by Mike Welch and Renovations Band.

*WHEELSVILLE RECORDS, INC., 17544 Sorrento, Detroit MI 48235. (313)342-6884. Labels include Wheelsville and Purcal Records. President: Will Hatcher. Contact: Sharon Hatcher and Theresa Hatcher. Record company and music publisher.
**How to Contact:** Submit demo tape and lead sheet. Prefers cassettes with 2-4 songs on demo. SASE. Reports in 2 weeks.
**Music:** Dance, gospel, soul and top 40/pop.

**WHITE ROCK RECORDS, INC.,** 401 Wintermantle Ave., Scranton PA 18505. (717)343-6718. President: Phil Ladd. Record company, music publisher and record producer. Releases 4-16 singles and 2-4 albums/year.
**How to Contact:** Query or submit demo tape and lead sheet. Prefers cassette with 2 songs minimum on demo. SASE. Reports in 3 weeks.
**Music:** Children's, C&W, easy listening, R&B, rock and top 40/pop. Recently released "Drummer," by Frantic Freddy (rock single); and "Ain't Misbehavin'," by Evra Bailey (MOR single).

**MARTY WILSON PRODUCTIONS, INC.,** 185 West End Ave., New York NY 10023. (212)580-0255. Labels include D&M Sound and Cyma Records. Assistant to the President: Janet J. Eddy. Record company and music publisher. Works with songwriters on contract; musicians on salary for in-house work. Payment varies for artists on contract; pays standard royalty to songwriters on contract.
**How to Contact:** Submit demo tape and lead sheet. Prefers 7 1/2 or 15 ips reel-to-reel or cassette with 1-3 songs on demo. SASE. Reports in 1 month.
**Music:** Easy listening, jazz, MOR and top 40/pop. Recently released "Love for Sale," by the Vast Majority (single); "Boop Boop a Hustle," by Camp Galore (single); and "Help Is on the Way," by Tanden Hayes (single).

**WILWIN RECORDS**, Box 1669, Carlsbad CA 92008. (619)729-8406. Contact: Denny Tymer. Record company and music publisher (Tymer Music/BMI). Works with artists and songwriters on contract. Pays 5-9% royalty to artists on contract; standard royalty to songwriters on contract; pays statutory rate to publishers for each record sold.
**How to Contact:** Arrange personal interview or submit demo tape and lead or lyric sheet. Prefers 7½ ips reel-to-reel or cassette with 1-3 songs on demo. "Demos should be simple and each song should not be over 3 minutes, 20 seconds long. Put leader between each song on tape." SASE. Reports in 3 weeks.
**Music:** C&W and top 40/pop. Recently released *It's About Tymer*, by Denny Tymer (C&W LP).
**Tips:** "We work with musicians according to the American Federation of Musicians (AFM) Phonographic Labor Agreement, and with vocal background singers in agreement with the American Federation of Television and Radio Artists (AFTRA). Listen to current country chart songs, especially the ballad type and write songs with simple, but strong lyrics that fit the trends. We are looking for original commercial country songs not only for Wilwin Records, but also for other artists and non-affiliated record labels."

***THE WORD RECORD AND MUSIC GROUP**, Box 2130, North Hollywood CA 91602. (213)5808-5550. A&R Director: Gary Whitlock. Record company and music publisher (Word Music/ASCAP, Dayspring Music/BMI). Member RIAA, NARAS. Releases 70 albums/year. Works with artists and songwriters on contract. Pays statutory rate to publishers for each record sold.
**How to Contact:** Call about your interest—"*no* unsolicited tapes, please." Prefers cassette with maximum of 3 songs on demo. SASE. Reports in 1 month.
**Music:** Mostly contemporary gospel; also choral and church/religious. Recently released "Age to Age," by Amy Grant; "Home Where I Belong," by B.J. Thomas; and "Stand By the Power," by the Imperials (all contemporary gospel). Other artists include Bill Gaither, Trio, Mighty Clouds of Joy, Dion, Maria Muldaur, Leon Patillo and Benny Hester.
**Tips:** "Study the contemporary Christian market first. The lyrical and musical expectations are much greater than most people perceive gospel music to be."

***WOULD'N SHOE/L'ORIENT**, Box H, Harvard MA 01451. (617)456-8111. Labels include Would'n Shoe, L'Orient, Greenpeace, New Moon. A&R Coordinator: Joshua Green. Record company and music publisher (Bullet Management, It's A Hit Productions). Releases 2-5 singles and 2-3 albums/year. Works with artists and songwriters on contract. Pays minimum of 2% royalty to artists on contract; statutory rate to publishers for each record sold.
**How to Contact:** Submit demo tape and lyric sheet; write about your interest. Prefers 7½ ips reel-to-reel or cassette with 3-8 songs on demo. Does not return unsolicited material. Reports in 1 month.
**Music:** Mostly pop rock and country rock; also C&W and MOR. Recently released "Are Your Afraid of Falling?," by Estes Boys; and "Keep on Singing," by Dean Adrian. Recently distributed "Save the Whales," by Allen Estes (all pop singles). Other artists include Andy Watson Band.
**Tips:** Looking for "professionalism, hook, structure and presentation."

**XL RECORDS**, Box 14671, Memphis TN 38114. (901)774-1720. Labels include Jenny Records. A&R Director: Errol Thomas. Record company, record producer and music publisher (Beckie Music). Member NARAS. Releases 3 singles/year. Works with artists and songwriters on contract. Pays 3%-6% royalty to artists on contract; statutory rate to publisher for each record sold.
**How to Contact:** Submit demo tape and lyric sheet. Prefers 7½ ips reel-to-reel or cassette with 4-10 songs on demo. SASE. Reports in 2 weeks.
**Music:** R&B and soul. Recently released "Everybody Cried," and "I'd Love to Love You," by Rufus Thomas (R&B singles); and "Goodbye Lady," by Rayner Street Band (R&B single). Other artists include Louis Williams and the Ovations.

**YATAHEY RECORDS**, Box 31819, Dallas TX 75231. (214)750-0720. Contact: Pat McKool. A&R: Mike Anthony. Record company and music publisher. Works with artists and songwriters on contract. Pays 8% royalty to artists on contract.
**How to Contact:** Submit demo tape and lead sheet or submit demo tape and lyric sheet. Prefers 7½ ips reel-to-reel with 1-4 songs on demo. SASE. Reports in 1 month.
**Music:** C&W and gospel. Recently released "Catching Fire" and "Bluebirds," by Angela Kay (C&W single); and "Stompin' on My Heart," by Glen Bailey (C&W single).

**ZZYZX RECORDS**, Box 23, Sun Valley CA 91352. (213)982-2174. Contact: J. Eric Freedner. Record company and music producer (Boss Tweed Music). Releases 1 album/year. Works with songwriters on contract. Pays negotiable royalty to songwriters on contract; statutory rate to publishers for each record sold.

**How to Contact:** Write about your interest. Prefers 7½ ips reel-to-reel or cassettes with 1-5 songs on demo. SASE. Reports in 3 weeks.
**Music:** Folk, rock, country/humorous and novelty. Recently released *How'd We Ever Get Stuck Listening to This Guy?* by J. Eric Freedner (novelty LP); "Give Me All Your Love" (rock/new wave single); and "Goodbye" (rock/single), by Windjammer. Other artists include Larry Treadwell.

---

# Geographic Index

The US section of this handy geographic index will quickly give you the names of record companies located in the music centers of Los Angeles, Nashville and New York. The International section lists, geographically, markets for your songs in Australia, England and New Zealand.

Find the names of companies in this index, and then check listings within the Record Companies section for addresses, phone numbers and submission details.

## UNITED STATES

### LOS ANGELES
A&M Records, Inc.
Ambiente Music Productions, Inc.
Arista Records Inc.
Atlantic Recording Corp.
AVI Records, Inc.
Backstreet Records
Bee Gee/Birthright Records
Blue Island Records
Boyce & Powers Music
Capitol Records, Inc.
Carousel Records, Inc.
Chattahoochee Records
The Chu Yeko Musical Foundation
Creative Sound, Inc.
Dupuy Records/Productions/Publishing, Inc.
Grass Roots Record & Tape/LMI Records
Gule Record
Kneptune International Records
L.M.I. (Lee Magid, Inc.)
Little David Records, Inc.
Longhorn Records
Message Records
Music Adventures Records, Inc.
Mystic Records, Inc.
Pepp Records
RCA Records
Rockin! Records
Rollin' Rock Records
Slash Records
Sound Image Records
Starborn Records
Velvet Productions
Warner Brothers Records, Inc.
Watts City Records
The Word Record and Music Group

### NASHVILLE
AMI
Carrie Records Co.
Charta Records
Country International
Curtiss Records
Dimension Records
Door Knob Records
F&L Records
50 States Records & Tapes
Forever Records
Jalyn Recording Company
Landmark (Audio of Nashville)
The Little Giant Record Company
MCA Records
Melodee Records
Moon Shine Records
Morningstar Records
Nashboro Records
Plantation Records
Priority Records/CBS
R.E.F. Records
Rustic Records
Shiloh Records
Stargem Records, Inc.
Sun International Corp.
Susan Records
Terock Records
Triangle Records, Inc.

### NEW YORK
A&M Records Inc.
Anamaze Records
Apon Record Company, Inc.
Arista Records
Bente Record
Big Mike Music
Blue Sky Records
Buddah Records, Inc.
Bulldog Records
Capitol Records
Chrysalis Records, Inc.
Clearinghouse Records Corp.
Coast to Coast Records
Courrier Records
Date Line International Records
De-Lite Records
Factory Beat Records, Inc.
Glad-Hamp Records, Inc.
Jody Records
MCA Records
Millennium Records
Mustevic Sound, Inc.
Oat Willie Productions
Polygram Records
Prelude Records
Ra Jo International
RBI/Record Breakers International
Relix Records, Inc.
RFC Records
Right On Records
Salsoul Records
Sam Records
Sandcastle Records
Sire Records
SMI Records, Corp.
Spring Records
Starburst Records Inc.
Urban Rock Records
Marty Wilson Productions, Inc.

## INTERNATIONAL

**AUSTRALIA**
Laser Records
W&G Record Processing Co., Pty.

**ENGLAND**
Arista/Ariola Records
Bam-Caruso Records
Big Bear Records
CBS Records
Creole Records Ltd.
Dansan Records
Dawn Promotions and Agency, Ltd.
Esquire Records Talent Ltd.
The Flying Record Company Ltd.
Heavy Metal Records
Highway Records Ltd.
Jive Records
Le Matt Music Ltd.
Magnum Force Records and Music Ltd.
Nervous Records
New Hormones
New Music Enterprises
Oakwood Audio Productions
Orbit Records
Precious Records
Red Bus Records (International) Ltd.
Rondercrest Ltd.
Royal Records
Rutland Records
Scratch Records Ltd.
Street Tunes Ltd.
The Surrey Sound Record Label Ltd.

## The Quiet Types

In preparing *Songwriter's Market 1984*, we contacted all major American and Canadian record companies at least once—and in some cases, two or three times. Most responded. Some, however, did not give us information for one of the following reasons:
* They are not actively seeking new artists or material from songwriters.
* They *will* listen to material, but believe that they receive sufficient material without listing in *Songwriter's Market*.
* They are a branch office that concentrates on marketing or other business endeavors, and leaves selection of artists and songs to branches in other cities.
* They work only with artists or songwriters recommended to them from other sources.
* They are staffed with inhouse songwriters.
* They don't have a staff large enough to handle the increased number of submissions a listing would create.
* They are concerned with copyright problems that might result if they record a song similar to one they've reviewed and rejected.
* They have once listed with another songwriter directory and were deluged with inappropriate submissions.

Though some of the following firms will review material, we suggest that you *not* send demo tapes. Write a brief query letter describing your material and asking about the company's current submission policies. Always use a self-addressed, stamped envelope or post card for such queries (see sample reply form in "The Business of Songwriting").

ARC (see CBS).
Arista Records, Inc., 6 W. 57th St., New York NY.
Asylum (see Elektra/Asylum/Nonesuch).
Atlantic Recording Group, 75 Rockefeller Plaza, New York NY 10019.
Badlands (see CBS).
Birthright Records, 3101 S. Western Ave., Los Angeles 90018.
The Boardwalk Entertainment Co., 9884 Santa Monica Blvd., Beverly Hills CA 90212.
The Boardwalk Entertainment Co., 200 W. 58th St., New York NY 10019.
Capitol Records Inc., 29 Music Square E., Nashville TN 37203.
CBS Records Group, 1801 Century Park W., Los Angeles CA 90067.
CBS Records, Inc., 51 W. 52nd St., New York NY 10019.
CBS Records, Inc., 49 Music Square W., Nashville TN 37203.
Century Records, 6550 Sunset Blvd., Hollywood CA 90028.
Columbia (see CBS).
Elektra/Asylum/Nonesuch Records, 962 N. La Cienega, Los Angeles CA 90069.
Elektra/Asylum/Nonesuch Records, 1216 17th Ave. S., Nashville TN 37212.

# Record Companies 205

Elektra/Asylum/Nonesuch Records, 665 5th Ave., New York NY 10022.
EMI-America/Liberty Records, 6920 Sunset Blvd., Los Angeles CA 90028.
EMI-United Artists Records, 29 Music Square E., Nashville TN 37203.
EMI America/Liberty Records, 1370 Avenue of the Americas, New York NY 10019.
Epic (see CBS).
Full Moon (see CBS).
Geffen Records, 9130 Sunset Blvd., Los Angeles CA 90069.
Island Records, Inc., 444 Madison Ave., New York NY 10022.
Liberty (see EMI-America/Liberty).
MCA Records, 70 Universal City Plaza, Universal City CA 91608.
MCA Records, 10 E. 53rd St., New York NY 10022.
Mercury (see Polygram).
Modern Records, Suite 1102, 2 W. 45th St., New York NY 10036.
Monitor Recordings, Inc., 156 Fifth Ave., New York NY 10010.
Monument Record Corp., 21 Music Square E, Nashville TN 37203.
Motown Records Group, 6255 Sunset Blvd., Los Angeles CA 90028.
Planet Records, 5505 Melrose Ave., Los Angeles CA 90038.
Polydor Records, Inc. (see PolyGram Records, Inc.)
PolyGram Records, Inc., 3940 Overland Ave., Culver City CA 90230.
Polygram Records, Inc., 10 Music Circle S., Nashville TN 37203.
RCA Records, 1133 Avenue of the Americas, New York NY 10036.
RCA Records, 30 Music Square W., Nashville TN 37203.
Riva (see Polygram).
Rolling Stones (see Atlantic).
RSO Records, Inc., 1775 Broadway, New York NY 10019.
Tamla (see Motown).
Virgin (see CBS).
Warner Brothers Records, Inc., 1706 Grand, Nashville TN 37203.
Warner Brothers Records, Inc., 3 E. 54th St., New York NY 10022.

# Record Producers

The independent producer can best be described as a creative coordinator. He finds talented artists and songs for those artists to record. He handles every aspect of the recording session and pays for all this with his own money, hoping to recoup his costs by selling the finished master to a record company. For information on contracts between an independent producer and a recording artist, see "Contracts" in the Appendix of this book.

Since independent producers are well-acquainted with the record company executives and artists with whom they deal, they can often get your material through doors that are not open to you. This is especially important if you are an artist-songwriter looking for a recording contract.

The fact that an independent producer works for himself means he can be open to a variety of styles in material. And since he makes all the decisions in a project, you will usually be told right away if he does or doesn't like your songs and if he can use them in an upcoming session.

Many producers listed here are publishers and some also have management firms. This can work to your advantage in several ways. Those who are publishers will be looking for good songs, whether or not they need it for a particular artist—they can always shop it to another producer or record company. Those who are managers can easily recognize material one of their acts could use, and will have a good deal of influence in suggesting your material to them.

Some of the producers listed here are also record companies. These producers not only have their own recording facilities, but can also release your songs on their label.

Appearing in this section for the first time—as well as in the Music Publishers and Record Companies sections—are producers located in England. Each has expressed a willingness to work with songwriters and artists from the US (most already have); some indicate in their listings that they have not yet, but would be willing to listen to material from US songwriters and artists.

Individual listings will tell you what a producer is looking for and the artists he is working with. *Billboard* and *Cash Box* list the producers' names on their weekly top song charts.

If there is a producer whose name you can't find among the listings in this section, see "How to Be a Music Market Detective" in the Appendix of this book. There you can learn how to successfully track down any record producer, music publisher, record company, or even recording artist you think might be interested in your song.

\*ACCENT RECORDS, 71906 Highway 111, Rancho Mirage CA 92270. (619)346-0075. President: Scott Seely. Record producer and music publisher (S&R Music). Deals with artists. Produces 10 singles and 5 albums/year. Fee derived from sales royalty.
**How to Contact:** Submit demo tape and lyric sheet. Prefers cassette with any amount of songs on demo. SASE. Reports in 3 weeks.
**Music:** Mostly C&W and MOR; also all types. Recently produced *Armendares*, by J. Armendares (contemporary gospel, JRA Records); *Along the Line*, by Richard Christopher (pop, Accent Records); and *Upbeat MOR*, by Buddy Merrill (instrumental MOR, Accent Records). Other artists include Linn Phillip, Chante, Kirby Hamilton, Eddie Rose and Chet Demilo.

ACCLAIM RECORDS, INC., Unit 401, 3500 Glen Erin Dr., Mississauga, Ontario, Canada L5L 1W6. (416)820-7788. Vice President: Stan Campbell. Record producer and music publisher (Veron Music/PROCAN and World Acclaim Music/CAPAC). Estab. 1981. Deals with artists and songwriters. Produces 12-15 singles and 5 albums/year. Fee derived from sales royalty.
**How to Contact:** Call first about your interest. Prefers cassette with 2-5 songs on demo. SASE, "but I prefer not to have to return material." Reports in 3-4 weeks.

**Music:** Mostly country, country pop and MOR; also gospel, rock (country) and top 40/pop. Recently produced *True Blue*, by Orval Prophet (country LP, Acclaim Records); "Born to Booze," by O. Prophet (country single, Acclaim Records); and "Wish I Had a Dollar," by Morn'n Sun (country single). Other artists include Iris Larratt.
**Tips:** Looking for "professional attitude with international appeal."

**AIRWAVE PRODUCTIONS**, (formerly Without Fail Productions), 1806 N. Normandie Ave., Los Angeles CA 90027. (213)669-1404. Producers: E.J. Emmons and Troy Mathisen. Deals with artists and songwriters. Produces 3 singles and 2 albums/year. Fees derived from sales royalty and/or outright fee from record company.
**How to Contact:** Write first about your interest then submit demo tape and lyric sheet. Prefers cassette with 3-25 songs on demo. SASE. Reports within 2 weeks.
**Music:** Mostly new wave; also progressive, rock, soul, funk and top 40/pop. Recently produced *Suburban Lawns*, by Suburban Lawns (new-wave LP, IRS Records); and *Better Luck*, by The Plugz (new wave LP, Fatima Records).

**ALDOUS DEMIAN PUBLISHING, LTD.**, Radio City Station, Box 1348, New York NY 10101. (212)375-2639, (212)824-7842. Branch offices: 819 F St., Sacramento CA 95814; 3250 Ocean Pk. Blvd., Suite 200, Santa Monica Ca 90405; 2255 E. 89th St., Cleveland OH 44106. Vice President: Harold Weber. Record producer, music publisher (Aldous Demian Publishing, Ltd.), management firm and record distributor. Deals with artists and songwriters. Produces 4 singles and 3 albums/year. Fee derived from sales royalty.
**How to Contact:** Submit demo tape and lyric sheet. Prefers "best quality metal or chrome" cassette with 3-10, "preferably 5" songs on demo. "Include resume, photo (if possible) and brief statement of goals." SASE. Reports in 6 weeks.
**Music:** C&W, dance-oriented, easy listening, folk, gospel, jazz, MOR, progressive, R&B, rock (preferred), top 40/pop and new wave. Recently produced *John Lennon for President*, by David Peel (folk LP); *King of Punk*, by D. Peel (punk LP); "Junk Rock," by D. Peel (new wave single); *Bring Back the Beatles*, by D. Peel (pop/MOR LP); *Rock & Roll Crucifix*, by Tommy Acosta (rock opera LP); *Campaign Promises*, by Dawn Huston and Campaign featuring River (rock LP); and *Angel in Black Leather*, by Phyllis Lee and Lightning Force (rock LP). Other artists include Joe Yussi, Joe Meyers Dorf, Paul Ferrar, Ann Marie Mitti, Mozart's People, Steve Alan Pros, Starshine and Fame.

*****ALLEN & MARTIN PRODUCTIONS**, 9701 Taylorsville Rd., Louisville KY 40299. (502)267-9658. Producer: S.D. Miller. Major productions include national and regional jingles and exclusive song demo production for Full City Music. Deals with artists, songwriters and singers. Fee derived from sales royalty or by outright fee from songwriter/artist or record company.
**How to Contact:** Submit demo tape and lyric sheet. Prefers 7½ ips reel-to-reel or cassette with 3-5 songs on demo. Does not return unsolicited material. Reports in 2 weeks.
**Music:** Mostly country crossover rock; also bluegrass, jazz, progressive and top 40/pop. Recently produced "Bondarz Superstarz," by Al Bondar (top 40, Starsongz Records); *Walker, Pietius & Kays*, by Walker, Pietius & Kays (jazz vocal, Bridges Records); and "Remaining Faithful," by Monks of St. Meinrad (religious, Abbey Press Records). Other artists include Free Fall, Bill Owens and Quick Draw.

**AMALISA**, Box 4559, Long Island City NY 11104. (212)361-2582. Contact: Charles Lucy. Record producer, music publisher, record company and theater/film production. Deals with artists, songwriters, and theater and film people. Produces 4 singles and 2 albums/year. Fee derived from sales royalty or outright fee from artist/songwriter or record company.
**How to Contact:** Submit demo tape and lyric sheet. Prefers cassette with 1-10 songs on demo. SASE. Reports in 3 weeks.
**Music:** Children's, C&W, dance-oriented, jazz, progressive, rock (hard), top 40/pop, satire, new wave, theater and electronic. Recently produced "Kangaroos, Koalas and Kids," by Dr. Ron Becks (title song for children's TV show, Amalisa Records); "Frustration," by Lucy (punk/satire single, Amalisa Records); and "It's My Turn for the Winner," by Zenda Check (50s satire single, Amalisa Records).

**AMBIENTE MUSIC PRODUCTIONS, INC.**, Box 91120, Worldway Postal Center, Los Angeles CA 90009. (213)641-0178. President: Philip Sonnichsen. Chairman: Edward "Lalo" Guerrero. Record producer, record company and music publisher (Ladera Music Publishing/BMI). Estab. 1981. Deals with artists and songwriters.
**How to Contact:** Write first about your interest, then submit demo tape and lyric sheet. Prefers 7½ ips reel-to-reel or cassette with 1-4 songs on demo. SASE. Reports in 1 month.
**Music:** "We are a Chicano/Latin-oriented company. New material should be primarily in English or Spanish."

**\*THE AME CORPORATION**, Suite 108, 3701 Twin Lakes Court, Baltimore MD 21207. (800)638-5700. President: Edward Astri. Vice President: Yigal Bosch. Record producer. Estab. 1982. Deals with artists, songwriters and producers. Produces 40 singles and 40 albums/year. Fee derived from sales royalty or outright fee from artist/songwriter or record company.
**How to Contact:** Submit demo tape and lyric sheet. Prefers 15 or 30 ips reel-to-reel or cassette with 6-12 songs as demo. SASE. Reports in 1 month.
**Music:** Mostly rockabilly, pop rock and C&W (crossover and hardcore); also classical, gospel, progressive and Spanish. Recently produced "This Time We're Winning," by Little Anthony (top 40/black/crossover single, PCM Records); "Dreams and Themes," by Patrick Williams (top 40/black/crossover single, PCM Records); "Blondes," by John Stewart (rock single, Allegiance Records); *Friend Lover Wife*, by Johnny Paycheck (country, Allegiance Records); and *Steppenwolf*, by Steppenwolf (rock LP, Allegiance Records).
**Tips:** "Be flexible and cooperative; don't be the temperamental artist type."

**AMERICAN CREATIVE ENTERTAINMENT, LTD.**, Suite 818, 1616 Pacific Ave., Atlantic City NJ 08401. (609)347-0484. Vice President: Danny Luciano. Associate Producer: Armand Cucinotti. Record producer and music publisher (Donna Marie Music/ASCAP). Deals with artists and songwriters. Produces 2 singles and 1 album/year. Fee derived from sales royalty.
**How to Contact:** Submit demo tape and lyric sheet. Prefers 7½ ips reel-to-reel or cassette with 4-8 songs on demo. "No 8 track." SASE. Reports in 6 weeks.
**Music:** MOR, R&B, rock (all types), soul and top 40/pop. Recently produced "Ting-A-Ling Doubleplay," by Larry Bowa and Dave Cash of the Philadelphia Phillies (top 40 single, Molly Records).

**\*AMI**, 111 Free Hill Rd., Hendersonville TN 37075. (615)822-6786. Vice President: Kenneth Bridger. Record producer and music publisher (Bridger Publishing). Deals with artists. Produces 22 singles and 6 albums/year. Fee derived from sales royalty.
**How to Contact:** Submit demo tape and lyric sheet; write about your interest. Prefers cassette with 2-5 songs on demo. SASE. Reports in 3 weeks.
**Music:** Mostly C&W; also classical, easy listening and gospel.

**APON RECORD COMPANY, INC.**, Box 3082, Steinway Station, Long Island City NY 11103. (212)721-5599. Manager: Don Zemann. Record producer and music publisher (Apon Publishing/ASCAP). Deals with artists and songwriters. Produces 20 albums/year. Fee derived from outright fee from record company.
**How to Contact:** Submit demo tape and lyric sheet. Prefers cassette with 2-6 songs on demo. SASE. Reports in 1 month.
**Music:** Classical, folk, Spanish, Slavic, polkas, and Hungarian gypsy. Recently produced *Czech Polka Festival* and *Polka Fever*, by Kunst (polka LPs, Apon Records); and *Holiday in Spain*, by Yavaloyas Orchestra (songs and dances LP, Apon Records).

**APPROPRIATE PRODUCTIONS**, 474 Atchison St., Pasadena CA 91104. (213)463-3400. Producer: Ben Brooks. Record producer and music publisher (Tantalizing Tunes/BMI and Atomic Tunes/ASCAP. Deals with artists and songwriters. Produces 2 singles/year. Fee derived from outright fee from artist/songwriter.
**How to Contact:** Submit demo tape and lyric sheet. Prefers cassette with 1-3 songs on demo. SASE. Reports in 3 weeks.
**Music:** Rock, R&B, C&W and MOR. Recently produced "Conscience of Man," and "Keep It All to Yourself" by Oscar Scotti (rock singles, Appropriate Records); and "Trip You in Love," and "Fixer Up" by T.M. Kenefick. Other songwriters include Dennis FitzGerald, K.A. Parker and David Fertitta.
**Tips:** "Be professional and learn the business and music well enough to create in the market place."

**\*ARZEE, ARCADE AND CLYMAX RECORDS**, 3010 N. Front St., Philadelphia PA 19133. (215)426-5682. Production Manager: Lucky Taylor. Record producer and music publisher (Rex Zario Music/BMI, Seabreeze Music/BMI, Jack Howard Publishing/BMI, Arcarde Music Co./ASCAP, Valley Brook Publishing/ASCAP). Deals with artists and songwriters. Produces 8-12 singles and 1-3 albums/year. Fee derived from sales royalty.
**How to Contact:** Submit demo tape and lyric sheet. Prefers 7½ ips reel-to-reel or cassette with 4-6 songs on demo. SASE. Reports in 1 month.
**Music:** Mostly C&W; also bluegrass, MOR and rock 'n' roll. Recently produced "Ten Gallon Stetson," by Bill Haley (C&W, Arzee Records); "This World of Mine," by Shorty Long (C&W, Arzee Records); and "Blues on the Block," by Charlie Stone (MOR, Arzee Records). Other artists include Dick Thomas, Rusty Wellington, Al Taber, Ben Taber, Willis Meyers, James E. Myers, Al Rex, Frank Marshall, Ray Coleman, Ray Hatcher, Bob Saver, Tex Carson, Eddie Thompson, Dallas Turner, Tommy Carr, Bob Dean, Jimmy Collett and Rex Zario.

## Record Producers 209

**ASTRAL PRODUCTIONS, INC.**, (A division of the Barancorp), First National Bank Towers, Box 4527, Topeka KS 66604. (913)233-9716. Executive Vice President: Kent Raine. Record producer and talent promoters. Other corporate divisions include record companies, music publishers and a management and booking firm. Deals with artists and songwriters. Produces 8-12 singles and 4-6 albums/year. Fee derived from sales royalty.
**How to Contact:** Submit demo tape and lead sheet. Prefers cassette with 2-6 songs on demo. SASE. Reports in 2 weeks.
**Music:** Rock, country rock, C&W, dance, jazz, MOR, blues, soul and top 40/pop.

**\*TOM ATOM PRODUCTIONS**, 28B Howden Rd., Toronto, Ontario, Canada M1R 3E4. (416)535-3717. Producer: Tom Atom. Record producer, music publisher and record company. Deals with artists and songwriters. Produces 2 singles and 2 albums/year. Fee derived from sales royalty.
**How to Contact:** Submit demo tape and lyric sheet. Prefers cassette with 1-5 songs on demo. SASE. Reports in 3 weeks.
**Music:** Mostly pop; also MOR, rock (heavy metal) and top 40. Recently produced *Neon*, by Neon (wave EP, Chameleon Records); "Instructions," by Instructions (wave single, Chameleon Records); and "Music for Subways," by Varios (MOR single, Foxtrot Records). Other artists include The Instructions, Rapid Tears, O.A. Bachlow and Winston.

**AZTEC PRODUCTIONS**, 20531 Plummer St., Chatsworth CA 91311. (213)998-0443. General Manager: A. Sullivan. Record producer, music publisher (Amiron Music/ASCAP) and management firm. Deals with artists and songwriters. Produces 2 singles and 1 album/year. Fee derived from sales royalty.
**How to Contact:** Submit demo tape and lead sheet. Prefers 7½ ips reel-to-reel or cassette with 6 songs maximum on demo. SASE. Reports in 2 weeks.
**Music:** Blues, dance, easy listening, MOR, rock and top 40/pop. Recently produced "Midnite Flite," by Papillon (MOR single, AKO Records); "El Chicano" (top 40 single, Dorn Records); "With You," by Abraxas (top 40 single, Dorn Records); and "Summer Nites," by Newstreet (rock single, Dorn Records). Other artists include Julie Reina, El Chicano and Jacqueleen Clifford.

**AZURE RECORDS**, 1450 Terrell, Beaumont TX 77701. (713)832-0748. President: Don Gilbert. Record producer and music publisher (Don Gilbert Music/BMI) and record company. Deals with artists and songwriters. Produces 10 singles/year. Fee derived from sales royalty.
**How to Contact:** Submit demo tape and lyric sheet. Prefers 7½ ips reel-to-reel with 2-10 songs on demo. SASE. Reports in 1 month.
**Music:** C&W and MOR. Recently produced "Sweet and Simple," by Randy McClain (country MOR single, Azure Records); "Take Your Memories Too," by Sherry Black (country MOR single, Gold Guitar Records); and "Cajun Lullaby," by Jesse Stuart (country MOR single, Gold Guitar Records). Other artists include Silver Strings and Don Gilbert.

**B.C. ENTERPRISES OF MEMPHIS, INC.**, 726 E. McLemore Ave., Memphis TN 38106. (901)947-2553. Administrative Assistant: Nat Engleberg. Record producer and music publisher (Colca Music, Epitome Music, Insight Music/BMI). Deals with artists and songwriters. Produces 2 singles and 1 album/year. Fee derived from sales royalty.
**How to Contact:** Submit demo tape and lyric sheet. Prefers cassette with 1-3 songs on demo. SASE. Reports in 1 week.
**Music:** Mostly R&B and pure blues; also gospel and soul. Recently produced "You Must Be Gravity," by Sir Henry Ivy (R&B single, Brian Manor Records); and "LOve Me At Own Risk," by Curtis Davis (R&B single, Brian Manor Records). Other artists include Calvin Leavy and the Larry Gibson Group.

**\*BARSONGS LTD.**, 4 Cheniston Gardens, London, W86TQ England. 44-01-937-2252. Director: Alan Barson. Record producer and music publisher (Barsongs, Ltd.). Estab. 1981. Deals with artists and songwriters. Fee derived from sales royalty.
**How to Contact:** Submit demo tape and lyric sheet. Prefers reel-to-reel or cassette with 3-7 songs on demo. SAE and IRC. Reports in 1 month.
**Music:** Mostly rock and top 40/pop; also children's, dance-oriented and MOR. Recently produced "Let The Heartaches Begin," by Chris Farlowe (rock single, CBS Records); "Man to Man," by Wayne Sleep (pop/dance single, Gravity Records); "Don't Take Away," by Jonathan Gregg (soft rock single, Polydor Records); "Legends," by Profit (electronic pop single, Hansa Records); and *Trials and Crosses*, by Cuddly Toys (pop LP, Fresh/Jungle Records). Other artists include Ian Gibbons, Pete Thompson, Keff McCulloch, Jackie (Pass The Dutchie) Mattoo, Dollar, Geoff Deane (Modern Romance), INDIPOP, Steve Coe, China Burton, Freddie Waite, The Cure, Simon May, Martha Ladley, Fashion, Zeus B. Held and Billy Lyall.

**BASIC RECORDS**, 1309 Celesta Way, Sellersburg IN 47172. (812)246-2959. Contact: Buddy Powell. Record producer and music publisher (Hoosier Hills Publishing). Deals with artists and songwriters. Produces 15 singles and 7 albums/year. Fee derived from outright fee from artist/songwriter.
**How to Contact:** Submit demo tape and lyric sheet. Prefers 7½ ips reel-to-reel or cassette with 2-4 songs on demo. SASE. Reports in 2 weeks.
**Music:** Bluegrass, C&W and gospel.

**BEE/ALEXANDER PRODUCTIONS, INC.**, Suite 2129, 1100 Glendon, Los Angeles CA 90024. (213)208-7871. Contact: Morey Alexander or Jimmy Bee. Record producer, music publisher (Bee/Mor Music/BMI, Pepper & Salt Music/ASCAP) and management firm. Deals with artists, songwriters and managers. Produces 3-5 albums/year. Fee derived from sales royalty.
**How to Contact:** Submit demo tape and lyric sheet. Prefers cassette with 4-8 songs on demo. Does not return unsolicited material. Reports in 1 week.
**Music:** Blues, C&W, dance-oriented, jazz, R&B, rock, soul and top 40/pop. Recently produced *Magic Man*, by Robert Winters (R&B LP, Arista Records); *Aurora Borealis*, by Aurora Borealis (jazz fusion LP, in foreign release only); and *Louisiana Fog*, by Charlie Musselwhite (blues LP, Cherry Red Records).

**BEE HIVE JAZZ RECORDS**, 1130 Colfax St., Evanston IL 60201. (312)328-5593. Producer: Susan Neumann. Record producer and music publisher. Deals with artists and songwriters. Fee derived from sales royalty.
**How to Contact:** Call or write first about your interest or submit demo tape and lyric sheet. Prefers cassette. SASE. Reports in 1 month.
**Music:** Jazz. Recently produced "Baritone Madness," by Nick Brignola; "Juicy Lucy," by Ed Salvador; and "Neo-Nistico," by Sal Nistico (jazz single, Beehive Records).

**BEE JAY RECORDING STUDIOS**, 5000 Eggleston Ave., Orlando FL 32810. (305)293-1781. President: Eric T. Schabacker. Record producer and music publisher (Schabraf Music/BMI). Deals with artists and songwriters. Produces 18 singles and 10 albums/year. Fee derived from sales royalty.
**How to Contact:** Submit demo tape and lyric sheet. Prefers cassette with 1-4 songs on demo. SASE. Reports in 2 weeks.
**Music:** Dance-oriented, easy listening, MOR, progressive, rock, soul, top 40/pop and contemporary Christian. Recently produced *Xavier*, by Xavier (top 40 LP, Xavier Records).

**THE BERKLEY MUSIC GROUP**, 108 Berkley Dr., Madison TN 37115. (615)868-3407. Producers: Bill Anderson, Jr. or D.D. Morris. Record producer, music publisher (Newcreature Music/BMI) and TV/radio syndication. Deals with artists and songwriters. Produces 4 singles and 4 albums/year. Fee derived from sales royalty.
**How to Contact:** Submit demo tape and lyric sheet. Prefers 7½ ips reel-to-reel or cassette with 4-10 songs on demo. SASE. Reports in 1 month.
**Music:** Blues, C&W, gospel, jazz, rock and top 40/pop. Recently produced *Teddy Nelson*, by T. Nelson (country LP, EMI Records); *Little Richard*, by Little Richard (gospel LP, Landmark Records); and "Nights Alone" and "Unchain My Heart," by Sheri Hare (top 40/pop singles, Landmark Records).

*****BIG BEAR**, 190 Monument Rd., Birmingham, B16 8UU, England. (021)454-7020. Managing Director: Jim Simpson. Record producer, music publisher (Bearsongs) and record company (Big Bear Records). Deals with artists. Produces 15 singles and 10 albums/year. Fee derived from sales royalty.
**How to Contact:** Write first about your interest, then submit demo tape and lyric sheet. Reports in 2 weeks.
**Music:** Blues, jazz, R&B and soul.

**BIG DEAL RECORDS CO.**, Box 60-A, Cheneyville LA 71325. President: Launey Deal. Record producer, music publisher, booking agency and management firm. Deals with artists and songwriters. Produces 30 singles and 3 albums/year. Fee derived from sales royalty or outright fee from songwriter/artist.
**How to Contact:** Query, arrange personal interview, submit demo tape or submit demo tape and lead sheet. Prefers 7½ ips reel-to-reel or cassette with 4-20 songs on demo. SASE. Reports in 1 week.
**Music:** Mostly soul, R&B and rock; also blues, C&W, disco and gospel. Recently produced "Go Ahead, Go Ahead and Party," b/w "Pride & Joy," by Rockin' Guitar Loni (R&B single, Soul Cat Records); and *Sensational Golden Links*, by Sensational Golden Links (gospel LP, Gospel Soul Train Records).

**BIRC**, 601 E. Blacklidge Dr., Tucson AZ 85705. (602)882-9016. President: Joe Bidwell. Record producer and music publisher (Autograph Music/BMI). Deals with artists and songwriters. Produces 6-8

# Close-up

**Ron Blackwood**
Publisher/Producer/Manager

Memphis-based producer/publisher/manager Ron Blackwood is shown here with friends Jerry Lee Lewis, left, and Charlie Rich, who began their music careers in Memphis.

Blackwood, a member of the family that founded the famous Blackwood Singers, is involved in both Christian and secular music as president of the music conglomerate Blackwood Music/Memphis Management.

"I'm one of the few who does everything from A to Z," says Blackwood, meaning that within his organization of companies he functions as a publisher, producer, manager and booking agent, and also has professional studio recording facilities.

Blackwood has managed or booked exclusively top artists and groups including Hank Williams, Jr., Moe Bandy, R.W. Blackwood, Tommy Overstreet, Vern Gosdin, The Blackwood Singers, Ronnie McDowell and J.D. Sumner and the Stamps Quartet. Among his greatest accomplishments to date, however, is co-producing "In the Misty Moonlight" for Jerry Wallace whom he was also managing.

Experience in the music business has taught Blackwood the importance of listening to song demos with the ears of a DJ, rather than just the ears of a publisher or producer. "DJs who get from two- to three-hundred songs a week only listen to eight to ten seconds of a song, particularly if it's a release by a new artist," says Blackwood. "That's why, when I listen to a song for an artist, it has to grab me in the first ten or fifteen seconds. If it's not a song the DJs will play, it's not a song we can use."

Blackwood thinks talented songwriters have an advantage—at least an advantage of numbers—over aspiring artists. "Everybody's a singer," he says. "I have more good artists than I have enough good songs for them to record."

Blackwood says a songwriter's chance of getting songs cut by one of those artists is greater if the demo is of master or near master quality.

"The competition to get songs recorded has become fierce. When artists and producers listen to a song and all of a sudden hear a professional, studio-quality demo, it certainly makes them pay more attention to the song, I think that, if a songwriter believes in his songs, he should somehow get the money to record them in a good studio."

Blackwood's answer to songwriters who ask if they need to move to Los Angeles, or Nashville or New York to become successful is short and to-the-point: "I haven't."

singles and 2-3 albums/year. Fee derived from sales royalty.
**How to Contact:** Submit demo tape and lyric sheet. Prefers cassette with 1-3 songs on demo. SASE. Reports in 1 month.
**Music:** C&W and top 40/pop. Recently produced "Natchez Trace," by Don Shipley; "I Smile (But You Know It Ain't Easy)," by Erin Brooks; "Tonight You Might Find a Friend," by Duncan Stitt (country singles, Birc Records); and "My Time Has Come and Gone," by Jack Barron (country single, Birc Records).

**\*BLACK & WHITE MUSIC PRODUCTIONS LTD.**, 9 Devonport, 23 Southwick St., London, W2 England. 44-01-402-9750. Director: Tim Knight. Record producer and music publisher (Black & White Music Corp. Ltd.). Affiliate/US: Crystal Jukebox Inc. Estab. 1981. Works with artists and songwriters. Releases 3 singles/year. Fee derived from sales royalty.
**How to Contact:** Submit demo tape and lyric sheet. Prefers cassette with 1-3 songs on demo. SAE and IRC. Reports in 1 month.
**Music:** Mostly top 40/pop; also dance-oriented, MOR, rock and soul. Recently produced "You You You," by Loose Talk (pop single, Jet Records); and "Judge Dredd," by Loose Talk (pop single, K-Tel Records).

**BLACK DIAMOND MUSIC PUBLISHING & PRODUCTION CO.**, Box 28800, Philadelphia PA 19151. (215)623-1549. President: Allen Gabriel. Record producer and music publisher (Black Diamond Music/BMI). Estab. 1981. Deals with artists, songwriters and musicians. Fee derived from sales royalty or outright fee from record company.
**How to Contact:** Write first about your interest, then submit demo tape and lyric sheet. Prefers cassette with 2 songs on demo. "Demo tape must be of good quality, lyric sheets must be clearly printed." Does not return unsolicited material. Reports in 3 weeks.
**Music:** Children's, church/religious, dance-oriented, easy listening, gospel, jazz, MOR, progressive, Spanish, R&B, rock, soul, top 40/pop and reggae.

**BLACKWOOD MUSIC/MEMPHIS MANAGEMENT CORP.**, Box 17272, Memphis TN 38187-0272. (901)767-2220. Contact: Ron Blackwood. Record producer and music publisher (Memphis Management Music). Deals with artists and songwriters. Produces 50 singles and 10 albums/year. Fee derived from sales royalty.
**How to Contact:** Submit demo tape and lyric sheet. Prefers cassette with 1-5 songs on demo. Does not return unsolicited material. Reports in 1 month; "only if we're interested in material."
**Music:** C&W, gospel, MOR and top 40/pop. Recently released *Let Jesus Happen*, by R.W. Blackwood and the Blackwood singers (contemporary gospel LP, Capitol records); *Jerry Wallace*, by J. Wallace (country pop LP, MCA Records); and *Roger McDuff*, by R. McDuff (MOR/gospel LP, Benson Records). Other artists include Tanya Tucker, Willie Nelson, Jimmy Dean and Wink Martindale.

**BLIND PIG RECORDS**, 208 S. 1st St., Ann Arbor MI 48103. (313)428-7216. A&R Director: Jerry Del Giuduce. Record producer, music publisher (Viper Music/BMI) and record company. Deals with artists. Produces 3-6 albums/year.
**How to Contact:** Submit demo tape and lyric sheet. Prefers cassette with 2-4 songs on demo. SASE. Reports in 2-3 months.
**Music:** Blues, R&B (40s, 50s) and rock (rockabilly). Recently produced *It's All Rock & Roll*, by Steve Nardella (rock/rockabilly LP, Blind Pig Records); *Comin' Your Way*, by John Mooney; and *Fine Cuts*, by Walter Horton (blues LPs, Blind Pig Records).

**BLUE CHEK MUSIC, INC.**, Box 74, Saw Mill River Rd., Ardsley NY 10502. (914)592-3479. Contact: A&R Department. Record producer. Deals with artists. Produces 30 singles and 15 albums/year. Fee derived from sales royalty.
**How to Contact:** Submit demo tape and lyric sheet. Prefers 7½ ips reel-to-reel or cassette with 1-3 songs on demo. SASE. Reports in 1 week.
**Music:** Church/religious, C&W, easy listening, gospel and MOR.

**BLUE ISLAND INDUSTRIES**, Unit 3, 1446 N. Martel, Los Angeles CA 90046. (213)851-3733. Contact: Bob Gilbert. Record producer and music publisher (Blue Island, Rock Island and Fleming Enterprises). Deals with artists and songwriters. Produces 5 singles/year. Fee derived from sales royalty.
**How to Contact:** Submit demo tape and lyric sheet. Prefers cassette with 3-6 songs on demo. SASE. Reports in 3 weeks.
**Music:** C&W, MOR, rock and top 40/pop. "We are a new organization and our artist list is growing with new talent."
**Tips:** "We listen to *all* material presented. Many companies only listen to a few songs. We give everyone a fair chance to be heard. Anyone can write a hit song."

## Record Producers 213

**BOUQUET-ORCHID ENTERPRISES**, Box 18284, Shreveport LA 71138. (318)686-7362. President: Bill Bohannon. Record producer and music publisher (Orchid Publishing). Deals with artists and songwriters. Produces 5 singles/year. Fee derived from sales royalty.
**How to Contact:** Submit demo tape and lyric sheet. Prefers cassette with 3-5 songs on demo. "Include brief background information. Make lyrics clear and the demos as strong as possible." SASE. Reports in 1 month.
**Music:** C&W, MOR and top 40/pop. Recently produced "The Touch of You," by Adam Day; and "I Need You Today," by Shan Wilson (C&W singles, Bouquet Records).

**BOBBY BOYD PRODUCTIONS**, 2609 NW 36th St., Oklahoma City OK 73112. (405)942-0462. Producer: Bobby Boyd. Record producer (Boyd Records) and music publisher (Watonga Publishing/ASCAP; Catalpa Publishing/BMI). Deals with artists and songwriters. Produces 10 singles/year.
**How to Contact:** Submit demo tape and lyric sheet "that need not be returned." Prefers 7½ ips reel-to-reel or record with 3-12 songs on demo. Does not return unsolicited material. Reports in 2 weeks "if interested."
**Music:** C&W, R&B, rock, soul and top 40/pop. Recently produced *Trucking Truth*, by Marvin Ray (country LP, Boyd Records). Artists include Dale Greear.

**BROADWAY PRODUCTION, INC.**, 1307 Broadway St., Box 551, Sheffield AL 35660. (205)381-1833. President: David Johnson. Record producer and music publisher (Love House Music/ASCAP, Tired Iron Publishing/BMI). Deals with artists and songwriters. Produces 10+ singles and 3-5 albums/year. Fee derived by sales royalty "and fees for work.".
**How to Contact:** Submit demo tape and lyric sheet. Prefers 7½ ips reel-to-reel or cassette with 1-3 songs on demo. SASE. Reports in 2 weeks.
**Music:** Mostly R&B and country; also rock, soul and top 40/pop. Recently produced *She's Too Pretty to Cry*, by Percy Sledge (R&B crossover LP, Monument Records); and *Percy* by Percy Sledge (R&B LP, Monument Records). Other artists include James Govan and the Debow Brothers.

**BROTHER LOVE PRODUCTIONS**, Box 852, Beverly Hills CA 90213. (213)980-3812. Producer: Jeremy McClain. Secretary: S. Roshay. Record producer and music publisher (Pratt & McClain Music/ASCAP, Happy Days Music/BMI). Deals with artists and songwriters. Produces 5-8 singles and 1-2 albums/year. Fee derived by royalty or outright fee from record company.
**How to Contact:** Query with letter of introduction, arrange personal interview or submit demo tape and lead sheet. Prefers cassette with 4 songs on demo. SASE. Reports in 3 weeks.
**Music:** Mostly top 40; also C&W, dance, easy listening, MOR, rock pop and religious music. Recently produced "Happy Days," by Pratt and McClain (top 40, Warner Bros. Records); "What Ever Happened," by Tom Gillon (country, Brother Love Records); *Pratt & McClain*, by Pratt and McClain (top 40, ABC Records); and "Summertime in the City," by Pratt and McClain (rock). Other artists include Ocean (Warner Bros. Records, MCA Records, and Songbird Records).

**RON BROWN MANAGEMENT**, Box 15375, Pittsburgh PA 15237. (412)486-7740. Producer: Ron Brown. Record producer and music publisher (Etna Music/BMI). Produces 5-15 singles and 3 albums/year. Deals with artists and songwriters. Fee derived from sales royalty or outright fee from record company.
**How to Contact:** Submit demo tape or submit demo tape and lead sheet. "Submit only cassette tapes. Reel-to-reel and 8 track tapes will not be accepted." SASE. Reports in 2 weeks.
**Music:** Blues, dance, easy listening, MOR, progressive, rock, soul and top 40/pop. Recently produced *Give Me Love* and *Stay Awhile With Me*, by Shaker (top 40/R&B LPs, Pittsburg Records); and *More Title Town USA*, by Acappella Gold (Acappella LP, Iron City Records). Other artists include the El-Monacs, Fun, Patchwork and Centerfold.

**BENNIE BROWN PRODUCTIONS**, 3011 Woodway Lane, Box 5702, Columbia SC 29206. (803)788-5734. Contact: Bennie Brown Jr. Deals with artists, songwriters and music publishers. Produces 10 singles and 4-6 albums/year. Fee derived from sales royalty.
**How to Contact:** Query, submit demo tape, or submit demo tape and lead sheet. Prefers cassette with 2-4 songs on demo. SASE. Reports in 3 weeks.
**Music:** Mostly C&W (pop country); also dance, gospel, MOR, soul, and top 40/pop. Recently produced "Hold On," by Five Sing Stars (gospel, Nutone Records); "For Your Love," by Freestyle (disco, Nutone Records); and "I'll Keep On Lovin' You," by Twana Tolbert (top 40/R&B, Nutone Records).

*****BILL BYRON PRODUCTIONS**, 1727 Elm St., Bethlehem PA 18017. (215)865-1083. Project Coordinator: J. Peterson. Record producer and record company (Mystic Oak Records). Deals with artists. Produces 2-6 singles and 2-12 albums/year. Fee derived from sales royalty.

**How to Contact:** Write about your interest. Prefers 15 ips reel-to-reel or cassette with 3-9 songs on demo. SASE. Reports in 1 month.
**Music:** Mostly synthesized rock; also new wave and experimentals. Recently produced "Set the Trend," by Trendsetters (rock, Mystic Oak Records); "Among the Ruins," by Psychic Warriors (rock, Mystic Oak Records); and "In Your Dreams," by Office Toys (synthesized rock, Mystic Oak Records). Other artists include Even Stephen, Ego, the BBC and Steve Brosky.
**Tips:** "We are looking for artists with both good studio ability and a good live show. Inform us of any performance dates you might have in the northeast region."

**CADENCE JAZZ RECORDS, LTD.**, Cadence Bldg., Redwood NY 13679. (315)287-7852. Record producer and record company (Cadence Jazz Records). Deals with artists and songwriters. Produces 10-15 albums/year. Fee derived from sales royalty.
**How to Contact:** Submit demo tape and lyric sheet. Prefers cassette. SASE. Reports in 1 week.
**Music:** Blues and jazz. Recently produced *Beaver Harris Live at Nyon*, by Harris; *Saheb Sarbib Live at the Public Theatre*, by Sarbib; and *Skizoke*, by Frank Lowe (jazz LPs, Cadence Records). Other artists include Larry Gelb, Barbara Donald, Dwight James, Hugh Brodie and J.R. Monterose.

**CHARLES CALELLO PRODUCTIONS, LTD.**, Box 2127, Beverly Hills CA 90213. (213)275-8248. President: Charles Calello. Music arranger and music publisher. Deals with artists and songwriters. Produces 2-4 albums/year. Fee derived from royalties or outright fee from record company.
**How to Contact:** Submit demo tape and lead sheet. Prefers cassette with 1-2 songs on demo. SASE. Reports in 2 weeks.
**Music:** Pop songs. Recently produced "On the Heels of Love," by Roger Voudouris (Boardwalk Records); "Welcome to the Phunktion," by Ellis Hall; and "Never Forget Your Eyes" and *Victory* by Larry Graham (Warner Bros. Records). Other artists include Debra Allen, Frankie Valli, Larry Graham and Pia Zadora.

*****CALIFORNIA INTERNATIONAL RECORDS & VIDEO**, Box 2818, Newport Beach CA 92663. Vice President/Co-Producer: Cheryl Nicoletti. Record producer, music publisher (Joseph Nicoletti Music) and record company. Deals with artists and songwriters. Produces 2-3 singles/year. Fee derived from sales royalty.
**How to Contact:** Call about your interest; submit demo tape and lyric sheet. Cassette only with 1-4 songs on demo. SASE. Reports in 1 month.
**Music:** Mostly rock and top 40; also MOR, rock (new wave, pop and classical) and rockabilly. Recently publishsed *Child of Technology*, by Joseph Nicoletti (rock LP, California International Records); *Streetwise*, by Nicoletti (rock LP, California International Records); *Fantasy Dancer*, by Nicoletti (ballad LP, California International Records); and *Children Are the Future*, by J. Nicoletti (instrumental ballad, TV theme song, Nicoletti Music Co.).
**Tips:** "Have a strong belief in the material you send."

*****CAPITOL STAR ARTIST ENT., INC.**, Box 11276, Rochester NY 14611. (716)328-5565. Contact: Donald Redanz. Record producer and music publisher (Red Plow). Deals with artists and songwriters. Produces 20 singles and 4 albums/year. Fee derived from sales royalty.
**How to Contact:** Submit demo tape and lyric sheet. Prefers 7½ ips reel-to-reel or cassette for demo.
**Music:** Bluegrass, church/religious, C&W and gospel.

*****DON CASALE MUSIC, INC.**, 377 Plainfield St., Westbury NY 11590. (516)333-7898. President: Don Casale.
**How to Contact:** Call or write (SASE) *before* submitting.

**CASTALIA PRODUCTIONS**, Box 11516, Milwaukee WI 53211. (414)272-0963. President: Jim Spencer. Promotions Director: Dave Luhrssen. Record producer and music publisher (Castalia Music/BMI). Deals with artists and songwriters. Produces 2 singles and 6 albums/year.
**How to Contact:** Submit demo tape and lyric sheet or call about your interest. Prefers cassette with 1-6 songs on demo. SASE. Reports in 1 month.
**Music:** All types. Recently produced "Sunset Lady," by Marvell Love (R&B single); *Put Your Trust In God*, by Phebe Holmes and Darrell Hines (gospel LP); *Doctor Yah Yah*, by Suspence (blues/rock); and *Thought I Wasn't Going to Make It Back*, by the Viceroys (R&B single).

**CASTLE PRODUCTIONS**, Box 7574, Tulsa OK 74105. (918)587-1515. President: Ben Ferrell. Record producer and music publisher (Spirit & Soul Publishing Co./ASCAP, Mighty Song Publishing Co./BMI). Estab. 1981. Deals with artists and songwriters. Produces 15 albums/year. Fee derived from sales royalty or outright fee from record company.
**How to Contact:** Arrange personal interview to play demo tape or submit demo tape and lyric sheet.

Prefers cassette with 2-10 songs on demo. SASE. Reports in 3 weeks.
**Music:** Choral, church/religious, gospel and MOR. Artists include Vicki Jamison, Followers of Christ, Ron Perry and Doyle Tucker.

**CHICAGO KID PRODUCTIONS**, 2228 Observatory, Los Angeles CA 90027. (213)666-0494. Contact: John Ryan. Record producer and music publisher (Cottage Grove Music). Deals with artists and songwriters. Produces 10 singles and 6 albums/year.
**How to Contact:** Submit demo tape and lyric sheet. Prefers cassette with 4 songs on demo. SASE. Reports in 3 weeks.
**Music:** Rock and top 40/pop. Artists include Allman Brothers Band, Greg Guidry, The Hawks, Bill Wray, Styx, Climax Blues Band, Pure Prairie League, Rare Earth, States, Doucette, Tantrum, Blackoak Arkansas and The Gap Band.

**THE CHU YEKO MUSICAL FOUNDATION**, Box 10051, Beverly Hills CA 90213. (213)761-2646; messages (213)998-9839. Branch: Box 1314, Englewood Cliffs, NJ 07632. Messages: (201)567-5524. Producer: Doris Chu Yeko. Record producer and music publisher (The Chu Yeko Musical Foundation/BMI). Deals with artists and songwriters. Produces 4 albums/year. Fee derived from sales royalty; by outright fee from songwriter/artist; by outright fee from record company.
**How to Contact:** Submit demo tape and lyric sheet or "phone on Tuesday or Friday. Vacation: July and August." Prefers cassette with any number songs on demo. SASE.
**Music:** Children's, choral, church/religious, classical, C&W, dance-oriented, easy listening, jazz, MOR, musicals, R&B, rock and top 40/pop. Recently produced *Ka-Boom!*, by Original Cast (Broadway musical LP, The Chu Yeko Musical Foundation Records); and *Fly with Me*, by Original Cast (off-Broadway musical LP, The Chu Yeko Musical Foundation Records).
**Tips:** "We will co-produce records with songwriter/artist."

**LOU CICCHETTI**, 211 Birchwood Ave., Upper Nyack NY 10960. (914)358-0861. Contact: Lou Cicchetti. Record producer and music publisher (Cousins Music). Deals with artists and songwriters. Produces 1-2 singles/year. Fee derived from sales royalty.
**How to Contact:** Submit demo tape and lyric sheet. Prefers 7½ or 15 ips reel-to-reel or cassette with any number songs on demo. SASE. Reports in 3 weeks.
**Music:** C&W and rock. Recently produced "Your Honor," by Koko (country single, Daisy Records).
**Tips:** "We produce mostly demos (8-track) and try to find major labels who will sign the acts directly. But, if all else fails, we will release on our own labels."

**CLAY PIGEON PRODUCTIONS**, Box 20346, Chicago IL 60620. (312)778-8760. A&R Director: V. Beleska. Record producer. Deals with artists and songwriters. Produces 10-25 singles and 5-15 albums/year. Fee derived from sales royalty or outright fee from record company.
**How to Contact:** "We cannot consider any material without a written inquiry first, describing self and material in some depth. Do not phone." Prefers 7½ ips reel-to-reel or cassette with 1-5 songs on demo. SASE. Reports in 2-8 weeks.
**Music:** Bluegrass, blues, children's, choral, church/religious, classical, C&W, dance, easy listening, folk, gospel, jazz, MOR, progressive, rock, soul, top 40/pop, avant-garde and punk rock. Recently produced "All for You," by Christopher (MOR single, Clay Pigeon International Records); "Disco People," by Roto Applicators (punk rock single, Broken Records); and *Tricentennial 2076*, by Vyto B (avant-garde LP, Clay Pigeon International Records).
**Tips:** "Cover letter should explain songwriter's background, type of songs written and why songs are unique enough to be listened to."

*****CLOUDBURST RECORDS**, Box 31, Edmonton KY 42129. (502)432-3183. President: W. Junior Lawson. Record producer, music publisher (Holy Spirit Music) and record company. Deals with artists and songwriters. Produces 3 singles and 4 albums/year. Fee derived from sales royalty.
**How to Contact:** Submit demo tape and lyric sheet. Prefers 7½ ips reel-to-reel or cassette for demo. SASE. Reports in 3 weeks.
**Music:** Mostly southern gospel; also MOR. Recently produced "I Went to Jesus," by the Servants; "Don't Let the Ship Sail Without You," by the New Apostles; and "When I See the Great King," by the Helmsmen (all southern gospel singles, Cloudburst Records).
**Tips:** "Be honest. Submit material with less volume on instruments and more volume on voices."

**COUNTRY STAR PRODUCTIONS**, 439 Wiley Ave., Franklin PA 16323. (814)432-4633. President: Norman Kelly. Record producer and music publisher (Country Star Music/ASCAP, Kelly Music/BMI and Process Music/BMI). Deals with artists and songwriters. Produces 2-4 albums/year. Fee derived from outright fee from artist/songwriter or record company.

**How to Contact:** Submit demo tape and lyric sheet. Prefers 7½ ips reel-to-reel or cassette with 2-4 songs on demo. SASE. Reports in 2 weeks.
**Music:** Mostly country; also bluegrass, easy listening, folk, gospel, MOR, rock and top 40/pop. Recently produced "My Love Rolls Over," by Valerie Anderson; "Siempre," by Doc Holiday (both country singles, Country Star Records); and "Radar," by Rose Marie (rock single, Mersey Records). Other artists include Rube Schafer, Debbie Sue, Patty Cottrill, Junie Lou, Virge Brown and Junior Norman.
**Tips:** "Submit only your best efforts."

**COUNTRYSIDE RECORDING**, Rt. 2, Crookston MN 56716. (218)281-6450. Contact: Gary Emerson. Record producer and music publisher (Gentilly Music/BMI). Deals with artists and songwriters. Produces 8 singles and 4 albums/year. Fee derived from sales royalty.
**How to Contact:** Submit demo tape and lyric sheet. Prefers cassette with 2-5 songs on demo. SASE. Reports in 1 month.
**Music:** Bluegrass, C&W and gospel. Recently produced "Nothing's Gonna' Come Better," by Darcy Hagen (country single, Glade Records). Other artists include Steve Lockman.

**COUSINS MUSIC**, 211 Birchwood Ave., Upper Nyack NY 10960. President: Lou Cicchetti. Produces 5 singles/year. Fee derived from sales royalty.
**How to Contact:** Submit demo tape only. Prefers 7½ or 15 ips reel-to-reel or cassette with 2 songs minimum on demo. SASE. Reports in 2 weeks.
**Music:** C&W (any) and rock. Recently produced "Wall between Us," by the Earls (soul/rock, Dakar Records) and "One More Heartache," by CoCo (C&W, Daisy Records).

*****COWBOY JUNCTION PUBLISHING CO.**, Hwy. 44 W., Lecanto FL 32661. (904)746-4754. Contact: Elizabeth Thomson. Record producer and music publisher (Cowboy Junction). Deals with artists and songwriters. Fee derived from sales royalty.
**How to Contact:** Submit demo tape and lyric sheet. Prefers 7½ reel-to-reel or cassette with 1-4 songs on demo. SASE. Reports ASAP.
**Music:** Mostly C&W; also bluegrass. Recently produced "The Story of Barney Clark," "Flea Market Cowboy," and "The Great Nashville Star," by Buddy Max (country singles, Cowboy Junction Records).

**THE EDDIE CROOK COMPANY**, Box 213, Hendersonville TN 37075. (615)822-1360. Contact: Eddie Crook. Record producer and music publisher (Pleasant View Music/ASCAP and Chestnut Mound Music/BMI). Deals with artists and songwriters. Produces 10 singles and 25 albums/year. Fee derived from sales royalty.
**How to Contact:** Submit demo tape and lyric sheet. Prefers cassette with 1-3 songs on demo. Does not return unsolicited material. Reports in 1 month.
**Music:** Gospel. Recently produced *Solid as a Rock*, by Mid-South Boys; *Keeping It Gospel*, by the Sego Brothers and Naomi; and *Assurance*, by the Dixie Echoes.

**CROSS-OVER ENTERPRISES, INC.**, 880 NE 71st St., Miami FL 33138. (305)759-1405. President: Carlos Oliva. Record producer, music publisher (Avilo Music/BMI, Santa Clara Music/ASCAP and Oliva Music/SESAC), and booking agency. Deals with artists and songwriters. Produces 10 singles and 7 albums/year. Fee derived from sales royalty.
**How to Contact:** Submit demo tape and lyric sheet. Prefers cassette with any number songs on demo. SASE. Reports in 2 weeks.
**Music:** Dance-oriented, Spanish and rock. Recently produced *Llegamos*, by Clouds and *Hermanos*, by Judge's Nephews (rock/salsa LPs, Common Cause Records); and *Salsa Express*, by Salsa Express (salsa LP, Common Cause Records). Regularly produces Spanish rock, Spanish love ballads and salsa groups.

**CUMMINGS PRODUCTIONS**, Suite 303, 14045 S. Main, Houston TX 77035. (713)645-5391; 641-0793. A&R Director: Roger L. Cummings. Branch: 5019 Boeingshier, Memphis TN 38116. A&R Director: Robert Jackson. Record producer, music publisher (Sirloin Music Publishing), and record company (Happy Beat and MSB Records). Deals with artists and songwriters. Produces 12 singles and 4 albums/year. Fee derived from sales royalty or outright fee from artist/songwriter.
**How to Contact:** Write first about your interest, then submit demo tape and lyric sheet. Prefers cassette with 3-6 songs on demo. SASE. Reports in 1 month.
**Music:** Blues, C&W, dance-oriented, gospel, jazz, R&B, rock, soul and top 40/pop. Recently produced albums by Friction (dance/soul/funk, Happy Beat Records); Carl Stewart (soul/R&B, Happy Beat Records); Ralph Lowe (country, Columbine Records); Richey Cee (soul, Fox Century Records); and Carl Adams (jazz, Venus Records). Other artists include Invasion.

Record Producers **217**

**\*DAN THE MAN PRODUCTIONS**, 3094 W. 101 St., Cleveland OH 44111. (216)631-6553. President: Daniel L. Bischoff. Record producer, music publisher (Dan the Man Music Publishing Co./ASCAP) and record company. Deals with artists, songwriters and producers. Produces 6 singles/year; several albums now pending. Fee derived from sales royalty.
**How to Contact:** Submit demo tape and lyric sheet. Prefers cassette or demo record with 2-4 songs on demo. SASE. Reports in 3 weeks.
**Music:** Mostly country, top 40, R&B and novelty; also easy listening, folk, rock and soul. Recently produced "Reagan-omics," "High Priced Gasoline," "Iran Crisis," "Collect," "E.T. Interview," "Buzzard Man," "Job-less" and "Checks" all by Dan the Man (novelty singles, Dan the Man Records); and "Just a Simple Bouquet," by Johnny Wright (country single, Dan the Man Records).

**\*DAWN PRODUCTIONS**, 108 Morning Glory Ln., Manheim PA 17545. President: Joey Welz. Record producer, music publisher and record company. Deals with artists, songwriters and producers. Produces 4 singles and 2 albums/year. Fee derived from outright fee from record company.
**How to Contact:** Submit demo tape and lyric sheet. Prefers cassette with 3-6 songs on demo. Does not return unsolicited material. "We hold submissions for consideration."
**Music:** Mostly R&R; also C&W, dance-oriented, easy listening, folk, MOR and top 40/pop. Recently produced "Rock Around the Clock" b/w "I Remember Rock 'n Roll," by Joey Welz (Fraternity Records); "Bring Back the Music" b/w "The Hawk Talks," by Bill Haleys Comets (Music City Records); and *American Made Rock 'n Roll*, by J. Welz (R&R LP, Fraternity Records). Other artists include Roy Smith.

**DAWN PROMOTIONS AND AGENCY, LTD.**, 10 St. Mary's Hill, Stamford, PE92DP, England. 44-0780-51736. Managing Director: Ken Cox. Record producer, music publisher (Pixie Music Co. Ltd.) and record company (Soul Stop, Buffalo and Weasel). Works with artists and songwriters. Produces 20 singles and 2 albums/year. Fee derived from sales royalty.
**How to Contact:** Submit demo tape and lyric sheet. Prefers cassette with 2-6 songs on demo. SAE and IRC. Reports in 2 weeks.
**Music:** Mostly C&W and up-tempo soul; also top 40/pop. Recently produced "Nine Times Out of Ten," by M. Day (soul single, Soul-Stop Records); "All You Got Your Ears On," by R. Ryan (C&W single, Buffalo Records); and "Crystal Chandeliers," by Mahana (reggae single, Weasel Records).

**\*DAZIA PRODUCTIONS**, 13033 W. McNichols, Detroit MI 48235. (313)342-9692. Business Manager: Jacqueline Harris. Record producer, music publisher (Dazia Music) and record company. Estab. 1981. Works with artists. Produces 8 singles/year. Fee derived from sales royalty; or outright fee from songwriter/artist or record company.
**How to Contact:** Write first about your interest; submit demo tape and lyric sheet. Prefers 7½ ips reel-to-reel or cassette with 1-4 songs on demo. Include photos and bio. SASE. Reports in 1 month.
**Music:** Mostly R&B and pop; also children's, dance-oriented, easy listening and soul. Recently produced "Do Me Baby Do Me," by Somerset (dance single, Dazia Records); "I'm in Love With You," by Somerset (pop/top 40 single, Dazia Records); and "Do Anything for You," by Somerset (pop/easy listening single, Dazia Records).

**\*DESTINY PRODUCTIONS, INC.**, 117 W. Rockland Rd., Box 615, Libertyville IL 60048. (312)362-4060. Vice President: Rick Johnson. Record producer and music publisher (Amalgamated Tulip Corp.). Deals with artists and songwriters. Produces 2 singles and 1 album/year. Fee derived from sales royalty.
**How to Contact:** Submit demo tape and lyric sheet; write about your interest. Prefers cassette with 3-5 songs on demo. SASE. Reports in 1 month.
**Music:** Mostly hard rock; also blues, C&W, MOR, progressive, Spanish rock and top 40/pop. Recently published *Conrad Black*, by Conrad Black (rock/R&B LP, Dharma Records); *Dancexercise*, by Johnson & Poole (exercise LP, Homexercise Records); "Last Chance," by Gabriel Bondage (progressive rock single, Dharma Records); and *Not Marmosets Yet*, by Conrad Black (hard rock LP, Dharma Records).

**\*DESTINY RECORDS**, 31 Nassau Ave., Wilmington MA 01887. (617)658-8391. Contact: Larry Feeney. Record producer and music publisher (Seismic Music). Works with artists and songwriters. Produces 3-5 singles/year. Fee derived from sales royalty.
**How to Contact:** Call first about your interest. Prefers cassette with maximum 2 songs on demo. "Artists must be currently performing." Does not return unsolicited material. Reports in 1 month.
**Music:** Mostly rock; also bluegrass, blues, C&W, dance-oriented, easy listening, folk, jazz, MOR, progressive, R&B, soul and top 40/pop. Recently produced "Push It to the Limit," by The Wages (pop/rock single, Destiny Records); and "She'll Drive You Crazy," by Wild Turkey (R&R single, Destiny Records).

**STEVE DIGGS PRODUCTIONS**, 1110 16th Ave. S., Nashville TN 37212. (615)259-4024. Producer: Steve Diggs. Record producer, music publisher and jingle producer. Deals with artists and songwriters, and clients looking for musical advertising. Fee derived from sales royalty or outright fee from record company.
**How to Contact:** Query or submit demo tape and lead sheet. Prefers 7½ ips reel-to-reel with 2-4 songs on demo. SASE. Reports in 1 month.
**Music:** Bluegrass, children's, church/religious, C&W, easy listening, folk, MOR, rock and top 40/pop.

**DMI PRODUCTIONS**, #1911, 6255 Sunset Blvd., Hollywood CA 90028. (213)462-1922. Managing Director: Christian de Walden. Record producer and music publisher (De Walden Music International, Inc./BMI, ASCAP). Estab. 1981. Deals with artists and songwriters. Produces 6-7 singles and 3-4 albums/year. Fee derived from sales royalty.
**How to Contact:** Arrange personal interview if in the area or submit demo tape and lyric sheet. Prefers cassette with 2-5 songs on demo. SASE. Reports in 2-3 weeks or ASAP.
**Music:** Country (pop), easy listening, MOR, Spanish, soul and top 40/pop. Recently produced "Never Say Goodbye," by Sally Kellerman (country crossover single); "Love Party," by the Honey B's (black dance single); *John Rowles*, by J. Rowles (MOR ballads LP, RCA Records/Australia, EMI Records/New Zealand); "Dynamite," by Dick St. John (gimmick single, WEA Records-BeneLux Victor Records); "Mina" (POW Records/Italy); "Hornettes" (Jupiter Records/Germany); and "Trini Lopez" (Bogart EMI Records, worldwide).
**Tips:** "My companies are specialized in international recordings. Right now some songs in our publishing catalog have been recorded by such top artists as Demis Roussos, Barry White (soon to be released), Jeane Manson (CBS France), etc."

**JOHN DOELP ASSOCIATES**, Suite 7S, 1 Astor Place, New York NY 10003. (212)242-4782. President/Producer: John McL. Doelp. Record producer. Deals with artists, songwriters and record companies. Produces 2 singles and 2 albums/year. Fee derived from sales royalty or outright fee from record company.
**How to Contact:** Submit demo tape and lyric sheet. Prefers 7½ ips reel-to-reel or cassette with 2-4 songs on demo. "Include supporting information, i.e., resume, reviews, picture, bio, etc." SASE. Reports in 2 weeks.
**Music:** Mostly new wave and pop; also rock (country or hard), soul and top 40/. Recently produced "She Had to Go," and "Rubber Rodeo" by Rubber Rodeo (country western/new wave, EAT Records).
**Tips:** "Looking for originality with a popular twist."

**DOOR KNOB RECORDS**, 2125 8th Ave. S., Nashville TN 37204. (615)383-6002. President: Gene Kennedy. Vice-president: Karen Jeglum. Director of Promotions: Joe Carroll. Record producer, music publisher, distributor and promoter. Deals with artists and songwriters. Fee derived by sales royalty.
**How to Contact:** Submit demo tape and lyric sheet or call first about your interest. Prefers 7½ ips reel-to-reel or cassette with 4 songs maximum on demo. SASE. Reports in 1-3 month.
**Music:** C&W, gospel and MOR. Recently released "Back in Debbie's Arms" and "Green Eyes," by Tom Carlile; and "A Thing or Two On My Mind," by Gene Kennedy and Karen Jeglum. Other artists include Thomas Riley, Shirley Parker, Kris Carpenter and Dealer's Choice.

**BARRY DRAKE ENTERPRISES**, Red Kill Rd., Fleischmanns NY 12430. (914)254-4565. Record producer, music publisher (Sweet Swamp Music/BMI) and record company (Catskill Mountain Records). Deals with artists and songwriters. Produces 2 singles and 2 albums/year. Fee derived from sales royalty.
**How to Contact:** Submit demo tape and lyric sheet. Prefers cassette with 1-3 songs on demo. SASE. Reports in 1 month.
**Music:** Bluegrass, blues, C&W, folk, MOR, rock (soft, country) and top 40/pop. Recently released *Roadsongs*, by Barry Drake (LP, CatskillMountain Records). Other artists include Jon Ims.

*****PETE DRAKE PRODUCTIONS, INC.**, 809 18th Ave. S, Nashville TN 37203. (615)327-3211. Professional Manager: Ron Cornelius. Record producer and music publisher (The Drake Music Group, Window Music Pub. Co., Inc.). Deals with artists and songwriters. Produces 6-10 singles and 12-15 albums/year. Fee derived from sales royalty.
**How to Contact:** Call or write about your interest. Prefers cassette with 2-4 songs on demo. SASE. Reports in 3 weeks.
**Music:** Mostly country and MOR; also church/religious, easy listening, gospel and top 40/pop. Recently produced *Amazing Grace*, by B.J. Thomas (gospel LP, World Records); "Whatever Happened to Old Fashioned Love," by B.J. Thomas (country single, CBS-Cleveland International Records); and "If Drinkin' Don't Kill Me," by George Jones (country single, Epic Records). Other artists include Slim

Whitman, Ray Pillow and Melba Montgomery.
**Tips:** "Submit only your best material and only for the artists we handle."

**DUANE MUSIC, INC.**, 382 Clarence Ave., Sunnyvale CA 94086. (408)739-6133. President: Garrie Thompson. Record producer and music publisher. Deals with artists and songwriters. Fee derived from sales royalty.
**How to Contact:** Submit demo tape only. Prefers cassette with 1-5 songs on demo. SASE. Reports in 1 month.
**Music:** Blues, C&W, rock, soul, and top 40/pop. Recently produced "Wichita," (C&W single, Hush Records); and "Syndicate of Sound," (rock single, Buddah Records).

**DUPUY RECORDS/PRODUCTIONS/PUBLISHING, INC.**, Suite 200, 10960 Ventura Blvd., Studio City CA 91604. (213)980-6412). President: Pedro Dupuy. Record producer and music publisher (Dupuy Publishing, Inc./ASCAP). Estab. 1981. Deals with artists, songwriters, music arrangers, copyists, musicians, background vocalists, singers and recording engineers. Produces 5 singles and 5 albums/year. Fee derived from sales royalty; differs with each artist.
**How to Contact:** Write or call first about your interest, arrange personal interview or submit demo tape and lyric sheet. Prefers cassette with 2-4 songs on demo. SASE. Reports in 1 month.
**Music:** Easy listening, jazz, MOR, R&B, soul and top 40/pop. Artists include Gordon Gilman.
**Tips:** "Artists and songwriters should have strong songs, versatility, and open minds."

**EARTH AND SKY RECORDS**, Box 4157, Winter Park FL 32793. Manager/Producer: William (Bill) Winborne. Record producer and music publisher (Earth and Sky Music Publishing, Inc./BMI). Deals with artists and songwriters. Produces 6 singles and 4 albums/year. Fee derived from sales royalty per standard contract.
**How to Contact:** Write first about your interest; submit demo tape and lyric sheet. "Do not phone." Prefers cassette with 1-3 songs on demo. "Songwriters should send *only* copyrighted material with good lead sheets and demos." SASE. Reports ASAP.
**Music:** Mostly pop, adult contemporary and country; also bluegrass, easy listening, jazz, MOR, progressive, R&B, rock and top 40. Recently produced "Mountain Song," by the Stallion Band (country single, Les Records); *Late Night Lullaby*, by Jack McIntosh (pop LP, Earth and Sky Records); *Goodby Lady Jane*, by Trans Atlantic (mellow rock LP, Les Records); and *That's How Fresh Your Love Is*, by Mark Christopher (pop single, Earth and Sky Records).
**Tips:** "Interested in new talent. Send photo if available and any other informaton you'd like us to be aware of. Send as many songs as you like."

**EASTEX MUSIC**, #2, 8537 Sunset Blvd., Los Angeles CA 90069. (213)657-8852. Contact: Travis Lehman. Record producer and music publisher. Deals with songwriters and artists. Fee derived from sales royalty plus advance.
**How to Contact:** Submit demo tape. Prefers cassette. SASE. Reports in 3 weeks.
**Music:** R&R and country.

**EBB-TIDE PRODUCTIONS**, Box 2544, Baton Rouge LA 70821. (504)924-6865 (24 hrs.). President: E.K. Harrison. Record producer and music publisher (Harrison Music Publishing Company, Inc./BMI, Cryin' in the Streets Music Publishers/ASCAP). Deals with artists and songwriters. Produces 12 singles and 12 albums/year. Fee derived from sales royalty.
**How to Contact:** Submit demo tape and lead sheet. Prefers cassette with 4-6 songs on demo. SASE. Reports in 2 weeks.
**Music:** Bluegrass, church/religious, C&W, and folk. Recently produced *Cryin' in the Streets*, by George Perkins and The Silver Stars, and *The Mighty-Chevelles*, by Disco Music (soul LPs, C.I.T.S. Records); and "Doggie-Dog World," by Willie-Joe (soul single, P.B.S. Records). Other artists include Jimmy and Joanie Angel, Pamla-Marie, George Hickory, Richard Jones, and Wylie and Truth (group).

**EB-TIDE MUSIC/YOUNG COUNTRY MUSIC**, Box 5412, Buena Park CA 90620. (213)864-6302. Contact: Leo J. Eiffert, Jr. Record producer and music publisher (Eb Tide Music Co./BMI, Young Country Music Co./BMI). Deals with artists. Produces 20 singles and 4 albums/year. Fee derived from sales royalty.
**How to Contact:** Call or write first about your interest, then submit demo tape and lyric sheet. Prefers 7½ ips reel-to-reel as demo. SASE. Reports in 3 weeks.
**Music:** C&W. Recently produced "She's a Texas Redneck," by Leo J. Eiffert, Jr.; "Street Lights and White Lines," by Jodie Scarberry; and "Woman, Give Him to Me," by Pamela Jean (country singles, Plain Country Records). Other artists include Crawfish, Billy Smith, Al Bruno, Jack Tucker, Bobby Bee, Cleat Wooley and Larry Settle.
**Tips:** "All songs must be copyrighted and open for publishing."

**ECHO RECORDS**, 824 83rd St., Miami Beach FL 33141. (305)865-8960. Record producer and music publisher (Dana Publishing). Deals with artists. Produces 2 singles and 1 album/year.
**How to Contact:** Write first about your interest. Prefers 7½ or 15 ips reel-to-reel or cassette as demo. SASE.
**Music:** Classical and Polish. Recently produced "God's Children," by Don Bennett; "We Want God," by Regina Kujawa (religious singles, Echo Records); *Chor Dana*, by Chor Dana (Polish pop LP, Echo Records); *Polish Dances Opus 40, 41, 43, 44*, by Walter Dana (piano solo and classical form of Polish dances); and "Come Back Lost Day," by Stas Jaworski (Polish pop single, Echo Records).

**EN POINTE PRODUCTIONS**, Box 1451, Beverly Hills CA 90213. (805)497-1584. President: Jeff Weber. Record producer. Deals with artists. Produces 3-7 albums/year. Fee derived from sales royalty, by outright fee from record company or royalty advance from labels or private companies.
**How to Contact:** Write first about your interest. Prefers cassette with 2-4 songs on demo. "Record on the best tape available utilizing the best means available." SASE. Reports in 2 weeks "or less."
**Music:** Bluegrass, classical, jazz, R&B, rock, soul, and top 40/pop. Recently produced *Desire*, by Tom Scott (Elektra/Musician Records); *Ride Like the Wind*, by Freddie Hubbard (commercial jazz LP, Elektra/Musician Records); and *Night Plane*, by Haden Gregg/Jim Dykann (contemporary pop/rock LP, Handshake Records).
**Tips:** "My work is primarily involved with audiophile recording techniques (i.e., direct to disc, digital and live to the two track). My recordings accentuate artistry as well as emotional involvement."

*****ENCHANTED DOOR, INC.**, Box 1235, New Rochelle NY 10802. (914)834-5676. Manager: Joe Chanler. Record producer, music publisher (Cap-Orion Music), record company and artist management firm. Works with artists and songwriters. Produces 6 singles and 2 albums/year. Fee derived from sales royalty.
**How to Contact:** Submit demo tape and lyric sheet. Prefers cassette with 2-4 songs on demo. Include photos, bio and itinerary. Does not return unsolicited material. Reporting time varies.
**Music:** *Makin' Wowii*, by Wowii (top 40 LP, Elektra Records); *Struck by Lightnin'*, by Rat Race Choir (pop LP, Crescent Records); and "Forever," by Wowii (pop single, Cartoon Records). Other artists include Beth Ames, Spyder Turner and Precious.

**ENTERTAINMENT COMPANY**, 40 W. 57th St., New York NY 10019. (212)265-2600. Contact: Publishing Department. Record producer and music publisher. Deals with artists and songwriters.
**How to Contact:** Submit demo tape and lyric sheet. Prefers cassette with 1-2 songs on demo. SASE. Reports in 1-3 months.
**Music:** Country/pop, MOR, R&B, crossover rock and top 40/pop. Artists include Dolly Parton, Cher, The Four Tops, Tanya Tucker and Barbra Streisand.

**ESQUIRE INTERNATIONAL**, Box 6032, Station B, Miami FL 33123. (305)547-1424. President: Jeb Stuart. Record producer, music publisher and management firm. Deals with artists and record labels. Produces 5 singles/year. Fee derived from sales royalty or independent leasing of masters and placing songs.
**How to Contact:** Query, submit demo tape and lead sheet or telephone. Prefers cassette with 2-4 songs on demo, or disc. SASE. Reports in 1 month.
**Music:** Blues, church/religious, C&W, dance, gospel, jazz, rock, soul and top 40/pop. Recently produced "Can't Count the Days" (R&B single, Kent Records); "Sitba" (R&B single, King Records); and "Hung Up on Your Love" (disco single, Esquire Records), all by Jeb Stuart.

**FACTORY BEAT RECORDS, INC.**, 663 5th Ave., New York NY 10022. (212)757-3638. Record producer and music publisher (Ren-Maur Music/BMI). Produces 6 singles and 2 albums/year. Fee derived from sales royalty.
**How to Contact:** Submit demo tape and lyric sheet only. Prefers cassette with 2-4 songs on demo. SASE. Reports in 3 weeks.
**Music:** R&B, rock, soul and top 40/pop. Recently produced "Let's Slip Away" and "Everybody's Doin' It," by Charles T. Hudson (R&B/funk singles, Factory Beat Records); "I Love Your Beat" and "Dance It Off," by Rena (dance singles, Factory Beat Records); and "Do It to Me and I'll Do It to You," by Rena Romano.
**Tips:** "Have a finished product, ready to master and press for commercial use."

*****FANTASY WORKSHOP**, 3156 Gifford Lane, Coconut Grove FL 33133. (305)448-2735. Producer: Jim Rudd. Record producer and music publisher (Snoopy Music/BMI). Deals with artists, songwriters and financeers. Produces 1-2 singles and 1-2 albums/year. Fee derived from sales royalty or outright fee from songwriter/artist for professional consultation or from record company. "Our subsidiary, FatCat

Productions, seeks and finds financial backers for artists."
**How to Contact:** Submit demo tape and lyric and lead sheet. Prefers cassette with 1-3 songs on demo. SASE. Reports in 1 month.
**Music:** Mostly mellow rock and rockabilly; also C&W, dance-oriented, easy listening, MOR and R&B. Recently produced *The Clown*, by Toni Bishop (A/C LP, Revolution Records); *Las Vegas Lady*, by Romeo (Latin rock LP, Revolution Records); and *Loving You*, by Kim Russell (rockabilly LP, Revolution Records). Other artists include Ken Jinks (ballad collection) and Spinnaker (jazz/rock).

**\*DON FELT/OVERTON LEE**, 10051 Green Leaf, Santa Fe Spring CA 90670. (213)946-1524. President: Overton Lee. Record producer and music publisher (Boggy Depot, Overton Lee Music). Deals with artists and songwriters. Produces 6 singles and 2 albums/year. Fee derived from sales royalty.
**How to Contact:** Submit demo tape and lyric sheet. Prefers cassette with 1-3 songs on demo. SASE. Reports in 4 months.
**Music:** Mostly country; also bluegrass, blues, C&W and gospel. Recently produced *Hard On the Heart* and *Some Where in Houston*, both by Johnny Blankenship (Overton Lee Records); and *May You Never Be Alone*, by Overton Lee (Overton Lee Records). Other artists include Alan Lee Blackwell, Gene Davis and Eddie Marie.

**\*FOLK ARTS PRODUCTIONS**, Box 155, Huntington NY 11743. (516)231-0497. President: Tom Pomposello. Record producer and TV/radio production. Deals with artists, producers and film and video people. Produces 6 albums/year. Fee derived from sales royalty.
**How to Contact:** Submit demo tape and lyric sheet. Prefers cassette with 1-3 songs on demo. SASE. Reports in 3 weeks.
**Music:** Bluegrass, blues, folk, R&B and "classic" R&R (e.g. Chuck Berry, Fats Domino, Carl Perkins). Recently produced *American Music: A Journal*, by Honest Tom Pomposello (folk/blues LP, Folk Arts Records); *Shake 'em on Down*, by Mississippi Fred McDowell (folk/blues LP, Labor Records); and *Can't Find a Friend*, by Dee Harris (folk/blues LP, Absolute Records).

**FULL CIRCLE PRODUCTIONS, INC.**, 80 E. San Francisco St., Santa Fe NM 87501. (505)982-2900. President: Reno Myerson. Record producer and music publisher (Full Cycle Publishing Co./BMI, ASCAP). Deals with artists and songwriters. Produces 3 singles and 3 albums/year. Fee derived from sales royalty or outright fee from record company.
**How to Contact:** Submit demo tape and lyric sheet or call for appointment. Prefers cassette with 4-10 songs on demo. SASE. Reports in 1 month.
**Music:** Bluegrass, blues, C&W, dance-oriented, folk, jazz, progressive, R&B, rock (country and hard) and soul. Recently produced *Burn You with Cold*, by the Grandmothers (rock/jazz fusion LP and single, Helios Records). Other artists include Richard Moon, Jimmy Carl Black and Joey Bradley.
**Tips:** "Groups should have a business manager; artists should have *original* material."

**FUTURE 1 PRODUCTIONS**, 8924 E. Calle Norlo, Tucson AZ 85710. (602)885-5931. Producers: James M. Gasper and Thomas M. Dukes. Record producer and music publisher (Myko Music/BMI). Estab. 1981. Deals with artists and songwriters. Produces 2 singles and 2 albums/year. Fee derived from sales royalty.
**How to Contact:** Call first about your interest, then submit demo tape and lyric sheet. Prefers 7½ ips reel-to-reel or cassette with 3-5 songs on demo. SASE. Reports in 1 month.
**Music:** Easy listening, R&B, rock, top 40/pop and poprock. Recently produced "Siren's Song" and "Just Arrived," by Gasper & Dukes (pop/rock EP, Ariana Records); "She's on Fire," by The Band-Aids (new wave/rock single, Ariana Records); and "Just an Hour a Day," by Happy Leggs (power pop, Ariana Records).

**FYDAQ PRODUCTIONS**, 240 E. Radcliffe Dr., Claremont CA 91711. (714)624-0677. President: Gary K. Buckley. Record producer. Deals with artists, songwriters and record companies. Produces 2-5 singles and 4-5 albums/year. Fee derived from sales royalty, outright fee from record company, or outright fee from songwriter/artist.
**How to Contact:** Query, submit demo tape, or submit demo tape and lead sheet. Prefers 7½ ips reel-to-reel or cassette with 1-4 songs on demo. SASE. Reports in 3 weeks.
**Music:** C&W, easy listening, folk, gospel, MOR, rock, soul and top 40/pop. Recently produced *Buche*, by Rick Buche (top 40/MOR LP, Paradise Records); *To God, with Love*, by Jerry Roark (gospel LP, Majega Records); *Country Love*, by J. Roark (C&W LP, Majega Records); *Sending A Copy Home*, by Jody Barry (gospel LP, Majega Records); "Is It Right," by Borderline (top 40/AOR single, Majega Records); "Touch Me Now," by Borderline (top 40/single, Majega Records); *Sky's the Limit*, by Michael Noll (top 40/pop LP, Gottabehit Records); and *My Simple Song*, by Debbie Norheim (gospel LP, DNC Records).

**GEE PRODUCTIONS-DON LEONARD PRODUCTIONS**, 8 Cherry Hill Court, Reisterstown MD 21136. (301)883-3816. Producer: Don Leonard. (Leonard-Gee Music/BMI). Deals with artists and songwriters. Fee derived from sales royalty. Changes fee "if hired to produce and the artist or writer wants to pay for own session. I do not charge if I see a strong potential in an artist—no fee for songs of chart possibility."
**How to Contact:** Query, arrange personal interview, submit demo tape only or submit demo tape and lead sheet. Prefers cassette or 8-track cassette. SASE. Reports in 1 month.
**Music:** C&W, disco, easy listening, jazz, MOR, progressive, rock, soul and top 40/pop. Recently produced "Roll Away Heartaches," by Eddie Farrel.

*****GET RICH MUSIC/STAY RICH MUSIC**, Suite 608, 1650 Broadway, New York NY 10019. (212)245-9055. President: David Nelson Askew. Record producer and music publisher (Get Rich Music/BMI, Stay Rich Music/ASCAP). Deals with artists, songwriters, staff writers and producers. Produces 12 12" singles and 6 albums/year. Fee derived from sales royalty.
**How to Contact:** Submit demo tape and lyric sheet; write about your interest. Prefers 7½ ips reel-to-reel or cassette with 1-3 songs on demo. SASE. Reports in 6 weeks.
**Music:** Mostly dance, up-tempo funky music and adult contemporary for radio formats; also R&B, soul and rap. Recently produced "Happiness" and "Take Your Time," by The Conservatives (dance singles, On Time Records and SMI Records); and "Reality," by The Bangies (rap single, SMI Records).

**GOLDBAND RECORDING STUDIO**, 313 Church St., Lake Charles LA 70601. (318)439-8839. Contact: Eddie Shuler. Record producer. Deals with artists and songwriters. Fee derived from sales royalty.
**How to Contact:** Prefers 7½ ips reel-to-reel or cassette with 1-10 songs on demo. SASE. Reports in 2 months.
**Music:** All types. Recently produced "Things I Used to Do," by Katie Webster (R&B single, Goldband Records); "Cajun Disco," by La Salle Sisters (disco single, Goldband Records); and "Ole Billy Hell," by Rickey Kelley (country single, Goldband Records).

**GOLLY MUSIC**, Suite 8Q, 12 Marshall St., Irvington NJ 07111. (201)373-6050. Executive Director: Walt Gollender. Record producer, music publisher and management firm. Deals with artists and songwriters. Produces 2-3 singles and 1 album/year. Fee derived from sales royalty, outright fee from record company, or outright management fee from songwriter/artist.
**How to Contact:** Arrange personal interview or submit demo tape. Prefers 7½ ips mono reel-to-reel or cassette with 1-4 songs on demo. SASE. Reports in 1 month.
**Music:** Mostly soft to medium rock, soul and C&W; also blues, dance, easy listening, folk, MOR and top 40/pop. Artists include Tommy Boyce, Fire, Irwin Levine and Lee Shapiro.
**Tips:** "Write songs as good or better than what is on the top record charts. Be willing to re-write and take constructive criticism."

**GOSPEL EXPRESS**, 1899 S. 3rd, Box 2194, Memphis TN 38101. (901)774-5689. President: Bishop Cole. Deals with artists and songwriters. Produces 5-8 albums/year. Fee derived from sales royalty.
**How to Contact:** Submit demo tape and lead sheet. Prefers cassette. SASE. Reports in 3 weeks.
**Music:** Blues, church/religious, dance and gospel. Recently produced "Phone Call From God," by The Bishop (gospel, Michal Records); "Tell Heaven," by Gospel Songbirds (gospel, Gospel Express Records); and "Save A Seat for Me," by Shirly James (gospel, Michal Records).

**GOSPEL RECORDS, INC.**, Box 90, Rugby Station, Brooklyn NY 11203. (212)773-5910. President: John R. Lockley. Record producer and music publisher (Gospel Clef Music/BMI). Deals with artists, songwriters and musicians. Fee derived from sales royalty.
**How to Contact:** Write for permission to send demo. Reports in 1 month.
**Music:** Spirituals. Recently produced "Everytime I Feel the Spirit," by Glorytone (spiritual single, Gospel Records, Inc.); *Jesus* and *Glorifying Jesus*, by The Lockley Family Gospel Ensemble (spiritual LPs, Gospel Records, Inc.).

**GRASSROOTS PROJECTS UNLIMITED**, Box 4689, San Francisco CA 94101. Contact: James L. Heisterkamp. Record company and music publisher (Grassroots Projects Unlimited/BMI). Fee derived from sales royalty.
**How to Contact:** Write first about your interest. "We are really not looking for new talent at this time. We have an in-house operation and use San Francisco talent when needed." SASE.
**Music:** Ragtime, songs about San Francisco by San Francisco writers, and gospel by Bay area talent. Recently produced *Echoes from Lulu White's Mahogany Hall*, by Dick Kroeckel (ragtime LP, Ragtime Records); "A Cable Car Special," by Jack Bryson Bowden (local appeal single, Cable Car Records);

and "I'll Be in My Dixie Home Again Tomorrow," by J.C. Munns & His Boys (ragtime single, Cable Car Records).

**MILES GRAYSON PRODUCTIONS**, 1159 S. LaJolla Ave., Los Angeles CA 90035. (213)938-3531. Musical Director: Lerman Horton. Deals with artists and songwriters. Fee derived from sales royalty.
**How to Contact:** Submit demo tape and lyric sheet. Prefers cassette with 2-4 songs on demo. SASE. Reports in 2 weeks and "sometimes minutes."
**Music:** Dance, MOR, R&B, soul and top 40/pop. Recently produced *What Time It Is*, by Jackie Payne (RCA Victor/Mojo Records); and *Mojo Power*, by Julie Clark (top 40 LP, Columbia/Warner Bros. Records).

**GREAT PYRAMID, LTD. MUSIC**, 10 Waterville St., San Francisco CA 94124. Contact: Joseph Buchwald. Record producer, music publisher (Great Pyramid Music/BMI) and management firm. Deals with artists and songwriters. Produces 2 singles and 1-2 albums/year. Fee derived from sales royalty, outright fee from record company, outright fee from songwriter/artist or commissions.
**How to Contact:** Query or submit demo tape and lead sheet. Prefers cassette with 3-6 songs on demo. Does not return unsolicited material. Reports "as soon as possible."
**Music:** Mostly MOR. Recently produced "What Love Is," "Do It for Love," and "Hearts," by Balin (ballad singles, EMI Records).

**GRUSIN/ROSEN PRODUCTIONS/GRP RECORDS**, Suite 1228, 558 W. 57th St., New York NY 10019. (212)245-7033. Contact: Dave Grusin, Larry Rosen, Peter Lopez. Deals with artists and songwriters. Releases 10 albums/year. Fee derived from sales royalty or outright fee from record company.
**How to Contact:** Query. Prefers reel-to-reel or cassette with 2-5 songs on demo. SASE.
**Music:** Jazz, R&B and pop. Recently released albums by Angela Bofill, Tom Browne, Dave Valentin, Scott Jarrett, Gerry Mulligan, Dave Grusin and the Glen Miller Orchestra.

**GST MUSIC PRODUCTIONS**, 17 Ponca Trail, St. Louis MO 63122. (314)821-2741. Producer: Gregory Trampe. Record producer and music publisher (Tragrey Music Publishing/BMI). Deals with artists and songwriters. Produces 10-12 singles and 2 albums/year. Fee derived from sales royalty or outright fee from record company.
**How to Contact:** Write or call first about your interest, arrange personal interview or submit demo tape and lyric sheet. Prefers 7½ ips reel-to-reel or cassette with 2-4 songs on demo. SASE. Reports in 1 month.
**Music:** C&W, dance-oriented, gospel, jazz, MOR, progressive, R&B, rock (all types), soul, top 40/pop and contemporary gospel. Recently produced "Stealin' the Feelin'," by Terry Aden; "Don't Start Something You Can't Finish," by Terry Ray Bradley; and "Given' up Easy," by Susan Anderson (country singles, BB Records). Other artists include Shannon, Kim Bridger and Ron Head.

**GEORGE GUESS PRODUCTIONS**, 2250 Bryn Mawr Ave., Philadelphia PA 19131. (215)477-7122. A&R Director: Ted Brown. Record producer. Deals with artists and songwriters. Produces 3-5 singles and 2-3 albums/year. Fee derived from sales royalty, outright fee from artists or record company.
**How to Contact:** Query with letter of introduction or submit demo tape. Prefers 7½ ips reel-to-reel or cassette with 5 songs on demo. SASE. Reports in 3 weeks.
**Music:** Dance, soul, and top 40/pop. Recently produced "Bus Stop," by the Lambchops; *Dreams & Nightmares*, by Dream Merchants (R&B LP, Dazz Records); "Lovin Kind of Love," by Vee Vee and "Roadrunner," by Satins Breed (rock singles, Sin Records); and "God Only Knows," by Donald Reeves (gospel single, Heaven Records). Other artists include Day One and George Guess.
**Tips:** "If a writer, be consistent with creativity of original compositions. Stay on top of what's musically happening."

**JIM HALL & GIDGET STARR PRODUCTIONS**, 5 Aldom Circle, West Caldwell NJ 07006. (201)226-0035. Contact: Jim Hall or Gidget Starr. Record producer and music publisher (Cactus Music and Gidget Publishing/ASCAP). Deals with artists and songwriters. Fee derived from sales royalty.
**How to Contact:** Write first about your interest then submit demo tape and lyric sheet. Prefers 7½ ips reel-to-reel, cassette or 8-track tapes with 5 songs minimum on demo. Does not return unsolicited material. Reports in 3 weeks.
**Music:** Bluegrass, blues, church/religious, C&W, easy listening, gospel, R&B, rock and soul. Artists include Doc Hopkins, The Tune Twisters.

**HALLWAYS TO FAME PRODUCTIONS**, Box 18918, Los Angeles CA 90018. (213)935-7277. General Manager: Al Hall, Jr. Record producer and music publisher (Aljoni Music Co./BMI, Hallmar-

que Musical Works, Ltd./ASCAP). Deals with artists and songwriters. Produces 10 singles and 2-4 albums/year. Fee derived from sales royalty.
**How to Contact:** Submit demo tape and lyric sheet. Prefers cassette, (7½ ips reel-to-reel is OK), with 5-10 songs on demo. Does not return unsolicited material. Reports in 1 month.
**Music:** Jazz, R&B, rock (soft), soul and top 40/pop. Recently produced *Splash*, by Freddie Hubbard (R&B/jazz LP, Fantasy Records); "You're Gonna Lose Me," by F. Hubbard (R&B single, Fantasy Records); and "Bip Bam," by Bill Brown (R&B/pop single, Brownstone Records).
**Tips:** "We seek artists with strong direction and positive attitude; songs with good melodies, slick lyrics (hooks) and nice chord progressions."

***HALNAT PUBLISHING CO.**, Box 37156, Cincinnati OH 45222. (513)891-2300, 2301; 531-7605. Contact: Saul Halper. Record producer and music publisher (Halnat). Works with artists and songwriters. Produces 4 singles/year. Fee derived from sales royalty.
**How to Contact:** Submit demo tape and lyric sheet. Prefers cassette with 4-5 songs on demo. SASE. Reports in 2 weeks.
**Music:** Bluegrass, blues, gospel, R&B and soul.

**HALPERN SOUNDS**, #9, 1775 Old County Rd., Belmont CA 94002. (415)592-4900. President: Steven Halpern. Record producer. Deals with artists and songwriters. Produces 4 albums/year. Fee derived from sales royalty.
**How to Contact:** Submit demo tape and lyric sheet. Prefers cassette with 4-8 songs on demo. "Songs should have *uplifting* lyrics." SASE. Reports in 3 months.
**Music:** Easy listening and MOR. Recently produced *Dawn*, and *Eventide*, by Steven Halpern (soothing and uplifting LPs, Halpern Sounds Records).

**RL HAMMEL ASSOCIATES**, Box 531, Alexandria IN 46001-0531. (317)642-7030. Contact: Randal L. Hammel. Record producer, music publisher (Ladnar Music/ASCAP) and consultants. Deals with artists and songwriters. Produces 3-4 singles and 10 albums/year. Fee derived from sales royalty, outright fee from artist/songwriter or record company, or negotiable fee per project.
**How to Contact:** Write first about your interest and send brief resume (including experience, age, goal). Prefers cassette with 3 songs maximum on demo. "Lyrics (preferably typed) *must* accompany tapes!" SASE. Reports ASAP.
**Music:** Blues, church/religious, C&W, dance, easy listening, gospel, MOR, progressive, R&B, rock (usually country), soul and top 40/pop. Recently produced *The Glove*, by Jeff Steinberg (religious LP, GlovePrints Records); *Reason for the Season*, by David Clydesdale (religious LP, Benson Records); *Morning Sun*, by Ronn Koerper (big band/religious LP); *Singing a Love Song*, by Gary Floyd (Christian LP, Custom Records); *Longtime Friends*, by Morris Chapman (Word Records); and *Word and Song*, by Judy Foskey (Christian LP, Custom Records). Other artists include Overeasy and Heigh-Liters.
**Tips:** "Though there are certain stigmas that go along with being from the Midwest, we still maintain that quality work can be done, and our good reputation with the 'biggies' in Chicago, Los Angeles, Nashville, etc. will bear us out. Only those who have a full knowledge of the sacrifice involved with this industry (or those willing to hear it) should consider contacting this office. We will shoot straight, and it is *always* explained that our observations are just that—'ours', and another company/production team/etc. might be interested."

**HAM-SEM RECORDS, INC.**, 541 S. Spring St., Los Angeles CA 90013. (213)627-0557. A&R Director: Dianna Green. Record producer (Four Buddies/ASCAP). Deals with artists and songwriters. Produces 4 singles and 1 album/year. Fee derived from sales royalty or outright fee from artist/songwriter.
**How to Contact:** Call first about your interest. Prefers cassette with 4-10 songs on demo. Does not return unsolicited material. Reports in 1 month.
**Music:** Church/religious, gospel (contemporary), MOR, R&B and top 40/pop. Recently produced *Secret Love*, by Charles Scott (disco LP, Ham-Sem Records); and "Share Your Love," by C. Scott (ballad single, Ham-Sem Records).

**HANSEN-O'BRIEN MUSIC, PRODUCTIONS**, (formerly O'Brien Productions), #8, 234 5th Ave., Redwood City CA 94063. (415)367-0298. President: E.J. O'Brien. Record producer and music publisher (O'Brien Publishing & Record Co.). Estab. 1981. Deals with artists and songwriters. Produces 10 singles and 1 album/year. Fee derived from sales royalty.
**How to Contact:** Submit demo tape and lyric sheet. Prefers cassette with 2-4 songs on demo. SASE. Reports in 2 weeks.
**Music:** Blues, C&W, MOR, R&B and rock. Recently produced "Give It Up," by Paul Hanson (R&B

single, Duck Records); "The Devils Dues," by P. Hanson (C&W single, O'Brien Records); and "Enough Is Enough," by Dale Hanson (MOR single, O'Brien Records).

**HAPPY DAY PRODUCTIONS, INC.**, 800 N. Ridgeland, Oak Park IL 60302. (312)848-3322. Vice President: Vince Ippolito. Record producer and music publisher. Deals with artists.
**How to Contact:** Submit demo tape and lyric sheet. Prefers 7½ ips reel-to-reel or cassette with 2-3 songs on demo. SASE.
**Music:** MOR, progressive, R&B, rock, soul and top 40/pop. Recently produced "Disco Fairyland" and "Rock Me Baby," by Kitty & Haywoods (disco/R&B single, Capital Records); and "Fightin' Jane," by Frank Pisani (C&W/MOR single, Happy Day Records).

**HARD HAT PRODUCTIONS**, 519 N. Halifax Ave., Daytona Beach FL 32018. (904)252-0381. President/producer: Bobby Lee Cude. Record producer and music publisher (Cude & Pickens Publishing). Deals with artists and songwriters. Produces 12 singles and 6 albums/year. Fee derived from sales royalty or outright fee from artist/songwriter or record company.
**How to Contact:** "Write first telling me about yourself—what type artist etc." Prefers cassette with 1-6 songs on demo. SASE. Reports ASAP.
**Music:** C&W, easy listening, gospel, MOR, top 40/pop and Broadway Show. Recently produced "Heard You Married Him Today," by Blue Bandana Country Band (country single, Hard Hat Records); "The Island Song," by Caribbean Knights (salsa single, Hard Hat Records); "Where These Big City Lights Shine," by Cityfolks Country Band (salsa single, Hard Hat Records); and "It's Twelve O'Clock! Do You Know Where Your Children Are?," by Watie Riley the Piano Man.

**HARD-BOILED RECORDS (PHIL PHILLIPS-PRODUCER)**, 484 Lake Park Ave., Box 6, Oakland CA 94610. (415)482-4854. A&R Director: Dan Orth. Record producer and music publisher (Dynamo Publishing Co./BMI). Deals with artists, songwriters and musicians. Produces 1 single/year. Fee derived from sales royalty.
**How to Contact:** Write or call first about your interest, then submit demo tape and lyric sheet. Prefers cassette with 1-3 songs on demo. SASE. Reports in 1 month.
**Music:** C&W, easy listening, folk, R&B, rock (hard, soft, pop), top 40/pop and new wave. Recently produced "Cruisin' the Strip" (hard rock single, Hard-Boiled Records); and "It Takes More," by Phil Phillips (pop rock single, Hard-Boiled Records).

**\*HEAVY METAL RECORDS PRODUCTIONS**, 165 Wolverhampton Road, Sedgley, Dudley, DY31QR, England. 44-09073-2211-3356. Managing Director: Paul Bireut. Record producer, music publisher (Andersong Music) and record company (Heavy Metal Records and Heavy Metal Worldwide). Works with artists, songwriters and label producers. Produces 3-4 singles and 20 albums/year.
**How to Contact:** Submit demo tape. Prefers 7½ or 15 ips reel-to-reel, cassette or record with 1 song on demo. Does not return unsolicited material. Reports in 1 month.
**Music:** Mostly rock; also progressive. Recently produced "Restless and Wild," by Accept (heavy metal single, Heavy Metal Records); "Lonesome Crow," by Scorpions (heavy metal single, Heavy Metal Worldwide Records); and "Against All Odds," by Quartz (heavy metal single, Heavy Metal Records). Other artists include Santers, Shiva, Witchfinder and General Eloy.
**Tips:** "Send good photographs, short bio (50-100 words maximum); and *relevant* press clippings, i.e., charts, etc."

**JOHN HILL MUSIC, INC.**, 116 E. 37th St., New York NY 10016. (212)683-2448. President: John Hill. Record producer and music publisher (Salami Music/ASCAP). Deals with artists and songwriters. Produces 3 singles and 1 album/year. Fee derived from royalty of sales when song or artist is recorded or by outright fee from record company.
**How to Contact:** Submit demo tape and lyric sheet. Prefers cassette with 3 songs on demo. SASE. Reports in 1 month.
**Music:** Mosty pop; also dance-oriented and rock (punk, new wave). Recently produced *City Kids*, by Sterling (top 40/new wave LP, A&M Records); *Pacific Gas & Electric*, by Pacific Gas & Electric (pop/R&B LP, ABC Records); and *I'm Gonna' Getcha*, by Jimmy Maelen (disco LP, Epic Records).

**HOLY SPIRIT PRODUCTIONS, INC.**, 27335 Penn St., Inkster MI 48141. (313)595-8247. President: Elder Otis G. Johnson. Record producer and music publisher (God's World/SESAC, Manfield Music/BMI, Stephen Enoch Johnson Music/ASCAP). Deals with artists and songwriters. Produces 5 singles and 5 albums/year. Fee derived from sales royalty.
**How to Contact:** Write first about your interest, submit demo tape and lyric sheet. Prefers 7½ ips reel-to-reel or cassette with 3 songs on demo. SASE. Reports in 1 month.
**Music:** Church/religious, C&W, easy listening, gospel and jazz. Recently produced *To Be with You*,

(single and LP); and "Sing from the Center World" and "Ladybug," by Karen Bouchard (Aspro Records). Other artists include Marcello Ratliff, Angela Snodgrass and Linda Strong.

**HOMETOWN PRODUCTIONS, INC.**, 1625 Woods Dr., Los Angeles CA 90069. (213)656-8490. President: Ken Mansfield. Record producer and music publisher (Frontlawn Music/BMI and Backyard Music/ASCAP). Deals with artists and songwriters.
**How to Contact:** Submit demo tape and lyric sheet. Prefers cassette. SASE. Reporting time varies.
**Music:** C&W, easy listening, folk, MOR, progressive, rock and top 40/pop. Recently produced *Rock America*, by Nick Gilder (rock LP, Casablanca Records); *Diamond In the Rough*, by Jessi Colter (C&W LP, Capitol Records); *Greatest Hits*, by Waylon Jennings (C&W LP, RCA Records); and *Changin' All the Time*, by LaCosta (MOR LP, Capitol Records).

**HOPSACK AND SILK PRODUCTIONS INC.**, Suite 1A, 254 W. 72nd St., New York NY 10023. (212)873-2179. Associate Director: Ms. Tee Alston. Music publisher (Nick-O-Val Music). Deals with artists and songwriters.
**How to Contact:** "Not accepting unsolicited material at this time."
**Music:** R&B.

*****IF PRODUCTIONS, INC.**, 15 Glenby La., Brookville NY 11545. (516)626-9504. Branch: 22240 Schoenborn St., Canoga Park CA 91304. (213)883-4865. New York Contact: Tom Ingegno. California Contact: Mike Frenchik. Record producer and music publisher (Beautiful Day Music). Works with artists. Producers 3-5 singles and 2 albums/year. Fee derived from sales royalty or outright fee from record company.
**How to Contact:** Submit demo tape and lyric sheet. Prefers cassette with minumum 3 songs on demo. SASE. Reports in 3 weeks.
**Music:** R&R and top 40/pop. Recently produced "First Thrills," "Front Page News," and "Thrills Three," by Thrills (rock singles, G&P Records).

*****INTERNATIONAL MUSIC CONSULTANT**, Suite 503, 6000 Cavendish Blvd., Cote Str., Quebec, Canada H4W 2Y2. (514)487-1573. President: Michel Zgarka. Record producer, music publisher (Simone Publishing/CAPAC, Mekla Publishing/PROCAN) and international music consultant. Deals with artists, songwriters, managers and independent producers. Produces 10 singles and 2 albums/year. Fee derived from sales royalty.
**How to Contact:** Submit demo tape and lyric sheet. Prefers 7½ reel-to-reel or cassette with 2-8 songs on demo. Include bio and photo. SAE and IRC. Reports in 3 weeks.
**Music:** Mostly dance-oriented and R&B; also soul, top 40/pop and French. Recently produced *Give Me Some* and *Hold on Tight*, by Linda Singer (dance LP, TransCanada Records); *Hooked On a Feeling*, by Jose Avalar (AOR LP, TransCanada Records); and *Nite Life*, by Peter King (dance/R&B LP, GAM Records). Other artists include Cheri, Claudja Barry and Ronnie Jones.

*****I'VE GOT THE MUSIC COMPANY**, Box 2631, Muscle Shoals AL 35662. (205)381-1455. Professional Manager: Richard Butler. Record producer, music publisher (Song Tailors Music Co./BMI, Terry Woodford Music/ASCAP and Creative Source Music/BMI) and video production company (Flying Colors Video). Produces varied number of singles and albums/year. Works with songwriters.
**How to Contact:** Submit demo tape and lyric sheet. Prefers cassette with 1-3 songs on demo. SASE "for returned material." Reports ASAP.
**Music:** Mostly top 40/pop; also C&W, dance-oriented, easy listening, MOR, progressive, R&B, rock and soul. Recently producer "After I Cry Tonight," by Lanier & Co. (ballad single, LARC/MCA Records); "Minimum Love," by Mac McAnally (top 40/pop single, Geffen Records); and "Old Flame," by Alabama (country single, RCA Records).

**J.K. PRODUCTIONS**, 1140 Rosalie St., Philadelphia PA 19149. (215)535-4231. President: Jack Kolber. Record producer. Deals with artists and songwriters. Fee negotiable per contract.
**How to Contact:** Submit demo tape and lyric sheet. Prefers 7½ ips reel-to-reel or cassette with 2-4 songs on demo. Does not return unsolicited material. Reports in 3 weeks.
**Music:** Rock (hard). "We need good hard rock songs for our artists."

**JAMAKA RECORD CO.**, 3621 Heath Ln., Mesquite TX 75150. (214)279-5858. Contact: Jimmy Fields or Joe Bill. Record producer, music publisher (Cherie Music Co./BMI) and record company. Deals with artists, songwriters and record companies. Produces 10 singles and 3 albums/year. Fee derived from sales royalty.
**How to Contact:** Submit demo tape and lyric sheet. Prefers 7½ ips reel-to-reel or cassette with 5 songs on demo. SASE. Reports in 2 months.

**Music:** Bluegrass, church/religious, C&W, easy listening, progressive country, R&B, rock (hard) and top 40/pop. Recently produced *Heart Achin' Blues*, by Suzan Stotts (progressive country LP, Jamaka Records); *Sissie Mae*, by Bill Lowery (R&B LP, Kick Records); and *Boots Bourguin*, by Boots & His Buddies (country LP, Jamaka Records). Other artists include Saucers and Billy Taylor.

**BRUCE JAMES COMPANY,** Box 439, Lyndonville VT 05851. (802)626-3317. President: Bruce James. Record producer. Deals with artists. Produces 5 singles and 1 album/year. Fee derived from outright fee from artist/songwriter.
**How to Contact:** Submit demo tape and lyric sheet. Prefers cassette with 1-5 songs on demo. SASE. Reports in 3 weeks.
**Music:** Rock (top 40/AOR) and top 40/pop. Recently produced "Take It All" and "Old Paree," by Fox (rock singles, Prime Cut Records); "Heartless," by Fox (ballad single, Prime Cut Records); and "Trying to Get the New Wave," by Rockestra. Other artists include Littlewing.
**Tips:** "Songs should be hit material no longer than 3½ minutes and consist of verse and 2 choruses; lyrics should be personal and intimate."

**JESSE JAMES PRODUCTIONS, INC.,** Box 128, Worcester PA 19470. (215)424-0800. President: Mr. J. James. Record producer and music publisher (James Boy Publishing Co./BMI). Deals with artists and songwriters. Fee derived from sales royalty.
**How to Contact:** Submit demo tape and lyric sheet. Prefers cassette with any number songs on demo. SASE. Reports in 1 month.
**Music:** C&W, dance-oriented, easy listening, folk, gospel, MOR, R&B and soul. Recently produced *Super You*, by Chee Chee and Peppy (R&B LP, Branding Iron Records); "So Glad You Came My Way" and "The Way You Do the Things You Do," by Chee Chee and Peppy (R&B singles, Branding Iron Records).

**\*JAMESTUNE RECORDS PRODUCTIONS,** Box 121, Waterville OH 43566. (419)535-7900. A&R Director: D. Larue. Record producer and music publisher (Keeny-York). Works with artists and songwriters. Producers 6-15 singles and 2 albums/year. Fee derived from sales royalty.
**How to Contact:** Submit demo tape and lyric sheet. Prefers cassette with 5-10 songs on demo. SASE. Reports in 1 month.
**Music:** C&W, easy listening, MOR and to 40/pop. Artists include Belle Starr and Jackass Flatts.

**ALEXANDER JANOULIS PRODUCTIONS (AJP),** Box 13584, Atlanta GA 30324. (404)872-6000. Independent record producer and video producer. Deals with artists and songwriters. Produces 6-10 singles and 2-3 albums/year. Fee derived "depends on particular situation and circumstance. If the songwriter/artist is not signed to me, a minimum fee of $600/song or $6,000/album plus travel expenses is charged."
**How to Contact:** Query or submit demo tape. Prefers cassette with 2-3 songs on demo. Does not return unsolicited material. Reports in 6 weeks.
**Music:** Blues, C&W, dance, jazz, MOR, progressive, rock (new wave) and top 40/pop. Recently produced "So Much" and "The Way It Used to Be," by Little Phil and the Night Shadows (top 40/pop singles, ABC Dot Records); "Babylon" and "Take It or Leave It," by Starfoxx (top 40/new wave singles, Hottrax Records); and "Love Generator" and "Silver Grill Blues," by Diamond Lil (disco, Glamour & Grease Records). Produced music videos on The Aztex, Cold Duck, The Bop, Diamond Lil, Starfoxx, New Money, Darryl Rhoades, Little Phil & The Night Shadows, and Central Park West.

**JED RECORD PRODUCTION,** 39 Music Square E., Nashville TN 57203. (615)255-6535. President: John E. Denny. Record producer and production company. Deals with artists and songwriters. Fee derived from sales royalty, production, publishing and management.
**How to Contact:** Submit demo tape and lead sheet. Prefers 7½ ips mono reel-to-reel with 4 songs on demo. SASE. Reports in 6 weeks.
**Music:** Bluegrass, C&W, gospel and MOR.

**\*JOHN & KARIN,** Bente Record, 382 Central Park W., New York NY 10025. (212)749-2267. President: Karin Mann. Record producer and music publisher (Jorin Music). Deals with artists. Fee derived from sales royalty.
**How to Contact:** Submit demo tape and lyric sheet. Prefers cassette with 3-5 songs on demo. SASE. Reports in 1 month.
**Music:** R&B and soul.

**LITTLE RICHIE JOHNSON PRODUCTIONS,** Box 3, 1700 Plunket, Belen NM 87002. (505)864-7441. President: Little Richie Johnson. Record producer and music publisher (Little Richie Johnson

Music/BMI and Little Cowboy Music/ASCAP). Deals with artists and songwriters. Produces 25 singles and 6 albums/year. Fee derived from outright fee from songwriter/artist or record company.
**How to Contact:** Call first about your interest. Prefers 7½ ips reel-to-reel with 4-8 songs on demo. SASE. Reports in 2 weeks.
**Music:** C&W, gospel and Spanish. Recently produced *Always Late*, by Lennie Bowman (C&W LP, Snapp Records); *I Don't Want to Cry*, by Carol Roman (C&W LP, LRJ Records); and *Helpless*, by Ronnie Smith (C&W LP, Little Richie Records).

**\*JUNE PRODUCTIONS LTD.**, Toftrees Church Rd., Weldingham, Surrey, England. Managing Director: David Mackay. Record producer.
**How to Contact:** Submit demo tape and lyric sheet. Prefers cassette with 1-4 songs on demo. SAE and IRC. Reports in 2 weeks.
**Music:** MOR, rock and top 40/pop. Recently produced "Its A Heartache," by Bonnie Tyler (top 40/ rock single, RCA Records); "I'd Like to Teach the World to Sing," by The New Seekers (MOR single, Elektra Records); and "Look What You've Done to My Song, Ma," by The New Seekers (MOR/pop single, Elektra Records).

**KAT FAMILY PRODUCTIONS**, Suite B-130, 5775 Peachtree Dunwoody Rd. NE, Atlanta GA 30342. (404)252-5800. President: Joel A. Katz. Vice President and General Manager: Mike Sullivan. Record producer and music publisher (Kat Family Music Company/BMI). Fee derived by sales royalty.
**How to Contact:** Submit demo tape and lyric sheet. Prefers cassette with 5-10 songs on demo. SASE. Reports in 1 month.
**Music:** Rock, top 40/pop and contemporary gospel. Recently produced *Teddy Baker and Friends*, by Teddy Baker (rock LP, Casablanca Records); *Darryl Kutz*, by Darryl Kutz (rock LP, Mercury Records); and *Billy Joe Royal*, by Billy Joe Royal (soft rock LP, Mercury Records). Other artists include Darts, Smashers, James Anderson, Bertie Higgins and Unipop.

**GENE KENNEDY ENTERPRISES, INC.**, 2125 8th Ave. S., Nashville TN 37204. (615)383-6002. President: Gene Kennedy. Vice President: Karen Jeglum. Director of Promotion for Door Knob Records: Joe Carroll. Record producer, independent distribution and promotion firm and music publisher (Chip 'N' Dale Music Publishers, Inc./ASCAP, Door Knob Music Publishing, Inc./BMI and Lodestar Music/SESAC). Deals with artists and songwriters. Produces 40-50 singles and 3-5 albums/year. Fee derived from outright fee from songwriter/artist or record company.
**How to Contact:** Submit demo tape and lyric sheet or arrange for personal interview. Prefers 7½ ips reel-to-reel or cassette with up to 4 songs on demo and lyric sheets. SASE. Reports in 1-3 weeks.
**Music:** C&W, easy listening and MOR. Recently produced "Green Eyes" and "Back in Debbie's Arms," by Tom Carlile; and "A Thing or Two on My Mind," by Gene Kennedy and Karen Jeglum. Other artists include Bonnie Shannon, Shirley Parker, Kris Carpenter and Thomas Riley.
**Tips:** "We are looking for hit songs and good talent."

**KEYNOTE PRODUCTIONS**, Box 4185, Youngstown OH 44515. (216)793-7295. Executive Producer: Richard Hahn. Record producer and music publisher (Al-Kris Music/BMI). Deals with artists and songwriters. Produces 5 singles and 2 albums/year. Fee derived from sales royalty or outright fee from songwriter/artist.
**How to Contact:** Query by mail, then submit demo tape and *neat* lyric sheet. Prefers cassette with 3-5 songs on demo. SASE. Reports in 3 weeks.
**Music:** C&W, gospel, MOR and top 40/pop. Recently produced "Here Come the Browns," by Kardiak Kids (MOR single, Keynote Records); "Help Me I'm Falling," by Kirsti Manna (MOR single, Genuine Records); "Teach Me Lovely Lady," by Jim Stack (C&W single, Peppermint Records); and "The San Francisco 49er's Fight Song" and "Prom Night," by the B-Minors (MOR singles). Other artists include Phil Hickman.
**Tips:** "The artist or writer should be willing to compromise on creative decisions by the producer to achieve the best possible product."

**KIDERIAN RECORDS PRODUCTIONS**, 4926 W. Gunnison, Chicago IL 60630. (312)545-0861. President: Raymond Peck. Record producer. Deals with artists and songwriters. Fee derived from sales royalty and outright fee from record company.
**How to Contact:** Submit demo tape and lyric sheet. Prefers cassette with 4-6 songs on demo. SASE. Reports in 1 month.
**Music:** Blues, C&W, dance, MOR, new wave, power pop, R&B, hard rock, soul and top 40/pop. Recently produced "Boy I Need You," by Nadine Herman (new wave single, Stang Records); and "Tribute to John Lennon," by Torn Orphan (rock single, Kiderian Records). Other artists include Boyz and Mammoth.

# Close-up

**David Mackay**
Producer

"I produced a record for EMI Records in Australia at the age of nineteen and have been producing ever since," says David Mackay, managing director of June Productions, Ltd., Woldingham, Surrey, England. Mackay started studying music at age ten, learning theory and harmony. Later he studied sound and TV/radio techniques and spent a year in the theater—"a valuable experience in understanding audience reaction," he says.

"I enjoy all my work in the studio. I arrange, engineer and produce, and while I don't claim this to be a great achievement, it is rewarding artistically."

Among the well-known songs and acts Mackay has produced are "It's a Heartache," by Bonnie Tyler on RCA Records; and "I'd Like to Teach the World to Sing" and "Look What They've Done to My Song, Ma," both recorded by The New Seekers on Elektra Records.

As a producer, Mackay works for more than just money. "Some of my hits while financially rewarding have not given any more satisfaction than less successful ones. However, my first big single, 'Look What They've Done to My Song, Ma' was probably the most exciting as far as marrying artist and song."

If there's one quality producers look for, no matter where they're located, it's *originality*—the new treatment of an old theme. For instance, more songs are written about "love"—possibly the oldest and most universal feeling—than any other subject. That will most likely continue to be the case. The wise songwriter then, whether writing in English, French, German, Spanish, Japanese, or, for whatever strange reason, even in the archaic Swahilian, looks for that different angle, a unique way of approaching the old subject of matters of the human heart. And today more than ever before, it's common practice to translate the lyrics of one *good, original* song into many languages.

When Mackay listens to a demo, he, like any good producer who is thinking of songs that could become world-wide hits, listens for that special song with a unique, universal appeal. "I don't think there should be any rules about what makes a song good or bad. The quality I most look for in a demo is imagination—musically and lyrically. It's particularly great to find a lyricist who can put across ideas in a fresh way."

Mackay doesn't like a demo that is produced to the point of possibly hiding something that might be fresh and unique. "I like demos sparse so I can hear the song, not the production. Then I can adapt the material to suit various artists."

Mackay believes a songwriter need not move to a music center to be successful. The influences of the home environment which are different than those of a music center can actually aid the songwriter in discovering and maintaining his identity as a distinctive writer.

**KING HENRY PRODUCTION**, 1855 Fairview Ave., Easton PA 18042. (215)258-4461. President: Henry Casella. Record producer and music publisher (King Henry Music/BMI). Deals with artists and songwriters. Produces 4 singles and 1 album/year. Fee derived from sales royalty or outright fee from songwriter/artist.
**How to Contact:** Submit demo tape and lead sheet. Prefers cassette with 2-4 songs on demo. SASE. Reports in 1 month.
**Music:** Mostly contemporary pop; also bluegrass, C&W, dance, easy listening and MOR. Recently produced *Video Wars*, by various artists (contemporary LP, KHP Records); "Calling All Spies," by King Henry; and "We Play Them All," by the American Show Band (contemporary singles, KHP Records). Other artists include Philly Cream.
**Tips:** "A good song can stand on its own merits—not on an elaborate production. A good song should be creative and easily remembered."

**KNOWN ARTIST PRODUCTIONS**, 1219 Kerlin Ave., Brewton AL 36426. (205)867-2228. President: Roy Edwards. Record producer and music publisher (Cheavoria Music Co./BMI and Baitstring Music/ASCAP). Deals with artists and songwriters. Produces 12 singles and 3 albums/year. Fee derived from sales royalty or outright fee from record company.
**How to Contact:** Write first about your interest, then submit demo tape and lyric sheet. Prefers cassette with 3-5 songs on demo. SASE. Reports in 1 month.
**Music:** C&W, easy listening, MOR, R&B and soul. Recently produced "Music Inside," by Roy Edwards (MOR single, Bolivia Records); "Make Me Forget," by Bobby Roberson; and "Always and Forever," by Jim Portwood (country singles, Bolivia Records).
**Tips:** "Write a good song that tells a good story."

**FREDDIE KOBER PRODUCTIONS**, Box 11967, Houston TX 77016. (713)694-2971. President: Freddie Kober. Record producer and music publisher (Anode Music/BMI and Claudia Bee Music/ASCAP). Deals with songwriters. Produces 2 singles/year. Fee derived from sales royalty.
**How to Contact:** Submit demo tape and lyric sheet. Prefers cassette with 1-3 songs on demo. SASE. Reports in 2 weeks.
**Music:** Gospel and soul. Recently produced "Do's and Don't," by Sonny Tippitt; "I Wanna Be There," by Teddy Reynolds; and "God Is (So Wonderful)," by Ken Raines.

**ROBERT R. KOVACH**, Drawer 1967, Warner Robins GA 31099. (912)953-2800. Producer: Robert R. Kovach. Record producer. Deals with artists and songwriters. Produces 2 singles/year. Fee derived from sales royalty, or outright fee from songwriter/artist or record company.
**How to Contact:** Submit demo tape and lyric sheet. Prefers 7½ ips reel-to-reel or cassette with 3-5 songs on demo. SASE. Reports in 1 month.
**Music:** C&W, easy listening, R&B, rock, soul and top 40/pop. Recently produced "Easy on Your Feet," by Justice (easy listening, Sacramouche Records). Other artists include Justice with Theresa Queen of the Drums and Napoleon Starke.

***KRAUSE & REMAL MUSIC, INC.**, Suite 414, 680 Beach St., San Francisco CA 94109. (415)673-4544. Contact: Gary S. Remal or Bernie Krause. Record producer and music publisher (Parasound Publishing, Wild Sanctuary Music). Deals with artists and songwriters. Produces 1 album/year. Fee derived from sales royalty.
**How to Contact:** Write about your interest. Prefers cassette with 2-4 songs on demo. SASE. Reports in 3 months.
**Music:** Mostly electronic new wave; also top 40/pop, MOR, R&B, rock and soul. Recently produced *Citadels of Mystery*, by Bernie Krause (electronic jazz LP, Mobile Fidelity Sound Labs Records); and *The New Nonesuch Guide to Electronic Music*, by Bernie Krause (electronic LP, Nonesuch Records).
**Tips:** "We write our own music. However, we would be open to listening to other people's music. We're very interested in lyrics and soon will get into more record production of other artists."

**GREG LADANYI**, 1592 Crossroads of the World, Hollywood CA 90028. (213)462-6156. Manager: Bill Siddons. Record producer. Deals with artists. Produces 8 albums/year. Fee derived from sales royalty.
**How to Contact:** Submit demo tape and lyric sheet. Prefers cassette with 1-3 songs on demo. SASE. Reports in 1 month.
**Music:** Rock. Recently produced *El Rayo X*, by David Lindley; *Hold Out*, by Jackson Browne; *Bad Luck Streak in Dancing School*, by Warren Zevon (rock LPs, Elektra Records); *Can't Stand Still*, by Don Henley; and "7 to IV" by Greg Ladanyi.

**LAS VEGAS RECORDING STUDIO, INC.**, Box 42937, Las Vegas NV 89116. (702)457-4365. Vice President: Hank Castro. Producers: Eli Anderson and Michael Hufford. Record producer, music

publisher, management firm and record company. Deals with artists and songwriters. Fee derived from sales royalty, outright fee from record company, or outright fee from songwriter/artist. "We do not charge songwriters for their demos, but we do ask for publishing if we place the material."
**How to Contact:** Arrange personal interview, or submit demo tape and lead sheet. Include lyric sheet. Prefers reel-to-reel or cassette. SASE. Reports ASAP.
**Music:** Bluegrass, blues, church/religous, C&W, disco, easy listening, folk, gospel, jazz, MOR, progressive, rock, soul, top 40/pop and instrumental. Recently produced Ronnie Fuller, Joy Britton, JoAnna Neal and Terry Richards for ECR Records.

**LAST MINUTE PRODUCTIONS**, c/o Bette Hisiger, 320 E. 23rd St., New York NY 10010. (212)254-9338. Contact: Bette Hisiger. Record producer and music publisher (Minute by Minute Publishing) and management firm. Deals with artists and songwriters. Produces 5 singles and 10 albums/year. Fee derived from sales royalty.
**How to Contact:** Submit demo tape and lyric sheet. Prefers cassette with 3-8 songs on demo. SASE. Reports in 1 month.
**Music:** C&W, dance-oriented, MOR, R&B, rock (hard) and top 40/pop. Recently produced *Non-Fiction*, by Non-Fiction (AOR rock LP, Mega Records); "Low-Budget," by The Kinks (AOR rock single, Arista Records); and *Oz-Knozz*, by Oz-Knozz (AOR rock LP).

**LAURIE RECORDS, INC.**, 20 F. Robert Pitt Dr., Monsey NY 10952. (914)425-7000. Vice President: Gene Schwartz. Record producer and music publisher (Vibar Music/ASCAP, Rogelle Music/BMI). Deals with artists and songwriters. Produces 12 singles and 5 albums/year. Fee derived from sales royalty.
**How to Contact:** Submit demo tape and lyric sheet. Prefers cassette. SASE. Reports in 2 weeks.
**Music:** Dance-oriented and top 40/pop.

**LAZER RECORDS**, 7330 Sycamore Ave., Philadelphia PA 19126. (215)635-6921. President: A. Gravatt. Record producer and music publisher (Lazer Music/BMI). Estab. 1981. Deals with artists and songwriters. Produces variable number singles and albums/year. Fee derived from sales royalty or outright fee from artist/songwriter.
**How to Contact:** Write first about your interest, then submit demo tape and lyric sheet. Prefers cassette with limit of 1 song on demo. SASE. Reports in 1 month.
**Music:** Dance-oriented, jazz, MOR, progressive, R&B, rock, soul and top 40/pop. Recently produced "Tight Money," by CE Rock (R&B/pop single, Lazer Records); and "I Want You (So Bad)," by Latita (pop single, Lazer Records).

**ROOSEVELT LEE INTERNATIONAL RECORDS**, 3966 Standish Ave., Cincinnati OH 45213. (513)793-8191. President: Roosevelt Lee. Record producer and music publisher (Citiy Music). Deals with artists and songwriters. Produces 4 singles and 2 albums/year. Fee derived from sales royalty.
**How to Contact:** Submit demo tape and lyric sheet. Prefers cassette with 4 songs on demo. SASE. Reports in 1 month.
**Music:** C&W, R&B and soul. Recently produced "Love City," by Larry Daby (soul single, Wes World Records); and "Come Home to Me," by Mike Ellis (C&W single, Wes World Records).

*****LEGEND RECORDS AND PROMOTIONS**, 1102 Virginia St. SW, Lenoir NC 28645. (704)758-4170. President: Mike McCoy. Record producer and music publisher (Nancy Jane Publishing/BMI). Estab. 1982. Works with artists and songwriters. Produces 1 single and 1 album/year. Fee derived from sales royalty.
**How to Contact:** Submit demo tape and lyric sheet. Prefers cassette with 1-4 songs on demo. SASE. Reports in 1 month.
**Music:** Mostly C&W, church/religious, gospel, R&B and outlaw C&W. Recently produced "Music City," and "Cinderella," by Mike McCoy (C&W singles, Legend Records); and "Old Fashion Preacher," by M. McCoy (gospel single, Legend Records).

**TY LEMLEY MUSIC**, 430 Pearce Rd., Pittsburgh PA 15234. (412)341-0991. President: Ty Lemley. Vice-President: Tolema Lemley. General Manager: Bud Lemley. Record producer. Deals with songwriters. Fee derived from sales royalty.
**How to Contact:** Submit demo tape or 45 record and lyric sheet. Prefers cassette. SASE. Reports in 1 month.
**Music:** C&W, easy listening, MOR and top 40/pop. Recently produced "Ramblin' Ways," by Ty Lemley (C&W single, Tymena Records); "One Day at a Time," and "Happy Willow-Bee," by T. Lemley (children's singles, Tymena Records).

**LEMON SQUARE PRODUCTIONS**, Box 31819, Dallas TX 75231. (214)750-0720. Producer: The General. Record producer. Deals with artists and songwriters. Fee derived from sales royalty.
**How to Contact:** Query or arrange personal interview. Prefers 7½ ips reel-to-reel with 2-4 songs on demo. Include lyric or lead sheet. SASE. Reports in 1 month.
**Music:** Church/religious, C&W, and gospel. Recently produced "Bluejeaned Bandits" and "Designer Jeans," by Glen Bailey (C&W singles, Yatahey Records); "Barstool Cowboy," by David Denman (C&W single, Yatahey Records); "Woman Needs Love (Just Like You Do)," by Brooks Brothers (Primiero Records); and "Too Many Rainbows," by D. Denman (Yatahey Records).

**LEONARD PRODUCTIONS, INC.**, Suite 104, 11258 Goodnight Lane, Dallas TX 75229. (214)241-0254. Record producer and music publisher. Deals with artists and songwriters. Fee derived by sales royalty.
**How to Contact:** Write first about your interest. Prefers cassette. SASE. Reports in 2 weeks.
**Music:** C&W and top 40/pop.

**LIFESINGER PRODUCTIONS**, Suite #902, 50 Music Square W., Nashville TN 37203. (615)329-2278. President: Bobby Fischer. Record producer, music publisher (Bobby Fischer Music Group), record company (F & L Records) and distribution and promotion firm. Deals with artists and songwriters. Produces 10 singles and variable number of albums/year. Fee derived from record company.
**How to Contact:** Submit demo tape and lyric sheet. Prefers cassette with 2-3 songs on demo. SASE. Reports "when time permits."
**Music:** C&W and progressive. Recently produced "An Afternoon of Love," by Clifford Russell and Mary Lou Turner (love song single, Sugartree Records); "Cheater's Last Chance," by Larry Riley (love song single, F & L Records); and "Somebody's Darlin', Somebody's Wife," by Dottsy (love song single, Tanglewood Records).

*****LIL' WALLY MUSIC PRODUCTIONS**, 35 NE 62nd St., Miami FL 33138. (305)258-0000. President: Walter Jagiello. Record producer and music publisher (Jay Jay Publishing/BMI). Deals with songwriters. Produces 10 singles and 6 albums/year. Fee derived from sales royalty.
**How to Contact:** Submit demo tape and lyric sheet. Prefers 15 ips reel-to-reel with 2-6 songs on demo. SASE. Reports in 1 month.
**Music:** Mostly polkas, waltzes and C&W; also easy listening.

*****SONNY LIMBO INTERNATIONAL, LTD.**, Box 9869, Atlanta GA 30319. (404)633-4659. President: Sonny Limbo. Record producer and music publisher (Sonny Limbo Music/BMI). Deals with artists and songwriters. Produces 10 singles and 5 albums/year. Fee derived from sales royalty.
**How to Contact:** Submit demo tape and lyric sheet. Prefers cassette with 1-3 songs on demo. SASE. Reports in 2 weeks.
**Music:** Mostly top 40 and MOR; also C&W, easy listening and rock. Recently produced *Key Largo*, by Bertie Higgins (top 40/MOR LP, CBS Records); *What If*, by Unipop (top 40/rock LP, CBS Records); and *I Wanna' Come Over*, by Alabama (country/top 40, RCA Records).

**LITTLE GIANT ENTERPRISES**, Box 205, White Lake NY 12786. (914)583-4471. President: Mickey Barnett. Record producer and music publisher (Karjan Music Publishing Co./SESAC). Deals with artists and songwriters. Produces 3 singles and 5 albums/year. Fee derived from outright fee from artist/songwriter.
**How to Contact:** Submit demo tape and lyric sheet. Prefers cassette with 1-3 songs on demo. SASE. Reports in 3 weeks.
**Music:** Blues, C&W, easy listening, MOR, R&B and top 40/pop. Recently produced *Country Songs and Dreams*, by Chuck Wilson (country LP, Killer Records); *Valley View House Presents*, by T. Barry Kaminski (MOR LP, Little Giant Records); and *Young and Polish*, by Kenny Adams (comedy single, Killer Records). Other artists include Jayson Ross, The Third Edition, Mickey Barnett and The Little Giants.

**MICK LLOYD PRODUCTIONS**, 1014 16th Ave. S., Nashville TN 37212. (615)244-1630. President: Mick Lloyd. Director of Publishing: Ken Jones. Record producer, music publisher (Kelly & Lloyd/ASCAP, Jerrimick/BMI and Mick Lloyd/SESAC) and record company. Deals with artists and songwriters. Fee derived from sales royalty.
**How to Contact:** Call first about your interest. Prefers 7½ ips reel-to-reel or cassette with 1 song on demo. SASE. Reports in 3 weeks.
**Music:** Mostly country; also easy listening, folk, gospel, MOR, progressive, and top 40/pop. Recently produced "Come On Out to California," by Billy Sea (C&W single, Little Giant Records); "Worlds,"

by Jerri Kelly (MOR/pop single, 21 Records); and "Just Another Night in New York City," by Melissa Prewitt (rock single, Little Giant Records). Other artists include the Nashville Music Machine.

**\*LONSONG MUSIC INC.**, Suite 600, 1055 Wilson Ave., Toronto, Ontario, Canada M3K 1Y9. (416)630-2973. President: Frank Longo. Record producer and music publisher (Lonsong Music, Inc./CAPAC). Deals with artists and songwriters. Produces 4 singles and 2 albums/year. Fee derived from sales royalty.
**How to Contact:** Submit demo tape and lyric sheet. Prefers cassette with 1-3 songs on demo. SASE. Reports in 2 weeks.
**Music:** Mostly R&B and MOR; also dance-oriented, easy listening and top 40/pop. Recently produced *Patti Jannetta*, by Patti Jannetta (pop/MOR LP, Janta Records); "In the Middle of the Night," by Jill Vogel (R&B single, People City Music); "The Nightlife," by Wayne St. John (R&B single, People City Music); "Easy Life," by Jim Mancel (pop single, People City Music); and "Coast to Coast," by Longo Brothers (pop single, People City Music).

**HAROLD LUICK & ASSOCIATES**, 110 Garfield St., Box B, Carlisle IA 50047. (515)989-3679. Record producer and music publisher. Deals with artists and songwriters. Produces 30 singles and 12 albums/year. Fee derived from sales royalty, outright fee from artist/songwriter or record company, and from retainer fees.
**How to Contact:** Call or write first about your interest then submit demo tape and lyric sheet. Prefers cassette with 3-5 songs on demo. SASE. Reports in 3 weeks.
**Music:** Bluegrass, C&W, dance-oriented, easy listening, gospel, MOR, R&B, rock and top 40/pop. Recently produced *Brand of a Country Man*, by Darrell C. Thomas (country LP, Ozark Opry Records); "House of Memories," by Bob Schirmer (country single, RDS Records); "What You Do to Me," by Linda Cooper (pop single, LC Records); and *Proud to be a Mother*, by June Murphy (country LP, Jay/Bee Records). Other artists include Ray Faubus and the Kenny Hofer Orchestra.
**Tips:** "Producers are becoming more and more independent (this means not having to rely on a big record company) and they can be more creative. This means they have use for more song material than ever before. Keep writing commercial material that has possibilities, let the producer work the 'probabilities.' Don't 'hype' a producer about your song. This is one of the biggest turnoffs that amateurs use."

**AL McKAY**, Suite 205, 19301 Ventura Blvd., Tarzana CA 91356. (213)708-1300. Manager: Zachary Glickman. Record producer and music publisher. Deals with artists and songwriters.
**How to Contact:** Submit demo tape and lyric sheet. Prefers cassette. SASE. Reports in 1 month.
**Music:** Church/religious, dance-oriented, easy listening, gospel, R&B, soul and top 40/pop. Recently produced "Cloudburst," by the Mighty Clouds of Joy (single, Myrrh Records); "Out of the Woods," by Ren Woods (single, ARC Records); and "Boogie Wonderland," by Earth Wind and Fire (single, ARC Records).

**LEE MAGID PRODUCTIONS**, Box 532, Malibu CA 90265. (213)858-7282. President: Lee Magid. Record producer and music publisher (Alexis Music, Inc./ASCAP, Marvelle Music Co./BMI). Deals with artists, songwriters and producers. Produces 12 singles and 6 albums/year. Fee derived from sales royalty and "advance fee against royalties"; sometimes pays a flat outright sum.
**How to Contact:** Write first about your interest giving address and phone number; include SASE. Submit demo tape and lyric sheet. Prefers cassette with 3-6 songs on demo. SASE. Reports "as soon as we can after listening."
**Music:** Mostly country, rock, jazz, blues and pop; also bluegrass, church/religious, easy listening, folk, gospel, MOR, progressive, soul, instrumental and top 40. Recently produced "Too Many Women," by Windstorm (R&B single, LMI Records); *From the Heart*, by Ernie Andrews (jazz R&B LP, Discovery Records); and *Rags Waldorf Live*, by R. Waldorf (R&R/R&B LP, Judgement Records).
**Tips:** "The visual effect is just as important as the audio. An act should have theatrical as well as musical ability."

**MAINLINE PRODUCTIONS**, Box 902, Provo UT 84603. President: Richard D. Rees. Record producer, music publisher (Scarlet Stallion Music/BMI, Contractor Music Inc./ASCAP), concert promoter and personal management company. Deals with artists and songwriters. Produces 2 singles and 2 albums/year. Fee derived from sales royalty.
**How to Contact:** Submit demo tape and lyric sheet; include photo. Prefers cassette with 4-6 songs on demo. SASE. Reports in 3 weeks.
**Music:** Progressive, rock, and top 40/pop. Recently produced *Hot Kids From City Time*, by Mannequin (rock LP, Record Records); *Dave Boshard*, by Dave Boshard, (country crossover LP, ML Records); *Slyder*, by Slyder (hard rock LP, ML Records); and *Tyrant*, by Tyrant (hard rock LP, Mainline Records). Other artists include Rick Jackson, The Tools and Moon Dog.

**MAINROADS PRODUCTIONS, INC.**, 100 Huntley St., Toronto, Ontario, Canada M4Y 2L1. (416)961-8001. Manager: Paul Kelly. Record producer, music publisher (Mainroads Publishing/CAPAC, Bruce W. Stacey Publishing/PRO). Deals with artists and songwriters. Produces 3 albums/year. Fee derived from sales royalty.
**How to Contact:** Write first about your interest. Prefers cassette with 3 songs on demo. SASE. Reports in 1 month.
**Music:** Children's, choral, church/religious and gospel.

**MANQUIN**, Box 2388, Toluca Lake CA 91602. (213)985-8284. Contact: Quint Benedetti or Mannie Rodriquez. Deals with artists, songwriters and writers of musical comedy. Fee derived from sales royalty.
**How to Contact:** Submit demo tape and lyric sheet. Prefers cassette with 2-6 songs on demo. SASE. Reports in 1 month.
**Music:** Christmas songs, musical comedy and C&W novelty only. Recently produced *Topsy or Sorry About That Harriett*, by the original cast (musical comedy LP, Quinto Records); and *Lavendar Lady*, by Agnes Moorehead and the original cast.

**PETE MARTIN/VAAM MUSIC PRODUCTIONS**, Suite C-114, 3740 Evans St., Los Angeles CA 90027. (213)664-7765. President: Pete Martin. Record producer and music publisher (Vaam Music/BMI, Pete Martin Music/ASCAP). Deals with artists and songwriters. Produces 5-10 singles and 2-8 albums/year. Fee derived from sales royalty.
**How to Contact:** Submit demo tape and lyric sheet. Prefers 7½ ips reel-to-reel or cassette with 1-4 songs on demo. SASE. Reports in 1 month.
**Music:** C&W, easy listening, MOR, rock (general), soul and top 40/pop. Recently produced "Secrets Are for Telling," by Meza (rock single, Blue Gem Records); "Shattered, Tattered & Battered," by Joe Ward (C&W single, Blue Gem Records); "Here Is Happiness," by Reynolds & Nalani (pop single, Hi-Lute Records); *I've Got the Country in Me*, by Kamie Redell (C&W LP, Blue Gem Records). Other artists include P.S. Lambert, Flashback and Wayne Allen Anderson.

**MARULLO PRODUCTIONS**, 1121 Market St., Galveston TX 77550. President: A.W. Marullo Sr. Vice President: A.W. Marullo Jr. Record producer (Red Dot and Rotab Records) and music publisher (Marullo Music/BMI). Deals with artists, songwriters and master owners. Produces 4-7 singles/year. Fee derived from sales royalty.
**How to Contact:** Submit demo tape. Prefers 7½ ips reel-to-reel, cassette or demo dub with 12 songs maximum on demo. SASE. Reports in 1 month.
**Music:** C&W, dance, rock, soul and top 40/pop.
**Tips:** "You record it, we will lease it. We hold consultations and negotiations to place your masters with the major record companies and the music publishers."

**MASTER AUDIO, INC.**, 1227 Spring St. NW, Atlanta GA 30309. (404)875-1440. President: Bob Richardson. Record producer and music publisher. Deals with artists and songwriters. Fee derived from sales royalty.
**How to Contact:** Arrange personal interview or submit demo tape and lead sheet. Prefers cassette with 2-5 songs on demo. SASE. Reports in 1 month.
**Music:** Dance, easy listening, gospel (traditional or contemporary), MOR, rock and top 40/pop. Recently produced *Troy Ramey & Soul Searchers*, by Troy Ramey and the Soul Searchers (gospel LP, Nashboro Records); and *Ivory Roads*, by Mac Frampton (MOR/easy listening LP, Triumvirate Records).

**MASTERSOURCE PRODUCTIONS**, 704 N. Wells, Chicago IL 60610. (312)922-0375. Executive Producer: Charles Thomas. Sales and Marketing: Debbie Birkey. Music producer. Deals with artists and songwriters. Produces 8-12 albums/year. Fee is negotiable. "We desire long-term artist relationships."
**How to Contact:** Query or submit demo tape and lyric or lead sheet. Prefers cassette with 3 songs on demo. Does not return unsolicited material. Reports in 3 weeks.
**Music:** Rock, adult contemporary, jazz and Christian rock. Recently produced "I Turn to You," by Marianne McCall (MSM/Angelaco Records); "The Feeling Doesn't Go Away," by Maurice Spiccia (MasterSource/Angelaco Records); "Super Star," by Carma Wood; and "The Boy Can't Help Himself," by Steve Padgett (PKB/MasterSource Records). Other artists include Relayer and Ronnii Tog.

**MASTERVIEW MUSIC PUBLISHING CORP.**, Ridge Rd. and Butler Lane, Perkasie PA 18944. (215)257-9616. General Manager: Thomas Fausto. President: John Wolf. Record producer, music publisher (Masterview Music/BMI), record company and management firm. Deals with artists and songwriters. Produces 12 singles and 3-4 albums/year. Fee derived from sales royalty.
**How to Contact:** Arrange personal interview or submit demo tape and lead sheet. Prefers 7½ or 15 ips

reel-to-reel with 2-6 songs on demo. SASE. Reports in 2 weeks.
Music: Disco, folk, gospel, and rock. Recently produced "Up North to Bluegrass," by Country Boys (bluegrass); "I Am Happen," by El Botteon (Rheta Records); and "Footprints," by Charles Newman (religious single, Masterview Records). Other artists include Sugarcane.

**MBA PRODUCTIONS**, 8914 Georgian Dr., Austin TX 78753. (512)836-3201. General Manager: Shirley Montgomery. Record Producer and music publisher. Deals with artists and songwriters. Fee derived from sales royalty.
**How to Contact:** Submit demo tape and lyric sheet. Prefers 7½ ips reel-to-reel with 1-3 songs on demo. SASE. Reports in 2 weeks.
**Music:** All types. Recently produced "The Shootist," by Eli Worden (C&W, Darva Records); "Country Girl," by Nona Stacey (C&W, Darva Records); and "Times Are Changing," by Steve Douglas (C&W, Darva Records). Other artists include Bill Henderson (C&W), Sue Creech (C&W), Wilson Family (gospel), Tommy Hodges (C&W) and Grassfire (bluegrass).

**MCI PRODUCTIONS/MICHAEL BERMAN PRODUCTIONS**, Suite 308, 20 E. 1st St., Mt. Vernon NY 10550. (914)699-4003. Chief of Production: Michael Berman. President: Chip Rigo. Record producer, music publisher (MCI Music/BMI) and booking and management firm. Deals with artists and songwriters. Produces 5-6 singles and 2-3 albums/year. Fee derived from sales royalty or outright fee from record company.
**How to Contact:** Call first about your interest or submit demo tape and lyric sheet. Prefers cassette with 3-6 songs on demo. SASE. Reports in 3 weeks.
**Music:** Dance-oriented, easy listening, R&B, rock (all styles) and top 40/pop. Recently produced "Fallen Angels," by Allan Corby (rock/disco single, Mercury Records/Polygram Europe); *Sunrise*, by Sunrise (jazz/pop-rock LP, Buddah Records); "Go Crazy" b/w "I Know," by Vixen; and "Who is Gonna Love Me," by Alfie Davison (R&B/disco single, RCA Records). Other artists include Jailbait, Lotus and Michael Berman.

**MCP/DAVISOUND**, Bypass 76/Sunset, Box 521, Newberry SC 29108. (803)276-0639. Studio Manager: Polly Davis. Producer/Director: Hayne Davis. Record producer, music publisher and production company. Deals with artists and songwriters. Produces 5-6 singles and 2-3 albums/year. Fee derived from sales royalty, outright fee from record company, or outright fee from songwriter/artist. Charges for some services: "In special cases, where the songwriter/artist is simply booking our studio facilities, there is a charge. Also, if an artist/writer wishes us to produce him with himself as co-producer, we share profits on a 50/50 basis but at the same time, expenses of production are also shared 50/50."
**How to Contact:** Submit demo tape. Prefers 7½ ips reel-to-reel or cassette with 4-8 songs on demo. SASE. Reports in 2 weeks.
**Music:** C&W (contemporary), dance, easy listening, MOR, rock (all) and top 40/pop (all). Recently produced "Sheila," by James Meadows (C&W/rock single, Mother Cleo Records); "Too Far Gone," by Curt Bradford (C&W/rock single, Mother Cleo Records); and "Brainwasher," by J. Teal Band (rock single, Mother Cleo Records). Other artists include Raw Material and Sugar & Spice.

**MELODEE ENT., INC.**, Box 1010, Hendersonville TN 37075. (615)329-9492. General Manager: Dee Mullins. Record producer and music publisher (Dee Mullins Music, Mel Dee Music/BMI). Deals with artists and songwriters. Produces 10-20 singles and 20-30 albums/year. Fee derived from sales royalty.
**How to Contact:** Write or call first about your interest, then submit demo tape and lyric sheet or arrange personal interview to play demo tape. Prefers 7½ ips reel-to-reel or cassette with 1-4 songs on demo. SASE. Reports in 1 month.
**Music:** Bluegrass, C&W, folk, gospel, MOR, rock (country) and top 40/pop. Recently produced "I Can't Keep My Hands Off of You," by Dee Mullins (country/pop, Melodee Records); "Yesterday Today," by Rommie Osbahr (country, Son-Circuit Records); and "Circle Me," by D. Mullins (country/pop, Triune Records). Other artists include Hank Marshall and Suzann Sunday.

**MERCANTILE MUSIC**, Box 2271, Palm Springs CA 92263. (619)320-4848. President: Kent Fox. Record producer and music publisher (Mercantile Music/BMI and Blueford Music/ASCAP). Deals with artists and songwriters. Fee derived from sales royalty.
**How to Contact:** Submit demo tape and lyric sheet. Prefers cassette with 3-5 songs on demo. SASE. Reports in 1 month.
**Music:** C&W, easy listening and top 40/pop. Recently produced "Keeping the Tradition Alive" and "Heart."

***MIGHTY "T" PRODUCTIONS**, Box 1869, Hollywood CA 90078. (213)564-1008. Producers: Philip Nicholas or Kent Washburn. Record producer and music publisher (Highest Praise Publishing/

BMI). Deals with songwriters. Produces 2 albums/year. Fee derived from sales royalty.
**How to Contact:** Submit demo tape and lyric sheet. Prefers cassette with 2-4 songs on demo. SASE. Reports in 1 month.
**Music:** Mostly gospel; also choral and church/religious. Recently produced *Tell the World*, by Nicholas (gospel LP, Message/Impact Records). Other artists include Rodney Friend and Vernessa Mitchell.
**Tips:** "Know the artist that you are submitting the material for."

**JAY MILLER PRODUCTIONS**, 413 N. Parkerson Ave., Crowley LA 70526. (318)783-1601. Contact: Jay Miller. Manager: Mark Miller. Record producer and music publisher. Deals with artists and songwriters. Produces 50 singles and 10 albums/year. Fee derived from sales royalty.
**How to Contact:** Arrange personal interview or submit demo tape. Prefers 7½ ips reel-to-reel or cassette for audition. SASE. Reports in 1 month.
**Music:** Blues, C&W, Cajun, disco, folk, gospel, MOR, rock, top 40/pop, and comedy. Recently produced *Cajun Gentleman*, by Douct Cet; *Blues Attack*, by Sonny Landreth; *The Green Acres Goodtime Album*, by Paul Marks; *Cruisin' On*, by Sam Brothers; and *Louisianna Cajun Music*, by Pat Sabent and the Louisiana Playboys.
**Tips:** "Inquiries are invited."

**MOBY DICK RECORDS**, 2354 Market St., San Francisco CA 94114. (415)861-0476. Contact: Producer. Record producer, record company and music publisher (Moby Dick Publishers/ASCAP). Deals with artists and songwriters. Produces 10 singles and 5 albums/year. Fee derived from sales royalty.
**How to Contact:** Call first about your interest, then submit demo tape and lyric sheet. Prefers cassette with 2-3 songs on demo. SASE. Reports in 3 weeks.
**Music:** Dance-oriented, R&B, disco and high-energy dance music. Recently produced *Signed, Sealed, Delivered*, by Boystown Gang (R&B LP, Moby Dick Records); *Ain't No Mountain High Enough*, by Boystown Gang (disco LP, Moby Dick Records); and *Dance with Me*, by Crystal & the Team (dance LP, Moby Dick Records).

**MOM AND POP PRODUCTIONS, INC.**, Box 96, El Cerrito CA 94530. Executive Vice President: James Bronson, Jr. Record producer, record company and music publisher (Toulouse Music/BMI). Deals with artists, songwriters and music publishers. Fee derived from sales royalty.
**How to Contact:** Submit demo tape and lyric sheet. Prefers cassette with 2-4 songs on demo. SASE. Reports in 1 month.
**Music:** Bluegrass, gospel, jazz, R&B and soul. Artists include Les Oublies du Jazz Ensemble.

**MONOTONE RECORDS**, 281 E. Kingsbridge Rd., Bronx NY 10458. (212)582-3240. President: Murray Fuller. Record producer and music publisher (Sun Island Music Publishing Co.). Deals with artists and songwriters. Produces 1 single/year. Fee derived from sales royalty.
**How to Contact:** Submit demo tape and lyric sheet. Prefers cassette with 3-5 songs on demo. SASE. Reports in 6 weeks.
**Music:** Blues, dance-oriented, easy listening, jazz, R&B, soul and top 40/pop.

***MONTICANA PRODUCTIONS**, Box 702, Snowdon Station, Montreal, Quebec, Canada H3X 3X8. Executive Producer: D. Leonard. Record producer. Deals with artists, songwriters and artists' managers. Fee derived from sales royalty.
**How to Contact:** Submit demo tape and lyric sheet. Prfers 7½ or 15 ips reel-to-reel, cassette, phonograph record or video cassette (VHS) with maximum 10 songs on demo. "Demos should be as tightly produced as a master." Does not return unsolicited material.
**Music:** Mostly top 40; also bluegrass, blues, C&W, dance-oriented, easy listening, folk, gospel, jazz, MOR, progressive, R&B, rock and soul.

**THE MORGAN MUSIC GROUP**, Box 2388, Prescott AZ 86302. (602)445-5801. Contact: Michael D. Morgan. Record producer and music publisher (The Morgan Music Group, Hollydale Music/ASCAP, Winteroak Music/ASCAP, Chromewood Music/BMI). Deals with artists, songwriters and labels. Produces 10 singles and 5 albums/year. Fee derived from sales royalty.
**How to Contact:** Submit demo tape and lyric sheet only. Prefers cassette with 3 songs on demo. "Include cover letter with past experience, photo, bio and future expectations." SASE. Reports in 1 month.
**Music:** C&W, jazz, rock (country) and top 40/pop (country). Recently produced *Songs of the Concrete Cowboys*, by various artists (country LP, Big Wheels Records); and "California Time Again," by Michael Hollister Morgan (country single, Quarter Moon Records). Other artists include Garry Greer and Skyquake.
**Tips:** "We are interested in working with artists who have a lifelong commitment to the music industry—meaning, no matter what, they will continue in the business."

**\*MOSEKA RECORDS**, 110 N. Main, Fostoria OH 44830. (419)455-6525. Contact: Ronald Hanson. Record producer, music publisher (Fresh Air Music/BMI, Son-Ton Music/ASCAP), arranger and engineer. Deals with artists and songwriters. Produces 6 singles and 3 albums/year. Fee derived from sales royalty.
**How to Contact:** Submit demo tape and lyric sheet; call or write about your interest. Prefers cassette with 2-4 songs on demo. SASE. Reports ASAP.
**Music:** Mostly rock (all types); also C&W, dance-oriented, easy listening, folk, MOR, progressive, R&B, soul, top 40/pop and jingles. Recently produced "Runnin Through the Night," by Risque (rock single, Moseka Records; *Steal Your Heart*, by Partners Band (rock LP, Moseka Records); and *Take Me to the City*, by Rize Band (rock LP, Moseka Records). Other artists include The Exception, Tresle, The Other Half, Nobody's Kids, Flying Steel and Snatch.

**RON MOSS PRODUCTION SERVICES & MANAGEMENT**, (formerly Nots Productions), 11257 Blix St., North Hollywood CA 91602. (213)508-9865. Record producer. Estab. 1981. Deals with artists and songwriters. Produces 4 singles and 4 albums/year. Fee negotiable.
**How to Contact:** Submit demo tape and lyric sheet. Prefers cassette with 3-5 songs on demo. SASE. Reports in 1 month.
**Music:** Jazz, MOR, progressive, R&B, rock, soul and top 40/pop. Recently produced *Ivanhoe*, by Bunny Brunel (jazz LP, Headfirst Records); and *Red Metal*, by Allen Vizzutti (jazz/rock LP, Headfirst Records).
**Tips:** "We are looking for commercially-minded, high-quality musicians who are personable and willing to work toward producing a good product."

**MUSIC RESOURCES INTERNATIONAL CORP.**, 5th Floor, 21 W. 39th St., New York NY 10018. (212)869-2299. President: Andy Hussakowsky. Director: A&R: Gene O'Brien. Record production company and music publisher (MRI Music/ASCAP). Deals with artists and songwriters. Produces 5 singles and 5 albums/year. Fee derived from sales royalty or outright fee from record company.
**How to Contact:** Submit demo tape and lead sheet. Prefers cassette with 1-3 songs on demo. SASE. Reports in 3 months.
**Music:** R&B, rock, soul and top 40/pop. Past hits include: "More, More, More," "New York You Got Me Dancing," and "What's Your Name, What's Your Number," by Andrea True Connection (Buddah Records); "Jack in the Box," by David Morris (Buddah Records); "You're My Super Hero," by Everlife (Clearinghouse Records); and "Just One More Time," by Johnny Pinna and Salvation (Clearinghouse Records).
**Tips:** "MRI has negotiated leases with Buddah, Polydor, Polygram, Casablanca, AVI and other major labels."

**\*NERVOUS MUSIC**, 4/36 Dabas Hill Lane, Northout, Middlesex, London, England. 44-01-422-3462. Managing Director: R. Williams. Record producer, music publishing (Nervous Publishing) and record company (Nervous Records). Works with artists. Produces 1 single and 10 albums/year. Fee derived from sales royalty.
**How to Contact:** Submit demo tape and lyric sheet. Prefers cassette with 3-10 songs on demo. "Include photo and a letter giving your age and career goals." SAE and IRC. Reports in 2 weeks.
**Music:** Mostly rockabilly; also blues, C&W, R&B and 50s R&R. Recently produced *Buzz & the Flyers*, by Buzz and the Flyers (R&R/rockabilly LP, Nervous/Rockhouse Records); *Stack-A-Records*, by various artists (R&B LP, Nervous/Rockhouse Records); and *Phantom Rockers*, by Sharks (psychobilly LP, Nervous/Rockhouse Records). Other artists include the Deltas and the Restless.

**\*NEW DAWN PRODUCTIONS/SOUTH BOUND PRODUCTIONS**, Box 186, Cedarburg WI 53012. (414)673-5091. Producer: Robert Wiegert. Record producer and music publisher (RobJen Music, Trinity Music and Great Northern Lights Music). Works with artists and songwriters. Fee derived from sales royalty.
**How to Contact:** Submit demo tape and lyric sheet. Prefers 7½ ips reel-to-reel or cassette with 3 songs on demo. Does not return unsolicited material. Reports in 1 month.
**Music:** "Any and all types of commercial music." Recently produced "I Believed In You," by Cathy Bemis (MOR/pop single, Abacus Records); "I Think It's Gonna Rain," by Stills & Scott (country rock single, Abacus Records); and "Far Far Cry," by Gregg Scott (MOR/pop single, Abacus Records). Other artists include Katie McGivin.
**Tips:** "If we feel a song is a hit, we do everything possble to get it cut. But writers must be self critical and write, write, write."

**NEW WORLD RECORDS**, Suite 11, 2309 N. 36th St., Milwaukee WI 53210. (414)445-4872. President: Marvell Love. Record producer and music publisher (Jero Limited Music). Deals with artists and

songwriters. Produces 8 singles and 2 albums/year. Fee derived from sales royalty.
**How to Contact:** Submit demo tape and lyric sheet. Prefers cassette with 3-5 songs on demo. SASE. Reports in 3 weeks.
**Music:** Mostly R&B and soul ballads; also church/religious, gospel, soul and top 40/pop. Recently produced "Sunset Lady," by Marvell Love (love ballad single, New World Records); "Thought I Wasn't Gonna Make It Back," by the Viceroys (love ballad single, Castalia Records); "I'll Miss You," by Jim Spencer (easy listening single, New World Records); "Red Tape," by Tony Dawkins and "Oh, What a Friend," by Phebe and Darrell Hines. Other artists include the Majestics and Danny Finckley.

**NISE PRODUCTIONS, INC.**, Suite 101, 413 Cooper St., Camden NJ 08102. (215)276-0100. President: Michael Nise. Record producer and music publisher. Deals with artists and songwriters. Produces 10 singles and 10 albums/year. Fee derived from sales royalty.
**How to Contact:** Submit demo tape and lyric sheet. Prefers cassette with 1-3 songs on demo. SASE. Reports in 1 month.
**Music:** Children's, church/religious, C&W, dance-oriented, easy listening, folk, gospel, jazz, R&B, rock, soul and top 40/pop.
**Tips:** "Starting record label in May—seeking masters."

**NORTH AMERICAN LITURGY RESOURCES**, 10802 N. 23rd Ave., Phoenix AZ 85029. (602)864-1980. Record Producer: Paul Quinlan. Music Editor: Henry Papale. Record producer and music publisher. Deals with artists and songwriters and arrangers/conductors. Produces 10 albums/year. Fee derived from sales royalty.
**How to Contact:** Submit demo tape and lyric sheet. Prefers cassette with 5-12 songs on demo. SASE. Reports in 1 month.
**Music:** Children's, choral, church/religious, liturgical and Christian rock and inspirational. Recently produced "Lord of Light," by St. Louis Jesuits; "Color the World with Song," by Rev. Carey Landry; "Path of Life," and "Reflections," by the Dameans; and "Awaken My Heart/The Dawn of Day," by Lucien Deiss (all NALR Records). Other artists include Al Valverde, Victor Cabrera, Tom Kendzia, Michael Joncas, Daniel Consiglio, Joe Pinson, Jack Miffleton, Paul Contio, Timoth Crawley, Jerry Goebel and Marcy Tinger.
**Tips:** "Be familiar with our recordings. Free catalogs and brochures are supplied on request."

*****NORTHERN COMFORT PRODUCTIONS**, 10 Erica Ave., Toronto, Ontario, Canada M3H 3H2. (416)923-5717. President: J. Allan Vogel. Record producer and music publisher (Northern Comfort Music/CAPAC and Sacro-Iliac Music/PROCAN). Deals with artists and songwriters. Produces 4 singles and 1 album/year. Fee derived from sales royalty.
**How to Contact:** Submit demo tape and lyric sheet. Prefers 7½ ips reel-to-reel or cassette with 3-5 songs on demo. SAE and IRC. Reports in 3 weeks.
**Music:** Mostly pop, rock and top 40; also R&B and soul. Recently produced *Flux*, by Flux (NCP Records).
**Tips:** "Write honest, hook-laden songs about city life!"

**O.T.L. PRODUCTIONS**, Suite 5, 74 Main St., Maynard MA 01754. (617)897-8459. Producer-in-Chief: David Butler. Record producer. Deals with artists, songwriters, publishers and managers. Produces 6 singles and 3 albums/year. Fee determined by outright fee and/or royalty from label and/or artist per negotiation.
**How to Contact:** Arrange personal interview after submitting demo tape only. "Personal contact necessary to serious consideration. Audition live if possible." Prefers cassette with 3-6 songs on tape. SASE. Reports in 6-8 weeks. Tapes are not returned; no report unless interested in submitted material.
**Music:** Rock, country rock, MOR/pop, R&B, disco/funk, jazz and folk. Recently produced "Face in the Photograph," by Tragus (heavy metal single, TBA Records); and "Ina's Song," by Limbo Race (new wave single, Limbouations Records). Other artists include Midnight Traveler, Ictus and Gary Boigon.
**Tips:** "Submit material that shows an awareness of the marketplace!"

*****OAKWOOD AUDIO PRODUCTIONS**, Reed Ave., Canterbury, Kent, CT11ET, England. 44-0227-50033. Producer: G. Quinton-Jones. Record producer and music publisher (Oakwood Music). Works with artists and songwriters. Fee derived from sales royalty or outright fee from songwriter/artist or record company.
**How to Contact:** Submit demo tape and lyric sheet. Prefers cassette with 1-4 songs on demo. SASE. Reports in 1 month.
**Music:** Mostly pop; also dance-oriented and top 40. Recently produced "Overtures," by Choir (rock single, A&M Records/England); "Shanghai," by Syncopated Orchestra (1920s single, Astra Records); and "Here Comes the Night," by Rivals (punk single, Oakwood Records). Other artists include Desadi.

# Record Producers 239

**OLD HAT RECORDS/THE WIND MILL**, 3442 Nies, Ft. Worth TX 76111. (817)838-8189. President: J. Taylor. Record producer and music publisher (Royal T. Music/ASCAP). Deals with artists and songwriters. Produces 2 singles and 1 album/year. Fee derived from sales royalty.
**How to Contact:** Submit demo tape and lyric sheet. Prefers cassette with at least 1 song on demo. SASE. Reports in 1 month.
**Music:** Children's, choral, C&W, easy listening, folk, MOR, rock (all kinds) and top 40/pop. Recently produced *(Texas) Water Under the Bridge*, by Texas Water (country pop LP, Old Hat Records); "Memories Don't Grow Old," by James Michael (country single, Old Hat Records); and "One More," by Texas Water (country single, Old Hat Records). Other artists include Peggy Souix.

*__PANIO BROTHERS LABEL__, Box 99, Montmartre, Saskatchewan, Canada, S0G 3M0. Executive Director: John Panio, Jr. Record producer. Deals with artists and songwriters. Produces 1 album/year. Fee derived from sales royalty.
**How to Contact:** Submit demo tape and lyric sheet or write first about your interest. Prefers 7¾ ips reel-to-reel with any number of songs on demo. SASE. Reports in 1 month.
**Music:** C&W, dance-oriented, easy listening and Ukrainian. Recently produced "Celebrate Saskatchewan," by Panio Brothers (dance music, PB Records); and "Dance Music," by Panio Brothers (dance music, PB Records).

**PARASOUND, INC.**, Suite 414, 680 Beach St., San Francisco CA 94109. (415)673-4544. President: Bernie Krause. Vice President: Gary Remal. Record producer and music publisher. Deals with artists and songwriters. Produces 1-4 singles/year. Fee derived from sales royalty.
**How to Contact:** Submit demo tape and lead sheet. Prefers cassette with 3-6 songs on demo. SASE. Reports in 3 weeks.
**Music:** Top 40/pop, electronic and new wave.

**THE PASHA MUSIC ORG., INC.**, 5615 Melrose Ave., Hollywood CA 90038. (213)466-3507. General Manager: Carol Peters. Record producer, music publisher and personal artist manager. Deals with artists and songwriters. Fee derived by sales royalty.
**How to Contact:** Write first about your interest. Prefers cassette with 1-3 songs on demo. SASE. Reports in 3 weeks.
**Music:** Progressive, rock and top 40/pop.

**DAVE PATON**, 9502 Harrell St., Pico Rivera CA 90660. (213)692-1472. Contact: Dave Paton. Record producer and music publisher (Heaven Songs/BMI). Deals with artists and songwriters. Produces 20 singles and 3-5 albums/year. Fee negotiable.
**How to Contact:** Write first about your interest, then submit demo tape and lyric sheet. Prefers 7½ ips reel-to-reel or cassette with 3-6 songs on demo. SASE. Reports in 2 weeks.
**Music:** C&W, dance-oriented, easy listening, jazz, MOR, progressive, R&B, rock and top 40/pop.

*__RAY PAUL RECORD COMPANY__, Box 1406, Brea CA 92621. (714)595-6925. Contact: Ray Paul or Arlene Silvergleid. Record producer and music publisher (Permanent Pop Music). Deals with artists and songwriters. Produces 4 singles and 1-2 albums/year. Fee derived from sales royalty or outright fee from artist/songwriter or record company.
**How to Contact:** Call or write about your interest; submit demo tape and lyric sheet. Prefers cassette or previously recorded records with 3-5 songs on demo. SASE. Reports in 1 month.
**Music:** Mostly top 40, rock, pop and dance-oriented 80s music; also easy listening and MOR. Recently produced "How Do You Know," by Ray Paul (top 40/pop rock single, Permanent Press Records); "Complicated Girl," by Puppet Rulers (rock/top 40 single, Permanent Press Records); *Go Time*, by R. Paul & RPM (top 40 rock LP, Muscle Recordworks); and "Lady Be Mine Tonight," by R. Paul (top 40 rock single, Euphoria Records). Other artists include Memo and Nick Name.

**PCRL**, 2364 Sherbrooke East, Montreal, Quebec, Canada H2K 1E6. (514)526-2831. Contact: Carole Risch. Record producer and music publisher (Editeurs Associes). Deals with artists. Produces 15-20 singles and 5-10 albums/year. Fee derived from sales royalty.
**How to Contact:** Submit demo tape and lyric sheet. Prefers 7½ ips reel-to-reel or cassette with 3-5 songs on demo. SAE and IRC. Reports in 3 weeks.
**Music:** Easy listening, MOR and top 40/pop.

*__DON PERRY PRODUCTIONS, INC.__, 2974 Parkview Dr., Thousand Oaks CA 91362. (805)497-4738. President: Don Perry. Record producer and music publisher. Deals with artists, songwriters and film composers. Produces 4-6 singles and 1-2 albums/year. Fee derived from sales royalty.
**How to Contact:** Submit demo tape and lyric sheet. Prefers cassette with 2-4 songs on demo. SASE. Reports in 1 month.

**Music:** Mostly top 40/pop and country; also rock (country/soft). Recently produced *Instant Hero*, by Doug Kershaw (country LP, Scotti Brothers/CBS Records); "I Used To Be Her," by Lyndsey Edwards (country single, Monument Records); and *Maybe*, by Thom Pace (top 40 LP, Capitol Records).

**POSITIVE PRODUCTIONS**, Box 1405, Highland Park NJ 08904. Contact: J. Vincenzo. Record producer and music publisher. Deals with songwriters. Payment negotiable.
**How to Contact:** Submit demo tape and lyric sheet. Prefers 7½ ips reel-to-reel with 2-4 songs on demo. SASE. Reports in 1 month.
**Music:** Children's, easy listening, folk, and MOR. Other artists include Wooden Soldier and Joe Cory.

**\*PRAISE INDUSTRIES CORP.**, 7802 Express St., Burnaby, British Columbia, Canada V5A 1T4. (604)421-3441. Manager: Paul Yaroshuk. Record producer. Deals with artists. Produces 30 singles and 24 albums/year. Fee derived from sales royalty.
**How to Contact:** Submit demo tape and lyric sheet. Prefers cassette with 1-12 songs on demo. SAE and IRC. Reports in 2 weeks.
**Music:** Bluegrass, children's, choral, church/religious, C&W, folk and gospel.

**THE PRESCRIPTION CO.**, 70 Murray Ave., Port Washington NY 10050. (516)767-1929. President: David F. Gasman. Record producer, record company, and music publisher (Prescription Co./BMI). Deals with artists and songwriters. Fee derived from sales royalty or outright fee from record company.
**How to Contact:** Write or call first about your interest then submit demo tape or acetate disk and lyric sheet. Prefers cassette with any number songs on demo. Does not return unsolicited material. Reports in 1 month.
**Music:** Bluegrass, blues, children's, C&W, dance-oriented, easy listening, jazz, MOR, progressive, R&B, rock, soul and top 40/pop. Recently produced "You Came In" and "Rock 'n' Roll Blues," by Medicine Mike (pop singles, Prescription Records); and *Just What the Doctor Ordered*, by Medicine Mike (LP, Prescription Records).
**Tips:** "We want quality—fads mean nothing to us. Familiarity with the artist's material helps too."

**PREWITT ROSE PRODUCTIONS**, Box 372, Antioch TN 37013. (615)331-2378. Director: Terry Rose. Record producer and music publisher (Pocket-Money Music). Deals with artists. Produces 15-20 singles and 10 albums/year. Fee derived from sales royalty.
**How to Contact:** Write first about your interest. Prefers cassette with 2 songs maximum on demo. SASE. Reports in 3 weeks.
**Music:** Blues, C&W, dance-oriented, easy listening, gospel, MOR, new wave, R&B, rock, soul and top 40/pop. Recently produced *Working Country*, by Ralph Hollis (C&W LP, Sunbelt Records); *Coast To Coast*, by Dixie Echoes (gospel LP, Supreme Records) and *The Minerals*, by The Minerals (rock LP, Heat Wave Records). Other artists include The Magics, Wally Willette, Purvis Pickett, Marcel Grantello, Mouse and the Traps (Smudge Records).

**PRITCHETT PUBLICATION**, 38603 Sage Tree St., Palmdale CA 93550. Branch: 171 Pine Haven Dr., Daytona Beach FL 32014. (904)252-4849. President: Leroy Pritchett (California). A&R Director: Charles Vickers (Florida). Record producer and music publisher (BMI). Deals with artists and songwriters. Fee derived from sales royalty.
**How to Contact:** Submit only lead sheet first. SASE. Reports in 1 month.
**Music:** Church/religious, dance, easy listening, gospel and top 40/pop. Recently produced *Another Dawn*, (gospel LP); *Heaven Is Just Over the Hill*, (gospel LP); *Charles Vickers Does Disco* (disco LP); *Disco Pop for the 80's*, (pop-disco LP), all by Charles Vickers.

**PRODIGY PRODUCTIONS LTD./BURNT OUT MUSIC**, Suite 205, 323 E. 23rd St., Chicago IL 60616. (312)225-2110. President: Donald Burnside. Record producer and music publisher (Burnt Out Music/BMI). Deals with artists and songwriters. Produces 2 singles and 2 albums/year. Fee derived from sales royalty.
**How to Contact:** Write first about your interest. Prefers cassette with 4-6 songs on demo. SASE. Reports in 3 weeks.
**Music:** Dance, R&B, soul and top 40/pop. Recently produced "Sir Jam Alot," by Capt. Sky (R&B single, WMOT Records); *Concerned Party #1*, by Capt. Sky (R&B LP, WMOT Records); and "Don't Say Goodnight," by First Love (dance single, Brunswick Records). Other artists include Superior Movement and O.C. Smith, Jr.

**\*PRODUCTION CONNECTION**, 408 St. Gabriel, Montreal, Quebec, Canada H2Y 2Z9. (514)866-2021. Secretary: Yves Godin. Record producer and music publisher (Les Editions la Bobine). Deals with artists and songwriters. Produces 15 singles/year. Fee derived from sales royalty.

**How to Contact:** Submit demo tape and lyric sheet. Prefers cassette with minimum of 5 songs on demo. SASE. Reports in 2 weeks.
**Music:** Mostly pop and dance; also easy listening and rock. Recently produced "If You Can Count," by Cesarez (electro pop single, Bobinason Records); "Snap," by Beau Flash (electro rock single, Focus Records); and "SOS Anonyme," by Dwight Druick (pop rock single, Bobinason Records).

**QUINTO RECORDS**, Box 2388, Toluca Lake CA 91602. (213)985-8284. Producer: Quint Benedetti. Produces 1-2 singles and 2 albums/year. Deals with artists and songwriters. Fee derived from sales royalty.
**How to Contact:** Submit demo tape and lead sheet. Prefers cassette with 2-4 songs on demo. SASE. Reports in 1 month.
**Music:** Seasonal and Christmas songs only. Recently produced "Christmas Is for Children" and "Christmas Presents," (Quinto Records).

**R.E.F. RECORDS**, 404 Bluegrass Ave., Madison TN 37115. (615)865-6380. President: Bob Frick. Manager: Shawn Frick. A&R Director: Scott Frick. Record producer and music publisher (Frick Music Publishing Co./BMI). Deals with artists, songwriters and producers. Produces 10 albums/year. Fee derived from sales royalty.
**How to Contact:** Write or call first about your interest, then submit demo tape and lyric sheet. Prefers 7 1/2 ips reel-to-reel or cassette with 2-10 songs on demo. SASE. Reports in 1 month.
**Music:** C&W, gospel, rock and top 40/pop. Recently produced *Imgenes*, by Francisco Morales (gospel LP, R.E.F. Records); *Live in Nashville*, by Larry Ahlborn (gospel LP, Love Notes Records); and *I Can't Help Myself*, by Bob Scott and Family (gospel LP, R.E.F. Records).

**CAROL J. RACHOU, SR.**, 711 Stevenson St., Lafayette LA 70501. (318)234-5577. President: Carol J. Rachou, Sr. Record producer, music publisher (La Lou Music/BMI), record company, recording studio and distributing company. Deals with artists and songwriters, musicians, promoters, agents and managers. Produces 10-20 singles and 6-8 albums/year. Receives negotiable royalty.
**How to Contact:** Submit demo tape and lyric sheet. Prefers 7 1/2 ips reel-to-reel or cassette with 1-6 songs on demo. SASE. Reports in 2 weeks.
**Music:** Produces primarily Cajun/French; also some bluegrass, blues, church/religious, classical, comedy C&W, folk, gospel, jazz, MOR, progressive, R&B, rock and top 40/pop. Recently produced "Lache Pas La Patate," (Gold Record in Canada) and "The Saints (in French)," by Jimmy C. Newman (Cajun singles, La Louisianne Records); *That Cajun Country Sound*, by Eddy Raven (Cajun English LP, La Louisianne Records); and "Cajun Fiddle," by Rufus Thibodeaux (Cajun/instrumental, La Louisianne Records). Other artists include Ambrose Thibodeaux, Merlin Fontenot, Nathan Abshire, L.J. Foret, Blackie Forestier, The Dusenbery Family, Vin Bruce, Doc Guidry, Aldus Roger, Bud Fletcher, Alex Broussand and others.

**RADIO MAGIC PRODUCTIONS**, (formerly Frequency Productions), Via C Modestino 64, Paternopoli, 83052 (Avelino), Italy. 39-0827-71073. US Office: 2695 Carrell Lane, Willow Grove PA 19090. (215)674-0562. President and General Manager: Sal Barbieri. A&R Manager: Raffaele Barbieri. US Office Manager: Ciro Schiano. Record producer, music publisher (Conypol Music/BMI) and radio station. Deals with artists and songwriters. Produces 15 singles and 8 albums/year. Fee derived from sales royalty or outright fee from record company.
**How to Contact:** "All tapes must be sent to our main office in Italy." Submit demo tape and lyric sheet. Prefers cassette with 1-4 songs on demo. SASE. Reports in 2 weeks.
**Music:** C&W, dance-oriented, easy listening, MOR, R&B, rock (soft and hard), soul and top 40/pop. Recently produced "Feeling Good," by Sal Barbieri (dance rock single, Mercury Records); "Beatrice," by S. Barieri (top 40/R&B single, BSO Records); and "I Love You," by D. McCain (top 40/pop single, BSO Records). Other artists include The Royal Company, Bianca, La Dolce Vita and Gus Manuel.

**RADMUS PRODUCTIONS, INC.**, 164 Onderdonck Ave., Manhasset NY 10030. (212)957-9330. Contact: General Manager. Record producer and music publisher (Radmus Publishing, Inc./ASCAP). Deals with artists and songwriters. Produces 5-10 singles and 2-3 albums/year. Fee derived from sales royalty.
**How to Contact:** Submit demo tape and lyric sheet. Prefers 7 1/2 or 15 ips reel-to-reel or cassette with 2-5 songs on demo. SASE. Reports in 3 weeks "or longer depending on work load."
**Music:** C&W, dance, easy listening, folk, jazz (fusion), MOR, progressive, R&B, new wave rock, soul and top 40/pop. Recently produced "First Time" and "One Good Reason," by M. Lewis (country singles, Door Knob records); "Guilty with an Explanation," by M. Lewis (country single, Warner/Curb Records); and *In the Crowd*, by VOG (rock LP, CBS Records).

**RAINBOW RECORDING STUDIOS**, 2322 S. 64th Ave., Omaha NE 68106 (402)554-0123. Producer: Lars Erickson. Record producer and music publisher (Thomas Jackson Publishing/BMI). Deals with artists, songwriters in production of "commercial jingles." Produces 12 singles and 2 albums/year. Fee derived from outright fee from client, record company or songwriter/artist.
**How to Contact:** Query or submit demo tape and lyric sheet. Prefers 7½ ips reel-to-reel or cassette with 4 songs maximum on demo. SASE. Reports in 1 month.
**Music:** Any style acceptable. Recently produced "We Can Be" b/w "Don't Fade Away," by Tommy Jackson (MOR singles, Jacksongs Records); and "I Live For You," by John Fischer (MOR single, Jacksongs Records). Other artists include The Group, Beebe Runyon & the Furniture and Skuddur.

**RAINBOW ROAD RECORDS**, 1212 Bell Grimes Ln., Nashville TN 37207. (615)865-0653. Contact: Glenn Summers. Record producer, music publisher (Caress Me Publishing Co./BMI) and record company. Produces 1 single/year. Fee derived from royalty from air play.
**How to Contact:** Write first about your interest, then submit demo tape and lyric sheet. Prefers cassette or 8-track tape with 2-3 songs on demo. SASE. Reports in 1 month.
**Music:** Bluegrass, C&W, folk and gospel. Recently produced "Disco Bells," and "My Blues," (disco singles, Rainbow Road Records); and "When You Caress Me," (country ballad single, PAD Records).

*****RAINFIRE MUSIC PRODUCTION**, 15217 Otsego St., Sherman Oaks CA 91403. (213)784-0388. A&R Director: Billy Goodman. Record producer and music publisher (Rainfire Music/BMI). Deals with artists and songwriters. Produces 3 singles and 2 albums/year. Fee derived from sales royalty.
**How to Contact:** Submit demo tape and lyric sheet. Prefers cassette with 3-5 songs on demo. SASE. Reports in 1 week.
**Music:** Mostly pop and rock; also C&W, dance-oriented, MOR and R&B. Artists include Rita Jenrette and Rhonda Silver.

*****RA-JO INTERNATIONAL RECORDS & TAPES**, Box 214, Co. Op. City Station, Bronx NY 10475. (212)379-2593. Executive Producers: J or Ace Adams. Record producer and music publisher (Ace Adams Music, Adam Puertas Music, Bill Ace Music). Deals with artists and songwriters. Produces 5 singles and 2 albums/year. Fee derived from sales royalty or outright fee from artist/songwriter or record company.
**How to Contact:** Call or write first about your interest; submit demo tape and lyric sheet. Prefers cassette with 4-8 songs on demo. SASE. Reports in 2 weeks.
**Music:** Mostly R&B, country and dance; also children's, progressive, soul, top 40/pop and punk. Recently produced "Zoot Zoot Zoot," by Tiny Tim (children's Christmas single, Ra-Jo Records); and "Honky Tonk," by Bill Doget (dance single, King Records).

*****RANDALL PRODUCTIONS**, Box 11960, Chicago IL 60611. (312)561-0027. President: Mary Freeman. Record producer and music publisher (Billetdoux Music/BMI). Deals with artists and songwriters. Produces 5 singles and 2 albums/year. Fee derived from sales royalty.
**How to Contact:** Submit demo tape and lyric sheet. Prefers cassette with 3-6 songs on demo. SASE. Reports in 1 month.
**Music:** Gospel, jazz, MOR, R&B, rock, soul and top 40/pop. Recently produced "I Wanna Be with You," by Mickey Dee (R&B dance single, Grandville Records); "I'm Gonna Love You," by Randy Terry (country/rock/pop single, Grandville Records); and *Journey to Beyond*, by Duncan Pryce Kirk (country rock single, Grandville Records). Other artists include Shannon Band and Emett Beard.

*****RAWLS BROTHERS PRODUCTIONS CO.**, c/o Fun City Record Co., 281 W. 6th St., Mansfield OH 44903. (419)524-2141. Executive Producer: L.A. Rawls. Record producer. Deals with artists. Produces 2 singles and 2 albums/year. Fee derived from sales royalty.
**How to Contact:** Submit demo tape and lyric sheet. Prefers cassette with 3-5 songs on demo. Does not return unsolicited material. Reports in 3 weeks.
**Music:** Gospel, R&B and top 40/pop.

**RICK RHODES PRODUCTIONS**, 11800 Mayfield Ave., Los Angeles CA 90049. President: Rick Rhodes. Record producer, music publisher (Captain Nemo) and record company. Deals with artists and songwriters. Produces 2 singles/year. Fee derived from sales royalty.
**How to Contact:** Submit demo tape and lyric sheet. Prefers cassette with 3-6 songs on demo. SASE. Reports in 1 month.
**Music:** Top 40/pop. Recently produced "One More Miracle" and "It's All Downhill from Here," by Rick Rhodes (pop singles).

**RICHEY RECORDS**, #118, 7121 W. Vickery, Ft. Worth TX 76116. (817)731-7375. Contact: D.M. (Slim) Richey. Record producer and music publisher (Ridge Runner Publishing/ASCAP, Grass Moun-

tain Publishing/BMI). Deals with artists and songwriters. Produces 6 albums/year. Fee derived from sales royalty.
**How to Contact:** Submit demo tape and lyric sheet. Prefers cassette with 3-6 songs on demo. Does not return unsolicited material. Reports in 1 month.
**Music:** Bluegrass, blues, C&W, rock and top 40/pop. Recently produced "Still Flyin'," by Bugs Henderson (rock/blues single, Flying High Records); "Texas Boogie Blues," by Ray Sharpe (R&B single, Flying High Records); and *Festival Favorites*, by Alan Munde (bluegrass banjo LP, Ridge Runner Records). Other artists include Country Gazette.

**RICOCHET RECORDS**, Suite 22-1A, 600 Pine Hollow Rd., E. Norwich NY 11732. (516)922-6980. President: Andy Marvel. Record producer and music publisher (Bing, Bing, Bing Music/ASCAP), Droopy Tunes/BMI) and record company. Estab. 1981. Deals with artists and songwriters. Fee derived from sales royalty.
**How to Contact:** Submit demo tape and lyric sheet or arrange personal interview to play demo tape. Prefers 7½ ips reel-to-reel or cassette with 3-5 songs on demo. SASE. Reports in 2 weeks.
**Music:** C&W, MOR, rock and top 40/pop.

**RMS TRIAD PRODUCTIONS**, 6267 Potomac Circle, West Bloomfield MI 48033. (313)661-5167. Contact: Bob Szajner. Record producer, record company and music publisher (RMS Triad Publishing/ASCAP). Deals with artists and songwriters (instrumental). Produces 3 albums/year. Fee derived from outright fee from artist/songwriter or record company for services.
**How to Contact:** Write first about your interest. Prefers cassette with 1-3 songs on demo. SASE. Reports in 3 weeks.
**Music:** Jazz and instrumental. Recently produced *Jazz Opus 20/40, Detroit Jazz Center* and *1981 Montreaux/Detroit Live*, by Triad (jazz instrumental LPs, RMS Records); *Are You Glad to Be in America*, by James "Blood" Ulmer; and *Where Flamingos Fly*, by Gil Evans (jazz instrumental LPs, Artist's House Records). Other artists include Frank Isola and Ray Brooks.
**Tips:** "We are currently associated with John Snyder and Artist's House, Inc./BMI, 40 W. 37th St., New York NY 10018. (212)594-9435. This joint venture is promoting the releases of artists such as Ornette Coleman, Art Pepper, Chet Baker, Mel Lewis, Thad Jones, James 'Blood' Ulmer, Jim Hall, Paul Desmond and others."

**ANGELO ROMAN ENTERPRISES**, Box 3144, Covina CA 91723. (213)967-1451. Producer: Angelo Roman. Management/consultant and music publisher (Laughing Bird Songs). Primarily deals with singer-songwriters. Fee derived from "various arrangements with artists and production companies."
**How to Contact:** Submit demo tape and lyric sheet. Prefers cassette with 1-3 songs on demo. Include bio and photos. SASE. Reports in 1 month.
**Music:** C&W, easy listening, jazz, MOR, rock, soul and top 40/pop. Artists include Mercy Rongel and Venette Glsud.

**ROSE HILL PRODUCTIONS**, 3929 New Seneca Tpk., Marcellus NY 13108. (315)673-1117. A&R: Vincent Taft. Record producer and music publisher (Katch Nazar Music/ASCAP). Deals with artists and songwriters. Fee derived from sales royalty and outright fee from songwriter/artist.
**How to Contact:** Submit demo tape and lyric sheet. Prefers cassette with 3 songs maximum on demo. SASE. Reports in 2 weeks.
**Music:** Jazz, MOR, progressive, R&B, rock, soul and top 40/pop. Recently produced *Time*, by Taksim (jazz LP); "Too Much," by Foxy (pop single, Sunday Records); and "Rock & Roll Shoes," by Dan Eaton (rock single, Star City Records).
**Tips:** "Songs should have a beginning, middle and end; melodic and strong, real lyrics. They should be concise; every note should count. Less is more."

**ROSEMARY MELODY LINE CO.**, 633 Almond St., Vineland NJ 08360. (609)696-0943. Producer: Dennis Link. Record producer and recording studios. Deals with artists and songwriters. Produces 5 singles and 5 albums/year. Fee derived from outright fee from artist/songwriter.
**How to Contact:** Write first about your interest. Prefers cassette with 3-5 songs on demo. SASE. Reports in 2 weeks.
**Music:** Bluegrass, church/religious, gospel, rock and top 40/pop. Recently produced *Wings of Love*, by Juan and Jenny Avila and Smoked County Jam (folk/bluegrass LP, Goodworks Records); *Eternal Light*, by Eugene Palow (gospel LP, RML Records); and *Getting Our Feet Wet*, by Northwind (pop LP, RML Records). Other artists include Ned Stites, Mark Uncle, Buddy Leonetti and Vanessa Beals.

**BRIAN ROSS PRODUCTIONS**, Box 2950, Hollywood CA 90028. (213)851-2500 (studio); 662-3121 (office). A&R Producer: Brian Ross. Record producer and music publisher (Brian Ross Music/

BMI); also international music representation in all foreign countries. Deals with artists, songwriters, attorneys, agents and managers. Produces 15 singles and 15-20 albums/year. Fee derived from sales royalty.
**How to Contact:** Submit demo tape and lyric sheet. Prefers cassette with 1-4 songs on demo; also include photo and bio (if artist) "giving details about management, performances, etc. Be professional. Pick your 2-4 best songs, enclose SASE, and label clearly." Reports in 1 week, "24 hours if good."
**Music:** Mostly top 40/pop, contemporary and MOR; also all types of music including techno-pop and new wave. "Foreign releases are our specialty." Recently produced "Talk Talk," by Music Machine (new wave single, Rhino Records); "I'm on Fire," by the Muglestons (pop ballad, Starborn Records); "I Wish You the Best," by Robert Jason (MOR ballad, Starborn Records); and "Cry Like a Baby," by Didi Anthony (R&B ballad, Starborn Records). Other artists include El Chicano, Lance Powers, Fire and Ice, Dick Gesswein, Dove, Squeezer, Great Western, Mouse, Jensen Interceptor (Canada), Chakra, The Light and Rain.

**ROYAL K PRODUCTIONS**, 6 Melrose Dr., Livingston NJ 07039. (201)533-0448. President: Marc Katz. Record producer and music publisher (Royal K Music). Deals with artists, songwriters and producers. Produces 16 singles and 4 albums/year. Fee derived from sales royalty.
**How to Contact:** Write first about your interest then submit demo tape and lyric sheet. Prefers cassette with 1-5 songs on demo. "Include resume and pertinent background information." SASE. Reports in 3 weeks.
**Music:** Bluegrass, C&W, dance-oriented, gospel, MOR, R&B, rock, soul and top 40/pop. Recently produced *Living in Paradise*, by Rea (pop LP, Musique de Soleil Records); *Arcade*, by Chakraes (rock LP, Musique de Soleil Records) and *Steppin'*, by Charles Stewart (rock/gospel LP, Musique de Soleil Records). Other artists include Williams Brothers, Race, Score, Hip and Frozen Image.
**Tips:** "Artist or group should be professional, solid musically and have potentially commercial songs."

**RUSTRON MUSIC PRODUCTIONS**, 200 Westmoreland Ave., White Plains NY 10606. (914)946-1689. Executive Director: Rusty Gordon. Director A&R: Ron Caruso. Independent record producer and music publisher (Rustron Music Publishers/BMI). Deals with artists and songwriters. Produces 3-4 albums and 3-8 singles/year. Fee derived from sales royalty and outright fee from record company.
**How to Contact:** Query, arrange personal interview or submit demo tape and lead/lyric sheet. Include promotional material and photos. Prefers 7 1/2 ips reel-to-reel, "with leader tape between all songs and at beginning and end of tape" or cassette with 3-6 songs on demo. "Interviews are held in the evenings Monday through Thursday from 7-10 p.m. We specialize in singer/songwriter package for promotion and publishing. We will also review songs from non-performing writers." SASE. Reports in 1 month.
**Music:** R&B, country (popular and progressive), disco (salsa, popular, swing), easy listening, folk (rock and folk/country), MOR, rock (country/rock and R&R), and pop (standards). Recently produced *Lois Britten Project #2*, by Lois Britten (pop/rock/disco LP, Rustron Records); "Sign Painter," *Everything She Touches*, and "Llguste, Llguste," and "El Amor," by Christian Camilo and the Tingalayo Rhythm Band (international Hispanic release, FM Records); "Amor Mio," by Christian Camilo and the Tingalayo Rhythm Band (Spanish ballad single, FM Records); "Live Cabaret Album," by Richard Collins; *Street Singer*, by Lynn Haney & Co.; and "Where Love Can Go," by Dianne Mower & Jasmine.
**Tips:** "Write commercially marketable songs with strong hooks. We want professional stage presence levels, good vocal continuity and range, and excellent musicianship."

**S.P.Q.R. MUSIC**, 69 Robinhood Rd., Clifton NJ 07013. (201)778-6759. General Manager: Fausto Lucignani. Record producer and music publisher. Deals with artists, songwriters and record companies. Produces 2 singles and 1 album/year. Fee derived from sales royalty.
**How to Contact:** Submit demo tape and lyric sheet. Prefers cassette with 2-4 songs on demo. "Beneath the voice, each song should be played by at least 4 musicians." SASE. Reports in 3 weeks.
**Music:** Dance/pop and top 40/pop.
**Tips:** "Songwriters should always keep in mind they write for the public; not for themselves."

**SAGITTAR RECORDS**, Box 210636, Dallas TX 75211. (214)298-9576. President: Paul Ketter. Record producer, record company and music publisher. Deals with artists and songwriters. Produces 12 singles and 3 albums/year.
**How to Contact:** Submit demo tape and lead sheet. Prefers cassette with 3-12 songs on demo. SASE. Reports in 1 month.
**Music:** Mostly C&W; also folk, MOR (country), and progressive (country). Recently produced "Stay Till I Don't Love You Anymore," "I Wanna Say 'I Do'," and "Lovin' Bound," by P.J. Kamel (C&W singles, Sagittar Records); "Theodore Csanta's Right-Hand-Man," by Dave Gregory (C&W single, Sagittar Records); and *Only A Woman* by Bunnie Mills (C&W LP, Sagittar Records). Other artists include Jay Douglas, Sandra Storm, Jackie Rosser, Buddy Howard, Joe Johnson and Jodi Witt.
**Tips:** "Be familiar with the top 10 songs on C&W charts."

**Record Producers 245**

***SAIN RECORDIAU CVF**, Llandwrog, Caernarfon, Gwynedd, LL54 5TG, United Kingdom. Directors: Hefin Elis and Davydd Iwan. Record producer, music publisher (Cyhoeddiadau Sain) and record company (Sain). Deals with artists and songwriters. Produces 10 singles and 40 albums/year. Fee derived from sales royalty. Listens only to material submitted by songwriters and artists in the U.K.
**How to Contact:** Submit demo tape and lyric sheet. Prefers cassette with 3-6 songs on demo. SAE and IRC. Reports in 1 month.
**Music:** Mostly choral and folk; also children's, church/religious, C&W, rock and Welsh language. Recently produced *Shampw*, by Bando (rock/MOR LP, Sain Records); *Pererinion*, by Pendyrus Choir (choral LP, Sain Records); and *Ychydig Hedd*, by Trebor Edwards (MOR LP, Sain Records). Other artists include Ar Log, The Llanelli Male Choir and Geraint Jarman.

**SAMARAH PRODUCTIONS, INC.**, Box 2501, Columbia SC 29202. (803)754-3556. President: Daniel Hodge, Jr. Record producer, music publisher (Jemiah Publishing/BMI) and artist management. Deals with artists, songwriters and record companies. Produces minimum of 4 singles/year. Fee derived from sales royalty or outright fee from record company.
**How to Contact:** Submit demo tape and lyric sheet, "and lead sheet if possible." Prefers 7½ ips reel-to-reel or cassette with 3-6 songs on demo. SASE. Reports in 1 month.
**Music:** Church/religious, C&W, gospel, MOR, R&B, rock (top 40), soul and top 40/pop. Recently produced "I Who Have Nothing," by Midnight Blue (R&B/pop single, Motown Records); "Wishing" and "Feel It and Groove Together," by Midnight Blue (both R&B singles, Samarah Records).
**Tips:** "Rhythm tracks and vocals on tape must be tight. Before sending tape compare the *feel* of your song to the *feel* of a successful artist's song in the same market."

**SANSU ENTERPRISES**, 3809 Clematis Ave., New Orleans LA 70122. (504)949-8386. Contact: Clarence Toussaint. Record producer and music publisher (Marsaint Music, Inc./BMI, Rhilander Music/BMI, Martu Music/ASCAP). Deals with artists. Produces 10 singles and 6 albums/year. Fee derived from sales royalty or outright fee from record company.
**How to Contact:** Submit demo tape and lyric sheet. Prefers cassette with 3-5 songs on demo. SASE. Reports in 2 months.
**Music:** Blues, gospel, country, jazz, R&B, rock and soul. Recently produced *Touch of Silk*, by Eric Gale (jazz LP, Columbia Records); *Routes*, by Ramsey Lewis (jazz LP, Columbia Records); and *Released*, by Pat Labelle (soul LP, Epic Records). Other artists include Allen Toussaint, Lee Dorsey, Earl King and Ernie K. Doe.

**SAPPHIRE RECORD CO.**, 2815 Octavia St., New Orleans LA 70115. (504)866-3478. Contact: Lou Welsch. Record producer and music publisher (Sapphire Music Publishers/BMI). Deals with artists and songwriters. Produces 2-4 singles/year. Fee derived from sales royalty.
**How to Contact:** Call to arrange interview to play demo tape. Prefers cassette with 4 songs on demo. SASE. Reports in 3 weeks.
**Music:** Bluegrass, blues, C&W, easy listening, MOR, R&B, rock, soul and top 40/pop. Recently produced "Crying the Blues," by the Moon Beams (blues single, Sapphire Records). Other artists include Mike Lord.

**STEVEN C. SARGEANT**, 31632 2nd Ave., South Laguna Beach CA 92677. (714)499-4409. Producer: Steven C. Sargeant. Record producer. Deals with artists and songwriters. Produces 4 singles/year. Fee derived from sales royalty. Demo studio facility available (8 track, 2 track, dolby, etc.).
**How to Contact:** Query or submit demo tape. Prefers 7½ ips reel-to-reel or cassette with 3-5 songs on demo. SASE. Reports in 3 weeks.
**Music:** Folk, jazz and rock (country, hard). Recently produced "Rocky and the Rancher," by McMahon and Sargeant (country rock single, Black Rose Records); "Catcher in the Rye" and "Stranded," by McMahon and Sargeant (rock singles, Black Rose Records).

**STEVE SCHARF**, Double Header Productions, 61 Jane St., New York NY 10014. (212)929-2068. Contact: Steve Scharf. Record producer, music publisher (Weeze Music Co./BMI) and independent record producer. Produces 4 singles and 4 albums/year. Deals with artists and songwriters. Fee derived from sales royalty and outright fee from songwriter/artist and record company. Production fees charged for demos and records.
**How to Contact:** Call first about your interest. Submit demo tape and lyric sheet. Prefers 7½ ips reel-to-reel or cassette with maximum 4 songs on demo. SASE.
**Music:** Mostly rock, pop and R&B; also adult contemporary and top 40. Recently produced *The Markley Band*, by The Markley Band (jazz, funk, pop LP, Townhouse/Capitol Records); *Pictures*, by Pictures (mainstream pop/rock LP, United Artists Records); and "Let's Eat Our Fast Food Slow," by

Tony Schaeffer Project (pop/rock single, Night Train Records). Produces "local rock and pop bands developing in New York City.
**Tips:** "Songwriters must have great attitudes as people, then original hit material."

**SEASUN EXPERIENCE MUSIC PRODUCTIONS**, Box 1725, Daytona Beach FL 32015. (904)255-4891. Creative Manager: T. Patrick Brown. Record producer. Deals with songwriters and owners of master tapes. Produces 1-3 singles and 1 album/year. Fee derived from sales royalty or outright fee from record company.
**How to Contact:** Submit demo tape and lyric sheet. Prefers cassette with 1-3 songs on demo. SASE. Reports in 3 months.
**Music:** Children's, classical, dance-oriented, easy listening, jazz, MOR, progressive, R&B, soul and top 40/pop. Recently produced "Time Gets Away," by Raw Honey (single ballad, Seasun Experience Records); "Honey," by Reginald Asberry (MOR single, Seasun Experience Records); and "The Jam," by Bruce Allen (jazz/funk single, Seasun Experience Records). Other artists include Flarre, Magic Band, James Smith, Rozlyn Walker and Derrick James.
**Tips:** "Send only songs with catchy melodies, harmonies and clear lyrics. Don't be too kinky or negative and aim for the heart of the market with a large amount of originality to boot."

**SECOND SUN PRODUCTIONS**, Rt. 2, Box 133, Vashon Island WA 98013. (206)463-2850. Producer: Robert Krinsky. Record producer and music publisher (Ferry Boat Music/ASCAP, Thea Music/BMI). Record labels include Second Sun and Pinup. Deals with artists and songwriters. Produces 1-2 singles and 3-5 albums/year. Fee derived from sales royalty or outright fee from record company.
**How to Contact:** Submit demo tape and lyric sheet. Prefers cassette with 1-4 songs on demo. "Include cover letter stating whether you are submitting for artist or publishing consideration. Artists should be regionally located." Does not return unsolicited material.
**Music:** Blues, jazz, rock and top 40/pop. Recently published *Lonesome City Kings*, by the Lonesome City Kings (rock LP, First American Records); *Big Time Blues Man*, by Isaac Scott (blues LP, Music Is Medicine Records); and *Diane Schuur I and II*, by Diane Schuur (jazz vocal LP, First American Records).

**SEVEN HILLS RECORDING & PUBLISHING CO., INC.**, 905 N. Main St., Evansville IN 47711. (812)423-1861. President: Ed Krietemeyer. Record producer and music publisher. Deals with artists and songwriters. Produces 3 singles/year. Fee derived from sales royalty.
**How to Contact:** Write first about your interest. Prefers cassette as demo. SASE. Reports in 1 month.
**Music:** Bluegrass, blues, C&W, easy listening, folk, gospel and R&B.

**SHEKERE PRODUCTIONS**, Box 26034, Richmond VA 23260. (804)355-3586. President: Plunky Nkabinde. Record producer and music publisher (Shekere Music/BMI). Produces 3 singles and 6 albums/year. Deals with artists and songwriters. Fee derived by outright fee from record company or outright fee from songwriter/artist.
**How to Contact:** Submit demo tape and lyric sheet. Prefers cassette with 2-5 songs on demo. SASE. Reports in 3 weeks.
**Music:** Blues, dance, jazz, progressive, R&B, and soul. Recently produced *Make a Change*, by Oneness of Juju (jazz, funk, reggae LP, Blackfire Records); "SABI," by O. Asante (African disco single, Atampan Records); and *Larry Bland and the Volunteer Choir*, by Larry Bland and the Volunteer Choir (gospel LP).
**Tips:** "Have good material, experience, contacts and be willing to work. It would be extremely helpful if you have an orientation towards African music, jazz or reggae."

**MICKEY SHERMAN PRODUCTIONS**, Division of Music Syndications, Inc., 2108 NW 115th St., Oklahoma City, OK 73120. (405)751-8954. Producer: Mickey Sherman. Record producer, music publisher (Okisher/BMI) and record company. Deals with artists and songwriters. Produces 15-20 singles and 6-10 albums/year. Fee derived from sales royalty.
**How to Contact:** Submit demo tape and lyric sheet. Prefers cassette with 1-3 songs on demo. Does not return unsolicited material. Reports in 1 month.
**Music:** Mostly blues and C&W; also children's, easy listening, jazz, MOR and R&B. Recently produced "A Bad Case of the Blues," by Janjo (easy listening single, Seeds Records); "Tulsa on a Saturday Night," by Benny Kabiak (C&W single, Homa Records); and "Last Call," by Ronny McClendon (C&W single, Seed Records). Other artists include Charley Shaw and Rebecca Mavity.

**\*SHETLAND SOUND**, Box 120023, Nashville TN 37212. President: Gregory Lucas. Record producer and music publisher (Shetland Enterprises, International/ASCAP and Little David Music, Inc./BMI). Deals with artists and songwriters. Produces 4 singles and 1 album/year. Fee derived from sales royalty.

**How to Contact:** Write first about your interest. Prefers cassette with 2-3 songs on demo. SASE. Reports "immediately if we hold it. Otherwise, no report."
**Music:** Mostly country; also easy listening, folk and MOR. Recently produced "Facets of Love," "Passing in the Night," "Things That Lady Did to Me," "Darling, Brandy" and "Arizona Lady," by Greg Lucas (country singles, Shetland Sound Records). Other artists include Little David Wilkins.

**SHOWCASE OF STARS**, 310 Franklin St., Boston MA 02110; Suite 805, 77 Summer St., Boston MA 02110. (617)396-0751. Director: Marv Cutler. Record producer, music publisher (Maric Music/ASCAP), management firm and talent agent. Deals with artists and songwriters. Produces 25 singles and 25 albums/year. Fee derived from sales royalty.
**How to Contact:** Query or submit demo tape and lead sheet. Prefers 7½ ips reel-to-reel or cassette with 2-6 songs on demo. Does not return unsolicited material. Reports in 1 month.
**Music:** Blues; children's; C&W; easy listening; jazz; MOR; progressive; rock (light); soul; and top 40/pop. Recently produced "What am I Doing Here?" and "The Color of Neil's Eyes," by Boston Harbour (soft rock/top 40); and "Without Boundaries," by Channel One (fusion). Other artists include Cecil Payne, Makoto Takenaka Trio and Tiny Grimes.

**SHU-QUA-LOK RECORDS & ACORN RECORDS**, 233 Penner Dr., Pearl MS 39208. (601)939-6616. 939-5975. Contact: George W. Allen. Record producer and music publisher (Galyn Music/BMI). Deals with artists and songwriters. Produces 10 singles and 1 album/year. Fee derived from sales royalty.
**How to Contact:** Submit demo tape and lyric sheet; write or call about your interest or arrange personal interview. Prefers 7½ ips reel-to-reel or cassette with 2-6 songs on demo. SASE. Reports in 3 weeks.
**Music:** Bluegrass, blues, C&W, gospel, MOR, progressive, R&B, soul and top 40/pop. Recently produced "Play Me a Cheating Song," by Keith Lamb (country single, Acorn Records); "Please Don't Lead Me On," by Jackie Pearson (MOR single, Shu-Qua-Lok Records); "Just Let Me Love You," by Ted Holman (country single, Acorn Records); and "Pleasant State of Mind" and "Reminiscing," by Bobby Souls (Acorn Records). Other artists include Larry Brock, J.D. Martin, David Dunn, Deby Gooch and Larry Jenkins.
**Tips:** "We are able to co-write on lyrics, set melodies to words, and work with songwriters on a percentage basis at no cost to the writer."

***SIGHT AND SOUND MARKETING**, 1037 E. Parkway South, Memphis TN 38104. (901)276-2113. A&R Director: Bill Lusk. Record producer and music publisher (Rocken Rythmn Publishing). Estab. 1981. Deals with artists, songwriters, producers and promoters. Fee derived from sales royalty or outright fee from artist/songwriter or record company.
**How to Contact:** Submit demo tape and lyric sheet. Prefers cassette with 1-4 songs on demo. Specify the number of songs on the tape. SASE, but "we would like the option to keep the tape on file." Reports in 1 month.
**Music:** Mostly rock, pop, R&B and blues; also MOR and soul. Recently produced "Where You Want Me," by Bill Lusk (pop single, Rocken Rythmn Records); and "Straight and Narrow Line," by B. Lusk (R&B single, Rocken Rythmn Records). Other artists include Delta Project and Blues Rambles.

**SILVER BLUE PRODUCTIONS**, Suite 31M, 211 W. 56th St., New York NY 10019. (212)586-3535. Contact: Joel Diamond. Record producer and music publisher. Deals with artists and songwriters. Fee derived by sales royalty.
**How to Contact:** Submit demo tape and lyric sheet. Prefers cassette with 1-3 songs on demo. SASE.
**Music:** MOR, dance, easy listening, C&W, R&B, rock, soul and top 40/pop. Recently produced "After the Lovin'," by Engelbert Humperdinck (top 40 single, Epic Records); "You're All I Need to Get By," by Gloria Gaynor (R&B single, Polydor Records); *Joel Diamond Experience*, by Joel Diamond Experience (disco/top 40 LP, Casablanca Records); and Helen Reddy album.

**SILVER BULLET PRODUCTIONS/TRULY FINE RECORDS**, Box 423, Station F, Toronto, Ontario, Canada M4Y 2L8. Professional Manager: Allen Shechtman. Record producer and music publisher (Sidewalk Sailor Music/CAPAC, Scales of My Head Music/PROCAN, Etheric Polyphony/CAPAC, Cumulonimbus Music/PROCAN). Deals with artists, songwriters, labels, producers and publishers. Produces maximum 2 singles and 1 album/year. Fee derived from sales royalty or by outright fee from record company.
**How to Contact:** Write first about your interest, then submit demo tape. Prefers 7½ or 15 ips reel-to-reel or cassette with 3 songs minimum on demo. Does not return unsolicited material. Reports in 3 months.
**Music:** Mostly crossover pop, C&W and R&B. Recently produced *Dorothea's Dream*, by Graeme Card (concept LP, Change Records/MCA Records); "Supernatural One," by G. Card (AOR/MOR sin-

gle, Change Records/MCA Records); *Graeme Card*, by G. Card (LP, Truly Fine Records); *Saskatoon*, by Humphrey and Dumptrucks, (bluegrass LP, United Artists Records); and "Do Not Leave Us if You Love Us," by Mark Labelle (AOR/ballad single, Apex/InterDisc/MCA Records).

**SKYS THE LIMIT PRODUCTIONS, INC.**, 400 Main St., Reading MA 01867. (617)944-0423. President: Carl Strube. Record producer, music publisher, management firm and promoter. Deals with artists and songwriters. Fee derived by sales royalty.
**How to Contact:** Submit demo tape and lyric sheet. Prefers 7½ ips reel-to-reel or cassette with 1-3 songs on demo. SASE. Reports in 1 month.
**Music:** C&W, MOR, R&B, rock, soul and top 40/pop. Recently published "This Is Love" and "Draw the Line," by Oak (top 40 singles, Mercury Records); and "Where Is the Woman," by Chip Harding (top 40 single, RSO Records). Other artists include Blend (MCA Records).

**SONGCO PRODUCTION CO., INC.**, 10802 N. 23rd Ave., Phoenix AZ 85029. (602)864-1980. Director: Tom Kendzia. Record producer, music publisher (Epoch Universal Publications, NALR. Epoch Music Corp.) and recording studio (Epoch Sound). Deals with artists and songwriters. Produces 5 singles and 10-20 albums/year. Fee derived from sales royalty or outright fee from artist/songwriter or record company.
**How to Contact:** Call or write first about your interest. Prefers 7½ ips reel-to-reel or cassette with 3-20 songs on demo. SASE. Reports in 1 week.
**Music:** Considers all types. Recently produced *Christmas With Friends*, by Ed McMahon and Doc Severinsen (Christmas LP, Sounds of Hope Records); *Rob Taylor*, by R. Taylor (country/rock LP); and *Land of Love*, by Marcy Tigner (children's LP, Livingsong Records). Other artists include St. Louis Jesuits, Carey Landry, and the *Tonight Show* Orchestra.

**\*SOUND IMAGE PRODUCTIONS**, 6556 Wilkinson, N. Hollywood CA 91606. (213)762-8881. Vice President: David Chatfield. Record producer, music publisher (Sound Image Publishing) and record company. Deals with artists, songwriters and producers. Produces 12 singles and 6 albums/year. Fee derived from sales royalty or outright fee from artist/songwriter or record company or by combination of the above.
**How to Contact:** Submit demo tape and lyric sheet. Prefers cassette with 2-6 songs on demo. Does not return unsolicited material. Reports in 1 month.
**Music:** Dance-oriented, R&B, rock (mainstream), top 40/pop and reggae. Recently produced *The Secrets*, by The Secrets (techno-pop LP, Sound Image Records); *George Faber & Stronghold*, by G. Faber & Stronghold (R&B/pop LP, Sound Image Records); and *Jah Moon*, by Jah Moon & Stronghold (reggae LP, Sound Image Records).

**SOUNDS OF WINCHESTER**, Box 574, Winchester VA 22601. (703)667-9379. Contact: Jim McCoy. Record producer and music publisher (New Edition Music, Jim McCoy Music and Alear Music/BMI). Deals with artists and songwriters. Produces 20 singles and 10 albums/year. Fee derived from sales royalty.
**How to Contact:** Submit demo tape and lead sheet. Prefers 7½ ips reel-to-reel with 4-10 songs on demo. SASE. Reports in 1 month.
**Music:** Bluegrass, C&W, gospel, MOR and rock. Recently produced "One More Time," by Earl Howard (country single, Alear Records); and *Thank-You Jesus*, by Jubilee Travelers (gospel LP, Faith Records). Other artists include Dave Elliott, Alvin Kesner, Carroll County Ramblers and Jim McCoy.

**\*THE SOURCE UNLIMITED**, 331 East 9th St., New York NY 10003. (212)473-7833. Vice President: S.J. Mollica. Record producer. Estab. 1981. Deals with songwriters. Produces 2 singles and 4 EPs/year. Outright fee from record company.
**How to Contact:** Write first about your interest; submit demo tape and lyric sheet. Prefers cassette with 3-6 songs on demo. SASE. Reports in 1 month.
**Music:** Folk, gospel, jazz, progressive, R&B and rock. Recently produced *Music from the Street*, by Santo (Store Front Records); and "Son of a Working Man," (Music House Records).

**SOUTHERN SOUND PRODUCTIONS**, 100 Labon St., Tabor City NC 28463. (919)653-2546. President: Elson H. Stevens. Record producer, music publisher (Creekside Music/BMI) and record company. Deals with artists, songwriters and radio stations. Produces 15-20 singles and 4 albums/year. Fee derived from sales royalty.
**How to Contact:** Write first about your interest, then submit demo tape and lyric sheet. Prefers cassette or 8-track tape with 1-3 songs on demo. SASE. Reports in 1 month.
**Music:** Mostly country; also bluegrass, gospel, rock (country and hard) and beach music. Recently produced "Nightime Lady," by T. Jay Jon; "Happy Endings," by Sheila Gore (both country singles, Sea-

side Records); and "Cheap Imitation," by J.C. Batchelor (country single, JCB Records). Other artists include Mitch Todd, Copper Creek and The Entertainers.
**Tips:** "Please make sure that all songs submitted have a very strong hook. Limit of 3 songs per submission."

**SPARROW RECORDS, INC.**, 8025 Deering Ave., Canoga Park CA 91304. (213)703-6599. A&R Assistant Director: Ken Pennell. Record producer. Produces 20 albums/year. Fee derived from sales royalty.
**How to Contact:** Submit demo tape and lyric sheet. Prefers cassette with 1-3 songs on demo. SASE. Reports in 1 month.
**Music:** Children's, choral, church/religious, contemporary, Christian and Spanish. Recently produced *Antshillvania*, by various artists (children's LP, Birdwing Records); *Town to Town*, by Phil Keaggy (rock/gospel LP, Sparrow Records); and *Finer than Gold*, by Barry McGuire (country/pop/gospel LP, Sparrow Records). Other artists include Candle, 2nd Chapter of Acts and John Michael Talbot.

*****SPINN RECORDS**, R.F.D. 3, Box 100-N, Stuart VA 24171. (703)694-6128. Contact: Frank W. Singleton. Record producer and music publisher (WilSing Music). Deals with artists and songwriters. Pays outright fee from songwriter/artist or record company.
**How to Contact:** Submit demo tape. Prefers 7½ or 15 ips reel-to-reel or cassette with any number of songs on demo. SASE. Reports in 1 month.
**Music:** Mostly C&W; also bluegrass, church/religious, folk and gospel. Recently produced "Live Here with the Blues" and "Papa Papa Da Da He Calls Me," recorded by Tommy Riddle (C&W singles, Spinn Records); and "I'll Cry Again" and "I Feel Another Heartbreak," by Norman Wade (C&W singles, Spinn Records).

*****SPRING/POSSE RECORDS**, 161 W. 54 St., New York NY 10019. (212)581-5398. President: Jules Rifkind. Vice President: Bill Spitalsky. Treasurer: Roy Rifkind. Record producer and music publisher (Possie Music Corp.). Deals with artists and songwriters. Produces 12 singles and 2-3 albums/year. Fee derived by sales royalty or outright fee from record company.
**How to Contact:** Submit demo tape and lyric sheet. Prefers cassette with 2-4 songs on demo. "Masters appreciated." SASE. Reports in 3 weeks.
**Music:** Mostly R&B; also gospel. Recently produced *Joe Simon's Greatest Hits*, by Joe Simon (R&B LP, Posse Records); *Hard Times*, by Millie Jackson (R&B LP, Spring Records); *Is This the Future?*, by Fatback Band (R&B LP, Spring Records); and *Lay My Burden Down*, by Jackie Verdell (gospel LP). Other artists include Fonda Rae and Joe Simon.

**SQUILLIT PRODUCTIONS, INC.**, Box 98, Forest Hills NY 11375. (212)261-1111. President: K.Z. Purzycki. Record producer and music publisher (Memnon, Ltd./ASCAP, Tithonus Music, Ltd./BMI). Deals with artists and songwriters. Produces 3 singles and 1 album/year. Fee derived from royalty or outright fee from record company.
**How to Contact:** "We are open to review new artists; you must include a demo tape, photo and bio." Prefers cassette with 3-5 songs on demo, "leader between songs, if on reel." SASE. Reports in 1 month.
**Music:** C&W and top 40/pop. Recently produced "You Are Queen of My Heart," by Happy End (top 40/pop single, Memnon Records); "Was Young Love Born to Die," by Bobbie Roberson (C&W single, Bolivia Records); *Swing with the King*, by King Edward and his Orchestra (polka LP, Polamart Records); and "All My Life," by The Sound Alternative (top 40 single, Memnon Records). Other artists include Donna Sands.

*****SSS, INTERNATIONAL**, 3106 Belmont Blvd., Nashville TN 37212. (615)385-1960. Producer: Billy Self. Record producer. Deals with artists and songwriters. Produces 8 singles and 6 albums/year. Fee derived from sales royalty or outright fee from songwriter/artist or record company.
**How to Contact:** Submit demo tape and lyric sheet; call about your interest. Prefers cassette with 1-3 songs on demo. Does not return unsolicited material. Reports in 1 month.
**Music:** Mostly country and MOR; also easy listening, gospel and top 40/pop. Recently produced "Bogalusa," by Jim Owen (country single, Sun Records); "Barbara's Daughter," by Patti Page (MOR/country single, Plantation Records); *Aces*, by P. Page (MOR/country LP, Plantation Records); and *Double Winners*, by Ken Lowery (country LP, Plantation Records). Other artists include Paul Martin, Norris Treat and Rita Remington.
**Tips:** "We (the act and myself) must be in total agreement in our direction and have the utmost mutual trust in our abilities."

**STACHE RECORDS, INC.**, #208, 4050 Buckingham Rd., Los Angeles CA 90008. (213)290-2262. Record producer and music publisher (Atjack Music/BMI).

**How to Contact:** Submit demo tape and lyric sheet. Prefers cassette. SASE. Reports in 3 weeks.
**Music:** Gospel, jazz, R&B, soul and top 40/pop.

**THE STACY-LEE LABEL**, Box 711, Hackensack NJ 07602. (201)488-5211. President: Johnny Miracle. Record producer, music publisher (Miracle-Joy/BMI), record company (Stacy-Lee, Banana, Inner Circle, Joy, Lions Den, Lotus, Lybra, Riot, Vanishing Point, S.A.M.). Deals with artists and songwriters. Fee derived from sales royalty.
**How to Contact:** Submit demo tape and lyric sheet. Prefers cassette with 1-6 songs on demo. SASE. Reports in 3 weeks.
**Music:** Children's, church/religious, C&W, easy listening, folk, gospel and MOR. Recently produced "Memories," by Sam Starr; "Ashes Are Still Warm," by Duo (country singles, Stacy-Lee Records); and "Pizza Man," by Tiny (novelty single, Banana Records).

**STAIRCASE PROMOTION**, Box 211, E. Prairie MO 63845. (314)649-2211. Manager: Tommy Loomas. Record producer and music publisher. Deals with artists and songwriters.
**How to Contact:** Write first about your interest or submit demo tape and lyric sheet. Prefers cassette with 2-4 songs on demo. SASE. Reports in 1 month.
**Music:** C&W, easy listening, MOR, country rock and top 40/pop. Recently produced "Best of All," by Mary Nichols (easy listening single, Onie Records); "Stay Baby Stay," by Shuri Castle (country rock single, Capstan Records); and "Country Boy," by Alden Lambert (C&W single, Capstan Records).

**WADE STALEY PRODUCTIONS**, Box 5712, High Point NC 27262. (919)885-0263. President: W.C. Staley. Record producer and music publisher (Staley Music Publishing). Estab. 1981. Deals with artists and songwriters. Produces 10 singles and 25 albums/year. Fee derived from sales royalty or outright fee from artist/songwriter.
**How to Contact:** Submit demo tape and lyric sheet. Prefers cassette with 3-7 songs on demo. SASE. Reports in 1 month.
**Music:** Bluegrass, church/religious, C&W, folk, gospel, MOR, R&B, rock, soul and top 40/pop. Recently produced *Here and Now*, by Blueridge Rangers (western LP, Deka Records); and *The Harvesters*, by Harvesters (gospel LP, Mecca Records).

*****STARBURST RECORDS, INC.**, Box 3072, Brooklyn NY 11202. (212)774-1008. President: Wallace D. Garrett. Record producer and music publisher (Nelter Music Publishing Co.). Estab. 1982. Deals with artists and songwriters. Fee derived from sales royalty.
**How to Contact:** Submit demo tape and lyric sheet; or "we will attend showcases where songwriters and artists are performing." Prefers cassette with 3-5 songs on demo. SASE. Reports in 3 months.
**Music:** Mostly R&B, soul and dance; also C&W, jazz, punk, funk and Spanish.

**STARGEM RECORD PRODUCTIONS**, 43 Music Square E, Nashville TN 37203. (615)244-1025. President/A&R Director: Wayne Hodge. Record producer and music publisher (Newwriters Music/BMI and Timestar Music/ASCAP). Deals with artists and songwriters.
**How to Contact:** Call first about your interest then submit demo tape and lyric sheet. Prefers cassette with 1-4 songs on demo. SASE. Reports in 1 week.
**Music:** C&W and MOR.

**STARMAN RECORDS**, Box 20604, Sacramento CA 95820. (916)446-6301. Vice President: Marsha Ann Covington. Record producer, music publisher (Ultima Thule Music/BMI) and record company (Starman Records). Deals with songwriters. Produces 1-2 singles and 1 album/year.
**How to Contact:** Submit demo tape and lyric sheet. Prefers cassette with 6-10 songs on demo. SASE. Reports in 6 weeks.
**Music:** Church/religious, C&W, easy listening, gospel, jazz, MOR, R&B, rock (soft), soul and top 40/pop. Recently produced "Going to Triangle" by A.V. Covington (ballad single, Starman Records); "Ocean Tune," by Ray Raymond (easy listening single, Starman Records); "Lifting Up Jesus," by New Testament Choir #II (gospel single, Starman Records); and "What'cha Gonna Do, When the Nights Are Long," by Sunlight (R&R single, Starman Records). Other artists include The V.C. Pyramid Principle.
**Tips:** "Be experienced in working in a studio and in working with others."

*****STARSOUND RECORDS**, Division of Starsound Broadcasting Network, Box 3664, Davenport IA 52808. (309)794-1968. National Promotion Manager: Gary Unger. Record producer and music publisher (Sugarvine Music/BMI, Groovesonic Music/BMI, Starsound Records/ASCAP). Estab. 1983. Deals with artists, songwriters, co-producers and independent labels. Produces 7 singles and 3 albums/year. Co-master lease fee is 50% from co-producers, producers, independent labels and production firms.
**How to Contact:** Write first about your interest or send test pressing or master tape for release consider-

ation. Prefers 7½ ips reel-to-reel or cassette, or sample pressing or master tape with 4-10 songs on demo. SASE. Reports in 1-3 months.
**Music:** C&W, dance-oriented, easy listening, rock and top 40/pop. Recently produced "Lucky In Love" b/w "Love Me or Leave Me," by Paul Gregory (pop single, Grovesong Records); "Alive Again" b/w "Steppin Stone," by Dane Weiner (pop single); "Cry," by Betty Parsons (pop single, Americangroove Records); "Give A Care," by Alan Hale (pop single, ACI International Records); "Long Long Time," by Dolly Coulter (pop/country/AC single, ECI/Starsound Records); and *Ten Jewels*, by The Union (rock LP, ACI International Records).

**\*STARTIME MUSIC**, Box 643, LaQuinta CA 92253. (714)564-4823. President: Fred Rice. Record producer, music publisher and record company.
**How to Contact:** Submit demo tape and lead sheet. Cassette only with 1-2 songs on demo. SASE. Reports in 6 weeks.
**Music:** Mostly novelty; also country, rock and top 40/pop. Recently produced "White Lady," "Somebody Cares" and "Love Is Just a Touch Away," by Rob Carter (MOR contemporary singles, Startime Records).
**Tips:** "A song has to be built on 'flesh and blood'—the rhythm is the skeleton, the musical theme is the flesh and the lyrics are the blood (the soul). The song must have a *provocative* title, *repetitive* musical theme with *simple* word phrase lyrics, *identifiable* melody line, a *different* sound and always the proverbial 'hook'."

**STARTOWN ENTERPRISES**, 1037 E. Parkway S., Memphis TN 38104. (901)725-7019. President: Allen White. Record producer (Dewaun Music/SESAC). Deals with artists, songwriters and producers. Produces 5 singles and 2 albums/year. Fee derived from sales royalty.
**How to Contact:** Submit demo tape and lyric sheet. Prefers cassette with 4-8 songs on demo. SASE. Reports in 1 month.
**Music:** Blues, church/religious, C&W, gospel, R&B, rock, soul and top 40/pop. Artists include Ike Strong, Mack Banks, Joyce Young, Chick Willis, True Image, Bill Lusk, Circle, The Majestics, J.J. Daniels, The Jubirt Sisters and The Jam Conductors.

**A. STEWART PRODUCTIONS**, 22146 Lanark St., Canoga Park CA 91304. (213)704-0629. President: Art Stewart. Record producer and music publisher (Famosonda Music/BMI). Deals with artists and songwriters. Produces 4 singles and 2 albums/year. Fee determined by sales royalty.
**How to Contact:** Submit demo tape and lyric sheet. Prefers 7½ ips reel-to-reel or cassette with 1-4 songs on demo. SASE. Reports in 1 month.
**Music:** Soul. Recently produced "Eboni Band," by Eboni Band (Afro/American, Eboni Records); *Cherry*, by Platypus (soul LP, Casablanca Records); "Same Old Story," by Sai Whatt (soul single, Stache Records); "Got to Give It Up," by Marvin Gaye; and "You and I," by Rich James. Other artists include Charades and Randie Coulter.

**STONEDOG PRODUCTIONS**, 1819 W. Thome, Chicago IL 60660. (312)869-0175. Vice President: Stoney Phillips. Record producer and music publisher (Hannan-Phillips Music/BMI). Deals with artists and songwriters. Produces 2-4 singles and 1 album/year. Fee derived from sales royalty.
**How to Contact:** Submit demo tape and lyric sheet. Prefers cassette with 1-3 songs on demo. SASE. Reports in 3 weeks.
**Music:** Mostly country crossover and MOR; also country rock. Recently produced "Ain't Got Sense Enough," "Sometimes I Can't Be There," and "Favorite Lady," by Ronnie Rice (country crossover singles, Stonedog Records).

**STONE-HIGH RECORDS, INC.**, Box 2544, Baton Rouge LA 70821. (504)924-6865 (24 hrs.). A&R Director: E.K. Harrison. Record producer.
**How to Contact:** Submit demo tape and lyric sheet. Cassette only with 2-6 songs on demo. Include photos and bio. SASE. Reports in 1 month.
**Music:** Rock and punk.
**Tips:** "We are an exclusive rock and foreign label dealing strictly with rock and punk acts, groups and songwriters."

**STONY PLAIN RECORDING CO., LTD.**, Box 861, Edmonton, Alberta, Canada T5J 2L8. (403)477-6844. Managing Director: Holger Petersen. Record producer and music publisher (Kitchen Table Music/Procan, Gimbleco West Music/PROCAN and Eyeball Wine Music/CAPAC). Deals with artists and songwriters. Produces 4-6 singles and 12-15 albums/year. Fee derived by outright fee from record company.

**How to Contact:** Call or write first about your interest. Prefers cassette with 1-4 songs on demo. SAE and IRC. Reports in 3 weeks.
**Music:** Mostly bluegrass; also folk, MOR, progressive, rock and top 40/pop. Recently produced "Amos Behavin'," by Amos Garrett (R&B single, Stony Plain Records); "Anything You Want," by Bim (folk single, Stony Plain Records); and "Branded," by Diamond Joe White (country single, Stony Plain Records). Other artists include The Reds.

**\*STREET TUNES LIMITED**, 81 Harley House, Marylebone Road, London, NW1, England. 44-01-486-1816. Manager: John Glover. Record producer, music publisher (Street Tunes Publishing, Ltd.), and record company (Street Tunes Records, Ltd.). Deals with artists, songwriters and overseas affiliates. Produces 3 singles and 5 albums/year. Fee derived from sales royalty.
**How to Contact:** Submit demo tape and lyric sheet. Prefers reel-to-reel or cassette with 2-4 songs on demo. SAE and IRC. Reports in 2 weeks.
**Music:** Mostly progressive, R&B and rock (all types); also blues, dance-oriented, soul and top 40/pop. Recently produced "Casual Tease," by Techno Orchestra (progessive single, Street Tunes Records); "Technostalgia," by Techno Twins (progressive single, P.R.T. Records); and "Nicky Moore," by Nicky Moore (rock single, Street Tunes Records). Other artists include Zen Attack, Black Alice, Tweets and HGV.

**SUNBURST MUSIC PRODUCTIONS**, Suite 203, 26949 Chagrin Blvd., Beachwood OH 44122. Executive Producer: Jim Quinn. Associate Producer: Otto F. Neuber. Record producer, music publisher (Solarium Music/ASCAP) and management firm. Deals with artists and songwriters. Produces 3 singles and 1 album/year. Fee derived from outright fee from record company and/or royalty on sales.
**How to Contact:** Submit demo tape. Cassette only with 1-3 songs on demo. SASE. Reports in 3 weeks.
**Music:** AOR and top 40/pop. Recently produced *Love Affair*, *L.A.*, and "Mama Sez" by Love Affair (rock/top 40, Radio/Atlantic Records); and "Go For The Money," by Charlie Weiner (White Light Records). Other artists include Champion and Alexander and Savannah.

**SUN-RAY RECORDS**, 1662 Wyatt Parkway, Lexington KY 40505. (606)254-7474. President: James T. Price. Record producer, music publisher (Jimmy Price Music Publishing/BMI) and music printer. Deals with artists, songwriters and musicians. Produces 7 singles/year. Fee derived from sales royalty.
**How to Contact:** Submit demo tape and lyric sheet. Prefers 7½ ips reel-to-reel or cassette with 1-6 songs on demo. SASE. Reports in 1 month.
**Music:** Bluegrass, blues, church/religious, C&W and gospel. Recently published "Country Waltz" (waltz single, Sun-Ray Records); "Where the Music Plays Sweetly" and "Beautiful Love" by Charles Stephens, (country singles, Sun-Ray Records). Other artists include Virgil Vickers.

**\*SUNSET PRODUCTIONS**, 15 Albert Crescent, Penarth, South Glamorgan, South Wales, United Kingdom. 44-0222-704279. Director: Paul Barrett. Record producer. Estab. 1981. Deals with artists and songwriters. Fee derived from sales royalty. Royalties paid directly to US songwriters and artists. Has not yet, but would listen to material from US songwriters and artists.
**How to Contact:** Submit demo tape and lyric sheet. Prefers cassette for demo. SAE and IRC. Reports in 3 weeks.
**Music:** 50s music only: C&W, R&B andR&R. Recently produced *Tiger*, by Shakin' Stevens and Sunsets (R&R LP); *Unleashed*, by Blue Caps (R&R LP); and *Greasy Kids Only*, by Johnny Storm and Sunsets (R&R LP). Other artists include Nervous Breakdown, Questionaires, Haley & The Hailstones, Rockin' Louie, Questionaires and Phil Fernando.

**SUNSET RECORDS, INC.**, 1577 Redwood Dr., Harvey LA 70058. (504)367-8501. President: George Leger. Record producer and music publisher (Country Legs Music/ASCAP and Golden Sunburst Music/BMI). Deals with artists and songwriters. Produces 5 singles and 1 album/year. Fee derived by outright fee from record company.
**How to Contact:** Submit demo tape and lyric and lead sheet. Prefers 7½ ips reel-to-reel or cassette (if very clear) with 3-5 songs on demo. SASE. Reports in 1 month.
**Music:** Mostly hard country; also gospel, progressive country and R&B. Recently produced "Oh Lonely Heart," by Sonny Tears (country/uptempo single, Sunset Records); "Let's Put Christ in Christmas Again," by George Leger (country Christmas single, Sunset Records); and "We're Changing," by Larry Maynard (country/pop single, Sunburst Records).
**Tips:** "Always looking for new artists."

**THE SUNSHINE GROUP**, 800 S. 4th St., Philadelphia PA 19147. (215)755-7000. President: Walter Kahn. Promotion: Tom Kennedy. Publicity: Michele Quigley. Record producer (Sunshine, Grand Prix Records) and music publisher (Scully Music/ASCAP). Works with artists and songwriters on contract.

Produces 8 singles and 3 albums/year. Pays standard royalty.
**How to Contact:** Submit demo tape and lyric sheet. Prefers 7½ ips reel-to-reel or cassette with 1-4 songs on demo. SASE. Reports in 1 month.
**Music:** Mostly pop, R&B and dance; also top 40 and rock. Recently recorded "Detour" and "Expressway to Your Heart," by Karen Young (pop/dance singles, Atlantic Records); "The Flute," by Pipedream (pop/dance single, CBS/Epic Records); "You Don't Know What You Got," by K. Young (Boardwalk Records); "Dr. Jam," by Men At Play (rap single, Sunshine Records); and "Dirty Looks," by Dick Tracey (rock single, Sunshine Records). Other artists include Ronni Anderson, Danny Paradise and Pretty Slick.

**SWEETSONG PRODUCTIONS**, Box 2041, Parkersburg WV 26102. (304)489-2911. Contact: Roger Hoover. Record producer and music publisher (Sweetsong Productions). Deals with artists and songwriters. Produces 10 singles and 20 albums/year. Fee derived from sales royalty.
**How to Contact:** Submit demo tape and lyric sheet. Prefers cassette with 1-3 songs that doesn't have to be returned. SASE. Reporting time varies.
**Music:** Contemporary gospel only. Recently produced *He's the One*, by Light (gospel LP); "You Have His Promises," by Virginia Pryor (gospel single); and *Jazzaway*, by Murmac Jr (exercise LP). Other artists include Mona Freshour, Mike McGuire, The Gospelaires, Pam Gordon and Miltonberges and Clark.

**SWORD & SHIELD RECORDS**, Box 211, Arlington TX 76010. (817)572-1414. Contact: Calvin Wills. Record producer. Deals with artists. Produces 8 singles and 100 albums/year. Fee derived from outright fee from artist/songwriter.
**How to Contact:** Call first about your interest. Prefers cassette with 2-6 songs on demo. Does not return unsolicited material. SASE. Reports in 1 month.
**Music:** Mostly southern gospel and contemporary Christian music. Recently produced "Heaven on Your Mind," by Sam Nix (contemporary Christian single, S&S Records); "O Glorious Love," by Ysis Espana (contemporary inspirational single, S&S Records); and "Slow Down," by Laury Ann Thurier (country gospel single, S&S Records). Other artists include Janie White, Gary Gibson and the Wills Family Singers.

***RICH SZABO**, Box 262, Livingston NJ 07039. (201)994-1195. Producer: Rich Szabo. Record producer and arranger. Deals with artists, songwriters and record companies. Produces 2 singles and 1 album/year. Fee derived from sales royalty or outright fee from record company.
**How to Contact:** Submit demo tape and lyric sheet. Prefers cassette with 3-5 songs on demo. Include biographical information. SASE. Reports in 3 weeks.
**Music:** Mostly jazz, jazz fusion and big band; also MOR and top 40/pop. Recently produced *Best of Both Worlds*, by Rich Szabo (big band LP, BBW Records); "Jumpin' on the Bandstand," by R. Szabo (pop single, BBW Records); "Ikyat," by Rich Acciavatti (fusion single, BBW Records); and "Smooth," by R. Szabo (big band single, Big Bands' '80s). Other artists include the Music Men, Mark Friedman and Robert Pollack.
**Tips:** "Send in material that is commercially viable. A good attitude is more important than anything else."

***TABITHA PRODUCTIONS**, 39 Cordery Road, St. Thomas, Exeter, Devon, EX2 9DJ, England. 0392-79914. Producer: Graham Sclater. Record producer, music publisher (Tabitha Music, Ltd.) and record company (Tabitha/Willow Records). Works with artists and songwriters. Produces 4 singles and 2 albums/year. Fee derived from sales royalty or outright fee from artist/songwriter or record company.
**How to Contact:** Submit demo tape and lyric sheet. Prefers cassette with 2-6 songs on demo. SAE and IRC. Reports in 3 weeks.
**Music:** C&W, dance-oriented, MOR, rock, soul and top 40/pop. Recently produced *Shades*, by Shades (R&R LP, Ach/Chiswick Records); *Mountain Call*, by Bobby Arnst (pop LP, Willow Records); *Key West*, by Key West (pop LP, Epic Records); and *Tina*, by The Smith (pop LP, Barn Records).

**TAKE HOME TUNES! RECORD CO.**, Box 10051, Beverly Hills CA 90213. (213)761-2646. Branch: Box 1314, Englewood Cliffs NJ 07632. Messages: (201)567-5524. Box 1314, Englewood Cliffs NJ 07632. Messages: (201)567-5524. Producer: Doris Chu Yeko. Record producer and music publisher (The Chu Yeko Musical Foundation/BMI and Broadway/Hollywood International Music/ASCAP). Deals with artists and songwriters. Produces 8 albums/year. Fee derived from sales royalty.
**How to Contact:** Call first about your interest then submit demo tape and lyric sheet. Prefers cassette with any number songs on demo. SASE. Reports in 1 month.
**Music:** Children's, classical, C&W, easy listening, jazz, MOR, musicals, R&B and top 40/pop. Recently produced *King of Hearts*, by Millicent Martin and Don Scardino; *Lovesong*, by the original cast

(musical LPs, Original Cast Records); *Ka-Boom!* and *Fly with Me*, by the original cast (musical LPs, Chu Yeko Musical Foundation Records); and *Christy (Playboy of the Western World)*, by the original cast (musical LP, Original Cast Records).
**Tips:** "We're interested in the 'top 10' pop types of songs; original cast musicals that had a production somewhere; and R&B songs sung by new singers, groups, etc. Co-production possible with financial backing."

**TEROCK RECORDS**, Box 4740, Nashville TN 37216. President: Wade Curtiss. Record producer and music publisher. Deals with artists and songwriters. Fee derived from sales royalty.
**How to Contact:** Submit demo tape and lyric sheet. Prefers 7½ ips reel-to-reel with 2-6 songs on demo. SASE. Reports in 3 weeks.
**Music:** Bluegrass, blues, C&W, dance, easy listening, folk, gospel, progressive, R&B, hard rock, soul and top 40/pop.

**THIRD STORY RECORDING**, 3436 Sansom St., Philadelphia PA 19104. (215)386-5998. Contact: Scott Herzog and John Wicks. Record producer, record company and music publisher (City Surfer Music, Inc./ASCAP and TSR Music, Inc./ASCAP). Deals with artists and songwriters. Produces 5 singles and 10 albums/year. Fee derived from sales royalty or outright fee from artist/songwriter or record company.
**How to Contact:** Call or submit demo tape and lyric sheet. Prefers cassette with 1-4 songs on demo. SASE. Reports in 3 weeks.
**Music:** Blues, church/religious, C&W, dance-oriented, easy listening, folk, gospel, MOR, R&B, rock, soul and top 40/pop. Recently produced "Crash Course In Science" and "Basement Culture" (new wave rock singles, TSR Records). Other artists include The Benders, The Insiders and The Stickmen.

***THOMPSON-FRIDAY PRODUCTIONS**, 4637 Verdugo Rd., Los Angeles CA 90065. (213)257-0454. Producers: Mick Thompson and Bill Friday. Record producer, music publisher (Hard Ten Music) and manager. Estab. 1982. Deals with artists. Produces 6 singles and 2 albums/year. Fee derived from sales royalty or outright fee from artist/songwriter.
**How to Contact:** Call or write first about your interest; submit demo tape and lyric sheet. Prefers 7½ or 15 ips reel-to-reel or cassette with 3-5 songs on demo. SASE. Reports in 1 month.
**Music:** Mostly rock, top 40/pop and new wave; also jazz, MOR, R&B and soul.
**Tips:** "Send your best hit material that is competitive with what is on the charts."

**3B MUSIC CORP.**, 437 5th Ave., New York NY 10016. (212)679-3701. Vice President: Richard Berardi. Record producer and music publisher (3B Music Corp./ASCAP, Bernardi Bros. Music, Inc./BMI). Deals with artists and songwriters. Produces 10 singles and 3 albums/year. Fee derived from sales royalty or outright fee from artist/songwriter or record company.
**How to Contact:** Submit demo tape and lyric sheet. Prefers cassette with 1-3 songs on demo. SASE. Reports in 3 weeks.
**Music:** Children's, C&W, dance-oriented, easy listening, gospel, MOR, R&B, rock (all kinds), soul and top 40/pop. Recently produced "In You I Found Me," by Pia Zadora and Billy Preston (Elektra Records); and "Just Another Heartbreak," by Hank Marvin (Polydor Records). Other artists include Line Drive.

**TIGER RECORDS**, C.I.T.S. Records, Box 2544, Baton Rouge LA 70821. (504)924-6865. Producer/A&R Director: "Ebb-Tide." Director: E.K. Harrison. Record producer, music publisher (Cryin' in the Streets Music Publishers/ASCAP, Dan-Rite Publishers/BMI and Church of "Gospel" Ministry Music Publishers/BMI) and record company. Deals with artists, songwriters and composers. Publishes 6 singles and 6 albums/year. Fee derived from sales royalty.
**How to Contact:** Submit demo tape and lead sheet. Prefers cassette with 4-6 songs on demo. SASE. Reports in 2 weeks.
**Music:** Folk, MOR, rock (pop) and top 40/pop. Recently produced "Millie the Pro," by Rodeo (rock single, Stone-High Records); "Where Is Justice," by Jimmy Angel (rock/pop single, Stone-High Records); "Fire-Woman," by Gary Angelo (rock single, Stone-High Records); and "Butterfly," by Sweden (rock single, Stone-High Records).

**RIK TINORY PRODUCTIONS**, Box 311, Cohasset MA 02025. (617)383-9494. Artist Relations: Claire Babcock. Record producer and music publisher (Old Boston Publishing). Deals with artists. Produces 20 singles and 15 albums/year. Fee derived from standard publishing royalties.
**How to Contact:** Call first about your interest. Prefers cassette with 1-3 songs on demo. Does not return unsolicited material.
**Music:** Recently produced *Scollay Square*, by Rik Tinory (dixie/nostalgia LP, Old Boston Records);

*Live on Boston Common*, by Pope John Paul II (religious LP, Old Boston Records); and *Martha's Vineyard*, by R. Tinory (folk rock LP, Old Boston Records).
**Tips:** "We are looking for master recordings with strong material ready for release."

**TITO PRODUCTIONS/TEE-WEB PRODUCTIONS**, 12842 Fenkell Ave., Detroit MI 48227. President: Tito Lewis. Record producer, music publisher (Teebo Publishing and Tee-Web Music Co./ASCAP), promotion company. Deals with artists, songwriters, producers and record companies. Produces 5 singles and 4 albums/year. Fee derived from sales royalty or outright fee from record company.
**How to Contact:** Submit demo tape and lyric sheet. Prefers cassette with 2-10 songs on demo. SASE. Reports in 1 month.
**Music:** Children's, church/religious, dance-oriented, gospel, R&B, soul and top 40/pop. Recently released *Big Apple Rappin*, by Spyder B (dance rap LP, Newtroit Records); and *I Thank You Lord*, by Jan Winshell (gospel LP).

*****TMC PRODUCTIONS**, 3800 San Pedro Ave., San Antonio TX 78212. (512)735-3322. Producer: Joe Scates. Record producer, music publisher (Axbar Productions/BMI, Axe Handle Music/ASCAP) and record distributor. Deals with artists and songwriters. Produces 12-15 singles and 3-6 albums/year. Fee derived from sales royalty.
**How to Contact:** Submit demo tape and lyric sheet. Prefers 7½ ips reel-to-reel or cassette with 1-5 songs on demo. SASE. Reports "as soon as possible, but don't rush us."
**Music:** Blues, country, MOR and rock (soft). Recently produced "Today Just Ain't the Day," by Mark Nesler (country single, Axbar Records); "Love Letters in My Mind," by Juni Moon (country single, Axbar Records); "Pack Up all Your Memories," by the Davenports (country single, JATO Records); and "Full Blooded Texan," by Mark Chesnutt (country single, Axbar Records). Other artists include Joe's Studio Band, Steve Kendrick and J'Anna Tebbs.
**Tips:** "Availability in South Texas area helps those who want to work with us."

**TREND PRODUCTIONS**, Box 201, Smyrna GA 30080. (404)432-2454. Manager: Tom Hodges. Record producer, music publisher and artist manager. Deals with artists, songwriters and musicians. Fee derived from sales royalty.
**How to Contact:** Submit demo tape and lyric sheet. Prefers cassette with 3-10 songs on demo. SASE. Reports in 3 weeks.
**Music:** Bluegrass, blues, C&W, gospel, MOR, R&B, rock, soul and top 40/pop. Recently produced "Sugar Daddy Man," by Frank Brannon (C&W single); "To See the Kids," by Jo Ann Johnson (C&W single); and "Be Bop A Lula," by Dempsey (C&W single). Other artists include Terry Brand.

*****TRIBAL RECORDS**, Box 6495, Buena Park CA 90620. (714)554-0851. Contact: Jerry Wood. Record producer. Deals with artists and songwriters. Fee derived from sales royalty or outright fee from record company.
**How to Contact:** Submit demo tape and lyric sheet. Prefers 7½ ips reel-to-reel or cassette with 3 songs on demo. SASE. Reports in 2 weeks.
**Music:** C&W, easy listening and MOR. Recently produced "Many Are the Colors," by Roy Dee (country, Tribal Records); "99 Years," by Ron Hayden (country, Tribal Records); and "Gold Plated Boy Scout Knife," by Jeanne Taylor (country, Tribal Records).

**TROD NOSSEL ARTISTS**, 10 George St., Box 57, Wallingford CT 06492. (203)269-4465, ext. 66. Executive Director: Thomas 'Doc' Cavalier. Record producer, music publisher (Rohm Music, Linesider Music, BIG Music) and record company manager. Produces 6-9 albums/year. Fee derived from sales royalty.
**How to Contact:** Submit demo tape and lyric sheet. Include statement of goals and purposes. Prefers cassette with 2-6 songs on demo. SASE. Reports in 1 month.
**Music:** Blues, R&B, rock (all kinds), soul and top 40/pop. Recently produced *Worlds Favorite Songs*, by B. Willie Smith Band (roots/R&R/R&B LP, TNA Records). Other artists include Christine Ohlman and the Soul Rockers, Bob Mel and The Chryslers.

*****TSR INC.**, 3436 Sansom, Philadelphia PA 19104. (215)386-5998. Producers: John O. Wicks III and Scott M. Herzog. Record producer and music publisher (TSR Music, City Surfer Music). Deals with artists and songwriters. Produces 2 singles and 3 albums/year. Fee derived from sales royalty or outright fee from record company.
**How to Contact;** Submit demo tape and lyric sheet. Prefers cassette with 2-3 songs on demo. "Studio demo please." SASE. Reports in 1 month.
**Music:** MOR and easy listening; also C&W, dance-oriented, gospel, progressive, rock, soul, top 40/pop, funk and rap. Recently produced *John Scott Mottinger*, by John Scott Mottinger (country/MOR LP,

TSR Inc. Records); *Carl Bright Unltd.*, by Carl Bright (gospel LP, TSR Inc. Records); and *City Surfer*, by The Benders (new wave rock single, TSR, Inc. Records).

**TUMAC MUSIC**, 2097 Vistadale Ct., Tucker GA 30084. (404)938-1210. Professional Manager: Phil McDaniel. Record company, music publisher and record producer. Produces 3 singles/year. Deals with artists and songwriters on contract.
**How to Contact:** Submit demo tape and lyric sheet. Prefers cassette with 1-3 songs on demo. SASE. Reports in 3 weeks.
**Music:** Blues, C&W, easy listening, country jazz, MOR, R&B, country and soft rock and top 40/pop. Recently produced "In Love with Today," by Connie Johnson; and "Why Couldn't I Just Love You," by Ron Perrault.

**SCOTT TURNER PRODUCTIONS**, 524 Doral Country Dr., Nashville TN 37221. Executive Producer: Scott Turner. Record producer and music publisher (Buried Treasure/ASCAP, Captain Kidd/BMI). Deals with artists and songwriters. Fee derived from sales royalty or outright fee from record company "plus override percentage. I will only produce a new act, financially aided by a backer, if the artist can compete, and has 'on stage' experience. It depends on whether or not I am producing a major act for a major label, or if I place a custom session with a label. There is a standard fee for producing the session, plus a percentage. Sessions are produced through A.F. of M. only, and every expenditure is accounted for honestly."
**How to Contact:** Submit demo tape and lead sheet. Prefers cassette with 1-4 songs on demo. SASE. Reports in 2 weeks.
**Music:** Mostly country, progressive country, rockabilly and MOR; also easy listening, folk, progressive, rock, and top 40/pop. Recently produced "When the Wind Blows in Chicago," by Robert Bouchard (country single, Clearwood Records); "(We Make) A Great Country Song" and "Talk Back Tremblin' Lips," by Bobby Lewis (country singles, Ventura Records). Other artists include Tony Graham, Nilsson, Jerry Wallace, Denny Ray Lamson and El Paso Country.
**Tips:** "Do your homework, study the pros and pay your dues. I have produced over 70 artists, and the 'overnight success' (record-wise) of any of them has taken from 5 to 6 years. Your demo tape can be as simple as possible, but the artist and song must get to me in the first 8 bars. Also must have a qualified CPA handling all funding so that every dime can be accounted for. Many 'hopefuls' do not realize that Superstars are 'created', not born, and they don't know the intricate workings within the record industry. Records are only a stepping-stone to personal appearances, where the bulk of an artist's money is made, but in order to reach that status it takes a group of hard-working honest professionals."

\***TWO STAR PRODUCTIONS**, 15 King George's DR., Toronto, Ontario, Canada M6M 2H1. (416)656-1566. Producer: Bob Johnston. Record producer. Deals with artists and songwriters. Produces 1-2 singles and 1 album/year. Fee derived from outright fee from songwriter/artist.
**How to Contact:** Call or write first about your interest. Prefers cassette with 2-4 songs on demo. SAE and IRC. Reports in 2 weeks.
**Music:** Mostly country crossover; also easy listening, MOR and rock (commercial). Recently produced "The Same Mistake," by Skyliner (country crossover single, MBS Records); "Give Me a Chance," by Skyliner (country pop single, MBS Records); and *Saturday Night at the Perriers*, by the Perrier Family (bluegrass LP, Goldtown Records). Other artists include Dusty Shelf.
**Tips:** "Send only good material with a good hook."

**TYMENA MUSIC (TY LEMLEY MUSIC)**, 430 Pearce Rd., Baldwin Township, Pittsburgh PA 15234. (412)341-0991. General Manager: Bud Lemley. President: Ty Lemley. Vice President: Tolmena Lemley. Record producer. Deals with artists and songwriters. Fee derived from sales royalty.
**How to Contact:** Submit lyric sheet, 45 demo record or cassette. Reports in 1 month.
**Music:** C&W, easy listening, MOR and top 40/pop. Recently produced "One Day At A Time," (MOR single); "You and Me," (top/40 rock single); "Ramblin' Ways" and "Offer Me Your Love," (C&W singles), all by Ty Lemley (Tymena Records).

**VAMPLE RECORD, INC.**, Box 23152, Kansas City MO 64141. President: Jerry Vample. Record producer and music publisher (Jerry Vample Publishing Co./BMI). Deals with artists and songwriters. Produces 4 singles and 2 albums/year. Fee derived from sales royalty.
**How to Contact:** Write first about your interest, then submit demo tape and lyric sheet. Prefers 7½ ips reel-to-reel or cassette with 2-4 songs on demo. SASE. Reports in 1 month.
**Music:** Church/religious, easy listening and gospel. Artists include Michael Charles and Zenobia Smith.

**VENTURE PRODUCTIONS**, 121 Meadowbrook Dr., Somerville NJ 08876. (201)359-5110. Producers: Tony Camillo, Cecile Barker. Record producer, music publisher and production company. Deals

with artists and songwriters. Produces 21-25 singles and 5-8 albums/year. Fee derived from sales royalty or outright fee from record company.
**How to Contact:** Query or submit demo tape and lead sheet. "Send as complete a package as possible." Prefers cassette with 2-5 songs on demo. SASE. Reports in "1 month or longer depending on schedule."
**Music:** Dance, soul, MOR and top 40/pop; "excellent material only." Recently produced *Let's Burn*, by Clarence Carter; "Without You" and *Don't Make Me Eat*, by Pendullum; "Body Bait," by Symba (disco single); and "Once a Night," by Charlie English (single from the movie, *Hopscotch*).

**CHARLES VICKERS MUSIC ASSOCIATION**, 171 Pine Haven, Daytona Beach FL 32014. (904)252-4849. President/Producer: Dr. Charles H. Vickers D.M. Record producer and music publisher (Pritchett Publication/BMI and Alison Music/ASCAP). Deals with artists and songwriters. Produces 90 singles and 4 albums/year. Fee derived from sales royalty.
**How to Contact:** Write first about your interest. Prefers 7 1/2 ips reel-to-reel or cassette with 1-6 songs on demo. SASE. Reports in 1 week.
**Music:** Bluegrass, blues, church/religious, classical, C&W, easy listening, gospel, jazz, MOR, progressive, reggae (pop), R&B, rock, soul and top 40/pop. Recently produced *Charle Vickers Does Disco*, by C. Vickers (disco LP, Tropical Records); *Charles Vickers*, by C. Vickers (country/pop/disco LP, Tropical Records); *Disco Pop of the 80's*, by C. Vickers (ballad/rock LP, Tropical Records); *Another Dawn*, by C. Vickers (gospel LP, Accent/King of Kings Records); and *Heaven Is Just Over the Hill*, by C. Vickers (gospel LP, King of Kings/L.A. International and Pickwick International Inc. Records).

**VOICE BOX RECORDS**, 5180-B Park Ave., Memphis TN 38122. (901)761-5074. President: Mark Blackwood. Record producer and music publisher (Songs From The Box/BMI, Voice Of Paradise/ASCAP). Deals with artists and songwriters. Produces 10 singles and 6 albums/year. Fee derived from sales royalty.
**How to Contact:** Submit demo tape and lyric sheet. Prefers cassette. Does not return unsolicited material. Reports in 1 month.
**Music:** Gospel. "We are primarily interested in Christian MOR songs and artists." Recently produced "Following You," by Blackwood Brothers; "Vessel of Love," by Lindy Hearne; and "Lord, I Need Your Love," by Jeanne Johnson.

*****WAM RECORDS, LTD.**, 901 Kenilworth Rd., Montreal, Quebec, Canada H3R 2R5. (514)341-6721. President: Leon Aronson. Record producer and music publisher (Think Big Music). Deals with artists and songwriters. Produces 10 singles and 6 albums/year. Fee derived from sales royalty.
**How to Contact:** Submit demo tape and lyric sheet. Prefers cassette with 6 songs on demo. SASE. Reports in 1 month.
**Music:** Mostly pop/rock; also dance-oriented. Recently produced *Marty Butler*, by Marty Butler (pop/rock LP, RCA Records); *Good Girl Gone Bad*, by Terry Crawford (rock LP, RCA Records); and *Larry Patten*, by Larry Patten (pop/rock LP, WAM Records).

**KENT WASHBURN**, 10622 Commerce Ave., Tujunga CA 91042. Contact: Kent Washburn. Record producer and music publisher (Monard Music/ASCAP). Deals with artists and songwriters. Produces 5 singles and 3-4 albums/year. Fee derived from sales royalty or outright fee from record company.
**How to Contact:** Query or submit demo tape and lead sheet. Prefers 7 1/2 ips reel-to-reel or cassette with 1-4 songs on demo. SASE. Reports in 1 month.
**Music:** Dance, easy listening, jazz, MOR, soul and top 40/pop. Recently produced "Tell the World," by Nicholas (Impact Records); "Plugged In," by Randy Matthews (Spirit Records); "Weary Child," by Pamela Hart (Spirit Records); and "Energizin Love," by Paul Davis (Spirit Records).
**Tips:** "Understand the artists before submitting material."

*****WATTS CITY RECORDS & PRODUCTION CO.**, 11211 Wilmington Ave., Los Angeles CA 90059. (213)566-9982. Executive Producer: Joe Fornis. Record producer and music publisher (Watts City Production/ASCAP). Deals with artists and songwriters. Produces 5 singles and 2 albums/year. Fee derived from sales royalty.
**How to Contact:** Submit demo tape and lyric sheet. Prefers cassette with 4-12 songs on demo. SASE. Reports in 3 weeks.
**Music:** R&B, soul and top 40/pop.

*****WEBCO RECORDS & RECORDING STUDIO**, 8705 Deanna Dr., Gaithersburg MD 20879. (301)253-5962. President: Wayne E. Busbice. Record producer and music publisher (Old Home Place Music). Deals with artists and songwriters. Produces 4 singles and 8-10 albums/year. Fee dervied from sales royalty.

**258** Songwriter's Market '84

**How to Contact:** Write first about your interest. Prefers cassette with 3-5 songs on demo. "It helps if an artist is referred to me by an already-known artist." SASE. Reports in 1 month.
**Music:** Mostly bluegrass; also C&W. Recently produced *The Bluegrass of Buzz Busby*, by Buzz Busby (bluegrass LP, WEBCO Records); *Carl Nelson & His Fiddle*, by Carl Nelson (bluegrass LP, WEBCO Records); and *West Virginia Style*, by Darrell Sanders (banjo/bluegrass LP, WEBCO Records). Other artists include Bill Rouse & The Up Town Grass Band, The Grass Reflection, the Busby Brothers and Jack Fincham and The Dixie Grass.
**Tips:** "Be referred by established artist."

*****W/G RECORDS**, 991 Oak St., West Barnstable MA 02668. (617)362-4908. President: Michael Welch. Record producer and music publisher (Welchy Grape Publishing). Deals with artists and songwriters. Produces 2 singles and 1 album/year. Fee derived from sales royalty.
**How to Contact:** Submit demo tape and lyric sheet or write first about your interest. Prefers cassette or record with 10 songs on demo. SASE. Reports in 1 month.
**Music:** C&W, easy listening, folk, MOR, rock (country/hard) and top 40/pop. Recently produced *Renovations*; *Resurgence*; *Turning Point*; *You Are My Destiny*; and *Everybody Knows*, all by Mike Welch (W/G Records).

**WHITEWAY PRODUCTIONS, INC.**, 65 W. 55th St., New York NY 10019. (212)757-4317. President: Eddie White. Vice President: Peter White. Record, play, film and concert producer. Deals with artists and actors. Fee derived from sales royalty.
**How to Contact:** Query, arrange personal interview or submit demo tape. "We advertise or send out calls when we are doing a show." Does not return unsolicited material.
**Music:** Musical shows. Recently produced *Birmingham Rag* and *Dixieland Blues*, by Sunny Gale.

**SHANE WILDER PRODUCTIONS**, Box 3503, Hollywood CA 90028. (213)762-1613. President: Shane Wilder. Record producer and music publisher. Deals with artists and songwriters. Produces 25-30 singles and 10-15 albums/year. Fee derived from sales royalty plus production fee.
**How to Contact:** Submit demo tape and lyric sheet. Prefers cassette with 6-8 songs on demo. SASE. Reports in 2 weeks.
**Music:** C&W, easy listening, MOR, rock and top 40/pop. Recently produced "Part Time Love," by Crystal Blue (disco single); and "Old Liars, Umpires and a Woman Who Knows," by Mike Franklin (country single, N.S.D. Records). Other artists include Priscilla Emerson, Laurie Loman (MCA recording artist) and Terry Brooks (rock artist, Jet Records).

**DON WILLIAMS MUSIC GROUP**, Suite 1106, 1888 Century Park E., Los Angeles CA 90067. (213)556-2458. Contact: D.W. Hathaway. Music publishing/administration and record production. Deals with artists and songwriters. Fee derived from sales royalty.
**How to Contact:** Submit demo tape and lyric sheet. Prefers 2-3 songs on demo. List name, address and telephone number on package. SASE. Reports in 4-6 weeks.
**Music:** All types.

*****WISHBONE, INC.**, Box 2631, Muscle Shoals AL 35662. (205)381-1455. President: Terry Woodford. Professional Manager: Richard Butler. Record producer, music publisher (I've Got The Music Co./ASCAP, Song Tailors Music Co./BMI, Terry Woodford Music/ASCAP and Creative Source Music/BMI) and video producer. Deals with artists and songwriters.
**How to Contact:** Submit demo tape and lyric sheet. Prefers cassette with 1-3 songs on demo. SASE. Reports ASAP.
**Music:** Mostly top 40/pop; also C&W, dance-oriented, easy listening, MOR, progressive, R&B, rock and soul. Recently produced *Nothing But the Truth*, by Mac Mcanally (top 40/pop/easy listening/rock LP, Geffen Records).

*****WORDS OF WISDOM PRODUCTION**, 3403 N. Ralston Ave., Indianapolis IN 46218. (317)926-6271. Producer: Rickie Clark. Record producer and music publisher (Clark Publishing, Tyscot, Inc.). Deals with artists. Produces 4 singles and 2 albums/year. Fee derived from sales royalty or outright free from record company.
**How to Contact:** Submit demo tape and lyric sheet. Prefers cassette with 6 songs on demo. SASE. Reports in 1 month.
**Music:** Mostly soul, R&B and gospel; also church/religious, dance-oriented, jazz and top 40/pop. Recently produced "Hold Out," by Robert Turner (gospel single, Tyscot Records); "I Wish" b/w "Come On Around," by Terry Huff (soul singles, Circle City Records); "Flam," by Ricky Clark (soul single, Circle City records); and "Lady's Right," by R. Clark (soul single, Indy 5 Records). Other artists include Circle City Band, Truth & Devotion and Redd Hott.

# Close-up

**Tom Snow**
Songwriter/Publisher/Performer

"Simplicity and economy of style are the secrets that make great art," says hit songwriter Tom Snow. "I wish I'd learned about the economy of structure and melody sooner, how to be to the point within the framework of the song. I finally learned it from people saying 'we like this song, but it's too long,' or 'it seems too wordy.'

"Songwriting is somewhat like painting a picture. An artist spends years refining his compositional ability and his technique. As I developed as a songwriter, I learned to work within the artistic framework of a song."

Tom Snow came to L.A. in 1969, shortly after graduating second in his class with a Bachelor's of Music in Composition from Berklee School of Music. Since then, he has recorded four albums and established, with wife Mary Belle, the successful publishing house of Snow Music. But songwriting, says Snow, "is my absolute, passionate love."

Today Snow is one of the most successful writers in the music industry with well over 100 of his songs recorded by almost every major recording artist. Among his million-selling hits are "He's So Shy," by the Pointer Sisters; "Deeper than the Night," by Olivia Newton-John; and "You," by Rita Coolidge. Other artists recording Snow songs include Barry Manilow, Dolly Parton, Kenny Rogers, and Melissa Manchester, just to name a few.

Snow who finds himself more prolific with melodies than words says, "I'm always looking for a co-writer." The list of his collaborators includes names as famous as the acts who've recorded the songs: Barry Mann, Cynthia Weil, John Farrar, Leo Sayer and many others.

As a trained composer, Snow sees the recent changes in the music scene as positive ones very much to his liking. "I've never been more excited about the possibilities open to songwriters than I am right now. The public's tastes in music are becoming more sophisticated. Music is not as monolithic as it was in the seventies. That got me down, because I had lots of training and couldn't use it.

"Music will always change and grow," says Snow. "To be a successful songwriter you must be aware of that, and adapt. Learn to write in different styles and formats. Bring yourself and your music to what's going on—it's not going to come to you."

How does a songwriter adapt his material to today's music market without compromising his craft completely? "Compromise, but be honest with yourself," says Snow. "Ask yourself if what you've written is the best representation of your work, but yet contemporary enough for today."

As a further guideline to evaluating your own work, Snow paraphrases the writer who said: "Evaluating your writing is to sit in judgment on yourself. If it is not right for you, then it can't be right for anybody else."

**BARRY YEARWOOD ENTERPRISES**, 200 W. 51st St., New York NY 10019. (212)245-3939. Vice President and General Manager: Barry Yearwood. Record producer and music publisher (Mega-Star Music/BMI). Estab. 1982. Deals with artists and songwriters. Produces 4 singles/year. Fee derived from sales royalty.
**How to Contact:** Submit demo tape and lyric sheet. Prefers cassette with 4-8 songs on demo. Does not return unsolicited material. Reports in 1 month.
**Music:** Gospel, jazz, MOR, progressive, R&B, rock, soul and top 40/pop.

**PAUL ZALESKI**, Box 34032, Bartlett TN 38134. (901)377-1439. Contact: Paul Zaleski. Record producer and music publisher (Apache's Rhythm/ASCAP). Deals with artists and songwriters. Produces 4 singles and 3 albums/year. Fee derived from sales royalty or outright fee from record company or record artist.
**How to Contact:** Submit demo tape and lyric sheet. Prefers cassette with 4-10 songs on demo. SASE. Reports in 2-3 weeks.
**Music:** C&W, easy listening, contemporary Christian and R&R. Recently produced "Follow Me," by Ellason Castiglione (contemporary Christian single, Blackwood Records); "(I Don't Believe) We Can Make It Without You," by Chuck Bell (country single, Blackwood Records); and "Slow Motion," by Park Avenue (R&B single, Atlantic Records). Other artists include Johnny Nash, Flaming Aces, Jim Dandy with Black Oak and R.W. Blackwood.
**Tips:** "Submit good songs with structure and good easy hook."

**DAN ZAM PRODUCTIONS**, 183 Thompson St., New York NY 10012. (212)982-1374. President: Dan Zam. Record producer. Deals with artists and songwriters. Fee derived from sales royalty or outright fee from songwriter/artist or record company.
**How to Contact:** Submit demo tape or submit demo tape and lead sheet. Prefers cassette (with Dolby) or 7½ or 15 ips reel-to-reel (no Dolby) with 3 songs minimum on tape. SASE. Reports in 3 weeks.
**Music:** New music, avante-pop and rock.
**Tips:** "Send demos that are simple, not over-produced. Lyric, melody, hook are basic. Leave some room for approach to the producer."

*****ZIPP-ZAPP RECORDS CORP.**, 744 Joppa Farm Rd., Joppa MD 21085. (301)679-2262. A&R/Promotion Manager: Ernest W. Cash. Record producer and music publisher (Guerriero Music/BMI). Estab. 1981. Deals with artists and songwriters. Produces 10 singles and 5 albums/year. Fee derived from sales royalty.
**How to Contact:** Submit demo tape and lyric sheet. Prefers cassette with 4-10 songs on demo. SASE. Reports in 1 month.
**Music:** C&W and gospel. Recently produced *Just Us Three*, by Glen Justice (C&W LP, Zipp-Zapp Records); "Let Me Love You Where It Hurts," and "Time for Lettin' Go," by Billy Buck (C&W singles, Zipp-Zapp Records). Other artists include Ernie Cash and Ernie C. Penn.

# Advertising Agencies

Songwriters with the desire and ability to write jingles, songs and background music for commercials need look no farther than their home town for good markets in the advertising field. It's true that the greatest concentrations of major advertising agencies are in New York, Chicago and other large commercial centers. But, no matter what size the town, wherever there are car dealerships, grocery stores and other retail businesses, there are agencies to provide individualized advertising campaigns for TV and radio. Many top agencies also have branches in cities across the country.

The agencies listed here tell exactly what type of clients they serve—many are willing to send you a specific list of their clients—and how songwriters should submit examples of their work. Most ad agencies who like what you present them will want to keep your demo on file for possible future assignment. Many will return your tape at your request, however, if you have enclosed a SASE.

Read James Dearing's article on "Writing for the Local Alternative Music Markets" in the front of this book to learn all you need to know about making money in the advertising field: the theory and craft of writing jingles, how to find markets in your own home town, how to make your own markets, and how to submit your work *and* get assignments.

Check the Yellow Pages for names and addresses of agencies in your area. Additional names and addresses of agencies along with specific clients of each company may be obtained from *The Standard Directory of Advertising Agencies* (National Register Publishing Company).

**ADELANTE ADVERTISING, INC.**, Suite 807, 386 Park Ave. S., New York NY 10016. (212)696-0855. Executive Vice President: David Krieger. Ad agency. Serves soft goods, entertainment, wine, financial and other consumer products clients. Uses jingles and background music in commercials, demonstration and sales films and audiovisuals. Commissions 6-10 songwriters and 6-10 lyricists/year. Pays $25-3,000/job. "Speculative demos to be determined." Buys all rights.
**How to Contact:** Submit demo tape of previously aired work. Prefers 7½ ips reel-to-reel or cassette with 3-15 songs on tape. SASE, but prefers to keep material on file. Reports in 2 weeks or as need arises.
**Music:** "We are an ethnic advertising agency. Our needs are to fulfill the music needs of the black and Spanish communities to enforce sales via radio and TV. We use R&B, jazz, disco, salsa, merenque, etc."

**ADVERTISING & MARKETING, INC.**, 1 LeFleur's Square, Box 873, Jackson MS 39205. (601)981-8881. Contact: Creative Director. Advertising agency. Serves financial, service and package goods clients. Uses services of songwriters and lyricists for industrial films and AV shows. "The lyricist gets campaign theme, sample copy for print, and our creative rationale plus any suggested lines we might have. It is then his job to turn our ideas into a song." Commissions 10-15 pieces/year. Pays $1,000-15,000/job. Prefers to buy all rights, but will negotiate for top quality work. Prefers to use production house lyricist and purchase music "packages" of lyrics, arrangements, recordings, etc., ready for broadcast.
**How to Contact:** Submit demo tape of previously aired work or tape demonstrating jingle/composition skills. Prefers 7½ ips reel-to-reel with 5-15 songs on demo. "Where possible, identify cost of production for each piece of music on reel." SASE, but prefers to keep material on file. "As a project comes up that we think is up their alley, we call a jingle production house and ask it to spec a demo." Reports "as needed."
**Music:** Both long-term corporate jingles and short-term music for single campaigns. Adamantly opposed to re-treads. "We look for songwriters who can demonstrate a variety of styles and musical configurations—country and western alone will not get it. The good song impresses us, not necessarily the good production."
**Tips:** "Avoid condescension; we may be in Jackson, Mississippi, but we know what's good and what isn't. We have used major national sources in the past, and will in the future. Be able to provide turnkey job—with singers, instrumentation, recording—ready to air. Be familiar with campaign needs of agencies."

**ADVERTISING COMMUNICATIONS, INC.**, Suite #715, 111 E. Third St., Davenport IA 52801. (319)326-4055. Broadcast Creative Director: Dean Teeselink. Advertising agency. Uses services of songwriters. Commissions 2-3 songwriters/year. Pays by the job. Buys all rights or one-time rights.
**How to Contact:** Submit demo tape of previous work. Prefers 7½ ips reel-to-reel or cassette with 4-10 songs on demo. Does not return unsolicted material; prefers to keep on file.
**Music:** "Music varies with each client and promotion."

**ALPINE ADVERTISING, INC.**, 2639 St. Johns Ave., Box 30895, Billings MT 59817. (406)652-1630. President: James F. Preste. Ad agency. Serves financial, automotive and food clients. Uses jingles. Commissions 20 pieces/year. Pays $650-3,500/job. Buys all rights.
**How to Contact:** Submit demo tape of previously aired work. Prefers 7½ ips reel-to-reel with 5-12 songs on demo. Does not return unsolicited material. Reports in 1 month.

**AMVID COMMUNICATION SERVICES, INC.**, Box 577, Manhattan Beach CA 90266. (213)545-6691. Contact: Production Manager or Producer. Uses services of music houses for background music. Pays by the job.
**How to Contact:** Query with resume of credits or submit demo tape of previously aired work. Prefers 7½ ips reel-to-reel or cassette. SASE. Reports in 10 days.
**Music:** Background music written to convey specific moods.

*****N. ARMSTRONG ADVERTISING AGENCY**, Suite 223, 3610 Avenue Q, Lubbock TX 79412. (806)765-6283. Contact: Nelda Armstrong. Advertising agency. Uses services of jingle companies for jingles. Commissions 1 songwriter/year. Pays by the job. Buy all rights.
**How to Contact:** Arrange personal interview or query with resume of credits. Prefers cassette with 2-4 songs on demo. SASE.
**Music:** Country and contemporary. Jingles: 60- and 30-seconds and music bed. "Present lyrics (without music) that could be produced using various types of music formats."

**BALLARD CANNON, INC.**, 506 2nd W., Box 9787, Seattle WA 98119. (206)284-8800. Vice President/Creative Director: Dick Rosenwald. Ad agency. Serves financial, retail, electronics, travel, entertainment/food and insurance clients. Uses services of songwriters for jingles and background music for commercials. Commissions 5 pieces/year. Pays $1,500 minimum/job. Rights purchased vary.
**How to Contact:** Query with resume of credits or submit demo tape of previously aired work. Prefers 7½ ips reel-to-reel with 4-12 songs on demo. "Include a brief description of involvement in each project, total costs, objectives and use of material." SASE. Reports in 1 month, if requested.
**Tips:** "Do not try to prepackage jingles. You must approach each one individually to solve specific communication/image needs."

*****BANANAS INC.**, Box 347, Hales Corners WI 53130. Vice President/Marketing: Bill Eisner Jr. Recording studio and production company. Uses services of songwriters and staff writers for jingles and background music in commercials. Pays $150-1,500/job.
**How to Contact:** Submit demo tape of previous work ("by mail only—no calls"). Prefers cassette as demo. Does not return unsolicited material; prefers to keep on file. "We will phone you when we can utilize your talents on a job."
**Music:** Jingles and film scores.

**BATTEN, BARTON, DURSTINE & OSBORN, INC.**, Lutheran Brotherhood Bldg., Minneapolis MN 55402. (612)338-8401. Broadcast Production Manager: Marge Austin. Ad agency. Uses services of individual songwriters and music houses for jingles and background music in commerials. "We generally do not use lyricists. Our copywriters would compose the lyrics/copy." Commissions about 10-20 songwriters/year. Pays negotiated creative fee and production fee. Buys all rights.
**How to Contact:** Submit demo tape of previously aired work (if no previously aired work, samples OK). SASE; prefers to keep tape on file for contact "if a project develops which we would like songwriter to consider."
**Music:** Music varies. "Can be country oriented; sophisticated; tricky jingles; or polished compositions."
**Tips:** "Present only the very best and most professionally produced material possible."

**BATZ-HODGSON-NEUWOEHNER, INC.**, VFW Bldg., 406 W. 34th St., Kansas City MO 64111. (816)561-7568. Creative Director: Jim Sheiner. Ad agency. Uses jingles and background music in commercials. Commissions 1 piece/year. Payment arranged through AFTRA. Rights purchased vary.
**How to Contact:** Submit demo tape of previously aired work. Prefers 7½ ips reel-to-reel with 7-8 songs on demo. SASE. Reports in 1 week.

# Advertising Agencies

**BBDO**, 410 N. Michigan Ave., Chicago IL 60611. (312)337-7860. Producer: Hank Sadian. Ad Agency. Serves food clients. Uses music houses for jingles. Commissions 75 pieces/year. Pays fair price for demonstration; asks what creative fee is wanted. Buys all rights.
**How to Contact:** Arrange personal interview or submit demonstration tape of previous work; or submit demo tape showing jingles/composition skills. Prefers 7 1/2 ips reel-to-reel; wants to hear instrumental first. Returns material if requested with SASE; prefers to keep tape on file.
**Music:** Likes melodies "such as in the Juicy Fruit gum commercial." Once a melody is achieved, does own variations.

**BBDO WEST**, 10960 Wilshire Blvd., Los Angeles CA 90024. (213)479-3979. Producer: Jim Baier. Ad agency. Uses jingles and background music for commercials. Pays by the job.
**How to Contact:** Submit demo tape of previously aired work. Prefers 7 1/2 ips reel-to-reel. SASE.

**BEAR ADVERTISING**, 1424 N. Highland Ave., Los Angeles CA 90028. (213)466-6464. Vice President: Bruce Bear. Serves sporting goods, fast food and industrial clients. Uses jingles and background music in commercials. Pays by the job.
**How to Contact:** Submit demo tape of previously aired work. Prefers cassette. SASE. Reports "as soon as possible."
**Music:** Needs vary.

**BELL OF THE CAPE ADVERTISING**, Box 23, East Dennis MA 02641. (617)385-2334. Vice President: Diane King. Ad agency. Serves amusement, financial, insurance, light industry, cable TV, furniture and restaurant clients. Uses jingles and background music for commercials. Commissions 3 pieces/year. Pays $300 minimum/job. "We purchase only when the client accepts." Buys all rights.
**How to Contact:** Submit demo tape of previously aired work or of jingles/compositions for a specific client. Prefers 7 1/2 ips reel-to-reel with 5-15 songs on demo. SASE, but prefers to keep material on file. Reports in 2 weeks.
**Music:** "We work with jingles and one-shot or full series music backgrounds. Persons willing to work on spec are most valuable to us. We deal with a medium market and most clients prefer specs. Closings are better following such specs."

**BERGER, STONE & PARTNERS, INC.**, 666 5th Ave., New York NY 10103. (212)977-7474. Broadcast Production Manager: Sara Neiditz. Broadcast Copy Supervisor: Steve Miller. President and Director of Creative Services: Joseph Stone. Ad agency. Serves automobile, bank, jewelry, optical, corporate financial, packaged goods and institutional clients. Uses jingles and background music for commercials. Commissions 10 pieces/year. Pays $1,000-4,000/job. "We mainly buy orchestration and production of commercials we write." Buys all rights.
**How to Contact:** Query with resume. Prefers reel-to-reel or cassette, or videotape or 16mm film. Does not return unsolicited material. "Never reports, unless interested in the material."
**Tips:** "Realize that jingles are advertising; they must fill marketing needs within marketing plans. Learn what makes advertising work, and write that kind of material into the jingle."

**DOYLE DANE BERNBACH ADVERTISING LTD.**, 2 Bloor St. W, Toronto, Ontario, Canada M4W 1G4. (416)925-8911. Contact: Rick Davis. Ad agency. Serves all types of clients. Uses services of songwriters for jingles and background music in commercials. Commissions 1-10 pieces/year. Pays by union scale. Usually buys all rights.
**How to Contact:** Submit any type demo tape of previously aired work. Prefers maximum 10 minutes on demo. SAE and IRC, but prefers to keep material on file. Responds as need arises.
**Music:** All types.

**BERNSTEIN & REIN**, 800 W. 47th St., Kansas City MO 64112. (816)756-0640. Creative Director: Jeff Bremser. Ad agency. Uses services of songwriters for jingles and background music in commercials. Commissions 10-20 pieces/year from 3-5 songwriters. Pays $15,000 maximum/job. "We buy complete production, not just songs."
**How to Contact:** Submit demo tape of previously aired work. Prefers reel-to-reel with 5 songs minimum on tape. SASE. "We keep tapes on file; we do not report."
**Music:** "All styles for use as jingles and commercial scores."

*****RALPH BING ADVERTISING CO.**, 16109 Selva Dr., San Diego CA 92128. (619)487-7444. President: Ralph S. Bing. Ad agency. Uses the services of independent producers for jingles. Commissions 1 songwriter and 1 lyricist/year. Pays by the job as determined by the producer. Buys all rights.
**How to Contact:** Query first. Prefers cassette with 3-6 songs on demo. SASE, but prefers to keep material on file.
**Music:** Easy listening.

**BLAIR ADVERTISING, INC.**, subsidiary of BBDO International, 96 College Ave., Rochester NY 14607. (716)473-0440. Vice President: John R. Brown. Ad agency. Serves financial, industrial and consumer clients. Uses jingles, background music for commercials and music for sales meeting presentations. Commissions 10 pieces/year. Pays $5,000-20,000/job. Buys all rights.
**How to Contact:** Query. Prefers 7½ ips reel-to-reel with 5-20 songs on demo. Does not return unsolicited material.
**Music:** "We need every type. Often lyrics will be supplied. We're seriously interested in hearing from good production sources. We have at hand some of the world's best working for us, but we're always ready to listen to fresh, new ideas."

***GEORGE BLAKE & ASSOC.**, 912 Magellan Dr., Sarasota FL 33580. President: George Blake. Ad agency. Uses the services of songwriters for jingles. Pays by the job. Buys all rights.
**How to Contact:** Query first. Prefers cassette with 3-6 songs on demo. Does not return unsolicited material; prefers to keep on file. Responds in 1 month-3 years.
**Music:** Various types.

**JOHN BORDEN ADVERTISING AGENCY**, #102, 5841 73rd Ave. N., Brooklyn Park MN 55429. (612)566-4515. Account Executive: John Borden. Serves recruitment, industrial, hotel, financial, medical, insurance and food manufacturing clients. Uses services of songwriters and lyricists for jingles. Commissions 1-3 songwriters and 1-3 lyricists/year. Pay varies. Rights purchased vary.
**How to Contact:** Submit demo tape of previously aired work. Prefers cassette. Does not return unsolicited material. SASE, but prefers to keep material on file. Reports "when material fits need."
**Tips:** "Our specialty is recruitment advertising (sales, data processing personnel, nurses, electronic technicians, engineers and bank personnel). Get product platform before writing."

**BOZELL & JACOBS, INC.**, 2440 Embarcadero Way, Palo Alto CA 94303. (415)856-9000. Broadcast Supervisor: Scott McSwain. Ad agency. Serves consumer, hi-technology and industrial. Uses primarily music houses, some individual songwriters for jingles, background music in commercials and audiovisual shows for sales meetings. Commissions 4 jingles and 4 pieces for audiovisual shows per year. Negotiates price when union is not involved. Buys all rights.
**How to Contact:** Send reel or information. Prefers ¼" reel-to-reel or cassette. Tape should have variety of music. Does not return material; keeps tape on file.
**Music:** All types.

**BOZELL & JACOBS, INC.**, 360 N. Michigan, Chicago IL 60601. (312)580-4600. Broadcast Production Manager: Gail Duyckinck. Ad agency. Serves utility and cosmetic clients. Uses individual songwriters and music houses for jingles and background music in commercials. Commissions 10 pieces/year. Pays $2,400 minimum/job. Buys all rights.
**How to Contact:** Submit demo tape of previously aired work (if no previously aired work, samples OK). Prefers 7½ ips reel-to-reel. Tape should be about 3 minutes in length. SASE; prefers to keep tape on file.

**BOZELL & JACOBS/PACIFIC**, 10850 Wilshire Blvd., Los Angeles CA 90024. (213)879-1800. Producer: Jan Rosenthal. Ad agency and public relations firm. Serves financial, food and realty clients. Uses individual songwriters for jingles and background music in commercials. Pays according to client's budget. Buys all rights.
**How to Contact:** Submit demo tape of previously aired work (if no previously aired work, samples OK). Prefers reel-to-reel. Wants a representative amount of songs. If songwriter has 10 award winning commercials, wants to hear them all. If has only 1 that has been sold, wants to hear that one and then some other work, too. SASE; prefers to keep tape on file.
**Music:** All types.

**BOZELL & JACOBS/PR**, Suite 2000, 1200 Smith, 2 Allen Center, Houston TX 77002. (713)651-3114. Contact: Creative Director. Ad agency. Serves industrial, packaged goods, service and banking clients. Uses music houses for jingles, background music in commercials, TV, slide shows and audiovisual presentations. Commissions 12-15 packages/year. Pays $500-1,000 for working demo. Buys all rights, then pays talent residuals and musician residuals.
**How to Contact:** Submit demo tape of previous work or demo tape showing jingle/composition skills. Prefers 7½ ips reel-to-reel. Tapes should be a maximum of 6 minutes. SASE; prefers to keep tape on file.

***BOZELL & JACOBS/SOUTHWEST**, 201 E. Carpenter Freeway, Box 61200, DFW, Airport TX 75261. (214)239-4639. Executive Producer: Bill Duryea. Ad agency. Uses the services of songwriters and lyricists for jingles, background music and sales films. Commissions 20-30 songwriters and 5-10

lyricists/year. Pays by the job plus negotiable royalties. Buys all rights.
**How to Contact:** Query with resume of credits. Prefers cassette with 8-15 songs on demo. Does not accept unsolicited material; prefers to keep on file.
**Music:** "Various types for TV and radio commercials; assignment will be rough lyric or lyric idea to be polished."

*****BRANDON/RAY & ASSOCIATES, INC.**, 515 Rock Street, Box 1433, Little Rock AR 72203. (501)374-3789. President: Jim Brandon. Ad agency. Uses the services of songwriters for jingles and background music. Commissions 1 songwriter and 1 lyricist/year. Pays by the job. Buys one-time rights.
**How to Contact:** Submit demo tape of previous work. Prefers cassette with 3-5 songs on demo. SASE, but prefers to keep on file. "We review and choose from most recent material on file when music and jingles are needed."
**Tips:** "Keep the material short, to the point and memorable. Repetition is important. Also, send recent accomplishments at least once a year."

**BROOKS, JOHNSON, ZAUSMER ADVERTISING**, Suite 240, Milam Bldg., San Antonio TX 78205. (512)227-3454. Contact: Rick Neff. Ad agency. Uses music houses for jingles and background music in commercials. Commissions 7-10 songwriters/year. Payment based on bids. Buys all rights.
**How to Contact:** Submit demo tape of previously aired work or "call to see if we have work coming up you want to bid on." Prefers any type tape, although "it's easier to file cassettes" with 7-10 songs on demo. SASE but prefers to file submissions. Responds as needs arise.
**Music:** Uses all types according to client's needs.
**Tips:** "Submit demo of work done for others."

**BRUCE-GREEN ADVERTISING, LTD.**, #3 Felton Place, Box 549, Bloomington IL 61701. (309)827-8081. Vice President: Gina Ready. Ad agency. Serves consumer, industrial and agricultural clients. Uses services of songwriters for jingles and background music in commercials; lyricists for jingle lyrics. Commissions 2 songwriters and 1 lyricist/year. Pays $100 minimum/job. Buys all rights.
**How to Contact:** Query with resume or submit demo tape showing jingle/composition skills. Prefers cassette. SASE, but prefers to keep material on file. Reports as soon as possible by mail or phone.

**SAL BUTERA ASSOCIATES ADVERTISING**, 1824 Whipple Ave. NW, Canton OH 44708. Broadcast Services Supervisor/President: Sal Butera. Ad agency. Serves consumer clients. Uses jingles and background music for commercials. Commissions 5 pieces/year. Pays on a per-bid basis. Buys all rights or one-time rights.
**How to Contact:** Query with resume of credits, submit demo tape of previously aired work or submit demo tape showing jingle/composition skills. Prefers 7½ ips reel-to-reel with 6-12 songs on demo. Does not return unsolicited material. Reports in 1 month.

**CALEP, HIRSCH, KURNIP & SPECTOR, INC.**, 135 W 50th, New York NY 10020. (212)489-9390. Producers: Frank DiSalvo, Valerie Hutchinson and Ron Weber. Ad agency. Uses jingles and background music for commercials. Pays $5,000-7,500/job. Buys all rights.
**How to Contact:** Submit demo tape of previously aired work, submit demo tape of jingle/compositions for a particular client or submit demo tape showing jingle/composition skills. Prefers 7½ ips reel-to-reel with 1-12 songs on demo. Does not return unsolicited material. Material kept on file for future reference.
**Music:** Background and underscore for TV commercials.
**Tips:** "Being too aggressive will turn people off. Show consistent good work, with a successful track record."

*****CARAVETTA ALLEN KIMBROUGH/BBDO**, Suite 825, 255 Alhambra Cicle, Coral Gables FL 33134. (305)448-4741. Senior Vice President/Creative Director: Thomas Scharre. Ad agency. Uses the services of songwriters for jingles and background music. Commissions 3-4 songwriters/year. Pays flat fee, negotiated by project. Buys all rights.
**How to Contact:** Submit demo tape of previous work. Prefers cassette with 3-15 songs on demo. Does not return unsolicited material; prefers to keep on file. "We respond by telephone, but only if we are requesting a bid on a project."
**Music:** Background music for TV commercials, post-scored to picture; and occasional jingles for TV and radio.

*****CARTER ADVERTISING INC.**, 800 American Tower, Shreveport LA 71101. (318)227-1920. Creative Director: Fair Hyams. Ad agency. Uses the services of songwriters and lyricists for jingles, back-

ground music and audiovisual films. Commissions 2-3 songwriters and 1 lyricist/year. Pays by the job or as negotiated. Rights negotiable.
**How to Contact:** Submit demo tape of previous work. Prefers cassette with 3-5 songs on demo. SASE, but prefers to keep on file. "We usually phone when projects come up."

**CHIAT/DAY ADVERTISING,** 517 S. Olive, Los Angeles CA 90013. (213)622-7454. Vice President/Creative Director: Lee Clow. Creative Secretaries: Diana Barton and Virginia Trujillo. Serves stereo equipment, home loan, life insurance, food, beverage and hotel clients. Uses background music in commercials. Commissions 1 piece/year. Pays by the job.
**How to Contact:** Submit demo tape of previously aired work. Prefers 7 1/2 ips reel-to-reel. SASE. Reports "as soon as possible."

*****CLELAND, WARD, SMITH & ASSOCIATES,** #301, 201 N. Broad St., Winston-Salem NC 27101. (919)723-5551. A/V Director: Roger Shaver. Ad agency. Uses the services of jingle producers for jingles. Pays by the job. Buys all rights.
**How to Contact:** Query with resume of credits. Prefers 7 1/2 ips reel-to-reel with 2-5 songs on demo. SASE, prefers to keep on file.
**Music:** Jingles for a wide variety of accounts: car dealers, insurance companies, department stores, etc.
**Tips:** "Be willing to submit piano and voice demos. Be patient, not pushy, and give reasonable quotes based on our budget."

**COAST TO COAST ADVERTISING, INC.,** 1500 N. Dale Mabry, Box 22601, Tampa FL 33622. (813)871-4731. Vice President: Charles R. Bisbee Jr. Ad agency. Serves retail clients. Uses jingles. Commissions 3 pieces/year. Pays by the job. Buys all rights.
**How to Contact:** Query with resume of credits, submit demo tape of previously aired work or submit demo tape showing jingle/composition skills. Prefers reel-to-reel or cassette. SASE. Reports "immediately if material is solicited. If it's unsolicited, I may not report back."

**COMMUNICATIONS TEAM, INC.,** 3848 Sheffield Dr., Huntingdon Valley PA 19006. (215)947-2400. President: Charles Tucker. Ad agency. Serves real estate, graphics, casino, perfume, insurance, automobile, paint and varnish manufacturer and hospital clients. Uses services of songwriters for jingles and background music. Commissions 3 songwriters and 1-2 lyricists/year. Pays $500-5,000/job. Buys all rights.
**How to Contact:** Query with resume of credits or submit demo tape of previously aired work. Prefers cassette with 4-6 songs on demo. SASE, but prefers to keep material on file. Reports when needs arise.
**Music:** "We need jingles for our accounts, many of whom are real estate oriented, selling entire communities."

**CONRADI, JOHNSON AND ASSOCIATES, INC.,** Suite 1010, 7777 Bonhomme, St. Louis MO 63105. Media Director: Donna Vorhies. Creative Director: Don McKenna. Producer: Richard Ohms. Ad agency, public relations firm and marketing firm. Serves financial, automotive, industrial, hotel and retail clients. Uses services of songwriters and lyricists for jingles and background music for commercials. Commissions 2 songwriters/year. Payment negotiable. Buys all rights.
**How to Contact:** Submit resume of credits or submit demo tape showing jingle/composition skills. Prefers cassette with 4-5 songs on demo. SASE, but prefers to keep material on file. "When the need arises, we'll phone."
**Tips:** "Basically, we look for music, and supply a good portion of the lyrics ourselves. Don't get so involved in the piece that you lose sight of what you're actually selling."

**THE CRAMER-KRASSELT CO.,** 733 N. Van Buren, Milwaukee WI 53202. (414)276-3500. Contact: Creative Director. Serves consumer, financial and service accounts. Uses services of songwriters and music production companies for jingles and background music in commercials. Commissions 5-6 songwriters/year. Pays $2,500-14,000 per job. Usually buys all rights.
**How to Contact:** Send sample reel with cover letter; "everyone in the firm who would be a potential purchaser is made aware of it." Prefers 7 1/2 ips reel-to-reel. Prefers to keep material on file. Responds as needed.

**CREATIVE HOUSE ADVERTISING, INC.,** Suite 200, 24472 Northwestern Hwy., Southfield MI 48075. (313)353-3344. Vice President/Creative Director: Robert G. Washburn. Ad agency and graphics studio. Serves commercial, retail, consumer, industrial and financial clients. Uses services of songwriters and lyricists for jingles and background music for radio and TV commercials. Commissions 1 songwriter and 1 lyricist for 2 pieces/year. Pays $40-60/hour depending on job involvement. Buys all rights.

## Advertising Agencies 267

**How to Contact:** Query with resume of credits, submit tape demo showing jingle/composition skills. Prefers 7½ ips reel-to-reel with 6-12 songs on demo. SASE, but would prefer to keep material on file. Reports in 1 month, if requested.
**Music:** "The type of music we need depends on clients. The range is multi, from contemporary to disco, rock, MOR and traditional."

**CRESWELL, MUNSELL, FULTZ & ZIRBEL, INC.**, Box 2879, Cedar Rapids IA 52406. (319)395-6500. Executive Producer: Terry Taylor. Serves agricultural, retail and industrial clients. Uses individual songwriters and music houses for jingles and background music in commercials and multi-image soundtracks. Commissions 7-8 songwriters for 15 pieces/year. Pays union rate. Buys rights on talent residuals.
**How to Contact:** Submit demo tape of previously aired work. Prefers 7½ or 15 ips reel-to-reel with 7-8 songs maximum on demo. SASE, prefers to keep tape on file. Reports "when we want figures on a job."
**Music:** All types. Likes to hear a good range of music material. Will listen to anything from "small groups to full orchestration."
**Tips:** "Create unique, recognizable melodies."

**JOHN CROWE ADVERTISING AGENCY**, 1104 S. 2nd St., Springfield IL 62704. (217)528-1076. President: John F. Crowe. Ad agency. Clients include industrial, financial, commercial, aviation, retail, state and federal agencies. Uses jingles and background music in commercials. Commissions 3-6 pieces/year. Pays $500-3,000/job. Buys all rights.
**How to Contact:** Submit demo tape of previously aired work. Prefers cassette with 2-4 songs on demo. Does not return unsolicited material. Reports in 1 month.

**CUMMINGS/McPHERSON/JONES & PORTER, INC.**, Suite 204, 510 N. Church St., Rockford IL 61103. (815)962-0615. President: W.W. Jones. Ad agency. Serves business clients. Uses background music in commercials.
**How to Contact:** Submit demo tape showing jingle/composition skills. Prefers 7½ ips reel-to-reel or cassette. SASE. Reports in 1 week.

**\*D'ARCY-MacMANUS & MASIUS, INC.**, Suite 1901, 400 Colony Square, Atlanta GA 30361. (404)892-8722. Ad agency. Serves dairy products, real estate and sports equipment clients. Uses jingles and background music in commercials. Commissions 5-6 pieces/year. Payment based on "budget". Buys copyrights on all material.
**How to Contact:** Submit demo tape of previously aired work. Prefers 7½ ips reel-to-reel. SASE.
**Music:** "About 50% of commissions are for background music and 50% utilize thematic singing."

**D'ARCY-MacMANUS & MASIUS, INC.**, Gateway Tower, 1 Memorial Dr., St. Louis MO 63102. (314)342-8600. Sr. Vice President/Director of Creative Services: Carl Klinghammer. Ad agency. Serves all types of clients. Uses staff for music, but occasionally uses outside material. Uses jingles and background music for commercials. Commissions 30 pieces/year.
**How to Contact:** Submit demonstration tape of previously aired work. Will listen to music done for someone else, but will "*absolutely not* listen to anything done specifically for one of our clients."
**Music:** All types.

**\*DE MARTINI ASSOCIATES**, 414 4th Ave., Haddon Heights NJ 08035. President: Alfred De Martini. Ad agency. Serves industrial, consumer and food clients. Uses services of songwriters and lyricists for jingles, background music for commercials and educational filmstrips. Commissions 4 songwriters and 2 lyricists for 12-15 pieces/year. Pays $50-1,000/job. Buys all rights.
**How to Contact:** Query with resume of credits or submit demo tape showing jingle/composition skills. "Include typewritten or printed lyric sheet." Prefers cassette with 5-10 songs on demo. SASE. Reports "when services are required."
**Music:** Background music for filmstrips and audiovisual purposes, and jingles. "Synthesizer music welcome."
**Tips:** "Be original. Have style. Be industrious. Be brief. Be humble."

**DELTA DESIGN GROUP, INC.**, 518 Central, Greenville MS 38701. (601)335-6148. President: Noel Workman. Ad agency. Serves industrial, financial, agricultural and retail commercial clients. Uses jingles and background music for commercials. Commissions 6 pieces/year. Pays $500-1,500/job. Buys "rights which vary geographically according to client. Some are all rights; others are rights for a specified market only."
**How to Contact:** Submit demo tape showing jingle/composition skills. Prefers 7½ ips reel-to-reel with

3-6 songs on demo. "Include typed sequence of cuts on tape on the outside of the reel box." SASE. Reports in 2 weeks.
**Music:** Needs "30- and 60-second jingles for banks, savings and loans, home improvement centers, fertilizer manufacturers, auto dealers, furniture retailers and chambers of commerce."

**W.B. DONER & CO.**, 2305 N. Charles, Baltimore MD 21218. (301)338-1600. Contact: Jim Dale. Ad agency. Serves consumer product clients. Uses music production houses for jingles and background music in commercials and films for sales meetings. Commissions 12 pieces/year. Pays creative fee and union rates. Rights negotiable.
**How to Contact:** Call for appointment to play tape. Prefers 7½ ips reel-to-reel; 5 minutes maximum. Prefers to keep tape on file.
**Music:** Uses wide range of music.

**EASTMAN ADVERTISING AGENCY**, Suite 601, 6842 Van Nuys Blvd., Van Nuys CA 91405. (213)787-3120. Radio Production Director: Sharon Capell. Ad agency. Serves savings and loan and industrial clients. Uses jingles and background music for commercials. Commissions 1 piece/year. Pays $5,000 maximum/job. Buys all rights.
**How to Contact:** Query, submit demo tape of previously aired work or submit demo tape showing jingle/composition skills. Prefers cassette. SASE. Reports in 2 weeks.
**Music:** "Big beat or country rock orchestration acceptable for presentation, but we prefer upbeat full orchestral arrangements. No rock." Agency sets slogan line or theme for campaign. "Vocals open and close music beds for announcer/copy inserts."
**Tips:** Target audience is 25-55.

**EHRLICH-MANES & ASSOCIATES**, 4901 Fairmont Ave., Bethesda MD 20814. (301)657-1800. Creative Director: Lee Blom. Ad agency. Serves a wide variety of local, regional and national accounts. Uses jingles and background music for commercials. Commissions 5-10 pieces/year. Pays $1,000-6,000/job. Rights purchased vary.
**How to Contact:** Query with resume, submit demo tape of previously aired work or submit demo tape showing jingle/composition skills. Prefers cassette. Does not return unsolicited material. "Submissions kept on file. We will contact with specific jobs in mind."
**Music:** "Musical identity packages for both radio and TV use. Style and instrumentation will vary depending upon the client and use."

*****ESTEY-HOOVER, INC.**, 3300 Irvine Ave, Newport Beach CA 06032. (714)549-8651. Creative Director: Bernie Feldman. Ad agency. Uses the services of songwriters for jingles and background music. Commissions 2 songwriters and 1 lyricist/year. Pays by the job. Buys all rights.
**How to Contact:** Query first; submit demo tape of previous work. Prefers cassette with 5-7 songs on demo. SASE, but prefers to keep on file. Responds as need arises.
**Music:** "Depends upon the specific assignment. We have used, for example, heavy romantic schmaltz and also upbeat middle-of-the-road."
**Tips:** "Get samples on your reel ASAP. Sell yourself as a bargain when you're starting out just to build a reel. In time you'll make plenty of money if you're good."

**DAVID W. EVANS/ATLANTIC, INC.**, 550 Pharr Rd. NE, Atlanta GA 30305. (404)261-7000. Creative Director: Tom Deardorff. Ad agency. Serves primarily industrial and consumer clients. Uses songwriters and music houses for jingles and background music in commercials. Commissions 2 pieces/year. Pays per hour, job or royalty.
**How to Contact:** Submit demo tape of previously aired work. SASE, but prefers to keep material on file.
**Music:** All types.

*****EVANS/CICCARONE, INC.**, 420 NW 42 Ave., Miami FL 33126. (305)445-1433. President: Peter Evans. Ad agency. Uses the services of songwriters and lyricists for jingles and background music. Commissions 3 songwriters and 1 lyricist/year. Payment negotiated. Buys all rights.
**How to Contact:** Query with resume of credits or submit demo tape of previous work. Prefers cassette with 3-6 songs on demo. SASE, but prefers to keep on file. Responds as needs arise.
**Music:** All kinds.

**EXCLAMATION POINT ADVERTISING**, Suite 424, 424 Hart-Albin Bldg., Billings MT 59101. (406)245-6341. Media Director: Corby Skinner. President: Janet Cox. Ad agency. Serves financial, real estate, retail clothing and lumber clients. Uses jingles. Pays on a per-job basis. Buys all rights.
**How to Contact:** Submit demo tape of previously aired work or submit demo tape showing jingle/com-

position skills. Prefers reel-to-reel or cassette. SASE. Reports in 1 month.
**Music:** 30-second jingles.

**\*FAULKNER & ASSOCIATES**, 1601 Broadway, Little Rock AR 72201. (501)375-6923. Creative Director: Ben Hogan. Copywriter: Bob Goss. Ad agency. Uses the services of songwriters, lyricists and music production houses for jingles and background music. Commissions 1-3 songwriters and 1-3 lyricists/year. Payment negotiated. Buys all rights (30% of the time) or one-time rights (70% of the time).
**How to Contact:** Query first; submit demo tape of previous work and arrange a personal interview. Prefers 7½ ips reel-to-reel with 3-6 songs on demo. Does not return unsolicited material; prefers to keep on file. Responds "when the writer's product suits our needs."
**Music:** Suitable work for financial institutions (to project an image), fast food restaurants and retail merchants.
**Tips:** "Know your target market; be creative, but don't obscure your message with too much flash and dash. Also, be patient, be flexible, and keep your prices realistic."

**FREMERMAN-MALCY SPIVAK ROSENFIELD, INC.**, 106 W. 14th St., Kansas City MO 64105. (816)474-8120. Ad agency. Chairman: Marvin Fremerman. Serves consumer, financial and public service clients. Uses jingles and background music in commercials. Commissions 5-7 pieces/year. Pays $500-3,800/job. Buys all rights.
**How to Contact:** Submit demo tape of previously aired work. Prefers 7½ ips reel-to-reel with 8-10 songs on demo. Does not return unsolicited material; keeps material on file.

**FROZEN MUSIC, INC.**, 1169 Howard St., San Francisco CA 94103. (415)626-0501. Production Director: Don Goldberg. Media consultants. Serves entertainment, industrial and recreational clients. Uses services of songwriters for jingles and background music for commercials and theme songs. Commissions 4-5 songwriters and 4-5 lyricists/year. Pays $100 minimum/job. Buys all rights.
**How to Contact:** Query with resume, submit demo tape of previously aired work or submit demo tape showing jingle/composition skills for particular client. "Have commercial experience! No beginners." Prefers cassette with 5-15 songs on demo. "Send only high quality tapes, edited for time and content. No splices. We prefer examples which have been used in productions, with a list of credits." SASE, but prefers to keep material on file. Reports in 4 weeks.
**Music:** "Hard/soft rock, jazz, MOR and country rock. Assignments are mostly commercials for the radio market, with some TV and independent movie scoring."
**Tips:** "Do freebies for experience. Be different, yet commercial."

**GALLAGHER GROUP, INC.**, 1250 Broadway, New York NY 10001. (212)563-3611. President: James Gallagher. Ad agency. Serves automotive, entertainment and other clients. Uses jingles and background music in commercials. Commissions 5-6 pieces/year. Pays $500-2,000/job. Buys all rights.
**How to Contact:** Query with resume of credits. Prefers 7½ ips reel-to-reel.

**GARNER & ASSOCIATES, INC.**, Suite 350, 3721 Latrobe Dr., Charlotte NC 28211. (704)365-3455. Creative Director: Tim Farney. Ad agency. Serves a wide range of clients; client list available on request. Uses services of songwriters for jingles. Pays by the job. Buys all rights.
**How to Contact:** Arrange personal interview or submit demo tape of previous work. Prefers 7½ ips reel-to-reel with enough songs to showcase best work. SASE.
**Music:** All types.

**GEER, DuBOIS, INC.**, 114 5th Ave., New York NY 10017. (212)741-1900. Contact: Ethel Rubinstein. Ad agency. Serves all types of clients including financial, industrial, fashion and packaged goods. Uses music houses for jingles and background music for commercials. Buys original and stock pieces. Commissions 5-6 pieces/year. Buys all rights.
**How to Contact:** Submit demonstration tape of previously aired work. Prefers 7½ ips reel-to-reel. SASE, but prefers to keep tape on file.
**Music:** All types.

**GILLHAM ADVERTISING**, 5th Floor, Desert Plaza, 15 E. 1st S., Salt Lake City UT 84111. (801)328-0281. Producers: Katherine Gygi and Greg McFarlane. Ad agency. Serves financial, real estate, fast food, mall and automobile dealer clients. Uses services of songwriters and local production companies for jingles and background music in commercials and for radio. Commissions 4-6 songwriters and 2 lyricists/year. Payment negotiable. Buys all rights.
**How to Contact:** Submit demo tape of previously aired work. Prefers 7½ ips reel-to-reel with 6-12 songs on demo. Does not return unsolicited material. "Please don't call twice a month. If you're good enough we both know it and we'll call for bids."

**Music:** "Easy, inexpensive 'identity' jingles for a variety of clients."
**Tips:** "Keep us up-to-date on your work with occasional demo tapes and inquiries about our needs. We may be looking for economical, quick turnaround on unique jingles for short term use."

**GOODWIN, DANNENBAUM, LITMAN & WINGFIELD, INC.**, 7676 Woodway, Houston TX 77063. (713)977-7676. Creative Director: Wayne Franks. Ad agency. Serves multi-market, retail, financial, real estate and food products clients. Uses services of songwriters and production companies for jingles, background music for commercials and audiovisual presentations. Commissions 10-15 songwriters/year. Pays $2,500-5,000/job. Buys commercial use rights.
**How to Contact:** Submit demo tape of previously aired work and price structure. Prefers 7½ ips reel-to-reel with 10-20 songs on demo. SASE, but prefers to keep material on file. Responds as needs arise.
**Music:** "We want music that enhances the selling message or image building efforts for our clients. Send proof of performance on tape, showing how you helped solve a marketing problem with your music. Include costs."
**Tips:** "We use lyricists to supply marketing info, idea of style and theme line where applicable."

**GREY ADVERTISING**, 1000 Midwest Plaza E., Minneapolis MN 55402. (612)341-2701. Creative Director: Judy Kirk. Serves retail department store, bookseller, jeweler, bedding, television, media, business, machine and airline clients. Uses songwriters and music houses for jingles and background music in commercials.
**How to Contact:** Submit demo tape of previous work or submit demo tape showing jingle/composition skills. Prefers 7½ ips reel-to-reel with 5-10 songs on demo. SASE, prefers to keep on file.
**Music:** All types.

**GRIFFITH & SOMERS ADVERTISING AGENCY, LTD.**, Suite 2, 1615 Douglas, Sioux City IA 51105. (712)277-3343. President: Margaret Holtze. Ad agency. Uses jingles. Commissions 4 pieces/year. Pays $700-5,000/job.
**How to Contact:** Submit demo tape of previously aired work. Prefers reel-to-reel or cassette with 3-5 songs on demo. SASE. Reporting time varies.
**Music:** 30- to 60-second jingles.

**GROUP TWO ADVERTISING**, 2002 Ludlow St., Philadelphia PA 19103. (215)561-2200. Creative Director: Fred Lavner. Ad agency. Serves industrial, entertainment, financial, real estate, hotel/motel and retail clients. Uses jingles. Commissions 1 songwriter/year. Pays $1,000-4,000/job. Buys one-time rights.
**How to Contact:** Submit demo tape of previously aired work. Prefers 7½ ips reel-to-reel with 5 songs minimum on demo. SASE. "We prefer to keep material on file for future reference. We'll contact the person when a job comes up. A price list (no matter how general) is also helpful for us to keep on file."
**Music:** "Due to the variety of clients we handle, with various budgets, assignments can be of any nature."

*****HART/CONWAY COMPANY, INC.**, 300 Triangle Building, Rochester NY 14604. (716)232-2930. Producer/Director: Peter Tonery. Ad agency. Uses the services of songwriters for jingles. Commissions 2 songwriters and 2 lyricists/year. Pays by the job. Buys all rights.
**How to Contact:** Submit demo tape of previous work. Prefers cassette with 4-9 songs on demo. Does not return unsolicited material; prefers to keep on file. Responds as needs arise.
**Music:** Commercial.
**Tips:** "Keep mailing tapes."

**HEPWORTH ADVERTISING CO.**, 3403 McKinney Ave., Dallas TX 75204. (214)526-7785. President: S.W. Hepworth. Ad agency. Serves financial, industrial and food clients. Uses jingles. Pays by the job. Buys all rights.
**How to Contact:** Query by phone or submit demo tape of previously aired work. Prefers cassette. SASE. Reports in 1 week.

**HERMAN ASSOCIATES**, 488 Madison Ave., New York NY 10022. (212)935-1730. Creative Director: Richard Murnak. Ad agency. Serves industrial, travel, insurance, fashion, electronics and photographic clients. Uses background music for commercials and audiovisual presentations. "To date, we have never purchased original music." Pays $250 minimum/job. Buys one-time rights.
**How to Contact:** Query with resume of credits. Prefers cassette with 3-6 songs on demo. SASE. Reports in 3 weeks.
**Music:** Possible assignments related to travel, photography or fashion; "primarily speculative generic music is also of interest. Music influenced by foreign destinations might be needed."

**Tips:** "Don't over-orchestrate. The simpler, the better. Plan pieces that are adaptable to audiovisuals, not simply commercials."

**HOOD, HOPE & ASSOCIATES**, 8023 63rd Place, Box 35408, Tulsa OK 74153. (918)749-4454. Senior Vice President/Creative Director: J.B. Bowers. Ad agency and public relations firm. Serves industrial, entertainment and financial clients. Uses jingles, background music in commercials and original tracks for sales films. Commissions 3-4 pieces/year. Pays by the job. Buys all rights.
**How to Contact:** Submit demo tape of previously aired work. Prefers 7½ ips reel-to-reel. SASE.

**HOUCK & HARRISON ADVERTISING**, (formerly Claude Harrison and Co.), Box 12487, Roanoke VA 24026. President: Claude Harrison. Ad agency and public relations firm. Serves consumer, industrial and financial clients. Uses services of songwriters for jingles and background music for commercials. "Our copy staff usually writes needed lyrics." Commissions 4-5 songwriters/year. Pays $1,000-6,000/job, "depending on the client's budget. Fee must include scratch track, which must be approved by the client." Buys all rights.
**How to Contact:** Query, submit demo tape of previously aired work or submit demo tape of jingles/compositions for specific client. Prefers reel-to-reel. SASE, but prefers to keep material on file. Reports when needs arise; "depends on decision by client."

*****HUME SMITH MICKELBERRY**, 1000 Brickell Ave., Miami FL 33131. (305)377-8361. Creative Director: Bob Wright. Producer: Juan Gato. Ad agency. Uses the services of songwriters for jingles. Commissions 10 songwriters/year. Pays by the job or by royalty as negotiated. Buys all rights or one-time rights.
**How to Contact:** Submit demo tape of previous work. Prefers 7½ ips reel-to-reel with 6-12 songs on demo. Does not return unsolicited material; prefers to keep on file. Responds as needs arise.
**Music:** All kinds.
**Tips:** "Include all types of music on the demo tape. Call on us personally."

**INGALLS ASSOCIATES, INC.**, 857 Boylston St., Boston MA 02116. (617)437-7000. Broadcast Manager: Beverly Monchun. Ad agency. Serves industrial, financial and retail clients. Commissions 10-15 pieces/year. Pays $7,500 maximum/creative job.
**How to Contact:** Submit demo tape of previously aired work, then call. Prefers 7½ ips reel-to-reel with 5-12 songs on demo. SASE.
**Music:** Needs commercial jingles in all styles.
**Tip:** "Put together a demo which reflects an ability to write a variety of types of commercial music."

**JOHN PAUL ITTA, INC.**, 680 5th Ave., New York NY 10019. (212)541-4460. Contact: Administrative Assistant. Ad agency. Serves package goods clients. Uses jingles and background music for commericals. Commissions 15 pieces/year. Payment negotiable. Rights purchased vary.
**How to Contact:** Submit demo tape of previously aired work. Prefers 7½ ips reel-to-reel. Does not return unsolicited material.

*****THE JAYME ORGANIZATION**, 23200 Chagrin Blvd., Cleveland OH 44122. (216)831-0110. Creative Supervisor: Merritt Johnquest. Ad agency. Uses the services of songwriters and lyricists for jingles and background music. Pays by the job. Buys all rights.
**How to Contact:** Query first; submit demo tape of previous work. Prefers cassette with 4-8 songs on demo. SASE. Reponds by phone as needs arise.
**Music:** Jingles.

**JONATHAN ADVERTISING, INC.**, 205 E. 42nd St., New York NY 10017. President: Jonathan Gubin. Ad agency. Serves consumer products clients. Uses services of songwriters for jingles and background music for commercials. Commissions 2 lyricists/year. Pays by the job.
**How to Contact:** Submit demo tape showing jingle/composition skills. Prefers cassette. Prefers to keep material on file. Responds when the needs arise.
**Tips:** "Keep in touch."

**KETCHUM COMMUNICATIONS**, 4 Gateway Center, Pittsburgh PA 15222. (412)456-3500. Contact: Raymond Werner. Ad agency. Serves consumer and business clients. Uses services of production houses for jingles, background music for commercials and "sometimes" films. Supplies lyricists with "basic strategic directions and background and often excellent lyrics as well." Commissions 10-15 songwriters and 10-15 lyricists for 15-20 pieces/year. Pays $500 minimum/job, "depending on markets." Buys all rights.
**How to Contact:** Query with resume of credits or submit demo showing jingle/composition skills. Pre-

fers 7½ ips reel-to-reel with 7-15 songs on demo. Does not return unsolicited material. "Material is kept on file in our creative department. Will respond only if writer calls."
**Music:** "We use a wide range of styles with memorable melodies and excellent production. Assignments are generally original, specific and with excellent lyrics supplied as a direction."
**Tips:** "Be simple. Be original. Be around."

**DENNIS KING KIZER**, Box 14207, Oklahoma City OK 73113. (405)478-3343. President/Creative Director: Dennis Kizer. Ad agency and production service. Serves fast food, food service and financial clients. Uses jingles. Commissions 5 pieces/year. Pays $500-5,000/job. Buys all rights or one-time rights.
**How to Contact:** Query with resume of credits or submit demo tape of previously aired work. Prefers 7½ ips reel-to-reel. SASE. Reports in 2 weeks.
**Tips:** "Don't be too persistent. We'll yell when we're ready."

**LA GRAVE KLIPFEL CLARKSON, INC., ADVERTISING, PUBLIC RELATIONS, MARKETING**, 1707 High St., Des Moines IA 50309. (515)283-2297. President: Mary Langen. Serves wide range of clients including financial, industrial and retail; client list available on request. Uses services of songwriters for jingles and other needs. Commissions 0-5 songwriters and lyricists/year. Pays by the job. Rights negotiable.
**How to Contact:** "Telephone first then follow up with mailed information." Prefers reel-to-reel or cassette with any number songs on demo. SASE, but prefers to keep material on file.
**Music:** Primarily interested in jingles.

**LANE & HUFF ADVERTISING**, Suite 1200, 707 Broadway, San Diego CA 92101. (619)234-5101. Executive Vice President: Robert V. Maywood. Creative Directors: Bob Nelson and Chuck Dykes. Ad agency. Serves financial clients. Uses services of songwriters for jingles and background music in commercials. Commissions 4 songwriters and 4 lyricists/year. Pays $2,500-30,000/job. Buys all rights.
**How to Contact:** Submit demo tape of previously aired work. Prefers reel-to-reel with 8 pieces on demo. Prefers to keep material on file. Reports in 1 month.
**Music:** Full lyric jingles.
**Tips:** "Include only your best work, even if it is only a few selections."

**LAURENCE, CHARLES & FREE, INC.**, 261 Madison Ave., New York NY 10016. (212)661-0200. Contact: Ellen Goldschmidt. Ad agency. Serves all types of consumer clients. Uses music houses, songwriters and lyricists for jingles and background music in commercials. Pays by the job. Buys all rights.
**How to Contact:** Query. Prefers 7½ ips reel-to-reel; 5 minutes maximum. SASE, but prefers to keep material on file.
**Music:** Music depends on job.

**LD&A ADVERTISING CORP.**, 717 Main St., Batavia IL 60510. (312)879-2000. President: Leo Denz. Ad agency, public relations firm and audiovisual company. Serves consumer and industrial clients. Uses jingles and background music for commercials and audiovisual shows. Payment depends on use. Buys one-time rights or all rights.
**How to Contact:** Query with resume of credits or submit demo tape of previously aired work. Prefers cassettes. "Don't mix 'types' on a single cassette; for example, don't put jingles on the same tape as background music." SASE. "We'll keep material on file for client review. We like to let our clients have a hand in choosing talent for their commercials and films. Usually we select 3 and let them make the final choice."
**Music:** "Jingles: We will furnish the points to cover and their relative importance. Background: We will furnish the edited film with a description sheet of what the music is to accomplish."

**AL PAUL LEFTON CO.**, 71 Vanderbilt Ave., New York NY 10169. (212)867-5100. Director of Broadcast: Joe Africano. Ad agency. Clients include financial, industrial and consumer products clients. Uses jingles and background music for commercials. Commissions 15 pieces/year. Buys all rights.
**How to Contact:** Submit demo tape of previously aired work. Prefers 7½ ips reel-to-reel with 5 songs minimum on demo. SASE. Reports in 3 weeks.

***THE LEMPERT CO.**, Box 61, Belleville NJ 07109. (201)759-2927. Creative Director: Philip Lempert. Ad agency. Uses the services of songwriters and lyricists for jingles. Commissions 5 songwriters/year. Pays by the job. Buys all rights.
**How to Contact:** Submit demo tape of previous work. Prefers cassette with 10-15 songs on demo. SASE, but prefers to keep on file. Responds by phone as needs arise.
**Music:** For commercials for food products.
**Tips:** "Be creative and easy to understand."

## Advertising Agencies 273

**S.R. LEON COMPANY, INC.**, 111 Great Neck Rd., Great Neck NY 11021. (516)487-0500. Contact: Creative Director. Ad agency. Serves industrial, drug, automotive and dairy product clients. Uses jingles and background music for commercials. Commissions vary. Rights purchased are limited to use of music for commercials.
**How to Contact:** Submit demo tape of previously aired work. Prefers 7½ ips reel-to-reel with no length restrictions on demo.
**Music:** Uses all types.

**LEWIS, GILMAN & KYNETTE, INC.**, 1700 Market St., Philadelphia PA 19103. (215)208-3775. Production Head: John Whitaker. Ad agency. Serves industrial and consumer clients. Uses music houses for jingles and background music in commercials. Commissions 4 pieces/year. Pays creative fee asked by music houses.
**How to Contact:** Submit demo tape of previously aired work. "If songwriter has no previous work bought by ad agency, it's OK to submit samples of work." Prefers 7½ ips reel-to-reel. Will return with SASE if requested, but prefers to keep on file.
**Music:** All types.

**LONG, HAYMES & CARR, INC.**, 2006 S. Hawthorne Rd., Box 5627, Ardmore Station, Winston-Salem NC 27103. (919)765-3630. Vice President/Creative Director: Bill Kent. Ad agency. Clients cover "broad spectrum: food, hosiery, banking, industrial." Uses jingles and background music in commercials and films. Commissions 10-15 pieces/year. Pays by the job. Buys all rights.
**How to Contact:** Query with resume of credits. Prefers 7½ ips reel-to-reel. SASE. Reports "as soon as possible."
**Music:** "Primarily jingles for TV; usually for 30-second spots."

**LORD, SULLIVAN & YODER, INC.**, 196 S. Main St., Marion OH 43302. (614)387-8500. Producer: Neil Pynchon. Ad agency. Serves industrial and consumer clients. Uses services of songwriters and music producers for jingles and background music for commercials plus scores for industrial films. Commissions 5-6 songwriters for 6-10 pieces/year. Pays $5,000-20,000/job. Buys all rights.
**How to Contact:** Query with resume of credits, submit demo tape of previously aired work or submit demo tape of jingles/compositions for particular client. Prefers 7½ ips reel-to-reel with 6-12 songs on demo. SASE. Reports "when job possibility arises."
**Music:** Jingles, TV post-scores, movie scores.
**Tips:** "Submit fresh, non-jingly ideas. Show an understanding of what commercial music should do. Stress strong enunciation in lyrics. We welcome—and can sell—totally new ideas as well as unusual adaptations of old forms and techniques. We don't welcome the jingle-mill sound; nothing dull, nothing trite."

***LUNCH TIME PRODUCTIONS**, 66 Centre St., Woodmere NY 11598. Producer: Robert Edelstein. Video production house. Estab. 1983. Uses the services of songwriters, lyricists and independent record labels for complete musical score or song. "We conceive and produce music videos for distribution to sources such as USA Network's NightFlight and MTV." Commissions 3-4 songwriters/year. Payment negotiable. Buys no rights.
**How to Contact:** Query first. Prefers cassette with 4-12 songs on demo. SASE. Responds by phone or letter as needs arise. "Don't call us; we'll call you."
**Music:** "Unique, artistic sound, not heavily influenced by any one artist. Should have something to say lyrically so we may translate that visually. Band should have a developed personality or self-conception to show the world."
**Tips:** "Be unique; do the outrageous and you'll be noticed. Style should be dictated by inner feelings and not outside comparisons. Lyrics and performances should lend themselves to a visual type image where the words bring pictures to life; not just literal descriptions, though. Songs should have a bite to them, something meaningful that adds to the groups' overall effect."

**McCANN-ERICKSON/LOUISVILLE OFFICE**, 1469 S. 4th St., Louisville KY 40208. (502)636-0441. Creative Administrator: Emery Lewis. Ad agency. Serves packaged goods, industrial, service, race track, etc. clients. Uses jingles and background music in commercials. Commissions about 12 pieces broadcast music/year. Buys rights on "13 week or yearly cycles according to AFM codes, etc."

**McCANN-ERICKSON WORLDWIDE**, 201 California St., San Franciso CA 94111. (415)981-2262. Contact: Broadcasting Department. Ad agency. Serves food, chemical, agricultural, industrial and banking clients. Uses music houses mostly; some individual songwriters for jingles and background music in commercials. Commissions 20-25 pieces/year. Pays "by the union." Usually buys all rights.
**How to Contact:** Submit demonstration tape of previously aired work. Prefers 7½ ips reel-to-reel or

cassette. SASE, but prefers to keep material on file.
**Music:** All types.

**McCANN-ERICKSON WORLDWIDE**, Briar Hollow Bldg., 520 S. Post Oak Rd., Houston TX 77056. (713)965-0303. Creative Director: Jesse Caesar. Ad agency. Serves all types of clients. Uses services of songwriters for jingles and background music in commercials. Commissions 10 songwriters/year. Pays production cost and registered creative fee. Arrangement fee and creative fee depend on size of client and size of market. "If song is for a big market, a big fee is paid; if for a small market, a small fee is paid." Buys all rights.
**How to Contact:** Submit demonstration tape of previously aired work. Does not like to deal with agents. Prefers 7½ ips reel-to-reel. "There is no minimum or maximum length for tapes. Tapes may be of a variety of work or a specialization. Very open on tape content; agency does own lyrics." SASE, but prefers to keep material on file. Responds by phone when need arises.
**Music:** All types.

**AL MAESCHER ADVERTISING, INC.**, 25 S. Bemiston, Clayton MO 63105. (314)727-6981. President: Al Maescher. Ad agency. Serves industrial, retail and financial clients. Uses services of songwriters for jingles. Pays by the job. Buys one-time rights, for exclusive use in service area.
**How to Contact:** Submit demo tape of previously aired work. Prefers 7½ ips reel-to-reel or cassette. SASE, but prefers to keep material on file. Responds as needs arise.

**MAISH ADVERTISING**, 280 N. Main, Marion OH 43302. (614)382-1191. Contact: Creative Director. Ad agency. Serves industrial, financial and home building products clients. Uses jingles. Payment negotiable for complete packages, including production. Buys all rights.
**How to Contact:** Submit demo tape of previously aired work. Prefers 7½ ips reel-to-reel.

**MANDABACH & SIMMS, INC.**, Suite 3600, 20 N. Wacker Dr., Chicago IL 60606. (312)236-5333. Creative Director: Burt Bentkover. Copy Director: Linda Masterson. Ad agency. Serves industrial, financial and consumer clients. Uses jingles and background music for commercials. Commissions 5-10 songwriters/year. Pays union scale. "We normally work with complete production houses, not individuals." Rights purchased dependent upon client's needs.
**How to Contact:** Submit demo tape of previously aired work. Prefers 7½ ips reel-to-reel with 6 songs minimum on demo. Does not return unsolicited material.
**Music:** All types for TV, radio and audiovisual presentations.
**Tips:** "Make sure tapes are labeled and dated. We normally don't acknowledge or comment on unsolicited material. We contact only if needed."

*****MASLOW, GOLD & ROTHSCHILD**, 1220 Statler Office Bldg., Boston MA 02116. (617)482-7700. Vice President/Creative: Alan Joseph. Ad agency. Uses the services of production companies for jingles.
**How to Contact:** Query with resume of credits; submit demo tape of previous work. Prefers 7½ ips reel-to-reel or cassette with 7-12 songs on demo. Does not return unsolicited material; prefers to keep on file. Responds by mail, "when I feel we can use the writer."
**Music:** "Types of needs vary by individual needs of client, account, etc."

**METCALFE-COOK & SMITH, INC.**, 4701 Trousdale Dr., Nashville TN 37220. (615)834-6323. Contact: Betty Cook Sanders. Serves industrial and entertainment clients. Uses jingles and background music in commercials. Commissions 2 pieces/year. Payment depends on pre-determined budget.
**How to Contact:** Query first by mail. Prefers 7½ ips reel-to-reel with 3 songs minimum on demo. SASE. Reports in 2 weeks.

**MINTZ & HOKE, INC.**, 10 Tower Lane, Avon CT 06001. (203)678-0473. Creative Director: Dik Haddad. Ad agency and public relations firm. Serves industrial, retail, financial, telephone company and entertainment clients. Uses jingles. Payment depends on client's budget. Buys all rights.
**How to Contact:** Submit demo tape of previously aired work or submit demo tape showing jingles for a particular client. Prefers 7½ ips reel-to-reel or cassette with 5-10 songs on demo. "Tape submitted should show a wide variety of styles." Does not return unsolicited material. "We want to keep tapes on file so that when a jingle comes up, we can refer to tapes to find someone who has the style we need."
**Music:** "We give writers the type of feeling that we want, the slogan and, possibly, all the lyrics."
**Tips:** "We'll call when and if we have something."

**MOHAWK ADVERTISING CO.**, 1307 6th St. SW, Box 1608, Mason City IA 50401. (515)423-1354. President: Jim Grossman. Ad agency. Serves financial and industrial clients, agricultural indus-

tries, fast food restaurants and insurance companies. Uses services of independent songwriters and lyricists for jingles and background music in commercials, films and slide shows. Commissions 6 songwriters and 6 lyricists/year. Pays $1,000-15,000/job; supply fee estimate. Prefers to buy one-time rights.
**How to Contact:** Submit demo tape of previously aired work or submit demo tape showing jingles/compositions for a particular client. Prefers 7½ ips reel-to-reel or cassette with 5-10 songs on demo. Material kept on file for reference.

**MONTGOMERY, ZUKERMAN, DAVIS, INC.**, (formerly MZB Inc.), 1812 N. Meridian St., Indianapolis IN 46202. (317)924-6271. Contact: Creative Director. Ad agency. Uses jingles. Commissions 10-15 pieces/year. Pays $500-1,000/year for demo only. Package payment for final versions needed from demo. Buys all rights.
**How to Contact:** Submit demo tape showing jingle/composition skills. Prefers 7½ ips reel-to-reel with 10-15 songs on demo. SASE. Reports "as needed."
**Music:** Needs vary.

**MOSS ADVERTISING**, Room 1205, 370 Lexington Ave., New York NY 10017. (212)696-4110. Contact: Michael Carieri. Ad agency. Serves all type of clients including utility and restaurant. Uses services of songwriters and lyricists for jingles and background music in commercials. Commissions 2 songwriters and 2 lyricists for about 10 pieces/year. "I give lyricists a rough of the concept, then they come back to me with possibilities and roughs. We work together toward a finished product." Pays by the hour; "negotiates if work particularly desired." Usually buys all rights.
**How to Contact:** Arrange personal interview with M. Carieri and/or submit demo tape of previously aired work. Prefers 10-15 minute cassette which can be kept on file. Does not return unsolicited material and reports "if needs arise and I like what I hear."
**Music:** Uses all types.
**Tips:** Looking for "original sounds with strong, positive sense of harmony."

*****FRANK C. NAHSER, INC.**, 18th Floor, 10 S. Riverside Plaza, Chicago IL 60606. (312)845-5000. Art Buyer: Linda Uhlir. Ad agency. Uses the services of songwriters for jingles and background music. Pays by the job. Buys all rights.
**How to Contact:** Submit demo tape of previous work. Prefers cassette as demo. Does not return unsolicited material; prefers to keep on file.

**NOWAK/BARLOW/JOHNSON ADVERTISING**, 117 Highbridge St., Fayetteville NY 13066. (315)637-9895. Broadcast Production Director: Patrick Scullin. Ad agency. Serves retail, industrial and financial clients. Uses jingles. Commissions 5 pieces/year. Buys all rights.
**How to Contact:** Query with resume of credits or submit demo tape of previously aired work. Prefers 7½ ips reel-to-reel or cassette with 3 songs minimum on demo. SASE. Reports in 1 month.

**OGILVY & MATHER, INC.**, 735 Battery, San Francisco CA 94111. (415)397-1020. Production/Broadcasting Department: Carol Lee Kelliher. Ad agency. Serves financial, entertainment, outdoor apparel and consumer product clients. Uses songwriters and music houses for jingles and background music in commercials. Commissions 20 pieces/year. Pays per job. Buys all rights.
**How to Contact:** Submit demo tape of previously aired work. Prefers 7½ ips reel-to-reel. Returns material if requested with SASE; prefers to keep tape on file.
**Music:** Usually sophisticated.

**OGILVY & MATHER INC.**, 2 E. 48th St., New York NY 10017. (212)907-3895. Vice President/Director of Music: Faith Norwick. Ad agency. Serves all types of clients. Uses services of songwriters for jingles and background music for commercials; uses services of lyricists for jingles. Commissions 20-30 songwriters and 5-10 lyricists for about 50 pieces/year. Pays by the job. "A nationally used jingle pays $5,000-10,000."
**How to Contact:** Send demo tape of previously aired work or demo tape showing jingle/composition skills. Do not include unsolicited jingles relating to clients because of possible legal implications. Prefers 7½ ips reel-to-reel with "bits of songs, 2 minutes is enough. 10 pieces on a jingle demo is sufficient." Likes to file tapes for later review. Does not return unsolicited material. Reports "when something comes up."
**Music:** Uses all types.

**OGILVY & MATHER (CANADA) LTD.**, 1401 McGill College Ave., Montreal, Quebec, Canada H3A 1Z4. (514)849-3601. Contact: Micheline LaRoche. Ad agency. Primarily uses jingles. Commissions 10 pieces/year. Buys all rights.

**How to Contact:** Arrange personal interview to play demo. Prefers 7½ ips reel-to-reel demo.
**Music:** Uses all types depending on client's needs.

**\*OWENS & ASSOCIATES**, #1200, 3443 N. Central, Phoenix AZ 85012. (602)264-5691. Creative Director: Loren Markus. Advertising agency. Uses the services of songwriters for jingles and background music. Commissions 3-6 songwriters/year. Pays $400-10,000/job. Buys all rights.
**How to Contact:** Submit demo tape of previous work. Prefers 7½ ips reel-to-reel or cassette with 5-10 songs on demo. Does not return unsolicited material; prefers to keep on file. Responds as needs arise.
**Music:** All types of music "based on marketing strategies and objectives. We prefer to deal with music people who think advertising."
**Tips:** "Learn advertising communication and strategy."

**\*PACE ADVERTISING**, 260 Amity Rd., Woodbridge CT 06525. Production Manager: Ariana Eaton. Ad agency. Uses the services of lyricists for jingles and background music (radio and TV). Commissions 3 lyricists/year. Pays $200-5,000/job. Buys all rights.
**How to Contact:** Submit demo tape of previous work. Prefers cassette with 3-7 songs on demo. SASE, but prefers to keep on file. Responds by phone as needs arise.
**Music:** Jingles for public transit, real estate, health and banks.

**PEARSON, CLARKE & SAWYER ADVERTISING & PUBLIC RELATIONS**, Suite 681, 5401 W. Kennedy Blvd., Lincoln Center, Tampa FL 33609. (813)877-2425. Copywriter: Bill Brown. Ad agency and public relations firm. Serves industrial, financial, fast food, shelter and packaged goods clients. Uses services of songwriters for jingles and music for audiovisual presentations. Commissions 1-3 songwriters/year. Pays $500-10,000/job. Prefers to buy all rights.
**How to Contact:** Submit demo tape of previously aired work. SASE, but prefers to keep material on file. Reports by phone or mail as needs arise.
**Tips:** "Be willing to work with us on a spec basis; if the client buys, we buy."

**POMEROY PRODUCTIONS**, Division of American Filmworld Company, Suite 179, 8033 Sunset Blvd., West Hollywood CA 90046. Vice President/Media & Music Director: Chip Miller. Motion picture and TV development agency. Serves film and entertainment industry. Uses jingles and background music for commercials and films. Uses services of songwriters and lyricists for film scenes. Commissions 4-6 songwriters and 2-4 lyricists for 10 pieces/year. Pays $60 minimum/hour. Buys all rights.
**How to Contact:** Query with resume, submit demo tape of previously aired work or submit tape demonstrating jingle/composition skills. Prefers cassette with 3-6 songs on demo. "Send lyric sheets, when applicable." SASE, but prefers to keep material on file. Reports in 2-4 weeks.
**Music:** Needs jingles ("catchy, good solid lyrics; contemporary, folk- or rock-oriented, with hooks"); and film and commercial scoring (dramatic or lightly orchestrated arrangements). Avoid "overproduction, pretentiousness and slickness."
**Tips:** "Compose with a market in mind not limited to your own artistic liking."

**PRINGLE DIXON PRINGLE**, 3340 Peachtree Rd. NE, Atlanta GA 30026. (404)261-9542. Creative Director: Dan Scarlotto. Broadcast Producer/Copywriter: Daniel Russ. Ad agency. Serves fashion, financial, fast food and industrial clients; client list available on request. Uses services of songwriters for jingles and background music. Pays by the job. Rights vary, depending on job.
**How to Contact:** Submit tape of previous work. Prefers 7½ ips reel-to-reel. SASE.
**Music:** All types.

**PRO/CREATIVES**, 25 W. Burda Place, Spring Valley NY 10977. President: David Rapp. Ad and promotion agency. Serves consumer products and services, sports and miscellaneous clients. Uses background music in TV and radio commercials. Payment negotiable.
**How to Contact:** Query with resume of credits. SASE.

**\*RAUH, GOOD & DARLO ADVERTISING ASSOC., INC.**, 142 S. Santa Cruz Ave., Los Gatos CA 95030. (408)354-5555. Vice President, Account Services: James Barnes. Ad agency. Uses services of songwriters, lyricists and in-house writers for jingles and background music. Commissions 2 songwriters and 2 lyricists/year. Pays by the job. Buys all rights.
**How to Contact:** Submit demo tape of previous work. Prefers cassette with 5 songs on demo. Does not return unsolicited material; prefers to keep on file. Responds as needs arise.
**Music:** Commercial beds and lyrics; also vocalists.

**READ POLAND, INC.**, Suite 901, 807 Brazos St., Austin TX 78701. Associates/Account Executive: Howard Adkins. Communications consultants. Serves political, corporate, public service, retail and

trade clients. Uses jingles and background music for commercials. Payment negotiable; "it depends on the job and the client—we usually aim for mid-range prices." Rights purchased vary.
**How to Contact:** Query with resume; "include information so that sample tapes can be obtained when and if we have a need." Prefers cassette with 30-second to 2-minute songs on demo. SASE. Reports in 1 month.

**RIVES, SMITH, BALDWIN & CARLBERG, T&R**, Box 27359, Houston TX 77027; 6363 Richmond Ave., Houston TX 77057. (713)783-7640. Contact: Dick Sinreich. Ad agency. Serves primarily consumer, financial and industrial (oil-related) clients. Uses music houses for jingles and background music in commercials. Commissions 25+ pieces/year. Pays by the job. Purchase of rights depends on job.
**How to Contact:** Submit demo tape of previously aired work. Prefers 7½ ips reel-to-reel with 6-7 songs on demo. Returns video tapes with SASE; does not return radio tapes.
**Music:** All types.

**ALBERT JAY ROSENTHAL & CO.**, 400 N. Michigan Ave., Chicago IL 60611. (312)337-8070. Group Creative Director: Harvey Rubin. Ad agency. Serves fashion, consumer foods, kitchen utensils, automotive repair and cosmetics clients. Uses jingles and background music for commercials and sales films. Commissions 15-20 pieces/year. Pays by the job. Buys all rights.
**How to Contact:** Submit demo tape of previously aired work. Prefers 7½ ips reel-to-reel demo 3-5 minutes long. SASE, but prefers to keep material on file.
**Music:** Uses all types; currently has needs for modern and jazzy renditions.

**CHUCK RUHR ADVERTISING, INC.**, 10709 Wayzata Blvd., Box 9375. Minneapolis MN 55440. (612)546-4323. Contact: Art Director. Ad agency. Serves consumer and industrial clients; client list available on request. Uses services of songwriters for jingles and background music. Commissions 5-10 songwriters and 2-5 lyricists/year. Initial fee negotiated, after that pays union scales. Pays residuals for subsequent use of material.
**How to Contact:** Submit demo tape of previous work. Prefers cassette as demo. Reports "when needed."
**Tips:** "Be good and be flexible."

***THE SAVAN COMPANY, INC.**, 670 Community Federal Center, St. Louis MO 63131. (314)965-6565. Creative Director: Glenn Savan. Ad agency. Uses services of songwriters for jingles and background music. Pays by the job. Buys all rights.
**How to Contact:** Query first; submit demo tape of previous work. Prefers 7½ ips reel-to-reel tape or cassette with 2 songs on demo. Does not return unsolicited material; prefers to keep on file.

***SCG ADVERTISING**, Suite 400, 6901 W. 63rd St., Overland Park KS 66202. (913)384-4444. Senior Senior Writer/Associate Creative Director: Liz Craig. Ad agency. Uses services of arrangers and production houses for jingles and background music. Commissions 3 songwriters/year. Pays by the job. Buys all rights.
**How to Contact:** Submit demo tape of previous work. Prefers 7½ ips reel-to-reel tape with 6-15 songs on demo. SASE, but prefers to keep on file. Responds as needs arise.
**Music:** "Jingle beds, electronic 'mood' music keyed to visuals, classical sounds, Gilbert & Sullivan type tunes—maybe anything at all, even black funk or Italian opera style; 30 seconds (for TV); 30 and 60 seconds (radio)."
**Tips:** "Let love of music and your personality be expressed in your work. A style that people will remember is an asset. Gutless, soulless *muzak* is easy to find—be better; dare to be audacious. Don't send standard-sounding commercial music. We have plenty that all sound alike. Send samples of unique styles of music and arrangements showing a range of solutions to ad problems. Vitality, dynamics, and a sense of humor are all important."

**ROBERT D. SCHOENBROD, INC.**, 919 N. Michigan Ave., Chicago IL 60611. (312)944-4774. Vice President: Jerry R. Germaine. Ad agency. Serves all types of clients. Uses services of songwriters for jingles and background music in commercials, trade shows and presentations. "Generally write guide for lyricist listing points to cover and/or emphasize." Payment negotiable; "usually music writers have their own schedules." Buys all rights.
**How to Contact:** Query, submit demo tape of previously aired work or submit demo tape showing jingle/composition skills. Prefers 7½ ips reel-to-reel or cassette. "Do not submit unsolicited material."
**Tips:** "Shun the ordinary. Use simple, clear melody line and lyrics people can understand at first hearing."

**\*SHAFFER SHAFFER SHAFFER, INC.**, 226 Hanna Bldg., Cleveland OH 44115. (216)566-1188. President: Harry Gard Shaffer, Jr. Ad agency. Uses services of songwriters and lyricists for jingles and background music. Commissions 8-14 songwriters and 3-7 lyricists/year. Pays $1,000-12,500 + /job. Buys all rights.
**How to Contact:** Query with resume of credits. Prefers 7½ ips reel-to-reel with 6-12 songs on demo. SASE, but prefers to keep on file. Responds as needs arise.

**SHAILER DAVIDOFF ROGERS, INC.**, Heritage Square, Fairfield CT 06430. (203)255-3425. Broadcast Manager: Barbara Boyd. Ad agency. Serves consumer and financial clients. Uses jingles and background music for commercials. Commissions 6-8 pieces/year. Pays $400-4,500/job. Rights purchased vary.
**How to Contact:** Submit demo tape of previously aired work. Prefers 7½ ips reel-to-reel with 4 songs on demo. Does not return unsolicited material.

**SIMONS ADVERTISING & ASSOCIATES**, 29200 Southfield Rd., Southfield MI 48076. (313)559-7977. Creative Director: Bill Keller. Ad agency. Serves retail clients. Uses jingles and background music for commercials. Pays $750 minimum/job. Buys all rights.
**How to Contact:** Query with resume or submit demo tape of previously aired work. Prefers 7½ ips reel-to-reel.

**EDGAR S. SPIZEL ADVERTISING, INC.**, 1782 Pacific Ave., San Francisco CA 94109. (415)474-5735. President: Edgar S. Spizel. Ad agency, public relations firm and TV/radio production firm. Serves consumer clients "from jeans to symphony orchestras, from new products to political." Uses background music in commercials. Pays $1,500 minimum/job. Buys all rights.
**How to Contact:** Query. Prefers cassette with 3-5 songs on demo. Does not return unsolicited material.

**STAUCH-VETROMILE, INC.**, 55 S. Brow St. E., Providence RI 02914. (401)438-0614. Creative/Copy Director: Kathy Silvestri. Ad, marketing and public relations firm. Serves industrial, financial, retail and consumer clients. Uses services of songwriters and sound production companies for jingles and background music in commercials. Pays by the hour or job. Rights purchased negotiable.
**How to Contact:** Query with resume, or submit demo tape of previously aired work. Prefers reel-to-reel or cassette with 1-10 songs on demo. SASE, but prefers to keep material on file. Reports in 2-3 weeks or "in most cases, following a decision to use a particular sound(s) for a client. Material is returned to songwriters if agency is provided with SASE and the songwriter requests return of material."
**Tips:** "Keep plugging. Learn to tap the market's attitude toward certain products and/or services to grasp the music and lyrics that are best for convincing the buyers."

**STEVENS, INC.**, 809 Commerce Bldg., Grand Rapids MI 49502. (616)459-8175. Creative Director: Burl Robins. Ad agency. Uses jingles and background music for commercials. Commissions 1-3 pieces/year. Pays $2,000 minimum/job. Buys all rights.
**How to Contact:** Submit demo tape of previously aired work. Prefers 7½ ips reel-to-reel with 5 songs on demo. SASE. Reports in 3 weeks.

**STOLZ ADVERTISING CO.**, 7701 Forsyth Blvd., St. Louis MO 63105. (314)863-0005. Contact: Marv Gold. Ad agency. Serves consumer product clients. Will provide names of clients on request but has no formal list prepared. Uses services of songwriters for jingles and background music in commercials. Commissions 3 songwriters/year. Pays by the job. Rights purchased varies.
**How to Contact:** Submit demo tape of previous work. Prefers ¼" reel-to-reel or cassette with enough songs to showcase songwriter's best work. SASE, but prefers to keep material on file. Reports "when needed."
**Music:** Needs vary.

**STONE & ADLER, INC.**, 150 N. Wacker Dr., Chicago IL 60606. (312)346-6100. Vice Chairman/Chief Creative Officer: William Waites. Ad agency and direct marketing firm. Serves industrial, entertainment and financial clients. Uses music houses for background music in commercials. Commissions 3-4 pieces/year. Pays according to budget. Usually buys one-time rights.

---

**Market conditions are constantly changing! If this is 1985 or later, buy the newest edition of *Songwriter's Market* at your favorite bookstore or order directly from Writer's Digest Books.**

**How to Contact:** Submit demo tape of previously aired work. Prefers reel-to-reel or cassette. Returns material if requested with SASE; prefers to keep tape on file.
**Music:** All types.

**SULLIVAN & BRUGNATELLI**, 300 E. 42nd St., New York NY 10017. (212)986-4200. Contact: John Benetos. Ad agency. Serves beverage, food, medicinal and cosmetic clients. Uses music houses and songwriters for jingles. Usually buys all rights.
**How to Contact:** Arrange personal interview to play tape. Prefers 1/4" reel-to-reel; 15 minutes maximum. SASE, but prefers to keep tape on file.
**Music:** All types.

**SULLIVAN AND/OR HAAS**, (formerly Bozell & Jacobs), 1177 Virginia Ave., Atlanta GA 30306. (404)874-2330. Contact: Ken Haas. Creative and production firm. Serves consumer, packaged goods, financial and banking clients. Uses services of independent songwriters and lyricists. "I never use 'jingles.' I use music. And there *is* a difference." Uses music houses for "musical beds and full songs depending upon the concept." Commissions 4-5 songwriters and 3-4 lyricists/year.
**How to Contact:** "Representative should call and set up appointment to play reel. If no reel is available, don't bother." Prefers cassette. SASE, but prefers to keep material on file. Responds if and when the needs arise.
**Music:** Type of music needed depends upon project.
**Tips:** "Just be great at what you do. Act like mensch."

**THOMAS ADVERTISING**, Box 1327, Studio City CA 91604. (213)908-9080. President: Thomas Waller. Media Buyer: Sandy Ward. Ad agency. Serves entertainment and publishing clients. Uses jingles, background music for commercials and movie scores. Commissions 50 pieces/year. Pays $125 minimum/job or 1-2% royalty. Buys all rights.
**How to Contact:** Submit demo tape showing jingle/composition skills. Prefers cassette with minimum 3 songs on demo. SASE. Reports "as soon as possible."
**Music:** C&W and MOR.

**J. WALTER THOMPSON CO.**, 2828 Tower Place, 3340 Peachtree Rd. NE, Atlanta GA 30026. (404)266-2828. Creative Director/Vice President: Bruce Levitt. Ad agency. Serves financial, automotive, sporting goods and pest control clients. Uses music houses for jingles and background music in commercials.
**How to Contact:** Submit demo tape of previously aired work or demo tape showing jingles/composition skills. Prefers 7 1/2 ips reel-to-reel with 6 songs maximum. Returns material if requested with SASE; prefers to keep tape on file.
**Music:** Types vary with needs and campaign. Sometimes wants music plus lyrics, and sometimes needs just music for lyrics written inhouse.

**J. WALTER THOMPSON CO.**, 17000 Executive Plaza Dr., Dearborn MI 48126. (313)336-6900. Executive Producer: Jerry Apoian. Ad agency. Serves industrial, recreational, banking, media clients and major car companies. Uses music houses and individual songwriters for jingles (often writes own lyrics) and background music in commercials. Commissions 30-40 pieces/year. Pays union rates. "If music is written for specific needs of client, buys all rights."
**How to Contact:** Call first about demo tape. Prefers 7 1/2 ips reel-to-reel. Use best works. SASE.
**Music:** All types.

**JERRE R. TODD & ASSOCIATES**, 1800 Texas Bldg., Fort Worth TX 76102. (817)429-0348. Contact: Creative Director. Ad agency and public relations firm. Serves financial, oil, gas and automobile dealership clients. Uses jingles. Commissions 5-6 pieces/year. Pays $1,000-15,000/job. Buys all rights.
**How to Contact:** Submit demo tape of previously aired work. Prefers 7 1/2 ips reel-to-reel or cassette. Does not return unsolicited material. "We might hold for future use."
**Music:** "Needs jingles for financial, car dealers and other clients with assortment of full-sing and donuts in both 30- and 60-second lengths."

*****TRIAD**, 124 N. Ontario St., Toledo OH 43624. (419)241-5110. Creative Writer: Karen Hamer. Ad agency. Uses services of songwriters for jingles. Commissions 1-2 songwriters/year. Pays $1,500 maximum/job. Buys all rights or territorial rights.
**How to Contact:** Submit demo tape of previous work. Prefers cassette with 5-12 songs on demo. SASE, but prefers to keep on file. Responds by phone as needs arise.
**Music:** Jingles in varied styles.
**Tips:** "Be willing to do work on speculation."

**CALDWELL VAN RIPER**, 1314 N. Meridian, Indianapolis IN 46202. (317)632-6501. Executive Creative Director: Deborah Karnowsky. Ad agency and public relations firm. Serves industrial, financial and consumer/trade clients. Uses jingles and background music for commercials. Commissions 25 pieces/year. Buys all rights.
**How to Contact:** Submit demo tape of previously aired work or submit demo tape showing jingle/composition skills. Prefers 7½ ips reel-to-reel. SASE. Reports "as soon as possible."

**VANDECAR, DEPORTE & JOHNSON**, 255 Lark St., Albany NY 12210. (518)463-2153. Production Director: Marc W. Johnson. Ad agency. Serves financial, automotive, consumer and other clients. Uses services of lyricists and music houses for jingles, background music in commercials and filmtracks. Commissions 15 pieces/year. Pays by the job. Rights purchased vary.
**How to Contact:** Submit demo tape showing jingle/composition skills. Prefers 7½ ips reel-to-reel with 3 songs minimum on demo. SASE, but prefers to keep material on file "but will dub off and send back if specified." Responds by phone when needs arise.
**Music:** Jingle work, music tracks, demo work, chart writing, conceptualization and assistance on assignments.

**VANGUARD ASSOCIATES, INC.**, 15 S. 9th St., Minneapolis MN 55402. (612)338-5386. Creative Director: Christopher Schmitz. Account Executive: Thornton Jones. Ad agency. Serves consumer product clients; client list available on request. Uses services of songwriters "mostly for the arranging of jingles; some background music for commercials." Pays creative fee on project basis plus more, depending on number of musicians, singers, etc. Buys all rights.
**How to Contact:** Submit demo tape of previous work. Prefers 7½ ips reel-to-reel with enough songs to display best work. SASE, but prefers to keep material on file.
**Music:** All types but "we do a lot of radio work aimed at the black market so that black sound is important with us."

*****VANSANT DUGDALE**, World Trade Center, Baltimore MD 21202. (301)539-5400. Broadcast Producer: Sherie Levin. Ad agency. Uses services of songwriters for jingles and background music. "Generally, the composer writes or has a lyricist who works with him on lyrics or agency works on lyrics." Commissions 5-10 songwriters/year. Pays $2,000-20,000/job. Buys one-time rights.
**How to Contact:** Submit demo tape of previous work. Prefers 7½ ips reel-to-reel tape with 10-20 songs on demo. Does not return unsolicited material; prefers to keep on file. Responds "when we are considering a writer for an assignment."
**Music:** All types. "We describe concept and 'feel' of what we are looking for; sometimes, we provide lyric concept lines."
**Tips:** "Remember that work must communicate product, service and the name as well as concept."

**STERN WALTERS/EARLE LUDGIN, INC.**, 150 E. Huron St., Chicago IL 60611. (312)642-4990. Broadcast Production Supervisor: Marsha Pollock. Ad agency. Serves consumer clients. Uses services of songwriters for jingles and background music in commercials. Commissions 10 songwriters/year. Pays $500 minimum/job.
**How to Contact:** Arrange personal interview or submit demo tape. Prefers 7½ ips reel-to-reel. SASE, but prefers to keep material on file. "We respond when we need information, when songwriters ask for something or when we want their services."

**WARWICK, WELSH & MILLER**, 875 3rd Ave., New York NY 10022. (212)751-4700. Broadcast Manager: Lou Kohuth. Ad agency. Serves consumer products clients. Uses jingles and background music for commercials. Commissions 50 pieces/year. Pays $250-7,500/job. Buys all rights.
**How to Contact:** Submit demo tape of previously aired work. Prefers 7½ ips reel-to-reel tape, 5-7 minutes long. Does not return unsolicited material.

**TUCKER WAYNE & CO.**, Suite 2700, 230 Peachtree St. NW, Atlanta GA 30303. (404)522-2383. Contact: Mr. McNulty or Markay Wiley. Serves financial, industrial, software, textile, food and tobacco clients. Uses services of songwriters and lyricists for jingles and background music in commercials. Commissions 5-50 pieces/year. Pays by the job. Buys all rights.
**How to Contact:** Call for appointment to listen to demo. Prefers 7½ ips reel-to-reel; tape should be no longer than 7-8 minutes. Prefers to keep tape on file.
**Music:** All types.

**WEBER, COHN & RILEY**, 444 N. Michigan Ave., Chicago IL 60611. (312)527-4260. Contact: Creative Director. Ad agency. Serves real estate, financial and food clients. Uses jingles and background music for commercials. Commissions 3-5 pieces/year. Pays $1,000 minimum/job. Rights purchased vary.

**How to Contact:** Submit demo tape of previously aired work. Prefers 7½ ips reel-to-reel with 3-8 spots on tape. "We listen to and keep a file of all submissions, but generally do not reply unless we have a specific job in mind."
**Music:** "We expect highly original, tight arrangements that contribute to the overall concept of the commercial. We do not work with songwriters who have little or no previous experience scoring and recording commercials."
**Tips:** "Don't aim too high to start. Establish credentials and get experience on small local work, then go after bigger accounts. Don't oversell when making contacts or claim the ability to produce any kind of 'sound.' Producers only believe what they hear on sample reels."

**WEBSTER & HARRIS ADVERTISING AGENCY**, Suite 1, 1313 Broadway, Lubbock TX 79401. (806)747-2588. Contact: Account Executive. Ad agency and public relations firm. Serves financial, industrial, automobile and agricultural clients. Uses jingles and background music for commercials. Commissions 5 pieces/year. Pays $1,200-2,000 maximum/job. Buys all rights.
**How to Contact:** Submit demo tape of previously aired work or demo tape showing jingle/composition skills. Prefers 7½ ips reel-to-reel with 1-10 songs on demo. SASE. Reports in 1 week.
**Music:** "We need all types of music—C&W, top 40, etc. Before any songwriter could begin working for us, they'd have to know the client inside out, the problems involved and what type of background music/jingles would fit the products. To gain this, they would have to work closely with us and the client."

**WILDRICK & MILLER, INC.**, 350 5th Ave., New York NY 10118. President: Donald Wildrick. Ad agency. Serves industrial clients. Uses background music in commercials. "We have just begun to buy music." Pays by the job. Buys all rights.
**How to Contact:** Query. "We do not accept unsolicited material and we neither evaluate it nor return it."

**WILK & BRICHTA ADVERTISING**, 875 N. Michigan, John Hancock Center., Chicago IL 60611. (312)280-2836. Director of Broadcast Production: Mr. Clair Callihan. Uses services of songwriters for jingles, background music in commercials and longer films/filmstrips. Commissions 2-4 songwriters for 3-4 pieces/year. Pays per job. Buys all rights.
**How to Contact:** Query by mail or phone, then submit by mail demonstration tape of previous work with cover letter. Will also review video cassettes and 16mm film but *call* before submitting. Prefers ¼" audio reel-to-reel. Does not return unsolicited material. Reports "only if interested in specific material.".
**Music:** All types.

***WOLKCAS ADVERTISING**, 8 Wade Rd., Latham NY 12201. (518)783-5151. Creative Director: Stewart Sacklow. Ad agency. Uses the services of songwriters and lyricists for jingles, background music and slide shows. Commissions 4-6 songwriters and 3-4 lyricists/year. Pays by the job and buy out. Buys all rights.
**How to Contact:** Submit demo tape of previous work. Prefers 7½ ips reel-to-reel with 3-5 songs on demo. Does not return unsolicited material; prefers to keep on file. Responds when needs arise.
**Music:** Various types depending on client—"from full string orchestra to hard rock and synthesizers."
**Tips:** "Keep submitting updated work; we are always looking for something new and fresh for our clients. Also, we need more short music to accompany IDs for TV."

**WOMACK/CLAYPOOLE/GRIFFIN**, Suite 125, 2997 LBJ Business Park, Dallas TX 75234. (214)620-0300. Contact: Nancy Tharp. Ad agency. Serves petroleum, aviation, financial, insurance and retail clients. Uses services of songwriters for jingles and background music in commercials. Pays by the job. Buys all rights.
**How to Contact:** Submit demo tape of previous work. Prefers reel-to-reel. SASE, but prefers to keep on file.
**Music:** Radio spots and TV background.

**ED YARDANG & ASSOCIATES**, 1 Romana Plaza, San Antonio TX 78205. (512)227-8141. Contact: Creative Director. Ad agency. Uses services of songwriters for jingles. Sometimes uses services of lyricists. Commissions 10-15 pieces/year. Payment varies with job. Buys all rights.
**How to Contact:** Query with resume of credits or submit demo tape of previously aired work. Prefers 7½ ips reel-to-reel or cassette with 2-10 songs on demo. Does not return unsolicited material. Reports in 3 weeks. "If we don't like the material, it is unlikely that we'll report back."
**Music:** Jingles and instrumentals. "We're especially interested in Latin and Hispanic ethnic style. We like jingles with a lot of liveliness and memorability."

**Tips:** "We like lyricists and songwriters who are willing to work very closely with us and are sensitive to our needs."

**YECK BROTHERS GROUP,** Box 225, Dayton OH 45406. (513)294-4000. Ad agency. Serves retail, industrial and financial clients. Uses jingles and background music in commercials and audiovisual productions. Commissions 3-5 pieces/year. Pays $800-4,000/job. Buys all rights.
**How to Contact:** Submit demo tape of previously aired work. Prefers cassette or 7½ ips reel-to-reel with 6-8 songs on demo. Does not return unsolicited material.
**Music:** "Types vary. We provide a guideline sheet that specifies the types of products wanted. Don't try to sell us a stock track or rewrite to some other hot jingle in another market."

**YOUNG & RUBICAM,** 3435 Wilshire Blvd., Los Angeles CA 90010. (213)736-7400. Contact: Marcy Weimberg. Ad agency. Serves financial, food, beverage, and various product clients. Uses the services of independent songwriters for jingles and background music in commercials; lyricists to work with established arranger/composers. Commissions 6-7 songwriters and 1-2 lyricists/year. Pays by royalty and creative service. Buys all rights.
**How to Contact:** Submit demo tape of previously aired or publicly performed work showing variation of composition skills. Prefers reel-to-reel. Does not return material; prefers to keep tape on file.
**Music:** All types.

# Audiovisual Firms

There are many opportunities for the songwriter in the audiovisual field. Schools, government, business and industry, advertising agencies, libraries, publishers and organizations use audiovisuals to teach, inform or sell. Other audiovisual presentations are meant primarily to entertain and are geared with the mass audience in mind: documentary films; network, syndicated and local television; and feature-length movies.

Companies listed in this section are open to the fresh material of top-notch songwriters. Listings for specific companies will tell you what facet of the audiovisual field and what type of clients they serve.

To learn all you need to know about writing for and working with audiovisual markets, read James Dearing's article on "Writing for the Local Alternative Music Markets" in front of this book.

Additional names of audiovisual firms can be found in the *Audiovisual Market Place* (R.R. Bowker) and *Audio-Visual Communications* magazine (United Business Publications, Inc.).

**\*ADCO PRODUCTIONS**, 7101 Biscayne Blvd., Miami FL 33138. (305)751-3118. Creative Director: Bob Arbogast. Clients includes TV, business and industry. Uses the services of music houses for scoring of videotape, films and slide presentations. Commissions 20-30 composers/year. Pays $500-2,500/job. Buys all rights or one-time rights.
**How to Contact:** Submit demo tape of previous work. Prefers 7½ ips reel-to-reel or cassette with 3-10 songs on demo. SASE. Reports in 3 weeks.

**ARZTCO PICTURES, INC.**, 15 E. 61st St., New York NY 10021. (212)753-1050. President/Producer: Tony Arzt. Clients include industry, government and advertising agencies. "We're currently producing feature films." Uses services of music houses and songwriters for film scores. Commissions 20-50 pieces/year. Pay negotiable "depending on composer and the project." Buys all rights or one-time rights.
**How to Contact:** Submit demo tape of previously aired work or submit demo tape of composition skills. Prefers cassette with 6-12 songs on demo. "We prefer to keep tapes on file, then review them when a project comes up." Reports "immediately, if appropriate for a job on hand."
**Music:** "We generally prefer small group sound—no large orchestras with too much brass and strings. Good beat and melody are important."

**CLIFF AYERS ENTERPRISES**, 62 Music Square W., Nashville TN 37203. (615)327-4538 and 361-7902. President: Cliff Ayers. Audiovisual firm, music publisher and record company. Uses services of songwriters and lyricists for music and lyrics for commercials. Commissions 200 pieces/year. Pays 50% minimum royalty.
**How to Contact:** Submit demonstration tape of previous work or tape demonstrating composition skills. Prefers cassette with 3 songs on demo. SASE. Reports in 2 weeks. Free book catalog.
**Music:** C&W, pop, R&B and R&R.

**BACHNER PRODUCTIONS, INC.**, 360 1st Ave., New York NY 10010. (212)354-8760. President: A. Bachner. Motion picture production company. Clients include users of TV film and videotape commercials and industrial and sales training films. Uses services of music houses and songwriters for commercial jingles and background music for TV and inhouse use. "Assignments are for music only or music and lyrics for commercials. Background music is scored to film." Commissions 6-10 pieces/year. Pays $750-5,000/job. Buys all rights or one-time rights.
**How to Contact:** Query with resume of credits. Prefers 7½ or 15 ips reel-to-reel. Does not return unsolicited material. Reports in 1 month.
**Tips:** "Be able to supply complete package."

**BELLE STREET PRODUCTIONS, INC.**, 3620 Bell St., Kansas City MO 64111. (816)753-4376. Producer: Bill Foard. Chief Engineer: Larry Johnson. Clients include business and promotional firms. Uses services of songwriters for music in radio and TV commercials. Payment negotiable. Rights purchased vary.

**How to Contact:** Submit demo tape of previously aired work. Prefers 7½ ips reel-to-reel or cassette with 4-5 songs on demo. SASE. Reports in 1 week.

**ROBERT BERNING-FILM PRODUCTIONS**, 710 Papworth Ave., Metairie LA 70005. (504)834-8811. Audio Director: Gary Holland. Motion picture production company. Clients include advertising agencies, industrial firms and corporations. Uses services of music houses and songwriters for background music, musical scores in films, original songs for themes, music scoring, TV and radio commercials, international sales films, and safety/training films; uses lyricists for lyrics and themes. Commissions 10 composers and 4 lyricists/year for 10 pieces/year. Pays by the job, $1,000-10,000. Buys all rights or one-time rights.
**How to Contact:** Submit demo tape of previous work or query with resume of credits. Prefers 7½ ips reel-to-reel with 4 songs minimum on tape. SASE. Reports in 1 month.
**Music:** Uses music for TV and radio commercials, multi-media productions and films.
**Tips:** "Submit examples of past work and work within budgetary range."

*__BURST/GOSA PRODUCTIONS, INC.__*, Box 5354, Atlanta GA 30307. (404)523-8023. Vice President: Cheryl Gosa. Audiovisual firm and motion picture production company. Estab. 1981. Clients include business, industry, churches, schools, hospitals, government. Uses the services of music houses, songwriters and composers for musical backgrounds for filmstrips and slide shows, film scores and theme songs; and music with an international feel by country; rarely uses lyricists, but possibly for public service announcements. Commissions 10-20 composers/year. Pays $500 minimum/job. Buys all rights.
**How to Contact:** Query with resume of credits; submit demo tape of previous work. Prefers cassette with 5-10 songs on demo. Does not return unsolicited material; "we like to keep material on file until a job requiring music arises."
**Music:** "Upbeat, light, industrial, contemporary, lyrical, sensitive, subtle and compassionate. Usually for 1-5 instruments. Rarely use lyrics. A typical filmstrip or slide show assignment would be 3-5 short (4 minutes) pieces of a genre, but each unique. Film tracks are more complex with needs according to individual films (14-90 minutes)."
**Tips:** "Be pleasantly available, i.e., check in periodically, but don't call every month. Exhibit flexibility and creativity in intuiting the musical needs of a script. Be open to changes—we rarely go with first drafts on anything."

*__CINE DESIGN FILMS__*, 255 Washington St., Denver CO 80203. (303)777-4222. Producer: Jon Husband. Motion picture production company. Clients include business, industry and documentaries. Uses the services of music houses and songwriters. Commissions 10 composers and 2 lyricists/year. Pays by the job. Buys all rights or one-time rights.
**How to Contact:** Query with resume of credits; submit demo tape of previous work. Prefers 7½ ips reel-to-reel or cassette; finished, film or tape with 5-15 songs on demo. Does not return unsolicited material.
**Music:** "Our needs could be from a full score to an individual cut—depending on our needs at the time."
**Tips:** "Keep in touch and be flexible."

**CINETUDES FILM PRODUCTIONS**, 293 W. 4th St., New York City NY 10014. (212)966-4600. Producer: Christine Jurzykowski. Motion picture production company. Clients include television. Uses services of songwriters for musical scores in films. Commissions variable number pieces/year. Pays by the job. Buys all rights.
**How to Contact:** Submit tape demonstrating composition skills. Prefers reel-to-reel with 2-4 songs on demo. "Recommendations are helpful." SASE. Reports in 2 weeks.
**Music:** Film music.

**CLARUS MUSIC, LTD.**, 340 Bellevue Ave., Yonkers NY 10703. (914)591-7715. President: Selma Fass. Contact: New Product Department. Music publisher and record company (educational). Clients include educational and retail markets. Uses services of songwriters and lyricists for musical plays (script and songs) for the educational market. Commissions 2-3 composers and 2-3 lyricists/year. Pays standard royalties. Buys all rights.
**How to Contact:** Query with resume of credits or submit demo tape of previously aired work or submit demo tape showing flexibility of composition skills. Prefers 7½ ips reel-to-reel or cassette with 3-20 songs on the tape. SASE. Reports in 3 weeks. Free book catalog.
**Music:** Various kinds of music.
**Tips:** "Submit material for consideration; no assignments until we've communicated and an agreement is made between our company and the writer(s)."

# Close-up

**Alan and Marilyn Bergman**
Lyricists

Alan and Marilyn Bergman ask, in a lyric, *how do you keep the music playing?* For them, keeping the music playing means writing lyrics for movies like *Tootsie* and *Yentl*, the Oscar-winning *The Way We Were* and *The Windmills of Your Mind*. It also means hard work, research, and sometimes round-the-clock writing. "Nobody even hears a song until we are happy with it," says Mrs. Bergman.

With three of the five Oscar nominations for best song in 1983, the Bergmans say lyrics demand continuous writing and rewriting. "The more you write, the more you find the alternatives are endless," says Mr. Bergman.

Each director, producer and film gives the lyricists a new set of demands, but rarely do film producers or directors ever suggest changes in Bergman lyrics once they're written. That's because, says Mrs. Bergman, "By the time they do hear them, they're hearing something that is the result of a distillation process and of exploring a lot of possibilities."

The Bergmans wrote the lyrics for nine songs in *Yentl* in four months but spent nearly a year of research before writing these words. For other films, like *Tootsie* for instance, they had five days to write two songs.

"The first criterion is that the song serves the film, that it be an extension of the screenplay," says Mrs. Bergman.

Does that pose problems, one asks. "That's what it's all about. That's why we choose to do it. That's the challenge," she says.

The Bergmans stress lyricists must know the film/theater music classics but must find their own style and voice. "The most common mistake young writers make is that they imitate what they hear. You have to say it your way," says Mr. Bergman.

As aspiring songwriters, the Bergmans musicalized dramatic moments from books and plays—before landing any assignments. "Just as an actor has to go to class and work on scenes before he's actually hired to act in a production, so lyric writers have to go to class, or create their own class, and work on song scenes and dramatic writing to prepare themselves for that kind of work."

Mrs. Bergman admits there are moments when the blank pages can stare at a lyricist. But then writing lyrics brings a "joy at having created something that wasn't there before."

In conversation, the Bergmans take turns, enhancing one another's words as if singing a duet. They admit that this is also the case when they write.

"You have to *need* to write. Wanting is not enough. Needing to write gives you a protective coverage," says Mr. Bergman.

"Otherwise," adds Mrs. Bergman. "There are too many deterrents."

—Paula Deimling

**COCONUT GROVE PRODUCTIONS**, Suite 104, 3100 Carlisle Plaza, Dallas TX 75204. (214)748-2755. Producers: Tim Pugliese and Bruce Halford. Clients include business firms. Uses services of music houses for film and TV scores, business communications films, TV commercials and TV programs. Commissions 1 lyricist for 2 pieces/year. Pays $250-10,000/job. Buys all rights.
**How to Contact:** Submit demo tape of previously aired work with cover letter explaining prices. Prefers cassette with 5-10 songs on demo. Does not return unsolicited material. Reports "only if we are going to use the person."
**Music:** Uses soundtracks for business films. Needs "anything from full instrumentals to synthesized music."

**THE CREATIVE ESTABLISHMENT**, 115 W. 31st St., New York NY 10001. (212)563-3337. Vice President and General Manager: Ron Osso. Audiovisual firm and motion picture production company. Clients include business and industry. Uses services of music houses, songwriters for scores in films, themes for business meetings; lyricists for writing lyrics for themes. Commissions 10-15 pieces/year. Pays by the job. Buys all rights and one-time rights.
**How to Contact:** Query with resume of credits; submit demonstration tape of previous work or tape demonstrating composition skills. Prefers 7½ ips reel-to-reel with 5-10 songs on demo. "All material is kept on file."

*****D.S.M. PRODUCERS**, Suite #602, 161 W. 54th St., New York NY 10019. (212)245-0006. Contact: Suzan Bader. Scoring service, music/sound effects library and record production. Clients include industrial (Motorola), publishers (song demos), groups (recording) and commercials (radio and TV). Uses the services of songwriters and lyricists. Payment negotiable "as per agreement with D.S.M. producers." Rights purchased depends on client.
**How to Contact:** Submit demo tape of previous work. Prefers cassette or video cassette with 1-4 songs on demo. SASE. Reports in 3 weeks. Catalog $3.60.
**Music:** Country, rock, R&B, urban contemporary, AOR, classical, etc.

**DCA FILM/VIDEO PRODUCTIONS**, 424 Valley Rd., Warrington PA 18976. (215)343-2020. Executive Producer: Hal Fine. Audiovisual firm and motion picture production company. Clients include business, industry and advertising agencies. Uses services of music houses for musical scores in film, TV commercials, background music, etc. Commissions 3-4 pieces/year. Pays by the job. Rights vary, depending on job.
**How to Contact:** Submit demo tape of previous work or tape demonstrating composition skills. Prefers 7½ ips reel-to-reel as demo. SASE. Reports in 3 weeks. Free catalog.

*****DEL PAESKE PRODUCTIONS, INC.**, 5820 W. St. Paul Ave., Milwaukee WI 53213. (414)257-3321. Senior Producer/President: Del Paeske. Audivisual firm and slides, film and video producer. Clients include industry, commercial and advertising agencies. Uses the services of songwriters for scoring and background music. Commissions 5-6 composers/year. Pays $150-1,000/job. Buys all rights.
**How to Contact:** Query with resume of credits; submit demo tape of previous work. Prefers 7½ ips reel-to-reel or cassette with 3-7 songs on demo. SASE. Reports in 1 month.
**Music:** Uses music "to back electro-mechanical machinery operations or to set a mood;" 5-6 minutes.

*****DEPT. OF MEDIA SERVICES, DIMOND LIBRARY**, University of New Hampshire, Durham NH 03824. (603)862-2240. Filmmaker: Gary Samson. Educational media producer. Clients include schools and colleges. Uses the services of songwriters for music scores for 16mm films and slide tapes. Commissions 4 composers/year. Pays $300-1,200/job. Buys all rights.
**How to Contact:** Submit demo tape of previous work or tape demonstrating composition skills. Prefers cassette with 4-9 songs on demo. SASE. Reports in 1 month. Free catalog.
**Music:** Scores for films which deal with New England history and culture; period music as well as contemporary.
**Tips:** "Be versatile and reasonably priced. Also, research music possibilities for a project before meeting with us."

**D4 FILMS STUDIOS, INC.**, 109 Highland Ave., Needham Heights MA 02194. (617)444-0226. President: Stephen Dephoure. Clients include educational, industrial and medical firms, and governmental agencies. Uses services of music houses and songwriters for background music. "We only use one or two songwriters a year."
**How to Contact:** Submit resume of credits. Prefers cassette. Reports in 10 days.

*****THE DURASELL CORP.**, 16th Floor, 360 Lexington Ave., New York NY 10017. (212)687-1010. Director Production Services: Ms. Bibi Damon. Senior Producer/Acct. Services: Pat Jacoby. Audiovi-

sual firm. Clients include package goods manufacturers, magazines, pharmaceutical, liquor, tobacco and food manufacturers. Uses the services of music houses and songwriters for background music for sales meetings, sound filmstrips, musical scores in films, originals songs for themes and music scoring; lyricists for writing lyrics for themes and other music. Pays by the job. Buys all rights on originals or one-time rights for existing tracks.
**How to Contact:** Query with resume of credits—"a letter is a *must*." Prefers cassette as demo. Does not return unsolicited material.
**Music:** Upbeat, tuneful, show tune-oriented material for major sales meetings.

**ENTERTAINMENT PRODUCTIONS, INC.**, Box 554, Malibu CA 90265. (213)456-3143. Motion picture production company. President: Edward Coe. Clients include distributors/exhibitors. Uses services of music houses and songwriters for background and theme music for films. Commissions/year vary. Pays scale/job. Rights purchased vary.
**How to Contact:** Query with resume of credits. Prefers reel-to-reel. Demo should show flexibility of composition skills. "Demo records/tapes sent at own risk—returned if SASE included." Reports in 1 month.
**Tips:** "Have resume on file."

**EPIGRAM MUSIC**, Box 7962, Ann Arbor MI 48107. Contact: Michael Fishbein. Scoring service and marketing agent. Clients include publishers, film companies and performers. Uses services of songwriters for film-background and educational music. Pays by the job. Buys all rights.
**How to Contact:** Submit demo tape of previous work or tape demonstrating composition skills. Prefers cassette with 3-8 songs on demo. SASE. Reports in 3 weeks.

**MARTIN EZRA & ASSOCIATES**, 48 Garrett Rd., Upper Darby PA 19082. (215)352-9595 or 9596. Producer: Martin Ezra. Audiovisual firm and motion picture production company. Clients include business, industry and education. Uses services of music houses, songwriters and stock music for background music for sound filmstrips, musical scores in films, and original songs for themes; uses lyricists for movie themes. Commissions 5-6 compositions/year and 1-2 lyricists/year. Pays $100-2,000/job. Buys all rights or one-time rights.
**How to Contact:** Submit demo tape of previous work. "We do not return tapes." Prefers cassette with 1-20 songs on demo. Reports in 3 weeks.
**Music:** Uses music for film and audiovisual production.

*****SHELDON FREUND PRODUCTIONS**, Suite 1527, 250 W. 57th St., New York NY 10019. (212)581-0190. President: Sheldon Freund. Music producer and publisher. Clients include business and industry. Uses the services of songwriters for jingles; lyricists for writing lyrics for themes and other music. Commissions 12 composers/year. Pays 50% maximum royalty. Buys all rights.
**How to Contact:** Submit tape demonstrating composition skills. Prefers cassette with 1-5 songs on demo. SASE. Reports in 1 month.
**Music:** Pop, R&B, jingles, etc.
**Tips:** "Submit hit-oriented material."

**INDIANER MULTI-MEDIA**, 16201 SW 95th Ave., Box 550, Miami FL 33157. (305)235-6132. Vice President Systems: David Gravel. President: Paul Indianer. Uses services of music houses and songwriters for background music scored to action. Commissions 40 pieces/year. Pays $50/finished minute. Buys all rights or one-time rights.
**How to Contact:** Query with resume of credits or submit demo tape showing flexibility of composition skills. Prefers 7½ ips reel-to-reel with 5 songs minimum on tape. SASE. Reports in 3 weeks.

*****INSIGHT! INC.**, 100 E. Ohio St., Chicago IL 60611. (312)467-4350. Audiovisual firm. Clients include business and industry. Uses the services of music houses, songwriters and lyricists. Commissions 20 composers and 15 lyricists/year. Pays by the job; "usually a bid figure—no set minimum." Buys all rights.
**How to Contact:** Submit demo tape of previous work or tape demonstrating composition skills. Prefers 7½ ips reel-to-reel or cassette as demo. SASE.
**Music:** Film scores; industrial show music.

*****INTERAND CORP.**, Suite 1100, 666 N. Lakeshore Dr., Chicago IL 60611. (312)943-1200. Director of Multimedia Productions: Linda T. Phillips. Audiovisual firm. Clients include schools, publishers, business and industry. Uses the services of songwriters and music libraries for background music for sound filmstrips and videotapes; some multi-image shows. Commissions 1-2 composers/year. Pays by the job. Buys all rights.

**How to Contact:** Query with resume of credits. Prefers cassette, "but only after we've requested a submission." SASE. Reports in 2 weeks.
**Music:** Varies, depending on individual projects.
**Tips:** "Be patient. We deal on a contract basis with outside clients and only require songwriters on a minimal basis at present."

**JACOBY/STORM PRODUCTIONS, INC.**, 101 Post Rd. E., Westport CT 06880. President: Doris Storm. Clients include schools, publishers, business and industrial firms. Uses services of music houses and songwriters for film scores, background music and an occasional theme song. Commissions 2-3 pieces/year. Payment negotiable. Buys all rights or one-time rights.
**How to Contact:** Query with resume of credits or submit demo tape of previously aired work. Prefers 7½ or 15 ips reel-to-reel. SASE. Reports in 2 weeks. "Don't send any material without querying first."
**Music:** Needs songs and background music for films geared to elementary or high school students; also suitable for industrial and documentary films.

**KEN-DEL PRODUCTIONS INC.**, 111 Valley Rd., Wilmington DE 19804-1397. (302)655-7488. A&R Director: Shirley Kay. General Manager: Ed Kennedy. Clients include publishers, schools, industrial firms and advertising agencies. Uses services of songwriters for film scores and title music. Pays by the job. Buys all rights.
**How to Contact:** Submit demo of previously aired work. Prefers acetate discs, but will accept tapes. SASE; "however, we prefer to keep tapes on file for possible future use." Reports in 2 weeks.

**KEY PRODUCTIONS, INC.**, Box 2684, Gravois Station, St. Louis MO 63116. President: John E. Schroeder. Audiovisual firm. Clients include churches, colleges, church schools, industry and festivals. Uses services of songwriters for stage and educational TV musical dramas, background music for filmstrips, some speculative collaboration for submission to publishers and regional theatrical productions. Commissions "10 pieces/year, but selects up to 50 songs." Pays $50 minimum/job or by 10% minimum royalty. Buys one-time rights or all rights.
**How to Contact:** Query with resume of credits or submit demo tape showing flexibility of composition skills. "Suggest prior fee scales." Prefers cassette with 3-8 songs on demo. SASE. Reports in 1 month.
**Music:** "We mostly use religious material, some contemporary Biblical opera, some gospel, a few pop, blues, folk-rock and occasionally soul."

**KIMBO EDUCATIONAL UNITED SOUND ARTS, INC.**, 10-16 N. 3rd Ave., Box 477, Long Branch NJ 07740. (201)229-4949. Producers: James Kimble or Amy Laufer. Audiovisual firm and manufacturer of educational material: records, cassettes and teacher manuals or guides. Clients include schools and stores selling teachers' supplies. Uses services of music houses, songwriters, and educators for original songs for special education, early childhood, music classes, physical education and pre-school children; lyricists for lyrics to describe children's activities centering on development of motor skills, language, fitness or related educational skills. Commissions 12-15 pieces and 12-15 lyricists/year. Pays by the job or royalty. Buys all rights.
**How to Contact:** Submit demo tape of previous work, tape demonstrating composition skills, manuscript showing music scoring skills or lead sheet with lyrics. Prefers 7½ or 15 ips reel-to-reel or cassette with 1-12 songs on demo. "Upon receipt of a demo tape and/or written material, each property is previewed by our production staff. The same chances exist for any individual if the material is of high quality and we feel it meets the educational goals we are seeking." Reports in 1 month. Free catalog.
**Music:** "Contemporary sounds with limited instrumentation so as not to appear too sophisticated nor distracting for the young or special populations. Lyrics should be noncomplex and repetitive."

**SID KLEINER MUSIC ENTERPRISES**, 3701 25th Ave. SW, Naples FL 33999. (813)455-2693 or 455-2696. Managing Director: Sid Kleiner. Audiovisual firm. Clients include the music industry. Uses services of music houses, songwriters and inhouse writers for background music; lyricists for special material. Pays $25 minimum/job. Buys all rights.
**How to Contact:** Query with resume of credits or submit demo tape of previously aired work. Prefers cassette with 1-4 songs on demo. SASE. Reports in 3-5 weeks.
**Music:** "We generally need soft background music, with some special lyrics to fit a particular project. We also assign country, pop, mystical and metaphysical."

***KOCH/MARSCHALL PRODUCTIONS, INC.**, 1718 N. Mohawk St., Chicago IL 60614. (312)664-6482. President: Phillip Koch. Motion picture production company. Clients include schools, hospitals and theaters. Uses services of songwriters for musical scores in films, mostly music only, no lyrics. Commissions 2 composers/year. Pays $300-2,000/job. Buys all rights.
**How to Contact:** Query with resume of credits. "Always write first; never call." Prefers cassette with

Audiovisual Firms **289**

2-10 songs on demo. Does not return unsolicited material. Reports in 1 month.
**Music:** "We commission scores—original music only—for films, both dramatic and comedic."
**Tips:** "The songwriter must be technically proficient and creatively inspired. We are impressed by freshness, style and feeling."

**KOESTER AUDIO-VISUAL PRESENTATIONS**, Box 336, Far Hills NJ 07931. (201)766-2143. President: Ralph Koester. Clients include industrial and sales firms, schools and museums. Uses services of music houses and songwriters for opening, closing and background music for slide shows and films. Pays by license fee or contract. Buys all rights or nonexclusive one-time rights.
**How to Contact:** Contact by phone, query with resume of credits, submit demo tape of previously aired compositions, submit demo tape of compositions for particular client or submit demo tape showing flexibility of composition skills. Prefers 7½ ips reel-to-reel or cassette with 3-10 songs on demo. Does not return unsolicited material. "Leave demo tape, and we will call when the need arises."
**Music:** "We need openings, closings and backgrounds in both modern and classical moods. Usually, we use no vocals."

**LAVIDGE & ASSOCIATES, INC.**, 409 Bearden Park Circle, Knoxville TN 37919. (615)584-6121. Account Executive: R. Lyle Lavidge. "Full-service advertising agency with complete in-house film production facility." Uses services of music houses for jingles, musical commercials and audiovisual/film scores. Payment negotiable. Buys all rights or one-time rights, "depending on the client, market, etc."
**How to Contact:** Arrange personal interview or submit demo tape of previously aired work. Prefers 7½ ips reel-to-reel or cassette with 4-12 songs on demo. SASE. Reports if interested.

**JACK LIEB PRODUCTIONS**, 200 E. Ontario, Chicago IL 60611. (312)943-1440. Contact: Susan Schrier. President: W.H. Lieb. Clients include governmental agencies and industrial firms. Uses services of music houses and songwriters for background music and public service announcements. Pays by the job. Buys all rights.
**How to Contact:** Query with resume of credits, submit demo tape of previously aired compositions, or submit demo tape showing flexibility of composition skills. Prefers 7½ ips reel-to-reel. Does not return unsolicited material.

**LONGBRANCH STUDIO**, 6314 E. 13th St., Tulsa OK 74112. (918)832-7640. Manager: Walt Banfield. Scoring service and music/sound effects library. Clients include schools, producers, industry, business and advertising agencies. Uses services of songwriters, lyricists and inhouse writers to provide ideas or concepts; lyricists to provide ideas, concepts or musical content. Commissions 5 lyricists/year for 20 pieces. Pays $100-800/job, or 50% royalty. Buys all rights or one-time rights.
**How to Contact:** Query with resume of credits and submit demo tape of previously aired work or submit demo tape showing flexibility of composition skills. Prefers 7½ or 15 ips reel-to-reel or cassette with 3-6 songs on demo. SASE. Reports in 10 days.
**Music:** Needs vary with client's desires.

*****LYONS STUDIOS INC.**, 200 W. 9th St., Wilmington DE 19801. (302)654-6146. Audio Producer, Engineer: James Heffernan. Audiovisual firm and video production company. Clients include industrial, training and entertainment. Uses the services of music houses, songwriters; some in-house writing for background music (film, video, AV); logos-video (10 seconds or less); and some jingle work (radio, TV); lyricists for possible lyrics for industrial (live or canned) shows, or jingle lyrics. (Commissions 10 composers and 1-5 lyricists/year. Pay "depends on budget and circumstances." Buys all rights, except demo and publicity use by songwriter.
**How to Contact:** Submit demo tape of previous work or tape demonstrating composition skills. Prefers cassette with 3-10 songs on demo. SASE; returns material only "if requested." Reports as needs arise. Catalog for SASE (11x14) and $1.
**Music:** Synthesizer, rhythmic, orchestral, piano/bass/drums. "Much of our music is either mysterious (mood-setting) or proud upbeat 'on the move' music."
**Tips:** "Learn to put visual suggestions into sound (think visually); and learn to take intense direction without letting your pride interfere."

**MAJOR MEDIA, INC.**, Box 209, Deerfield IL 60015. (312)498-4610. President: Jay Steinberg. Audiovisual firm. Clients include educational and industrial firms. Uses services of music houses, songwriters and lyricists for filmstrips, slides, audio tapes, micro-computer disks, live shows and packaged audiovisual modual productions. Commissions 3-4 pieces and 2 lyricists/year. Payment negotiable. Buys all rights.

**How to Contact:** Submit tape demonstrating composition skills. Prefers 7½ ips reel-to-reel. SASE. Reports in 3 months.
**Music:** Industrial show themes.

**\*MARTIN/ARNOLD COLOR SYSTEMS, INC.**, 150 5th Ave., New York NY 10011. (212)675-7270. Contact: Martin Block. Audiovisual firm. Clients include schools, publishers, business and industry. Uses services of music houses for background music. Pays by the job. Rights purchased depends on assignment.
**How to Contact:** Query with resume of credits or submit demo tape of previously aired work. Prefers cassette as demo. SASE. Reports in 2 weeks.

**MAXFILMS**, 2525 Hyperion Ave., Los Angeles CA 90027. (213)662-3285. Vice President, Production: Sid Glenar. Production Assistant: Y. Shinn. Audiovisual firm and motion picture production company. Clients include corporations, nonprofit organizations and schools. Also produces films for theatrical and television release. Uses services of songwriters "for background on a theatrical or television film. Occasionally, an original score will be contracted for use in a corporate or educational film." Commissions 8-10 pieces/year. Pays $500-10,000/job. Buys all rights.
**How to Contact:** Submit demo tape of previously aired work, submit demo tape of composition for particular client or submit demo tape showing flexibility of composition skills. Prefers 7½ ips reel-to-reel or cassette with 1-6 songs on demo. "Tapes submitted should have some background as to the type of picture or presentation the music was scored for." SASE. Reports in 3 weeks.
**Music:** "Complete scoring, or a title song or intro to a film or audiovisual presentation. State complete capabilities in terms of composing, arranging and performing with some indication of the type of music that you handle best."

**MEDIA DEPT.**, Box 1006, St. Charles IL 60174. (312)377-0005. General Manager: Bruce Meisner. Audiovisual firm. Clients include business and industry. Uses services of music houses and lyricists for backgrounds and themes for AV multi-image productions. Pays minimum $500/job. Buys all rights.
**How to Contact:** Query with resume of credits, submit demo tape of previous work or tape demonstrating composition skills. Prefers cassette with minimum 2 songs on demo. SASE. Reports in 3 weeks.
**Music:** Uses "short 3-7 minute multi-image business presentations."

**FORNEY MILLER FILM ASSOCIATES**, 5 Timber Fare, Spring House PA 19477. (215)643-4167. Contact: Forney Miller. Clients include institutions, industrial and business firms. Uses services of songwriters and composers for film scores and background music. Pays $200 minimum "for open/close music." Buys all rights or one-time rights.
**How to Contact:** Submit demo tape of previously aired work. Prefers cassette. SASE. Reports "as soon as possible."
**Music:** Uses background music for business, promotional and documentary films.

**WARREN MILLER PRODUCTIONS**, 505 Pier Ave., Hermosa Beach CA 90254. (213)376-2494. Production: Robert Knop. Clients include industrial, sports, resort and airline firms. Uses services of music houses for background music in films. Commissions 1 piece/year. Pays $2,000 minimum/job; $50/needle drop. Buys one-time rights.
**How to Contact:** Submit demo tape of previously aired work. Prefers cassette with 1-10 songs on demo or disc. SASE. Reports in 3 weeks.
**Music:** Needs action, outdoors, symphonic, soft rock, "energy music that is light and youthful."
**Tips:** "It is important to be in this area to score a film. The musician must work closely with the editor. Be adept at scoring several instruments. Instrumentals will be better for us than vocals."

**MONUMENTAL FILMS & RECORDINGS**, 2160 Rockrose Ave., Baltimore MD 21211. (301)462-1550. President: John A'Hern. Audiovisual firm and motion picture production company. Clients include business and industry. Uses services of music houses for background music for sound filmstrips and musical scores in films; lyricists for writing lyrics for themes and other music and translations. Commissions 10 pieces and 10 lyricists/year. Pays by the job. Buys all rights.
**How to Contact:** Arrange personal interview, submit demo tape of previous work or tape demonstrating composition skills. Prefers reel-to-reel or cassette with 5-10 songs on demo. SASE. Reports in 2 weeks. Free book catalog.
**Music:** Musical background for documentary films.

**\*MOTIVATION MEDIA, INC.**, 1245 Milwaukee Ave., Glenview IL 60025. (312)297-4740. Vice President Production Operations: Paul C. Snyder. Audiovisual firm, motion picture production compa-

ny, business meeting planner and video producer. Clients include business and industry. Uses services of music houses, songwriters and composers "mostly for business meetings and multi-image production;" lyricists for writing lyrics for business meeting themes, audience motivation songs and promotional music for new product introduction. Commissions 4 lyricists for 6-10 pieces/year. Pays minimum $200/job. Buys all rights.
**How To Contact:** Query with resume of credits; submit demo tape of previous work. Prefers cassette with 5-7 songs on demo. Does not return unsolicited material. Reports in 1 month.
**Music:** Uses "up-beat contemporary music that motivates an audience of sales people."
**Tips:** "Keep in touch—let us know what new and exciting assignments you have undertaken."

**\*MULTI IMAGE PRODUCTIONS,** 8849 Complex Dr., San Diego CA 92123. (619)560-8383. President: Fred Ashman. Audiovisual firm and multi-media producer. Clients include major corporations and industries. Uses services of songwriters for original songs for themes and music arrangements for live entertainment; lyricists for theme songs for sales meetings, conventions and multi-media productions. Commissions 4-6 lyricists for 6-8 pieces/year. Pays by the job. Buys all rights.
**How to Contact:** Submit demo tape of previous work. Prefers 15 ips reel-to-reel or cassette tape with 3-8 songs on demo. SASE. Reports in 3 weeks.
**Music:** Uses material for multi-image shows.

**MULTIVISION OF DENVER, INC.,** 1121 S. Pearl, Denver CO 80210. (303)698-0420. President: Robert J. Taylor. Audiovisual firm and recording/broadcast production house. Clients include business, industry, state and federal government. Uses music houses and composers/arrangers for background music for sound filmstrips, sound logos, radio/TV jingles, background music, musical scores in films and original songs for album and demo projects. Commissions 5 composers/year. Pays $100-1,000/job. Buys all rights and one-time rights.
**How to Contact:** Query with resume of credits, arrange personal interview or submit demo tape showing flexibility of composition skills. Prefers 7½ reel-to-reel or cassette with 3 songs on demo. SASE. Reports in 1 week.
**Music:** "Radio/TV commercial cuts, station and product sound logos, media backgrounds, industrial, promotional and commercial arrangements."
**Tips:** "Be available and be easy to talk to. Be intelligently persistent and open to any associated work."

**OCEAN REALM VIDEO PRODUCTIONS,** 2333 Brickell Ave., Miami FL 33129. President/Producer: Richard Stewart. Video picture production company. Clients include ABC, "Good Morning America," and Home Box Office. Uses services of music houses for background music for TV series. Commissions 3 pieces/year. Pays $250 minimum/job. Buys all rights and one-time rights.
**How to Contact:** Submit demo tape of previous work. Prefers cassette for demo. SASE. Reports in 2 weeks.
**Music:** Ocean-related.

**ORIGIN, INC.,** 4466 Laclede, St. Louis MO 63108. (314)533-0010. Creative Director: George Johnson. Audiovisual firm, scoring service and music contractor. Clients include business, industry, government, agricultural conglomerates and hospitals. Uses services of songwriters and lyricists for music for conventions, industrial shows, films, video, etc. Payment negotiable. Rights purchased as requested by client.
**How to Contact:** Query with resume of credits; submit demonstration tape of previous work or tape demonstrating composition skills or manuscript showing music scoring skills. Prefers cassette with any number of songs on demo. SASE. Reports in 2 weeks.
**Music:** Depends on client's needs.

**PADDOCK PRODUCTIONS, INC.,** 9101 Barton, Shawnee Mission KS 66214. (913)492-9850. Sound Engineer: Fred Paddock. President: Chuck Paddock. Clients include industrial and educational firms. Uses services of music houses and songwriters for filmstrips, films, commercials and jingles. Commissions 50 pieces/year. Pays by the job. Buys one-time rights or all rights.
**How to Contact:** Submit demo tape showing flexibility of composition skills. Prefers 7½ ips reel-to-reel with 5 songs minimum on demo. SASE. Reports "as soon as possible."

**POP INTERNATIONAL CORPORATION,** 253 Closter Dock Rd., Box 527, Closter NJ 07624. (201)767-8030. Producers: Augie Borghese, Arnold De Pasquale and Peter DeCaro. Motion picture production company. Clients include "political campaigns, commercial spots, business and industry concerns as a production service; feature films and documentaries as producers." Uses services of music houses and songwriters for "mood purposes only on documentary films. However, Pop International Productions does conceptualize major theatrical and/or album musical projects." Commissions com-

mercial and soundtrack pieces for entertainment specials; commissions 2-3 lyricists/year. Pays $75-200/hour; minimum $500/job; 10% minimum royalty. Buys all rights and one-time rights.
**How to Contact:** Submit demo tape of previously aired work. Prefers cassette with 2-4 songs on demo. "We review tapes on file, speak with agents and/or referrals, then interview writer. Once committee approves, we work *very* closely in preproduction." SASE. Reports in 3 weeks.
**Music:** Uses "mood music for documentaries, occasionally jingles for spots or promotional films or theme music/songs for dramatic projects (the latter by assignment only from producers or agencies). Some material is strictly mood, as in documentary work; some is informative as in promotional; some is motivating as in commercial; some is entertaining as in theatrical/TV."
**Tips:** "Be persistent and very patient. Try to get an agent, use demos and build a reputation for working very closely with scriptwriters/producers/directors."

**HENRY PORTIN MOTION PICTURES**, 709 Jones Bldg., Seattle WA 98101. (206)682-7863. Producer: Henry Portin. Motion picture production company. Clients include industrial, airline and touring firms. Uses services of songwriters for original songs for themes and scoring. Commissions 2 pieces and 1 lyricist/year. Pays $500 minimum/job. Buys all rights.
**How to Contact:** Query with resume of credits. Prefers cassette with 2-4 songs on demo. SASE. Reports in 1 month. Free catalog.
**Music:** Background music for documentaries.

**PREMIER FILM AND RECORDING CORP.**, 3033 Locust St., St. Louis MO 63103. (314)531-3555. President: Wilson Dalzell. Secretary/Treasurer: Grace Dalzell. Audiovisual firm and motion picture production company. Uses services of songwriters for original background music and lyrics to reinforce scripts. Commissions 6-10 pieces and 5-10 lyricists/year. Pays according to the maximum contribution of the music to the total production. Buys all rights and "occasionally one-time rights with composer retaining title."
**How to Contact:** Query with resume of credits. Prefers 7½ or 15 ips reel-to-reel or cassette with any number of songs on demo. SASE. Reports "as soon as possible."
**Tips:** "Be sure a resume is direct, to-the-point and includes an honest review of past efforts."

**JOHN M. PRICE FILMS, INC.**, Box 81, Radnor PA 19087. (215)687-6699. President: John M. Price. Clients include business, government and ad agencies. Uses music houses for occasional background music and musical scores for films. Pays $100-500/job. Buys one-time rights.
**How to Contact:** "Mail description of work, and we will file information for future reference." Prefers 7½ ips reel-to-reel tape "but none until requested."

**PROTESTANT RADIO & TV CENTER, INC.**, 1727 Clifton Rd. NE, Atlanta GA 30329. (404)634-3324. Chief Engineer: Jim Hicks. Clients include denominational projects, local churches, schools and colleges (educational needs), and social campaigns. Uses services of songwriters for film scores, commercials and radio programs. Payment negotiable. Rights purchased vary.
**How to Contact:** Query or submit demo tape of previously aired work. Prefers 7½ or 15 ips reel-to-reel or cassette with 2-8 songs on demo. Does not return unsolicited material. Reports in 1 month.
**Music:** Themes for radio, TV, film and audiovisual productions.

**RICHTER PRODUCTIONS, INC.**, 330 W. 42nd St., New York NY 10036. President: Robert Richter. Motion picture production company. Clients include public and commercial TV, government agencies and nonprofit organizations. Uses services of music houses, songwriters and composers/arrangers for film scores and background music. Commissions 2 pieces/year. Pays by the job. Buys all rights or one-time rights.
**How to Contact:** Submit demo and resume of previously aired work. Prefers cassette with 2-5 songs on demo. SASE. "Also, put name, return address and phone number on the tape itself." Reporting time varies "according to our business rush."
**Music:** "We have varying needs—sometimes we need a musical score to which we cut the film; at other times, we need music for already edited film."

**SEVEN OAKS PRODUCTIONS**, 9145 Seigo Creek Pkwy., Silver Spring MD 20901. (301)587-0030. Production Manager: Marcia Marlow. Production Chief: M.A. Marlow. Audiovisual firm and motion picture production company. Clients include blue chip companies, government agencies and foreign film producers. Uses services of music houses and songwriters for film scores and background music; lyricists to help develop musical narratives or themes and title songs for features and educational films. "Often a ballad can create mood and tone better than an all-knowing narrator." Commissions 10-30 composers and 2-6 lyricists/year. Payment negotiable. Buys all rights or one-time rights.
**How to Contact:** Query with resume of credits or submit demo tape showing flexibility of composition

## Audiovisual Firms 293

skills. "If possible, submit a film with soundtrack so we can judge if the score fits the film's mood." Prefers 7½ ips reel-to-reel or cassette tape with 3 songs minimum to 1 hour long maximum, or 16mm film. SASE. "We prefer to keep tapes on file to select potential composers for our projects." Reporting time varies "with the demands of the project."
**Music:** Needs scores and theme songs for "family-type feature films and educational, documentary productions. Our production people rely heavily upon music to raise audience interest and make even the most pedantic subjects interesting. We are interested in working with male and female composers and arrangers on future children's feature projects."

**SILVER BURDETT COMPANY**, 250 James St., CN 018, Morristown NJ 07960. (201)285-8002. Assistant Music Editor: Donald Scafuri. Publisher of textbooks and records for kindergarten through 8th grade. "Our books and records are sold directly to schools and are evaluated and chosen for use according to the adoption procedures of a particular school district." Uses services of music houses and songwriters for original songs for children K-8; lyricists for translating foreign lyrics into a singable English version and "writing original lyrics to a folk tune or a melody composed by someone else." Commissions 0-20 lyricists for 0-20 pieces/year. Pays $55 for lyrics and arrangements; $150 for original compositions (reprint rights plus statutory record royalty). Buys one-time rights.
**How to Contact:** Submit lead sheets of previous work. Prefers cassette as demo. "If song is not copyrighted, author should write first to Music Editorial Department for Idea Submission Form to submit with song." SASE. Reports in 1 month. Free catalog.
**Music:** "We seek virtually any kind of song that is suitable both in words and music for children to sing. We are particularly interested in songs that are contemporary pop or folk-like in style. We are also interested in choral compositions for upper grades."
**Tips:** "Become acquainted with teachers and students in elementary or junior high classrooms. Find out what music they are presently using and what they would like to use."

**PHOEBE T. SNOW PRODUCTIONS, INC.**, 240 Madison Ave., New York NY 10016. (212)679-8756. Creative Director: Beth Bagnold. Audiovisual firm. Clients include business and industry. Uses services of songwriters and lyricists for original music and songs for business shows. Commissions 5-10 lyricists for 10 pieces/year. Pays minimum $500/job. Buys all rights.
**How to Contact:** Query with resume of credits, then arrange personal interview. SASE. Reports in 1 month.
**Music:** Needs theme music for business shows.

**THE SOUND SERVICE**, 860 2nd St., San Francisco CA 94107. (415)433-3674. Staff Composer: Steven Shapiro. Music/sound effects library. Clients include business and TV. Uses the services of staff writers for commercials and audiovisual shows. Buys all rights.
**How to Contact:** Submit demo tape of previous work. Prefers 7½ or 15 ips reel-to-reel with 3-8 songs on demo. SASE. Reports "as soon as possible, depending on work load."
**Music:** Needs "instrumental only—industrial synthesizer music wanted."

**SPACE PRODUCTIONS**, 451 West End Ave., New York NY 10024. (212)986-0857. Producer: J. Alexander. Motion picture production company. Clients include broadcast, commercial and corporate clients. Uses music houses and songwriters for music for sound filmstrips, musical scores in films, original songs for themes and music scoring, etc. Commissions 6-10 pieces/year. Pays $250-5,000/job, depending on assignment. Rights purchased depend on assignment.
**How to Contact:** Query with resume of credits, submit demo tape of previous work or submit tape demonstrating composition skills. Prefers 7½ ips reel-to-reel, cassette or video (if scored to picture) with a representative sampling of songwriter's work. Include a resume. SASE. Reports in 2-8 weeks.
**Music:** Commercial and theme music for commercial and industrial features.

**STAGE 3 SOUND PRODUCTIONS**, 1901 W. 43rd St., Kansas City KS 66103. (913)384-9111. President: Don Warnock. Clients include business and advertising agencies. Uses services of songwriters for background music in productions. Pays AFTRA scale. Buys all rights.
**How to Contact:** Query. Prefers 7½ ips reel-to-reel or cassette. SASE. Reports "as soon as possible."

**CARTER STEVENS STUDIOS, INC.**, 269 W. 25th St., New York NY 10001. President: Carter Stevens. Produces theatrical feature films and business documentaries. Uses services of music houses and songwriters for film scores. Commissions 40-60 pieces/year. Pays $250-1,000/job. Buys all rights or one-time rights.
**How to Contact:** Submit demo tape of previous work or query with resume of credits. "Do not call our office." Prefers cassette with 2-8 songs on demo. SASE. Returns material if totally unusable; "we keep everything for future reference if we feel the writer has any potential. Send a sample of as many styles and moods of music as possible."

**Tips:** "There is a 3- to 6-month lag time on our projects, as we are working at least one to two films ahead at all times."

**E.J. STEWART INC.**, 525 Mildred Ave., Primos PA 19018. (215)626-6700. Creative Director: David Lindquester. Audiovisual firm and video tape production company. Clients include broadcasting companies, cable TV, advertising agencies, schools, business, industry, government and the medical profession. Uses services of music houses and songwriters for background music for commercials and programs. Commissions 50 pieces and 5 lyricists/year. Payment negotiable by the job. Buys all rights.
**How to Contact:** Query with resume of credits or submit demo tape of previous work. Prefers reel-to-reel or cassette with any number of songs on demo. SASE. Reports "when needed."

*****SUNSET FILMS**, 625 Market St., San Francisco CA 94105. (415)495-4555. Producer: Greg Bezat. Motion picture production company. Clients include business and industry. Uses services of music houses and songwriters for background scores for films and TV shows. Commissions 2 pieces/year. Pays $10,000-30,000/job. Buys all rights.
**How to Contact:** Query with resume of credits; submit demo tape of previous work. Prefers cassette as demo. SASE.
**Music:** "Sponsored films use a bouncy, up-beat flavor; the emotional qualities are secondary most of the time although they're what make films tick."
**Tips:** "It really is the personality mix that helps get your foot in the door as well as being a strong, confident musician."

*****TELEMATION PRODUCTIONS, INC.**, 3210 W. West Lake, Glenview IL 60025. (312)729-5215. Producer: Jeanni McCormick. Videotape production house. Clients include advertising clients and industrial programs. Uses services of network and music libraries for jingles and background music for industrials; lyricists for jingles. Pays by the job. Buys all rights.
**How to Contact:** Submit demo tape of previous work, along with resume. Prefers 7½ ips reel-to-reel with 3-10 songs on demo. SASE. "We return tapes if requested. However, we like to keep tapes on file for future reference." Reports in 3 weeks.
**Music:** Uses "up-tempo music that can be faded out smoothly to fit time alloted for commercials for industrial clients; some easy listening, mostly instrumental."

**TELECINE SERVICES & PRODUCTION LTD.**, 11 Ely Place, Dublin 2, Ireland. 353-01-763188. Telex 92309 PAVEL. Director: Anabella Jackson. Audiovisual firm and video productions. Clients include advertising and commercial business. Uses services of songwriters and music houses for original songs for TV commercials and audiovisual and video programs; lyricists for writing lyrics for commercials and conference themes. Commissions 3 lyricists for 20 pieces/year. Pays $1,250 minimum/job. Buys all rights or rights within one country.
**How to Contact:** Query with resume of credits or submit tape demonstrating composition skills. Prefers 15 ips reel-to-reel or cassette with 3-10 songs on demo. SASE. Reports in 1 month.
**Music:** Scoring for TV commercials.

*****TULCHIN PRODUCTIONS**, 240 E. 45th St., New York NY 10016. (212)986-8270. Executive Producer: Louis Georgaras. Motion picture production company. Clients include advertising agencies, business and industry. Uses services of music houses and songwriters for background music and musical scores for commercials and industrials, etc.; lyricists for writing lyrics for commercials. Pays by the job per agreement. Buys all rights.

**WING PRODUCTIONS**, 1600 Broadway, New York NY 10019. (212)265-5179. President: Jon Wing Lum. Clients include NBC and the New York State Education Department. Uses services of songwriters for scores for film and tape. Commissions 20 lyricists for 40 pieces/year. Pays $500 minimum/job. Buys all rights.
**How to Contact:** Submit demo tape of previously aired work or submit demo tape showing flexibility of composition skills. Prefers 7½ or 15 ips reel-to-reel or cassette with 5 songs on demo. SASE. Reporting time "depends on need." Free catalog.
**Music:** Needs all types of music.

*****ZELMAN STUDIOS**, 623 Cortelyoo Rd., Brooklyn NY 11218. (212)941-5500. Assistant Manager of Sound Services: Ann Shira. Audiovisual firm. Clients include schools, business and industry. Uses services of music houses and songwriters for background music and musical scores in films. Commissions 6-8 lyricists for 6-8 pieces/year. Pays $100-500/job. Buys one-time rights.
**How to Contact:** Submit demo tape of previous work. Prefers cassette with minimum 3 songs on demo. SASE. Reports in 1 month.

**ZM SQUARED**, 903 Edgewood Lane, Box C-30, Cinnaminson NJ 08077. (609)786-0612. Clients include colleges, schools, businesses and AV producers. Uses services of songwriters "for themes for our no-needledrop music library and background for AV presentations. We prefer to work with composer/arranger/performer and use primarily background music." Commissions 2-3 albums with 10 cuts each/year; 1-2 lyricists/year. Pays 10-35% royalty. Buys all rights.
**How to Contact:** Submit demo tape of previous work. Prefers cassette with 4-6 songs on demo. SASE. Reports in 3 weeks. Free catalog.
**Music:** "We require a variety of background music—educational and industrial for general use with audiovisual programs."
**Tips:** "Know what we want and be able to produce what you write."

# Managers & Booking Agents

The manager is a valuable contact, both for the songwriter trying to get songs to a particular artist, and for the songwriter-performer. Often the manager is the person closest to the artist. He functions as a confidant who guides and promotes the artist's career, even helping in the choice of new material for performance and recording. Some of the managers in this section also operate as booking agents—finding work for their artists—or even as publishers and record companies.

Managers of nationally-known acts are usually located in Los Angeles, Nashville or New York, and many have branch offices located in all three music centers. Don't expect these "big time" managers to be the easiest people to approach. Because of their proximity to the famous people they represent, they must, along with all their other managerial functions, act as a shield between their artists and the public. In some cases the manager may even be nearly as famous as the artists he represents, and you'll need to get past at least a receptionist or a secretary just to talk with him by phone.

Still, the main function of the manager is to *represent* the artist. Even the managers of superstars *will* listen to anything that can benefit their clients—especially if it's a hit song! Most of the managers in this section review material for their clients (listings will say if they do). Listings also tell you the types of acts the manager handles, the types of music he's looking for, and specific artists he represents. Reading the listings you'll see the names of some of today's biggest stars: Pat Benatar, Rick James—also featured as a Close-up in the Record Companies section—The Charlie Daniels Band, and more.

You needn't go farther than your home town, however, to find talented artists needing material. Managers of local acts will often have more to say in the choice of material their clients perform and record than managers located in music centers where the producer often makes the final decision about which songs an artist records. Locally, it could be the manager who not only chooses songs for a recording session, but picks the producer, studio, and musicians as well.

Just as with superstars, your songs for local and regional acts *must* be the best. Local acts work hard to make a reputation for themselves in hope of someday being superstars themselves. Today's top acts were in most cases yesterday's local entertainers. If and when the artist goes on to bigger things, it could be that you—the songwriter—will go on with him. To learn more about successfully writing songs for local artists, see James Dearing's article on "Writing for the Local Alternative Music Markets" in the front of this book.

If you are a performer-songwriter, your most important consideration is finding a manager who unfailingly believes in your ability and your future—both as a performer and as a writer. His job is to promote you as a first-class artist. Your job is to prove him right. (For information on contracts between manager and performer, see "Contracts" in the Appendix of this book.)

Talent, originality, credits, dedication, self-confidence and professionalism are things that will attract a manager to you. Your press kit should contain a high-quality, interesting, professional 8x10 publicity photo; a three- to four-paragraph biographical data sheet; a list of songs (both copy songs and original material) performed; a list of engagement credits; a current itinerary; any relevant press clippings; and a live, unedited cassette tape of an actual performance. Your package to managers and booking agencies will resemble your material for record companies and producers. In each case, you are auditioning. You want to include your best material, the most exciting part of your act.

If there is an artist or manager whose name you can't find among the listings in tis section, see "How to Be a Music Market Detective" in the Appendix of this book. There you can learn how to track down any artist, manager, record company, publisher or record producer you think might be interested in your songs.

**ACE PRODUCTIONS**, 3407 Green Ridge Dr., Nashville TN 37214. (615)883-3480. Contact: Jim Case. Management firm and booking agency. Represents artists, groups and songwriters; currently handles 12 acts. Receives 15-20% commission. Reviews material for acts.
**How to Contact:** Submit demo tape and lead sheet. Prefers cassette with 3-6 songs on demo. SASE. Reports in 1 month.
**Music:** Mostly C&W; also rock (hard and country) and top 40/pop. Works primarily with show, dance and bar bands. Current acts include Little David Wilkins, Jimmy Case, Dennis Seymore, Cedar Creek, Jerry Wallace, Johnny Carver, J.D. Bell & the Silver Spurs Band, Kent Westberry & the Memory Makers, Suzi Deveraux & the Nashville Expressions, Lorrie Morgan, Doug Lavalley & Elisa Gerard and David Rogers.

\***ACT "1" ENTERTAINMENTS**, Box 1079, New Haven CT 06504. (203)776-2847. President: Johnny Parris. Management firm, booking agency and record company. Represents artists, groups and songwriters; currently handles 20-25 acts. Reviews material for acts.
**How to Contact:** Query by mail or submit demo tape and lead sheet; arrange personal interview. Prefers cassette with 5-10 songs on demo. SASE. Reports in 2 weeks.
**Music:** Mostly hard rock, top 40/pop, soul and R&B; also dance-oriented, easy listening, jazz, MOR and rock. Current acts include Roxx (hard rock); Bob Mel (top 40/pop); Jeff Michaels (top 40/pop); and Half Moon (rock and top 40/pop).
**Tips:** "I'm looking for people who are ethical and not into drugs."

\***ACTION TICKET AGENCY AND PROMOTIONS**, 2609 NW 36th St., Oklahoma City OK 73112. (405)942-0462. Manager: Bobby Boyd. Management and booking agency and promotions firm. Represents individual artists from anywhere; currently handles 4 acts. Receives 25% minimum commission. Reviews material for acts.
**How to Contact:** Query by mail, then submit demo tape only. Prefers 7½ ips reel-to-reel with 3-12 songs on demo. Does not return unsolicited material. Reports in 2 weeks.
**Music:** C&W, R&B, rock and top 40/pop. Current acts include Dale Greear, Faye Haley and Bobby Barnett (all country acts).

**ADORATION, INC. (aka The Tatom Agency)**, Suite 2-A, 6750 W. 75th St., Overland Park KS 66204. (913)384-1050. Vice-President: Betty Tatom. Management firm, booking agency and public relations company. Represents artists, groups and songwriters—"all are nationally known." Currently handles 10 acts. Receives "fee or love offering plus expenses" as commission. Reviews material for acts.
**How to Contact:** Query by mail, then submit demo tape and lead sheet. Prefers cassette. Does not return unsolicited material. Reports "when various artists need material to record."
**Music:** Bluegrass, C&W, easy listening, gospel, MOR, progressive, Spanish and top 40/pop. Works primarily with "live bands (4-8 instruments plus vocals); solo artists; some symphony orchestra (big band sound)." Current acts include Sue Ellen Chenault (gospel singer); Kathie Sullivan (gospel singer); Gordon Jensen (songwriter/artist); Eternity (brass section, group of 15); The Mercy River Boys (country group of nine); Steve and Maria Gardner (duo); Kathie Lee Johnson (Coke spokeswoman, solo; duo with sister Michie Mader); and Dave Boyer (solo artist).

**AJAYE ENTERTAINMENT CORP.**, 2181 Victory Pkwy., Box 6568, Cincinnati OH 45206. (513)221-2626. Artist Relations: Suzy Evans. Booking agency. Represents artists and groups; currently represents 33 acts. Receives 10-20% commission.
**How to Contact:** Submit demo tape and write or call to explain the purpose of submission. Prefers 7½ ips reel-to-reel or cassette with 3-6 songs on demo. SASE. Reports in 1 week.
**Music:** Progressive, rock, soul and top 40/pop. Current acts include Bell Jar, Relay, The Raisins, Hyroller, The Young Invaders, Spike, Buster Brown, Prizoner, Elaine and the Biscaynes, Asher, Tangent and Swan (all rock groups).

**ALAMO TALENT AND PRODUCTIONS**, 217 Arden Grove, San Antonio TX 78215. (512)225-6294. President: Carl Mertens. Management firm and booking agency. Represents artists and groups; currently handles 57 acts. Receives 15-25% commission. Reviews material for acts.
**How to Contact:** Query by mail. Prefers 7½ ips reel-to-reel or cassette with 3-5 songs on demo. Does not return unsolicited material.
**Music:** Mostly C&W; also folk, MOR and Spanish. Works primarily with dance bands. Current acts include Lisa Lopez (Spanish artist); Janie C. Ramirez & Cactus Country; and American Express (C&W group).

**\*WILLIE LOCO ALEXANDER/SOMOR MUSIC**, #22, 399 Broadway, Cambridge MA 02139. Contact: Willie Loco Alexander. Represents artists, groups and songwriters in the northeastern US. Reviews material for acts.
**How to Contact:** Query by mail or submit demo tape and lead sheet. Prefers cassette as demo. SASE. Reports in 1 month.
**Music:** Mostly rock and top 40/pop; also dance-oriented. Current acts include Willie Loco Alexander (vocalist/songwriter).

**ALIVE ENTERPRISES**, Suite 525, 9000 Sunset Blvd., Los Angeles CA 90069. (213)276-4500. Director of Business Affairs: Bob Emmer. Management agency. Represents artists, groups and songwriters; currently represents 7 acts. Receives 20% minimum commission.
**How to Contact:** Submit demo tape and lead sheet. Prefers cassette with 2-4 songs on demo. SASE. Reports in 3-5 weeks.
**Music:** Rock (all types), soul and top 40/pop. Works with "major record company signed artists." Current acts include Alice Cooper (rock); and Teddy Pendergrass (R&B).

**ALL NIGHT ENTERTAINMENT**, 1207 E. 27th Place, Tulsa OK 74114. (918)743-1262. President: Scott Hurowitz. Management firm and production company. Estab. 1981. Represents artists, groups and songwriters; currently handles 3 acts. Receives 15-20% commission. Reviews material for acts.
**How to Contact:** Phone in advance, then submit demo tape and lead sheet. Prefers cassette with 3-5 songs on demo. Does not return unsolicited material. Reports in 3 weeks.
**Music:** Mostly rock (all types) and top 40/pop; also C&W, dance-oriented and easy listening. Works primarily with rock and pop artists. "We deal with strictly original artists who understand the patience and hard work they must be willing to put forth." Current acts include Jeff Gibson (rock/pop artist); GEO (rock/pop artist); Jef Scott (rock artist); and Gary Knutson (country/pop artist).
**Tips:** "Please call first and follow up with a tape containing 3-5 of your best songs. Call in 2-3 weeks if we have not yet responded. Photos are always helpful, as are details of background, past music ventures, and career plans for the future."

**ALL STAR TALENT AGENCY**, Box 82, Greenbrier TN 37073. (615)643-4644. Agent: Joyce Brown. Booking agency. Represents professional individuals, groups and songwriters; currently handles 12 acts. Receives 15% commission. Reviews material for acts.
**How to Contact:** Submit demo tape and lead sheet. Prefers reel-to-reel or cassette with 1-4 songs on demo. SASE. Reports ASAP.
**Music:** Bluegrass, C&W, gospel, MOR, rock (country) and top 40/pop. Works primarily with dance, show and bar bands, vocalists, club acts and concerts. Current acts include Bill Carlisle and the Carlisles (C&W group); Ronnie Dove (MOR/C&W artist); Randy Parton (pop artist); Charlie McCoy (instrumentalist); Tommy Overstreet (C&W artist); and Del Wood (Grand Ole Opry star).

**\*ALL STAR TALENT & PROMOTIONS**, 2028 Chestnut St., Philadelphia PA 19103. (215)561-5822. President: Ron Russen. Management firm and booking agency. Estab. 1981. Represents artists and musical groups in Philadelphia and the surrounding area only; currently handles 15 acts. Receives 4-6% commission. Reviews material for acts.
**How to Contact:** Query by mail or submit demo tape and lyric sheet. Prefers cassette with 2-6 songs on demo. Does not return unsolicited material. Reports in 2 weeks.
**Music:** Dance-oriented, R&B, rock, soul and top 40/pop. Works primarily with self-contained groups and vocal groups. Current acts include the Coasters (vocal group) and the Tokens (vocal group).

**ALLIED BOOKING CO.**, Suite J, 2321 Morena Blvd., San Diego CA 92110. (619)275-5030. Associate: Jim Deacy. Booking agency. Deals with individuals in California and Arizona. Receives 10-20% commission.
**How to Contact:** Query or submit demo tape. Prefers cassette with 5-10 songs on demo. SASE. Reports in 2 weeks.
**Music:** Mostly dance-oriented; also bluegrass, blues, C&W, easy listening, folk, jazz, MOR, R&B, rock (50's or MOR) and top 40/pop. Works primarily with dance bands or groups with vocalists included. "We book all types of musical groups, and many different ones throughout the year."

**AMERICAN ARTISTS**, Suite 110, 430 Oak Grove, Minneapolis MN 55403. (612)871-6200. Contact: Owen Husney or Peter Martinsen. Management firm and recording studio. Represents artists, groups and songwriters; currently handles 2 acts. Receives variable commission. Reviews material for acts.
**How to Contact:** Submit demo tape only or demo tape and lead sheet. Prefers cassette with maximum 4

songs on demo. SASE. Reports in 1 month.
**Music:** Dance-oriented, jazz, R&B, rock (all types), soul and top 40/pop. Current acts include Sue Ann (R&B artist/Warner Bros. Records); and Andre Cymone (rock/R&B artist/Columbia Records).

**AMERICAN CREATIVE ENTERTAINMENT LTD.**, Professional Arts Bldg., Suite 818, 1616 Pacific Ave., Atlantic City NJ 08401. (609)347-0484. Vice President: Danny Luciano. Booking agency and record producer. Represents artists, groups and songwriters from anywhere. Receives 10-25% commission. Reviews material for acts.
**How to Contact:** Submit demo tape and lead sheet. Prefers 7½ ips reel-to-reel or cassette with 4-8 songs on demo. "No 8-tracks. Include picture and promotion package if self-contained performing artist." SASE. Reports in 6 weeks.
**Music:** C&W, MOR, R&B, soft country rock and top 40/pop. Works primarily with dance bands, bar bands, show groups and recording artists. Current acts include Steve Jason and Diane Richards; Dan Nelson Show, Sheeva & Company, Atlantic City III, Mixx and Focus.

**AMJ INTERNATIONAL/JACKSON ENTERPRISES**, 9000 Sunset Blvd., West Hollywood CA 90069. (213)550-0397. General Manager: Alice M. Jackson. Management firm, booking agency and music publisher. Represents artists, groups and songwriters; currently handles 20 acts. Receives 10% commission. Reviews material for acts.
**How to Contact:** Submit demo tape and lead sheet. Prefers cassette ("copy only—do not send original") with 2-4 songs on demo. SASE. Reports in 3 weeks.
**Music:** Blues, C&W, dance-oriented, MOR, R&B, rock (country), soul and top 40/pop. Works primarily with "dance bands, combos, lounge groups, concert artists and singles." Current acts include Shane Barmby (country/pop artist); Jerri C. Carroll (MOR artist); Eddie Simpson (R&B singer, ESP Records); and Eddie Jay (soul artist).
**Tips:** "Be different. Present something unique in sound. Have good lyrics that tell a story."

**ARCEE PRODUCTIONS**, Suite 214, 1680 N. Vine St., Hollywood CA 90028. (213)871-8787. Talent Agent: Jim Roberts. Represents artists, groups and songwriters. Currently handles 73 acts. Receives 10% commission. Reviews material for acts.
**How to Contact:** "Submit photo, resume and demo tape." Prefers 7½ ips reel-to-reel or cassette with 3-5 songs on demo. SASE. Reports ASAP.
**Music:** C&W, dance-oriented, easy listening, gospel, MOR, R&B, soul and top 40/pop. Works primarily with "solo artists and groups such as duos and trios; all have label affiliation or are being shopped at this time." Current acts include Sylvester (dance, R&B); The Weather Girls (dance-oriented music, duo); and Linda Clifford (dance, R&B artist).
**Tips:** "Be as courteous and polite to us as you want us to be to you. Keep in mind that there are many other songwriters and artists vying for the same opportunity to submit their work so be patient and professional."

**ARISTO MUSIC ASSOCIATES, INC.**, Box 22765, Nashville TN 37202. (615)320-5491. President: Jeff Walker. Public relations and media consulting firm. Represents artists, groups and songwriters. "We deal with artists on a national and international level." Currently handles 8 clients. Receives negotiable commission—"based on estimated time and services involved." Reviews material for acts.
**How to Contact:** Query by mail. "At present we are only interested in artists with national distribution." Prefers cassette with 3-5 songs on demo. Prefers a "low-key, patient approach." SASE. Reports in 1 month.
**Music:** C&W, easy listening, MOR, rock and top 40/pop. Works primarily with country groups and artists. Current acts include Karen Taylor-Good (Mesa Records); Gary Goodnight (Soundwaves Records); Rich Landers (AMI Records); Darlene Austin (Myrtle Records); Cedar Creek (country vocal group); the Nashville Roster of the Shorty Lawander Talent Agency; and Terri Hollowell (female country solo artist).
**Tips:** Songwriters "need to be professional in their approach to the music business. Presently establishing affiliated publishing companies."

**PAT ARMSTRONG & ASSOCIATES, INC.**, Suite 202, 1500 Lee Rd., Lee Square Bldg., Orlando FL 32810. (305)299-0077. President: Pat Armstrong. Vice President: Jack Armstrong. Management firm, production company and music publisher. Represents artists, groups and songwriters; currently handles 5 acts. Receives 20% commission. Reviews material for acts.
**How to Contact:** Query by phone or submit demo tape and lead sheet. Prefers cassette with 4-6 songs on demo. SASE. Reports in 2 weeks.
**Music:** Progressive, rock (hard, country, heavy), top 40/pop and modern music. Works primarily with developing artists and bands. Current acts include Molly Hatchet (Southern rock group/Epic Records);

Riggs (rock group/Warner Bros. Records); Susan Lynch (rock group/CBS Records); Stranger (rock group/Epic Records); and Four In Legion (modern music/Elektra/Asylum Records).

**CLIFF AYERS PRODUCTIONS**, 62 Music Square W., Nashville TN 37203. (615)361-7902. Vice President: Chris Ostermeyer. Management firm, booking agency, record production and distribution company, publisher. "We publish *Music City Entertainer* newspaper." Represents artists, groups and songwriters; currently represents 79 acts. Receives 15-20% minimum commission. Reviews material for acts.
**How to Contact:** Submit demo tape and lead or lyric sheet. Prefers cassette with a maximum of 2 songs on demo. SASE. Reports in 1 week.
**Music:** Church/religious, C&W, disco, gospel, MOR, soft rock and top 40/pop. Current acts include Ernie Ashworth (C&W, Grand Old Opry star); Vicki Knight (rock); and Teddy Burns (French rock).
**Tips:** "Submit material as soon as you have it."

*****AZTEC PRODUCTIONS**, 20531 Plummer St., Chatsworth CA 91311. (213)998-0443. General Manager: A. Sullivan. Management firm and booking agency. Represents individuals, groups and songwriters; currently handles 7 acts. Receives 10-25% commission.
**How to Contact:** Submit demo tape and lead sheet. Prefers 7½ ips reel-to-reel or cassette. SASE. Reports in 3 weeks.
**Music:** Blues, C&W, disco, MOR, rock, soul and top 40/pop. Works primarily with club bands, show groups and concert groups. Current acts include El Chicano (Latin/rock); Abraxas (MOR); Storm (show group); Tribe (soul/R&B); New Street, Kelly Lynn, Ako, Zaral and Debbie Rockwell.

**BOBBY BAKER ENTERPRISES**, Box 684, Des Moines IA 50303. (515)282-8421. Contact: Bobby Baker. Management firm and booking agency. Represents artists, groups and songwriters; currently handles 5 acts. Receives 15-20% commission. Reviews material for acts.
**How to Contact:** Submit demo tape and short bio. Prefers cassette with 3-6 songs on demo. SASE. Reports in 2 weeks.
**Music:** Bluegrass, C&W, easy listening, gospel, MOR and top 40/pop. Works primarily with "convention groups (trios, etc.), singles and groups for fairs." Current acts include Two for the Show Trio (musical comedy); Robbie Wittkowski (country trio); The Johnsons (musical comedy); and The Swinging Ambassadors (musical comedy).
**Tips:** "Good quality tape and professional attitude desirable."

**BARNARD MANAGEMENT SERVICES (BMS)**, 2219 Main St., Santa Monica CA 90405. (213)392-4539. Agent: Russell Barnard. Management firm. Represents artists, groups and songwriters; currently handles 3 acts. Receives 10-20% commission. Reviews material for acts.
**How to Contact:** Query by mail, then submit demo tape and lead sheet. Prefers cassette with 3-10 songs on demo. SASE. Reports in 1 month.
**Music:** Bluegrass, blues, C&W, folk, R&B, rock, soul and top 40/pop. Works primarily with country crossover singers/songwriters. Current acts include Helen Hudson (singer/songwriter); Mark Shipper (songwriter/author); and Sally Spurs (singer/songwriter).

**BAUER-HALL ENTERPRISES**, 138 Frog Hollow Rd., Churchville PA 18966. (215)357-5189. Contact: William B. Hall III. Booking agency. Represents individuals and groups; currently handles 12 acts. Receives 10-15% commission. Reviews material for acts, depending on engagement.
**How to Contact:** Query ("include photos, promo material, and record or tape") or submit demo tape and lyric sheet. Prefers cassette with 2-3 songs on demo. "Letter of inquiry preferred as initial contact." Does not return unsolicited material. Reports in 1 month.
**Music:** Circus, ethnic and polka. Works primarily with "unusual or novelty attractions in musical line, preferably those that appeal to family groups." Current acts include Coco's Musical Comix (all clown band); Philadelphia Mummers' String Bands (string bands); Ruth Daye (novelty xylophonist); Fred Wayne (circus bandmaster); Joseph Kaye (one-man band); Loki Ontai (Hawaiian revue); Jos. Dallas-Dan Conn (show-circus band); Bobby Burnett (harmonica virtuoso-comedian-emcee); Steel Band; Greater Pottstown Concert Band; Organ Grinder & Monkey; and Bill (Boom-Boom) Browning (circus bandmaster); calliope specialties; and Verdi Band of Greater Norristown, Pennsylvania.

**BEACON INTERNATIONAL ARTISTS**, (A division of Beacon International Entertainment Corporation), Rt. #4, Box 184, Quakerstown PA 18951. Regional Manager: R.W. Augstroze. Management agency and record producer and promoter. Represents artists, groups, songwriters, actors, popular personalities and writers (screenplays novels) worldwide; currently handles 30 acts. Receives 15-25% commission. Reviews material for acts.

**How to Contact:** Query by mail then submit demo tape and lead sheet. Prefers cassette with 2-5 songs on demo. SASE. Reports in 2-3 weeks.
**Music:** Choral, church/religious, classical, easy listening, gospel, jazz, MOR, progressive, R&B, rock (all types), soul and top 40/pop. Works primarily with classical singers, rock groups and classical/religious choirs; opening acts for top 40 bands, and top 40 groups and vocalists. Current acts include Silvia Erdmanis (classical soprano); Equinox (rock group); and Surface (rock/jazz group).
**Tips:** "Submit no information without the inclusion of a tape. Material should be original—no top 40 impersonators. Emphasize your strong points and advantages; written descriptions should be short and concise. Be professional and tell it straight—no hype."

**THE BELKIN MADURI ORGANIZATION**, Suite 205, 28001 Chagrin Blvd., Cleveland OH 44122. (216)464-5990. A&R Department: Chris Maduri or Carl Maduri. Management firm and production company. Represents artists, groups and songwriters; currently handles 6 acts. Reviews material for acts.
**How to Contact:** Query or submit demo tape and lyric sheet. Prefers 7½ or 15 ips reel-to-reel or cassette with 2-4 songs on demo. "Send a tape and follow up with a phone call." SASE. Please call back for report.
**Music:** Mostly top 40/pop, rock and dance-oriented; also R&B and church/religious. Works with commercial pop, R&B artists/songwriters, R&R/adult contemporary artists and black acts. "Would like to pursue disco acts much more aggressively. We are involved in crossover acts." Current acts include The Michael Stanley Band (rock/pop/top 40); Donnie Iris (rock/pop); B.E. Taylor Group (rock/pop); Karen Jackson (AC/Christian contemporary); and Swankk (R&B).

**FRED BERK ARTIST MANAGEMENT/TOP DOG PRODUCTIONS/TOP DOG MUSIC**, 71 Boylston St., Brookline MA 02147. (617)739-2010. President: Fred Berk. Management firm, record producer and music publisher. Represents artists, groups and songwriters; currently handles 6 acts. Receives variable commissions, fees and royalties. Reviews material for acts.
**How to Contact:** Submit demo tape. Prefers cassette with 1-6 songs on demo. Does not return unsolicited material.
**Music:** Mostly rock, country rock, rockabilly and C&W; also bluegrass, R&B and top 40/pop. Works primarily with recording acts. Current acts include Jeanne French (rock/C&W artist); Bobby Keyes (rock artist); Scott Anderson (rockabilly artist); Kenny Girard (C&W artist); and Northern Tier (rock artist).

***RICHARD BERNSTEIN PERSONAL MANAGEMENT**, Suite 119, 1585 Crossroads of the World, Hollywood CA 90028. (213)469-4631. President: Richard Bernstein. Management firm. Represents artists, musical groups and songwriters from anywhere; currently handles 8 acts. Receives 15-20% commission. Reviews material for acts.
**How to Contact:** Query by mail. Prefers cassette with minimum of 3 songs on demo. SASE. Reports in 1 month.
**Music:** Mostly C&W, MOR, rock and R&B; also folk, gospel, jazz, Spanish, soul and top 40/pop. Works with all types of artists and groups. Current acts include Diana Davies (C&W); Ace Jacks (C&W); Jack Powers (pop); and The Now Band (rock).

**J. BIRD BOOKING AGENCY**, Box 1036, Daytona Beach FL 32019. (904)767-4707. Contact: John Bird. Booking agency. Represents artists and groups from anywhere; currently handles 104 acts. Receives 15-25% commission.
**How to Contact:** Submit demo tape and lead sheet. Prefers cassette with 3-4 songs on demo. "Initial interview is usually by phone; after demo material is received we usually ask person to contact us again in 1 week-10 days." Does not return unsolicited material.
**Music:** Bluegrass, blues, church/religious, C&W, dance-oriented, easy listening, folk, jazz, R&B, soul, country rock and top 40/pop. Works primarily with "top 40 dance and show bands, rock bands (dance and concert), and concert groups (major label touring bands). Particularly active in national college concerts. Most of our demand is for dance bands since we generally work with high schools and universities." Current acts include Terry Brooks (R&B, Star People Records); Nantucket (Epic Records, rock/college concerts); Brewed (Atlantic Records, soul/dance and concerts); James Durst (Phoenix Songs Records, contemporary folk/concerts); Gypsychild (R&R/top 40 band); and Gina Crute & Tasty (top 40/group).
**Tips:** "We solicit established professional acts interested in touring full time. The groups should have or be willing to prepare a promotional package containing audio and/or videotape, photos, song, personnel, and equipment lists. Since we are the largest 'one nighter' agency in the Southeast, providing entertainment to colleges nationwide, artists submitting materials should be geared for that market."

**BLACK HILLS TALENT & BOOKING**, Box 603, Rapid City SD 57709. (605)341-5940. Agent: Darla Drew. Booking agency. Represents groups in South Dakota, Wyoming and Nebraska; currently handles 15 acts. Receives 10-20% commission.
**How to Contact:** Submit demo tape. Prefers cassette with 3-7 songs on demo. SASE. Reports in 1 week "if genuinely interested in material."
**Music:** C&W, rock (hard, country, new wave) and top 40/pop. Works primarily with "3-6 piece rock or country rock bands and bands for bars, schools and public dances." Current acts include Asia (hard rock group—equal amount of cover and original); Ivory (top 40/hard rock group—some originals); and Tryx (hard rock group).
**Tips:** "I would only suggest commercial sounding material to my bands (AM radio)."

**BLADE AGENCY**, Box 1550, Gainesville FL 32602. (904)372-8158 and 377-8158. General Manager: Charles V. Steadham Jr. Management firm and booking agency. Represents professional individuals and groups; currently handles 36 acts. Reviews material for acts.
**How to Contact:** Query or submit demo tape, publicity materials and itinerary. Prefers cassette with 2-5 songs on demo. Does not return unsolicited material. Reports as soon as possible on solicited material.
**Music:** Bluegrass, blues, C&W, dance-oriented, easy listening, folk, MOR, rock (country), soul and top 40/pop. Current acts include Gamble Rogers (C&W/folk artist); Tom Parks (comedian); Mike Cross (country/folk artist); Mike Reid (MOR/pop); Truc of American (R&R/comedy); Paul Zimmerman (comedy/variety); Robert Nelson (comedy variety); Judy Carter (comedy); and Barbara Bailey Hutchison (folk/pop).

**WILLIS BLUME AGENCY**, Box 509, Orangeburg SC 29115. (803)536-2951. President: Willis Blume. Management firm and booking agency. Represents artists and groups in the southeast; currently handles 13 acts. Receives minimum 15% commission. Reviews material for acts.
**How to Contact:** Query by mail. Prefers cassette with 4 songs maximum on demo. SASE.
**Music:** Mostly beach music and dance-oriented; also easy listening, MOR, R&B, soul and top 40/pop. Works primarily with show and dance bands. Current acts include Shagtime, The O'Kaysions, and The Swingin' McDallons; (all beach/top 40 show acts); Maurice Williams & the Zodiacs; and the Tams (beach/top 40/pop artists).

*****BOBBY BOYD**, 2609 NW 36th St., Oklahoma City OK 73112. (405)942-0462. President: Bobby Boyd. Management agency. Represents artists and songwriters. Receives minimum 25% commission.
**How to Contact:** Submit demo tape and lead sheet. Prefers 7½ ips reel-to-reel with 5-6 songs on demo. "Send tapes that do not have to be returned." Does not return unsolicited material. Reports in 2 weeks.
**Music:** C&W, rock, soul and top 40/pop. Current acts include Jim Whitaker (single); Dale Greear (single); and Belinda Eaves (single).

**BRANCHING-OUT PRODUCTION**, 281 E. Kingsbridge Rd., Bronx NY 10458. (212)733-5342. President: Murray Fuller. Management firm. Represents artists, groups and songwriters; currently handles 5 acts. Receives 10-20% commission. Reviews material for acts.
**How to Contact:** Submit demo tape and lead sheet. Prefers cassette with 3-6 songs on demo. SASE. Reports in 1 month.
**Music:** Dance-oriented, easy listening, jazz, R&B, rock and soul. Works primarily with dance and bar bands, and bands for concert support. Current acts include Ray Rivera (jazz artist); Boncellia Lewis (contemporary vocalist); and Tony Graye (jazz artist).

**BREAKTHROUGH ENTERTAINMENT CORPORATION**, Box 354, Durham CT 06422. (203)349-9637. President: Randall Coates. Management firm, music publisher and record company. Estab. 1982. Represents artists, groups and songwriters in northeast US; currently handles 6 acts. Receives 10-25% commission. Reviews material for acts.
**How to Contact:** Submit demo tape and lead sheet. Prefers 7½ ips reel-to-reel or cassette with 1-3 songs on demo. SASE. Reports in 1 month.
**Music:** C&W, easy listening, MOR, rock and top 40/pop. Current acts include Morningstar (AC, MOR, top 40 group); Prisoners (new wave group); and Allies (rock group).
**Tips:** "We represent artists with purpose and are not interested in copy bands. We are looking for acts we consider to be 'artists' in the true sense of the word."

**BUG MUSIC**, 9th Floor, 6777 Hollywood Blvd., Hollywood CA 90028. Contact: Fred Bourgoise. Music publisher. Represents songwriters from anywhere; currently publishes and administers over 200 publishers and artists. "Sometimes" reviews material for acts.
**How to Contact:** Submit demo tape only. Prefers cassette with 2 songs on demo. SASE. Reports ASAP.

**Music:** All types, including C&W, easy listening, R&B, rock (all), soul and top 40/pop. Current acts include Blasters, Iggy Pop, Del Shannon, Moon Martin, John Hiatt, T. Bone Burnett, Tom Kelly, Jack Nitzsche, Shoes, Craig Leon, Commander Cody, Asleep at the Wheel, Stooges, Richie Cole, Dwight Twilley, Los Lobos, Surf Punks, Nicky Hopkins and Mose Allison.

**AL BUNETTA MANAGEMENT, INC.**, Suite 215, 4121 Wilshire Blvd, Los Angeles CA 90010. (213)385-0882. President: Al Bunetta. Management firm. Represents artists and songwriters; currently handles 6 acts. Receives variable commission. Reviews material for acts.
**How to Contact:** Submit demo tape and lead sheet. Prefers cassette with 1-5 songs on demo. SASE. Reports in 1 month.
**Music:** R&B, rock, new music, top 40/pop and adult contemporary. Works primarily with national recording artists. Current acts include John Prine and Steve Goodman (both singer/songwriter/recording artists).

**C.A. MUSIC**, Box 1990, Thousand Oaks CA 91360. Representative: Rick Logan. Management firm. Represents songwriters; currently handles 15 artists. "Artist receives royalties from publishing and recordings."
**How to Contact:** Submit demo tape and lead sheet. Prefers cassette with 1-3 songs on demo. Does not return unsolicited material. "Allow 3-5 weeks."
**Music:** Mostly gospel and contemporary Christian; also children's, choral and church/religious. Works primarily with contemporary and traditional gospel writers, vocalists and instrumentalists. Current artists include Cam Floria, Jeff Kennedy, Tim Hosman, Claire Cloninger and David Graham.

**C.M. MANAGEMENT**, Box 2999, San Rafael CA 94912. (415)457-5474. President: Craig Miller. Management firm, booking agency and music publisher. Represents artists, groups, producers and publishers; currently handles 6 acts. Receives 10-20% commission—"occasional flat fee."
**How to Contact:** Query by mail, then submit demo tape and lead sheet. Prefers cassette with 3-5 songs on demo. Submit material "with the best package, (i.e., representation) possible." SASE. Reports in 3 weeks.
**Music:** Jazz, rock and fusion. Works primarily with acoustic musicians and composers. Current acts include David Grisman (popular recording quartet); Anger-Marshall (popular recording duo); and Rob Wasserman (popular recording artist).
**Tips:** "Send an interesting and complete package. If a song works with just a vocal and accompaniment of just one instrument, then it should be great when produced."

*****CACTUS INDUSTRIES MUSIC INC.**, 870 Woodland Rd., Ingomar PA 15127. (412)364-5095. President: Chuck Surman. Management firm, publisher and record producer. Represents artists, musical groups and songwriters from anywhere; currently handles 25 acts. Receives administration fee plus percentage of artist's earnings. Reviews material for acts.
**How to Contact:** Submit demo tape only. Prefers 7½ ips reel-to-reel or cassette with 5-15 songs on demo. Writers should include a short bio. SASE. Reports ASAP.
**Music:** C&W, dance-oriented, MOR, R&B, rock (all types) and top 40/pop. Works primarily with solo artists (vocal) and self contained groups; no instrumental acts. Current acts include the X-15 (hard rock group, Precision Records); Silencers (hard rock group, Precision Records); and David Kent (easy rock group, Epic Records).

**CALIFORNIA MUSIC PRESENTATIONS**, #200, 8831 Sunset Blvd., Los Angeles CA 90069. (213)704-1764. President: Robert E. Brondell. Management firm. Represents artists, groups and songwriters; currently handles 7 acts. Receives 10-25% commission. Reviews material for acts.
**How to Contact:** Query by mail, arrange personal interview or submit demo tape and lead sheet. Prefers cassette with 3-5 songs on demo. SASE. Reports in 1 month.
**Music:** Bluegrass, blues, C&W, dance-oriented, jazz, MOR, progressive, rock, soul and top 40/pop. Current acts include Paul Sober, Elixir Trip, Sweet Magnolia (all R&B); and Caryn Robin & Ice (top 40/pop).

**CAN'T STOP PRODUCTIONS, INC.**, 65 E. 55th St., New York NY 10022. (212)751-6177. International Manager: Hope Goering. Management firm, production company and music publisher. Represents artists, groups and songwriters. Receives variable commission. Reviews material for acts.
**How to Contact:** Submit demo tape and lead sheet. Prefers cassette with 1-4 songs on demo. SASE. Reports in 1 month.
**Music:** Dance-oriented, MOR, progressive, R&B, rock (no hard or country) and top 40/pop. Current acts include Ritchie Family and Village People.

**CAPITOL BOOKING SERVICE, INC.**, 11844 Market St., North Lima OH 44452. (216)549-2155. President: David Musselman. Booking agency. Represents show groups; currently handles 7 acts. Receives maximum 15% commission. Reviews material for acts "on occasion."
**How to Contact:** Query. Prefers cassette with 3 songs minimum on tape. "We would like references. We also have video equipment, and if artist has videotape, we would like to see this." SASE. Reports ASAP.
**Music:** Mostly MOR; also C&W, dance-oriented, easy listening, folk, gospel, patriotic and top 40/pop. Works primarily with "self-contained musical groups that play all-around music for mixed audiences; young American or Las Vegas-type show reviews, some country and the New Seekers who are, of course, a name act from the '70s." Current acts include Life, Sunshine Express, Higher Power, New(est) Seekers (all show groups); Alann & Hays Show (show and dance group); Eddie Jaye (ventriloquist and comedy M.C.); and JoAnn Castle (formerly of Lawrence Welk Show).
**Tips:** "Acts should have good literature, well choreographed and produced show."

**CAROLINA ATTRACTIONS, INC.**, 203 Culver Ave., Charleston SC 29407. (803)766-2500. President: Harold Thomas. Vice President, A&R: Michael Thomas. Management firm. Represents only nationally known individuals, groups and songwriters; currently handles 3 acts. Receives 10-25% commission. Reviews material for acts.
**How to Contact:** Submit demo tape. Cassette only as demo. "Send cover letter with tape and any additional promo material (pictures, news releases, etc.) available. Bio if possible." SASE. Reports in 3 weeks.
**Music:** R&B, beach and top 40/pop. Works primarily with artists for show and dance groups and concerts. Current acts include the Tams (show/concert group); Cornelius Brothers and Sister Rose (show/concert group); and the Original Drifters (show/concert group).

**BUDD CARR**, Box U, Tarzana CA 91356. (213)705-2717. Managers: Budd Carr or Marlene Bitters. Management firm. Represents artists, groups, songwriters and producers; currently handles 6 acts. Receives variable commission. Reviews material for acts.
**How to Contact:** Query by mail, then submit demo tape and lead sheet. Prefers cassette with 1-5 songs on demo. "Photographs, a bio and resume along with tape submissions are appreciated." SASE. Reports in 2 weeks or "as soon as the group has been contacted."
**Music:** R&B, rock (pop) and top 40/pop. Works primarily with pop and rock artists. Current acts include Kansas (pop/rock group); Le Roux (pop/rock group); Jay Ferguson (pop/rock artist); Brick; and Total Coelo (all girl band from England).

**RICHARD CARR PRODUCTIONS, INC.**, 1 Court Dr., Lincoln RI 02865. (401)333-0700. Artist Development: Bruce Marshall. Management firm and booking agency. Represents artists and groups; currently handles 20 acts. Receives maximum 15% commission. Reviews material for acts.
**How to Contact:** Query by mail; "submit press kit (promotional pictures, song list and tape)." Prefers cassette with 2-10 songs on demo. Does not return unsolicited material. Reports in 2 weeks.
**Music:** Mostly rock; also dance-oriented, top 40/pop and FM commercial. Works primarily with "dance bands playing a majority of cover/copy material in the commercial FM rock market plus national acts for night clubs and colleges." Current acts include P.F. & The Flyers (sophisticated rock group); Strutt (dance/rock group); Touch (production/rock group); English, Radiostar and Fallen Angel (dance rock groups).
**Tips:** "Artists should have established track record. Original material must have definite 'hit' potential."

**DON CASALE MUSIC, INC.**, 377 Plainfield St., Westbury NY 11590. (516)333-7898. President: Don Casale. Music publisher.
**How to Contact:** "Call or write before submitting." SASE.

**CELEBRITY ENTERPRISES, INC./MUSIC MARKETING INTERNATIONAL, INC.**, Box 390, Hollywood CA 90028. (213)366-1289. President: Buz Wilburn. Management firm, music publisher, record company and TV/movie production company. Represents artists, groups and songwriters; currently handles 6 acts. Receives minimum 20% commission. Reviews material for acts.
**How to Contact:** Submit demo tape and lead sheet, include "brief information sheet about act or writer." Prefers cassette with 3-6 songs on demo. "All submissions should be brief and concise." SASE. Reports in 2 weeks.
**Music:** C&W, easy listening, gospel, MOR, R&B, soul and top 40/pop. Works primarily with "individual artists who have a background of performing and can write. We are not interested in any act that doesn't have recording possibilities." Current acts include Sam Neely (performer/songwriter); Alex

Harvey (performer/songwriter); Chris David (C&W/recording artist); and Calamity Jayne (songwriter/recording artist).
**Tips:** "We are only looking for dedicated and professional acts who are multi-talented. Send complete (but brief) information and we will give an immediate answer as to whether or not our company can work with the act."

**CLARK MUSICAL PRODUCTIONS**, Box 299, Watseka IL 60970. President: Dr. Paul E. Clark. Management firm, booking agency and music publisher. Deals with artists in the Midwest and South. Represents individuals, groups and songwriters; currently handles 8 acts. Receives 10-20% commission.
**How to Contact:** Query or submit demo tape and lead sheet. Prefers cassette with 1-3 songs on demo. Does not return unsolicited material.
**Music:** Church/religious, C&W, gospel, rock (soft) and top 40/pop. Works primarily with acts for concerts, dances and club dates. Current acts include Pat Gould (top 40/pop solo artist).

**CLOCKWORK ENTERTAINMENT MANAGEMENT AGENCY**, Box 1600, Haverhill MA 01831. (617)373-6010. President: Bill Macek. Management firm and booking agency. Deals with artists throughout New England. Represents groups and songwriters; currently handles 6 acts. Receives 10-15% commission. Reviews material for acts.
**How to Contact:** Query or submit demo tape only. Include "interesting facts about yourself in a cover letter." Prefers cassette with 3-12 songs on demo. "Also submit promotion and cover letter with tape." Does not return unsolicited material unless accompanied with a SASE. Reports in 2 weeks.
**Music:** Rock (all types) and top 40/pop. Works primarily with bar bands and original acts. Current acts include Renegade (FM rocker); Gail Savage (4-piece rocker group); Bogash (4-piece FM rocker); The Suspects (5-piece FM rocker); The Street Rockers (5-piece FM rocker); and Familiar Faces (4-piece high energy top 40/rock).

**STEVE COHEN & ASSOCIATES**, Suite 502, 9000 Sunset Blvd., Los Angeles CA 90069. (213)275-7329. Director, Artist Development: David Cook. Management firm. Represents artists, groups, songwriters and producers "mostly in our West Coast region, but could represent hit talent from anywhere;" currently handles 4 acts. Receives 15-20% commission. Reviews material for acts.
**How to Contact:** Query by mail, then submit demo tape. Prefers cassette with 2-3 songs on demo. "Send photo, resume or any other relevant materials." SASE. Reports in 1 month or "1 day, depending on level of interest."
**Music:** Dance-oriented, R&B, rock, soul and top 40/pop. Works primarily with "recording artists, songwriters, soloists and bands." Current acts include Mary Wells (pop/R&B artist/Epic-CBS Records); Greg Watson (arranger, writer, producer, performer, overseas performance tours, publishing, Fantasy Records); and Paulette McWilliams (solo and background singer and MCA Records recording artist working with Quincy Jones, Luther Vandress, Lionel Ritchie and Marvin Gaye).
**Tips:** "Submit hit songs only, i.e., "A" side, top 10 record. No ballads, please."

**COLLINS/BARRASSO AGENCY**, 280 Lincoln St., Allston MA 02134. (617)783-1100. Contact: Steve Barrasso. Management firm. Represents artists, groups and songwriters. Receives variable commission. Reviews material for acts.
**How to Contact:** Submit demo tape. Prefers cassette with 2-6 songs on demo. SASE. Reports in 1 month.
**Music:** C&W, rock and top 40/pop. Current acts include Jonathan Edwards and Joe Perry.

**BURT COMPTON AGENCY**, Box 160373, Miami FL 33116. (305)238-7312. Contact: Burt Compton. Booking agency. Represents groups; currently handles 36 acts. Receives 10-20% commission. Reviews material for acts.
**How to Contact:** Query by mail, then submit demo tape. Prefers cassette with 3-6 songs on demo. "Include complete repertoire, 8x10 photo and resume." Does not return unsolicited material. Reports in 1 month.
**Music:** Mostly top 40/pop; also rock (hard/dance). Works primarily with dance and bar bands. Current acts include Heroes (dance band); Fantasy (recording/concert group); and Wildlife (recording/concert group).
**Tips:** "Have your promotional materials professionally packaged. We don't like having to decipher handwritten resumes with misspelled words and incomplete sentences."

*****CONCERT IDEAS**, Box 669, Woodstock NY 12498. (914)679-6069 or 679-2458. President: Harris Goldberg. Vice President: Tom Akstens. Management and book agency. Represents artists, groups and songwriters; currently handles 4 acts. Receives 10-20% commission. Reviews material for acts.

**How to Contact:** Query by mail, then submit demo tape and lead sheet. Prefers cassette with 2-4 songs on demo. SASE. Reports in 3 weeks.
**Music:** Easy listening, rock and top 40/pop. Works primarily with singer/songwriter. Current acts include Artie Traum/Pat Alger (singer, songwriter); Tim Moore (singer/songwriter); Robert Dupree ("We co-publish his writing through Oozle Music"); and Mark Black.

**\*CONTEMPORARY ARTIST MANAGEMENT,** Box 220, Altamonte Springs FL 32701. (305)834-6677. Artist Management: Terrie Miner. Management firm. Represents musical groups from anywhere; currently handles 12 acts. Receives 10-15% commission. Reviews material for acts.
**How to Contact:** Query by mail or submit demo tape and lyric sheet. Prefers cassette with 4-6 songs on demo. SASE. Reports in 3 weeks.
**Music:** Mostly dance-oriented and top 40/pop; also MOR, R&B, rock and soul. Works primarily with high-energy show acts, including dance acts. Current acts include Apple Band, Coast to Coast and Strut (show groups).

**CONTI PRODUCTION STUDIO,** Box 968, Edgewater FL 32032. (904)427-2480. President: Dick Conti. Recording/video studio and management firm. Represents artists, groups and songwriters; currently handles 5 acts. Commission "negotiated by what we can do." Reviews material for acts, commercials and jingles.
**How to Contact:** Query or submit demo tape and lead sheet. Prefers 7½ ips reel-to-reel or cassette. SASE. Reports in 1 month.
**Music:** Mostly C&W and top 40/pop; also blues, children's, church/religious, easy listening, folk, gospel, R&B, MOR, rock and soul. Works primarily with large "Mike Curb Congregation" type groups, rock groups, show bands (new Christian), vocalists (R&B), church groups (children) and commercial/ jingle writers and arrangers. Current acts include the Conti Family (family variety); Gino Conti (Gino Vannelli type); and Britton (metal rock group).

**\*CONTINENTAL TALENT AGENCY,** 1425 Key Highway, Baltimore MD 21230. (301)837-5570. Booking agency. Estab. 1981. Represents artists; currently handles 20 acts. Receives 15-20% commission. Reviews material for acts.
**How to Contact:** Query by mail; submit demo tape and lead sheet or arrange personal interview. Prefers reel-to-reel or cassette with 1-12 songs as demo. SASE. Reports in 1 week.
**Music:** Mostly country and country rock; also bluegrass, gospel and top 40/pop. Works primarily with show bands. Current acts include Just Us Three (show group); Warren Blair and Southland (bluegrass show group); and The Ernie C. Penn Show (country show act).
**Tips:** "We are going into markets in Japan and other foreign countries. We welcome newcomers to our business."

**\*WAYNE COOMBS AGENCY,** Suite 11, 75 Malaga Cove Plaza, Palos Verdes Estates CA 90274. (213)377-0420. Executive Vice President & Artist Representative: Marc Whitmore. Artist Representative: Jacqueline Macklem. Booking agency. Represents artists and musical groups from anywhere; currently handles 12 acts. Receives 10% minimum commission. Reviews material for acts.
**How to Contact:** Query by mail. Prefers cassette with 3-5 songs on demo. SASE. Reports in 1 month.
**Music:** Mostly top 40 and gospel; also C&W, easy listening, MOR and rock. Works primarily with vocalists and recording groups. Current acts include Debby Boone; Dan Peek (rock/soft rock); and Reba Rambo (contemporary gospel).

**TIM COULTER & ASSOCIATES,** Box 24172, Columbus OH 43224. (614)261-1107. President: Tim D. Coulter. Management firm, booking agency and public relations firm. Represents artists and groups; currently handles 3 acts. Receives 10-20% commission. Reviews material for acts.
**How to Contact:** Submit demo tape with background information and resume. Prefers cassette with 3-5 songs on demo. SASE. Reports in 1 month.
**Music:** Church/religious, C&W, gospel, MOR, soul and top 40/pop. Works primarily with show bands and concert acts. Current acts include Ransom (art rock group); Dave Fullen (contemporary Christian artist); and Chuck Childers and Surrender (contemporary Christian group).

**\*COUNTRY STAR ATTRACTIONS,** 439 Wiley Ave., Franklin PA 16323. (814)432-4633. Contact: Norman Kelly. Booking agency. Represents artists and musical groups; currently handles 10 acts. Receives 10-15% commission. Reviews material for acts.
**How to Contact:** Submit demo tape and lyric sheet. Prefers 7½ ips reel-to-reel and cassette with 1-4 songs on demo; include photo. SASE. Reports in 2 weeks.
**Music:** Mostly C&W; also bluegrass, gospel, rock and top 40/pop. Works primarily with vocalists accompanied by band for shows. Current acts include Junie Lou (country); Virgie Brown (country); Rose-Marie (rock); and Debbie Sue (country).

## Managers & Booking Agencies

**CRASH PRODUCTIONS,** Box 40, Bangor ME 04401-0040. (207)794-6686. Manager: Jim Moreau. Booking agency. Represents individuals and groups; currently handles 5 acts. Receives 10-25% commission.
**How to Contact:** Query. Prefers cassette with 4-8 songs on demo. Include resume and photos. "We prefer to hear groups at an actual performance." SASE. Reports in 2 weeks.
**Music:** Bluegrass, C&W, dance-oriented, easy listening, 50s & 60s, folk, MOR, rock (country) and top 40/pop. Works primarily with groups who perform mainly at night clubs and outdoor events (festivals and fairs). Current acts include Band of Gold (50s & 60s); Dirigo (50s and 60s); Bushwhack (country rock); Coyote (rock); and Inn Country Band featuring the Two of Us (country rock).

*****CROSBY MUSIC AGENCY,** 7730 Herschel Ave., La Jolla CA 92037. (619)454-0383. Agent: Douglas Friedman. Booking agency. Deals primarily with regional artists. Represents artists and groups; currently handles 80+ acts. Receives 10-20% commission.
**How to Contact:** Submit demo tape, photo and song list. "Evaluation usually within 2 weeks. SASE for return of material."
**Music:** Jazz, rock (hard rock and country rock), top 40 and new wave. Works with wide variety of performers; show bands, dance bands, bar bands and duos. Current acts include Snails (new wave); Bob Crosby Orchestra (jazz); and Freddie Martin Orchestra (big band).
**Tips:** "Send a complete promotional package including a good photo, complete song list, and clear demo tape."

**CROSSLIGHT MANAGEMENT, LTD.,** 1592 Crossroads of the World, Hollywood CA 90028. (213)462-6156. Associate: Debbie Fletcher. Management firm. Represents artists, groups and songwriters; "It's most convenient to deal with local talent, but we will consider any gifted artist/writer;" currently handles 10 acts. Receives minimum 15% commission. Reviews material for acts.
**How to Contact:** Submit demo tape and lyric sheet. Prefers cassette with 1-3 songs on demo. "Please have identification on the cassette itself. Also, do not send masters." Does not return unsolicited material. Reports in 3 weeks.
**Music:** C&W, easy listening, MOR, R&B, rock and top 40/pop. Works primarily with "rock, acoustic rock and country rock acts." Current acts include Jackson Browne, David Lindley, Poco and Cosby, Stills & Nash.

**ARTHUR CRUME & THE SOUL STIRRERS,** Box 42606, Chicago IL 60642. (512)231-4740. Manager: Arthur Crume. Management firm. Currently handles only The Soul Stirrers group. Receives 5-10% commission. Reviews material for act.
**How to Contact:** Submit demo tape and lead sheet. Prefers cassette with 3-5 songs on demo. SASE. Reports in 1 month.
**Music:** Church/religious and gospel. Especially interested in "good lyrics." Works with gospel groups only.

*****JOE DEANGELIS MANAGEMENT,** 79 Kingsland Ave., Brooklyn NY 11211. (212)389-2511. President: Joe DeAngelis. Management agency. Represents artists, groups and songwriters; currently handles 10 acts. Receives 10-15% commission. Reviews material for acts.
**How to Contact:** Query by mail. Prefers cassette with 10 songs on demo. SASE. Reports in 2 weeks.
**Music:** Blues, C&W, R&B, soul and top 40/pop. Works primarily with female groups and single artists. Current acts include Devonnes (lounge group); Hill Twins (lounge group); Pat Core (solo artist); and Traci Core (dancer-model).
**Tips:** "Have great tunes and good lyrics."

*****DIVERSIFIED MANAGEMENT AGENCY,** 17650 W. Twelve Mile Rd., Southfield MI 48076. (313)559-2600. Midwest and East Coast Agent: Trip Brown. Booking agency. Represents groups; currently handles 30 acts. Receives 10-20% commission.
**How to Contact:** Submit "promo pack, demo tape and photo of act." Prefers cassette with 2-4 songs on demo. Does not return unsolicited material. Reports in 3 weeks "if interested."
**Music:** Rock (hard or new music). Works primarily with concert acts. Current acts include Aerosmith, Scorpions, Romantics, Payolas and Nazareth.

**DMR AGENCY,** Suite 316, Wilson Bldg., Syracuse NY 13202. (315)471-0868. Contact: David M. Rezak. Booking agency. Represents individuals and groups; currently handles 75 acts. Receives 10-15% commission.
**How to Contact:** Submit demo tape and press kit. Prefers cassette with 1-4 songs on demo. SASE.
**Music:** Mostly rock (all styles); also jazz, R&B and progressive. Works primarily with bar and concert bands; all kinds of rock for schools, clubs, concerts, etc. Current acts include New York Flyers (rock);

Alecstar, (rock); Mr. Edd . . . of course (comedy-rock); Joe Whiting (rock); the Velcros (rockabilly group); the Keyes (vocal rock); Atlas Linen Company (jazz rock); and 805 (progressive rock).

*DOUBLE EAGLE MUSIC ORGANIZATION, 29 Commonwealth Ave., Boston MA 02116. (617)267-7189. Contact: Peter Lembo. Management firm. Represents musical groups; currently handles 2 acts. Receives 15-20% commission. Reviews material for acts.
**How to Contact:** Query by mail or submit demo tape and lyric sheet. Prefers cassette as demo. SASE. Reports in 3 weeks.
**Music:** Mostly rock; also R&B and top 40/pop. Current acts include The Stompers; and John A's Hidden Secret (rock acts, Boardwalk Records).

DOUBLE TEE PROMOTIONS, Suite B, 712 SW Salmon, Portland OR 97205. (503)221-0288. Contact: Carole Pucik. Management firm. Represents artists, groups and songwriters; currently handles 5 acts. Receives minimum 15% commission. Reviews material for acts.
**How to Contact:** Query by mail. Prefers cassette with minimum 2 songs on demo. Does not return unsolicited material. Reports in 1 month.
**Music:** Mostly rock; also blues, dance-oriented, R&B and top 40/pop. Works primarily with show bands. Current acts include Taxxi (rock group); Shock (funk group); Sequel (top 40); The Robert Cray Band (blues); and Marlon McClain (R&B artist).

THE BOB DOYLE AGENCY, Box 1199, State College PA 16801. (814)238-5478, 237-3746 or 234-1647. President: Bob Doyle. Booking agency. Deals with artists in Pennsylvania and neighboring states. Represents groups and singles; currently handles 50 acts. Receives 15-25% commission. Reviews material for acts.
**How to Contact:** Submit demo tape, lead sheet and promo photograph. Prefers cassette with 3-5 songs on demo. Does not return unsolicited material. Reports in 1 week. "I prefer a phone call first to see if this agency can work with the group. Then we like to have the promo and tape. We need to know if the group can work the markets we are involved with."
**Music:** Bluegrass, folk (American, ethnic), rock (country) and C&W. Works college markets and some clubs; "bluegrass, old-time, folk and ethnic, plus some R&R, mainly dance-oriented groups." Current acts include Whetstone Run (traditional bluegrass); Jim Corr & Friends (Irish); Hat Trick (R&R/funk); and The Allegheny String Band (old-time and square-dance).

TIM DRAKE PRESENTS, Box 602, Woodcliff Lake NJ 07675. (201)666-5553. Vice President: Pat Schiavino. Management, concert promotion and talent buying agent for universities and clubs. Represents artists, groups and songwriters; currently handles 5 acts. Receives 10-20% commission. "If we manage and also act as booking agent the commission will be 20%." Reviews material for acts.
**How to Contact:** "Please submit a well recorded demo. If artist is well known, telephone call will do. If unknown, submit tape, biography, press clippings, etc." Prefers cassette with 3-5 songs on demo. SASE. Reports in 2 weeks.
**Music:** Rock (all types) and top 40/pop. Works with touring rock acts, solo acoustic artists, jazz fusion artists and groups. "We deal primarily with concert acts, as our main business is concert promotion. However, on the booking and management end of things we have helped develop some very talented and commercially potential artists. We don't look for new, undeveloped acts, but if we see or hear something sensational, we'll pursue it." Current acts include John Macey (jazz fusion artist, CBS Records); The Hurt (new wave act); Phil Garland (rock act, Atlantic Records); and Billy Falcon Group (rock act, MCA Records).
**Tips:** "Take the time to carefully prepare your submitted tape. Try to make your presentation as professional as possible."

DYNAMIC TALENT AGENCY, Box 13584, Atlanta GA 30324. (404)872-6000. Vice President, Promotions: Marie Sutton. President: Alex Janoulis. Booking agency. Represents individuals and groups; currently handles 6 acts. Receives 10-15% commission.
**How to Contact:** Submit demo tape. Prefers cassette with 2-3 songs on demo. "Send photos and bio." Reports ASAP.
**Music:** Blues, jazz and rock (new music). Works with top 40 bands and rock and blues bands.. Current acts include The Bop (top 40/pop); Starfoxx (top 40/rock); The Night Shadows (new wave); Diamond Lil (female impersonator); and The Heaters (top 40/new music).

*T.O. EARNHEART AGENCY, Suite 700, 2500 Mt. Moriah, Memphis TN 38115. (901)794-4011. Contact: T.O. Earnheart. Booking agency. Represents artists and musical groups; currently handles 25 acts. Receives 15-20% commission. Reviews material for acts.

**How to Contact:** Query by mail or call first. Prefers cassette with 1-6 songs on demo. SASE. Reports in 1 week.
**Music:** Mostly C&W; also MOR, R&B, rock, soul and top 40/pop. Works primarily with vocalists and recording bands. Current acts include the Gentrys (top 40/pop act); The Diamonds (oldies act); and In Pact (soul act).

**EBB-TIDE BOOKING AGENCY,** Box 2544, Baton Rouge LA 70821. (504)924-6865 (24 hrs.). Director: E.K. Harrison. Booking agency. Represents professional individuals and groups; currently handles 12 acts. Receives 15-25% commission. Reviews material for acts.
**How to Contact:** Query or submit demo tape along with photographs and biographical information. Prefers cassette tape. SASE. Reports in 1 month.
**Music:** Bluegrass, blues, children's, church/religious, C&W, dance-oriented, easy listening, gospel, jazz, MOR, progressive, R&B, rock (hard or punk), soul and top 40/pop. Works primarily with "commercial/selling acts and talents; show bands, vocalists, dance bands and concert groups (no bar or lounge gigs). They have to be good and commercial for today's market." Current acts include George Perkins and the Silver-Stars (soul/gospel); Pamla-Marie (country pop/rock); Larry Hobbs (soul); George Hickory (C&W); and Jimmy Angel (pop/C&W/gospel).
**Tips:** "Submit your best 4-6 commercial songs. Our 'doors' are always open for new hit material."

***MARSH EDELSTEIN & ASSOCIATES, INC.,** 1704 W. Lake St., Minneapolis MN 55408. (612)827-4611. President: Marsh Edelstein. Management fim. Represents artists and musical groups; currently handles 3 acts. Receives maximum 20% commission. Reviews material for acts.
**How to Contact:** Query by mail, arrange personal interview or submit demo tape and lyric sheet. Prefers cassette with 3-4 songs on demo. SASE. Reports in 2 weeks.
**Music:** Dance-oriented, easy listening, MOR, R&B, rock and top 40/pop. Current acts include Dez Dickerson (rock act and lead guitar player for Prince); Paradox (hard rock); and Diamonds (MOR).

**STEVE ELLIS AGENCY, LTD.,** Suite 330, 250 W. 57th St., New York NY 10019. (212)757-5800. President: Steve Ellis. Vice President: Nanci Linke. Agent: Paul Zukoski. Booking agency. Represents individuals and groups; currently handles 10 acts. Receives 10% commission. Reviews material for acts.
**How to Contact:** Query. Prefers cassette with 2-3 songs on demo. Does not return unsolicited material. Reports in 3 weeks.
**Music:** Dance-oriented, R&B, rock (mainstream) and soul. Works with one night concert groups (vocalists with band). Current acts include Chic (pop/soul/R&B/dance group); and Jerry Butler (pop/R&B).

**RICHARD LEE EMLER ENTERPRISES,** Suite 1000, 8601 Wilshire Blvd., Beverly Hills CA 90211. (213)659-3932. Contact: Richard Lee Emler. Management firm. Represents professional artists and songwriters; currently handles 16 acts. Receives 15-25% commission. Reviews material for acts.
**How to Contact:** Query. Prefers cassette as demo. SASE. Reports in 1 month.
**Music:** Mostly MOR and C&W; also classical, jazz, disco, folk, rock, soul, top 40/pop and music for films and TV. "Work is primarily film scoring and song writing." Current acts include Bob Alcivar, Johnny Harris, Michael J. Lewis, Peter Matz, Gil Melle, Nelson Riddle, George Romanis, Michel Rubini, Denny Jaeger, Misha Segal, Stephen Seretan, Tim Simon, Fred Thaler, Robert Webb (composers/arrangers/conductors/music directors); and Richard & Donald Addrisi, Harriet Schock and Molly Ann Leikin (songwriters/lyricists).
**Tips:** "Get as much experience as possible, wherever possible."

**EMPIRE AGENCY, INC.,** Box 1343, Marietta GA 30061. (404)427-1200. Agent: Carole Kinzel. Booking agency. Represents artists and groups; currently handles 25 acts. Receives 10-15% commission. Reviews material for acts.
**How to Contact:** Query by mail, then submit demo tape. Prefers cassette with 2-4 songs on demo. SASE. Reports in 1 month.
**Music:** Mostly rock; also dance-oriented, R&B and top 40/pop. Works primarily with modern rock and country rock bands. Current acts include The Charlie Daniels Band, The Gregg Allman Band, BHLT, David Allan Coe, Delbert McClinton, The Look, Greg Douglass, Peter Rowan, Norman Nardini and the Tigers, Asleep at the Wheel, The Brains, Rick Derringer, Stevie Ray Vaughan & Double Trouble and Ronnie Hammond.

***ENCHANTED DOOR MANAGEMENT CO., INC.,** Box 1235, New Rochelle NY 10802. (914)834-5676. President: Joe Messina. Vice President/General Manager: Kerry McNamara. Management firm. Represents individual artists, groups, songwriters and film writers and directors; currently

handles 6 acts. Receives 10-25% commission. Reviews material for acts.
**How to Contact:** Submit demo tape and lyric sheet; include bio, photo and resume. Prefers cassette with 2-3 songs on demo. SASE. Reports ASAP.
**Music:** Mostly top 40/pop; also dance-oriented, MOR, R&B and rock (all types). Current acts include Rat Race Choir (hard rock concert act, Crescent Records); David Chmela (top songwriter); and Precious (female dance/rock group, Cartoon Records).

*****BOB ENGLAR THEATRICAL AGENCY**, 2466 Wildon Dr., York PA 17403. (717)741-2844. President: Bob Englar. Booking agency. Represents individuals and groups. Receives 10-15% commission.
**How to Contact:** Query or submit demo tape. Prefers 8-track cartridge with 5-10 songs on demo, or disc. Include photo. SASE. Reports in 3 weeks.
**Music:** Bluegrass, blues, children's, choral, church/religious, classical, C&W, disco, folk, gospel, jazz, polka, rock (light), soul and top 40/pop. Works primarily with string quartets and dance bands.

*****ENTERTAINMENT AGENCY UNLTD.**, Suite 101, 9777 Harwin, Houston TX 77036. (713)782-1783. Booking Agent/Talent Scout: Sirron Kyles. Management firm and booking agency. Represents artists and musical groups; currently handles 500 acts. Receives 15-20% commission. Reviews material for acts.
**How to Contact:** Query by mail. Prefers cassette as demo.
**Music:** All types.

*****ENTERTAINMENT MANAGEMENT ENTERPRISES**, 454 Alps Rd., Wayne NJ 07470. (201)694-3333. President: Richard Zielinski. Management firm. Estab. 1982. Represents artists and musical groups; currently handles 5 acts. Receives minimum of 20% commission. Reviews material for acts.
**How to Contact:** Submit demo tape and lyric sheet; include 8x10 glossy and bio. Prefers cassette or if possible, send VHS or ¾" video tape (if possible) with 4-6 songs on demo. "Let us know, by mail or phone, about any New York area performances so we can attend." SASE. Reports in 2 weeks.
**Music:** Mostly rock (hard and new wave). Works primarily with rock groups with vocals, synthesized rock and contemporary singers. Current acts include One & One (synthesized, improvisational, original dance/rock group with vocals); This Part of the Body (original rock group); Don Massi (pop, soul, blues singer); and Dee Hart (R&R, top 40).
**Tips:** "A good press kit is important."

**ENTERTAINMENT SERVICES CONCEPT**, Box 2501, Des Moines IA 50315. (515)285-6564. President: Art Smart Stenstrom. Management firm, booking agency, record company and music publisher. Represents groups and songwriters; currently handles 2 acts and books 10-20 acts. "We generally deal only with regional attractions, primarily Iowa groups. Receives 7½-20% commission. Reviews material for acts.
**How to Contact:** Submit all promotional materials available, with song list and demo tape. Prefers cassette tape. "On a demo tape of a live performance, any number of songs. Telephoning prior to sending materials will ensure that materials get attention." SASE. Reports in 2 weeks.
**Music:** Rock (only material that is recognizable), easy listening, MOR and top 40/pop (commercial or nostalgia shows). Works primarily with "regional attractions that work club, small concert, college, high school and ballroom gigs." Current acts include Colt .45 (original country-rock/top 40); Spencer (top 40/rock); and Hard Times (country rock/top 40).

**ENTERTAINMENT UNLIMITED**, 1701 Banksville Rd., Pittsburgh PA 15216. Contact: Manager. Management firm and booking agency. Represents artists and groups in eastern US; currently handles 50 acts. Receives 10-20% commission.
**How to Contact:** Query by mail, then submit demo tape and lead sheet. Prefers cassette (sound or video) with 6-10 songs on demo. Does not return unsolicited material. Reports "as soon as possible but only if interested."
**Music:** Bluegrass, C&W, dance-oriented, easy listening, R&B and top 40/pop. Works primarily with dance and bar bands. Current acts include Madhatters (top 40/dance, funk group); Nite Life (top 40/dance group); and Masquerade (top 40/dance group).

**EPICENTER**, Box 92266, Milwaukee WI 53202. (414)645-3133. Agents: JoAnn or Stephen Grimm. Management firm, booking agency and record company. Estab. 1981. Represents artists, groups and songwriters in Milwaukee region. Receives minimum 15% commission. Reviews material for acts—"assuming there is no lengthy response required."
**How to Contact:** Submit demo tape and lead sheet. Prefers cassette with 2-4 songs on demo. SASE. "Send only your best." Reports in 1 month.

**Music:** R&B, rock and top/40 pop. Works primarily with rock dance bands on the bar circuit with strong original songs. Current acts include White Lie and Bad Boy.
**Tips:** "Give us a memorable melody plus chorus with a beat that won't quit."

**FAR WEST ENTERPRISES,** Box 4546, Downey CA 90241. (213)862-7548. President: Tom Plummer. Management firm, booking agency, music publisher and record company. Represents artists, groups and songwriters; currently handles 15 acts. Receives 10-15% commission. Reviews material for acts.
**How to Contact:** Submit demo tape and lead sheet "or typed copy of words." Prefers cassette with 1-5 songs on demo. SASE. Reports in 1 month.
**Music:** Mostly C&W, country rock and rock; also bluegrass, blues, gospel, R&B and top 40/pop. Works primarily with "single acts, show bands with featured star, dance groups and bar bands." Current acts include Ray Sanders (show act with group, Hillside Records); Miss Eddie Marie (floor show with groups, DL Records); Steve Spurgin (dinner house act, 3J Records); Tex Williams (single, Shasta Records); Mike Posey (bar/club band, Titan Records); and Dick Miller (single vocalist, Blue Chip Records).
**Tips:** "We offer a full service operation to the new artist who is trying to get started. We welcome inquiries from anyone who feels they have what it takes to make it. Be sincere, know your limitations, have confidence and believe in yourself."

**FARRIS INTERNATIONAL TALENT,** 821 19th Ave. S., Nashville TN 37203. (615)329-9264. Contact: Molly Thomas. Management firm, booking agency and recording studio. Represents artists, groups and songwriters; currently handles 3 acts. Receives variable commission. Reviews material for acts.
**How to Contact:** Submit demo tape and lead sheet. Prefers cassette with 2-4 songs on demo. SASE. Reports in 1 week.
**Music:** Blues, C&W and top 40/pop. Current acts include Carl Perkins (rockabilly); and Jacky Ward (country/pop artist).

**FIELD HARDWICK PRODUCTIONS,** 7th Floor, 770 Lexington Ave., New York NY 10021. (212)838-7521. Business Manager: Richard McNerney. Management firm, booking agency and record company. Represents artists, groups and songwriters; currently handles 4 acts. Receives 15-20% commission. Reviews material for acts.
**How to Contact:** Submit demo tape. "No phone calls from songwriters." Prefers cassette with 1-2 songs on demo. SASE. Reports in 6 weeks.
**Music:** Classical, C&W, dance-oriented, easy listening, folk, jazz, MOR, R&B, rock, soul and top 40/pop. Works primarily with dance bands, rock groups and individual singers. Current acts include The Bob Hardwick Sound (dance orchestra); Bob Hardwick (rock/MOR artist, songwriter); and Music on the Move (disco band).

**FIREBALL MANAGEMENT,** Box 588, Freeport NY 11520. (516)223-1244. President: Joel Peskin. Management firm. Represents groups; currently handles 1 act. Receives 20-25% commission. Reviews material for acts.
**How to Contact:** Query by mail, then submit demo tape and lead sheet. Prefers cassette with 2-5 songs on demo. SASE. Reports in 2 weeks.
**Music:** Rock (hard). Works primarily with hard rock concert groups. Current acts include Cintron (hard rock concert group).
**Tips:** "Be dedicated and hardworking."

**FISHER & ASSOCIATES ENTERTAINMENT, INC.,** Box 240802, Charlotte NC 28224. (704)525-9220. Agent: Ed Duncan. Booking agency. Represents musical groups in the Southeastern states including North Carolina, South Carolina, Virginia, Georgia, Tennessee, Alabama, Mississippi and Florida; currently handles 60 groups. Receives 15-20% commission. Reviews material for acts.
**How to Contact:** Submit demo tape, include resume, bio, references and publicity photos. Prefers cassette with 6-10 songs on demo. SASE. Reports in 1 month.
**Music:** Dance-oriented, R&B, rock (commercial and danceable) and top 40/pop and variety groups. Works primarily with club and lounge groups (4 to 8 pieces), bar bands, and dance groups suitable for the young adult market (ages 16-40). Current acts include Sugarcreek (top 40/rock); Phenix (top 40/rock); Shuffle (top 40/variety); and Lyrics (top 40/variety).
**Tips:** "We are interested in self-contained, commercial, outfitted shows (if possible)."

**JOAN FRANK PRODUCTIONS,** Suite 101, 9550 Forest Lane, Dallas TX 75343. (214)343-8737. Manager: R.D. Leonard. Booking agency. Represents individuals and groups; currently handles 6 acts.

Receives 10-15% commission. Reviews material for acts.
**How to Contact:** Query. Prefers cassette tapes. SASE. Reports in 2 weeks.
**Music:** Mostly dance-oriented; also C&W and easy listening. Works primarily with dance bands, show bands, combos and singles. Current acts include the Gary Lee Orchestra (big band); The Nat "King" Cohen Combo (combo); The Dave Harris Orchestra (dance band); Texas (C&W show and dance group); and Chuck Pangburn & His Men of the West (C&W group).

**THE FRANKLYN AGENCY,** #312, 1010 Hammond St., Los Angeles CA 90069. (213)272-6080. President: Audrey P. Franklyn. Management agency, public relations firm and American Song Festival judge. Represents artists, musical groups and businesses; currently handles 7 acts. Receives 5-15% commission. Reviews material for acts.
**How to Contact:** Query by mail, arrange personal interview or submit demo tape and lead sheet. Prefers cassette or video cassette. SASE. Reports in 1 month.
**Music:** Blues, easy listening, gospel, jazz, MOR, progressive, R&B, rock and top 40/pop. Works primarily with rock bands and single soloist singers. Current acts include Talisman Band (jazz/rock); Merrell Frankhauser (environmental rock); Marilyn Johnson (pop singer); Marco Valenti (pop and semi-classical); Lennart Flindt (jazz pianist).

**FREDDIE CEE ATTRACTIONS,** 370 Market St., Box 333, Lemoyne PA 17043. (717)761-0821. Contact: Fred Clousher. Booking agency. Represents groups and comedy and novelty acts in Pennsylvania, Maryland, Virginia, West Virginia, New York, New Jersey and Ohio; currently handles approximately 75 acts. Receives 10-20% commission.
**How to Contact:** Query or submit demo tape. Include "photos, list of credits, etc." Prefers cassette or 8-track cartridge with 5-10 songs on demo. Does not return unsolicited material. Reports in 3 weeks.
**Music:** Mostly country and dance-oriented; also bluegrass, gospel, easy listening, top 40/pop, Hawaiian, German and ethnic. Works primarily with "marketable groups in country, country rock, bluegrass, gospel, variety show groups, etc." Current acts include the Hawaiian Revue '84 (show and dance act); Showdown (country/rock); Sound Foundation (variety dance group); Stony Ridge (bluegrass act); Jay Wamsley (country, country rock artist); J.D. Brothers (country rock group); Rosiers (magic/illusions act); and Harmonica Rascals (vaudeville).
**Tips:** "We obtain employment for marketable groups and performers. Those desiring to use our services should submit complete promo material (demo tape, photos, credits, etc.)"

**FREEDOM PRODUCTIONS,** Box 20005, Westland Station, Jackson MS 39209. (601)366-9450. Manager: Jesse Thompson, Jr. Management firm, booking agency and production company. Represents artists, groups and songwriters; currently handles 3 acts. Receives 15-20% commission. Reviews material for acts.
**How to Contact:** Query by mail. Prefers cassette with 3-7 songs on demo. SASE. Reports in 3 weeks.
**Music:** R&B and soul. Works primarily with dance, show groups and single performers. Current acts include Freedom (self-contained show group); Ray and James (duo act); and Pat Franklin (single artist).

**FRO RECORDS (HARVEST GROUP),** 317 Taft Ave., West Paterson NJ 07424. (201)278-3735. Contact: Frank Galardi or Frank Russell. Record label and artist agency. Represents artists, groups and songwriters. Receives 10-50% commission. Reviews material for acts.
**How to Contact:** Query by mail, then submit demo tape. Prefers cassette with 2-7 songs on demo. "No return on demos." Does not return unsolicited material. Reports in 3 weeks.
**Music:** Church/religious and gospel. Works primarily with solo and vocal groups. Current acts include Harvest (vocal group); Sojo (male vocal group); and Cendy Zefereno (female vocalist).

**FROST & FROST ENTERTAINMENT,** 3985 W. Taft Dr., Spokane WA 99208. (509)325-1777. Agent: Dick Frost. Booking agency. Represents individuals and groups; currently handles 10-15 acts. Receives 10-15% commission.
**How to Contact:** Query or submit demo tape and lyric sheet. Prefers cassette with 5 songs on tape. Include information on past appearances, as well as list of references. SASE. Reports in 2 weeks.
**Music:** C&W, dance-oriented, easy listening, MOR, rock (country and 50s) and top 40/pop. Works primarily with dance bands, show bands and individual artists. Currently some acts include Tex Williams (western act); Kay Austin (C&W/MOR act); Big Tiny Little, Kenny O & Rhinestone, Stagecoach West, and High Country (show and/or dance).

**FTM ENTERPRISES, INC.,** 9165 Sunset Blvd., Los Angeles CA 90069. (213)550-0130. President: Toby Mamis. Management firm. Represents artists, groups, songwriters and producers. Receives 15-25% commission. Reviews material for acts.
**How to Contact:** Submit demo tape and lead sheet. "If writer is also an artist/performer, enclose photo,

Managers & Booking Agencies **313**

bio and press clips." SASE. Prefers cassette with 3-6 songs on demo. "Reporting time varies."
**Music:** C&W, dance-oriented, easy listening, MOR, rock and top 40/pop. Works primarily with mass appeal, commercial pop/rock, some country and adult contemporary artists.

**GAIL AND RICE PRODUCTIONS**, 11845 Mayfield, Livonia MI 48150. (313)427-9300. Account Representative: Chris Nordman. Booking agency. Represents individuals and groups; currently handles 25 acts. Receives 10-20% commission.
**How to Contact:** Submit demo tape and lead sheet. Prefers cassette with 3-6 songs on demo. Does not return unsolicited material. Reports in 3 weeks.
**Music:** Bluegrass, children's, C&W, dance-oriented, jazz and top 40/pop. Works primarily with "self-contained groups (1-8 people), show and dance music, listening groups, and individual name or semi-name attractions." Current acts include 21st Century Steel Drum Band (show group); the Dazzlers (vocal/dance act); and Glenn Haywood (comedian/ventriloquist).

*** MICK GAMBILL ENTERPRISES, INC.**, Suite 12, 1617 N. El Centro, Hollywood CA 90028. (213)466-9777. President: Mick Gambill. Management firm and booking agency. Represents West Coast groups; currently handles 30 acts. Receives 15-20% commission. Reviews material for acts.
**How to Contact:** Submit demo tape. Prefers cassette with 3-6 songs on demo. SASE. Reports in 2 weeks.
**Music:** Dance-oriented, rock and top 40/pop. Works primarily with top 40 groups. Current acts include Whizz Kidds (rock); Frontseat (top 40/pop); Keeper (top 40); Singles (rock); and Bachelors (top 40).

**KEN GAUB MINISTRIES**, Box 1, Yakima WA 98907. (509)575-1965. Manager: Ron Thomasson. Management firm and booking agency. Represents groups, songwriters and comedy acts; currently handles 8 acts.
**How to Contact:** Query by mail or call. "We represent songwriters. Artists looking for songs should check with us." SASE.
**Music:** Rock (gospel). Works primarily with concert Christian rock bands, and songwriters who write Christian rock and Christian comedy. Current acts include Ken Gaub (comedy single); Eternity Express (Christian rock group); and Nathan Gaub (songwriter).
**Tips:** "We are not looking for songs but have a lot of songs looking for artists."

**PETER GOLDEN & ASSOC./CROSSLIGHT MANAGEMENT, LTD.**, 1592 Crossroads of the World, Hollywood CA 90028. (213)462-6156. Contact: Bill Siddons. Management firm. Represents artists, songwriters, and producers/engineers; currently handles 6 acts. Receives negotiable commission. Reviews material for acts.
**How to Contact:** Query by mail, then submit demo tape. Prefers cassette with 2-4 songs on demo. Does not return unsolicited material. Reports in 2 months.
**Music:** Blues, R&B, rock (country), and top 40/pop. Current acts include Jackson Browne; Poco; Graham Nash; David Lindley, Greg Copeland, The Hollies and Jesse Colin Young.

*** GOLDMAN-DELL MUSIC PRODUCTIONS**, 421 W. 87th St., Box 8680, Kansas City MO 64114. (816)333-8701. Contact: Irv Goldman. Management firm and booking agency. Represents individuals, groups and songwriters; currently handles over 30 acts. Receives "commission as set by the union." Also contract producer of shows with local or national acts. Operates Deggis Music Co. (BMI) with (ASCAP) co-publishing available.
**How to Contact:** Songwriters—submit demo tape and lead sheet or contact by phone. Bandleaders or acts—send cassette tape, photo, bio and typical song list. Prefers cassette with 2 songs minimum on tape. "Allow 4-6 weeks for reply on songs submitted for publishing/recording. Material returned only if SASE is included. Tapes must be labeled with name, address and phone number on cassette."
**Music:** Mostly top 40/pop, jazz and R&B; also "big band sound," blues, C&W, dance-oriented, easy listening, jazz, MOR, rock (hard) and variety. Works primarily with variety and dance bands but accepts all types. Current acts include Photofinish (variety dance band); Harbour (easy rock, top 40); Dynastar ("boys & girls, together!"); Brothers Heritage (show-dance-stage band); Two/Twenty; Wildfire; Reunion (all 5-man variety dance bands); and Virgil Hill (oldtime black jazz and blues to top 40 one-man band). Also handles some national, Nashville and TV performers, musical or not. To other qualified agents and managers or producers: "I am your man in Kansas City." Also provides direction for Bruce Gordon ("Frank Nitti") character on *The Untouchables* for musical and non-musical sketches or plays, plus TV commercials and other acts. Can produce original music for any commercial situation.
**Tips:** "Songwriters: Identify (label) all tapes sent to us. Artists: Be outstanding, have wardrobe and good stage presence."

**DAVID GOLIATH AGENCY**, Box 11960, Chicago IL 60611. (312)561-0027. Booking Manager: Tony Apostolopoulos. Management and booking agency. Represents artists and musical groups; cur-

rently handles 12 acts. Receives 15-20% commission. Reviews material for acts.
**How to Contact:** Query by mail; submit demo tape, song list, 8x10 glossy photo, biography. Prefers cassette with 3-6 songs on demo. "Good promo material or at least the desire or ability to gather and process this information is most important." Does not return unsolicited material. Reports in 1 month.
**Music:** Blues, dance-oriented, MOR, rock (soft), top 40/pop and soul (funk). Has international bookings secured for Canada and Japan. Works primarily with show bands, dance bands, bar bands and road bands. Current acts include Cupid (funk/top 40/R&B); New Experience (pop/R&B); Shannon Band (R&B/funk); and Main Foundation (funk/top 40/R&B/disco).

**WALT GOLLENDER ENTERPRISES**, Suite 8Q, 12 Marshall St., Irvington NJ 07111. (201)373-6050. Executive Director: Walt Gollender. Management firm. Represents artists and songwriters. Receives sales royalty, outright fee from record company or outright fee from songwriter/artist.
**How to Contact:** Submit demo tape and lyric sheet, or arrange personal interview. Prefers 7½ ips reel-to-reel (mono mix) or cassette with a maximum of 4 songs on demo. "Call any evening 5-8 p.m. EST." SASE. Reports in 1 month.
**Music:** Blues, C&W, dance, easy listening, folk, MOR, rock (light), soul and top 40/pop. Works primarily with rock groups, vocalists, small combos, songwriters and C&W vocalists. Current acts include Fire (all girl rock band).
**Tips:** "Seeking top rate singers, songwriters and musical acts. New record production company being established with funding and international outlets."

**GOOD KARMA PRODUCTIONS, INC.**, 2 W. 43rd St., Kansas City MO 64111. (816)531-3857. Co-Owner: Paul Peterson. Management agency. Deals with Midwest artists only. Represents artists and groups; currently handles 3 acts. Receives 20% commission. Reviews material for acts.
**How to Contact:** Submit demo tape and lyric sheet. Prefers cassette with 2-4 songs on demo. SASE. Reports in 2-3 weeks.
**Music:** Rock (hard and country) and top 40/pop. Works with rock and country rock bands, concert and recording artists only and songwriters. Current acts include the Ozark Mountain Daredevils (country-rock group, Columbia Records); The Clocks (pop rock band, Epic Records); and Larry Lee (pop vocalist, Columbia Records).

***GARY GOOD MANAGEMENT**, 2500 NW 39th St., Oklahoma OK 73112. (405)947-1503. Contact: Gary Good. Management firm. Represents artists, groups and songwriters mainly from Oklahoma; currently handles 8 acts. Receives 15% commission. Reviews material for acts.
**How to Contact:** Submit demo tape and lyric sheet. Prefers cassette with 1-5 songs on demo. SASE. Reports ASAP.
**Music:** Mostly C&W and MOR; also dance-oriented, easy listening and top 40/pop. Works primarily with pop bands. Current acts include The Sullivans (band); Steve Rhodes (band); and John Webster (solo act).

***GOOD MUSIC MANAGEMENT**, Box 437, Excelsior MN 55331. (612)474-2681. Secretary/Treasurer: Doug Brown. Booking agent. Estab. 1981. Represents artists, groups and songwriters; currently handles 30 acts. Receives 15-30% commission. Reviews material for acts.
**How to Contact:** Submit demo tape and lead sheet. Prefers cassette with 1-3 songs on demo. SASE. Reports in 2 months.
**Music:** Mostly rock, R&B, C&W and top 40; also dance-oriented, R&B and soul. Works primarily with bands. Current acts include John Thoennes (singer/songwriter, pop band); Dave Toland (singer/songwriter, C&W); Montana (rock/C&W/bluegrass); and Daisy Dillmand Band (rock/C&W).

**THE GOSPEL ROAD**, Box 6865, Irondale AL 35210. (205)491-5821. Director of New Talent: Marsha Moore. President: Buddy Poe. Management firm, booking agency and music publisher. Represents artists, groups and songwriters; currently handles 5 acts. Receives minimum 15% commission or pays negotiable royalty. Reviews material for acts.
**How to Contact:** Submit demo tape, resume and photo. Prefers cassette with 3-5 songs on demo. SASE. Reports in 1 month.
**Music:** Mostly gospel (southern, contemporary); also church/religious, choral, folk and soul. Works primarily with gospel quartets, trios and solo artists. Current acts include The Connections (southern gospel quartet); Buddy Burton (gospel artist); Sabrina (contemporary artist); and Mellissa (contemporary artist).
**Tips:** "Get as much experience as possible in local area."

***BILL GRAHAM MANAGEMENT**, 201 11th St., San Francisco CA 94103. (415)864-0815. Creative Development: Mick Brigden and Bonnie Simmons. Management firm. Represents artists and groups; currently handles 2 acts. Reviews material for acts.

**How to Contact:** Submit demo tape and lead sheet. Prefers cassette. SASE. Reports as soon as possible.
**Music:** Progressive, R&B, rock and top 40/pop. Works primarily with R&R bands. Current acts include Santana; and Eddie Money.

**GRAND TALENT INTERNATIONAL,** Suite 605, 1750 Kalakaua Ave., Honolulu HI 96826. (808)955-5758. President: Mark Nishimoto. Booking agency. Represents artists and groups. Receives 10-15% commission. Reviews material for acts.
**How to Contact:** Query by mail. Prefers cassette with minimum 4 songs on demo. SASE. Reports in 2 weeks.
**Music:** R&B, rock and top 40/pop.

**JOE GRAYDON & ASSOCIATES,** Box 1, Toluca Lake CA 91602. (213)769-2424. President: Joe Graydon. Management firm. Represents artists, groups, songwriters and package shows for tours; currently handles 12 acts. Receives 10-15% commission.
**How to Contact:** Submit demo tape and lyric sheet. Prefers cassette tape with 3-10 songs on demo. SASE. Reports in 1 week.
**Music:** Bluegrass, C&W, dance, MOR, soul and primarily top 40/pop. Works with show groups that play Nevada lounges and individual singers, male and female. Current acts include Helen Forrest (singer); The Boos Brothers (show group); Connie Haines, (singer); The Pied Pipers (vocal group); The Big Band Cavalcade & Big Band Show; Concert Attraction; and Jody Donovan (singer). Also screens tapes for acts produced by Jay Graydon.

**GREAT PLAINS ASSOCIATES, INC.,** Box 634, Southern Hills Shopping Center, Lawrence KS 66044. (913)841-4444. Contact: Scott Winters, Mark Swanson, Stuart Doores or Gary Mackender. Booking agency. Represents groups in Midwest; currently handles 30 acts. Receives 10-20% commission. Reviews material for acts.
**How to Contact:** Submit demo tape. Prefers cassette with 3-5 songs on demo. SASE.
**Music:** C&W, R&B, rock and soul. Works primarily with dance bands "for college mini-concerts to bar band dances." Current acts include Think Pink (new music); Blue Wave (beach music); Astra (contemporary rock); Kelley and the Kinetics (new music); and Kokomo (contemporary rock).
**Tips:** "We are constantly looking for and expect our artists to have a *definite* idea of what they want and where they are going."

**GREAT PYRAMID MUSIC,** 10 Waterville St. San Francisco CA 94124. Administrator: Joseph Buchwald. Management firm. Represents artists, groups and songwriters; currently handles 12 acts. Receives 10-25% commission. Reviews material for acts.
**How to Contact:** Query by mail, submit demo tape and lead sheet. Prefers cassette with 3-5 songs on demo. SASE. Reports as soon as possible.
**Music:** Mostly MOR; also R&B, top 40/pop and ballads. Works primarily with vocalists, songwriters and groups. Current acts include Marty Balin (solo artist).
**Tips:** "Don't pressure."

***GREIF-GARRIS MANAGEMENT,** 8467 Beverly Blvd., Los Angeles CA 90048. (213)653-4780. Vice President: Sid Garris. Management firm. Represents artists, groups and songwriters; currently handles 3 acts. Receives minimum 15% commission. Reviews material for acts.
**How to Contact:** Query by mail. Prefers cassette with 3-5 songs on demo. SASE. Reports ASAP.
**Music:** All types of "good music." Current acts include The Crusaders (jazz/pop); The New Christy Minstrels (folk); and Michael Smotherman (pop).
**Tips:** "Artists should be critical enough to ensure that what is being sent is the *best* of their possible ability."

**THE GROUP, INC.,** 1957 Kilburn Dr., Atlanta GA 30324. (404)872-6000. General Manager: Hamilton Underwood. Vice President: Marie Sutton. Management agency. Represents individuals and groups. Receives 15-25% commission.
**How to Contact:** Submit demo tape only. Prefers cassette with 2-3 songs on demo. Include photo and bio. Does not return unsolicited material. Reports ASAP.
**Music:** Blues, jazz, progressive, rock and top 40/pop. Works with total package groups (artists and songwriters). Current acts Starfoxx (group/rock, Hottrax Records); and Little Phil and The Night Shadows (artist-songwriter/rock, ABC/Dot Records).

**BOB HALE TALENT/JESTER SOUND,** 423 Kuhlman Dr., Billings MT 59101. (406)245-2174. President: Bob Hale. Management firm, booking agency, record label, music publisher and recording studio. Represents artists, groups and songwriters; currently handles 15 acts. Receives 15% (booking)

to 20% (management). Pays standard royalty to songwriters; negotiable royalty to artists on recording contract. Reviews material for acts.
**How to Contact:** Submit demo tape. Prefers 7½ ips reel-to-reel or cassette with 5 songs maximum on demo. "Demo should emphasize vocal with minimum amount of production." SASE. Reports in 2 weeks.
**Music:** Bluegrass, C&W, dance-oriented, easy listening, rock (hard, country), MOR and top 40/pop. Works primarily with C&W, bluegrass and top 40/pop. Current acts include Prairie Fire (C&W show group); Lost Highway Band (rock/country rock group); Linda Jordan (country/country rock artist); Clint Jackson (country single); Back to Back (C&W group); The Brothers Plus (C&W show group); and Your Move (rock group).

**GEOFFREY HANSEN ENTERPRISES, LTD.**, Box 63, Orinda CA 94563. (415)937-6469. Artist Relations: J. Malcom Baird. Management agency. Represents artists, groups and songwriters; currently handles 10 acts. Receives 15-25% commission. Also paid on a contract basis. Reviews material for acts.
**How to Contact:** Submit demo tape, lead sheet and cover letter. Prefers cassette. SASE. Reports in 1 month or longer.
**Music:** C&W, MOR, French, Spanish, R&B, rock (and country rock), top 40/pop, 50s R&R and comedy/novelty tunes. Works with top 40 and C&W artists; recording acts and overseas stars. Current acts include Johnny Hallyday (French MOR); Yves Montand (French MOR); Gene Vincent, Jr. (C&W recording artist); Mari Asakaze (top 40 Japanese recording artist and TV performer); Aabci (studio band); and Bert Friel (MOR/Hawaiian artist).
**Tips:** "Send letter—if it is interesting and there is possible talent . . ."

***HARMONY ARTISTS, INC.**, Suite 200, 8833 Sunset Blvd., Los Angeles CA 90069. (213)659-9644. President: Michael Dixon. Booking agency. Represents groups; currently handles 100 acts. Receives 15% commission. Reviews material for acts.
**How To Contact:** Submit demo tape and lyric sheet and photo. Prefers cassette with 3-5 songs on demo. Reports in 2 weeks.
**Music:** Easy listening, MOR, progressive, rock and top 40/pop. Current acts include Shakee Jake and Rave-Up.

**HARVEST AGENCY**, 317 Taft Ave., West Paterson NJ 07424. (201)278-3735. Manager: Frank Galardi. Represents artists and groups in New York and New Jersey area only; currently handles 4 acts. Receives 10-15% commission.
**How to Contact:** Query by mail, submit demo tape and lead sheet. Prefers cassette with 3-6 songs on demo. SASE. Reports in 2 weeks.
**Music:** Church/religious and gospel—"must be in the gospel style." Works primarily with gospel groups and solo artists. Current acts include Cindy Zaforanio; Ronny G.; and Sojournors.

***HAT BAND MUSIC**, Sound 70 Suite, 210 25th Ave. N., Nashville TN 37203. (615)327-1711. Project Manager: Douglas Casmus. Management firm and publishing company. Represents artists, groups and songwriters; currently handles 6 acts. Reviews material for acts.
**How to Contact:** Query by mail or submit demo tape and lyric sheet. Prefers cassette with 1-2 songs on demo. SASE. Reports in 3 weeks.
**Music:** C&W, progressive, rock and top 40/pop. Works primarily with major recording artists. Current acts include Charlie Daniels Band (country rock); Dobie Gray (pop); and McGuffy Lane (C&W) (publishing only).

***HEAVY WEATHER MUSIC**, Box 1338, Merchantville NJ 08109. (215)561-5822. Vice President: Bob Francis. Management firm and publishing company. Represents groups; currently handles 10 acts. Receives 4-6% commission. Reviews material for acts.
**How to Contact:** Submit demo tape and lyric sheet. Prefers cassette with 2-6 songs on demo. Does not return unsolicited material. Reports in 1 month.
**Music:** Mostly funk, R&B and soul; also dance-oriented. Current acts include Phoenix (funk); Heavy Weather (funk); Philly Cream (R&B); and Grumpy Brogsdale (R&B).

**GLENN HENRY ENTERTAINMENT AGENCY**, Suite 9, 55 S. LaCumbre Rd., Santa Barbara CA 93105. (805)687-1131. Contact: Glenn Henry. Booking agency. Represents individuals and groups; currently handles 16 acts. Receives 10-15% commission. Reviews material for acts.
**How to Contact:** Query or arrange personal interview. Prefers 8-track cartridge with 3-6 songs on demo. Artist may submit 8x10 promo pictures and/or credits. SASE. Reporting time varies.
**Music:** C&W (modern), MOR, rock and top 40/pop. Works with lounge and hotel bands (all top 40/MOR) with female vocalist if possible and/or modern country dance groups. At present, needs pop rock

band with female vocalist. Current acts include Passion (top 40/variety group); Waterfall (dance/lounge); Sizzle (dance/lounge); and Double or Nothin' (modern country).

**GARY HILLS, LTD.**, (formerly Blast From The Past Productions), 10 James St., New Providence NJ 07974. (201)464-3832 and 541-9422. President: Gary Hills. Management firm and booking agency. Represents groups; currently handles 88 acts. Receives 15-20% commission. Reviews material for acts.
**How to Contact:** Submit demo tape and lead sheet. Prefers 7½ ips reel-to-reel or cassette with 6-12 songs on demo. SASE. Reports in 1 month.
**Music:** Bluegrass, blues, C&W, dance-oriented, easy listening, folk, gospel, jazz, MOR, progressive, Spanish, R&B, rock (country), soul, top 40/pop and Polish. Works primarily with show bands, dance groups and all-occasion type artists. Current acts include The Moonglows, The Coasters, Frankie Lymon's Teenagers (all oldies groups); Bobby Valli and the New Daze (MOR); and Louie Lymon's Teencords (oldies).
**Tips:** "Always looking for tomorrow's stars today. We need new and fresh talent for tomorrow's music."

*****HODGMAR PRODUCTIONS, INC. (BIZ FLAKES MUSIC)**, 120-09 84th Ave., Queens NY 11415. (212)441-0906. President: Mark D. Hodgson. Management firm and publisher. Estab. 1981. Represents artists, groups, songwriters, poets and playwriters; currently handles 3 acts. Receives 15-50% commission. Reviews material for acts.
**How to Contact:** Submit demo tape and lyric sheet. Prefers 7½ ips reel-to-reel or cassette with 2-3 songs on demo. Demos should be a finished product, i.e., drum, bass, vocal, keyboard, one lead instrument, etc. SASE. Reports in 3 weeks.
**Music:** Mostly blues (urban and rural) and C&W; also dance-oriented, easy listening, folk, rock (pop, rockabilly), top 40/pop and tape synthesis with words. Works primarily with singers, songwriters and performing artists. Current acts include Jonathan Wild (contemporary dance); The Rootie Tootie Band (show group, "primarily Blue-Eyed soul"); and Mar Corvair (avante garde tape synthesis with words).
**Tips:** "We are new and extremely disciplined. We have major contacts within the industry, and know the NYC Showcase situations."

**HOFFMAN TALENT, INC.**, 7432 Landau Curve, Bloomington MN 55438. Manager/Publisher: Dave Hoffman. Management firm, booking agency and music publisher (Ottertail). Represents artists, groups and songwriters; currently handles 6 acts. Receives 10-20% commission. "Ottertail receives publishing royalties—writer receives writer's royalties, etc." Reviews material for acts. Also reviews albums.
**How to Contact:** Submit demo tape and lead sheet. Prefers cassette with 1-3 songs on demo. SASE. Reports in 1 month.
**Music:** Blues, bluegrass, choral, church/religious, jazz, C&W, dance-oriented, easy listening, folk, gospel, MOR, progressive, R&B, rock (all), soul and top 40/pop. Works primarily with dance/show bands. Current acts include Johnny Holm Band, Bobby Vee and Tommy Roe (all dance/show acts).

**ICR INTERNATIONAL CELEBRITY REGISTER, INC.**, First National Bank Towers, Box 4527, Topeka KS 66604. (913)233-9716. Executive Vice President in Charge of Entertainment: Kent Raine. Management firm and booking agency. Represents artists, groups and songwriters; currently handles 8 acts. Receives 10-25% commission.
**How to Contact:** Query or submit demo tape and lead sheet. Photos and short biography helpful. Prefers cassette with 2-6 songs on demo. SASE. Reports in 2 weeks.
**Music:** Blues, C&W, dance, jazz, MOR, rock (and country rock), soul and top 40/pop. Works with artists for concert attractions and recording groups.

*****IF PRODUCTIONS, INC.**, 15 Glenby Lane, Brookville NY 11545. (516)626-9504. Branches: 22240 Schoenborn St., Canoga Park CA 91304. (213)883-4865. New York: Producer/Staff writer: Tom Ingegno. Los Angeles: Producer/Staff writer: Mike Frenchik. Management agency and production company. Represents individuals, groups and songwriters; currently handles 4 acts. Receives 15-20% commission. Reviews material for acts.
**How to Contact:** Query or submit demo tape and lyric sheet. Prefers cassette with 3-5 songs on demo. SASE. Reports in 3 weeks.
**Music:** MOR, progressive, rock and top 40/pop. Works primarily with recording acts and solo performers. Current acts include Thrills (rock act); Tony Monaco (songwriter/recording artist); Dave Fullerton (songwriter/recording artist); and Pat O'Brien (songwriter/recording artist).

**INTERMOUNTAIN TALENT**, Box 942, Rapid City SD 57709. (605)348-7777. Contact: Ron Kohn. Management firm and concert production agency. Deals with artists from the upper-midwest region.

Represents artists and groups; currently handles 14 acts. Receives 10-25% commission. Reviews material for acts.
**How to Contact:** Query or submit demo tape and lyric sheet. Prefers cassette with 3-5 songs on demo. SASE. Reports in 2 weeks.
**Music:** Mostly rock; also soul and top 40/pop. Current acts include Bold Lightning; Hod Rod Dee Luzz; Doctor K and the Shantays; and Chariot (rock bands).

**JACKSON ARTISTS CORP.**, Suite 200, 7251 Lowell Dr., Shawnee Mission KS 66204. Management firm, booking agency and music publisher. Represents individuals and songwriters; currently handles 40 acts. Receives 10-20% minimum commission from individual artists and groups; 10% from songwriters. Reviews material for acts.
**How to Contact:** Query, arrange personal interview, submit demo tape and lead sheet or phone. Prefers cassette with 2-4 songs on demo. "Mark names of tunes on cassettes. May send up to 4 tapes. We do most of our business by phone." Will return material if requested with SASE. Reporting time varies.
**Music:** Bluegrass, blues, C&W, easy listening, disco, MOR, progressive, rock (soft), soul and top 40/pop. Works with dance, bar and show bands and vocalists; lounge acts primarily. Current acts include "Ragtime Bob" Darch (ASCAP songwriter/entertainer, Universal Records); Mark Baysinger (songwriter); The Moon Glows (8-piece top/40/soul/variety band); The Romeo Sisters (band); The Mark Sexton Show (band); Mark Valentine (trio); Bob Marriott Band (5-piece lounge act, vocal group).
**Tips:** "Although it's not necessary, we prefer lead sheets with the tapes—send 2 or 3 that you are proud of. Also note what 'name' artist you'd like to see do the song."

*****JMAR PRODUCTIONS**, Box 678, Van Nuys CA 91408. President: Jeff Rizzotti. Management firm, booking agency and sales and distribution firm. Represents artists, groups and songwriters; currently handles 12 acts. Reviews material for acts.
**How to Contact:** Query by mail. Prefers cassette with 3-6 songs on demo. SASE. Reports in 2 weeks.
**Music:** Mostly C&W and soul; also top 40/pop.
**Tips:** "We look for total honesty, individuality, patience and people who are workaholics."

**KATONA PRODUCTIONS, INC.**, Box 100, Toccoa GA 30577. (404)779-2711. President: Tommy Scott. Management firm. Represents artists and songwriters. Receives variable commission. Reviews material for acts.
**How to Contact:** Query by mail. Prefers cassette demos. SASE. Reporting time varies.
**Music:** C&W.

**KINETIC RECORDS, LTD.**, Suite 914, 8033 Sunset Blvd., Los Angeles CA 90046. President: Luke O'Reilly. Management firm, booking agency and record production company. Represents artists, groups and songwriters "preferably from southern California;" currently handles 9 acts. Reviews material for acts.
**How to Contact:** Submit demo tape, lead sheet and "any other pertinent information." Prefers cassette with minimum 5 songs on demo. Does not return unsolicited material. Reports in 2 weeks.
**Music:** Rock. Works primarily with new music acts and songwriters. "If we are unable to secure a recording or publishing contract within a reasonable time, artists are dropped." Current acts and songwriters include Al Stewart (Arista Records recording artist); The Fixx (new music group); Shot in the Dark (RSO Records recording artist); and Pete White (songwriter, co-writer of "Time Passages," recorded by Al Stewart).
**Tips:** "Good songs are imperative."

**BOB KNIGHT AGENCY**, 185 Clinton Ave., Staten Island NY 10301. (212)448-8420. General Manager: Bob Knight. Management firm, booking agency, music publishing and royalty collection firm. Represents artists, groups and songwriters; currently handles 15 acts. Receives 10-25% commission. Reviews material for acts.
**How to Contact:** Submit demo cassette tape and lead sheet. "Phone calls accepted 6-9 p.m." Prefers cassette with 3-10 songs on demo "with photo, bio and references." SASE. Reports in 1 month.
**Music:** Mostly top 40/pop; also easy listening, MOR, R&B, soul and rock. Works primarily with lounge groups, high energy dance, 50's acts and show groups. Current acts include The Elegants (oldie show); Ad-Libs (60s group); and Superbold (grease show).

**L & R PRODUCTIONS, LLEANA PRODUCTIONS AND DOC DICK ENTERPRISES**, 16 E. Broad St., Mt. Vernon NY 10552. (914)668-4488 and 528-8249. President: Richard Rashbaum. Vice President: Elizabeth Rashbaum. Management firm and music publisher. Represents artists, groups and songwriters; currently handles 12 acts. Receives 10-20% commission. Reviews material for acts.

**How to Contact:** Submit demo tape and lead sheet. Prefers 7½ ips reel-to-reel or cassette with 1-4 songs on demo. SASE. Reports in 2 weeks.
**Music:** Mostly R&B and top 40/pop; also light rock and soul. Works with dance and show bands, vocalists, lounge acts, recording artists and groups, songwriters and producers. Current acts include Daybreak (dance band/recorded act); Network (rock band); MTV (dance band); and Alfie Davison (recorded single artist and writer).

**\*L.D.F. PRODUCTIONS**, Box 406, Old Chelsea Station, New York NY 10011. (212)925-8925. President: Mr. Dowell. Management firm and booking agency. Represents artists and choirs in the New York area. Receives 15-25% commission.
**How to Contact:** Query by mail or submit demo tape and lyric sheet. Prefers cassette with 2-8 songs on demo. SASE. Reports in 1 month.
**Music:** Mostly gospel; also choral and church/religious. Works primarily with vocalists and choirs. Current acts include L.D. Frazier (gospel artist/lecturer); and Frazier's (gospel workshop choir).
**Tips:** "Those interested in working with us must be original, enthusiastic and persistent."

**LANDSLIDE MANAGEMENT**, 928 Broadway, New York NY 10010. Principals: Ted Lehrman and Libby Bush. Management firm. Represents actors, singers and songwriters. Receives 15% commission. Reviews material for acts.
**How to Contact:** Submit demo tape and lead sheet "of potential hit singles only—not interested in album cuts." SASE. "Include picture and resume."
**Music:** C&W, dance-oriented, easy listening, MOR, R&B, rock (soft, pop), soul and top 40/pop. Works primarily with vocalists. Current acts include Susie Raney, Robert Bendall, C.J. Critt, Barry Tarallo, Debra Whitfield, Jack Parrish, Adam Baum and the Explosions.

**THE CHARLES LANT AGENCY**, 569 Lynwood Dr., Box 1085, Cornwall, Ontario, Canada K6H 5V2. (613)938-1532. Contact: Charles W. B. Lant. Booking agency. Represents individuals and groups. Receives 10-20% commission.
**How to Contact:** Query or phone. Prefers cassette with 3-10 songs on demo. SAE and IRC. Reports ASAP.
**Music:** C&W and big bands. Works primarily with C&W groups. Current acts include The Stardusters Orchestra (17-piece band); the Gilles Godard Show (C&W); Foxx (4-piece group); and Bernadette Van Loon (5-piece group).

**\*STAN LAWRENCE PRODUCTIONS**, 191 Presidential Blvd., Bala Cynwyd PA 19004. (215)664-4959. Production Coordinator: Mitchem Newman. Management firm and booking agency. Represents artists and groups in Pennsylvania, New Jersey and Delaware. Receives 10-20% commission. Reviews material for acts.
**How to Contact:** Query by mail or submit demo tape and lyric sheet. Prefers cassette with 2-5 songs on demo. SASE. Reports in 3 weeks.
**Music:** Mostly top 40 pop; also dance-oriented and easy listening. Works primarily with vocalists and dance bands.

**GARY LAZAR MANAGEMENT**, 3222 Belinda Dr., Sterling Heights MI 48077. (313)977-0645. Contact: Gary Lazar. Management firm, booking agency and music publisher. Represents artists, groups and songwriters; currently handles 4 acts. Receives 10-20% commission. Reviews material for acts.
**How to Contact:** Submit demo tape and lead sheet. Prefers cassette with 3 songs maximum on demo. Does not return unsolicited material. Reports in 1 month.
**Music:** Rock (hard), children's and top 40/pop. Works primarily with recording artists, club bands and songwriters/lyricists. Current acts include The Rockets (rock band/recording artists, Capitol Records); Don Wellman (songwriter/lyricist); Frankie LaMarr (songwriter/lyricist); and Letter O (pop/rock band, Polygram Records).

**BUDDY LEE ATTRACTIONS, INC.**, Suite 300, 38 Music Square E., Nashville TN 37203. (615)244-4336. Artists and Groups Contact: Tony Conway. Songwriters Contact: Nancy Dunn. Management firm and booking agency. Represents individuals and groups; currently handles 60 acts. "Principally, we deal with established name acts who have recording contracts with major labels." Receives 10-15% commission. Reviews material for acts.
**How to Contact:** Submit demo tape and lead sheet. Prefers 7½ ips reel-to-reel with 4 songs minimum on tape. Does not return unsolicited material. Reports as soon as possible on solicited material.
**Music:** Bluegrass, C&W, MOR, rock, soul and top 40/pop. Works primarily with concert attractions. Current acts include Danny Davis and the Nashville Brass (C&W/MOR instrumental); Willie Nelson

and Family; John Conlee (C&W/pop); Mitch Ryder (pop/rock); Freddy Fender, Johnny Paycheck, Ed Bruce, George Strait, Bill Monroe and Porter Wagoner (all C&W artists).

**LEMON SQUARE MUSIC**, Box 31819, Dallas TX 75231. (214)750-0720. A&R Director: Mike Anthony. Production company. Represents artists, groups and songwriters; currently handles 7 acts. Reviews material for acts.
**How to Contact:** Query by mail, then submit demo tape. Prefers 7½ ips reel-to-reel or cassette with 2-4 songs on demo. SASE. Reports in 1 month.
**Music:** C&W and gospel. Works primarily with show bands. Current acts include Brooks Brothers (C&W group); Glen Bailey (progressive country artist); Steve Reed (songwriter); Denman & Clark Band (country band/show band); Craig Solieau (comedy act); Millie Collise (country singer); and Nancy Eisen (progressive country singer).

*****LESTER PRODUCTIONS**, 13 Wall St., Rockaway NJ 07866. (201)627-0690. Theatrical Agent: Nancy Sloan. Booking agency. Represents artists, groups and lecture demonstrators; currently handles 15-20 acts. Receives 15-20% commission. Reviews material for acts.
**How to Contact:** Submit demo tape and lyric sheet. Prefers cassette with 5-10 songs on demo. Send complete promotional package. SASE. Reports in 1-2 weeks.
**Music:** Mostly rockabilly, top 40, country rock and progressive rock; also bluegrass, blues, church/religious, classical, C&W, dance-oriented, easy listening, folk, gospel, jazz, R&B and soul. Works primarily with dance bands (rock and country) and vocalists (all types). Current acts include Saturday Nite Special (tribute to Lynyrd Skynyrd); Mantis (progressve rock band); and Gangbusters (rockabilly show band).

**JOHN LEVY ENTERPRISES, INC.**, Suite 101, 181 S. Sycamore Ave., Los Angeles CA 90036. (213)934-0255. President: John Levy. Management agency. Represents individuals and songwriters; currently handles 3 acts. Receives 10-20% commission.
**How To Contact:** Submit demo tape only or demo tape and lead sheet. Prefers 7½ ips or cassette with 1-5 songs on demo. SASE. Reports in 2 weeks.
**Music:** Jazz, soul and top 40/pop. Current acts include Nancy Wilson, Joe Williams and Benard Ighner (all vocalists).

*****LEW LINET MANAGEMENT**, 7225 Hollywood Blvd., Hollywood CA 90046. (213)876-4071. President: Lew Linet. Management agency and independent record producer. Represents artists, groups and songwriters; currently handles 1 act. Receives maximum 20% commission. Reviews material for acts.
**How To Contact:** Submit demo tape and lyric sheet. Prefers cassette with 3 songs on demo. Include lyric sheet. SASE. Reports in 1 month.
**Music:** Mostly pop rock; also folk, rock (country or soft) and top 40/pop. Works with recording artists. Current acts include Noel Butler (pop rock).

**LINGERING MUSIC, INC.**, 2 Bay St., Thomaston ME 04861. (207)354-8928. President: Chuck Kruger. Management firm and booking agency. Represents artists, groups and songwriters in the Northeast; currently handles 3 acts. Receives 10-15% commission. Reviews material for acts.
**How to Contact:** Query by mail, submit demo tape. Prefers 7½ ips reel-to-reel or cassette with 2-5 songs on demo. "Brief biography okay, but let material speak for itself." SASE. Reports in 1 month.
**Music:** C&W, dance-oriented, easy listening, folk, gospel, jazz, MOR, progressive, R&B, rock, soul, top 40/pop, calypso and reggae. Works primarily with soloists, trios and dance bands. Current acts include Chuck Kruger (singer/songwriter); The Fabulous Prizes (club trio); and Cruzan Confuzion Band (dance and college concert band).

*****LOCONTO PRODUCTIONS**, 7766 NW 44th St., Sunrise FL 33321. (305)741-7766 or (305)940-2626 (Miami). President: Frank X. Loconto. Management firm and booking agency. Represents artists and groups; currently handles 5 acts. Receives 10-25% commission. Reviews material for acts.
**How to Contact:** Submit demo tape. Prefers 7½ ips reel-to-reel or cassette with 2-6 songs on demo. "We are looking primarily for C&W artists and songs with strong hooks and crossover potential." SASE. Reports in 1 month.
**Music:** Mostly country; also bluegrass, blues, children's, choral, church/religious, classical, C&W, dance-oriented, easy listening, folk, gospel, jazz, MOR, progressive, Spanish, R&B, rock, soul and top 40/pop. Works primarily with country vocalists, country bands, MOR vocalists and bluegrass artists. Current acts include J.J. Brotherton; Frank X. Loconto; and Janet Falcone.

*****LOCUST, INC.**, #101, 3875 Lone Pine, W. Bloomfield MI 48037. (313)851-6244. A&R Director: Mimi LePage. Management firm and production company. Represents artists, groups and songwriters;

currently handles 5 acts. Receives 12½-25% commisson. Reviews material for acts.
**How to Contact:** Query by mail, submit demo tape and lyric sheet or "send completed record projects for placement." Prefers cassette with 1-4 songs on demo. SASE. Reports in 1 month.
**Music:** Mostly R&B, top 40/pop, rock and soul; also blues, children's, church/religious, dance-oriented, gospel and MOR. Works primarily with vocalists, groups, self-contained groups. Current acts include Cut Glass (R&B); Jack Dalton (pop); and Edjo (rock/pop).

**LOGSDON ASSOCIATES,** Box 137, New Providence PA 17560. (717)284-2063. President: Paul K. Logsdon. Management firm and booking agency. Represents artists, groups and songwriters. Represents 4 northeast based artists who tour nationally; currently handles 4 acts. Receives 20-25% commission. Reviews material for acts.
**How to Contact:** Query by mail, submit demo tape and lead sheet. Prefers cassette with 1-3 songs on demo. SASE. Reporting time varies—"usually 3 weeks."
**Music:** Mostly top 40/pop Christian rock; also gospel rock and Christian MOR. Works primarily with Christian rock artists; groups with a mellow to progressive rock style, able to play the college circuit, concert halls, 'Jesus Festivals,' conventions and related outlets. Current acts include GLAD (5-man band; jazz/pop/rock blend); Pete Carlson (pop soloist); Lou Gibilisco (pop soloist); and Kathy Troccolli (pop soloist).
**Tips:** "Material must have Christian appeal (not 'churchy,' but morality conscious) and be inspirational or uplifting in attitude. The best example of what we are looking for is 'Captured In Time,' by GLAD, Greentree Records (The Benson Co.-R3941)."

*****LOVELAND MINISTRIES-CHRISTINE WYRTZEN MINISTRY,** 6278 Branch Hill-Guinea Rd., Loveland OH 45140. (513)683-3168. Executive Director: Paula J. Bussard. Management firm, booking agency and publishing company. Estab. 1981. Represents artists and songwriters. "Payment for services mutually agreed upon." Reviews material for acts.
**How to Contact:** Submit demo tape and lyric sheet. Prefers cassette as demo. SASE, "but we prefer to keep material on file." Reports in 1 month.
**Music:** Mostly MOR; also children's, choral, church/religious, easy listening, gospel and top 40/pop. Current artists include Christine Wyrtzen (female MOR vocalist).

**LS TALENT,** 120 Hickory St., Madison TN 37115. (615)868-7172. Managers: Lee Stoller or Harold Hodges. Management firm. Represents artists and groups; currently handles 4 acts. Receives 10-25% commission. Reviews material for acts.
**How to Contact:** Submit demo tape and lead sheet, "include bio and press kit." Prefers cassette with 2 songs on demo. "We only want artists capable of writing their own material—at least initially. No 'outlaw' or 'corn country' acts. Today's modern country only." SASE. Reports in 3 weeks.
**Music:** C&W and easy listening. Works primarily with "individuals with back-up groups and artists with records charted." Current acts include Cristy Lane, Anne Marie and Daniel (all country artists with back-up groups).
**Tips:** "We're looking for a hot country group to develop."

**RON LUCIANO MUSIC CO.,** Box 263, Hasbrouck Heights NJ 07604. (201)288-8935. President: Ron Luciano. Management firm and booking agency. Represents artists, group and recording/specialty acts; currently handles 7-8 acts. Receives 10-20% commission. Reviews material for artists.
**How To Contact:** Query or submit picture and biography. Prefers 7½ ips reel-to-reel or cassette with 4-8 songs on demo. "Can also approach by sending a copy of their record release." SASE. Reports in 2-6 weeks.
**Music:** Disco, MOR, rock, soul and top 40/pop. Works with 4- or 5- piece, self-contained groups "that play in Holiday Inns, Sheratons, etc. We also book a lot of oldie groups like the Belmonts and Flamingos." Current acts include Voyage (top 40/disco); Legz (R&R); Spit-N-Image (R&R group); and Charles Lamont.

**RICHARD LUTZ ENTERTAINMENT AGENCY,** 5625 0 St., Lincoln NE 68510. (402)483-2241. General Manager: Cherie Hanfelt. Management firm and booking agency. Represents individuals and groups; currently handles 200 acts. Receives 15-20% minimum commission. Reviews material for acts.
**How to Contact:** Query by phone or submit demo tape and lead sheet. Prefers cassette with 5-10 songs on demo. SASE. Reports in 1 week.
**Music:** Mostly MOR and C&W; also dance-oriented and top 40/pop. Works primarily with show and dance bands for lounge circuit. "Acts must be uniformed." Current acts include Miller and Meyer (MOR); Rainbow Express (C&W group); and Forty Karat (top 40 group).
**Tips:** "Send photo, resume, tape, partial song list and include references."

**LEE MAGID, INC.**, Box 532, Malibu CA 90265. (213)858-7282. President: Lee Magid. Management firm and music publisher. Record labels include LMI (jazz) and Grassroots (blues and country). Represents artists, groups, songwriters and comics, etc.; currently handles 10 acts. Receives 20-25% commission. Reviews material for acts.
**How to Contact:** Submit demo tape. Prefers cassette with 3-4 songs on demo. SASE. Reports in 3 weeks—"sometimes longer."
**Music:** Blues, C&W, gospel, jazz, R&B, rock and soul. Works primarily with self-contained and solo singers and instrumental jazz groups. Current acts include Gloria Lynne (jazz vocalist); Ernie Andrews (pop/jazz vocalist); Rags Waldorf (rock/jazz vocalist and keyboard); Becky Bishop (C&W artist); and Big Joe Turner (blues artist).

**ED MALHOIT AGENCY**, Box 2001, Claremont NH 03743. (603)542-8777. Agents: Ed Malhoit, Kathy Shull, Jason Farrell. Management firm and booking agency. Represents groups in eastern US; currently handles 60 acts. Receives 15-25% commission. Reviews material for acts.
**How to Contact:** Query by mail. Prefers cassette with minimum 5 songs on demo. SASE. Reports in 1 month.
**Music:** Rock. Current acts include Stone Cross, Laquidara and Whisper (all rock concert/club acts).

**MARS TALENT AGENCY**, 168 Orchid Dr., Pearl River NY 10965. (914)735-4569. Contact: Arnie Kay. Management firm and booking agency. Represents artists and groups; currently handles 7 acts. Receives 10-20% commission. Reviews material for acts.
**How to Contact:** Query by mail, then submit demo tape and lead sheet. Prefers cassette. SASE. Reports in 3 weeks.
**Music:** Easy listening, MOR and R&B. Works primarily with artists and groups from the 50s and 60s era. Current acts include Crystals, Duprees, Earls, Freddy Cannon, Regents, Cleftones and Reparata and the Delrons.

**MARSH PRODUCTIONS, INC.**, 1704 W. Lake St., Minneapolis MN 55408. (612)827-6141. President: Marshall Edelstein. Management firm, booking agency and promotion company. Represents artists and groups; currently handles 44 exclusive acts and 25 songwriters. Receives 15-20% commission. Reviews materials for acts.
**How To Contact:** Query, arrange personal interview, submit demo tape or submit demo tape and lead sheet. Prefers 7½ ips reel-to-reel or cassette with 3-6 songs on demo. SASE. Reports in 2-4 weeks.
**Music:** Bluegrass, blues, C&W, dance-oriented, easy listening, jazz, MOR, progressive, R&B, rock (all types), soul and top 40/pop. "We have eight fulltime agents who have all been in the rock industry; that's our specialty." Works with dance, party, bar (rock); wedding and concert bands; single, duos and specialized acts. Current acts include White Raven (rock); Hot Ash (rock); Counter Attack (rock); Hickory Wind (country rock); and Dare Force (rock).
**Tips:** "Always looking for that top 40 rock, original clothing, stage presence."

**MASADA MUSIC, INC.**, 888 8th Ave., New York NY 10019. (212)757-1953. President: Gene Heimlich. Management consultant firm and production house. Deals with artists in East Coast region only. Represents artists, groups and songwriters; currently handles 3 acts. Receives 10-15% commission or salary against commission. Reviews material for acts.
**How To Contact:** Query or arrange personal interview. Prefers 7½ ips reel-to-reel with 2-5 songs on demo. SASE. Reports in 3 weeks.
**Music:** Mostly R&B, pop and country; also blues, dance-oriented, easy listening, folk, jazz, MOR, progressive, rock, soul and top 40/pop. Works with singer/songwriters and self-contained bands. Current acts include Jeff Tozer (pop act); Tucker Smallwood (blues act); and Vince Montana Orchestra (contemporary).
**Tips:** "Present clean simple demos and focus on your market."

**MBA PRODUCTIONS**, 8914 Georgian Dr., Austin TX 78735. (512)836-3201. President: Roy J. Montgomery. Management firm and booking agency. Represents artists, groups and songwriters; currently handles 20 acts. Receives 10-15% commission. Reviews material for acts.
**How to Contact:** Submit demo tape. Prefers cassette with 1-3 songs on demo. SASE. Reports in 1 month.
**Music:** C&W, easy listening, MOR and rock (country). Works primarily with dance bands and recording artists. Current acts include Eli Worden (MOR artist); Suzanne Carlson (country artist); Joe Montgomery (rock group); The Price Sisters (C&W singing duo); and Jody Jay (C&W).

***MEADOWLARK VENTURERS**, Box 7218, Missoula MT 59807. (406)728-2180. Contact: Chris Roberts or David Englund. Management firm and booking agency. Represents groups in the western

US; currently handles 62 acts. Receives 15-20% commission. Reviews material for acts.
**How to Contact:** Query by mail or arrange personal interview. Prefers cassette with 3-7 songs on demo. SASE. Reports in 2 weeks.
**Music:** Mostly rock; also MOR, R&B and top 40/pop. Works primarily with bands. Current acts include Prophecy (top 40 rock); Boy Toast (new wave rock); and David LaFlamme (rock).

*MECCA INTERNATIONAL, 1 Comanche Dr., Middeltown NJ 07748. (201)291-0204. President: Stu Ric. Management firm and booking agency. Represents artists and groups; currently handles 2 acts. Receives 10-20% commission. Reviews material for acts.
**How to Contact:** Query by mail or phone or submit demo tape and lyric sheet. Prefers cassette with 2-5 songs on demo. SASE. Reports in 2 weeks.
**Music:** Bluegrass, C&W, MOR, R&B, rock and soul. Current acts include Prophet (rock); Redd Foxx (comedian); and Smash Palace (rock).

**MEDIA CONCEPTS, INC.**, Suite 308, 20 E. 1st St., Mt. Vernon NY 10550. (914)699-4003. President: Chip Rigo. Producer/Manager: Michael Berman. Management firm, booking agency, music publisher (MCI Music) and production company. Represents artists, groups and songwriters; currently handles approximately 25 acts. Receives 10-25% commission. Reviews material for acts.
**How to Contact:** Arrange personal interview or submit demo tape. Prefers 7½ ips reel-to-reel or cassette with 3-8 songs on demo. "Include photo and press kit; lyric sheets are helpful for song demos." SASE. Reports in 3 weeks.
**Music:** C&W, dance-oriented, easy listening, R&B, rock (all styles) and top 40/pop. Works primarily with dance bands, club groups, concert attractions and recording acts. "We specialize in female bands or groups with female singers." Current acts include Jailbait (concert concept attraction); Lotus (commercial rock group); Regina Richards (A&M recording artist); Chubby Checker (MCA recording artist); and Guy and Pipp Gillette (R&B recording act).

**MEDLAND MANAGEMENT**, 334 Dufferin St., Toronto, Ontario, Canada. (416)536-4882. President: John Medland. Represents local artists and musical groups; currently handles 3 acts. Receives 10-20% commission. Reviews material for acts.
**How to Contact:** Submit demo tape only. Prefers cassette with 1-5 songs on demo. SAE and IRC. Reports in 1 month.
**Music:** Mostly top 40/pop; also rock, dance-oriented and 50s R&R. Works primarily with full time traveling bands (bars, high schools, etc.). Current acts include Joey Rodes (top 40/pop/Bowie); S.X.S. (top 40/pop) and The Willies (folk/pop).

**MEGA-STAR MUSIC (Division of Norby Walters Associates)**, 200 W. 51st St., New York NY 10019. (212)245-3939. General Manager: Barry Yearwood. Management firm and music publisher. Represents artists, groups, songwriters and producers. "We work on commissions but percentages vary as we consider all factors involved to make it fair to those we represent and ourselves." Reviews material for acts.
**How to Contact:** Query by mail. Prefers cassette with 1-4 songs on demo. Does not return unsolicited material. Reports in 1 month.
**Music:** C&W, dance-oriented, easy listening, gospel, jazz, MOR, progressive, R&B, rock, soul and top 40/pop. Works primarily with dance bands and bar bands. Current acts include Henderson and Whitfield (R&B duo); Monica Neal (pop artist); and Conway and Temple (R&B duo).
**Tips:** "Make sure your songs have good hooks and that what is being said is understood."

**BARRY MENES & ASSOCIATES**. #1240, 901 Avenue of the Stars, Los Angeles CA 90067. (213)277-4895. Attorney: Barry Menes. Law firm; some artist management. Represents artists, groups and songwriters; currently handles over 100 acts. Receives "15% contingency or pay by the hour." Reviews material for acts.
**How to Contact:** Submit demo tape and bio. Prefers cassette. SASE. Reports in 1 month.
**Music:** All types. Works primarily with bands, solo artists and songwriters. Current acts include Lee Ritenour (jazz/pop band); and Four Tops (R&B/pop band).

**GREG MENZA ARITIST MANAGEMENT**, (formerly Come Alive Artist Management), Box 222, Marlton NJ 08053. (609)596-1590. Director: Greg Menza. Management firm, booking agency and concert producers. Represents artists, groups, songwriters, speakers and DJ's exclusively; currently handles 8 acts. Receives 10-20% commission. Reviews material for acts.
**How to Contact:** Query by mail. Prefers cassette with 3-6 songs on demo. Reports in at least 1 month. "Include SASE if you wish material returned. Send only high quality finished demos."
**Music:** Gospel, rock (contemporary Christian), church/religious and secular. Works primarily with

contemporary Christian rock artists. Current acts include Christian Stephens (duo); Harry Thomas; Rick & Shelley Poole; Gary Rand (Christian rock, folk artist); Mylon LeFevre & Broken Heart (contemporary Christian rock); David & the Giants (contemporary Christian rock); First Love Band (contemporary Christian rock); and Hosanna Sacred Dance (dance group).

**MERCANTILE MUSIC**, Box 2271, Palm Springs CA 92263. (619)320-4848. President: Kent Fox. Management firm and booking agency. Represents artists, groups and songwriters; currently handles 2 acts. Receives 10-25% commission. Reviews material for acts.
**How to Contact:** Submit demo tape. Prefers cassette with 3-12 songs on demo. SASE. Reports in 1 month.
**Music:** C&W, easy listening, MOR, R&R and top 40/pop. Works primarily fair dates.

*****JOSEPH C. MESSINA**, 80 West Garden Road, Larchmont NY 10538. (914)834-5676. Attorney/manager. Represents artists, groups and songwriters; currently handles 12 acts. Receives negotiable commission.
**How to Contact:** Submit demo tape and lead sheet. Prefers cassette with 1-2 songs on demo. Does not return unsolicited material.
**Music:** Mostly top 40; also jazz. Works primarily with male and female vocal/dance soloists. Current acts include Spyder Turner (R&B/top 40); Natalie Sands (top 40); and Mob Violence (jazz).

**MIDDLETON'S PUBLIC RELATIONS & MANAGEMENT**, 322 Smith Rd., Polk City FL 33868. (813)984-1286. President: Ben Middleton. Management and booking agency. Represents artists, groups and songwriters; currently handles 20 acts. Receives 10-20% commission. Reviews material for acts.
**How to Contact:** Submit demo tape. Prefers cassette with 3-5 songs on demo. SASE. Reports in 1 month.
**Music:** C&W, dance-oriented, easy listening, gospel, R&B, soul and top 40/pop. Works primarily with dance bands and vocal groups. Current acts include Genobia Jeter (contemporary gospel artist, Arista Records); Glenn Jones (R&B/top 40 artist, RCA Records); and Isaac Douglas (gospel artist, Savoy-Arista Records).

**MILLER BOOKING & MANAGEMENT**, 581-D Old Hickory Blvd., Jackson TN 38301. (901)668-1404. Contact: Bill W. Miller. Management firm and booking agency. Represents artists, groups and songwriters; currently handles 5 acts. Negotiates payment. Reviews material for acts.
**How to Contact:** Submit demo tape and lead sheet. Prefers cassette with 4-12 songs on demo. SASE. Reports in 1 month.
**Music:** C&W, R&B, rock, soul and top 40/pop. Works primarily with "artists, groups and songwriters who play for clubs and have enough recording and songwriting talent to get a deal from a record company. We prefer writer/singer or groups." Current acts include Wolfpack Band, Steve Mallard and James (Poly) Stanfield (all pop rock, country rock artists).
**Tips:** "Have good commercial material."

**MINIMUM MUSIC/JOSEPH CASEY MANAGEMENT**, 739 Astor Station, Boston MA 02123. Contact: Joseph Casey. Management (US and International) booking for clubs, promoters, schools, video production and brokerage firm. Represents artists, groups and songwriters; currently handles 4 acts. Receives 15% commission; "all arrangements are particular to each artist's career needs." Reviews material for acts.
**How to Contact:** Submit demo tape. Prefers cassette with 2-6 songs on demo. SASE. Reports in 1 month.
**Music:** Dance-oriented (rock) and new wave. Works primarily with rock and new wave writers and performers for touring and management/artist development. Current acts include The Neighborhoods (3-piece original rock band and recording group); Boys Life (young, 4-piece original rock band and recording group); Willie Alexander (songwriter/appears with 4-piece rock band and recording group, Willie Alexander and "The Confessions"); and The Outlets (4-piece original rock band and recording group).

**MOTOBOY MOTIONS**, 1st Floor, 1216 Cottman Ave., Philadelphia PA 19111. (215)342-6757. President: Alan Moss. New Talent A&R Representative: Karen Leto. Management firm, booking agency and promoter. Represents artists and groups. Receives 10-20% commission. "Most business commands the standard industry rates." Reviews material for acts.
**How to Contact:** Query by mail, arrange personal interview. "Include bio material." Prefers cassette with 2 songs minimum on demo. SASE. Reports in 6 weeks.
**Music:** Bluegrass, blues, C&W, dance-oriented, easy listening, folk, jazz, MOR, new wave, progres-

sive, R&B, rock and top 40/pop. Works primarily with bar, club and dance bands. Current acts include Chronicles (hard rock/new wave); The Tones (top 40 rock-cover and original); Rob Sukol (single act-sometimes with backup group); and The Plyers (top 40 rock cover and original).

**MPL ASSOCIATES, LTD.**, Box 2108, Phoenix AZ 85001. President: Louis P. Goldstein. Management firm. Represents artists and songwriters; currently handles 2 acts. Receives 10-20% commission. Reviews material for acts.
**How to Contact:** Submit demo tape and lead sheet. Prefers cassette with 1-5 songs on demo. "Be sure that any tapes submitted have clear vocals and be sure to include a lead sheet for each song . . . and a current picture if possible." SASE. Reports within 2 weeks to 1 month.
**Music:** C&W, easy listening, MOR and top 40/pop. Works primarily with songwriters and songwriting performers. Current acts include Jack Wright and Keira Hayes (vocalists/songwriters).

***ALEXANDER MURPHY, JR., ESQUIRE**, 225 Church St., Philadelphia PA 19106. (215)592-9710. Contact: Alexander Murphy. Attorney. Represents artists, groups and songwriters; currently handles 25 acts. Receives 5-10% commission or hourly rate (for consultation). Reviews material for acts.
**How to Contact:** Query by mail. Prefers cassette with 3-4 songs on demo. Include bio. SASE. Reports in 1 month.
**Music:** Mostly rock and top 40/pop; also easy listening, jazz and MOR. Works primarily with bands, solo performers and songwriters. Current acts include John Flynn (songwriter); Johnny Neel (band); The Stickmen (band); and Jack of Diamonds (band).

**MUSKRAT PRODUCTIONS, INC.**, 44 N. Central Ave., Elmsford NY 10523. (914)592-3144. Contact: Bruce McNichols. Represents individuals and groups; currently represents 11 acts. Deals with artists in the New York City area. Reviews material for acts.
**How to Contact:** Query. Prefers cassette with 3 songs minimum on tape. SASE. Reports "only if interested."
**Music:** "We specialize in old-time jazz, dixieland and banjo music and shows;" also C&W and jazz." Works primarily with dixieland, banjo/sing-along groups to play parties, specialty acts for theme parties, dances, shows and conventions. Current acts include Smith Street Society Jazz Band (dixieland jazz); Your Father's Mustache (banjo sing-along); and Harry Hepcat and the Boogie Woogie Band (50s rock revival).

**MUTUAL MANAGEMENT ASSOCIATES/COMSTOCK RECORDS, LTD.**, Box 3247, Shawnee KS 66203. (913)631-6060. General Manager: Frank Fara. Management agency, music publisher, record producer and promotion firm. Represents artists, musical groups and songwriters primarily from Canada and the US; currently handles 3 acts. Receives 10-15% commission. Reviews material for acts.
**How to Contact:** Check by phone for specific needs, then arrange personal interview or submit demo tape only. Prefers cassette with 1-5 songs on demo. "After phone call, submit bio, tape, photo, etc." SASE. Reports in 2 weeks.
**Music:** C&W, gospel and pop. Works primarily with 2-6 member self-contained groups for concert or club appearances primarily in support of artists' record releases in the US and Canada. Current acts include The O'Roark Brothers (high energy country show/dance act); Doc & Dusty Holliday (country/pop duo); Steve Gray & Jubilation (contemporary gospel); Don TeBeaux; Anne Lord; Buddy Day and Bill Hersh.

**MYRIAD PRODUCTIONS**, Suite 402, 1314 N. Hayworth Ave., Los Angeles CA 90046. (213)851-1400. President/Executive Producer: Ed Harris. Multimedia production company, providing performing arts services to professional performers, groups and industrial show productions. "We work with entertainers, management companies and record companies in producing live stage acts and in record production in studio and location situations." Payment varies per assignment or show/record.
**How to Contact:** Submit demo tape and lead sheet. "*No telephone inquiries!*" Prefers 7½ ips reel-to-reel or cassette with 1-4 songs on demo. "We keep extensive files of submitted material for the artists we work with and refer to them for live stage acts as well as recording dates. Should an artist pick a song on file, we then contact the songwriter/publishing company to arrange royalties for the songwriter. *We do not return submitted material for this reason.*"
**Music:** Blues, country, easy listening, folk, jazz, AOR, progressive, Latin, R&B, rock (hard, country, folk, etc.), soul and top 40/pop. Works with all performing artists and groups as well as corporate clientele in writing and producing industrial shows (live industrial theater and multimedia A/V productions). "We are constantly looking for new musical material for our varied clientele in all areas of music."

**FRANK NANOIA MANAGEMENT**, 1999 N. Sycamore Ave., Los Angeles CA 90068. (213)874-8725. President: Frank Nanoia. Management firm. Represents artists, groups and songwriters; currently handles 11 acts. Receives 15-20% commission. Reviews material for acts.

**How to Contact:** Submit demo tape and lead sheet. Prefers 7½ or 15 ips reel-to-reel or cassette with 3-5 songs on demo. Does not return unsolicited material. Reports "only if material is above average."
**Music:** Mostly R&B, top 40/pop and jazz; also C&W, dance-oriented, easy listening, MOR, gospel and soul. Works primarily with vocalists and show groups. Current acts include Marc Allen Trujillo (top 40/pop, R&B artist); Paramour (R&B show group), and The Tim & Dan Show.

**NEW IMAGE ARTIST AND MODELS GUILD,** Box 3702, Hollywood CA 90028. (213)465-5236. Contact: Wally Eagler. Management firm, promotion and marketing company. Estab. 1981. Represents local artists, groups, songwriters and dancers; currently handles 60 acts. Receives 10-15% commission or "$50-150/month per individual or group acts for promotion and marketing services." Reviews material for acts.
**How to Contact:** Query by mail or arrange personal interview. Prefers 2 cassettes with maximum 3 top 40/standard and 3 original songs on demos. Submit only your very best." Does not return unsolicited material. Reports in 1 week.
**Music:** C&W, dance-oriented, easy listening, MOR, progressive, R&B, rock (all kinds) and top 40/pop. Works primarily with songwriters, bands and singers for clubs, movies and TV shows.
**Tips:** "Send enough good quality tapes to send around to our buyers. Include good pictures (in performance) and complete resume with all pertinent information in order to hire for openings."

**NEW VINTAGE MANAGEMENT,** Box 716, Ojai CA 93023. (805)646-8156. Contact: Kim Ferguson or Stuart Ross. Management firm. Represents artists and groups; currently handles 1 act. Receives minimum 10-20% commission. Reviews material for acts.
**How to Contact:** Query by mail, then submit demo tape and lead sheet. Prefers cassette with 3-8 songs on demo. SASE. Reports in 3 weeks.
**Music:** Jazz, rock and top 40/pop. Current acts include Maynard Ferguson (jazz artist).

**MIKE NICHOLS PRODUCTIONS,** #309, 2130 E. Crawford, Salina KS 67401. (913)825-1124. President: Mike Nichols. Assistant Producer: Jim Beilman. Management firm, booking agency and concert promotion. Represents artists and groups; currently handles 10 acts. Receives 15-20% commission. Reviews material for acts.
**How to Contact:** Query by mail. Prefers cassette with 3-4 songs on demo. Include "club references and an 8x10 photo." SASE. Reports ASAP.
**Music:** Mostly rock (new wave) and top 40/pop; also easy listening, MOR, progressive and heavy metal rock. Works primarily with bar and dance bands. Current acts include Shagnasty (heavy metal, rock band); Still Nobody (post modern pop); and Voices (mainstream pop).
**Tips:** "You must be willing to promote yourself as well as using the promotion techniques of the agency."

*****NIGHTSTREAM MUSIC,** 670 Lindsay Rd., Carnegie PA 15106. A&R Director: Tom Balistreri. Management firm, recording company and music publisher. Works with artists, groups and songwriters; currently handlers 5 acts. Recieves 10-25% commission. Reviews material for acts.
**How to Contact:** Submit demo tape and lead sheet. Prefers cassette with 1-5 songs on demo. SASE. Reports in 1 month.
**Music:** Mostly top 40/pop; also dance-oriented, easy listening, MOR, R&B and R&R. Works primaily with vocalists and pop bands for concert, club and recording work. Current acts include Nightstream (pop band); Tom Balistreri (singer/songwriter); and Gary Gallagher (singer/songwriter).

**NORTH-SOUTH ARTSCOPE,** 1914 White Plains Rd., Chapel Hill NC 27514. (919)929-5508. Personal Representative: Mary Nordstrom. Personal representative of performing artists and attractions. Represents artists, groups, conductors and music directors. Receives 10-20% commission. "We charge an annual career development fee for artists or ensembles with concert fees below $2,500."
**How to Contact:** Query by mail, arrange personal interview. Prefers cassette with 2-4 songs on demo. Does not return unsolicited material. Reports in 1 month "or more."
**Music:** Classical and contemporary. Works primarily with chamber music ensembles, classical music soloists and special attractions featuring classical music. "Material may be submitted on speculation to Ken Moses, Owner/Director, Pickwick Puppet Theatre for possible cable TV shows and concert tours." Current roster includes Pickwick Puppet Theatre (concert puppetry); Bryant Hayes (clarinetist); An Evening with the Poets (vocal settings); and Chansonet (trio—clarinet, voice, piano).
**Tips:** "If you already have a publisher who needs outstanding musicians to record promotional material we are interested in mutual benefits at moderate performance fees for recording purposes."

*****N2D BREEZEWAY PUBLISHING COMPANIES,** Box 23684, Nashville TN 37202. Contact: Douglas Casmus. Management firm and publisher. Estab. 1981. Represents artists, groups, songwriters and comedians; currently handles 4 acts. Reviews material for acts.

**How to Contact:** Submit demo tape and lyric sheet. Prefers cassette with 1-2 songs on demo. SASE. Reports in 1 month.
**Music:** Mostly country and top 40/pop; also new wave, progressive, rock and comedy. Works primarily with country, rock and top 40/pop writers and artists.

**OHIO RECORDS**, Box 655, Hudson OH 44236. (216)650-1330. A&R Director: Russ Delaney. Management firm. Represents artists and groups; currently handles 6 acts. "We are an independent label (BMI affiliated) and if we record material we handle the publishing gratis." Reviews material for acts.
**How to Contact:** Submit demo tape and lead sheet. Prefers cassette with 6-10 songs on demo. SASE. "Do not expect your material back immediately. If we are looking for material for our artists we would be happy to review new material. Sometimes we review only at time of recording sessions. Don't call us, we'll call you."
**Music:** C&W. Works primarily with theater/stage artists and groups. Current acts include Ethel Delaney (songwriter/singer/rhythm guitar artist); Buckeye Strings (vocalists and instrumentalists); and Russ Thomas (vocalist/drummer).

*****OPEN BOOKING AGENCY**, 5601 Odana Rd., Madison WI 53719. (608)271-1190. Contact: Nels Christiansen. Booking agency. Represents artists and groups mainly from the midwest but also from other locales; currently handles 50-60 acts. Receives 15-20% commission. Reviews material for acts.
**How to Contact:** Submit demo tape and lyric sheet. Prefers cassette with 5-10 songs on demo. Include biography of band, photo and references. Does not return unsolicited material. Reports in 2 weeks.
**Music:** Mostly rock, country, variety and 50s/60s music; also bluegrass, blues, dance-oriented, easy listening, folk, jazz, R&B, soul, top 40/pop and reggae. Works primarily with 4-6 piece bands. Current acts include Piper Road Spring Band (bluegrass band); The Cheeters (50s/60s); and Wet Behind the Ears (country).
**Tips:** "Have a good commercial sound, be business-minded, and a good promotional package."

*****OPERATION MUSIC ENTERPRISES**, 233 W. Woodland Ave., Ottomwa IA 52501. (515)682-8283. President: Nada C. Jones. Management firm and booking agency. Represents artists, groups and songwriters; currently handles 7 acts. Receives 15-20% commission. Reviews material for acts.
**How to Contact:** Submit demo tape and lyric sheet. Prefers cassette as demo. Artists should include references. SASE. Reports in 6-8 weeks.
**Music:** Mostly C&W; also blues. Works primarily with vocalists and show-lounge and concert groups. Current acts include Reesa Kay Jones (country vocalist and recording artist); Prairie Fire (country show group); and Hugo J. Huck (songwriter).

**ORANGE BLOSSOM PRODUCTIONS**, Suite 1119, 380 Lexington Ave., New York NY 10017. (212)687-9000. President: Douglas Tuchman. Booking agency and production company. Represents groups; currently handles 4 acts. Receives minimum 15% commission. Reviews material for acts.
**How to Contact:** Submit demo tape of performance recorded "live." Prefers 7½ ips reel-to-reel or cassette with 4-8 songs on demo. "Make package as complete as possible." SASE. Reports in 2 weeks.
**Music:** Mostly bluegrass; also traditional C&W. Works primarily with touring show bands (concerts, festivals, etc). Current acts include Bill Harrell and The Virginians (bluegrass band); John Herald Band (bluegrass, country); The Dixie Doughboys (C&W swing band); and Pat Cannon & Foot & Fiddle (clog dancing troupe).
**Tips:** "We will not accept for consideration any songs sent us that writer has not copyrighted for his/her protection. Only video tapes and/or in-concert cassette (or reel-to-reel) tapes accepted for consideration. Return postage must accompany material sent us."

**ORGANIC MANAGEMENT**, 745 5th Ave., New York NY 10151. (212)751-3400. Contact: A&R Director. Management and record company. Currently handles 6 acts. Receives 25% maximum commission. Reviews material for acts.
**How to Contact:** Submit demo tape and lyric sheet. Prefers cassette with 1-3 songs on demo. SASE. Reports in 1 month "or more."
**Music:** Blues, MOR, R&B, rock and top 40/pop. Works primarily with concert attractions, club acts and solo artists. Current acts include Dan Hartman (pop artist); Edgar Winter (pop/rock artist); and David Johansen (pop/rock artist).

**ORPHEUS ENTERTAINMENT**, Box 647, Orange NJ 07015. (201)677-1090. Contact: A&R Department. Management firm, booking agency and production company. Represents artists, groups and songwriters; currently handles 15 acts. Receives 10-20% commission. Reviews material for acts.
**How to Contact:** Query by mail, then submit demo tape and lead sheet. Prefers cassette with 2-6 songs on demo. Does not return unsolicited material. Reports in 1 month.

**Music:** Jazz, MOR, progressive, R&B, rock, soul, top 40/pop and fusion. Works primarily with national and regional recording and concert artists. Current acts include Teruo Nakamura and The Rising Sun Band (fusion/progressive rock); Jimmy Ponder (guitar jazz); Reach (jazz fusion/progressive rock); and Michal Urbaniak and UBX (fusion/jazz).

*P. D. Q. DIRECTIONS, INC., 1474 N. Kings Rd., Los Angeles CA 90048. (213)656-4870. President: Leo Leichter. Management agency and production company. Represents artists and musical groups from anywhere; currently handles 5 acts. Receives 15-25% commission. Reviews material for acts (cassettes and videos only).
**How to Contact:** Submit demo tape and lead sheet. Prefers cassette with 4-6 songs on demo. Does not return unsolicited material. Reports in 1 month.
**Music:** C&W, rock (country), top 40/pop and MOR. Current acts include Johnny Guitar Watson (R&B); Herman Brood (rock); Society of Seven (MOR); Glen Yarbrough (contemporary); The Limeliter (contemporary); and The Diamonds (50s rock).
**Tips:** "Artists should be earning at least $100,000/year and have strong work experience and professional stage presence."

**PELICAN PRODUCTIONS**, Room 10, 3700 East Ave., Rochester NY 14618. President: Peter Morticelli. Management firm and publishing company; currently handles 3 acts. Receives 15-25% commission. Reviews material for acts.
**How to Contact:** Submit demo tape. Prefers cassette with 3 songs on demo. SASE. Reports in 1 month.
**Music:** Mostly rock (all kinds); also C&W, dance-oriented, soul and top 40/pop. Works with "any type of act as long as the songwriting ability is very strong." Currently represents Duke Jupiter (mainstream rock artist); The Rods (heavy metal trio); and Bartolo (R&R).

**PEOPLE SONG, INTERNATIONAL**, Rt. 3, Sweeney Hollow, Franklin TN 37064. (615)794-5712. General Manager: Jeff Engle. Artist Relations: Ti Buckman. Management agency, booking agency and music publisher. Represents artists, musical groups and songwriters from anywhere; currently handles 10 acts. "The agency end charges 10% flat; the management end charges 15% flat." Reviews material for acts.
**How to Contact:** Submit demo tape and lead sheet. Prefers cassette with 1-4 songs on demo. SASE. Reports in 1 month.
**Music:** MOR, progressive rock, rock, and top 40/pop. Current acts include Gene Cotton (pop/rock singer-songwriter); Oliver (pop/rock singer-songwriter); Dianne Darling (pop/rock singer-songwriter); Marc Speer and Hot Rocks (R&R act); and American Ace (R&R band).
**Tips:** "We are not currently looking to sign new artists, but we are looking for good songs."

**PERFECTION LIGHT PRODUCTIONS**, Box 690, San Francisco CA 94101. (415)626-0655. Vice President: Gregory DiGiovine. Management agency and production company. Represents artists, groups and producers in Northern California; currently handles 2 acts. Receives negotiable commission. Reviews material for acts.
**How to Contact:** Submit demo tape and lyric sheet. Prefers cassette with 1-4 songs on demo. Does not return unsolicited material.
**Music:** Dance-oriented, R&B, rock, soul and top 40/pop. Works primarily with R&B/pop solo artists and groups. Current acts include Narada Michael Walden and Wanda Walden (R&B/pop artists).

**PIZAZZ PRODUCTIONS**, 35 Hambly Ave., Toronto, Ontario, Canada M4E 2R5. (416)699-3359. Manager: Craig Nicholson. Management agency. Represents musical groups and songwriters from anywhere; currently handles 7 acts. Receives 12-25% commission. Reviews material for acts.
**How to Contact:** Submit demo tape only. Prefers cassette with 2-4 songs on demo. SAE and IRC. Reports in 1 month.
**Music:** Top 40/rock and pop. Works primarily with top 40/rock and pop groups with recording contracts with independent labels and producers. Current acts include Robbie Rae (top 40/rock); Crackers (original rock); Mama Coco (top 40/pop/theatrical rock); Angel Fever (3-girl front-pop act); and Biko (progressive new music).

**RICK POPPELL PRODUCTION**, 103 Jamie Ct., West Columbia SC 29169. (803)359-7014. President: Rick C. Poppell. Management firm, booking agency and music publisher. Represents artists, groups and songwriters; currently handles 6 acts. Receives 10% commission for booking; 20-35% for group/artist management; and 50% for publishing. Reviews material for acts.
**How to Contact:** Submit demo tape. Prefers cassette with 3-6 songs on demo. SASE. Reports in 3 weeks.
**Music:** C&W, MOR, R&B and soul. Works primarily with night club artists and groups. Current acts

include Maxwell (R&B/funk group); Corby Myers (artist/songwriter); and Hank Marshall (artist/songwriter).

**PREFERRED ARTIST MANAGEMENT, INC.**, Box 99035, Louisville KY 40299. (502)267-5466. President: Dan Green. Secretary: David H. Snowden. Management agency. Deals with artists in eastern United States and Midwest states. Represents artists and groups; currently handles 9 acts. Receives 10-25% commission. Reviews material for acts.
**How to Contact:** Query or submit demo tape and lead sheet. Prefers cassette with 3-5 songs on demo. SASE. Reports in 2 weeks.
**Music:** Dance, rock (funk, medium) and top 40/pop. Works with bar artists ranging from bar bands to both single and group concert acts. Current acts include Free Fall (rock/show act); New Horizon (country/bluegrass act); Ambush (original artists); Peaches (MOR/original act); Bob Brickley Band (top 40/original artists); Jubilation (top 40/original artists); Sue Powell (pop/country artist, RCA Records); and Circus (rock/original act).

**PRO TALENT CONSULTANTS**, Box 29543, Atlanta GA 30359. (404)424-1684. Coordinator/Product Manager: John Eckert/Glenn Elliott. Management agency and public relations firm. Represents artists, groups and songwriters; currently handles 7 acts. Receives 15-20% commission. Reviews material for acts.
**How to Contact:** Submit demo tape. Prefers cassette with 4-6 songs on demo. SASE. Reports in 2 weeks.
**Music:** C&W, easy listening, folk, jazz, MOR, rock (top 40/country), comedy and top 40/pop. Works primarily with bar bands, novelty/comedy acts and top 40 club bands. Current acts include Glenn Elliott Band (rock group); Tristan (vocal group); Tommy Wells (artist/songwriter); Ron Young (country balladeer); and Simeaul (artist/songwriter).

**PROCESS TALENT MANAGEMENT**, 439 Wiley Ave., Franklin PA 16323. (814)432-4633. Contact: Norman Kelly. Management agency. Represents artists and groups; currently handles 10-15 acts. Receives 10-15% commission. Reviews material for acts.
**How to Contact:** Query. Prefers 7½ ips reel-to-reel, cassette or 8-track cartridge with 2-6 songs on demo. SASE. Reports in 2 weeks.
**Music:** Mostly country; also bluegrass, C&W, gospel, jazz and rock. Works with C&W artists (70%), gospel (10%) and pop/rock, etc. (20%). Current acts include Junie Lou (C&W); Debbie Sue (C&W); Glen Lucas Family (gospel); Bonnie Baldwin (C&W); Virge Brown (C&W); Junior Norman (country); Lady Brown Sugar (rock); Tessa Carol (soul and jazz); and Valerie Anderson (country rock).

*****PROFESSIONAL ARTISTS**, Rustic Acres, Jasper IN 47546. (812)482-6823. Contact: Jerry J. Fuhs. Management firm and promoter. Represents artists; currently handles 3 acts. Receives negotiable commission. Reviews material for acts.
**How to Contact:** Query by mail. Prefers 7½ ips reel-to-reel or cassette with 1-2 songs on demo. SASE. Reports in 3 weeks.
**Music:** C&W and country rock. Works primarily with national country stars. Current acts include George Jones and David Allan Coe.

**PROGRESS ENTERTAINMENT**, 5500 Avion Park Dr., Highland Heights OH 44143. (216)461-7880. President: Ray Calabrese. Management firm and label placement. Represents artists, groups and songwriters; currently handles 6 acts. Receives 20% commission. Reviews material for acts.
**How to Contact:** Submit demo tape and lead sheet. Prefers cassette with 4 songs on demo. SASE; "will return material upon request." Reports in 2 weeks.
**Music:** Mostly R&B; also rock, soul and top 40/pop. Prefers "marketable music and artists." Current acts include Dazz Band (R&B, Motown Records); Sekou (R&B); Tony Evan (top 40/pop); Jonah Koslin (pop/rock—"The Latest" R&B); and Candela (R&B/Latin, Arista Records).
**Tips:** "Exceptional talent can only succeed with exceptional management."

**PROGRESSIVE TALENT MANAGEMENT, INC.**, 2014 W. 8th St, Erie PA 16505. (814)455-3042. President: Daniel F. Lewis. Management firm and booking agency. Represents artists, groups and songwriters; currently handles 10 acts. Receives 10-20% commission. Reviews material for acts.
**How to Contact:** "Phone me to discuss what you have in mind," query by mail, or submit demo tape and lead sheet. "One-half inch VHS videotape is desirable if the artist is a writer/performer." SASE. Reports in 1 week "unless we are very busy."
**Music:** R&B, rock (top 40), soul and top 40/pop. Works primarily with "groups that are very top 40 oriented and career minded." Current acts include Friction (top 40/rock group); Tite Endz (top 40/rock group); Georgia Michels Band (top 40/soul artists); Splash (top 40/rock); Prophecy (top 40/rock);

A.T.V (top 40/rock); Crossfire (top 40/rock); Kramer & Doris (acoustic duo); Laura Presutti (acoustic); Riverside (acoustic); Marty O'Connor (acoustic); and the Moonlighters, (wave and contour, top 40/lounge act).
**Tips:** "We take pride in representing truly professional artists and we are very selective. We look for people who are intelligent, cooperative, and willing to be dedicated to the pursuit of their goals."

**\*PRO-TALENTS, INC.**, Suite 920, 414 Walnut St., Cincinnati OH 45202. (513)241-7767. President: Bill Waller Jr. Management firm. Represents artists, groups, songwriters, magicians and comedians; currently handles 32 acts. Receives 5-15% commission.
**How to Contact:** Query by mail. Prefers cassette with 2-5 songs on demo. SASE. Reports in 2 weeks.
**Music:** Mostly R&B and top 40; also blues, children's, church/religious, dance-oriented, gospel, MOR, progressive, rock and soul. Works primarily with vocalists and bands. Current acts include General Crook (R&B); Joel Davis (songwriter); and Meditation (gospel).
**Tips:** "Identify your strongest talents, and work hard to develop those strengths."

**QUADRANGLE MANAGEMENT, INC.**, Suite 611, 9000 Sunset Blvd., Los Angeles CA 90069. (213)550-1010. President: Ronald Domont. Vice President: Joel Brandes. Management agency, music publisher and production company. Estab. 1981. Represents artists, groups and songwriters.
**How to Contact:** Inquire about your interest by mail. Prefers cassette with 1-4 songs on demo. SASE. Reports in 4 weeks.
**Music:** Easy listening, progressive and rock (hard). Works primarily with touring bands and songwriters. Artists include David Pomeranz (songwriter); Jerry Corbetta (songwriter); YST (heavy metal rock); Glenn Hughes (heavy metal rock); Osamo Kitajima (guitar, koto & biwa); Judy Roberts (jazz/pop singer); Terry Gregory (country singer); and Hughes and Thrall (rock band).

**QUEST TALENT MANAGEMENT CO.**, #220, 9100 Sunset, Los Angeles CA 90069. (213)550-1799. A&R Director: Adrienne Weisman. Management firm. Represents artists, groups and songwriters; currently handles 20 acts. Receives 15-20% commission. Reviews material for acts.
**How to Contact:** Query by mail, then submit demo tape. Prefers cassette with 3-5 songs on demo. "No demo tapes will be returned without SASE." Reports in 1 month.
**Music:** C&W, gospel, rock and top 40/pop. "Our prime interest is in rock and top 40 originals." Works primarily with rock groups. Current acts include OXO, Sherie Currie, and 7th Heaven (all recording rock acts).

**THE RAINBOW COLLECTION, LTD.**, 101 W. 57th St., New York NY 10019. (212)765-8160. A&R Director: Ray Wilson. Management firm. Represents artists, groups and songwriters; currently handles 6 acts. Receives 20% commission. Reviews material for acts.
**How to Contact:** Submit demo tape. Prefers cassette with 3 songs on demo. Does not return unsolicited material. Reports in 4-6 weeks.
**Music:** Rock, pop and dance-oriented. Works "almost exclusively with strong songwriters whether they are solo artists or bands." Current acts include Don McLean, Andy Breckman and Tony Bird.
**Tips:** "Don't necessarily worry about current trends in music. Just do what you do to the best of your ability. With our company the song is the thing even if production-wise it's in its infant stages."

**\*THE RECORD COMPANY OF THE SOUTH (RCS)**, 5220 Essen Ln, Baton Rouge LA 70898. (504)766-3233. President: Cyril E. Vetter. Management agency, music publisher and record company. Represents artists, groups and songwriters; currently handles 5 acts. Receives 20-25% commission. Reviews material for acts.
**How to Contact:** Submit demo tape and lyric sheet. Prefers cassette with 2-6 songs on demo. SASE. Reports in 6 weeks.
**Music:** C&W, R&B, rock, soul and top 40/pop. Works primarily with artists, bands and songwriters. Current acts include Irma Thomas (top 40/pop and R&B); Luther Kent (top 40/pop and R&B); Butch Hornsby (country); and Floyd Brown (pop/country).

**RECORD MUSIC, INC.**, Box 182, Middle Village, New York NY 11379. (212)898-3027. President: Peter Paul. Management firm, record promoter, music publisher and record producer. Represents artists, groups and songwriters worldwide. Reviews material for acts.
**How to Contact:** Submit demo tape. Prefers cassette. SASE. Reporting time "varies."
**Music:** Bluegrass, blues, C&W, dance-oriented, easy listening, jazz, MOR, progressive, R&B, rock, soul, top 40/pop and novelty.

**REDBEARD PRESENTS PRODUCTIONS, LTD.**, 1061 E. Flamingo Rd., Box 19114, Las Vegas NV 89112. (702)361-4875. President: Robert Leonard. Management firm, booking agency, production

company and music publisher. Represents individuals, groups and songwriters; currently handles 12 acts. Receives 10-15% commission. Reviews material for acts.
**How to Contact:** Query or submit demo tape and lyric sheet. Prefers cassette with 4-8 songs on demo. "It is most helpful if the artist or group can arrange for me to see them work if they are interested in my overseas bookings in Europe, South Africa and the Far East." SASE. Reports in 3 weeks.
**Music:** MOR, jazz, blues, dance-oriented, progressive, rock (soft, country), soul and top 40/pop. Works primarily with "jazz 'names,'" celebrity performers, MOR main room performers, record name artists, show bands with international appeal, cabaret singers for South Africa, Europe and the Far East, and exciting attractions for gambling spots in the US." Current acts include Karen Nelson (singer/keyboard/songwriter, RCA-Finland Records and Chameleon Records); Marlena Shaw (blues cabaret singer, Columbia-Blue Note Records); Timi Yuro (United Artists and Mercury Records); Odia Coates (cabaret performer, RCA Records); Doris Troy (Brunswick Records); Bob Anderson (singer/impressionist); Billy Eckstine (Mercury-MGM Records); and Dakota Staton (blues cabaret singer, Capital Records).
**Tips:** "I look for professionalism in groups or songwriters. Groups should have solid variety of entertainment suitable for a worldwide market, be costumed, choreographed, double instruments, and contain plenty of group vocals for Nevada and Atlantic City work. A polished show group without hit records can work all over the world with the right attitude! Songwriters should be writing about positive, good and loving thoughts for the 80s."

**RODGERS REDDING & ASSOCIATES**, Box 4603, Macon GA 31208. (912)742-8771. President: Rodgers Redding. Booking agency. Represents artists and groups; currently handles 13 acts. Receives 15-20% commission. Reviews material for acts.
**How to Contact:** Query by mail, then submit demo tape. Prefers cassette with 4-12 songs on demo. SASE. Reports in 1 month.
**Music:** Mostly R&B; also soul, blues and top 40/pop. Works primarily with dance and bar bands. Current acts include Clarence Carter (male vocalist/musician); Tyrone Davis (male vocalist); Brick (5-piece self-contained R&B group); Z.Z. Hill; Denise La Salle; Latimore; Lanier & Co.; and Percy Sledge.
**Tips:** "Be yourself."

*****REED SOUND RECORDS, INC.**, 120 Mikel Dr., Summerville SC 29483. (803)873-3324. Contact: Haden Reed. Management agency. Represents artists; currently handles 3 acts. Receives 2-4% commission. Reviews material for acts.
**How to Contact:** Query by mail. Prefers cassette with 1-4 songs on demo. SASE. Reports in 1 month.
**Music:** Mostly C&W; also church/religious, easy listening and gospel. Current acts include Becky Knowles and The Country Blues; Haden Reed (songwriter/country); Vocalettes (gospel); and Country Blues (show band).

**JOANNE RILE MANAGEMENT**, Box 27539, Philadelphia PA 19118. President: Joanne Rile. Management firm, booking agency, promotion firm and consultant. Represents artists, groups, novelty acts (magic show) and dance and theater presentations; currently handles 50 acts. Receives 20% commission; "fees are used for preparation of promotional work." Reviews material for acts.
**How to Contact:** Query by mail. "Send reviews and brochures with letter of inquiry." Prefers cassette with 6-10 songs on demo. SASE. Reports between June and August.
**Music:** Mostly classical; also bluegrass, choral, folk, gospel and jazz. Works primarily with classical, soft rock and folk soloists and brass ensembles (quartets, trios, quintets). Current acts include Chestnut Brass Co. (classical brass ensemble); Ed McDade (soft rock/folk singer/songwriter); and Leon Bates (classical pianist).
**Tips:** "We deal with experienced artists who have been performing and have reviews, brochures, glossy photos, records or tapes (or some professional bio material)."

*****RISING STAR ENTERPRISES**, Suite 1000, 157 W. 57th St., New York NY 10019. Music Department: Tim Wright. Management firm, music publisher and video and TV producer. Represents artists, groups and songwriters; currently handles 3 acts. Receives negotial commission. Reviews material for acts.
**How to Contact:** Submit demo tape and lead sheet. Prefers cassette as demo. Does not return unsoliced material. Reporting time varies.
**Music:** Mostly rock; also blues, dance-oriented, folk, MOR, progressive, R&B and top 40/pop. Current acts include Pat Benatar (rock); Steve Forbert (rock/country); and George Sanders (rock/pop).
**Tips:** "Will listen to all tapes submitted."

*****ROADWORK, INC.**, 1475 Harvard St. NW, Washington DC 20009. (202)234-9308. Director: Amy Horowitz. Booking agency. Represents artists, groups, songwriters, and performing artists (dance,

mime, poetry)—"women only;" currently represents 2-5 acts. Receives 10-20% commission.
**How to Contact:** Query by mail or submit demo tape and lead sheet. Prefers cassette with 2-5 songs on demo. Does not return unsolicited material.
**Music:** Blues, dance-oriented, gospel, jazz, Spanish, R&B, rock and soul. Current acts include Sweet Honey in the Rock (black acappella singers); Ferron (folk); and Robin Flower (bluegrass).

**\*ROB-LEE MUSIC**, Box 1338, Merchantville NJ 08109. (215)561-5822. President: Rob Russen. Management firm, booking agency, publishing company and record company. Represents artists, groups and songwriters; currently handles 20 acts. Receives 4-6% commission. Reviews material for acts.
**How to Contact:** Submit demo tape and lyric sheet. Prefers cassette with 2-6 songs on demo. Does not return unsolicited material. Reports in 1 month.
**Music:** Mostly dance-oriented, R&B and rock; also easy listening, jazz, MOR, soul and top 40/pop. Current acts include The All Stars (R&B/blues); Thelma Price (R&B); Snow (rock); and Big El (top 40).

**ROCKFEVER PRODUCTIONS**, 535 Broadway, Lawrence MA 01841. (617)682-7085. Contact: Neil Schneider, or Bruce Houghton. Management firm and booking agency. Represents artists and groups; currently handles 7 acts. Receives 10-25% commission. Reviews material for acts.
**How to Contact:** Submit demo tape and lead sheet. Prefers cassette with 2-4 songs on demo. SASE. Reports in 2 weeks.
**Music:** Mostly rock; also blues, folk, progressive, jazz, rock and new wave. Works primarily with rock dance bands and recording artists. Current acts include B Street Bombers, Eric Preston's Purple Haze, Grand Slamm, Trapper, Jon Butcher Axis, Lipstick, The Meetings, New Models, Gary Shane and The Detour (all rock acts); and Country Joe McDonald (folk).
**Tips:** "We do review all material."

**\*RODANCA MUSIC**, 3627 Park Ave., Memphis TN 38111. (901)454-0700. Music publisher. Represents songwriters from anywhere; currently handles 40 acts. Receives standard royalty. Reviews material for acts.
**How to Contact:** Submit demo tape and lead sheet. Prefers 7½ ips reel-to-reel or cassette with 4 songs on demo. Does not return unsolicited material. Reports in 2 weeks.
**Music:** Gospel and R&B.

**SY ROSENBERG ORGANIZATION**, 140 N. Third, Memphis TN 38103. (901)527-1588. Contact: Sy Rosenberg. Management firm. Represents artists, groups and songwriters; currently handles 5 acts. Receives 10-25% commission. Reviews material for acts.
**How to Contact:** Submit demo tape. Prefers cassette with 4-10 songs on demo. SASE. Reports in 2 weeks.
**Music:** C&W, rock, R&B and top 40/pop. Works primarily with recording acts. Current acts include Rufus Thomas; Jimmy Hart; Cathy Wyatt; and The Kids.

**JEFFREY ROSS MUSIC**, Box D, Seattle WA 98109. (206)285-6838. Contact: Jeffrey Ross or Jan Charkow. Management agency. Represents artists, groups and songwriters; currently handles 3 acts. Receives 15% minimum commission. Reviews material for acts.
**How to Contact:** Submit demo tape. Prefers cassette with 4-6 songs on demo. SASE. Reports in 3 weeks.
**Music:** Jazz, progressive, R&B, soul and top 40/pop. Works primarily with touring bands with members that write their own music. Current acts include Jeff Lorber Fusion (jazz/R&B fusion); Jeff Lorber (songwriter); Kenny G (writer/multi-reedist); and Jay Hoggard (writer/vibist).
**Tips:** "It is important to set your goals based on what you do best. If you write well in a certain idiom, concentrate and develop what you do best before trying other directions. A strong intention to be successful in this business is fueled by acquired knowledge of how the music business operates."

**ROYAL T MUSIC**, 3442 Nies, Fort Worth TX 76111. (817)834-3879. President: James Michael Taylor. Management and booking agency and music publisher. Represents local artists, groups and songwriters, but "considers material from anyone, anywhere;" currently handles 3 acts. Receives 10-15% commission. Reviews material for acts.
**How to Contact:** Query by mail, then submit demo tape and lyric sheet. Prefers cassette with any number of songs on demo. Include photo and statement of goals. SASE. Reports in 1 month.
**Music:** Bluegrass, blues, choral, C&W, folk, MOR, progressive, Spanish, R&B, rock (any), soul (any) and top 40/pop. Works primarily with bar and folk bands for colleges; rock and pop bands that can do concert work. Current acts include TxH2o (Texas water) (country/pop trio); and James Michael Taylor (contemporary folk single).

## Managers & Booking Agencies   333

**RUSTRON MUSIC PRODUCTIONS**, 200 Westmoreland Ave., White Plains NY 10606. (914)946-1689. Artists' Consultant: Rusty Gordon. Composition Management: Ron Caruso. Management firm, booking agency, music publisher and record producer. Represents individuals, groups and songwriters; currently handles 6 acts. Receives 10-25% commission for management and/or booking only. Reviews material for acts.
**How to Contact:** Query, arrange personal interview, or submit in person or by mail demo tape and lead sheet. Prefers 7½ ips reel-to-reel or cassette with 3-6 songs on demo. SASE. Reports in 1 month.
**Music:** Blues (country & rock), C&W (rock, blues, progressive), easy listening (ballads), folk/rock (contemporary/topical), MOR (pop style), rock (folk/pop), top 40/pop and salsa/disco. Current acts include Lynn Haney (blues/rock singer, songwriter); Gordon and Caruso (songwriter/producers); Lois Britten (disco/rock/pop/singer/songwriter); Christian Camilo and the Tingalayo Rhythm Band (salsa-disco/pop); Dianne Mower and Jasmine (modern jazz instrumental and vocal); Orfen Annie Band (country blues/rock); and Casse Culver and the Belle Starr Band (progressive country).

**THE S.R.O. GROUP OF COMPANIES**, 189 Carleton St., Toronto, Ontario, Canada M5A 2K7. (416)923-5855. President: Ray Danniels. A&R Director: Val Azzoli. Represents individuals, groups and songwriters; currently handles 6 acts. Receives commission based on individually negotiated contracts. Reviews material for acts.
**How to Contact:** Solicited demo tapes only and lyric sheet with bio material. Prefers cassette with maximum 3 songs on demo. SAE and IRC. Reports in 8 weeks.
**Music:** Progressive, rock and top 40/pop. Works primarily with rock concert acts. Current acts include Rush; Kim Mitchell Band; Ian Thomas; Coney Hatch; Larry Gowan; and Boys' Brigade.

**SAGITTARIAN ARTISTS INTERNATIONAL**, 970 Aztec Dr., Muskegon MI 49444. (616)733-1152. Coordinator/Director: G. Loren Ruhl. Management firm. Represents individuals and songwriters; currently handles 6 acts. Receives 15-25% commission. Reviews material for acts.
**How to Contact:** Query or submit demo tape and lead sheet. Prefers cassette with 2-4 songs on demo, or record. SASE. Reports in 1 month.
**Music:** Top 40/pop, blues, easy listening and jazz. Works primarily with dance and bar bands. Current acts include Ricky Briton (pop vocalist); Les Basilio (vocalist); and Tobie Columbus (pop vocalist).
**Tips:** "Material must be nightclub oriented."

*****SAGUARO BOOKING AGENCY**, 2609 NW 36th St., Oklahoma City OK 73112. (405)942-0462. General Manager: Bobby Boyd. Management firm and booking agency. Represents artists, groups and songwriters. Receives 25% commission. Reviews material for acts.
**How to Contact:** Query by mail or submit demo tape and lyric sheet. Prefers 7½ ips reel-to-reel tape with 3-5 songs on demo. Does not return unsolicited material. Reports in 1 month.
**Music:** Mostly country; also R&B, rock and soul. Current acts include Dale Greear, Bobby Barnett, and Rebel Lee.

**SAMARAH PRODUCTIONS, INC.**, Box 2501, Columbia SC 29202. (803)754-3556. President: Daniel Hodge Jr. Vice President: Myron Alford. Management firm, booking agency, music publisher and record production company. Estab. 1981. Represents artists, groups and songwriters primarily from the southeast; currently handles 2 acts. Receives 20-25% commission. Reviews material for acts.
**How to Contact:** Query by mail, then submit demo tape. Prefers 7½ ips reel-to-reel or cassette with 4-8 songs on demo. "Will only negotiate with serious and dedicated people." SASE. Reports in 3 weeks.
**Music:** C&W, R&B, rock (top 40), soul and top 40/pop. Works primarily with "self-contained dance/show bands; solo, duet, trio, or quartet performers." Current acts include Midnight Blue (R&B self-contained band); Joannie Dickens (country artist); Distance; and Saffire (R&B bands).
**Tips:** "Have patience, dedication and of course, *talent*."

**BEN SANDMEL (INDEPENDENT)**, 1154 W. Lill, Chicago IL 60614. (504)899-6601. Contact: Ben Sandmel. Management firm and booking agency. Represents groups; currently handles 4 acts. Receives 5-20% commission. Reviews material for acts.
**How to Contact:** Submit demo tape. Prefers cassette with maximum 5 songs on demo. SASE. Reports "usually in two weeks, depending on schedule."
**Music:** Blues, C&W, R&B, rock and soul. Current acts include Jimmy Johnson Blues Band (blues group); Luther "Guitar Junior" Johnson (blues artist); and Bob Margolin (blues artist).

**THE AL SCHULTZ AGENCY**, 38328 N. Sheridan Rd., Waukegan IL 60087. (312)244-1550. Agent: John Hall. Booking agency. Represents artists and groups; currently handles 30 acts. Receives 15-20% commission. "Club pays band and then band pays agent."
**How to Contact:** "Submit full promotional package with tape, song list, photos and all other related in-

formation. Follow-up by phone in 7-8 days." Prefers cassette—"no overdubs" with 10-15 songs on demo. SASE. "If no follow-up by artist, material may be disregarded."
**Music:** C&W, dance-oriented, easy listening, MOR, rock and top 40/pop. Works primarily with dance bands. Current acts include Monopoly (show/dance group); Streetwise (rock/variety group); and Salt Creek (C&W group).
**Tips:** "Present yourself in the most professional manner and always follow up your submittals."

**SEA CRUISE PRODUCTIONS**, Box 1830, Gretna LA 70053. (504)392-4615. President: Ken Keene. Management firm and booking agency. Represents artists, groups and songwriters; currently handles 4 acts. Receives minimum 25% commission. Reviews material for acts.
**How to Contact:** Submit demo tape. Prefers 7½ ips (5" or 7" reel only) reel-to-reel, photo records or cassette with 1-10 songs on demo. "Artists should submit any 45 singles/albums they've already recorded, along with complete press/bio info, including photos, when available. Otherwise a tape with complete info can be submitted." SASE. Reports in 1 month.
**Music:** C&W and rock. Works primarily with country and/or rock single artists or groups and show groups with recording potential. Current acts include Frankie Ford—Mr. "Sea Cruise" (50's R&R artist); Matt Lucas—"Movin' On" (blue-eyed soul artist); Jimmy Payne (country artist); and Johnny Pennino (tenor sax instrumentalist).
**Tips:** "We prefer artists with hit records or potential for recording hits who have a good show appearance for worldwide bookings."

***SEEDS, INC.**, Box 220601, Charlotte NC 28222. (704)376-4388. President: Bob Ferster. Management firm. Represents artists, groups and speakers from the southeast; currently handles 5 acts. Receives 10-20% commission. Reviews material for acts.
**How to Contact:** Query by mail or submit demo tape and lyric sheet. Prefers 15 ips reel-to-reel tape or cassette with 3-6 songs on demo. SASE. Reports in 1 month.
**Music:** Mostly comtemporary Christian; also bluegrass, easy listening, gospel, MOR, rock (hard and pop) and top 40/pop. Works primarily with 4-7 member Christian rock bands. Current acts include Don Hall (MOR); Deliverance (gospel); and Heir Express (rock).

***WILLIAM SEIP MANAGEMENT, INC.**, 104 King St. S, Waterloo, Ontario, Canada N2J 1P5. (519)885-6570. President: William Seip. Managment agency. Represents musical groups from the Ontario region (at present); currently handles 9 groups. Receives 10-25% commission. Reviews material for acts.
**How to Contact:** Query by mail or phone, then arrange personal interview. Prefers cassette with 1-10 songs on demo. SAE and IRC. Reporting time varies.
**Music:** Mostly commercial rock; also C&W, MOR, rock (heavy) and top 40/pop. Works primarily with bar bands and concert acts. Current acts include Helix (heavy R&R); Tracy Kane (commercial R&R); Mike Biker & Kickstands (50s and 60s group); and Keith Gallagher (commercial top 40).

***MICKEY SHERMAN ARTIST MANAGEMENT & DEVELOPMENT**, Box 20814, Oklahoma City OK 73120. (405)751-8954. President: Mickey Sherman. Management firm. Represents artists, groups and songwriters; currently handles 30 acts. Receives minimum 15% commission. Reviews material for acts.
**How to Contact:** Submit demo tape and lead sheet. Prefers cassette with 1-3 songs on demo. Does not return unsolicited material. Reports in 1 month.
**Music:** Mostly blues and ballads; also C&W, easy listening, jazz and R&B. Works primarily with vocalists. Current acts include Janjo (blues); Benny Kubiak (fiddler/western swing band); and Charley Shaw (country singer).

**SHINDLER & ASSOC., INC.**, Box 381585, Memphis TN 38138. (901)761-3709. President: Robert Shindler. Management firm, music publisher and production company. Represents artists, groups and songwriters; currently handles 3 acts. Receives 15-25% commission. Reviews material for acts.
**How to Contact:** Submit demo tape and lead sheet. Prefers cassette with 3-4 songs on demo. Does not return unsolicited material. Reports in 1 month.
**Music:** MOR, R&B, rock, soul and top 40/pop. Current acts include Lonnie Franklin (R&B artist); and Tom Jones III (songwriter).

**SHOWCASE ATTRACTIONS**, Box 6687, Wheeling WV 26003. (614)758-5812. President: R.H. Gallion. Management firm and booking agency. Represents individuals, groups and songwriters; currently handles 44 acts. Receives 15% minimum commission.
**How to Contact:** Query or submit demo tape. Prefers 7½ ips reel-to-reel with 2 songs minimum on demo. Does not return unsolicited material. Reports in 1 month.

Music: Bluegrass, C&W, folk, gospel, MOR and top 40/pop. Works primarily with C&W and gospel artists and groups. Current acts include Bob Gallion (C&W); Patti Powell (C&W); and The Younger Brothers Band.

**SHOWCASE TALENT PRODUCTIONS, INC.**, Box 172, Madison NJ 07940. (201)377-9535. President: Jerry Stanley. Assistant: Barbara Fritts. Booking agency. Represents "mostly freelance" artists, groups and comedians. Receives 10-15% commission. Reviews material for acts.
How to Contact: Submit demo tape, audio, video (¾") or VHS (½") tape. Prefers cassette with 3-6 songs on demo. SASE. Reports in 1 month.
Music: Classical, MOR, R&B, rock (hard, rockabilly) and comedy. Works primarily with bar and studio bands. Current acts include Billy Jayne Band (top 40 dance band); Jump Johnson (rock artist); and Mission (rock group).
Tips: "Artists should have good management."

**SIDARTHA ENTERPRISES, LTD.**, Suite 101, 1504 E. Grandriver Ave., East Lansing MI 48823. (517)351-6780. President: Thomas R. Brunner. Management firm and booking agency. Represents artists and groups; currently represents 30 acts. Receives 15-25% commission. Reviews material for acts.
How to Contact: "Always make phone contact first." Submit demo tape and lyric sheet. Prefers cassette tape with at least 4 songs on demo. SASE. Reports in 1 month.
Music: Rock and top 40/pop. Works primarily with bar bands and recording acts.

**BRAD SIMON ORGANIZATION**, 445 E. 80th St., New York NY 10021. (212)988-4962. President: Brad Simon. Represents individual artists, record producers, musical groups and songwriters; currently handles 7 acts. Receives 20% commission. Reviews material for acts.
How to Contact: Arrange personal interview by mail or phone after submission of demo cassette. Prefers cassette with 3 songs minimum on demo. SASE. Reports in 4 weeks.
Music: C&W/pop, easy listening, jazz, MOR, progressive, rock (all types) and top 40/pop. Works with artists, groups and songwriters in contemporary rock, pop, jazz with strong commercial appeal and crossover potential, vocal and instrumental artists with strong performing and writing skills. Current acts include Architectural Romance (rock); and Kilimanjaro (pop/jazz).
Tips: "Songwriters and artists must have original and distinctive material with strong commercial appeal."

**SKORMAN/WEISS**, 2362 Barbados Dr., Winter Park FL 32792. (305)677-5995. Management firm. Represents groups; currently handles 25 acts. Receives 10-30% commission. Reviews material for acts.
How to Contact: "Phone for permission to send tape." Prefers cassette with 3 songs on demo. Does not return unsolicited material. Reports in 1 month.
Music: Mostly top 40 and rock; also dance-oriented, MOR and pop. Works primarily with show and rock bands. Current acts include Smiles (top 40/show group); The Pact (top 40/rock group); and Hi-Rize (top 40/show group).
Tips: "We need commercial hit material with a visual aspect."

***SOUND '86 TALENT MANAGEMENT**, Box 222, Black Hawk SD 57718. (605)343-3941. Contact: Ron Kohn. Management firm. Represents artists and groups; currently handles 4 acts. Receives 5-10% commission. Reviews material for acts.
How to Contact: Query by mail or submit demo tape and lyric sheet. Prefers cassette with 3-8 songs on demo. SASE. Reports in 1 month.
Music: Mostly rock (all types); also bluegrass, C&W, dance-oriented, easy listening and top 40/pop. Works primarily with bands. Current acts include Hot Rod De Luxx (rock); WPFM Band (rock); and Bold Lightning (rock).

**SOUTH PRODUCTIONS, LTD.**, Box 227, Chicago Ridge IL 60415 (312)636-1253. Contact: Bud Monaco or Jerry Gamauf. Management firm and artist development firm. Represents artists and groups in the local region; currently handles 4 acts. Receives maximum 20% commission. Reviews material for acts.
How to Contact: Query by mail, then submit demo tape and lead sheet. Prefers cassette with 3-6 songs on demo. Does not return unsolicited material. Reports in 2 weeks.
Music: Mostly blues; also R&B, MOR, progressive, rock, dance-oriented and top 40/pop. Works primarily with concert rock bands. Current acts include John Hunter (rock/dance); Rich Hazdra; Tony Wilson (top 40/rock); and Don Griffin (rock/R&B).

**SOUTHERN CONCERTS**, 3279 Hickory View Place, Memphis TN 38115. (901)363-6773. President: Buddy Swords. Management firm and record company. Represents artists; currently handles 4 acts. Receives 15% commission. Reviews material for acts.

**How to Contact:** Submit demo tape. Prefers cassette with maximum 4 songs on demo. Does not return unsolicited material. Reports in 1 week.
**Music:** C&W and top 40/pop. Current acts include Wendel Adkins, Tony Joe White; Billy Herbert (all country artists); and Dennis James.

**SOUTHERN GRASS BOOKING**, Box 262, RD 2, Landenberg PA 19350. (215)268-8166. Manager: Bob Paisley. Booking agency. Represents artists and groups in the northeast US only; currently handles 7 acts. Receives 10-20% commission. Reviews material for acts.
**How to Contact:** Query by mail, then submit demo tape and lead sheet. Prefers cassette with 1-3 songs on demo. SASE. Reports in 3 weeks.
**Music:** Bluegrass and gospel. Works primarily with groups at festivals, shows and bars. Current acts include Southern Grass, Dixie Rebels and Clay Creek Ramblers.

**\*SOUTHERN TALENT INTERNATIONAL**, 2925 Fallowridge, Snellville GA 30278. (404)979-0847. President: John M. Titak. Management and booking agency. Represents groups and songwriters; currently handles 76 acts. Receives 10-15% commission. Reviews material for acts.
**How to Contact:** Submit demo tape and lead sheet. Prefers cassette with 3 songs on demo. SASE. Reports in 1 month.
**Music:** Mostly rock; also bluegrass, dance-oriented, easy listening, R&B, rock, soul and top 40/pop. Works primarily with bar bands and recording artists. Current acts include Trixx, Hunter, Bounty Hunters, Passendger, Zeus, Lizzy Borden, Centurian, Myth and Joshua Page.

**SPIDER ENTERTAINMENT CO.**, Box 133LV, Lathrup Village MI 48076. President: Arnie Tencer. Vice President: Joel Zuckerman. Management firm. Represents artists, groups and songwriters; currently handles 2 acts. Receives minimum 20% commission. Reviews material for acts.
**How to Contact:** Submit demo tape. Prefers cassette with 3-6 songs on demo. Does not return unsolicited material. Reports in 3 weeks.
**Music:** Rock (hard) and top 40/pop. Works primarily with "R&R bands with good songs and great live shows." Current acts include The Romantics (R&R band, Nemperor-Epic Records); and Deserters (R&R band, Capitol Records).
**Tips:** Artists "must have commercially viable material."

**SPOTLITE ENTERPRISES, LTD.**, 9th Floor, 221 W. 57th St., New York NY 10019. (212)586-6750. Assistant to the President: Valerie Koob. Management firm and booking agency. Represents performers on an international basis. Receives minimum 15% commission. Reviews material for acts.
**How to Contact:** Submit "a brief yet complete presentation by mail only;" include demo tape and lead sheet. Prefers cassette with 3-5 songs on demo. Does not return unsolicited material. Reports "only if interested."
**Music:** Classical, C&W, folk, jazz, MOR, rock, soul, top 40/pop and variety. Works primarily with "name artists."

**\*SRO ARTISTS**, Box 9532, Madison WI 53715. (608)256-9000. President: Jeff Laramie. Booking agency. Represents artists and groups; currently handles 15 acts. Receives 10-20% commission. Reviews material for acts.
**How to Contact:** Query by mail. Prefers cassette with 1-5 songs on demo. SASE. Reports in 2 weeks.
**Music:** Mostly classical; also jazz. Works primarily with artists and groups who are willing to tour colleges. Current acts include George Winston (solo pianist); Javier Calderon (classical guitarist); and The Free Hot Lunch Band (three-part acoustic group).

**STAGE II ATTRACTIONS**, Box 344, Nolensville TN 37135. (615)776-2600. Agents: Norm or Mandy Forrest. Management firm, booking agency and music publisher. Represents artists, groups and songwriters; currently handles 50 acts. Receives 10-20% commission. Reviews material for acts.
**How to Contact:** Query by mail, arrange personal interview or submit demo tape. Prefers 7½ ips reel-to-reel, 8 track or cassette. Include "photos, bio and song list with live tape or video." Does not return unsolicited material. Reports in 2 weeks or "as soon as possible."
**Music:** Mostly C&W and top 40; also dance-oriented, easy listening, MOR and pop. Works primarily with dance bands, show groups, R&R and country acts. Current acts include Sandra Kaye (country/show and dance artist); Ottice Yawn (top 40/show artist); and Marty Martel (country/show and dance artist).
**Tips:** "Send as much information as possible including photo, bio and previous employment. Be cleancut, strictly professional and want to work."

**STAR ARTIST MANAGEMENT INC.**, Box 114, Fraser MI 48026. (313)979-5115. President: Ron Geddish. Director of Canadian Operations: Brian Courtis. House Producers: Gary Spaniola. Directors

Managers & Booking Agencies **337**

of Public Relations: Rikki Hansen and John Sands. General Counselor: Tom Werner. West Coast Counselor: S.D. Ashley. House Label: USA Records. Management firm. Represents individuals, groups and songwriters; currently handles 10 acts. Receives 10-20% commission. Reviews material for acts.
**How to Contact:** Submit demo tape. Prefers cassette with 3-5 songs on demo. SASE. Reports in 2 weeks.
**Music:** Modern music, progressive, rock and top 40/pop. Works primarily with new music and rock groups. Current acts include Toby Redd (modern music); Doug Kahan; Bitter Sweet Alley (rock); The Act (modern music); Switch (rock); and Red Alert (rock).

**STAR DRIVE MANAGEMENT**, 12645 Chandler Blvd., North Hollywood CA 91607. (213)508-5856. President: David Kuck. Management firm. Represents groups; currently handles 2 acts. Receives 10-20% commission. Reviews material for acts.
**How to Contact:** Query by mail, then submit demo tape. Prefers cassette with 3-5 songs on demo. SASE. Reports in 3 weeks.
**Music:** Blues, R&B, rock, soul and top 40/pop. Works primarily with "artists who have had experience in dance/lounges and are ready to move into recording; and those who have original, or access to, original material." Current acts include Santa Fe, Headliners and The Mix; andKirk Arnold and Bill Deloach (songwriters).
**Tips:** "We like artists who have been around for a long time and are not afraid to pay their dues."

*****STAR REPRESENTATION**, 4026 Bobby Lane, Schiller Park IL 60176. (312)678-2755. President: James Stella. Management firm and production company. Represents artists, groups and songwriters; currently handles 9 acts. Receives 15-25% commission.
**How to Contact:** Arrange personal interview or submit demo tape and lead sheet. Prefers 7½ ips reel-to-reel or cassette with 2-6 songs on demo. SASE. Reports in 2-3 weeks.
**Music:** Children's, dance, MOR, progressive, rock (hard or melodic rock), soul and top 40/pop. Works with bands "looking for national potential." Current act includes Steve Busa (songwriter/artist).
**Tips:** "We are dealing with new record labels—Vinage Records, which deals with oldies, and Our Gang Records, which deals wih all new talent and placement of new talent."

*****STARTIME MUSIC**, Box 643, LaQuinta CA 92253. (714)564-4873. President: Fred Rice. Management firm. Music publisher, record company.
**How to Contact:** Submit demo tape and lead sheet. Prefers cassette with 1-2 songs on demo. SASE. Reports in 6 weeks.
**Music:** Mostly novelty; also C&W, rock and top 40/pop.

**BILL STEIN**, Box 1516, Champaign IL 61820. Artists Manager: Bill Stein. Management firm. Represents artists and groups; currently handles 2 acts. Receives variable commission. Reviews material for acts.
**How to Contact:** Submit demo tape and promotional material. Prefers cassette with 3-6 songs on demo. SASE. Reports in 1 month.
**Music:** Mostly C&W, top 40/pop and rock; also dance-oriented, progressive, R&B, rock and soul. Works primarily with bar and dance bands and concert groups. Current acts include Appaloosa (country rock act); and Atlantic Mine (modern metal).

**DEL SUGGS/SALTWATER MUSIC**, 1811 Jackson Bluff, Tallahassee FL 32304. (904)575-2328. Contact: Del Suggs. Management firm and booking agency. Represents artists; currently handles 6 acts. Pays "variable commission; determined by amount of time and money expended by us—generally runs around 10%." Occasionally reviews material for acts.
**How to Contact:** Query by mail "first to see if we are presently reviewing material." Prefers cassette with 2-6 songs on demo. SASE. Reports in 2 weeks.
**Music:** Folk (contemporary), MOR (contemporary) and top 40/pop. Works primarily with "single artists who are often songwriters. We also work with single artists and their bands, but less often, and occasionally we look for new outside material for our artists as a supplement to their own writing." Current acts include Del Suggs (folk/rock artist); Johnny Gilliam (country artist); and Fred Slade (traditional fingerstyle guitarist).
**Tips:** "Drop us a line and we will respond as soon as possible. We are not generally looking for new artists, but will listen and give what advice and help we can."

**GREG SULLIVAN MANAGEMENT**, Suite 116, 6625 Clayton Ave., St. Louis MO 63139. (314)647-5366. President: Greg Sullivan. Management firm. Represents groups; currently handles 4 acts. Receives 10-20% commission. Reviews material for acts.

**How to Contact:** Query by mail, then submit demo tape and lead sheet. Prefers cassette as demo. SASE. Reports in 3 weeks.
**Music:** Rock (new wave, R&R) and top 40/pop. Works primarily with bar bands and "bands interested in becoming national bands with recording contracts, etc." Current acts include Chris Casamento, Mark Evans, Scott Nienhaus and Mike Ritter (new wave rock bands).

**SUNBELT MANAGEMENT GROUP,** Box 2000, Jenks OK 74037. (918)446-3446. President: Steven C. Wyer. Management firm and production company. Represents artists, groups and songwriters; currently handles 5 acts. Receives 10-20% commission. Reviews material for acts.
**How to Contact:** Query by mail, then submit demo tape. Prefers cassette with 3-5 songs on demo. "Include bio material." Does not return unsolicited material. Reports in 1 month.
**Music:** Church/religious, folk, gospel, R&B and top 40/pop. Works primarily with contemporary Christian music, soloists or bands. Current acts include Steve Camp (pop gospel); Carman (pop gospel); and The Latinos (contemporary gospel and Spanish music).

**T.D.I. DIRECTION & MANAGEMENT DIVISION,** 4100 W. Flagler St., Miami FL 33134. (305)446-1900. Manager: Larry Brahms. Management firm, publishing and production company. Represents artists, groups, songwriters and record producers; currently handles 6 acts. Receives 10-20% commission. Reviews material for acts.
**How to Contact:** Query or submit demo tape and lyric sheet. Prefers cassette with 3-4 songs. SASE. Reports in 2 weeks.
**Music:** Mostly dance-oriented; also C&W, country rock, MOR, rock, R&B, soul and top 40/pop. Works primarily with studio musicians, local musicians and major recording artists. Looking for additional artists. Current acts include Ritchie Family (vocal group); Celi Bee (vocalist); Hot Walker Band (country); Ray Martinez & Friends; Amant; Passion (vocal group); Dorothy Moore (vocalist); O'Mercedes (vocalist); and Darylle Rice (songwriter).
**Tips:** "Any background information (e.g., press kit) is always helpful but not essential. Make sure material is copyrighted."

**TALENT ATTRACTIONS,** Box 8542, Asheville NC 28814. (704)253-4161. President: Larry Phillips. Management firm and booking agency. Represents artists, groups and songwriters; currently handles 4 acts. Receives 10-20% commission. Reviews material for acts.
**How to Contact:** Submit demo tape and lead sheet. Prefers cassette with 3-5 songs on demo. SASE. Reports in 3 weeks.
**Music:** C&W, rock and top 40/pop. Works primarily with 4-6 piece groups and single vocal artists. Current acts include Southern Breeze (southern rock, country band); Natalie Nugent (C&W, top 40/pop vocalist); Johnny Weathers (MOR and classic country); and Justice (top 40/pop, C&W band).
**Tips:** "At present I am only interested in original copyrighted songs. An inexpensive cassette is sufficient. If I like the songs, I will ask for a studio demo."

**TALENT MASTER,** Suite 507, 50 Music Sq., W., Nashville TN 37203. (615)320-0881. President: Steve Bess. Vice President: Charli McMillan. Booking agency. Represents artists and musical groups from Tennessee and surrounding states; currently handles 14 acts. Receives 15-20% commission. Reviews material for acts.
**How to Contact:** Prefers personal interview (artist/group only) or submit demo tape with good promo kit. Prefers live cassette with 1-3 songs on demo. Does not return unsolicited material. Reports in 2-3 weeks.
**Music:** C&W, dance-oriented, easy listening, MOR and rock (top 40, country). Works primarily with recording artists and dance and show bands. Current acts include Glass Hammer (dance and show group); John Wesley Riles (country recording artist); and Steve Bess Show (dance and show group).

**TEAHOUSE MUSIC,** (formerly Baby Whale Music), Box 46035, Los Angeles CA 90046. (213)876-9971. Executive Producer: Ron Nadel. Management firm, music publisher and production company. Represents artists, groups, songwriters and producers. Receives 20-50% commission. "If songwriters, we publish material; if artist, we may secure production deals." Reviews material for acts.
**How to Contact:** Query by phone, submit demo tape or demo tape and lead sheet. SASE. "We try to return material, but no promises." Reports "when the producer or artist gets back to us."
**Music:** Blues, dance-oriented, easy listening, MOR, R&B, rock (soft, hard, new wave), soul (up- and mid-tempo, ballads) and top 40/pop. Current acts include Larry Graham, Roger Voudouris, Janis Jan, and Charlie Calello.

**MIKE THOMAS MANAGEMENT,** Box 70486, Charleston SC 29405. (803)797-6298. President: Mike Thomas. Management and booking agency and record company. Represents artists, groups, song-

Managers & Booking Agencies **339**

writers and lighting companies; currently handles 3 acts. Receives 10-15% commission. Reviews material for acts.
**How to Contact:** Query by mail, then submit demo tape. Prefers cassette with 1 song on demo. Include photo and bio. SASE. Reports in 3 weeks.
**Music:** Mostly soul; also reggae and top 40/pop. "We work with anyone who is serious about what they do." Current acts include The Tymes (oldies singing group); Natural Light Band (top 40 band); The Charleston Connection (R&B-oriented singing group); and Sparkle (top 40 group).
**Tips:** "The tapes you send need not be finished masters. We do, however, give consideration to finished material for release on our WAHR label."

\*TOTAL ENTERTAINMENT CONCEPT (T.E.C.), Suite M, 6045 Kimberly Blvd., North Lauderdal FL 33068. (305)974-0001. Contact: Vic Beri or Kevin Anderson. Management firm. Estab. 1981. Represents artists, groups and songwriters; currently handles 15 acts. Receives 10-20% commission.
**How to Contact:** Query by mail. Prefers 7½ ips reel-to-reel tape or cassette as demo. Does not return unsolicited material. Reports ASAP.
**Music:** C&W, easy listening, MOR, rock and top 40/pop. Current acts include Michael Iceberg and Iceberg Machine (concert act); Dan Riley (crossover country); and Ferguson and Taylor (top 40/pop and rock).

\*TRIANGLE TALENT, INC., 9701 Taylorsville Rd., Box 99035, Louisville KY 40299. (502)267-5466. President: David H. Snowden. Booking agency. Represents artists and groups; currently handles 90 acts. Receives 10-20% commission. Reviews material for acts.
**How to Contact:** Query or submit demo tape. Prefers cassette with 2-4 songs on demo. SASE. Reports in 2 weeks.
**Music:** Mostly rock and top 40; also bluegrass, C&W and pop. Current acts include Free Fall (rock/concert); Pure Pleasure (disco/top 40); Epics (show/concert); Sue Powell (pop/country); and Circus (rock).

UMBRELLA ARTISTS MANAGEMENT, INC., 2181 Victory Pkwy., Box 6507, Cincinnati OH 45206. (513)861-1500. President: Stan Hertzman. Management agency. Represents artists, groups and songwriters; currently handles 4 acts.
**How to Contact:** Submit demo tape and lyric sheet. Prefers cassette with 3 songs on demo. SASE. Reports in 1 month.
**Music:** Progressive;,rock and top 40/pop. Works with contemporary/progressive pop/rock artists and writers. Current acts include The Young Invaders, (AOR rock group); Charlie Fletcher (pop rock, artist-songwriter); and Adrian Belew (artist/guitarist/songwriter). Credits include: Frank Zappa, David Bowie, Talking Heads, Garland Jeffreys, Tom Tom Club, Herbie Hancock, and presently a member of King Crimson.

VALEX TALENT AGENCY, 105 E. Clinton St., Ithaca NY 14850. (607)273-3931. Publishing President: John Perialas. Booking Vice President: Tom McNerney. Management firm, booking agency and publishing house. Deals with artists in northeast US only. Represents artists, groups and songwriters; currently handles 25 acts. Receives 15-25% commission. Reviews material for acts.
**How to Contact:** Submit demo tape and lead sheet. Prefers 7½ ips reel-to-reel or cassette with 3-6 songs on demo. SASE. Reports in 1 month. "Songwriters please send material in care of John Perialas, Copper John Music; also send cassettes or 7½ ips tapes to same."
**Music:** Country pop, dance-oriented, easy listening, MOR, R&B, rock, soul and top 40/pop. Works with vocalists, show, dance and bar bands. Current acts include Charlie Starr (single, guitar and vocals); Bobby Comstock (rock); Small Change (top 40/pop); Tokyo (rock/new wave); The Peter Lovi Band (rock/top 40/pop); RBT Band (rock); and The Choice (rock).

VELVETT RECORDING COMPANY, 517 W. 57th St., Los Angeles CA 90037. (213)753-7893. Manager: Aaron Johnson. Management firm and record company. Represents artists, groups and songwriters; currently handles 7 acts. Receives minimum 10-20% commission. Reviews material for acts.
**How to Contact:** Submit demo tape only or demo tape and lead sheet. Prefers cassette with 2-3 songs on demo. SASE.
**Music:** Blues, gospel, church/religious, R&B, rock, soul and top 40/pop. Works primarily with show and dance bands and vocalists. Current acts include Arlene Bell (soul/top 40/pop artist); Chuck Willis (blues artist); and Gifled Group (top 40/pop artists).

VOKES BOOKING AGENCY, Box 12, New Kensington PA 15068. (412)335-2775. President: Howard Vokes. Booking agency. Represents individuals, groups and songwriters; currently handles 25 acts. Receives 10-20% commission.

**How to Contact:** Query or submit demo tape and lead sheet. Cassette only with 3-6 songs on demo. SASE. Reports in 2 weeks.
**Music:** Bluegrass, C&W and gospel. "We work with bluegrass and hard country bands who generally play bars, hotels and clubs. However, we also book in ole-time artists as singles. We want nothing to do with hard rock or country rock." Current acts include Bluefield Boys (bluegrass); and Country Boys (C&W).

**\*WILLIAM F. WAGNER AGENCY**, 14343 Addison St., Suite 218, Sherman Oaks CA 91423. (213)501-4161. Owner: Bill Wagner. Management agency and record producer. Represents artists and groups; currently handles 5 acts. Receives 15% commission. "For recording production of artists other than my own clients I receive $100/hour, live studio time; $50/hour overdub, editing and mix-down time." Reviews material for acts.
**How to Contact:** Submit demo tape and lyric sheet. Prefers 7½ or 3¾ ips reel-to-reel (2- or 4-track) or cassette with 15 minutes maximum on tape. SASE. Reports in 2 weeks.
**Music:** Blues, choral, C&W, dance-oriented, easy listening, jazz, MOR, progressive, Spanish, R&B, rock (all kinds), soul and top 40/pop. Works with singers, songwriter-singers, instrumentalists and 2- to 19-piece groups. Current acts include JoAnne Kurman (country/pop vocalist); L.A. Jazz Choir; Sandy Graham (jazz vocalist); Frank Sinatra Jr.; Margie Gibson (pop/contemporary vocalist); Pat Longo Super Big Band; and Mark Vogel (contemporary/pop singer).

**\*WAILING WALL PRODUCTIONS**, 281 E. Kingsbridge Road, Bronx NY 10458. (212)733-5342. President: Murray Fuller. Booking agency. Estab. 1981. Currently handles 6 acts. Recieves 10-25% commission. Reviews material for acts.
**How to Contact:** Submit demo tape and lead sheet. Prefers cassette with 3-5 songs on demo. SASE. Reports in 6 weeks.
**Music:** Mostly soul; also jazz and R&B. Works primarily with vocalists. Current acts include The Essence of Sound (R&B); Boncellia Lewis (R&B/contemporary); and Opus and Personal Touch (R&B).

**NORBY WALTERS ASSOCIATES**, 1650 Broadway, New York NY 10015. (212)245-3939. President: Norby Walters. Management firm and booking agency. Represents individuals and groups; currently handles 50 acts. Receives 10-20% commission. Reviews material for acts.
**How to Contact:** Submit demo tape and lyric sheet. Prefers reel-to-reel or cassette tape with 1-3 songs on demo. Does not return unsolicited material. Reports in 2 weeks.
**Music:** Mostly R&B; also dance-oriented, MOR, soul and top 40/pop. Works primarily with R&B/pop crossover artists. Current acts include Kool and the Gang (pop/R&B group, Delite Records); Dionne Warwick (pop, Arista Records); Rick James; and Peaches & Herb (R&B/pop group, Polygram Records).

**WALTNER ENTERPRISES**, 14702 Canterbury Ave., Tustin CA 92680. (714)731-2981. President: Steve Waltner. Management firm, music publisher and record company. Represents artists, groups and songwriters; currently handles 5 acts. Pays by "standard artist recording contract and standard songwriters contract." Reviews material for acts.
**How to Contact:** Submit demo tape and lead sheet. Prefers cassette with 2-4 songs on demo. SASE. Reports in 1 month.
**Music:** C&W, MOR and top 40/pop. Current acts include Tim Morgon, Jason Chase, Jay Daniel and Steve Shelby (all country, pop artists).

**JOEY WELZ MUSIC COMPLEX**, 108 Morning Glory Lane, Manheim PA 17545. Gretna PA 17064. President: Joey Welz. Management firm, booking agency and record company. Represents artists, groups and songwriters; currently handles 3 acts. Receives variable commission. Reviews material for acts.
**How to Contact:** Submit demo tape. Prefers cassette with 4-8 songs on demo. Does not return unsolicited material. Reports in 1 month "if we can use material."
**Music:** C&W, easy listening, R&B, rock and top 40/pop. Works primarily with standard entertainers. Current acts include Link Wray, Bill Haley's Comets, Jimmy Velvet, Joey Welz, Gerry Granahan, Gary Conahan and Roy Smith.

**WINTERSWAN**, Division of Great Plains Associates, Box 634, Lawrence KS 66044. (913)841-4444. Presidents: Mark Swanson, Scott Winters. Management firm. Represents groups; currently handles 1 act. Receives 10-20% commission. Reviews material for acts.
**How to Contact:** Submit demo tape and lyric sheet. Prefers cassette with 3-7 songs on demo. SASE. Reports in 1 week.

Music: C&W, R&B, rock (straight) and soul. Works primarily with dance/concert bands, for small college circuit and dance halls. Current acts include Blue Wave (beach music).

**BILLY WOLFE & ASSOCIATES**, Box 262, Abe Lincoln Station, Carteret NJ 07008. (201)541-9422. President: Billy Wolfe. Vice President: Gary Hills. Management firm, booking agency and record producer. Represents individuals, groups, songwriters and show and oldie acts from the US, Canada, Japan, England, France, Sweden, Belgium and Holland; currently handles 60 acts. "We try to locate outlets for all material we receive in our agency." Receives 15-20% commission; "the artist picks up his money directly — we receive deposits only with signed contracts." Reviews material for acts.
**How to Contact:** Submit demo tape and lyric sheet. Prefers 7½ ips reel-to-reel or cassette with 6-12 songs on demo. "Send material with demo, photographs and short bio on yourself to get a better idea of the sender." SASE. Reports in 1 month.
Music: Mostly rock, MOR, soul and R&B; also C&W, dance-oriented, easy listening, folk, progressive, rock (country), Polish, French and top 40/pop. Works primarily with dance and show bands, some polka dance bands, show groups and singles. Current acts include The Moonglows; The Teenagers; and Danny & The Juniors (all oldies).
**Tips:** "We welcome new songwriters as well as new groups; we want to develop tomorrow's hit artist as well as our agency's future."

*****RICHARD WOOD ARTIST MANAGEMENT**, 42 Clinton Ave., Staten Island NY 1-301. (212)981-0641. Contact: Richard Wood. Management firm. Represents musical groups. Currently handles 2 acts. Receives 10-15% commission. Reviews material for acts.
**How to Contact:** Query by mail or submit demo tape and lead sheet. Prefers cassette as demo. SASE. Reports in 2 weeks.
Music: Mostly R&B and top 40/pop; also MOR. Works primarily with "high energy" show bands. Current acts include Hot Pepper; and Onyz (show bands).
**Tips:** "Please be versatile and able to make changes in material to suit the type of acts I book."

**WORLD WIDE MANAGEMENT**, 1767 Front St., Yorktown Heights NY 10598. (914)962-2727. A/R Director: Mr. Stevens. Management firm and booking agency. Represents artists, groups, songwriters and actors. Receives 15-40% commission. Reviews material for acts.
**How to Contact:** Query by mail, arrange personal interview or submit demo tape. Prefers cassette with 3-5 songs on demo. SASE. Reports in 1 month.
Music: Bluegrass, blues, C&W, folk, jazz, R&B and rock.

*****YBARRA MUSIC**, Box 665, Lemon Grove CA 92045. (714)462-6538. Contact: D. Braun. A&R Director: R. William. Booking agency, music publisher and record company. Deals with artists from Southern California. Represents groups; currently handles 4 acts. Receives 5-20% commission.
**How to Contact:** Query. Prefers cassette. Does not return unsolicited material. Reports in 1 month.
Music: Blues, classical (chamber, woodwind or strings), folk and jazz (swing, dixieland, progressive or big band). Works primarily with dance-oriented dixieland, traditional jazz and swing acts. Currently represents the Dick Braun Big Band; and Dixieland Band (dance and show bands).

*****DOUGLAS A. YEAGER PRODUCTIONS**, 300 W. 55th St., New York NY 10019. (212)245-0240. Manager: Jerry Burnham. Management firm. Represents artists; currently handles 6 acts. Receives 15-25% commission. Reviews material for acts.
**How to Contact:** Submit demo tape and lyric sheet. Prefers cassette with 2-4 songs on demo. SASE. Reports in 1 month.
Music: Mostly R&B and dance; also soul. Works primarily with female R&B singers. Current acts include Clare Bathe (R&B dance jazz vocalist); Ange Ward (R&B dance vocalist); Josh White, Jr. (R&B MOR/jazz vocalist); and Guthrie Thomas (country vocalist).

**BARRY YEARWOOD ENTERPRISES**, 100 Rutland Rd., Hempstead NY 11550. (516)245-3939. President: Barry Yearwood. Management firm. Estab. 1982. Represents artists, groups, songwriters and producers; currently handles 7 acts. Receives 20-25% commission. Reviews material for acts.
**How to Contact:** Query by mail or submit demo tape and lead sheet. Prefers cassette with 4-8 songs on demo. Does not return unsolicited material. Reports in 1 month.
Music: Gospel, jazz, MOR, progressive, R&B, rock, soul and top 40/pop.

**ZANE MANAGEMENT, INC.**, 700-703 Penn Center, Philadelphia PA 19102. (215)563-1100. President: Lloyd Zane Remick. Represents artists, songwriters and athletes; currently handles 5 acts. Receives variable commission.

**How to Contact:** Submit demo tape and lyric sheet. Prefers cassette as demo. SASE. Reports in 3-4 weeks.
**Music:** Children's, dance, easy listening, folk, gospel, jazz (fusion), MOR, rock (hard and country), soul and top 40/pop. Current acts include Phil Hurtt; Bunny Sigler (disco/funk); Spaces (jazz fusion); Pieces of a Dream (consultant); and Grover Washington, Jr. (management).

# Play Producers & Publishers

Today's wise playwright keeps it simple: shows with uncomplicated sets and small casts are a must for little theaters with limited facilities and funds. Even on Broadway, rising costs force producers and directors to seek material that can be produced unpretentiously and inexpensively.

However, Broadway need not be—and should not be—your only goal. Many local groups—dinner theaters, children's theaters, high school and college groups, and community theaters—provide outlets for musicals.

To learn more about writing for and working with theater groups right in your own home town, see James Dearing's article on "Writing for the Local Alternative Music Markets" in the front of this book.

**AMERICAN THEATRE ARTS**, Play Development Program, 6240 Hollywood Blvd., Hollywood CA 90028. (213)466-2462. Play Development Director: Pamela Bohnert. Mounts 9 productions per year (5 Main Stage, 4 Second Stage). Ideally, two are original plays. ATA houses 2 Equity-waiver theaters, plus a conservatory. Shows run 6-8 weeks; Thursday, Friday, and Saturday nights and Sunday matinee. Royalty varies, especially if work goes on to Equity houses. Submit complete manuscript and cassette tape of songs. Tape need not be elaborate—just piano and voice are OK. SASE. Reports in 3-4 months.
**Musicals:** "Musicals with 8-12 characters maximum. One-set shows."
**Recent Productions:** *Richards' Cork Leg*, by Brendan Beehan (Irish satire); *River Wind*, by John Jennings (young love; mid-life crisis); and *The All Star Radio Broadcast of 1939*, by John Terry Bell and Rolly Fanton (old-time radio).

**ARENA PLAYERS REPERTORY THEATRE**, 296 Route 109, East Farmingdale NY 11735. (516)293-0674. Producer: Frederic De Feis. Play producer. Produces 13 plays (2 musicals and 3 originals)/year. Plays performed in a "professional, arena-style repertory theater playing to a broad cross-section of teenagers to senior citizens, drawn from all over Long Island as well as Manhattan." Pays royalty averaging $600-1,200. Query with synopsis. SASE. Reports in 1 month.
**Musicals:** "We are particularly interested in full-length intimate musicals which can be mounted with minimal orchestration and are well-suited to production in a small, arena-style theater."
**Recent Productions:** *Sweeney Todd, The Barber*, by Burton (a new adaptation of the original script with new musical numbers and full new score).

**ARKANSAS STATE UNIVERSITY-BEEBE CAMPUS**, Box H, Beebe AR 72012. (501)882-6452. Director of Theater: L.R. Chudomelka. Play producer. Produces 6 plays (3-4 musicals)/year. Plays are performed in a "600 seat theater (proscenium) in a city of 4,000, 30 miles from metropolitan area of more than 200,000." Payment $25-100/performance. Submit complete manuscript and score. SASE. Reports in 2 weeks.
**Musicals:** "Material should be within the ability of traditional community college with traditional and non-traditional students: simple dancing, innovative and traditional, not over-sophisticated (somewhat family oriented). Variety of music styles. Flexible cast size, props, staging, etc. We do not want extremes, unnecessary profanity or 'operatic' material."
**Recent Productions:** *Working*; *Grease*; *Rainbow Jones*; and *Show Me Where The Good Times Are*.
**Tips:** "Music should be singable and vary in style. Songs should be an intricate part of the show and not just put in for spectacle. Major roles should be balanced between 4 or 5 characters, rather than one-character shows with chorus."

**ASOLO STATE THEATER**, Drawer E, Sarasota FL 33578. (813)355-7115. Literary Manager. Play producer. Produces 11 plays (1 musical)/year. Plays are performed at the Asolo Theater (325-seat proscenium house) or by the Asolo Touring Theater (6-member company touring the Southeast). Pays 5% minimum royalty. Query. SASE.
**Musicals:** "We want nonchorus musicals only. They should be full-length, any subject, with not over 6 in the cast. There are no restrictions on production demands; however, musicals with excessive scenic requirements may be difficult to consider. Submit finished works only."
**Recent Productions:** *A Midsummer Night's Dream*, by Shakespeare; *Mrs. Warren's Profession*, by G.B. Shaw; *The Song Is Kern!*, *Tintypes*, and *The Show Off*, by George Kelly; and *Charley's Aunt*, by Brandon Thomas.

**Tips:** "Musicals are produced infrequently here due to the 'classical' basis of Asolo's repertory and inability to 'job-in' musical-theater talent."

**BARTER THEATRE, STATE THEATRE OF VIRGINIA**, Abingdon VA 24210. (703)628-2281. Producing Director: Rex Partington. Business Manager: Pearl Hayter. Play producer. Produces 12 plays (2 musicals)/year. Plays performed in Barter Theatre. Pays minimum 5% royalty. SASE. Reports in 6 months.
**Musicals:** Full length, all styles and topics, small casts, basic instrumentation and minimal set requirements. "Keep it small. Think in relevant and romantic subjects."
**Recent Productions:** *Tintypes*; *Oh Coward*; and *The Apple Tree*.

**\*QUENTIN C. BEAVER**, 32 Horatio St., Yonkers NY 10710. (914)968-0488. Producer: Q.C. Beaver. Produces 6 plays (3 musicals)/year. Plays presented at Fort Salem Theatre, Salem NY—summer stock in Saratoga Springs area. Pays $50-200/performance. Query with synopsis. SASE. Reports in 1 month.
**Musicals:** Musicals should be "full-length, contemporary, entertaining (not heavy) and include comedy (most important) and good chorus numbers. Sets must be simple and cast should include no more than 4 principals, 10 secondary leads and 8 dancers." Does not want "historic, period, overly dramatic or absurd material."
**Recent Productions:** *Exit Who*, by Fred Carmichael; and *Fox Trot by the Bay*, by M.H. Appleman.

**DAVID BLACK**, 251 E. 51st St., New York NY 10022. (212)753-1188. Producer/Director: David Black. Play producer. Produces 2 plays/year. Plays are performed on Broadway, Off-Broadway and in London. Pays 2% royalty of "gross weekly box office plus $500 average advance." Query with synopsis. SASE. Reports in 2 weeks.
**Musicals:** "I'm interested in all types of musicals. Playwrights should write for themselves, not me."
**Recent Productions:** *The Guys In The Truck* (Broadway).

**CALIFORNIA STATE COLLEGE, BAKERSFIELD, DEPARTMENT OF FINE ARTS**, 9001 Stockdale Hwy., Bakersfield CA 93309. (805)833-3093. Associate Professor of Theater: Peter Grego. Chairman, Fine Arts: Jerome Kleinsasser. Play producer. Produces 5 plays/year (1 musical every other year). Plays performed in the 500-seat Dore Theatre to the college community and the community at large. Pays minimum $25/performance. Query. Does not return unsolicited material. Reports in 1 month.
**Musicals:** Looking for "exciting plays with unit set and small casts."
**Recent Productions:** *Trial By Jury*, by Gilbert and Sullivan (punk/new wave treatment of operetta); *Camelot*, by Lerner and Lowe; and *The Threepenny Opera*, by Brecht and Weill.

**WILLIAM CAREY COLLEGE DINNER THEATRE**, William Carey College, Hattiesburg MS 39401. (601)582-5051, ext. 228. Managing Director: O.L. Quave. Play producer. Produces 2 plays (2 musicals)/year. "Our dinner theater operates only in summer and plays to family audiences." Payment negotiable. Submit complete manuscript and score. SASE. Reports as soon as possible.
**Musicals:** "Plays should be simply-staged, have small casts (8-10), and be suitable for family viewing; two hours maximum length. Score should require piano only, or piano, electric piano, and drums."
**Recent Productions:** *Ernest in Love*; and *Rodgers and Hart: A Musical Celebration*; plus several musical revues.

**CARROLL COLLEGE**, Little Theatre, Helena MT 59625. (406)442-3450, ext. 276. Director of Theater: Jim Bartruff. Play producer. Produces 4-5 plays (1 musical)/year. "Our plays are produced in our Little Theatre for campus and community. The Little Theatre is a small proscenium house with flexible seating (90-120)." Pays $25-75/performance. Query or submit complete manuscript score and tape of songs. SASE. Reports in 2 weeks.
**Musicals:** "We consider all types of plays geared for small cast (15-18 people) and minimal settings (unit preferred). Scoring should be for piano and percussion. Also considers arrangement for quitar—keyboards—piano. Original material is preferred, but not readily available." Does not want musicals based on other musicals or musicals based on non-musical material, e.g., tragedy.
**Recent Productions:** *Celebration*, by Tom Jones and Harvey Schmidt (ritual love story); *Kiss Me, Kate*, by Spewack and Porter; *Threepenny Opera*, by Bertolt Brecht and Kurt Weill (capitalism); and *Working*, by Stephen Schwartz, Nina Faso and Studs Terkel and others (working people).
**Tips:** "Find a place, any place, to do it and get it done. Stay involved with the production. Don't be afraid to make changes if you need to. The best way to discover 'what works' is to get it done. There are literally thousands of little markets yearning for new and good material."

# Close-up

**Stephen Schwartz**
Composer/Lyricist

For the aspiring composer/lyricist—before "you pack up your boots and bluejeans and your records and your pride"—have a musical in the works, something to show when you get to New York. Stephen Schwartz followed the advice he gave in his lyrics from "West End Avenue," a song in *The Magic Show*. His showcase musical, *Pippin, Pippin* (written wile he was in college) kept him busy, even after he arrived in the Big Apple. By the time *Pippin* opened on Broadway, he had changed every note and lyric.

The musical (six years in the works) and the people he met in New York ultimately led to more work: the title song for *Butterflies are Free*, the music and lyrics for *Godspell*, directing and writing four songs for *Working*, and collaboration with Leonard Bernstein on the texts for *Mass*. Schwartz is now writing lyrics for a new show, *Rags* that he will also direct.

Writing a musical, though demanding, is the easiest entrée into the theatrical field. The aspiring composer/lyricist has an advantage over a would-be director (who needs a show to be able to direct) or an actor (who needs a part *to act*). "All a writer has to do is sit in his room and write," Schwartz says. "Then when you have something good enough, you can start showing it."

Producers, theaters and agents or their staffs generally take the time to hear new works. "Everyone is constantly on the lookout for new talent. I've never found it difficult for anyone to get people to listen. It is difficult after that sometimes to get people to spend some money or to actually go forward, but it's really not hard to get people to listen."

Working with aspiring composers/lyricists in colleges, Schwartz sees them making the same mistakes he did as a newcomer in the theater world—using elaborate rhyme schemes and strange rhythms and chords.

"Young writers try to be *too* clever for their own good," he says. "It's fine to have your own style, but when it becomes a self-conscious attempt to be different or to call attention to yourself—which you often wind up doing—you're undercutting the *emotional* quality."

Composers/lyricists with a talent for theater writing need "an ability to understand the dramatic demands of a situation." That is what makes composing for stage and popular recordings so different. By his own admission, Schwartz can't write pop music or dialogue but has "a dramatic sense of what a scene needs or a theatrical moment means to really make it work. And I try to bring that to the songs I use in shows."

Now, after his years of experience and two Grammys, Schwartz's style is to let an idea ripen naturally, to combine words, lists of ideas and phrases until an emotional and dramatic, as well as a musical, framework for a song becomes clear. "The longer I take in *not* forcing it, the longer I can work on something without trying to finish it, the better ultimately it gets to be," he says.

Still, he acknowledges a "point where you have to say now I'm ready to sit down and do it. The key is not to sit around and say, 'gee, I would like to do this but how can I get started.' Write. That is a cliché, but the fact it's a cliché doesn't make it any less true."

—*Paula Deimling*

*Photo by Peter Fink*

**CIRCLE IN THE SQUARE THEATRE**, 1633 Broadway, New York NY 10019. (212)581-3270. Literary Manager: ElizaBeth King. Play producer. Produces 3 plays/year; occasionally produces a musical. Query with a letter and script. Reports in 3-4 months.
**Musicals:** "We are actively looking for original material."

**COCKPIT IN COURT SUMMER THEATRE**, Essex Community College, Baltimore MD 21237. (301)682-6000. Managing Director: F. Scott Black. Play producer. Produces 7 plays/year. "We operate three separate theaters on our campus. Broadway type musicals are performed in a well-equipped, beautiful theater. Cockpit, upstairs, is a cabaret theater. Classics are performed outdoors in the courtyard with stylized sets and full makeup." Pays through rental and royalty agreement with firms who control rights. Submit complete ms and score. SASE. Reports in 1 month.
**Musicals:** "Wholesome shows which are suitable for audiences of all ages. Musical score should be of top quality. We use a full orchestra in the pit. Large casts are OK. We like good leading and supporting roles. We prefer a cast of 20-30 for most of our summer musicals with some doubling. We use wagon sets, no turntables or revolving stages. We are also looking for small cabaret musicals or musical reviews."
**Recent Productions:** *My Fair Lady*; and *Merrily We Roll Along*.

**DAVID J. COGAN**, 350 5th Ave., New York NY 10003. Contact: David Cogan. Play producer. Produces 1 play/year. Produces musical comedy, straight comedy, and drama in New York. Pays on a royalty basis, or buys script outright for $5,000 maximum. Query. SASE. Reports in 1 month.
**Musicals:** Interested only in completed projects.
**Recent Productions:** *A Raisin in the Sun*, by Hannesbury (drama); and *The Odd Couple*, by Neil Simon (comedy).

**CONSERVATORY OF THEATRE ARTS AT WEBSTER COLLEGE**, 470 E. Lockwood Ave., St. Louis MO 63119. (314)968-6929. Chairman: Peter E. Sargent. Play producer. Produces 10 plays (2-3 musicals)/year. "Our plays are performed in the Loretto Hilton Center for the Performing Arts in the 500-seat Main Stage, the 150-seat Studio Theater and also in a space and schedule called Stage 3, a 125-seat proscenium house." Pays 3-5% royalty or $15-200/performance "depending on the space." Query with synopsis. SASE. Reports in 1 month.
**Musicals:** "The Conservatory has a training program in musical theatre and, as a result, would be interested in musicals of all types and performance needs. Send a letter including a statement of production needs, scale of orchestration and such elements that would include cast size, nature of vocal skills and anything the author might consider unusual, within the normal needs of musical productions. Our audience is a midwestern one and we consider that when we choose scripts. However, we would welcome most scripts and would make that judgement upon reading the material."
**Recent Productions:** *Fiddler on the Roof*, by Stein, Bock and Harnick; *Once Upon a Mattress*, by Mary Rodgers and M. Bauer; and *Carnival* by Merrick and Stuart.
**Tips:** "Make the musical for a general appeal and include the potential for some strong dance. The story must always be interesting. Do not rely on heavy production values to make the play successful. A strong story with supporting music can work."

**GLENN CRANE**, 6260 Birdland Dr., Adrian MI 49221. (517)263-3411. Producing Director: Glenn Crane. Play producer. Produces 2-4 plays (2-4 musicals)/year. Pays 15-20% royalty; $50-200 outright purchase; $50-200/performance or $1,000 for 1 year option. Submit complete ms, score and tape of songs. Prefers 7½ ips reel-to-reel or cassette. SASE. Reports in 1 month.
**Musicals:** "Any creative, clever, original treatment—full-length or 1-act. We are especially interested in children's musicals with large cast; adult musicals with small cast, but can give first class production to large scale musicals after laboratory production proves worth."
**Recent Productions:** *Sound of Music*; *Rodgers and Hammerstein: A Musical Celebration*; and *Oklahoma* (Rodgers and Hammerstein).
**Tips:** "I am planning to move to Hawaii to produce musicals for chidren *and* reviws for the tourist trade" Looking for "thorough preparation of scores and arrangements that are readable and proofed."

**THE CRICKET THEATRE**, Hennepin Center for the Arts, 528 Hennepin Ave., Minneapolis MN 55403. (612)333-5241. Associate Artistic Director: Sean Michael Dowse. Play producer. Produces 12-14 plays (1-2 musicals)/year. Pays negotiable royalty; or per diem, honorarium or commission. Submit complete ms and cassette tape of songs. SASE. Reports in 6 months.
**Musicals:** "We seek chamber musicals with small cost and small orchestra—mainstream yet adventurous. New American playwrights and songwriters can use our Works-In-Progress program to develop new work."
**Recent Productions:** *Billy Bishop Goes to War*, by John Gray with Eric Peterson (WWI Ace); and *Tin-*

*types* (immigrants in early 20th century US).
**Tips:** "Try to get a workshop of play done at the theatre you wish to work with."

**CYPRESS COLLEGE THEATER ARTS DEPARTMENT**, 9200 Valley View St., Cypress CA 90630. (714)821-6320. Theater Arts Department Chairman: Kaleta Brown. Play producer. Produces 6-7 plays (2 musicals)/year. "Our audience at Cypress College is basically a middle-class, suburban audience. We have a continuing audience that we have built up over the years. Our plays now are produced in our Campus Theater (seating capacity 623) or workshop theater (maximum seating capacity 250)." Payment varies with each production. Submit complete ms, score and 7½ ips reel-to-reel tape of songs. SASE. Reports in 1 month.
**Musicals:** "We must do large-cast shows, generally, because the shows are done as a class. Because we are on a slightly limited budget, we must look carefully at scenery requirements, costume requirements and props.
**Recent Productions:** *Damn Yankees*; *A Funny Thing Happened on the Way to the Forum*; *Mans a Man*; and *Music Man*.
**Tips:** "Open show with a large group, energetic number. Intersperse dance (especially tap) throughout shows and end with a 'ripping' choral number."

**DEPARTMENT OF THEATRE, MICHIGAN STATE UNIVERSITY**, 149 Auditorium, East Lansing MI 48824. (517)353-5169. Director: Dr. Jon Baisch. Play producer. Produces 15 plays (1-2 large scale and 4-6 small revue musicals/year. "Our audiences are students, faculty, and members of the Lansing community. We use 6 theatres, ranging from 100 to 2,500 seats, including proscenium, platform, arena, and cabaret dinner theatre types. We stage everything from large-scale productions with orchestra and large casts to small-cast, intimate shows and cabaret entertainment." Performance rights negotiable. Query with synopsis and production specifications. SASE. Reports in 1 month.
**Musicals:** "We are interested in all types of new musicals. However, we are especially interested in small cast revues and book shows for cabaret and dinner theatre productions, and unusual material for our small arena and studio theatres."
**Recent Productions:** *Godspell*; *Oliver*; and *Man of LaMancha*.
**Tips:** "Write a good, modern show. Either write a good story or find one to adapt. The public—much of it—still wants a story."

**DEPARTMENT OF THEATRE, SOUTHERN CONNECTICUT STATE COLLEGE**, New Haven CT 06515. (203)397-4431. Chairman: Daniel E. Cashman. Play producer. Produces 4-6 plays (1-2 musicals)/year. Plays performed to general audiences and college students. Pays $25/performance or standard royalty. Submit cassette and/or manuscript. SASE. Reports ASAP—"depends on time of year."
**Musicals:** "We are interested in any musicals as long as they are not religious or polemical in a narrow sense." Should require small cast, props, staging, etc. Does not want "big, old-fashioned musicals."
**Recently Produced:** *Three Penny Opera*, by Brecht and Weil; and *The Boy Friend*, by Wilson.

**EAST WEST PLAYERS**, 4424 Santa Monica Blvd., Los Angeles CA 90029. (213)660-0366. Artistic Director: Mako. Administrator: Janet Mitsui. Play producer. Produces 6 plays/year. "We have produced original musical revues and some children's musicals in our theater which is a 99-seat Equity waiver house. Our actors are professional actors. We are an Asian-American theater and consequently the audience is primarily ethnic in makeup." Pays 5% minimum royalty. Query with synopsis. SASE. Reports in 2 months.
**Musicals:** "We look for material dealing with Asian-American culture and produce adult and children's musicals in book and/or revue form. We make no limitations on the writing approach. We look for theme and above all originality. We primarily produce shows with casts under 15. The stage is not huge and has certain limitations; however, we do have a turntable at our disposal."
**Recent Productions:** *Godspell*, by Tebelak/Schwartz (Jesus Christ); *Happy End*, by Brecht/Weil (Salvation Army vs. hoods); *Pacific Overtures*, by Sondheim/Weidman (opening of Japan) and *Christmas in Camp*, by Dom Magwili (Japanese internment camps).

**ETC. COMPANY**, Michigan School of The Arts, 2111 Emmons Rd., Jackson MI 49203. (517)787-0800. Director: G.L. Blanchard. Play producer. Produces 10-11 plays (2-3 musicals)/year. Plays are produced in a new proscenium theater with thrust capabilities seating 367, or a multiform theater seating 100-200 depending on arrangement. Pays $100-200 outright purchase or by agreement. Query with synopsis. SASE. Reports in 2 weeks.
**Recent Productions:** *Starting Here, Starting Now* (musical revival); *Antigone* (Greek tragedy); *Nuts* (drama); and *The Birthday Party*.

**Tips:** "We lean in the direction of shows with casts in the area of 20 or under, with 'moderately sensible staging."

**THE FIRST ALL CHILDREN'S THEATRE, INC.,** 37 W. 65th St., New York NY 10023. (212)873-6400. Producer: Meridee Stein. Produces 5 plays (4 musicals)/year. "For children, ages two and up, teenagers and their families. These plays are developed with and for our special company to appeal to an audience of young theatergoers." Pays 5% maximum royalty; buys script outright for $750 maximum, or pays $15/performance. Query or submit complete ms and score; "outline is best. If we like it, then we help develop it with the author. All pieces must be created especially for our company." SASE. Reports in 8-10 weeks.
**Musicals:** "ACT musicals are 45-50 minutes in length and include 8-10 songs with incidental music. We do plays in all genres featuring many kinds of music, i.e., commedia dell' arte, baroque musical fairy tales, modern pop, old tales made new, and originals with challenging, meaningful messages. We do not want material unsuitable for children and their families. The music must be a very important part of the work. Harmonies, arrangements and selection of a band are all done later. Plays include 15-35 children and teenagers. Props, staging can be creative and challenging, though not unrealistic. We have as many as nine pieces in our orchestra. We seldom produce completed scripts. We prefer to develop works from an outline in a cooperative effort between writer, composer, artistic director and staff."
**Recent Productions:** *Nightingale*, by Charles Strause; and *The Children's Crusade*, by Kenneth Cavender and Richard Peaslee.
**Tips:** "Our theater stresses excellence and professionalism. Flexibility on everybody's part is the key to our success. The work we produce is extremely creative and highly original. Each production is developed and nurtured over a long period of time—sometimes as long as two years. Each show has a team of adult theater professionals who direct and supervise the entire production."

**FOOLKILLER ETC.,** 2 W. 39th St., Kansas City MO 64111. (816)756-3754. Contact: Theater Council. Play producer. Produces 7-15 plays/year. Pays negotiable royalties. "Foolkiller is an excellent exposure showcase for new talent." Query with synopsis or contact by phone. SASE. Reports in 2 months.
**Musicals:** "We consider everything but prefer topics dealing with problems aimed at working and middle-class people —comedies and political and social commentaries. We prefer material that doesn't last more than one hour. Our stage is about 15x35; cast should be 2-15 people. We don't want to see any slick, sophisticated kinds of writing that may go over everyone's head, or anything terribly pessimistic."
**Recent Productions:** *Hughie*, by Eugene O'Neill; and *After the Fall*, by Arthur Miller.
**Tips:** "The Foolkiller is an organization that has many facets. It is a showcase for new talent. Musicians have frequent public jam sessions and walk-on talent is encouraged. Freedom of expression is emphasized in all activities. There is a large public following and community support. All material is original."

**SAMUEL FRENCH, INC.,** 25 W. 45th St., New York NY 10036-4982. (212)382-0800. Editor: Lawrence R. Harbison. Play publisher. Publishes about 80 scripts (8 musicals)/year. Plays used by community, stock and dinner theaters, regional repertories, and college and high school markets. Pays 10% royalty on play scripts sold, generally an advance against future royalties, and a per-performance royalty depending on various factors. "We take 10-20% agency fee. Submit only the libretto (book). If we like it, we may ask to see and/or hear music." SASE. Reports in 6 weeks minimum. If the work has been recommended for further consideration, the process may take considerably longer.
**Musicals:** "We publish primarily New York-produced musicals, though we do occasionally bring out a show which has not had a New York City production (1 in 1980). These are intended primarily, but not necessarily, for children's and community or dinner theaters. No religious material, or anything unstageworthy. We are particularly looking for small-cast, easy-to-produce musicals with good female roles. We are not interested in publishing big, splashy 'Broadway' musicals—unless they have been done on Broadway. Send us only the book of your musical. The music seems to be the easiest part of a musical; the book, the most difficult. Musicals succeed or fail on the basis of their book, not their music. If we like the book, we may ask to hear a tape of the score."
**Recent Publications:** *The First*, by Joel Siegel, Martin Charnin and Bob Brush (Broadway musical about Jackie Robinson); *The Best Little Whorehouse in Texas*, by Carol Hall, Larry King & Peter Masterson (Broadway); and *The Saloonkeeper's Daughter*, by Jack Sharkey and Dave Reiser (musical melodrama).
**Tips:** "Start small. Do a small-cast, easy-to-produce, inexpensive show. Then, once you have achieved a 'track record,' only then, try your Broadway musical. Never, ever, imitate what you think is 'commercial'—it never *will* be. Remember that musicals today are practically operas. Work with a director to develop concept."

**GEORGIA COLLEGE THEATRE**, Box 654, Milledgeville GA 31061. (914)453-5139. Director: John P. Blair Jr. Play producer. Produces 3-4 plays (1 musical)/year. "Plays are presented in 1,100 capacity proscenium to small-town, provincial audience whom we are trying to educate." Pays 50% royalty. Submit complete manuscript and score. SASE. Reports in 1 month.
**Musicals:** "We like serious topics and intents, but with color, humor and lots of life—like *Fiddler on the Roof*, *3 Penny Opera* and *Man of La Mancha*. We are catholic in our tastes. We cannot handle casts of more than 35 comfortably. Our space is limited with no fly or wing space to speak of. We don't want bright, happy, nonsensical pieces (*Brigadoon* is about as much like that as we intend to get)."
**Recently Produced:** *3 Penny Opera*; *Man of La Mancha*; *Camelot*; *Brigadoon*; *Fiddler on the Roof*; and *Jesus Christ, Superstar*.

**GREEN MOUNTAIN GUILD**, White River Junction VT 05001. (802)295-7016. Managing Director: Marjorie O'Neill-Butler. Play producer. Produces 18 plays (8-10 musicals)/year. Produces plays for a summer theater audience in 4 locations in Vermont: Stowe, White River Junction, Killington and Mt. Snow. Pays $75 minimum/performance. Query with synopsis. Send script and cassette with music. SASE. Reports in 1 month.
**Musicals:** "We are looking for musicals with a small cast, a good story line, well-developed characters, songs and music that come naturally out of the story and music that works with piano and drums only." No frivolous material. Prefers one-set shows.
**Recent Productions:** *Jenny Lind*, by David Harlay (an original play); *Sweeney Todd*, by Stephen Sondheim; *Student Prince*, by Sigmund Romberg; and *Naughty Marietta*, by Victor Hubert.

**HOWARD UNIVERSITY DEPARTMENT OF DRAMA**, Washington DC 20059. (202)636-7050. Chairperson: Dr. Geoffrey Newman. Play producer. Produces 1 play/year. Pays $75-100/performance. Submit complete ms and cassette of songs. SASE. Reports in 4 months.
**Recent Productions:** *Black Images/Black Reflections*, by Kelsey Collie; *The Whiz* by Charlie Smalls, choreographed by Lewis Johnson; *Strike Heaven on the Fall*, by Richard Wesley; and *Black Orpheus*, by Laverne Reed.

**HUDSON GUILD THEATRE**, 441 W. 26 St., New York NY 10001. (212)760-9810. Producing Director: David Kerry Heefner. Play producer. Produces 5 plays (1 musical)/year. "Plays are done at the Hudson Guild Theatre to very diverse audiences, ages 25-65." Pays $500 for a limited run. Submit complete manuscript and tape. SASE. Reports in about 2 months.
**Musicals:** "The only limitation is that material should *not* have been performed in New York before." Maximum cast size should be 20 people.
**Recent Productions:** *Hooters*, by Ted Tally; *Breakfast with Les and Bess* by Lee Kalcheim; *Blood Relations* by Sharon Pollock; and *Vamps and Rideouts*, by Julie Styne and Phyllis Newman.
**Tips:** "Don't imitate. Stretch the bounds of musical theatre."

**INTAR, INTERNATIONAL ARTS RELATIONS, INC.**, Box 788, New York NY 10108. (212)695-6134. Artistic Director: Max Ferra. Play producer. Produces 3 plays (1-2 musicals)/year. Plays are performed in New York City. Pays maximum $500 outright purchase. Query, submit complete ms and score, and/or send resume. SASE. Reports in 1 month.
**Musicals:** "We are seeking material for small cast musicals with a Latin theme or flavor." Length: 1-1½ hours.
**Recent Productions:** *Crisp!*, by Dolores Prida and Max Ferra (two adventurers con a town); and *Exiles* by Ana Maria Simo (woman exiled from Cuba).

**INTERLOCHEN ARTS ACADEMY PLAYWRIGHT PROJECT**, Interlochen MI 49643. (616)276-9221. Contact: Denny Bechtelheimer. Play producer. Produces 4 plays (1 musical)/every other year. "We are an every-other-year project. We plan no plays for 1982-83. We hope, however, to carry on the project in 1983-84."
**Recent Productions:** *Pippin*; and *As You Like It*.

**JEKYLL ISLAND MUSIC THEATRE**, 181 Old Plantation Rd., Jekyll Island GA 31520. (912)635-3378. Resident Manager: Ms. Leila El-Bisi. Musical play producer. Produces 1 musical/year. "Musicals are produced for either educational or entertainment purposes and often both. Audiences are conservative middle- or upper-middle-class. New musicals we produce are workshop productions that should help the creators as much as educate our students or entertain our patrons. The composer-lyricist-writer is hired for 3 months at $125-200/week, plus room." Query with synopsis. SASE. Reports whenever possible and as soon as possible.
**Musicals:** "We use musicals involving a relatively young cast (teenage to mid-twenties). Lengths have never been past 2½ hours. Musicals have ranged in subject matter from fantasy to an adaptation of an F.

Scott Fitzgerald short story. Periods of particular interest are the gay nineties through the roaring twenties. We perform new works on a workshop basis and are more interested in the developmental phase of a new musical than anything else. We work with very limited production budgets on new works. We want the writers to hear and see their work and *change* it—*rework* it, free from final production constraints. We don't want perfect sets to obscure flaws that need to be corrected in the material. We are sensitive to language, vulgarity for its own sake is useless to us."

**Recent Productions:** *Soap* (soap operas), (produced in 1977, before the TV show); *Bernice Bobs Her Hair*, by Bob McDowell (based on F. Scott Fitzgerald short story); and *Pisbee Cocola*, (a musical fantasy).

**Tips:** "Work on your script and music for a long time anywhere and with anyone you can with no sets, costumes, lights, etc. That way you find out how good your work is. There are a lot of 'this is what the theater is really like' musicals being written—it's getting redundant and self-indulgent. Musical writers should go outside the theater and find material in the streets, the schools, history, people. Musical writers should not be afraid to draw on the techniques and styles of past musical traditions."

**JITASCA,** 313 Heston Ave., Norristown PA 19403. (215)539-9284. Play producer. Produces 1 play/year. "We need a composer to set lyrics to music. *Experienced only please.*" Pays 2% minimum royalty. Query. SASE. Reports in 1 week.

**LOS ANGELES (INNER CITY) CULTURAL CENTER,** 1308 S. New Hampshire Ave., Los Angeles CA 90006. (213)387-1161. Executive Director: C. Bernard Jackson. Administrative Director: Elaine Kashiki. Branch: Inner City Cultural Center Bay Area, 762 Fulton St., San Francisco CA 94102. (415)929-7586. Artistic Director: John Thorpe. Produces 6-8 plays (3 musicals)/year. A "multi-ethnic, multi-cultural arts organization." Pays 6% royalty. Query with synopsis. Does not return unsolicited material. Reports in 3 months.

**Musicals:** "Those with a point of view that lend themselves to utilizing people of all ethnic backgrounds."

**Recent Productions:** *Showgirls*, by Victoria Hood, based on an idea by Ebony Wright (a contemporary look at the struggles of black women in show business); *Sleep No More*, by Felton Perry (a comedie noir musical inspired by Shakespeare's MacBeth); and *Proud* by C. Bernard Jackson (a one-man show starring Glynn Turman).

**Tips:** "Have something to say."

**LYRIC THEATER OF NEW YORK,** 8J, 363 E. 76th St., New York NY 10021. Artistic Director: Neal Newman. Play producer. Produces 6-10 plays (6-10 musicals)/year. Plays presented in "small off-off Broadway theater in New York; during summer in a lovely old playhouse in North Conway, New Hampshire." Pays $25-55/performance. Query with synopsis. SASE. Reports in 3 months.

**Musicals:** "We consider anything that is not a typical commercial Broadway-type musical. We search for works that advance the musical theater as an artform. Strong characters, situations, and individual expression in play, lyrics and music. Full length works are preferred but one acts are occasionally done. Any topic or type, but we are always searching for a great dramatic musical. Any format is possible providing music is used in some way to tell the story. Cast size is not a problem. Due to budget limitations, however, we are unable to present works calling for many or elaborate settings and properties. Costumes are always first rate. We don't want commercial musicals (*Sugar, No, No, Nanette*), non-musicals or revues."

**Recent Productions:** *Sweeney Todd*, by Sondheim; *Carnival*, by Bob Merrill; *Fantastiks*, by Jones and Schmidt; *Once Upon Many Times*, by Rhona Roberts and Ken Jacobson (musical of country wife); and *Damon's Song*, by William Brown and George Robertson (original rock fairy tale).

**Tips:** "Don't expect Broadway for a long, long time. If it's good it will get done eventually. Strong characters and situations are better than big budgets. Also, know what market you are writing for: opera house, Broadway, summer stock, etc."

**MANHATTAN THEATRE CLUB,** 321 E. 73 St., New York NY 10021. (212)288-2500. Literary Manager: Jonathan Alper. Play producer. Produces 10 plays (1-2 musicals)/year. Plays are performed at the Manhattan Theatre Club before varied audiences. Pays negotiated fee. Send synopsis first *or* a letter of recommendation with the manuscript or "send a cassette of several of your songs." SASE. Reports in 6 months.

**Musicals:** Small cast, original work. "Small scale musicals—revue types are best because of theatre's limited space. *No* historical drama, verse drama or children's plays."

**Recent Production:** *Real Life Funnies*, by Alan Menken and Howard Ashman (topical New York City); *Livin' Dolls*, by Scott Wittman and Marc Shaiman; *Ain't Misbehavin'*, by Fats Waller and Richard Maltby; *On the Swing Shift*, by Michael Dansicker and Sarah Schlesinger; and *New Tunes*, by Jonathon Sheffer and Alan Paul (revue).

**MID-PLAINS COMMUNITY COLLEGE**, State Farm Rd., North Platte NE 69101. (308)532-8980. Chairman, Communication and Drama Department: Colin Taylor. Play producer. Produces 3-4 plays (1 musical)/year. Plays performed "at the college auditorium (small house and on tour to area schools." Query with synopsis or submit complete manuscript and score. SASE. Reports in 1 month.
**Musicals:** Needs musicals, prefers to work with a small cast, "flexible staging a necessity. Beginning singers need consideration. We cannot fly scenery, but use free-standing sets and projections in a 'theatre of light.' We work with a limited budget and unlimited imagination."
**Recent Productions:** *Fiddler on the Roof*, (musical); *Paint Your Wagon*, (musical); and *The Children's Hour*, (drama).

**MILWAUKEE REPERTORY THEATER**, 929 N. Water St., Milwaukee WI 53202. (414)273-7121. Artistic Director: John Dillon. Play producer. Produces 12 plays (1 musical)/year. "We have mainly a subscription audience." Pays negotiable royalty. Submit ms and cassette tape of songs. SASE. Reports "as soon as possible."
**Musicals:** "We seek small cast musicals suitable for resident theater productions. We're interested in quality material (not froth) performable in a 500-seat three-quarter round theater."
**Recent Productions:** *Miss LuLu Bett*, by Zona Gale; *Buried Child*, by Sam Shepard; *The Glass Menagerie*, by Tennessee Williams; and *The Foreigner*, by Larry Shue (resident playwright).

**NASHVILLE ACADEMY THEATRE**, 724 2nd Ave. S., Nashville TN 37210. (615)254-9103. Director: Guy Keeton. Play producer. Produces 4 plays/year. Plays are performed in a 696-seat theater for audiences ranging in age from kindergarten through high school. Pays $15-50/performance. Submit complete ms and score. SASE. Reports "after play-reading committee is through."
**Musicals:** "We want wholesome entertainment for various age groups, e.g. *Cinderella* for the very young, *Tom Sawyer* for teens and pre-teens and *Man of La Mancha* for high schoolers. Average cast size is 15. We do not want to see any poorly written, sensational or pornographic materials."
**Recent Productions:** *1984*, by George Orwell (future); *Ten Little Indians*, by Agatha Christie (revenge); and *Really Rosie*, by Maurice Sendak (imagination).

**NEGRO ENSEMBLE COMPANY**, Suite 800, 165 W. 46th St., New York NY 10036. (212)575-5860. Artistic Director: Douglas Turner Ward. Play producer. Produces 4 plays/year. Pays by percentage of box office take. Submit complete manuscript and score. SASE. Returns material "only if writers insists, otherwise, play is kept on file."
**Musicals:** "Submit only plays that deal with black life and the black experience."

**THE NEW PLAYWRIGHT'S THEATRE OF WASHINGTON**, 1742 Church St. NW, Washington DC 20036. (202)232-1122. Literary Manager: Ms. Lloyd Rose. Play producer. "We do developmental work with playwrights." Produces 5 plays (1 musical)/year. For general audience with interest in new works. Payment individually negotiated. Submit complete ms and cassette tape of music. Score is optional. SASE. Reports in 4-6 months.
**Musicals:** Seeks all types: revues, musical comedies and musical theater with strong story line. Does not want material that has had major, fully professional prior production. "Instrumental forces should be chamber-size; no more than 12 musicians. Cast can be up to 15."
**Recent Productions:** *Out of the Reach of Children*, by Cornelia Ravenal.

**THE NICOLET PLAYERS**, Nicolet College, Box 518. Rhinelander WI 54501. (715)369-4476. Play producer. Produces 6 plays (2 musicals)/year. "Nicolet College is a small community college of about 1,000 students, in a town of about 10,000 people." Pays $25-100/performance. Query with synopsis. SASE. Reports in 1 weeks.
**Musicals:** "We consider musicals that are interesting and theatrical. We have a small stage, a ¾ thrust, which is approximately 25-feet in diameter and limited backstage area. No fly space, just a ceiling 12 feet above the stage. Keep it small and simple."
**Recent Productions:** *The Fantasticks*, by Schmidt and Jones; *A Funny Thing Happened on the Way to the Forum*, by Sondheim, Shevelove and Gelbert; *The Apple Tree*, by Feiffer, Bock and Harnick; and *Diamond Studs*, by Wann and Simpson.

**NORTH CAROLINA CENTRAL UNIVERSITY, DEPARTMENT OF DRAMATIC ART**, Box 19593, Durham NC 27707. (919)683-6242. Chairperson: Linda Kerr Norflett, Ph.D. Play producer. Produces 4 plays (1-2 musicals)/year. "North Carolina Central University is a traditionally black university but the theater faculty is racially mixed. We put great emphasis on producing new works by black playwrights as well as other minorities. Pays by royalty. Query with synopsis or submit tape of songs with or without manuscript and score. SASE. Reports in 2 weeks.
**Musicals:** "We are looking for plays that are preferably non-racial or racial with clean humanistic

themes, music and dance compilations (revue styles), musical dramas, and experimental performance pieces. Be as creative and experimental as your talent will allow and don't underestimate the power of metaphor. Keep staging simple, props at a minimum and cast size below 20." Does not want culturally limiting material.

**Recent Productions:** *Don't Bother Me, I Can't Cope*, by Micki Grant (race relations); *Guys and Dolls*; *Purlie* (race relations); *Deadwood Dick, The Legend of the West*; *Black Nativity*; and *Death and the King's Horseman* (Nigerian).

**PERFORMANCE PUBLISHING CO.**, 978 N. McLean Blvd., Elgin IL 60120. (312)697-5636. Editor: Virginia Butler. Play publisher. Publishes 30 plays (4-6 musicals)/year. Plays are used by children's theaters, junior and senior high schools, colleges and community theaters. Pays standard nonprofessional royalty/performance. Submit complete ms, score and cassette tape of songs. SASE. Reports in 3 months.

**Musicals:** "We prefer large cast, contemporary musicals which are easy to stage and produce. We like children's musicals if the accompaniment is fairly simple. Plot your shows strongly, keep your scenery and staging simple, your musical numbers and choreography easily explained and blocked out. Originality and style are up to the author. We want innovative and tuneful shows but no X-rated material. We are very interested in the new writer and believe that, with revision and editorial help, he can achieve success in writing original musicals for the non-professional market."

**Recent Publications:** *Nashvile Jamboree*, by Tim Kelly, Jim and Mary Stuart (country and rock musical); *Musical Pied Piper*, by Bob Noll; and *How The West Was Fun*, by James L. Seay and Dave Ellis (musical).

**PERFORMING ARTS DEPARTMENT**, Avila College, 11901 Wornall Rd., Kansas City MO 64145. (816)942-8408. Chairman, Performing Arts: Dr. William J. Louis. Play producer. Produces 8 plays (1 musical)/year. Four plays are produced in a 500-seat thrust stage theater and four in Actors Laboratory Theatre (250 seat theatre-in-the-round). "To date, only well known musicals have been produced. Original shows would have to be individually contracted for." Submit through agent. Pays 75% royalty. SASE. Reports in 2 months.

**Musicals:** "We prefer shows 2 hours in length and topics for a liberal arts school and a Catholic-sponsored institution, family audience-oriented, cast perferably 25 or below."

**Recent Productions:** *110 in the Shade*; *The Fantastiks*, by Jones/Schmidt; *Company*, by Sondheim; and *Paint Your Wagon*, (romantic comedy).

**Tips:** "Return to romantic plot of substance, like *110 in the Shade*, *Man of LaMancha* or *West Side Story*. Strive for memorable times but first and foremost, keep vulgarity out of scipt."

**SHOWBOAT MAJESTIC**, Foot of Broadway, Cincinnati OH 45202. (513)241-6550. Producing Director: F. Paul Rutledge. Play producer. Produces 10 plays (3-5 musicals)/year. Plays are produced on the Showboat Majestic, the last of the original floating theaters located on the Ohio River. Pays $75-110/performance. "Most musicals are rented through New York. We follow regular royalty rental plan from them." Query. SASE. Reports in 1 month.

**Musicals:** "We are seeking original songs, musical comedies no longer than two hours with an intermission, revues and small cast shows." No avant-garde or experimental scripts. Cast should be less than 10.

**Recent Productions:** *The Fantastiks*, by Schmidt and Jones; *Gold Dust*, by Wann; *I Do! I Do!*, by Schmidt and Jones; and *Show Me Where the Good Times Are.*

**Tips:** "Begin with an acknowledged good story line. Find a play in the public domain that could be turned into a musical."

**SUSQUEHANNA UNIVERSITY THEATRE**, Susquehanna University, Selinsgrove PA 17870. (717)374-9700. Producer: Larry D. Augustine. Play producer. Produces 13 plays (1-2 musicals)/year. Plays are produced in 1,500-seat auditorium and in a 160-seat theater to a general audience of high school students through senior citizens. Pays royalty. Query with synopsis. SASE. Reports in 3 weeks.

**Recent Productions:** *Mame*, by Jerry Herman.

**THEATRE DEPARTMENT**, Centenary College, Shreveport LA 71104. (318)869-5242. Chairman: Robert R. Buseick. Play producer. Produces 6 plays (3 musicals)/year. Plays are presented in a 350-seat playhouse to college and community audiences. Submit ms and score. SASE. Reports in 1 month.

**Recent Productions:** *Annie*; *Trixie True, Teen Detective*; and *The Unsinkable Molly Brown*.

**THEATRE FOR THE NEW CITY**, 162 2nd Ave., New York NY 10003. (212)254-1109. Director: George Bartenieff. Play producer. Produces 40-50 plays (6 musicals)/year. Plays are performed for a mixed audience. "Some writers are commissioned; others share the box office take with actors." Submit complete manuscript with lyrics. SASE. Reports in 12-18 months.

**Musicals:** No limitations òn cast size, props, staging, etc. "No children's plays with bunny rabbit feel."
**Recent Productions:** *Rosetti's Apologetic*, by Leonard Melfi; *Starburn*, by Rosalyn Drexler; and *The Danube*, by Marie Irene Fones.

**THEATRE FOR YOUNG AMERICA**, 7204 W. 80th St., Shawnee Mission KS 66208. Artistic Director: Gene Mackey. Play producer. Produces 8 plays (2-3 musicals)/year. For children, preschool to high.school. Pays $10-25/performance. Query with synopsis. SASE. Reports in 1 month.
**Musicals:** 1-1½ hour productions with small cast oriented to children and high-school youths. "A clear, strong, compelling story is important; a well known title is very important."
**Recent Productions:** *Androcles and the Lion*, by Aurand Harris and Glen Mack (music); *The Tale of Peter Rabbit*, by Rita Lovett and Gene Mackey (adapted from Beatrix Potter's *Peter Rabbit*); *The Hare and the Tortoise*, by Cheryl O'Brien and Gene Mackey (adapted from Aesop's fable); and *Tom Sawyer*, by Michael Dansicker and Sarah Marie Schlesinger (adapted from Mark Twain's novel).

**THEATRE OF THE RIVERSIDE CHURCH**, 490 Riverside Dr., New York NY 10027. (212)864-2929. Coordinating Director: David Manion. Play producer. Produces 6 plays/year. Plays are produced for black and Hispanic audiences in New Jersey and New York. Pays $125. Submit complete ms, score and tape of songs. Prefers cassette. SASE. Reports in 1-3 months.
**Musicals:** "All types are accepted, full-evening or one-act. We are very involved·with Hispanic and black themes and are specifically searching for an American Indian show. We favor smaller casts (under ten) and do not want to see sexual overtness or nudity for no purpose."
**Recent Productions:** *Fixed*, by Robert M. Riley (a beauty parlor in Detroit in the 1930s); *Breaking Light*, by Marcus Hemphill; *A Broadway Musical*, by William F. Brown, Charles Strouse and Lee Adams; *Abdul and the Night Visitors*; and *Godspell*.
**Tips:** All submissions should be as brief as possible and include a resume and synopsis.

**13th STREET THEATRE REPERTORY CO.**, 50 W. 13th St., New York NY 10011. (212)741-9282. Artistic Director: Edith O'Hara. Play producer. Produces 20 plays (3 musicals)/year. Pays 6% royalty for off-Broadway productions; does not pay for workshop productions. Submit complete ms, score and cassette or reel-to-reel tape of songs. SASE. Reports in 3-6 months.
**Musicals:** "Open to anything but prefer small casts, and simple sets, costumes and technical requirements. However, we will do anything if it's good enough. We'd love to see some experimental musicals that work. The writer should keep in mind current producing costs, if he has an expectation of the show moving off-Broadway. We are the only nonprofit theater in New York dedicated to producing original works for the American musical theater as a primary focus. We do not want musicals on a gay theme, unless they're exceptionally well-done."
**Recent Productions:** *Boy Meets Boy*, by B. Solly and D. Ward ('30s spoof); *Empire Laughs Back*, by Nancy Rodgers (children's musical); *Snow White Show*, by Jerry Coben and Mark Saltzman; *Joan and the Devil*, by S. Reiter and D. Hyman (Americana satire); and *Movie Buff*, by J. Raniello and H. Taylor ('30s movies).

**UNIVERSITY OF MAINE AT FORT KENT**, Pleasant St., Fort Kent ME 04743. (207)834-3162. Director of Performing Art: Charles Closser. Play producer. Produces 5 plays (1 musical)/year. Plays are produced in a university theater to university and community audience. Pays $300 maximum for royalty or $100 maximum/performance. Query with synopsis. SASE. Reports in 1 month.
**Musicals:** We are looking for musicals of 2 hours "for general audience family theater. No strong language, nudity or shows with more than six sets."
**Recent Productions:** *Anthing Goes*, by Cole Porter (musical comedy); *Applause*; and *I Do! I Do!*.

**UNIVERSITY THEATRE**, Oregon State University, Corvallis OR 97331. Coordinator, Theatre Arts: C.V. Bennett. Play producer. Produces 6-8 plays/year and 1 musical every 2 years. Produces plays in 2 theaters seating 80 and 426 to an audience of faculty, students and townspeople. Pays flat royalty fee of $25-150 and by performance: $25-50 for first performance and $10-35 for each additional performance. Pays "standard quotation from French, DPS, MTI, etc. We seldom premier a new script—seldom receive them." Submit complete ms and score. SASE. Reports in 2 weeks.
**Musicals:** "Usually small cast/small orchestra. We will probably do a standard big cast musical in 1983-84 ."
**Recent Productions:** *The Fantasticks*, by Schmidt and Jones; *Something's Afoot*, (satire); *Stop the World*; and *Cabaret*, by Bricusse and Newley.
**Tips:** "Get an agent or representation of some kind."

**CEDRIC VENDYBACK**, Brandon University, Brandon, Manitoba, Canada R7A 6A9. (204)727-9662. Professor: C. Vendyback. Play producer. Produces 2-6 plays/year. Rarely produces musicals. Audience is urban and rural, middle-class, faculty and students. Pays $25-75/performance. Query with synopsis. SASE. Reports in 1 month.

**Musicals:** Prefers "one- to three-act; social comment, smallish cast. We also like simple props and staging. Nothing lavish, possibly revue style."

**Recent Productions:** *All My Sons*, by Miller (social conscience); *The Love of Four Colonels*, by Ustinov (good vs. evil); and *Getting Married*, by Shaw (social awareness).

**Tips:** "Study Rodgers and Hart for good melody and witty lyrics. Also study *The Music Man*, *Pal Joey*, *Guys and Dolls*, etc. Eschew *bleak* melodies and lyrics of recent times. Audiences are pining for and in need of warmth and quality."

**WABASH COLLEGE THEATER**, Wabash College, Crawfordsville IN 47933. (317)362-0677. Chairman/Theater Department: James Fisher. Play producer. Produces 4 plays (1 musical)/year. "Musicals are produced occasionally as schedule and personnel permit. Audience is small college town and the male student body of the college. We have two theaters: a 370-seat intimate proscenium with lift for stage; and a black box, seating up to 150. Looking for plays with moderate size cast with more male than female roles." Pays standard royalty. Query with synopsis or submit complete ms and score. SASE. Reports as soon as possible.

**Musicals:** Any type. Plays require mostly male characters with small- to medium-size orchestra and up to 25-30 in cast.

**Recent Productions:** *Guys and Dolls*; *Cabaret*; *Fantastiks*; *Canterbury Tales*; *The Crimson Bird*, by Strawn and Enenbach (medieval French nightingale legend); and *S.H. Ades*, by Seward (ghosts and aspiring showbiz hopeful).

**WALDO ASTORIA PLAYHOUSE**, 5028 Main, Kansas City MO 64112. Producer: Richard Carothers. Play producer. Produces 12 plays (1 musical)/year. For general audience. Pays negotiable royalty. Submit complete ms. SASE. Reports in 1 month.

**Musicals:** Wants musical comedy. "No special format, just appeal to public taste. Three acts, 40-40-40 maximum, rated G. Do not exceed 15 in cast with minimal orchestra; we have a relatively small stage. Not interested in burlesque."

**Recent Productions:** *The Owl and the Pussycat*; *Hello Dolly*; *Charlie's Aunt*; *The Unsinkable Molly Brown*; and *Dames at Sea*.

**Tips:** "Don't over write. Don't become too attached to any particular song. Be open minded in working with the director and producers."

**WATERLOO COMMUNITY PLAYHOUSE**, Box 433, Waterloo IA 50704. (319)235-0367. Managing Director: Charles Stilwill. Play producer. Produces 6-7 plays (1-2 musicals)/year. "Our audience prefers solid, wholesome entertainment, nothing risque or with strong language. We perform in Hope Martin Theatre, a 368-seat house." Pays $25-150/performance. Submit complete ms, score and tape of songs on cassette. SASE.

**Musicals:** "Casts may vary from as few as 6 people to 54. We are producing children's theater as well."

**Recent Productions:** *Sing Ho for a Prince*; *Brigadoon*; *The Music Man*; *Oklahoma*; and *Man of La Mancha*.

**YELLOW BRICK PROMISES**, Suite 23, 19270 Colima Rd., Rowland Heights CA 91748. (213)912-0741. Creative Coordinator: Michael Ricciardi. Play publisher. "We are also a writers' organization in the process of developing a creative repertory company." Estab. 1981. Publishes 4 musicals/year. "We are a young organization of writers looking to expand. We have been producing our own work in equity-waiver type theatres and local high schools. Now we are looking for new writers (composers and librettists) to work with us. By offering our work as well as that of others, we can begin to be the creative 'umbrella' organization we desire to become. We are also looking for good tech people to create our costume, choreography, and lighting and sound guides we want to bring out with each show. We have a standard royalty schedule and at present work on 50/50 split." Query with synopsis. Include tape of show's opening number, best ballad, and "11 o'clock song (a song like 'Everything's Coming Up Roses' from *Gypsy*)." SASE, but use a pre-printed reply form or postcard. Reports ASAP: synopsis with 3-song tape, usually within 1 month; complete manuscript with score, usually within 3 months.

**Musicals:** "Any audience-pleasing, well-plotted show with a good story line—anything creative without being vulgar. We prefer musicals in two acts, but would like to see musical one-acts, thematically related. Show ideas should be *universally* appealing: we don't want to see any regional characters, stereotyped story lines or reworks of tired formulas. Be original. Work with a classic story first to get your feet wet. Go from there to conceive new ideas. There *is* room in theater for original story lines. Also, keep it simple. Excecssive sets, costumes, and scenery don't make the show. Casts should be 5-18 people with good roles for both men and women. (There are always exceptions, of course. A way to understand this is to read the Moss Hart comedy *Light Up the Sky*, available from the Dramatists

# Close-up

**Jeff Jones**
Composer/Arranger/Musician

"When I am in need of inspiration, I find musical ideas in ordinary sounds," says composer/musician Jeff Jones. "Perhaps it's nothing more than a street worker, traffic humming, bird songs, or a busy typewriter. I simply listen for inspiration in the sound itself."

Some of the common sounds Jones talks about have inspired incredibly uncommon works. Three of Jones' compositions have been published—in New York, Paris and Milan—and two of his most ambitious works, *Ambiance* and *Pieces Mouvantes*, have been recorded respectively on Nonesuch and CRI Records and Tapes.

Jones' success has come from more than just inspiration, however. He studied music on a Fulbright Scholarship at the famous Accademia di Santa Cecilia in Rome, where he ultimately earned their Diploma of Perfection. In 1972, he went on to win the coveted Rome Prize for Creative Competition, then the BMI Award to Student Composers, followed by the Bonaventura Somma Prize, the D'atri Prize, and First Prize in the International Competition of Sound. He plays fourteen instruments, has mastered the technologies of electronic instruments and synthesizers, and was the assistant instructor for the Electronic Music Lab at Brandeis University, where he was also choral conductor.

Jones often uses his knowledge of composition and instrumentation to overcome what's commonly known as *writer's block*. "When I can't find the idea for what I want, I rely on my craft. I take a melodic structure apart, or turn a melody around. Because I practice my craft every day, I renew everything I have learned by both education and experience."

Although Jones has an excellent classical background, he certainly doesn't consider himself locked into the stereotyped "baton-wielding, long-hair moody maestro with chewed-off fingernails and his head up his Bach." He has moved to Hollywood with the purpose of writing, arranging and conducting for films, television, and commercials. Already he has arranged music for producer Paul Gilman, songwriter Freeman King, and June Pointer of the Pointer Sisters, and edited the music for the TV series, *Insights*. He is also working with the Yellow Brick Promises organization (see listing in this section) on material destined for the musical theater.

To understand the motivation behind Jones is to understand the driving desire behind any great creative artist: "If the great composers had been satisfied with what they heard in their lifetimes, they would have never created the masterpieces they did. I write and don't quit because I'm not satisfied. I'm always trying to open new doors in music."

Play Service, 440 Park Ave. S., New York NY 10016. 212/683-8960.) Submit standard script format with all lyrics printed or within the scripts. When we ask for a script, be sure to include a character description, a list of scenes, and a summary of musical numbers and which characters sing them."

**Recent Productions:** *The Wizard of Oz* (original adaptation of classic story with new original score); *Skylark*, (a teenager growing up in Shakespeare's time); and *Christmas Belongs to You* (a musical trilogy that explores what Christmas means to different people), all by Ricciardi, Ames and Clement.

**Tips:** "Don't ever give up. Develop your craft every single day. Keep writer's notebooks. We want to work with new writers and possibly bring them directly into our organization working with us in a collaborative association. Those who live in the California area might do well by writing us a letter about themselves, their skills, and their aspirations to write musicals."

# Services & Opportunities

## Contests and Awards

Songwriter or musician competitions can be pleasant and sometimes lucrative endeavors. What's more, participation in contests is a good way to expose your work and your talents. Some contests—the American Song Festival and Music City Song Festival, for instance—are judged by music publishers and other industry officials, guaranteeing a professional hearing for your material. Contacts, and sometimes contracts, result from a good showing in a major competition.

Contests may not seem to be a good "market" in the usual sense, yet you are selling yourself and your work. Thus, marketing techniques shouldn't be forgotten. Each contest you enter, for example, should be studied so that you can slant your material to the award you seek.

Contests listed here encompass all types of music and all levels of composition expertise: some are on a level requiring a degree in music while others require only talent to write strong lyrics and melodies that touch people's hearts (and the judges') and have great commercial appeal. Most of these contests are annual. Read each listing carefully and write a letter to any that interest you, asking that you be put on the list to receive information about upcoming competitions.

**AMERICAN SONG FESTIVAL**, Box 57, Hollywood CA 90028. (213)464-8193. An international songwriting competition. Offers lyric, vocal and song competitions for amateur and professional songwriters and performers. Query for complete information and official entry form.

**BMI AWARDS TO STUDENT COMPOSERS**, 320 W. 57th St., New York NY 10019. (212)586-2000. Director: James G. Roy Jr. For composers of "serious concert music." Annual. Purpose: "to pick outstanding young (25 or under) composers and make cash awards for furthering their musical education."
**Requirements:** Applicants must not have reached their 26th birthday by Dec. 31 of the year preceding the Feb. 15th contest deadline. "Serious concert music is preferred to popular songs, but all music is considered. All geographic locations of the world, but applicant must be a citizen or permanent resident of the western hemisphere enrolled in an accredited public, private or parochial secondary school, in an accredited college or conservatory of music, or engaged in private study with recognized music teachers." Deadline: Feb. 15. One entry per student. Send for free application and rules. Rights retained. Entries returned, include SASE.
**Awards:** BMI Awards to Student Composers: "prizes totaling $15,000 ranging from $500 to $2,500 may be given to winning students, by check, with certificate of honor." Contest judged by "outstanding composers, music publishers and musicologists."

**COMPOSERS GUILD**, 2333 Olympus Dr., Salt Lake City UT 84117. (801)278-1745. President: Sharon Nielson. For songwriters and composers. "We are a nonprofit organization working to help the composer/songwriter. Each year we sponsor classes, workshops, seminars, a composition contest, and a performance at the Symphony Hall."

**Requirements:** "Annual dues of $25 entitles members to reduced entry fee for contest plus invaluable information kit. Cassette demo and lead sheet required for all *jazz* and *popular* entries only. No other restrictions." Deadline: August 31. Send for application.

**Awards, Grants:** $3,000 distributed among 7 categories: keyboard, popular, choral, vocal solo, jazz, instrumental and children's music. The best-of-the-show (can be from any music category) is awarded $1,000. "Detailed critique is given to every contest entry. Applicants judged by professional, usually head of university music department or firmly established producer of performed music."

**Tips:** "Be as professional as possible—clear, neat manuscript. Have music taped on cassette. Sloppy manuscripts will not be accepted by Composers Guild."

**MUSIC CITY SONG FESTIVAL**, 1014 16th Ave. S, Box 17999, Nashville TN 37217. (800)251-1791. Festival Directors: Roy Sinkovich, Mick Lloyd. Country, easy listening, gospel, pop/R&B songwriting and performance competitions for amateurs and professionals. Deadline: November. Write or call for complete information.

**Awards:** Separate awards in country, easy listening, gospel, and pop/R&B categories will be given for songwriting, lyric writing and vocal performance. Prizes for a single award range from $50-5,000 with over $40,000 in cash and recording prizes to be awarded. Contest judged by persons active in the industry (disc jockeys, publishers and record company executives).

**RICHARD RODGERS PRODUCTION AWARD**, American Academy and Institute of Arts and Letters, 633 W. 155th St., New York NY 10032. (212)368-5900. Assistant to the Executive Director: Lydia Kaim. "This award subsidizes a production in New York City by a nonprofit theater group or professional school of a musical play by composers and writers who are not already established in this field."

**Requirements:** Applicants must be citizens or permanent residents of US. Only one submission per group/writer. Work must be of significant length, but may consist of a group of smaller, related pieces. Deadline: November 1. SASE for application form and instructions. Material cannot be accepted unless accompanied by an application form.

**Awards:** Production award of $80,000 to be used within the year the award is granted.

**SONGSEARCH CONTEST & CONCERT**, 6772 Hollywood Blvd., Hollywood CA 90028. (213)463-7178. SongSearch Director: Billy James. Presented annually by Songwriters Resources and Services. Different sponsors each year; the 1982 competition was sponsored by International Creative Management, Shure, and the BAM music magazine network. Deadline: September. Open to everyone. Nominal entry fee. For more information, send a self-addressed stamped envelope marked "SongSearch entry" after April.

**Purpose:** To draw national attention to the emergence of new music in our culture, and to give new songwriters the opportunity to have their work evaluated by professionals and presented to the industry and the general public as the best of America's new songs. Highlight of the contest is a concert where SongSearch winners perform their songs (or hear them performed).

**Requirements:** "A song is defined as being words and music. Any new song is eligible if a recorded version has not been released for sale to the public before the winners are notified, on or about November 1."

**Categories:** Rock/new wave (from rock-and-roll to country rock to heavy metal to the most urban new wave songs); gospel/inspirational (songs of a religious or spiritual nature); pop/adult contemporary (pop songs with a softer sound that might appeal to an older audience; includes crossover type songs that might be performed by Anne Murray, Kenny Rogers, Lionel Richie, Dan Fogelberg and Little River Band); country/folk (songs in the style of Johnny Cash, Tammy Wynette, Waylon Jennings, Dolly Parton, Oak Ridge Boys and the like, as well as folk songs, bluegrass songs and songs on traditional instruments such as autoharps, zithers and dulcimers); black-oriented (songs with funky rhythms and/or black dialect in the style of Kool & The Gang, Shalamar and some Doobie Brothers; also includes blues and reggae, as well as songs in a jazz vocal style); and topical (songs of a topical nature or that have social relevance in the styles of Bob Dylan, Tom Lehrer, Malvina Reynolds, The Clash, and Phil Ochs; winner will receive the special Helen King Award, given in memory of Helen King, founder of SRS). Please refer to these descriptions, as any song may be entered in more than one category.

**Awards:** Six category winners will receive $1,000 cash awards and certificates. One grand prize winner, selected from the six category winners, will receive a major sponsor award of an additional $4,000.

**THE UNIVERSITY OF MICHIGAN PROFESSIONAL THEATRE PROGRAM**, The Marshall Award, The Michigan League, Ann Arbor MI 48109. (313)763-5213. Contact: Associate Director. Musical theater contest. Gives 1 or more major award each year.

**Awards:** $2,000 maximum to writers of an original full-length musical theater script. Submit 3 manuscripts and cassettes of songs. Does not return unsolicited material. Reports in May of each year. Deadline: January 31 (each year).

**WORLD POPULAR SONG FESTIVAL**, Yamaha Music Foundation, 3-24-22, Shimo Meguro, Meguro-ku, Tokyo, 153, Japan. Contact: Festival Committee.
**Requirements:** Entry must be an original song, which has never been published or performed in public. Send for deadlines and application.
**Awards:** Awards include Grand Prize, Best Song Awards, Most Outstanding Performance Awards and Outstanding Song Awards. Cash award, cetificate of honor and medallion are given to the winners.
**Tips:** "Irrespective of categories of the application songs, quality of the song and the excellence of singer's interpretation are accounted much of."

# Organizations and Clubs

A major benefit of membership in a club or professional organization is access to specialized information and publications. Organizations often serve as information clearinghouses, forums for idea exchanges among members, and sources of market information. Some organizations also sponsor workshops, conferences and seminars; some make grants to songwriters; some sponsor contests; and the Nashville Songwriters Association International (NSAI) even critiques members' songs by mail—free. Read the Close-up of Doug Thiele in this section. A songwriter and member of the Board of Directors of Songwriters Resources and Services (SRS), Thiele talks about what an organization can do for songwriters."

The problem is that there are not nearly enough local songwriter clubs. If there is one in your town you can learn about it from other songwriters or musicians. If there is none in your town, why not start one? SRS and the NSAI are both National organizations that will forward information on starting a songwriting group in your area.

Since success as a songwriter depends on national acceptance, it's very important that you consider joining at least one national organization or club. Association with professional groups sometimes helps build your professional image. Their newsletters will keep you informed of happenings and trends in the industry that affect you as a songwriter. Annual (sometimes more frequent) get-togethers for seminars, workshops, awards dinners, etc. are informative and inspiring and give you a chance to meet songwriters from across the US and foreign countries as well. What's more, an organization can serve as a liaison between you and some of the people you deal with, and can sometimes act as your representative in certain kinds of disputes.

To choose the national organization(s) of most benefit to you, read each listing carefully, noticing the membership description and programs offered. Each lists its services, activities and requirements for membership. For more information, write to the individual organizations that interest you.

**THE ACADEMY OF COUNTRY MUSIC,** #915, 6255 Sunset Blvd., Box 508, Hollywood CA 90028. (213)462-2351. Executive Secretary: Fran Boyd. For "professional persons connected with the country music industry. We have a separate membership for fans. For professional membership the person must be affiliated with the country music industry in some manner." Offers newsletter and showcases. "Purpose is to promote country music."

**AMERICAN FEDERATION OF MUSICIANS,** 1500 Broadway, New York NY 10036. (212)869-1330. Membership available to all qualified musicians and vocalists in the United States and Canada. "The American Federation of Musicians of the United States and Canada is the largest entertainment union in the world and exists solely for the advancement of live music and the benefit of its 280,000 members. In addition to enhancing employment opportunities for members the AFM aids members in negotiating contracts; enforces employers' observance of working conditions and wage scales; arbitrates members' claims at no cost to members; protects musicians from unfavorable legislation at the federal, state and local levels; negotiates pension, welfare and retirement benefits; offers instrument insurance to members; offers free job referral service to members who are seeking employment with traveling groups; and keeps membership informed of happenings in the business through its publication *International Musician*. Members also receive numerous benefits provided by each local." Initiation fees vary; a small percentage of work dues are contributed by members and local dues average $24/year. Write for further information or contact AFM local nearest you."

**THE AMERICAN GUILD OF AUTHORS & COMPOSERS (AGAC/The Songwriters Guild),** Suite 1113, 6430 Sunset Blvd., Hollywood CA 90028. (213)462-1108. Regional Director: Jack Segal. Serves songwriters. Members are pre-professional and professional songwriters, composers, lyricists, melodists, film and TV scorers. No eligibility requirements other than the "desire to be a songwriter."

Applications accepted year-round. Offers instruction, lectures, newsletter and workshops. "AGAC is a protective and advisory agency for songwriters."

**AGAC/The Songwriters Guild**, 40 W. 57th St., New York NY 10019. (212)757-8833. West Coast: 6430 Sunset Blvd., Hollywood CA 90028. (213)462-1108. Nashville: United Artist Tower, 50 Music Square W., Nashville TN 37203. (615)329-1782. Founded as the Songwriter's Protective Association in 1931, name changed to American Guild of Authors and Composers in 1958. The name was expanded to AGAC/The Songwriters Guild in 1982. President: George David Weiss. Executive Director: Lewis M. Bachman. National Projects Director: Bob Leone. West Coast Regional Director: Jack Segal. Nashville Regional Director: Susan Loudermilk. "A full member must be a published songwriter. An associate member is any unpublished songwriter with a desire to learn more about the business and craft of songwriting. The third class of membership comprises estates of deceased writers. The AGAC contract is conceded to be the best available in the industry, having the greatest number of built-in protections for the songwriter. The guild's Royalty Collection Plan makes certain that prompt and accurate payments are made to writers. The ongoing Audit Program makes periodic checks of publishers' books. For the self-publisher, the Catalogue Administration Plan (CAP) relieves a writer of the paperwork of publishing for a fee lower than the prevailing industry rates. The Copyright Renewal Service informs members a year in advance of a song's renewal date. Other services include workshops in New York and Los Angeles, free ASKAPRO rap sessions with industry pros (see Workshops), critique sessions, collaborator service and newsletters. In addition AGAC reviews your songwriter contract on request (AGAC or otherwise); fights to strengthen songwriters' rights and to increase writers' royalties by supporting legislation which directly affects copyright; offers a group medical and life insurance plan; issues news bulletins with essential information for songwriters; provides a songwriter collaboration service for younger writers; financially evaluates catalogs of copyrights in connection with possible sale and estate planning; operates an estates administration service; and maintains a nonprofit educational foundation (The AGAC Foundation)."

**AMERICAN GUILD OF MUSIC**, Box 3, Downers Grove IL 60515. (312)968-0173. Executive Secretary: Elmer Herrick. For musicians and students. Members are music studio operators, teachers, students all interested in teaching and performing. Offers competitions, instruction, lectures, newsletter, performance opportunities and workshops. "Purpose is to improve teaching methods, promote interest in string instruments, accordion, etc."

**AMERICAN MECHANICAL RIGHTS ASSOCIATION**, 250 W. 57th St., New York NY 10107. (212)246-4077. Executive Director: Mrs. R.W. Miller. Members include songwriters and music publishers from the US, Canada and 18 European countries. Applicants must have a record released in the US. Purpose is to collect mechanical, synchronization and background royalties.

**AMERICAN MUSIC CENTER, INC.**, Room 300, 250 W. 54th St., New York NY 10019. (212)247-3121. Executive Director: Margaret Jory. For musicians and composers. Members are "composers of American music, as well as critics, publishers and performers and others interested in supporting AMC's purposes." Offers newsletter, workshops, library of classical music and reference services. Purpose is "to increase knowledge about and interest in serious American contemporary music." Members receive AMC *Newsletter* quarterly, discounts on other AMC publications and invitation to annual members party.

**AMERICAN MUSIC CONFERENCE**, 1000 Skokie Blvd., Wilmette IL 60091. (312)251-1600. President: Bill Peterson. Executive Director: J. Roman Babiak. National nonprofit association for expanding the future of music. Membership includes companies and associations from musical instrument manufacturers and music publishers to educators and organizations of professional musicians. Offers competitions, publications and music promotional materials. "Purpose is to educate the public in the benefits of lifetime participation in music; to foster interest in the extension of music education in the schools; to increase appreciation of the value of music in the home, the church and the community; and to give recognition to the development of musical activities." Co-sponsor of the Original Song Festival, an annual songwriting competition.

**AMERICAN SOCIETY OF COMPOSERS, AUTHORS AND PUBLISHERS**, 1 Lincoln Plaza, New York NY 10023. (212)595-3050. Director of Membership: Paul S. Adler. Membership Department Staff: Lorraine Gillan, Rick Morrison, Lisa Schmidt, Bill Velez. Members are songwriters, composers and music publishers. Applicants must "have at least one song copyrighted for associate membership; have at least one song published, commercially recorded, or performed in media licensed by the Society for full membership." Purpose: "ASCAP is a nonprofit, membership-owned, performing right licensing organization that licenses its members' nondramatic musical compositions for public

performance and distributes the fees collected from such licensing to its members based on a scientific random sample survey of performances." Primary value is "as a clearinghouse, giving users a practical and economical bulk licensing system and its members a vehicle through which the many thousands of users can be licensed and the members paid royalties for the use of their material.".
**Tips:** "The Society sponsors a series of writers' workshops in Los Angeles, Nashville and New York; open to members and nonmembers. Grants to composers available to members and nonmembers. Contact the public relations or membership departments of the New York office or the following branch offices: 6430 Sunset Blvd., Los Angeles CA 90028; 2 Music Square W., Nashville TN 37203; 52 Haymarket St., London, SW1Y4RP, England."

**ARIZONA SONGWRITERS ASSOCIATION**, Box 678, Phoenix AZ 85001. (602)841-6397. Membership Director: Joanne Sherwood. Serves songwriters and musicians. Our members are ages 14-73. Most are both lyricists and composers; some are lyricists only. Many are artist/songwriters. Members should have a real interest in music and be willing to contribute talent and time to some of our special events. Applications accepted year-round. Offers competitions, instruction, lectures, library (limited), newsletter, performance opportunities and workshops (monthly); and two 6-8 week showcases (spring and fall) that include performer/songwriter competitions. "Our purpose is educational: to teach all phases of songwriting."

**BLACK MUSIC ASSOCIATION**, 1500 Locust St., Philadelphia PA 19102. (215)545-8600. President: Dick Griffey. Executive Director: George Ware. For songwriters, musicians and anyone interested in music, entertainment, and arts industries. Members are individuals, companies and organizations involved in the music industry. Offers lectures, newsletter, workshops, industry contact resource center, seminars and an annual conference. "Purpose is the dedication to the advancement, enrichment, encouragement and recognition of black music."

**CANADIAN ACADEMY OF RECORDING ARTS & SCIENCES (CARAS)**, 89 Bloor St. E., Toronto, Ontario, Canada M4W 1A9. (416)922-5029. National Co-ordinator: Daisy C. Falle. Serves songwriters and musicians. Membership is open to all employees (including support staff) in: broadcasting, record companies and producers, personal managers, recording artists, recording engineers, arrangers, composers, music publishers, album designers, promoters, talent and booking agents, record retailers, rack jobbers, distributors, recording studios and other music industry related professions (on approval). Applicants must be affliliated with the recording industry. Applications accepted year-round. Offers newsletter, performance opportunities, social outings, workshops and annual Juno Awards show. "CARAS strives to foster the development of the Canadian music and recording industries and to contribute toward higher artistic standards." Fees: $30/year.

**CANADIAN RECORDING INDUSTRY ASSOCIATION**, 89 Bloor St. E., Toronto, Ontario, Canada M4W 1A9. (416)967-7272. President: Brian Robertson. Membership open to record company executives, independent record producers and recording studios (engineers and producers). Applications accepted year-round. "CRIA is the 'voice' of the recording industry in Canada. Its 40 members represent over 98% of the sound recordings manufactured and sold in this country. The association represents the industry on many levels including communication with government, international liaison with music and recording industry organizations around the world, the control of record and tape piracy and other legal matters, and the direction of industry marketing programs such as the certification of gold and platinum records."

**CANADIAN SONGWRITERS ASSOCIATION**, Suite 1400, 1 Nicholas St., Ottawa, Ontario, Canada K1N 7B7. (613)234-7839. President: Robert Dunn. "We have an open-door policy to all songwriters and to those people in the industry who are not songwriters but who take an interest in the songwriter and his work. We offer a newsletter, seminars, forums, and multi-day workshops, as well as educate aspiring songwriters in how to best reach their goals in the music business."

**COMPOSERS, ARRANGERS AND SONGWRITERS OF KANSAS**, 117 W. 8th St., Hays KS 67601. (913)625-9634. Administrator: Mark Meckel. Serves songwriters, musicians, arrangers and lyricists. Membership open to "anyone desiring information on the business of songwriting, copyrights or marketing—from professional musicians to housewives." No eligibility requirements other than "a desire for a career in the music industry." Applications accepted year-round. Offers competitions, library, newsletter, personal consultations and demo tape discounts. "Our purpose is to educate members about the business end of the music industry. Our newsletter profiles markets and offers technical articles." Fees: $15/year.
**Tips:** "We are working toward area song contests in conjunction with local radio stations and also have a *homegrown* album project in the works."

## Organizations and Clubs 363

**CONNECTICUT SONGWRITERS ASSOCIATION**, Box 544, Waterford CT 06385. (203)447-3665. President: Don Donegan. "We are an educational, nonprofit organization dedicated to improving the art and craft of original music. We offer a monthly newsletter (subscription rate for non-Connecticut residents is $15 per year/12 issues), monthly seminars and song critique sessions, performing opportunities at songwriter showcases, song screening service, song tape library, discounts, awards and social outings. No eligibility requirements. Applications accepted year round. Ages range from 12 to 70. Annual membership categories are: Individual $30, Student and Senior Citizen $20, Organizations $60, Sustaining $100, Benefactor $250, Lifetime $500. ("All memberships include newsletter subscription and are tax deductible to the extent allowed by law.")
**Tips:** "Members can learn about the music business, improve their songcrafting skills, gain performing opportunities and make collaboration contacts."

**COUNTRY MUSIC FOUNDATION OF COLORADO**, Box 19435, Denver CO 80219. (303)936-7762. President: Gladys Hart. Serves songwriters and musicians, promoters, publishers and record companies to assist them in learning the proper method of presenting new material to the publisher. "The membership roster comes from the country music industry in general with special interest in the annual Colorado Country Music Festival." Offers lectures, newsletter, performance opportunities and an annual convention. Purpose is "to promote country music in all facets of the industry. The association provides new artists with information on the basic fundamentals essential for career advancement. Songwriters Day will be scheduled to include songwriter/publisher meeting. The evening show will be dedicated to the presentation of new material by bands and artists."
**Tips:** "The Songwriter Award has been added to the presentations at the Annual Colorado Country Music & Trade Convention and is voted on performance and recorded material."

**THE DRAMATISTS GUILD, INC.**, 234 W. 44th St., New York NY 10036. (212)398-9366. Membership Coordinator: Jeremiah Williamson. Membership: over 6,000 playwrights, composers, lyricists and librettists nationwide. "To be a member of the Dramatists Guild, you must have completed a dramatic work (a one-act or full-length play or component part—book, music or lyrics—of a musical), whether produced or not. Offers field trips, lectures, library, newsletter, seminars and workshops, and legal advice and counseling on business problems related to playwright's work. "As the professional association of playwrights, composers, and lyricists, the Guild protects the rights of all theater writers, and improves the conditions under which they work. Additionally, the Guild encourages and nurtures the work of dramatists in the US through its program of seminars and workshops."

**GOSPEL MUSIC ASSOCIATION**, 38 Music Square W., Nashville TN 37203. (615)242-0303. Executive Director: Don Butler. For songwriters, broadcasters, musicians, merchandisers, promoters, performance licensing agencies, church staff musicians, talent agencies, record companies and publishers. Offers lectures, newsletter, workshops and awards programs.

**THE LOS ANGELES SONGWRITERS SHOWCASE**, (formerly The Alternative Chorus Songwriters Showcase), 6772 Hollywood Blvd., Hollywood CA 90028. (213)462-1382. Co-Directors: Len H. Chandler Jr. and John Braheny. General Manager: Lynda Careb. "The Los Angeles Songwriters Showcase (LASS), a nonprofit service organization for songwriters, auditions more than 150 songwriters/month, both live and by tape. Less than 6% of the songs auditioned are presented in a showcase, making it a focus for record industry people looking for new songs and writer/artists. Writers must participate in the performances of their own material. This unique service is free and is sponsored by Broadcast Music, Inc. (BMI). LASS Also provides counseling, conducts lectures, and interviews top music industry professionals at the Showcase. Two new features have been added to the Wednesday night Showcase: Cassette Roulette in which a different publisher every week critiques songs submitted on cassette that night; and Pick-A-Thon in which a different producer every week screens songs for his/her current recording projects. Both events take place at 6353 Hollywood Boulevard every Wednesday night in front of an audience of songwriters and music industry; there is no prescreening necessary for either. LASS also produces an annual Songwriters Expo in November." Membership: $40/year. Included in both "general" and "professional" membership benefits are: priorities to have tapes listened to first at Pitch-A-Thon sessions; discounts on numerous items such as blank tapes, books, demo production services, tapes of Songwriters Expo sessions and other seminars; and discounts on admission to the weekly showcase as well as $1 off on each $4/per song critiquing fee. Professional membership is by invitation or audition only and features special private Pitcha-A-Thon sessions and referrals.

**MEMPHIS SONGWRITERS ASSOCIATION**, 1024 Whitehaven Pk. Circle, Memphis TN 38116. President: Ken Thomas. Vice President: Mary Sandridge. Secretary: Joyce Goodwin. For songwriters, musicians and artists; "we have people from all walks of life, including amateur and professional songwriters, publishing company executives and recording company people." Offers competitions, lec-

tures, newsletter, performance opportunities, social outings and contact lists and guides. Purpose is to "assist the songwriter in contact information and to guide and direct the songwriter in the basic steps of songwriting." Fees: $15/year.
**Tips:** "We have an annual competition in which we have awards for the best original songs members have written. We solicit tapes for this once a year and 12 songs are chosen from this screening to be presented before a panel of judges."

**MISSOURI SONGWRITERS ASSOCIATION, INC.**, 3711 Andora Pl., St. Louis MO 63125. (314)894-3354. President: John G. Nolan, Jr. Serves songwriters and musicians. "We have members ranging from ages 14 through 87, which includes professionals, amateurs and people who write songs just for the enjoyment it provides." No eligibility requirements. Applications accepted year-round. Offers competitions, field trips, instruction, lectures, library, newsletter, performance opportunities, social outings, workshops, seminars, showcases, collaborator referral and musician referral. "The main purpose of our nonprofit organization is to educate our members with respect to the business and the artistic sides of the craft of songwriting. Songwriters gain support from their fellow members when they join the MSA and the organization provides 'strength in numbers' when approaching music industry professionals, along with (of course) the promotional and educational benefits we offer." Fees: $15/year.

**MUSCLE SHOALS MUSIC ASSOCIATION**, Box 2009, Muscle Shoals AL 35662. (205)381-1442. Executive Director: William M. "Bill" Jarnigan. For songwriters, musicians, publishers, promoters, engineers, artists, producers, studio owners and "others interested in music and recording." Members are "from all over the world. Age limits run from 14 to 82 years old. We have over 400 active members with our board of directors meeting monthly. There are no limitations on membership if applications are approved by the board of directors." Offers competitions, newsletter, performance opportunities, social outings, workshops and seminars. "We have an annual songwriter's showcase for songwriters who belong to the association. We have a monthly songwriter's workshop and our newsletter is quarterly." Purpose is to "assist our membership in obtaining employment; hold workshops; present at least four concerts yearly using our own members; and to hold an annual seminar with top record executives and independent producers giving lectures and serving on panels. We have proven instructors at the workshops who have a minimum of 10 songs published and who have written at least 3 chart tunes." Fee: $100/year for professional and associate firms; $25/year for professional and associate individuals; and $10/year for students. "Our year runs from January 1 to December 31. Applications are accepted any time but we do not prorate dues, that is, the appropriate fee is due regardless of the date joined."

**MUSIC INDUSTRY EDUCATORS ASSOCIATION (MIEA)**, Suite 301, 1435 Bleury St., Montreal, Quebec, Canada H3A 2H7. Purpose: to establish and maintain standards of music industry education throughout the world; to encourage and facilitate interaction between the educational community and the music industry; to foster interaction among individuals involved with music industry education; to assist institutions involved in the development of programs in music industry education; and to promote music industry related research, scholarship and outstanding achievement. Offers quarterly newsletter, seminars and workshops, annual conventions in major recording center, e.g. Nashville. Membership: individual, $25/year; student, $5/year; pre-college or 2-year colleges, $50/year; 4-year and graduate colleges, $100/year; national or international commercial music industry, $250/year; regional commercial music industry, $150/year; and local commercial music industry, $75/year. Write for application and more information.

*****MUSICIANS CONTACT SERVICE**, 6605 Sunset Blvd., Hollywood CA 90028. (213)467-2191. For songwriters, musicians, agents, managers, production companies, record labels and recording studios seeking each other for collaboration. Average age of members is 25-35 (any age acceptable); any and all styles of music are acceptable. Offers performance opportunities. "We are a placement/referral service for musical performance where groups can reach musicians and vice versa. We have hundreds of resumes of composers and lyricists seeking one another—a way for them to find each other for collaboration."

**NASHVILLE SONGWRITERS ASSOCIATION, INTERNATIONAL**, 803 18th Ave. S, Nashville TN 37203. (615)361-5004. Executive Director: Maggie Cavender. For songwriters. Applicants may apply for 1 of 2 memberships; "active membership is having had at least one song published with an affiliate of BMI, ASCAP or SESAC. An associate membership is for the yet-to-be-published writer and others interested in the songwriter." Offers newsletter, counseling, seminars, symposium, workshop, showcases and awards. "Purpose is to gain recognition for the songwriter, to serve any purpose toward this recognition and to pursue this on a worldwide basis."

# Close-up

**Doug Thiele**
Songwriter

"Songwriter organizations take songwriters out of the subjective closet, where we all start writing, and show them a more objective picture of not only how songs are written, but how the business operates," says songwriter Doug Thiele. "Also, whether aspiring, professional, or amateur songwriters, the larger organizations have a range of helpful services to make things easier for them in this very difficult business."

Thiele, whose songs have been recorded by artists such as Dolly Parton, Cristy Lane and Mary MacGregor, is on the staff of Songwriters Resources and Services, a member of the board of directors of the Academy of Country Music, and director of the songwriter program at Dick Grove Music Workshops.

Although Thiele relocated to L.A. from the Midwest several years ago, he says songwriters can pursue their craft, successfully, without moving to a music center. "Regional cable TV, advertising and recording activities are becoming increasingly important," says Thiele. "In the near future it may even be that major labels in the music centers will look to the best acts in Minneapolis or Phoenix or Tallahassee for the artists they sign, because those acts will already have a proven regional track record. That means writers for those acts will have a greater chance of attaining national success than ever before."

Thiele also sees foreign markets as a viable alternative to submitting songs to the US music centers. "The bottom line is that it's getting more difficult to shop and place songs in the music centers of this country. But a songwriter can send a great song with universal appeal to a publisher or record company in England or Australia or New Zealand. There's even a market for English-language songs in non-English-speaking countries—Japan, for instance, and European countries.

"When submitting songs to foreign markets, the rules are pretty much the same as for the US. But foreign markets do have their own trends and fads and their own lyrical attitudes. English-speaking countries looking for songs from the US are at least partially looking for American sounds. Demo the song so that it sounds like an American tune, but an American tune that an act like Little River Band or Abba might perform.

"These are interesting times for the music industry," says Thiele. "The wheat is being separated from the chaff. Songwriters who are serious about their craft—addicted, as many of us are—will continue whether the industry has trouble or not. My best advice is keep writing songs you believe in, keep pitching them, and let the industry go where it will."

**NATIONAL ACADEMY OF POPULAR MUSIC**, 1 Times Square, New York NY 10036. (212)221-1252. General Manager: W. Randall Poe. President: Sammy Cahn. Curator: Oscar Brand. Manager/Archives: Frankie MacCormick. Serves songwriters, musicians, school groups and other visitors to the Songwriters' Hall of Fame Museum. Members are songwriters and those interested in songwriting. Offers library, research on songs and songwriters, special exhibits honoring songwriters and newsletter. Purpose: To honor and recognize the creators of American popular songs, to call attention to the important role of popular music in American life and history and to maintain a library and archive of music and music-related material. Membership year: July 1-June 30.

**NATIONAL MUSIC PUBLISHERS' ASSOCIATION, INC.**, 110 E. 59th St., New York NY 10022. (212)751-1930. Chairman: Salvatore T. Chiantia. President: Leonard Feist. Trade association for popular music publishers. Eligible members include "any person, firm, corporation or partnership actively engaged in the business of publishing music in the U.S.A. for a period of at least one year, whose musical publications have been used or distributed on a commercial scale or who assumes the financial risk involved in the normal publication of musical works." Offers newsletter, workshops, special reports and information.

**PACIFIC NORTHWEST SONGWRITERS ASSOCIATION**, Box 98324, Seattle WA 98188. (206)824-1568. "We are a nonprofit association, dedicated to serving the songwriters of the Pacific Northwest. Our focus is on professional songwriting for today's commercial markets. We offer monthly workshops, newsletters and a music directory. Membership: $15/year.

**PERFORMING RIGHTS ORGANIZATION OF CANADA LIMITED**, 41 Valleybrook Dr., Don Mills, Ontario, Canada M3B 2S6. (416)445-8700. Writer/Publisher: Charlie Gall. Publicity Manager: Nancy Gyokeres. For Canadian songwriters and publishers. Offers competitions, magazine, workshops, advice and direction. Purpose is to collect performance royalties and distribute them to songwriters and publishers.

**SANTA BARBARA SONGWRITERS' GUILD**, Box 2238, Santa Barbara CA 93120. (805)962-9333. President: Steven A. Williams. Estab. 1981. The Guild is a nonprofit organization for aspiring songwriters, performers, those interested in the music industry and anyone interested in original music. The Guild sponsors monthly showcases and songwriting workshops, plus classes and lectures on studio recording, music and copyright law, record production, song marketing, music composition, lyric writing, songwriting and also provide a directory of music services and organizations. Membership is $25/year.

**SESAC, INC.**, 10 Columbus Circle, New York NY 10019. (212)586-3450. Branches: 11 Music Circle S., Nashville TN 37203; 9000 Sunset Blvd., Los Angeles CA 90069. Vice President of Affiliation: Vincent Candilora, New York. Membership Director, Los Angeles: Kathy Cooney. Vice President/Director of Country Music: Dianne Petty, Nashville. Vice President/Director of Gospel Music: Jim Black, Nashville. For writers and publishers who have their works performed by radio, television, nightclubs, cable TV, etc. in all types of music. "Prospective affiliates are requested to present a demo tape of their works which is reviewed by our Screening Committee." Purpose of organization is to collect and distribute prformance royalties to all active affiliates. Send membership applications to New York or Los Angeles for all types of music; contact Nashville office for country or gospel music."

**SONGWRITERS RESOURCES AND SERVICES**, 6772 Hollywood Blvd., Hollywood CA 90028. (213)463-7178. President: Pat Luboff. A nonprofit organization dedicated to the protection and education of songwriters. Membership is $30/year. Offers songbank, group legal services, hotline, counseling, forums, song review, songwriters network, tip sheets, workshops, pamphlets and newsletter. Some services restricted to members and include workshops on lyric writing, harmony and composition, songwriting, song evaluation, performance and others as the need and interest develop; counseling, hotline, library, *Open Ears* (bimonthly listing of publishers and producers, type of material they're looking for, and how and whom to present it to), collaborator's and artist's directories, lead sheet service and a group legal plan. "We answer any of our members' music-related questions; as the nation's largest organization exclusively for songwriters, we speak on their behalf."

**SOUTH BAY SONGWRITERS ASSOCIATION**, Box 50643, Palo Alto CA 94303. (415)327-8296. Director: Sandra Schwab. Serves songwriters and musicians. "Our 350 members are lyricists and composers from ages 16-70 who have varied backgrounds. There are several professional songwriters along with those people who are at the earliest stages of writing. We also have several businesses in the community that have joined SBSA to further advance the strength of the music community." No eligibility

requirements. Applications accepted year-round. Offers annual Northern California Songwriting Conference and Contest, instruction, lectures, library, newsletter, performance opportunities and workshops. "Our purpose is to teach the songwriter as much about the art and craft of songwriting (as well as the business of music) as is needed to promote himself and his songs."
**Tips:** "Personal contacts are essential in this business; SBSA's functions draw both local talent and nationally recognized names together. This is a trememdous value to writers outside a major music center. It is an organization where all types of talent can team up for virtually any project."

**THEATRE COMMUNICATIONS GROUP, INC.**, 355 Lexington Ave., New York NY 10017. (212)697-5230. Serves composers, lyricists, librettists for the theater. "TCG has a constituency of nonprofit professional theaters for which it is the national organization. It provides services in casting, personnel and management, as well as numerous publications and literary services, to organizations and individuals. TCG publishes a monthly journal, *TheatreCommunications*, *New Plays USA* (anthology series); *Artsearch* (biweekly newsletter), and provides employment information for theater artists, managers and technicians. The Literary Services department publishes the yearly *Dramatists Sourcebook* and also operates *Plays in Process* (a script distribution service). Writers of musicals may benefit from this program if their works receive full production at a TCG constituent theater and have not been otherwise published. The Publications Department is reponsible for *Theatre Profiles*, the biennial reference guide to America's nonfprofit professional theatre, and *Theatre Directory*, the annual pocket-sized contact resource of theatres and related organizations. Criteria for membership in the TCG include longevity of operation, professional orientation and standards, and size of operating budgets. Membership benefits include discounts on TCG publications and services; free subscriptions to *TheatreCommunications*; invitations to TCG workshops and conferences; access to TCG personnel files and information services. While individuals cannot become members, TCG's many publications are available to all."

**VOLUNTEER LAWYERS FOR THE ARTS**, Suite 711, 1560 Broadway, New York NY 10036. (212)575-1150. Administrator: Barbara Sieck Taylor. For songwriters, musicians and all performing, visual, literary and fine arts and artists. Offers legal assistance and representation to eligible individual artists and arts organizations who are unable to afford private counsel. Also provides a growing list of manuals and guides on arts-related issues. In addition, there are affiliates nationwide who handle local arts organizations and artists and their problems in their immediate areas." Offers conferences lectures, library and workshops.

# Publications of Interest

This section is divided into two groups. The first lists magazines that inform songwriters about songwriting and the music industry in general. These periodicals contain articles on songwriters, publishers, record company executives, how-to pieces and trends in the industry.

Before investing in a subscription, read what each editor says about his magazine. Some are of great interest to musicians as well as songwriters while others are aimed at only songwriters or a particular type of music (e.g., country, rock).

Many of these magazines can be purchased at newsstands. This gives you a chance to look first, then decide which benefit you as a songwriter or songwriter/musician. If you can't find a certain publication on the newsstand, write the publisher for more information.

Books are the second part of the section and answer many questions about the actual process of writing songs, along with detailed information on different aspects of the industry (contracts, copyright, etc.). Some may be available at your local library or bookstores. If not, write the publisher whose name is listed with each book.

# Periodicals

**BILLBOARD**, (The International Music/Record/Tape Newsweekly), Billboard Publications, Inc., 12th Floor, 9000 Sunset Blvd., Los Angeles CA 90069. (213)273-7040. Subscription address: Billboard Subscriber Service, Box 1413, Riverton NJ 08077. (609)786-1669. Vice President of Circulation: Ann Haire. Promotion Director: Elvira Lopez. Weekly magazine; 108 pages. "*Billboard* documents the most recent developments in the music business, every week." Includes record charts, industry information, and "the thousands of weekly events" that tell what is happening in the music business.

**CASH BOX MAGAZINE**, Cash Box Publishing Co., Inc., Suite 930, 6363 Sunset Blvd., Hollywood CA 90028. (213)464-8241. Circulation Manager: Theresa Tortosa. Subscription address: 1775 Broadway, New York NY 10019. Weekly magazine; 75 pages. "*Cash Box* is an international music trade weekly. We provide record charts, news and information on executives, companies and artists that are making news, as well as an all-inclusive radio section. We also provide features for new and developing artists."

**MUSIC CITY NEWS**, Suite 601, 50 Music Square W., Box 22975, Nashville TN 37202. Monthly country music publication focusing on the Nashville music scene; 40 pages. Circulation: 100,000. Host of the Music City News Cover Awards and the Top Country Hits of the Year Awards for songwriters, both nationwide television programs. Also publishes articles on Nashville songwriters and one songwriters special issue each year.

**THE MUSIC CONNECTION**, Suite 201, 6640 Sunset Blvd., Hollywood CA 90028. (213)462-5772. Contact: Subscription Dept. Biweekly magazine; 48 pages. "*The Music Connection* is a local musicians' trade magazine. Departments include a gig guide connecting musicians and songwriters with agents, producers, publishers and club owners; a free classified section; music personal ads; interviews with music industry executives and major artists; and articles on songwriting, publishing and the music business."

**MUSIC MAKERS**, The Sunday School Board of the Southern Baptist Convention, 127 9th Ave. N, Nashville TN 37234. (615)251-2000. Contact: Church Music Dept. Music Editor: Vicki Hancock Wright. Quarterly magazine; 36 pages. Publishes "music for use by 1st, 2nd and 3rd graders in choir at church. Includes spiritual concept and musical concept songs, plus stories and musical activities."

**MUSICIAN MAGAZINE**, Amordian Press, Inc., Billboard Publications, Inc. Box 701, Gloucester MA 01930. (617)281-3110. President: Gordon P. Baird. Executive Editor: Sam Holdsworth. Magazine published 12 times/year; 108 pages. "The editorial thrust is directed at the generation of young and old rockers who have grown into more mature forms of rock, jazz and jazz/rock. This is a magazine for those who are serious about their music, both as a player and as a listener."

**SIGMA ALPHA IOTA QUARTERLY: PAN PIPES**, Sigma Alpha Iota, National Music Fraternity for Women, 2820 Webber St., Sarasota FL 33579. National Executive Offices: 4119 Rollins Ave., Des Moines, IA 50312. Editor: Margaret Maxwell. For musicians at undergraduate, graduate and professional levels. Magazine published 4 times/year (Fall, Winter, Spring and Summer); 24 pages except 48 pages/Winter issue. "We cover articles with the emphasis on the American composer. The Winter issue is devoted to American Music and the American composers, with a section devoted to the latest publications of their music."

**TRUSTY TIPS FROM THE COLONEL**, Trusty International, Rt. 1, Box 100, Nebo KY 42441. (502)249-3194. President: Elsie Childers. Monthly 1-page newsletter. "Producers and artists who need material contact us and we fill an 8½x11 sheet full of names and addresses of people needing songs for recording sessions or shows and types of song material needed. Subscribers to our sheet have been placing their songs regularly through tips from our tip sheet. Sample copy for SASE and 25¢."

**WASHINGTON INTERNATIONAL ARTS LETTER**, Allied Business Consultants, Inc., 325 Pennsylvania Ave., Washington DC 20003. (202)488-0800. Business Manager: T. Snyder. Publisher: Daniel Millsaps. Magazine published 10 times/year; 8 pages. "WAIL concentrates on discovering new sources of funding for the arts and keeping up with policy changes in funding by governments, private foundations, and businesses which give out grants to individual creative and performing artists. We publish in addition, the Arts Patronage Series, which are directories where all this information is under one cover and updated periodically. We are the major source of information about funding for the arts in the US. Songwriters and composers can get grants for their work through our information and keep informed about Congressional actions which affect their lives. Areas covered include vexatious problems of taxation, etc. as well as how to get money for projects."

**YOUNG MUSICIANS**, The Sunday School Board of the Southern Baptist Convention, 127 9th Ave. N., Nashville TN 37234. (615)251-2000. Contact: Church Music Dept. Music Editor: Vicki Hancock Wright. Quarterly magazine; 52 pages. Publishes music for use by 4th, 5th and 6th graders in church choirs. Includes spiritual and musical concept songs and activities, plus music insert containing four or five anthems. "This is an excellent publication to which songwriters whose interests and skills lie in the area of composing for children may submit their original manuscripts."

# Books

**ARRANGING POPULAR MUSIC**, edited by Genichi Hawakami. 657 pages. Price: $25. Direct orders to Mike Honda, Foundation Liason, Music Education Division of Yamaha International Corp., 6600 Orangethorpe Ave., Buena Park CA 90620.

**BREAKIN IN TO THE MUSIC BUSINESS**, by Alan H. Siegel, entertainment attorney for over 25 years. Published: 1983. 274 pages. Price: $8.95. Talks about how to prepare and present professional quality demo tapes, choosing a competent lawyer and manager, the copyright laws and how they affect the songwriter, royalties, advances and contracts (the economics of the music business), and more. Includes interviews with some of the most influential people in the music business. Published by Cherry Lane Books, Port Chester NY 10573.

**BRINGING IT TO NASHVILLE**, by Michael J. Kosser. The inside information on what it's like to make it as a songwriter in Nashville. Available through the Nashville Songwriter's Association, 25 Music Square W., Nashville TN 37203.

**THE ENCYCLOPEDIA OF THE MUSIC BUSINESS**, by Harvey Rachlin. Published: 1981. 524 pages. Price: $18.95. A comprehensive and lucid reference work with more than 450 entries that cover in meticulous detail all facets of the music business: The Copyright Law, contracts, recording and production, the recording industry, unions and trade associations, technology, and much more. Includes photos, charts, tables, diagrams, and other illustrative material. Published by Harper & Row, 10 E. 53rd St., New York NY 10022.

**IF THEY ASK YOU, YOU CAN WRITE A SONG**, by Al Kasha & Joel Hirschhorn. The A-Zs of how to write songs from two Academy Award-winning songwriters. Published by Simon and Schuster, Inc., 1230 Avenue of the Americas, New York NY 10020.

**HOW I WRITE SONGS (WHY YOU CAN)**, by Tom T. Hall. Tom T. uses his own experiences as a songwriter to demonstrate how you can write songs too. Available through the Nashville Songwriter's Association, 25 Music Square W., Nashville TN 37203.

**HOW TO BE A SUCCESSFUL SONGWRITER**, by Kent McNeel and Mark Luther. Mac Davis, Paul Williams, Henry Mancini and twenty other successful songwriters tell you how they do it. Published by St. Martin's Press, 175 5th Ave., New York NY 10010.

**MAKING IT WITH MUSIC**, by Kenny Rogers and Len Epand. Practical information on forming a group and making it succeed: equipment, recording, touring, songwriting and taking care of your money. Published by Harper & Row, 10 E. 53rd St., New York NY 10022.

**MORE ABOUT THIS BUSINESS OF MUSIC**, by Sidney Shemel and M. William Krasilovsky. A practical guide to five additional areas of the music industry not treated in *This Business of Music*: serious music, background music and transcriptions, tape and tape cartridges, production and sale of printed music, and live performances. Published by Billboard Publications, Inc., 1 Astor Plaza, New York NY 10036.

**THE MUSIC BUSINESS: CAREER OPPORTUNITIES AND SELF-DEFENSE**, by Dick Weissman. Covers all facets of the music industry: how record companies operate, the functions of agents and personal managers, the field of commercials, the roles of the performing and the studio musician, music publishing, contracts, record production, unions, radio, using your college education, and careers in music. Published by Crown Publishers, Inc., 1 Park Ave., New York NY 10016.

**MUSIC TO SELL BY: THE CRAFT OF JINGLE WRITING**, by Antonio Teixeira, Jr. A valuable, easy to read, how-to book on the preparation of jingles and compositions for radio and TV commercials. Published by Berklee Press Publications, 1265 Boylston St., Boston MA 02215.

**THE PLATINUM RAINBOW (How to Succeed in the Music Business Without Selling Your Soul).** "*The Platinum Rainbow* (updated 1982, 239 pages. Price: $9.95) by Grammy Award-winning record producer Bob Monaco and nationally syndicated music columnist James Riodan, gives you an inside look at the recording industry and tells you how to think realistically in a business based on fantasy; how to promote yourself, how to get a manager, producer or agent; how to get free recording time, how to make a deal, how to recognize and record a hit song, how to be a session musician, how to kick your brother out of the band, how to put together the six key elements a record company looks for. There are quotes from some of the biggest names in pop music and a complete analysis of: *The Song*; *The Studio*; *The Stage*; *Demo Or Master*; *Cutting A Record*; *Hooks And Arrangements*; *The Producer*; *The Engineer*; *The Budget*; *The Basic Track*; *Vocals*; *Overdubs*; *The Mix*; *The 24 Track Monster*; *Things You Can Hear But Can't See*; *The Deal*; *The Creative Businessman*; *The Music Attorney*; *The Manager, Agent, Promoter*; *The Artist As Vendor*; *Leverage, Clout And The Ladder*; *Getting A Job With A Record Company*; *Gigs*; *The Golden Reel To Reel And The Platinum Turntable*; *Staying Happy*; *Waiting To Be Discovered And Nine Other Popular Myths About The Music Business*. Also included is a complete and updated directory of record companies, producers, managers, publishers, agents, studios, engineering schools, concert promoters, all the names, addresses and phone numbers of who to contact." Published by Swordsman Press, 15445 Ventura Blvd., Suite 10, Box 5973, Sherman Oaks CA 91413.

**SO YOU WANT TO BE IN MUSIC!**, by Jesse Burt and Bob Ferguson. An inside look at songwriting and the music industry by two Nashville professionals. Available through the Nashville Songwriter's Association, 25 Music Square W., Nashville TN 37203.

**THE SONGWRITER'S GUIDE TO CHORDS AND PROGRESSIONS**, by Joseph R. Lilore. Published: 1982. 48 pages. Price: $4.95. 58 chord outlines, each showing a different principle frequently used in popular music. Includes easy-to-understand charts and all major and minor scales and keys to help give songwriters countless ideas for new and commercially proven chords and progressions. Companion manuscript paper and cassette tape also available. Published by Lionhead Publishing, Box 1272, Clifton NJ 07012.

**THE SONGWRITER'S RHYMING DICTIONARY**, by Sammy Cahn. Published: 1983. 162 pages. Price: $17.95. Cahn gives his ingenious system for organizing end rhymes, and also insights from his own experience as a multi-award-winning legend among songwriters. Published by Facts on File Publications, 460 Park Ave. S., New York NY 10016.

**THE SONGWRITER'S HANDBOOK**, by Harvey Rachlin. Starts with the basic components of a song and covers the entire spectrum of the profession—from the conception of an idea for a song to getting it recorded. Published by Funk & Wagnalls, 10 E. 53rd St., New York NY 10022.

**THE SONGWRITERS' SUCCESS MANUAL**, by Lee Pincus. Answers to many questions including do-it-yourself publishing, how much a songwriter can earn, and four ways songwriters lose money. Published by Music Press, Box 1229, Grand Central Station, New York NY 10017.

**THIS BUSINESS OF MUSIC**, by Sidney Shemel and M. William Krasilovsky. Edited by Paul Ackerman. A practical guide to the music industry for publishers, songwriters, record companies, producers, artists and agents. Published by Billboard Publications, Inc., 1 Astor Plaza, New York NY 10036.

# Workshops

The value of workshops as a source of tips, instruction, evaluation and constructive criticism cannot be emphasized too much. The workshops listed here offer all these things to you and other songwriters who are trying to become better at their craft.

The music centers—Los Angeles, Nashville, and New York—in particular offer workshop opportunities to songwriters. You may want to plan a vacation around attending a workshop in one of these cities and also "pitching" your songs while you're in the area. Some workshops are purposely planned for the summer months just so you can combine vacation time and workshop training.

There may be a university near you which offers workshops and classes (both credit and noncredit) in songwriting. Check the bulletin of one near you. Some of the songwriter organizations listed in this section (AGAC, NSAI and SRS) offer traveling workshops. Contact them for more information about bringing the expertise of top songwriters and industry professionals into or near your own hometown.

To choose a workshop wisely you must know where your weaknesses as a songwriter lie and seek a workshop with a program that can complement the abilities you already have. To help you make that decision, the following workshops describe programs offered, costs, available facilities, program length and average class size.

Most want you to write or call about your interest. They will then reply with brochures giving complete details of their particular programs and an application or registration form.

**AGAC WORKSHOPS**, 40 W. 57th St., New York NY 10019. (212)757-8833. Director of Special Projects: Bob Leone.
**Ask-a-pro:** "2 hour weekly music business rap session to which all writers are welcome. It features industry professionals—publishers, writers, producers, artists—fielding questions from new songwriters." Offered year-round. 40-50/meeting. Each session lasts 2 hours. Charge: free to member, $2 to nonmembers. Phone reservation necessary.
**Hit Songwriting Workshop:** "This workshop is designed to introduce the songwriter to the basics of writing commercial songs, with focus on both lyrics and music. Pop, soul, rock, dance and country songwriting will be discussed. Areas to be covered include formats, titles, themes, hooks, concept records, melody writing and the making of demos." Offered year-round with 10 to 12 in each workshop. Instructor for the Hit Songwriting Workshop is Lou Stallman whose songs have been recorded by Aretha Franklin, Deniece Williams, Laura Nyro, The Supremes, Robert John and many more. Cost: $100 to AGAC members, $130 for non-members to cover ten 2-hour sessions.
**The Craft of Lyric Writing:** Conducted by NYU Adjunct Professor Sheila Davis who has a book in progress on lyric writing soon to be published by Writer's Digest Books. In the college-accredited Basics Course—designed for the new professional, as well as the pre-professional—students learn the 3 classic song forms, the 5 components of a well-written lyric and the top-10 writing principles. Weekly assignments require writing to a form, a title, a theme and a melody, and techniques are stressed that lead to craftsmanship. Beyond The Basics is a continuing seminar/workshop for "graduates" of the Basics Course who have made a career committment to lyric writing. Challenging assignments are criticized in depth and re-writing is required to achieve recordable results. Students receive special exercises to overcome individual writing problems, expand productivity, and develop the third eye of self-criticism. Unique music industry tie-ins afford class members opportunities to write special assignments. Applications to the year-round, 10-week courses must be accompanied by two typed lyrics. Classes are limited to 10-12 students. Cost: $100 to AGAC members; $130 for non-members.
**Song Critique:** Published and ready to be published AGAC songwriters can play one song every other session at the Guild's New York headquarters, 40 W. 57th St., New York NY. These weekly 2 hour sessions start at 5 pm every Thursday night and writers interested in performing their songs must call the Guild (212)757-8833 on Wednesdays between 11 am and 12:30 pm to make an appointment. All other writers are invited to attend and help provide feedback. Critique sessions are also held in Los Angeles. Call (213)462-1108 for more information. In New York, the host of the song critique is Jonathan Holtzman whose credits include everything from the music to "Foxfire," a Broadway show starring Hume Cronyn and Jessica Tandy, to the music to Jon Bishop's "Jedidiah Kohler" with William Hurt; to records by Laurie Beechman (Atlantic) and Pure Energy (Prism).

**AMERICAN GUILD OF AUTHORS AND COMPOSERS (AGAC/The Songwriters Guild) WORKSHOPS**, Suite 1113, 6430 Sunset Blvd., Hollywood CA 90028. (213)462-1108. Regional Director: Jack Segal.
**ASKAPRO:** "2-hour music business rap session to which all writers are welcome held on the first Tuesday of each month. Features industry professionals—publishers, writers, producers, artists—fielding questions from new songwriters." Offered year-round. 100-150/meeting. Each session lasts 2 hours. Free to all AGAC members, $2 non-members. Reservations necessary. Phone for more information.
**Jack Segal's Songwriting Workshop:** "designed to give the songwriter additional techniques to write for today's song market. Both lyrics and music will be treated in terms of contemporary content and form. Song evaluation at every meeting. Workshop activities will include: the basics—form, content, design; tools; collaboration; the demo; the lyric and lead sheet; and the music business. Offered year-round. 12-15/class. Each session lasts 2 hours. Cost: $70 to AGAC members, $85 to nonmembers. Classes held in private home in Hollywood. All applicants must submit a tape and Jack Segal will make final selection."

**ASCAP "Welcomes Songwriters" Series**, c/o ASCAP, 2nd Floor, 6430 Sunset Blvd., Hollywood CA 90028. (213)466-7681. ASCAP Western Executive Director: Todd Brabec. Workshop Director: Julie Horton. Offers programs for songwriters: "ASCAP offers a tuition-free, 8-week workshop series during which songs are performed and evaluated a well-known songwriter or publisher guest moderator. Song casting and placing are discussed. The various song markets are analyzed. Additional workshops include The Business and Creative Sides of Writing for Film and Television; Black Contemporary Music; and Symphonic Music. Class size: 25-40 students in each workshop. Length: approximately 2 hours. Workshop classes take place at ASCAP as well as at outside forums. A piano and stereo and cassette tape playback system are among the facilities. Applicants are selected by the workshop director based on material submitted on cassette by prospective members. Write or phone ASCAP for information.

**DICK GROVE SCHOOL OF MUSIC**, 12754 Ventura Blvd., Studio City CA 91604. (213)985-0905 and (800)423-2283. Contact: Thom Sharp. Offers programs for songwriters in lyric writing, composition, harmony, theory, and rhythmic dictation. All classes are taught by professional musicians. Workshops are offered for guitarists, bassists, drummers, keyboardists, vocalists and brass, reed and string players. Other classes include arranging, conducting, ear-training, improvisation, film scoring, music preparation and sight-singing." Four 10-week terms/calendar year. Enrollment is 800/term; average class size is 15. Classes range from $70-140 covering five-ten 2-hour sessions. Some classes require texts or materials that are not included in the tuition fee. Complete classroom facilities. "We offer year long, full-time programs for arrangers/composers, vocalists and players. We also offer The Composition and Musicianship Program (COMD) for students wishing a primary career as songwriter and the related experience in record producing, the record industry and publishing. Students will obtain in-depth experience in all styles of song composition and concept from both the lyrical and compositional aspects." Applicants must be "interviewed prior to enrolling for placement. Certain classes require auditions." Request current catalog by mail or telephone.

**FRANKS SILVERA WRITERS' WORKSHOP**, 3rd Floor, 317 W. 125 St., New York NY 10027. (212)662-8463. Contact: Garland Lee Thompson. "Our workshop is open to *all* writers who are prepared to participate by reading their work. Each year 70-80 plays are read. Third World and women writers are especially encouraged."

**SONGWRITER SEMINARS AND WORKSHOPS**, 928 Broadway, New York NY 10010. (212)505-7332. President: Ted Lehrman. Vice President: Libby Bush. Offers programs for songwriters: intermediate pop songwriting; advanced workshop; and at-home songwriter workshop. Year-round with cycles beginning in September, January, March and June. Approximately 12 in each songwriter workshop. Each cycle lasts eight weeks. "Our programs stress the craft and business realities of *today's* pop music industry. We guide our members in the writing of the hit single song (both lyrics and music) for those recording artists who are open to outside material. We also share with them our considerable experience and expertise in the marketing of commercial pop music product. Our instructors, Ted Lehrman and Libby Bush, both members of ASCAP, have had between them more than 80 songs recorded and commercially released here and abroad. They continue to be highly active in writing and placing pop songs for publication." Workshops: Pop Songwriting—Preparing for the Marketplace; Advanced Songwriter Seminar and Workshop—Ready for the Marketplace. Cost of 8 week workshops: $135-140. Cost of at-home songwriter workshop: $12.50/lyric; $15/song. Private song and career consultation sessions: $35/hour. Top 40 single stressed. Collaboration opportunities available. No housing provided. Interviews/auditions held for songwriters and singer/songwriters to determine which workshop would be most helpful. Call for free brochure and/or set up interview.

**THE SONGWRITERS ADVOCATE (TSA)**, 47 Maplehurst Rd., Rochester NY 14617. (716)266-0679. Director: Jerry Englerth. TSA is a non-profit educational organization that is striving to fulfill the needs of the songwriter. "We are co-sponsored by the Greece Central Continuing Education Division directed by Dwayne Rupert. Jointly we offer three opportunities for songwriters including: 1) A complete 10-week course, Songwriting: Craft/Business, which covers copyright law, methods and procedures of songwriting, home and professional demo recording, publishing and co-publishing, song sharks, functions of ASCAP, BMI, SESAC, AGAC etc.; 2) song evaluation workshops that afford songwriters the opportunity to bounce their songs off other songwriters and receive an objective critique and improve their craft; and 3) the Songwriters Collaboration Workshop, a 4-week course designed to expose the songwriter to new and different material by fellow songwriters. The Songwriters Advocate also publishes an international newsletter to inform, protect and nurture the songwriter in hopes that the necessary skills will be honed and sharpened to facilitate the pursuit of songwriting as a worthwhile and satisfying craft. TSA evaluates tapes and lyric sheets via the mail. In addition, for those of you who wish to have a demo made, TSA will also be able to accommodate you." Price list is available upon request. Cost: newsletter—4 issues $6; tape evaluations by mail $1/song; "Please add $1 if outside USA."
**Tips:** "We do not measure success on a monitary scale, ever. It is the craft of songwriting that is the primary objective. If a songwriter can arm himself with knowledge about the craft and the business, it will increase his confidence and effectiveness in all his dealings."

**SONGWRITING WORKSHOP AND THE BUSINESS OF MUSIC**, Rustron Music Productions, 200 Westmoreland Ave., White Plains NY 10606. (914)946-1689. Course Instructor: Rusty Gordon. Offers programs for songwriters "about the music industry and how it works. Lecture material is very specific and complete, covering all areas of the subject. Includes instruction in the techniques of the craft and the mechanics needed to write commercially marketable songs. We teach from both the lyrical and musical points of view. We specify universality, concept uniqueness and mood development for clearcut media marketing." Year-round. 10 students/class. 2½-hour evening classes meet once/week for 8 weeks. "The entire course including workbook/folder and all additional printed material is $150. We have a payment plan requiring $45 paid at the first class and $15 paid at each successive class. Group discount available. We have no boarding facilities. Classes are held at main office and at sites in NYC. Applicants must be at least 16 years old. This is a college-level course. In-depth personal songwriting critiques for up to 6 songs available in 3-hour sessions and/or in-depth music business informative consultations also available in 3-hour sessions. Reasonable fees. Evening appointment only. For specifics and course information write or call 6-11 p.m., Monday-Thursday."

**SRS WORKSHOPS**, 6772 Hollywood Blvd., Hollywood CA 90028. (213)463-7178. Staff Members: Kathy Gronau, Joan Goodstein, Billy James, Pat Luboff, Bruce Kaplan, Doug Thiele and Doug Trazzare. Offers programs for songwriters: performers workshop, song evaluation workshop, lyric writing, songwriting, music theory, harmony and theory, composers workshop, demo production, and voice, business and band workshops. Offers programs year-round. Attendance: up to 25/workshop. Length: 2-4 hours/workshop. "Some of our workshops are available to members only for a nominal $1. Others are open to everyone." Membership is $40." Send for application. "SRS is a nonprofit membership organization dedicated to the protection and education of songwriters. We also provide an 'Open Ears' Tip Sheet telling members which publishers, producers and artists are looking for material."

# Appendix

## The Business of Songwriting

Being creative is not enough to assure success as a songwriter. A little business savvy is a great advantage when you approach music executives who may themselves be more business-oriented than creative.

The articles in this section give you insights into the structure and operation of the music business as well as detailed information on contracts, copyright, submitting your songs, and more.

### The Structure of the Music Business

Los Angeles, New York City and Nashville claim the largest concentrations of companies involved in the music business. There are, of course, companies in cities across the country which continue to make important contributions to today's music scene. But it's the decisions made in the three music centers that determine the direction the industry takes: which songs are published, which artists are signed to recording contracts and which records are released.

No matter which city you're dealing in, the chart showing the structure of the music business (Chart 1, on the front leaves of this book) shows the possible routes a song can take to becoming published, recorded and released. Those routes include taking your songs to the A) artist; B) artist's manager; C) music publisher; D) independent record producer; or E) the record company.

Choosing where to submit your songs depends on many things. If you know a recording artist (A) personally and have a song you think would suit him, approach the artist first. If he likes the song he will take it to his producer and, if the producer agrees, it will be scheduled for the artist's recording session.

If you don't know an artist personally, you might try to contact the artist's personal manager (B). You can also submit your songs to the independent record producer (D), or the A&R director of a record company (E). They are always looking for songs for the artists they produce. If they and their artists think your song is a hit, it will be recorded and released.

If the artist being produced by the independent producer is already signed to a recording contract, the song will be released on that record company's label. Many times, however, the independent producer will pay for and produce a session by an artist who is not yet under contract to a recording company. The producer then tries to sell the master tape of that session to the A&R directors of various recording companies. If he sells the master and negotiates a contract for the artist, the record is released on that label.

Each of the above approaches to the music industry requires that, somewhere along the line, someone either publishes your song or recommends a publisher. The advantage to those approaches is that many artists, producers, and record companies *do* have their own publishing companies. Since publishing means money if the song is successful and more money if it is recorded by other artists, a good song can have even greater appeal to artists, producers and record companies if the publishing is "open" (if the song has not yet been published).

There is much to be said, however, for taking your songs to a publisher (C) *first*. The publisher pitches (an industry term meaning to play your songs for artists and producers who might record them) your songs to artists, producers and A&R directors. Major publishers in music centers are regularly sent notification of who will be recording and when.

The greatest advantage, then, to approaching a music publisher first is his know-how and clout with the industry as a whole. You can concentrate on your business—writing songs—while the publisher works on getting cuts (recordings) on the songs you write. Some publishers do encourage their writers to do some pitching. That is not necessarily bad since it keeps the writer even closer to what's happening in the industry.

Any one (or a combination) of these ways of getting your song heard, published, recorded and released is the best way if it works for you. In this book are listed music publishers, record companies, record producers and managers with specifications on how to submit your material to each. The choice is yours.

## Submitting Your Songs

Here are guidelines to help when submitting material to companies listed in this book:

- Read the listing and submit exactly what a company asks for and exactly how it asks that it be submitted.
- Listen to each demo before submitting to make sure the quality is satisfactory.
- Enclose a brief, neat cover letter of introduction. Indicate the types of songs you're submitting and, if you wish, recording artists you think they might suit.
- Include typed or legibly printed lyric sheets. If requested, include a lead sheet. Place your name, address and phone number on each lead or lyric sheet.
- Label neatly each tape and tape box with your name, address, phone number and the names of songs on the tape in the sequence in which they appear.
- Keep a record of the date, the names of the songs and the company to which you are submitting.
- Include a SASE for the return of your material. Your return envelope to companies based in countries other than your own should contain a SAE and International Reply Coupons.
- Wrap and tie the package neatly and write or type the address and your return address so they are clearly visible. Your package is the first impression a company has of you and your songs, so neatness is very important.
- Mail First Class. Stamp or write "First Class Mail" on the package and on the SASE you enclose. Don't send by registered mail. The recipient must interrupt his day to sign for it and many companies refuse all registered mail.

If a company is not listed in *Songwriter's Market*, or if, at the end of the Music Publisher or Record Company section, it is noted as a company that does not usually accept unsolicited material, don't submit to them without first writing and receiving a reply to a query.

The query letter should be neat (preferably typewritten), brief and pleasant. Explain the type of material you have and ask about their needs and current submission policy.

To expedite a reply, you can enclose a self-addressed stamped postcard asking the information you need to know. Your typed questions (see Sample Reply Form) should be direct and easy for the receiver to answer. Don't forget to include a line for the respondent's name and title. Also remember to place the company's name and address in the upper left-hand space on the front of the postcard so you'll know what company it was you queried. Queries, like tape submissions, should be recorded for future reference.

---

**Sample Reply Form**

I would like to hear:

( ) "Name of Song"     ( ) "Name of Song"     ( ) "Name of Song"

I prefer:

( ) reel-to-reel      ( ) cassette          ( ) either

With:

( ) lyric sheet   ( ) lead sheet    ( ) either      ( ) both

( ) I am not looking for material at this time, try me later.

( ) I am not interested.

Name                                    Title

---

## Submitting in Person

A trip to Los Angeles, New York or Nashville can give you an inside glimpse of the music business at work. If you've planned ahead, outlined your schedule, made appointments, and carefully prepared demos, you have only to reap the rewards of first-hand reaction to your material. Use the geographic index at the end of both the Music Publishers and Record Companies sections to contact, before you leave home, companies you'd like to visit.

Take several reel-to-reel and cassette copies and lyric sheets of each of your songs. More than one of the companies you visit may ask that you leave a copy with them. If the person who's reviewing material likes a song, he may want to play it for someone else. There's also a good chance the person you have the appointment with will have to cancel (expect that occasionally), but wants you to leave a copy of your songs and he will contact you later.

Listen attentively to what the reviewers say. When you return home, summarize their reactions to your material and look for similarities in their critiques. That information will be invaluable as you continue to submit material to the people who now know you personally.

## The Money

The songwriter's money comes in the form of royalty checks. Unless your contract (see "Contracts" in this book) stipulates you will receive a salary or advance on future royalties, you shouldn't expect your first money before three to six months after the song is released.

A look at the royalties chart (Chart 2, on the book leaves of this book) shows that the songwriter receives:

- Mechanical royalties from the sale of records and tapes.

- Performance royalties for airplay on radio and TV, plays on jukeboxes and live performances.
- Foreign royalties from foreign sub-publishers.
- Money for sheet music, choral arrangements and folio sales.

*Mechanical royalties* are due the songwriter and the publisher every time a recorded copy of your song is sold and not returned. You and the publisher split a portion of that revenue (50-50 is standard). The Copyright Royalty Tribunal has set maximum royalty at 4¢/song.

The money for mechanical royalties flows from retail record shops to the record company. The record company then pays the music publisher 4¢ per record *sold*. You and the publisher split the 4¢ less reasonable publisher's expenses. Reasonable publisher's expenses means only the cost incurred for that particular song: phone calls, postage, etc.

The songwriter also shares 50-50 in any royalties the publisher receives from the sub-publisher who collected the publishing monies generated by your songs in the foreign music market.

The publisher pays you a share of the profit from the sale of sheet music, orchestrations, choral arrangements and folio sales. You earn 3-8% for each sheet of piano music sold and about 10% of the wholesale price of orchestrations, choral arrangments and folios.

Periodically (usually every six months) the publisher sends the songwriter a check that reflects his share of the mechanical royalties, foreign sub-publishing royalties, and sheet music, orchestrations, choral arrangments and folio sales.

*Performance royalties* are collected from radio and television stations, night clubs and jukeboxes by the performance rights organizations (ASCAP, BMI and SESAC). A published songwriter *must* belong to the same organization to which the publisher belongs. You'll notice that many publishers listed in this book have affiliate companies belonging to a different performance rights organization. That allows the publisher to deal with writers of more than one affiliation.

Each performance rights organization has its own unique method of determining how many times your song is performed during a given period. Their primary difference is *how* they make that determination. ASCAP monitors individual radio and television stations as well as concerts and clubs where music is performed. BMI uses logs sent them from radio and TV stations. SESAC uses the charts of the trade magazines (*Billboard* and *Cash Box*) to determine the popularity of individual songs. ASCAP charges a membership fee. BMI and SESAC do not.

The songwriter receives a statement of performances and a royalty check from his chosen performance rights organization quarterly. The amount earned depends on how many times the organization determined the song was performed.

ASCAP, BMI and SESAC are highly professional and reputable friends of the songwriter. To look into the specific policies, procedures, benefits and requirements of each before joining, use the addresses given in our Organizations & Clubs section to write them. Also, consult the chapter on these organizations in *This Business of Music* by Sidney Shemel and M. William Kasilovski (Billboard Publications).

## Copyright

One of the questions songwriters frequently ask is, "How do I protect my songs?" The answer is that since the new copyright law went into effect January 1, 1978, your songs are automatically copyrighted for life plus fifty years the moment you put them to paper or tape. To ascertain and protect your ownership of that copyright, however, you must register your songs. To register your song(s) send the following to the Register of Copyrights, Library of Congress, Washington DC 20559:

- a tape or lead sheet of your song(s).
- a government form PA, available on request from the Copyright Office or your local Federal Information Center.
- $10 registration fee which will cover the cost of registering as many songs (by

the same writers) as you wish to submit for registration at one time.
It may take as long as four months before you receive your certificate of registration from the Copyright Office. However, since your songs are copyrighted from the moment of creation, you may use the copyright symbol immediately, affixing it to all written and taped copies of your songs. That is a "c" with a circle around it, followed by the date the song was written and your name (©1984 John Doe).

Write the Copyright Office for more information and/or a copy of the Copyright Law. All information is free.

## Record Keeping

Your record keeping should include a list of income from royalty checks as well as expenses incurred as a result of your songwriting business: cost of tapes, demo sessions, office supplies, postage, traveling expenses, dues to songwriting organizations, class and workshop fees, and publications of interest. It's also advisable to open a checking account exclusively for your songwriting activities, not only to make record keeping easier, but to establish your identity as a business for tax purposes.

## The Rip Offs

There are those who use the music business as a means to unfairly exploit others. Here are some guidelines to help you recognize when you've come upon such a person or company:

- *Never pay* to have your songs published. A reputable company interested in your songs assumes the responsibility and cost of promoting your material. That company invests in your material because it expects a profit once the song is recorded and released.
- Never pay to have your music "reviewed." Reviewing material—free of charge—is the business of a reputable company.
- Never pay to have your lyrics or poems set to music. "Music mills"—for a price—may use the same melody for hundreds of lyrics and poems. Publishers can recognize one of these melodies as soon as it hits their tape player.
- Read *all* contracts carefully before signing and don't sign any contract you're unsure about or that you don't understand.
- Don't pay a company to pair you up with a collaborator. Better ways include contacting organizations which offer collaboration services to their members (see the Organizations and Clubs section in this book).
- Don't "sell your songs outright." It's unethical for anyone to offer you such a proposition.
- If you are being offered a "recording contract" you should not be expected to pay upfront for the session, musicians, promotion, etc. Major record companies recoup such expenses from record sales. If you *are* asked to pay expenses upfront, beware. No matter how much is promised to you verbally or in your contract, you will probably never see a return on your money. With such companies, it's a good idea to ask to speak with other artists who have signed such contracts with them before signing one yourself. And if, after weighing expenses, you think you can afford the longshot, then it's your decision. Read the stipulations of the contract carefully, however, and go over them with an attorney.
- Verify any situation about a company or individual if you have doubts: 1) contact the performance rights organization with which they are affiliated; 2) check with the Better Business Bureau in the town where they're located; 3) contact professional organizations listed in our Organization and Clubs section.

## Co-Writing

A quick check of the charts in *Billboard* or *Cash Box* will show that collaboration is not just an alternative way of writing—it's the most popular way. Among its advantages is the instant feedback and criticism of the songs you're writing. Another plus for collaboration is the talent that each songwriter brings to the task.

Where do you find collaborators? Check the bulletin board at your local musician's union hall. Professional organizations like Songwriter's Resources and Services (SRS) in Los Angeles, The American Guild of Authors and Composers (AGAC) in New York City and Los Angeles, and The Nashville Songwriters Association International (NSAI) in Nashville offer collaboration services. Check the Organizations and Clubs section for addresses.

For more information on collaborator's agreements between writers, see "Contracts" in this book.

## Alternatives

Alternatives a songwriter might consider other than the popular music market are advertising agencies, audiovisual firms, the theater and writing songs for local and regional performers. Each is a specialized market requiring not only talent, but technical knowledge of that particular field.

For more information about these read "Writing for the Local Alternative Music Markets" in the front of this book.

# Use an up-to-date Market Directory!

### Don't let your Songwriter's Market turn old on you.

You may be reluctant to give up this copy of Songwriter's Market. After all, you would never discard an old friend.

But resist the urge to hold onto an old Songwriter's Market! Like your first guitar or your favorite pair of jeans, the time will come when this copy of Songwriter's Market will have to be replaced.

In fact, if you're still using this 1984 Songwriter's Market when the calendar reads 1985, your old friend isn't your best friend anymore. Many of the buyers listed here have moved or been promoted. Many of the addresses are now incorrect. Rates of pay have certainly changed, and even the record company's music needs are changed from last year.

You can't afford to use an out-of-date book to plan your marketing efforts. But there's an easy way for you to stay current — order the 1985 Songwriter's Market. All you have to do is complete the attached post card and return it with your payment or charge card information. Best of all, we'll send you the 1985 edition at the 1984 price — just $13.95. The 1985 Songwriter's Market will be published and ready for shipment in October 1984.

Make sure you have the most current marketing information — order the new edition of Songwriter's Market now.

---

**To order, drop this post-paid card in the mail:** ➡

☐ **YES!** I want the most current edition of Songwriter's Market Please send me the 1985 Songwriter's Market at the 1984 price — $13.95. I have included $1.50 for postage and handling. (Ohio residents add 5½% sales tax.)

☐ Payment enclosed (Slip this card and your payment into an envelope.)

☐ Charge my:   ☐ Visa   ☐ MasterCard   ☐ Interbank # _____

Account # _____ Exp. Date _____

Signature _____

Name _____

Address _____

City _____ State _____ Zip _____

(This offer expires August 1, 1985. Please allow 30 days for delivery.)
NOTE: 1985 Songwriter's Market will be ready for shipment in October 1984.

**Writer's Digest Books**
9933 Alliance Road
Cincinnati, Ohio 45242

# Make sure you have a current edition of Songwriter's Market

Songwriter's Market has been the song writer's bible for years. Each edition contains hundreds of changes to give you the most current information to work with. Make sure your copy is the latest edition.

## This card will get you the 1985 edition... at 1984 prices! ⬇

---

**BUSINESS REPLY CARD**
FIRST CLASS   PERMIT NO. 17   CINCINNATI

POSTAGE WILL BE PAID BY ADDRESSEE

NO POSTAGE
NECESSARY
IF MAILED
IN THE
UNITED STATES

**Writer's Digest Books**

9933 Alliance Rd.
Cincinnati, Ohio 45242

# Contracts

BY BOB LEONE

Maybe you never *really* thought it would happen. Oh, you knew it *could* happen, that someday someone might like one or more of your songs enough to ask you to sign a contract. Now here you are, holding a contract in your hand, squinting at the percent and dollar signs scattered throughout the lines of fine print. Your reaction, if it's like that of most never-before-published songwriters, is to panic. You ask yourself: Should I sign or shouldn't I? Is this a good contract or a bad one? Do I need an attorney?

The purpose of this article is to answer those questions and many others about contracts, to give you—the unpublished songwriter—all the information you need to make an informed decision when you're asked to sign a contract. The emphasis here will be on publishing contracts, in particular the "single song" contract, but other types of contracts with which a songwriter might be confronted will also be reviewed.

## The "Song Sharks"

First of all, it is imperative that you be able to ascertain that you are dealing with a legitimate publisher, not with what is unaffectionately referred to in the music business as a "song shark." As Director of Special Projects for AGAC/the songwriters guild, I have heard from many unhappy, disillusioned songwriters who have paid out hundreds, and sometimes thousands of dollars to have lyrics reworked, melodies composed, and records made.

There are guidelines to help you determine the legitimacy of a publisher. No songwriter should ever have anything to do with a company that requires a fee to publish or record a song. Many of you, no doubt, have received literature through the mail, or have seen magazine advertisements offering to "set your poem to music" or "get your song recorded by a top artist."

The song shark never promises (on paper, that is) that your song will be played widely, if at all. He has but one interest—to extract as much money from you, the writer, as he can. You won't find these companies listed on the *Billboard* or *Cash Box* charts as publishers of songs for top artists. Their track record is usually recorded only in one-sided, fast-moving conversations scattered with big names: "I saw Barry just yesterday" or "Dolly was in town last week." Don't be intimidated by these big-name droppers. If they saw Barry it was probably on TV. And, if Dolly was in town, it was most probably not to see Mr. Name-dropping Publisher. Instead, ask for the names of songwriters and artists the publisher has dealt with before. Then check them out. (Read more about song sharks in "The Rip Offs" section in the Appendix of this book.)

A legitimate publisher, producer, or record company, on the other hand, only takes a song in the expectation that it will make money for all concerned. This, of course, includes the writer.

## The AGAC Popular Songwriters Contract

What actually happens when you assign your song to a music publisher? It is

---

**Bob Leone** *is Director of Special Projects for American Guild of Authors and Composers (AGAC)/the songwriters guild. He is also a composer/keyboardist who has worked with such artists as Stevie Nicks, Patti Smith, Joey Heatherton and Pam Johnson, and was principal writer and player for the former RCA recording group, Flame.*

important to realize that in signing a publishing contract you are not "selling" your song. Rather, you are assigning your rights to a particular song (or songs) to the publisher for a designated number of years. The contract, moreover, sets forth the royalties to be paid to you for various types of uses of the song.

An example of the "single song" contract is the AGAC Popular Songwriters Contract (see the contract and a detailed explanation at the end of this article). Prepared by AGAC/the songwriters guild and its legal counsel, Linden and Deutsch, this contract represents what the Guild and many music industry professionals believe to be the best minimum songwriter contract available.

AGAC/the songwriters guild is not a union, but rather a voluntary association of songwriters (see their listing in the Organizations and Clubs section of this book). Therefore, the AGAC Contract is not a negotiated contract between publishers and the Guild. We strongly encourage Guild members, and all songwriters, to request the AGAC Contract whenever a publisher expresses an interest in their material. While not every publisher will grant you this contract, a large and ever-growing number of music publishers will do so if you request it. In those instances when a publisher refuses the AGAC Contract (publishers have contracts of their own), the Guild will review and evaluate for its members, at no charge, whatever contract is offered by the publisher, and will advise how it measures up to the AGAC Contract.

Songwriters who are not Guild members are strongly advised to retain an attorney who specializes in entertainment law to do a contract review before signing. Rates for such a service generally begin at around $100 per hour. If cost is a problem, contact Volunteer Lawyers for the Arts (see their listing in the Organizations and Clubs section of this book).

## The Basics

Those elements that a songwriter must consider when deciding whether a particular publishing contract should or should not be signed fall under at least one of three categories: basic, critical, and negotiable. The basic features of a contract include the name of the publisher, the name(s) of the writer(s), the title of the song to be assigned, and the date of the agreement. Also included among a contract's basic features is its purpose. It must be stated with clarity that the writer is assigning his song to the publisher for use throughout a specific territory (the United States, the world, or the universe, as the case may be) for a designated number of years. Also among the basic features is a statement by the writer to the effect that he or she is, in fact, the author of the song, that the song is original, and that rights to the song may be freely assigned to the publisher. While it is certainly expected that you will shop a song to more than one publisher at a time, you cannot assign exclusive rights to a song to more than one publisher at a time.

## The Critical and the Negotiable

The critical aspects of a publishing contract are those which relate to payments, or royalties, to be made to the songwriter by the publisher for various types of uses of the song. These uses include commercial sound recordings; piano sheet music, song books, and folios; arrangements (orchestral, vocal, band, and the like); concerts; synchronization with motion pictures; television, including pay-TV, cable, and video; radio broadcasting; and any uses not specifically set forth (see paragraph 4m of the AGAC Contract). The provisions for royalty payments, and the specific amounts for each of these song uses, must be set forth in the contract—and they are negotiable. This leads us to our third category of contract terms.

The negotiable elements of any contract are the most important ones. They are what make a contract great or horrendous, fair or unfair, acceptable or unacceptable. It is up to you to get the best deal that you can get, but remember that negotiation invariably means compromise.

When you read through the AGAC Contract notice that, with respect to the negotiable/critical elements, suggested royalty percentages are indicated. Anything less than these percentages are deemed by the Guild to be below generally accepted industry standards.

Another negotiable feature would be an advance on royalties. The amounts offered vary widely depending on your track record (chart success), or the impact the song has had on your publisher ("I haven't been able to get that hook out of my head!"). Generally, advances are in the $100 to $250 range. The publisher can recoup this sum by deducting the amount of the advance from your royalties, starting with the "mechanical" royalties. By definition, mechanical royalties are earned whenever records or tapes or print music are sold. If your publisher fails to obtain a release of a commercial sound recording of your song, or if he gets a release but it does not sell and so fails to produce any income, then you are not obliged to return the royalty advance. Under these circumstances, the advance is not recoupable.

Some publishers may attempt to deduct demo costs against future royalties, but most publishers agree to take full responsibility for paying all demo costs. We wholeheartedly agree with that point of view.

The songwriter should receive no less than 50% of the gross receipts that the song earns in domestic royalties from mechanical reproductions, electrical transcriptions and synchronization licenses. The songwriter's 50% is called, quite appropriately, the "writer's share." The remaining 50% is referred to as the "publisher's share." When a publisher's share is 50%, it means that he has *all* the publishing, 100% of it.

In some instances, the songwriter may negotiate what is referred to as a "split publishing" deal. In such a situation, the publisher does not get all the publishing. Instead, he gets half the publishing, or 25% of the royalties, while the writer (if he is the sole writer) gets the remaining half of the publishing, in addition to his writer royalties—a total of 75% of the royalties earned by the song. Unless you have already had a hit song or two, do not expect a publisher to split publishing with you. Such a request from an unpublished songwriter almost inevitably, and justifiably, gets rejected.

With respect to sheet music and arrangements, a good contract will provide for the writer to receive no less that 10% of the retail selling price. In the AGAC Contract, the greater the number of copies sold, the greater the songwriter's percentage, up to a maximum of 15% on copies in excess of 500,000.

Where your song is used in synchronization with sound motion pictures, your share should be equal to the publisher's share. The same is true when your song is being marketed in a country outside the United States.

A songwriter without a track record should not expect to get more, nor should he or she settle for less than what we have outlined above. As we have pointed out previously, when you have achieved some chart success, you have earned the right to negotiate for larger percentages.

Be sure the contract is specific and clear with regard to how and when you will receive your royalty payments. Some publishers pay quarterly (four times a year, or once every three months), while others prefer to pay semi-annually (twice a year, or once every six months). Whatever the case, spell it out in the contract. Related to this is your right to inspect or audit your publisher's books. This right should exist for you or your accountant. The authority to audit your publisher's books is to be considered a critical feature of the contract, not a negotiable one. It should be part of any acceptable contract.

The performing rights organizations—ASCAP, BMI, and SESAC—pay the songwriter and publisher with separate checks. These performance royalties represent the money earned whenever a particular song or songs is played on radio, on television, or in concert. Both writer and publisher must belong to the same performing rights organization. AGAC/the songwriters guild collects, on the writer's behalf, all royalties payable by the publisher according to the terms of the contract—which excludes performance royalties.

A good contract will also contain provisions that define whose responsiblity it is to bring lawsuits against copyright infringers, and how the cost is to be handled. Furthermore, the contract should cover defending against lawsuits in the event that someone claims that your song infringes upon one of their copyrights. What this means, in essence, is that your song sounds an awful lot like someone else's (refer to paragraphs 15 and 16 of the AGAC Contract).

Provision should also be made for arbitration, should a dispute develop between you and your publisher which the two of you simply cannot resolve (see paragraph 17 of the AGAC Contract).

A good contract places restrictions on the publisher's right to sell your song to another publisher. Unless a publisher's entire catalogue of songs is being transferred or assigned to another publisher, the contract should provide for your prior written consent to the sale or transfer of your material to another publisher.

The final negotiable feature we will review is the "reversion of rights" clause. Reversion means that for any one of a number of reasons specified in the contract, the contract is no longer binding and rights to the contracted song revert to the songwriter. For example, if the contract stipulates that you or your accountant have the right to inspect your publisher's books (and, as mentioned above, it certainly should), and your publisher refuses to allow you to do so, then copyright ownership reverts to you and the contract is terminated. Another example: if your publisher transfers only your song, of all those in his catalogue, to someone else without your permission, then again the contract terminates and you get back the rights to your song.

The most essential type of reversion is the one that occurs when a publisher fails to obtain a commercial sound recording of your song within a specified period of time. A song is not "published" merely because you have signed a contract assigning the rights to that song to a publisher. A song becomes a published song only when it is released on a commercial sound recording for sale to the general public. We recommend that a publisher be granted no more than one year to obtain a commercial sound recording of your song, after which time one of two things should happen. Either the song reverts to you, the writer; or, the publisher must pay you at least $250 for the right to extend this period.

As you can see, there are at least three negotiable features involved in any reversion of ownership for failure to publish: first, there is the initial time period; second, there is the amount of money to be paid to the writer for an extension of the initial period; and, third, there is the amount of time stipulated for the extension (usually six months).

Something else to consider when negotiating a contract is how you feel about publisher rewriting. Unless you feel otherwise, specify that without your permission no changes can be made in your song (music, title, lyric, and so forth), or you may find yourself sharing royalties with someone you have never even met.

Lastly, under the Copyright Law, various uses of a song, such as sound recordings and arrangements, are considered "derivative works." Frequently, such derivative works have more of a monetary value than the original sheet music. Be sure to include a provision stipulating that when the contract terminates, the publisher loses all rights to such derivative works, as well as to the original version of the song.

Your publisher may disagree with any of the negotiable or critical elements discussed here. Ultimately, you, the writer, must decide whether or not the contract offered to you is a fair and acceptable one. Do not make the mistake of thinking that any contract is better than no contract at all; if you do, you will very likely live to regret your decision. There are a lot of publishers out there, and they are all looking for material. After all, songs are the very lifeblood of the music industry. So shop around until you get a deal that meets at least your minimal expectations.

It should be noted that not all publishing contracts are of the "single song" variety. Some publishing companies will sign songwriters to exclusive contracts. In exchange for a weekly royalty advance, starting generally around $125, the rights to all the songs written by the writer within a specified time period (usually a year with company's option to renew for four more years) are assigned to that company. Exclusive contracts are usually offered only to songwriters who have shown genuine promise in the form of chart success.

## Other Contracts

Other types of contracts a songwriter might be asked to sign:

*Artist/Record Company*: The basic album deal (if such an animal truly exists) is generally for a period of one year with company's option to renew the contract each year for a specified number of years (usually five). As a rule, you will be expected to record one album per year, but this can vary. The record company owns the masters that you record as an exclusive service for them. In return for this service, you, the artist, can expect to receive an advance of several thousand dollars (or millions, depending on your "star status"), and a percentage of whatever money is earned from the sale of your records and tapes.

You will not receive any royalties until all of the money advanced to you by the record company has been recouped by the company. Any money paid out to cover studio recording costs, producer fees, musician fees, touring (hotels, food, transportation, etc.) is paid by the artist from royalties.

Record company contracts are usually much more complex than publishing agreements, but look for many of the same rights that we explored in relation to the latter: the right not to be assigned to another company without your written consent and the right to audit the company books are good examples. By all means, find yourself the very best entertainment lawyer available.

*Artist/Producer*: This should be a percentage, not a fee, arrangement. I would like to reiterate what I said at the beginning of this article: *never* have anything to do with a company that charges you a fee to publish or produce your songs. A typical production agreement allows a producer to produce your song, or a number of your songs, and to attempt to obtain a publishing or a recording contract, or both. Set forth in the contract is the period of time during which the producer does his shopping (one year is standard). As with publishers, the deal will be exclusive in that only he will be shopping your material during that time. If he gets you a deal, his share can be a piece of your publishing and record royalties and even a piece of your advances. It all depends, of course, on how the contract is negotiated.

*Artist/Manager*: A standard management contract stipulates that, in exchange for personal career counseling, a personal manager takes a percentage of your earnings as an artist. The standard is 20%, but some managers take only 10%, while others insist on 25%. Contracts usually run for one year.

*Writer/Writer*: A collaborator's agreement specifies each writer's share of royalties and control of copyright. Generally, each collaborator gets an equal share of royalties, and equal control of copyright, but provisions should be included to guide all parties involved in the event of the death of one of the writers.

## International Markets

You may have noticed that a considerable number of foreign publishers and record companies (mostly located in England, Australia and New Zealand) appear in this edition of *Songwriter's Market*. You should be aware that the laws governing copyright, contracts, royalties, and so forth, can vary enormously from country to country. I will not discourage you from sending your material to foreign companies because many of these companies are highly competitive in regard to obtaining the rights to songs written by American songwriters. And some of your material may, in fact, be better suited to the Asian or European marketplace. If you consider signing a contract with an enthusiastic publisher from a country outside the US, use the same criteria that we discussed previously when making a decision as to the contract's acceptability.

One final statement: never send out any of your songs anywhere unless they have been copyrighted with the Register of Copyrights. Copyright forms can be obtained by writing to Register of Copyrights, Library of Congress, Washington DC 20559.

## 386 Songwriter's Market '84

For more information on the subject matter covered in this article, we recommend the following:
*This Business of Music*, Billboard Books, 1515 Broadway, New York NY 10036.
*More About This Business of Music*, Billboard Books, 1515 Broadway, New York NY 10036.
*An Introduction to Popular Music Publishing in America*, National Music Publishers Association, 110 East 59th St., New York NY 10022.
*The Musician's Manual*, Beverly Hills Bar Association, 606 South Olive, Bevery Hills CA 90014.

For more information about the organizations mentioned in this article, write to:
AGAC/the songwriters guild, Suite 410, 40 West 57th St., New York NY 10019.
BMI, 320 West 57th St., New York NY 10019.
ASCAP, One Lincoln Plaza, New York NY 10023.
SESAC, 10 Columbus Circle, New York NY 10019.

# Overview of the AGAC Popular Songwriters Contract

**Paragraph 1**

Writer assigns his song to the Publisher throughout the world for a designated number of years, not to exceed forty (40) (or thirty-five (35) years from the date of first release of a commercial sound recording). (The term reflects the provisions of the 1976 Copyright Revision Law.) The shorter the term, the better for the Writer, because if the song is successful, he/she can re-negotiate more favorable financial terms at an earlier time. The length of the term would depend on the bargaining strength and reputation of the Writer.

**Paragraph 2**

This recognizes that the Writer is a member of a particular performing rights society (either ASCAP, BMI, or SESAC) and that this Contract will not interfere with the Writer's collection of performing rights proceeds directly from his/her performing rights society. It is crucial that the Writer and Publisher are members of the same performing rights society.

**Paragraph 3**

Writer warrants that the song was written by him/her, is original, and that Writer has the right to enter into the agreement.

**Paragraph 4**

Sets forth royalties to be paid for various types of uses of the song. Note that the Contract sets forth *minimum* amounts that Writer must receive. Of course, Writer is free to attempt to negotiate for higher royalty rates. If no amounts are filled in, the minimum amounts apply (see Paragraph 20 of the initial contract). Paragraph 4(k) provides that the initial publisher, may not, without the Writer's written consent, grant certain licenses not specifically permitted by the contract (e.g., use of the title of the song; to give a dramatic representation of the song; synchronization, licenses, etc.).

**Paragraph 5**

This applies if there is more than one Writer. If so, each Writer will share royalties equally, unless specified otherwise in Paragraph 23.

**Paragraph 6**

This requires the Publisher to have a commercial sound recording of the song made and released within twelve (12) months from the date of the Contract or to pay Writer a sum of not less than Two Hundred and Fifty ($250.00) Dollars for the right to extend this period for not more than six (6) months. If Publisher does not comply, the Contract terminates and all rights return to Writer.

When the sound recording is cut, Publisher is required to give Writer six (6) copies of the sound recording.

Under Paragraph 6(c), Publisher must either (i) publish and offer for sale regular piano copies of the song within thirty (30) days of release of the sound recording; or (ii) make a piano arrangement or lead sheet of the song within thirty (30) days of execution of the Contract (with six (6) copies to be given to the Writer). The parties must select which of the above alternatives will apply.

**Paragraph 7**

Deals with the Publisher's sub-licensing of the song in foreign countries. It guarantees that the Writer will receive no less than 50% of the revenue by the Publisher from rights licensed outside the U.S.

**Paragraph 8**

Explains what happens when the Contract terminates (i.e. all rights revert to Writer, subject to any outstanding licenses issued by the Publisher and the latter's duty to account for monies received after termination).

**Paragraph 9**

Deals with exploitation of the song in a manner not yet contemplated and thus not specifically covered in the Contract. Any such exploitation must be mutually agreed upon by the Writer and the Publisher.

**Paragraphs 10, 11 and 12**

Deal with the method of payment of royalties to the Writer and the Writer's right to inspect Publisher's books.

**Paragraph 13**

Various uses of the song, such as sound recordings and arrangements, are considered "derivative works" under the Copyright Law. Often, such derivative works can have more financial value than the original sheet music. This provision provides that when the Contract terminates, the Publisher loses all rights in such derivative works, as well as in the original version of the song.

**Paragraphs 15 and 16**

Deal with bringing lawsuits against infringers and defending lawsuits in the event someone claims that the Writer's song infringed a copyright.

**Paragraph 17**

In the event there is a dispute between the Writer and the Publisher and they cannot resolve it, such dispute is to be settled by arbitration (generally considered a more expeditious and inexpensive means of settling claims).

**Paragraph 18**

This places restrictions on Publisher's rights to sell the Writer's song to another publisher other than as part of the Publisher's entire catalog.

# AGAC/the songwriters guild
American Guild of Authors and Composers

NOTE TO SONGWRITERS: (A) DO NOT SIGN THIS CONTRACT IF IT HAS ANY CHANGES UNLESS YOU HAVE FIRST DISCUSSED SUCH CHANGES WITH AGAC; (B) FOR YOUR PROTECTION PLEASE SEND A FULLY EXECUTED COPY OF THIS CONTRACT TO AGAC.

## POPULAR SONGWRITERS CONTRACT
© Copyright 1978 AGAC

AGREEMENT made this .......... day of .........., 19 ...., between

................................................................

(hereinafter called "Publisher") and ................................................................

(Jointly and/or severally hereinafter collectively called "Writer");

WITNESSETH:

**Composition** (Insert title of composition here) → 1. The Writer hereby assigns, transfers and delivers to the Publisher a certain heretofore unpublished original musical composition, written and/or composed by the above-named Writer now entitled ................................................................ (hereinafter referred to as "the composition"), including the title, words and music thereof, and the right to secure copyright therein throughout the entire world, and to have and to hold the said copyright and all rights of whatsoever nature thereunder existing, for **(Insert number of years here)** → not more than 40 ...... years from the date of this contract or 35 years from the date of the first release of a commercial sound recording of the composition, whichever term ends earlier, unless this contract is sooner terminated in accordance with the provisions hereof.

2. In all respects this contract shall be subject to any existing agreements between the parties hereto and the following small **Performing Rights Affiliation (Delete Two)** → performing rights licensing organization with which Writer and Publisher are affiliated: ................................................................ (ASCAP, BMI, SESAC). Nothing contained herein shall, or shall be deemed to, alter, vary or modify the rights of Writer and Publisher to share in, receive and retain the proceeds distributed to them by such small performing rights licensing organization pursuant to their respective agreement with it.

**Warranty** 3. The Writer hereby warrants that the composition is his sole, exclusive and original work, that he has full right and power to make this contract, and that there exists no adverse claim to or in the composition, except as aforesaid in Paragraph 2 hereof and except such rights as are specifically set forth in Paragraph 23 hereof.

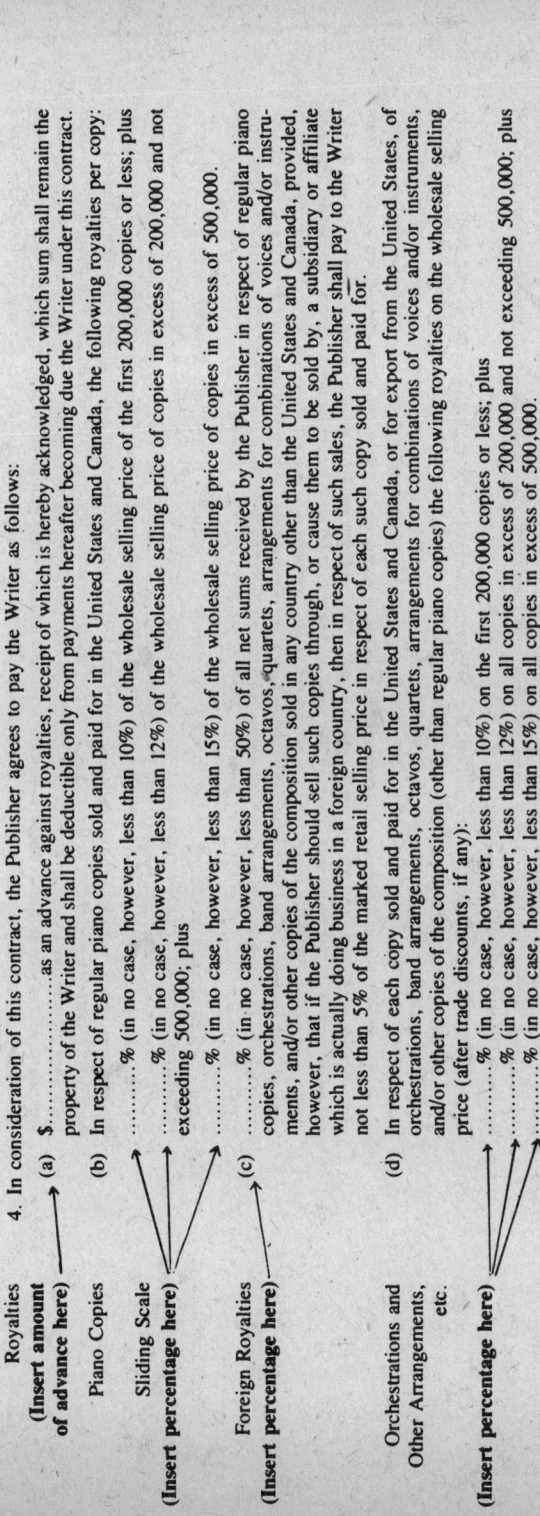

# The AGAC Popular Songwriters Contract

4. In consideration of this contract, the Publisher agrees to pay the Writer as follows:

Royalties  
**(Insert amount of advance here)** → (a) $............ as an advance against royalties, receipt of which is hereby acknowledged, which sum shall remain the property of the Writer and shall be deductible only from payments hereafter becoming due the Writer under this contract.

Piano Copies (b) In respect of regular piano copies sold and paid for in the United States and Canada, the following royalties per copy:

Sliding Scale → ............% (in no case, however, less than 10%) of the wholesale selling price of the first 200,000 copies or less; plus  
**(Insert percentage here)** → ............% (in no case, however, less than 12%) of the wholesale selling price of copies in excess of 200,000 and not exceeding 500,000; plus  
→ ............% (in no case, however, less than 15%) of the wholesale selling price of copies in excess of 500,000.

Foreign Royalties  
**(Insert percentage here)** → (c) ............% (in no case, however, less than 50%) of all net sums received by the Publisher in respect of regular piano copies, orchestrations, band arrangements, octavos, quartets, arrangements for combinations of voices and/or instruments, and/or other copies of the composition sold in any country other than the United States and Canada, provided, however, that if the Publisher should sell such copies through, or cause them to be sold by, a subsidiary or affiliate which is actually doing business in a foreign country, then in respect of such sales, the Publisher shall pay to the Writer not less than 5% of the marked retail selling price in respect of each such copy sold and paid for.

Orchestrations and Other Arrangements, etc. (d) In respect of each copy sold and paid for in the United States and Canada, or for export from the United States, of orchestrations, band arrangements, octavos, quartets, arrangements for combinations of voices and/or instruments, and/or other copies of the composition (other than regular piano copies) the following royalties on the wholesale selling price (after trade discounts, if any):

**(Insert percentage here)** → ............% (in no case, however, less than 10%) on the first 200,000 copies or less; plus  
→ ............% (in no case, however, less than 12%) on all copies in excess of 200,000 and not exceeding 500,000; plus  
→ ............% (in no case, however, less than 15%) on all copies in excess of 500,000.

Publisher's Song Book, Folio, etc. (e) (i) If the composition, or any part thereof, is included in any song book, folio or similar publication issued by the Publisher containing at least four, but not more than twenty-five musical compositions, the royalty to be paid by the Publisher to the Writer shall be an amount determined by dividing 10% of the wholesale selling price (after trade discounts, if any) of the copies sold, among the total number of the Publisher's copyrighted musical compositions included in such publication. If such publication contains more than twenty-five musical compositions, the said 10% shall be increased by an additional ½% for each additional musical composition.

Licensee's Song Book, Folio, etc. (ii) If, pursuant to a license granted by the Publisher to a licensee not controlled by or affiliated with it, the composition, or any part thereof, is included in any song book, folio or similar publication, containing at least four musical compositions, the royalty to be paid by the Publisher to the Writer shall be that proportion of 50% of the gross amount received by it from the licensee, as the number of uses of the composition under the license and during the license period, bears to the total number of uses of the Publisher's copyrighted musical compositions under the license and during the license period.

(iii) In computing the number of the Publisher's copyrighted musical compositions under subdivisions (i) and (ii) hereof, there shall be excluded musical compositions in the public domain and arrangements thereof and those with respect to which the Publisher does not currently publish and offer for sale regular piano copies.

(iv) Royalties on publications containing less than four musical compositions shall be payable at regular piano copy rates.

**Professional Material and Free Copies**

(f) As to "professional material" not sold or resold, no royalty shall be payable. Free copies of the lyrics of the composition shall not be distributed except under the following conditions: (i) with the Writer's written consent; or (ii) when printed without music in limited numbers for charitable, religious or governmental purposes, or for similar public purposes, if no profit is derived, directly or indirectly; or (iii) when authorized for printing in a book, magazine or periodical, where such use is incidental to a novel or story (as distinguished from use in a book of lyrics or a lyric magazine or folio), provided that any such use shall bear the Writer's name and the proper copyright notice; or (iv) when distributed solely for the purpose of exploiting the composition, provided, that such exploitation is restricted to the distribution of limited numbers of such copies for the purpose of influencing the sale of the composition, that the distribution is independent of the sale of any other musical compositions, services, goods, wares or merchandise, and that no profit is made, directly or indirectly, in connection therewith.

**Mechanicals, Electrical Transcription, Synchronization, All Other Rights**

(g) ........% (Insert percentage here) (in no case, however, less than 50%) of:

All gross receipts of the Publisher in respect of any licenses (including statutory royalties) authorizing the manufacture of parts of instruments serving to mechanically reproduce the composition, or to use the composition in synchronization with sound motion pictures, or to reproduce it upon electrical transcription for broadcasting purposes; and of any and all gross receipts of the Publisher from any other source or right now known or which may hereafter come into existence, except as provided in paragraph 2.

**Licensing Agent's Charges**

(h) If the Publisher administers licenses authorizing the manufacture of parts of instruments serving to mechanically reproduce said composition, or the use of said composition in synchronization or in timed relation with sound motion pictures or its reproduction upon electrical transcriptions, or any of them, through an agent, trustee or other administrator acting for a substantial part of the industry and not under the exclusive control of the Publisher (hereinafter sometimes referred to as licensing agent), the Publisher, in determining his receipts, shall be entitled to deduct from gross license fees paid by the Licensees, a sum equal to the charges paid by the Publisher to said licensing agent, provided, however, that in respect to synchronization or timed relation with sound motion pictures, said deduction shall in no event exceed $150.00 or 10% of said gross license fee, whichever is less; in connection with the manufacture of parts of instruments serving to mechanically reproduce said composition, said deductions shall not exceed 5% of said gross license fee; and in connection with electrical transcriptions, said deduction shall not exceed 10% of said gross license fee.

**Block Licenses**

(i) The Publisher agrees that the use of the composition will not be included in any bulk or block license heretofore or hereafter granted, and that it will not grant any bulk or block license to include the same, without the written consent of the Writer in each instance, except (i) that the Publisher may grant such licenses with respect to electrical transcription for broadcasting purposes, but in such event, the Publisher shall pay to the Writer that proportion of 50% of the gross amount received by it under each such license as the number of uses of the composition under each such license during each such license period bears to the total number of uses of the Publisher's copyrighted musical compositions under each such license during each such license period; in computing the number of the Publisher's copyrighted musical compositions for this purpose, there shall be excluded musical compositions in the public domain and arrangements thereof and those with respect to which the Publisher does not currently publish and offer for sale regular piano copies;

**Television and New Uses**

(ii) that the Publisher may appoint agents or representatives in countries outside of the United States and Canada to use and to grant licenses for the use of the composition on the customary royalty fee basis under which the Publisher shall receive not less than 10% of the marked retail selling price in respect of regular piano copies, and 50% of all other revenue; if, in connection with any such bulk or block license, the Publisher shall have received any advance, the Writer shall not be entitled to share therein, but in part of said advance shall be deducted in computing the composition's earnings under said bulk or block license. A bulk or block license shall be deemed to mean any license or agreement, domestic or foreign, whereby rights are granted in respect of two or more musical compositions.

(j) Except to the extent that the Publisher and Writer have heretofore or may hereafter assign to or vest in the small performing rights licensing organization with which Writer and Publisher are affiliated, the said rights or the right to grant licenses therefor, it is agreed that no licenses shall be granted without the written consent, in each instance, of the Writer for the use of the composition by means of television, or by any means, or for any purposes not commercially established, or for which licenses were not granted by the Publisher on musical compositions prior to June 1, 1937.

**Writer's Consent to Licenses**

(k) The Publisher shall not, without the written consent of the Writer in each case, give or grant any right or license (i) to use the title of the composition, or (ii) for the exclusive use of the composition in any form or for any purpose, or for any period of time, or for any territory, other than its customary arrangements with foreign publishers, or (iii) to give a dramatic representation of the composition or to dramatize the plot or story thereof, or (iv) for a vocal rendition of the composition in synchronization with sound motion pictures, or (v) for any synchronization use thereof, or (vi) for the use of the composition or a quotation or excerpt therefrom in any article, book, periodical, advertisement or other similar publication. If, however, the Publisher shall give to the Writer written notice by certified mail, return receipt requested, or telegram, specifying the right or license to be given or granted, the name of the licensee and the terms and conditions thereof, including the price or other compensation to be received therefor, then, unless the Writer (or any one or more of them) shall, within five business days after the delivery of such notice to the address of the Writer hereinafter designated, object thereto, the Publisher may grant such right or license in accordance with the said notice without first obtaining the consent of the Writer. Such notice shall be deemed sufficient if sent to the Writer at the address or addresses hereinafter designated or at the address or addresses last furnished to the Publisher in writing by the Writer.

**Trust for Writer**

(l) Any portion of the receipts which may become due to the Writer from license fees (in excess of offsets), whether received directly from the licensee or from any licensing agent of the Publisher, shall, if not paid immediately on the receipt thereof by the Publisher, belong to the Writer and shall be held in trust for the Writer until payment is made; the ownership of said trust fund by the Writer shall not be questioned whether the monies are physically segregated or not.

**Writer Participation**

(m) The Publisher agrees that it will not issue any license as a result of which it will receive any financial benefit in which the Writer does not participate.

**Writer Credit**

(n) On all regular piano copies, orchestrations, band or other arrangements, octavos, quartets, commercial sound recordings and other reproductions of the composition or parts thereof, in whatever form and however produced, Publisher shall include or cause to be included, in addition to the copyright notice, the name of the Writer, and Publisher shall include a similar requirement in every license or authorization issued by it with respect to the composition.

**Writers'**

5. Whenever the term "Writer" is used herein, it shall be deemed to mean all of the persons herein defined as "Writer" and any

| | |
|---|---|
| Respective Shares | and all royalties herein provided to be paid to the Writer shall be paid equally to such persons if there be more than one, unless otherwise provided in Paragraph 23. |
| Release of Commercial Sound Recording (Insert period not exceeding 12 months) | 6. (a) (i) The Publisher shall, within...............months from the date of this contract (the "initial period"), cause a commercial sound recording of the composition to be made and released in the customary form and through the customary commercial channels. If at the end of such initial period a sound recording has not been made and released, as above provided, then, subject to the provisions of the next succeeding subdivision, this contract shall terminate. |
| (Insert amount to be not less than $250) (Insert period not exceeding six months) | (ii) If, prior to the expiration of the initial period, Publisher pays the Writer the sum of $........(which shall not be charged against or recoupable out of any advances, royalties or other monies theretofor paid, then due, or which thereafter may become due the Writer from the Publisher pursuant to this contract or otherwise), Publisher shall have an additional..........months (the "additional period") commencing with the end of the initial period, within which to cause such commercial sound recording to be made and released as provided in subdivision (i) above. If at the end of the additional period a commercial sound recording has not been made and released, as above provided, then this contract shall terminate. |
| | (iii) Upon termination pursuant to this Paragraph 6(a), all rights of any and every nature in and to the composition and in and to any and all copyrights secured thereon in the United States and throughout the world shall automatically re-vest in and become the property of the Writer and shall be reassigned to him by the Publisher. The Writer shall not be obligated to return or pay to the Publisher any advance or indebtedness as a condition of such re-assignment; the said re-assignment shall be in accordance with and subject to the provisions of Paragraph 8 hereof, and, in addition, the Publisher shall pay to the Writer all gross sums which it has theretofore or may thereafter receive in respect of the composition. |
| Writer's Copies | (b) The Publisher shall furnish, or cause to be furnished, to the Writer six copies of the commercial sound recording referred to in Paragraph 6(a). |
| Piano Copies, Piano Arrangement or Lead Sheet (Select (i) or (ii) | (c) The Publisher shall <br> ☐ (i) within 30 days after the initial release of a commercial sound recording of the composition, make, publish and offer for sale regular piano copies of the composition in the form and through the channels customarily employed by it for that purpose; <br> ☐ (ii) within 30 days after execution of this contract make a piano arrangement or lead sheet of the composition and furnish six copies thereof to the Writer. <br> In the event neither subdivision (i) nor (ii) of this subparagraph (c) is selected, the provisions of subdivision (ii) shall be automatically deemed to have been selected by the parties. |
| Foreign Copyright | 7. (a) Each copyright on the composition in countries other than the United States shall be secured only in the name of the Publisher, and the Publisher shall not at any time divest itself of said foreign copyright directly or indirectly. |

# The AGAC Popular Songwriters Contract 393

Foreign Publication
(b) No rights shall be granted by the Publisher in the composition to any foreign publisher or licensee inconsistent with the terms hereof, nor shall any foreign publication rights in the composition be given to a foreign publisher or licensee unless and until the Publisher shall have complied with the provisions of Paragraph 6 hereof.

Foreign Advance
(c) If foreign rights in the composition are separately conveyed, otherwise than as a part of the Publisher's current and/or future catalog, not less than 50% of any advance received in respect thereof shall be credited to the account of and paid to the Writer.

Foreign Percentage
(d) The percentage of the Writer on monies received from foreign sources shall be computed on the Publisher's net receipts, provided, however, that no deductions shall be made for offsets of monies due from the Publisher to said foreign sources; or for advances made by such foreign sources to the Publisher, unless the Writer shall have received at least 50% of said advances.

No Foreign Allocations
(e) In computing the receipts of the Publisher from licenses granted in respect of synchronization with sound motion pictures, or in respect of any world-wide licenses, or in respect of licenses granted by the Publisher for use of the composition in countries other than the United States, no amount shall be deducted for payments or allocations to publishers or licensees in such countries.

Termination or Expiration of Contract
8. Upon the termination or expiration of this contract, all rights of any and every nature in and to the composition and in and to any and all copyrights secured thereon in the United States and throughout the world, shall re-vest in and become the property of the Writer, and shall be re-assigned to the Writer by the Publisher free of any and all encumbrances of any nature whatsoever, provided that:

(a) If the Publisher, prior to such termination or expiration, shall have granted a domestic license for the use of the composition, not inconsistent with the terms and provisions of this contract, the re-assignment may be subject to the terms of such license.

(b) Publisher shall assign to the Writer all rights which it may have under any such agreement or license referred to in subdivision (a) in respect of the composition, including, but not limited to, the right to receive all royalties or other monies earned by the composition thereunder after the date of termination or expiration of this contract. Should the Publisher thereafter receive or be credited with any royalties or other monies so earned, it shall pay the same to the Writer.

(c) The Writer shall not be obligated to return or pay to the Publisher any advance or indebtedness as a condition of the re-assignment provided for in this Paragraph 8, and shall be entitled to receive the plates and copies of the composition in the possession of the Publisher.

(d) Publisher shall pay any and all royalties which may have accrued to the Writer prior to such termination or expiration.

(e) The Publisher shall execute any and all documents and do any and all acts or things necessary to effect any and all re-assignments to the Writer herein provided for.

Negotiations for New or Unspecified Uses
9. If the Publisher desires to exercise a right in and to the composition now known or which may hereafter become known, but for which no specific provision has been made herein, the Publisher shall give written notice to the Writer thereof. Negotiations respecting all the terms and conditions of any such disposition shall thereupon be entered into between the Publisher and the Writer and no such right shall be exercised until specific agreement has been made.

Royalty
10. The Publisher shall render to the Writer, hereafter, royalty statements accompanied by remittance of the amount due at the

**Statements and Payments**

times such statements and remittances are customarily rendered by the Publisher, provided, however, that such statements and remittances shall be rendered either semi-annually or quarterly and not more than forty-five days after the end of each such semi-annual or quarterly period, as the case may be. The Writer may at any time, or from time to time, make written request for a detailed royalty statement, and the Publisher shall, within sixty days, comply therewith. Such royalty statements shall set forth in detail the various items, foreign and domestic, for which royalties are payable thereunder and the amounts thereof, including, but not limited to, the number of copies sold and the number of uses made in each royalty category. If a use is made in a publication of the character provided in Paragraph 4, subdivision (e) hereof, there shall be included in said royalty statement the title of said publication, the publisher or issuer thereof, the date of and number of uses, the gross license fee received in connection with each publication, the share thereto of all the writers under contract with the Publisher, and the Writer's share thereof. There shall likewise be included in statement a description of every other use of the composition, and if by a licensee or licensees their name or names, and if said use is upon a part of an instrument serving to reproduce the composition mechanically, the type of mechanical reproduction, the title of the label thereon, the name or names of the artists performing the same, together with the gross license fees received, and the Writer's share thereof.

**Examination of Books**

11. (a) The Publisher shall from time to time, upon written demand of the Writer or his representative, permit the Writer or his representative to inspect at the place of business of the Publisher, all books, records and documents relating to the composition and all licenses granted, uses had and payments made therefor, such right of inspection to include, but not by way of limitation, the right to examine all original accountings and records relating to uses and payments by manufacturers of commercial sound recordings and music rolls; and the Writer or his representative may appoint an accountant who shall at any time during usual business hours have access to all records of the Publisher relating to the composition for the purpose of verifying royalty statements rendered or which are delinquent under the terms hereof.

(b) The Publisher shall, upon written demand of the Writer or his representative, cause any licensing agent in the United States and Canada to furnish to the Writer or his representative, statements showing in detail all licenses granted, uses had and payments made in connection with the composition, which licenses or permits were granted, or payments were received, by or through said licensing agent, and to permit the Writer or his representative to inspect at the place of business of such licensing agent, all books, records and documents of such licensing agent, relating thereto. Any and all agreements made by the Publisher with any such licensing agent shall provide that any such licensing agent will comply with the terms and provisions hereof. In the event that the Publisher shall instruct such licensing agent to furnish to the Writer or his representative statements as provided for herein, and to permit the inspection of the books, records and documents as herein provided, then if such licensing agent should refuse to comply with the said instructions, or any of them, the Publisher agrees to institute and prosecute diligently and in good faith such action or proceedings as may be necessary to compel compliance with the said instructions.

(c) With respect to foreign licensing agents, the Publisher shall make available the books or records of said licensing agents in countries outside of the United States and Canada to the extent such books or records are available to the Publisher, except that the Publisher may in lieu thereof make available any accountants' reports and audits which the Publisher is able to obtain.

(d) If as a result of any examination of books, records or documents pursuant to Paragraphs 11(a), 11(b) or 11(c) hereof, it is determined that, with respect to any royalty statement rendered by or on behalf of the Publisher to the Writer, the Writer is owed a sum equal to or greater than five percent of the sum shown on that royalty statement as being due to the Writer, then the Publisher shall pay to the Writer the entire cost of such examination, not to exceed 50% of the amount shown to be due the Writer.

## The AGAC Popular Songwriters Contract 395

(e) (i) In the event the Publisher administers its own licenses for the manufacture of parts of instruments serving to mechanically reproduce the composition rather than employing a licensing agent for that purpose, the Publisher shall include in each license agreement a provision permitting the Publisher, the Writer or their respective representatives to inspect, at the place of business of such licensee, all books, records and documents of such licensee relating to such license. Within 30 days after written demand by the Writer, the Publisher shall commence to inspect such licensee's books, records and documents and shall furnish a written report of such inspection to the Writer within 90 days following such demand. If the Publisher fails, after written demand by the Writer, to so inspect the licensee's books, records and documents, or fails to furnish such report, the Writer or his representative may inspect such licensee's books, records and documents at his own expense.

(ii) In the further event that the Publisher and the licensee referred to in subdivision (i) above are subsidiaries or affiliates of the same entity or one is a subsidiary or affiliate of the other, then, unless the Publisher employs a licensing agent to administer the licenses referred to in subdivision (i) above, the Writer shall have the right to make the inspection referred to in subdivision (i) above without the necessity of making written demand on the Publisher as provided in subdivision (i) above.

(iii) If as a result of any inspection by the Writer pursuant to subdivisions (i) and (ii) of this subparagraph (e) the Writer recovers additional monies from the licensee, the Publisher and the Writer shall share equally in the cost of such inspection.

**Default in Payment or Prevention of Examination**

12. If the Publisher shall fail or refuse, within sixty days after written demand, to furnish or cause to be furnished, such statements, books, records or documents, or to permit inspection thereof, as provided for in Paragraphs 10 and 11 hereof, or within thirty days after written demand, to make the payment of any royalties due under this contract, then the Writer shall be entitled, upon ten days' written notice, to terminate this contract. However if the Publisher shall:

(a) Within the said ten-day period serve upon the Writer a written notice demanding arbitration; and

(b) Submit to arbitration its claim that it has complied with its obligation to furnish statements, books, records or documents, or permitted inspection thereof or to pay royalties, as the case may be, or both, and thereafter comply with any award of the arbitrator within ten days after such award or within such time as the arbitrator may specify;

then this contract shall continue in full force and effect as if the Writer had not sent such notice of termination. If the Publisher shall fail to comply with the foregoing provisions, then this contract shall be deemed to have been terminated as of the date of the Writer's written notice of termination.

**Derivative Works**

13. No derivative work prepared under authority of Publisher during the term of this contract may be utilized by Publisher or any other party after termination or expiration of this contract.

**Notices**

14. All written demands and notices provided for herein shall be sent by certified mail, return receipt requested.

**Suits for Infringement**

15. Any legal action brought by the Publisher against any alleged infringer of the composition shall be initiated and prosecuted at its sole cost and expense, but if the Publisher should fail, within thirty days after written demand, to institute such action, the Writer shall be entitled to institute such suit at his cost and expense. All sums recovered as a result of any such action shall, after the deduction of the reasonable expense thereof, be divided equally between the Publisher and the Writer. No settlement of any such action may be made by either party without first notifying the other; in the event that either party should object to such settlement, then such

settlement shall not be made if the party objecting assumes the prosecution of the action and all expenses thereof, except that any sums thereafter recovered shall be divided equally between the Publisher and the Writer after the deduction of the reasonable expenses thereof.

Infringement Claims

16. (a) If a claim is presented against the Publisher alleging that the composition is an infringement upon some other work or a violation of any other right of another, and because therof the Publisher is jeopardized, it shall forthwith serve a written notice upon the Writer setting forth the full details of such claim. The pendency of said claim shall not relieve the Publisher of the obligation to make payment of the royalties to the Writer hereunder, unless the Publisher shall deposit said royalties as and when they would otherwise be payable, in an account in the joint names of the Publisher and the Writer in a bank or trust company in New York, New York, if the Writer on the date of execution of this contract resides East of the Mississippi River, or in Los Angeles, California, if the Writer on the date of execution of this contract resides West of the Mississippi River. If no suit be filed within nine months after said written notice from the Publisher to the Writer, all monies deposited in said joint account shall be paid over to the Writer plus any interest which may have been earned thereon.

(b) Should an action be instituted against the Publisher claiming that the composition is an infringement upon some other work or a violation of any other right of another, the Publisher shall forthwith serve written notice upon the Writer containing the full details of such claim. Notwithstanding the commencement of such action, the Publisher shall continue to pay the royalties hereunder to the Writer unless it shall, from and after the date of the service of the summons, deposit said royalties as and when they would otherwise be payable, in an account in the joint names of the Publisher and the Writer in a bank or trust company in New York, New York, if the Writer on the date of execution of this contract resides East of the Mississippi River, or in Los Angeles, California, if the Writer on the date of execution of this contract resides West of the Mississippi River. If the said suit shall be finally adjudicated in favor of the Publisher or shall be settled, there shall be released and paid to the Writer all of such sums held in escrow less any amount paid out of the Writer's share with the Writer's written consent in settlement of said action. Should the said suit finally result adversely to the Publisher, the said amount on deposit shall be released to the Publisher to the extent of any expense or damage it incurs and the balance shall be paid over to the Writer.

(c) In any of the foregoing events, however, the Writer shall be entitled to payment of said royalties or the money so deposited at and after such time as he files with the Publisher a surety company bond, or a bond in other form acceptable to the Publisher, in the sum of such payments to secure the return thereof to the extent that the Publisher may be entitled to such return. The foregoing payments or deposits or the filing of a bond shall be without prejudice to the rights of the Publisher or Writer in the premises.

Arbitration

17. Any and all differences, disputes or controversies arising out of or in connection with this contract shall be submitted to arbitration before a sole arbitrator under the then prevailing rules of the American Arbitration Association. The location of the arbitration shall be New York, New York, if the Writer on the date of execution of this contract resides East of the Mississippi River, or Los Angeles, California, if the Writer on the date of execution of this contract resides West of the Mississippi River. The parties hereby individually and jointly agree to abide by and perform any award rendered in such arbitration. Judgment upon any such award rendered may be entered in any court having jurisdiction thereof.

Assignment

18. Except to the extent herein otherwise expressly provided, the Publisher shall not sell, transfer, assign, convey, encumber or otherwise dispose of the composition or the copyright or copyrights secured thereon without the prior written consent of the Writer. The Writer has been induced to enter into this contract in reliance upon the value to him of the personal service and ability of the Publisher

## The AGAC Popular Songwriters Contract

in the exploitation of the composition, and by reason thereof it is the intention of the parties and the essence of the relationship between them that the rights herein granted to the Publisher shall remain with the Publisher and that the same shall not pass to any other person, including, without limitations, successors to or receivers or trustees of the property of the Publisher, either by act or deed of the Publisher or by operation of law, and in the event of the voluntary or involuntary bankruptcy of the Publisher, this contract shall terminate, provided, however, that the composition may be included by the Publisher in a bona fide voluntary sale of its music business or its entire catalog of musical compositions, or in a merger or consolidation of the Publisher with another corporation, in which event the Publisher shall immediately give written notice thereof to the Writer; and provided further that the composition and the copyright therein may be assigned by the Publisher to a subsidiary or affiliated company generally engaged in the music publishing business. If the Publisher is an individual, the composition may pass to a legatee or distributee as part of the inheritance of the Publisher's music business and entire catalog of musical compositions. Any such transfer or assignment shall, however, be conditioned upon the execution and delivery by the transferee or assignee to the Writer of an agreement to be bound by and to perform all of the terms and conditions of this contract to be performed on the part of the Publisher.

**Subsidiary Defined** 19. A subsidiary, affiliate, or any person, firm or corporation controlled by the Publisher or by such subsidiary or affiliate, as used in this contract, shall be deemed to include any person, firm or corporation, under common control with, or the majority of whose stock or capital contribution is owned or controlled by the Publisher or by any of its officers, directors, partners or associates, or whose policies and actions are subject to domination or control by the Publisher or any of its officers, directors, partners or associates.

**Amounts** 20. The amounts and percentages specified in this contract shall be deemed to be the amounts and percentages agreed upon by the parties hereto, unless other amounts or percentages are inserted in the blank spaces provided therefor.

**Modifications** 21. This contract is binding upon and shall enure to the benefit of the parties hereto and their respective successors in interest (as hereinbefore limited). If the Writer (or one or more of them) shall not be living, any notices may be given to, or consents given by, his or their successors in interest. No change or modification of this contract shall be effective unless reduced to writing and signed by the parties hereto.

The words in this contract shall be so construed that the singular shall include the plural and the plural shall include the singular where the context so requires and the masculine shall include the feminine and the feminine shall include the masculine where the context so requires.

**Paragraph Headings** 22. The paragraph headings are inserted only as a matter of convenience and for reference, and in no way define, limit or describe the scope or intent of this contract nor in any way affect this contract.

**Special Provisions** 23.

Witness: ..................................... Publisher ......................................
                                              By ..............................................
Witness: ..................................... Address .......................................
                                              Writer ..................................(L.S.)
Witness: ..................................... Address .......................................
                                              Soc. Sec. #
                                              Writer ..................................(L.S.)
Witness: ..................................... Address .......................................
                                              Soc. Sec. #
                                              Writer ..................................(L.S.)
                                              Address .......................................
                                              Soc. Sec. #

• • • • •

FOR YOUR PROTECTION,
SEND A COPY OF THE FULLY SIGNED CONTRACT TO AGAC.

Special Exceptions to apply only if filled in and initialed by the parties.
☐ The composition is part of an original score (not an interpolation) of
  ☐ Living Stage Production   ☐ Motion Picture   ☐ Night Club Revue
  ☐ Televised Musical Production
which is the subject of an agreement between the parties dated _____, a copy of which is hereto annexed. Unless said agreement requires compliance with Paragraph 6 in respect of a greater number of musical compositions, the Publisher shall be deemed to have complied with said Paragraph 6 with respect to the composition if it fully performs the terms of said Paragraph 6 in respect of any one musical composition included in said score.

# Home Demos that "Sell" Songs

BY MICHAEL J. KOSSER

Can you make a demo at home with your guitar (or piano) and a $50 cassette recorder that is good enough to interest a publisher in your song?

The answer, of course, is, "yes, if. . . ." Successful songwriters have had many of their songs recorded by submitting a simple voice/guitar tape to a producer or artist. However, you must be your own toughest critic in deciding when your demo is good enough to submit. To increase your chances of making a good voice/instrument demo at home:

- Put your cassette recorder in order (you can use a reel-to-reel recorder, of course, but you'll probably want to transfer the finished product to a cassette because that's what most publishers and producers listen to). Clean the recording heads and make sure it is recording properly.
- Make sure your musical instrument is properly tuned. Yes, it does make a difference. People with musical ears generally HATE demos with badly tuned instruments.
- Set up your "studio." The room should be free of background noise. This is very important. Whether it is a live room (bare walls and some echo) or a dead room (lots of drapes and no echo) is up to you. I believe a dead room is better, particularly for a piano demo.
- For a guitar demo, an armless chair in front of a table piled with books as a mike stand might be sufficient, but for a piano demo, a mike stand might be necessary. DO NOT use the condenser mike built into most of today's cassette recorders. It tends to pick up noise from the machine and is difficult to position for a proper voice-instrument mix. No, I take that back—partially. Sometimes you can make it work. But you're better off with a separate mike. In any event, DO NOT try a piano demo with the mike laying on top of the piano. That won't work and here's why: All publishers and producers have their own horror stories about the hundreds of home tapes they receive on which the piano or guitar is so loud they can hardly hear the melody being sung, much less the lyric. Your biggest technical challenge in doing your home demo is to get the right "mix" between your instrument and your voice—too much instrument and you lose the song. Too little instrument and you can lose the feel. In this case you get the right mix by positioning your mike closer or farther away from your mouth in proportion to the instrument. Make several trial "takes," adding and subtracting books, or raising and lowering the mike stand, until the mix sounds right.
- Now you have to think about "dynamics," which essentially is the variation of intensity within a song. "Work" the mike by pulling your head back when you're belting out a high note, and move in close when your voice becomes soft and intimate. Move your guitar a little closer when you're playing a little arpeggio fill between lines or, in the case of piano, play a little louder when the arrangement calls for it.

**Mike Kosser** *is a songwriter, journalist, lecturer, member of the NSAI Board of Directors, and author of* Bringing It to Nashville. *Along with Tom C. Armstrong and Beverly Beard, he also wrote* The History of Country Music, *a 52-hour presentation syndicated to date on over one-hundred twenty five radio stations.*

- Pay attention to the way you sing your song. None of us has a perfect voice, and our demos become much better once we learn our own limitations. If you can't hold a certain note without blaring it out unpleasantly or fading flat, find a way to soften it, or shorten it. You can hold a note more easily on some vowels than others. And if you're having trouble playing certain rhythms and singing at the same time, well, a little practice ought to take care of that.
- If you pay too much attention to getting every note right, of course, you're liable to lose the feeling. After all, you are trying to "sell" the song to your listener, so once you feel like you know your material, try to perform it on tape as naturally as possible. This is not as easy as it sounds. After your fifth fluff or so, there's a tendency to tighten up when you're nearing the place in the song where you keep making your mistake, or when you're nearing the end of the take. Just keep reminding yourself that music is supposed to be fun, take a few deep breaths, relax, and try again.
- Since few of us can edit a cassette, make sure that you do not have pieces of previous takes lurking on the tape before your new take begins, and let the tape run a few seconds after you finish recording your song for the same reason.

## Judging Your Demo

In listening to your home demo, you must be the one to judge whether or not you've done the job.
- Is your singing too bland? Or is it too emotional? Is the phrasing sloppy, tense or sing-songy?
- If you put in a long instrumental break, do the song over again, and leave out the break. Publishers and producers want to hear the song.
- Have you recorded at too low a level, so that the tape hiss is too high? Or too high a level so there is distortion on the tape?
- Are there any distracting noises on the tape, like, say, foot-stomping, or the sound of your clothes rubbing against the table?
- If you used a piano, have you placed the microphone off the piano, so the tape is free of piano vibrations?
- Most important, do you like the way it sounds? If the feeling is there, it can make up for a dozen minor glitches.

## Upgrading Your Home Demo

Some of us can sing well, and play an instrument well. Others of us cannot. Most songwriters who do both lyrics and melodies can do both, at least a little. It is my belief that if you learn to do it a little, you should be able to learn to do it a lot better. Don't say you can't. The more you are able to do yourself, the better your chances of success. So sharpen your musical skills. No matter how much time it takes, it's time well spent.

As you gain experience you might want to upgrade your home demoing capability. One to two thousand dollars could give you a four-track reel-to-reel or cassette system that translates into ten tracks once you become skillful in the art of "ping-ponging."

With this new added dimension, you'll find yourself learning to play new rhythm instruments, searching for new sounds, and experimenting in harmony. It's all a lot of fun, but don't forget that most songs are sold by simplicity, and that overbusy and clashing sounds often detract from the feel of a recording.

However you are doing your home demos, remember that you are not only the songwriter and performer, but the producer, which means you're the sole judge of when a demo is ready to be presented. If you're too easy on yourself your song might not have the showcase it deserves. If you're too hard on yourself, your song might *never* have a chance to be heard. Only one thing is virtually certain: Given an average amount of talent, the more you work at it, the better you'll get.

# How to Be a Music Market Detective

BY BARBARA NORTON KUROFF

Today's top acts don't advertise for songs, and stars aren't listed in telephone books and rarely in any other directory, including *Songwriter's Market*. So if you've written what you think could be a hit for a specific recording artist, how do you get your song to him?

Fortunately, the producers, publishers and managers around star performers *are* accessible. They are the people who play a big part in decisions concerning the stars' careers, including the choice of material for recording sessions. Get your song to one of these people and you get your song to the artist, assuming, of course, that the people around the artist think your song is good. This is not to say these people are easy to reach—they are not—but a music market detective can ferret them out.

## Your Music Market Notebook

Begin your search by assigning one page of a notebook for each artist you think you might have songs for; these pages are your artist information sheets. Use each sheet to record the names, addresses and phone numbers of the artist's record companies, producers, publishers and managers. To get this information begin by looking around your home. Do you own albums by any of the artists you've listed in your notebook? If so, their covers and labels are loaded with clues.

Album covers give the name (and possibly address) of an artist's record company and also the name of the producer. If song titles and their writers and publishers are not listed on the album covers, they can be found on the record label. Album liner notes might also reveal valuable information about an artist or group: how a particular song came to their attention or why they recorded it; or a new musical or career direction the act might be undertaking.

Check album dates, however. Since we're talking about popular artists, you can assume if albums are more than a year old, there may be a more recent one available in your local record shop with new information.

Once you've found the names of record companies and publishers of the artists you wish to submit songs to, be sure to check the index of *Songwriter's Market*. If you don't find the companies listed, then refer to the "Quiet Types" at the end of both the Music Publishers and Record Companies sections. There you will find the addresses of many top companies, but no phone numbers or submission information.

## The Corner Newsstand

Your next stop should be your local magazine stand, if they carry the weekly music industry trade magazines, *Billboard* or *Cash Box*.

The charts in *Billboard* and *Cash Box* list today's most popular songs in a variety of musical categories—Adult Contemporary, Hot 100, Country, Black, Jazz, Classical, etc. At the top of each chart is a guide to reading the information given in the entries: producer, writer, label, publisher, etc. *Cash Box* does not list producers, but otherwise the charts in both publications give information in a somewhat similar format.

The trades also offer the songwriter information about what's happening in the music business in Los Angeles, Nashville, New York City, and across the US and around the world: industry events, new companies, executive changes, artist news, new releases. This is all information you can use in your songwriting career. Read the ads, too, especially those announcing an artist's newest release. Often the name and perhaps the address and phone number of the artist's manager can be found there.

Although the charts change weekly, songs by top artists climb and then fall slowly back down the charts for weeks. Therefore, for your purpose of finding the names of labels, producers and publishers of particular artists, it is sufficient to purchase a trade magazine once every few weeks. (Don't forget to keep the receipts to claim as a business expense when song royalties start coming in.)

Annual subscriptions to the trades are expensive (see the Publications of Interest section of this book for ordering information), but keep in mind the value of other publications included in the subscription rate. A *Billboard* subscription includes their annual *International Buyer's Guide*, selling separately for $50. *Cash Box* automatically sends subscribers their *Annual Directory*, selling separately for $17.50 if purchased by mail. Included in these directories are the names, addresses and phone numbers of hundreds of music publishers and record companies, but no submission information.

## The Local Library

Both publications can be found in the music sections of many libraries. They're usually available for reference only and can't be checked out. Libraries subscribing to either trade magazine should also have that publication's annual directory of publishers and record companies.

Even if your library does not subscribe to *Billboard* or *Cash Box*, they probably do have phone directories for cities across the country—including Los Angeles, New York (Manhattan), and Nashville. Unlike the famous artists they represent, music publishers and record companies *are* listed in phone books, not only with their phone numbers but also their addresses.

Phone books don't include zip codes with the addresses, but you can refer to the *Zip Code and Post Office Directory*, published annually by the US Postal Service. There should be one in the library; if not, you will find one in your local post office.

If you call and ask, most libraries will even look up a company's address and phone number for you, or you can use the phone company's directory service, usually limited to answering a certain number of requests per call.

## Getting Closer

Your music market notebook by now should pin-point your artists and the names, addresses and phone numbers of their record companies and publishers; the names of their producers; and possibly the names of their managers. What you don't know is which of those names would be the best to first submit material to.

My advice would be to work toward getting your material to the person with the most to say in the artist's choice of material—the producer. Unfortunately, so far you only have the names of the artists' producers—no addresses or phone numbers. You will have obtained some information from *Songwriter's Market* and might have been observant enough to notice some producers listed in *Billboard International Buyer's Guide* as the A&R director of record companies. You might also have been lucky enough to find some in the L.A., Nashville or Manhattan phone books. But the producer who does not always work out of an office but spends most of his time in various recording studios is not an easy person to track down. You must now find another route to them.

The addresses and phone numbers of all the artists' record companies and many of their publishers that you *do* have in your music market notebook will become your key to getting your songs to the producers who can get them to the artists.

## Zeroing In

For several reasons the record company is the best place to start tracking a producer. Record companies are big-business operations with regular hours; receptionists and secretaries are paid to answer phones and handle mail. It's been my experience that these front desk people are amiable, capable and helpful, as long as you don't abuse their good qualities by being overly demanding, calling every other day, or keeping them on the phone too long.

When you get someone on the phone, be upfront and to the point. Know what you intend to say: "I'm (*your name*) and I'm trying to contact (*the producer's name*), or the person who reviews material for (*the artist's name*). If the producer has an office in the studio—many times he will—you may be switched there immediately. If he doesn't have an office in the studio, the receptionist may give you an address and phone number where the producer can be contacted. If she doesn't volunteer this valuable information, be sure to ask for it.

On the other hand, you could get no farther than: "I'm sorry, we aren't allowed to give out that information," or "We don't accept any outside material." Don't get discouraged. Remember you also have names and addresses of several publishers of the artist's recently recorded songs. The producer may have worked closely with these publishers. It could even be that the artist or the producer owns one of the publishing houses. So try the same routine with the music publishers written in your notebook.

Whomever you talk with at recording companies or publishing houses, make notes in your notebook on when you called, whom you talked with, and what was said. Jot down things like "He's in Europe at Midem" or "He'll be tied up for the next few weeks producing a session on Linda Ronstadt." This could be valuable information later, even as conversation, when you finally do talk with the big, busy producer.

If the person on the other end of the line gives you permission to submit material, establish some way your package can be easily identified when it arrives at the office. Often a receptionist—let's call her Susan—will tell you to write her name on your package. When your tape arrives at the office, Susan sees her name, knows she must have talked with you, and so lays it on the producer's desk (or at least sees it's somewhere near the top of the unsolicited tapes). I'm not saying this procedure works every time. What I am saying is that it has worked many times for unknown songwriters. Even well-known songwriters use it as a way of seeing that their material is heard.

When calling long distance, remember time differences. When it's 9 a.m. in New York City and people are already at their desks with their fourth coffee, it's 8 a.m. in Nashville, where many music industry people don't arrive in their offices until 10, and only 6 a.m. in Los Angeles where a producer may just be finishing up an all-night recording session.

## In Conclusion

If you've been a diligent music market detective, you may find yourself invited to submit songs to people who spend thousands of dollars just on the production of one song. Your submissions cannot be mediocre songs only your family and friends like. Your songs must be worked and honed until they are better than the best. If they are not, all your detective work will have been in vain.

I think that by keeping a music market notebook you will no longer feel helpless in an industry that can often intimidate beginners (and even those who are successful). Recognize your own ability to dig for information and use resources that help get your songs to anyone in any music center without leaving your own home town.

# Glossary

**A&R director.** Record company employee who deals with new artists, songs and masters coordinating the best material with a particular artist.
**A/C.** Adult contemporary.
**Acetate dub.** A demonstration record that is individually cut, often referred to as a disc.
**Advance.** Money paid to the songwriter or recording artist before regular royalty payments begin. Sometimes called "upfront" money, advances are deducted from royalties.
**AFM.** American Federation of Musicians. A union for musicians and arrangers.
**AFTRA.** American Federation of Television and Radio Artists.
**AGAC.** American Guild of Authors and Composers.
**AIMP.** Association Independent Music Publishers.
**AOR.** Album-oriented rock.
**Arrangement.** Adapting a composition for performance by other instruments, voices or performers.
**ASCAP.** American Society of Composers, Authors and Publishers.
**A-side.** Side one of a single promoted by the record company to become a hit.
**Assignment.** Transfer of rights to a song from writer to publisher.
**Audiovisual.** Presentations using audio backup for visual material.
**Bed.** Prerecorded music used as background material in commercials.
**BMI.** Broadcast Music, Inc.
**Booking agent.** Solicits work and schedules performances for entertainer.
**b/w.** Backed with.
**C&W.** Country and western.
**CAPAC.** Composers, Authors & Publishers of Canada Ltd.
**CARAS.** Canadian Academy of Recording Arts and Sciences.
**Catalog.** The collected songs of one writer, or all songs handled by one publisher.
**CCC.** California Copyright Conference.
**Chart.** The written arrangement of a song.
**Charts.** The weekly trade magazines' lists of the bestselling records.
**CIRPA.** Canadian Independent Record Producers Association.
**CMRRA.** Canadian Musical Reproduction Rights Association.
**Collaborator.** Person who works with another in a creative situation.
**CMA.** Country Music Association.
**CMPA.** Church Music Publishers Association.
**Copy song.** A song already released and made popular by another act.
**Copyright.** Legal protection given authors and composers for an original work.
**Cover record.** A new version of a previously recorded song.

**CPM.** Conference of Personal Managers.
**CRIA.** Canadian Musical Reproduction Rights Association.
**Crossover.** A song that becomes popular in two or more music fields.
**Cut.** Any finished recording; a selection from an LP; or to record.
**C&W.** Country and western.
**Demo.** A rough recording, usually a tape, of a song.
**Disc.** A record.
**Distributor.** Sole marketing agent of a record in a particular area.
**Donut.** Jingle with singing at the beginning and end and only instrumental background in the middle.
**Engineer.** A specially trained individual who operates all studio recording equipment.
**Evergreen.** Any song that remains popular year after year.
**EP.** Extended play.
**FICAP.** Federation of International Country Air Personalities.
**Folio.** A softcover collection of songs prepared for sale.
**GMA.** Gospel Music Association.
**Harry Fox Agency.** Organization that collects mechanical royalties.
**Hook.** A memorable "catch" phrase or melody line which is repeated in a song.
**ILA.** Independent Record Labels Association.
**IMU.** International Musicians Union.
**IPS.** Inches per second; a speed designation for reel-to-reel tape.
**IRMA.** International Record Manufacturers Association.
**Jingle.** Usually a short verse set to music designed as a commercial message.
**LP.** Designation for long-playing record synonomous with album and played at 33 1/3 rpm.
**Lead sheet.** Written version (melody, chord symbols and lyric) of a song.
**Leader.** Tape at the beginning and between songs for ease in selection.
**Lryic sheet.** A typed copy of a song's lyrics.
**Manager.** Guides and advises artist in his career.
**Market.** A demographic division of the record-buying public.
**Master.** Edited and mixed tape used in the pressing of records.
**MCA.** Music Critics Association.
**Mechanical right.** The right to profit from the reproduction of a song.
**Mechanical royalty.** Money earned from record and tape sales.
**MIEA.** Music Industry Educators' Association.
**Mix.** To blend a multi-track recording into the desired balance of sound.
**MOR.** Middle of the road. A song considered "easy listening."
**Ms.** Manuscript.
**Music publisher.** A company that evaluates songs for commercial potential, finds artists to record them, finds other uses such as TV or film for the songs, collects income generated by the songs and protects copyrights from infringement.
**NAIRD.** National Association of Independent Record Distributors.
**NARAS.** National Academy of Recording Arts and Sciences.
**NARM.** National Association of Record Merchandisers.
**Needle-drop.** Use of a prerecorded cut from a stock music house in an audiovisual soundtrack.
**NMA.** Nashville Music Assocation.
**NMPA.** National Music Publishers Association
**NSAI.** Nashville Songwriters Association International.
**NSG.** National Songwriters' Guild.
**Performing rights.** A specific right granted by US copyright law that protects a composition from being publicly performed without the owner's permission.
**Performing rights organization.** An organization that collects income from the public performance of songs written by its members and then proportionally

distributes this income to the individual copyright holder based on the number of performances of each song.
**Pitch.** To attempt to sell a song by audition; the sales talk.
**Playlist.** List of songs, usually top 40, that a radio station will play.
**Plug.** A favorable mention, broadcast or performance of a song. Also means to pitch a song.
**Points.** Percentage paid to producers and artists for records sold.
**Press.** To manufacture a record from the master tape.
**PROCAN.** Performing Rights Organization of Canada Ltd.
**Production company.** Company that specializes in producing jingle packages for advertising agencies. May also refer to companies that specialize in audiovisual programs.
**Professional manager.** Member of a music publisher's staff who screens submitted material and tries to get the company's catalog of songs recorded.
**Producer.** Person who controls every aspect of recording a song.
**Program director.** Radio station employee who screens records and develops a playlist of songs that station will broadcast.
**Public domain.** Any composition with an expired, lapsed or invalid copyright.
**Purchase license.** Fee paid for music used from a stock music library.
**Query.** A letter of inquiry to a potential song buyer soliciting his interest.
**R&B.** Rhythm and blues.
**R&R.** Rock and roll.
**Rate.** The percentage of royalty as specified by contract.
**Release.** Any record issued by a record company.
**Residuals.** In advertising, payments to singers and musicians for subsequent use of a commercial.
**Rhythm Machine.** An electronic device that provides various tempos for use as background rhythm for other instruments or vocalists.
**RIAA.** Recording Industry Association of America.
**Royalty.** Percentage of money earned from the sale of records or use of a song.
**SASE.** Abbreviation for self-addressed stamped envelope.
**SBSA.** Santa Barbara Screenwriters' Association.
**SBSG.** Santa Barbara Songwriters' Guild.
**Scratch track.** Rough working tape demonstrating idea for a commercial.
**SESAC.** Performing rights organization.
**Shop.** To pitch songs to a number of companies or publishers.
**Single.** 45 rpm record.
**SIRMA.** Small Independent Record Manufacturers Association.
**Song shark.** Person who deals with songwriters deceptively for his own profit.
**Soundtrack.** The audio, including music and narration, of a film, videotape or audiovisual program.
**Split Publishing.** To divide publishing rights between two or more publishers.
**SRS.** Songwriters Resources and Services.
**Staff writer.** A salaried songwriter who writes exclusively for one publishing firm.
**Standard.** A song popular year after year; an evergreen.
**Statutory royalty rate.** The minimum payment for mechanical rights guaranteed by law that a record company must pay the songwriter and his publisher for each record or tape sold.
**Stiff.** The first recording of a song that commercially fails.
**Subpublishing.** Certain rights granted by a US publisher to a foreign publisher in exchange for promoting the US catalog in his territory.
**Synchronization.** Technique of timing a musical soundtrack to action on film.
**Synchronization rights.** Right to use composition in timed-relation to action on film.
**TMA.** Texas Music Association.

**Track.** Portions of a recording tape (e.g., 24-track tape) that can be individually recorded in the studio, then mixed into a finished master.
**Trades.** Publications that cover the music industry.
**U/C.** Urban contemporary.
**Work.** To pitch or shop a song.

# Index

## A

A&M Records, Inc. (Los Angeles) 125
A&M Records, Inc. (New York) 125
A&M Records of Canada, Ltd. 125
Abacus 125
Able Music, Inc. 12
Academy of Country Music, The 360
Accent Records 206
Acclaim Records, Inc. 125, 206
Ace Adams Music, Adam Puertas Music 13
Ace Productions 297
ACI International/Groovesong Records 125
Acoustic Music, Inc. 12
Act "1" Entertainments 297
Action Ticket Agency and Promotions 297
Adco Productions 283
Adelante Advertising, Inc. 261
Adoration, Inc. 297
Advertising & Marketing, Inc. 261
Advertising Communications, Inc. 262
Aferton Records 126
AGAC Workshops 372
AGAC/The Songwriters Guild (see The American Guild of Authors and Composers) 361
Airwave Productions 207
Ajaye Entertainment Corp. 297
ALAB 126
Alamo Talent and Productions 297
Aldous Demian Publishing, Ltd. 13, 207
Alear Music (see Jim McCoy Music) 65
Alear Records 126
Aleph-Baze Music & Strangeland Music 13
Alexander/Somor Music, Willie Loco 298
Alexis 13
Alive Enterprises 298
Aljoni Music Co. 13
Al-Kris Music 14
All Night Entertainment 298
All Star Talent Agency 298
All Star Talent & Promotions 298
Allen & Martin Productions 207
Allied Booking Co. 298
Alpha-Robinson Music 14

Alpine Advertising, Inc. 262
Alternative Chorus Songwriters Showcase, The (See The Los Angeles Songwriters Showcase) 363
Alternative Direction Music Publishers 14
Amalgamated Tulip Corp. 14, 126
Amalisa 207
Ambiente Music Productions, Inc. 126, 207
AME Corporation, The 126, 208
American Artists 298
American Broadcasting Music, Inc. 14
American Creative Entertainment, Ltd. 208, 299
American Entertainment General 14
American Federation of Musicians 360
American Guild of Authors and Composers 360, 373
American Guild of Music 361
American Mechanical Rights Association 361
American Music Center, Inc. 361
American Music Company 127
American Music Conference 361
American Society of Composers, Authors and Publishers 361
American Song Festival 357
American Theatre Arts 343
Americus Music 14
AMI 15, 127, 208
Amiron Music 15, 127
AMJ International/Jackson Enterprises 299
Amvid Communication Services, Inc. 262
Anamaze Records 127
Anderson Enterprises, Lee 127 (also see Calwest Songs/Lee Anderson Enterprises 28)
Anderson Music 15
Andrea Record Co. 127
Andustin Music 15
Anode Music 15
Anthem Records of Canada 128
Apon Publishing Co. 15
Apon Record Company, Inc. 128, 208
Apple-Glass Music 15
Appropriate Productions 208

April Records 128
April/Blackwood Music Canada, Ltd. 16
Aquarius Records 128
Aquila Records 128
Arby Records 128
Arcade Music Co. 16
Arcade Records (see Arzee Records 208)
Arcee Productions 299
Arena Players Repertory Theatre 343
Argus Record Productions 129
Ariana Records 129
Ariola Records (see Arista Records, England 129)
Arista Music Publishing Group 16
Arista Records Inc. (Los Angeles) 129
Arista Records (England) 129
Aristo Music Associates, Inc. 299
Arizona Songwriters Association 362
Arkansas State University—Beebe Campus 343
Arlo Records 129
Armstrong Advertising Agency, N. 262
Armstrong & Associates, Inc., Pat 299
Arnold Color Systems, Inc. (See Martin/Arnold Color Systems, Inc. 290)
Arranging Popular Music 369
Art Attact Records, Inc. 131
Art Audio Publishing Co. 16
Arzee Records 208
Arztco Pictures, Inc. 283
ASC Music Co. 16
ASCAP "Welcomes Songwriters" Series 373
Asilomar/Dreena Music 16
Asolo State Theater 343
Associated Recording Companies 131
Astral Productions, Inc. 209
Atjack Music 17
Atlantic Recording Corp. 131
Atom Productions, Tom 209
Attic Publishing Group 17
Attic Records Ltd. 131
ATV Music Corp. (Los Angeles) 17
ATV Music Corp. (Nashville) 17
ATV Music Corp. (New York) 17
Audio Arts Publishing 17
Audio Fidelity Enterprises, Inc. 131
Aura Records & Music Ltd. 17
Autograph Music 18
AVI Records, Inc. 131
Avilo Music 18
Axbar Productions 18
Axbar Records 132
Ayers Enterprises, Cliff 283, 300
Azra Records 132
Aztec Productions 209, 300 (also see Amiron Music 127)
Azure Records 209

## B

B.C. Enterprises of Memphis, Inc. 18, 209
Baby Huey Music 18

Baby Whale Music (see Teahouse Music)
Bachner Productions, Inc. 283
Bagatelle Record Company 132
Bal & Bal Music Publishing Co. 19
Bal Records 132
Ballard Cannon, Inc. 262
Baker Enterprises, Bobby 300
Bam-Caruso Records 133
Bananas Inc. 262
Band of Angels, Inc. 19
B&C Musical Services 132
B&D Publishing 18
Barnard Management Services 300
Barrasso Agency (see Collins/Barrasso Agency) 305
Barsongs Limited 19, 209
Barter Theatre, State Theatre of Virginia 344
Baruth Music 19
Basic Records 210
Bass Clef Music 19
Batten, Barton, Durstine & Osborn, Inc. 262
Batz-Hodgson-Neuwoehner, Inc. 262
Bauer-Hall Enterprises 300
BBDO 263
BBDO West 263
BBW Records 133
Beacon International Artists 300
Beantown Publishing Co. (see Sunbonnet Publishing Co. 105)
Beantown Records (see Sunbonnet Records 194)
Bear Advertising 263
Bearce Publishing 19
Bearsongs 20
Bearsville Records 133
Beautiful Day Music 20
Beaver, Quentin C. 344
Bee Gee 133
Bee Hive Jazz Records 133, 210
Bee Jay Recording Studios 210
Bee Mor Music 20
Bee/Alexander Productions 210
Beechwood (Los Angeles) 20
Beechwood Music (Nashville) 20
Beechwood Music Corp. (New York) 20
Believe in a Dream Records, Inc. 133
Belkin Maduri Organization, The 301
Bell of the Cape Advertising 263
Belle Street Productions, Inc. 283
Belwin-Mills Publishing Corp. 20
Benedetti Music, Quint 22
Bente Records 134
Berandol Music Ltd. 22
Berger, Stone & Partners, Inc. 263
Berk Artist Management/Top Dog Productions/Top Dog Music, Fred 301
Berkley Music Group, The 210
Berman Productions, Michael (see MCL Productions 235)
Bernard Enterprises, Inc., Hal 22
Bernbach Advertising, Ltd., Doyle Dane 263
Berning-Film Productions, Robert 284
Bernstein & Rein 263

Index **411**

Bernstein Personal Management, Richard 301
Better-Half Music Co. 22
BGS Productions Ltd. 134
Big Bear 210
Big Bear Records 134
Big Deal Records Co. 210
Big Heart Music 22
Big Mike Music 22
Big Secret Music Ltd. 23
Big Spliff Music Ltd. 23
Big Wheels 134
Billboard 368
Billetdoux Music Publishing 23
Bing Advertising Company, Ralph 263
Biograph Records, Inc. 23, 134
Birc 210
Birc Records 135
Bird Booking Agency, J. 301
Birdwing Music (See Sparrow/Birdwing Music 103)
Birthright Music (see Chinwah Songs/Birthright Music 32)
Birthright Records (see Bee Gee 133)
Biz Flakes Music (see Hodgmar Productions, Inc. 317)
Black & White Music Productions Ltd. 23, 212
Black, David 344
Black Diamond Music Publishing & Productions Co. 212
Black Hills Talent & Booking 302
Black Music Association 362
Black Stallion Country Publishing 23
Blackwood Music (see April/Blackwood Music Canada, Ltd. 16)
Blackwood Music 24, 212
Blade Agency 302
Blair Advertising, Inc. 264
Blake & Assoc., George 264
Blast from the Past Productions (see Gary Hills, Ltd. 317)
Blind Pig Records 135, 212
Blue Chek Music, Inc. 212
Blue Island Industries 212
Blue Island Publishing 24
Blue Island Records 135
Blue Sky Records 135
Blue Umbrella Music Publishing Co. 24
Blume Agency, Willis 302
BMI Awards to Student Composers 357
Bo Gal Music 24
Bocu Music Ltd. 24
Boggy Depot Music 24
Bolivia Records 135
Boot Records, Ltd. 135
Borden Advertising Agency, John 264
Boss Tweed Music 24
Bouquet Records 136
Bouquet-Orchid Enterprises 213
Bourne Music 25
Boyce & Melvin Powers Music Enterprises, Tommy 25, 136

Boyd, Bobby 213, 302
Boyd Records 136
Bozell & Jacobs, Inc. (California) 264
Bozell & Jacobs, Inc. (Chicago) 264
Bozell & Jacobs, Inc. (see Sullivan and/or Haas 279)
Bozell & Jacobs/Pacific 264
Bozell & Jacobs/PR 264
Bozell & Jacobs/Southwest 264
Branch International Music 25
Branch International Records 136
Branching-Out Productions 302
Brandon/Ray & Associates, Inc. 265
Brandwood Music, Inc. 25
Brave New Music 25
Bread 'N Honey Records 136
Breakin in to the Music Business 369
Breakthrough Entertainment Corporation 302
Breakthrough Quality Music 25
Briarmeade Records 137
Bringing It to Nashville 369
Brittell Music (see Brown Moon/Brittell Music 26)
Broad River Publishing Co. 26
Broadman Press 26
Broadway Production, Inc. 213
Brooklyn Country Music 26
Books Brothers Publishers 26
Books, Johnson, Zausmer Advertising 265
Brother Love Productions 213
Brown Management, Ron 213
Brown Moon/Brittell Music 26
Brown Productions, Bennie 213
Bruce-Green Advertising, Ltd. 265
Brumley & Sons, Albert E. 26
Brut Music Publishing 26
BSO Records, Inc. 137
Buddah Records, Inc. 137
Bug Music 302
Bulldog Records 137
Bullet Management/Its a Hit Productions 27
Bunetta Management Inc., Al 303
Buried Treasure Music 27
Burnt Out Music (see Prodigy Productions Ltd. 240)
Burst/Gosa Productions, Inc. 284
Busch Country Records 137
Bush/Lehrman Productions 27
Business of Music, The 371
Butera Associates Advertising, Sal 265
Buttermilk Sky Associates 27
Byron Productions, Bill 213

# C

C.A. Music 303
C.M. Management 303
Cactus Industries Music Inc. 303
Cactus Music and Gidget Publishing 27
Cadence Jazz Records, Ltd. 137, 214
Calello Productions, Ltd., Charles 214
Calep, Hirsch, Kurnip & Spector, Inc. 265

California International Records & Video 138
California Music Presentations 303
California State College, Bakersfield, Department of Fine Arts 344
Caligula, Inc. 27
Calvary Records, Inc. 28
Calwest Songs/Lee Anderson Enterprises 28
Camerica Music 28
Cameron Organisation, Inc., The 28
Camillo, Tony (see Venture 199)
Campbell Enterprises, Ltd., Glen 28
Can You Hear Me Music 28
Canadian Academy of Recording Arts & Sciences 362
Canadian Recording Industry Association 362
Canadian Songwriters Association 362
Canal Publishing, Inc. 28
Candlestick Publishing Co. 29
Candy Records 138
Can't Stop Music 29
Can't Stop Productions, Inc. 303
Capitol Booking Service, Inc. 304
Capitol Records, Inc. (New York) 138
Capitol Records, Inc. (Los Angeles) 138
Capitol Star Artist Ent. Inc. 29,138, 214
Cap-Orion Music Publ. Co., Inc. 29
Capstan Record Production 138
Caravetta Allen Kimbrough/BBDO 265
Carey College Dinner Theatre, William 344
Carolina Attractions, Inc. 304
Carousel Records, Inc. 138
Carr, Budd 305
Carr Productions, Inc., Richard 304
Carrie Records Co. 139
Carroll College 344
Carter Advertsing Inc. 265
Cartoon Records (see Crescent Records 144)
Casa Grande Records 139
Casale Music, Inc., Don 29, 214, 304
Casey Management, Joseph (see Minimum Music/Joseph Casey Management) 324
Cash Box Magazine 368
Casino Records 139
Castalia Music 29
Castalia Productions 214
Castalia Records 139
Castle Music, Inc. 139
Castle Productions 214
Catalpa Publishing Co. 29
Cats Whiskers Music Ltd. 29
CBS Records 139
CBS Songs 30
Celebrity Enterprises, Inc./Music Marketing International, Inc. 304
Cha-Cha Records 140
Chapie Music 30
Chapman Records 140
Chappell & Co. (Aust.) Pty Ltd. 30
Charade Records 140
Charisma Music Publishing Co. Ltd. 30

Charta Records 140
Chartbound Music Publications, Ltd. 30
Chascot Music Publishing 31
Chase Music Productions, C. 31
Chattahoochee Records 140
Chatterbox Music 31
Cheavoria Music Co. 31
Cheri Music Co. 31
Cherokee Sound Recording 140
Cherry Lane Music Publishing Co., Inc. 31
Cherry Red Music Ltd. 32
Chestnut Mound Music 32
Chiat/Day Advertising 266
Chicago Kid Productions 215
Chinwah Songs/Birthright Music 32
Chip 'N' Dale Music Publishers, Inc. 32
Chris Music Publishing 32
Christy Records 141
Chromewood Music 33
Chrysalis Records, Inc. 141
Chu Yeko Musical Foundation, The 33, 141, 215
Ciano Publishing 33
Cicchetti, Lou 215
Cine Design Films 284
Cinetudes Film Productions 284
Circle in the Square Theatre 346
City Publishing Co. 33
Clark Music Publishing 33
Clark Musical Productions 305
Clarus Music, Ltd. 33, 141, 284
Clay Pigeon Productions 215
Clay Pigeon Records 141
Clearinghouse Records Corp. 141
Cleland, Ward, Smith & Associates 266
Clockwork Entertainment Management Agency 305
Cloudburst Records 142, 215
Club of Spade Records (see Longhorn Records 165)
Clymax Records (see Arzee Records 208)
Coast to Coast Advertising, Inc. 266
Coast to Coast Records 142
Cockpit in Court Summer Theatre 346
Coconut Grove Productions 286
Cogan, David J. 346
Cohen & Associates, Steve 305
Cohn Music, Bruce 33
Colgems (see Screen Gems/Colgems/EMI Music, Inc. 98)
Collbeck Publishing Co. 34
Collings Music Ltd., Barry 34
Collins/Barrasso Agency 305
Come Alive Artist Management (see Greg Menze Artist Management 323)
Communications Team, Inc. 266
Compo Record and Publishing Co. 142
Composers, Arrangers and Songwriters of Kansas 362
Composers Guild 357
Compton Agency, Burt 305
Comstock Records, Ltd. 142 (also see Mutual Management Associates 325)
Concert Ideas 305

Index **413**

Connecticut Songwriters Association 363
Connel Publishing 34
Conradi, Johnson and Associates, Inc. 266
Conservatory of Theatre Arts at Webster College 346
Contemporary Artist Management 306
Conti Production Studio 306
Continental Talent Agency 306
Coombs Agency, Wayne 306
Copyright Service Bureau Ltd. 34
Cosmic Records of Canada 143
Cotillion Music, Inc. 34
Coulter & Associates, Tim 306
Counterpart Creative Studios 143
Counterpop Music Group 34
Country Classics Music Publishing Co. 34
Country International 143
Country Legs Music 35
Country Music Foundation of Colorado 363
Country Star Attractions 306
Country Star, Inc. 143
Country Star Music 35
Country Star Productions 215
Countryside Recording 216
Courrier Records 143
Cousins Music 35, 216
Covered Bridge Music 35
Cowboy Junction Publishing Co. 35, 216
Cramer-Krasselt Co., The 266
Crane, Glenn 346
Crash Prodctions 307
Crazy Cajun Music, Inc. 36
Cream Publishing Group 36 (also see Music Publishing Corporation/Cream Publishing Group 76)
Creative Corps 36
Creative Establishment, The 286
Creative House Advertising, Inc. 266
Creative Sound, Inc. 144
Creekside Music 36
Creole Music Ltd. 36
Creole Records Ltd. 144
Crescent Records 144
Creswell, Munsell, Fultz & Zirbel, Inc. 267
Cricket Theatre, The 346
Crimson Dynasty Records Corp. 36, 144
Crook Company, The Eddie 37, 216
Crosby Music Agency 307
Crosslight Management, Ltd 307 (also see Peter Golden & Assoc./Crosslight Management, Ltd. 313)
Cross-Over Enterprises, Inc. 216
Crowe Advertising Agency, John 267
Crume & The Soul Stirrers, Arthur 307
"Cryin in the Streets" Record Company 144
Cuca Record and Cassette Manufacturing (see American Music Company 127)
Cude & Pickens Publishing 37
Cummings Productions 216
Cummings/McPherson/Jones & Porter, Inc. 267
Curtiss Records 144
Cutler Music Co., V&M 37

Cyhoeddiadau Sain 37
Cypress College Theatre Arts Department 347

**D**

D.S.M. Producers 286
Da Car Recording 145
Dallas Star Records 145
Dan the Man Music Pub. Co. 37
Dan the Man Productions 217
Dan the Man Records Co. 145
Dana Publishing Co. 37
Danboro Publishing Co. 38
Dance-a-thon Records 145
Dansan Records 145
D'Arcy-MacManus & Masius, Inc. (Georgia) 267
D'Arcy-MacManus & Masius, Inc. (Missouri) 267
Date Line International Records 146
David Music 38
Davike Music Co. 38
Dawn Productions 146, 217
Dawn Promotions and Agency, Ltd. 146, 217
Dawn Treader Music 38
Dazia Music Publishing Company 38
Dazia Productions 217
Dazia Records 146
DCA Film/Video Productions 286
De Martini Associates 267
De Walden Music International, Inc. 38
Deangelis Management, Joe 307
Deercreek Publishing Co. 39
Deka Records 146
Delightful Music Ltd. 39
De-Lite Records 147
Delta Design Group, Inc. 267
Delta Sound Records 147
Dept. of Media Services, Dimond Library 286
Department of Theatre, Michigan State University 347
Department of Theatre, Southern Connecticut State College 347
Derby Music 39
Desk Drawer Publishing (see Kicking Mule Publishing/Desk Drawer Publishing 60)
Destiny Records 147, 217
Dew Music (see Don White Publishing/Dew Music) 116
D4 Films Studios, Inc. 286
Dharma Records 147
Diamond in the Rough Music 39
Diamondback Music 39
Diggs Productions, Steve 218
Dimension Records 147
Diversified Management Agency 307
Diversified Management Group (see The Hit Machine Music Co. 54)
Diversified Music, Inc. 39
Dixon Music, Inc., Hugh 40
DMI Productions 218

DMR Agency 307
Doc Dick Enterprises 40 (also see L&R Productions 318)
Doelp Associates, John 218
Domino Records, Ltd. 147
Don-Del Music/Don-De Music 40
Doner & Co., W.B. 268
Donna Marie Music 40
Donna Music Publishing Co. 40
Dooms Music Publishing Co. 40
Door Knob Music Publishing, Inc. 40
Door Knob Records 148, 218
Double Eagle Music Organization 308
Double Header Productions (see Weeze Music Co. & Double Header Productions 114)
Double Tee Promotions 308
Doyle Agency, The Bob 308
Dragon Fly Music 40
Dragon International Music 41
Drake Enterprises, Barry 218
Drake Music Group, The 41
Drake Presents, Tim 308
Drake Productions, Inc., Pete 218
Dramatists Guild, Inc., The 363
Dreena Music (see Asilomar Music 16)
Duane Music, Inc. 41, 219
Dupuy Records/Productions/Publishing 41, 148, 219
Durasell Corp., The 286
Dynamic Artists Records 148
Dynamic Talent Agency 308
Dynamite 148
Dynamo Publishing Co. 41

# E

E.L.J. Record Co. 41, 148
Eagle Rock Music Co. 42
Early Bird Music 42
Earnheart Agency, T.O. 308
Earth and Sky Music Publishing, Inc. 42
Eary and Sky Records 219
Earthscream Music Publishing Co. 42
East West Players 347
Eastex Music 219
Eastman Advertising Agency 268
Easy Chair Records 149
Eat Records 149
Ebb-Tide Booking Agency 309
Ebb-Tide Music 219
Ebb-Tide Productions 219
Echo Records 149, 220
Eclipse Records 149
Edelstein & Associates, Inc., Marsh 309
Edgar Music, Don 42
Editions la Bobine, Les 43
Editions Nahej 43
Educator Records, Inc. 149
Ehrlich-Manes & Associates 268
El Chicano Music 43
Ellis Agency, Ltd., Steve 309

EMI Music, Inc. (see Screen Gems/Colgems/EMI Music, Inc. 98)
Emkay Records 149
Emler Enterprises, Richard Lee 309
Empire Agency, Inc. 309
En Avant Music Co. 43
En Pointe Productions 220
Enchanted Door, Inc. 220
Enchanted Door Management Co., Inc. 309
Enchantment Music Co. 43
Encyclopedia of the Music Business, The 369
Englar Theatrical Agency, Bob 310
English Mountain Publishing Co. 43
Enterprize Records 150
Entertainment Agency Unltd. 310
Entertainment Co. Music Group 43
Entertainment Company 220
Entertainment Management Enterprises 310
Entertainment Productions, Inc. 287
Entertainment Services Concept 310
Entertainment Unlimited 310
Epicenter 310
Epigram Music 287
Epoch Universal Publications, Inc. 44, 150
Equa Music 44
Equa Records 150
Equinox Music 44
Esquire International 220
Esquire Records Talent Ltd. 150
Essex Music of Australia Pty. Ltd. 44
Estey-Hoover, Inc. 268
Etc. Company 347
ETS Record Company 150
Etude/Bakcan 44
Evans/Atlantic, Inc., David W. 268
Evans/Ciccarone, Inc. 268
Exlamation Point Advertising 268
Ezra & Associates, Martin 287

# F

Factory Beat Records, Inc. 151, 220
Fairchild Music Publishing 44
Fame Publishing Co., Inc. 45
Famous Door Publishing Co. 151
Famous Door Records 151
F&L Records 150
Fanfare Records 151
Fantasy Records 151
Fantasy Workshop 220
Far East Records 151
Far West Enterprises 311
Farr Records 151
Farris International Talent 311
Faulkner & Associates 269
Felt, Don 221
Ferry Boat Music 45
Field Hardwick Productions 311
50 States Records & Tapes 151
Fireball Management 311

# Index

Firelight Publishing 45
First All Children's Theatre, Inc., The 348
Fisher & Associates Entertainment, Inc. 311
Flin-Flon Music 45
Flowers Records 152
Flying Music Company Ltd., The 45
Flying Record Company Ltd. The 152
Focal Point Music Publishers 45
Fold Arts Productions 221
Foolkiller Etc. 348
Force Records 152
Forever Records 152
Forrest Hills Music, Inc. 46
415 Records 152
Fourth Corner Music 46
Frank Productions, Joan 311
Franklyn Agency, Inc. 312
Franne Records 153
Freckle Records 153
Freddie Cee Attractions 312
Free & Show Music 46
Freedom Productions 312
Fremerman-Marcy Spivak Rosenfield, Inc. 269
French, Inc. Samuel 348
Freund Productions, Sheldon 287
Frick Music Publishing 46
Friendly Finley Music 46
Fro Records (Harvest Group) 312
Frost & Frost Entertainment 312
Frozen Inca Music 47
Frozen Music, Inc. 269
FTM Enterprises, Inc. 312
Full Circle Productions, Inc. 221
Full Circle Records 153
Full Cycle Music Publishing Co. 47
Full Sail Records 153
Fun City Records Co. 153
Funky Acres Music Co. 47
Future 1 Productions 221
Fydaq Music 47
Fydaq Productions 221

# G

G. G. Music, Inc. 47
Gabrielli, Chris 48
Gail and Rice Productions 313
Gallagher Group, Inc. 269
Gallico Music Corp., Al (Los Angeles) 48
Gallico Music Corp., Al (Nashville) 48
Galyn Music 48
Gambill Enterprises, Inc., Mick 313
Gamma Records Ltd. 153
Gammill-Murphy Music 48
Gammon Records 153
Garner & Associates, Inc. 269
Garrett Music Enterprises 48
Garron Music 49
Gaub Ministries, Ken 313
GCS Records 154
Gee Productions 222
Geer, DuBois, Inc. 269

Georgia College Theatre 349
Get Rich Music 222
Ghost Records 154
Gilday Publishing Co., Gill 49
Gillham Advertising 269
Glad-Hamp Records Inc. 154
Glen Eagle Publishing Company 49
Global Record Co. 154
God's World 49
Gold Guitar Records 154
Gold Street, Inc. 49, 154
Goldband Recording Studio 222
Goldband Records 154
Golden & Assoc./Crosslight Management, Ltd., Peter 313
Golden Dawn Music 49
Golden Guitar Music 50
Goldman-Dell Music Productions 313
Goldust Record Co. 155
Goliath Agency, David 313
Gollender Enterprises, Walt 314
Golly Music 222
Good Karma Productions, Inc. 314
Good Management, Gary 314
Good Music Management 314
Goodwin, Dannenbaum, Litman & Wingfield, Inc. 270
Gopam Enterprises, Inc. 50
Gordon Music Co., Inc. 50
Gosa Productions, Inc. (see Burst/Gosa Productions, Inc. 284)
Gospel Clef 50
Gospel Express 222
Gospel Music Association 363
Gospel Records, Inc. 222
Gospel Road, The 314
Graham Management, Bill 314
Grand Pasha Publisher, The 50 (also see Sasha Songs, Unltd. and The Grand Pasha Publisher 97)
Grand Talent International 315
Grandville Record Corp. 155
Grass Roots Record and Tape 155
Grassroots Projects Unlimited 222
Gravenhurst Music 50
Grawick Music 51
Graydon & Associates, Joe 315
Grayson Productions, Miles 223
Great Plains Associates, Inc. 315
Great Pyramid Music 223, 315
Great Southern Record Co., Inc 155
Greater Songs 51
Green Mountain Guild 349
Greif-Garris Management 315
Grey Advertising 270
Griffith & Somers Advertising Agency, Ltd. 270
Groovesville Music 51
Group, Inc., The 315
Group Two Advertising 270
Grove School of Music, Dick 373
GRP Records (see Grusin/Rosen Productions 223)

Grusin/Rosen Productions 223
GST Music Productions 223
Gubala Music, Frank 51
Guess Productions, George 223
Gule Record 51, 156

# H

Halben Music Publishing Co. 57
Hale Talent/Jester Sound, Bob 315
Hall & Gidget Starr Productions, Jim 223
Hallways to Fame Productions 223
Halnat Music Publishing Co. 51
Halnat Publishing Co. 224
Halpern Sounds 156, 224
Hamman Publishing Co. 52
Hammel Associates, R.L. 224
Ham-Sem Records, Inc. 224
Hansen Enterprises, Ltd., Geoffrey 316
Hansen-O'Brien Music 52, 156
Hansen-O'Brien Music Productions 224
Happy Beat Records 156
Happy Day Music Co. 52
Happy Day Productions, Inc. 225
Happy Day Records, Inc. 156
Hard Hat Productions 225
Hard Hat Records and Cassettes 156
Hard Ten Music 52
Hard-Boiled Records 156, 225
Harmony Artists, Inc. 316
Harrison Music Corp. 52
Hart/Conway Company, Inc. 270
Harvest Agency 316
Harvey Publishing Co., John 52
Hat Band Music 316
Haystack Publishing Company 53
Heart Records & Tapes of Canada Ltd. 157
Heaven Songs 53
Heavy Metal Records 157
Heavy Metal Records Productions 225
Heavy Weather Music 316
Hedley Music Group 53
Helios Music Corporation 53
Helping Hand Music Ltd. 53
Henry Entertainment Agency, Glenn 316
Hepworth Advertising Co. 270
Herald Association, Inc., The, 54, 157
Herman Associates 270
Highest Praise Publishing 54
Highway Music 54
Highway Records, Ltd. 157
Hill Music, Inc., John 225
Hills, Ltd., Gary 317
Hit Machine Music Co., The 54
Hodgman Productions, Inc. 317
Hoffman Talent, Inc. 317
Hollyrock Records 157
Holy Spirit Music 54
Holy Spirit Productions, Inc. 225
Holy Spirit Records, Inc. 158
Hometown Productions, Inc. 226
Hoochie Coochie Music (see Monona Music 72)

Hood, Hope & Associates 271
Hoosier Hills Publishing 54
Hopsack and Silk Productions Inc. 226
Hot Gold Music Publishing Co. 55
Houck & Harrison Advertising 271
House of Diamonds Music 55
How I Write Songs (Why You Can) 370
How to be a Successful Songwriter 370
Howard University Department of Drama 349
Hudson Guild Theatre 349
Hula Records Inc. 158
Hume Smith Mickelberry 271
Hungaria Records, Inc. 158
Huntley Street Publishing 55

# I

I.A.M. Music 55
ICR International Celebrity Register, Inc. 317
If Productions, Inc. 226, 317
If They Ask You, You Can Write a Song 370
Iffin Music Publishing Co. 55
IGL Audio 158
Ileana Productions (see L&R Productions 318)
Image Music Pty., Ltd. 55
Impact Records 158
Incidental Music 56
Indianer Multi-Media 287
Ingalls Associates, Inc. 271
Insight! Inc. 287
Intar, International Arts Relations, Inc. 349
Interand Corp. 287
Interlochen Arts Academy Playwright Project 349
Intermountain Talent 317
International Music Consultant 226
Interplanetary Music 56
It's a Hit Productions (see Bullet Management/It's a Hit Productions 27)
Itta, Inc., John Paul 271
I've Got the Music Company 56, 226

# J

J.K. Productions 226
Jackpot Music 56
Jackson Artists Corp. 318
Jackson Enterprises (see AMJ International/Jackson Enterprises 299)
Jaclyn Music 56
Jacoby/Storm Productions, Inc. 288
Jalyn Recording Company 158
Jamaka Record Co. 159, 226
James Boy Publishing Co. 56
James Company, Bruce 227
James Music, Inc., Dick 57
James Productions, Inc., Jesse 227
Jamestune Records Productions 227
Janell Music Publishing/Tiki Enterprises 57

Index **417**

Janoulis Productions, Alexander 227
Jansen Music, Doug 57
Jason Music/Mooreside Music 57
Jay Jay Publishing 57, 159
Jayme Organization, The 271
Jed Record Production 227
Jekyll Island Music Theatre 349
Jemiah Publishing 57
Jerjoy Music 57
Jero Music Ltd. 58
Jersey Coast Agents, Ltd. 159
Jester Sound (see Bob Hale Talent/Jester Sound 315)
Jewel Record Corp. 159
Jibaro Music Co., Inc. 58
Jitasca 350
Jive Records 159
JMAR Productions 318
JMR Enterprises 58
Jody Records, Inc. 159
John & Karin 227
Jon 58
Jonan Music 58
Jonathan Advertising, Inc. 271
Jorin 59
JRM Records 159
June Productions Ltd. 228

## K

K and R Music, Inc. 59
K and R Records 160
Kack Klick, Inc. 59
Kamakazi Music Corporation 59
Kapri Records, Inc. 160
Karjan Music Publishing Co. 59
Kat Family Music Publishing Co. 59
Kat Family Productions 228
Kat Family Records 160
Katch Nazar Music 59
Katona Productions, Inc. 318
K-D Music Co. Division of KDP Inc. 160
Keene Music Co., Joe 59
Keeny-York Publishing 60
Kelly & Lloyd Music 60
Ken-Del Productions Inc. 288
Kennedy Enterprises, Inc., Gene 60, 228
Ketchum Communications 271
Key Productions, Inc. 288
Keynote Productions 228
Keynote Records 160
Kicking Mule Publishing/Desk Drawer Publishing 60
Kicking Mule Records, Inc. 160
Kiderian Record Products 161
Kiderian Records Productions 228
Kimbo Educational United Sound Arts, Inc. 288
Kinetic Records, Ltd. 318
King Henry Production 230
King of Kings Record Co. 161
King-J Record Co. 161

Kirtland Music Ltd., Lorna 60
Kitchen Table Music 60
Kizer, Dennis King 272
Kleiner Music Enterprises, Sid 161, 288
Kneptune International Records 161
Knight Agency, Bob 318
Known Artist Productions 230
Kober Productions, Freddie 230
Koch/Marschall Productions, Inc. 288
Koester Audio-Visual Presentations 289
Kovach, Robert R. 230
Krause & Remal Music, Inc. 230
KRPCO Music 61

## L

L.D.F. Productions 319
L.M.I. (Lee Magid, Inc.) 162
L.P.S. Records, Inc. 162
La Grave Klipfel Clarkson, Inc., Advertising, Public Relations, Marketing 272
La Lou Music 61
La Louisianne Records 162
Lackey Publishing Co. 61
Ladanyi, Greg 230
Ladd Music Co. 61, 162
Ladera Music Publishing 61
Lake Country Records 162
Lance Jay Music 61
Landers Music, Jay 62
Landmark (Audio of Nashville) 163
L & R Productions 318
Landslide Management 319
Landslide Records 163
Lane & Huff Advertising 272
Lanis Music, Inc., Stuart 62
Lanor Records 163
Lant Agency, The Charles 319
Lardon Music 62
Lareo Music, Inc. 62
Lar-Jo Records, Inc. 163
Larkspur Music Publishing 62
Las Vegas Recording Studio, Inc. 230
LaSalle Recording Co. 163
Laser Records 163
Last Minute Productions 231
Laughing Bird Songs Publishing Co. 62
Laurence, Charles & Free, Inc. 272
Laurie Records, Inc. 231
Lavidge & Associates, Inc. 289
Lawrence Productions, Stan 319
Lazar Management, Gary 319
Lazar Music 62
Lazer Records 231
LD&A Advertising Corp. 272
Le Matt Music, Ltd. 63, 164
Lee International Productions, Roosevelt 231
Lee, Overton (see Don Felt 221)
Lefton Co., Al Paul 272
Legend Records and Promotions 164, 231
Legnick & Co., Ltd. Alfred 63

**418** Songwriter's Market '84

Lehrman Productions (see Bush/Lehrman Productions 27)
Lemley Music, Ty 164, 231
Lemon Square Music 320
Lemon Square Productions 232
Lempert Co., The 272
Leon Company, Inc., S.R. 273
Leonard Productions, Don (see Gee Productions 222)
Leonard Productions, Inc. 232
Les Attractions, Inc., Buddy 319
Lester Productions 320
Levy Enterprises, Inc., John 320
Lewis, Gilman & Kynette, Inc. 273
Lieb Productions, Jack 289
Lifesinger Productions 232
Lil' Wally Music Productions 232
Lillenas Publishing Co. 63
Limbo International, Ltd., Sonny 232
Lineage Publishing Co. 63
Linet Management, Lew 320
Lingering Music, Inc. 320
Little David Records, Inc. 164
Little Giant Enterprises 232
Little Giant Record Company, The (Nashville) 164
Little Giant Records (White Lake, New York) 164
Little Joe Music Co. 63
Little Otis Music 63
Little Richie Johnson Music 58
Little Richie Johnson Productions 227
Little Things Music 63
Lloyd Productions, Mick 232
LMI Records (see Grass Roots Record & Tape 155)
Lock Record Co. 165
Loconto Productions 320
Locust, Inc. 320
Lodestar Music 64
Logo III 165
Logsdon Associates 321
Lone Lake Songs, Inc. 64
Long, Haymes & Carr, Inc. 273
Longbranch Studio 289
Longhorn Records 165
Look Hear Music 64
Lord, Sullivan & Yoder, Inc. 273
Lorenz Corporation, The 64
Lorenz Creative Services 64
Los Angeles (Inner City) Cultural Center 350
Los Angeles International Music 64
Los Angeles Songwriters Showcase, The 363
Loveland Ministries—Christine Wyrtzen Ministry 321
Lowery Music Co., Inc. 65
LS Talent 321
Luciano Music Co., Ron 321
Lucifer Records, Inc. 165
Luick & Associates, Harold 233
Luick & Associates Music Publisher, Harold 65

Luna Records Co. 165
Lunch Time Productions 273
Lutz Entertainment Agency, Richard 321
Lyons Studios Inc. 289
Lyric Theater of New York 350

# M

M.R.C. Records 166
McCann-Erickson/Louisville Office 273
McCann-Erickson Worldwide (Houston) 274
McCann-Erickson Worldwide (San Francisco) 273
McCoy Music/Alear Music, Jim 65
Mace's Ozark Opry Records, Inc., Lee 175
MacHarmony Music 65 (also see Date Line International Records 146)
McKay, Al 233
Maescher Advertising, Inc., Al 274
Magid, Inc., Lee 322
Magid Productions, Lee 233
Magnum Force Records and Music Ltd. 166
Mainline Productions 233
Mainroads Productions, Inc. 234
Mainroads Publishing 65
Maish Advertising 274
Majego Records 166
Major Label, A (see Castalia Records 139)
Major Label Record Co. 166
Major Media, Inc. 289
Making it with Music 370
Malaco, Inc. 65
Malaco Records 166
Malhoit Agency, Ed 322
Mandabach & Simms, Inc. 274
Manfield Music 66
Manhattan Theatre Club 350
Manna Music, Inc. 66
Manquin 166, 234
Marielle Music Co. 66
Marmik 167
Marmik Music, Inc. 66
Mars Talent Agency 322
Marsaint Music, Inc. 66
Marschall Productions (see Koch/Marschall Productions, Inc. 288)
Marsh Productions, Inc. 322
Marshall Street Melodies 66
Martin Productions, Pete 234
Martin/Arnold Color Systems, Inc. 290
Marullo Master Leasing Co. 167
Marullo Music Publishers 68
Marullo Productions 234
Marvel Music, Andy 68
Marvel Records Co. 167
Masada Music, Inc. 322
Maslow, Gold & Rothschild 274
Master Audio, Inc. 234
Master Trak Sound Recorders 167
Masterlease Music Publications 68
Master's Collection Limited, The 167

Index **419**

Master's Collection Publishing and T.M.C. Publishing 68
Mastersource Productions 234
Masterview Music Publishing Corp. 234
Matthews Music Pty., Ltd. 68
Maui Music 68
Maxfilms 290
MBA Productions 235, 322
MCA Music 69
MCA Music Australia Pty., Ltd. 69
MCA Records (Nashville) 167
MCA Records (New York) 168
MCI Productions 235
MCP/Davisound 168, 235
MDS—Northcoast 168
Me Music 69
Meadowlark Ventures 322
Mecca International 323
Meda Record Co. 168
Media Concepts, Inc. 323
Media Concepts, Inc./MCI Music 69
Media Dept. 290
Media Interstellar Music 69
Medland Management 323
Mega-Star Music 69, 323
Melodee Ent., Inc. 235
Melodee Records 168
Memnon, Ltd. 70
Memnon Records 169
Memphis Management Corp (see Blackwood Music 211)
Memphis Management Music 70
Memphis Songwriters Association 363
Menes & Associates, Barry 323
Menza Artist Management, Greg 323
Mercantile Music 70, 235, 324
Mercantle Records 169
Mertis Music Co. 70
Merit Music Corporation 70
Message Records 169
Messina, Joseph C. 324
Metcalfe-Cook & Smith, Inc. 274
Michal Recording Enterprises 169
Michavin Music 70
Mid America Music 70
Middleton's Public Relations & Management 324
Mideb Music 71
Mid-Plains Community College 351
Mighty "T" Productions 235
Mighty Three Music Group, The 71
Mighty Twinns Music 71
Milestone Records (see Fantasy Records 151)
Millan Music Corp., Brian 71
Millennium 169
Miller Booking & Management 324
Miller Film Associates, Forney 290
Miller Productons, Jay 236
Miller Productions, Warren 290
Milwaukee Repertory Theater 351
Mimic Music 71

Minimum Music/Joseph Casey Management 324
Mintz & Hoke, Inc. 274
Miracle-Joy Publications 72
Mirror Records, Inc. 169
Missouri Songwriters Association 364
Mr. Mort Music 72
Moby Dick Records 169, 236
Mogull Music Corp., Ivan 72
Mohawk Advertising Co. 274
Mom and Pop Productions, Inc. 236
Monard Music 72
Monkey Music, Inc. 72
Monona Music 72
Monotone Records 236
Montace Records 170
Montgomery Publishing 73
Montgomery, Zukerman, Davis, Inc. 275
Monticana Productions 236
Monticana Records 170
Montina Music 73
Monumental Films & Recordings 290
Moody Music, Doug. 73
Moon June Music 73
Moon Shine Records 170
Mooreside Music (see Jason Music/Mooreside Music 57)
More About this Business of Music 370
Morgan Music Group, The 73, 236
Morningstar Records 170
Morris Music, Inc. 73
Morrison Hill Music 73
Moseka Records 237
Moss Advertising 275
Moss Production Services & Management, Ron 237
Motivation Media, Inc. 290
Motoboy Motions 324
Motorbeat Music 74
Mountain Railroad Music 74
Mountain Railroad Records, Inc. 170
Mountain Willie Music 74
MPL Associates, Ltd. 325
Multi Image Productions 291
Multimedia Music Group 74
Multivision of Denver, Inc. 291
Murphy, Jr., Esquire, Alexander 325
Muscle Shoals Music Association 364
Musedco Publishing Co. 74
Music A.D. Records 170
Music Adventures Records, Inc. 172
Music Anno Domini 74
Music Business: Career Opportunities and Self-Defense, The 370
Music City News 368
Music City Records 172
Music City Song Festival 358
Music City Concepts International 75
Music Connection, The 368
Music Copyright Holding Corporation 75
Music Craftshop 75
Music Designers 75
Music for Percussion, Inc. 75

Music Industry Educators Association 364
Music Makers 368
Music Management 75
Music Marketing International, Inc. (see Celebrity Enterprises, Inc./Music Marketing International Inc. 304)
Music Publishing Corp. (see Merit Music Corp. 70)
Music Publishing Corp./Cream Publishing Group 76
Music Resources International Corp. 76, 237
Music to Sell by: The Craft of Jingle Writing 370
Musicanza Corporation 172
Musician Magazine 368
Musicians Contact Service 364
Musinfo Publishing Groupe Inc. 76
Muskrat Productions, Inc. 325
Mustevic Sound Inc. 76
Mutual Management Associates/Comstock Records, Ltd. 325
Myriad Productions 325
Mystic Oak Records 172
Mystic Records, Inc. 172
MZB Inc. (see Montgomery, Zukerman, Davis, Inc. 274)

# N

Nahser, Inc., Frank C. 275
Nancy Jane Publishing Co. 76
Nanoia Management, Frank 325
Narrowroad Records/Music 76
Nashboro Records 173
Nashcal Music 77
Nashville Academy Theatre 351
Nashville Songwriters Association, International 364
National Academy of Popular Music 366
National Music Publishers' Association, Inc. 366
Nelter Music Publishing 77
Negro Ensemble Company 351
Nervous Music 237
Nervous Publishing 77
Nervous Records 173
Never Ending Music 77
Neverland Music Publishing Co. 77
New Dawn Productions 237
New Dawning Records (see Cherokee Sound Recording 140)
New Playwright's Theatre of Washington, The 351
New Vintage Management 326
New World Records 173, 237
Newcreature Music 78
Newwriters Music 78
New England Record Company 173
New Hormones 173
New Image Artist and Models Guild 326
New Music Enterprises 77, 173

Nichols Productions, Mike 326
Nick-O-Val Music 78
Nicolet Players, The 351
Night Food Music (see Impact Records 158)
Nightstream Music 326
Nirvana Records 174
Nise Productions, Inc. 78, 238
Nocoletti Music, Joseph 78
Nonpareil Music 78
North American Liturgy Resources 174, 238
North Carolina Central University, Department of Dramatic Art 351
North Ranch Music 80
Northern Comfort Music 80
Northern Comfort Productions 238
North-South Artscope 326
Notable Music Co. Inc. 80
Noteworthy Publishing Co. 80
Nowak/Barlow/Johnson Advertising 275
NRP Music Group 80
Nucleus Records 174
Nu-Trayl Publishing Co. 80
NZD Breezeway Publishing Companies 326

# O

O.A.S. Music Group 81
O.A.S. Music Publishing (see Counterpop Music Group) 34
O.L. Records, Inc. 174
O.T.L. Productions 238
Oak Springs Music 81
Oakridge Music Recording Service 81
Oakwood Audio Productions 174, 238
Oakwood Music 81
Oat Willie Productions 174
O'Brien Publishing Co. (see Hansen-O'Brien Music 52)
Ocean Realm Video Productions 291
O'Connor Music, Michael 81
Odle Recording & Publishing Co., Mary Francis 81
Ogilvy & Mather Inc. (New York) 275
Ogilvy & Mather Inc., (San Francisco) 275
Ogilvy & Mather Inc. (Canada) Ltd. 275
Ohio Records 175, 327
O'Keefe Music Ltd., Trisha 82
Okisher Music 82
Okoboji Music 82
Old Boston Publishing 82
Old Hat Records 175, 239
Old Home Place Music 82
Olofsong Music 82
O'Lyric Music 83
On the Wing Music Publishing Co. 83
Oneida Music Publishing Co. 83
Open Booking Agency 327
Operation Music Enterprises 327
Orange Blossom Productions 327
Orbit Records 175
Orchid Publishing 83
Organic Management 327

Orient, L. (see Would'n Shoe/L'Orient 202)
Origin, Inc. 291
Orpheus Entertainment 327
Otto Publishing Co. 83
Overholt Music, Ray 84
Owens & Associates 276
Ozark Opry Music Publishing, Lee Maces 84

## P

P.D.O. Directions, Inc. 328
P.M. Records 175
Pace Advertising 276
Pacific Northwest Songwriters Association 366
Paddock Productions, Inc. 291
Paeske Productions, Inc., Del 286
Palamar Music Publishers 84
Panio Brothers Label 239
Parasound, Inc. 175
Pasha Music Organization, Inc., The 239
Paton, Dave 239
Paul Record Production, Ray 239
Pavillion Productions/Promotion, Inc. 84
Payton Place Publishing 84
PCRL 176, 239
Pearson, Clarke & Sawyer Advertising & Public Relations 276
Peer-Southern Organization (Hollywood) 85
Peer-Southern Organization (Nashville) 85
Peer-Southern Organization (New York) 85
Peer-Southern Organization (Toronto) 85
Pegasus Music 85
Pelican Productions 328
Peliperus Music Co. 85
Penny Pincher Publishing, Inc. 85
People City Music Publishing Inc. 86
People Song, International 328
Pepp Records 176
Perfection Light Productions 328
Performance Publishing Co. 352
Performing Arts Dept., Avila College 352
Performing Rights Organization of Canada Limited 366
Perla Music 86
Permanent Pop Music 86
Permanent Press Records 176
Perry Productions, Inc., Don 86, 239
Peyton Records 176
Philippopolis Music 86
Phillips-Producer, Phil (see Hard Boiled Records 225)
Philo Records, Inc. 176
Phonetones 87
Pilgrim International Ltd. 87
Pine Island Music 87
Pineapple Music Publishing Co. 87
Pixie Music Co. Ltd. 87
Pizazz Productions 328
Plantation Records 177
Plastic Records 177
Platinum Rainbow, The 370

Pleiades Music 87, 177
Polka Towne Music 88
Polka Towne Records 177
Polygram Records 177
Pomeroy Productions 276
Pop International Corp. 291
Poppell Productions, Rick 328
Portin Motion Pictures, Henry 292
Positive Productions 88, 240
Praise Industries Corp. 177, 240
Precious Records 177
Preferred Artist Management, Inc. 329
Prelude Records 178
Premier Film and Recording Corp. 292
Prescription Co., The 88, 178, 240
Prestige Records (see Fantasy Records 151)
Prewitt Rose Productions 240
Price Films, Inc., John M. 292
Price Music Publishing, Jimmy 88
Primero Records 178
Pringle Dixon Pringle 276
Priority Records/CBS 178
Priority/Preference Music—CBS Songs 88
Pritchett Publications 88, 240
Pro Talent Consultants 329
Process Talent Management 329
Pro/Creatives 276
Prodigy Productions Ltd. 240
Production Connection 178, 240
Progress Entertainment 329
Progressive Talent Management, Inc. 329
Prophecy Publishing, Inc. 89
Pro-Talents, Inc. 330
Protestant Radio & TV Center, Inc. 292
Publicare Music, Ltd. 89
Publishing Ventures, Inc. 89
Purcell Associates, Gerald W. 89
Pyramid Records 89

## Q

Quadrangle Management, Inc. 330
Quality Music Publishing 89
Quality Records 178
Quantum Records, Ltd. 179
Quarter Moon Records (see Big Wheel 134)
Queen of Hearts 90
Quest Talent Management Co. 330
Quinones Music Co. 90
Quinto Record Productions 179
Quinto Records 241

## R

R.E.F. Records 179, 241
Ra Jo International Records & Tapes 179, 242
Rachou, Sr., Carol J. 241
Racouillat Music Enterprises, Rac 90
Radio Magic Productions 241
Radmus Productions, Inc. 241

Rainbow Collection, Ltd., The 330
Rainbow Recording Studios 242
Rainbow Road Records 242
Rainbow Sound Inc. 179
Rainfire Music 90
Rainfire Music Production 242
Rainfire Records 179
Randall Productions 242
Rauh, Good & Darlo Advertising Assoc. Inc. 276
Raven Music 90
Raven Records 91
Rawls Bros. Productions Co. 242
Raybird Music 90
RBI Records/Rowalba Publishing 91
RBI/Record Breakers International 180
RCA Records, Inc. 180
RCI Records, Inc. 180
RCS Publishing Co. 91
Read Poland, Inc. 276
Record Company of the South (RCS) 180, 330
Record Music, Inc. 330
Red Bus Music International, Ltd., 91, 180
Red Horse Records 181
Red Tennies Music 91
Redbeard Presents Productions, Ltd. 330
Redding & Associates, Rodgers 331
Redick Music Publishing Co., Jack 91
Reed Sound Records, Inc. 331
Reeves Enterprises, Jim 91
Rego Irish Records & Tapes, Inc. 181
Release Records 181
Relix Records, Inc. 181
Ren Maur Music Corp. 91
Revel Music, Gary 91
Revolution Records 181
Revonah Records 181
Rezey Music Co., Wm. 92
RFC Records 182
Rhodes Productions, Rick 242
Rhythms Productions 92
Richey Records 182, 242
Richter Productions, Inc. 292
Ricochet Records 243
Ricochet Records, Ltd. 182
Right on Records 182
Rile Management, Joanne 331
Ripsaw Record Co. 182
Rising Star Enterprises 331
Rives, Smith, Baldwin & Carlberg, T & R 277
RMS Triad 92, 182, 243
Roadwork, Inc. 331
Rob Lee Music 183, 332
Robbins Records 183
Robjen Music 92
Rocken Rythmn Publishing 92
Rocket Publishing 92
Rockfever Productions 332
Rockmore Music 93
Rocky Bell Music 93
Rocky's Ragdoll Publishing 93
Rodanca Music 332

Rodgers Production Award, Richard 358
Rogersound Records 183
Rohm Music 93
Rollin' Rock Records 184
Roman Enterprises, Angelo 243
Rondor Music (Australia) Pty., Ltd. 93
Rondercrest Ltd. 184
Rooftop Records 184
Roots Music 93
Rose Hill Productions 243
Rosemary Melody Line Co. 243
Rosenberg Organization, Sy 332
Rosenthal & Co., Albert J. 277
Ross Music, Brian 94
Ross Music, Jeffrey 332
Ross Productions, Brian 243
Rothstein Music, Ltd. 94
Rough Trade, Inc. 184
Roulette (see Buddah Records, Inc. 137)
Round Sound Music 94
Rounder Records Corp. 184
Rowalba Publishing (see RBI Records/Rowalba Publishing) 91
Rowilco 94
Royal Flair Publishing 94
Royal K Productions 244
Royal Records 184
Royal T Music 185, 332
Royalty Records of Canada, Ltd. 185
Rubicon Music 94
Ruhr Advertising, Inc., Chuck 277
Rustic Records 185
Rustron Music Productons 244, 333
Rustron Music Publishers 96
Rutland Records 185
RWP Records Group 185

S

S.M.C.L. Productions, Inc. 96
S.P.Q.R. Music 244
S.R.O. Group of Companies, The 333
S.R.O. Publishing Group, The 96
S & R Music Publishing Co.
Sabre Music 96
Safmar Publishing Co. 96
Sagittar Records 244
Sagittarian Artists International 333
Saguaro Booking Agency 333
Sain Recordian CYF 186, 245
Salsoul Records 186
Saltwater Music (see Del Suggs/Saltwater Music) 337
Sam Records 186
Samarah Productions, Inc. 245, 333
Sandcastle Records 186
Sandmel (Independent), Ben 333
Sansu Enterprises 245
Santa Barbara Songwriters' Guild 366
Sapphire Record Co. 186, 245
Sargeant, Steven C. 245
Sasha Songs, Unltd. & The Grand Pasha Publisher 97

Index **423**

Sasnras Music 97
Saul Avenue Music Publishing 97
Savan Company, Inc., The 277
Savgos Music, Inc. 97
Savoy Records 186
Scarlet Stallion Music 97
Scene Productions 187
SCG Advertising, Inc. 277
Schabraf Music 97
Scharf, Steve 245
Schoenbrod, Inc., Robert D. 277
Schultz Agency, The Al 333
Scotti Brothers Music Publishing 97
Scratch Records Ltd. 187
Screen Gems/Colgems/EMI Music, Inc. 98
Scully Music Co. 98
Sea Cruise Productions 98, 187, 334
Seaside Records 187
Seasun Experience Music Productions 246
Second Sun Productions 246
Seeds, Inc. 334
Seeds Records 187
Seip Management, Inc., William 334
Seismic Music 98
September Music Corp. 98
SESAC, Inc. 366
Seven Hills Recording & Publishing Co., Inc. 246
Seven Oaks Productions 292
Seyah Music 99
Shaffer Shaffer Shaffer, Inc. 278
Shailer Davidoff Rogers, Inc. 278
Shawnee Press, Inc. 99
Shayne Enterprises, Larry 99
Shekere Productions 246
Shelton Associates 99
Sherman Artist Management & Development, Mickey 334
Sherman Productions, Mickey 246
Shetland Sound 99, 246
Shiloh Records 188
Shindler & Assoc., Inc. 334
Short Pump Records 188
Showboat Majestic 352
Showcase Attractions 334
Showcase of Stars 247
Showcase Talent Productions, Inc. 335
Shu-Qua-Lok Records & Acorn Records 188, 247
Sidartha Enterprises, Ltd. 335
Sidewalk Sailor Music 99
Sight and Sound Marketing 247
Sigma Alpha Iota Quarterly: Pan Pipes 369
Silhouette Music 100
Silicon Music Publishing Co. 100
Silver Blue Productions 100, 247
Silver Bullet Productions 247
Silver Burdett Company 293
Silvera Writers' Workshop, Frank 373
Simon Organization, Brad 335
Simons Advertising & Assoc. 278
Singleton Music Inc., Shelby 100
Singspiration Music 100, 188

Sire Records 188
Sirloin Music Publishing Co. 100
Sivatt Music Publishing Co. 100, 189
Skafish Music (see Monona Music 72)
Skorman/Weiss 335
Skylight Records 189
Skys the Limit Productions, Inc. 248
Slash Records 189
SMI Records Corp. 189
Smith Music, Mack 101
Snapfinger Music 101
Snoopy Music 101
Snow Productions, Inc., Phoebe T. 293
So You Want to Be in Music 371
Solid Gold Records 189
Solid Records 190
Somor Music (see Willie Loco Alexander/Somor Music 298)
Sonata Records 190
Sone Songs 101
Song Farm Music 101
Song of Songs Music 101
Song Tailors Music Co. 102
Songco Production Co., Inc. 248
Songline Music 102
Songs from the Box 102
Songwriter Seminars and Workshops 373
Songwriters Advocate, The 374
Songwriter's Guide to Chords and Progressions, The 370
Songwriter's Handbook 371
Songwriters Resources and Services 366
Songwriter's Rhyming Dictionary, The 371
Songwriter's Success Manual, The 371
Songwriting Workshop and the Business of Music 374
Soro Publishing 102
Soul Sounds Unlimited Recording Co. 190
Sound '86 Talent Management 335
Sound Image Productions 248
Sound Image Publishing 102
Sound Image Records 190
Sound Service, The 293
Sound South Records 190
Sounds of Hope, Inc. 190
Sounds of Winchester 190, 248
Source Unlimited, The 248
South Bay Songwriters Association 366
South Bound Productions (see New Dawn Productions 237)
South Productions, Ltd. 335
Southern Concerts 335
Southern Crescent Publishing 103
Southern Grass Booking 336
Southern Sound Productions 248
Southern Talent International 336
Southern Writers Group USA 103
Space Productions 293
Sparrow Records, Inc. 249
Sparrow/Birdwing Music 103
Speer Music, Ben 103
Spider Entertainment Co. 336
Spinn Records 249

Spirit and Soul Publishing Co. 103
Spizel Advertisng, Inc., Edgar S. 278
Spotlite Enterprises, Ltd. 336
Spring Records 191
Spring/Posse Records 249
Squillit Productions, Inc. 249
SRO Artists 336
SRS Workshops 374
SSS, International 249
Stache Records, Inc. 249
Stacy-Lee Label, The 250
Stacy-Lee, The 191
Stage One Music 104
Stage 3 Sound Productions 293
Stage II Attractions 336
Staircase Promotion 250
Staley Music, Wade 104
Staley Productions, Wade 250
Standy Records Inc. 191
Star Artist Management, Inc. 336
Star Drive Management 337
Star Jazz Records, Inc. 191
Star Representation 337
Star Song Records 191
Starborn Records 191
Starburst Records, Inc. 250
Starfox Publishing 104
Stargem Record Productions 250
Stargem Records, Inc. 193
Stark Records & Tape Co. 193
Starman Records 193, 150
Starsound Records 250
Startime Music 104, 251, 337
Startown Enterprises 251
Stauch-Vetromile, Inc. 278
Stax Records (see Fantasy Records 151)
Stay Rich Music (see Get Rich Music 222)
Stein, Bill 337
Stevens, Inc. 278
Stevens Studios, Inc., Carter 293
Stewart, Inc., E.J. 294
Stewart Productions, A. 251
Stolz Advertising Co. 278
Stone & Adler, Inc. 278
Stone Row Music Co. 104
Stonebess Music Co. 104
Stonedog Productions 251
Stone-High Records, Inc. 251
Stony Plain Recording Co., Ltd. 251
Storm Productions, Inc. (see Jacoby/Storm Productions) 288
Strawberry Patch 104
Street Tunes Limited 104, 194, 252
Stuart Music Co., Jeb 105
Sugarplum Music Co. 105
Suggs/Saltwater Music, Del 337
Sullivan & Brugnatelli 279
Sullivan and/or Haas 279
Sullivan Management, Greg 337
Su-Ma Publishing Co., Inc. 105
Sun International Corp. 194
Sun-Bear Corporation 105
Sunbelt Management Group 338
Sunbonnet Publishing Co. 105
Sunbonnet Records 194
Sunbury/Dunbar Music Canada, Ltd. 106
Sundowner Music (Australia) Pty., Ltd. 106
Sun-Ray Records 194, 252
Sunset Films 294
Sunset Productions 252
Sunset Records, Inc. 194, 252
Sunshine Country Enterprises, Inc. 106
Sunshine Group, The 252
Sunshine Sound Enterprises, Inc. 194
Surrey Sound Record Label Ltd., The 195
Susan Records 195
Susquehanna University Theatre 352
Sugarplum Music co. 105
Sweet Bernadette (see Mountain Willie Music 74)
Sweet City Records 195
Sweet Polly Music 106
Sweet Singer Music 106
Sweet Swamp Music 106
Sweet Tooth Music Publishing 107
Sweetsong Productions 253
Sword & Shield Records 253
Szabo, Rich 253

# T

T.D.I. Direction & Management Division 338
T.M International Records (see Famous Door Publishing Co. 151)
Tabitha Music, Ltd. 107
Tabitha Productions 253
Take Home Tunes 195
Take Home Tunes! Record Co. 253
Tal Music, Inc. 107
Talent Attractions 338
Talent Master 338
Tatom Agency, The (see Adoration, Inc. 297)
Teahouse Music 338
Tedesco Music Co., Dale 107
Tee-Web Productions (see Tito Productions 255)
Telecine Services & Productions Ltd. 294
Telematin Productions, Inc. 294
Teleson-America 195
Televox Music 107
Tell International Record Co. 196
Terock Records 196, 254
Theatre Communications Group, Inc. 367
Theatre Department 352
Theatre for the New City 352
Theatre for Young America 353
Theatre of the Riverside Church 353
Think Big Music 107
Third Story Music, Inc. (Los Angeles) 108
Third Story Music, Inc. (Philadelphia) 108
Third Story Recording 254
13th Street Theatre Repertory Co. 353
Thomas Advertising 279
Thomas Management, Mike 338
Thompson Co., J. Walter (Georgia) 279

Index **425**

Thompson Co. J. Walter (Michigan) 279
Thompson-Friday Productions 254
3 G's Industries 196
3 H's Music 108
3B Music Corp. 254
Tiger Records 254
Tiki Enterprises (see Janell Music Publishing/Tiki Enterprises 57)
Tinory Productions, Rik 254
Tito Productions 255
TMC Productions 255
TNA Records 196
Todd & Associates, Jerre R. 279
Tom Tom Publishing Co. 108
Tompaul Music Co. 108
Top Dog Productions (see Fred Berk Artist Management/Top Dog Productions/Top Dog Music 301)
Topsail Music 108
Total Entertainment Concept 339
Touche Records 196
Toulouse Music Publishing Co., Inc. 108
Transatlantic Music 109
Transcity Records 196
Tree Publishing Co., Inc. 109
Trend Productions 255
Trend Records 197
Triad 279
Triangle Records, Inc. 197
Triangle Talent, Inc. 339
Tribal Records 255
Trod Nossel Artists 255
Trucker Man Records 197
True North Records 197
Truly Fine Records (see Silver Bullet Productions 247)
Trusty Publications 109
Trusty Records 197
Trusty Tips from the Colonel 369
TSR Inc. 198, 255
TSR, Inc. & City Surfer Music 109
Tteltrab Music (see Date Line International Records 146)
Tulchin Productions 294
Tumac Music 256
Tumac Music Publishing 109
Turner Productions, Scott 256
Tutch Music Publishing 109
Twist and Shout Music 110
Two Sisters (see Mountain Willie Music 74)
Two Star Productions 256
Tymena Music 198
Tymena Music (Ty Lemley Music) 256
Tyner Music 110
Tyscot, Inc. 110
Tyscot Records 198

## U

Ultima Thule Music Publishing Co. 110
Umbrella Artist Management, Inc. 339
Universal Stars Music 110
Universal-Athena Records 198
University of Maine at Fort Kent 353
University of Michigan Professional Theatre Program, The 358
University Theatre 353
Unregulated Music 111
Unregulated Record Co., Inc. 198
Upstart Music 111
Upstart Records 198
Urban Rock Records 198
Ursula Music 111

## V

Vaam Music 111 (also see Pete Martin Productions 234)
Vado Music 111
Valex Talent Agency 339
Vample Publishing Co., Jerry 111
Vample Record, Inc. 199, 256
Van Riper, Caldwell 280
Vandecar, Deporte & Johnson 280
Vanguard Associates, Inc. 280
Vansant Dugdale 280
Vector Music 111
Velvet Productions 199
Velvett Recording Company 339
Vendyback, Cedric 353
Venture 199
Venture Productions 256
Veron Music/World Acclaim Music 112
Vickers Music Association, Charles 257
Village Records, Inc. 199
Virginia Arts Publishing Companies, The 112
Voice Box Records 199, 257
Vokes Booking Agency 339
Vokes Music Publishing 112
Vokes Music Publishing & Record Co. 199
Volunteer Lawyers for the Arts 367

## W

Wabash College Theatre 354
Wagner Agency, William F. 340
Wailing Wall Productions 340
Waldo Astoria Playhouse 354
Walters Associates, Norby 340 (also see Mega-Star Music 323)
Walters/Earle Ludgin, Inc., Stern 280
Waltner Enterprises 200, 340
WAM Music Corp., Ltd. 200
Wam Records 257
W&G Record Processing Co. Pty. 200
Warner Bros Music Australia Pty., Ltd. 112
Warner Brothers Records, Inc. 200
Warwick, Welsh & Miller 280
Washburn Productions, Kent 112, 257
Washington International Arts Letter 369
Waterhouse Music, Inc. 114

## 426 Songwriter's Market '84

Waterloo Community Playhouse 354
Watertoons Music (see Monona Music 72)
Watonga Publishing Co. 114
Watts City Productions 114
Watts City Records 200
Watts City Records & Production Co. 257
Wayne & Co., Tucker 280
Wayne Music Publishing Ltd., Jeff 114
Wea Music of Canada, Ltd. 200
Web IV Music Publishing 114
Webco Records & Recording Studio 201, 257
Weber, Cohn & Riley 280
Webster & Harris Advertising 281
Weeze Music Co. & Double Header Productions 114
Weiser Publishing, Ron 114
Welchy Grape Publishing 114
Weldee Music Company, The 115
Welz Music Complex, Joey 340
Wesjac Music 115
Wesjac Record Enterprises 201
Weyand Music Publishing 115
W/G Records 201, 258
Wheelsville Records, Inc. 201
White Cat Music 115
White Clay Productions, Inc. 115
White Publishing, Don/Dew Music 116
White Rock Records, Inc. 201
White Way Music Co. 116
Whiteway Productions, Inc. 258
Wilder Productions, Shane 258
Wildrick & Miller, Inc. 281
Wilk & Brichta Advertising 281
Will-Du Music Publishers 116
Williams Music Group, Don 116, 258
Wilsing Music Publishers 116
Wilson Music Co., Luther 116
Wilson Productions, Inc. Marty 201
Wilwin Records 202
Wind Mill, The (see Old Hat Records 239)
Window Music Publishing Co., Inc. 117
Wing Productions 294
Winterswan 340
Wishbone, Inc. 117, 258
Wolfe & Associates, Billy 341
Wolkcas Advertising 281

Womack/Claypoole/Griffin 281
Wood Artist Management, Richard 341
Woodrich Publishing Co. 117
Woomera Music Pty. Ltd. 117
Word Music 117
Word Record and Music Group, The 202
Words of Wisdom Production 258
Work Music Publishing Company 118
World Acclaim Music (see Veron Music/World Acclaim Music) 112
World Popular Song Festival 359
World Wide Management 341
Would'n Shoe 202
Wyrtzen Ministry, Christine (see Loveland Ministries) 321

## X

XL Records 202

## Y

Yardang & Associates, Ed 281
Yatahey Records 202
Ybarra Music 341
Yeager Productions, Douglas A. 341
Yearwood Enterprises, Barry 260, 341
Yeck Brothers Group 282
Yellow Brick Promises 354
Young & Rubicam 282
Young Country Music (see Eb-Tide Music 219)
Young Musicians 369

## Z

Zaleski, Paul 260
Zam Productions, Dan 260
Zane Management, Inc. 341
Zario Music, Rex 118
Zelman Studios 294
Zip-Zapp Records Corp. 260
ZM Squared 295
ZZYZX Records 202

# Other Writer's Digest Books

**Music**
  Making Money Making Music, by James Dearing (paper) $12.95
**Art/Photography**
  Artist's Market, $14.95
  British Journal of Photography Annual, $24.95
  Developing the Creative Edge in Photography, by Bert Eifer (paper) $14.95
  How to Create and Sell Photo Products, by Mike and Carol Werner (paper) $14.95
  How You Can Make $20,000 a Year With Your Camera, by Larry Cribb (paper) $9.95
  Photographer's Market, $14.95
  Sell & Resell Your Photos, by Rohn Engh $14.95
  Starting—And Succeeding In—Your Own Photography Business, by Jeanne Thwaites $17.95
**General Writing**
  The Complete Guide to Writing Nonfiction, edited by Glen Evans $24.95
  Getting the Words Right: How to Revise, Edit, and Rewrite, by Theodore Cheney $13.95
  How to Get Started in Writing, by Peggy Teeters $10.95
  International Writers' & Artists' Yearbook, (paper) $10.95
  Law and the Writer, edited by Polking and Meranus (paper) $7.95
  Make Every Word Count, by Gary Provost (paper) $6.95
  Writer's Encyclopedia, edited by Kirk Polking $19.95
  Writer's Market, $18.95
  Writer's Resource Guide, $16.95
  Writing for the Joy of It, by Leonard Knott $11.95
**Fiction Writing**
  Fiction Is Folks: How to Create Unforgettable Characters, by Robert Newton Peck $11.95
  Fiction Writer's Market, $17.95
  How to Write Best-Selling Fiction, by Dean R. Koontz $13.95
  How to Write a Play, by Raymond Hull $13.95
  Writing the Novel: From Plot to Print, by Lawrence Block $10.95
  Writing Romance Fiction, by Helene S. Barnhart $14.95
**Special Interest Writing**
  Children's Picture Book: How to Write It, How to Sell It, by Ellen E.M. Roberts $17.95
  Complete Book of Scriptwriting, by J. Michael Straczynski $14.95
  How to Make Money Writing . . . Fillers, by Connie Emerson $12.95
  How to Write and Sell Your Personal Experiences, by Lois Duncan $10.95
  How to Write and Sell Your Sense of Humor, by Gene Perret $12.95
  How to Write "How-To" Books and Articles, by Raymond Hull (paper) $8.95
  The Poet and the Poem, by Judson Jerome $13.95
  The Poet's Handbook, by Judson Jerome $11.95
  Programmer's Market, edited by Brad M. McGehee (paper) $16.95
**The Writing Business**
  Complete Handbook for Freelance Writers, by Kay Cassill $14.95
  How to Be a Successful Housewife/Writer, by Elaince Fantle Shimberg $10.95
  How You Can Make $20,000 a Year Writing, by Nancy Hanson (paper) $6.95
  Jobs for Writers, edited by Kirk Polking $11.95
  Writer's Survival Guide: How to Cope with Rejection, Success, and 99 Other Hang-Ups of the Writing Life, by Jean and Veryl Rosenbaum $12.95

To order directly from the publisher, include $1.50 postage and handling for 1 book and 50¢ for each additional book. Allow 30 days for delivery.

Writer's Digest Books, Department B
9933 Alliance Road, Cincinnati OH 45242

Prices subject to change without notice.